FOR REFERENCE

Do Not Take From T

INDEX TO
POETRY
for CHILDREN *and*
YOUNG PEOPLE

1982–1987

VOLUMES IN THIS SERIES

INDEX TO
POETRY
for CHILDREN *and*
YOUNG PEOPLE
1982–1987

A TITLE, SUBJECT, AUTHOR, AND FIRST LINE INDEX

TO POETRY IN COLLECTIONS

FOR CHILDREN AND YOUNG PEOPLE

Compiled by
G. Meredith Blackburn III

THE H. W. WILSON COMPANY • NEW YORK 1989

International Standard Book Number 0-8242-0773-4

Printed in the United States of America

Library of Congress Cataloging-in-Publication Data

Blackburn, G. Meredith.
    Index to poetry for children and young people, 1982–1987 : a title, subject, author, and first line index to poetry in collections for children and young people / compiled by G. Meredith Blackburn III.
        p.   cm.
    ISBN 0-8242-0773-4 : $48.00
    1. Children's poetry—Indexes.   I. Title.
PN1023.B68   1989
016.821′008′09282—dc 19   89-5342
                                            CIP

CONTENTS

INTRODUCTION

The *Index to Poetry for Children and Young People: 1982–1987* is a dictionary index—with title, subject, author, and first line entries—to 125 collections of poetry for children and young people. Most of the collections were published between 1982 and 1987, inclusive; a few were issued at an earlier date but omitted from earlier editions of the *Index*. In this edition, more than 8,500 poems by approximately 2,000 authors and translators are classified under some 1,500 subjects.

One of a series, this volume is the third supplement to the *Index to Poetry for Children and Young People: 1964–1969*. The series was initiated in 1942 with the publication of the *Index to Children's Poetry*, compiled by John E. and Sara W. Brewton. Additional volumes are listed on page ii.

Scope. The carefully-selected books of poetry that are indexed here include collections for the very young child (e.g., books classified as "Easy Books" in *Children's Catalog*, Mother Goose rhymes, etc.); collections for the elementary school grades (e.g., the range of collections in class 811 in *Children's Catalog*); and collections suitable for junior and senior high school students (e.g., such collections as are found in class 821.08 in *Junior High School Library Catalog* and in *Senior High School Library Catalog*). In addition to anthologies or collections of poetry by more than one poet, volumes by individual poets (e.g., books by N. M. Bodecker, Nikki Giovanni, Ted Hughes) and selections from the works of a single author (e.g., *How Pleasant to Know Mr. Lear: Edward Lear's Selected Works*, edited by Myra Cohn Livingston) are also included. Poems that appear in anthologies that also contain prose selections (e.g., *Snowy Day; Stories and Poems*, edited by Caroline F. Bauer) are indexed, as well as those that appear in collections of poetry devoted to a single subject (e.g., *Dinosaurs*, compiled by Lee Bennett Hopkins). The inclusion of comprehensive collections (e.g., *The World Treasury of Children's Literature*, edited by Clifton Fadiman and *The Oxford Book of Children's Verse in America*, compiled by Donald Hall) give the index a wide range.

Selection of Collections Included. Selection of the 125 collections indexed here is based on a list of titles voted on by consulting librarians and specialists in various parts of the United States. A comprehensive list of anthologies and volumes of poetry by individual authors was sent to the consultants, their advice secured, and the final selections made. A list of consultants follows this Introduction.

Entries. Entries are of four types: title, subject, author, and reference from first line to title. The addition of collection symbols to title, subject, and author entries makes these complete within themselves, thus obviating the necessity for cross references.

1. TITLE ENTRY. The fullest information is given in this entry. Although the symbols designating the books in which the poems are to be found are also given in the author and subject entries, the title entry is the only one which gives the full name of the

author, when known, and the full name of the translator, if any. References to the title entry have been made both from first lines (e.g., "Up the airy mountain." See The fairies) and from variant titles (e.g., His highness' dog. See Engraved on the collar of a dog which I gave to his royal highness).

The title entry includes:

(a) Title, followed by first line in parentheses when needed to distinguish between poems with the same title. If a poem is untitled, the first line is treated as the title.

(b) Variant titles, indented under the main title. When the same poem appears in different books with different titles, one title, generally the one most frequently used, has been chosen as the title entry and all variations have been listed under this title.

(c) Full name of author, when known.

(d) Full name of translator, if any.

(e) Symbols for collections in which the poem is found.

In order to bring together selections from a single source, selections are listed under source titles, as well as individually. An example follows:

> As you like it, sels. William Shakespeare
> "It was a lover and his lass."—HoUn
> "Under the greenwood tree."—KoT

All entries subordinated under source titles in this manner are also entered in their own alphabetical position, and identified as to source. An example follows:

> "It was a lover and his lass." From As you like
> it. William Shakespeare.—HoUn

A group title (e.g., Tender buttons) under which several poems appear has been treated as a source title. An example follows:

> Tender buttons. Gertrude Stein
> An umbrella.—KoT

2. SUBJECT ENTRY. Entries are listed alphabetically by title under various subject headings. For example, under **Animals** are listed the poems about animals in general or in variety, while poems about specific animals are grouped under the names of types of animals, as **Apes and monkeys.** A single poem is often classified under a number of subject headings (e.g., The poem Popsicles is listed under the subject headings **Summer, Lips, Kissing,** and **Ice cream**).

Both *See* and *See also* references have been made freely to and from related subjects. These are filed at the beginning of the entries for the subject. Examples follow:

> **Honesty.** See Truthfulness and falsehood
> **Honey.** See also Bees

In order that individual poems or selections from longer poems which have been subordinated to source titles may be classified according to subject and may also be readily identified as to sources, they have been entered under subject headings as follows:

> **Soup**
> Turtle soup. From Alice's adventures in Wonderland.
> L. Carroll.—HoMu

The subject entry gives under the subject heading:

(a) Title, followed by first line in parentheses when needed to distinguish between poems with the same title.

(b) Last name and initials of author.

(c) Symbols for collections in which the poem is to be found.

3. AUTHOR ENTRY. All titles are listed alphabetically under the name of the author. Titles of selections subordinated under source titles are also entered in their proper alphabetical place and referred to the source title; variant titles are cross-referenced to main titles when necessary.

The author entry gives, under the full name of the author:

(a) Title, followed by first line in parentheses when needed to distinguish between poems with the same title.

(b) Symbols for collections in which the poem is to be found.

(c) Cross references from variant titles to main titles, as needed.

(d) Cross references from titles of selections to source titles.

4. FIRST LINE REFERENCES. The first line is always given in quotation marks, even when it is also the title. When the title differs from the first line, reference is made from first line to title. An example follows.

"**Consider** the calamity." See Floradora Doe

Arrangement. The arrangement is alphabetical. Articles are always retained at the beginning of title and first line, but these articles (in English, in foreign languages, and in dialect) are disregarded in alphabetizing. Such entries are alphabetized by the word following the article, and this word is printed in **boldface** (e.g., The **cat,** is filed under C; La **belle** dame sans merci, under B; and "Der **spring** is sprung" under S). Abbreviations are filed as if spelled in full (e.g., St is filed as Saint). Contractions are filed as one word (e.g., I'd is filed as **Id**). Hyphenated compounds are filed as separate words (e.g., **Bed-time** precedes **Bedtime**). To facilitate quick use, the entries beginning with **O** and **Oh** have been filed together under **Oh.** Likewise, names beginning **Mac** and **Mc** have been filed together as **Mac.** Punctuation within a title or first line has been regularized to facilitate mechanical filing. Where the wording is the same, entries have been arranged in the following order: author, subject, title, first line used as title, first line.

Grades. The books have been graded, and the grades are given in parentheses in the Analysis of Books Indexed and in the Key to Symbols. The grading is only approximate and is provided to indicate in general the grades for which each book is suitable. Open-ended grades (e.g., A child's treasury of poems, k–up) are used to establish a minimum age of readership even though some of the material indexed may appeal to older students as well. A book that is comprehensive in nature and is suitable for a wide range of grades up to and beyond the twelfth is designated (r), reference.

Uses. The *Index to Poetry for Children and Young People* should serve as a practical reference book for all who desire to locate poems for children and young people by subject, author, title, or first line. It should prove especially useful to librarians, teachers in elementary and secondary schools, teachers and students of literature for children and young people, radio and television artists, parents, young people, and children. The variety of subject classifications should be helpful to anyone preparing programs for special occasions, to teachers planning activities around the interests of children and young people, to parents who desire to share poetry, and to anyone searching for poems on a given topic. The Analysis of Books Indexed, which gives in detail the contents of each book, number of poems included, number of authors represented, and number of poems in each group or classification, should prove valuable in the selection of collections for purchase or use. The comprehensiveness of the books indexed insures the usefulness of the Index to those interested in poetry from the nursery level through secondary school and beyond.

Acknowledgments. The compiler would like to thank the consultants who cooperated in checking lists of titles to be included, especially Linda Lapides. Grateful recognition is given to John Edmund Brewton and Sara Westbrook Brewton, my grandparents, who were the originators and compilers of the first five volumes in this series and assisted in the preparation of the sixth. Thanks are also due the many publishers who kindly provided copies of their books for indexing, and Bruce Carrick and Norris Smith of the H. W. Wilson Company, who worked diligently and with much patience throughout this project.

GEORGE MEREDITH BLACKBURN III

CONSULTANTS

Dr. Caroline Feller Bauer
Specialist, Children's Literature
Huntington Beach, California

Terese Bigelow
Children's and YA Librarian
Charles H. Taylor Memorial Library
Hampton, Virginia

Elizabeth Breting
Director, Children's Services
Kansas City Public Library
Kansas City, Missouri

Laurie Dudley
Special Services Librarian
Abilene Public Library
Abilene, Texas

Evaluation Committee
The Newton Public Schools
Newtonville, Massachusetts

Sally Holmes Holtze
Editor and Critic of Children's and
   YA Literature
New York, New York

Amy Kellman
Coordinator, Children's Services
Carnegie Library of Pittsburgh
Pittsburgh, Pennsylvania

Linda F. Lapides
Head, Materials Management Office
Enoch Pratt Free Library
Baltimore, Maryland

Joyce W. Mills
Assistant Professor
School of Library and Information Studies
Atlanta University
Atlanta, Georgia

Bonnie O'Brian, Shirley Porter, Nancy
   Reich, Marilyn Robertson, and Joe
   Saraci
Library Services
Los Angeles Unified School District
Los Angeles, California

Linda Perkins
Supervising Program Librarian
Young People's Services
The Berkeley Public Library
Berkeley, California

Dr. Henrietta M. Smith
Instructor, Children's Literature
School of Library and Information Science
University of South Florida
Tampa, Florida

Divna Todorovich
Subject Cataloger
Library of Congress
Washington, DC

Arrolyn H. Vernon
Head Librarian
Beaver Country Day School
Chestnut Hill, Massachusetts

Caroljean Wagner
Central Library, Children's Room
Milwaukee Public Library
Milwaukee, Wisconsin

ANALYSIS OF BOOKS OF POETRY INDEXED

Adoff, Arnold. All the colors of the race: illustrated by John Steptoe. Lothrop 1982 (3–up).
   Contents—38 poems, ungrouped.

Alderson, Brian, comp. The Helen Oxenbury nursery rhyme book; illustrated by Helen Oxenbury. Morrow 1986 (k).
   Contents—56 nursery rhymes, ungrouped.

Angelou, Maya. Shaker, why don't you sing, more poems. Random House 1983 (7-up).
   Contents—28 poems, ungrouped. Table of contents.

Bauer, Caroline Feller, ed. Snowy day, stories and poems; illustrated by Margot Tomes. Lippincott 1986 (3–6).
   Contents—32 poems by 27 authors, ungrouped. Table of contents.

Bayley, Nicola, comp. Hush-a-bye-baby and other bedtime rhymes; illustrated by the compiler. Macmillan 1986 (k).
   Contents—12 nursery rhymes, ungrouped.

Bennett, Jill, comp. Days are where we live and other poems; illustrated by Maureen Roffey. Lothrop 1982 (k–3).
   Contents—24 poems by 18 poets, ungrouped.

Bierhorst, John, ed. The sacred path, spells, prayers and power songs of the American Indians. Morrow 1983 (r).
   Contents—109 poems grouped as follows: Birth and infancy, 14; Growing up, 12; Love songs and love magic, 14; For the traveler, 8; Against sickness and evil, 13; Controlling the weather, 12; Planting and gathering, 11; For the hunter, 13; For the dying and the dead, 12. Introduction by the editor; glossary of tribes, cultures, and languages.

Blake, Quentin, comp. Quentin Blake's nursery rhyme book; illustrated by the author. Harper and Row 1983 (k–3).
   Contents—18 nursery rhymes, ungrouped.

Blegvad, Lenore, ed. The parrot in the garret and other rhymes about dwellings; illustrated by Erik Blegvad. Atheneum 1982 (k–3).
Contents—26 rhymes, ungrouped.

Blishen, Edward, ed. Oxford book of poetry for children; illustrated by Brian Wildsmith. Oxford University Press 1984 (k–5).
Contents—169 poems by 64 authors, grouped as follows: The moon's in a fit, 21; Children you are very little, 8; There I met a pretty miss, 12; The world of waters is our home, 12; What bird so sings, 10; A story I'll to you unfold, 7; O'er ditches and mires, 5; Sweet sprites, tiger, 10; Other creatures, 19; We'll let each other alone, 5; O'er vales and hills, 16; A chip hat she had on, 11; Sigh as you sing, 7; With sweet-briar and bonfire, 5; Rock them, rock them, lullaby, 3. Indexed by authors and first lines. Introduction by the editor.

Bodecker, N. M. Pigeon cubes and other verse; illustrated by the author. Atheneum 1982 (k–up). A Margaret K. McElderry book.
Contents—45 poems, ungrouped.

Bodecker, N. M. Snowman sniffles and other verse; illustrated by the author. Atheneum 1983 (k–up).
Contents—51 poems, ungrouped.

Brewton, John E. and **Blackburn, Lorraine A.,** comps. They've discovered a head in the box for the bread and other laughable limericks; illustrated by Fernando Krahn. Crowell 1978 (3–6).
Contents—231 limericks by 64 authors, grouped as follows: Leaning on a limerick, 5; Of creatures and people, capricious and peculiar, 15; The troupial and other distinguished beasts, 12; Animal antics, 15; Funny folk, frivolous and frenzied, 34; Mind your manners, 9; Puns, atrocious and otherwise, 24; There's nothing like food, 22; On music I dote, 14; Schoolish, or foolish, 13; Bell cords and other finery, 7; It was love at first sight, 6; Such silly mistakes, 22; Can you read these, they're especially tricky, 21; Write the last line yourself, 12. Indexed by authors, first lines, and titles.

Cassedy, Sylvia. Roomrimes; illustrated by Michelle Chessare. Crowell 1987 (3–7).
Contents—26 poems, ungrouped. Table of contents.

Chapman, Jean, comp. Cat will rhyme with hat, a book of poems; illustrated by Peter Parnall. Scribners 1986 (5–up).
Contents—61 poems by 49 authors, ungrouped. Indexed by authors, first lines, and titles.

Chorao, Kay, comp. The baby's bedtime book; illustrated by the compiler. Dutton 1984 (k–3).
Contents—27 poems, ungrouped. Table of contents.

Chorao, Kay, comp. The baby's good morning book; illustrated by the compiler. Dutton 1986 (k–3).
    Contents—26 poems by 16 authors, ungrouped. Table of contents and index to first lines. Color illustrations.

Ciardi, John. Doodle soup; illustrated by Merle Nacht. Houghton Mifflin 1985 (3–up).
    Contents—38 poems, ungrouped. Table of contents.

Cole, Joanna, comp. A new treasury of children's poetry, old favorites and new discoveries; illustrated by Judith Gwyn Brown. Doubleday 1984 (k–5).
    Contents—211 poems by 112 authors, grouped as follows: First poems of childhood, 31; People and portraits, 16; Animal fair, 28; Silly time, 41; Come play with me, 15; When I went out to see the sun, 17; Celebrate the time, 27; A different way of seeing, 16; Inside myself, 20. Introduction by the editor; index to authors and titles.

Corrin, Sara and **Corrin, Stephen,** eds. Once upon a rhyme, 101 poems for young people; illustrated by Jill Bennett. Faber 1982 (3–6).
    Contents—101 poems by 56 authors, grouped as follows: Puffing along and shooting up, 5; Viewpoints, 8; Creatures great and small, 12; Wind and weather, 17; Odd and funny, 13; The importance of me, 9; If you should meet, beware, 6; Isn't it mysterious, 11; Tickle your fancy, 19; Piper, pipe that song again, 1. Table of contents and indexes to authors and first lines.

De Regniers, Beatrice Schenk. This big cat and other cats I've known; illustrated by Alan Daniel. Crown 1985 (3–up).
    Contents—17 poems, ungrouped. Color illustrations.

Daniel, Ed, ed. A child's treasury of poems; illustrated with color and black and white reproductions of Victorian and Edwardian era paintings and drawings. Dial 1986 (k–up).
    Contents—136 poems by 29 authors, grouped as follows: Daybreak, 19; The classroom, 18; Playtime, 19; Sunny days, 19; All creatures great and small, 21; Some old friends, 20; Sweet dreams, 20. Table of contents and index to first lines. Biographical sketches of authors and list of artists.

Demi, ed. Dragon kites and dragonflies, a collection of Chinese nursery rhymes; illustrated by the editor. Harcourt 1986 (k–3).
    Contents—22 Chinese nursery rhymes, ungrouped.

DePaola, Tomie, comp. Tomie dePaola's Mother Goose; illustrated by the compiler. Putnam 1985 (k–3).
    Contents—199 nursery rhymes, ungrouped. Index of first lines.

Downie, Mary Alice and **Robertson, Barbara,** comps. The new Wind has wings, poems from Canada; illustrated by Elizabeth Cleaver. Oxford (Canada) 1984 (1–5).

    Contents—90 poems by 56 authors, ungrouped. Table of contents and index of poets. Color illustrations.

Esbensen, Barbara Juster. Cold stars and fireflies, poems of the four seasons; illustrated by Susan Bonners. Crowell 1984 (5–up).

    Contents—43 poems grouped as follows: Autumn, 10; Winter, 12; Spring, 11; Summer, 10. Table of contents. Indexed by first lines.

Fadiman, Clifton, ed. The world treasury of children's literature; illustrations by Leslie Morrill. Little, Brown 1984 (r).

    Contents—151 poems by 132 authors, ungrouped. Table of contents. Indexed by authors, first lines, and titles; two volumes.

Farber, Norma and **Livingston, Myra Cohn,** eds. These small stones. Harper 1987 (3–7).

    Contents—60 poems by 52 authors, grouped as follows: In my hand, 10; On the ground, 10; In the air, 10; Outside, 10; On the table, 10; A piece of it all, 10. Indexed by authors, first lines, titles, and translators.

Farjeon, Eleanor. Eleanor Farjeon's poems for children. Lippincott 1984 (4–up).

    Contents—293 poems grouped as follows: Meeting Mary, 20; Sing for your supper, 80; Over the garden wall, 104; Joan's door, 57; Come Christmas, 32. Index to titles.

Fisher, Aileen. When it comes to bugs, poems by Aileen Fisher; illustrated by Chris and Bruce Degen. Harper and Row 1986 (k–3).

    Contents—16 poems, ungrouped. Table of contents.

Fleischman, Paul. I am phoenix, poems for two voices; illustrated by Ken Nutt. Harper and Row 1985 (k–up). A Charlotte Zolotow book.

    Contents—15 poems, ungrouped, written for two voices. Black and white illustrations.

Frank, Josette, ed. Poems to read to the very young; illustrated by Eloise Wilkin. Random House 1982 (k–3).

    Contents—70 poems, ungrouped. Index to first lines.

Frost, Robert. A swinger of birches, poems of Robert Frost for young people; illustrated by Peter Koeppen with an introduction by Clifton Fadiman. Stemmer House 1982 (5–up).

    Contents—38 poems, ungrouped. Table of contents and glossary. Color illustrations.

Giovanni, Nikki. Spin a soft black song, poems for children; illustrated by Charles Bible. Hill and Wang 1971 (k–up).
Contents—35 poems, ungrouped. Introduction.

Glenn, Mel. Class dismissed, high school poems; photographs by Michael J. Bernstein. Houghton 1982 (7–up).
Contents—70 poems, ungrouped. Table of contents.

Glenn, Mel. Class dismissed II, more high school poems; photographs by Michael J. Bernstein. Houghton 1986 (7–up).
Contents—70 poems, ungrouped. Table of contents.

Griego, Margot C.; Bucks, Betsy L.; Gilbert, Sharon S.; and **Kimball, Laurel H.,** comps. Tortillitas para mama and other nursery rhymes, Spanish and English; illustrated by Barbara Cooney. Holt 1981 (k–up).
Contents—13 nursery rhymes and lullabies, ungrouped, in Spanish and English. Color illustrations.

Hall, Donald, comp. The Oxford book of children's verse in America. Oxford University Press 1985 (r).
Contents—263 poems by 99 authors, ungrouped. Table of contents, indexed by authors, first lines, and titles. Also notes on authors and introduction by the editor.

Harrison, Michael and **Stuart-Clark, Christopher,** eds. The Oxford book of Christmas poems. Oxford University Press 1984 (r).
Contents—121 poems by 98 authors, grouped as follows: The sky turns dark, the year grows old, 10; This was the moment when before turned into after, 45; Glad Christmas comes, and every hearth makes room to bid him welcome now, 54; Open you the east door and let the new year in, 12. Table of contents. Indexed by first lines and titles.

Heaney, Seamus and **Hughes, Ted,** eds. The rattle bag. Faber 1982 (7–up) (r).
Contents—483 poems by 138 authors, ungrouped. Table of contents. Index to authors and a glossary.

Holdridge, Barbara, comp. Under the greenwood tree, Shakespeare for young people; illustrated by Robin and Pat Dewitt. Stemmer House 1986 (r).
Contents—39 selections from Shakespeare, ungrouped. Table of contents and glossary. Color illustrations each page.

Hopkins, Lee Bennett, comp. Best friends; illustrated by James Watts. Harper and Row 1986 (3–6).
Contents—18 poems by 17 authors, ungrouped.

Hopkins, Lee Bennett, comp. Click, rumble, roar, poems about machines; photographs by Anna Held Audette. Crowell 1987 (2–6)
   Contents—18 poems, ungrouped. Table of contents and index to first lines.

Hopkins, Lee Bennett, comp. Creatures; illustrated by Stella Ormi. Harcourt 1985 (3–6).
   Contents—18 poems by 13 authors, ungrouped. Indexed by authors, first lines, and titles.

Hopkins, Lee Bennett, ed. Crickets and bullfrogs and whispers of thunder, poems and pictures by Harry Behn. Lothrop 1982 (5–up).
   Contents—50 poems grouped as follows: Every bright beautiful wonderful thing, 17; I made believe, 12; This hill is mine, 21. Table of contents and indexes to first lines and titles.

Hopkins, Lee Bennett, comp. Dinosaurs; illustrated by Murray Tinkelman. Harcourt 1987 (k–up).
   Contents—18 poems by 16 authors, ungrouped. Table of contents. Index to authors.

Hopkins, Lee Bennett, ed. A dog's life; illustrated by Linda Rochester Richards. Harcourt 1983 (k–up).
   Contents—23 poems by 21 authors, ungrouped. Table of contents and indexes to authors, first lines, and titles.

Hopkins, Lee Bennett, ed. Munching, poems about eating; illustrated by Nelle Davis. Little, Brown 1985 (k–5).
   Contents—23 poems by 21 authors, ungrouped. Table of contents.

Hopkins, Lee Bennett, ed. Rainbows are made, poems by Carl Sandburg; illustrated with wood engravings by Fritz Eichenberg. Harcourt 1982 (5–up).
   Contents—64 poems grouped as follows: Poetry is a series of explanations of life, 18; Poetry is a search for syllables, 11; Poetry is a shuffling of boxes of illusions, 12; Poetry is a section of river-fog, 8; Poetry is a sequence of dots and dashes, 9. Table of contents and indexes to first lines and titles.

Hopkins, Lee Bennett, comp. The sea is calling me; illustrated by Walter Gaffney-Kessell. Harcourt 1986 (3–up).
   Contents—21 poems by 17 authors, ungrouped. Indexed by authors, first lines, and titles.

Hopkins, Lee Bennett, comp. The sky is full of song; illustrated by Dirk Zimmer. Harper 1983 (3–up).
   Contents—38 poems by 27 authors, grouped as follows: Autumn, 9; Winter, 10; Spring, 9; Summer, 10.

Hopkins, Lee Bennett, comp. A song in stone, city poems; illustrated with photographs by Anna Held Audette. Crowell 1983 (4–up).
Contents—20 poems by 18 authors, ungrouped. Table of contents.

Hopkins, Lee Bennett, comp. Surprises; illustrated by Megan Lloyd. Harper 1984 (k–3).
Contents—32 poems by 28 authors grouped as follows: Who to pet, 6; Creep, crawl and fly, 6; At the top of my voice, 6; Boats, trains and planes, 7; Rain, sun and snow, 7; Good night, 6. Indexed by authors and titles.

Hughes, Langston. The dream keeper; illustrated by Helen Sewell. Knopf 1986 (5–up).
Contents—59 poems grouped as follows: The dream keeper, 11; Sea charm, 11; Dressed up, 15; Feet o' Jesus, 8; Walkers with the dawn, 14. Introduction by Augusta Baker and table of contents.

Hughes, Ted. Under the north star; illustrated by Leonard Baskin. Viking 1981 (5–up).
Contents—24 poems, ungrouped. Table of contents.

Janeczko, Paul B., comp. Don't forget to fly, a cycle of modern poems. Bradbury 1981 (7–up).
Contents—130 poems by 73 authors, ungrouped. Table of contents and index to authors.

Janeczko, Paul B., comp. Going over to your place, poems for each other. Bradbury 1987 (7–up).
Contents—131 poems by 78 authors, ungrouped. Table of contents and index to authors.

Janeczko, Paul B., comp. Pocket poems, selected for a journey. Bradbury 1985 (7–up).
Contents—120 poems by 78 authors, ungrouped. Table of contents and index to authors.

Janeczko, Paul B., ed. Poetspeak, in their work, about their work. Bradbury 1983 (r).
Contents—148 poems by 62 authors, ungrouped. Comments by the poets. Table of contents and index to authors.

Janeczko, Paul B., comp. Strings, a gathering of family poems. Bradbury 1984 (7–up).
Contents—127 poems by 86 authors, grouped as follows: Strings, from wives and husbands, 8; Strings, from parents, 27; Strings, from children, 46; Strings, from brothers and sisters, 9; Strings, from cousins, 4; Strings, from nieces and nephews, 13; Strings, from grandchildren, 20. Table of contents and index to authors.

Janeczko, Paul B., comp. This delicious day, 65 poems. Orchard Books 1987 (7–up).

> *Contents*—65 poems by 55 authors, ungrouped. Table of contents and index to authors.

Kennedy, X. J. Brats; illustrated by James Watts. Atheneum 1986 (3–6). A Margaret K. McElderry book.

> *Contents*—42 poems, ungrouped.

Kennedy, X. J. The forgetful wishing well, poems for young people; illustrated by Monica Incisa. Atheneum 1985 (4–up).

> *Contents*—70 poems grouped as follows: Growing pains, 7; Creatures, 14; People I know, 5; Family matters, 7; Wonders, 13; In the city, 8; All around the year, 16. Table of contents.

Kennedy, X. J. and **Kennedy, Dorothy,** comps. Knock at a star, a child's introduction to poetry; illustrated by Karen Ann Weinhaus. Little, Brown 1982 (3–6).

> *Contents*—163 poems by 119 authors, grouped as follows: What do poems do, 53; What's inside a poem, 46; Special kinds of poetry, 59; Do it yourself, 3. Table of contents. Indexed by authors, first lines, and titles.

Koch, Kenneth and **Farrell, Kate,** eds. Talking to the sun, an illustrated anthology of poems for young people; illustrated with paintings from the Metropolitan Museum of Art, in color. Henry Holt 1985 (5–up).

> *Contents*—175 poems by 138 authors, grouped as follows: Hymn to the sun, 9; Come unto these yellow sands, 13; All the pretty little horses, 15; Come live with me and be my love, 21; When the green woods laugh, 14; A rabbit as king of the ghosts, 34; The world's wanderers, 20; For the moment, 23; Sleeping on the ceiling, 15; Tender buttons, 11. Index to authors, first lines, and titles.

Larrick, Nancy, comp. Tambourines, tambourines to glory, prayers and poems; illustrated by Geri Greinke. Westminster 1982 (k–5).

> *Contents*—76 poems and prayers by 46 authors, grouped as follows: Get out your rainbow colors, 15; God bless all those I love, 11; The animals I love, 9; Be good to me, 18; Light a candle within my heart, 15; Yet certain am I, 8. Indexed by authors, first lines, and titles.

Larrick, Nancy, comp. When the dark comes dancing, a bedtime poetry book; illustrated by John Wallner. Philomel 1983 (k–5).

> *Contents*—45 poems by 24 authors, grouped as follows: Little creatures everywhere are settling down to sleep, 6; The stars danced over the daisies, 9; There's nothing sweeter than the middle of the night, 12; The moon will weave sweet dreams, 6; Singing you their lullabies, 12. Indexed by authors, first lines, and titles. Table of contents.

Livingston, Myra Cohn, comp. Cat poems; illustrated by Trina Schart Hyman. Holiday House 1987 (k–up).
Contents—19 poems by 18 authors, ungrouped. Table of contents.

Livingston, Myra Cohn. Celebrations; illustrated by Leonard Everett Fisher. Holiday House 1985 (k–up).
Contents—16 poems, ungrouped. Table of contents.

Livingston, Myra Cohn, ed. Christmas poems; illustrated by Trina Schart Hyman. Holiday House 1984 (3–up).
Contents—18 poems by 15 authors, ungrouped. Table of contents.

Livingston, Myra Cohn. A circle of seasons; illustrated by Leonard Everett Fisher. Holiday House 1982 (3–up).
Contents—12 poems, ungrouped. Color illustrations.

Livingston, Myra Cohn, comp. Easter poems; illustrated by John Wallner. Holiday House 1985 (3–up).
Contents—18 poems by 18 authors, ungrouped. Table of contents.

Livingston, Myra Cohn, ed. How pleasant to know Mr. Lear, Edward Lear's selected works; illustrations by Edward Lear. Holiday House 1982 (3–up).
Contents—130 limericks and poems, grouped as follows: Ill tempered and queer, 11; His nose is remarkably big, 10; His visage is more or less hideous, 11; His beard it resembles a wig, 10; One of the singers, 16; One of the dumbs, 18; A runcible hat, 9; He weeps, 10; By the side of the ocean, 10; Pancakes and chocolate shrimps, 18; The days of his pilgrimage, 7. Index to titles.

Livingston, Myra Cohn, comp. I like you, if you like me, poems of friendship. Macmillan 1987 (5–up). A Margaret K. McElderry book.
Contents—87 poems by 59 authors, grouped as follows: Lonesome all alone, 8; Would you come and be my friend, 8; The friendly beasts, 8; One good friendship, 9; Come over, 12; We're going to be good friends, 9; As happy as happy could be, 13; The scratches are always there, 10; Missing you, 12. Indexed by authors, first lines, titles, and translators.

Livingston, Myra Cohn. Monkey puzzle and other poems; illustrated with woodcuts by Antonio Frasconi. Atheneum 1984 (7–up). A Margaret K. McElderry book.
Contents—30 poems, ungrouped. Table of contents.

Livingston, Myra Cohn, comp. New Year's poems; illustrated by Margo Tomes. Holiday House 1987 (k–up).
Contents—17 poems by 15 authors, ungrouped. Table of contents.

Livingston, Myra Cohn, comp. Poems for Jewish holidays; illustrated by Leonard Bloom. Holiday House 1986 (3–up).
Contents—16 poems by 12 authors, ungrouped. Table of contents.

Livingston, Myra Cohn. Sky songs; illustrated by Leonard Everett Fisher. Holiday House 1984 (5–up).
> *Contents*—14 poems, ungrouped. Table of contents.

Livingston, Myra Cohn, comp. Thanksgiving poems; illustrated by Stephen Gammell. Holiday House 1985 (5–up).
> *Contents*—16 poems by 14 authors, ungrouped. Table of contents.

Livingston, Myra Cohn, comp. Valentine poems; illustrated by Patience Brewster. Holiday House 1987 (5–up).
> *Contents*—20 poems by 15 authors, ungrouped. Table of contents.

Livingston, Myra Cohn, ed. Why am I grown so cold, poems of the unknowable. Atheneum 1982 (5–up). A Margaret K. McElderry book.
> *Contents*—151 poems by 80 authors, grouped as follows: Fears, nightmares, portents, warnings and imaginings, 13; Spells, charms, incantations, omens, curses and abracadabra, 13; Voices, whispers, cries, siren songs and echoes, 13; Haunts, illusions, dreams, faraway and miraculous places, 13; Enchantment, witchery, sorcery, allurement and necromancy, 10; Fairies, dwarves, goblins, trolls and elves, 14; Phantoms, wraiths, spectres, ghosts and spirits, 13; Mermaids, mermen, sea monsters and other denizens of the deep, 15; Witches, sorceresses, enchantresses, hags and crones, 13; Devils, fiends, giants, ogres and wizards, 12; White wands, a haunted oven, the mewlips and other strange matters, 13; Metamorphoses, transformations and disguises, 9. Table of contents. Indexed by authors, first lines, titles, and translators.

Livingston, Myra Cohn. Worlds I know and other poems; illustrated by Tim Arnold. Atheneum 1984 (5–up). A Margaret K. McElderry book.
> *Contents*—42 poems, ungrouped. Table of contents.

Lobel, Arnold. The book of pigericks; illustrated by the author. Harper and Row 1983 (k–5).
> *Contents*—38 limericks, ungrouped. Table of contents.

Lobel, Arnold, comp. The Random House book of Mother Goose; illustrated by the editor. Random House 1986 (k–3).
> *Contents*—307 nursery rhymes, ungrouped. Index to first lines. Color illustrations.

Lobel, Arnold. Whiskers and rhymes; illustrations by the author. Greenwillow 1985 (k–3).
> *Contents*—35 nursery rhymes, ungrouped. Table of contents. Color illustrations.

Margolis, Richard J. Secrets of a small brother; illustrated by Donald Carrick. Macmillan 1984 (3–6).
> *Contents*—22 poems, ungrouped.

McCord, David. All small; illustrated by Madelaine Gill Linden. Little, Brown 1986 (3–6).
>   *Contents*—25 poems, ungrouped. Table of contents.

McCullough, Frances, comp. Love is like the lion's tooth, an anthology of love poems. Harper 1984 (r).
>   *Contents*—86 poems by 55 authors, ungrouped. Table of contents. Indexed by authors, first lines, and titles.

Merriam, Eve. Blackberry ink; illustrated by Hans Wilhelm. Morrow 1985 (k–3).
>   *Contents*—24 poems, ungrouped.

Merriam, Eve. Fresh paint; illustrated with woodcuts by David Frampton. Macmillan 1986 (5–up).
>   *Contents*—45 poems, ungrouped.

Merriam, Eve. Halloween ABC, poems by Eve Merriam; illustrated by Lane Smith. Macmillan 1987 (k–up).
>   *Contents*—26 poems, ungrouped. Alphabet book.

Merriam, Eve. A sky full of poems; illustrated by Walter Gaffney-Kessell. Dell 1986 (3–6). A Yearling book.
>   *Contents*—66 poems grouped as follows: Poet's play, 19; Poet's tools, 13; Poet's talk, 9; Poet's people, 11; A sky full of poems, 14. Table of contents and a special section, "Writing a poem."

Moore, Lilian. Something new begins, new and selected poems. Atheneum 1982 (3–up).
>   *Contents*—85 poems grouped as follows: Something new begins, 15; I thought I heard the city, 13; Little raccoon and poems from the woods, 9; I feel the same way, 8; See my lovely poison ivy, 8; Think of shadows, 12; Sam's place, 20. Table of contents and index to first lines.

Patz, Nancy, ad. Moses supposes his toeses are roses, and seven other silly old rhymes; illustrated by the adaptor. Harcourt 1983 (k–3).
>   *Contents*—8 rhymes, ungrouped.

Plotz, Helen, comp. As I walked out one evening, a book of ballads. Morrow 1976 (r).
>   *Contents*—138 poems by 51 authors, grouped as follows: Magic and miracles, 28; Narratives, 31; Broadsides and satires, 17; War, 15; Work, 17; Love, 30. Indexed by authors, titles, and first lines.

Plotz, Helen, comp. Eye's delight, poems of art and architecture. Greenwillow 1983 (r).
>   *Contents*—114 poems by 74 authors, grouped as follows: Pictures, 38; Sculpture, 24; Dwelling places, 17; Public architecture, 35. Indexed by authors, first lines, and titles.

Plotz, Helen, comp. Saturday's children, poems of work. Greenwillow 1982 (r).
    Contents—122 poems by 81 authors, grouped as follows: When Adam
delved, 25; Let her own work praise her, 30; A long way we come, a long
way to go, 38; What a prodigious step to have taken, 29. Indexed by
titles, first lines, and authors.

Pomerantz, Charlotte. All asleep; illustrated by Nancy Tafuri. Greenwillow
    1984 (k–5).
    Contents—15 poems, ungrouped. Table of contents.

Pomerantz, Charlotte, comp. If I had a paka, poems in eleven languages;
    illustrated by Nancy Tafuri. Greenwillow 1982 (k–3).
    Contents—12 poems, ungrouped. Illustrated in color.

Prelutsky, Jack. The baby uggs are hatching; illustrated by James Stevenson.
    Greenwillow 1982 (3–6).
    Contents—12 poems, ungrouped. Table of contents.

Prelutsky, Jack. It's snowing, it's snowing; illustrated by Jeanne Titherington.
    Greenwillow 1984 (k–5).
    Contents—17 poems, ungrouped.

Prelutsky, Jack. It's Thanksgiving; illustrated by Marylin Hafner. Greenwillow
    1982 (k–3).
    Contents—12 poems, ungrouped.

Prelutsky, Jack. It's Valentine's day; illustrated by Yossi Abolafia. Greenwillow
    1983 (k–3).
    Contents—14 poems, ungrouped. Table of contents.

Prelutsky, Jack. My parents think I'm sleeping; illustrated by Yossi Abolafia.
    Greenwillow 1985 (k–5).
    Contents—14 poems, ungrouped. Table of contents.

Prelutsky, Jack. The new kid on the block; illustrations by James Stevenson.
    Greenwillow 1984 (3–up).
    Contents—107 poems, ungrouped. Indexed by first lines and titles.

Prelutsky, Jack, ed. The Random House book of poetry for children; illustrated
    by Arnold Lobel. Random House 1983 (k–5).
    Contents—572 poems by 261 authors, grouped as follows: Nature is,
44; The four seasons, 48; Dogs and cats and bears and bats, 49; The ways
of living things, 50; City, oh, city, 33; Children, children everywhere,
47; Me I am, 38; Home, you're where it's warm inside, 33; I'm hungry,
26; Some people I know, 37; Nonsense, nonsense, 45; Alphabet stew,
30; Where goblins dwell, 40; The land of potpourri, 39. Indexed by
authors, first lines, titles, and subjects. Also table of contents.

Prelutsky, Jack, comp. Read-aloud poems for the very young; illustrated by Marc Brown. Knopf 1986 (k).
  Contents—187 poems by 119 authors, ungrouped. Indexed by authors, first lines, and titles. Color illustrations each page.

Prelutsky, Jack. Ride a purple pelican; illustrated by Garth Williams. Morrow 1986 (k–3).
  Contents—28 poems, ungrouped. Tale of contents. Color illustrations each page.

Prelutsky, Jack. The sheriff of Rottenshot; illustrated by Victoria Chess. Greenwillow 1982 (k–5).
  Contents—16 poems, ungrouped. Table of contents.

Prelutsky, Jack. What I did last summer; illustrated by Yossi Abolafia. Greenwillow 1984 (3–6).
  Contents—13 poems, ungrouped. Table of contents.

Prelutsky, Jack. Zoo doings; illustrated by Paul O. Zelinsky. Greenwillow 1984 (3–up).
  Contents—46 poems, ungrouped.

Provensen, Alice and **Provensen, Martin,** comps. Birds, beasts and the third thing, poems by D. H. Lawrence; illustrated by the editors. Viking 1982 (5–up).
  Contents—23 poems, ungrouped. Introduction by Donald Hall. Color illustrations.

Ra, Carol F., comp. Trot, trot, to Boston, play rhymes for baby; illustrated by Catherine Stock. Lothrop 1987 (k).
  Contents—22 nursery rhymes, ungrouped.

Royds, Caroline, comp. The Christmas book, stories, poems and carols for the twelve days of Christmas; illustrated by Annabel Spenceley. Putnam 1985 (3–up).
  Contents—24 poems. Table of contents.

Russo, Susan, comp. The ice cream ocean and other delectable poems of the ocean; illustrated by the editor. Lothrop 1984 (k–5).
  Contents—20 poems by 18 authors, ungrouped. Table of contents.

Rylant, Cynthia. Waiting to waltz, a childhood; illustrated by Stephen Gammell. Bradbury 1984 (5–up).
  Contents—30 poems, ungrouped. Table of contents.

Streich, Corrine, ed. Grandparents' houses, poems about grandparents; illustrated by Lillian Hoban. Greenwillow 1984 (3–up).
  Contents—15 poems by 12 authors, ungrouped. Illustrations in color.

Sutherland, Zena and **Livingston, Myra Cohn,** eds. The Scott, Foresman anthology of children's literature; illustrated by Jean Helmer, Dick Martin, and Margaret Briody. Scott, Foresman 1984 (r).

Contents—430 poems by 331 authors, grouped as follows: About you, no one but me, 25; Friends and family, you always come back to my thoughts, 19; Poems of the spirit, who makes much of a miracle, 14; School, counting, and alphabets, 13; Objects around us, 19; Travel, 19; Riddles, 22; Small creatures, insects, and rodents, 20; Dogs and cats, 21; Animals, 29; Birds, 20; Nonsense, 15; Food, 18; Play and sports, 17; Music and dance, 21; Magic people, 19; Nonsense people, 29; The seasons, 26; The world around us, 30; Holidays, 24. Table of contents. Indexed by authors and titles.

Tripp, Wallace, comp. Marguerite, go wash your feet; illustrated by the compiler. Houghton 1985 (k–5).

Contents—58 poems by 47 authors, ungrouped. Color illustrations.

Turner, Ann. Street talk; illustrated by Catherine Stock. Houghton 1986 (3–7).

Contents—29 poems, ungrouped. Table of contents.

Viorst, Judith. If I were in charge of the world and other worries, poems for children and their parents; illustrated by Lynne Cherry. Atheneum 1982 (3–up).

Contents—46 poems grouped as follows: Wishes and worries, 5; Cats and other people, 5; Nights, 4; Spring fever, 2; Facts of life, 4; Fairy tales, 9; Words, 4; Thanks and no thanks, 4; Wicked thoughts, 3; Good-byes, 6. Table of contents.

Watson, Clyde. Catch me & kiss me & say it again; illustrated by Wendy Watson. Collins 1978 (k–2).

Contents—31 rhymes, ungrouped.

Worth, Valerie. Small poems again; illustrated by Natalie Babbit. Farrar 1986 (k–up).

Contents—25 poems, ungrouped. Table of contents.

Yolen, Jane. Ring of earth, a child's book of seasons; illustrated by John Wallner. Harcourt 1986 (3–up).

Contents—4 poems in seasonal order. Color illustrations each page.

Zolotow, Charlotte. Everything glistens and everything sings; illustrated by Margot Tomes. Harcourt 1987 (k–up).

Contents—69 poems grouped as follows: Observing the world, 8; The sea, 7; Colors, 8; People and friendship, 12; Animals, 10; The seasons, 12; Growing things, 8; Bedtime thoughts, 6. Indexed by authors, first lines, titles, and translators.

KEY TO SYMBOLS FOR BOOKS
INDEXED

Grades are given in parentheses at the end of each entry: (k), kindergarten or preschool grade; (1), first grade; (2), second grade, etc. Comprehensive general collections are designated (r), reference.

AdA   Adoff, A. comp. All the colors of the race. Lothrop 1982 (3–up)

AlH   Alderson, B. comp. The Helen Oxenbury nursery rhyme book. Morrow 1986 (k)

AnS   Angelou, M. Shaker, why don't you sing. Random House 1983 (7–up)

BaH   Bayley, N. comp. Hush-a-bye-baby. Macmillan 1986 (k)

BaS   Bauer, C. F. ed. Snowy day. Lippincott 1986 (3–6)

BeD   Bennett, J. comp. Days are where we live. Lothrop 1982 (k–3)

BiSp   Bierhorst, J. ed. The sacred path. Morrow 1983 (r)

BlO   Blishen, E. ed. Oxford book of poetry for children. Oxford 1984 (k–5)

BlPi   Blegvad, L. ed. The parrot in the garret. Atheneum 1982 (k–3)

BlQ   Blake, Q. Quentin Blake's nursery rhyme book. Harper 1983 (k–3)

BoPc   Bodecker, N. M. Pigeon cubes and other verse. Atheneum 1982 (k–up)

BoSs   Bodecker, N. M. Snowman sniffles. Atheneum 1983 (k–up).

BrT   Brewton, J. E. and Blackburn, L.A. comps. They've discovered a head. Crowell 1978 (3–6)

CaR   Cassedy, S. Roomrimes. Crowell 1987 (3–7)

ChB   Chorao, K. comp. The baby's bedtime book. Dutton 1984 (k–3)

ChC   Chapman, J. comp. Cat will rhyme with hat. Scribners 1986 (5–up)

ChG   Chorao, K. comp. The baby's good morning book. Dutton 1986 (k–3)

CiD   Ciardi, J. Doodle soup. Houghton 1985 (3–up)

CoN   Cole, J. comp. A new treasury of children's poetry. Doubleday 1984 (k–5)

CoOu   Corrin, S. and Corrin, S. eds. Once upon a rhyme. Faber 1982 (3–6)

DaC   Daniel, E. ed. A child's treasury of poems. Dial 1986 (k–up)

DeD   Demi. ed. Dragon kites and dragonflies. Harcourt 1986 (k–3)

DeM   DePaola, T. comp. Tomie dePaola's Mother Goose. Putnam 1985 (k–3)

DeT   De Regniers, B. S. This big cat and other cats I've known. Crown 1985 (3–up)

DoNw   Downie, M. A. and Robertson, B. comps. The new Wind has wings, poems from Canada. Oxford 1984 (1–5)

EsCs   Esbensen, B. J. Cold stars and fireflies. Crowell 1984 (5–up)

FaE   Farjeon, E. Eleanor Farjeon's poems for children. Lippincott 1984 (4–up)

FaTh   Farber, N. and Livingston, M. C. eds. These small stones. Harper 1987 (3–7)

FaW Fadiman, C. ed. The world treasury of children's literature. Little 1984 (r)

FiW Fisher, A. When it comes to bugs. Harper 1986 (k–3)

FlI Fleischman, P. I am phoenix, poems for two voices. Harper 1985 (k–up)

FrP Frank, J. ed. Poems to read to the very young. Random House 1982 (k–3)

GiSp Giovanni, N. Spin a soft black song. Hill and Wang 1971 (k–up)

GlC Glenn, M. Class dismissed, high school poems. Houghton 1982 (7–up)

GlCd Glenn, M. Class dismissed II, more high school poems. Houghton 1986 (7–up)

GrT Griego, M. C.; Bucks, B. L.; Gilbert, S. S.; and Kimball, L. H. comps. Tortillitas para mama. Holt 1981 (k–up)

HaO Harrison, M. and Stuart-Clark, C. eds. The Oxford book of Christmas poems. Oxford 1984 (r)

HaOf Hall, D. comp. The Oxford book of children's verse in America. Oxford 1985 (r)

HeR Heaney, S. and Hughes, T. eds. The rattle bag. Faber 1982 (7–up) (r)

HoBf Hopkins, L. B. comp. Best friends. Harper 1986 (3–6)

HoCb Hopkins, L. B. ed. Crickets and bullfrogs and whispers of thunder. Lothrop 1982 (5–up)

HoCl Hopkins, L. B. comp. Click, rumble, roar, poems about machines. Crowell 1986 (2–6)

HoCr Hopkins, L. B. comp. Creatures. Harcourt 1985 (3–6)

HoDi Hopkins, L. B. comp. Dinosaurs. Harcourt 1987 (k–up)

HoDl Hopkins, L. B. ed. A dog's life. Harcourt 1983 (k–up)

HoMu Hopkins, L. B. comp. Munching, poems about eating. Little 1985 (k–5)

HoRa Hopkins, L. B. ed. Rainbows are made, poems by Carl Sandburg. Harcourt 1982 (5–up)

HoSe Hopkins, L. B. comp. The sea is calling me. Harcourt 1986 (3–up)

HoSi Hopkins, L. B. comp. The sky is full of song. Harper 1983 (3–up)

HoSs Hopkins, L. B. comp. A song in stone, city poems. Crowell 1983 (4–up)

HoSu Hopkins, L. B. comp. Surprises. Harper 1984 (k–3)

HoUn Holdridge, B. comp. Under the greenwood tree, Shakespeare for young people. Stemmer House 1986 (r)

HuDk Hughes, L. The dream keeper. Knopf 1986 (5–up)

HuU Hughes, T. Under the north star. Viking 1981 (5–up)

JaD Janeczko, P. comp. Don't forget to fly. Bradbury 1981 (7–up)

JaG Janeczko, P. comp. Going over to your place. Bradbury 1987 (7–up)

JaPi Janeczko, P. comp. Poetspeak, in their work, about their work. Bradbury 1983 (r)

JaPo Janeczko, P. comp. Pocket poems. Bradbury 1985 (7–up)

JaS Janeczko, P. comp. Strings, a gathering of family poems. Bradbury 1984 (7–up)

JaT Janeczko, P. comp. This delicious day. Orchard 1987 (7–up)

KeB Kennedy, X. J. Brats. Atheneum 1986 (3–6)

KeF Kennedy, X. J. The forgetful wishing well. Atheneum 1985 (4–up)

KeK Kennedy, X. J. and Kennedy, D. comps. Knock at a star. Little 1982 (3–6)

KoS Frost, R. A swinger of birches. Stemmer House 1982 (5–up)

KoT Koch, K. and Farrell, K. eds. Talking to the sun. Metropolitan Museum of Art and Henry Holt 1985 (5–up)

LaT Larrick, N. comp. Tambourines, tambourines to glory. Westminster 1982 (k–5)

LaW Larrick, N. comp. When the dark comes dancing. Philomel 1983 (k–5)

LiCa Livingston, M. C. comp. Cat poems. Holiday 1987 (k–up)

LiCe Livingston, M. C. Celebrations. Holiday 1985 (k–up)

LiCp Livingston, M. C. ed. Christmas poems. Holiday 1984 (3–up)

LiCs Livingston, M. C. A circle of seasons. Holiday 1982 (3–up)

LiE Livingston, M. C. comp. Easter poems. Holiday 1985 (3–up)

LiH Livingston, M. C. ed. How pleasant to know Mr. Lear. Holiday 1982 (3–up)

LiIl Livingston, M. C. comp. I like you, if you like me. Macmillan 1987 (5–up)

LiMp Livingston, M. C. Monkey puzzle. Atheneum 1984 (7–up)

LiNe Livingston, M. C. comp. New Year's poems. Holiday 1987 (k–up)

LiPj Livingston, M. C. comp. Poems for Jewish holidays. Holiday 1986 (3–up)

LiSf Sutherland, Z. and Livingston, M. C. eds. The Scott, Foresman anthology of children's literature. Scott, Foresman 1984 (r)

LiSi Livingston, M. C. Sky songs. Holiday 1984 (5–up)

LiTp Livingston, M. C. comp. Thanksgiving poems. Holiday 1985 (5–up)

LiVp Livingston, M. C. comp. Valentine poems. Holiday 1987 (5–up)

LiWa Livingston, M. C. ed. Why am I grown so cold, poems of the unknowable. Atheneum 1982 (5–up)

LiWo Livingston, M. C. Worlds I know and other poems. Atheneum 1984 (5–up)

LoB Lobel, A. The book of pigericks. Harper 1983 (k–5)

LoR Lobel, A. comp. The Random House book of Mother Goose. Random House 1986 (k–3)

LoWr Lobel, A. Whiskers and rhymes. Greenwillow 1985 (k–3)

MaS Margolis, R. J. Secrets of a small brother. Macmillan 1984 (3–6)

McAs McCord, D. All small. Little 1986 (3–6)

McL McCullough, F. comp. Love is like the lion's tooth. Harper 1984 (r)

MeBl Merriam, E. Blackberry ink. Morrow 1985 (k–3)

MeF Merriam, E. Fresh paint. Macmillan 1986 (5–up)

MeHa Merriam, E. Halloween ABC, poems by Eve Merriam. Macmillan 1987 (k–up)

MeSk Merriam, E. A sky full of poems. Dell 1986 (3–6)

MoSn Moore, L. Something new begins. Atheneum 1982 (3–up)

PaM Patz, N. ad. Moses supposes his toeses are roses. Harcourt 1983 (k–3)

PlAs Plotz, H. comp. As I walked out one evening. Morrow 1976 (r)

PlEd Plotz, H. comp. Eye's delight, poems of art and architecture. Greenwillow 1983 (r)

PlSc Plotz, H. comp. Saturday's children, poems of work. Greenwillow 1982 (r)

PoA Pomerantz, C. All asleep. Greenwillow 1984 (k–5)

PoI Pomerantz, C. comp. If I had a paka, poems in eleven languages. Greenwillow 1982 (k–3)

PrB Prelutsky, J. The baby uggs are hatching. Greenwillow 1982 (3–6)

PrBb Provensen, A. and Provensen, M. comps. Birds, beasts and the third thing. Viking 1982 (5–up)

PrIs Prelutsky, J. It's snowing, it's snowing. Greenwillow 1984 (k–5)

PrIt Prelutsky, J. It's Thanksgiving. Greenwillow 1982 (k–3)

PrIv Prelutsky, J. It's Valentine's day. Greenwillow 1983 (k–3)

PrMp Prelutsky, J. My parents think I'm sleeping. Greenwillow 1985 (k–5)

PrNk Prelutsky, J. The new kid on the block. Greenwillow 1984 (3–up)

KEY TO ABBREVIATIONS

ad. adapted
at. attributed
bk. book
comp. compiler, compiled
comps. compilers
ed. edition, editor
eds. editors
il. illustrated, illustrator
ils. illustrators
jt. auth. joint author
jt. auths. joint authors
k kindergarten or preschool grade

pseud. pseudonym
pseuds. pseudonyms
r reference
rev. revised
rev. ed. revised edition
sel. selection
sels. selections
tr. translator
tr. fr. translated from
trs. translators
unat. unattributed
wr. at. wrongly attributed

DIRECTIONS FOR USE

The Title Entry is the main entry and gives the fullest information, including title (with first line in parentheses when needed to distinguish between poems with the same title); variant titles; full name of author; translator; and symbols for collections in which the poem is to be found. Variant titles and titles with variant first lines are also listed in their alphabetical order, with attribution to the main title. If a poem is untitled, the first line is treated as the title.

> The **little** mute boy. Federico Garcia Lorca, tr. fr.
>   the Spanish by W. S. Merwin.—HeR
> A **peanut**. Unknown.—HoSu
>   Toot, toot.—PrRh
> **Toot**, toot. See A peanut
> "**What** is the opposite of two." Richard Wilbur.—LiIl

Titles of poems are grouped according to subject, in alphabetical order under a subject heading. Each Subject Entry gives the title of the poem, the last name of the author with initials, the first line where needed for identification, the source title for subordinate selections, and the symbols for the collections in which the poem is to be found.

> **Beauty, of nature or art**
>   "It is not growing like a tree." B. Jonson.—HeR
>   My cat, Jeoffrey. From Jubilate Agno. C. Smart.—HeR

The Author Entry gives the full name of the author, title of poem with its variants (first line in parentheses when needed for identification), and the symbols for the collections in which the poem is to be found. Included under the author entry are references from variant titles and from titles of selections to the source title.

> Carroll, Lewis, pseud. (Charles Lutwidge Dodgson)
>   Alice's adventures in wonderland, sels.
>   Turtle soup.—HoMu
>   "Beautiful soup, so rich and green."—BlO
>   "Beautiful soup, so rich and green." See
>   Alice's adventures in wonderland—Turtle soup

First lines of poems, enclosed in quotation marks, are listed in their alphabetical order with references to the title entry where all the information may be found. First lines are enclosed in quotation marks even when used as titles.

> "Once I saw a little bird." See Little bird
> "Will there really be a morning." Emily Dickinson.—ChG

When the source of a poem is more familiar than the title of a poem, or when only selections from a longer work are given, such titles are grouped under the same source title. All titles subordinated to source titles also appear as individual entries in their alphabetical order with references to the source title.

"Come unto these yellow sands." From The tempest.
 William Shakespeare.—KoT
"Full fathom five thy father lies." From The tempest.
 William Shakespeare.—HoUn

The tempest, sels. William Shakespeare
 "Come unto these yellow sands."—KoT
 "Full fathom five thy father lies."—HoUn

INDEX TO POETRY FOR CHILDREN AND YOUNG PEOPLE

A

Achievement—*Continued*
"The hand that rounded Peter's dome." From The problem. R. W. Emerson.—PlEd
Hayes Iverson. M. Glenn.—GlCd
Jessica Berg. M. Glenn.—GlCd
Joel Feit. M. Glenn.—GlC
Lance Perkins. M. Glenn.—GlCd
Mandy Bailer. M. Glenn.—GlCd
Miguel DeVega. M. Glenn.—GlCd
Min Trang. M. Glenn.—GlCd
A psalm of life. H. W. Longfellow.—HaOf
Rhonda Winfrey. M. Glenn.—GlC
Robin Gold. M. Glenn.—GlC
Ronnie Evans. M. Glenn.—GlCd
Susan Tulchin. M. Glenn.—GlC
What price glory. J. Viorst.—ViI
Acoma Indians. See Indians of the Americas—Acoma
Acorn, Milton
Poem in June.—DoNw
"An **acorn**." See Acorn
Acorn. Valerie Worth.—FaTh
Acorns
Acorn. V. Worth.—FaTh
October ("The whole world dances"). S. Hahn.—JaPo
"**Acorns** drop." See October nights in my cabin
Acquainted with the night. Robert Frost.—KoS
Acrobats
"The acrobats are jumping around." Unknown.—DeD
Hazardous occupations. C. Sandburg.—PlSc
Real talent. S. L. Nelms.—JaT
Somersaults. J. Prelutsky.—PrRa
"The **acrobats** are jumping around." Unknown.—DeD
"**Across**." See The planets
"**Across** cold, moon bright." From The seasons. Harry Behn.—HoDl
"**Across** the highway, low and slow." See Close call
"**Across** the lonely beach we flit." See The sandpiper
"**Across** the plains one Christmas night." See The three drovers
"**Across** the river is Iowa." See From Council Bluffs to Omaha
"**Across** the world." See Columbus day
The **actor.** Paul Fleischman.—FlI
Actors and acting
The actor. P. Fleischman.—FlI
"All the world's a stage." From As you like it. W. Shakespeare.—HeR—HoUn
Christmas play. M. C. Livingston.—LiWo
The fourteenth day of Adar. B. J. Esbensen.—LiPj
Gus, the theatre cat. T. S. Eliot.—HaOf
"I was Harriet." A. Adoff.—AdA
"If we shadows have offended." From A midsummer night's dream. W. Shakespeare.—HoUn
Minstrel man. L. Hughes.—HuDk
The mummers. E. Farjeon.—FaE
"Our revels now are ended." From The tempest. W. Shakespeare.—HeR
Pantomime. E. Farjeon.—FaE
Rachel Ferrara. M. Glenn.—GlCd
Adam and Eve. See also Eden, Garden of
When Adam delved. Unknown.—PlSc
Adam Whitney. Mel Glenn.—GlC
Adams, John Quincy (about)
John Quincy Adams. S. V. Benét, and R. C. Benét.—HaOf

Adam's apple. Coleman Barks.—JaPo
"**Add** them up." See Pocket calculator
Address to a child during a boisterous winter evening. Dorothy Wordsworth.—BlO
Ade, George
"Early to bed and early to rise."—TrM
Adelaide. Jack Prelutsky.—LiSf
"**Adelaide** was quite dismayed." See Adelaide
"**Adieu,** farewell earth's bliss." From Summer's last will and testament. Thomas Nashe.—HeR
Adler, Carol
Havdalah.—LiPj
Adlestrop. Edward Thomas.—BlO
Adoff, Arnold
All the colors of the race.—AdA
"All the colors of the race are."—AdA
"At the meeting."—AdA
Bad guys.—AdA
Borders.—AdA
"Chocolate."—LiSf
Chocolate chocolate.—PrRh
Flavors (1) ("Mama is chocolate, you must be swirls").—AdA
Flavors (2) ("Daddy is vanilla, you must be mean").—AdA
Flavors (3) ("Me is better").—AdA
For every one.—AdA
Four foot feat.—AdA
Friend dog.—HoDl
Great Grandma Ida.—AdA
I am.—AdA
"I am learning."—HoMu
"I am making a circle for myself."—AdA
"I am the running girl."—LiSf
I can do my hair.—AdA
I know the rules.—AdA
I know we can go back so far.—AdA
"I think the real color is behind the color."—AdA
"I was Harriet."—AdA
"If they hate me."—AdA
"In both the families."—AdA
In our one family.—AdA
The lady said.—AdA
My mouth.—PrRh
Night ("Up to bed, your head").—BeD
Of the race.—AdA
On my applications.—AdA
Passing.—AdA
Past ("I have all these parts stuffed in me").—AdA—JaT
Remember.—AdA
Some old ones.—AdA
A song ("I am of the earth and the earth is of me").—AdA
A song ("I have the fore").—AdA
Still finding out.—AdA
Sum people.—AdA
"Sunny side up."—LiSf
"There is so much."—AdA
Trilingual.—AdA
"The way I see any hope for later."—AdA
"We are talking about."—AdA
"When they asked."—AdA
Adolescence. Gregory Orr.—JaPi
The **adoration** of the Magi. Christopher Pilling.—HaO
Advent, a carol. Patric Dickinson.—HaO
Advent 1955. Sir John Betjeman.—HaO
"The **Advent** wind begins to stir." See Advent 1955
Adventure. Harry Behn.—HoCb

Adventure and adventurers. See also Camping and hiking; Explorers and exploration; Frontier and pioneer life; Heroes and heroines; Seafaring life; Space and space travel

Adventures of Isabel. O. Nash.—CoN—CoOu—HaOf—PrRh

Excelsior. H. W. Longfellow.—HaOf

The jungle husband. S. Smith.—HeR

"Off we go on a piggyback ride." C. Watson.—WaC

The purist. O. Nash.—HaOf

Robin Hood and the Bishop of Hereford. Unknown.—BlO

The train to Glasgow. W. Horsburgh.—CoOu

The wanderer. W. H. Auden.—HeR

Adventures of Isabel. Ogden Nash.—CoN—CoOu—HaOf—PrRh

The **adversary.** Phyllis McGinley.—HaOf

Advertisement for a divertissement. Eve Merriam.—MeSk

Advertising

Clarence. S. Silverstein. HaOf

The codfish. Unknown.—PrRh

Song of the open road. O. Nash.—JaPo

Advice

Advice from Poor Robin's almanack. Unknown.—HaO

Advice to my son. P. Meinke.—JaPi

Advice to small children. E. Anthony.—PrRh

Advice to travelers. W. Gibson.—JaPo

Before starting.—KeK

Alphabet 1727. From The New England Primer. Unknown.—HaOf

Ambition. N. P. Willis.—HaOf

As much as you can. C. P. Cavafy.—HeR

Beware, or be yourself. E. Merriam.—MeSk

The drum. N. Giovanni.—GiSp—LiSf

"Early to bed and early to rise." G. Ade.—TrM

Ellen Winters. M. Glenn.—GlC

"A father sees a son nearing manhood." C. Sandburg.—HoRa

The fist upstairs. W. Dickey.—JaPi

For the young who want to. M. Piercy.—JaPi

Fraulein reads instructive rhymes. M. Kumin.—JaPi

How to solve a problem. E. Merriam.—MeF

"If you wish to live and thrive." Mother Goose.—LoR

John Rogers' exhortation to his children. J. Rogers.—HaOf

"Little girl, be careful what you say." C. Sandburg.—HoRa

Mary Louise Donahue. M. Glenn.—GlCd

Mother to son. L. Hughes.—CoN—HaOf—HuDk—LiSf

New year's advice from my Cornish grandmother. X. J. Kennedy.—LiNe

Noah. R. Daniells.—DoNw

Nolan Davis. M. Glenn.—GlCd

"The pobble who has no toes." E. Lear.—FaW—LiH

The pobble.—BlO

Primer lesson. C. Sandburg.—HoRa

A psalm of life. H. W. Longfellow.—HaOf

Rules ("Do not jump on ancient uncles"). K. Kuskin.—PrRh

The seventh. A. József.—HeR

Sir Walter Ralegh to his son. Sir W. Raleigh.—HeR

A smugglers' song. R. Kipling.—BlO

Some sound advice from Singapore. J. Ciardi.—LiSf

Song ("Lovely, dark, and lonely one"). L. Hughes.—HuDk

"To give advice I hesitate." R. Beasley.—TrM

Warning to children. R. Graves.—BlO

"When in danger." Unknown.—TrM

Advice from Poor Robin's almanack. Unknown.—HaO

Advice to my son. Peter Meinke.—JaPi

Advice to small children. Edward Anthony.—PrRh

Advice to travelers. Walker Gibson.—JaPo

Before starting.—KeK

AEIOU. Jonathan Swift.—BlO

"Aer, aer." See Concrete cat

Afreet. David McCord.—LiWa

"Afreet I am afraid of." See Afreet

Africa

African Christmas. J. Press.—HaO

African Christmas. John Press.—HaO

African dance. Langston Hughes.—HuDk

African peoples—Ambo

"Ah, the roofs." From Five ghost songs. Unknown, fr. the Ambo people of Africa.—KoT

"The dove stays in the garden." From Five ghost songs. Unknown, fr. the Ambo people of Africa.—KoT

"The ghost is gone in rags." From Five ghost songs. Unknown, fr. the Ambo people of Africa.—KoT

"I have no rattles." From Five ghost songs. Unknown, fr. the Ambo people of Africa.—KoT

"See how it circles." From Five ghost songs. Unknown, fr. the Ambo people of Africa.—KoT

African peoples—Azande

Song ("Desire for a woman took hold of me in the night"). Unknown, tr. fr. the Azande.—McL

African peoples—Dinka

The magnificent bull. Unknown, fr. the Dinka people of Africa.—KoT

African peoples—Fang

Hymn to the sun. Unknown, fr. the Fang people of Africa.—KoT

African peoples—Galla

"If I might be an ox." Unknown, from the Ethiopian Galla tribe.—HeR

African peoples—Hottentot

Song for the sun that disappeared behind the rainclouds. Unknown, fr. the Hottentot people of Africa.—KoT

African peoples—Swahili

Swahili love song. Unknown.—McL

African peoples—Tuareg

Girl's song. Unknown.—McL

African peoples—Yoruba

Baboon. Unknown.—HeR

Blue cuckoo. Unknown.—HeR

Buffalo. Unknown.—HeR

Chicken. Unknown.—HeR

Colobus monkey. Unknown.—HeR

Elephant. Unknown.—HeR

The elephant ("Elephant, who brings death"). Unknown, fr. the Yoruba people of Africa.—KoT

Hyena. Unknown.—HeR

Kob antelope. Unknown.—HeR

Leopard ("Gentle hunter"). Unknown.—HeR

Red monkey. Unknown.—HeR

After a bath. Aileen Fisher.—BeD—FrP

"After a bitter cold night." See Winter's tale

After Christmas. Michael Richards.—HaO

"**After** Christmas." See New year

"**After** Eli Whitney's gin." See Southeast Arkanasia

After his death. Norman MacCaig.—HeR

"**After** I got religion and steadied down." See Butch Weldy

"**After** it happened." See Poem for a suicide

"**After** it snows." See Lying on things

After looking into a book belonging to my great-grandfather, Eli Eliakim Plutzik. Hyam Plutzik.—HeR

After many springs. Langston Hughes.—HuDk

After midnight. D. G. (Douglas Gordon) Jones.—DoNw

"**After** my bath." See After a bath

"**After** our moon mother." See From a prayer summoning the novice for his initiation

After rain. Eleanor Farjeon.—FaE

After tea. Eleanor Farjeon.—FaE

After the dentist. May Swenson.—JaD

"**After** the doctor checked to see." See First practice

"**After** the explosion or cataclysm, that big." See The eternal city

"**After** the midnight unfolding of the white rose." See The feast of Stephen

"**After** the palaces." From A nobleman's house. May Sarton.—PlEd

"**After** the rains." N. M. Bodecker.—BoSs

"**After** the snow stopped." See The cardinal

"**After** waiting up." See Midnight

"**After** weeks of watching the roof leak." Gary Snyder.—KeK

Afternoon
    Abracadabra. D. Livesay.—DoNw
    Afternoon on a hill. E. S. Millay.—CoN—HaOf—KoT

Afternoon. Donald Hall.—JaS

Afternoon in Waterloo Park, sels. Gerald Dumas
    "I look at this picture of that old man".—StG
    "Oma was sixty three when I was born".—StG

Afternoon on a hill. Edna St. Vincent Millay.—CoN—HaOf—KoT

Afterthought. Elizabeth Jennings.—HaO

Afterwards. Thomas Hardy.—HeR

"**Aga**." See Aunts and uncles

The **Aga** Khan. Steve Orlen.—JaPi

"**Again**." See Dry spell

Again, good night. Charlotte Zolotow.—ZoE

"**Again** heavy rain drives him home." See Stepfather, a girl's song

"**Again** the belt was off the flywheel." See The musician at his work

"**Again** today." See A valentine birthday

Against idleness. Unknown.—DaC

"**Against** the great darkness looming up armed." See Magic spell for an approaching storm

Age. See Birthdays; Old age; Youth and age

"**Age** may bring wisdom." See Is it nice to be wise

Agincourt, Battle of
    "Now entertain conjecture of a time." W. Shakespeare.—HeR
    "This day is call'd the feast of Crispian." From Henry V. W. Shakespeare.—HoUn

The **aging** poet, on a reading trip to Dayton, visits the Air Force Museum and discovers there a plane he once flew. Richard Snyder.—JaPi

"An **agitation** of the air." See End of summer

"**Agnes** looks through the window." See The home place

Agnes Snaggletooth. X. J. Kennedy.—KeF—LiIl

Agnew, Edith
    Los pastores.—LiCp

Ago. Elizabeth Jennings.—JaG

"**Ah**, a monster's lot is merry." Jack Prelutsky.—PrNk

"**Ah**, did you once see Shelley plain." See Memorabilia

"**Ah** leave my harp and me alone." Unknown.—PlSc

Ah, sunflower. William Blake.—HeR

"**Ah**, sunflower, weary of time." See Ah, sunflower

"**Ah**, the roofs." From Five ghost songs. Unknown.—KoT

"**Ah**, welcome to my chamber." See The cave beast greets a visitor

"**Ahi** viene la luna." See La luna

Aiken, Conrad
    The mandrill.—PrRh
    Who shapes a balustrade.—PlEd

Aiken, Joan
    Air on an escalator.—LiSf
    The ballad of Newington Green.—LiSf
    Do it yourself.—KeK
    Down below.—LiWa
    Fable ("Pity the girl with the crystal hair").—LiWa
    The fisherman writes a letter to the mermaid.—LiWa
    Footprints.—LiSf
    In the old house.—LiWa
    Kyrie Eleison.—LiE

Aiken Drum. Mother Goose.—BlO—BlPi

Air balloons. Eleanor Farjeon.—FaE

"**The air** is like a butterfly." See Easter

Air on an escalator. Joan Aiken.—LiSf

Air raid. Peter Wild.—JaPi

Air traveler. Lillian Morrison.—PrRh

The **airplane**. Rowena Bennett.—FrP

"**The airplane** taxis down the field." See Taking off

Airplanes and aviators
    The aging poet, on a reading trip to Dayton, visits the Air Force Museum and discovers there a plane he once flew. R. Snyder.—JaPi
    Air traveler. L. Morrison.—PrRh
    The airplane. R. Bennett.—FrP
    The biplane. S. Orlen.—JaG
    Darius Green and his flying-machine. J. T. Trowbridge.—HaOf
    The death of the ball turret gunner. R. Jarrell.—HeR
    The dying airman. Unknown.—HeR
    The flying cat. N. S. Nye.—JaT
    "Flying for the first time." E. Merriam.—MeF
    A hikoka in hikoki. C. Pomerantz.—PoI
    Jetstream. L. Moore.—MoSn
    My brother flies over low. D. Huddle.—JaT
    "Night settles on earth." From From an airplane. H. Behn.—HoSs
    "Panic struck flight nine oh nine." X. J. Kennedy.—KeB
    Prayer for the pilot. C. Roberts.—LaT
    "Rickenbacker flew a Spad Thirteen." L. C. Briggs.—TrM
    "See how it circles." From Five ghost songs. Unknown, fr. the Ambo people of Africa.—KoT
    Taking off. Unknown.—HoSu
    To an aviator. D. W. Hicky.—PrRh
    Uncle. H. Graham.—PrRh
    Up in the air. J. S. Tippett.—HoSu
    The world ("I move back by shortcut"). V. Rutsala.—JaPi

"All things bright and beautiful." Cecil Frances Alexander.—DaC—PrRh

All through the night ("Sleep, my babe, lie still and slumber"). Unknown.—DaC

All through the night ("Sleep, my child, and peace attend thee"). Sir Harold Boulton.—ChB

"All tucked in and roasty toasty." Clyde Watson.—LaW—WaC

"All week long I sit in class counting the hours." See Julie Snow

"All winter long I slept below." See Song of the spring peeper

"All winter your brute shoulders strained against collars, padding." See Names of horses

"All work and no play makes Jack a dull boy." Mother Goose.—LoR

"All you Southerners now draw near." See The Battle of Shiloh

The **Allansford** pursuit. Robert Graves.—HeR

Allen, Elizabeth Akers
Rock me to sleep.—HaOf
A toad.—HaOf

Allen, Marie Louise
First snow ("Snow makes whiteness where it falls").—BaS—HoSu—PrRa—PrRh
Five years old.—FrP—PrRa
The mitten song.—CoN—PrRa

Allen, Sarah Van Alstyne
Song for a surf rider.—HoSe

Allen Greshner. Mel Glenn.—GlC

Alley cat school. Frank Asch.—PrRh

An **alley** cat with one life left. Jack Prelutsky.—PrNk

The **alligator**. Mary Macdonald.—PrRh

"The **alligator** chased his tail." See The alligator

Alligator pie. Dennis Lee.—FaW—JaT—PrRh

"**Alligator** pie, alligator pie." See Alligator pie

Alligators
The alligator. M. Macdonald.—PrRh
Alligator pie. D. Lee.—FaW—JaT—PrRh
"Alligators are unfriendly." J. Prelutsky.—PrNk
The careless zookeeper. Unknown.—BrT
Mr. 'Gator. N. M. Bodecker.—CoN—CoOu—FaW—LiSf
The purist. O. Nash.—HaOf

"**Alligators** are unfriendly." Jack Prelutsky.—PrNk

Allingham, William
The fairies ("Up the airy mountain").—BlO—LiWa—PrRh
"Four ducks on a pond."—BlO
A swing song.—FrP

Allman, John
You owe them everything.—PlSc

"**Allow** me just one short remark." See The boa

"**Allthegirlsarebunched**." See Crystal Rowe

Alma-Tadema, Laurence
"If no one ever marries me."—DaC—PrRh—TrM

Almedingen, Edith Martha
Gifts from my grandmother.—StG

"**Almost** every day." See Let's take a nap

"**Almost** reluctant, we approach the block." See Thumbprint

Alone ("Alone is delicious"). Jonathan Holden.—JaPi

Alone ("I was alone the other day"). Dorothy Aldis.—FaW

"**Alone** at the end of green allees, alone." See The statues in the public gardens

"**Alone** is delicious." See Alone

"**Along** a road." See Rain clouds

"**Along** the cement walkway I pick up." See Markings

"**Along** the line of smoky hills." See Indian summer

Along the river. J. D. Enright.—JaD

"**Along** the sea edge, like a gnome." See The sandpiper

"**Along** the wall." See Attic

Alonso, Ricardo
Tiempo muerto.—PlSc

Alphabet
"A, B, C, tumble down D." Mother Goose.—AlH
The A B C bunny. W. Gág.—LiSf
"A was an apple pie." Mother Goose.—LoR
"A was an archer." Unknown.—DaC
AEIOU. J. Swift.—BlO
Alphabet. E. Farjeon.—FaE
Alphabet 1727. From The New England Primer. Unknown.—HaOf
Alphabet stew. J. Prelutsky.—PrRh
An animal alphabet, complete. E. Lear.—HeR
"Apple-pie, pudding and pancake." Mother Goose.—AlH
"As I was crossing Boston Common." N. Farber.—FaW
Beautiful Bella. Unknown.—BrT
A beggarly bear. C. Wells.—BrT
C is for charms. E. Farjeon.—LiWa
Curious Charlie. I. F. Bellows.—BrT
E. P. McGinley.—FrP
G. H. Belloc.—FaW
G is for Gustave. I. F. Bellows.—BrT
"Great A, little a." Mother Goose.—DeM—LoR
A grumbler gruff. O. Herford.—BrT
Halloween ABC. E. Merriam.—MeHa
Ignorant Ida. I. F. Bellows.—BrT
"J's the jumping jay walker." P. McGinley.—PrRh
The letters at school. M. M. Dodge.—HaOf
Naughty young Nat. I. F. Bellows.—BrT
Operatic Olivia. I. F. Bellows.—BrT
An ossified oyster. C. Wells.—BrT
Poet ("At his right hand"). L. Pastan.—JaD
A quoter. O. Herford.—BrT
R. From A bestiary of the garden for children who should know better. P. Gotlieb.—DoNw
S. From A bestiary of the garden for children who should know better. P. Gotlieb.—DoNw
Vowels. A. Rimbaud.—KoT
W ("The wasp's a kind of buzzing cousin"). From A bestiary of the garden for children who should know better. P. Gotlieb.—DoNw
W ("The king sent for his wise men all"). J. Reeves.—CoN—FaW
A well informed wight. O. Herford.—BrT
A wild worm. C. Wells.—BrT
Winter alphabet. E. Merriam.—MeSk
Z. From A bestiary of the garden for children who should know better. P. Gotlieb.—DoNw
Z is for Zoroaster ("How mighty a wizard"). E. Farjeon.—LiWa

Alphabet. Eleanor Farjeon.—FaE

Alphabet 1727. From The New England Primer. Unknown.—HaOf

Alphabet stew. Jack Prelutsky.—PrRh

"**Alphonse** arrives as a fifth season." See A visit from Alphonse

"**Although** he didn't like the taste." Arnold Lobel.—LoWr

"**Although** I conquer all the earth." Unknown.—KoT

"**Although** my father's only child." See Cecilia
"**Always,** I tell you this they learned." See House fear
Always room for one more. Sorche Nic Leodhas.—LiSf
Amanda ("Amanda was an alley cat"). Karla Kuskin.—LiCa
Amanda ("This girl, Amanda"). Ann Turner.—TuS
Amanda Butler. Mel Glenn.—GlCd
"**Amanda** was an alley cat." See Amanda
The **ambiguous** dog. Arthur Guiterman.—HoDl
Ambition
  Ambition. N. P. Willis.—HaOf
  Anna Montalvo. M. Glenn.—GlC
  Application for a grant. A. Hecht.—PlSc
  Basketball star. K. Fufuka.—PrRh
  Donna Vasquez. M. Glenn.—GlC
  Eleanor Paine. M. Glenn.—GlC
  "I love you." C. Sandburg.—HoRa
  Kevin McDonald. M. Glenn.—GlC
  Min Trang. M. Glenn.—GlCd
  Ronnie Evans. M. Glenn.—GlCd
  Sharon Vail and. M. Glenn.—GlCd
  Stuart Rieger. M. Glenn.—GlC
  Tina DeMarco. M. Glenn.—GlC
  What price glory. J. Viorst.—ViI
  What Zimmer would be. P. Zimmer.—JaPi
Ambition. N. P. Willis.—HaOf
"An **ambitious,** and young, Ph.D." See Bad manners
The **ambitious** ant. Amos R. Wells.—HaOf
"The **ambitious** ant would a-travelling go." See The ambitious ant
Ambush. Eleanor Farjeon.—FaE
"**Amelia** mixed the mustard." Alfred Edward Housman.—PrRh
An **American** boyhood. Jonathan Holden.—JaPi
The **American** dilemma. N. M. Bodecker.—BoPc
American Indians. See Indians of the Americas
American revolution. See United States—History—Revolution
Amichai, Yehuda
  A painful love song.—McL
  To carry on living.—McL
Ammons, Archie Randolph
  Bay bank.—JaD
  The eternal city.—PlEd
  Spruce woods.—KeK
  Windy trees.—JaPo
Amoeba. Valerie Worth.—WoSp
Amoebaean for daddy. Maya Angelou.—AnS
Amoebas
  Amoeba. V. Worth.—WoSp
  A microscopic topic. J. Prelutsky.—PrNk
"**Among.**" See The locust tree in flower
Among his effects we found a photograph. Ed Ochester.—JaS
"**Among** the flowers I am moving reverently." See Songs of the corn dance
"**Among** the hills of St Jerome." See At St. Jerome
"**Among** the iodoform, in twilight-sleep." See The leg
Among the millet. Archibald Lampman.—DoNw
Among the narcissi. Sylvia Plath.—HeR
"**Among** the rain." See The great figure
"**Among** the taller wood with ivy hung." See The vixen
"**Among** these North Shore tennis tans I sit." See Commencement, Pingree School
"**Among** twenty snowy mountains." See Thirteen ways of looking at a blackbird
The **amorous** señor. Ogden Nash.—BrT

Amputation
  The amputation. H. Sorrells.—JaD
  The amputee soldier. P. Dacey.—JaG
  Forget about it. R. Currie.—JaS
  The leg. K. Shapiro.—JaD
The **amputation.** Helen Sorrells.—JaD
The **amputee** soldier. Philip Dacey.—JaG
Amtrak. Elliot Fried.—JaPo
Amulet. Ted Hughes.—HuU
Amy Pines. Mel Glenn.—GlC
Analysis of baseball. May Swenson.—KeK
Anambe Indians. See Indians of the Americas—Anambe
Anatomy. See names of parts of the body, as Hands
Ancestry. See also Heritage
  All the colors of the race. A. Adoff.—AdA
  Borders. A. Adoff.—AdA
  Both my grandmothers. E. Field.—JaS
  I am. A. Adoff.—AdA
  "I am making a circle for myself." A. Adoff.—AdA
  "I look at this picture of that old man." From Afternoon in Waterloo Park. G. Dumas.—StG
  "In both the families." A. Adoff.—AdA
  The mendacious mole. O. Herford.—BrT
  Of the race. A. Adoff.—AdA
  Rutherford McDowell. E. L. Masters.—PlEd
  The string of my ancestors. N. Nyhart.—JaS
  Sum people. A. Adoff.—AdA
  There was a man. D. Lee.—KeK
"**Anchises,** Paris, and Adonis too." See Spoken by Venus on seeing her statue done by Praxiteles
"The **ancient** armadillo." See The armadillo
Ancient history. Arthur Guiterman.—HaOf—KeK
"**Ancient** pool." Basho, tr. by Olivia Gray.—KeK
The **ancients** of the world. Ronald Stuart Thomas.—HeR
And although the little mermaid sacrificed everthing to win the love of the prince, the prince, alas, decided to wed another. Judith Viorst.—ViI
"**And** can the physician make sick men well." Unknown.—BlO
"**And** did those feet in ancient time." See Jerusalem
"**And** did you know." See Snowflakes
"**And** every time I pass." See Construction
"**And** God stepped out on space." See The creation, complete
"**And** God stepped out on space." From The creation. James Weldon Johnson.—LaT
"**And** here's the happy, bounding flea." See The flea
"**And** Hiram of Tyre sent his servants unto Solomon, for he had." From Kings. Bible/Old Testament.—PlEd
"**And** I say nothing, no, not a word." See My sister Jane
"**And** I'm thinking how to get out." See History
And in the 51st year of that century, while my brother cried in the trench, while my enemy glared from the cave. Hyam Plutzik.—HeR
"**And** let me the canakin clink, clink." From Othello. William Shakespeare.—PlAs
"**And** my love has come to me." From Verses of the same song. Wendell Berry.—McL
"**And** now the dark comes on, all full of chitter noise." See The sound of night
"**And** now the den, a warm retreat." See Den

"**And** now when the branches were beginning to be heavy." See Bird talk

"**And** oh, the jayour nest did yield." See Day's work a-done

And some more wicked thoughts. Judith Viorst.—ViI

And stands there sighing. Elizabeth Coatsworth.—KeK

And suddenly spring. Margaret Hillert.—HoSi

And the. Prince Redcloud.—BaS

"**And** the days are not full enough." Ezra Pound.—HeR

And the princess was astonished to see the ugly frog turn into a handsome prince. Judith Viorst.—ViI

"**And** the whole earth was of one language, and of one speech." From Genesis. Bible/Old Testament.—PlEd

And then the prince knelt down and tried to put the glass slipper on Cinderella's foot. Judith Viorst.—ViI

"**And** there goes the bell for the third month." See The fight of the year

"**And** there were in the same country shepherds." From Gospel according to Luke. Bible/New Testament.—LiCp

"**And** to think that I saw it on Mulberry Street." Dr. Seuss.—FaW

"**And** when the rain had gone away." See The bug

"**And** you, big rocket." See November the fifth

Anderson, Gordon
The first hunt.—JaPo

Anderson, Marjorie Allen
A new friend.—FrP

Anderson, Mildred Leigh
I can be a tiger.—PrRa

"**Andrew** was an apple thief." Arnold Lobel.—LoWr

"An **angel** came to me." See O simplicitas

"The **angel** that presided o'er my birth." William Blake.—HeR

Angelica the doorkeeper. Unknown, tr. by Anne Pennington.—HeR

Angelino Falco. Mel Glenn.—GlCd

Angelou, Maya
Amoebaean for daddy.—AnS
Arrival.—AnS
Avec merci, mother.—AnS
Awakening in New York.—AnS
Brief innocence.—AnS
Caged birds.—AnS
Changes.—AnS
Contemporary announcement.—AnS
Family affairs.—AnS
A Georgia song.—AnS
A good woman feeling bad.—AnS
The health-food diner.—AnS
Impeccable conception.—AnS
Insomniac.—AnS
The last decision.—AnS
The lie ("Today, you threaten to leave me").—AnS
Martial choreograph.—AnS
My life has turned to blue.—AnS
A plagued journey.—AnS
Prelude to a parting.—AnS
Prescience.—AnS
Recovery.—AnS
Remembering.—JaPo
Shaker, why don't you sing.—AnS
Slave coffle.—AnS
Song for the old ones.—PlSc

Southeast Arkanasia.—PlSc
Starvation.—AnS
To a suitor.—AnS
Unmeasured tempo.—AnS
Weekend glory.—AnS
Woman work.—PlSc

Angels
"And there were in the same country shepherds." From Gospel according to Luke. Bible/New Testament.—LiCp
"The angel that presided o'er my birth." W. Blake.—HeR
Angel's song. C. Causley.—HaO
Arrival. M. Angelou.—AnS
Early morning. P. Dow.—JaD
Father Gilligan. W. B. Yeats.—PlAs
"Matthew, Mark, Luke and John, bless the bed that I lie on." Mother Goose.—DaC—DeM
Questions for an angel. From A throw of threes. E. Merriam.—MeF
Tom's angel. W. De la Mare.—PlAs
Witness. E. Merriam.—MeSk

"**Angels** gather." See Arrival

Angel's song. Charles Causley.—HaO

Anger
"Anger lay by me all night long." E. Daryush.—HeR
An angry valentine. M. C. Livingston.—LiVp
Aunt Julia. N. MacCaig.—HeR
"Do not go gentle into that good night." D. Thomas.—HeR
Franz Dominguez. M. Glenn.—GlC
"I wonder why Dad is so thoroughly mad." J. Prelutsky.—PrNk
Listening to grownups quarreling. R. Whitman.—CoN—KeK
Mean song. E. Merriam.—LiSf
A poison tree. W. Blake.—HeR
Spray. D. H. Lawrence.—PrBb
Spring storm ("He comes gusting out of the house"). J. W. Miller.—JaG
Strike me pink. E. Merriam.—MeF
Sulk. F. Holman.—PrRh
"There was an old person of Bangor." E. Lear.—LiH
"Trouble, oh trouble." A. Lobel.—LoWr

"**Anger** lay by me all night long." Elizabeth Daryush.—HeR

Anglund, Joan Walsh
Ladybug ("A small speckled visitor").—PrRh
"We built a castle near the rocks."—PrRa

"**Anguilla**, Adina." See A sea-chantey

An **animal** alphabet, complete. Edward Lear.—HeR

An **animal** alphabet, sels. Edward Lear
"The fizzgiggious fish".—LiH
"The judicious jubilant jay".—LiH
"The melodious meritorious mouse".—LiH
"The rural runcible raven".—LiH
"The scroobious snake".—LiH
"The tumultuous tom-tommy tortoise".—LiH
"The umbrageous umbrella maker".—LiH
"The worrying whizzing wasp".—LiH
"The zigzag zealous zebra".—LiH

Animal crackers. Christopher Morley.—FrP

"**Animal** crackers, and cocoa to drink." See Animal crackers

The **animal** fair. Unknown.—CoN—PrRh

The **animal** store. Rachel Field.—LiSf

Annar-Mariar's Christmas shopping. Eleanor Farjeon.—FaE

"**Anne** says she dreams sometimes, and so do I." See Silent hill

"**Anne** told Beth." See Secrets

Annie Scarella. Mel Glenn.—GlC

The **anniversary**. William Dickey.—JaG

"**Annoying** Miss Tillie McLush." See Miss Tillie McLush

Ann's house. Dick Lourie.—JaD

Anonymous drawing. Donald Justice.—PlEd

Another epitaph on an army of mercenaries. Hugh MacDiarmid.—HeR

"**Another** nickel in the slot." See A hero in the land of dough

"**Another** road, it seems sometimes." See The idiot

Another Sarah. Anne Porter.—KoT

Answer to a child's question. Samuel Taylor Coleridge.—BlO

Answers. Aileen Fisher.—LiSf

Ant ("An ant works hard"). X. J. Kennedy.—KeF

Ant-hills. Marian Douglas.—HaOf

"An **ant** on the tablecloth." See Departmental

"An **ant** works hard." See Ant

The **anteater** ("An anteater can't eat a thing but an ant"). Jack Prelutsky.—PrSr

Anteater ("Imagine overturning"). Valerie Worth.—WoSp

"An **anteater** can't eat a thing but an ant." See The anteater

Anteaters
The anteater ("An anteater can't eat a thing but an ant"). J. Prelutsky.—PrSr
Anteater ("Imagine overturning"). V. Worth.—WoSp

Antelopes
The gazelle calf. D. H. Lawrence.—HeR
Kob antelope. Unknown.—HeR

Anthony, Edward
Advice to small children.—PrRh
Let others share.—PrRh

Anthony. Jane Shore.—JaD

Anticipations. From A throw of threes. Eve Merriam.—MeF

Antonio. Laura E. Richards.—BrT—HaOf—PrRh

"**Antonio**, Antonio." See Antonio

Antony and Cleopatra, sels. William Shakespeare
"The barge she sat in, like a burnish'd throne".—HoUn
"Come, thou monarch of the vine".—HoUn

Ants
A. From A bestiary of the garden for children who should know better. P. Gotlieb.—DoNw
The ambitious ant. A. R. Wells.—HaOf
Ant ("An ant works hard"). X. J. Kennedy.—KeF
Ant-hills. M. Douglas.—HaOf
Anteater ("Imagine overturning"). V. Worth.—WoSp
Ants. M. A. Hoberman.—PrRa
Ants, although admirable, are awfully aggravating. W. R. Brooks.—PrRh
The ants at the olympics. R. Digance.—PrRh
"Ants live here." L. Moore.—PrRa
The carpenter rages. J. Prelutsky.—PrNk
Departmental. R. Frost.—KoS
The humorous ant. O. Herford.—BrT

Ants. Mary Ann Hoberman.—PrRa

Ants, although admirable, are awfully aggravating. Walter R. Brooks.—PrRh

"The **ants** are walking under the ground." See The people

The **ants** at the olympics. Richard Digance.—PrRh

"**Ants** live here." Lilian Moore.—PrRa

"**Ants** look up as I trot by." See Dog's song

"**Anyone** could hunt the old dog." See The one to grieve

"**Anyone** lived in a pretty how town." Edward Estlin Cummings.—HeR

"**Anyone** with quiet pace who." See Walking west

Ap Gwilym, Dafydd
The rattle bag.—HeR

Apache Indians. See Indians of the Americas—Apache

"**Apartment** houses, as a rule." See Vestibule

Apartments and apartment life. See also Cities and city life; Houses and dwellings
Gift with the wrappings off. M. E. Counselman.—PrRh
The people upstairs. O. Nash.—PrRh
A sad song about Greenwich Village. F. Park.—PrRh
Zebra ("White sun"). J. Thurman.—PrRh

Apes and monkeys
"All around the cobbler's bench." Mother Goose.—LoR
Autumn cove. Li Po.—KoT
Baboon. Unknown.—HeR
Before the monkey's cage. E. Becker.—PrRa
Colobus monkey. Unknown.—HeR
"I went up one pair of stairs." Mother Goose.—DeM—LoR
The kept secret. Unknown.—BrT
"Look at all those monkeys." S. Milligan.—CoOu
The mandrill. C. Aiken.—PrRh
The monkey puzzle. M. C. Livingston.—LiMp
Monkeyland. S. Weöres.—HeR
The prayer of the monkey. C. B. de Gasztold.—LaT
Red monkey. Unknown.—HeR
The surgeon and the ape. Unknown.—BrT
"When you talk to a monkey." R. Bennett.—PrRa

"**Apes**, may I speak to you a moment." See Is wisdom a lot of language

Apollinaire, Guillaume
Heart crown and mirror.—KoT
It's raining.—KoT

Apology ("It's hard to say I'm sorry"). Judith Viorst.—ViI

Apology ("A word sticks in the wind's throat"). Richard Wilbur.—JaPi

The **apparition**. Theodore Roethke.—PlAs

Apple ("At the center, a dark star"). Nan Fry.—JaPo

The **apple**. Bruce Guernsey.—JaPo

"**Apple**." Eve Merriam.—MeHa

An **apple** a day ("I must eat an apple, said Link"). Lee Blair.—BrT

"An **apple** a day." Mother Goose.—LoR

Apple blossom. Louis MacNeice.—HeR

"**Apple** in the morning." Mother Goose.—LoR

Apple joys. From A throw of threes. Eve Merriam.—MeF

Apple pie. Ivy O. Eastwick.—HoMu

"**Apple-pie**, pudding and pancake." Mother Goose.—AlH

The **apple** tree. Charlotte Zolotow.—ZoE

Apple trees
Another Sarah. A. Porter.—KoT
Apple blossom. L. MacNeice.—HeR

Apple trees—*Continued*
The apple tree. C. Zolotow.—ZoE
Dancer. R. Scheele.—JaG
"Dear, dear, what can the matter be." Mother Goose.—DeM
He was. R. Wilbur.—PlSc
"Here's to thee." Unknown.—BlO
New Hampshire. From Landscapes. T. S. Eliot.—HeR
Patriarchs. L. Moore.—MoSn
Pick your own. X. J. Kennedy.—KeF
St. Paul's steeple. Unknown.—DaC
"Up in the green orchard there is a green tree." Mother Goose.—LoR
Windfalls. E. Farjeon.—FaE
"The **Apple** Valley School has closed its books." See Country school
Apples. See also Apple trees
"Apple." E. Merriam.—MeHa
Apple ("At the center, a dark star"). N. Fry.—JaPo
The apple. B. Guernsey.—JaPo
"An apple a day." Mother Goose.—LoR
An apple a day ("I must eat an apple, said Link"). L. Blair.—BrT
"Apple in the morning." Mother Goose.—LoR
Apple joys. From A throw of threes. E. Merriam.—MeF
Apple pie. I. O. Eastwick.—HoMu
Cider inside her. Unknown.—BrT
Crabapples. C. Sandburg.—HoRa
"Eat an apple going to bed." Mother Goose.—LoR
A kitchen memory. R. Scheele.—JaS
Pick your own. X. J. Kennedy.—KeF
"Roast apple at night." Mother Goose.—LoR
Application for a grant. Anthony Hecht.—PlSc
The **approach** of the storm. Unknown.—KoT
April
April ("Rain is good"). L. Clifton.—HoSi—PrRa
April ("The young cherry trees"). L. Pastan.—JaPi
April rain song. L. Hughes.—CoN—HaOf—HuDk—LiSf—PrRh
"April weather." Mother Goose.—LoR
Canticle of spring. H. Behn.—HoCb
Crows ("So, nine crows to this April field"). P. Booth.—JaD
Heigh ho April. E. Farjeon.—FaE
"March winds and April showers." Mother Goose.—DaC—DeM
Morning ("The April day"). B. J. Esbensen.—EsCs
Spring storm ("Our old fat tiger cat"). X. J. Kennedy.—KeF
April ("Rain is good"). Lucille Clifton.—HoSi—PrRa
April ("The young cherry trees"). Linda Pastan.—JaPi
"The **April** day." See Morning
April fool. Myra Cohn Livingston.—LiCe
April Fool's Day
April fool. M. C. Livingston.—LiCe
Oh have you heard. S. Silverstein.—LiSf
April rain song. Langston Hughes.—CoN—HaOf—HuDk—LiSf—PrRh
"**April** weather." Mother Goose.—LoR
Arapaho Indians. See Indians of the Americas—Arapaho
"**Arbuckle** Jones." Peter Wesley-Smith.—JaT
The **archer.** Eleanor Farjeon.—FaE
Archers and archery. See also Bows and arrows
The archer. E. Farjeon.—FaE

"To become an archer." Lao Tse.—KeK
Archie B. McCall. Jack Prelutsky.—PrNk
Architect. Louise Townsend Nicholl.—PlEd
Architectural masks. Thomas Hardy.—PlEd
The **arctic** fox. Ted Hughes.—HuU
"The **Arctic** moon hangs overhead." See The wolf cry
"**Are** round and soft." See Barbara poems
"**Are** you asleep yet." See Questions
"**Are** you going to Whittingham Fair." See Whittingham Fair
Arekuna Indians. See Indians of the Americas—Arekuna
"**Aren't** you coming out, Mary." See Mary indoors
Arf, said Sandy. Charles Stetler.—JaPo
Argument. Eve Merriam.—MeSk
The **argument** of his book. Robert Herrick.—KoT
Arguments
Argument. E. Merriam.—MeSk
"Belly and Tubs went out in a boat." C. Watson.—PrRa
The blind men and the elephant. J. G. Saxe.—CoOu—HaOf
Gail Larkin. M. Glenn.—GlC
"Molly, my sister, and I fell out." Mother Goose.—DeM
"Mollie, my sister, and I fell out".—LoR
Never mince words with a shark. J. Prelutsky.—PrNk
Ariel's song. See "Full fathom five thy father lies"
Arikara Indians. See Indians of the Americas—Arikara
Arithmetic. See Mathematics
Arithmetic ("Arithmetic is where numbers fly like pigeons in and out of your head"). Carl Sandburg.—HoRa—LiSf—PrRh
Arithmetic ("Multiplication is vexation"). Unknown.—DaC
"**Arithmetic** is where numbers fly like pigeons in and out of your head." See Arithmetic
Arlene Lasky. Mel Glenn.—GlCd
Arm wrestling with my father. Jack Driscoll.—JaG
The **armadillo.** Jack Prelutsky.—PrZ
Armadillos
The armadillo. J. Prelutsky.—PrZ
Armor. See also Weapons
Armour, Richard
Good sportsmanship.—KeK
Arms. See Weapons
Arnold, Matthew
The forsaken merman.—BlO
"**Around** now." See Easter habits
Around the corner. From Forgotten girlhood. Laura Riding.—HeR
"**Around** the gleaming map of Europe." See Autobahnmotorwayautoroute
Around the kitchen table. Gary Gildner.—JaS
"**Around** the kitchen table we are never out." See Around the kitchen table
The **arrest** of Oscar Wilde at the Cadogan Hotel. Sir John Betjeman.—PlAs
Arrival. Maya Angelou.—AnS
The **arrival** of my mother. Keith Wilson.—JaD
Arrows. See Bows and arrows
Arson. Lilian Moore.—MoSn
Art. Herman Melville.—PlEd
Art and artists. See also Beauty, of nature or art; Painting and pictures
Art. H. Melville.—PlEd
Bridges and tunnels. B. Bentley.—PlEd
The Chicago Picasso. G. Brooks.—PlEd

Art and artists.—*Continued*

Death-bed reflections of Michelangelo. H. Coleridge.—PlEd

Epiphany, for the artist. E. Sewell.—PlEd

Epitaph on an unfortunate artist. R. Graves.—TrM

For the young who want to. M. Piercy.—JaPi

George. N. Giovanni.—GiSp

Heart crown and mirror. G. Apollinaire.—KoT

In galleries. R. Jarrell.—PlEd

The lion for real. A. Ginsberg.—HeR

Looking at quilts. M. Piercy.—PlSc

"The martyr poets, did not tell." E. Dickinson.—PlEd

Nancy Soto. M. Glenn.—GlC

The National Gallery. L. MacNeice.—PlEd

On the bust of Helen by Canova. Lord Byron.—PlEd

The paint box. E. V. Rieu.—PrRh

Poem to Franz Kline. F. O'Hara.—McL

Portrait by Alice Neel. A. Kramer.—PlEd

Portrait of the boy as artist. B. Howes.—JaD

To an artist. R. Burns.—PlEd

Vincent Van Gogh. W. J. Smith.—PlEd

When I buy pictures. M. Moore.—PlEd

Art class. X. J. Kennedy.—KeF

"Art thou pale for weariness." See To the moon

"Art thou poor, yet hast thou golden slumbers." See The happy heart

Art work. Ronald Wallace.—JaPo

Artic regions. See Polar regions

"An **artichoke.**" See Artichoke

Artichoke ("An artichoke"). Maxine Kumin.—HoMu

Artichoke ("Leaf"). Eve Merriam.—MeF

Artichokes

Artichoke ("An artichoke"). M. Kumin.—HoMu

Artichoke ("Leaf"). E. Merriam.—MeF

The **artist.** William Carlos Williams.—HeR

Artists. See Art and artists

Arullo. Unknown.—GrT

"As / big / as." See Balloon

"As a friend to the children commend me the Yak." See The yak

"As a head only, I roll around." See Dream songs

"As a rule." See Wanting

"As a sloop with a sweep of immaculate wing on her." See Buick

"As a white stone draws down the fish." See Behavior of fish in an English tea garden

"As fine a piece of furniture." See Central

"As free as a bird." See The cormorant's tale

"As from an ancestral oak." See Similes for two political characters of 1819

"As gardens grow with flowers." See English

"As I came in by Fiddich-side." Unknown.—HeR

"As I came to the edge of the woods." See Come in

As I grew older. Langston Hughes.—HuDk

"As I in hoary winter's night stood shivering in the snow." See The burning babe

"As I lay asleep in Italy." From The mask of anarchy. Percy Bysshe Shelley.—HeR

"As I lay, fullness of praise." See The rattle bag

"As I lie in bed I hear." See Winter night

"As I picked it up." Unknown, tr. by Peter Beilenson.—FaTh

"As I roved out on a May morning." See Johnny's the lad I love

"As I sat in the gloaming." See The voice

"As I sat on a sunny bank." Mother Goose.—DeM

"As I see them now and then." See Mardi Gras

"As I seize the ladder by its shoulder." See Remembering my father

"As I walked on the hills of Kerry." See The Kerry loon

"As I walked out in the streets of Laredo." See The streets of Laredo See The streets of Laredo ("As I walked out in the streets of Laredo")

"As I walked out one evening." Wystan Hugh Auden.—HeR—PlAs

"As I walked out one morning for pleasure." See Whoopee ti yi yo, git along little dogies

"As I walked over London Bridge." See Georgie

"As I was a-hoeing, a-hoeing my lands." See The six badgers

"As I was a-walking." See The pretty ploughboy

"As I was crossing Boston Common." Norma Farber.—FaW

"As I was fishing off Pondy Point." See Jim Desterland

"As I was going by Charing Cross." Mother Goose.—BlO

"As I was going out one day." Mother Goose.—LoR

"As I was going to Banbury." Mother Goose.—DeM

"As I was going to St. Ives." Mother Goose.—CoN—DeM—LoR

"As I was going to sell my eggs." Mother Goose.—DaC—LoR

"As I was going up Long Green Hill." See Long Green Hill

"As I was going up Pippen Hill." Mother Goose.—AlH—LoR

"As I was going up Pippin Hill".—BlO

"As I was going up Pippin Hill". See "As I was going up Pippen Hill"

"As I was going up the stair." See The little man

"As I was laying on the green." Unknown.—TrM

"As I was sitting in my chair." See The perfect reactionary

"As I was standing in the street." Unknown.—CoN—FaW

"As I was wa'king all alone." See The wee wee man

"As I was walking all alane." See The twa corbies

"As I was walking along-long-long." See Singing in the spring

"As I was walking down the lake." Unknown.—DaC

"As I was walking up the stair." See The little man

"As I watch the snow fall." See Contrast

"As I went out a crow." See The last word of a bluebird (as told to a child)

"As I went walking one fine Sunday." See Coati-mundi

As if you had never been. Richard Eberhart.—PlEd

"As in a thunderstorm at night." See Waiting

"As in old/mummy-times." See Beetle

"As it wanders." See The little brown celery

"As kingfishers catch fire, dragonflies draw flame." Gerard Manley Hopkins.—HeR

"As long as I live." See Me

"As May was opening the rosebuds." See Birth of the foal

As much as you can. Constantine P. Cavafy, tr. by Edmund Keeley and Philip Sherrard.—HeR

"As round as an apple, as deep as a cup."
  Mother Goose.—LiSf
"As the cat." See Poem
"As the days grow longer." Mother Goose.—LoR
"As the sun came up, a ball of red." Unknown,
  tr. by Robert Wyndham.—LiIl
"As the team's head-brass flashed out on the
  turn." Edward Thomas.—HeR
"As Tommy Snooks and Bessy Brooks." Mother
  Goose.—DeM—FaW—LoR
"As wishing all about us sweet." See On St.
  Winefred
"As you came from the holy land." Sir Walter
  Raleigh.—HeR
As you like it, sels. William Shakespeare
  "All the world's a stage".—HeR—HoUn
  "Blow, blow, thou winter wind".—HoUn
  "It was a lover and his lass".—HeR—HoUn—
    KoT
  "Under the greenwood tree".—HoUn—KoT—
    LiSf
The ascension, 1925. John Malcolm Brinnin.—JaS
Asch, Frank
  Alley cat school.—PrRh
  Leaves ("My green leaves are more
    beautiful").—CoN
  Play.—CoN
  The sugar lady.—PrRh
  Summer.—CoN—PrRh
  Sunflakes.—CoN
  Sunrise.—ChG—PrRh
Ashbery, John
  Meditations of a parrot.—KoT
  The thinnest shadow.—KoT
"Ashen man on ashen cliff above the salt halloo."
  See Statue against a clear sky
Ashes. Vasco Popa, tr. by Anne Pennington.—
  HeR
"Asleep he wheezes at his ease." See Roger the
  dog
Asparagus. Valerie Worth.—WoSp
"The aspens glisten." See Spring again
Aspiration. See Ambition
Asquith, Herbert
  The hairy dog.—PrRh
Asses. See Donkeys
"The Assyrian came down like the wolf on the
  fold." See The destruction of Sennacherib
Astronomy. See also Moon; Planets; Stars; Sun;
  Tides
  Dandelion ("Out of / green space"). V.
    Worth.—WoSp
  A marvel. C. Wells.—HaOf
  The universe ("There is the moon, there is the
    sun"). M. B. Miller.—PrRh
  Universe ("The universe is all the skies"). E.
    Farjeon.—FaE
  "When I heard the learn'd astronomer." W.
    Whitman.—LiSf
At a low mass for two hot rodders. X. J.
  Kennedy.—JaPi
At a modernist school. Morris Bishop.—BrT
"At a modernist school in Park Hill." See At a
  modernist school
At Annika's place. Siv Widerberg, tr. by Verne
  Moberg.—CoN
"At Autumn Cove, so many white monkeys." See
  Autumn cove
"At breakfast." See On certain mornings
  everything is sensual
At Candlemas. Charles Causley.—HaO

"At Christmas, when old friends are meeting." See
  Good will to men
"At dawn she lay with her profile at that angle."
  See Daybreak
"At de feet o' Jesus." See Feet o' Jesus
"At dusk the first stars appear." See Stars
"At dusk there are swallows." See Dusk
"At early morn the spiders spin." Mother
  Goose.—LoR
"At Easter dawn." See Kyrie Eleison
"At Easter wild grass is left to grow." See Easter,
  for Penny
"At evening when the lamp is lit." See The land
  of story books
"At first I thought it was the moon." See Night
  game
"At first light." See Bird theater
"At first light the finches." See Dawn
"At fourteen I went regularly to Beaver Baptist."
  See Saved
"At Gettysburg full anonymity." See Yugoslav
  cemetery
At grandfather's. Clara Boty Bates.—HaOf
At grass. Philip Larkin.—HeR
At Hannukah. Myra Cohn Livingston.—LiSf
"At Henry's market you could charge things." See
  Henry's market
"At his incipient sun." See First love
"At his right hand." See Poet
"At home at Annika's place." See At Annika's
  place
"At last I know a very good way." See Elves
  and goblins
"At last year's jungle olympics." See The ants at
  the olympics
"At least at night, a streetlight." See So long
"At low tide like this how sheer the water is."
  See The bight, on my birthday
"At mid-day then along the lane." See Old Jack
  Noman
At mid ocean. Robert Bly.—McL
At midnight. Ted Kooser.—JaG
At night ("In the dust are my father's beautiful
  hands"). Richard Eberhart.—JaS
At night ("When I am outdoors and begin"). John
  Ciardi.—CiD
At night ("When I go to bed at night"). Anne
  Blackwell Payne.—ChB
At night ("When night is dark"). Aileen Fisher.—
  LiSf—PrRa
"At night when grownups start to yawn." See
  How to stay up late
"At 9:42 on this May morning." See A house of
  readers
"At noon in the desert a panting lizard." See At
  the bomb testing site
At St. Jerome. Frances Harrison.—DoNw
"At sea in the dome of St. Paul's." See Homage
  to Wren
"At seven, on the dock next door." See In the
  shadows of early sunlight
At sunrise. N. M. Bodecker.—BoPc
"At sunset, when the night-dews fall." See The
  snail
At the Algonquin. Howard Moss.—JaPi
At the beach ("First I walked"). Sandra Liatsos.—
  HoSe
At the beach ("Johnny, Johnny, let go of that
  crab"). John Ciardi.—CiD
At the bomb testing site. William Stafford.—HeR
"At the center, a dark star." See Apple
"At the edge of tide." See The sandpiper

At the first Thanksgiving. X. J. Kennedy.—LiTp
"At the foot of the hill, the ice cream truck."
    See Doing a good deed
At the funeral of great aunt Mary. Robert Bly.—
    JaS
At the garden gate. David McCord.—LiIl
At the grave of my brother. William Stafford.—
    JaS
"At the grey round of the hill." See The dreaming
    of the bones
At the keyhole. Walter De la Mare.—BlO
"At the laundromat Liz Meyer." X. J. Kennedy.—
    KeB
"At the meeting." Arnold Adoff.—AdA
At the museum. John Malcolm Brinnin.—PlEd
"At the party honoring my father." See Jennie
    Tang
At the pool. Barbara Juster Esbensen.—EsCs
"At the rock club where I hang out." See Candie
    Brewer
At the St. Louis Institute of Music. Ronald
    Wallace.—JaG
"At the screen door." See Mrs. Green
At the sea-side. Robert Louis Stevenson.—CoN—
    FaW
At the table. Constance Andrea Keremes.—HoMu
"At the tennis court, Paul Pest." X. J.
    Kennedy.—KeB
At the top of my voice. Felice Holman.—HoSu
At the woodpile. Raymond Henri.—PlSc
At the zoo ("First I saw the white bear"). William
    Makepeace Thackeray.—CoN
At the zoo ("There are lions and roaring tigers,
    and enormous camels and things"). Alan
    Alexander Milne.—FrP
"At whim of winds." See Monterey cypress, Point
    Lobos
"At winter's end." See Snowman sniffles
"At Woodlawn I heard the dead cry." See The
    flight
Atharva Veda, sels. Unknown, tr. by A. A.
    MacDonnell
    An imprecation against foes and sorcerers.—
        LiWa
"An athlete, one vacation." See An
    accommodating lion
Athletes and athletics. See also names of sports,
    as Baseball
    The ants at the olympics. R. Digance.—PrRh
    Baseball. F. D. Sherman.—HaOf
    Crystal Rowe. M. Glenn.—GlCd
    In memory of the Utah stars. W. Matthews.—
        JaPi
    Jose Cruz. M. Glenn.—GlCd
Atomic age
    At the bomb testing site. W. Stafford.—HeR
    The horses. E. Muir.—HeR
    Ian Sinclair. M. Glenn.—GlCd
    A post-mortem. S. Sassoon.—JaD
    Relativity. D. H. Lawrence.—PrBb
    The third thing. D. H. Lawrence.—PrBb
Atoms. See Atomic age
Atop. Prince Redcloud.—HoBf
An atrocious pun. Unknown.—BrT—PrRh
"Attention, architect." See Message from a mouse,
    ascending in a rocket
Attic. Sylvia Cassedy.—CaR
Attics
    Attic. S. Cassedy.—CaR
    Ode to a dressmaker's dummy. D. Justice.—
        JaD

"Up in the attic there's a great big trunk." E.
    Merriam.—MeBl
Auctioneer. Carl Sandburg.—HoRa
Auden, Wystan Hugh
    "As I walked out one evening."—HeR—PlAs
    "Carry her over the water."—HeR
    Epitaph on a tyrant.—HeR
    For the time being, sels.
        "Well, so that is that, now we must
            dismantle the tree".—HaO
    "From gallery grave and the hunt of a wren
        king." See Thanksgiving for a habitat
    Horae Canonicae, sels.
        Sext.—PlSc
    I am not a camera.—PlEd
    "I cannot grow."—HeR
    "Lady, weeping at the crossroads."—PlAs
    Lullaby ("Lay your sleeping head, my love").—
        McL
    O, what is that sound.—PlAs
    Sext. See Horae Canonicae
    Song of the ogres.—PrRh
    "Stop all the clocks, cut off the telephone."—
        HeR
    Thanksgiving for a habitat, sels.
        "From gallery grave and the hunt of a wren
            king".—PlEd
    "This lunar beauty."—HeR
    The wanderer.—HeR
    "Well, so that is that, now we must dismantle
        the tree." See For the time being
Auguries of innocence, complete. William Blake.—
    HeR
Auguries of innocence, sels. William Blake
    "To see a world in a grain of sand".—PrRh
        To see a world.—KeK
August
    August ("Deep in the wood I made a house").
        K. Pyle.—HaOf
    August ("The sprinkler twirls"). J. Updike.—
        HaOf—PrRh
    August heat. Unknown.—HoSi—PrRa
    August 28. D. McCord.—HoSi—McAs
    Bats ("Versa says"). M. C. Livingston.—LiWo
    In August. M. Chute.—HoSu
    "My birthday's in August." J. Prelutsky.—PrWi
    On an August day. L. B. Hopkins.—HoSe
    Too hot. J. Prelutsky.—PrWi
August ("Deep in the wood I made a house").
    Katharine Pyle.—HaOf
August ("In waves of heat"). Roy Scheele.—JaPo
August ("The sprinkler twirls"). John Updike.—
    HaOf—PrRh
August heat. Unknown.—HoSi—PrRa
"August sun hangs low above the city." See
    Return
August 28. David McCord.—HoSi—McAs
"Augustus was a chubby lad." See The story of
    Augustus who would not have any soup
Auks
    The great auk's ghost. R. Hodgson.—KeK—
        PrRh
"Aunt Elsie hears." See Aunt Elsie's night music
Aunt Elsie's night music. Mary Oliver.—JaS
Aunt Evelyn. Myra Cohn Livingston.—LiWo
Aunt Flora (envoi). Myra Cohn Livingston.—
    LiWo
Aunt Gladys's home movie no. 31, Albert's
    funeral. Jim Wayne Miller.—JaS
Aunt Julia. Norman MacCaig.—HeR
"Aunt Julia spoke Gaelic." See Aunt Julia
Aunt Leaf. Mary Oliver.—JaT
Aunt Melissa. R. T. Smith.—JaS

B

Babies.—*Continued*
Dahn the plug 'ole. Unknown.—HeR
The first tooth. C. Lamb, and M. Lamb.—
    DaC—PrRh
"Hang up the baby's stocking." Unknown.—
    HaO
The inquest. W. H. Davies.—HeR
It really wasn't too bad. J. Ciardi.—CiD
"Johnnie Crack and Flossie Snail." From Under
    Milk Wood. D. Thomas.—LiSf—PrRh
Mothers. A. Sexton.—JaS
My baby brother. J. Prelutsky.—PrNk
My brother. M. Ridlon.—PrRh
On a child who lived one minute. X. J.
    Kennedy.—JaD
Peregrine White and Virginia Dare. S. V. Benét,
    and R. C. Benét.—HaOf
Poem for Ntombe Iayo (at five weeks of age).
    N. Giovanni.—GiSp
Six weeks old. C. Morley.—PrRh
Some things don't make any sense at all. J.
    Viorst.—PrRh—ViI
"There was a young pig by a cradle." A.
    Lobel.—LoB
Thumbs. S. Silverstein.—FaTh
Two sisters looking at baby brother. A. Barto.—
    FaW
"Where did you come from, baby dear." G.
    MacDonald.—DaC
"Where should a baby rest." Mother Goose.—
    BaH
Baboon. Unknown, tr. by Ulli Beier.—HeR
Baboons. See Apes and monkeys
Baby. Langston Hughes.—HuDk
"**Baby** and I." Mother Goose.—AlH
"A **baby** sardine." Spike Milligan.—CoOu
"**Baby,** sleep, sleep, sleep." See Lullaby
Baby song. Thom Gunn.—HeR
Baby stands. Eleanor Farjeon.—FaE
"**Baby** swimming down the river." See Lullaby
Baby talk. Anna Bird Stewart.—PrRh
"The **baby** uggs are hatching." Jack Prelutsky.—
    PrB
Baby's baking. Evaleen Stein.—PrRa
Baby's drinking song. James Kirkup.—CoN
Babysitters
    Holiness. C. Rylant.—RyW
    Miss Bitter. N. M. Bodecker.—CoN
"The **bachelor** growls when his peace is." See A
    token of attachment
Back country. Joyce Carol Oates.—JaPi
Back from the word processing course, I say to
    my old typewriter. Michael Blumenthal.—JaG
"**Back** in a melon pink." See Great-grandma
"**Back** to back, stud poker and an open." See
    Twin aces
Back to school. Aileen Fisher.—LiSf
Back yard, July night. William Cole.—KeK
"**Backpacking** Max." See The hiker
"**Backward,** turn backward, O time, in your
    flight." See Rock me to sleep
A **backwards** journey. Patricia K. Page.—DoNw
Bacmeister, Rhoda W.
    Galoshes.—CoN
    Icy.—PrRa
    Stars ("Bright stars, light stars").—FrP
    Under the ground.—PrRa
Bad and good. Alexander Resnikoff.—CoN
Bad day. Marci Ridlon.—HoBf
Bad guys. Arnold Adoff.—AdA
The **bad** kittens. Elizabeth Coatsworth.—HaOf
Bad manners. Unknown.—BrT
The **badger.** John Clare.—HeR

"The **badger** grunting on his woodland track." See
    The badger
Badgers
    The badger. J. Clare.—HeR
    The combe. E. Thomas.—HeR
    The six badgers. R. Graves.—LiSf—LiWa
    Walking west. W. Stafford.—HeR
    "White is my neck, head yellow, sides." From
        Three riddles from the Exeter book.
        Unknown.—HeR
Bagpipe music. Louis MacNeice.—HeR
Bags of meat. Thomas Hardy.—HeR
The **bailiff's** daughter of Islington. Unknown.—
    PlAs
The **baite.** John Donne.—HeR
Baker, Barbara
    A spike of green.—PrRa
Baker, Carlos
    A Chinese mural. See A visit to the art gallery
    On a landscape of Sestos. See A visit to the
        art gallery
    A visit to the art gallery, sels.
        A Chinese mural.—PlEd
        On a landscape of Sestos.—PlEd
Bakers and baking
    Baby's baking. E. Stein.—PrRa
    Baking day. R. Joseph.—JaS
    "Blow, wind, blow." Mother Goose.—DeM—
        LoR
    The loaves. R. Everson.—JaT
    "The moon's the north wind's cooky." V.
        Lindsay.—CoN—HaOf—LaW—LiSf—PrRa—PrRh
    "Pat-a-cake, pat-a-cake, baker's man." Mother
        Goose.—DeM—LoR—RaT
    Raisin bread. L. Blair.—BrT
    Yeast. E. Merriam.—MeHa
A **baker's** dozen of wild beasts, sels. Carolyn
    Wells
    The bath-bunny.—HaOf
    The corn-pone-y.—HaOf
    The cream-puffin.—HaOf
    The mince-python.—HaOf
Baking day. Rosemary Joseph.—JaS
Balada de la loca fortuna. Enrique Gonzales
    Martinez.—LiSf
Bald cypress. Myra Cohn Livingston.—LiMp
Ball, John
    When Adam delved, at. to.—PlSc
Ballad. John Hall Wheelock.—PlAs
A **ballad** maker. Padraic Colum.—PlAs
Ballad of a boneless chicken. Jack Prelutsky.—
    PrNk
The **ballad** of Befana. Phyllis McGinley.—PlAs
A **ballad** of Christmas. Walter De la Mare.—HaO
The **ballad** of mad fortune. Enrique Gonzales
    Martinez, tr. by Edna Worthley
    Underwood.—LiSf
The **ballad** of Newington Green. Joan Aiken.—
    LiSf
The **ballad** of Rudolph Reed. Gwendolyn
    Brooks.—HeR
The **ballad** of Semmerwater. William Watson.—
    BlO
Ballad of the bread man. Charles Causley.—HeR
The **ballad** of the harp-weaver. Edna St. Vincent
    Millay.—LiSf—LiWa
Ballad of the man who's gone. Langston
    Hughes.—PlAs
Ballad of the morning streets. Amiri Baraka.—
    KoT

Ballads

"As I walked out one evening." W. H. Auden.—HeR—PlAs

Balada de la loca fortuna. E. Gonzales Martinez.—LiSf

Ballad. J. H. Wheelock.—PlAs

A ballad maker. P. Colum.—PlAs

Ballad of a boneless chicken. J. Prelutsky.—PrNk

The ballad of Befana. P. McGinley.—PlAs

A ballad of Christmas. W. De la Mare.—HaO

The ballad of mad fortune. E. Gonzales Martinez.—LiSf

The ballad of Newington Green. J. Aiken.—LiSf

The ballad of Rudolph Reed. G. Brooks.—HeR

The ballad of Semmerwater. W. Watson.—BlO

Ballad of the bread man. C. Causley.—HeR

The ballad of the harp-weaver. E. S. Millay.—LiSf—LiWa

Ballad of the man who's gone. L. Hughes.—PlAs

Ballad of the morning streets. A. Baraka.—KoT

La belle dame sans merci ("O, what can ail thee, knight at arms"). J. Keats.—HeR—LiWa—PlAs

The brother ("O, know you what I have done"). T. Hardy.—PlAs

Canadian boat-song. Unknown, at. to John Galt.—PlAs

Casey Jones. T. L. Siebert.—BlO (unat.)—PlAs

The erl-king. J. W. von Goethe.—LiWa

Father Gilligan. W. B. Yeats.—PlAs

The highwayman. A. Noyes.—LiSf

How do you do, Alabama. F. Wilson.—PlAs

In Weatherbury stocks. T. Hardy.—PlAs

"It was a' for our rightfu' king." R. Burns.—PlAs

John Barleycorn. R. Burns.—HeR—PlAs

The juniper tree. W. Watson.—DoNw

The king's son. T. Boyd.—PlAs

Lochinvar. Sir W. Scott.—PlAs

The market. J. Stephens.—PlAs

"Oh, have you heard the gallant news." From Western star. S. V. Benét.—PlAs

O, what is that sound. W. H. Auden.—PlAs

"Oh, who will shoe your pretty little foot." K. Rexroth.—PlAs

Proud Maisie. Sir W. Scott.—BlO—PlAs

"Rapunzel, Rapunzel." M. Van Doren.—PlAs

The Saginaw song. T. Roethke.—HeR

The shooting of Dan McGrew. R. W. Service.—DoNw—HeR

Sing me a song. R. L. Stevenson.—PlAs

Song to the ninth grade. P. C. Holahan.—PlAs

The true ballad of the great race to Gilmore City. P. Hey.—JaPi

Truelove. M. Van Doren.—PlAs

"When I set out for Lyonesse." T. Hardy.—HeR

The wreck of the Hesperus. H. W. Longfellow.—HaOf

Ye ancient Yuba miner of the days of '49. S. C. Upham.—PlAs

Ballads—Traditional

"As I came in by Fiddich-side." Unknown.—HeR

The bailiff's daughter of Islington. Unknown.—PlAs

Barbara Allen's cruelty. Unknown.—PlAs

Barbara Ellen. Unknown.—PlAs

The Battle of Shiloh. Unknown.—PlAs

The big rock candy mountains ("On a summer's day in the month of May, a burly little bum come a-hiking"). Unknown.—KeK

The big rock candy mountains ("One evening as the sun went down").—KoT

Binnorie. Unknown.—PlAs

The bold pedlar and Robin Hood. Unknown.—PlAs

The bonny Earl of Moray ("Ye hielands and ye lawlands"). Unknown.—BlO

The bonny earl of Murray ("Ye highlands and ye lawlands").—PlAs

Bonny George Campbell. Unknown.—PlAs

Brennan on the moor. Unknown.—PlAs

The broken wedding ring. Unknown.—PlAs

The buffalo skinners. Unknown.—HeR

Cecilia. Unknown.—DoNw

The cherry-tree carol. Unknown.—LiE

"Joseph was an old man" .—HaO

Clementine. Unknown.—KeK—LiSf

Oh, my darling Clementine.—PlAs

Cocaine Lil and Morphine Sue. Unknown.—HeR

The curst wife. Unknown.—PlAs

The death of Admiral Benbow. Unknown.—BlO

The demon lover. Unknown.—PlAs

The devil's nine questions. Unknown.—LiWa

Edward, Edward. Unknown.—PlAs

The elfin knight. Unknown.—LiWa

The fair maid of Amsterdam. Unknown.—HeR

A farewell to Kingsbridge. Unknown.—PlAs

The farmer's curst wife. Unknown.—PlAs

Flowers in the valley. Unknown.—BlO

Frankie and Johnny. Unknown.—HeR

Georgie. Unknown.—PlAs

Get up and bar the door. Unknown.—BlO—PlAs

Go from my window. Unknown.—PlAs

"Going up the river." Unknown.—PlAs

The Golden Vanity ("A ship I have got in the north country"). Unknown.—BlO

The Golden Vanity ("Now Jack he had a ship in the north counterie").—PlAs

The green bushes. Unknown.—PlAs

The Green Willow Tree. Unknown.—PlAs

The Gresford disaster. Unknown.—PlAs

The gypsy laddies. Unknown.—BlO

Have over the water to Florida. Unknown.—PlAs

"I will give my love an apple without e'er a core." Unknown.—HeR

I will give my love an apple.—BlO

I'm going to Georgia. Unknown.—PlAs

Isabel. Unknown.—DoNw

Jamie Douglas. Unknown.—PlAs

Jesse James. Unknown.—PlAs

John Henry ("When John Henry was a little tiny baby"). Unknown.—KeK

John Henry ("John Henry was a lil baby").—PlAs

John Henry ("When John Henry was a little babe").—LiSf

"A knight came riding from the east." Unknown.—BlO

Lord Randal. Unknown.—PlAs

The lowlands of Holland. Unknown.—PlAs

The maid freed from the gallows. Unknown.—PlAs

Mary Hamilton. Unknown.—PlAs

Ballads—Traditional—*Continued*

Meet-on-the-road ("Now, pray, where are you going, said Meet-on-the-road"). Unknown.—BlO

Meet-on-the-road ("Now, pray, where are you going, child").—KoT

Mister Fox. Unknown.—BlO

The mouse's courting song. Unknown.—PlAs

Nottamun Town. Unknown.—BlO

"O, say my jolly fellow." Unknown.—PlAs

"O waly, waly, up the bank." Unknown.—PlAs

One morning in May (the nightingale). Unknown.—PlAs

The Queen of Elfan's nourice. Unknown.—PlAs

Rare Willie drowned in Yarrow. Unknown.—PlAs

Riddle song ("I gave my love a cherry that had no stone"). Unknown.—HeR

The riddling knight. Unknown.—LiSf—PlAs

Robin Hood and the Bishop of Hereford. Unknown. BlO

Roll, Alabama, roll. Unknown.—PlAs

Santa Ana. Unknown.—PlAs

The seeds of love. Unknown.—PlAs

Seeing the elephant. Unknown.—PlAs

Sir Patrick Spens ("The king sits in Dunfermline town"). Unknown.—BlO—PlAs

Sir Patrick Spens (". . . Dunfermline toun").—HeR

Sir Patrick Spence (". . . Dumferling town").—LiSf

"Soldier, soldier, won't you marry me." Unknown.—BlO

"Oh, soldier, soldier, will you marry me".—DeM

Soldier, won't you marry me.—PlAs

The sons of liberty. Unknown.—PlAs

Springfield Mountain. Unknown.—PlAs

Stormalong. Unknown.—PlAs

The streets of Laredo ("As I walked out in the streets of Laredo"). Unknown.—HeR—LiSf

"As I walked out in the streets of Laredo".—PlAs

Sweet William's ghost. Unknown.—PlAs

Tam Lin ("O, I forbid you, maidens a'"). Unknown.—PlAs

Tamlane (". . . maidens all").—LiWa

Tam Lin ("She's ta'en her petticoat by the band"). Unknown.—PlAs

Tarrier's song. Unknown.—PlAs

Thomas Rymer ("True Thomas lay on Huntlie bank"). Unknown.—HeR

Thomas Rymer (". . . o'er yond grassy bank").—PlAs

The three ravens. Unknown.—PlAs

The twa corbies. Unknown.—HeR—PlAs

The two sisters. Unknown.—PlAs

The unquiet grave ("So cold the wintry winds do blow"). Unknown.—PlAs

The unquiet grave ("The wind doth blow today, my love"). Unknown.—HeR

The Vicar of Bray. Unknown.—PlAs

Waily, waily. Unknown.—PlAs

The wearin' o' the green. Unknown.—PlAs

Whittingham Fair. Unknown.—PlAs

The wife of Usher's well ("There lived a lady, a lady gay"). Unknown.—PlAs

The wife of Usher's well ("There lived a wife at Usher's well"). Unknown.—HeR—PlAs

"A wife was sitting at her reel ae night." Unknown.—BlO

The wife wrapt in wether's skin. Unknown.—PlAs

The wild colonial boy. Unknown.—PlAs

The wild lumberjack. Unknown.—PlAs

Working in the mines. Unknown.—PlAs

Ballet. Unknown.—BrT

Balloon ("As / big / as"). Colleen Thibaudeau.—DoNw

The **balloon** ("I went to the park"). Karla Kuskin.—BeD

Balloons

Air balloons. E. Farjeon.—FaE

Balloon ("As / big / as"). C. Thibaudeau.—DoNw

The balloon ("I went to the park"). K. Kuskin.—BeD

"In just." E. E. Cummings.—KeK—LiSf

Saturday in the park. B. J. Esbensen.—EsCs

"There was an old man of the Hague." E. Lear.—LiH—LiSf

The old man of the Hague.—BrT

"What's the news of the day." Mother Goose.—LoR

Balls

"Over the garden wall." E. Farjeon.—FaE

"**Baloney** belly Billy." Jack Prelutsky.—PrNk

Banananananananana. William Cole.—PrRh

Bananas

"Bananas and cream." D. McCord.—FaW—HoMu

Forty performing bananas. J. Prelutsky.—PrNk

"**Bananas** and cream." David McCord.—FaW—HoMu

Band practice. Cynthia Rylant.—RyW

Bandit. Abraham Moses Klein.—DoNw

Bands. See Orchestras

"**Bang**, the starter's gun." Dorthi Charles.—KeK

Bangs, John Kendrick

The dreadful fate of naughty Nate.—HaOf

The hired man's way.—HaOf

If ("If I had a trunk like a big elephant").—HaOf

The little elf.—CoN—HaOf—PrRa

The little elfman.—CoOu—LiSf

"A **bantam** rooster." Kikaku, tr. by Harry Behn.—KeK

Baptisms. See Christenings

Baraka, Amiri

Ballad of the morning streets.—KoT

Song form.—KoT

Barbara Allen's cruelty. Unknown.—PlAs

Barbara Ellen. Unknown.—PlAs

Barbara Frietchie. John Greenleaf Whittier.—HaOf

Barbara poems. Nikki Giovanni.—GiSp

Barbara Sutton. Mel Glenn.—GlCd

"**Barbarians** must we always be." See Observing a vulgar name on the plinth of an ancient statue

Barbarossa. Friedrich Ruckert, tr. by John W. Thomas.—LiWa

"**Barber**, barber, shave a pig." Mother Goose.—AlH—DeM—FaW—LoR

Barbers. See also Hair

"Barber, barber, shave a pig." Mother Goose.—AlH—DeM—FaW—LoR

Barbershop. M. Gardner.—PrRh

The boy in the barbershop. N. Giovanni.—GiSp

"Whiskers of style." A. Lobel.—LoWr

Who's next. Unknown.—BrT

Barbershop. Martin Gardner.—PrRh

Barbie doll. Marge Piercy.—JaD

Barclay, William
  "O God, bless all the people for whom life is hard and difficult."—LaT
  "Oh God, I thank you that you have made me as I am."—LaT
The **bare** arms of trees. John Tagliabue.—JaPi
"**Bare** branches of trees." See Winter alphabet
"**Bare-handed** reach." See End of winter
The **barefoot** boy. John Greenleaf Whittier.—HaOf
"**Barely** a twelvemonth after." See The horses
"The **barge** she sat in, like a burnish'd throne." From Antony and Cleopatra. William Shakespeare.—HoUn
Baring-Gould, Sabine
  "Now the day is over."—DaC—LaW
Barker, David
  Packard.—JaD
Barker, George
  "The house I go to in my dream."—CoOu
Barks, Coleman
  Adam's apple.—JaPo
  Brain.—JaPo
  Bruises.—JaPo
The **barn** ("I am tired of this barn, said the colt"). Elizabeth Coatsworth.—HaO
The **barn** ("They should never have built a barn there, at all"). Edward Thomas.—PlEd
The **barn** ("While we unloaded the hay from the truck, building"). Wendell Berry.—PlEd
Barners, Dame Juliana
  The properties of a good greyhound.—HeR
Barnes, William
  Day's work a-done.—PlSc
Barns and stables
  The barn ("I am tired of this barn, said the colt"). E. Coatsworth.—HaO
  The barn ("They should never have built a barn there, at all"). E. Thomas.—PlEd
  The barn ("While we unloaded the hay from the truck, building"). W. Berry.—PlEd
  Country barnyard. E. Coatsworth.—ChC—PrRh
  Iowa land. M. Bell.—PlSc
  Loft. S. Cassedy.—CaR
  Old grey goose. H. Behn.—HoCb
  Recycled. L. Moore.—MoSn
  "There was a little boy went into a barn." Mother Goose.—DeM
Barnstone, Willis
  Changsha shoe factory.—PlSc
  Seizure, tr. by.—McL
  "Unknown love", tr. by.—McL
Baro, Gene
  The ferns.—PrRh
"A **baron** of the sea, the great tropic." See The marvel
"A **barrel** organ." See Cures for melancholy
Barrington, Patric
  I had a hippopotamus, sels.
    "I had a hippopotamus, I loved him as a friend".—LiIl
  "I had a hippopotamus, I loved him as a friend." See I had a hippopotamus
Barrows, Marjorie
  The bug ("And when the rain had gone away").—PrRh
Barry Owens. Mel Glenn.—GlC
"**Bartholomew** the hatter." N. M. Bodecker.—BoSs
Barto, Agnia
  Two sisters looking at baby brother.—FaW
Baruch, Dorothy
  Cat ("My cat").—ChC
Baruch, Dorothy W.
  To sup like a pup.—HoDl

The **base** stealer. Robert Francis.—CoN—LiSf—PrRh
Baseball
  The abominable baseball bat. X. J. Kennedy.—LiWa
  Analysis of baseball. M. Swenson.—KeK
  The base stealer. R. Francis.—CoN—LiSf—PrRh
  Baseball. F. D. Sherman.—HaOf
  The baseball player. J. Ciardi.—CiD
  Casey at the bat. E. L. Thayer.—HaOf
  Christopher Conti. M. Glenn.—GlC
  Danny Vargas. M. Glenn.—GlC
  History ("And I'm thinking how to get out") M. C. Livingston.—PrRh
  The hummer. W. Matthews.—JaT
  July the first. R. Currie.—JaPi
  The lady pitcher. C. Macdonald.—JaPi
  Mean Rufus throw-down. D. Smith.—JaT
  Neil Winningham. M. Glenn.—GlCd
  Night game. L. Morrison.—LiSf
  Rural recreation. L. Morrison.—KeK
  Two hopper. R. Ikan.—JaS
  We need a hit. J. Prelutsky.—PrWi
Baseball. Frank Dempster Sherman.—HaOf
The **baseball** player. John Ciardi.—CiD
Basement. Sylvia Cassedy.—CaR
Basho
  "Ancient pool."—KeK
  "Beside the road."—KoT
  "First cold rain."—KoT
  "How cool it feels."—KoT
  "An old silent pool."—LiSf
  Spider ("With what voice").—KoT
  "Well, let's go."—KoT
Basic for further irresponsibility. Eve Merriam.—MeSk
Basic for irresponsibility. Eve Merriam.—MeSk
Basket. Myra Cohn Livingston.—LiWo
Basketball
  Basketball. N. Giovanni.—GiSp—PrRh
  Basketball star. K. Fufuka.—PrRh
  Fernando. M. Ridlon.—CoN—PrRh
  Forms of praise. L. Morrison.—LiSf
  Foul shot. E. A. Hoey.—PrRh
  Hayes Iverson. M. Glenn.—GlCd
  Nocturn at the institute. D. McElroy.—JaPi
  Nothing but net. R. Scheele.—JaT
  Shooting. B. H. Fairchild.—JaT
  Stringbean Small. J. Prelutsky.—PrNk
Basketball. Nikki Giovanni.—GiSp—PrRh
"**Basketball** players." See Forms of praise
Basketball star. Karama Fufuka.—PrRh
Bat ("All day bats drowse in houses' eaves"). X. J. Kennedy.—KeF
The **bat** ("Bats are creepy, bats are scary"). Frank Jacobs.—PrRh
Bat ("Bats in the belfry"). Eve Merriam.—MeHa
The **bat** ("By day the bat is cousin to the mouse"). Theodore Roethke.—HaOf—LiSf—LiWa—PrRh
"**Bat,** bat, come under my hat." Mother Goose.—LoR
"A **bat** is born." See Bats
"**Batata** and rice." See Tiempo muerto
Bates, Clara Boty
  At grandfather's.—HaOf
  Gray thrums.—HaOf
The **bath-bunny.** From A baker's dozen of wild beasts. Carolyn Wells.—HaOf
"The **bath-bunny** is chubby and fat." See The bath-bunny

Bathing
After a bath. A. Fisher.—BeD—FrP
Before the bath. C. Marsh.—FrP—PrRa
"Bertie, Bertie." E. Merriam.—MeBl
Bethsabe's song. From The love of King David
and fair Bethsabe. G. Peele.—HeR
The dangers of taking baths. J. Ciardi.—CiD
The dirtiest man in the world. S. Silverstein.—
HaOf
"Happy winter, steamy tub." K.
Gundersheimer.—PrRa
If I were a fish. A. Winn.—BeD
Naughty soap song. D. Aldis.—PrRa
Peter. E. Farjeon.—FaE
A pig is never blamed. B. Deutsch.—PrRh
"Rub-a-dub-dub." Mother Goose.—DaC—
DeM—FaW—LoR—WaC
"Sing a song of soapsuds." C. Watson.—WaC
Soap ("Just look at those hands"). M.
Gardner.—PrRh
The story of Lava. D. A. Evans.—JaPi
"There was a small pig who wept tears." A.
Lobel.—LoB—PrRa
Trips. N. Giovanni.—GiSp
Water sport. N. M. Bodecker.—BoPc
"The way they scrub." A. B. Ross.—PrRa
"**Bathing** near Oahu, May." X. J. Kennedy.—KeB
Batki, John
The seventh, tr. by.—HeR
Bats
Bat ("All day bats drowse in houses' eaves").
X. J. Kennedy.—KeF
The bat ("Bats are creepy, bats are scary"). F.
Jacobs.—PrRh
Bat ("Bats in the belfry"). E. Merriam.—MeHa
The bat ("By day the bat is cousin to the
mouse"). T. Roethke.—HaOf—LiSf—LiWa—
PrRh
"Bat, bat, come under my hat." Mother
Goose.—LoR
Bats ("A bat is born"). R. Jarrell.—CoN—HaOf
Bats ("Versa says"). M. C. Livingston.—LiWo
"I wish." L. Moore.—MoSn
Loft. S. Cassedy.—CaR
Man and bat. D. H. Lawrence.—HeR
Twinkle, twinkle. From Alice's adventures in
Wonderland. L. Carroll.—PrRa
Bats ("A bat is born"). Randall Jarrell.—CoN—
HaOf
Bats ("Versa says"). Myra Cohn Livingston.—
LiWo
"**Bats** are creepy, bats are scary." See The bat
"**Bats** in the belfry." See Bat
The **Battle** of Shiloh. Unknown.—PlAs
"The **battle** rent a cobweb diamond-strung." See
Range-finding
Battles. See also War
The Battle of Shiloh. Unknown.—PlAs
Calling the roll. N. G. Shepherd.—HaOf
Carentan O Carentan. L. Simpson.—HeR
"For want of a nail the shoe was lost." Mother
Goose.—FaW—LoR
Grass. C. Sandburg.—HoRa
Memories of Verdun. A. Dugan.—HeR
"Now entertain conjecture of a time." W.
Shakespeare.—HeR
"Pensive, on her dead gazing, I heard the
Mother of All." W. Whitman.—HeR
Range-finding. R. Frost.—HeR
"This day is call'd the feast of Crispian." From
Henry V. W. Shakespeare.—HoUn
The Trojan Horse. W. Drummond.—PlEd

Vergissmeinicht. K. Douglas.—HeR
"Yon island carrions desperate of their bones."
From Henry V. W. Shakespeare.—HeR
Bauer, Grace
Spring and all.—JaPo
Bavarian gentians. David Herbert Lawrence.—KoT
"**Baxter** Bickerbone of Burlington." See On
learning to adjust to things
Bay bank. Archie Randolph Ammons.—JaD
Baylor, Byrd
Desert tortoise.—PrRh
BC, AD. U. A. Fanthorpe.—HaO
"**Be** glad your nose is on your face." Jack
Prelutsky.—PrNk
"**Be** gracious to me, my father, hold up the boat."
See Prayer for smooth waters
"**Be** kind and tender to the frog." See The frog
Be like the bird. Victor Hugo.—LiSf
"**Be** like the bird, who." See Be like the bird
Be merry. Unknown.—HeR
Be my non-Valentine. Eve Merriam.—MeSk
"**Be** not afeard, the isle is full of noises." From
The tempest. William Shakespeare.—HeR
"**Be** wary of the loathsome troll." See The troll
"The **beach** at this evening full." Unknown.—JaT
Beach stones. Lilian Moore.—FaTh—MoSn
Beaches. See Shore
The **bean** stalk. Edna St. Vincent Millay.—LiWa
Beans
"There was an old person of Dean." E. Lear.—
BlO—FaTh—LiH
Limerick.—HoMu
The woman cleaning lentils. Zehrd.—FaTh
The **bear.** Ann Stanford.—LiWa
The **bear** and the squirrels. C. P. Cranch.—HaOf
"A **bear,** however hard he tries." See Teddy bear
"**Bear** in mind." See Catmint
Beards
Beatnik limernik. N. R. Jaffray.—BrT
Porcupine pa. X. J. Kennedy.—KeF
"There was an old man in a tree." E. Lear.—
LiH—LiH—LiH—LiSf
"There was an old man with a beard." E.
Lear.—CoOu—FaW—LiH—LiSf—PrRh
Old man with a beard.—CoN
"There was an old man with a beard, who sat."
E. Lear.—LiH
"Whiskers of style." A. Lobel.—LoWr
Bearhug. Michael Ondaatje.—JaPo
Bears
Adventures of Isabel. O. Nash.—CoN—CoOu—
HaOf—PrRh
"Algy met a bear." Unknown.—PrRh
Algy.—KeK
Algie and the bear.—PaM
The bear. A. Stanford.—LiWa
The bear and the squirrels. C. P. Cranch.—
HaOf
A beggarly bear. C. Wells.—BrT
The black bear ("The bear's black bulk"). T.
Hughes.—HuU
The black bear ("In the summer, fall and
spring"). J. Prelutsky.—PrZ
Black bear ("Sweet-mouth, honey-paws, hairy
one!"). D. Lepan.—DoNw
"Camping in Grand Canyon Park." X. J.
Kennedy.—KeB
"The common cormorant or shag." Unknown.—
BlO
The common cormorant.—PrRh (at. to
Christopher Isherwood)

Bears—*Continued*

The dancing bear ("Oh, it's fiddle-de-dum and fiddle-de-dee"). A. B. Paine.—HaOf

The dancing bear ("Slowly he turns himself round and round"). R. Field.—CoN—KeK

The disobliging bear. C. Wells.—BrT

Excursion. E. Merriam.—MeF

Furry bear. A. A. Milne.—FrP

"Fuzzy Wuzzy was a bear." Unknown.—CoN

"Grandma Bear from Delaware." J. Prelutsky.—PrRi

Grandpa bear's lullaby. J. Yolen.—PrRh

The grizzly bear ("I see a bear"). T. Hughes.—HuU

Grizzly bear ("If you ever, ever, ever meet a grizzly bear"). M. Austin.—CoOu—LiSf

Hard to bear. T. Jenks.—HaOf

"In the summer we eat." Z. Gay.—PrRa

"Louise, a whiz at curling hair." X. J. Kennedy.—KeB

"Mama Bear, you'll never miss." X. J. Kennedy.—KeB

My teddy bear ("A teddy bear is a faithful friend"). M. Chute.—PrRa

My teddy bear ("A teddy bear is nice to hold"). M. Hillert.—PrRa

The polar bear ("The polar bear by being white"). J. Prelutsky.—PrZ

The polar bear ("The polar bear is unaware"). H. Belloc.—LiSf

Polar bear ("The secret of the polar bear"). G. Kredenser.—PrRa

Prayer of the black bear. Unknown, fr. the Kwakiutl Indian.—BiSp

The smart little bear ("Teacher Bruin said, cub, bear in mind"). M. Fenderson.—BrT

Teddy bear. A. A. Milne.—CoOu

Teddy bear poem. J. Viorst.—ViI

"Teddy bear, teddy bear." Unknown.—CoN—PrRa

"There was an old person of Ware." E. Lear.—LiH

    An old person of Ware.—PrRa

"To give advice I hesitate." R. Beasley.—TrM

Waiting ("Dreaming of honeycombs to share"). H. Behn.—HoCb—HoSi

Wake up call. B. J. Esbensen.—EsCs

"The **bear's** black bulk." See The black bear

Beasley, R.

"To give advice I hesitate."—TrM

"When Noah loaded the ark as bidden."—TrM

"Who are they who rudely jeer."—TrM

"**Beast** of the sea." See Words to call up game

"**Beat** the drum, beat the drum." Unknown.—DeD

Beatles

We four lads. Unknown.—KeK

Beatnik limernik. Norman R. Jaffray.—BrT

"**Beautification.**" N. M. Bodecker.—BoPc

"**Beautiful** beautiful Beverly." See Nightmare

Beautiful Bella. Unknown.—BrT

"A **beautiful** lady named Psyche." See A lady named Psyche

"**Beautiful** soup, so rich and green." From Alice's adventures in wonderland. Lewis Carroll.—BlO

Turtle soup.—HoMu—PrRh

"The **beautiful** thing is starting toward me." See It starts toward me

"**Beautifully** Janet slept." See Janet waking

Beauty, of nature or art

Afternoon on a hill. E. S. Millay.—CoN—HaOf—KoT

The argument of his book. R. Herrick.—KoT

"Beautification." N. M. Bodecker.—BoPc

Binsey poplars, felled 1879. G. M. Hopkins.—HeR

Cynthia in the snow. G. Brooks.—BaS—HoSi—LiSf

"How the old mountains drip with sunset." E. Dickinson.—HeR

I think. J. Schuyler.—KoT

"I wandered lonely as a cloud." From Daffodils. W. Wordsworth.—BlO—KoT

Immalee. C. G. Rossetti.—BlO

"In beauty may I walk." Unknown.—HeR

Interlude. K. Shapiro.—JaD

Inversnaid. G. M. Hopkins.—HeR

"It is not growing like a tree." B. Jonson.—HeR

It starts toward me. Unknown, fr. the Navajo Indian.—BiSp

"The lands around my dwelling." Unknown.—LiIl

Leaves ("My green leaves are more beautiful"). F. Asch.—CoN

Leaves compared with flowers. R. Frost.—KoS

"Loveliest of trees, the cherry now." A. E. Housman.—HeR

    Loveliest of trees.—BlO

Marigolds. C. Zolotow.—ZoE

My cat Jeoffrey. From Jubilate Agno. C. Smart.—BlO—HeR

    "For I will consider my cat Jeoffry".—KoT

Night ("Stars over snow"). S. Teasdale.—LiSf

"Oh I have dined on this delicious day." R. Snyder.—JaT

Pied beauty. G. M. Hopkins.—HeR—KoT

The rainbow ("Boats sail on the rivers"). C. G. Rossetti.—DaC

Requiem for Sonora. R. Shelton.—JaPi

Saint Francis and the sow. G. Kinnell.—HeR

Scotland small. H. MacDiarmid.—HeR

"Swift things are beautiful." E. Coatsworth.—LiSf

"This lunar beauty." W. H. Auden.—HeR

The windhover, to Christ our Lord. G. M. Hopkins.—HeR

Wonders of the world. R. Shelton.—JaD

A young birch. R. Frost.—KoS

Beauty, personal

Amy Pines. M. Glenn.—GlC

Aunt Sponge and Aunt Spiker. R. Dahl.—PrRh

Avec merci, mother. M. Angelou.—AnS

"The barge she sat in, like a burnish'd throne." From Antony and Cleopatra. W. Shakespeare.—HoUn

Behavior of fish in an English tea garden. K. Douglas.—HeR

Bethsabe's song. From The love of King David and fair Bethsabe. G. Peele.—HeR

Blackberry sweet. D. Randall.—KeK

Blue girls. J. C. Ransom.—HeR

An epitaph ("Here lies a most beautiful lady"). W. De la Mare.—HeR

"The fair maid who, the first of May." Mother Goose.—AlH

For young men growing up to help themselves. Unknown, fr. the Cherokee Indian.—BiSp

From my mother's house. L. Goldberg.—StG

Growing old. R. Henderson.—PrRh

Beauty, personal—*Continued*
He remembers forgotten beauty. W. B. Yeats.—
  McL
"I am the rose of Sharon, and the lily of the
  valleys." From The Song of Solomon.
  Bible/Old Testament.—McL
Lady Sara Bunbury sacrificing to the Graces,
  by Reynolds. D. Hine.—PlEd
Lauren Jones. M. Glenn.—GlC
Lullaby ("Lay your sleeping head, my love").
  W. H. Auden.—McL
Me ("My nose is blue"). K. Kuskin.—PrRh
"Mine eye and heart are at a mortal war."
  From Sonnets. W. Shakespeare.—PlEd
"Mirror, mirror, tell me." Mother Goose.—
  DaC—LoR
My people. L. Hughes.—HuDk
On the bust of Helen by Canova. Lord
  Byron.—PlEd
Seashell ("My father's mother"). V. Worth.—
  WoSp
"Shall I compare thee to a summer's day?"
  From Sonnets. W. Shakespeare.—HoUn
The sound of rain. D. A. Evans.—JaG
Teddy bear. A. A. Milne.—CoOu
"Thrice tosse these oaken ashes in the ayre."
  T. Campion.—LiWa
Upon Julia's clothes. R. Herrick.—KoT
Valentine thoughts for Mari. E. Di Pasquale.—
  LiVp
"Wash me and comb me." Unknown.—BaH
When Jane goes to market. E. Farjeon.—FaE
When Sue wears red. L. Hughes.—HuDk
"Who is Silvia, what is she." From The two
  gentlemen of Verona. W. Shakespeare.—HoUn
The **beaver** ("The beaver is fat"). Jack
  Prelutsky.—PrZ
Beaver ("Coming to it from the country").
  Cynthia Rylant.—RyW
"The **beaver** is fat." See The beaver
Beaver moon, the suicide of a friend. Mary
  Oliver.—JaG
Beavers
The beaver ("The beaver is fat"). J. Prelutsky.—
  PrZ
"**Because** I had failing grades in history." See
  Craig Blanchard
"**Because** I wanted life in the fast lane." See
  Sharon Vail and
"**Because** my mouth." See Minstrel man
"**Because** of the steepness." See Mountain brook
"**Because** of you, I'm an heiress." See A
  daughter's house
"**Because** this month, when napkins, pretty
  spoons." See Roman presents
"**Because** we do." See Together
"**Because** you are to me a song." See Passing love
Becker, Edna
  Before the monkey's cage.—PrRa
  Beside the line of elephants.—PrRh
Becker, John
  Feather or fur.—PrRh
The **bed**. Charlotte Zolotow.—ZoE
The **bed** book, sels. Sylvia Plath
  "These are the beds".—PrRh
Bed in summer. Robert Louis Stevenson.—DaC—
  FaW
Bed-time. See Bedtime
Beddoes, Thomas Lovell
  A crocodile.—HeR
Bedford, William
  The kitchen (for my grandmother).—StG

Bedtime. See also Lullabies
Again, good night. C. Zolotow.—ZoE
All asleep 1 ("A lamb has a lambkin"). C.
  Pomerantz.—PoA
All asleep 2 ("Hush, it's the hour"). C.
  Pomerantz.—PoA
"All tucked in and roasty toasty." C. Watson.—
  LaW—WaC
Arullo. Unknown.—GrT
At night ("When I am outdoors and begin").
  J. Ciardi.—CiD
At night ("When I go to bed at night"). A. B.
  Payne.—ChB
Bearhug. M. Ondaatje.—JaPo
The bed. C. Zolotow.—ZoE
Bed in summer. R. L. Stevenson.—DaC—FaW
Bedtime ("Five minutes, five minutes more,
  please"). E. Farjeon.—FaE—FrP—PrRa
Bedtime ("Good night"). M. L'Engle.—LaT
Bedtime ("Hop away"). P. Hubbell.—HoSu
Bedtime ("Now the mouse goes to his hole").
  T. Holman. LaW
Bedtime mumble. N. M. Bodecker.—BoSs
Bedtime stories. L. Moore.—BeD—CoN—HoCr
  Bedtime story.—MoSn—PrRa
Between the bars. E. Farjeon.—FaE
By the Exeter River. D. Hall.—PlAs
"Catch me the moon, daddy." G. Vitez.—LaW
Catsnest. X. J. Kennedy.—KeF—LiCa
Child's song. R. Lowell.—HeR
A chill. C. G. Rossetti.—ChB
Chocolate cake. J. Prelutsky.—PrMp
City under water. E. Farjeon.—FaE
"Come, let's to bed." Mother Goose.—BaH—
  FaW—LoR
The cottager to the infant. D. Wordsworth.—
  KoT
The country bedroom. F. Cornford.—BlO
Covers. N. Giovanni.—HoSu—PrRa
The crack of light. E. Farjeon.—FaE
A cradle song ("Sweet dreams, form a shade").
  W. Blake.—HaO—RoC
Cradle song for Christmas. E. Farjeon.—FaE
"Day is done." Unknown.—ChB
"Diddle, diddle, dumpling, my son John."
  Mother Goose.—BaH—DeM—FaW—LiSf—
  LoR
Disillusionment of ten o'clock. W. Stevens.—
  HeR—KoT
Don't make a peep. C. Pomerantz.—PoA
A drink of water. E. Farjeon.—FaE
Drowsy bees. C. Pomerantz.—PoA
"Eat an apple going to bed." Mother Goose.—
  LoR
Eight o'clock. C. Zolotow.—ZoE
Evening ("Prince Absalom and Sir Rotherham
  Redde"). Dame E. Sitwell.—PlAs
"The evening is coming, the sun sinks to rest."
  Unknown.—LaW—PrRa
Falling asleep. I. Serraillier.—FaW
Flashlight ("Tucked tight in bed, the day all
  gone"). X. J. Kennedy.—KeF
For good night. E. Farjeon.—FaE
"From ghoulies and ghosties." From A Cornish
  litany. Unknown.—HoCr—LiSf
  Things that go bump in the night.—CoN
  A Cornish litany.—LiWa
German slumber song. Unknown.—BaH
Ghost sounds. Unknown.—HoCr
"Go to bed first." Unknown.—BaH—FrP
"Go to bed late." Mother Goose.—LoR
Going to bed. E. Farjeon.—FaE

Behavior.—*Continued*
Taboo to boot. O. Nash.—HeR
Ten kinds. M. M. Dodge.—PrRh
"There was a little girl, and she had a little
curl." Mother Goose.—DeM—LoR
  Jemima.—DaC
  Jemima (". . . and she wore a little
    curl").—ChG
  "There was a little girl, who had a little
    curl".—PrRh (at. to H. W. Longfellow)
"There was a naughty boy." J. Keats.—CoOu
"This little fellow was naughty, they say."
  Unknown.—DeD
Threats. M. Ridlon.—FrP
"Thumbkin Bumpkin, jolly and stout." C.
  Watson.—WaC
Tired Tim. W. De la Mare.—CoN—PrRh
Tom. E. Farjeon.—FaE
Tom, Jill and Bob. Unknown.—DaC
Tony Baloney. D. Lee.—PrRh
Two people ("Two people live in Rosamund").
  E. V. Rieu.—PrRh
"Vince released a jar of vermin." X. J.
  Kennedy.—KeB
We real cool. G. Brooks.—KeK
"When Jacky's a good boy." Mother Goose.—
  DeM—FaW
  "When Jack's a very good boy".—LoR
  "When Jacky's a very good boy".—AlH
Whitley at three o'clock. J. Worley.—JaG
Why ("Fie, darling, why do you cry, why do
  you cry"). E. Farjeon.—FaE
"Why did the children." C. Sandburg.—HoRa
Wicked thoughts. J. Viorst.—ViI
Winifred Waters. W. B. Rands.—DaC
"With the garden sprinkler Brett." X. J.
  Kennedy.—KeB
The yak ("For hours the princess would not
  play or sleep"). V. Sheard.—DoNw
A young girl of Asturias. Unknown.—BrT
Behavior of fish in an English tea garden. Keith
  Douglas.—HeR
"Behind him spreads the horizoned shore." See
  On a landscape of Sestos
Behind the waterfall. Winifred Welles.—LiSf
Behn, Harry
  "Across cold, moon bright." See The seasons
  Adventure.—HoCb
  Autumn ("Summer's flurry").—HoCb
  Canticle of spring.—HoCb
  Christmas morning.—LiCp
  Circles.—LiSf
  Coloring.—HoCb
  Crickets ("We cannot say that crickets sing").—
    HoCb
  "Deep in a windless", tr. by.—LiWa
  Discovery.—HoCb
  The dream ("One night I dreamed").—HoCb—
    LiSf
  Elves and goblins.—HoCb
  Enchanted summer.—HoCb
  Enchantment.—HoCb
  The errand.—HoCb
  Evening ("Now the drowsy sun shine").—HoCb
  Fairies ("What could have frightened them
    away").—HoCb
  The fairy and the bird.—HoCb
  The first Christmas eve.—HoCb
  A friendly mouse.—HoCb
  From an airplane, sels.
    "Night settles on earth".—HoSs
  Ghosts ("A cold and starry darkness moans").—
    HoCr—PrRh

The gnome.—HoCb—HoCr
The golden hive.—HoCb
"The great sea", tr. by.—LiSf
Growing up.—HoCb—PrRh
Hallowe'en ("Tonight is the night").—HoCb
Hansi.—HoCb—HoDl
"I called to the wind", tr. by.—LiSf—LiWa
Indian summer ("These are the days when
  early").—HoCb
"It is nice to read", tr. by.—LiSf
The kite ("How bright on the blue").—HoCb—
  LiSf
The lake ("Rippling green and gold and
  brown").—HoCb
The last leaf.—HoCb
The little hill.—HoCb
Lost ("I shall remember chuffs the train").—
  HoCb
Make believe.—HoCb
March wind.—HoCb
Mr. Potts.—HoCb
Mr. Pyme.—HoCb
Morning magic.—HoCb
"Night settles on earth." See From an airplane
"O moon, why must you", tr. by.—LiSf
Old grey goose.—HoCb
"Once upon a time", tr. by.—LiWa
River's song.—HoCb
Roosters and hens.—HoCb
Ruins.—HoCb
The sea shell.—HoCb
The sea shore.—HoCb
The seasons, sels.
  "Across cold, moon bright".—HoDl
  "Small bird, forgive me", tr. by.—KeK
Spring flowers.—HoCb
Summer night.—HoCb
Sun tiger.—HoCb
Sunrise and sun.—HoCb
Tea party.—LiSf
"That duck, bobbing up", tr. by.—LiSf—LiWa
Thunder dragon.—HoCb
Thunderstorm.—HoCb
Tree song.—HoCb
Trees ("Trees are the kindest things I know").—
  HoCb
Undine's garden.—HoCb
Waiting ("Dreaming of honeycombs to
  share").—HoCb—HoSi
"Well, hello down there", tr. by.—FaTh—LiIl—
  LiSf
Winter night ("It is very dark").—HoCb
The wizard in the well.—HoCb
"Behold her, single in the field." See The solitary
  reaper
"Behold the duck." See The duck
"Behold the hippopotamus." See The
  hippopotamus
"Behold the wandering." See The wandering
  albatross
"Behold the wonders of the mighty deep." See
  The sea
Beier, Ulli
  Baboon, tr. by.—HeR
  Blue cuckoo, tr. by.—HeR
  Buffalo, tr. by.—HeR
  Chicken, tr. by.—HeR
  Colobus monkey, tr. by.—HeR
  Elephant, tr. by.—HeR
  Hyena, tr. by.—HeR
  Kob antelope, tr. by.—HeR
  Leopard ("Gentle hunter"), tr. by.—HeR
  Red monkey, tr. by.—HeR

Beilenson, Peter
  "As I picked it up", tr. by.—FaTh
  "For a companion", tr. by.—FaTh
  "Seeking in my hut", tr. by.—FaTh
Being sad. Orban Veli Kanik, tr. by Talât Sait
    Halman.—McL
"**Being** walkers with the dawn and morning." See
    Walkers with the dawn
Beissel, Henry
  The boar and the dromedar.—DoNw
Belief. See Faith
"**Belinda** lived in a little white house." See The
    tale of Custard the dragon
Belitt, Ben
  Charwomen.—PlSc
  The sand painters.—PlEd
Bell, J. J.
  The boa ("Allow me just one short remark").—
    PrRh
  The hedgehog.—PrRh
  The shark ("Oh what a lark to fish for
    shark").—PrRh
Bell, Marvin
  Iowa land.—PlSc
  Reflexes.—JaS
  To Dorothy.—JaPi
  What do they do to you in distant places.—
    JaPi
The **bell** hill. Julia Fields.—LiNe
"**Bell** horses, bell horses." Mother Goose.—LoR
The **bell** in the leaves. Eleanor Farjeon.—FaE
Bell song. Eleanor Farjeon.—FaE
Bella by the sea. Leroy F. Jackson.—PrRh
"**Bella** had a new umbrella." Eve Merriam.—MeBl
La **belle** dame sans merci ("O, what can ail thee,
    knight at arms"). John Keats.—HeR—LiWa—
    PlAs
Belloc, Hilaire
  The elephant ("When people call this beast to
    mind").—LiSf
  The frog ("Be kind and tender to the frog").—
    CoN—LiSf—PrRh
  G.—FaW
  Ha'nacker Mill.—HeR
  The   hippopotamus   ("I   shoot   the
    hippopotamus").—FaW
  Jim, who ran away from his nurse, and was
    eaten by a lion.—LiSf
  The lion ("The lion, the lion, he dwells in the
    waste").—FaW
  Matilda, who told lies, and was burned to
    death.—BlO
  The microbe.—LiSf
  The polar bear ("The polar bear is unaware").—
    LiSf
  Tarantella.—HeR
  The tiger ("The tiger, on the other hand, is
    kittenish and mild").—FaW
  The vulture.—PrRh
  The yak ("As a friend to the children commend
    me the Yak").—BlO—FaW
Bellows, Isabel Frances
  Curious Charlie.—BrT
  G is for Gustave.—BrT
  Ignorant Ida.—BrT
  Naughty young Nat.—BrT
  Operatic Olivia.—BrT
Bells
  The bell in the leaves. E. Farjeon.—FaE
  Bell song. E. Farjeon.—FaE
  The bells. E. A. Poe.—HaOf
  "The bells in the valley." E. Farjeon.—FaE
  Bethlehem bells. E. Farjeon.—FaE

  Church bells. B. Braley.—BrT
  Easter ("On Easter morn"). H. Conkling.—LiE—
    LiSf
  Easter song. B. Nims.—LiE
  "I heard the bells on Christmas Day." H. W.
    Longfellow.—CoN
      Christmas bells.—HaO
  "Merry are the bells, and merry would they
    ring." Mother Goose.—LiSf—LoR
  "Oranges and lemons, say the bells of St
    Clement's." Mother Goose.—DaC
  "Ring out, wild bells, to the wild sky." From
    In memoriam. A. Tennyson.—LiNe
  School bell. E. Farjeon.—FaE
The **bells.** Edgar Allan Poe.—HaOf
Bells for John Whiteside's daughter. John Crowe
    Ransom.—HeR
"The **bells** in the valley." Eleanor Farjeon.—FaE
"The **bells** of waiting advent ring." See Christmas
"**Belly** and Tubs went out in a boat." Clyde
    Watson.—PrRa
The **belly** dancer in the nursing home. Ronald
    Wallace.—JaG
"A **bellyfull** and the fire." See Inside
"**Below** the bluffs." See Old Sam
"**Below** the thunders of the upper deep." See The
    kraken
Belting, Natalia
  "Once, when the sky was very near the
    earth."—LiSf
  "Put the pine tree in its pot by the
    doorway."—LiIl
  "Some say the sun is a golden earring."—LiS
Bembo, Pietro
  Cardinal Bembo's epitaph on Raphael.—PlEd
"**Beneath** a bush, the zoosher lies." See The
    zoosher
"**Beneath** the pine tree where I sat." See All day
    long
"**Beneath** the waters." See Undersea
"**Beneath** the willow, wound round with ivy." See
    Hops
Benét, Rosemary Carr See Benét, Stephen Vincent,
    and Benét, Rosemary Carr
Benét, Stephen Vincent. See also next entry
  Daniel Boone.—KeK
  The innovator.—PlEd
  John Brown's body, sels.
      Melora's song.—PlAs
  Melora's song. See John Brown's body
  Nightmare number three.—PlSc
  "Oh, have you heard the gallant news." See
    Western star
  Western star, sels.
      "Oh, have you heard the gallant news".—
        PlAs
**Benét, Stephen Vincent, and Benét, Rosemary
Carr**
  Abraham Lincoln 1809-1865.—LiSf
  Captain Kidd.—RuI
  John Quincy Adams.—HaOf
  Nancy Hanks, 1784-1818.—CoN
  Peregrine White and Virginia Dare.—HaOf
Bengal. Unknown.—CoOu
The **Bengal** tiger. Jack Prelutsky.—PrZ
"The **Bengal** tiger likes to eat." See The Bengal
    tiger
Benjamin Heywood. Mel Glenn.—GlC
Bennett, John
  The merry pieman's song.—LiIl
  A tiger tale.—HaOf

Bible/New Testament—*Continued*
  Gospel according to Luke, sels.
    "And there were in the same country shepherds".—LiCp
Bible/Old Testament
  "And Hiram of Tyre sent his servants unto Solomon, for he had." See Kings
  "And the whole earth was of one language, and of one speech." See Genesis
  The book of psalms, sels.
    Psalm 23 ("The Lord is my shepherd, I shall not want").—LiSf
    Psalm 23 ("The Lord to me a shepherd is").—HaOf
    Psalm 24.—LiSf
    Psalm 100.—LiSf—LiTp
    Psalm 103.—LiSf
    Psalm 121.—HaOf
  Genesis, sels.
    "And the whole earth was of one language, and of one speech".—PlEd
  "I am the rose of Sharon, and the lily of the valleys." See The Song of Solomon
  Job, sels.
    "Surely there is a mine for silver".—PlSc
  Kings, sels.
    "And Hiram of Tyre sent his servants unto Solomon, for he had".—PlEd
  Proverbs, sels.
    "Who can find a virtuous woman, for her price is far above rubies".—PlSc
  Psalm 23 ("The Lord is my shepherd, I shall not want"). See The book of psalms
  Psalm 24. See The book of psalms
  Psalm 100. See The book of psalms
  Psalm 103. See The book of psalms
  Psalm 121. See The book of psalms
  The Song of Solomon, sels.
    "I am the rose of Sharon, and the lily of the valleys".—McL
  "Surely there is a mine for silver." See Job
  "Who can find a virtuous woman, for her price is far above rubies." See Proverbs
Bicycles and bicycling
  Bike ride. L. Moore.—LiSf—MoSn
  The centipede ("The centipede with many feet"). J. Prelutsky.—PrSr
  Lament. G. Roberts.—JaG
  "Michael built a bicycle." J. Prelutsky.—PrNk
  Two wheels. R. J. Margolis.—MaS
  "Under the dawn I wake my two-wheel friend." From On a bicycle. Y. Yevtushenko.—LiIl
Bierhorst, John
  Friendship ("Like a quetzal plume, a fragrant flower"), tr. by.—LiIl
  The song of a dream, tr. by.—LiIl
Bifocal. William Stafford.—HeR
"**Big**." See Move over
Big. Dorothy Aldis.—PrRa
"The **big** brown hen and Mrs. Duck." See A little talk
Big friend of the stones. Steve Orlen.—JaPi
Big house. Myra Cohn Livingston.—LiWo
"**Big** Ralph from Rolfe had a black Corvette." See The true ballad of the great race to Gilmore City
The **big** rock candy mountains ("On a summer's day in the month of May, a burly little bum come a-hiking"). Unknown.—KeK
The big rock candy mountains ("One evening as the sun went down").—KoT

The **big** rock candy mountains ("One evening as the sun went down"). See The big rock candy mountains ("On a summer's day in the month of May, a burly little bum come a-hiking")
"**Big** rocks into pebbles." See Rocks
A **big** turtle. Unknown.—PrRa
"A **big** turtle sat on the end of a log." See A big turtle
"**Big** wings dawns dark." See Eagle
"The **bigger** the box the more it holds." See Boxes and bags
The **bight,** on my birthday. Elizabeth Bishop.—HeR
Bijou. Vern Rutsala.—JaD
Bike ride. Lilian Moore.—LiSf—MoSn
"**Bill** Bubble in a bowler hat." See All the way back
"**Bill** learned to play tunes on a comb." See A nuisance at home
"**Billy,** in one of his nice new sashes." See Tender heartedness
Billy Paris. Mel Glenn.—GlC
Bingo. Unknown.—KoT
Binnorie. Unknown.—PlAs
Binsey poplars, felled 1879. Gerard Manley Hopkins.—HeR
The **biplane.** Steve Orlen.—JaG
"The **birch** begins to crack its outer sheath." See A young birch
Birch trees
  Birch trees. J. R. Moreland.—PrRh
  Birches. R. Frost.—HeR—KoS
  Birches, Doheny Road. M. C. Livingston.—LiMp
  A young birch. R. Frost.—KoS
Birch trees. John Richard Moreland.—PrRh
Birches. Robert Frost.—HeR—KoS
Birches, Doheny Road. Myra Cohn Livingston.—LiMp
A **bird.** See "A bird came down the walk"
"A **bird** came down the walk." Emily Dickinson.—HaOf
  A bird.—CoN
The **bird** of night. Randall Jarrell.—KeK—LiSf
Bird talk ("And now when the branches were beginning to be heavy"). Carl Sandburg.—HoRa
Bird talk ("Think, said the robin"). Aileen Fisher.—FrP
Bird theater. Robert Wallace.—JaT
Bird watcher. Ronald Wallace.—JaPo
"A **birdie** with a yellow bill." See Time to rise
Birds. See also names of birds, as Sparrows
  The actor. P. Fleischman.—FlI
  Baby talk. A. B. Stewart.—PrRh
  Be like the bird. V. Hugo.—LiSf
  The bight, on my birthday. E. Bishop.—HeR
  "A bird came down the walk." E. Dickinson.—HaOf
    A bird.—CoN
  Bird talk ("And now when the branches were beginning to be heavy"). C. Sandburg.—HoRa
  Bird talk ("Think, said the robin"). A. Fisher.—FrP
  Bird theater. R. Wallace.—JaT
  Bird watcher. R. Wallace.—JaPo
  The birds know. E. Farjeon.—FaE
  "Birds of a feather flock together." Mother Goose.—DaC
    "Birds of a feather will flock together".—LoR

Birds—Migration—*Continued*
"How do they know." A. Fisher.—HoSi
The last word of a bluebird (as told to a child).
R. Frost.—KoS—LiSf
Lost ("What happened in the sky"). L.
Moore.—MoSn
Prayer to the migratory birds. Unknown, fr. the
Kwakiutl Indian.—BiSp
"Something told the wild geese." R. Field.—
CoN—CoOu—HaOf—LiSf—PrRh
They've all gone south. M. B. Miller.—PrRh
"The **birds**." See December eclipse
"**Birds** and leaves disconnect in Fall." See
Zimmer in fall
"The **birds** are gone to bed, the cows are still."
See Hares at play
"**Birds** are known to cheep and chirp." See The
multilingual mynah bird
"The **birds** are still out of town." See Just before
springtime
"The **birds**, are they worth remembering." See
Wingtip
"The **birds** go fluttering in the air." See The silent
snake
"**Birds** in the sea." See Beyond sci-fi
The **birds** know. Eleanor Farjeon.—FaE
"The **birds** know, you can hear they know." See
The birds know
The **bird's** nest. Unknown.—DaC
"**Birds** of a feather flock together." Mother
Goose.—DaC
"Birds of a feather will flock together".—LoR
"**Birds** of a feather will flock together". See "Birds
of a feather flock together"
"**Birds** will be house hunting." See House hunters
Birth
"The angel that presided o'er my birth." W.
Blake.—HeR
Baby song. T. Gunn.—HeR
Birth. G. E. Lyon.—JaS
Birth of the foal. F. Juhasz.—HeR
The egg ("If you listen very carefully, you'll
hear the"). J. Prelutsky.—PrZ
For my son, born during an ice storm. D.
Jauss.—JaS
The hen and the carp. I. Serraillier.—CoOu—
LiSf
Infant sorrow. W. Blake.—HeR
Introduction to life. Unknown, fr. the Iglulik
Eskimo.—BiSp
Magic spell for a difficult birth. Unknown, fr.
the Arejuna Indian.—BiSp
Mary's burden. E. Farjeon.—FaE
Melora's song. From John Brown's body. S. V.
Benét.—PlAs
Mother's prayer for a girl. Unknown, fr. the
Navajo Indian.—BiSp
The new mothers. C. Shields.—JaS
On a child who lived one minute. X. J.
Kennedy.—JaD
Poem in which my legs are accepted. K.
Fraser.—McL
Prayer of the midwife to the Goddess of Water.
Unknown, fr. the Aztec Indian.—BiSp
Song to a son. Unknown, fr. the Kwakiutl
Indian.—BiSp
Song to the child. Unknown, fr. the West
Greenland Eskimo.—BiSp
When the child is named. Unknown, fr. the
Tewa Indian.—BiSp
Woman's prayer to the sun, for a newborn girl.
Unknown, fr. the Hopi Indian.—BiSp

Birth. George Ella Lyon.—JaS
Birth of the daisies. Ruth Krauss.—HoBf
Birth of the foal. Ferenc Juhasz, tr. by David
Wevill.—HeR
A **birthday** ("My heart is like a singing bird").
Christina Georgina Rossetti.—BlO—KoT
Birthday ("Today I'm a year older."). Richard J.
Margolis.—MaS
Birthday ("When he asked for the moon"). Myra
Cohn Livingston.—LiCe
The **birthday** child. Rose Fyleman.—FrP
Birthdays
Betsy Jane's sixth birthday. A. Noyes.—LiIl
Between birthdays. O. Nash.—CoOu
The bight, on my birthday. E. Bishop.—HeR
A birthday ("My heart is like a singing bird").
C. G. Rossetti.—BlO—KoT
Birthday ("Today I'm a year older."). R. J.
Margolis.—MaS
Birthday ("When he asked for the moon"). M.
C. Livingston.—LiCe
The birthday child. R. Fyleman.—FrP
Birthdays. M. A. Hoberman.—PrRa
Buying a puppy. L. Norris.—LiIl—LiSf
Five years old. M. L. Allen.—FrP—PrRa
Goodbye six, hello seven. J. Viorst.—ViI
Happy birthday, dear dragon. J. Prelutsky.—
PrNk
If we didn't have birthdays. Dr. Seuss.—PrRh
"I'm disgusted with my brother." J. Prelutsky.—
PrNk
Jane Seagrim's party. L. Nathan.—JaG
"Monday's child is fair of face." Mother
Goose.—DaC—DeM—FaW—LoR
"My birthday's in August." J. Prelutsky.—PrWi
Poem for Ntombe Iayo (at five weeks of age).
N. Giovanni.—GiSp
Poem for Shane on her brother's birthday. D.
T. Sanders.—KoT
Poem in October. D. Thomas.—HeR
A valentine birthday. B. J. Esbensen.—LiVp
What someone said when he was spanked on
the day before his birthday. J. Ciardi.—PrRh
The wish ("Each birthday wish"). A. Friday.—
PrRa
Birthdays. Mary Ann Hoberman.—PrRa
The **birthplace**. Robert Frost.—PlEd
Bishop, Elizabeth
The bight, on my birthday.—HeR
The burglar of Babylon.—HeR
The fish ("I caught a tremendous fish").—HeR
Insomnia ("The moon in the bureau mirror").—
McL
Large bad picture.—PlEd
Manners ("My grandfather said to me").—
HeR—JaG
Sandpiper ("The roaring alongside he takes for
granted").—HeR
Sleeping on the ceiling.—KoT
Songs for a colored singer.—HeR
Bishop, John Peale
John Donne's statue.—PlEd
Bishop, Morris
At a modernist school.—BrT
The car's in the hall.—BrT
Hog calling competition.—BrT—PrRh
How to treat elves.—HaOf
Opportunity's knock.—BrT
A sensitive man.—BrT
The sick shark.—BrT
Song of the pop-bottlers.—FaW—KeK
A strong minded lady.—BrT
A vaporish maiden.—BrT

Bisons. See Buffaloes

"Biting air." See Winter days

"Bitter batter boop." See The last cry of the damp fly

Black (color)
What is black. M. O'Neill.—CoN

"Black A, white E, red I, green U, blue O, vowels." See Vowels

The **black** bear ("The bear's black bulk"). Ted Hughes.—HuU

The **black** bear ("In the summer, fall and spring"). Jack Prelutsky.—PrZ

Black bear ("Sweet-mouth, honey-paws, hairy one!"). Douglas Lepan.—DoNw

"The **black** cat yawns." See Cat

The **black** cloud. William Henry Davies.—HeR

"The **black** cock crowed." See Two o'clock

Black dog. Charlotte Zolotow.—ZoE

"Black-eyed Susan." N. M. Bodecker.—BoSs

The **black** fern. Leslie Norris.—LiSf

"Black girl black girl." See Blackberry sweet

Black heritage. See Heritage—Black

"Black is the night." See What is black

"Black lake, black boat, two black, cut-paper people." See Crossing the water

"The **black** man." See Sum people

A **black** Pierrot. Langston Hughes.—HuDk

Black rock of Kiltearn. Andrew Young.—HeR

"Black spirits and white, red spirits and gray." From The witch. Thomas Middleton.—LiWa

"Black swallows swooping or gliding." See The skaters

Blackberries
Meeting Mary. E. Farjeon.—FaE

Blackberry sweet. Dudley Randall.—KeK

The **blackbird.** Humbert Wolfe.—LiSf—PrRh

Blackbirds
Bay bank. A. R. Ammons.—JaD
The blackbird. H. Wolfe.—LiSf—PrRh
The first blackbird. E. Farjeon.—FaE
The red-wing blackbird. W. C. Williams.—JaD
"Sing a song of sixpence." Mother Goose.—AlH—DaC—DeM—FaW—LoR
Singing in the spring. I. O. Eastwick.—PrRa
Thirteen ways of looking at a blackbird. W. Stevens.—HeR

Blackfeet. See Indians of the Americas—Blackfeet

Blacklisted. Carl Sandburg.—PlSc

Blacks. See also Heritage—Black; Race relations; Slavery
African dance. L. Hughes.—HuDk
Amoebaean for daddy. M. Angelou.—AnS
As I grew older. L. Hughes.—HuDk
The ballad of Rudolph Reed. G. Brooks.—HeR
Blackberry sweet. D. Randall.—KeK
Bound no'th blues. L. Hughes.—HuDk
Dance poem. N. Giovanni.—GiSp—LiSf
Dream variation. L. Hughes.—HuDk
I, too. L. Hughes.—HuDk
Martin Luther King. M. C. Livingston.—LiSf—PrRh
Montgomery. S. Cornish.—JaPi
My people. L. Hughes.—HuDk
Negro dancers. L. Hughes.—HuDk
The Negro speaks of rivers. L. Hughes.—HaOf—HuDk—LiSf
Po' boy blues. L. Hughes.—HuDk
Prayer meeting. L. Hughes.—HuDk
Psalm of a black mother. T. Greenwood.—LaT
Share-croppers. L. Hughes.—PlSc
Some things are funny like that. N. Giovanni.—GiSp

Song ("Lovely, dark, and lonely one"). L. Hughes.—HuDk
Songs for a colored singer. E. Bishop.—HeR
To a suitor. M. Angelou.—AnS
The weary blues. L. Hughes.—HuDk
Weekend glory. M. Angelou.—AnS
"Yvonne." N. Giovanni.—GiSp

"The **blackshawled** women of New Mexico." See Old women beside a church

Blacksmiths
The blacksmiths. Unknown.—HeR
The village blacksmith. H. W. Longfellow.—HaOf

The **blacksmiths.** Unknown.—HeR

"The **blacksmith's** boy went out with a rifle." See Legend

Blair, Lee
An apple a day ("I must eat an apple, said Link").—BrT
Raisin bread.—BrT
Stop.—BrT

Blake, William
Ah, sunflower.—HeR
"The angel that presided o'er my birth."—HeR
Auguries of innocence, complete.—HeR
Auguries of innocence, sels.
"To see a world in a grain of sand".—PrRh
To see a world.—KeK
The chimney sweeper ("A little black thing among the snow").—HeR—PlSc
The chimney sweeper ("When my mother died I was very young").—PlSc
The clod and the pebble.—HeR
A cradle song ("Sweet dreams, form a shade").—HaO—RoC
The crystal cabinet.—PlAs
A divine image.—HeR
Eternity.—HeR
The fly ("Little fly").—BlO
The garden of love.—HeR
"Hear the voice of the Bard."—HeR
Infant sorrow.—HeR
Introduction to Songs of innocence. See "Piping down the valleys wild"
Jerusalem. See Milton
The lamb ("Little lamb, who made thee").—LiSf
London.—HeR
Long John Brown and little Mary Bell.—HeR
Milton, sels.
Jerusalem.—HeR
Night ("The sun descending in the west").—ChB
"Piping down the valleys wild."—CoOu—LiSf
Introduction to Songs of innocence.—PrRh
A poison tree.—HeR
The sick rose.—HeR
The smile.—HeR
Spring ("Sound the flute").—FrP—KoT—LiSf
The tiger. See The tyger
"To see a world in a grain of sand." See Auguries of innocence
The tyger.—BlO—HeR—KoT
The tiger.—LiSf
"When old corruption first begun."—HeR
"When the green woods laugh."—KoT

Blake, William (about)
Blake leads a walk on the Milky Way. N. Willard.—HaOf
Blake leads a walk on the Milky Way. Nancy Willard.—HaOf

Blasing, Randy
Things I didn't know I loved, tr. by.—McL

Bleezer's ice cream. Jack Prelutsky.—PrNk

"**Bless** the four corners of this house." See House blessing
"**Bless** the Lord, O my soul." See Psalm 103
"**Blessed** Lord, what it is to be young." David McCord.—CoN—KeK
"**Blessed** Saint George." See Prayer of the Mexican child
A **blessing**. James Wright.—McL
Blessings. N. M. Bodecker.—BoPc
Blessings on gentle folk, sels. Unknown, tr. by Arthur Waley
    "The locusts' wings say, throng, throng".—StG
"**Blessings** on thee, little man." See The barefoot boy
Blind
    The blind men and the elephant. J. G. Saxe.—CoOu—HaOf
    "I asked the little boy who cannot see." Unknown.—CoOu
    "Three blind mice." Mother Goose.—AlH—DeM—LoR
    To a blind student who taught me to see. S. Hazo.—JaG
Blind alley. Eleanor Farjeon.—FaE
The **blind** men and the elephant. John Godfrey Saxe.—CoOu—HaOf
Bliss. Eleanor Farjeon.—FaE—PrRh
Blizzard. Barbara Juster Esbensen.—EsCs
Block city. Robert Louis Stevenson.—CoN—PlEd
Blocks. See Toys
"The **bloders** are exploding." Jack Prelutsky.—PrNk
Blok, Alexander
    Little catkins.—LiE
Blood
    For every one. A. Adoff.—AdA
    Great and strong. M. Holub.—HeR
    The mosquito knows. D. H. Lawrence.—HeR—PrBb
    "When Dracula went to the blood bank." J. Prelutsky.—PrNk
"A **bloody** and a sudden end." See John Kinsella's lament for Mrs. Mary Moore
Blossoms. Frank Dempster Sherman.—HaOf
Blount, Roy
    A hearty cook.—BrT
    Hog calling.—BrT
    A lady track star.—BrT
    Song against broccoli.—JaPo
Blount, Roy, Jr.
    A strong feeling for poultry.—BrT
"**Blow**, blow, thou winter wind." From As you like it. William Shakespeare.—HoUn
Blow, bugle, blow. See "The splendour falls on castle walls"
Blow the stars home. Eleanor Farjeon.—FaE
"**Blow** the stars home, wind, blow the stars home." See Blow the stars home
Blow up. X. J. Kennedy.—KeF
"**Blow**, wind, blow." Mother Goose.—DeM—LoR
Blowin' in the wind. Bob Dylan.—KeK
Blowing bubbles. Margaret Hillert.—PrRa
Blubber lips. Jim Daniels.—JaT
"**Blubber** lips, blubber lips." See Blubber lips
Blue (color)
    Bavarian gentians. D. H. Lawrence.—KoT
    Blue. C. Zolotow.—ZoE
    How violets came blue. R. Herrick.—KoT
    "Touch blue." Mother Goose.—LoR
Blue. Charlotte Zolotow.—ZoE
"The **blue** cuckoo." See Blue cuckoo
Blue cuckoo. Unknown, tr. by Ulli Beier.—HeR
"A **blue** day." See March

Blue-eyed Mary. Mary E. Wilkins Freeman.—HaOf
"The **blue** gate in the wall." See The gate in the wall
Blue girls. John Crowe Ransom.—HeR
"**Blue** is a good color." See Blue
Blue jays. See Jays
"**Blue** mountains to the north of the walls." See Taking leave of a friend
Blue sparks in dark closets. Richard Snyder.—JaPi
Blue Springs, Georgia. Ree Young.—JaG
"**Blue**, the sky." See Questions for September
"**Bluebird** and." See Spring
Bluebirds
    The last word of a bluebird (as told to a child). R. Frost.—KoS—LiSf
Blues (music)
    Bound no'th blues. L. Hughes.—HuDk
    Dressed up. L. Hughes.—HuDk
    A good woman feeling bad. M. Angelou.—AnS
    Homesick blues. L. Hughes.—HuDk
    Night and morn. L. Hughes.—HuDk
    Po' boy blues. L. Hughes.—HuDk
    The weary blues. L. Hughes.—HuDk
"The **blues** may be the life you've led." See A good woman feeling bad
The **bluffalo**. Jane Yolen.—PrRh
Blum. Dorothy Aldis.—FrP—LiSf
Blumenthal, Michael
    Back from the word processing course, I say to my old typewriter.—JaG
Bly, Robert
    At mid ocean.—McL
    At the funeral of great aunt Mary.—JaS
    Breathing space July, tr. by.—HeR
    The cable ship, tr. by.—HeR
    Cotton, tr. by.—HeR
    Dusk in the country, tr. by.—HeR
    The earthworm, tr. by.—HeR
    In a train.—KoT
    Masses, tr. by.—HeR
    On the Congo, tr. by.—HeR
    The radiance, tr. by.—McL
    Solitude ("Right here I was nearly killed one night in February"), tr. by.—HeR
    Track, tr. by.—HeR
Blyth, R. H.
    "The wren", tr. by.—CoN
The **boa** ("Allow me just one short remark"). J. J. Bell.—PrRh
Boa constrictors. See Snakes
The **boar** and the dromedar. Henry Beissel.—DoNw
Boasting. Eleanor Farjeon.—FaE
A **boat** ("O beautiful"). Richard Brautigan.—KeK
The **boat** ("Oh, see my little boat"). Caroline Gilman.—HaOf
Boat stealing. From The prelude. William Wordsworth.—HeR
"A **boat** steams slowly down the river." See I wonder
Boatman's prayer for smooth waters. Unknown.—BiSp
The **boats**. Charlotte Zolotow.—ZoE
Boats and boating. See also Canoes and canoeing; Ferries; Ships; Toys
    "The barge she sat in, like a burnish'd throne." From Antony and Cleopatra. W. Shakespeare.—HoUn
    "Belly and Tubs went out in a boat." C. Watson.—PrRa
    Bermudas. A. Marvell.—HeR

Boats and boating.—*Continued*
The boat ("Oh, see my little boat"). C. Gilman.—HaOf
Boat stealing. From The prelude. W. Wordsworth.—HeR
The boats. C. Zolotow.—ZoE
Bulgy Bunne. J. Prelutsky.—PrNk
Canadian boat-song. Unknown, at. to John Galt.—PlAs
Crossing the water. S. Plath.—HeR
"Dear God." Unknown.—LaT
"The dragon boats, there they go." Unknown.—DeD
"Gaily afloat." A. Lobel.—LoWr
"Going up the river." Unknown.—PlAs
A good play. R. L. Stevenson.—DaC
"I am going to California." Unknown.—PlAs
I wonder. C. Zolotow.—HoSu
The jumblies. E. Lear.—BlO—LiH
"Little Tee Wee." Mother Goose.—DeM—FaW—LoR—RuI
Love at sea. J. P. Lewis.—LiVp
Max Schmitt in a single scull. R. Lattimore.—PlEd
Mississippi sounding calls. Unknown.—LiSf
Moon boat. C. Pomerantz.—PoA—PrRa
My bed is a boat. R. L. Stevenson.—ChB
The old salt. J. Ciardi.—CiD
Out for a ride. C. Lewis.—HoSu
The owl and the pussycat. E. Lear.—BlO—CoN—FaW—KoT—LiH—LiSf—PrRh
Pirate story. R. L. Stevenson.—DaC
Prayer for smooth waters. Unknown, fr. the Yahgan Indian.—BiSp
Queens of the river. C. Lewis.—HoCl—LiSf
The rapid. C. Sangster.—DoNw
Rowing. E. Ochester.—JaS
"Rub-a-dub-dub." Mother Goose.—DaC—DeM—FaW—LoR—WaC
Sonnet. Dante Alighieri.—HeR—KoT
"A strong nor'wester's blowing, Bill." W. Pitt.—TrM
A tail of the see. E. T. Corbett.—HaOf
"There was an old person of Grange." E. Lear.—LiH
"Though pleased to see the dolphins play." M. Green.—TrM
"Three wise men of Gotham." Mother Goose.—DeM—FaW—LoR
"Two robins from Charlotte." J. Prelutsky.—PrRi
Where go the boats. R. L. Stevenson.—CoN
Wynken, Blynken, and Nod. E. Field.—CoN—DaC—HaOf
"Boats sail on the rivers." See The rainbow
Bobadil. James Reeves.—LiSf
Bobbily Boo and Wollypotump. Laura E. Richards.—LiSf
"Bobbily Boo, the king so free." See Bobbily Boo and Wollypotump
"Bobby Shaftoe's gone to sea". See "Bobby Shafto's gone to sea"
"Bobby Shafto's gone to sea." Mother Goose.—LoR
"Bobby Shaftoe's gone to sea".—DeM
Bobolinks
Robert of Lincoln. W. C. Bryant.—HaOf
Bodecker, N. M.
"After the rains."—BoSs
"Alicia Patricia."—BoSs
The American dilemma.—BoPc
At sunrise.—BoPc
Awake.—BoPc

"Bartholomew the hatter."—BoSs
"Beautification."—BoPc
Bedtime mumble.—BoSs
"Beware of dog."—BoSs
Beware of speaker.—BoPc
"Black-eyed Susan."—BoSs
Blessings.—BoPc
Bumble bee.—BoSs
Camel ("The camel is.").—BoSs
Cats and dogs ("Some like cats, and some like dogs.").—BoSs
Chameleon.—BoSs
Chipmunk.—BoSs
City dawn.—BoPc
Cityscape.—BoPc
Cockatoo.—BoSs
Crocodile ("I trust you not").—BoSs
Crustration.—BoPc
D.A.R.—BoPc
Development.—BoPc
Don't leave the spoon in the syrup.—BoSs
First snowflake.—BoSs
Floundering.—BoPc
"Footprints of a sparrow."—BaS—BoSs
Frog.—BoSs
Giraffe ("I like.").—BoSs
Glass walling.—BoPc
Gloire.—BoPc
Good chew.—BoPc
Good egg.—BoPc
"Goodby my winter suit."—PrRh
"Harry Perry Boysenberry."—BoSs
Hedgehog.—BoSs
"Heigh ho, mistletoe."—BoSs
Hippopotamus ("The hippopotamus").—BoSs
If ("If the pie crust").—BoPc
"I'm never as good as I want to be."—BoSs
In the field of clover by the river Charles.—BoSs
Is it nice to be wise.—BoPc
"The island of Yorrick."—LiWa
J. Prior, Esq.—LiSf
John.—PrRh
Journey's end.—BoPc
Know him.—BoPc
Lamb ("In Noah's").—BoSs
"Let's marry said the cherry."—LiSf
Lion ("The lion").—BoSs
A matter of principle.—BoPc
Miss Bitter.—CoN
Mr. 'Gator.—CoN—CoOu—FaW—LiSf
Mr. Skinner.—FaW—LiSf
Morning at the Post Office.—BoPc
Mosquito ("A mosquito.").—BoSs
My girl Maggie.—BoSs
My trouble with porringers and oranges.—BoSs
"Never mind the rain."—HoSu
New day.—BoPc
New England road.—BoPc
Newbread.—BoPc
"Night crawler."—JaT
Number two.—BoPc
Nut.—BoSs
"Oases."—BoSs
October nights in my cabin.—BoSs
Orbit's end.—BoPc
Order.—BoSs
Pelican.—BoSs
Pigeon hole.—BoPc
Possum.—BoSs
Radish.—BoSs
Rain in the city.—BoPc
Relations.—BoPc

Bodecker, N. M.—*Continued*
Rooster.—BoSs
Ruth Luce and Bruce Booth.—BoSs
Sensible Sue.—BoPc
Signs.—BoPc
A simple need.—BoPc
Sing me a song of teapots and trumpets.—PrRh
Single.—BoPc
Small rains.—BoSs
Snapshots.—BoPc
Snowman sniffles.—BoSs
A sparrow in winter.—BoSs
Spring gale.—BoSs
Spring morning in Boston's south end.—BoPc
Sweet history.—BoPc
Terror.—BoPc
"There once was a king", tr. by.—FaW
"This life."—BoPc
Town meeting or 'hey man, don't speak so good'.—BoPc
Traffic rule I.—BoPc
Trustworthiness.—BoPc
"Two cats were sitting in a tree", tr. by.—FaW
Up north.—BoPc
Warthog.—BoSs
Water sport.—BoPc
Weevil.—BoSs
When all the world is full of snow.—PrRh
"When skies are low."—BoSs
"Why do weeping willows weep."—BoSs
Windy day.—BoPc
Zebra and leopard.—BoSs
A zoo without bars.—BoSs
Body, Human. See also names of parts of the body, as Hands
"Be glad your nose is on your face." J. Prelutsky.—PrNk
Heart. J. LaBombard.—JaPo
"Here all we see." W. De la Mare.—PrRa
"Here is the nose that smelled something sweet." C. Watson.—WaC
"I like my body when it is with your." E. E. Cummings.—McL
I've got an itch. J. Prelutsky.—PrNk
Lauren Jones. M. Glenn.—GlC
The leg. K. Shapiro.—JaD
"Loose and limber." A. Lobel.—LoWr
One of the problems of play. N. Giovanni.—GiSp
Bog-face. Stevie Smith.—HeR
Bogan, Louise
The alchemist ("I burned my life, that I might find").—McL
Betrothed.—McL
Statue and birds.—PlEd
The **bogeyman.** Jack Prelutsky.—PrRh
Bogin, George
Abraham.—JaG
"The **bogus** boo." James Reeves.—PrRh
"**Boing,** boing, squeak." Jack Prelutsky.—PrNk
The **bold** pedlar and Robin Hood. Unknown.—PlAs
Bombs and bombing
Air raid. P. Wild.—JaPi
At the bomb testing site. W. Stafford.—HeR
The fury of aerial bombardment. R. Eberhart.—HeR
Bond, Ruskin
For silence.—LaT
Bones
At the keyhole. W. De la Mare.—BlO
Ballad of a boneless chicken. J. Prelutsky.—PrNk

Binnorie. Unknown.—PlAs
The collarbone of a hare. W. B. Yeats.—HeR
Dinosaurs ("Their feet, planted into tar"). M. C. Livingston.—HoDi
The dreaming of the bones. From Song for the cloth. W. B. Yeats.—HeR
Flies. V. Worth.—WoSp
Perfect. H. MacDiarmid.—HeR
Song for the clatter-bones. F. R. Higgins.—HeR
The stone troll. J. R. R. Tolkien.—LiSf
To the skeleton of a dinosaur in the museum. L. Moore.—HoDi
The tree on the corner. L. Moore.—MoSn
The wishbone. J. Prelutsky.—PrIt
Xylophone. E. Merriam.—MeHa
The **bonfire.** Eleanor Farjeon.—FaE
"**Bonny** bride, bonny bride, mind how you tread." See The bonny bride of Kent
The **bonny** bride of Kent. Eleanor Farjeon.—FaE
The **bonny** Earl of Moray ("Ye hielands and ye lawlands"). Unknown.—BlO
The **bonny** earl of Murray ("Ye highlands and ye lawlands").—PlAs
The **bonny** earl of Murray ("Ye highlands and ye lawlands"). See The bonny Earl of Moray ("Ye hielands and ye lawlands")
Bonny George Campbell. Unknown.—PlAs
"**Bonny** lass, pretty lass, wilt thou be mine." See A proposal
"The **bonsai** tree." See A work of artifice
Bontemps, Arna
Southern mansion.—LiWa
"A **book** is a place." Clyde Watson.—BeD
The **book** of psalms, sels. Bible/Old Testament
Psalm 23 ("The Lord is my shepherd, I shall not want").—LiSf
   Psalm 23 ("The Lord to me a shepherd is").—HaOf
Psalm 24.—LiSf
Psalm 100.—LiSf—LiTp
Psalm 103.—LiSf
Psalm 121.—HaOf
Booker, Betty
David in April.—JaPo
Bookish. Aileen Fisher.—FiW
Books. Eleanor Farjeon.—FaE
Books and reading
And the. P. Redcloud.—BaS
"As I was laying on the green." Unknown.—TrM
"A book is a place." C. Watson.—BeD
Bookish. A. Fisher.—FiW
Books. E. Farjeon.—FaE
"Books fall open." D. McCord.—HaOf
"Books to the ceiling, books to the sky." A. Lobel.—LoWr
Cats love books. B. S. De Regniers.—DeT
"Curiosity's not in my head." From On reading, four limericks. M. C. Livingston.—MeF
Dear reader. P. Meinke.—JaPi
"Doris Drummond sneaked a look." X. J. Kennedy.—KeB
The fly ("I was sitting on the porch"). C. Zolotow.—ZoE
Franz Dominguez. M. Glenn.—GlC
A house of readers. J. W. Miller.—JaPo
"If you don't know the meaning of snook." From On reading, four limericks. M. C. Livingston.—MeF—MeF
"If you're apt to be ravenous, look." From On reading, four limericks. M. C. Livingston.—MeF—MeF

Books and reading—*Continued*
In the library ("You're right"). M. P. Hearn.—
CoN
"It is nice to read." Onitsura.—LiSf
The land of story books. R. L. Stevenson.—
DaC
The library ("It looks like any building"). B.
A. Huff.—PrRh
Library ("No need even"). V. Worth.—WoSp
Lincoln. N. B. Turner.—PrRh
Mary indoors. E. Farjeon.—FaE
My fishbowl head. X. J. Kennedy.—KeF
My, oh wow, book. J. Viorst.—ViI
Now lift me close. W. Whitman.—JaD
The omnivorous bookworm. O. Herford.—BrT
Paul Hewitt. M. Glenn.—GlCd
Read. A. Turner.—TuS
Reading room the New York Public Library.
R. Eberhart.—JaG
Saul Steiner. M. Glenn.—GlC
Ten years old ("I paid my 30¢ and rode by
the bus"). N. Giovanni. GiSp LiSf
"There is no frigate like a book." E.
Dickinson.—HaOf
"What if." I. J. Glaser.—HoDi
White autumn. R. Morgan.—JaS
Worlds I know. M. C. Livingston.—LiWo
"A young person of precious precocity." From
On reading, four limericks. M. C.
Livingston.—MeF
'**Books** fall open." David McCord.—HaOf
'**Books** to the ceiling, books to the sky." Arnold
Lobel.—LoWr
'**Boom**, boom." Arnold Lobel.—LoWr
'A **boot** and a shoe and a slipper." See High and
low
Booth, Philip
Crows ("So, nine crows to this April field") —
JaD
Heron ("In the copper marsh").—JaPo
How to see deer.—JaPi
A late spring.—JaPi
Photographer.—PlEd
Thanksgiving ("The tides in my eyes are
heavy").—JaS
"**Boots**." See Downpour
Boots and shoes
Before I count fifteen. M. Rosen.—FaW
"Cobbler, cobbler, mend my shoe." Mother
Goose.—DaC—DeM—LoR
"Diddle, diddle, dumpling, my son John."
Mother Goose.—BaH—DeM—FaW—LiSf—
LoR
First day of school. B. J. Esbensen.—EsCs
Footnote. N. Smaridge.—PrRa
Galoshes. R. W. Bacmeister.—CoN
High and low. J. B. Tabb.—BrT
High heeled shoes. K. C. Goddard.—FrP
How much is a gross. J. Ciardi.—CiD
In Pete's shoes. J. Ciardi.—CiD
"It was a cold and wintry night." Unknown.—
TrM
"Left foot." E. Merriam.—MeBl
"Little Betty Blue lost her holiday shoe."
Mother Goose.—DeM—LoR
Muddy sneakers. X. J. Kennedy.—KeF
New shoes ("The first time in new shoes"). E.
Merriam.—MeF
New shoes ("My shoes are new and squeaky
shoes"). Unknown.—BeD
New shoes ("When I am walking down the
street"). M. S. Watts.—FrP
The sad boy. L. Riding.—HeR

Shoes. V. Worth.—JaT
Sole-hungering camel. O. Herford.—BrT
Squeaky shoes. Unknown.—BrT
Teresa's red Adidas. P. B. Janeczko.—JaT
"There was a young lady of Twickenham." O.
Herford.—KeK
"There was an old man from Peru."
Unknown.—CoOu—KeK
An old man from Peru.—BrT—CoN
"There was an old man of Toulouse." E.
Lear.—LiH
"There was an old woman who lived in a
shoe." Mother Goose.—AlH—DeM—FaW—
LoR
"There was an old woman, she lived in
a shoe".—BlPi
Unusual shoelaces. X. J. Kennedy.—JaT—LiSf
Borders. Arnold Adoff.—AdA
The **bored** ostrich. Unknown.—BrT
Boredom
The bored ostrich. Unknown.—BrT
Boredom. E. Farjeon.—FaE
Boring. J. Prelutsky.—PrWi
Disillusionment of ten o'clock. W. Stevens.—
HeR—KoT
Ennui. L. Hughes.—HaOf
Faith Plotkin. M. Glenn.—GlC
Gary Irving. M. Glenn.—GlCd
Harvey Persky. M. Glenn.—GlCd
History ("And I'm thinking how to get out").
M. C. Livingston.—PrRh
"It's eleven o'clock." N. Chambers.—PrRa
Michelle Church. M. Glenn.—GlCd
The pessimist. B. King.—BlO
Russell Hodges. M. Glenn.—GlCd
Tired Tim. W. De la Mare.—CoN—PrRh
"Today is very boring." J. Prelutsky.—PrNk
Yawning. E. Farjeon.—FaE—PrRh
Boredom. Eleanor Farjeon.—FaE
Boring. Jack Prelutsky.—PrWi
Borson, Roo
In the cafe.—JaPo
The transparence of November.—JaPo
The **boss**. James Russell Lowell.—PlSc
Boston, Ruth
First night of Hanukkah.—LiPj
Boston, Massachusetts
"I come from the city of Boston." Unknown.—
TrM
Botany. See Plants and planting; Science
"**Both** my grandmas came from far away." See
Both my grandmothers
Both my grandmothers. Edward Field.—JaS
"**Bottle**, coarse tumbler, loaf of bread." See Still
life
"The **boughs** do shake and the bells do ring."
Mother Goose.—DeM—LoR
Boulder, Colorado. X. J. Kennedy.—KeF
Boulder dam. May Sarton.—PlSc
Boulton, Sir Harold
All through the night ("Sleep, my child, and
peace attend thee").—ChB
"**Bouncing**, bouncing, on the beds." See In the
motel
Bound no'th blues. Langston Hughes.—HuDk
"**Bound** with." See New planting, shopping mall
Bouquets. Robert Francis.—JaD
Bourinot, Arthur S.
Fish ("The little fish are silent").—PrRa
"**Bow**, wow, wow." Mother Goose.—DeM—LiSf
"**Bowed** by the weight of centuries he leans." See
The man with the hoe

Boys and boyhood.—*Continued*
　While dissecting frogs in biology class Scrut discovers the intricacies of the scooped neckline in his lab partner's dress. G. Roberts.—JaG
　The wind is blowing west. J. Ceravolo.—KoT
　The worm ("When the earth is turned in spring"). R. Bergengren.—ChG—PrRh
　Wrestling. K. Fraser.—HoBf—PrRh
"**Boys** and girls, come out to play." Mother Goose.—DeM—LiSf—LoR
　"Girls and boys, come out to play".—AlH—ChB—DaC
"The **boys** I meet want just one thing only." See Alison Ford
Boys' names. Eleanor Farjeon.—FaE—LiSf
A **boy's** song. James Hogg.—BlO—CoOu—LiIl
Boy's will, joyful labor without pay, and harvest home, sels. Robert Penn Warren
　Work.—PlSc
Bracker, Milton
　A troupial.—BrT
Bradley, Edward
　A queer fellow named Woodin.—BrT
Brady, June
　Far trek.—PrRh
Brain. Coleman Barks.—JaPo
The **brain** surgeon. Cynthia Rylant.—RyW
Brains
　Brain. C. Barks.—JaPo
　My fishbowl head. X. J. Kennedy.—KeF
Braley, Berton
　Church bells.—BrT
　The twins ("When twins came, their father, Dan Dunn").—BrT
"The **branchy** leafy oak-tree." See Sweeney praises the trees
Brandon Dale. Mel Glenn.—GlCd
"The **brass** band blares." See Circus
Brautigan, Richard
　A boat ("O beautiful").—KeK
　The pumpkin tide.—HoSi
　Surprise ("I lift the toilet seat").—KeK
"**Brave** as a postage stamp." See Sporting goods
A **brave** knight. Mary Mapes Dodge.—BrT
The **brave** man. Wallace Stevens.—LiSf
"**Brave** news is come to town." Mother Goose.—DeM—LoR
Bravery. Eleanor Farjeon.—FaE
Bread
　"Hot cross buns, hot cross buns." Mother Goose.—DeM—FaW—LoR
　Newbread. N. M. Bodecker.—BoPc
"**Break,** break, break." Alfred Tennyson.—BlO—HeR
Breakfast
　Breakfast. E. Farjeon.—FaE
　Early breakfast. B. S. De Regniers.—DeT
　"I never had a piece of toast." J. Payn.—TrM
　"I want my breakfast." E. Merriam.—MeBl
　The king's breakfast. A. A. Milne.—FaW—LiSf
　The meal. K. Kuskin.—PrRa
　"Mix a pancake." C. G. Rossetti.—CoN—FrP—LiSf—PrRa
　　The pancake.—ChG
　Mummy slept late and Daddy fixed breakfast. J. Ciardi.—LiSf—PrRh
　Toaster time. E. Merriam.—BeD—PrRa
Breakfast. Eleanor Farjeon.—FaE
Breakin'. Ann Turner.—TuS
Breath and breathing
　Dragon smoke. L. Moore.—LiSf—MoSn—PrRa
　Snow stars. B. J. Esbensen.—EsCs

"**Breathe** and blow." See Dragon smoke
"**Breathing** something German at the end." See The gift to be simple
Breathing space July. Tomas Tranströmer, tr. by Robert Bly.—HeR
Brecht, Bertolt
　Of poor B. B.—HeR
Breek, Lily
　Thank you.—LaT
"The **breeze** stops, the afternoon heat rises." See The field
"A **breeze** wipes creases off my forehead." See Poem in June
"The **breezes** taste." See September
Brenda Stewart. Mel Glenn.—GlC
Brennan, Martin
　Benue lullaby.—LaW
Brennan on the moor. Unknown.—PlAs
Breton, André
　Free union, sels.
　　"My wife whose hair is a brush fire".—KoT
　"My wife whose hair is a brush fire." See Free union
Breton, Nicholas
　Phillida and Coridon.—KoT
Brian Nichols. Mel Glenn.—GlCd
Brian O'Linn. Unknown.—HeR
"**Brian** O'Linn was a gentleman born." See Brian O'Linn
The **bride** ("I wonder if ever"). Charlotte Zolotow.—ZoE
The **bride** ("In she goes"). Eleanor Farjeon.—FaE
Brides and bridegrooms. See Weddings
"A **bridge.**" See The bridge
The **bridge** ("A bridge"). Lilian Moore.—MoSn
The **bridge** ("Glittering bridge"). Charlotte Zolotow.—ZoE
"A **bridge** engineer, Mister Crumpett." Edward Lear.—KeK
The **bridge** from Brooklyn, sels. Raymond Henri
　"Roebling, his life and mind reprieved enough".—PlEd
Bridges, Robert
　Noel, Christmas eve, 1913.—HaO
Bridges
　The bridge ("A bridge"). L. Moore.—MoSn
　The bridge ("Glittering bridge"). C. Zolotow.—ZoE
　"A bridge engineer, Mister Crumpett." E. Lear.—KeK
　Bridges and tunnels. B. Bentley.—PlEd
　Brooklyn bridge. W. J. Smith.—KeK
　Brooklyn Bridge at dawn. R. Le Gallienne.—LiSf
　Composed upon Westminster bridge, Sept. 3, 1802. W. Wordsworth.—PlEd
　　Composed on Westminster bridge.—LiSf
　From Council Bluffs to Omaha. M. C. Livingston.—LiWo
　"If you chance to be crossing." Unknown.—DeD
　"London Bridge is falling down." Mother Goose.—PlEd
　　"London bridge is broken down".—LoR
　"My London Bridge." A. Lobel.—LoWr
　The old bridge at Florence. H. W. Longfellow.—PlEd
　On the bridge. K. Greenaway.—PrRh
　"Roebling, his life and mind reprieved enough." From The bridge from Brooklyn. R. Henri.—PlEd
　To Brooklyn Bridge. H. Crane.—PlEd

Bridges—*Continued*
The troll bridge. L. Moore.—MoSn
Bridges and tunnels. Beth Bentley.—PlEd
Bridgman, L. J. (Lewis Jesse)
The hare and the pig.—PrRh
Brief encounter. Winfield Townley Scott.—JaG
Brief innocence. Maya Angelou.—AnS
Briggs, L. C.
"A dog is a pal, so friendly and fun."—TrM
"Rickenbacker flew a Spad Thirteen."—TrM
"The Texan was mighty hungry."—TrM
"**Bright** clasp of her whole hand around my finger." See To my daughter
Bright conversation with Saint-Ex, sels. Carl Sandburg
"When the smoke of the clouds parted".—HoRa
"A **bright** little maid in St. Thomas." See St. Thomas
"**Bright** stars, light stars." See Stars
"**Bring** an old towel, said Pa." See Buying a puppy
"**Bring** me all of your dreams." See The dream keeper
"**Bring** out the tall tales now that we told." See Ghost story
"**Bring** salad or sausage or scone." From The clean platter. Ogden Nash.—HoMu
"**Bring** the holy crust of bread." See Charmes
Bringing up babies. Roy Fuller.—PrRh
Brinnin, John Malcolm
The ascension, 1925.—JaS
At the museum.—PlEd
Girl in a white coat.—PlSc
Letter to statues.—PlEd
With a posthumous medal.—PlSc
Bristlecone pine. Myra Cohn Livingston.—LiMp
Broccoli
Song against broccoli. R. Blount.—JaPo
"The **broken** mirror." See X, oh X
"The **broken** pillar of the wing jags from the clotted shoulder." See Hurt hawks
The **broken** wedding ring. Unknown.—PlAs
Broken wing. Eleanor Farjeon.—FaE
"**Bronosaurus**, thunder lizard." See Plant-eater
Brontë, Emily
Ladybird, ladybird.—CoOu
Brontë, Charlotte (about)
Charlotte Bronte. S. Coolidge.—HaOf
Brontosaurus. Gail Kredenser.—PrRh
"**Brontosaurus**, diplodocus, gentle trachodon." See When dinosaurs ruled the earth
Bronzes. Carl Sandburg.—PlEd
The **brook**. Alfred Tennyson.—BlO
The **brook** in February. Charles G. D. Roberts.—DoNw
Brooke, L. Leslie
Johnny Crow's garden.—FaW
Brooklyn bridge. William Jay Smith.—KeK
Brooklyn Bridge at dawn. Richard Le Gallienne.—LiSf
"**Brooklyn** bridge, Brooklyn bridge." See Brooklyn bridge
Brooks, Gwendolyn
The ballad of Rudolph Reed.—HeR
The Chicago Picasso.—PlEd
Cynthia in the snow.—BaS—HoSi—LiSf
De koven.—HoSu
Gertrude.—LiSf
Keziah.—PrRa—PrRh
Maurice.—HoBf
Narcissa.—CoN
Old people working (garden, car).—PlSc
Otto.—LiSf

Pete at the zoo.—LiIl
Robert, who is often a stranger to himself.—PrRa
Rudolph is tired of the city.—PrRh
Tommy.—HoSi
Vern.—HoDl—LiIl—LiSf
We real cool.—KeK
Brooks, Noah
"Conductor, when you receive a fare."—TrM
Brooks, Phillips
"O little town of Bethlehem."—RoC (unat.)
Brooks, Shirley
What Jenner said on hearing in Elysium that complaints had been made of his having a statue in Trafalgar Square.—PlEd
Brooks, Walter R.
Ants, although admirable, are awfully aggravating.—PrRh
Ode to spring.—PrRa—PrRh
Ode to the pig, his tail.—PrRh
Thoughts on talkers.—PrRh
Brooks. See Streams
Brooktrout. Ted Hughes.—HuU
"The **brooktrout**, superb as a matador." See Brooktrout
Broom. Valerie Worth.—WoSp
Broom balancing. Kathleen Fraser.—PrRh
Brooms
Broom. V. Worth.—WoSp
For the little girl who asked why the kitchen was so bright. J. Ulmer.—JaT
Moon witches. T. Hughes.—LiWa
"She sweeps with many-colored brooms." E. Dickinson.—PlSc
Brooms. X. J. Kennedy.—KeF
"The **broomstick** bat." See Stickball
The **brother** ("O, know you what I have done"). Thomas Hardy.—PlAs
Brother ("You still carry"). Richard Shelton.—JaS
Brother, can you spare a dime. E. Y. Harburg.—PlAs—PlSc
Brotherhood
Some old ones. A. Adoff.—AdA
Brothers. Robert Currie.—JaPi
Brothers and sisters
Abraham. G. Bogin.—JaG
Alex Garber. M. Glenn.—GlCd
All I did was ask my sister a question. J. Ciardi.—CiD
"All my hats." R. J. Margolis.—MaS
Angelino Falco. M. Glenn.—GlCd
At the grave of my brother. W. Stafford.—JaS
Basketball. N. Giovanni.—GiSp—PrRh
Binnorie. Unknown.—PlAs
Birthday ("Today I'm a year older."). R. J. Margolis.—MaS
The brother ("O, know you what I have done"). T. Hardy.—PlAs
Brother ("You still carry"). R. Shelton.—JaS
Brothers. R. Currie.—JaPi
Can't win. R. J. Margolis.—MaS
Cold potato. R. J. Margolis.—MaS
Danielle O'Mara. M. Glenn.—GlCd
The dead sister. C. Gilman.—HaOf
Dinnertime. R. J. Margolis.—MaS
Downhill. R. J. Margolis.—MaS
The dual site. M. Hamburger.—PlAs
The first tooth. C. Lamb, and M. Lamb.—DaC—PrRh
For my brother who died before I was born. B. Wormser.—JaG
Gathering the bones together. G. Orr.—JaPi
His dog. R. J. Margolis.—MaS

Brothers and sisters—*Continued*

Icicle ("I smacked you in the mouth for no good reason"). D. Huddle.—JaS

"I'm disgusted with my brother." J. Prelutsky.—PrNk

In the motel. X. J. Kennedy.—JaS—PrRh

It really wasn't too bad. J. Ciardi.—CiD

Jodi Kurtz. M. Glenn.—GlC

"Joseph fell a'dreaming." E. Farjeon.—FaE

A July goodbye. R. J. Margolis.—MaS

Kate and I. S. N. Tarrant.—JaT

Keziah. G. Brooks.—PrRa—PrRh

Lament. G. Roberts.—JaG

Last word. R. J. Margolis.—MaS

Lil' bro'. K. Fufuka.—PrRh

Little ("I am the sister of him"). D. Aldis.—CoN

The little brother poem. N. S. Nye.—JaS

Little brother puts his doll to sleep. C. Pomerantz.—PoA

The little maid. A. M. Wells.—HaOf

Maria Preosi. M. Glenn.—GlC

Mary Stuart. E. Muir.—HeR

Mean Maxine. J. Prelutsky.—PrNk

Mixed-up kid. X. J. Kennedy.—KeF

"Molly, my sister, and I fell out." Mother Goose.—DeM

"Mollie, my sister, and I fell out".—LoR

My baby brother. J. Prelutsky.—PrNk

My brother. M. Ridlon.—PrRh

My brother flies over low. D. Huddle.—JaT

"My brother's head should be replaced." J. Prelutsky.—PrNk

"My little sister." W. Wise.—PrRh

"My sister is a sissy." J. Prelutsky.—PrNk

My sister Jane. T. Hughes.—CoOu—LiSf

My sister Laura. S. Milligan.—CoN—FaW—PrRa

"My sister would never throw snowballs at butterflies." J. Prelutsky.—PrIs

On the sidelines. R. J. Margolis.—MaS

"One purple summer eve." R. J. Margolis.—MaS

The quarrel. E. Farjeon.—FaE

Regrets. R. J. Margolis.—MaS

Rhinos purple, hippos green. M. P. Hearn.—PrRh

Rima de la hermana vistiendose. Unknown.—GrT

Rosemarie Stewart. M. Glenn.—GlC

School mornings. R. J. Margolis.—MaS

Scott Garber. M. Glenn.—GlCd

Sisters. E. Farjeon.—FaE

Sister's dressing rhyme. Unknown.—GrT

Some things don't make any sense at all. J. Viorst.—PrRh—ViI

Soups and juices. R. J. Margolis.—MaS

Stars ("In science today we learned"). N. Giovanni.—GiSp—KeK

Stella Kolsky. M. Glenn.—GlC

Teased. R. J. Margolis.—MaS

To my blood sister. C. E. Hemp.—JaS

Triolet against sisters. P. McGinley.—HaOf—KeK

The twins ("In form and feature, face and limb"). H. S. Leigh.—PrRh

Two in bed. A. B. Ross.—CoN

The two sisters. Unknown.—PlAs

Where am I. R. J. Margolis.—MaS

The wishbone. J. Prelutsky.—PrIt

Brown, Abbie Farwell

The peach ("There once was a peach on a tree").—BrT

Brown, Alice

The sensitive cat.—BrT

Brown, Audrey Alexandra

The strangers.—DoNw

Brown, Beatrice Curtis

Jonathan Bing.—PrRh

A new song to sing about Jonathan Bing.—FaW

Brown, George Mackay

The hawk.—HeR

Shroud.—HeR

Brown, Margaret Wise

Goodnight moon.—FaW

Green stems.—PrRh

"Little black bug."—CoN—FrP

Little donkey close your eyes.—LaW

The rabbit skip.—FrP

The secret song.—HaOf—PrRh

Brown, Palmer

"The spangled pandemonium."—PrRh

Brown, Thomas Edward

I bended unto me.—CoN

Brown, Capability (about)

Capability Brown. W. Cowper.—PlSc

"**Brown** and furry." See Caterpillar See Caterpillar

The **brown** birds. Eleanor Farjeon.—FaE

"A **brown** old man with a green thumb." See He was

"The **brown** owl sits in the ivy bush." Mother Goose.—LoR

Brown penny. William Butler Yeats.—McL

The **brown** thrush. Lucy Larcom.—HaOf

Brownies. See Fairies

The **brownies'** celebration. Palmer Cox.—HaOf

Browning, Robert

Memorabilia.—HeR

The pied piper of Hamelin.—LiSf

Pippa passes, sels.

"The year's at the spring".—ChG—LaT

Pippa's song.—CoN

"The year's at the spring." See Pippa passes

Brownjohn, Alan

Camel ("I am a camel in all the sand").—PrRh

Cat ("Sometimes I am an unseen").—ChC

Elephant ("It is quite unfair to be").—CoOu

Brownjohn, John

The schoolmaster and the truants.—HaOf

Bruises. Coleman Barks.—JaPo

Bruno. Unknown.—BrT

"**Brusque** shoulders and bluff beard." See Tudor portrait

Bryant, William Cullen

The death of the flowers.—HaOf

Robert of Lincoln.—HaOf

Bubbles

Blowing bubbles. M. Hillert.—PrRa

Bubbles. C. Sandburg.—HoRa—JaT

"Happy winter, steamy tub." K. Gundersheimer.—PrRa

Bubbles. Carl Sandburg.—HoRa—JaT

Buckingham Palace. Alan Alexander Milne.—FaW

"The **bud**." See Saint Francis and the sow

"**Budging** the sluggard ripples of the Somme." See Hospital barge at Cerisy

Buds. Elizabeth Coatsworth.—FaTh

Buffalo. Unknown, tr. by Ulli Beier.—HeR

"**Buffalo** Bill's." Edward Estlin Cummings.—HeR

Buffalo dusk. Carl Sandburg.—HaOf—HoRa—LiSf—PrRh

Buffalo girls. Unknown.—LiSf

"**Buffalo** girls, ain't you coming out tonight." See Buffalo girls

"The **buffalo** is the death." See Buffalo

The **buffalo** skinners. Unknown.—HeR

Buffaloes
Buffalo. Unknown.—HeR
Buffalo dusk. C. Sandburg.—HaOf—HoRa—
LiSf—PrRh
The buffalo skinners. Unknown.—HeR
The flower-fed buffaloes. V. Lindsay.—HaOf—
HeR
A song of buffalo dance. Unknown, fr. the
Pawnee Indian.—BiSp
A song of the buffalo dance ("In the north").
Unknown, fr. the Sioux Indian.—BiSp
A song of the buffalo dance ("One I have
wounded, yonder he moves"). Unknown, fr.
the Omaha Indian.—BiSp
"The **buffaloes** are gone." See Buffalo dusk
The **bug** ("And when the rain had gone away").
Marjorie Barrows.—PrRh
Bug in a jug. Unknown.—PrRh
"A **bug** sat in a silver flower." Karla Kuskin.—
PrRh
Bugles
"The **splendour** falls on castle walls." From The
princess. A. Tennyson.—LiWa
Blow, bugle, blow.—LiSf
Song.—BlO
Bugs. See Insects
Bugs. Karla Kuskin.—HoSu
Buick. Karl Shapiro.—JaD
Build-on rhymes
"As I was going to St. Ives." Mother Goose.—
CoN—DeM—LoR
Fiddle-i-fee ("Had me a cat, the cat pleased
me"). Mother Goose.—LiSf
"I had a cat and the cat pleased me".—
DeM
"For want of a nail the shoe was lost." Mother
Goose.—FaW—LoR
"Hush, little baby, don't say a word." Mother
Goose.—BaH—ChB—DeM—LaW—LoR
The mocking bird ("Hush up, baby").—LiSf
An only kid. From Haggadah. Unknown.—LiPj
Poor old lady. Unknown.—HaOf—PrRh
"There was a crooked man." Mother Goose.—
DeM—FaW—LoR
"This is the house that Jack built." Mother
Goose.—LoR
"This is the key of the kingdom." Mother
Goose.—LoR
This is the key.—BlO
The tree in the wood. Unknown.—LiSf
The twelve days of Christmas. Unknown.—RoC
"The first day of Christmas".—LoR
"**Builder,** in building the little house." See The
kitchen chimney
Builders and building
"About an excavation." C. Reznikoff.—CoN—
KeK
Architect. L. T. Nicholl.—PlEd
The barn ("They should never have built a
barn there, at all"). E. Thomas.—PlEd
Block city. R. L. Stevenson.—CoN—PlEd
Boulder dam. M. Sarton.—PlSc
Building a skyscraper. J. S. Tippett.—CoOu
The building of a new church. Unknown.—PlEd
Bulgy Bunne. J. Prelutsky.—PrNk
Chant of the awakening bulldozers. P.
Hubbell.—HoCl
Cityscape. N. M. Bodecker.—BoPc
Construction ("And every time I pass"). M. C.
Livingston.—HoSs
Construction ("The giant mouth"). L. Moore.—
MoSn

Construction job. M. C. Livingston.—HoCl
Development. N. M. Bodecker.—BoPc
For the rebuilding of a house. W. Berry.—PlEd
For you. K. Kuskin.—LiVp
"From gallery grave and the hunt of a wren
king." From Thanksgiving for a habitat. W.
H. Auden.—PlEd
Giotto's tower. H. W. Longfellow.—PlEd
"The hand that rounded Peter's dome." From
The problem. R. W. Emerson.—PlEd
Homage to Paul Mellon, I. M. Pei, their gallery,
and Washington City. W. Meredith.—PlEd
Homage to Wren. L. MacNeice.—PlEd
In memory of George Whitby, architect. Sir J.
Betjeman.—PlEd
The kitchen chimney. R. Frost.—PlEd
Mending the adobe. H. Carruth.—JaPi—PlEd
Recycled. L. Moore.—MoSn
The riveter. M. Watts.—PrRh
The seven wonders of the ancient world.
Unknown.—PlEd
Skyscrapers. R. Field.—FrP
"This is my Carnac, whose unmeasured dome."
H. D. Thoreau.—PlEd
A time for building. M. C. Livingston.—HoSs
To build a poem. C. E. Hemp.—JaG
Who shapes a balustrade. C. Aiken.—PlEd
"**Building** a poem is like building a house." See
To build a poem
Building a skyscraper. James S. Tippett.—CoOu
The **building** of a new church. Unknown.—PlEd
Buildings. See names of kinds of buildings, as
Houses
The **buildings.** Wendell Berry.—PlEd
"The **buildings** are all womanly." See The
buildings
"**Bulging** in petticoats in May she comes." See
The dandelion gatherer
Bulgy Bunne. Jack Prelutsky.—PrNk
"**Bulgy** Bunne (the wonder builder)." See Bulgy
Bunne
"A **bull** voiced young fellow of Pawling." See Hog
calling competition
The **bulldozer.** Robert Francis.—JaPo
Bulldozers
The bulldozer. R. Francis.—JaPo
Chant of the awakening bulldozers. P.
Hubbell.—HoCl
Bullfight. Miroslav Holub, tr. by Ian Milner and
Jarmila Milner.—HeR
Bullfights
Bullfight. M. Holub.—HeR
Bullfrogs. David Allan Evans.—JaPi
"**Bullfrogs,** bullfrogs on parade." Jack Prelutsky.—
PrRi
"**Bulls** by day." See The bulldozer
Bumble bee. N. M. Bodecker.—BoSs
"A **bunch** of the boys were whooping it up in
the Malamute saloon." See The shooting of
Dan McGrew
Bundles. Carl Sandburg.—HoRa
"The **bunnies** are a feeble folk." See A bunny
romance
A **bunny** romance. Oliver Herford.—HaOf
"**Buns** harden like pomanders." See The great
aunts of my childhood
Burdette, Robert J.
Wilhelmj.—BrT
Burgess, Gelett
The goops. See Table manners ("The goops they
lick their fingers")

Burgess, Gelett—*Continued*
 "I never saw a purple cow". See The purple cow
 "I wish that my room had a floor."—HaOf
 A low trick.—HaOf
 The purple cow.—CoN—HaOf—LiSf—PrRh
  "I never saw a purple cow".—BlO
 Table manners ("The goops they lick their fingers").—FrP—HaOf—PrRa—PrRh
  The goops.—FaW
The **burglar** of Babylon. Elizabeth Bishop.—HeR
Burgunder, Rose
 Joyful.—PrRa—PrRh
 Upside down ("A field of clouds").—LiSf
Burials. See Funerals
The **burning** babe. Robert Southwell.—HaO—HeR
Burning bright. Lillian Morrison.—FaTh
Burning love letters. Howard Moss.—JaD
Burning the gate. Eleanor Farjeon.—FaE
Burns, Robert
 "It was a' for our rightfu' king."—PlAs
 John Barleycorn.—HeR—PlAs
 "My heart's in the Highlands, my heart is not here."—BlO
 A red, red rose.—LiSf
 To an artist.—PlEd
 "Up in the morning's no' for me."—BlO
"A **burro** once, sent by express." See Advice to travelers
Bursting. Dorothy Aldis.—HoBf
"**Bury** this old Illinois farmer with respect." See Illinois farmer
Buses
 School buses. R. Hoban.—LiSf
 The schoolbus comes before the sun. R. Currie.—JaT—JaT
 Sleepy schoolbus. X. J. Kennedy.—KeF
Business as usual. Mark Vinz.—JaS
Buson
 Conversation.—CoN
 "Deep in a windless."—LiWa
 "On the temple bell."—KoT
Busy. Alan Alexander Milne.—LiSf
"The **busy** ant works hard all day." See Ants, although admirable, are awfully aggravating
"**Busy** is the life of the weaving woman." See Song of the weaving woman
"**But** don't call Mother Damnable names." See Around the corner
"**But** don't you know it, my dear." See Looking at a picture on an anniversary
"**But** for the broken firing pin." See Spider Reeves
But I wonder. Aileen Fisher.—PrRa
"**But** that was nothing to what things came out." See Welsh incident
"**But** the most beautiful of all is the un-found island." See The most beautiful
"**Butch,** a black cocker spaniel, collected." See A history of the pets
Butch Weldy. Edgar Lee Masters.—PlSc
Butter
 "Betty Botter bought some butter." Mother Goose.—FaW—LoR
  Betty Botter.—PaM
 "Come, butter, come." Mother Goose.—DeM
 The king's breakfast. A. A. Milne.—FaW—LiSf
The **buttercup** field. Eleanor Farjeon.—FaE
"The **buttercup** field, oh the buttercup field." See The buttercup field
Buttercups
 The buttercup field. E. Farjeon.—FaE
 Buttercups. C. Zolotow.—ZoE
Buttercups. Charlotte Zolotow.—ZoE

Butterflies
 Blossoms. F. D. Sherman.—HaOf
 Butterflies. E. Merriam.—MeF
 Butterfly ("Butterfly, the wind blows sea-ward, strong beyond the garden wall"). D. H. Lawrence.—KoT
 "The butterfly." From Three animals. R. Padgett.—KoT
 The butterfly ("Up and down the air you float"). C. Scollard.—PrRa
 Cocoon. D. McCord.—HaOf—McAs
 Flying crooked. R. Graves.—HeR
 "For a companion." Shiki.—FaTh
 "Fuzzy wuzzy, creepy crawly." L. Schulz.—PrRa
 "The king of the yellow butterflies." V. Lindsay.—HaOf
 La mariposa linda. Unknown.—GrT
 "On the temple bell." Buson.—KoT
 The pretty butterfly. Unknown.—GrT
 "They look." Ryota.—KoT
 To a butterfly. W. Wordsworth.—DaC
 White oak. M. C. Livingston.—LiMp
Butterflies. Eve Merriam.—MeF
Butterfly ("Butterfly, the wind blows sea-ward, strong beyond the garden wall"). David Herbert Lawrence.—KoT
"The **butterfly.**" From Three animals. Ron Padgett.—KoT
The **butterfly** ("Up and down the air you float"). Clinton Scollard.—PrRa
"The **butterfly,** a cabbage-white." See Flying crooked
"**Butterfly,** the wind blows sea-ward, strong beyond the garden wall." See Butterfly
The **butterfly's** ball. William Roscoe.—CoOu—PrRh
"**Butterprint** knocks on the milkshop door." Clyde Watson.—WaC
"A **buttery,** sugary, syrupy waffle." See The groaning board
"**Buy** our little magazine." See Do it yourself
Buying a puppy. Leslie Norris.—LiIl—LiSf
Buying and selling. See Markets and marketing; Peddlers and vendors; Shops and shopkeepers
Buying the dog. Michael Ondaatje.—JaS
"The **buzz** saw snarled and rattled in the yard." See Out, out
"**By** and by." See Epitaph on a waiter
"**By,** baby bunting". See "Bye, baby bunting"
"**By** day the bat is cousin to the mouse." See The bat
"**By** death's favor." See Epitaph on an engraver
"**By** June our brook's run out of song and speed." See Hyla brook
"**By** Saint Mary, my lady." See To Mistress Isabel Pennell
"**By** sloth on sorrow fathered." See Lollocks
"**By** sundown we came to a hidden village." See Conquerors
By the Exeter River. Donald Hall.—PlAs
"**By** the fire, like drifting reddish goldfish." See Cat
By the Klondike River. Alan Coren.—CoOu
By the sea. Charlotte Zolotow.—ZoE
"**By** the shores of Lake Michigan." See Lake Michigan
"**By** the time that August ended." See Boring
"**By** the wave rising, by the wave breaking." See The crow
Bye, Reed
 Spring ("Bluebird and").—KoT

Bye, Reed—*Continued*
"**Bye,** baby bunting." Mother Goose.—LoR
"By, baby bunting".—DeM
Bye baby walnut. Norma Farber.—FaTh
Bye bye. Sean O'Huigin.—DoNw
The **Byfield** rabbit. Katherine Hoskins.—PlSc
"**By'm** bye." Unknown.—LaW
Bynner, Witter
A parting, tr. by.—LiIl
The sandpiper ("Along the sea edge, like a gnome").—PrRh
Byrom, John
"When things were as fine as could possibly be."—TrM
Byron, Lord (George Gordon Byron)
The destruction of Sennacherib.—HeR—PlAs
An ode to the framers of the Frame Bill.—PlSc
On the bust of Helen by Canova.—PlEd
"So, we'll go no more a-roving."—KoT
The wild, the free.—PrRh

C

C is for charms. Eleanor Farjeon.—LiWa
"**C** is for curious Charlie." See Curious Charlie
El **caballo.** Jose Maria Eguren.—LiSf
Cabbages
Nocturn cabbage. C. Sandburg.—HoRa
Old King Cabbage. R. K. Munkittrick.—HaOf
"**Cabbages** catch at the moon." See Nocturn cabbage
The **cable** ship. Harry Edmund Martinson, tr. by Robert Bly.—HeR
Cactus
"You need to have an iron rear." J. Prelutsky.—PrNk
Cadenza. Carl Sandburg.—HoRa
Caesar, Julius (about)
Latin. E. Farjeon.—FaE
Cagaba Indians. See Indians of the Americas—Cagaba
Caged birds. Maya Angelou.—AnS
Cake. David McCord.—HoMu
Cakes and cookies
Cake. D. McCord.—HoMu
Catherine. K. Kuskin.—CoN
"Chocolate cake." N. Payne.—PrRh
Chocolate cake. J. Prelutsky.—PrMp
"Clapcake, clapcake." C. Watson.—WaC
"Fee, fie, fo, fum a gingerbread baby." C. Watson.—WaC
The friendly cinnamon bun. R. Hoban.—LiIl
"Handy spandy, Jack-a-Dandy." Mother Goose.—BlQ—LoR
The merry pieman's song. J. Bennett.—LiIl
"The moon's the north wind's cooky." V. Lindsay.—CoN—HaOf—LaW—LiSf—PrRa—PrRh
My special cake. J. Prelutsky.—PrIv
"Pat-a-cake, pat-a-cake, baker's man." Mother Goose.—DeM—LoR—RaT
"Smiling girls, rosy boys." Mother Goose.—LoR
The gingerbread man.—DaC
Calculators
Pocket calculator. B. Katz.—HoCl
Calder, Alexander (about)
A Calder. K. Shapiro.—PlEd
A **Calder.** Karl Shapiro.—PlEd
A **calendar.** Sara Coleridge.—DaC—FrP
"January brings the snow".—LiSf (unat.)
The months.—PrRh
"**Calf-deep** in spruce dust." See Dulcimer maker

Caliban in the coal mines. Louis Untermeyer.—LaT
"**Calico** pie." Edward Lear.—BlO—LiH
California
"Johnny had a black horse." J. Prelutsky.—PrRi
"**Call** for the robin redbreast and the wren." From The white devil. John Webster.—HeR
A dirge.—BlO
"**Call** me the Valiant heading west on Fourteen into the frozen." See Ford pickup
Call them back. Chris Petrakos.—JaG
"**Call** us back, call us with your sliding silver." See Spring cries
Calling the roll. Nathaniel Graham Shepherd.—HaOf
"The **calm.**" See Suicide's note
"**Calm** weather in June." Mother Goose.—LoR
Calvary. From Song for the cloth. William Butler Yeats.—HeR
Camel ("The camel is."). N. M. Bodecker.—BoSs
Camel ("I am a camel in all the sand"). Alan Brownjohn.—PrRh
"The **camel** is." See Camel
"A **camel,** with practical views." See Sole-hungering camel
Camels
The boar and the dromedar. H. Beissel.—DoNw
Camel ("The camel is."). N. M. Bodecker.—BoSs
Camel ("I am a camel in all the sand"). A. Brownjohn.—PrRh
The camel's complaint. C. E. Carryl.—HaOf—PrRh
Camels of the kings. L. Norris.—HaO
"A dromedary standing still." J. Prelutsky.—PrZ
Sole-hungering camel. O. Herford.—BrT
The **camel's** complaint. Charles Edward Carryl.—HaOf—PrRh
Camels of the kings. Leslie Norris.—HaO
"The **camels,** the kings camels, haie-aie." See Camels of the kings
Camera. Ted Kooser.—JaPi
Cameron, Norman
The compassionate fool.—HeR
She and I.—HeR
Campbell, Alice B.
Sally and Manda.—FrP—PrRh
Campbell, Joseph
"I will go with my father a-ploughing."—LiSf
Campbell, Wilfred
Indian summer ("Along the line of smoky hills").—DoNw
Camping and hiking
"Camping in Grand Canyon Park." X. J. Kennedy.—KeB
Campsite. B. J. Esbensen.—EsCs
Eat-it-all Elaine. K. Starbird.—LiSf—PrRh
The hiker. E. Merriam.—LiSf
"Hiking in the Rockies, Midge." X. J. Kennedy.—KeB
"Humbert, hiking Moonshine Hill." X. J. Kennedy.—KeB
Sleeping outdoors. M. Chute.—LaW—PrRa
The sound of night. M. Kumin.—JaD
Where am I. R. J. Margolis.—MaS
"**Camping** in Grand Canyon Park." X. J. Kennedy.—KeB
Campion, Thomas
"Thrice tosse these oaken ashes in the ayre."—LiWa
Campsite. Barbara Juster Esbensen.—EsCs
"**Can** you dance." See Music

Canada—History
  Lake Michigan. From Great Lakes suite. J. Reaney.—DoNw
Canadian boat-song. Unknown, at. to John Galt.—PlAs
Canaries
  The canary. O. Nash.—JaD—PrRh
  "Mary had a pretty bird." Mother Goose.—DeM—LoR
  "When my canary." Shiki.—LiSf
  The **canary**. Ogden Nash.—JaD—PrRh
  "**Canary-birds** feed on sugar and seed." See The camel's complaint
  "A **canary**, its woe to assuage." See The conservative owl
Candie Brewer. Mel Glenn.—GlCd
"**Candlelight** and moth wings." Charlotte Zolotow.—ZoE
Candles
  "Jack be nimble." Mother Goose.—DeM—LoR
  Light another candle. M. Chaikin.—CoN
  Light the festive candles for Hanukkah. A. Fisher.—PrRh
  Little catkins. A. Blok.—LiE
  "Little Nanny Etticoat." Mother Goose.—DeM—LiSf—LoR
  "To make your candles last for aye." Mother Goose.—DeM
Candy
  Candy cane. V. Worth.—LiCp
  "Chocolate." A. Adoff.—LiSf
  Chocolate rhyme. Unknown.—GrT
  Conversation hearts. V. Worth.—LiVp
  Crunch and lick. D. Aldis.—PrRa
  The cupboard. W. De la Mare.—CoN
  "Handy spandy, Jack-a-Dandy." Mother Goose.—BlQ—LoR
  Molasses river. R. K. Munkittrick.—HaOf
  Mother's chocolate valentine. J. Prelutsky.—PrIv
  Patience. B. Katz.—PrRh
  Phantasus, 1, 8. A. Holz.—LiCp
  Rima de chocolate. Unknown.—GrT
  The sweetstuff wife. E. Farjeon.—FaE
  "This little house is sugar." L. Hughes.—CoN
  Winter sweetness.—HuDk—PrRa
  Valentine chocolates. V. Worth.—LiVp
Candy cane. Valerie Worth.—LiCp
Canis major. Robert Frost.—KeK—KoS
Canning time. Robert Morgan.—JaS
Canoes and canoeing
  The glass canoe. J. Ciardi.—CiD
  New moon. E. Merriam.—MeF
Canova, Antonio (about)
  On the bust of Helen by Canova. Lord Byron.—PlEd
"**Canst** thou imagine where those spirits live." From Prometheus unbound. Percy Bysshe Shelley.—LiWa
"**Can't** mutton be dull." See Food out of doors
Can't win. Richard J. Margolis.—MaS
Canticle. David Shapiro.—KoT
Canticle of spring. Harry Behn.—HoCb
The **cap** and bells. William Butler Yeats.—HeR—LiWa
Capability Brown. William Cowper.—PlSc
Cape Ann. From Landscapes. Thomas Stearns Eliot.—HeR
"A **capital** ship for an ocean trip." See The Walloping Window-Blind
Captain Kidd. Stephen Vincent Benét and Rosemary Carr Benét.—RuI
Captain Spud and his first mate, Spade. John Ciardi.—HaOf

"**Car**, I give you over to." See Car wash
Car wash. Myra Cohn Livingston.—CoN—HoCl
The **cardinal** ("After the snow stopped"). Charlotte Zolotow.—ZoE
Cardinal ("Red as a shout"). Barbara Juster Esbensen.—EsCs
Cardinal ("With deep snow"). Barbara Howes.—JaD
Cardinal Bembo's epitaph on Raphael. Pietro Bembo.—PlEd
Cardinal ideograms. May Swenson.—HaOf
Cardinals (birds)
  The cardinal ("After the snow stopped"). C. Zolotow.—ZoE
  Cardinal ("Red as a shout"). B. J. Esbensen.—EsCs
  Cardinal ("With deep snow"). B. Howes.—JaD
  Winter cardinal. L. Moore.—MoSn
"A **careless** young driver, McKissen." See Stop
"A **careless** young lad down in Natchez." See Ouch
The **careless** zookeeper. Unknown.—BrT
"A **careless** zookeeper named Blake." See The careless zookeeper
Carentan O Carentan. Louis Simpson.—HeR
Carl Immerman. Mel Glenn.—GlC
Carla Spooner. Mel Glenn.—GlCd
Carlile, Henry
  Dodo.—JaPi
  Grandmother.—JaD
  Listening to Beethoven on the Oregon coast.—JaPi
  Spider Reeves.—JaPi
Carlos Rodriguez. Mel Glenn.—GlCd
Carman, Bliss
  The ships of Yule.—DoNw
Carmichael, A.
  Omens ("Early on the morning of Monday"), tr. by.—HeR
  "The wicked who would do me harm", tr. by.—HeR
Carney, Julia A.
  Little things ("Little drops of water").—DaC
  "Little drops of water".—LoR (unat.)
Carol ("Deep in the fading leaves of night"). William Robert Rodgers.—HaO
Carol ("Mary laid her child among"). Norman Nicholson.—IlaO
A **carol** for Christmas eve. Eleanor Farjeon.—FaE
Carol for the last Christmas eve. Norman Nicholson.—HaO
Carol of patience. Robert Graves.—HaO
Carol of the birds. Unknown.—RoC
Carol of the brown king. Langston Hughes.—LiCp
Carol of the field mice. Kenneth Grahame.—RoC
The **carol** of the poor children. Richard Middleton.—HaO
Carol of the signs. Eleanor Farjeon.—FaE
"A **carol** round the ruddy hearth." See For Christmas day
The **carol** singers. Eleanor Farjeon.—FaE
Carolyn Warren. Mel Glenn.—GlCd
Carousels. See Merry-go-rounds
Caroutch, Yvonne
  "When we are like."—McL
Carpenter, William
  Autumn ("This morning they are putting away the whales").—JaPi
  Fire ("This morning on the opposite shore of the river").—JaPi
  The keeper.—JaPi
The **carpenter** rages. Jack Prelutsky.—PrNk

Cat ("Sometimes I am an unseen"). Alan Brownjohn.—ChC

The cat ("Within that porch, across the way"). William Henry Davies.—BlO—ChC

"Cat." Eleanor Farjeon.—BlO—CoOu—FaE

The cat and the moon. William Butler Yeats.—ChC—KoT—LiSf

Cat and the weather. May Swenson.—LiCa

Cat and wind. X. J. Kennedy.—KeF

The cat came back. Unknown.—ChC

"A cat came fiddling out of a barn." Mother Goose.—FaW

"Cat cat cat on the bed." Eve Merriam.—MeBl

Cat, Christmas. Valerie Worth.—LiCa

"The cat curls in a whorl." See Circle sleeper

"The cat has his sport." See The innocent

"A cat has prickly whiskers." See Cat's whiskers

The cat heard the cat-bird. John Ciardi.—LiCa

"Cat, if you go outdoors, you must walk in the snow." See On a night of snow

A cat in despondency. Unknown.—PrRh

"A cat in despondency sighed." See A cat in despondency

Cat in the moonlight. See White cat in moonlight

Cat in the snow. Aileen Fisher.—CoN

Cat kisses. Bobbi Katz.—PrRa

Cat mystery. Beatrice Schenk De Regniers.—DeT

The cat of cats. William Brighty Rands.—PrRh

Cat on couch. Barbara Howes.—JaD

"The cat sat asleep by the side of the fire." Mother Goose.—LoR

"Cat, scat." See Cat

"Cat takes a look at the weather." See Cat and the weather

Cat, Thanksgiving. Valerie Worth.—LiTp

"The cat that comes to my window sill." See That cat

"The cat that's inside." See Cat mystery

"Cat watched wind cross tall grass." See Cat and wind

"The cat went here and there." See The cat and the moon

The cat who aspired to higher things. X. J. Kennedy.—JaT

"The cat, who sleeps upon the mat." See The stray

"Cat will rhyme with hat." Spike Milligan.—ChC

Catalog. See Catalogue

Catalogue. Rosalie Moore.—ChC—CoN
  Catalog.—LiCa

"Catch a floater, catch an eel." See Bella by the sea

Catch a little rhyme. Eve Merriam.—HaOf

"Catch and shake the cobra garden hose." See Puppy

"Catch her, crow." Mother Goose.—RaT

Catch it. Eleanor Farjeon.—FaE

"Catch me and kiss me and say it again." Clyde Watson.—WaC

"Catch me the moon, daddy." Griger Vitez.—LaW

"Catch sun, catch sun." See Catch it

Catching quiet. Marci Ridlon.—HoSs

Catechisms, talking with a four year old. George Ella Lyon.—JaS

Caterpillar. Christina Georgina Rossetti.—FrP—PrRh
  "Brown and furry".—LiSf

"Caterpillar." Eve Merriam.—MeBl

"Caterpillar, have a care." See Woolly bear caterpillar

Caterpillars
  About caterpillars. A. Fisher.—FiW
  "Caterpillar." E. Merriam.—MeBl
  Caterpillar. C. G. Rossetti.—FrP—PrRh
    "Brown and furry".—LiSf
  Caterpillars. A. Fisher.—HoSu
  Cocoon. D. McCord.—HaOf—McAs
  Dora Diller. J. Prelutsky.—PrNk
  "Fuzzy wuzzy, creepy crawly." L. Schulz.—PrRa
  "How soft a caterpillar steps." E. Dickinson.—FaTh
  Jumping bean. M. A. Hoberman.—FaTh
  "Little silk worms, if you please." Unknown.—DeD
  Message from a caterpillar. L. Moore.—LiSf—MoSn
  Only my opinion. M. Shannon.—PrRa
  The tickle rhyme ("Who's that tickling my back, said the wall"). I. Serraillier.—CoN—CoOu—PrRh
  Woolly bear caterpillar ("Caterpillar, have a care"). A. Fisher.—FiW
  Woolly bear caterpillar ("Darkness comes early"). B. J. Esbensen.—EsCs

Caterpillars. Aileen Fisher.—HoSu

The catfish. Jack Prelutsky.—PrSr

"The catfish, far more fish than cat." See The catfish

Catherine. Karla Kuskin.—CoN

Catherine Heath. Mel Glenn.—GlC

"Catherine said, I think I'll bake." See Catherine

Catholics. Cynthia Rylant.—RyW

Catkin. Unknown.—DaC

Catmint. Eric Clough Taylor.—ChC

Catnip. Valerie Worth.—LiCa

Cats
  About claws and scratching. B. S. De Regniers.—DeT
  Alley cat school. F. Asch.—PrRh
  An alley cat with one life left. J. Prelutsky.—PrNk
  Amanda ("Amanda was an alley cat"). K. Kuskin.—LiCa
  At night ("When night is dark"). A. Fisher.—LiSf—PrRa
  The bad kittens. E. Coatsworth.—HaOf
  Cassius. C. Rylant.—RyW
  "Cat." E. Farjeon.—BlO—CoOu—FaE
  Cat ("The black cat yawns"). M. B. Miller.—ChC—LiSf—PrRh
  Cat ("By the fire, like drifting reddish goldfish"). J. Cocteau.—LiCa
  Cat ("Cat, scat"). E. Farjeon.—LiCa
  Cat ("The fat cat on the mat"). J. R. R. Tolkien.—ChC
  Cat ("My cat"). D. Baruch.—ChC
  Cat ("My cat has got no name"). V. Scannell.—ChC
  The cat ("One gets a wife, one gets a house"). O. Nash.—ChC
  A cat ("She had a name among the children"). E. Thomas.—BlO
  Cat ("Sometimes I am an unseen"). A. Brownjohn.—ChC
  The cat ("Within that porch, across the way"). W. H. Davies.—BlO—ChC
  The cat and the moon. W. B. Yeats.—ChC—KoT—LiSf
  Cat and the weather. M. Swenson.—LiCa
  Cat and wind. X. J. Kennedy.—KeF
  The cat came back. Unknown.—ChC

Cats—*Continued*

"A cat came fiddling out of a barn." Mother Goose.—FaW
"Cat cat on the bed." E. Merriam.—MeBl
Cat, Christmas. V. Worth.—LiCa
The cat heard the cat-bird. J. Ciardi.—LiCa
A cat in despondency. Unknown.—PrRh
Cat in the snow. A. Fisher.—CoN
Cat kisses. B. Katz.—PrRa
Cat mystery. B. S. De Regniers.—DeT
The cat of cats. W. B. Rands.—PrRh
Cat on couch. B. Howes.—JaD
"The cat sat asleep by the side of the fire." Mother Goose.—LoR
Cat, Thanksgiving. V. Worth.—LiTp
The cat who aspired to higher things. X. J. Kennedy.—JaT
"Cat will rhyme with hat." S. Milligan.—ChC
Catalogue. R. Moore.—ChC—CoN
   Catalog.—LiCa
Catmint. E. C. Taylor.—ChC
Catnip. V. Worth.—LiCa
The cats. S. Exler.—JaG
Cats ("Cats sleep"). E. Farjeon.—PrRh
Cats ("Cats walk neatly"). R. Francis.—JaD
Cats and dogs ("Some like cats, and some like dogs."). N. M. Bodecker.—BoSs
Cats are good for something. B. S. De Regniers.—DeT
Cats know what's good. B. S. De Regniers.—DeT
Cats love books. B. S. De Regniers.—DeT
Cat's menu. W. Crawford, at. to.—ChC
"Cat's tongue." E. Merriam.—LiCa—MeBl
Cat's whiskers. B. S. De Regniers.—DeT
Catsnest. X. J. Kennedy.—KeF—LiCa
Choosing their names. T. Hood.—DaC
The Christmas tree ("Outside the world was full, plural"). P. Beer.—HaO
Circle sleeper. J. H. Marvin.—ChC
Concrete cat. D. Charles.—KeK—LiSf
Country barnyard. E. Coatsworth.—ChC—PrRh
The curate's cat. Unknown.—BrT
Dad and the cat and the tree. K. Wright.—CoOu
"Dame Trot and her cat." Mother Goose.—DeM
Dedication. B. S. De Regniers.—DeT
Diamond cut diamond. E. Milne.—LiSf
"Diddlety, diddlety, dumpty." Mother Goose.—LoR
A different door. X. J. Kennedy.—ChC—KeF
"Ding dong bell." Mother Goose.—AlH—DaC—DeM—FaW—LiSf—LoR
"A dog is a pal, so friendly and fun." L. C. Briggs.—TrM
Double dutch. W. De la Mare.—ChC
The duel. E. Field.—FaW—HaOf—PrRh
Early breakfast. B. S. De Regniers.—DeT
Elegy ("My Thompson, least attractive character"). H. Nemerov.—JaPo
Elegy for Delina. A. Rowe.—ChC
Epitaph for a persian kitten. M. Vedder.—ChC
Feather or fur. J. Becker.—PrRh
Feline. R. Wallace.—JaT
Feline fine. J. P. Lewis.—JaT
"The fisherman's hands." N. Valen.—ChC
Five eyes. W. De la Mare.—ChC
The flying cat. N. S. Nye.—JaT
Fog. C. Sandburg.—HaOf—HoRa—KoT—LiSf—PrRh
Food for a cat. D. S. Jordan.—BrT
For a dead kitten. S. H. Hay.—ChC

For Mary and her kitten. E. Farjeon.—FaE
Fourteen ways of touching the Peter ("You can push"). G. MacBeth.—ChC
The genial grimalkin. J. G. Francis.—BrT
Gobbolino, the witch's cat. G. C. Westcott.—ChC
"God created cat and asked." Unknown.—ChC
The golden cat. E. Farjeon.—FaE
Goodbye ("Seven cats and seven mice"). J. Ciardi.—CiD
Gray thrums. C. B. Bates.—HaOf
"Great A, little a." Mother Goose.—DeM—LoR
Griselda Gratz. J. Prelutsky.—PrNk
Growltiger's last stand. T. S. Eliot.—HaOf
Gus, the theatre cat. T. S. Eliot.—HaOf
Halloween ("Green cat eyes"). M. C. Livingston.—LiCe
"Hoddley, poddley, puddles and fogs." Mother Goose.—LoR
   "Hoddley, poddley, puddle and frogs".—DeM
A home without a cat. M. Twain.—ChC
The house cat. A. Wynne.—PrRa
"I am the cat that walks by himself." R. Kipling.—ChC
"I like little pussy." Mother Goose.—LoR
   Pussy.—DaC
   "I love little pussy".—DeM
I wouldn't. J. Ciardi.—JaT
"If I lost my little cat, I should be sad without it." Mother Goose.—ChC
"In August once." K. Kuskin.—LiCa
In honour of Taffy Topaz. C. Morley.—ChC
The innocent. D. Levertov.—KeK
"It has a head like a cat, feet like a cat." Unknown.—CoN
The king of cats sends a postcard to his wife. N. Willard.—HaOf
A kitten ("He's nothing much but fur"). E. Farjeon.—ChC—FaE
The kitten ("The trouble with a kitten is that"). O. Nash.—ChC—JaD
The kitten and the falling leaves. W. Wordsworth.—BlO—ChC
Kittens. M. C. Livingston.—LiWo
Kitty. D. McLeod.—ChC
"Kitty caught a caterpillar." J. Prelutsky.—PrRi
Kitty cornered. E. Merriam.—ChC
The lazy pussy. P. Cox.—HaOf
Listening. A. Fisher.—CoN
The little cat. Unknown.—ChC
"Little orange cat." C. Zolotow.—ZoE
Loft. S. Cassedy.—CaR
Looks are deceiving. B. S. De Regniers.—DeT
The lost cat. E. V. Rieu.—ChC—LiSf
Macavity, the mystery cat. T. S. Eliot.—ChC—CoOu—HaOf—HeR—LiSf
Marmalade lost. R. Whitman.—LiCa
Midwife cat. M. Van Doren.—ChC
Milk for the cat. H. Monro.—BlO
Miss Tibbles. I. Serraillier.—LiCa
Mister alley cat. J. McGowan.—ChC
"Montague Michael." Unknown.—ChC
Moon ("I have a white cat whose name is Moon"). W. J. Smith.—ChC—LiCa—LiSf
Mother cat's purr. J. Yolen.—PrRa
Murgatroyd. C. T. Wright.—JaS
My cat. J. Viorst.—ViI
My cat Jeoffrey. From Jubilate Agno. C. Smart.—BlO—HeR
   "For I will consider my cat Jeoffry".—KoT
My cat Mrs. Lick-a-chin. J. Ciardi.—ChC
My cat, Robin Hood. E. Di Pasquale.—LiCa

Change—*Continued*
Buffalo dusk. C. Sandburg.—HaOf—HoRa—LiSf—PrRh
Changes. M. Angelou.—AnS
Changing. M. A. Hoberman.—HoBf—PrRh
"Full fathom five thy father lies." From The tempest. W. Shakespeare.—HoUn
Ariel's song.—BlO
Going away. H. Nemerov.—JaD
Humdrum. C. Sandburg.—HoRa
Journey of the Magi. T. S. Eliot.—HaO
Nothing gold can stay. R. Frost.—KoS
On learning to adjust to things. J. Ciardi.—HaOf—KeK
One-night fair. N. Price.—JaG
Passing love. L. Hughes.—HuDk
Ruins. H. Behn.—HoCb
Summer's end ("In the still pond"). E. Merriam.—MeF
Transformations. T. Hardy.—HeR
The view from father's porch. C. T. Wright.—JaS
Waiting both. T. Hardy.—KoT
"When I set out for Lyonesse." T. Hardy.—HeR
Change in the weather. Ilo Orleans.—HoSu
"The **changeable** chameleon." See The chameleon
Changes. Maya Angelou.—AnS
Changing. Mary Ann Hoberman.—HoBf—PrRh
Changsha shoe factory. Willis Barnstone.—PlSc
Channel firing. Thomas Hardy.—HeR
Chant of the awakening bulldozers. Patricia Hubbell.—HoCl
Ch'ao Li-houa
Thank you for your letter.—LiIl
"A **chap** has a shark up in Sparkill." See The sick shark
The **chap** who disappeared. John Ciardi.—CiD
Chapman, Jean
Territory.—ChC
Chappell, Fred
The lost carnival.—JaG
Character. See Conduct of life
Charity. See also Gifts and giving; Sympathy
"Christmas is coming, the geese are getting fat." Mother Goose.—DeM—LiCp—LiSf—LoR—RoC
"Christmas is a-coming".—CoN
In the workhouse. G. R. Sims.—HaO
Keeping Christmas. E. Farjeon.—HaO—RoC
Charles, Dorthi
"Bang, the starter's gun."—KeK
Concrete cat.—KeK—LiSf
"**Charley** Barley, butter and eggs." Mother Goose.—DeM
"**Charley** Coleman told me this." See Incident
Charlie Wallinsky. Mel Glenn.—GlC
"**Charlie** Warlie had a cow." Mother Goose.—DeM
Charlotte Bronte. Susan Coolidge.—HaOf
A **charm** ("O wen, wen, O little wennikins"). Unknown, tr. by Richard Hamer.—HeR
Charm ("With trembling eyes"). Miklós Radnóti, tr. by Steven Polgar and Stephen Berg and S. J. Marks.—McL
"**Charm**, dame, dame, the watch is set." See The witches' sabbath
A **charm** for our time. Eve Merriam.—MeSk
A **charm** for spring flowers. Rachel Field.—LiSf
Charmes. Robert Herrick.—LiWa
"**Charming**, the movement of girls about a May-pole in May." See Men working

Charms
The alchemist ("Sail of Claustra, Aelis, Azalais"). E. Pound.—LiWa
Alison Gross. Unknown.—LiWa
The Allansford pursuit. R. Graves.—HeR
The bear. A. Stanford.—LiWa
Black bear ("Sweet-mouth, honey-paws, hairy one!"). D. Lepan.—DoNw
"Black spirits and white, red spirits and gray." From The witch. T. Middleton.—LiWa
C is for charms. E. Farjeon.—LiWa
A charm ("O wen, wen, O little wennikins"). Unknown.—HeR
A charm for our time. E. Merriam.—MeSk
A charm for spring flowers. R. Field.—LiSf
Charmes. R. Herrick.—LiWa
"Come, butter, come." Mother Goose.—DeM
"Come the oak before the ash." Unknown.—DaC
Demon. E. Merriam.—MeHa
"Double, double, toil and trouble." From Macbeth. W. Shakespeare.—HoUn
Song of the witches.—PrRh
Edenhall. S. Coolidge.—HaOf
Fable ("Pity the girl with the crystal hair"). J. Aiken.—LiWa
For chest pain. Unknown, fr. the Aztec Indian.—BiSp
For putting a woman's family to sleep. Unknown, fr. the Cherokee Indian.—BiSp
For subduing a walrus. Unknown, fr. the Ammassalik Eskimo.—BiSp
Halloween ("Green cat eyes"). M. C. Livingston.—LiCe
"I sow hempseed." Unknown.—LiVp
An imprecation against foes and sorcerers. From Atharva Veda. Unknown.—LiWa
Incantation to Oedipus. J. Dryden.—LiWa
Korf's enchantment. C. Morgenstern.—LiWa
A legend of the Northland. P. Cary.—HaOf
"Lemonade ran out when the pitcher broke." E. Merriam.—MeBl
Magic spell for an approaching storm. Unknown, fr. the Arekuna Indian.—BiSp
Magic spell for finding a woman. Unknown, fr. the Aztec Indian.—BiSp
Magic spell to turn a woman's heart. Unknown, fr. the Arekuna Indian.—BiSp
Magic words to the gull. Unknown, fr. the Netsilik Eskimo.—BiSp
Merlin and the snake's egg. L. Norris.—LiWa
Midsummer eve. E. Farjeon.—FaE
"Mirror, mirror, tell me." Mother Goose.—DaC—LoR
"Put the pine tree in its pot by the doorway." N. Belting.—LiIl
St. Swithin's chair. Sir W. Scott.—LiWa
"Sea charm." L. Hughes.—HuDk
The spell. R. Herrick.—LiWa
This is to frighten a storm. Unknown, fr. the Cherokee Indian.—BiSp
"Thrice the brinded cat hath mew'd." From Macbeth. W. Shakespeare.—HeR—LiSf—LiWa
"Thrice tosse these oaken ashes in the ayre." T. Campion.—LiWa
To blow away a headache. Unknown, fr. the Uitoto Indian.—BiSp
To cure epilepsy. Unknown, fr. the Tzotzil Maya.—BiSp
To fix the affections. Unknown, fr. the Cherokee Indian.—BiSp

Child and dog. Eleanor Farjeon.—FaE
The **child** and the bird. Eleanor Farjeon.—FaE
"A **child** draws the outline of a body." See Portrait
The **child** dying. Edwin Muir.—HeR
Child frightened by thunderstorm. Ted Kooser.—KeK
The **child** in the rug. John Haines.—JaD
"**Child**, is thy father dead." See Song
"**Child** of maize." See Red monkey
The **child** on the shore. Ursula K. LeGuin.—KeK
Child on top of a greenhouse. Theodore Roethke.—KeK
"**Child**, take your basket down." See First gathering
"**Child**, when on this night you lie." See Cradle song for Christmas
Childhood. See Childhood recollections; Children and childhood
Childhood. Frances Cornford.—KeK
Childhood recollections
  Adolescence. G. Orr.—JaPi
  Air raid. P. Wild.—JaPi
  All. L. Gom.—JaS
  Amoebaean for daddy. M. Angelou.—AnS
  Among his effects we found a photograph. E. Ochester.—JaS
  Around the corner. From Forgotten girlhood. L. Riding.—HeR
  Around the kitchen table. G. Gildner.—JaS
  The arrival of my mother. K. Wilson.—JaD
  The ascension, 1925. J. M. Brinnin.—JaS
  At the St. Louis Institute of Music. R. Wallace.—JaG
  Aunt Julia. N. MacCaig.—HeR
  Autobiographia literaria. F. O'Hara.—KoT
  Autobiography. L. MacNeice.—HeR
  A backwards journey. P. K. Page.—DoNw
  Baking day. R. Joseph.—JaS
  Before breakup on the Chena outside Fairbanks. D. McElroy.—JaPi
  The biplane. S. Orlen.—JaG
  Block city. R. L. Stevenson.—CoN—PlEd
  Boat stealing. From The prelude. W. Wordsworth.—HeR
  Brothers. R. Currie.—JaPi
  The centaur. M. Swenson.—LiSf
  Chicago, summer past. R. Snyder.—JaPi
  Childhood. F. Cornford.—KeK
  Children ("Children sleep at night"). From Forgotten girlhood. L. Riding.—HeR
  Country school. T. Kooser.—KeK
  The days gone by. J. W. Riley.—HaOf
  Double feature. T. Roethke.—JaD
  The errand. H. Behn.—HoCb
  Everything we do. P. Meinke.—JaG
  Eviction. L. Clifton.—CoN
  Father ("You spent fifty-five years"). T. Kooser.—JaS
  First love ("I remember sadness"). P. Hubbell.—LiSf
  For Sue. P. Hey.—JaPo
  Frau Bauman, Frau Schmidt, and Frau Schwartze. T. Roethke.—PlSc
  From a childhood. R. M. Rilke.—KoT
  Ghost house. R. Frost.—LiWa
  The gold nest. R. Wallace.—JaPo
  "The grandfather I never knew." M. C. Livingston.—LiWo
  Grandmother Grace. R. Wallace.—JaG
  Grandmother Jackson. D. Jackson.—HaO
  Greener grass. F. Steele.—JaPi
  Gus, the theatre cat. T. S. Eliot.—HaOf

  He was. R. Wilbur.—PlSc
  Heather Yarnell. M. Glenn.—GlCd
  Helen's scar. A. Nowlan.—JaS
  His lunch basket. D. Cockrell.—JaPi
  A history of the pets. D. Huddle.—JaPo
  Houses ("Time and the weather wear away"). D. Justice.—JaPo—PlEd
  I, Icarus. A. Nowlan.—DoNw
  "I look at this picture of that old man." From Afternoon in Waterloo Park. G. Dumas.—StG
  "I remember, I remember." T. Hood.—DaC
  Ice cream. P. Wild.—JaPi
  In Laddery street herself. From Forgotten girlhood. L. Riding.—HeR
  In school-days. J. G. Whittier.—HaOf
  Incident ("Charley Coleman told me this"). K. Kopp.—JaG
  Incident ("Once riding in old Baltimore"). C. Cullen.—CoN—HaOf—KeK
  Into Laddery Street. From Forgotten girlhood. L. Riding.—HeR
  The journey. D. Ignatow.—JaPi
  July the first. R. Currie.—JaPi
  Kineo mountain. C. T. Wright.—JaPi
  The kitchen (for my grandmother). W. Bedford.—StG
  Kitchen tables. D. Huddle.—JaS
  Lantern. G. Soto.—JaS
  The late mother. C. Macdonald.—JaPi
  Laughing backwards. J. Hall.—JaG
  The legacy II. L. V. Quintana.—StG
  Lineage. M. Walker.—StG
  A man of action. C. Stetler.—JaG
  Manners ("My grandfather said to me"). E. Bishop.—HeR—JaG
  Mardi Gras. J. Nolan.—JaS
  The mill ("Over the harbor at St. James"). W. Heyen.—PlEd
  My father after work. G. Gildner.—JaPi
  "My father played the melodeon." From A Christmas childhood. P. Kavanagh.—HeR
  My grandfather burning cornfields. R. Sauls.—JaS
  My grandmother had bones. J. Hemschemeyer.—JaD
  Ode to a dressmaker's dummy. D. Justice.—JaD
  The old familiar faces. C. Lamb.—HeR
  Our mother's tunes. E. Farjeon.—FaE
  The oxen ("Christmas eve, and twelve of the clock"). T. Hardy.—HaO—HeR—RoC
  The painters. J. Hemschemeyer.—JaPi
  People ("Not all the time"). O. V. Kanik.—McL
  Poem ("O sole mio, hot diggety, nix, I wather think I can"). F. O'Hara.—KoT
  Poem in October. D. Thomas.—HeR
  The portrait ("My mother never forgave my father"). S. Kunitz.—JaPi
  Quilt song. M. Vinz.—JaG
  Return of the village lad. A. Lichtenstein.—StG
  The river-merchant's wife, a letter ("While my hair was still cut straight across my forehead"). E. Pound.—HeR—KoT
  Rock me to sleep. E. A. Allen.—HaOf
  The self-unseeing. T. Hardy.—HeR
  The sentimentalist. E. Farjeon.—JaPo
  The ships of Yule. B. Carman.—DoNw
  The sleeping giant. D. Hall.—JaPi
  Sleepless nights. Zolotow. Charlotte.—ZoE—ZoE
  The smell of old newspapers is always stronger after sleeping in the sun. M. Lowery.—JaPi

Children and childhood.—*Continued*
"A good child, a good child." Mother Goose.—LoR
A good play. R. L. Stevenson.—DaC
Grab-bag. H. H. Jackson.—HaOf
Harvey. J. Viorst.—ViI
Helen's scar. A. Nowlan.—JaS
Hide and seek ("When I am alone, and quite alone"). A. B. Shiffrin.—FrP—PrRa
Hiding. D. Aldis.—LiSf
How to get through the memorial service. R. J. Margolis.—LiPj
How to stay up late. X. J. Kennedy.—KeF
Hug o' war. S. Silverstein.—CoN—PrRh
I am. A. Adoff.—AdA
"I am cherry alive, the little girl sang." D. Schwartz.—KoT
  I am cherry alive.—PrRh
I can be a tiger. M. L. Anderson.—PrRa
I show the daffodils to the retarded kids. C. Sharp.—JaD
If I were a fish. A. Winn.—BcD
"If I were in charge of the world." J. Viorst.—ViI
I'm not. J. Viorst.—ViI
Incident ("Once riding in old Baltimore"). C. Cullen.—CoN—HaOf—KeK
"I've scratched the measles, itched the pox." Unknown.—TrM
Jimmy Jet and his TV set. S. Silverstein.—HaOf—LiSf—PrRh
Jittery Jim. W. J. Smith.—PrRh
Joan's door. E. Farjeon.—FaE
John. N. M. Bodecker.—PrRh
John Rogers' exhortation to his children. J. Rogers.—HaOf
Keziah. G. Brooks.—PrRa—PrRh
The knowledgeable child. L. Strong.—KeK
The lamplighter. R. L. Stevenson.—PlSc
The land of potpourri. J. Prelutsky.—PrRh
Latin. E. Farjeon.—FaE
Learning. J. Viorst.—ViI
Leave me alone. F. Holman.—PrRh
A lesson for mamma. S. Dayre.—HaOf
A lesson in manners. J. Ciardi.—CiD
Let's take a nap. N. Giovanni.—GiSp
Letty's globe. C. T. Turner.—CoOu
Listening to grownups quarreling. R. Whitman.—CoN—KeK
Little boy blue. E. Field.—HaOf
Little bush. E. M. Roberts.—LiSf
The little factory girl to a more fortunate playmate. Unknown.—PlSc
Living with children. J. W. Miller.—JaG
The Lizzie Pitofsky poem. J. Viorst.—ViI
"The locusts' wings say, throng, throng." From Blessings on gentle folk. Unknown.—StG
Looking forward. R. L. Stevenson.—DaC
Lullaby ("Someone would like to have you for her child"). Unknown, fr. the Akan people of Africa.—KoT—LaW
Mary indoors. E. Farjeon.—FaE
Mary's one. E. Farjeon.—FaE
Meet-on-the-road ("Now, pray, where are you going, said Meet-on-the-road"). Unknown.—BlO
  Meet-on-the-road ("Now, pray, where are you going, child").—KoT
Meeting Mary. E. Farjeon.—FaE
Mike and Major. C. Rylant.—RyW
Missing the children. P. Zimmer.—JaS
Mixed-up kid. X. J. Kennedy.—KeF
Mommies do. N. Giovanni.—GiSp

"Monday's child is fair of face." Mother Goose.—DaC—DeM—FaW—LoR
Moving ("Some of the sky is grey and some of it is white"). R. Jarrell.—JaD
Music ("When you wanted a piano"). N. S. Nye.—JaS
My cousin. J. Prelutsky.—PrWi
My house is red. Mother Goose.—BlPi
My shadow. R. L. Stevenson.—CoOu—FaW
The Myra song. J. Ciardi.—PrRh
Nan ("It's"). E. Farjeon.—FaE
Near and far. K. C. Goddard.—FrP
New Hampshire. From Landscapes. T. S. Eliot.—HeR
Nightmare ("Expecting to be put in a sack and dumped in a ditch"). E. Field.—JaS
Noises. A. Fisher.—HoBf
"Old Mother Goose." Mother Goose.—DeM—LoR
On Mother's Day. A. Fisher.—CoN—PrRh
Once. S. Widerberg.—CoN
One of the problems of play. N. Giovanni.—GiSp
"Out in the dark and daylight." A. Fisher.—BeD
"Over the garden wall." E. Farjeon.—FaE
A peck of gold. R. Frost.—KoS
Pink belly. C. Rylant.—RyW
Portrait ("A child draws the outline of a body"). L. Gluck.—JaS
Puppy and I. A. A. Milne.—CoOu—FrP
Reflexes. M. Bell.—JaS
Remember me. J. Viorst.—ViI
Rickie Miller. M. Glenn.—GlC
Robert, who is often a stranger to himself. G. Brooks.—PrRa
The runaway ("I made peanut butter sandwiches"). B. Katz.—PrRh
Runaway ("I think today"). W. Wise.—PrRa
Samantha speaking. D. McCord.—LiTp
Saturday's child. C. Cullen.—PlSc
A secret place. J. W. Steinbergh.—LiIl
September ("I already know where Africa is"). L. Clifton.—HoSi—LiSf
Shopping. N. Giovanni.—GiSp
Silly song. F. García Lorca.—KoT
"Simple Simon met a pieman." Mother Goose.—DeM—FaW—LiSf—LoR
"Sing for your supper." E. Farjeon.—FaE
Sleepless nights. Zolotow. Charlotte.—ZoE—ZoE
The snatchits. J. Prelutsky.—PrB
Some old ones. A. Adoff.—AdA
Some one to tea. E. Farjeon.—FaE
Some things are funny like that. N. Giovanni.—GiSp
Song form. A. Baraka.—KoT
The song of Kuk-ook, the bad boy. Unknown, fr. the Eskimo.—KoT
Song of triumph. L. Duncan.—HoBf
Song to the child. Unknown, fr. the West Greenland Eskimo.—BiSp
Spoilt child. E. Farjeon.—FaE
Springtime. N. Giovanni.—GiSp
Statues. R. Wilbur.—PlEd
Steve. C. Rylant.—RyW
The story of fidgety Philip. H. Hoffman.—DaC
A story that could be true ("If you were exchanged in the cradle and"). W. Stafford.—CoN
The string of my ancestors. N. Nyhart.—JaS
Sunday ("Up early while everyone sleeps"). V. Rutsala.—JaD
Susan Blue. K. Greenaway.—FrP

Children and childhood.—*Continued*
Susan Tulchin. M. Glenn.—GlC
"Suzanna socked me Sunday." J. Prelutsky.—PrNk
Swearing. C. Rylant.—RyW
Tag along. N. Payne.—PrRh
Teenagers. C. Rylant.—RyW
Television nose. X. J. Kennedy.—KeF
"Tell me, tell me, Sarah Jane." C. Causley.—HoSe—LiSf
Temple of the muses. B. Bentley.—PlEd
Ten kinds. M. M. Dodge.—PrRh
Ten years old ("I paid my 30¢ and rode by the bus"). N. Giovanni.—GiSp—LiSf
That's what we'd do. M. M. Dodge.—HaOf
They're calling. F. Holman.—LiSf—PrRh
"This is a poem to my son Peter." P. Meinke.—JaD
Threats. M. Ridlon.—FrP
Three children. Unknown.—DaC
Thumb. P. Dacey.—JaPo—KeK
Tired Tim. W. De la Mare.—CoN—PrRh
To L.B.S. W. T. Scott.—JaD
A token of attachment. J. A. Strawson.—BrT
Tom, Jill and Bob. Unknown.—DaC
The train to Glasgow. W. Horsburgh.—CoOu
"Trip upon trenchers, and dance upon dishes." Mother Goose.—AlH
Turkey in the corn. W. W. Guthrie.—KeK
The turn of the road. J. Stephens.—LiWa
Twinkletoes. A. A. Milne.—ChG
Two people ("Two people live in Rosamund"). E. V. Rieu.—PrRh
Two sisters looking at baby brother. A. Barto.—FaW
War ("With the open eyes of their dead fathers"). A. Voznesensky.—HeR
"We are talking about." A. Adoff.—AdA
"What in the world." E. Merriam.—PrRh
What I've been doing. E. Farjeon.—FaE
What someone said when he was spanked on the day before his birthday. J. Ciardi.—PrRh
"When I was a little boy." Mother Goose.—DeM—LoR
Whitley at three o'clock. J. Worley.—JaG
Who calls. F. C. Sayers.—LiSf
Why ("Fie, darling, why do you cry, why do you cry"). E. Farjeon.—FaE
"Why did the children." C. Sandburg.—HoRa
Willy wet-leg. D. H. Lawrence.—HeR
The windows. W. S. Merwin.—JaD
With my foot in my mouth. D. Lee.—LiIl
A work of artifice. M. Piercy.—JaPi
Zimmer in grade school. P. Zimmer.—KeK
"**Children**, children everywhere." Jack Prelutsky.—PrRh
"**Children**, if you dare to think." See Warning to children
Children not kept at home. Joyce Carol Oates.—JaD
"**Children** sleep at night." See Children
"**Children**, tonight is for Santa." See Christmas prayer
"The **children** wandered up and down." See The cruise of the Mystery
"**Children**, you are very little." See Good and bad children
The **children's** carol. Eleanor Farjeon.—FaE—PrRh
The **children's** hour. Henry Wadsworth Longfellow.—HaOf

"**Children's** voices in the orchard." See New Hampshire
Child's carol. Eleanor Farjeon.—FaE
A **child's** Christmas day. Unknown.—HaO
"The **child's** foot is not yet aware it's a foot." See To the foot from its child
A **child's** grave marker. Ted Kooser.—JaG
A **child's** pet. William Henry Davies.—HeR
A **child's** prayer. John Banister Tabb.—LaT
Child's song. Robert Lowell.—HeR
A **chill**. Christina Georgina Rossetti.—ChB
Chilly dawn. Eleanor Farjeon.—FaE
Chimes. See Bells
The **chimney** sweeper ("A little black thing among the snow"). William Blake.—HeR—PlSc
The **chimney** sweeper ("When my mother died I was very young"). William Blake.—PlSc
Chimney sweeps
   The chimney sweeper ("A little black thing among the snow"). W. Blake.—HeR—PlSc
   The chimney sweeper ("When my mother died I was very young"). W. Blake.—PlSc
   "Eaper Weaper, chimbley sweeper." Mother Goose.—AlH
   "Sweep, sweep." Mother Goose.—LoR
"**Chimneys**, colder." See Reindeer report
"**Chimnies** and wings." Edward Lear.—LiH
China
   Bronzes. C. Sandburg.—PlEd
   A Chinese mural. From A visit to the art gallery. C. Baker.—PlEd
Chinaware. See Tableware
A **Chinese** mural. From A visit to the art gallery. Carlos Baker.—PlEd
Chinese new year. Unknown.—LiNe
Chinese nursery rhymes. See Nursery rhymes—Chinese
"The **chipmunk**." See Chipmunk
Chipmunk. N. M. Bodecker.—BoSs
The **chipmunk.** Jack Prelutsky.—PrZ
Chipmunks
   Chipmunk. N. M. Bodecker.—BoSs
   The chipmunk. J. Prelutsky.—PrZ
   The chipmunk's day. R. Jarrell.—HaOf—PrRh
The **chipmunk's** day. Randall Jarrell.—HaOf—PrRh
"**Chipmunks** jump and." See Valentine
Chippewa Indians. See Indians of the Americas—Chippewa
Chiquita bonita. Unknown.—GrT
"**Chitchat**." See Ping-pong
"**Chitter** chatter, chitter chatter." See The chipmunk
Chivalry. See Knights and knighthood
"**Chock** full boxes, packages." See Kaleidoscope
"**Chocolate**." Arnold Adoff.—LiSf
Chocolate cake. Jack Prelutsky.—PrMp
"**Chocolate** cake." Nina Payne.—PrRh
Chocolate chocolate. Arnold Adoff.—PrRh
"**Chocolate** Easter bunny." See Patience
Chocolate milk. Ron Padgett.—KoT
Chocolate rhyme. Unknown.—GrT
"**Chook**, chook, chook, chook, chook." Mother Goose.—DeM—LoR—PrRa
Choose. Carl Sandburg.—HoRa
"**Choose** the darkest part o' the grove." See Incantation to Oedipus
Choosing
   Certain choices. R. Shelton.—JaPi
   Choose. C. Sandburg.—HoRa
   Choosing. E. Farjeon.—FaE
   "Handy-dandy, maple candy." C. Watson.—WaC

Choosing—*Continued*
  Minnie. E. Farjeon.—FaE
  Prayer ("I ask you this"). L. Hughes.—HuDk
  The road not taken. R. Frost.—KoS
Choosing. Eleanor Farjeon.—FaE
Choosing their names. Thomas Hood.—DaC
Choosing up rhymes. See Counting-out rhymes
"Chortling, ho ho, this'll learn us." X. J. Kennedy.—KeB
"The **Christ-child** lay on Mary's heart." See A Christmas carol
"The **Christ-child** lay on Mary's lap." See A Christmas carol
Christabel, sels. Samuel Taylor Coleridge
  "In the touch of this bosom there worketh a spell".—HeR
Christenings
  A testimony. G. E. Lyon.—JaG
  "When I was christened." D. McCord.—HaOf—KeK
Christgau, Ferdinand G.
  St. Thomas.—BrT
  Two jays at St. Louis.—BrT
Christianity. See also Jesus Christ (about)
  Carlos Rodriguez. M. Glenn.—GlCd
  Christine Leader. M. Glenn.—GlC
  Lepanto. G. K. Chesterton.—HeR
  Saved. C. Rylant.—RyW
Christine Leader. Mel Glenn.—GlC
Christmas. See also Christmas trees; Santa Claus
  The adoration of the Magi. C. Pilling.—HaO
  Advent, a carol. P. Dickinson.—HaO
  Advent 1955. Sir J. Betjeman.—HaO
  Advice from Poor Robin's almanack. Unknown.—HaO
  African Christmas. J. Press.—HaO
  After Christmas. M. Richards.—HaO
  Afterthought. E. Jennings.—HaO
  All on a Christmas morning. E. Coatsworth.—LiIl
  "And there were in the same country shepherds." From Gospel according to Luke. Bible/New Testament.—LiCp
  Angel's song. C. Causley.—HaO
  Annar-Mariar's Christmas shopping. E. Farjeon.—FaE
  "As I sat on a sunny bank." Mother Goose.—DeM
  "Away in a manger." Unknown.—RoC
  The ballad of Befana. P. McGinley.—PlAs
  A ballad of Christmas. W. De la Mare.—HaO
  The barn ("I am tired of this barn, said the colt"). E. Coatsworth.—HaO
  BC, AD. U. A. Fanthorpe.—HaO
  Bethlehem bells. E. Farjeon.—FaE
  The burning babe. R. Southwell.—HaO—HeR
  Camels of the kings. L. Norris.—HaO
  Candy cane. V. Worth.—LiCp
  Carol ("Deep in the fading leaves of night"). W. R. Rodgers.—HaO
  A carol for Christmas eve. E. Farjeon.—FaE
  Carol for the last Christmas eve. N. Nicholson.—HaO
  Carol of patience. R. Graves.—HaO
  Carol of the birds. Unknown.—RoC
  Carol of the brown king. L. Hughes.—LiCp
  Carol of the field mice. K. Grahame.—RoC
  The carol of the poor children. R. Middleton.—HaO
  Carol of the signs. E. Farjeon.—FaE
  The carol singers. E. Farjeon.—FaE
  Cat, Christmas. V. Worth.—LiCa

  Ceremony upon Candlemas eve. R. Herrick.—HaO
  The children's carol. E. Farjeon.—FaE—PrRh
  A child's Christmas day. Unknown.—HaO
  Christmas ("The bells of waiting advent ring"). Sir J. Betjeman.—HaO
  Christmas ("My goodness, my goodness"). M. Chute.—FrP
  Christmas ("What, do they suppose that everything has been said that can be said"). L. Hunt.—HaO
  Christmas bills. J. Hatton.—HaO
  Christmas card. T. Hughes.—HaO
  A Christmas carol ("The Christ-child lay on Mary's lap"). G. K. Chesterton.—HaO
    A Christmas carol ("The Christ-child lay on Mary's heart").—RoC
  Christmas chime. X. J. Kennedy.—LiCp
  "Christmas comes but once a year." Mother Goose.—DeM—LoR
  Christmas day ("Last night in the open shippen"). A. Young.—HaO—RoC
  Christmas day ("Nature's decorations glisten"). C. Smart.—HaO
  Christmas day ("Small girls on trikes"). R. Fuller.—HaO
  Christmas dinner. M. Rosen.—HaO
  Christmas eve ("He is coming"). M. C. Livingston.—LiCe
  Christmas eve ("The roofs over the shops"). P. Beer.—HaO
  A Christmas folk song. L. W. Reese.—HaOf
  A Christmas hymn. R. Wilbur.—HaO
  Christmas in Key West. J. Ciardi.—LiCp
  "Christmas is coming, the geese are getting fat." Mother Goose.—DeM—LiCp—LiSf—LoR—RoC
    "Christmas is a-coming".—CoN
  "Christmas is really for the children." S. Turner.—HaO
  Christmas kaleidoscope. X. J. Kennedy.—KeF
  Christmas landscape. L. Lee.—HaO
  A Christmas lullaby. E. Farjeon.—FaE
  Christmas morn. R. Sawyer.—HaO—RoC
  Christmas morning. H. Behn.—LiCp
  "Christmas morning i." C. Freeman.—KeK
  Christmas night. L. Sail.—HaO
  Christmas 1970. S. Milligan.—HaO
  Christmas, 1924. T. Hardy.—HaO
  Christmas play. M. C. Livingston.—LiWo
  Christmas prayer. D. McCord.—LiCp
  Christmas shopping. L. MacNeice.—HaO
  Christmas thank you's. M. Gowar.—HaO
  Cradle song for Christmas. E. Farjeon.—FaE
  The crib. R. Finch.—HaO
  The day after Christmas. L. B. Hopkins.—HoSi
  Day before Christmas. M. Chute.—CoN
  December ("All the months go past"). R. Fyleman.—PrRa
  December ("Glad Christmas comes, and every hearth"). J. Clare.—HaO
  Doll. M. C. Livingston.—LiWo
  The donkey ("When fishes flew and forests walked"). G. K. Chesterton.—DaC—HeR
  Don't tell. M. Rosen.—RoC
  Earth and sky. E. Farjeon.—FaE
  Eddi's service. R. Kipling.—HaO
  The feast o' Saint Stephen. R. Sawyer.—HaO
  The fire ("The fire with well dried logs supplied"). Sir W. Scott.—HaO
  The first Christmas eve. H. Behn.—HoCb
  For all. E. Farjeon.—FaE
  For Christmas day. E. Farjeon.—FaE

Christmas.—*Continued*

For the children or the grown-ups. Unknown.—HaO
For them. E. Farjeon.—FaE
The friendly beasts. Unknown.—LiIl
Ghost story. From From A child's Christmas in Wales. D. Thomas.—HaO
"God bless the master of this house." Mother Goose.—DeM
Good will to men. D. B. Thompson.—HaO
Grandmother Jackson. D. Jackson.—HaO
"Hang up the baby's stocking." Unknown.—HaO
Heap on more wood. Sir W. Scott.—HaO
Hob gobbling's song. J. R. Lowell.—HaOf
Holly and mistletoe. E. Farjeon.—FaE
"The holly and the ivy." Unknown.—RoC
The house of hospitalities. T. Hardy.—HeR
How to paint a perfect Christmas. M. Holub.—HaO
The Huron carol ("'Twas in the moon of winter time"). J. E. Middleton.—HaO
"I heard the bells on Christmas Day." H. W. Longfellow.—CoN
   Christmas bells.—HaO
I saw three ships. Unknown.—RoC
"I sing of a maiden." Unknown.—RoC
"In the bleak midwinter." C. G. Rossetti.—RoC
   A Christmas carol.—DaC
In the week when Christmas comes. E. Farjeon.—FaE—LiSf
In the workhouse. G. R. Sims.—HaO
"It blew." Mother Goose.—LoR
Journey back to Christmas. G. Denn.—HaO
Journey of the Magi. T. S. Eliot.—HaO
Kaleidoscope ("Chock full boxes, packages"). X. J. Kennedy.—LiCp
Keeping Christmas. E. Farjeon.—HaO—RoC
"Little Jack Horner." Mother Goose.—DeM—FaW—LoR
A manger song. E. Farjeon.—FaE
Mary's burden. E. Farjeon.—FaE
Men may talk of country Christmasses. P. Massinger.—HaO
Merry Christmas. A. Fisher.—PrRh
Mice in the hay. L. Norris.—HaO
Minstrel's song. T. Hughes.—HaO
The mistletoe. J. Prelutsky.—PrRa
Mrs. Kriss Kringle. E. M. Thomas.—HaOf
"Moonless darkness stands between." G. M. Hopkins.—HaO
The mother's song ("She knew, the maiden mother knew"). E. Farjeon.—FaE
The mother's tale. E. Farjeon.—FaE
The mummers. E. Farjeon.—FaE
My Christmas, mum's Christmas. S. Forsyth.—HaO
"My father played the melodeon." From A Christmas childhood. P. Kavanagh.—HeR
"My stocking's where." From A Christmas package. D. McCord.—PrRh
Noel. C. Zolotow.—ZoE
Noel, Christmas eve, 1913. R. Bridges.—HaO
North and south. C. Zolotow.—ZoE
"Now every man at my request." Unknown.—HaO
"O little town of Bethlehem." P. Brooks.—RoC (unat.)
"On the thirteenth day of Christmas." C. Causley.—HaO
"One Christmas-time." From The prelude. W. Wordsworth.—HeR
Otto. G. Brooks.—LiSf

The oxen ("Christmas eve, and twelve of the clock"). T. Hardy.—HaO—HeR—RoC
Los pastores. E. Agnew.—LiCp
Phantasus, 1, 8. A. Holz.—LiCp
Reindeer report. U. A. Fanthorpe.—HaO
The reminder. T. Hardy.—HaO
The riding of the kings. E. Farjeon.—FaE
The rocking carol. Unknown.—RoC
Sailor's carol. C. Causley.—HaO
"The shepherd and the king." E. Farjeon.—FaE
Shepherd's carol. N. Nicholson.—HaO
The shepherd's dog. L. Norris.—HaO
The shepherd's tale. R. Ponchon.—HaO
Silent night. J. Mohr.—RoC (unat.)
"Sing hey, sing hey." Mother Goose.—LiIl
Six green singers. E. Farjeon.—FaE
Stocking time. E. Farjeon.—FaE
A stocking to fill. E. Farjeon.—FaE
A summer Christmas in Australia. D. Sladen.—HaO
Take heart, sweet Mary. Unknown.—FaE
   In the town.—HaO
This holy night. E. Farjeon.—FaE
The three drovers. J. Wheeler.—RoC
Through a shop window. E. Farjeon.—FaE
Twelfth night ("Our candles, lit, re-lit, have gone down now"). P. Scupham.—HaO
The twelve days of Christmas. Unknown.—RoC
   "The first day of Christmas".—LoR
A visit from St. Nicholas ("'Twas the night before Christmas, when all through the house"). C. C. Moore.—CoN—HaO—HaOf—LiCp—LiSf—PrRh—RoC
Wassailing song. Unknown.—HaO
We three kings. Unknown.—RoC
The week after. E. Farjeon.—FaE
"Well, so that is that, now we must dismantle the tree." From For the time being. W. H. Auden.—HaO
What the donkey saw. U. A. Fanthorpe.—HaO
"When I was home last Christmas." R. Jarrell.—PlAs
The wise men ask the children the way. H. Heine.—HaO
Yule log. R. Herrick.—HaO

Christmas ("The bells of waiting advent ring"). Sir John Betjeman.—HaO
"The Christmas." See Doll
Christmas ("My goodness, my goodness"). Marchette Chute.—FrP
Christmas ("What, do they suppose that everything has been said that can be said"). Leigh Hunt.—HaO
"Christmas again." See North and south
Christmas bells. See "I heard the bells on Christmas Day"
"Christmas bells, awake and ring." See Christmas morning
Christmas bills. Joseph Hatton.—HaO
Christmas card. Ted Hughes.—HaO
A **Christmas** carol ("The Christ-child lay on Mary's lap"). Gilbert Keith Chesterton.—HaO
A Christmas carol ("The Christ-child lay on Mary's heart").—RoC
A **Christmas** carol, sels. Charles Dickens
   Tiny Tim's prayer.—LaT
A **Christmas** carol. See "In the bleak midwinter"
A **Christmas** carol ("The Christ-child lay on Mary's heart"). See A Christmas carol ("The Christ-child lay on Mary's lap")
A **Christmas** childhood, sels. Patrick Kavanagh
   "My father played the melodeon".—HeR

Christmas chime. X. J. Kennedy.—LiCp
"Christmas comes but once a year." Mother Goose.—DeM—LoR
Christmas day ("Last night in the open shippen"). Andrew Young.—HaO—RoC
Christmas day ("Nature's decorations glisten"). Christopher Smart.—HaO
Christmas day ("Small girls on trikes"). Roy Fuller.—HaO
Christmas dinner. Michael Rosen.—HaO
"The Christmas dinner was at two." See A summer Christmas in Australia
"Christmas eve." See Don't tell
Christmas eve ("He is coming"). Myra Cohn Livingston.—LiCe
Christmas eve ("The roofs over the shops"). Patricia Beer.—HaO
"Christmas eve, and twelve of the clock." See The oxen
A Christmas folk song. Lizette Woodworth Reese.—HaOf
"The Christmas hour I love the best." See Stocking time
A Christmas hymn. Richard Wilbur.—HaO
Christmas in Key West. John Ciardi.—LiCp
"Christmas is a-coming". See "Christmas is coming, the geese are getting fat"
"Christmas is coming, the geese are getting fat." Mother Goose.—DeM—LiCp—LiSf—LoR—RoC
   "Christmas is a-coming".—CoN
"Christmas is really for the children." Steve Turner.—HaO
Christmas kaleidoscope. X. J. Kennedy.—KeF
Christmas landscape. Laurie Lee.—HaO
A Christmas lullaby. Eleanor Farjeon.—FaE
Christmas morn. Ruth Sawyer.—HaO—RoC
Christmas morning. Harry Behn.—LiCp
"Christmas morning i." Carol Freeman.—KeK
Christmas night. Lawrence Sail.—HaO
Christmas 1970. Spike Milligan.—HaO
Christmas, 1924. Thomas Hardy.—HaO
A Christmas package, sels. David McCord
   "My stocking's where".—PrRh
Christmas play. Myra Cohn Livingston.—LiWo
Christmas prayer. David McCord.—LiCp
Christmas shopping. Louis MacNeice.—HaO
Christmas thank you's. Mick Gowar.—HaO
The Christmas tree ("I set a little Christmas tree"). Eleanor Farjeon.—FaE
The Christmas tree ("Outside the world was full, plural"). Patricia Beer.—HaO
Christmas tree ("Star over all"). Laurence Smith.—HaO
Christmas tree ("Stores and filling stations prefer a roof"). Stanley Cook.—HaO
Christmas trees
   African Christmas. J. Press.—HaO
   The Christmas tree ("I set a little Christmas tree"). E. Farjeon.—FaE
   The Christmas tree ("Outside the world was full, plural"). P. Beer.—HaO
   Christmas tree ("Star over all"). L. Smith.—HaO
   Christmas tree ("Stores and filling stations prefer a roof"). S. Cook.—HaO
   Come Christmas. D. McCord.—LiCp
   "Little tree." E. E. Cummings.—CoN—HaO—LiSf
   The song of the fir. E. Farjeon.—FaE
   Tinsel. V. Worth.—LiCp
   The tired tree. E. Farjeon.—FaE
Christopher Conti. Mel Glenn.—GlC

"Christopher Robin goes." See Hoppity
"Chuck-full boxes, packages." See Christmas kaleidoscope
Chums. Arthur Guiterman.—FrP—PrRa
"Chunks of night." See Shadows
Church bells. Berton Braley.—BrT
Churches
   "And Hiram of Tyre sent his servants unto Solomon, for he had." From Kings. Bible/Old Testament.—PlEd
   The building of a new church. Unknown.—PlEd
   Chartres. From View of the cathedral. R. Henri.—PlEd
   Duomo, Milan. From View of the cathedral. R. Henri.—PlEd
   Eddi's service. R. Kipling.—HaO
   For Wilma. D. Johnson.—JaG
   Holiness. C. Rylant.—RyW
   Homage to Wren. L. MacNeice.—PlEd
   In memory of George Whitby, architect. Sir J. Betjeman.—PlEd
   Journey back to Christmas. G. Denn.—HaO
   Mrs. Martha Jean Black. N. Giovanni.—GiSp
   Prayer meeting. L. Hughes.—HuDk
   Sunday ("Let me tell you"). A. Turner.—TuS
   Upon Fairford windows. R. Corbett.—PlEd
Chute, Marchette
   Christmas ("My goodness, my goodness").—FrP
   Crayons.—PrRa
   Day before Christmas.—CoN
   Drinking fountain.—FrP—PrRa
   In August.—HoSu
   In the night ("When I wake up and it is dark").—HoSu
   My dog ("His nose is short and scrubby").—FrP
   My kitten.—HoSu
   My teddy bear ("A teddy bear is a faithful friend").—PrRa
   Showers.—PrRa
   Sleeping outdoors.—LaW—PrRa
   Spring rain.—FrP—PrRh
   Undersea.—RuI
   Winter night ("As I lie in bed I hear").—LaW
   The wrong start.—PrRh
Ciardi, John
   About being very good and far better than most but still not quite good enough to take on the Atlantic Ocean ("There was a fine swimmer named Jack").—CiD
      On being much better than most and yet not quite good enough (". . . a great swimmer named Jack").—JaG
   About Indians.—CiD
   About the teeth of sharks.—HaOf
   About trapping in the North woods.—CiD
   All I did was ask my sister a question.—CiD
   At night ("When I am outdoors and begin").—CiD
   At the beach ("Johnny, Johnny, let go of that crab").—CiD
   The baseball player.—CiD
   The best part of going away is going away from you.—CiD
   Captain Spud and his first mate, Spade.—HaOf
   The cat heard the cat-bird.—LiCa
   The chap who disappeared.—CiD
   Christmas in Key West.—LiCp
   The dangers of taking baths.—CiD
   Ding-a-ling.—CiD
   Do you feel sorry for him.—CiD
   Doing a good deed.—CiD
   The dollar dog.—CiD

Cities and city life.—*Continued*
Flying uptown backwards. X. J. Kennedy.—KeF
For a quick exit. N. Farber.—HoCl—KeK
Forty Seventh Street crash. X. J. Kennedy.—KeF
Garage sale. K. Shapiro.—JaPi
Garbage truck. M. Ridlon.—HoCl
Get 'em here. L. B. Hopkins.—HoMu
Glass walling. N. M. Bodecker.—BoPc
The great figure. W. C. Williams.—KoT
Great things have happened. A. Nowlan.—JaG
Greener grass. F. Steele.—JaPi
Hello, graffiti. A. Turner.—TuS
The house-wreckers. C. Reznikoff.—HoSs—KeK
"In quiet night." M. C. Livingston.—LaW
"In the morning the city." From City. L. Hughes.—HoSs
Incident ("Once riding in old Baltimore"). C. Cullen.—CoN—HaOf—KeK
"It fell in the city." E. Merriam.—BaS—MeBl—PrRa
James Shell's snowball stand. N. Giovanni.—GiSp
Just for one day. L. Morrison.—PrRh
The lamplighter. R. L. Stevenson.—PlSc
The lights at night. E. Farjeon.—FaE
Litany. L. Hughes.—LaT
London. W. Blake.—HeR
Look up. A. Turner.—TuS
Manhattan lullabye. N. Farber.—HoSs
Mannahatta. W. Whitman.—PlEd
Mister alley cat. J. McGowan.—ChC
Mommies do. N. Giovanni.—GiSp
Morning ("Saw a play once"). A. Turner.—TuS
Mural on second avenue. L. Moore.—MoSn
The new kid on the block. J. Prelutsky.—PrNk
New York City, 1935. G. Corso.—JaPi
Night roof. A. Turner.—TuS
"Night settles on earth." From From an airplane. H. Behn.—HoSs
Nightfall. E. Olson.—JaD
Of poor B. B. B. Brecht.—HeR
Oil slick. J. Thurman.—HoSs—LiSf
Open hydrant. M. Ridlon.—PrRh
The park ("One day I so depressed"). A. Turner.—TuS
Parking lot full. E. Merriam.—HoCl
People leaves. A. Turner.—TuS
Pigeons. L. Moore.—HoSs—MoSn—PrRh
A piper. S. O'Sullivan.—LiSf
Rain in the city. N. M. Bodecker.—BoPc
Rainy nights. I. Thompson.—PrRh
Recuerdo. E. S. Millay.—LiSf
Red flower. A. Turner.—TuS
Reflections ("On this street"). L. Moore.—LiSf—MoSn
Roof. S. Cassedy.—CaR
Roofscape. X. J. Kennedy.—KeF
Rudolph is tired of the city. G. Brooks.—PrRh
A sad song about Greenwich Village. F. Park.—PrRh
Sentries. X. J. Kennedy.—KeF
Sidewalk measles. B. M. Hales.—HoSi—HoSs
"Sing a song of people." L. Lenski.—PrRh
"Sing a song of subways." E. Merriam.—KeK—PrRh
Skyscrapers. R. Field.—FrP
Smog. M. C. Livingston.—LiSi
Snowy morning. L. Moore.—BaS—MoSn
Song form. A. Baraka.—KoT
The sound of rain. D. A. Evans.—JaG
Spring morning in Boston's south end. N. M. Bodecker.—BoPc

Springtime. N. Giovanni.—GiSp
Statues. R. Wilbur.—PlEd
Steam shovel. C. Malam.—CoN—PrRh
Stickball. V. Schonborg.—PrRh
A street scene. L. W. Reese.—HaOf
The streets of Laredo ("O, early one morning I walked out like Agag"). L. MacNeice.—PlAs
Subway rush hour. L. Hughes.—KeK
Subway train. L. B. Jacobs.—HoCl—HoSu
Summer milk. X. J. Kennedy.—KeF
Sunrise. F. Asch.—ChG—PrRh
Taught me purple. E. T. Hunt.—LiSf
Taxis. R. Field.—LiSf
The telephone. E. Field.—JaPo
That May morning. L. B. Jacobs.—ChG—PrRh
Things to do if you are a subway. B. Katz.—HoSs—PrRh
Tiempo muerto. R. Alonso.—PlSc
Today is Saturday. Z. K. Snyder.—LiIl
Tom cat. A. Turner.—TuS
A tomcat is. J. P. Lewis.—LiCa
Trouble in town. X. J. Kennedy.—KeF
Tulips and addresses. E. Field.—JaPi
Umbrellas ("It's raining in the city"). M. Kumin.—HoSs
Umbrellas ("Umbrellas bloom"). B. J. Esbensen.—PrRa
Undefeated. R. Froman.—LiIl
Until we built a cabin. A. Fisher.—LaW
Vestibule. S. Cassedy.—CaR
Wash in the street. A. Turner.—TuS
Watch your step, I'm drenched. A. Mitchell.—HeR
Water-front streets. L. Hughes.—HuDk
Where are you now. M. B. Miller.—PrRh
Why ("Fumble-John they call him"). A. Turner.—TuS
Wind flowers. M. Lockwood.—JaD
With a posthumous medal. J. M. Brinnin.—PlSc
Witness. E. Merriam.—MeSk
Working girls. C. Sandburg.—PlSc
X. S. Cassedy.—CaR
Zimmer's street. P. Zimmer.—JaT
The city ("If the flowers want to grow"). David Ignatow.—HoSi
City, complete ("In the morning the city"). Langston Hughes.—FrP—PrRh
City, sels. Langston Hughes
"In the morning the city".—HoSs
"City asleep." See The city dump
City blockades. Lee Bennett Hopkins.—HoSs
The city child. Alfred Tennyson.—DaC
City, city 1 ("City, city, wrong and bad"). Marci Ridlon.—PrRh
City, city 2 ("City, city, golden clad"). Marci Ridlon.—PrRh
"City, city, golden clad." See City, city 2
"City, city, wrong and bad." See City, city 1
City dawn. N. M. Bodecker.—BoPc
The city dump. Felice Holman.—HoSs—PrRh
A city graveyard. Joyce Carol Oates.—JaD
"The city has streets." See City streets and country roads
City lights. Rachel Field.—PrRh
The city mouse and the garden mouse. Christina Georgina Rossetti.—CoN
"The city mouse lives in a house." See The city mouse and the garden mouse
"City, oh, city." Jack Prelutsky.—PrRh
The city show. Eleanor Farjeon.—FaE
City streets and country roads. Eleanor Farjeon.—FaE
City traffic. Eve Merriam.—LiSf—MeSk

City under water. Eleanor Farjeon.—FaE
"The city yawns." See Sunrise
Cityscape. N. M. Bodecker.—BoPc
Civil War. See United States—History—Civil War
Civilization
  "As I lay asleep in Italy." From The mask of
    anarchy. P. B. Shelley.—HeR
  A boat ("O beautiful"). R. Brautigan.—KeK
  Boulder dam. M. Sarton.—PlSc
  Homage to Paul Mellon, I. M. Pei, their gallery,
    and Washington City. W. Meredith.—PlEd
  "Make me feel the wild pulsation that I felt
    before the strife." From Locksley Hall. A.
    Tennyson.—PlSc
  The man with the hoe. E. Markham.—PlSc
  Metamorphoses ("These people, with their
    illegible diplomas"). H. Nemerov.—PlEd
  Nightmare number three. S. V. Benét.—PlSc
  The outwit song. D. Hoffman.—PlSc
  The passenger pigeon. P. Fleischman.—FlI
  Rain forest, Papua, New Guinea. M. C.
    Livingston.—LiMp
  Sext. From Horae Canonicae. W. H. Auden.—
    PlSc
  The streets of Laredo ("O, early one morning
    I walked out like Agag"). L. MacNeice.—PlAs
  Willis Beggs. E. L. Masters.—PlSc
"Clack clack clack." See Skeleton
Clairmont, Robert
  A hero in the land of dough.—KeK
Clams
  "From Table Isle." Unknown.—FaTh
  "On a bet, foolhardy Sam." X. J. Kennedy.—
    KeB
  Shell ("The shell"). S. Cassedy.—CaR
Clancy, Joseph
  The rattle bag, tr. by.—HeR
Clap your hands for Herod. Josef Hanzlik, tr. by
  Ian Milner.—HaO
"Clapcake, clapcake." Clyde Watson.—WaC
"Clapping the door to, in the little light." See
  Charwomen
Clara Cleech. Jack Prelutsky.—PrNk
"Clara, little curlylocks." Arnold Lobel.—LoWr
Clare, John
  Autumn ("Summer is gone and all the merry
    noise").—PlSc
  The badger.—HeR
  Clock-a-clay.—BlO
  December ("Glad Christmas comes, and every
    hearth").—HaO
  December ("While snows the window panes
    bedim").—HaO
  The flood.—HeR
  Grasshoppers.—KoT
  Hares at play.—HeR
  Little trotty wagtail.—BlO—CoOu—HeR
  Mouse's nest.—HeR
  The old year.—HaO
  Remembrances, sels.
    "When for school o'er Little Field with its
      brook and wooden brig".—PlSc
  Song ("I hid my love when young while I").—
    HeR
  Song's eternity.—PlAs
  The thrush's nest.—BlO
  The vixen.—HeR
  "When for school o'er Little Field with its
    brook and wooden brig." See Remembrances
Clarence. Shel Silverstein.—HaOf
"Clarence Lee from Tennessee." See Clarence
Clark, G. Orr
  "The night is a big black cat."—PrRh

Clark, Leonard
  House, for sale.—PrRh
  November the fifth.—CoOu
Clark, Tom
  Crows ("Like the shore's alternation of door
    wave").—JaD
Clarke, Austin
  The scholar.—HeR
  A strong wind.—HeR
Clarke, Pauline
  My name is.—PrRh
Class-room. Eleanor Farjeon.—FaE
Clay and water. Sandra Hochman.—JaS
Clean. Ann Turner.—TuS
The clean platter, sels. Ogden Nash
  "Bring salad or sausage or scone".—HoMu
Cleaning the well. Paul Ruffin.—JaS
Cleanliness. See also Bathing
  Car wash. M. C. Livingston.—CoN—HoCl
  "Cat's tongue." E. Merriam.—LiCa—MeBl
  Dainty Dottie Dee. J. Prelutsky.—PrNk
  The dirtiest man in the world. S. Silverstein.—
    HaOf
  Drumpp the grump. J. Prelutsky.—PrNk
  "Little Polly Flinders." Mother Goose.—AlH—
    DeM—FaW—LoR
  Meet neat Rosie De Fleet. Unknown.—BrT
  "Sing a song of soapsuds." C. Watson.—WaC
  "There was a messy gentleman." A. Lobel.—
    LoWr
  "There was a young lady of Crete."
    Unknown.—CoOu
      A young lady of Crete.—BrT
  "The tidy woman." Unknown.—DeD
  "Who are you." Mother Goose.—FaW
  "Who are you, a dirty old man." Mother
    Goose.—FaW—LoR
  "A wolf is at the laundromat." J. Prelutsky.—
    PrNk
  Your room. S. Cassedy.—CaR
"Clear and cool, clear and cool." See The river's
  song
"Clear river." Unknown.—BiSp
Cleghorn, Sarah N.
  The golf links.—KeK
Clementine. Unknown.—KeK—LiSf
  Oh, my darling Clementine.—PlAs
Cleopatra (about)
  "The barge she sat in, like a burnish'd throne."
    From Antony and Cleopatra. W.
    Shakespeare.—HoUn
Clergy
  Father Gilligan. W. B. Yeats.—PlAs
  The garden of love. W. Blake.—HeR
  The pious young priest. Unknown.—BrT
  Robin Hood and the Bishop of Hereford.
    Unknown.—BlO
  The Vicar of Bray. Unknown.—PlAs
"A clergyman told from his text." See Who's next
Clever Peter and the ogress. Katharine Pyle.—
  HaOf
A cliche. Eve Merriam.—MeSk
"Clickbeetle." Mary Ann Hoberman.—PrRh
"Clickety-clack." See Song of the train
Cliffs
  Beeny Cliff, March 1870–March 1913. T
    Hardy.—HeR
Clifton, Lucille
  April ("Rain is good").—HoSi—PrRa
  Everett Anderson's friend.—LiIl
  Eviction.—CoN
  "Let there be new flowering."—JaPo

Clifton, Lucille—*Continued*
The poet ("I beg my bones to be good but").—JaD
September ("I already know where Africa is").—HoSi—LiSf
Sunday morning lonely.—FaW
Climbing
The bean stalk. E. S. Millay.—LiWa
Black rock of Kiltearn. A. Young.—HeR
Child on top of a greenhouse. T. Roethke.—KeK
Do you feel sorry for him. J. Ciardi.—CiD
"Every time I climb a tree." From Five chants. D. McCord.—CoN—FaW—LiSf—PrRh
It makes no difference to me. J. Ciardi.—CiD
Song ("Up in the high"). D. H. Lawrence.—PrBb
Up in the pine. N. D. Watson.—PrRh
"**Climbing** through the January snow, into the Lobo canyon." See Mountain lion
Clint Reynolds. Mel Glenn.—GlCd
"**Clip clop,** clippity-clop." Clyde Watson. WaC
Clock. Valerie Worth.—LiSf
Clock-a-clay. John Clare.—BlO
"The **clock** stops ticking." See Stroke
The **clock** ticks. Eve Merriam.—MeSk
The **clock** tower. Colleen Thibaudeau.—DoNw
Clocks and watches
Alarm clock. E. Merriam.—MeSk
"Bell horses, bell horses." Mother Goose.—LoR
Clock. V. Worth.—LiSf
The clock ticks. E. Merriam.—MeSk
The clock tower. C. Thibaudeau.—DoNw
Cuckoo ("The cuckoo in our cuckoo clock"). J. Prelutsky.—PrNk
The gold nest. R. Wallace.—JaPo
Grandfather clock. M. C. Livingston.—LiWo
"Hickory dickory dock." Mother Goose.—DeM—FaW—LoR
A quick hush. X. J. Kennedy.—KeF
Telling time. L. Moore.—MoSn
"There was an old pig with a clock." A. Lobel.—LoB
Tide and time. R. McGough.—JaT
Time piece. W. Cole.—JaPo
"Two brothers are we." A. Lobel.—LoWr
Ways of winding a watch. E. Merriam.—MeSk
The wonderful clock. E. Farjeon.—FaE
The **clod** and the pebble. William Blake.—HeR
"**Close** by, / they're stolid." See Telephone poles
"**Close** by the basement door-step." See A toad
Close call. X. J. Kennedy.—KeF
Close of day. Eleanor Farjeon.—FaE
"**Close** the barbecue." See Now
"**Close** your eyes." See Grandma's lullaby
"**Close** your eyes." See Pussy willows
"**Closed,** it sleeps." See Safety pin
Closet. Sylvia Cassedy.—CaR
The **closing** of the rodeo. William Jay Smith.—PlSc
"**Clothes** make no sound when I tread ground." From Three riddles from the Exeter book. Unknown, tr. by Geoffrey Grigson.—HeR
Clothing and dress. See also names of clothing, as Boots and shoes
Amy Pines. M. Glenn.—GlC
An awful moment. X. J. Kennedy.—KeF
The ballad of Newington Green. J. Aiken.—LiSf
Brian O'Linn. Unknown.—HeR
Coat hangers. V. Worth.—WoSp
"Cockyolly Bumkin merry go bet." C. Watson.—WaC

"Daffy-down-dilly is new come to town." Mother Goose.—DeM—LoR
"Daffadowndilly".—CoN
Dinogad's petticoat. Unknown.—HeR
Double trouble. E. Merriam.—MeSk
Downpour. M. C. Livingston.—HoSu
Dressed up. L. Hughes.—HuDk
The Easter parade. W. J. Smith.—LiE
Fairies ("Out of the dust of dreams"). L. Hughes.—HuDk
"The fisherman's hands." N. Valen.—ChC
"Fritters used to say, there is poetry in neckties." From Heavy and light. C. Sandburg.—HoRa
"A hat to warm your topknot." C. Watson.—WaC
"Hector Protector was dressed all in green." Mother Goose.—AlH—DeM—LoR
Huswifery. E. Taylor.—PlSc
"I gathered mosses in Easedale." D. Wordsworth.—PlSc
Jenny. E. Farjeon. FaE
Joe's snow clothes. K. Kuskin.—BaS
John. N. M. Bodecker.—PrRh
Jonathan Bing. B. C. Brown.—PrRh
"A kind and gentle heart he had." From Elegy on the death of a mad dog. O. Goldsmith.—TrM
"Little Miss Lily." Mother Goose.—LoR
"Little Polly Flinders." Mother Goose.—AlH—DeM—FaW—LoR
"Lucy Locket lost her pocket." Mother Goose.—DeM—LoR
"Ma, don't throw that shirt out." J. Prelutsky.—PrNk
Meredith Piersall. M. Glenn.—GlCd
Mr. and Mrs. Spikky Sparrow. E. Lear.—LiH
The mitten song. M. L. Allen.—CoN—PrRa
Mixed-up kid. X. J. Kennedy.—KeF
"The morns are meeker than they were." E. Dickinson.—HaOf
"My brother lost his bathing suit." J. Prelutsky.—PrWi
My jacket old. H. Melville.—PlSc
"My mother's got me bundled up." J. Prelutsky.—PrIs
Nature and art. O. Herford.—BrT
New clothes and old. E. Farjeon.—BcD
New suit. E. Merriam.—MeF
The new vestments. E. Lear.—PrRh
Nightmare ("Beautiful beautiful Beverly"). J. Viorst.—ViI
Old clothes. P. Hey.—JaG
An old man of Toulon. W. J. Smith.—BrT
"The old woman must stand." Mother Goose.—DeM
"The old woman stands at the tub, tub, tub." Mother Goose.—LoR
Polar bear ("The secret of the polar bear"). G. Kredenser.—PrRa
"Poor old Robinson Crusoe." Mother Goose.—LoR
"Pussy cat Mole jumped over a coal." Mother Goose.—DeM
Rainy day. W. Wise.—PrRa
"Red stockings, blue stockings." Mother Goose.—LoR
"Said Dorothy Hughes to Helen Hocking." W. J. Smith.—KeK
Shirt. C. Sandburg.—HoRa
"There was a little woman." Mother Goose.—DeM

Clothing and dress.—*Continued*
"There was a man." A. Lobel.—LoWr
"There was a young belle of old Natchez." O. Nash.—KeK
"There was a young person in green." E. Lear.—LiH
"There was a young person of Crete." E. Lear.—LiH
"There was an old person of Bude." E. Lear.—LiH
"Those dressed in blue." Mother Goose.—LoR
A thrifty soprano. O. Nash.—BrT
A thrifty young fellow. Unknown.—BrT
Uncertain what to wear. W. J. Smith.—BrT
Upon Julia's clothes. R. Herrick.—KoT
"Vain, vain, Mister McLain." A. Lobel.—LoWr
Wendy in winter. K. Starbird.—PrRh
When Jane goes to market. E. Farjeon.—FaE
"When Molly Day wears yellow clothes." J. Prelutsky.—PrRi
When Sue wears red. L. Hughes.—HuDk
Winter clothes. K. Kuskin.—PrRh
"A **cloud**." See Pillows
"A **cloud** moved close, the bulk of the wind shifted." See The visitant
Cloud shadow. Lilian Moore.—JaT—MoSn
Clouds
Among the millet. A. Lampman.—DoNw
The black cloud. W. H. Davies.—HeR
Cloud shadow. L. Moore.—JaT—MoSn
Clouds ("These clouds are soft fat horses"). J. Reaney.—DoNw
Clouds ("Today"). M. C. Livingston.—LiSi
"The clouds I watched this afternoon." J. Prelutsky.—PrMp
Cumulus clouds. S. L. Nelms.—JaT
Definitions. X. J. Kennedy.—KeF
Footprints. J. Aiken.—LiSf
For a cloud. E. Farjeon.—FaE
"Have you noted the white areas." C. Reedy.—JaPo
The loaves. R. Everson.—JaT
The moon and a cloud. W. H. Davies.—HeR
Rags. J. Thurman.—HoSi—JaT
Rain clouds. E. E. Long.—PrRh
The rainbow ("Boats sail on the rivers"). C. G. Rossetti.—DaC
Stampede. L. Moore.—MoSn
Thunderstorm. H. Behn.—HoCb
"When clouds appear like rocks and towers." Mother Goose.—LoR
"A white cloud floated like a swan." J. Prelutsky.—PrRi
"White floating clouds." Unknown, fr. the Sia Indian.—LaT
Winter twilight. L. Lipsitz.—JaG
Clouds ("These clouds are soft fat horses"). James Reaney.—DoNw
Clouds ("Today"). Myra Cohn Livingston.—LiSi
"**Clouds** are swirling, clouds are swirling." See Phantoms on the steppe
"The **clouds** I watched this afternoon." Jack Prelutsky.—PrMp
"**Clownlike,** happiest on your hands." See Your're
Clowns
"Down derry down, my Pippin my clown." C. Watson.—WaC
Clumsy. J. B. Lee.—BrT
"A **clumsy** young laddie was Mulligan." See Clumsy
Coal
The black fern. L. Norris.—LiSf

First foot. I. Serraillier.—LiNe
"An old charcoal seller." Po Chu-yi.—PlSc
"**Coasting** down." See New England road
The **coasts** of high Barbary. Unknown.—BlO
Coat hangers. Valerie Worth.—WoSp
Coati-mundi. William Jay Smith.—LiIl
Coati-mundis
Coati-mundi. W. J. Smith.—LiIl
Coatsworth, Elizabeth
All on a Christmas morning.—LiIl
And stands there sighing.—KeK
The bad kittens.—HaOf
The barn ("I am tired of this barn, said the colt").—HaO
Buds.—FaTh
Country barnyard.—ChC—PrRh
Daniel Webster's horses.—HaOf
Field mouse to kitchen mouse.—FrP
"I like fish, said the Mermaid." See Song
March.—FaW—PrRh
Mountain brook.—PrRh
The mouse ("I heard a mouse").—HaOf
"No shop does the bird use."—HaOf
Nosegay.—HaOf
On a night of snow.—ChC—HaOf
The open door.—LiCa
Rhyme ("I like to see a thunder storm").—PrRh
Sea gull.—PrRh
Song, sels.
"I like fish, said the Mermaid".—HoCr
Song of the rabbits outside the tavern.—HaOf
The storm ("The fury and terror").—HaOf
Storm at night.—LaW
Sudden storm.—HoSu
"Swift things are beautiful."—LiSf
"This is the hay that no man planted."—HaOf
Three.—LiIl
The toad ("I met a little woman").—PrRa
The two cats.—JaT—LiIl
Witches' song.—HoCr
"**Cobalt** and umber and ultramarine." See The paint box
"**Cobbler,** cobbler, mend my shoe." Mother Goose.—DaC—DeM—LoR
Cobblers
"All around the cobbler's bench." Mother Goose.—LoR
At the keyhole. W. De la Mare.—BlO
"Cobbler, cobbler, mend my shoe." Mother Goose.—DaC—DeM—LoR
"The **Cobbles** live in the house next door." See Neighbors
Cobwebs
Gossamer. E. Farjeon.—FaE
A shower of cobwebs. G. White.—FaTh
Spider ("Spider's"). L. Moore.—MoSn
"**Cobwebs,** cobwebs." Clyde Watson.—WaC
Cocaine Lil and Morphine Sue. Unknown.—HeR
Coccimiglio, Vic
Visit.—JaS
"**Cock-a-doodle-do**". See "Cock-a-doodle-doo"
"**Cock-a-doodle-doo**." Mother Goose.—DaC—DeM
"Cock-a-doodle-do".—LoR
Cock-crow. Edward Thomas.—HeR
"The **cock** crows in the morn." Mother Goose.—DeM—LoR
"The **cock** is crowing." See Written in March
"**Cock** Robin got up early." Unknown.—DaC
"The **cockatoo**." See Cockatoo
Cockatoo. N. M. Bodecker.—BoSs
Cockatoos
Cockatoo. N. M. Bodecker.—BoSs
Cockpit in the clouds. Dick Dorrance.—PrRh

Cockrell, Doug
  Field work.—JaPi
  Fist fight.—JaPi
  His lunch basket.—JaPi
  Hunting at dusk.—JaS
Cockroach. Mary Ann Hoberman.—HaOf
Cockroaches
  Cockroach. M. A. Hoberman.—HaOf
  Cockroaches. K. Starbird.—PrRh
  Moon witches. T. Hughes.—LiWa
Cockroaches. Kaye Starbird.—PrRh
Cocks. See Chickens
"Cocks crow in the morning." Unknown.—DaC
"The **cock's** on the housetop blowing his horn".
    See "The cock's on the roof top blowing his
    horn"
"The **cock's** on the roof top blowing his horn."
    Mother Goose.—DeM
  "The cock's on the housetop blowing his
    horn".—LoR
"**Cockyolly** Bumkin merry go bet." Clyde
    Watson.—WaC
Coconuts
  King palm. M. C. Livingston.—LiMp
Cocoon. David McCord.—HaOf—McAs
Cocteau, Jean
  Cat ("By the fire, like drifting reddish
    goldfish").—LiCa
The **codfish.** Unknown.—PrRh
"The **codfish** lays ten thousand eggs." See The
    codfish
Cody, William Frederick (about)
  "Buffalo Bill's." E. E. Cummings.—HeR
Coffee
  "Molly, my sister, and I fell out." Mother
    Goose.—DeM
    "Mollie, my sister, and I fell out".—LoR
  Yes, it's raining. C. Pomerantz.—PoI
Cohn, Margit
  "My Shalom, my peace, is hidden in every
    broad smile."—LaT
"**Coins,** coins, coins." See Spendthrift
Cold
  December 21. L. Moore.—MoSn
  Dragon smoke. L. Moore.—LiSf—MoSn—PrRa
  The heron ("The sun's an iceberg"). T.
    Hughes.—HuU
  I am freezing. J. Prelutsky.—PrIs
  In like a lion. G. Hewitt.—JaPo
  The mitten song. M. L. Allen.—CoN—PrRa
  Mittens. B. J. Esbensen.—EsCs
  "The more it snows." A. A. Milne.—CoN—
    PrRa—PrRh
  The owl ("Downhill I came, hungry, and yet
    not starved"). E. Thomas.—HeR
  "There was an old person of Mold." E. Lear.—
    LiH
  Winter news. J. Haines.—JaPo
  Winter time. R. L. Stevenson.—DaC
"**Cold** and raw the north wind doth blow."
    Mother Goose.—DeM
"A **cold** and starry darkness moans." See Ghosts
"**Cold,** cold." See Weather incantation
"A **cold** coming we had of it." See Journey of
    the Magi
"A **cold** had a corpulent pig." See A corpulent
    pig
The **cold** heaven. William Butler Yeats.—HeR
Cold potato. Richard J. Margolis.—MaS
"**Cold** that day." See Toboggan ride, down Happy
    Hollow
Cole, Joanna
  Driving to the beach.—PrRh

Happy new year, anyway.—CoN
Hippopotamus ("See the handsome
    hippoppotamus").—CoN
Cole, William
  Back yard, July night.—KeK
  Banananananananana.—PrRh
  Did you.—PrRh
  Sneaky Bill.—PrRh
  Time piece.—JaPo
  Two sad.—PrRh
Coleridge, Hartley
  Death-bed reflections of Michelangelo.—PlEd
Coleridge, Mary Elizabeth
  I saw a stable.—HaO
Coleridge, Samuel Taylor
  Answer to a child's question.—BlO
  Christabel, sels.
    "In the touch of this bosom there worketh
      a spell".—HeR
  Hunting song.—BlO
  "In the touch of this bosom there worketh a
    spell." See Christabel
  The knight's tomb.—HeR
  Kubla Khan.—LiSf—LiWa—PlEd
  On a bad singer.—PrRh
  Work without hope.—PlSc
Coleridge, Sara
  A calendar.—DaC—FrP
    "January brings the snow".—LiSf (unat.)
  The months.—PrRh
  Trees ("The oak is called the king of trees").—
    DaC—PrRh
Colita de rana. Unknown.—GrT
The **collarbone** of a hare. William Butler Yeats.—
    HeR
"**Collectors** are abroad, the nets are spread." See
    At the museum
Collins, Ruth
  The song of the factory worker.—PlSc
Colobus monkey. Unknown, tr. by Ulli Beier.—
    HeR
Colonel Fazackerley. Charles Causley.—CoOu—
    PrRh
"**Colonel** Fazackerley Butterworth-Toast." See
    Colonel Fazackerley
Color. Eve Merriam.—MeSk
"A **coloratura** named Luna." J. F. Wilson.—BrT
Colored hats. From Tender buttons. Gertrude
    Stein.—KoT
"**Colored** hats are necessary to show that curls
    are worn." See Colored hats
Coloring. Harry Behn.—HoCb
"**Coloring** high means that the strange reason is
    in front." See An umbrella
Colors
  Colors. Y. Yevtushenko.—McL
  Crayons. M. Chute.—PrRa
  A factory rainbow. R. Saadi.—PlSc
  Fresh paint. E. Merriam.—MeF
  "I asked the little boy who cannot see."
    Unknown.—CoOu
  "If you love me, love me true." Mother
    Goose.—LoR
  The paint box. E. V. Rieu.—PrRh
  Pied beauty. G. M. Hopkins.—HeR—KoT
  Rhinos purple, hippos green. M. P. Hearn.—
    PrRh
  Sun on rain. L. Moore.—MoSn
  "Those dressed in blue." Mother Goose.—LoR
  Vowels. A. Rimbaud.—KoT
  "What happens to the colors." J. Prelutsky.—
    PrMp

Colors—*Continued*

What is pink. C. G. Rossetti.—CoOu—DaC—PrRh

"When Molly Day wears yellow clothes." J. Prelutsky.—PrRi

Yellow ("Green is go"). D. McCord.—FrP—PrRh

Colors. Yevgeny Yevtushenko, tr. by Robin Milner-Gulland and Peter Levi.—McL

Colum, Padraic

A ballad maker.—PlAs

A drover.—HeR

The knitters.—PlSc

She moved through the fair.—PlAs

The toy-maker.—PlSc

Columbus, Christopher (about)

Columbus day. M. C. Livingston.—LiCe

Columbus to Ferdinand. P. Freneau.—HaOf

12 October. M. C. Livingston.—CoN—LiSf—PrRh

Columbus day. Myra Cohn Livingston.—LiCe

Columbus to Ferdinand. Philip Freneau.—HaOf

The **combe.** Edward Thomas.—HeR

"The **combe** was ever dark, ancient and dark." See The combe

Combinations. Mary Ann Hoberman.—HaOf

"**Come** all you jolly cowboys and listen to my song." See The buffalo skinners

"**Come** all you rounders if you want to hear." See Casey Jones

"**Come** all you sailors bold." See The death of Admiral Benbow

"**Come** away, come away, death." From Twelfth night. William Shakespeare.—PlAs

"**Come,** bring with a noise." See Yule log

"**Come,** butter, come." Mother Goose.—DeM

Come Christmas. David McCord.—LiCp

"**Come,** cried Helen, eager Helen." See Sisters

"**Come,** dear children, let us away." See The forsaken merman

"**Come,** gentlemen all, and listen a while." See Robin Hood and the Bishop of Hereford

Come in. Robert Frost.—KoS

Come learn of Mary. Norma Farber.—LiCp

"**Come,** let us draw the curtains." From Autumn. Humbert Wolfe.—LiIl

"**Come,** let's to bed." Mother Goose.—BaH—FaW—LoR

"**Come** live with me and be my love." See The passionate shepherd to his love

"**Come** live with mee, and bee my love." See The baite

"**Come** Nataki dance with me." See Dance poem

"**Come,** nine times powdered ones, nine times crushed ones." See For chest pain

"**Come,** now a roundel and a fairy song." From A midsummer night's dream. William Shakespeare.—HoUn

"**Come** play with me." See To a squirrel at Kyle-na-no

"**Come** play with me said the sun." See Play

Come see the thing. Jack Prelutsky.—PrNk

"**Come** see the thing that Dad has caught." See Come see the thing

"**Come** soon." See Letter to a friend

"**Come,** stir the fire." See Safe

"**Come,** supper is ready." See The good mooly cow

"**Come** take up your hats, and away let us haste." See The butterfly's ball

"**Come** the oak before the ash." Unknown.—DaC

"**Come,** thou monarch of the vine." From Antony and Cleopatra. William Shakespeare.—HoUn

"**Come** to my window at two a.m." See Kurt Benoit

"**Come** trotting up." See Foal

"**Come** unto these yellow sands." From The tempest. William Shakespeare.—BlO—KoT

"**Come** visit my pancake collection." See The pancake collector

"**Come** with rain, O loud southwester." See To the thawing wind

"**Come,** ye thankful people, come." George J. Elvey.—LiTp

Comforting. Eleanor Farjeon.—FaE

"**Coming** back to this generous island." See Returning to Store Bay

Coming from Kansas. Myra Cohn Livingston.—LiWo

"**Coming** from the woods." Richard Wright.—KeK

The **coming** of light. Mark Strand.—JaPo

The **coming** of the cold. Theodore Roethke.—HaO

Coming storm. Myra Cohn Livingston.—LiSi

"**Coming** to it from the country." See Beaver

Commencement, Pingree School. John Updike.—JaS

The **common** cormorant. See "The common cormorant or shag"

"The **common** cormorant or shag." Unknown.—BlO

The **common** cormorant.—PrRh (at. to Christopher Isherwood)

The **common** egret. Paul Fleischman.—FlI

A **common** light. Steve Orlen.—JaS

Communication. See Conservation; Talking; Telephones

Comparatives. Unknown.—DaC

The **compassionate** fool. Norman Cameron.—HeR

"**Composed** in the Tower before his execution." See More light, more light

Composed on Westminster bridge. See Composed upon Westminster bridge, Sept. 3, 1802

Composed upon Westminster bridge, Sept. 3, 1802. William Wordsworth.—PlEd

Composed on Westminster bridge.—LiSf

Computers

Back from the word processing course, I say to my old typewriter. M. Blumenthal.—JaG

Neuteronomy. E. Merriam.—MeSk

No holes marred. S. Douglas.—PrRh

Nude reclining at word processor, in pastel. C. Conover.—JaG

Think tank. E. Merriam.—HoCl—MeSk

"**Con** el sol, el mar, el viento y la luna." See Balada de la loca fortuna

Conceit. See Pride and vanity

Concert. Robert Morgan.—JaT

Concrete cat. Dorthi Charles.—KeK—LiSf

Concrete mixers. Patricia Hubbell.—PrRh

Conduct of life. See also Behavior; Proverbs; also names of traits of character, as Perseverance

Advice to my son. P. Meinke.—JaPi

Alfred Corning Clark. R. Lowell.—HeR

"All work and no play makes Jack a dull boy." Mother Goose.—LoR

Ambition. N. P. Willis.—HaOf

Annie Scarella. M. Glenn.—GlC

The arrest of Oscar Wilde at the Cadogan Hotel. Sir J. Betjeman.—PlAs

"As kingfishers catch fire, dragonflies draw flame." G. M. Hopkins.—HeR

As much as you can. C. P. Cavafy.—HeR

Conduct of life.—*Continued*

Auguries of innocence, complete. W. Blake.—HeR

Basic for further irresponsibility. E. Merriam.—MeSk

Basic for irresponsibility. E. Merriam.—MeSk

Be like the bird. V. Hugo.—LiSf

Be merry. Unknown.—HeR

Beware, or be yourself. E. Merriam.—MeSk

Birches. R. Frost.—HeR—KoS

Brian O'Linn. Unknown.—HeR

The burglar of Babylon. E. Bishop.—HeR

Certain choices. R. Shelton.—JaPi

Choose. C. Sandburg.—HoRa

The clod and the pebble. W. Blake.—HeR

"The cock crows in the morn." Mother Goose.—DeM—LoR

"Cocks crow in the morning." Unknown.—DaC

Comparatives. Unknown.—DaC

The culprit. A. E. Housman.—PlAs

Dana Moran. M. Glenn.—GlCd

David Klein. M. Glenn. GlCd

Directions, please. Unknown.—LaT

"Don't ever cross a crocodile." K. Starbird.—LiSf

Dreams ("Hold fast to dreams"). L. Hughes.—HuDk—LiSf—PrRh

A drumlin woodchuck. R. Frost.—KoS

"Early to bed and early to rise." G. Ade.—TrM

Edenhall. S. Coolidge.—HaOf

Elegy for a diver. P. Meinke.—JaPi

Eternity. W. Blake.—HeR

The fairies ("If ye will with Mab find grace"). R. Herrick.—BlO

"A father sees a son nearing manhood." C. Sandburg.—HoRa

Fire ("This morning on the opposite shore of the river"). W. Carpenter.—JaPi

The fist upstairs. W. Dickey.—JaPi

For poets. A. Young.—JaD

Ghosts ("Those houses haunt in which we leave"). E. Jennings.—JaPo

The gift to be simple. H. Moss.—JaPi

"Go to bed late." Mother Goose.—LoR

Good and bad children. R. L. Stevenson.—BlO—DaC

Huswifery. E. Taylor.—PlSc

"I am the cat that walks by himself." R. Kipling.—ChC

"I never spake bad word, nor did ill turn." From Pericles. W. Shakespeare.—HoUn

"I think I could turn and live with animals." From Song of myself. W. Whitman.—LiSf

Ian Sinclair. M. Glenn.—GlCd

The idea of trust. T. Gunn.—JaPi

Idiosyncratic. E. Merriam.—MeSk

If ("If he could climb a tree"). N. Giovanni.—GiSp

"If only I may grow firmer, simpler." D. Hammarskjöld.—LaT

Invictus. W. E. Henley.—HeR

January one. D. McCord.—LiNe

Jill Le Claire. M. Glenn.—GlC

John Quincy Adams. S. V. Benét, and R. C. Benét.—HaOf

John Rogers' exhortation to his children. J. Rogers.—HaOf

"Keep a hand on your dream." X. J. Kennedy.—JaPi

Keeping Christmas. E. Farjeon.—HaO—RoC

Know him. N. M. Bodecker.—BoPc

Laughing backwards. J. Hall.—JaG

Lisa Goodman. M. Glenn.—GlC

"Little girl, be careful what you say." C. Sandburg.—HoRa

Little orphant Annie. J. W. Riley.—HaOf

Lollocks. R. Graves.—HeR

"Lord Jesus." G. Salmon.—LaT

Man. A. Turner.—TuS

"A man of words and not of deeds." Mother Goose.—AlH—BlO

A matter of principle. N. M. Bodecker.—BoPc

Mattie Lou at twelve. N. Giovanni.—GiSp

The Mayers' song. Unknown.—PlAs

Le medecin malgre lui. W. C. Williams.—PlSc

Miguel DeVega. M. Glenn.—GlCd

Mother to son. L. Hughes.—CoN—HaOf—HuDk—LiSf

The mouse and the cake. E. Cook.—DaC

Notice to myself. E. Merriam.—MeF

Number two. N. M. Bodecker.—BoPc

Of poor B. B. B. Brecht.—HeR

"O great spirit." Unknown, fr. the American Indian.—LaT

"O Lord, save us." P. Marshall.—LaT

The oratorical crab. O. Herford.—BrT

Pigeon hole. N. M. Bodecker.—BoPc

The pilgrim ("Father, I have launched my bark"). E. C. Embury.—HaOf

Prayer ("Dear heavenly Father, I often make mistakes"). E. M. Shields.—LaT

Prayer ("God, though this life is but a wraith"). L. Untermeyer.—LaT

Prayer ("I ask you this"). L. Hughes.—HuDk

"Put the pine tree in its pot by the doorway." N. Belting.—LiIl

Raccoon. K. Rexroth.—KeK

The Saginaw song. T. Roethke.—HeR

The scholar. A. Clarke.—HeR

Senex. Sir J. Betjeman.—HeR

Sensible Sue. N. M. Bodecker.—BoPc

The seventh. A. József.—HeR

Sinner. L. Hughes.—HuDk

Sir Walter Ralegh to his son. Sir W. Raleigh.—HeR

Song ("Lovely, dark, and lonely one"). L. Hughes.—HuDk

Song ("Sweet beast, I have gone prowling"). W. D. W. Snodgrass.—McL

Song for Dov Shamir. D. Abse.—LaT

The spider ("One biting winter morning"). H. F. Gould.—HaOf

Stopping by woods on a snowy evening. R. Frost.—CoN—HaOf—HeR—KoS—KoT—LiSf—PrRh

Stuart Rieger. M. Glenn.—GlC

"Think as I think, said a man." S. Crane.—KeK

Thoughts. P. Marshall, and C. Marshall.—LaT

Three children. Unknown.—DaC

The three little pigs. A. S. Gatty.—DaC

Tiger ("The paper tigers roar at noon"). A. D. Hope.—HeR

To a sad daughter. M. Ondaatje.—JaG

"To be, or not to be, that is the question." From Hamlet. W. Shakespeare.—HoUn

A toad. E. A. Allen.—HaOf

The true tale of grandfather Penny. E. Farjeon.—FaE

Two little kittens. Unknown.—DaC—HaOf

Usk. From Landscapes. T. S. Eliot.—HeR

Warning ("When I am an old woman I shall wear purple"). J. Joseph.—JaG

Warning to children. R. Graves.—BlO

We real cool. G. Brooks.—KeK

Weekend glory. M. Angelou.—AnS

The well rising. W. Stafford.—HeR

Cooks and cooking.—*Continued*
"Meaning well, Minerva Jean." X. J. Kennedy.—KeB
"Mix a pancake." C. G. Rossetti.—CoN—FrP—LiSf—PrRa
The pancake.—ChG
Mummy slept late and Daddy fixed breakfast. J. Ciardi.—LiSf—PrRh
My special cake. J. Prelutsky.—PrIv
The old lady from Dover. C. Wells.—BrT
The pumpkin. R. Graves.—LiWa—PrRh
Questions ("If cookies come in boxes"). L. B. Hopkins.—HoMu
Rima de chocolate. Unknown.—GrT
"Snowflake souffle." X. J. Kennedy.—BaS
Thanksgiving magic. R. Bennett.—PrRh
"There was a young lady of Poole." E. Lear.—LiH
"There was an old pig from Van Nuys." A. Lobel.—LoB
Toaster time. E. Merriam.—BeD—PrRa
"Two make it." Mother Goose.—LoR
"When good king Arthur ruled this land." Mother Goose.—AlH
"While the fruit boils, Mom sends Lars." X. J. Kennedy.—KeB
The **cooky-nut** trees. Albert Bigelow Paine.—HaOf
"A **cool** red rose and a pink cut pink, a collapse and ." See Red roses
Cool tombs. Carl Sandburg.—HoRa
Coolidge, Susan
Charlotte Bronte.—HaOf
Edenhall.—HaOf
Cooney Potter. Edgar Lee Masters.—PlSc
Coons. See Raccoons
Corbett, Elizabeth T.
A misspelled tail.—HaOf
A tail of the see.—HaOf
Three wise old women.—HaOf
Corbett, Richard
Upon Fairford windows.—PlEd
Coren, Alan
By the Klondike River.—CoOu
"The **cormorant** has." See Tails and heads
The **cormorant's** tale. Paul Fleischman.—FlI
Corn and beans. Carl Sandburg.—HoRa
Corn and cornfields
"Calm weather in June." Mother Goose.—LoR
Corn talk. L. Moore.—MoSn
Harvest. C. Sandburg.—HoRa
Harvester's prayer, with an offering of copal. Unknown, fr. the Kekchi Maya.—BiSp
Illinois farmer. C. Sandburg.—HoRa
Iowa land. M. Bell.—PlSc
My grandfather burning cornfields. R. Sauls.—JaS
"My great corn plants." Unknown, fr. the Navajo Indian.—LiSf
"Nicely while it is raining." Unknown, fr. the Acoma Indian.—LiSf
Prayer ("They have cleared away the place where the corn is to be"). Unknown, fr. the Arikara Indian.—BiSp
Prayer before felling to clear a cornfield. Unknown, fr. the Kekchi Maya.—BiSp
Prayer to the corn mothers. Unknown, fr. the Tewa Indian.—BiSp
"The sacred blue corn-seed I am planting." From Songs in the garden of the house god. Unknown.—LiTp
The skylark. C. G. Rossetti.—DaC
The song of a dream. Unknown.—LiIl

A song of the corn dance. Unknown, fr. the Papago Indian.—BiSp
Song of the Osage woman. Unknown.—LiTp
Songs of the corn dance. Unknown, fr. the Seneca Indian.—BiSp
Special request for the children of Mother Corn. Unknown, fr. the Zuni Indian.—BiSp
Ten billion crows. X. J. Kennedy.—KeF
There are no people song. Unknown, fr. the Navajo Indian.—KoT
To keep animals out of the cornfield. Unknown, fr. the Seneca Indian.—BiSp
The villain. W. H. Davies.—HeR
The **corn-pone-y.** From A baker's dozen of wild beasts. Carolyn Wells.—HaOf
Corn talk. Lilian Moore.—MoSn
Cornfields. See Corn and cornfields
Cornford, Frances
Childhood.—KeK
The country bedroom.—BlO
Cornish, Sam
Montgomery.—JaPi
When my grandmother died.—JaPi
A **Cornish** litany. See "From ghoulies and ghosties"
A **Cornish** litany, sels. Unknown
"From ghoulies and ghosties".—HoCr—LiSf
Things that go bump in the night.—CoN
A Cornish litany.—LiWa
"**Corporal** Green, the orderly cried." See Calling the roll
A **corpulent** pig. Marnie Wood and Harnie Wood.—BrT
Corso, Gregory
I met this guy who died.—JaPi
New York City, 1935.—JaPi
Cossante. Pero Meogo, tr. by Yvor Winters.—PlAs
The **cottager** to the infant. Dorothy Wordsworth.—KoT
Cotton
Cotton. H. E. Martinson.—HeR
Cotton. Harry Edmund Martinson, tr. by Robert Bly.—HeR
Could it have been a shadow. Monica Shannon.—PrRh
"**Could** mortal lip divine." Emily Dickinson.—HeR
"**Could** you indeed come lightly." See Song for a departure
Counselman, Mary Elizabeth
Gift with the wrappings off.—PrRh
"**Count** the white horses you meet on the way." See White horses
Counting. See also Counting-out rhymes
Arithmetic ("Arithmetic is where numbers fly like pigeons in and out of your head"). C. Sandburg.—HoRa—LiSf—PrRh
"Do the baby cake-walk." C. Watson.—CoN—WaC
Exactly. R. Metz.—FaTh
How much is a gross. J. Ciardi.—CiD
Numbers ("There are hundreds of numbers, they mount up so high"). E. Farjeon.—FaE
"One for the money." Mother Goose.—LoR
"One I love." Mother Goose.—DeM
"One, one." C. Watson.—LiSf—WaC
"One, two, buckle my shoe." Mother Goose.—AlH—DaC—DeM—FaW—LiSf—LoR
"One, two, three, four, five." Mother Goose.—DaC—DeM
"1, 2, 3, 4, 5".—AlH—LiSf
Ten to one. I. O. Eastwick.—PrRa

Counting.—*Continued*
"Twelve huntsmen with horns and hounds." Mother Goose.—AlH
Counting-out rhyme ("Grimes golden greening yellow transparent"). Eve Merriam.—KeK
Counting-out rhyme ("Silver bark of beech, and sallow"). Edna St. Vincent Millay.—KoT
Counting-out rhymes
Counting-out rhyme ("Grimes golden greening yellow transparent"). E. Merriam.—KeK
Counting-out rhyme ("Silver bark of beech, and sallow"). E. S. Millay.—KoT
"First in a carriage." Mother Goose.—DeM
"Wire, briar, limber lock." Mother Goose.—DaC
Countries. See names of countries, as Mexico
Country. See Country life
Country barnyard. Elizabeth Coatsworth.—ChC—PrRh
The **country** bedroom. Frances Cornford.—BlO
A **country** boy in winter. Sarah Orne Jewett.—HaOf
"**Country** bumpkin." Clyde Watson.—LiSf
Country greeting. Frank Steele.—JaPi
Country life. See also Farm life; Village life
Afternoon on a hill. E. S. Millay.—CoN—HaOf—KoT
Back country. J. C. Oates.—JaPi
Beaver ("Coming to it from the country"). C. Rylant.—RyW
Birches. R. Frost.—HeR—KoS
A boy's song. J. Hogg.—BlO—CoOu—LiIl
The buildings. W. Berry.—PlEd
Canning time. R. Morgan.—JaS
Central. T. Kooser.—JaPi
City streets and country roads. E. Farjeon.—FaE
Country barnyard. E. Coatsworth.—ChC—PrRh
A country boy in winter. S. O. Jewett.—HaOf
Country school. T. Kooser.—KeK
Dawn ("The soft grey of the distant hills"). Unknown.—PlSc
The days gone by. J. W. Riley.—HaOf
Day's work a-done. W. Barnes.—PlSc
Discovery. H. Behn.—HoCb
A drover. P. Colum.—HeR
Dusk ("Dusk over the lake"). J. Harrison.—JaT
Dusk in the country. H. E. Martinson.—HeR
Em. E. Farjeon.—FaE
The errand. H. Behn.—HoCb
An evening scene. C. Patmore.—DaC
The fallow deer at the lonely house. T. Hardy.—BlO—HeR—KoT
Farms. E. Farjeon.—FaE
Five eyes. W. De la Mare.—ChC
Fred. E. Farjeon.—FaE
A friendly mouse. H. Behn.—HoCb
Gathering leaves. R. Frost.—HeR—KoS
"The giggling gaggling gaggle of geese." J. Prelutsky.—PrZ
Going to sleep in the country. H. Moss.—JaD
The golden hive. H. Behn.—HoCb
Gone ("I've looked behind the shed"). D. McCord.—HoDl—JaT
"Humbert, hiking Moonshine Hill." X. J. Kennedy.—KeB
A late walk. R. Frost.—KoS
The lay of the labourer. T. Hood.—PlSc
The light heart. E. Farjeon.—FaE
The little old lady. Unknown.—GrT
Looking for a sunset bird in winter. R. Frost.—KoS
Mary's one. E. Farjeon.—FaE
Mending wall. R. Frost.—KoS

My grandfather in search of moonshine. G. E. Lyon.—JaG
Nan ("It's"). E. Farjeon.—FaE
Now close the windows. R. Frost.—KoS
Old Doc. M. Vinz.—JaPi
Out in the country, back home. J. D. Marion.—JaPo
Out in the dark. E. Thomas.—HeR
Out, out. R. Frost.—HeR
The ox-tamer. W. Whitman.—HeR
Psalm of the fruitful field. A. M. Klein.—DoNw
Raleigh was right. W. C. Williams.—HeR
Roosters and hens. H. Behn.—HoCb
"Running lightly over spongy ground." T. Roethke.—HeR
The snow ("It sifts from leaden sieves"). E. Dickinson.—DaC
The solitary reaper. W. Wordsworth.—BlO
Song for the sun that disappeared behind the rainclouds. Unknown, fr. the Hottentot people of Africa.—KoT
Spring ("Spring, the sweet spring, is the year's pleasant king"). T. Nashe.—BlO—CoOu
Spring, sweet spring.—KoT
"Sukey, you shall be my wife." Mother Goose.—DaC—DeM
Thanksgiving day. L. M. Child.—CoN—PrRh
The New England boy's song about Thankgiving day.—HaOf
Turkey in the corn. W. W. Guthrie.—KeK
Vegetables. E. Farjeon.—FaE
La viejita. Unknown.—GrT
The waking ("I strolled across"). T. Roethke.—KoT
"When icicles hang by the wall." From Love's labour's lost. W. Shakespeare.—HoUn
Winter.—BlO
Winding road. L. Moore.—MoSn
Written at the Po-shan monastery. Hsin Ch'i-chi.—LiIl
The **country** mouse and the city mouse. Richard Scrafton Sharpe.—DaC
Country school. Ted Kooser.—KeK
"The **country** vegetables scorn." See Vegetables
Couplet countdown. Eve Merriam.—MeSk
Courage. See also Conduct of life; Heroes and heroines; Perseverance
Adventures of Isabel. O. Nash.—CoN—CoOu—HaOf—PrRh
"As I lay asleep in Italy." From The mask of anarchy. P. B. Shelley.—HeR
The brave man. W. Stevens.—LiSf
Bravery. E. Farjeon.—FaE
Dauntless Dimble. J. Prelutsky.—PrNk
The death of Admiral Benbow. Unknown.—BlO
"Do not go gentle into that good night." D. Thomas.—HeR
Elizabeth McKenzie. M. Glenn.—GlCd
"Four and twenty tailors went to kill a snail." Mother Goose.—DaC
Hurt hawks. R. Jeffers.—HeR
"In white tie." D. Huddle.—JaS
Invictus. W. E. Henley.—HeR
Legend. J. Wright.—HeR
Lore. R. S. Thomas.—HeR
My old cat. H. Summers.—ChC—KeK
"O Lord, save us." P. Marshall.—LaT
"Once in the winter." From The forsaken. D. C. Scott.—DoNw
Peter. E. Farjeon.—FaE
Prayer ("Dear heavenly Father, I often make mistakes"). E. M. Shields.—LaT

Courage.—*Continued*
The tale of Custard the dragon. O. Nash.—HaOf
  Custard the dragon.—CoOu
Walkers with the dawn. L. Hughes.—HuDk
"Would you hear of an old-fashion'd sea-fight." From Song of myself. W. Whitman.—HeR
Youth ("We have tomorrow"). L. Hughes.—HuDk
Coursen, H. R.
Suburban.—JaG
The **court** jester's last report to the King. Jack Prelutsky.—PrSr
Court trials. See Law
Courtesy. See Kindness; Manners
Courtship
The baite. J. Donne.—HeR
Binnorie. Unknown.—PlAs
"Curly locks, curly locks." Mother Goose.—AlH—DeM—LoR
The king-fisher song. From Sylvie and Bruno. L. Carroll.—BlO
"A knight came riding from the east." Unknown.—BlO
The mouse's courting song. Unknown.—PlAs
"Old woman, old woman, shall we go a-shearing." Mother Goose.—FaW—LoR
The passionate shepherd to his love. C. Marlowe.—HeR—KoT
A proposal. Mother Goose.—DaC
The rattle bag. D. Ap Gwilym.—HeR
"Soldier, soldier, won't you marry me." Unknown.—BlO
  "Oh, soldier, soldier, will you marry me".—DeM
  Soldier, won't you marry me.—PlAs
The **courtship** of the Yonghy-Bonghy-Bo. Edward Lear.—LiH
Cousin Ella goes to town. George Ella Lyon.—JaS
The **cove.** David McCord.—McAs
"The **cove** is where the swallows skim." See The cove
Covell, Natalie Ann
Wiggly giggles, tr. by.—PrRh
"**Cover** my earth mother four times with many flowers." From Invocation of the U'wannami, Part III. Unknown.—LaT
Covers. Nikki Giovanni.—HoSu—PrRa
The **cow** ("The cow is of the bovine ilk"). Ogden Nash.—HeR—PrRh
The **cow** ("The cow mainly moos as she chooses to moo"). Jack Prelutsky.—PrRh—PrZ
The **cow** ("The friendly cow, all red and white"). Robert Louis Stevenson.—BlO—CoN—FrP
The **cow** ("There once was a cow with a double udder"). Theodore Roethke.—HaOf
The **cow-boy's** song. Anna Maria Wells.—HaOf
"The **cow** in the meadow." See Bravery
"The **cow** is of the bovine ilk." See The cow
"The **cow** mainly moos as she chooses to moo." See The cow
Coward, Noel
Convalescence.—KoT
"A **cowboy** with his sweetheart stood beneath a starlit sky." See The broken wedding ring
Cowboys
The broken wedding ring. Unknown.—PlAs
The buffalo skinners. Unknown.—HeR
The closing of the rodeo. W. J. Smith.—PlSc
The cow-boy's song. A. M. Wells.—HaOf
I ride an old paint. Unknown.—LiSf

"In the long flat panhandle of Texas." C. Sandburg.—HoRa
The streets of Laredo ("As I walked out in the streets of Laredo"). Unknown.—HeR—LiSf
  "As I walked out in the streets of Laredo".—PlAs
Tall. Unknown.—BrT
Whoopee ti yi yo, git along little dogies. Unknown.—LiSf
Cowley, Malcolm
The hill above the mine.—PlSc
Cowper, William
Capability Brown.—PlSc
Epitaph on a hare.—BlO
On his portrait.—PlEd
The sower.—PlSc
Cowper's tame hare. Norman Nicholson.—HeR
Cows. James Reeves.—BlO—CoN
A **cow's** outside. Jack Prelutsky.—PrNk
"A **cow's** outside is mainly hide." See A cow's outside
Cox, Kenyon
The wild boarder.—BrT
Cox, Palmer
The brownies' celebration.—HaOf
The lazy pussy.—HaOf
The mouse's lullaby.—HaOf
Crab. Francois Dodat, tr. by Bert Meyers and Odette Meyers.—FaTh
Crabapples. Carl Sandburg.—HoRa
Crabbe, George
"He built a mud-wall'd hovel, where he kept." See Peter Grimes
Peter Grimes, sels.
  "He built a mud-wall'd hovel, where he kept".—PlSc
"**Crabbed** age and youth cannot live together." From The passionate pilgrim. William Shakespeare.—HoUn
Crabs
At the beach ("Johnny, Johnny, let go of that crab"). J. Ciardi.—CiD
Crab. F. Dodat.—FaTh
The dead crab. A. Young.—HeR
The lobsters and the fiddler crab. F. J. Forster.—PrRh
The oratorical crab. O. Herford.—BrT
Sicilian thanksgiving on the feast of Saint John the Baptist. E. Di Pasquale.—LiTp
The **crack** of light. Eleanor Farjeon.—FaE
Cradle song ("From groves of spice"). Sarojini Naidu.—ChB
A **cradle** song ("Golden slumbers kiss your eyes"). Thomas Dekker.—BlO
A **cradle** song ("Sweet dreams, form a shade"). William Blake.—HaO—RoC
Cradle song for Christmas. Eleanor Farjeon.—FaE
Cradlesong ("Sleep, little one, your father is bringing"). Unknown.—BiSp
Cradlesong for Ahuitzotl. Unknown.—BiSp
Craig Blanchard. Mel Glenn.—GlCd
Cranch, C. P.
The bear and the squirrels.—HaOf
An old cat's confessions.—HaOf
Crane, Hart
To Brooklyn Bridge.—PlEd
Crane, Stephen
"There is a grey thing that lives in the tree tops."—LiWa
"Think as I think, said a man."—KeK
Crane, Walter
The crocus ("The golden crocus reaches up").—ChG—PrRh

"**Crane**, oh crane, your neck is long." See Construction job

Crapsey, Adelaide
The warning ("Just now").—LiWa

Crawford, Isabella V.
Love me, love my dog.—DoNw

Crawford, Winifred
Cat's menu.—ChC

"**Crawl** inside it." See How to solve a problem

Crawler. Eve Merriam.—MeHa

Crayon house. Muriel Rukeyser.—PlEd

Crayons. Marchette Chute.—PrRa

Crazy dog prayer. Unknown.—BiSp

Crazy dog song. Unknown.—BiSp

"The **crazy** ladies are singing again." See The belly dancer in the nursing home

The **cream-puffin.** From A baker's dozen of wild beasts. Carolyn Wells.—HaOf

"The **cream-puffin**, who lives upon custard." See The cream-puffin

Creation
"All things bright and beautiful." C. F. Alexander.—DaC—PrRh
"And God stepped out on space." From The creation. J. W. Johnson.—LaT
The creation, complete. J. W. Johnson.—LiSf
Makers. N. D. Watson.—PrRa
The mark. E. Farjeon.—FaE
The mole and the eagle. S. J. Hale.—HaOf
Mosquito ("To get into life"). T. Hughes.—HuU
My bath. M. L'Engle.—LaT
Song of creation. Unknown, fr. the Pima Indian.—LiSf
Song of the flood. Unknown, fr. the Navajo Indian.—KoT
Sporting goods. P. Soupault.—KoT
There are no people song. Unknown, fr. the Navajo Indian.—KoT
"There is only one horse on the earth." From Timesweep. C. Sandburg.—HoRa
They ask, is God, too, lonely. C. Sandburg.—LiIl
The third thing. D. H. Lawrence.—PrBb
The tyger. W. Blake.—BlO—HeR—KoT
The tiger.—LiSf

The **creation**, complete. James Weldon Johnson.—LiSf

The **creation**, sels. James Weldon Johnson
"And God stepped out on space".—LaT

Creativity
Art. H. Melville.—PlEd
The artist. W. C. Williams.—HeR
Drawing. M. L'Engle.—LaT
Elizabeth McKenzie. M. Glenn.—GlCd
Looking at quilts. M. Piercy.—PlSc
New day. N. M. Bodecker.—BoPc
Reply to the question, how can you become a poet. E. Merriam.—JaD
"This is my Carnac, whose unmeasured dome." H. D. Thoreau.—PlEd
When I buy pictures. M. Moore.—PlEd

The **creature** in the classroom. Jack Prelutsky.—PrB—PrRh

"A **creature** to pet and spoil." See Kob antelope

Creek Indians. See Indians of the Americas—Creek

Creeley, Robert
The conspiracy.—JaPo
"Love comes quietly."—McL

"**Creeping** Jenny." Eleanor Farjeon.—FaE

"**Creepy** crawlers." See Crawler

The **crib.** Robert Finch.—HaO

"**Crick**, crack." Eve Merriam.—MeBl

The **cricket** kept the house. Edith M. Thomas.—HaOf

"A **cricket** on a rubbish tip." See Winter cricket

Crickets
The cricket kept the house. E. M. Thomas.—HaOf
"Crickets." V. Worth.—HoSi—PrRh
Crickets ("All busy punching tickets"). D. McCord.—CoN—FaTh—LiSf—McAs
Crickets ("Of all the insects"). A. Fisher.—FiW
Crickets ("We cannot say that crickets sing"). H. Behn.—HoCb
Jack Frost ("Rustily creak the crickets, Jack Frost came down"). C. Thaxter.—HaOf
The little mute boy. F. García Lorca.—HeR
On the grasshopper and the cricket. J. Keats.—KoT
"On the top of a mountain." Unknown.—FaW
One guess. R. Frost.—KoS
"Seeking in my hut." Issa.—FaTh
Splinter. C. Sandburg.—HaOf—HoRa—KeK
Winter cricket. J. Heath-Stubbs.—HaO

Crickets ("All busy punching tickets"). David McCord.—CoN—FaTh—LiSf—McAs

Crickets ("Of all the insects"). Aileen Fisher.—FiW

Crickets ("We cannot say that crickets sing"). Harry Behn.—HoCb

"**Crickets**." Valerie Worth.—HoSi—PrRh

"The **crickets** in the thickets." See But I wonder

"**Cried** a man on the Salisbury Plain." Myra Cohn Livingston.—KeK

"**Cried** a scientist watching this creature dart by." See Hummingbird

Crime and criminals. See also Murder; Thieves
The arrest of Oscar Wilde at the Cadogan Hotel. Sir J. Betjeman.—PlAs
Bandit. A. M. Klein.—DoNw
Brennan on the moor. Unknown.—PlAs
The burglar of Babylon. E. Bishop.—HeR
The culprit. A. E. Housman.—PlAs
Cynthia Leonard. M. Glenn.—GlCd
Danny Deever. R. Kipling.—PlAs
The faking boy. Unknown.—HeR
The gallant highwayman. J. De Mille.—DoNw
Georgie. Unknown.—PlAs
The highwayman. A. Noyes.—LiSf
Jesse James. Unknown.—PlAs
Little Billee. W. M. Thackeray.—BlO
Macavity, the mystery cat. T. S. Eliot.—ChC—CoOu—HaOf—HeR—LiSf
More light, more light. A. Hecht.—HeR
The policeman's lot. From The pirates of Penzance. W. S. Gilbert.—PlSc
The rain it raineth. C. Bowen.—CoN
Rape poem. M. Piercy.—JaPi
The shooting of John Dillinger outside the Biograph Theater, July 22, 1934. D. Wagoner.—HeR
A smugglers' song. R. Kipling.—BlO
"Then to the bar, all they drew near." From The day of doom. M. Wigglesworth.—HaOf
The wild colonial boy. Unknown.—PlAs

Crint, Maude
"I saw a great scholar, apparently thinking."—TrM

Cripples
The amputation. H. Sorrells.—JaD

Crockett. William Jay Smith.—BrT

The **crocodile** ("Beware the crafty crocodile"). Jack Prelutsky.—PrZ

The **crocodile** ("A crocodile once dropped a line"). Oliver Herford.—BrT—HaOf
Crocodile ("The crocodile wept bitter tears"). William Jay Smith.—HaOf
A **crocodile**. Thomas Lovell Beddoes.—HeR
The **crocodile**. See "How doth the little crocodile"
Crocodile ("I trust you not"). N. M. Bodecker.—BoSs
"A **crocodile** once dropped a line." See The crocodile
"The **crocodile** wept bitter tears." See Crocodile
Crocodiles
  Bruno. Unknown.—BrT
  The considerate crocodile. A. R. Wells.—HaOf
  The crocodile ("Beware the crafty crocodile"). J. Prelutsky.—PrZ
  The crocodile ("A crocodile once dropped a line"). O. Herford.—BrT—HaOf
  Crocodile ("The crocodile wept bitter tears"). W. J. Smith.—HaOf
  A crocodile. T. L. Beddoes.—HeR
  Crocodile ("I trust you not"). N. M. Bodecker.—BoSs
  "Don't ever cross a crocodile." K. Starbird.—LiSf
  Fat Lena's recipe for crocodile soup. P. Janowitz.—JaT
  "How doth the little crocodile." From Alice's adventures in Wonderland. L. Carroll.—BlO—HeR—KoT—LiSf
    The crocodile.—PrRh
  "If you should meet a crocodile." Unknown.—CoOu
  The merry crocodile. G. E. Heath.—BrT
  The purist. O. Nash.—HaOf
The **crocus** ("The golden crocus reaches up"). Walter Crane.—ChG—PrRh
Crocus ("Little crocus"). Charlotte Zolotow.—ZoE
"A **crocus** tip in the snow." See Anticipations
Crocuses
  Autumn crocus. E. Farjeon.—FaE
  The crocus ("The golden crocus reaches up"). W. Crane.—ChG—PrRh
  Crocus ("Little crocus"). C. Zolotow.—ZoE
Croquet. David Huddle.—JaS
"A **cross-eyed** bee went looking for honey." See I know I'm sweet, but
"**Cross-patch**, draw the latch." Mother Goose.—DeM—LoR
Crossen, Stacy Jo
  Wiggly giggles.—PrRh
Crossing Ohio when poppies bloom in Ashtabula, sels. Carl Sandburg
  "Pick me poppies in Ohio".—HoRa
Crossing the Alps. From The prelude. William Wordsworth.—HeR
Crossing the water. Sylvia Plath.—HeR
The **crow** ("By the wave rising, by the wave breaking"). Patricia K. Page.—DoNw
The **crow** ("Flying loose and easy, where does he go"). Russell Hoban.—JaT—LiSf
Crow Indians. See Indians of the Americas—Crow
"**Crow** knows." See Crow wonders
Crow wonders. Lilian Moore.—MoSn
A **crowd**. Unknown.—LaT
Crowds
  Bouquets. R. Francis.—JaD
  A crowd. Unknown.—LaT
  Crowds. V. Schonborg.—PrRh
  Just for one day. L. Morrison.—PrRh
  "Sing a song of people." L. Lenski.—PrRh
Crowds. Virginia Schonborg.—PrRh

"**Crowds** pushing." See Crowds
Crows
  "A carrion crow sat on an oak." Unknown.—BlO
  The crow ("By the wave rising, by the wave breaking"). P. K. Page.—DoNw
  The crow ("Flying loose and easy, where does he go"). R. Hoban.—JaT—LiSf
  Crow wonders. L. Moore.—MoSn
  Crows ("Like the shore's alternation of door wave"). T. Clark.—JaD
  Crows ("So, nine crows to this April field"). P. Booth.—JaD
  Crows ("When the high/snows lie worn"). V. Worth.—WoSp
  Dust of snow. R. Frost.—KoS—LiSf—PrRh
  The first hunt. G. Anderson.—JaPo
  Flight ("All day long the clouds go by"). G. Johnston.—DoNw
  "Footprints of a sparrow." N. M. Bodecker.—BaS—BoSs
  "From a birch." P. Wolny. JaD
  The gnome. H. Behn.—HoCb—HoCr
  My sister Jane. T. Hughes.—CoOu—LiSf
  Night crow. T. Roethke.—JaD
  "On the first of March." Mother Goose.—DeM
  Poor crow. M. M. Dodge.—HaOf
  The raven. E. A. Poe.—HaOf
  Shooting crows. D. Huddle.—JaG
  The sycophantic fox and the gullible raven. G. W. Carryl.—HaOf
  Ten billion crows. X. J. Kennedy.—KeF
  The three ravens. Unknown.—PlAs
  To be or not to be. Unknown.—PrRh
  The twa corbies. Unknown.—HeR—PlAs
  X. S. Cassedy.—CaR
Crows ("Like the shore's alternation of door wave"). Tom Clark.—JaD
Crows ("So, nine crows to this April field"). Philip Booth.—JaD
Crows ("When the high/snows lie worn"). Valerie Worth.—WoSp
Crucifixion. See Easter
Cruelty
  Back country. J. C. Oates.—JaPi
  The badger. J. Clare.—HeR
  Barbara Allen's cruelty. Unknown.—PlAs
  Barbara Ellen. Unknown.—PlAs
  Blubber lips. J. Daniels.—JaT
  "He built a mud-wall'd hovel, where he kept." From Peter Grimes. G. Crabbe.—PlSc
  Hildy Ross. M. Glenn.—GlC
  The inquest. W. H. Davies.—HeR
  Joy McNair. M. Glenn.—GlC
  Teased. R. J. Margolis.—MaS
  Variations on a theme by William Carlos Williams. K. Koch.—KeK
"**Cruelty** has a human heart." See A divine image
The **cruise** of the Mystery. Celia Thaxter.—HaOf
Crunch and lick. Dorothy Aldis.—PrRa
Crusoe, Robinson
  "Poor old Robinson Crusoe." Mother Goose.—LoR
Crustration. N. M. Bodecker.—BoPc
Cruz, Victor Hernandez
  Spirits.—LiWa
Crying
  A boat ("O beautiful"). R. Brautigan.—KeK
  Bringing up babies. R. Fuller.—PrRh
  Crocodile ("The crocodile wept bitter tears"). W. J. Smith.—HaOf
  Crying. G. Kinnell.—CoN—KeK
  "Elizabeth cried." E. Farjeon.—FaE—LiIl

Crying—*Continued*
Foghorns. L. Moore.—HoSs—MoSn—PrRh
"Herons and sweeps." E. Lear.—LiH
"It's such a little thing to weep." E. Dickinson.—HeR
"Mr. Lizard is crying." F. García Lorca.—KoT
Small rains. N. M. Bodecker.—BoSs
Sometimes ("Sometimes I simply have to cry"). J. Prelutsky.—PrRa
"There was a small pig who wept tears." A. Lobel.—LoB—PrRa
"When my dog died." F. Littledale.—CoN
Why ("Fie, darling, why do you cry, why do you cry"). E. Farjeon.—FaE
Winifred Waters. W. B. Rands.—DaC
Crying. Galway Kinnell.—CoN—KeK
"**Crying** only a little bit." See Crying
The **crystal** cabinet. William Blake.—PlAs
Crystal Rowe. Mel Glenn.—GlCd
Crystals like blood. Hugh MacDiarmid.—HeR
Cuckoo ("The cuckoo in our cuckoo clock"). Jack Prelutsky.—PrNk
The **cuckoo** ("O, the cuckoo she's a pretty bird"). Mother Goose.—HeR
Cuckoo. See "Repeat that, repeat that"
"The **cuckoo** in our cuckoo clock." See Cuckoo
Cuckoos
Blue cuckoo. Unknown.—HeR
Carol of the birds. Unknown.—RoC
Cuckoo ("The cuckoo in our cuckoo clock"). J. Prelutsky.—PrNk
The cuckoo ("O, the cuckoo she's a pretty bird"). Mother Goose.—HeR
The koocoo. Unknown.—KoT
"Repeat that, repeat that." G. M. Hopkins.—HeR
    Cuckoo.—KoT
Weathers. T. Hardy.—BlO—DaC—HeR
What bird so sings. J. Lyly.—BlO
Cullen, Countee
Incident ("Once riding in old Baltimore").—CoN—HaOf—KeK
Saturday's child.—PlSc
The unknown color.—HaOf
The **culprit.** Alfred Edward Housman.—PlAs
Cummings, Edward Estlin
"Anyone lived in a pretty how town."—HeR
"Buffalo Bill's."—HeR
"Here's a little mouse."—KoT
"Hist whist."—LiSf—PrRh
"I like my body when it is with your."—McL
"I thank you God for most this amazing."—LaT
If there are any heavens.—JaD
"In just."—KeK—LiSf
"Little tree."—CoN—HaO—LiSf
"Maggie and Milly and Molly and May."—HeR—HoSe—PrRh
"Nobody loses all the time."—HeR
"(Sitting in a tree)."—FaTh
"Up into the silence the green."—KoT
"Your little voice."—McL
Cumulus clouds. Sheryl L. Nelms.—JaT
"**Cunning** and art he did not lack." See The Allansford pursuit
Cunningham, Allan
"A wet sheet and a flowing sea."—BlO
Cunningham, J. V.
Epigrams.—HeR
Cunningham, Julia
Little bird ("Little bird, little bird").—FaTh
Trapped mouse.—FaTh
The **cupboard.** Walter De la Mare.—CoN

The **curate's** cat. Unknown.—BrT
Cures for melancholy. From A throw of threes. Eve Merriam.—MeF
"**Curiosity's** not in me head." From On reading, four limericks. Myra Cohn Livingston.—MeF
Curious Charlie. Isabel Frances Bellows.—BrT
"**Curious,** curious Tiggady Rue." See Tiggady Rue
"**Curious** fly." See Bug in a jug
"**Curly** locks, curly locks." Mother Goose.—AlH—DeM—LoR
Curnow, Allen
Wild iron.—HeR
Currie, Robert
Brothers.—JaPi
Forget about it.—JaS
The home place.—JaPo
In the music.—JaT
July the first.—JaPi
The musician at his work.—JaS
Rope and drum.—JaS
The schoolbus comes before the sun.—JaT—JaT
What he saw.—JaS
Curses
The ballad of Semmerwater. W. Watson.—BlO
Curses to fling at a giant. From A throw of threes. E. Merriam.—MeF
A glass of beer. J. Stephens.—HeR
The reformed pirate. T. G. Roberts.—DoNw
Swearing. C. Rylant.—RyW
"The wicked who would do me harm." Unknown.—HeR
Curses to fling at a giant. From A throw of threes. Eve Merriam.—MeF
The **curst** wife. Unknown.—PlAs
"**Curtains** forcing their will." See Awakening in New York
"**Curves** of sand." See The sea shore
"A **curving,** leaping line of light." See Prairie fires
Custard the dragon. See The tale of Custard the dragon
Cut grass. Philip Larkin.—HeR
"**Cut** grass lies frail." See Cut grass
Cymbeline, sels. William Shakespeare
"Fear no more the heat o' the sun".—HeR—HoUn
    "Fear no more the heat o' th' sun".—PlAs
"Hark, hark, the lark at heaven's gate sings".—BlO—HoUn
"With fairest flowers".—HeR
Cynthia in the snow. Gwendolyn Brooks.—BaS—HoSi—LiSf
Cynthia Leonard. Mel Glenn.—GlCd

D

D., H. (Hilda Doolittle)
"O heart, small urn." See The walls do not fall
The walls do not fall, sels.
    "O heart, small urn".—McL
White world.—McL
D.A.R.. N. M. Bodecker.—BoPc
Dacey, Philip
The amputee soldier.—JaG
How I escaped from the labyrinth.—JaPo
One of the boys.—JaS
The poem as striptease.—JaPo
Prisms (altea).—JaPi
Small dark song.—JaPo
Thumb.—JaPo—KeK
Dad and the cat and the tree. Kit Wright.—CoOu
"**Dad** had some." See Real talent

Dandelions—*Continued*
"Gently, gently, the wind blows." K. Mizumura.—FaTh
"Who tossed those golden coins." K. Mizumura.—FaTh—LiSf
Dandelions. Howard Nemerov.—JaD
Dangel, Leo
Pa ("When we got home, there was our old man").—JaS
Dangerous. Dorothy Aldis.—PrRa
The **dangers** of taking baths. John Ciardi.—CiD
Daniel Boone. Stephen Vincent Benét.—KeK
Daniel Webster's horses. Elizabeth Coatsworth.—HaOf
Danielle O'Mara. Mel Glenn.—GlCd
Daniells, Roy
Noah.—DoNw
So they went deeper into the forest.—DoNw
Daniels, Jim
Blubber lips.—JaT
Danish nursery rhymes. See Nursery rhymes—Danish
Danny Deever. Rudyard Kipling.—PlAs
Danny Murphy. James Stephens.—CoOu
Danny Vargas. Mel Glenn.—GlC
Dante Alighieri
Sonnet.—HeR—KoT
Darcy Tanner. Mel Glenn.—GlC
Darius Green and his flying-machine. John Townsend Trowbridge.—HaOf
The **dark** ("I am glad of that other life"). William Heyen.—PlEd
The **dark** ("It's always"). Myra Cohn Livingston.—LiWo
"**Dark** brown is the river." See Where go the boats
"**Dark** clouds." See Stampede
"The **dark** danced over the daisies." See The stars, the dark, and the daisies
The **dark** house. Unknown.—CoN
"The **dark** is dreaming." See Good night, good night
"A **dark** November night, late, the back door wide." See Pets
"The **darkening** was like riches in the room." See From a childhood
The **darkling** elves. Jack Prelutsky.—PrRh
The **darkling** thrush. Thomas Hardy.—HeR
Darkness
Basement. S. Cassedy.—CaR
Bavarian gentians. D. H. Lawrence.—KoT
Good night ("We turn out the lights"). C. Zolotow.—ZoE
"It cannot be seen, cannot be felt." J. R. R. Tolkien.—LiSf
Nightfall. E. Olson.—JaD
Out in the dark. E. Thomas.—HeR
Sleep. N. Giovanni.—GiSp
The stars, the dark, and the daisies. I. O. Eastwick.—LaW
Stopping by woods on a snowy evening. R. Frost.—CoN—HaOf—HeR—KoS—KoT—LiSf—PrRh
Summer night. H. Behn.—HoCb
"**Darkness.**" See Beech, to owl
"**Darkness** begins a." See After Christmas
"**Darkness** can be a little too dark." See Summer night
"**Darkness** comes early." See Woolly bear caterpillar
"**Darkness** invades the shallows of the street." See Evening tide
Darley, George
The sea ritual.—LiWa

Siren chorus.—LiWa
"**Darling**, you are not at all." See Surfaces
Daryush, Elizabeth
"Anger lay by me all night long."—HeR
A **date.** Charlotte Zolotow.—ZoE
Dating (social)
Alison Ford. M. Glenn.—GlC
Angelino Falco. M. Glenn.—GlCd
Annie Scarella. M. Glenn.—GlC
Beth Rossiter and. M. Glenn.—GlCd
Candie Brewer. M. Glenn.—GlCd
Carrie Pearson. M. Glenn.—GlC
Douglas Kearney. M. Glenn.—GlCd
Eric Theodore. M. Glenn.—GlC
Julie Snow. M. Glenn.—GlC
Marcy Mannes. M. Glenn.—GlCd
Mario Benedetto. M. Glenn.—GlCd
Mary Gilardi. M. Glenn.—GlCd
Meredith Piersall. M. Glenn.—GlCd
Shari Morrow. M. Glenn.—GlC
Sharon Vail and. M. Glenn.—GlCd
Stacey Fowler. M. Glenn.—GlC
"The **daughter** of the farrier." Mother Goose.—DaC
"**Daughter** of the great earth." See Magic spell for a difficult birth
Daughters
Accomplishments. C. Macdonald.—JaD
Art work. R. Wallace.—JaPo
Cecilia. Unknown.—DoNw
The children's hour. H. W. Longfellow.—HaOf
Chiquita bonita. Unknown.—GrT
Cossante. P. Meogo.—PlAs
A date. C. Zolotow.—ZoE
A daughter's house. N. H. Richman.—JaG
Dora Antonopolis. M. Glenn.—GlC
A flower given to my daughter. J. Joyce.—HeR
For my daughter ("This is the summer storm"). E. Ochester.—JaS
Hildy Ross. M. Glenn.—GlC
"I was the child." V. S. Warren.—JaS
"If I should ever by chance grow rich." E. Thomas.—BlO
A lesson for mamma. S. Dayre.—HaOf
The lost girl. Unknown.—BrT
Louise Coyle. M. Glenn.—GlCd
Missing my daughter. S. Spender.—JaS
Monica Zindell. M. Glenn.—GlC
Poop ("My daughter, Blake, is in kindergarten"). G. Locklin.—JaS
Pretty little girl. Unknown.—GrT
"See this pretty little girl of mine." Mother Goose.—AlH
Smell my fingers. D. B. Axelrod.—JaS
To a sad daughter. M. Ondaatje.—JaG
To my daughter. S. Spender.—JaD
To my daughter riding in the circus parade. J. Labombard.—JaG
"When I have a little girl." C. Zolotow.—ZoE
The writer. R. Wilbur.—JaS
A **daughter's** house. Norma Hope Richman.—JaG
"A **daughter's** to her mother." See Relations
Dauntless Dimble. Jack Prelutsky.—PrNk
"**Dauntless** Dimble was the bravest." See Dauntless Dimble
Davey, Frank
The piano ("I sit on the edge").—DoNw
David. Eleanor Farjeon.—FaE
David Eberhoff. Mel Glenn.—GlC
David in April. Betty Booker.—JaPo
David Klein. Mel Glenn.—GlCd
Davies, Aneirin Talfan
Death, tr. by.—HeR

Davies, William Henry
The black cloud.—HeR
The cat ("Within that porch, across the way").—BlO—ChC
A child's pet.—HeR
The inquest.—HeR
The moon and a cloud.—HeR
Sheep ("When I was once in Baltimore").—HeR
A strange meeting ("The moon is full, and so am I").—BlO
The villain.—HeR

Davis, Helen Bayley
Jack Frost ("Someone painted pictures").—PrRa

Davison, Peter
Housing starts.—PlEd
The poem in the park.—JaG
"Davy Davy Dumpling." Mother Goose.—LoR
Davy Dumpling.—PrRa

Davy Dumpling. See "Davy Davy Dumpling"

Dawn. See also Morning
Brief innocence. M. Angelou.—AnS
Chilly dawn. E. Farjeon.—FaE
Dawn ("At first light the finches"). P. Fleischman.—FlI
Dawn ("I embraced the summer dawn"). A. Rimbaud.—KoT
Dawn ("The soft grey of the distant hills"). Unknown.—PlSc
Ducks at dawn. J. S. Tippett.—ChG
"Hark, hark, the lark at heaven's gate sings." From Cymbeline. W. Shakespeare.—BlO—HoUn
Sunrise and sun. H. Behn.—HoCb

Dawn ("At first light the finches"). Paul Fleischman.—FlI

Dawn ("I embraced the summer dawn"). Arthur Rimbaud.—KoT

Dawn ("The soft grey of the distant hills"). Unknown.—PlSc

"Dawn offers." See Brief innocence
"The **dawn** was apple green." See Green

Day. See also Afternoon; Bedtime; Dawn; Evening; Morning; Night
Bed in summer. R. L. Stevenson.—DaC—FaW
"Oh I have dined on this delicious day." R. Snyder.—JaT
Spring day. C. Zolotow.—ZoE
"What are days for." From The world is day breaking. S. Miyoshi.—BeD
"The **day**." See In the field of clover by the river Charles
The **day** after Christmas. Lee Bennett Hopkins.—HoSi
"The **day** after you left." See Disintegration
Day before Christmas. Marchette Chute.—CoN
A **day** begins. Denise Levertov.—JaD
"The **day** drags by with textbooks." See The schoolbus comes before the sun
"The **day** has come." Unknown.—DeD
A **day** in the country. Jack Prelutsky.—PrWi
"The **day** is done." See Evening hymn
"**Day** is done." Unknown.—ChB
"The **day** is past, the sun is set." See Evening
The **day** of doom, sels. Michael Wigglesworth
"Then to the bar, all they drew near".—HaOf
"The **day** they strung the cable from America to Europe." See Cotton
Day-time moon. Dorothy Aldis.—FrP
Daybreak. See Dawn
Daybreak. Stephen Spender.—JaD
"**Daybreak**." See Songs of the horse society
Daylight saving time. Phyllis McGinley.—PrRh

Dayre, Sydney
Grandma's lost balance.—HaOf
A lesson for mamma.—HaOf
Days. See Days of the week
Days. Philip Larkin.—HeR
"The **days** are cold, the nights." See The cottager to the infant
"The **days** are short." See January
The **days** gone by. James Whitcomb Riley.—HaOf
Days of the week
"As Tommy Snooks and Bessy Brooks." Mother Goose.—DeM—FaW—LoR
Days. P. Larkin.—HeR
"How many days has my baby to play." Mother Goose.—LoR
How to get there. B. Nims.—PrRh
"If you sneeze on Monday, you sneeze for danger." Mother Goose.—AlH
"Monday's child is fair of face." Mother Goose.—DaC—DeM—FaW—LoR
"On Saturday night shall be my care." Mother Goose.—AlH—LoR
"Solomon Grundy." Mother Goose.—AlH—FaW—LoR—PrRh
"Sunday is our roast beef day." From Munch. A. Wallner.—HoMu
"They that wash on Monday." Mother Goose.—BlO
Days of the week—Monday
Lonely Monday. J. P. Lewis.—LiIl
Days of the week—Saturday
Havdalah. C. Adler.—LiPj
"Sally go round the sun." Mother Goose.—DeM—FaW—LoR
Saturday. M. C. Livingston.—LiWo
Saturday's child. C. Cullen.—PlSc
Supermarket Shabbat. R. J. Margolis.—LiPj
Today is Saturday. Z. K. Snyder.—LiIl
Days of the week—Sunday
Coati-mundi. W. J. Smith.—LiIl
Homework ("Homework sits on top of Sunday, squashing Sunday flat"). R. Hoban.—PrRh
Morning after. M. Vinz.—JaPo
On a Sunday. C. Reznikoff.—JaD
Ploughing on Sunday. W. Stevens.—HeR—KoT
Sunday ("Let me tell you"). A. Turner.—TuS
Sunday ("The mint bed is in"). J. Schuyler.—KoT
Sunday ("Up early while everyone sleeps"). V. Rutsala.—JaD
Sunday funnies. A. Keiter.—JaD
Sunday morning lonely. L. Clifton.—FaW
Sunday rain. J. Updike.—JaD
"**Days** that the wind takes over." Karla Kuskin.—HoSi
Days through starch and bluing. Alice Fulton.—JaG
"**Days** when fir trees reared and shook." See Kate and I
Day's work a-done. William Barnes.—PlSc
De la Mare, Walter
Alas, alack.—LiSf
At the keyhole.—BlO
A ballad of Christmas.—HaO
The cupboard.—CoN
Done for.—BlO
Double dutch.—ChC
An epitaph ("Here lies a most beautiful lady").—HeR
Five eyes.—ChC
The fly ("How large unto the tiny fly").—CoOu
"Here all we see."—PrRa
The horseman.—PrRh

De la Mare, Walter—*Continued*
The huntsmen.—PrRa
John Mouldy.—HeR
The listeners.—LiWa
The magnifying glass.—BlO
Me ("As long as I live").—PrRh
Miss T.—CoN—CoOu—LiSf
Moonshine.—BrT
Napoleon.—HeR
Nicholas Nye.—BlO
Nothing ("Whsst, and away, and over the green").—LiWa
The old king.—PlAs
The shadow.—CoOu
The shubble.—BrT
Silly Sallie.—BlO
Silver.—KoT—PrRh
Snow ("No breath of wind").—CoOu
The snowflake.—FaTh—LiSf—PrRh
Some one.—FrP—LiSf—PrRh
Still life.—PlEd
The-ride-by-nights.—LiWa
Tired Tim.—CoN—PrRh
Tom's angel.—PlAs
The tryst.—PlAs
The voice.—LiWa
Where.—BaH
De Mille, James
The gallant highwayman.—DoNw
"Sweet maiden of Passamaquoddy."—DoNw
De Regniers, Beatrice Schenk
About claws and scratching.—DeT
Cat mystery.—DeT
Cats are good for something.—DeT
Cats know what's good.—DeT
Cats love books.—DeT
Cat's whiskers.—DeT
Dedication.—DeT
Early breakfast.—DeT
"I want to."—LaW
"Keep a poem in your pocket."—PrRh
Looks are deceiving.—DeT
"Night comes."—PrRa—PrRh
Poem about a special cat.—DeT
Poem by a cat.—DeT
Smart cat.—DeT
Some things I know about cats.—DeT
A special dictionary to help you understand cats.—DeT
"This big cat."—DeT
"This leaf."—HoSi
"This mother cat."—DeT
Three furry cats.—DeT
Too many cats.—DeT
De koven. Gwendolyn Brooks.—HoSu
"De las islas Puerto Rico." Unknown.—LiIl
The **deacon's** masterpiece. Oliver Wendell Holmes.—HaOf
The **dead** crab. Andrew Young.—HeR
"**Dead** in the cold, a song singing thrush." See Last rites
The **dead** sister. Caroline Gilman.—HaOf
Deafness
Miss Hartley. W. J. Smith.—BrT
"Old woman, old woman, shall we go a-shearing." Mother Goose.—FaW—LoR
"A **dear**." See Town meeting or 'hey man, don't speak so good'
"**Dear** Auntie." See Christmas thank you's
"**Dear** children, they asked in every town." See The wise men ask the children the way
"**Dear** Claudia, this is a love note written to you." See To Ellen

"**Dear** Dad." See Marcy Mannes
"**Dear**, dear, what can the matter be." Mother Goose.—DeM
"**Dear** Father." Unknown.—LaT
The **dear** girl. Sylvia Townsend Warner.—PlAs
"**Dear** God." See Prayer
"**Dear** God." See The prayer of the little ducks
"**Dear** God." See The prayer of the monkey
"**Dear** God." Unknown.—LaT
"**Dear** God, if there's one thing." See A crowd
"**Dear** God, my name's Samantha, and I'm seven." See Samantha speaking
"**Dear** God, thank you for our toys." Unknown.—LaT
"**Dear** heavenly Father." See Prayer
"**Dear** heavenly Father, I often make mistakes." See Prayer
"**Dear**, I'll gie ye some advice." See To an artist
"**Dear** little Bog-Face." See Bog-face
"**Dear** Lord my God." See Morning
"**Dear** mamma, if you just could be." See A lesson for mamma
"**Dear** Miss Miller." See Letter to a substitute teacher
"**Dear** Mr. Henderson." See Cecilia Dowling
Dear reader. Peter Meinke.—JaPi
"**Dear** sugar, dear tea, and dear corn." See The four dears
"**Dearest** Evelyn, I often think of you." See The jungle husband
Death. See also Grief; Immortality; Laments
Abraham. G. Bogin.—JaG
"Adieu, farewell earth's bliss." From Summer's last will and testament. T. Nashe.—HeR
After his death. N. MacCaig.—HeR
After looking into a book belonging to my great-grandfather, Eli Eliakim Plutzik. H. Plutzik.—HeR
Afterwards. T. Hardy.—HeR
The Aga Khan. S. Orlen.—JaPi
Alfred Corning Clark. R. Lowell.—HeR
"All the world's a stage." From As you like it. W. Shakespeare.—HeR—HoUn
Along the river. J. D. Enright.—JaD
Annabel Lee. E. A. Poe.—HaOf
Another epitaph on an army of mercenaries. H. MacDiarmid.—HeR
"Anyone lived in a pretty how town." E. E. Cummings.—HeR
The arrival of my mother. K. Wilson.—JaD
"As I walked out one evening." W. H. Auden.—HeR—PlAs
As if you had never been. R. Eberhart.—PlEd
"As the team's head-brass flashed out on the turn." E. Thomas.—HeR
At a low mass for two hot rodders. X. J. Kennedy.—JaPi
At night ("In the dust are my father's beautiful hands"). R. Eberhart.—JaS
At the grave of my brother. W. Stafford.—JaS
Aunt Julia. N. MacCaig.—HeR
Auto wreck. K. Shapiro.—HeR
"Aye, but to die, and go we know not where." From Measure for measure. W. Shakespeare.—HeR
The babes in the wood. Unknown.—BlO
Back country. J. C. Oates.—JaPi
The ballad of Rudolph Reed. G. Brooks.—HeR
Ballad of the man who's gone. L. Hughes.—PlAs
Barbara Allen's cruelty. Unknown.—PlAs
Barbara Ellen. Unknown.—PlAs

Death.—*Continued*

House, for sale. L. Clark.—PrRh
How to kill. K. Douglas.—HeR
Humdrum. C. Sandburg.—HoRa
Hurt hawks. R. Jeffers.—HeR
Hyena. Unknown.—HeR
"I had a young man." Mother Goose.—AlH
I met this guy who died. G. Corso.—JaPi
If there are any heavens. E. E. Cummings.—JaD
Illinois farmer. C. Sandburg.—HoRa
In grandfather's glasses. P. Peters.—JaS
In January, 1962. T. Kooser.—JaPi
"In the evening I would sit." From Journal. E. S. Millay.—PlSc
In the workhouse. G. R. Sims.—HaO
Interruption to a journey. N. MacCaig.—HeR
Irish wake. L. Hughes.—HuDk
"Is is far to go." C. D. Lewis.—PlAs
It was all very tidy. R. Graves.—HeR
"It's such a little thing to weep." E. Dickinson.—HeR
Janet waking. J. C. Ransom.—HeR
John Donne's statue. J. P. Bishop.—PlEd
John Kinsella's lament for Mrs. Mary Moore. W. B. Yeats.—HeR
John Rogers' exhortation to his children. J. Rogers.—HaOf
Judgement day. L. Hughes.—HuDk
Kineo mountain. C. T. Wright.—JaPi
Lament. G. Roberts.—JaG
Lament for Tadhg Cronin's children. M. Hartnett.—HeR
The last decision. M. Angelou.—AnS
"The last dinosaur." V. D. Najjar.—HoDi
Last rites. C. G. Rossetti.—PrRh
The last words of my English grandmother. W. C. Williams.—HeR
The late mother. C. Macdonald.—JaPi
Letter to a dead father. R. Shelton.—JaD
Light casualties. R. Francis.—JaPo
The lion for real. A. Ginsberg.—HeR
Little boy blue. E. Field.—HaOf
Little short legs. C. Rylant.—RyW
Looking at a picture on an anniversary. T. Hardy.—PlEd
"Looking at your face." G. Kinnell.—JaPo
Lore. R. S. Thomas.—HeR
Lowlands. Unknown.—PlAs
Mac. M. Vinz.—JaS
The man he killed. T. Hardy.—HeR
Martial choreograph. M. Angelou.—AnS
Masses. From España, aparta de me este Caliz. C. Vallejo.—HeR
"Methought that I had broken from the Tower." From Richard III. W. Shakespeare.—HeR
The mill ("The spoiling daylight inched along the bar-top"). R. Wilbur.—JaPi
Minstrel man. L. Hughes.—HuDk
Mitchell Chapin. M. Glenn.—GlC
More light, more light. A. Hecht.—HeR
Mountain lion. D. H. Lawrence.—HeR
The museum ("So we went to see this mummy"). A. Turner.—TuS
My father's ghost. D. Wagoner.—JaS
My father's heart. S. Friebert.—JaS
My grandfather dying. T. Kooser.—JaS
My grandmother had bones. J. Hemschemeyer.—JaD
"My mother had a maid call'd Barbara." From Othello. W. Shakespeare.—HoUn—PlAs
My mother's death. J. Hemschemeyer.—JaS

My old cat. H. Summers.—ChC—KeK
Names of horses. D. Hall.—McL
Neil Winningham. M. Glenn.—GlCd
New York City, 1935. G. Corso.—JaPi
Nightmare number three. S. V. Benét.—PlSc
Nocturn at the institute. D. McElroy.—JaPi
Ode to a nightingale. J. Keats.—HeR
O captain, my captain. W. Whitman.—HaOf
"Old Abram Brown is dead and gone." Mother Goose.—LoR
The old familiar faces. C. Lamb.—HeR
The old king. W. De la Mare.—PlAs
"An old man stirs the fire to a blaze." From Wanderings of Oisin. W. B. Yeats.—HeR
Old men ("People expect old men to die"). O. Nash.—HeR—JaD
The old men admiring themselves in the water. W. B. Yeats.—KeK
On a child who lived one minute. X. J. Kennedy.—JaD
On Addy Road. M. Swenson.—JaG
On seeing the Elgin Marbles. J. Keats.—PlEd
On the vanity of earthly greatness. A. Guiterman.—HaOf—TrM
"One Christmas-time." From The prelude. W. Wordsworth.—HeR
The one to grieve. R. Thomas.—JaG
Out, out. R. Frost.—HeR
Pardoner's tale blues. P. Beer.—PlAs
Parisian beggar woman. L. Hughes.—HuDk
Passage ("He was older and"). J. M. Roderick.—JaG
"Pensive, on her dead gazing, I heard the Mother of All." W. Whitman.—HeR
Poem ("I loved my friend"). L. Hughes.—CoN—HoBf—HuDk—JaD—LiII—LiSf
Poem about a special cat. B. S. De Regniers.—DeT
Poem for a suicide. G. Economou.—JaD
Poem for my father's ghost. M. Oliver.—JaS
The portrait ("My mother never forgave my father"). S. Kunitz.—JaPi
Posted as missing. J. Masefield.—BlO
Prayer for a dead buck. Unknown, fr. the Navajo Indian.—BiSp
Prayer to the deceased ("My child, you have toiled through life and come to the end"). Unknown, fr. the Aztec Indian.—BiSp
Prayer to the deceased ("Naked you came from Earth the mother, naked you return"). Unknown, fr. the Omaha Indian.—BiSp
Prayer to the deceased ("We have muddied the waters for you"). Unknown, fr. the Tewa Indian.—BiSp
Proud Maisie. Sir W. Scott.—BlO—PlAs
Rare Willie drowned in Yarrow. Unknown.—PlAs
Reflexes. M. Bell.—JaS
Rembrandt's late self portraits. E. Jennings.—PlEd
Request of a dying child. L. H. Sigourney.—HaOf
A room in the past. T. Kooser.—JaS
Rope and drum. R. Currie.—JaS
The sailor boy. A. Tennyson.—PlAs
Samuel. B. Katz.—PrRh
The sands of Dee. C. Kingsley.—BlO
"Sea charm." L. Hughes.—HuDk
The sea ritual. G. Darley.—LiWa
The self-unseeing. T. Hardy.—HeR
The shooting of Dan McGrew. R. W. Service.—DoNw—HeR

Death.—*Continued*

The shooting of John Dillinger outside the Biograph Theater, July 22, 1934. D. Wagoner.—HeR

Shroud. G. M. Brown.—HeR

"The silver swan, who living, had no note." O. Gibbons.—HeR

Slave coffle. M. Angelou.—AnS

"Small bird, forgive me." Unknown.—KeK

Solitude ("Right here I was nearly killed one night in February"). T. Tranströmer.—HeR

Some night again. W. Stafford.—JaG

Sometimes ("I am afraid of being crushed in the pincers"). G. Kuzma.—JaPi

Song ("Child, is thy father dead"). E. Elliot.—PlSc

Song ("I had a dove and the sweet dove died"). J. Keats.—BlO

Song ("Weep, weep, ye woodmen, wail"). A. Munday.—BlO

Song ("The world is rolling around for all the young people, so let's"). Unknown, fr. the Tlingit Indian.—BiSp

Song for the clatter-bones. F. R. Higgins.—HeR

Song of farewell to the deceased. Unknown, fr. the Quechua Indian.—BiSp

Song of the dying gunner A.A.I. C. Causley.—PlAs

Song Vu Chin. M. Glenn.—GlC

Songs my mother taught me. D. Wagoner.—JaS

Sonnet for my father. D. Justice.—JaD

The spider ("One biting winter morning"). H. F. Gould.—HaOf

Spider Reeves. H. Carlile.—JaPi

Springfield Mountain. Unknown.—PlAs

Stella Kolsky. M. Glenn.—GlC

Stopping by home. D. Huddle.—JaG

Stormalong. Unknown.—PlAs

Strange meeting ("It seemed that out of battle I escaped"). W. Owen.—HeR

The streets of Laredo ("As I walked out in the streets of Laredo"). Unknown.—HeR—LiSf
    "As I walked out in the streets of Laredo".—PlAs

The streets of Laredo ("O, early one morning I walked out like Agag"). L. MacNeice.—PlAs

Suburban. H. R. Coursen.—JaG

The suicide. J. C. Oates.—JaPi

Sundays visiting. A. Ríos.—JaS

The sweater. G. Orr.—JaPo

Sweet William's ghost. Unknown.—PlAs

Talk with a poet. H. Bevington.—PlSc

Thanksgiving ("The tides in my eyes are heavy"). P. Booth.—JaS

"That summer." J. Hemschemeyer.—JaPo

"Then to the bar, all they drew near." From The day of doom. M. Wigglesworth.—HaOf

"There's a certain slant of light." E. Dickinson.—HeR

Thistle. N. A. Zabolotsky.—HeR

The three ravens. Unknown.—PlAs

To a sad daughter. M. Ondaatje.—JaG

"To be, or not to be, that is the question." From Hamlet. W. Shakespeare.—HoUn

To daffodils. R. Herrick.—KoT

To Evan. R. Eberhart.—JaD

To L.B.S. W. T. Scott.—JaD

"Tomorrow, and tomorrow, and tomorrow." From Macbeth. W. Shakespeare.—HoUn

Transformations. T. Hardy.—HeR

Trapped mouse. J. Cunningham.—FaTh

Trees ("I am looking at trees"). W. S. Merwin.—JaPo

The true tale of grandfather Penny. E. Farjeon.—FaE

Tunes for bears to dance to. R. Wallace.—JaG

The twa corbies. Unknown.—HeR—PlAs

Two drops. Z. Herbert.—HeR

Uncle Julius. R. J. Margolis.—MaS

The unquiet grave ("So cold the wintry winds do blow"). Unknown.—PlAs

The unquiet grave ("The wind doth blow today, my love"). Unknown.—HeR

Ute Mountain. C. Tomlinson.—HeR

Vacation ("One scene as I bow to pour her coffee"). W. Stafford.—JaPi

The vacuum. H. Nemerov.—HeR

Vergissmeinicht. K. Douglas.—HeR

A walk. N. A. Zabolotsky.—HeR

War ("Each day the terror wagon"). R. Shelton.—JaPo

The wendigo. T. Hughes.—HuU

What he saw. R. Currie.—JaS

"When I was home last Christmas." R. Jarrell.—PlAs

"When my dog died." F. Littledale.—CoN

When my grandmother died. S. Cornish.—JaPi

When the ambulance came. R. Morgan.—JaS

While I slept. R. Francis.—KeK

"Who killed Cock Robin." Mother Goose.—LoR

The wife of Usher's well ("There lived a lady, a lady gay"). Unknown.—PlAs

The wife of Usher's well ("There lived a wife at Usher's well"). Unknown.—HeR—PlAs

The wild lumberjack. Unknown.—PlAs

With a posthumous medal. J. M. Brinnin.—PlSc

"Would you hear of an old-fashion'd sea-fight." From Song of myself. W. Whitman.—HeR

Yonosa house. R. T. Smith.—JaS

Death. Unknown, tr. by Aneirin Talfan Davies.—HeR

Death-bed reflections of Michelangelo. Hartley Coleridge.—PlEd

Death in Leamington. Sir John Betjeman.—HeR

The **death** of Admiral Benbow. Unknown.—BlO

Death of an old seaman. Langston Hughes.—HuDk

The **death** of the ball turret gunner. Randall Jarrell.—HeR

The **death** of the flowers. William Cullen Bryant.—HaOf

"Death, who one day taketh all." See Epitaph for a persian kitten

Death's blue-eyed girl. Linda Pastan.—JaPo

Deborah Delora. Unknown.—BeD

"Deborah Delora, she liked a bit of fun." See Deborah Delora

December

December ("All the months go past"). R. Fyleman.—PrRa

December ("Glad Christmas comes, and every hearth"). J. Clare.—HaO

December ("A little boy stood on the corner"). S. Vanderbilt.—HoSi

December ("While snows the window panes bedim"). J. Clare.—HaO

December days are short. J. Prelutsky.—PrIs

December hills. B. J. Esbensen.—EsCs

December leaves. K. Starbird.—BaS

December 21. L. Moore.—MoSn

"I heard a bird sing." O. Herford.—CoN—LiSf—PrRh

December ("All the months go past"). Rose Fyleman.—PrRa
December ("Glad Christmas comes, and every hearth"). John Clare.—HaO
December ("A little boy stood on the corner"). Sanderson Vanderbilt.—HoSi
December ("While snows the window panes bedim"). John Clare.—HaO
December days are short. Jack Prelutsky.—PrIs
"**December** days are short, and so." See December days are short
December eclipse. Margo Lockwood.—JaPi
December hills. Barbara Juster Esbensen.—EsCs
December leaves. Kaye Starbird.—BaS
December, prayer to St. Nicholas. John Heath-Stubbs.—HaO
December 21. Lilian Moore.—MoSn
"**Decorations** . . . climbing up to the loft on a wobbly ladder." See My Christmas, mum's Christmas
Dedication. Beatrice Schenk De Regniers.—DeT
"**Deena-gina.**" See For Deena
"**Deep** asleep, deep asleep." See The ballad of Semmerwater
"**Deep** in a windless." Buson, tr. by Harry Behn.—LiWa
"**Deep** in Alabama earth." See Alabama earth
"**Deep** in love." Bhavabbuti, tr. by William Stanley Merwin and Jeffrey Moussaieff Masson.—McL
"**Deep** in the fading leaves of night." See Carol
Deep in the mountains. Saibara, tr. by Hiroaki Sato.—StG
"**Deep** in the mountains, are you cutting trees, grandpa." See Deep in the mountains
"**Deep** in the rippling spring." May Ushida.—KeK
"**Deep** in the wood I made a house." See August
Deer
  Before butchering the deer. Unknown, fr. the Papago Indian.—BiSp
  Daniel Boone. S. V. Benét.—KeK
  Earthy anecdote. W. Stevens.—HeR—LiSf
  Encounter. L. Moore.—MoSn
  The fallow deer at the lonely house. T. Hardy.—BlO—HeR—KoT
  How to see deer. P. Booth.—JaPi
  Outside at night. C. Zolotow.—ZoE
  Prayer to a dead buck. Unknown, fr. the Navajo Indian.—BiSp
  Sentries. X. J. Kennedy.—KeF
  An unseen deer. J. Tagliabue.—JaPi
"The **deer** carcass hangs from a rafter." See Gathering the bones together
Defeat. See Failure
Definitions. X. J. Kennedy.—KeF
Defoe, Daniel
  "The labouring poor, in spite of double pay." See The true-born Englishman
  The true-born Englishman, sels.
    "The labouring poor, in spite of double pay".—PlSc
DeForest, Charlotte B.
  A lost snowflake.—BaS
Dehn, Paul
  "In a cavern, in a canyon."—KeK
Dekker, Thomas
  A cradle song ("Golden slumbers kiss your eyes").—BlO
  The happy heart.—HeR
Delander, Sonja
  The octopus ("The octopus would surely be").—RuI

Delayed action. Christian Morgenstern, tr. by William De Witt Snodgrass and Lore Segal.—HeR
"A **delicate** young Negro stands." See Anonymous drawing
Delight of being alone. David Herbert Lawrence.—PrBb
Demille, A. B.
  The ice-king.—DoNw
Demon. Eve Merriam.—MeHa
The **demon** lover. Unknown.—PlAs
Den. Sylvia Cassedy.—CaR
Denn, Gwen
  Journey back to Christmas.—HaO
Densmore, Frances
  I cannot forget you, tr. by.—LiIl—LiSf
Dentists
  After the dentist. M. Swenson.—JaD
  The poet's farewell to his teeth. W. Dickey.—JaD
Departing words to a son. Robert Pack.—JaG
Departmental. Robert Frost.—KoS
The **departure.** Frank Steele.—JaG—JaPo
"**Dependency.**" See Windy day
Der Hovanessian, Diana
  The woman cleaning lentils, tr. by.—FaTh
Desert places. Robert Frost.—HeR
Desert tortoise. Byrd Baylor.—PrRh
Deserts
  At the bomb testing site. W. Stafford.—HeR
  Desert tortoise. B. Baylor.—PrRh
  "Oases." N. M. Bodecker.—BoSs
  Requiem for Sonora. R. Shelton.—JaPi
"**Desire** for a woman took hold of me in the night." See Song
"**Desolate** and lone." See Lost
Despair
  A black Pierrot. L. Hughes.—HuDk
  Burning love letters. H. Moss.—JaD
  Carla Spooner. M. Glenn.—GlCd
  The chimney sweeper ("A little black thing among the snow"). W. Blake.—HeR—PlSc
  Disintegration. R. Shelton.—JaD
  "Don't touch me, I scream at passers by." N. Gorbanyevskaya.—McL
  Dressed up. L. Hughes.—HuDk
  First, goodbye. J. Smith.—JaG
  The fist upstairs. W. Dickey.—JaPi
  Going in ("Every day alone whittles me"). M. Piercy.—JaD
  A good woman feeling bad. M. Angelou.—AnS
  The grief of cafeterias. J. Updike.—JaPo
  "He built a mud-wall'd hovel, where he kept." From Peter Grimes. G. Crabbe.—PlSc
  "I am a little beggar girl." Mother Goose.—AlH
  I dreamed that I was old. S. Kunitz.—JaG
  "In Golden Gate Park that day." L. Ferlinghetti.—HeR
  "It is grey out." K. Kuskin.—LiSf
  Lines for a friend who left. J. Logan.—JaD
  "Misery is when your." L. Hughes.—LiIl
  Miss Blues'es child. L. Hughes.—KoT
  My life has turned to blue. M. Angelou.—AnS
  "My mother had a maid call'd Barbara." From Othello. W. Shakespeare.—HoUn—PlAs
  "Oh Pennington Poe." J. Prelutsky.—PrRi
  The park ("One day I so depressed"). A. Turner.—TuS
  The pessimist. B. King.—BlO
  A plagued journey. M. Angelou.—AnS
  Po' boy blues. L. Hughes.—HuDk
  The raven. E. A. Poe.—HaOf
  Robin Gold. M. Glenn.—GlC

Despair—*Continued*
The sad boy. L. Riding.—HeR
The shooting of Dan McGrew. R. W. Service.—
 DoNw—HeR
"The silver swan, who living had no note." O.
 Gibbons.—HeR
Sometimes ("Sometimes I simply have to cry").
 J. Prelutsky.—PrRa
Southeast Arkanasia. M. Angelou.—PlSc
"Stop all the clocks, cut off the telephone." W.
 H. Auden.—HeR
"There was an old man of Cape Horn." E.
 Lear.—LiH
"There was an old man whose despair." E.
 Lear.—LiH
"There was an old person of Fife." E. Lear.—
 LiH
Thistle. N. A. Zabolotsky.—HeR
Three moments. S. R. Sherman.—JaD
"To be, or not to be, that is the question."
 From Hamlet. W. Shakespeare.—HoUn
To carry on living. Y. Amichai.—McL
"Tomorrow, and tomorrow, and tomorrow."
 From Macbeth. W. Shakespeare.—HoUn
Vagabonds. L. Hughes.—PlSc
The weary blues. L. Hughes.—HuDk
"When, in disgrace with fortune and men's
 eyes." From Sonnets. W. Shakespeare.—HoUn
Work without hope. S. T. Coleridge.—PlSc
"Desperate Dan." Mother Goose.—AlH—FaW
Desserts
Apple pie. I. O. Eastwick.—HoMu
"Bananas and cream." D. McCord.—FaW—
 HoMu
Pie problem. S. Silverstein.—PrRh
"Destroying Jerusalem, burning Solomon's
 temple." See Tishab Be-Av
Destruction
The eternal city. A. R. Ammons.—PlEd
Fire and ice. R. Frost.—KoS
The sick rose. W. Blake.—HeR
The **destruction** of Sennacherib. Lord Byron.—
 HeR—PlAs
Deutsch, Babette
Little catkins, tr. by.—LiE
Phantasus, 1, 8, tr. by.—LiCp
A pig is never blamed.—PrRh
Development. N. M. Bodecker.—BoPc
Devil
The curst wife. Unknown.—PlAs
Demon. E. Merriam.—MeHa
The demon lover. Unknown.—PlAs
A devil. Z. Herbert.—HeR
The devil in Texas. Unknown.—HeR
The devil's bag. J. Stephens.—LiWa
The devil's nine questions. Unknown.—LiWa
The farmer's curst wife. Unknown.—PlAs
Fiend. E. Merriam.—MeHa
"A knight came riding from the east."
 Unknown.—BlO
Meet-on-the-road ("Now, pray, where are you
 going, said Meet-on-the-road"). Unknown.—
 BlO
 Meet-on-the-road ("Now, pray, where are
  you going, child").—KoT
The riddling knight. Unknown.—LiSf—PlAs
"St. Dunstan, as the story goes." Mother
 Goose.—DeM—LoR
The seven. Unknown.—HeR
"This is the foul fiend Flibbertigibbet, he begins
 at." From King Lear. W. Shakespeare.—LiWa

A **devil**. Zbigniew Herbert, tr. by Czesław
 Miłosz.—HeR
The **devil** in Texas. Unknown.—HeR
The **devil's** bag. James Stephens.—LiWa
The **devil's** nine questions. Unknown.—LiWa
Devotion. Robert Frost.—KoS
Dew
At sunrise. N. M. Bodecker.—BoPc
A dewdrop. Unknown.—ChG
For a dewdrop. E. Farjeon.—FaE
"The **dew** is gleaming in the grass." See Among
 the millet
"Dew on the bamboos." See Song
A **dewdrop**. Unknown.—ChG
Di Pasquale, Emanuel
First January walk.—LiNe
First surf.—JaS
Joy of an immigrant, a thanksgiving.—LiTp
Letters from Sicily.—LiIl
My cat, Robin Hood.—LiCa
Rain ("Like a drummer's brush").—KeK
Sicilian Easter Sunday.—LiE
Sicilian thanksgiving on the feast of Saint John
 the Baptist.—LiTp
Valentine thoughts for Mari.—LiVp
"Diabolic demons." See Demon
Dial tone. Felix Pollak.—JaPo
"Dialogue of the unspoken argument." See Gail
 Larkin
Diamond cut diamond. Ewart Milne.—LiSf
"Diamonds are forever so I gave you quartz." See
 The hardness scale
"Diamonds of brittle sugar." See An Easter present
"The diatonic dittymunch." Jack Prelutsky.—PrNk
Dickens, Charles
A Christmas carol, sels.
 Tiny Tim's prayer.—LaT
Tiny Tim's prayer. See A Christmas carol
"Dickery dickery dare." Mother Goose.—BlQ—
 DeM—LoR
Dickey, William
The anniversary.—JaG
The fist upstairs.—JaPi
Happiness.—JaPi
The poet's farewell to his teeth.—JaD
Tutankhamen.—JaPi
Dickinson, Emily
"Bee, I'm expecting you."—KoT
"A bird came down the walk."—HaOf
 A bird.—CoN
Certainty. See "I never saw a moor"
"Could mortal lip divine."—HeR
"Heart we will forget him."—McL
"How happy is the little stone."—HeR
"How soft a caterpillar steps."—FaTh
"How the old mountains drip with sunset."—
 HeR
"I know some lonely houses off the road."—
 LiWa
"I like to see it lap the miles."—HaOf
"I never saw a moor."—LaT—LiSf
 Certainty.—DaC
"I think that the root of the wind is water."—
 HeR
"I'm nobody, who are you."—HaOf—LiSf—
 PrRh—TrM
"It's such a little thing to weep."—HeR
"Like rain it sounded till it curved."—HeR
"The martyr poets, did not tell."—PlEd
"The morns are meeker than they were."—
 HaOf

Divorce
Jason Talmadge. M. Glenn.—GlC
Justin Faust. M. Glenn.—GlCd
Marcy Mannes. M. Glenn.—GlCd
A matter of principle. N. M. Bodecker.—BoPc
Rickie Miller. M. Glenn.—GlC
Dixon, Richard Watson
Song ("The feathers of the willow").—BlO
The **dizzy** giraffe. Unknown.—BrT
Dizzy McPete. Unknown.—PaM
"**Do** alley cats go." See Alley cat school
"**Do** fairies like a rainy day." See Do fairies like the rain
Do fairies like the rain. Barbara M. Hales.—HoCr
"**Do** I see a hat in the road, I said." See The old Sussex road
Do it yourself. Joan Aiken.—KeK
"**Do** not despise the breath of your fathers." See From a prayer for the novice at the close of his initiation
"**Do** not go gentle into that good night." Dylan Thomas.—HeR
"**Do** not harm us, If you have a son, I will marry him." See Girl's prayer to thunder during a storm
"**Do** not jump on ancient uncles." See Rules
"**Do** not suddenly break the branch, or." See Usk
"**Do** not think I shall harm you." See Prayer before killing an eagle
"**Do** not weep, little one." Unknown.—LiSf
Do oysters sneeze. Jack Prelutsky.—PrNk
"**Do** oysters sneeze beneath the seas." See Do oysters sneeze
"**Do** parks get lonely." See Snowy benches
"**Do** skyscrapers ever grow tired." See Skyscrapers
"**Do** the baby cake-walk." Clyde Watson.—CoN—WaC
"**Do** you ask what the birds say, the sparrow, the dove." See Answer to a child's question
"**Do** you ever." See Dreams
"**Do** you ever look in the looking-glass." See Robert, who is often a stranger to himself
"**Do** you ever see." See Look up
"**Do** you ever wonder." See Like a bug
Do you feel sorry for him. John Ciardi.—CiD
"**Do** you hear the cry as the pack goes by." See Wind wolves
"**Do** you know Paul, Paul Pine (he's nine)." See Friend
"**Do** you know the hour when all opposites meet." See The time is
"**Do** you know what is bad." See Bad and good
"**Do** you love me." See Question
"**Do** you remember." See Read
"**Do** you remember an inn." See Tarantella
"**Do** you take it off when you go to sleep." See Questions for an angel
"**Do** you write one every day, said Mary." See Mary's one
Dobbs, Jeannine
Kitchen song.—JaS
Doctor Emmanuel. James Reeves.—PrRh
"**Doctor** Emmanuel Harrison-Hyde." See Doctor Emmanuel
Dr. Foster. Unknown.—DaC
"**Doctor** Foster is a good man." See Dr. Foster
"**Doctor** Foster went to Gloucester." Mother Goose.—DaC—DeM—FaW—LoR
Doctors
"An apple a day." Mother Goose.—LoR
"Apple in the morning." Mother Goose.—LoR
The brain surgeon. C. Rylant.—RyW

Doctor Emmanuel. J. Reeves.—PrRh
"Doctor Foster went to Gloucester." Mother Goose.—DaC—DeM—FaW—LoR
"Eat an apple going to bed." Mother Goose.—LoR
"I do not like thee, Doctor Fell." Mother Goose.—DeM—LoR
Le medecin malgre lui. W. C. Williams.—PlSc
Old Doc. M. Vinz.—JaPi
"Roast apple at night." Mother Goose.—LoR
The surgeon and the ape. Unknown.—BrT
Vet. E. Farjeon.—FaE
"When old corruption first begun." W. Blake.—HeR
Dodat, Francois
Crab.—FaTh
Glowworm ("He studies very late").—FaTh
Ladybug ("A tiny island").—FaTh
Dodge, Mary Mapes
A brave knight.—BrT
The letters at school.—HaOf
Poor crow.—HaOf
Ten kinds.—PrRh
That's what we'd do.—HaOf
Dodo. Henry Carlile.—JaPi
Dodoes
Dodo. H. Carlile.—JaPi
"**Does** man love art, man visits art, but squirms." See The Chicago Picasso
"**Dog**." See Friend dog
A **dog** ("I am alone"). Charlotte Zolotow.—HoDl
A **dog** ("A little monkey goes like a donkey that means to say"). From Tender buttons. Gertrude Stein.—KoT
Dog ("Under a maple tree"). Valerie Worth.—HoDl
Dog ("Whether I'm Alsatian"). Eleanor Farjeon.—FaE
"The **dog** barks from a cloud." See Adolescence
"The **dog** beneath the cherry tree." See The ambiguous dog
A **dog** in San Francisco. Michael Ondaatje.—JaG
"A **dog** is a pal, so friendly and fun." L. C. Briggs.—TrM
"**Dog** means dog." See Blum
"The **dog** says bow wow." Unknown.—RaT
"The **dog** will come when he is called." Adelaide O'Keefe.—BlO
"The **dog** writes on the window with his nose." See Early spring
Dogs
"Across cold, moon bright." From The seasons. H. Behn.—HoDl
"All night I've kept an eye." From The old dog's song. L. Norris.—HoDl
The ambiguous dog. A. Guiterman.—HoDl
Arf, said Sandy. C. Stetler.—JaPo
At midnight. T. Kooser.—JaG
An awful moment. X. J. Kennedy.—KeF
Back country. J. C. Oates.—JaPi
Bengal. Unknown.—CoOu
"Beware of dog." N. M. Bodecker.—BoSs
Beware of the doggerel. E. Merriam.—MeSk
Bingo. Unknown.—KoT
Black dog. C. Zolotow.—ZoE
Bliss. E. Farjeon.—FaE—PrRh
Boasting. E. Farjeon.—FaE
"Bow, wow, wow." Mother Goose.—DeM—LiSf
Buying a puppy. L. Norris.—LiIl—LiSf
Buying the dog. M. Ondaatje.—JaS
Canis major. R. Frost.—KeK—KoS
Cats and dogs ("Some like cats, and some like dogs."). N. M. Bodecker.—BoSs

Dolls—*Continued*
Doll. M. C. Livingston.—LiWo
My cousins' dollhouse. M. C. Livingston.—LiWo
Night bear. L. B. Hopkins.—HoSu
Oh, teddy bear. J. Prelutsky.—PrNk
Dolphins and porpoises
"Though pleased to see the dolphins play." M. Green.—TrM
Dominique Blanco. Mel Glenn.—GlC
Donal Og. Unknown, tr. by Augusta Gregory.—HeR
Donald Kaminsky. Mel Glenn.—GlC
Done for. Walter De la Mare.—BlO
The **dong** with a luminous nose. Edward Lear.—LiH
The **donkey** ("I had a donkey, that was all right"). Theodore Roethke.—HaOf—PrRa
The **donkey** ("I saw a donkey"). Unknown.—PrRh
The **donkey** ("When fishes flew and forests walked"). Gilbert Keith Chesterton.—DaC—HeR
"The **donkey** doctor came covered with rain." See Big friend of the stones
"**Donkey**, donkey, old and gray." Mother Goose.—DaC—LoR
Donkey riding. Unknown.—DaC—DoNw
Donkeys
Advice to travelers. W. Gibson.—JaPo
Before starting.—KeK
Big friend of the stones. S. Orlen.—JaPi
The donkey ("I had a donkey, that was all right"). T. Roethke.—HaOf—PrRa
The donkey ("I saw a donkey"). Unknown.—PrRh
The donkey ("When fishes flew and forests walked"). G. K. Chesterton.—DaC—HeR
"Donkey, donkey, old and gray." Mother Goose.—DaC—LoR
Donkey riding. Unknown.—DaC—DoNw
The Erie Canal. Unknown.—LiIl
Kerr's ass. P. Kavanagh.—HeR
Nicholas Nye. W. De la Mare.—BlO
A prayer to go to paradise with the donkeys. F. Jammes.—HeR—LiSf
Sweet ass. E. Farjeon.—FaE
What the donkey saw. U. A. Fanthorpe.—HaO
Donna Vasquez. Mel Glenn.—GlC
Donne, John
The baite.—HeR
Witchcraft by a picture.—PlEd
Donne, John (about)
John Donne's statue. J. P. Bishop.—PlEd
Donnell, David
Open roads.—JaS
Donovan, Rhoda
Ten week wife.—JaS
"**Don't** ask me how he managed." See The worm
"**Don't** be polite." See How to eat a poem
"**Don't** begrudge." See Beware, or be yourself
"**Don't** Care didn't care." Mother Goose.—AlH—BlO
Don't Care ("Don't Care, he didn't care").—DaC
"**Don't** Care ("Don't Care, he didn't care"). See "Don't Care didn't care"
"**Don't** ever cross a crocodile." Kaye Starbird.—LiSf
"**Don't** ever make." See The snake
"**Don't** ever seize a weasel by the tail. Jack Prelutsky.—PrRh—PrZ
"**Don't** go, don't go, don't go, Jo." See Don't go, Jo

Don't go, Jo. Barbara Ireson.—BaS
"**Don't** go looking for fairies." See Fairies
Don't leave the spoon in the syrup. N. M. Bodecker.—BoSs
Don't let me. Ann Turner.—TuS
"**Don't** let my life grow dull, Lord." Elizabeth M. Shields.—LaT
"**Don't** let that horse." Lawrence Ferlinghetti.—HeR
"**Don't** look at his hands now." See Stonecarver
Don't make a peep. Charlotte Pomerantz.—PoA
"**Don't** procrastinate." See Notice to myself
"**Don't** shake this." See Message from a caterpillar
"**Don't** sleep, for your paddle fell into the water, and your spear." See Song of parents who want to wake up their son
"**Don't** snicker and sneer." See How to watch statues
Don't tell. Michael Rosen.—RoC
"**Don't** tell me that I talk too much." Arnold Spilka.—PrRh
"**Don't** touch me, I scream at passers by." Natalya Gorbanyevskaya, tr. by Daniel Weissbort.—McL
"**Don't** waste your time in looking for." See Long gone
"**Don't** worry if your job is small." Unknown.—PrRh
"**Don't** you ever." See Song
"**Don't** you go too near the sea." See The waves of the sea
"**Don't** you think it's probable." See Little talk
"**Doom** is dark and deeper than any sea-dingle." See The wanderer
The **door**. David McCord.—McAs
"The **door** is shut fast." See Who's in
Door number four. Charlotte Pomerantz.—LiIl—PoI
Doors
Angelica the doorkeeper. Unknown.—HeR
A different door. X. J. Kennedy.—ChC—KeF
The door. D. McCord.—McAs
Door number four. C. Pomerantz.—LiIl—PoI
Doors. C. Sandburg.—HoRa
Get up and bar the door. Unknown.—BlO—PlAs
Green candles. H. Wolfe.—PrRh
"I am running in a circle." J. Prelutsky.—PrNk
Joan's door. E. Farjeon.—FaE
"Knock on the door." Mother Goose.—DeM
Locked doors. From A throw of threes. E. Merriam.—MeF
The lockless door. R. Frost.—LiWa
The museum door. L. B. Hopkins.—HoDi
Open doors. From A throw of threes. E. Merriam.—MeF
Secret door. M. C. Livingston.—LiWo
Some one. W. De la Mare.—FrP—LiSf—PrRh
"There was a young lady of Norway." E. Lear.—FaW
Who's in. E. Fleming.—BlO—PrRh
Doors. Carl Sandburg.—HoRa
"The **doors** are locked." See House, for sale
Dora Antonopolis. Mel Glenn.—GlC
Dora Diller. Jack Prelutsky.—PrNk
"**Doris** Drummond sneaked a look." X. J. Kennedy.—KeB
"**Dormy**, dormy dormouse." Mother Goose.—BlPi
Dorothy Osmond. Mel Glenn.—GlCd
Dorrance, Dick
Cockpit in the clouds.—PrRh

Double barreled ding dong bat. Dennis Lee.—PrRh

"**Double,** double, toil and trouble." From Macbeth. William Shakespeare.—HoUn

Song of the witches.—PrRh

Double dutch. Walter De la Mare.—ChC

Double entendre. J. F. Wilson.—BrT

Double feature. Theodore Roethke.—JaD

"The **double** moon, one on the high backdrop of the west, one on the." See River moons

Double trouble. Eve Merriam.—MeSk

Douglas, Lord Alfred
 The hen ("The hen is a ferocious fowl").—PrRh
 The shark ("A treacherous monster").—PrRh

Douglas, Keith
 Behavior of fish in an English tea garden.—HeR
 How to kill.—HeR
 The marvel.—HeR
 Vergissmeinicht.—HeR

Douglas, Marian
 Ant-hills.—HaOf
 The snow-man.—HaOf

Douglas, Suzanne
 No holes marred.—PrRh

"**Douglas.**" See Beth Rossiter and

Douglas fir. Myra Cohn Livingston.—LiMp

Douglas Kearney. Mel Glenn.—GlCd

"The **dove** stays in the garden." From Five ghost songs. Unknown.—KoT

Doves. See Pigeons

Doves and starlings. Eleanor Farjeon.—FaE

Doves of Dodona. Paul Fleischman.—FlI

"The **doves** say, green leaves." See Doves and starlings

Dow, Philip
 Early morning.—JaD

"**Down.**" See The grasshopper

Down below. Joan Aiken.—LiWa

"**Down** by the gate of the orchard." See Spring whistles

"**Down** cellar, said the cricket." See The potatoes dance

"**Down** derry down, my Pippin my clown." Clyde Watson.—WaC

"**Down, down.**" Eleanor Farjeon.—CoN—FaE

"**Down** from the north on the north wind flying." See And stands there sighing

"**Down** in the Frantic Mountains." See A survey

"**Down** in yonder meadow where the green grass grows." Unknown.—DaC

Down on my tummy. Myra Cohn Livingston.—HoSi

"**Down** the blowhole of a whale." X. J. Kennedy.—KeB

"**Down** the close, darkening lanes they sang their way." See The send-off

"**Down** the hilly avenue." See Soldiers and horses

"**Down** with the rosemary, and so." See Ceremony upon Candlemas eve

Downhill. Richard J. Margolis.—MaS

"**Downhill** I came, hungry, and yet not starved." See The owl

Downpour. Myra Cohn Livingston.—HoSu

"**A dozen** machines." See A time for building

Dracula
 The Dracula vine. T. Hughes.—HoCr
 "When Dracula went to the blood bank." J. Prelutsky.—PrNk

The **Dracula** vine. Ted Hughes.—HoCr

The **dragon.** Carolyn Wells.—BrT

"The **dragon** boats, there they go." Unknown.—DeD

Dragon flies. See Dragonflies

Dragon smoke. Lilian Moore.—LiSf—MoSn—PrRa

"A **dragon,** who was a great wag." See The dragon

Dragonflies
 Dragonflies. A. Fisher.—FiW
 Dragonfly ("A dragonfly"). F. P. Jaques.—PrRa
 A dragonfly ("When the heat of the summer"). E. Farjeon.—CoOu—FaE—PrRh
 "Dragonfly, dragonfly." Unknown.—DeD
 Dragonfly's summer song. J. Yolen.—YoR
 I answer an SOS. X. J. Kennedy.—KeF

Dragonflies. Aileen Fisher.—FiW

"A **dragonfly.**" See Dragonfly

Dragonfly ("A dragonfly"). Florence Page Jaques.—PrRa

A **dragonfly** ("When the heat of the summer"). Eleanor Farjeon.—CoOu—FaE—PrRh

"**Dragonfly,** dragonfly." Unknown.—DeD

Dragonfly's summer song. Jane Yolen.—YoR

Dragons
 The dragon. C. Wells.—BrT
 Dragon smoke. L. Moore.—LiSf—MoSn—PrRa
 The gold-tinted dragon. K. Kuskin.—PrRa
 Happy birthday, dear dragon. J. Prelutsky.—PrNk
 Lost and found. L. Moore.—MoSn
 A modern dragon. R. Bennett.—PrRa
 My dragon. X. J. Kennedy.—PrRa
 Paper dragons. S. A. Schmeltz.—PrRh
 "Sir Eglamour, that worthy Knight." Unknown.—BlO
 The tale of Custard the dragon. O. Nash.—HaOf
  Custard the dragon.—CoOu
 Thunder dragon. H. Behn.—HoCb
 The toaster ("A silver-scaled dragon with jaws flaming red"). W. J. Smith.—LiSf—PrRa

Drawing. See Painting and pictures

Drawing. Madeleine L'Engle.—LaT

Drayton, Michael
 "Since there's no help, come, let us kiss and part."—HeR

The **dreadful** doings of Jelly Belly. Dennis Lee.—PrRa

The **dreadful** fate of naughty Nate. John Kendrick Bangs.—HaOf

The **dream** ("Last night I dreamed of you"). Unknown.—BiSp

"The **dream.**" See Martin Luther King day

The **dream** ("One night I dreamed"). Harry Behn.—HoCb—LiSf

The **dream,** sels. Theodore Roethke
 "I met her as a blossom on a stem".—McL
 "Love is not love until love's vulnerable".—McL
 "She came toward me in a flowing air".—McL
 "She held her body steady in the wind".—McL

Dream ("The sandman put it in his sack"). Myra Cohn Livingston.—LaW

The **dream** about our master, William Shakespeare. Hyam Plutzik.—HeR

Dream dog. Louis Phillips.—HoDl

"**Dream** dog leaps out of the moon with nothing." See Dream dog

The **dream** keeper. Langston Hughes.—HuDk

Dream songs. Unknown.—BiSp

Dream variation. Langston Hughes.—HuDk

"**Dreaming** of honeycombs to share." See Waiting

The **dreaming** of the bones. From Song for the cloth. William Butler Yeats.—HeR

Dreams. See also Ideals; Visions

Dreams.—*Continued*

Again, good night. C. Zolotow.—ZoE
Architect. L. T. Nicholl.—PlEd
As I grew older. L. Hughes.—HuDk
Aunt Leaf. M. Oliver.—JaT
Autobiography. L. MacNeice.—HeR
Ballad. J. H. Wheelock.—PlAs
"Be not afeard, the isle is full of noises." From The tempest. W. Shakespeare.—HeR
El beso de mama. Unknown.—GrT
Big house. M. C. Livingston.—LiWo
The biplane. S. Orlen.—JaG
Cat ("The fat cat on the mat"). J. R. R. Tolkien.—ChC
The chimney sweeper ("When my mother died I was very young"). W. Blake.—PlSc
City under water. E. Farjeon.—FaE
Cock-crow. E. Thomas.—HeR
Cowper's tame hare. N. Nicholson.—HeR
Cradle song for Christmas. E. Farjeon.—FaE
The dark ("I am glad of that other life"). W. Heyen.—PlEd
Dawn ("I embraced the summer dawn"). A. Rimbaud.—KoT
Daybreak. S. Spender.—JaD
Disillusionment of ten o'clock. W. Stevens.—HeR—KoT
The dream ("Last night I dreamed of you"). Unknown, fr. the Ammassalik Eskimo.—BiSp
The dream ("One night I dreamed"). H. Behn.—HoCb—LiSf
Dream ("The sandman put it in his sack"). M. C. Livingston.—LaW
The dream about our master, William Shakespeare. H. Plutzik.—HeR
Dream dog. L. Phillips.—HoDl
The dream keeper. L. Hughes.—HuDk
Dream songs. Unknown, fr. the Modoc Indian.—BiSp
Dream variation. L. Hughes.—HuDk
The dreaming of the bones. From Song for the cloth. W. B. Yeats.—HeR
Dreams ("Do you ever"). A. Fisher.—LaW
Dreams ("Here we are all, by day, by night we are hurled"). R. Herrick.—KeK
Dreams ("Hold fast to dreams"). L. Hughes.—HuDk—LiSf—PrRh
Dreams ("I get up at seven o'clock"). N. Giovanni.—GiSp
Dreamscape. L. M. Fisher.—HoDi
Evening ("Prince Absalom and Sir Rotherham Redde"). Dame E. Sitwell.—PlAs
"Evening hushes." E. Farjeon.—FaE
Fairies ("I cannot see fairies"). H. Conkling.—LiWa
Fairies ("Out of the dust of dreams"). L. Hughes.—HuDk
Fantasia ("I dream"). E. Merriam.—MeSk
The farm hands. D. Laing.—PlSc
Going into dream. E. Farjeon.—FaE
Good night, good night. D. Lee.—PrRa
How they sleep. Unknown.—ChB
"I dream'd a dream tonight." From Romeo and Juliet. W. Shakespeare.—HoUn
"I have been in bed for hours." J. Prelutsky.—PrMp
I hid you. M. Radnóti.—McL
"I met her as a blossom on a stem." From The dream. T. Roethke.—McL
"I picked a dream out of my head." J. Ciardi.—CiD

"If we shadows have offended." From A midsummer night's dream. W. Shakespeare.—HoUn
"In the pitch of the night." L. B. Hopkins.—HoCr
"Joseph fell a'dreaming." E. Farjeon.—FaE
"Keep a hand on your dream." X. J. Kennedy.—JaPi
Kubla Khan. S. T. Coleridge.—LiSf—LiWa—PlEd
The land of Nod. R. L. Stevenson.—ChB—DaC
Laurie Allen. M. Glenn.—GlC
Leopard in the zoo. C. Zolotow.—ZoE
Lowlands. Unknown.—PlAs
Mama's kiss. Unknown.—GrT
"Methought that I had broken from the Tower." From Richard III. W. Shakespeare.—HeR
Minstrel's song. T. Hughes.—HaO
Mirage. C. G. Rossetti.—McL
Mrs. Green. D. Huddle.—JaPo
My jacket old. H. Melville.—PlSc
Nightmare ("Beautiful beautiful Beverly"). J. Viorst.—ViI
Nightmare ("Expecting to be put in a sack and dumped in a ditch"). E. Field.—JaS
Nightmare ("Nay nay nay"). E. Merriam.—MeHa
Nightmares. S. C. Fox.—LiWa
The nine little goblins. J. W. Riley.—HaOf
The old king. W. De la Mare.—PlAs
The old salt. J. Ciardi.—CiD
"On the first snowfall." E. Merriam.—MeF
"Once I dreamt I was the snow." S. C. Fox.—LiSf
Once upon a great holiday. A. Wilkinson.—DoNw
"Our revels now are ended." From The tempest. W. Shakespeare.—HeR
The puffin ("Warm and plump as fresh baked muffins"). C. Pomerantz.—PoA
"Roll gently, old dump truck." C. Pomerantz.—PoA
The rumbly night train. C. Pomerantz.—PoA
School day. C. Zolotow.—ZoE
"The seafarers tell of the eastern Isle of Bliss." From His dream of the sky land, a farewell poem. Li Po.—LiWa
September ("It rained in my sleep"). L. Pastan.—JaPi
Shavuot, for Jessica. K. Hellerstein.—LiPj
"She is the fairies' midwife, and she comes." From Romeo and Juliet. W. Shakespeare.—HeR
"Silverly." D. Lee.—PrRa
Sleeping on the ceiling. E. Bishop.—KoT
The snail's dream. O. Herford.—PrRh
Some night again. W. Stafford.—JaG
Southern Pacific. C. Sandburg.—HoRa
The stray. B. E. Todd.—ChC
Suppressed. Unknown.—BrT
Teacher talk. A. Turner.—TuS
"There was an old man from Peru." Unknown.—CoOu—KeK
An old man from Peru.—BrT—CoN
"There was an old person of Rheims." E. Lear.—LiH
Three birds flying. E. Merriam.—MeSk
To dark eyes dreaming. Z. K. Snyder.—PrRh
To my daughter riding in the circus parade. J. Labombard.—JaG

Drummers and drums
"Beat the drum, beat the drum." Unknown.—DeD
The drum. N. Giovanni.—GiSp—LiSf
"Rumpitty Tumpitty Rumpitty Tum." J. Prelutsky.—PrRi
"Was ever a dream a drum." C. Sandburg.—HoRa

Drummond, William
The statue of Medusa.—PlEd
The Trojan Horse.—PlEd

Drumpp the grump. Jack Prelutsky.—PrNk
"**Drunk.**" See Last born
"The **drunks** like to sit beside Beaver Creek." See The brain surgeon
Dry spell. Lilian Moore.—MoSn
Dryads. See Fairies

Dryden, John
Incantation to Oedipus.—LiWa

Du Maurier, George
"I am gai, I am poet, I dwell."—TrM

The **dual** site. Michael Hamburger.—PlAs
The **duck** ("Behold the duck"). Ogden Nash.—HeR
Duck ("When the neat white"). Valerie Worth.—CoN
The **duck** ("When you're a duck like me it's impossible"). Richard Digance.—PrRh
"A **duck** and a drake." Mother Goose.—LoR
The **duck** and the kangaroo. Edward Lear.—LiH—LiIl
"**Ducklings.**" See Green

Ducks
"Charley Barley, butter and eggs." Mother Goose.—DeM
The duck ("Behold the duck"). O. Nash.—HeR
Duck ("When the neat white"). V. Worth.—CoN
The duck ("When you're a duck like me it's impossible"). R. Digance.—PrRh
"A duck and a drake." Mother Goose.—LoR
The duck and the kangaroo. E. Lear.—LiH—LiIl
Ducks. F. W. Harvey.—CoOu
Ducks at dawn. J. S. Tippett.—ChG
Ducks' ditty. K. Grahame.—CoN—LiSf—PrRh
Ducks in the rain. J. S. Tippett.—PrRa
Dumpy ducky. L. Larcom.—HaOf
The hunter. O. Nash.—JaPo
"I'm a yellow-bill duck." J. Prelutsky.—PrRi
"I've just come up." Joso.—KoT
A little talk. Unknown.—PrRa
Peter and Wendy. W. Garthwaite.—PrRa
The prayer of the little ducks. C. B. de Gasztold.—LaT
Quack, quack. Dr. Seuss.—PrRa
"That duck, bobbing up." Joso.—LiSf—LiWa
"There was an old lady of France." E. Lear.—LiH

Ducks. Frederick William Harvey.—CoOu
"**Ducks** are dabbling the rain." See Ducks in the rain
Ducks at dawn. James S. Tippett.—ChG
Ducks' ditty. Kenneth Grahame.—CoN—LiSf—PrRh
Ducks in the rain. James S. Tippett.—PrRa
The **duel.** Eugene Field.—FaW—HaOf—PrRh
"**Duérmete** mi niña." See Arullo

Dugan, Alan
Memories of Verdun.—HeR

Dugan, Michael
Gumble.—PrRh

Dulcimer maker. Carolyn Forché.—PlSc

Dumas, Gerald
Afternoon in Waterloo Park, sels.
"I look at this picture of that old man".—StG
"Oma was sixty three when I was born".—StG
"I look at this picture of that old man." See Afternoon in Waterloo Park
"Oma was sixty three when I was born." See Afternoon in Waterloo Park

Dumas, Henry
Valentines.—LiVp

Dumpy ducky. Lucy Larcom.—HaOf

Dunann, Louella
Hot line.—PrRh

Duncan, Lois
Song of triumph.—HoBf

Dunham, Vera
War ("With the open eyes of their dead fathers"), tr. by.—HeR

Dunn, Stephen
Poem for people who are understandably too busy to read poetry.—JaG

Duns Scotus's Oxford. Gerard Manley Hopkins.—PlEd

"The **duo** met to duel at dawn." See The mungle and the munn

Duomo, Milan. From View of the cathedral. Raymond Henri.—PlEd

Durán, Cheli
The horse, tr. by.—LiSf—LiWa
The mosquito ("A mosquito tried to provoke"), tr. by.—LiSf

D'Urfey, Thomas
"I'll sail upon the dog-star."—KoT

"**During** the early winter." See Poem for Shane on her brother's birthday

Durston, Georgia Roberts
The wolf ("When the pale moon hides and the wild wind wails").—PrRh

Dusk ("At dusk there are swallows"). Paul Fleischman.—FlI
Dusk ("Dusk over the lake"). James Harrison.—JaT
Dusk in the country. Harry Edmund Martinson, tr. by Robert Bly.—HeR
"**Dusk** over the lake." See Dusk
"**Dusk** was best, searching." See Shooting

Dust
A peck of gold. R. Frost.—KoS
"**Dust** always blowing about the town." See A peck of gold
Dust of snow. Robert Frost.—KoS—LiSf—PrRh

Dutch language
Trees ("Berkeboom"). C. Pomerantz.—PoI

Duty. See also Conduct of life
Noblesse oblige. C. T. Wright.—JaPi
Routine. A. Guiterman.—PrRh—TrM

Dwarfs
"Far over the misty mountains cold." J. R. R. Tolkien.—LiWa
"The giant is great." Unknown.—TrM

Dwellings. See Houses and dwellings

Dyer, Sir Edward
"The lowest of trees have tops, the ant her gall."—HeR

The **dying** airman. Unknown.—HeR
The **dying** child's request. Hannah F. Gould.—HaOf
The **dying** garden. Howard Nemerov.—JaPi

Dylan, Bob
Blowin' in the wind.—KeK

E

E. Phyllis McGinley.—FrP
"E is the escalator." See E
"Each birthday wish." See The wish
"Each day." See Separation
"Each day the terror wagon." See War
"Each of them must have terrified." See In
  memory of the Utah stars
"Each spring there was the well to be cleaned."
  See Cleaning the well
Eagle. Ted Hughes.—HuU
The eagle. Alfred Tennyson.—BlO—CoN—LiSf—
  PrRh
Eagle in New Mexico, sels. David Herbert
  Lawrence
  "Toward the sun, towards the south-west".—
  HeR
"An eagle is walking." See Eagle song
Eagle song. Unknown.—BiSp
Eagles
  Eagle. T. Hughes.—HuU
  The eagle. A. Tennyson.—BlO—CoN—LiSf—
  PrRh
  Eagle song. Unknown, fr. the Papago Indian.—
  BiSp
  The mole and the eagle. S. J. Hale.—HaOf
  Prayer before killing an eagle. Unknown, fr. the
  Yokuts Indian.—BiSp
  "Toward the sun, towards the south-west."
  From Eagle in New Mexico. D. H.
  Lawrence.—HeR
"Eaper Weaper, chimbley sweeper." Mother
  Goose.—AlH
Early breakfast. Beatrice Schenk De Regniers.—
  DeT
"Early, early, comes the dark." See Witches' song
"Early evening fear." See Fear
"Early May, after cold rain the sun baffling cold
  wind." See Dan
Early morning. Philip Dow.—JaD
"Early morning dawning green." See Song
"Early on the morning of Monday." See Omens
"Early one morning on Featherbed Lane." Jack
  Prelutsky.—PrRi
"Early Saturdays." See Rowing
Early spring. Philip Whalen.—JaT
"Early this morning." See The strangers
"Early to bed and early to rise." George Ade.—
  TrM
Ears
  Ears hear. L. Hymes, and J. L. Hymes.—PrRa
  The rabbit ("Hip hop hoppity, hip hop
  hoppity"). J. Prelutsky.—PrZ
Ears hear. Lucia Hymes and James L. Hymes.—
  PrRa
Earth
  The land of potpourri. J. Prelutsky.—PrRh
  The people. E. M. Roberts.—PrRh
  Under the ground. R. W. Bacmeister.—PrRa
  The underworld. M. Lavington.—PrRa
Earth (planet). See World
Earth and sky. Eleanor Farjeon.—FaE
"The earth grows green, the flowers bloom." See
  Song to the ninth grade
"Earth has not anything to show more fair." See
  Composed upon Westminster bridge, Sept. 3,
  1802

"The earth is the Lord's, and the fulness thereof."
  See Psalm 24
"The earth was green, the sky was blue." See The
  skylark
The earthworm. Harry Edmund Martinson, tr. by
  Robert Bly.—HeR
Earthy anecdote. Wallace Stevens.—HeR—LiSf
"The east is a clear violet mass." See A street
  scene
Easter
  The cherry-tree carol. Unknown.—LiE
    "Joseph was an old man" .—HaO
  "Christmas is really for the children." S.
  Turner.—HaO
  Easter ("The air is like a butterfly"). J.
  Kilmer.—PrRh
  Easter ("On Easter morn"). H. Conkling.—LiE—
  LiSf
  The Easter bunny. J. Ciardi.—LiE
  Easter disaster. J. P. Lewis.—LiE
  Easter, for Penny. M. C. Livingston.—LiCe
  Easter habits. F. Holman.—LiE
  The Easter parade. W. J. Smith.—LiE
  An Easter present. X. J. Kennedy.—LiE
  Easter song. B. Nims.—LiE
  Easter under the water. P. Neumeyer.—LiE
  Grandma's Easter bonnet. B. Katz.—LiE
  "Is Easter just a day of hats." From Easter
  morning. D. McCord.—LiE
  Kyrie Eleison. J. Aiken.—LiE
  Little catkins. A. Blok.—LiE
  Sicilian Easter Sunday. E. Di Pasquale.—LiE
  Some things that Easter brings. E. Parrish.—
  PrRa
  The sun on Easter day. N. Farber.—LiE
  These three. X. J. Kennedy.—LiE
  Written on an egg. E. Morike.—LiE
Easter ("The air is like a butterfly"). Joyce
  Kilmer.—PrRh
Easter ("On Easter morn"). Hilda Conkling.—
  LiE—LiSf
"The Easter bells are ringing." See Easter song
The Easter bunny. John Ciardi.—LiE
Easter disaster. J. Patrick Lewis.—LiE
"Easter duck and Easter chick." See Some things
  that Easter brings
Easter, for Penny. Myra Cohn Livingston.—LiCe
Easter habits. Felice Holman.—LiE
Easter morning, sels. David McCord
  "Is Easter just a day of hats".—LiE
The Easter parade. William Jay Smith.—LiE
An Easter present. X. J. Kennedy.—LiE
Easter song. Bonnie Nims.—LiE
Easter under the water. Peter Neumeyer.—LiE
Eastwick, Ivy O.
  Apple pie.—HoMu
  "The puppy chased the sunbeam."—PrRa
  Singing in the spring.—PrRa
  The stars, the dark, and the daisies.—LaW
  Ten to one.—PrRa
  Thanksgiving ("Thank you").—PrRh
"Eat an apple going to bed." Mother Goose.—
  LoR
Eat-it-all Elaine. Kaye Starbird.—LiSf—PrRh
"Eat no green apples or you'll droop." See Advice
  to small children
"Eat up your carrots and drink up your milk."
  See Sad sweet story
Eating. See Food and eating
Eating fish. George Johnston.—DoNw
Eberhart, Richard
  As if you had never been.—PlEd

Eberhart, Richard—*Continued*
   At night ("In the dust are my father's beautiful
      hands").—JaS
   Flux.—JaPi
   For a lamb.—HeR
   The fury of aerial bombardment.—HeR
   Gnat on my paper.—JaD
   Hardy perennial.—JaG
   On a squirrel crossing the road in autumn, in
      New England.—JaPi
   Reading room the New York Public Library.—
      JaG
   Sea-hawk.—HeR
   To Evan.—JaD
Echo echo. Eleanor Farjeon.—FaE
Echoes
   Advent, a carol. P. Dickinson.—HaO
   Echo echo. E. Farjeon.—FaE
   Heaven. G. Herbert.—KoT
   "The splendour falls on castle walls." From The
      princess. A. Tennyson.—LiWa
      Blow, bugle, blow.—LiSf
      Song.—BlO
Eclipse. Francis Reginald Scott.—DoNw
Eclipses
   December eclipse. M. Lockwood.—JaPi
   Eclipse. F. R. Scott.—DoNw
Ecology
   Ecology (for George Ember). L. Moore.—MoSn
   Recycled. L. Moore.—MoSn
Ecology (for George Ember). Lilian Moore.—
   MoSn
Economou, George
   Poem for a suicide.—JaD
Economy. Eleanor Farjeon.—FaE
"Eddi, priest of St. Wilfrid." See Eddi's service
"Eddie the spaghetti nut." See The spaghetti nut
Eddi's service. Rudyard Kipling.—HaO
Eddy, Mary Baker
   A verse.—LaT
Eden, Garden of
   Apple blossom. L. MacNeice.—HeR
Edenhall. Susan Coolidge.—HaOf
Edmondson, Madeleine
   Witches' spells.—CoN
Edser. Spike Milligan.—BrT
Education. Nikki Giovanni.—GiSp
Edward, Edward. Unknown.—PlAs
Edwin A. Nelms. Sheryl L. Nelms.—JaS
"Eeeveryyee time." See Trips
The eel. Ogden Nash.—CoN—RuI
Eels
   The eel. O. Nash.—CoN—RuI
   "The electric eel." From Three animals. R.
      Padgett.—KoT
   Electric eels. J. Prelutsky.—PrZ
The egg ("If you listen very carefully, you'll hear
   the"). Jack Prelutsky.—PrZ
Egg. Jay Macpherson.—DoNw
Egg talk. Michael Rosen.—BeD
Egg thoughts, soft boiled. Russell Hoban.—BeD—
   PrRh
   Soft boiled egg.—CoN
Eggs. See also Birds—Eggs and nests
   "As I was going to sell my eggs." Mother
      Goose.—DaC—LoR
   "A box without hinges, key, or lid." J. R. R.
      Tolkien.—LiSf
   The codfish. Unknown.—PrRh
   Easter disaster. J. P. Lewis.—LiE
   Easter, for Penny. M. C. Livingston.—LiCe
   An Easter present. X. J. Kennedy.—LiE

   The egg ("If you listen very carefully, you'll
      hear the"). J. Prelutsky.—PrZ
   Egg. J. Macpherson.—DoNw
   Egg talk. M. Rosen.—BeD
   Egg thoughts, soft boiled. R. Hoban.—BeD—
      PrRh
      Soft boiled egg.—CoN
   "Eggs." J. Prelutsky.—PrNk
   Finding an egg. Unknown.—GrT
   For a cock. E. Farjeon.—FaE
   Good egg. N. M. Bodecker.—BoPc
   Hallando un huevo. Unknown.—GrT
   The hen ("The hen is a ferocious fowl"). Lord
      A. Douglas.—PrRh
   The hen and the carp. I. Serraillier.—CoOu—
      LiSf
   "Hickety, pickety, my black hen." Mother
      Goose.—DeM—LoR
   "Humpty Dumpty sat on a wall." Mother
      Goose.—DeM—FaW—LoR
   "I bought a dozen new-laid eggs." Mother
      Goose. LoR
   "In marble halls as white as milk." Mother
      Goose.—FaTh
      A riddle.—BlPi
   "Little bits of soft boiled egg." F. Maschler.—
      PrRh
   "Little Blue Ben." Mother Goose.—BlQ—DeM
   Meg's egg. M. A. Hoberman.—PrRh
   "Sunny side up." A. Adoff.—LiSf
   Sunny-side-up. R. Hoban.—HoMu
   A war ("There set out, slowly, for a different
      world"). R. Jarrell.—JaD
   Written on an egg. E. Morike.—LiE
"Eggs." Jack Prelutsky.—PrNk
Egita, Charles J.
   Fruited rainbow.—HoMu
   Passing by the junkyard.—HoSs
Ego tripping. Nikki Giovanni.—JaPi
Egrets
   The common egret. P. Fleischman.—FlI
Eguren, Jose Maria
   El caballo.—LiSf
   The horse.—LiSf—LiWa
Eight o'clock. Charlotte Zolotow.—ZoE
Eight witches. B. J. Lee.—PrRh
"Eight witches rode the midnight sky." See Eight
   witches
Eleanor Paine. Mel Glenn.—GlC
"Elected silence, sing to me." See The habit of
   perfection
"The electric eel." From Three animals. Ron
   Padgett.—KoT
Electric eels. Jack Prelutsky.—PrZ
"Electric eels are rather rude." See Electric eels
Electricity
   "There was an old lady named Crockett." W.
      J. Smith.—KeK
Elegies. See Laments
Elegy ("Her face like a rain-beaten stone on the
   day she rolled off"). Theodore Roethke.—JaD
Elegy ("My Thompson, least attractive character").
   Howard Nemerov.—JaPo
Elegy for a diver. Peter Meinke.—JaPi
Elegy for a woman who remembered everything.
   David Wagoner.—JaD
Elegy for Delina. Albert Rowe.—ChC
Elegy for himself. Chidiock Tichborne.—HeR
Elegy on the death of a mad dog, complete.
   Oliver Goldsmith.—PlAs
Elegy on the death of a mad dog, sels. Oliver
   Goldsmith
   "A kind and gentle heart he had".—TrM

Elves and goblins. Harry Behn.—HoCb
Elvey, George J.
 "Come, ye thankful people, come."—LiTp
Em. Eleanor Farjeon.—FaE
"**Em** with her basket." See Em
Emanuel, James A.
 A small discovery.—LiSf
The **embarrassing** episode of Little Miss Muffet.
  Guy Wetmore Carryl.—HaOf
Embury, Emma C.
 The pilgrim ("Father, I have launched my
  bark").—HaOf
"An **emerald** is as green as grass." See Flint
Emerson, Ralph Waldo
 Beyond winter.—PrRh
 Fable ("The mountain and the squirrel").—HaOf
 "The hand that rounded Peter's dome." See The
  problem
 The problem, sels.
  "The hand that rounded Peter's dome".—
   PlEd
Emigration. See Immigration and emigration
Empty holds a question. Pat Folk.—JaG
The **empty** house. Russell Hoban.—LiWa
Emre, Yunus
 "The whole universe is full of God."—McL
Enchanted summer. Harry Behn.—HoCb
Enchantment. See also Charms; Magic
 La belle dame sans merci ("O, what can ail
  thee, knight at arms"). J. Keats.—HeR—
  LiWa—PlAs
 The crystal cabinet. W. Blake.—PlAs
 "Her strong enchantments failing." A. E.
  Housman.—KeK
 "In the touch of this bosom there worketh a
  spell." From Christabel. S. T. Coleridge.—
  HeR
 Tam Lin ("O, I forbid you, maidens a'").
  Unknown.—PlAs
   Tamlane (". . . maidens all").—LiWa
 Tam Lin ("She's ta'en her petticoat by the
  band"). Unknown.—PlAs
 Thomas Rymer ("True Thomas lay on Huntlie
  bank"). Unknown.—HeR
   Thomas Rymer (". . . o'er yond grassy
    bank").—PlAs
Enchantment. Harry Behn.—HoCb
Encounter. Lilian Moore.—MoSn
End of summer. Stanley Kunitz
End of winter. Eve Merriam.—MeSk
"The **end** of winter seeped up." See Julian barely
 misses Zimmer's brains
End song. Ruth Krauss.—McL
The **ending** of the year. Eleanor Farjeon.—FaE
The **enemy's** portrait. Thomas Hardy.—PlEd
England
 The four dears. E. Elliot.—PlSc
 Jerusalem. From Milton. W. Blake.—HeR
 Kerr's ass. P. Kavanagh.—HeR
 Teeth. S. Milligan.—TrM
 "Tommy waved his stick about." Unknown.—
  TrM
 What Jenner said on hearing in Elysium that
  complaints had been made of his having a
  statue in Trafalgar Square. S. Brooks.—PlEd
England—History
 "As I lay asleep in Italy." From The mask of
  anarchy. P. B. Shelley.—HeR
 The death of Admiral Benbow. Unknown.—BlO
 History ("Willy, Willy, Harry, Steve").
  Unknown.—DaC

 An ode to the framers of the Frame Bill. Lord
  Byron.—PlSc
 Song, to the men of England. P. B. Shelley.—
  PlSc
 "This day is call'd the feast of Crispian." From
  Henry V. W. Shakespeare.—HoUn
 Tudor portrait. R. Lattimore.—PlEd
 The Vicar of Bray. Unknown.—PlAs
"**England's** ingratitude still blots." See What
 Jenner said on hearing in Elysium that
 complaints had been made of his having a
 statue in Trafalgar Square
Engle, Paul
 Together.—PrRh
English. Eleanor Farjeon.—FaE
English language
 English. E. Farjeon.—FaE
English oak. Myra Cohn Livingston.—LiMp
"**English** teeth, English teeth." See Teeth
Engraved on the collar of a dog, which I gave
  to his Royal Highness. Alexander Pope.—KoT
 His highness's dog.—PrRh (unat.)
 Epigram engraved on the collar of a dog.—
  CoN—KeK
Engvik, William
 Where do you sleep.—LaW
Ennui. Langston Hughes.—HaOf
"**Enough** oil to last, they cry." See At Hannukah
Enright, J. D.
 Along the river.—JaD
"**Enthused** by flickers and coots." See Bird
 watcher
"**Enthusiastically** hurting a clouded yellow bud
 and." See A new cup and saucer
Envy. See also Jealousy
 Catholics. C. Rylant.—RyW
 Changing. M. A. Hoberman.—HoBf—PrRh
 The country mouse and the city mouse. R. S.
  Sharpe.—DaC
 "I raised a great hullabaloo." Unknown.—PrRh
 Mary Stuart. E. Muir.—HeR
 Overheard on a saltmarsh. H. Monro.—LiSf—
  LiWa
 Seizure. Sappho.—McL
 "When, in disgrace with fortune and men's
  eyes." From Sonnets. W. Shakespeare.—HoUn
"**Eons** ago, when the earth was still yeasty." See
 Leopard
Eoyang, Eugene
 "An old charcoal seller", tr. by.—PlSc
"An **epicure**, dining at Crewe." Unknown.—CoN
Epigram engraved on the collar of a dog. See
 Engraved on the collar of a dog, which I
 gave to his Royal Highness
Epigrams. J. V. Cunningham.—HeR
Epilogue. Denise Levertov.—McL
Epiphany. See Magi
Epiphany, for the artist. Elizabeth Sewell.—PlEd
An **epitaph** ("Here lies a most beautiful lady").
 Walter De la Mare.—HeR
Epitaph ("What is this stone he's laid upon my
 bones"). Eleanor Farjeon.—FaE
Epitaph for a persian kitten. Miriam Vedder.—
 ChC
Epitaph on a hare. William Cowper.—BlO
Epitaph on a tyrant. Wystan Hugh Auden.—HeR
Epitaph on a waiter. David McCord.—JaPo
Epitaph on an army of mercenaries. Alfred
 Edward Housman.—HeR—PlSc
Epitaph on an engraver. Henry David Thoreau.—
 PlEd

Epitaph on an unfortunate artist. Robert Graves.—TrM
Epitaph on Martha Snell. Unknown.—BlO
Epitaph on the Earl of Leicester. Sir Walter Raleigh.—HeR
Epitaphs
  Afterwards. T. Hardy.—HeR
  Another epitaph on an army of mercenaries. H. MacDiarmid.—HeR
  Cardinal Bembo's epitaph on Raphael. P. Bembo, Cardinal.—PlEd
  Death of an old seaman. L. Hughes.—HuDk
  Dirge. K. Fearing.—HeR
  An epitaph ("Here lies a most beautiful lady"). W. De la Mare.—HeR
  Epitaph ("What is this stone he's laid upon my bones"). E. Farjeon.—FaE
  Epitaph on a hare. W. Cowper.—BlO
  Epitaph on a tyrant. W. H. Auden.—HeR
  Epitaph on a waiter. D. McCord.—JaPo
  Epitaph on an army of mercenaries. A. E. Housman.—HeR—PlSc
  Epitaph on an engraver. H. D. Thoreau.—PlEd
  Epitaph on an unfortunate artist. R. Graves.—TrM
  Epitaph on Martha Snell. Unknown.—BlO
  Epitaph on the Earl of Leicester. Sir W. Raleigh.—HeR
  Here lies a lady. J. C. Ransom.—HeR
  "Here lies Fred." Unknown.—DaC
  "Here lies old Hobson, death hath broke his girt." J. Milton.—PlSc
  In memory of George Whitby, architect. Sir J. Betjeman.—PlEd
  Remember me. J. Viorst.—ViI
  "Solomon Grundy." Mother Goose.—AlH—FaW—LoR—PrRh
  Tombstone. L. Hymes, and J. L. Hymes.—PrRh
Eric Theodore. Mel Glenn.—GlC
The **Erie** Canal. Unknown.—LiIl
The **erl-king**. Johann Wolfgang von Goethe, tr. by Sir Walter Scott.—LiWa
Ernest Mott. Mel Glenn.—GlC
The **errand**. Harry Behn.—HoCb
Esau and Kate. Unknown.—PaM
Esbensen, Barbara Juster
  At the pool.—EsCs
  Blizzard.—EsCs
  Campsite.—EsCs
  Cardinal ("Red as a shout").—EsCs
  December hills.—EsCs
  Drought.—EsCs
  Exchange.—EsCs
  Fairy tale ("They don't tell you").—EsCs
  First day of school.—EsCs
  First snowfall ("Out of the grey").—BaS—EsCs
  The first Thanksgiving ("For a long time").—LiTp
  Flyaway.—EsCs
  The fourteenth day of Adar.—LiPj
  Fourth of July ("Tonight the air explodes").—EsCs
  A Halloween ghost story.—EsCs
  Icicles.—EsCs
  Indian summer ("Raise the curtain").—EsCs
  June ("Everything is light").—EsCs
  The lake ("This winter day").—EsCs
  Last day of school ("Look out").—EsCs
  Looking down in the rain.—EsCs
  March twenty-first.—EsCs
  May first, two inches of snow.—EsCs
  The Milky Way.—EsCs
  Mittens.—EsCs

  Morning ("The April day").—EsCs
  Mud ("Your fingers can take").—EsCs
  Nocturne for late summer.—EsCs
  Now that spring is here.—EsCs
  Passage ("Remember").—EsCs
  Perseid meteor shower.—EsCs
  Questions for September.—EsCs
  Saturday in the park.—EsCs
  Sled run.—EsCs
  Snow print one, mystery.—EsCs
  Snow print two, hieroglyphics.—EsCs—FaTh
  Snow stars.—EsCs
  Spring cleaning.—EsCs
  Spring fever.—EsCs
  Storm ("There has never been a wind").—EsCs
  Two ways to look at kites.—EsCs
  Umbrellas ("Umbrellas bloom").—PrRa
  A valentine birthday.—LiVp
  Wake up call.—EsCs
  Walking past the school at night.—EsCs
  Wind stories.—EsCs
  Woolly bear caterpillar ("Darkness comes early").—EsCs
Escalators
  Air on an escalator. J. Aiken.—LiSf
  E. P. McGinley.—FrP
  For a quick exit. N. Farber.—HoCl—KeK
Eskimo. See Indians of the Americas—Eskimo
Eskimo chant. Unknown, tr. by Knud Rasmussen.—DoNw
España, aparta de me este Caliz, sels. Cesar Vallejo, tr. by Robert Bly
  Masses.—HeR
"Este nino hallo un huevo." See Hallando un huevo
The **eternal** city. Archie Randolph Ammons.—PlEd
The **eternal** feminine. Oliver Herford.—BrT
Eternity. See also Infinity
  The ancients of the world. R. S. Thomas.—HeR
  Crazy dog song. Unknown, fr. the Kiowa Indian.—HeR
  Eternity. W. Blake.—HeR
  The muskellunge. T. Hughes.—HuU
  Song's eternity. J. Clare.—PlAs
Eternity. William Blake.—HeR
Euphonica Jarre. Jack Prelutsky.—PrNk
"Euphonica Jarre has a voice that's bizarre." See Euphonica Jarre
Evans, David Allan
  Bullfrogs.—JaPi
  Ford pickup.—JaPo
  Neighbors ("They live alone").—JaPi
  Retired farmer.—JaPi
  The sound of rain.—JaG
  The story of Lava.—JaPi
  Sunset ("Before I left my spot").—JaPo
  Uncle Claude.—JaS
Eve. See Adam and Eve
"Even if you can't shape your life the way you want it." See As much as you can
Even such is time. Sir Walter Raleigh.—HeR
"Even such is time, which takes in trust." See Even such is time
"Even the rainbow has a body." See The rainbow
"Even this late it happens." See The coming of light
Evening. See also Night
  Address to a child during a boisterous winter evening. D. Wordsworth.—BlO
  After tea. E. Farjeon.—FaE
  Again, good night. C. Zolotow.—ZoE
  The children's hour. H. W. Longfellow.—HaOf

"**Evicted** from sleep's mute palace." See Shaker, why don't you sing
Eviction. Lucille Clifton.—CoN
Evolution
Humming-bird ("I can imagine, in some otherworld"). D. H. Lawrence.—HeR—PrBb
Mosquito ("To get into life"). T. Hughes.—HuU
Sometimes ("Sometimes, when a bird cries out"). H. Hesse.—LiWa
Exactly. Roberta Metz.—FaTh
Excelsior. Henry Wadsworth Longfellow.—HaOf
Exchange. Barbara Juster Esbensen.—EsCs
"!! !! ! !" See Showers, clearing later in the day
The **exclusive** old oyster. Laura A. Steel.—BrT
Excursion. Eve Merriam.—MeF
Executions
Danny Deever. R. Kipling.—PlAs
Elegy for himself. C. Tichborne.—HeR
Georgie. Unknown.—PlAs
The maid freed from the gallows. Unknown.—PlAs
Mary Hamilton. Unknown.—PlAs
Exeunt. Richard Wilbur.—JaPi
Exler, Samuel
The cats.—JaG
"**Expecting** to be put in a sack and dumped in a ditch." See Nightmare
Expert. Unknown.—BrT
An **explanation** of the grasshopper. Vachel Lindsay.—PrRa
Exploding gravy. X. J. Kennedy.—LiSf
Explorers and exploration. See also names of explorers as Columbus, Christopher
Bermudas. A. Marvell.—HeR
Columbus to Ferdinand. P. Freneau.—HaOf
The **explosion.** Philip Larkin.—HeR
Exposure. Wilfred Owen.—HeR
"**Express** blizzards rumble, a horizontal snow-haulage." See The musk-ox
"An **extinct** old ichthyosaurus." See The ichthyosaurus
Extinction. See also names of extinct animals, as Auks
Buffalo dusk. C. Sandburg.—HaOf—HoRa—LiSf—PrRh
Dodo. H. Carlile.—JaPi
The flower-fed buffaloes. V. Lindsay.—HaOf—HeR
The great auk's ghost. R. Hodgson.—KeK—PrRh
How the end might have been. I. J. Glaser.—HoDi
"The last dinosaur." V. D. Najjar.—HoDi
Long gone. J. Prelutsky.—PrRh—PrZ
The passenger pigeon. P. Fleischman.—FlI
The whale ghost. L. Moore.—MoSn
"The **eye** can hardly pick them out." See At grass
Eyes
At night ("When night is dark"). A. Fisher.—LiSf—PrRa
At the keyhole. W. De la Mare.—BlO
Cat ("My cat"). D. Baruch.—ChC
The cat ("Within that porch, across the way"). W. H. Davies.—BlO—ChC
The dancing bear ("Slowly he turns himself round and round"). R. Field.—CoN—KeK
The fallow deer at the lonely house. T. Hardy.—BlO—HeR—KoT
Glass walling. N. M. Bodecker.—BoPc
Green ("The dawn was apple green"). D. H. Lawrence.—PrBb
The marvel. K. Douglas.—HeR
Night eyes. R. J. Margolis.—MaS

"**Paul**, in Aunt Pru's prune surprise." X. J. Kennedy.—KeB
"**Peep-eye**." C. Watson.—WaC
"**Poor** potatoes underground." J. Prelutsky.—PrRi
Rutherford McDowell. E. L. Masters.—PlEd
Sea-hawk. R. Eberhart.—HeR
Sunny-side-up. R. Hoban.—HoMu
"There was a young lady whose eyes." E. Lear.—LiH
True. L. Moore.—MoSn
The two cats. E. Coatsworth.—JaT—LiIl

F

Fable ("The mountain and the squirrel"). Ralph Waldo Emerson.—HaOf
Fable ("Once upon a time"). Janos Pilinszky, tr. by Ted Hughes.—HeR
Fable ("Pity the girl with the crystal hair"). Joan Aiken.—LiWa
Fables
A. From A bestiary of the garden for children who should know better. P. Gotlieb.—DoNw
Ants, although admirable, are awfully aggravating. W. R. Brooks.—PrRh
The blind men and the elephant. J. G. Saxe.—CoOu—HaOf
The country mouse and the city mouse. R. S. Sharpe.—DaC
Fable ("The mountain and the squirrel"). R. W. Emerson.—HaOf
Fable ("Once upon a time"). J. Pilinszky.—HeR
Fable ("Pity the girl with the crystal hair"). J. Aiken.—LiWa
The flattered flying fish. E. V. Rieu.—PrRh
The mouse and the cake. E. Cook.—DaC
The spider and the fly. M. Howitt.—CoOu—DaC
The sycophantic fox and the gullible raven. G. W. Carryl.—HaOf
"The **fabulous** wizard of Oz." Unknown.—BrT
The **face** of the horse. Nikolai Alekseevich Zabolotsky, tr. by Daniel Weissbort.—HeR
Faces
Art work. R. Wallace.—JaPo
The bat ("By day the bat is cousin to the mouse"). T. Roethke.—HaOf—LiSf—LiWa—PrRh
Bog-face. S. Smith.—HeR
Conversation with myself. E. Merriam.—MeSk
"Everybody says." D. Aldis.—HoSu—PrRh
The face of the horse. N. A. Zabolotsky.—HeR
Freckles. A. Fisher.—HoSu
Godmother. P. B. Morden.—PrRh
"Head bumper." Unknown.—RaT
"Here sits the Lord Mayor." Mother Goose.—RaT
Heredity. T. Hardy.—HeR
Horrible things. R. Fuller.—CoOu
Houses ("Houses are faces"). A. Fisher.—CoN
"I never forget a face." G. Marx.—TrM
"In the mirror." E. Fleming.—CoOu
"Looking at your face." G. Kinnell.—JaPo
The mandrill. C. Aiken.—PrRh
Mask. E. Merriam.—MeHa
"Mirror, mirror, over the sink." A. Lobel.—LoWr
Nature's lineaments. R. Graves.—HeR
Noses. A. Fisher.—FaW

Faces—*Continued*

The old familiar faces. C. Lamb.—HeR
"Oysters." J. Prelutsky.—PrZ—RuI
Pansies. C. Zolotow.—ZoE
Passing the Masonic home for the aged. H. Scott.—JaPo
Phizzog. C. Sandburg.—HoRa—LiSf
Portrait by Alice Neel. A. Kramer.—PlEd
The prayer of the monkey. C. B. de Gasztold.—LaT
"Ring the bell." Mother Goose.—RaT
Robert, who is often a stranger to himself. G. Brooks.—PrRa
Shagbark hickory. M. C. Livingston.—LiMp
Someone's face. J. Ciardi.—PrRa
A song ("I have the fore"). A. Adoff.—AdA
Spring storm ("He comes gusting out of the house"). J. W. Miller.—JaG
A strange meeting ("The moon is full, and so am I"). W. H. Davies.—BlO
"There was a young lady whose chin." E. Lear.—LiH
"There was an old person of Down." E. Lear.—LiH
A toad. E. A. Allen.—HaOf
"Two little eyes." Unknown.—RaT
Two masks unearthed in Bulgaria. W. Meredith.—PlEd
"**Faces,** voices, yes of course." See The house remembers

Factories

"Ah leave my harp and me alone." Unknown.—PlSc
Butch Weldy. E. L. Masters.—PlSc
Changsha shoe factory. W. Barnstone.—PlSc
Driving at dawn. W. Heyen.—PlSc
Factory girl ("No more shall I work in the factory"). Unknown.—PlSc
The factory girl ("She wasn't the least bit pretty"). J. A. Phillips.—PlSc
A factory rainbow. R. Saadi.—PlSc
"Factory windows are always broken." V. Lindsay.—HaOf
"In the coal pit, or the factory." J. Skipsey.—PlSc
"In the evening I would sit." From Journal. E. S. Millay.—PlSc
The little factory girl to a more fortunate playmate. Unknown.—PlSc
A lone striker. R. Frost.—PlSc
An ode to the framers of the Frame Bill. Lord Byron.—PlSc
"Oh, isn't it a pity, such a pretty girl as I." H. H. Robinson.—PlSc
Song of the factory girls. Unknown.—PlSc
The song of the factory worker. R. Collins.—PlSc
Willis Beggs. E. L. Masters.—PlSc
You on the tower. T. Hardy.—PlSc
Factory girl ("No more shall I work in the factory"). Unknown.—PlSc
The factory girl ("She wasn't the least bit pretty"). J. A. Phillips.—PlSc
A factory rainbow. Rose Saadi.—PlSc
"Factory windows are always broken." Vachel Lindsay.—HaOf

Failure

About being very good and far better than most but still not quite good enough to take on the Atlantic Ocean ("There was a fine swimmer named Jack"). J. Ciardi.—CiD
On being much better than most and yet not quite good enough (". . . a great swimmer named Jack").—JaG
Casey at the bat. E. L. Thayer.—HaOf
"Nobody loses all the time." E. E. Cummings.—HeR
The radiance. Kabir.—McL
Robin Gold. M. Glenn.—GlC
Trying. L. Nathan.—JaS
"**Fair** daffodils we weep to see." See To daffodils
The **fair** maid of Amsterdam. Unknown.—HeR
"The **fair** maid who, the first of May." Mother Goose.—AlH
Fair warning. Norah Smaridge.—HoSi

Fairchild, B. H.

Shooting.—JaT

Fairies

After many springs. L. Hughes.—HuDk
The beggar to Mab, the fairie Queen. R. Herrick.—LiWa
Behind the waterfall. W. Welles.—LiSf
La belle dame sans merci ("O, what can ail thee, knight at arms"). J. Keats.—HeR—LiWa—PlAs
Bobadil. J. Reeves.—LiSf
The brownies' celebration. P. Cox.—HaOf
"Canst thou imagine where those spirits live." From Prometheus unbound. P. B. Shelley.—LiWa
"Come, now a roundel and a fairy song." From A midsummer night's dream. W. Shakespeare.—HoUn
"Come unto these yellow sands." From The tempest. W. Shakespeare.—BlO—KoT
Could it have been a shadow. M. Shannon.—PrRh
The darkling elves. J. Prelutsky.—PrRh
Dinky. T. Roethke.—HaOf—LiSf—PrRh
Do fairies like the rain. B. M. Hales.—HoCr
Edenhall. S. Coolidge.—HaOf
Elf. E. Merriam.—MeHa
The elf and the dormouse. O. Herford.—PrRh
The elfin knight. Unknown.—LiWa
Elfin town. R. Field.—LiWa
Elves and goblins. H. Behn.—HoCb
Enchantment. H. Behn.—HoCb
The erl-king. J. W. von Goethe.—LiWa
An explanation of the grasshopper. V. Lindsay.—PrRa
Fairies ("Don't go looking for fairies"). E. Farjeon.—FaE—PrRa
Fairies ("I cannot see fairies"). H. Conkling.—LiWa
The fairies ("If ye will with Mab find grace"). R. Herrick.—BlO
Fairies ("Out of the dust of dreams"). L. Hughes.—HuDk
The fairies ("See the fairies dancing in"). P. Hubbell.—LiWa
The fairies ("Up the airy mountain"). W. Allingham.—BlO—LiWa—PrRh
Fairies ("What could have frightened them away"). H. Behn.—HoCb
The fairy and the bird. H. Behn.—HoCb
Fairy tale ("They don't tell you"). B. J. Esbensen.—EsCs
Fairyland. Sir R. Tagore.—LiWa

Fairies—*Continued*

For a mocking voice. E. Farjeon.—LiSf
The gnome. H. Behn.—HoCb—HoCr
The goblin. R. Fyleman.—CoN
Green riders. R. Field.—FaTh
Hob gobbling's song. J. R. Lowell.—HaOf
How to tell goblins from elves. M. Shannon.—PrRh
How to treat elves. M. Bishop.—HaOf
"I dream'd a dream tonight." From Romeo and Juliet. W. Shakespeare.—HoUn
"I know a bank where the wild thyme blows." From A midsummer night's dream. W. Shakespeare.—HoUn
"I see their knavery, this is to make an ass of me, to fright me." From A midsummer night's dream. W. Shakespeare.—HoUn
The king of the hobbledygoblins. L. E. Richards.—HaOf
The king's son. T. Boyd.—PlAs
Klabauterwife's letter. C. Morgenstern.—LiWa
The little elf. J. K. Bangs.—CoN—HaOf—PrRa
   The little elfman.—CoOu—LiSf
Little orphant Annie. J. W. Riley.—HaOf
Lollocks. R. Graves.—HeR
Midsummer eve. E. Farjeon.—FaE
Morning magic. H. Behn.—HoCb
"Ms. Whatchamacallit Thingamajig." M. Chaikin.—PrRh
"Musetta of the mountains." J. Reeves.—LiSf
The nine little goblins. J. W. Riley.—HaOf
"Now the hungry lion roars." From A midsummer night's dream. W. Shakespeare.—LiWa
"O, then, I see Queen Mab hath been with you." From Romeo and Juliet. W. Shakespeare.—LiWa
"Over hill, over dale." From A midsummer night's dream. W. Shakespeare.—BlO—HoUn
Overheard on a saltmarsh. H. Monro.—LiSf—LiWa
The plumppuppets. C. Morley.—PrRh
The pointed people. R. Field.—LiWa
The Queen of Elfan's nourice. Unknown.—PlAs
Sea fairies. P. Hubbell.—HoCr
The seven ages of elfhood. R. Field.—HoCr—PrRh
"She is the fairies' midwife, and she comes." From Romeo and Juliet. W. Shakespeare.—HeR
The song of wandering Aengus. W. B. Yeats.—BlO—KoT—LiWa
The stolen child. W. B. Yeats.—LiWa
The tale of Lilla. E. Farjeon.—FaE
Tam Lin ("O, I forbid you, maidens a'"). Unknown.—PlAs
   Tamlane (". . . maidens all").—LiWa
Tam Lin ("She's ta'en her petticoat by the band"). Unknown.—PlAs
"There was a ship a-sailing." Mother Goose.—RoC
   "I saw a ship a-sailing".—CoN
Thomas Rymer ("True Thomas lay on Huntlie bank"). Unknown.—HeR
   Thomas Rymer (". . . o'er yond grassy bank").—PlAs
"Thrice tosse these oaken ashes in the ayre." T. Campion.—LiWa
"Through the house give glimmering light." From A midsummer night's dream. W. Shakespeare.—HoUn
"Tippetty Witchet." E. Farjeon.—FaE

To mother fairie. A. Cary.—HaOf
The toadstool wood. J. Reeves.—FaTh—LiWa
The twelve elf. C. Morgenstern.—LiWa
The visitant. T. Roethke.—HeR
"What is the opposite of a prince." R. Wilbur.—LiSf—LiWa
Where goblins dwell. J. Prelutsky.—PrRh
"Where the bee sucks, there suck I." From The tempest. W. Shakespeare.—BlO—HoUn—KoT
"The wind blows out of the gates of the day." From The land of heart's desire. W. B. Yeats.—HeR
Wrimples. J. Prelutsky.—PrRh
"You spotted snakes with double tongue." From A midsummer night's dream. W. Shakespeare.—BlO—HoUn—LiWa
Fairies ("Don't go looking for fairies"). Eleanor Farjeon.—FaE—PrRa
Fairies ("I cannot see fairies"). Hilda Conkling.—LiWa
The **fairies** ("If ye will with Mab find grace"). Robert Herrick.—BlO
Fairies ("Out of the dust of dreams"). Langston Hughes.—HuDk
The **fairies** ("See the fairies dancing in"). Patricia Hubbell.—LiWa
The **fairies** ("Up the airy mountain"). William Allingham.—BlO—LiWa—PrRh
Fairies ("What could have frightened them away"). Harry Behn.—HoCb
Fairs

The animal fair. Unknown.—CoN—PrRh
"As I was going to Banbury." Mother Goose.—DeM
Between you and me. S. Hazo.—JaG
"Clip-clop, clippity-clop." C. Watson.—WaC
Excursion. E. Merriam.—MeF
The grand county fair. J. Prelutsky.—PrWi
"Jill came from the fair." E. Farjeon.—FaE
The market. J. Stephens.—PlAs
"Oh, dear, what can the matter be." Mother Goose.—FaW—LoR
   "O, dear, what can the matter be".—DeM
One-night fair. N. Price.—JaG
"Simple Simon met a pieman." Mother Goose.—DeM—FaW—LiSf—LoR
"Sue went to the fair." E. Farjeon.—FaE
"Tomorrow's the fair." Unknown.—PrRh
Whittingham Fair. Unknown.—PlAs
The **fairy** and the bird. Harry Behn.—HoCb
Fairy tale ("He built himself a house"). Miroslav Holub, tr. by George Theiner.—HeR
Fairy tale ("They don't tell you"). Barbara Juster Esbensen.—EsCs
Fairyland. Sir Rabindranath Tagore.—LiWa
Faith

Butch Weldy. E. L. Masters.—PlSc
Carlos Rodriguez. M. Glenn.—GlCd
Carol for the last Christmas eve. N. Nicholson.—HaO
Dandelions. H. Nemerov.—JaD
Death-bed reflections of Michelangelo. H. Coleridge.—PlEd
Grandfather's heaven. N. S. Nye.—JaS
Grandmother. H. Carlile.—JaD
The hammer. C. Sandburg.—HoRa
Huswifery. E. Taylor.—PlSc
"I never saw a moor." E. Dickinson.—LaT—LiSf
   Certainty.—DaC
January one. D. McCord.—LiNe
Journey of the Magi. T. S. Eliot.—HaO

Faith—*Continued*
The leg. K. Shapiro.—JaD
Lepanto. G. K. Chesterton.—HeR
Ma Lord. L. Hughes.—HuDk
Mashkin Hill. L. Simpson.—PlSc
Meet-on-the-road ("Now, pray, where are you going, said Meet-on-the-road"). Unknown.—BlO
    Meet-on-the-road ("Now, pray, where are you going, child").—KoT
The oxen ("Christmas eve, and twelve of the clock"). T. Hardy.—HaO—HeR—RoC
The pilgrim ("Father, I have launched my bark"). E. C. Embury.—HaOf
Prayer ("God, though this life is but a wraith"). L. Untermeyer.—LaT
Prayer to the moon. Unknown.—LaT
Psalm of a black mother. T. Greenwood.—LaT
Religion. M. Malloy.—LaT
Saved. C. Rylant.—RyW
Song for Dov Shamir. D. Abse.—LaT
Upon Fairford windows. R. Corbett.—PlEd
"Well, so that is that, now we must dismantle the tree." From For the time being. W. H. Auden.—HaO
"What can I give him." C. G. Rossetti.—LiCp
    My gift.—LaT
Faith Plotkin. Mel Glenn.—GlC
The **faking** boy. Unknown.—HeR
"The **faking** boy to the trap is gone." See The faking boy
"The **falcon** soars." See Angelica the doorkeeper
Fall. See Autumn
Fall journey. William Stafford.—JaS
Fall wind ("Everything is on the run"). Aileen Fisher.—HoSi
Fall wind ("Pods of summer crowd around the door"). William Stafford.—JaPo
"The **fallen** leaves are cornflakes." See December leaves
Falling asleep. Ian Serraillier.—FaW
The **falling** star. Sara Teasdale.—HaOf—LiSf
The **fallow** deer at the lonely house. Thomas Hardy.—BlO—HeR—KoT
False start. Charlotte Zolotow.—ZoE
Falsehood. See Truthfulness and falsehood
Fame
    Charlotte Bronte. S. Coolidge.—HaOf
    The codfish. Unknown.—PrRh
    "I'm nobody, who are you." E. Dickinson.—HaOf—LiSf—PrRh—TrM
    Soup. C. Sandburg.—HaOf—HoRa
Familiar friends. James S. Tippett.—HoDl
Family. See Children and childhood; Home and family life; Married life; Relatives
Family affairs. Maya Angelou.—AnS
Family cups. Steve Orlen.—JaS
Family needs. Unknown.—LiSf
Family reunion ("Sunlight glints off the chrome of many cars"). Jim Wayne Miller.—JaS
Family reunion ("Thanksgiving day, our family"). X. J. Kennedy.—LiTp
Fantasia ("I dream"). Eve Merriam.—MeSk
Fantasia ("The old grand piano"). Leonard Nathan.—JaPo
Fanthorpe, U. A.
    BC, AD.—HaO
    Reindeer report.—HaO
    What the donkey saw.—HaO
Far away. David McCord.—McAs
"**Far** different dejection once was mine." See Crossing the Alps
"**Far,** far will I go." Unknown.—LiSf

"**Far** from far." See Bobadil
"**Far** from home across the sea." Mother Goose.—LoR
"**Far** in the east, far below." See House song to the east
"**Far** out at sea the pretty mermaid." See Mermaid's music
"**Far** over the misty mountains cold." John Ronald Reuel Tolkien.—LiWa
Far trek. June Brady.—PrRh
Farber, Norma
    "As I was crossing Boston Common."—FaW
    Bye baby walnut.—FaTh
    Come learn of Mary.—LiCp
    For a quick exit.—HoCl—KeK
    In a starry orchard.—LiSf
    Manhattan lullabye.—HoSs
    Oh the toe test.—PrRh
    Spendthrift.—LiSf
    Sun after rain.—HoSu—PrRa
    Sun for breakfast.—HoSu
    The sun on Easter day.—LiE
    Winter's tale.—FaTh
"**Farewell,** thou child of my right hand, and joy." See On my first sonne
"**Farewell** to barn and stack and tree." Alfred Edward Housman.—PlAs
A **farewell** to Kingsbridge. Unknown.—PlAs
Farewell to the old year. Eleanor Farjeon.—FaE
Farewells. See also Parting
    "Adieu, farewell earth's bliss." From Summer's last will and testament. T. Nashe.—HeR
    Dido's farewell. L. Pastan.—JaG
    Different kinds of goodby. C. Sandburg.—HoRa
    "Farewell to barn and stack and tree." A. E. Housman.—PlAs
    A farewell to Kingsbridge. Unknown.—PlAs
    Farewell to the old year. E. Farjeon.—FaE
    Good night ("Many ways to spell good night"). C. Sandburg.—HoRa
    A July goodbye. R. J. Margolis.—MaS
    The lady's farewell. N. Fernandez Torneol.—PlAs
    On my first sonne. B. Jonson.—HeR
    The poet's farewell to his teeth. W. Dickey.—JaD
    Song of farewell to the deceased. Unknown, fr. the Quechua Indian.—BiSp
    Splinter. C. Sandburg.—HaOf—HoRa—KeK
    Woman's song. Unknown, fr. the Chippewa Indian.—BiSp
Farjeon, Eleanor
    After rain.—FaE
    After tea.—FaE
    Air balloons.—FaE
    Alphabet.—FaE
    Ambush.—FaE
    Annar-Mariar's Christmas shopping.—FaE
    The archer.—FaE
    Autumn crocus.—FaE
    Autumn rain.—FaE
    Baby stands.—FaE
    Bedtime ("Five minutes, five minutes more, please").—FaE—FrP—PrRa
    The bell in the leaves.—FaE
    Bell song.—FaE
    "The bells in the valley."—FaE
    Bethlehem bells.—FaE
    Between the bars.—FaE
    The birds know.—FaE
    Blind alley.—FaE
    Bliss.—FaE—PrRh
    Blow the stars home.—FaE

Farjeon, Eleanor—*Continued*
The lost farthing.—FaE
A manger song.—FaE
The mark.—FaE
Marmalade.—FaE
Mary indoors.—FaE
Mary's burden.—FaE
Mary's one.—FaE
May meadows.—FaE
Meeting Mary.—FaE
The mellow time.—FaE
Midsummer eve.—FaE
The milk cart pony.—FaE
Minnie.—FaE
Missy Sinkins.—FaE
"Mrs. Peck Pigeon."—CoN—CoOu—FaE—LiSf
Moon ("Who knows why I stand and bay at her").—FaE
"Moon-come-out."—FaE—PrRa
Moonlight ("Now, look, the big moon shines").—FaE
Morning glory.—FaE
Morning light.—FaE
The mother sings.—FaE
The mother's song ("She knew, the maiden mother knew").—FaE
The mother's tale.—FaE
The mummers.—FaE
Music ("Can you dance").—FaE
Nan ("It's").—FaE
Nearly.—FaE
Ned ("It's a singular thing that Ned").—FaE
New clothes and old.—BeD
News, news.—FaE
"The night will never stay."—CoN—FaE—FaW—LaW
Nine red horsemen.—FaE
Nothing ("He's gone").—FaE
Now every child.—FaE
Numbers ("There are hundreds of numbers, they mount up so high").—FaE
Oh hark.—FaE
Ol' red thief.—FaE
The old man's toes.—FaE
Old wife's song.—FaE
On the staircase.—FaE
Organ grinder.—FaE
Ornithology.—FaE
Our mother's tunes.—FaE
Outside.—FaE
"Over the garden wall."—FaE
Pantomime.—FaE
The pear tree.—FaE
The peddler.—FaE
Pencil and paint.—FaE
Penny royal.—FaE
Peter.—FaE
"Please God, take care of little things."—LaT
Poetry.—FaE—PrRh
The quarrel.—FaE
Questions ("The questions they ask").—FaE
Ragged robin.—FaE
Rainbow ("Oh, my pretty rainbow").—FaE
Rats.—FaE
Rhyme ("Two legs will bear a marching man").—FaE
Riding in Belmary.—FaE
The riding of the kings.—FaE
Robin to Jenny.—FaE
Rules ("All schools").—FaE
Sand ("The sand is the sand, till you take it").—FaE
School bell.—FaE

The second birth of roses.—FaE
Seven sisters roses.—FaE
"Shall I to the byre go down."—FaE
"The shepherd and the king."—FaE
"Sing for your supper."—FaE
Sisters.—FaE
Six green singers.—FaE
The smoke.—FaE
Snow ("Oh the falling snow").—FaE
Snow in the garden.—FaE
Snowfall.—FaE
Soldiers and horses.—FaE
Some one to tea.—FaE
The song of the fir.—FaE
"The sounds in the evening."—FaE
"The sounds in the morning."—FaE
Spoilt child.—FaE
Spring in Hampstead.—FaE
The start.—FaE
Stocking time.—FaE
A stocking to fill.—FaE
Strawberries ("Ripe, ripe strawberries").—FaE
The street fountain.—FaE
"Sue went to the fair."—FaE
Summer fountains.—FaE
Sun and wind.—FaE
Sweet ass.—FaE
Sweet herbs.—FaE
The sweetstuff wife.—FaE
Take heart, sweet Mary, tr. by.—FaE
The tale of Lilla.—FaE
The talking of the trees.—FaE
Teacher ("Teacher's tall and teacher's short").—FaE
There are big waves. See Waves ("There's big waves and little waves")
There isn't time.—FaE
This holy night.—FaE
This year, next year.—FaE
Through a shop window.—FaE
"The tide in the rive."—BlO
"Tippetty Witchet."—FaE
The tired tree.—FaE
To any garden.—FaE
To Michaelmas daisies.—FaE
Tom.—FaE
Treasure.—FaE
The true tale of grandfather Penny.—FaE
"Two penn'orth of chestnuts."—FaE
The two sweethearts.—FaE
Universe ("The universe is all the skies").—FaE
Vegetables.—FaE
Verbs.—FaE
Vet.—FaE
Victoria.—BlO
The village green.—FaE
Wake up, tr. by.—FaE
Waking at night.—FaE
Waves ("There's big waves and little waves").—FaE
    There are big waves.—CoOu
The waves of the sea.—FaE
The week after.—FaE
Welcome to the new year.—FaE
What I've been doing.—FaE
What should I see.—FaE
When Jane goes to market.—FaE
"When the almond blossoms."—FaE
White horses.—FaE
"Who'll buy my valley lilies."—FaE
Why ("Fie, darling, why do you cry, why do you cry").—FaE
Wild thyme.—FaE

Fathers and fatherhood—*Continued*
Rachel Ferrara. M. Glenn.—GlCd
Real talent. S. L. Nelms.—JaT
Remembering my father. J. Holden.—JaS
The river ("Winter"). D. Welch.—JaS
Rowing. E. Ochester.—JaS
Saturday. M. C. Livingston.—LiWo
Since you seem intent. G. Locklin.—JaG
Sir Walter Ralegh to his son. Sir W. Raleigh.—HeR
Sonnet for my father. D. Justice.—JaD
Stepfather, a girl's song. Y. Komunyakaa.—JaS
Stonecarver. C. Oles.—JaS
Stopping by home. D. Huddle.—JaG
The story of Lava. D. A. Evans.—JaPi
Subway psalm. A. Nowlan.—JaS
Sum. J. Nolan.—JaS
Sunday funnies. A. Keiter.—JaD
Sunday morning lonely. L. Clifton.—FaW
A testimony. G. E. Lyon.—JaG
That day. D. Kherdian.—PlSc
"There was an old man of Bohemia." E. Lear.—LiH
"This is a poem to my son Peter." P. Meinke.—JaD
Those winter Sundays. R. Hayden.—JaD
To a daughter with artistic talent. P. Meinke.—JaPi
To a sad daughter. M. Ondaatje.—JaG
To my daughter. S. Spender.—JaD
To my father. R. Pomeroy.—JaD
Toward dark. C. Zolotow.—ZoE
Tunes for bears to dance to. R. Wallace.—JaG
Twin aces. K. Wilson.—JaPi
Two hopper. R. Ikan.—JaS
Veronica Castell. M. Glenn.—GlCd
The view from father's porch. C. T. Wright.—JaS
War ("Each day the terror wagon"). R. Shelton.—JaPo
When father carves the duck. E. V. Wright.—CoN
Why I never went into politics. R. Shelton.—JaS
Zimmer and his turtle sink the house. P. Zimmer.—JaPi
Zoe and the ghosts. D. Weslowski.—JaPo
"Fathoms deep beneath the wave." See Song of the mermaids and mermen
"Fatty, Fatty, boom a latty." Unknown.—PrRh
Faust, sels. Johann Wolfgang von Goethe, tr. by Percy Bysshe Shelley
"The limits of the sphere of dream".—LiWa
Fear
Abracadabra. D. Livesay.—DoNw
Afreet. D. McCord.—LiWa
Autobiography. L. MacNeice.—HeR
"Aye, but to die, and go we know not where." From Measure for measure. W. Shakespeare.—HeR
Bad guys. A. Adoff.—AdA
Bat ("Bats in the belfry"). E. Merriam.—MeHa
Blind alley. E. Farjeon.—FaE
The brave man. W. Stevens.—LiSf
A bunny romance. O. Herford.—HaOf
Child frightened by thunderstorm. T. Kooser.—KeK
"Clara, little curlylocks." A. Lobel.—LoWr
Colors. Y. Yevtushenko.—McL
Crawler. E. Merriam.—MeHa
"Deep in a windless." Buson.—LiWa
Desert places. R. Frost.—HeR
Ding-a-ling. J. Ciardi.—CiD

Don't tell. M. Rosen.—RoC
Ernest Mott. M. Glenn.—GlC
Eskimo chant. Unknown.—DoNw
Fear. N. Giovanni.—GiSp
"Fear no more the heat o' the sun." From Cymbeline. W. Shakespeare.—HeR—HoUn
"Fear no more the heat o' th' sun".—PlAs
The flying cat. N. S. Nye.—JaT
"Give us courage, O Lord, to stand up." A. Paton.—LaT
Grace DeLorenzo. M. Glenn.—GlC
Hide and seek ("The trees are tall, but the moon small"). R. Graves.—CoN—KeK
Holiness. C. Rylant.—RyW
House fear. R. Frost.—LiWa
House noises. X. J. Kennedy.—KeF
"I am afraid." Unknown, fr. the Eskimo.—LiWa
I wouldn't be afraid. J. Viorst.—ViI
I'm bold, I'm brave. J. Prelutsky.—PrNk
In the night ("The light was burning very dim"). E. M. Roberts.—LiWa
Listening to grownups quarreling. R. Whitman.—CoN—KeK
"Little Miss Muffet." Mother Goose.—DeM—FaW—LiSf—LoR
Mad dog. C. Rylant.—RyW
Manerathiak's song. Unknown.—DoNw
Memories of Verdun. A. Dugan.—HeR
"My sister is a sissy." J. Prelutsky.—PrNk
"A narrow fellow in the grass." E. Dickinson.—HaOf—HeR—LiSf
Nightmare ("Nay nay nay"). E. Merriam.—MeHa
On the beach at Fontana. J. Joyce.—HeR
"Panic struck flight nine oh nine." X. J. Kennedy.—KeB
Phantoms on the steppe. A. Pushkin.—LiWa
Rape poem. M. Piercy.—JaPi
The raven. E. A. Poe.—HaOf
A riddle ("Once when I was very scared"). C. Zolotow.—CoN
The runaway ("Once, when the snow of the year was beginning to fall"). R. Frost.—KoS—LiSf
The secret. J. Stephens.—LiWa
Skeleton and spirit. Unknown.—HoCr
Sleep. N. Giovanni.—GiSp
"The snow-shoe hare." T. Hughes.—HuU
"Something is there." L. Moore.—LiWa—PrRh
Sometimes ("I am afraid of being crushed in the pincers"). G. Kuzma.—JaPi
Terror. N. M. Bodecker.—BoPc
"There came a gray owl at sunset." Unknown.—LiWa
"There is a grey thing that lives in the tree tops." S. Crane.—LiWa
To my children, fearing for them. W. Berry.—JaS
"Tommy's tears and Mary's fears." Mother Goose.—LoR
Vision by Sweetwater. J. C. Ransom.—HeR
The voice. W. De la Mare.—LiWa
The warning ("Just now"). A. Crapsey.—LiWa
"When in danger." Unknown.—TrM
Why run. N. Smaridge.—PrRh
Wild flowers ("Of what are you afraid, my child"). P. Newell.—PrRh
The wind has wings. Unknown.—DoNw
"A wolf." Unknown, fr. the Osage Indian.—PrRh
The wolverine. T. Hughes.—HuU
Zoe and the ghosts. D. Weslowski.—JaPo
Fear. Nikki Giovanni.—GiSp

"**Fear** no more the heat o' th' sun". See "Fear no more the heat o' the sun"
"**Fear** no more the heat o' the sun." From Cymbeline. William Shakespeare.—HeR—HoUn
"Fear no more the heat o' th' sun".—PlAs
"**Fear** not, shepherds, for I bring." See Angel's song
"The **fearful** night sinks." See Hymn to the sun
Fearing, Kenneth
Dirge.—HeR
The **feast** o' Saint Stephen. Ruth Sawyer.—HaO
The **feast** of Stephen. Kevin Nichols.—HaO
"A **feather** lifts." See Flyaway
Feather or fur. John Becker.—PrRh
Feathers
Tails and heads. S. Knowles.—HeR
"**Why** does it snow." L. E. Richards.—HaOf
"The **feathers** of the willow." See Song
February
The **brook** in February. C. G. D. Roberts.—DoNw
February. J. Heath-Stubbs.—HaO
February twilight. S. Teasdale.—HaOf—HoSi—PrRh
When. D. Aldis.—PrRh
"When skies are low." N. M. Bodecker.—BoSs
February. John Heath-Stubbs.—HaO
February twilight. Sara Teasdale.—HaOf—HoSi—PrRh
"**Fee**, fie, fo, fum a gingerbread baby." Clyde Watson.—WaC
"**Feeling** closed in and cut off from life." See Ellen Winters
"**Feeling** famished, Lester fried." X. J. Kennedy.—KeB
Feelings. See also specific emotional states as Fear, Happiness
Apology ("A word sticks in the wind's throat"). R. Wilbur.—JaPi
The bells. E. A. Poe.—HaOf
Brian Nichols. M. Glenn.—GlCd
City blockades. L. B. Hopkins.—HoSs
Dodo. H. Carlile.—JaPi
Dust of snow. R. Frost.—KoS—LiSf—PrRh
Ellen Winters. M. Glenn.—GlC
Epilogue. D. Levertov.—McL
Fire and ice. R. Frost.—KoS
Gary Irving. M. Glenn.—GlCd
Harvey Persky. M. Glenn.—GlCd
He sits down on the floor of a school for the retarded. A. Nowlan.—JaG
Jason Talmadge. M. Glenn.—GlC
On certain mornings everything is sensual. D. Jauss.—JaG
On the sidelines. R. J. Margolis.—MaS
Poet in residence at a county school. D. Welch.—JaG
Robert Ashford. M. Glenn.—GlCd
Rover. W. Stafford.—JaT
"Trying to say." From Nineteen pieces for love. S. Griffin.—McL
Trying to write thank-you letters. X. J. Kennedy.—KeF
The wind is blowing west. J. Ceravolo.—KoT
Feelings about words. Mary O'Neill.—PrRh
Feet
About feet. M. Hillert.—PrRh
"As I was going out one day." Mother Goose.—LoR
"Boom, boom." A. Lobel.—LoWr
First day of school. B. J. Esbensen.—EsCs
The house remembers. R. Francis.—JaD

In Pete's shoes. J. Ciardi.—CiD
"Left foot." E. Merriam.—MeBl
To the foot from its child. P. Neruda.—HeR
Feet o' Jesus. Langston Hughes.—HuDk
Feline. Ronald Wallace.—JaT
Feline fine. J. Patrick Lewis.—JaT
"A **fellow** named Dizzy McPete." See Dizzy McPete
A **fellow** named Hall. J. F. Wilson.—BrT
"A **fellow** who lived on the Rhine." See Invitation to a fish
The **feminine** seal. Oliver Herford.—BrT
Fence. Lilian Moore.—MoSn
Fences
After midnight. D. G. Jones.—DoNw
Fence. L. Moore.—MoSn
Knotholes. D. McCord.—McAs
Mending wall. R. Frost.—KoS
"The pickety fence." D. McCord.—BeD—CoN—FaW—LiSf
Road. W. S. Merwin.—JaPo
Snow fence. T. Kooser.—JaPo
Fenderson, Mark
The smart little bear ("Teacher Bruin said, cub, bear in mind").—BrT
Ferlinghetti, Lawrence
"Don't let that horse."—HeR
"In Golden Gate Park that day."—HeR
Fernandez Torneol, Nuno
The lady's farewell.—PlAs
Fernando. Marci Ridlon.—CoN—PrRh
"**Fernando** has a basketball." See Fernando
Ferns
The black fern. L. Norris.—LiSf
The ferns. G. Baro.—PrRh
The **ferns**. Gene Baro.—PrRh
Ferries
Recuerdo. E. S. Millay.—LiSf
"**Fetch** in the holly from the tree." See Holly and mistletoe
"A **few** leaves stay for a while on the trees." See The last leaf
"The **few** times back in the early fall." See Measles
"**Fickle** comfort steals away." See Changes
"**Fiddle-de-dee**, fiddle-de-dee." Mother Goose.—LoR
Fiddle-i-fee ("Had me a cat, the cat pleased me"). Mother Goose.—LiSf
"I had a cat and the cat pleased me".—DeM
The **fiddler** of Dooney. William Butler Yeats.—LiSf
Fiddlers and fiddling
The fiddler of Dooney. W. B. Yeats.—LiSf
"Friendly Fredrick Fuddlestone." A. Lobel.—LoWr
In the music. R. Currie.—JaT
"Old King Cole." Mother Goose.—DeM—FaW—LoR
One morning in May (the nightingale). Unknown.—PlAs
"Terence McDiddler." Mother Goose.—BlQ—DeM—LoR
A tiger tale. J. Bennett.—HaOf
Wilhelmj. R. J. Burdette.—BrT
"**Fie**, darling, why do you cry, why do you cry." See Why
"**Fie** fie." Eleanor Farjeon.—FaE
Field, Edward
Both my grandmothers.—JaS
Nightmare ("Expecting to be put in a sack and dumped in a ditch").—JaS
The sentimentalist.—JaPo

Fire—*Continued*

Fire ("This morning on the opposite shore of the river"). W. Carpenter.—JaPi

Fire and ice. R. Frost.—KoS

Flint. C. G. Rossetti.—PrRh

In bed. E. Farjeon.—FaE

"In the evening I would sit." From Journal. E. S. Millay.—PlSc

"Jeremiah, blow the fire." Mother Goose.—BlQ

"Ladybird, ladybird, fly away home/ Your house is on fire." Mother Goose.—LoR

Lament for Tadhg Cronin's children. M. Hartnett.—HeR

Lighting a fire. X. J. Kennedy.—FaTh—KeF

Matilda, who told lies, and was burned to death. H. Belloc.—BlO

A patriot. L. Reed.—BrT

The phoenix. P. Fleischman.—FlI

Prairie fires. H. Garland.—HaOf

Safe ("Come, stir the fire"). J. Walker.—HaO

"Shut in from all the world without." From Snowbound. J. G. Whittier.—HaO

"There's a fire in the forest." W. Ross.—DoNw

Two drops. Z. Herbert.—HeR

Yule log. R. Herrick.—HaO

The **fire** ("The fire with well dried logs supplied"). Sir Walter Scott.—HaO

Fire ("A new servant maid named Maria"). Unknown.—BrT

Fire ("This morning on the opposite shore of the river"). William Carpenter.—JaPi

Fire and ice. Robert Frost.—KoS

"The **fire** darkens, the wood turns black." See Song for the sun that disappeared behind the rainclouds

Fire escape. Sylvia Cassedy.—CaR

"**Fire-escape** time." See Fire escape

Fire-flies. See Fireflies

"**Fire** that cancels all that is." See Burning love letters

"The **fire** upon my ceiling glows." See In bed

"The **fire** with well dried logs supplied." See The fire

Fireflies

"As I picked it up." Unknown.—FaTh

The fireflies. C. Zolotow.—ZoE

"Fireflies, fireflies." Unknown.—DeD

Fireflies in the garden. R. Frost.—KoS—PrRh

Firefly ("A little light is going by"). E. M. Roberts.—CoN—FrP—LiSf—PrRa

Firefly, a song.—FaTh

Firefly ("On a June night"). C. Zolotow.—ZoE

Glowworm ("He studies very late"). F. Dodat.—FaTh

Glowworm ("Never talk down to a glowworm"). D. McCord.—CoN—FaW—McAs

The **fireflies.** Charlotte Zolotow.—ZoE

"**Fireflies,** fireflies." Unknown.—DeD

Fireflies in the garden. Robert Frost.—KoS—PrRh

Firefly ("A little light is going by"). Elizabeth Madox Roberts.—CoN—FrP—LiSf—PrRa

Firefly, a song. See Firefly ("A little light is going by")

Firefly ("On a June night"). Charlotte Zolotow.—ZoE

Firefly, a song. See Firefly ("A little light is going by")

"**Firefly,** airplane, satellite, star." See Back yard, July night

"**Firelight** and shadows." See Look

"**Firemen,** firemen." See Help

Firewood. See Wood

Fireworks

Fireworks ("First"). V. Worth.—CoN

Fireworks ("They rise like sudden fiery flowers"). J. Reeves.—CoOu

Fourth of July ("Hurrah for the fourth of July"). M. C. Livingston.—LiCe

Fourth of July ("Tonight the air explodes"). B. J. Esbensen.—EsCs

Fourth of July night ("Just see those pinwheels whirling round"). D. Aldis.—HoSi—LiSf

November the fifth. L. Clark.—CoOu

A rocket in my pocket. Unknown.—PrRh

"Summer blasts off fireworks, fuses them with red." M. C. Livingston.—LiCs

Fireworks ("First"). Valerie Worth.—CoN

Fireworks ("They rise like sudden fiery flowers"). James Reeves.—CoOu

"**First**." See The chestnuts are falling

"**First**." See Fireworks

The **first**. Lilian Moore.—MoSn

The **first** blackbird. Eleanor Farjeon.—FaE

"The **first** blossom was the best blossom." See Apple blossom

The **first** Christmas eve. Harry Behn.—HoCb

"**First** cold rain." Basho.—KoT

"The **first** day of Christmas". See The twelve days of Christmas

First day of school. Barbara Juster Esbensen.—EsCs

"The **first** day of spring." Eve Merriam.—MeF

"The **first** day of this month I saw." See Snowdrops

First foot. Ian Serraillier.—LiNe

First gathering. Eleanor Farjeon.—FaE

"The **first** girl I ever kissed was Sally Adams." See First kiss

First, goodbye. John Smith.—JaG

"**First** he drew a strike zone." See The hummer

"**First** hear the story of Kaspar the rosy cheeked." See Fraulein reads instructive rhymes

The **first** hunt. Gordon Anderson.—JaPo

"**First** I am frosted." Mary Austin.—LiSf

"**First** I saw the white bear." See At the zoo

"**First** I walked." See At the beach

"**First** in a carriage." Mother Goose.—DeM

First January walk. Emanuel Di Pasquale.—LiNe

First kiss. Jonathan Holden.—JaG

First love ("At his incipient sun"). Stanley Kunitz.—JaG

First love ("I remember sadness"). Patricia Hubbell.—LiSf

First love ("We fell in love at 'Journey for Margaret'"). Judith Hemschemeyer.—JaPi

"The **first** man, you are his child, he is your child." See Song of the flood

First night of Hanukkah. Ruth Boston.—LiPj

"The **first** night, the first night." See Carol for the last Christmas eve

First one out of bed. X. J. Kennedy.—KeF

First practice. Gary Gildner.—JaPi

"**First**, run around in circles." See Fat Lena's recipe for crocodile soup

First sight. Philip Larkin.—CoN

First snow ("Snow makes whiteness where it falls"). Marie Louise Allen.—BaS—HoSu—PrRa—PrRh

The **first** snow ("There is a special kind of quiet"). Charlotte Zolotow.—ZoE

"The **first** snow was sleet, it swished heavily." See Sleet

First snowfall ("Out of the grey"). Barbara Juster Esbensen.—BaS—EsCs

First snowflake. N. M. Bodecker.—BoSs
First song. Galway Kinnell.—JaG
First surf. Emanuel Di Pasquale.—JaS
The first Thanksgiving ("For a long time"). Barbara Juster Esbensen.—LiTp
The first Thanksgiving ("When the Pilgrims"). Jack Prelutsky.—CoN—PrIt
"First the clouds came." See Rain in the city
"The first thing I ever knew was funny." See Laughing backwards
"The first time I had sex with Raymond." See Carrie Pearson
"The first time I went to the fields alone." See Strawberries
"The first time in new shoes." See New shoes
The first tooth. Charles Lamb and Mary Lamb.—DaC—PrRh
"First, you will say goodbye, you will turn." See First, goodbye
Fish. See also names of fish, as Sharks
   Alas, alack. W. De la Mare.—LiSf
   "Alive without breath." J. R. R. Tolkien.—LiSf
   "A baby sardine." S. Milligan.—CoOu
   Behavior of fish in an English tea garden. K. Douglas.—HeR
   Brooktrout. T. Hughes.—HuU
   The catfish. J. Prelutsky.—PrSr
   The codfish. Unknown.—PrRh
   Easter under the water. P. Neumeyer.—LiE
   Eating fish. G. Johnston.—DoNw
   Fish ("Fish have fins"). J. Prelutsky.—FrP—PrZ
   The fish ("I caught a tremendous fish"). E. Bishop.—HeR
   Fish ("The little fish are silent"). A. S. Bourinot.—PrRa
   Fish ("Look at them flit"). M. A. Hoberman.—PrRa
   Fishes' evening song. D. Ipcar.—PrRh
   The fishvendor. W. Meredith.—PlSc
   "Fishy, fishy in the brook." Mother Goose.—LoR
   "The fizzgiggious fish." From An animal alphabet. E. Lear.—LiH
   The flattered flying fish. E. V. Rieu.—PrRh
   Floundering. N. M. Bodecker.—BoPc
   The hen and the carp. I. Serraillier.—CoOu—LiSf
   Into fish. S. L. Nelms.—JaG
   Little fish ("Little fish move in the water, swim, swim, swim"). Unknown.—GrT
   Little fish ("The tiny fish enjoy themselves"). D. H. Lawrence.—HeR—KoT—PrBb
   The maldive shark. H. Melville.—HeR
   The marvel. K. Douglas.—HeR
   The muskellunge. T. Hughes.—HuU
   "One, two, three, four, five." Mother Goose.—DaC—DeM
   "1, 2, 3, 4, 5".—AlH—LiSf
   Los pescaditos. Unknown.—GrT
   "There was once a fish." Mother Goose.—LoR
   Tip toe tail. D. Willson.—CoN
   "When howitzers began." H. Carruth.—JaPi
   Wish ("If I could wish"). D. B. Thompson.—PrRa
Fish ("Fish have fins"). Jack Prelutsky.—FrP—PrZ
The fish ("I caught a tremendous fish"). Elizabeth Bishop.—HeR
Fish ("The little fish are silent"). Arthur S. Bourinot.—PrRa
Fish ("Look at them flit"). Mary Ann Hoberman.—PrRa
"The fish has too many bones." See The old men

"Fish have fins." See Fish
"The fish lives in the brook." See The very nicest place
"A fish took a notion." See Tip toe tail
A fish who could not swim. Maxine Kumin.—RuI
Fishback, Margaret
   Lines on a small potato.—HoDi
Fisher, Aileen
   About caterpillars.—FiW
   After a bath.—BeD—FrP
   Answers.—LiSf
   At night ("When night is dark").—LiSf—PrRa
   Back to school.—LiSf
   Bird talk ("Think, said the robin").—FrP
   Bookish.—FiW
   But I wonder.—PrRa
   Cat in the snow.—CoN
   Caterpillars.—HoSu
   Centipede ("A centipede's a clever one").—FiW
   Crickets ("Of all the insects").—FiW
   Dragonflies.—FiW
   Dreams ("Do you ever").—LaW
   Drippy day.—FiW
   Drippy weather.—FrP
   Fall wind ("Everything is on the run").—HoSi
   Freckles.—HoSu
   Going barefoot.—FiW
   Good night ("This day's done").—FrP
   Houses ("Houses are faces").—CoN
   "How do they know."—HoSi
   Light the festive candles for Hanukkah.—PrRh
   Like a bug.—FiW
   Listening.—CoN
   Little talk.—FiW
   Merry Christmas.—PrRh
   Mrs. Brownish Beetle.—FiW
   Mouse dinner.—FaTh
   My puppy.—CoOu
   Noises.—HoBf
   Noses.—FaW
   On Halloween.—PrRa
   On Mother's Day.—CoN—PrRh
   Open house.—PrRa
   "Out in the dark and daylight."—BeD
   Point of view.—FiW
   Pussy willows.—PrRa
   Raindrops ("How brave a ladybug must be").—PrRa
   Right-of-way.—FiW
   The seed ("How does it know").—CoOu
   Sky net.—FiW
   Snail's pace.—PrRa
   Snowball wind.—BaS
   Snowy benches.—BaS—HoSi, KeK
   Spider ("I saw a little spider").—FiW
   Until we built a cabin.—LaW
   Upside down ("It's funny how beetles").—BeD—FiW
   "Waves of the sea."—HoSe
   Wearing of the green.—PrRh
   When it come to bugs.—FiW
   When mowers pass.—FiW
   Wings.—PrRa
   Woolly bear caterpillar ("Caterpillar, have a care").—FiW
Fisher, Lillian M.
   Dreamscape.—HoDi
   I'm glad I'm living now, not then.—HoDi
   To brontosaurus, a gentle giant dinosaur.—HoDi
Fisherman. Robert Francis.—JaPo
The fisherman writes a letter to the mermaid. Joan Aiken.—LiWa

"The **fisherman's** hands." Nanine Valen.—ChC
Fishers and fishing
  Autumn ("This morning they are putting away the whales"). W. Carpenter.—JaPi
  The baite. J. Donne.—HeR
  Bella by the sea. L. F. Jackson.—PrRh
  The cable ship. H. E. Martinson.—HeR
  Chester's wisdom. N. Giovanni.—GiSp
  The cormorant's tale. P. Fleischman.—FlI
  "Did you ever go fishing on a bright sunny day." Unknown.—PrRh
  The fish ("I caught a tremendous fish"). E. Bishop.—HeR
  Fisherman. R. Francis.—JaPo
  The fisherman writes a letter to the mermaid. J. Aiken.—LiWa
  "The fisherman's hands." N. Valen.—ChC
  Fishing Blue Creek. R. Scheele.—JaPo
  "Fishy, fishy in the brook." Mother Goose.—LoR
  The glass canoe. J. Ciardi.—CiD
  Heron ("Only / fools / pursue"). V. Worth.—WoSp
  I caught a fish. B. Murray.—CoOu
  In the deep channel. W. Stafford.—HeR
  In the shadows of early sunlight. R. Wallace.—JaT
  Jack was every inch a sailor. Unknown.—DoNw
  Jim Desterland. H. Plutzik.—HeR
  "Little Tommy Tittlemouse." Mother Goose.—AlH—BlPi—DeM—FaW—LoR
  "Once in the winter." From The forsaken. D. C. Scott.—DoNw
  "One, two, three, four, five." Mother Goose.—DaC—DeM
    "1, 2, 3, 4, 5".—AlH—LiSf
  The shark ("Oh what a lark to fish for shark"). J. J. Bell.—PrRh
  Sliding scale. N. R. Jaffray.—BrT
  "There was a young lady of Wales." E. Lear.—LiH
  "There was an old man in a barge." E. Lear.—FaW—LiH—RuI
  Tricia's fish. L. B. Hopkins.—HoBf
  Two of a kind. X. J. Kennedy.—KeF
  Wharf. M. C. Livingston.—HoSe
  When a jolly young fisher. Unknown.—RuI
  Wynken, Blynken, and Nod. E. Field.—CoN—DaC—HaOf
Fishes' evening song. Dahlov Ipcar.—PrRh
"**Fishes** swim in water clear." Mother Goose.—LoR
Fishing. See Fishers and fishing
Fishing Blue Creek. Roy Scheele.—JaPo
"The **fishing** boats sway." See Benue lullaby
The **fishvendor.** William Meredith.—PlSc
"**Fishy,** fishy in the brook." Mother Goose.—LoR
The **fist.** Derek Walcott.—McL
"The **fist** clenched round my heart." See The fist
Fist fight. Doug Cockrell.—JaPi
The **fist** upstairs. William Dickey.—JaPi
Five chants, sels. David McCord
  "Every time I climb a tree".—CoN—FaW—LiSf—PrRh
Five eyes. Walter De la Mare.—ChC
Five ghost songs, complete. Unknown
  "Ah, the roofs".—KoT
  "The dove stays in the garden".—KoT
  "The ghost is gone in rags".—KoT
  "I have no rattles".—KoT
  "See how it circles".—KoT
"**Five** hundred guests upon a summer's day." See The view from father's porch

Five little chickens. Unknown.—PrRa
"**Five** little monsters." Eve Merriam.—MeBl—PrRa
"**Five** little rabbits went out to walk." Unknown.—TrM
"**Five** minutes, five minutes more, please." See Bedtime
"**Five** times since July my father." See Stopping by home
Five years old. Marie Louise Allen.—FrP—PrRa
"**Five** years since you died and I am." See Letter to a dead father
"The **fizzgiggious** fish." From An animal alphabet. Edward Lear.—LiH
Flagg, James Montgomery
  Table manners ("When you turn down your glass it's a sign").—BrT
Flags
  Barbara Frietchie. J. G. Whittier.—HaOf
"**Flame** my." See Heart crown and mirror
Flame of the forest, midnight. Myra Cohn Livingston.—LiMp
Flanders, Michael
  The hummingbird ("The hummingbird, he has no song").—PrRh
  The walrus ("The walrus lives on icy floors").—PrRh
Flannan Isle. Wilfrid Wilson Gibson.—BlO
"A **flashlight.**" See Brain
Flashlight ("My flashlight tugs me"). Judith Thurman.—BeD—LiSf
Flashlight ("Tucked tight in bed, the day all gone"). X. J. Kennedy.—KeF
Flathead Indians. See Indians of the Americas—Flathead
The **flattered** flying fish. Emile Victor Rieu.—PrRh
Flavors (1) ("Mama is chocolate, you must be swirls"). Arnold Adoff.—AdA
Flavors (2) ("Daddy is vanilla, you must be mean"). Arnold Adoff.—AdA
Flavors (3) ("Me is better"). Arnold Adoff.—AdA
The **flea.** Roland Young.—PrRh
"A **flea** and a fly in a flue." Unknown.—PrRh
"A **flea** flew by a bee, the bee." See Combinations
Fleas
  Excursion. E. Merriam.—MeF
  The flea. R. Young.—PrRh
  "A flea and a fly in a flue." Unknown.—PrRh
  Fleas. V. Worth.—WoSp
  "Fleas interest me so much." From Bestiary. P. Neruda.—FaTh
  "A frog and a flea." C. Mitchell.—PrRa
  I've got a dog. Unknown.—PrRh
  Lines on a small potato. M. Fishback.—HoDi
Fleas. Valerie Worth.—WoSp
"**Fleas** interest me so much." From Bestiary. Pablo Neruda, tr. by Elsa Neuberger.—FaTh
"The **fledglings** have a language." See Baby talk
Fleischman, Paul
  The actor.—FlI
  The common egret.—FlI
  The cormorant's tale.—FlI
  Dawn ("At first light the finches").—FlI
  Doves of Dodona.—FlI
  Dusk ("At dusk there are swallows").—FlI
  Morning ("One waxwing's wakened").—FlI
  Owls ("Sun's down, sky's dark").—FlI
  The passenger pigeon.—FlI
  The phoenix.—FlI
  Sparrows.—FlI

Fleischman, Paul—*Continued*
The wandering albatross.—FlI
"Warblers."—FlI
The watchers.—FlI
"Whip-poor-will."—FlI
Fleming, Elizabeth
"In the mirror."—CoOu
Who's in.—BlO—PrRh
Fletcher, John Gould
The skaters.—KeK
Fletcher Avenue. Myra Cohn Livingston.—LiWo
"A **flicker** of blue." See Kingfisher
"A **flicker** with a broken neck." See On Addy Road
Flies
"At early morn the spiders spin." Mother Goose.—LoR
Bug in a jug. Unknown.—PrRh
"Fiddle-de-dee, fiddle-de-dee." Mother Goose.—LoR
"A flea and a fly in a flue." Unknown.—PrRh
Flies. V. Worth.—WoSp
The fly ("How large unto the tiny fly"). W. De la Mare.—CoOu
The fly ("I was sitting on the porch"). C. Zolotow.—ZoE
The fly ("Little fly"). W. Blake.—BlO
The fly ("She sat on a willow-trunk"). M. Holub.—HeR
"I wish I could meet the man that knows." J. Ciardi.—PrRh
Keeping a fly. Unknown, fr. the Quechua Indian.—BiSp
The last cry of the damp fly. D. Lee.—CoN
"Little black bug." M. W. Brown.—CoN—FrP
Math class. M. C. Livingston.—FaTh
My window screen. X. J. Kennedy.—KeF
Oh the toe test. N. Farber.—PrRh
"One person." Issa.—KoT
Spider ("Spider's"). L. Moore.—MoSn
The spider and the fly. M. Howitt.—CoOu—DaC
"There was an old person of Skye." E. Lear.—KeK—LiH
To the fly in my drink. D. Wagoner.—JaD
Flies. Valerie Worth.—WoSp
"**Flies** buzz." See Ears hear
"**Flies** wear." See Flies
Flight. See also Airplanes and aviators
The airplane. R. Bennett.—FrP
Alone ("Alone is delicious"). J. Holden.—JaPi
The butterfly ("Up and down the air you float"). C. Scollard.—PrRa
Cockpit in the clouds. D. Dorrance.—PrRh
The eagle. A. Tennyson.—BlO—CoN—LiSf—PrRh
Flight ("All day long the clouds go by"). G. Johnston.—DoNw
Flight ("A hound sound"). L. Moore.—MoSn
Flight of the roller-coaster. R. Souster.—DoNw
Flight plan. J. Merchant.—HoCl—PrRh
Flying ("When you fly in a plane"). E. Merriam.—HoSu
Flying crooked. R. Graves.—HeR
"Flying for the first time." E. Merriam.—MeF
"Flying-man, flying-man." Mother Goose.—LoR
Hummingbird ("Cried a scientist watching this creature dart by"). X. J. Kennedy.—KeF
"I am falling off a mountain." J. Prelutsky.—PrNk
I am flying. J. Prelutsky.—PrNk
I can fly. F. Holman.—CoN—PrRh

I, Icarus. A. Nowlan.—DoNw
If pigs could fly. J. Reeves.—CoOu
Laughter. M. Waddington.—DoNw
Night, landing at Newark. J. Holden.—JaPo
"Old Mother Goose." Mother Goose.—DeM—LoR
Questioning faces. R. Frost.—KoS
Reindeer report. U. A. Fanthorpe.—HaO
"Ride a purple pelican." J. Prelutsky.—PrRi
Sparrow in an airport. R. Snyder.—JaPo
The swallow ("Swallow, swallow, swooping free"). O. Nash.—PrRa
To an aviator. D. W. Hicky.—PrRh
Wingtip. C. Sandburg.—HoRa
The world ("I move back by shortcut"). V. Rutsala.—JaPi
Wouldn't you. J. Ciardi.—PrRa
Flight ("All day long the clouds go by"). George Johnston.—DoNw
The **flight** ("At Woodlawn I heard the dead cry"). From The lost son. Theodore Roethke.—HeR
Flight ("A hound sound"). Lilian Moore.—MoSn
Flight ("One day you were there, the next day gone"). Judith Hemschemeyer.—JaPo
Flight of the roller-coaster. Raymond Souster.—DoNw
Flight plan. Jane Merchant.—HoCl—PrRh
The **flimsy** fleek. Jack Prelutsky.—PrNk
"The **flimsy** fleek is mild and meek." See The flimsy fleek
"**Fling**." See To a red kite
Flint. Christina Georgina Rossetti.—PrRh
"**Flip** flop." See Fishes' evening song
Floccinaucinihilipilification. Eve Merriam.—MeSk
"A **flock** of swallows have gone flying south." See August 28
The **flood**. John Clare.—HeR
Floods
The flood. J. Clare.—HeR
Presents from the flood. X. J. Kennedy.—KeF
Song of the flood. Unknown, fr. the Navajo Indian.—KoT
The **floor** and the ceiling. William Jay Smith.—HaOf
"The **floor** was muddy with the juice of peaches." See Canning time
Floradora Doe. Jack Prelutsky.—PrNk
Florence, Italy
Giotto's tower. H. W. Longfellow.—PlEd
The old bridge at Florence. H. W. Longfellow.—PlEd
Florida
A Floridian museum of art. R. Whittemore.—PlEd
Have over the water to Florida. Unknown.—PlAs
A **Floridian** museum of art. Reed Whittemore.—PlEd
The **flotterzott**. Jack Prelutsky.—PrB
The **flotz**. Jack Prelutsky.—PrNk
Floundering. N. M. Bodecker.—BoPc
Flower, Robin
Pangur Ban, tr. by.—ChC—HeR
The **flower-fed** buffaloes. Vachel Lindsay.—HaOf—HeR
"The **flower-fed** buffaloes of the spring." See The flower-fed buffaloes
A **flower** given to my daughter. James Joyce.—HeR
"**Flower** in the crannied wall." Alfred Tennyson.—FaTh
The **flower** seller. Eleanor Farjeon.—FaE

"The **flower** seller's fat and she wears a big shawl." See The flower seller
Flowers. See also Gardens and gardening; Trees; also names of kinds of flowers, as Roses
Ann's house. D. Lourie.—JaD
Apple blossom. L. MacNeice.—HeR
Autumn crocus. E. Farjeon.—FaE
Autumn thought. L. Hughes.—HuDk
Bavarian gentians. D. H. Lawrence.—KoT
"Beside the road." Basho.—KoT
Blossoms. F. D. Sherman.—HaOf
Blue-eyed Mary. M. E. W. Freeman.—HaOf
Bouquets. R. Francis.—JaD
Caught stealing a dahlia. Unknown.—BrT
A charm for spring flowers. R. Field.—LiSf
The city ("If the flowers want to grow"). D. Ignatow.—HoSi
The crocus ("The golden crocus reaches up"). W. Crane.—ChG—PrRh
Crocus ("Little crocus"). C. Zolotow.—ZoE
The dancers. C. Zolotow.—ZoE
The death of the flowers. W. C. Bryant.—HaOf
First one out of bed. X. J. Kennedy.—KeF
Flame of the forest, midnight. M. C. Livingston.—LiMp
"Flower in the crannied wall." A. Tennyson.—FaTh
The flower seller. E. Farjeon.—FaE
"Flowers are a silly bunch." A. Spilka.—PrRh
Flowers by the sea. W. C. Williams.—HeR
Heigh ho April. E. Farjeon.—FaE
Hyla brook. R. Frost.—KoS
"I know a bank where the wild thyme blows." From A midsummer night's dream. W. Shakespeare.—HoUn
I show the daffodils to the retarded kids. C. Sharp.—JaD
I toss them to my elephant. J. Prelutsky.—PrNk
"If I should ever by chance grow rich." E. Thomas.—BlO
Jacaranda. M. C. Livingston.—FaTh—LiMp
Jack Frost ("Rustily creak the crickets, Jack Frost came down"). C. Thaxter.—HaOf
"March winds and April showers." Mother Goose.—DaC—DeM
Marigolds. C. Zolotow.—ZoE
Morning glory. E. Farjeon.—FaE
Nosegay. E. Coatsworth.—HaOf
Old florist. T. Roethke.—PlSc
Pansies. C. Zolotow.—ZoE
A passing glimpse. R. Frost.—KoS
Red flower. A. Turner.—TuS
The seeds of love. Unknown.—PlAs
Smells. K. Worth.—PrRh
Snowdrops. G. MacBeth.—HaO
A spike of green. B. Baker.—PrRa
Spring flowers. H. Behn.—HoCb
The start. E. Farjeon.—FaE
This year, next year. E. Farjeon.—FaE
To Michaelmas daisies. E. Farjeon.—FaE
To Mistress Isabel Pennell. J. Skelton.—KoT
Tulips and addresses. E. Field.—JaPi
"Who'll buy my valley lilies." E. Farjeon.—FaE
Wild flowers ("Of what are you afraid, my child"). P. Newell.—PrRh
Wildflowers ("We mustn't pick the garden flowers"). E. Farjeon.—FaE
Wind flowers. M. Lockwood.—JaD
Window boxes. E. Farjeon.—FaE
"With fairest flowers." From Cymbeline. W. Shakespeare.—HeR
Zinnias. V. Worth.—CoN
"**Flowers** are a silly bunch." Arnold Spilka.—PrRh

"**Flowers** are closed and lambs are sleeping." See Lullaby
"**Flowers** are happy in summer." See Autumn thought
Flowers by the sea. William Carlos Williams.—HeR
"The **flowers** get a darkening brilliance now." See The dying garden
Flowers in the valley. Unknown.—BlO
Flummery. Eve Merriam.—MeSk
Flux. Richard Eberhart.—JaPi
The **fly** ("How large unto the tiny fly"). Walter De la Mare.—CoOu
The **fly** ("I was sitting on the porch"). Charlotte Zolotow.—ZoE
The **fly** ("Little fly"). William Blake.—BlO
The **fly** ("She sat on a willow-trunk"). Miroslav Holub, tr. by George Theiner.—HeR
"**Fly** away, fly away, over the sea." See The swallow
"The **fly**, the fly." See Oh the toe test
Flyaway. Barbara Juster Esbensen.—EsCs
Flying ("I saw the moon"). J. M. Westrup.—CoOu
Flying ("When you fly in a plane"). Eve Merriam.—HoSu
The **flying** cat. Naomi Shihab Nye.—JaT
Flying crooked. Robert Graves.—HeR
"**Flying** for the first time." Eve Merriam.—MeF
"**Flying** loose and easy, where does he go." See The crow
"**Flying-man**, flying-man." Mother Goose.—LoR
Flying uptown backwards. X. J. Kennedy.—KeF
Foal. Mary Britton Miller.—LiSf
Fog
  Definitions. X. J. Kennedy.—KeF
  Fog. C. Sandburg.—HaOf—HoRa—KoT—LiSf—PrRh
  The fog. C. Zolotow.—ZoE
  Fog lifting. L. Moore.—MoSn
  Foghorns. L. Moore.—HoSs—MoSn—PrRh
  Grayness. C. Zolotow.—ZoE
  In the fog. L. Moore.—MoSn
  Uses for a fog. From A throw of threes. E. Merriam.—MeF
Fog. Carl Sandburg.—HaOf—HoRa—KoT—LiSf—PrRh
The **fog.** Charlotte Zolotow.—ZoE
"**Fog**, a cloud." See Definitions
"The **fog** comes." See Fog
"**Fog**, fog." From Songs of the ghost dance. Unknown.—LiWa
Fog lifting. Lilian Moore.—MoSn
"**Fog** on the river." See Grayness
"**Fog** smog, fog smog." See Windshield wiper
Foghorns. Lilian Moore.—HoSs—MoSn—PrRh
"The **foghorns** moaned." See Foghorns
Folk, Pat
  Empty holds a question.—JaG
Folk poetry. See Autograph album verses; Ballads—Traditional; Counting-out rhymes; Jump-rope rhymes
Folk tune. Richard Wilbur.—PlAs
"The **folk** who live in Backward Town." Mary Ann Hoberman.—HaOf—PrRh
Folklore. See also Superstitions
Follen, Eliza Lee
  The good mooly cow.—HaOf
"**Follow** me." See Key
Follow the leader. Kathleen Fraser.—PrRh
Food and eating. See also Cooks and cooking; also names of Food, also names of meals
  Accidentally. M. Kumin.—PrRh

Food and eating.—*Continued*
"Little bits of soft boiled egg." F. Maschler.—PrRh
The little brown celery. G. MacBeth.—FaTh
Little Dimity. W. J. Smith.—LiSf
"Little Jack Horner." Mother Goose.—DeM—FaW—LoR
"Little King Boggen, he built a fine hall." Mother Goose.—BlPi—LoR
"Little King Pippin." Mother Goose.—DeM
"Little Miss Muffet." Mother Goose.—DeM—FaW—LiSf—LoR
"Little Tom Tucker." Mother Goose.—AlH
"Little Tommy Tucker." Mother Goose.—DeM—FaW—LoR
Little tortillas. Unknown.—GrT
Lord Cray. E. Gorey.—PrRh
Mabel, remarkable Mabel. J. Prelutsky.—PrNk
Maple feast. F. Frost.—PrRh
Marmalade. E. Farjeon.—FaE
Master of arts. C. Monkhouse.—BrT
The meal. K. Kuskin.—PrRa
"Meaning well, Minerva Jean." X. J. Kennedy.—KeB
Meg's egg. M. A. Hoberman.—PrRh
Men may talk of country Christmasses. P. Massinger.—HaO
The merry pieman's song. J. Bennett.—LiIl
Mickey Jones. X. J. Kennedy.—KeF
Millions of strawberries. G. Taggard.—LiIl—LiSf
Minnie. E. Farjeon.—FaE
Miss T. W. De la Mare.—CoN—CoOu—LiSf
"Mr. East gave a feast." Mother Goose.—DeM
Mr. Pratt. M. C. Livingston.—PrRh
"Mix a pancake." C. G. Rossetti.—CoN—FrP—LiSf—PrRa
   The pancake.—ChG
"The moon's the north wind's cooky." V. Lindsay.—CoN—HaOf—LaW—LiSf—PrRa—PrRh
Ms. Minnie McFinney. Unknown.—BrT
Mummy slept late and Daddy fixed breakfast. J. Ciardi.—LiSf—PrRh
"My aunt kept turnips in a flock." R. Jarrell.—LiSf
My mouth. A. Adoff.—PrRh
The nine little goblins. J. W. Riley.—HaOf
"No, I won't turn orange." J. Prelutsky.—PrNk
"Oak leaf plate." M. A. Hoberman.—FaTh
"Oh I have dined on this delicious day." R. Snyder.—JaT
"Oh my goodness, oh my dear." C. Watson.—LiSf
An old man of Hawaii. Unknown.—BrT
The old men ("The fish has too many bones"). C. Reznikoff.—JaD
"One for me and one for you." C. Watson.—WaC
Oodles of noodles. L. Hymes, and J. L. Hymes.—PrRh
The pancake collector. J. Prelutsky.—HaOf
"Pass the plate." J. Yolen.—LiTp
Patience. B. Katz.—PrRh
"Paul, in Aunt Pru's prune surprise." X. J. Kennedy.—KeB
"Pease porridge hot." Mother Goose.—FaW—LiSf—LoR
The perfect turkey sandwich. S. Kroll.—HoMu
Pie problem. S. Silverstein.—PrRh
"A piggish young person from Leeds." Unknown.—KeK
The pious young priest. Unknown.—BrT
The pizza. O. Nash.—HoMu—PrRh

"Polly Barlor, in the parlor." A. Lobel.—LoWr
Poor old lady. Unknown.—HaOf—PrRh
Prayer before eating. Unknown, fr. the Arapaho Indian.—BiSp
A professor called Chesterton. W. S. Gilbert.—BrT
"Pumberly Pott's unpredictable niece." J. Prelutsky.—PrRh
Punkydoodle and Jollapin. L. E. Richards.—HaOf
Questions ("If cookies come in boxes"). L. B. Hopkins.—HoMu
"Robbin and Bobbin." Mother Goose.—LoR
"Robin the bobbin." Mother Goose.—BlQ
A round. E. Merriam.—MeSk
Sad sweet story. N. Smaridge.—HoMu
Sadie Snatt. J. Prelutsky.—PrSr
"Sammy Smith would drink and eat." Mother Goose.—FaW
Seven sisters roses. E. Farjeon.—FaE
Seymour Snorkle. J. Prelutsky. PrNk
"She said she wasn't hungry." Unknown.—TrM
Sidney Snickke. J. Prelutsky.—PrNk
"Sing for your supper." E. Farjeon.—FaE
Sneaky Bill. W. Cole.—PrRh
"Snowflake souffle." X. J. Kennedy.—BaS
Soup. C. Sandburg.—HaOf—HoRa
The spaghetti nut. J. Prelutsky.—PrSr
"Spaghetti, spaghetti." J. Prelutsky.—HoMu
Spring diet. N. D. Watson.—LiSf
The story of Augustus who would not have any soup. H. Hoffman.—PrRh
The story of fidgety Philip. H. Hoffman.—DaC
A summer Christmas in Australia. D. Sladen.—HaO
"Sunday is our roast beef day." From Munch. A. Wallner.—HoMu
"Sunny side up." A. Adoff.—LiSf
The sycophantic fox and the gullible raven. G. W. Carryl.—HaOf
Table manners ("The goops they lick their fingers"). G. Burgess.—FrP—HaOf—PrRa—PrRh
   The goops.—FaW
Taste of purple. L. B. Jacobs.—PrRh
Tea by the sea. E. Lear.—BrT
A ternary of littles, upon a pipkin of jelly sent to a lady. R. Herrick.—KoT
"The Texan was mighty hungry." L. C. Briggs.—TrM
Thanksgiving ("I feel so stuffed inside my skin"). M. Hillert.—HoSi
Thanksgiving magic. R. Bennett.—PrRh
"There was a young man so benighted." Unknown.—TrM
"There was an old man of Apulia." E. Lear.—LiH
"There was an old man of Calcutta." E. Lear.—LiH
"There was an old man of El Hums." E. Lear.—LiH
"There was an old man of the South." E. Lear.—LiH
"There was an old man of Tobago." Mother Goose.—LoR
"There was an old person of Bromley." E. Lear.—LiH
"There was an old person of Dean." E. Lear.—BlO—FaTh—LiH
   Limerick.—HoMu

Food and eating.—*Continued*
 "There was an old person of Ewell." E. Lear.—
  LiH
     Rice and mice.—BrT
 "There was an old person whose habits." E.
  Lear.—LiH
     Hurtful habits.—BrT
 "Thinking it hard candy, Rube." X. J.
  Kennedy.—KeB
 This is just to say. W. C. Williams.—KeK—
  PrRh
 "A thousand hairy savages." S. Milligan.—
  CoOu—PrRh
 "Three each day, seven days a week." Mother
  Goose.—LoR
 "Three little ghostesses." Mother Goose.—
  DeM—FaW
     Three ghostesses.—PrRh
 To a poor old woman. W. C. Williams.—KoT
 To sup like a pup. D. W. Baruch.—HoDl
 The toaster ("A silver-scaled dragon with jaws
  flaming red"). W. J. Smith.—LiSf—PrRa
 Tortillitas. Unknown.—GrT
 Toy tik ka. C. Pomerantz.—PoI
 Twickham Tweer. J. Prelutsky.—PrRh—PrSr
 "Two penn'orth of chestnuts." E. Farjeon.—FaE
 Two sad. W. Cole.—PrRa
 "The underwater wibbles." J. Prelutsky.—PrNk
 Vegetables. E. Farjeon.—FaE
 The visitor. K. Pyle.—CoOu
 The vulture. H. Belloc.—PrRh
 The walrus and the carpenter. From Through
  the looking glass. L. Carroll.—BlO—LiSf
 "What is the opposite of nuts." R. Wilbur.—
  LiSf
 "When daddy carves the turkey." J. Prelutsky.—
  PrIt
 When father carves the duck. E. V. Wright.—
  CoN
 "When Tillie ate the chili." J. Prelutsky.—PrNk
 "Wilburforce Fong." X. J. Kennedy.—KeF
 Witches' menu. S. Nikolay.—PrRh
 The worm ("When the earth is turned in
  spring"). R. Bergengren.—ChG—PrRh
 Yellow butter. M. A. Hoberman.—PrRa
 "You take the blueberry." C. Pomerantz.—PoI
 A young lady of Munich. Unknown.—BrT
 Yubbazubbies. J. Prelutsky.—PrNk
 Yule log. R. Herrick.—HaO
 A zoo without bars. N. M. Bodecker.—BoSs
 The zoosher. J. Prelutsky.—PrNk
Food for a cat. David Starr Jordan.—BrT
Food out of doors. Eleanor Farjeon.—FaE
Fools
 The cap and bells. W. B. Yeats.—HeR—LiWa
 The compassionate fool. N. Cameron.—HeR
 The court jester's last report to the King. J.
  Prelutsky.—PrSr
 Memorabilia. R. Browning.—HeR
 "Simple Simon met a pieman." Mother
  Goose.—DeM—FaW—LiSf—LoR
 "Three wise men of Gotham." Mother Goose.—
  DeM—FaW—LoR
Football
 An all American guard. Unknown.—BrT
 Daddy's football game. J. Prelutsky.—PrIt
 Football. W. Mason.—KeK
 A football game. A. Van Eck.—PrRh
 Lance Perkins. M. Glenn.—GlCd
 Marvin Pickett. M. Glenn.—GlC
Football. Walt Mason.—KeK
A **football** game. Alice Van Eck.—PrRh

Foote, Samuel
 The great panjandrum.—BlO
Footnote. Norah Smaridge.—PrRa
Footprints
 Cat in the snow. A. Fisher.—CoN
 Footprints. J. Aiken.—LiSf
 "Footprints of a sparrow." N. M. Bodecker.—
  BaS—BoSs
 The open door. E. Coatsworth.—LiCa
 The sandpiper ("Look at the little sandpiper").
  C. Zolotow.—FaTh—HoSe
 Snow print two, hieroglyphics. B. J. Esbensen.—
  EsCs—FaTh
Footprints. Joan Aiken.—LiSf
"**Footprints** I make, smoke arises from burning
 of the old stalks." See Song of the Osage
 woman
"**Footprints** of a sparrow." N. M. Bodecker.—
 BaS—BoSs
For a cloud. Eleanor Farjeon.—FaE
For a cock. Eleanor Farjeon.—FaE
"**For** a companion." Shiki, tr. by Peter
 Beilenson.—FaTh
"**For** a cough." See Remedies
For a dance. Eleanor Farjeon.—FaE
For a dead kitten. Sara Henderson Hay.—ChC
For a dewdrop. Eleanor Farjeon.—FaE
For a friend. Ted Kooser.—JaG
"**For** a harmless April rain." X. J. Kennedy.—
 KeB
For a lamb. Richard Eberhart.—HeR
"**For** a long time." See The first Thanksgiving
For a mocking voice. Eleanor Farjeon.—LiSf
For a quick exit. Norma Farber.—HoCl—KeK
"**For** a year had." See Swearing
For all. Eleanor Farjeon.—FaE
For chest pain. Unknown.—BiSp
For Christmas day. Eleanor Farjeon.—FaE
"**For** comfort and pleasure." See Zoo
For Deena. Nikki Giovanni.—GiSp
For every one. Arnold Adoff.—AdA
"**For** every one we know the inside." See For
 every one
"**For** going up or coming down." See For a quick
 exit
For good morning. Eleanor Farjeon.—FaE
For good night. Eleanor Farjeon.—FaE
For her. Mark Strand.—JaG
"**For** hours the princess would not play or sleep."
 See The yak
"**For** I will consider my cat Jeoffrey." See M
 cat Jeoffrey
"**For** I will consider my cat Jeoffry". See My ca
 Jeoffrey
For Laura. Myra Cohn Livingston.—HoBf
"**For** little beetles." See Point of view
"**For** love of lovely words, and for the sake." Se
 Skerryvore
For Mary and her kitten. Eleanor Farjeon.—Fa
For Mugs. Myra Cohn Livingston.—HoDl
For my brother who died before I was bor
 Baron Wormser.—JaG
For my daughter ("She often lies with her hand
 behind her head"). Ronald Koertge.—JaS
For my daughter ("This is the summer storm"
 Ed Ochester.—JaS
For my father on his birthday. Greg Kuzma.—Ja
For my son, born during an ice storm. Dav
 Jauss.—JaS
"**For** New Year, Postumus, ten years ago." S
 A Roman thank you letter
"**For** once he wanted." See My grandfather
 search of moonshine

For poets. Al Young.—JaD
"For printed instructions." See No holes marred
For putting a woman's family to sleep. Unknown.—BiSp
For Richard Chase. Jim Wayne Miller.—JaG
For silence. Ruskin Bond.—LaT
For subduing a walrus. Unknown.—BiSp
For Sue. Phil Hey.—JaPo
For the children or the grown-ups. Unknown.—HaO
For the little girl who asked why the kitchen was so bright. James Ulmer.—JaT
For the moment. Pierre Reverdy.—KoT
For the rebuilding of a house. Wendell Berry.—PlEd
For the sisters of the Hôtel Dieu. Abraham Moses Klein.—DoNw
"For the third time in ten years." See Tunes for bears to dance to
For the time being, sels. Wystan Hugh Auden
"Well, so that is that, now we must dismantle the tree".—HaO
For the young who want to. Marge Piercy.—JaPi
For them. Eleanor Farjeon.—FaE
"For wandering walks." See Joe's snow clothes
"For want of a nail the shoe was lost." Mother Goose.—FaW—LoR
"For weeks before it comes I feel excited, yet when it." See Afterthought
For Wilma. Don Johnson.—JaG
For you. Karla Kuskin.—LiVp
For young men growing up to help themselves. Unknown.—BiSp
The forbidden play. Robert Graves.—LiSf
"The force that through the green fuse drives the flower." Dylan Thomas.—HeR
Forché, Carolyn
Dulcimer maker.—PlSc
Ford pickup. David Allan Evans.—JaPo
Forest: an invitation. Myra Cohn Livingston.—LiMp
Forests and forestry. See also Trees
At St. Jerome. F. Harrison.—DoNw
The combe. E. Thomas.—HeR
Come in. R. Frost.—KoS
English oak. M. C. Livingston.—LiMp
Flame of the forest, midnight. M. C. Livingston.—LiMp
Forest: an invitation. M. C. Livingston.—LiMp
Gluskap's hound. T. G. Roberts.—DoNw
Hidden. E. Farjeon.—FaE
In hardwood groves. R. Frost.—KoS
The intruders. J. Reeves.—CoOu
Lair. E. Merriam.—MeHa
Narcolepsy. M. Owen.—KoT
Nutting. W. Wordsworth.—HeR
Progress. C. Martin.—JaPo
Rain forest, Papua, New Guinea. M. C. Livingston.—LiMp
So they went deeper into the forest. R. Daniells.—DoNw
Spring pools. R. Frost.—KoS
Spruce woods. A. R. Ammons.—KeK
Stopping by woods on a snowy evening. R. Frost.—CoN—HaOf—HeR—KoS—KoT—LiSf—PrRh
The tale of Lilla. E. Farjeon.—FaE
"There's a fire in the forest." W. Ross.—DoNw
The toadstool wood. J. Reeves.—FaTh—LiWa
"Under the greenwood tree." From As you like it. W. Shakespeare.—HoUn—KoT—LiSf
The wild lumberjack. Unknown.—PlAs
"The forests were on fire." See Two drops
Forever. Eve Merriam.—MeSk

Forget about it. Robert Currie.—JaS
Forget it. David McCord.—McAs
"Forget roadside crossings." See How to see deer
Forgetfulness
Grass. C. Sandburg.—HoRa
The keeper. W. Carpenter.—JaPi
Metamorphosis ("When water turns to ice does it remember"). C. Sandburg.—HoRa
Questions ("The questions they ask"). E. Farjeon.—FaE
"Twinkle Toes." A. Lobel.—LoWr
"Forgive me if I have not sent you." See Valentines
Forgiveness. See also Charity; Kindness
Clap your hands for Herod. J. Hanzlik.—HaO
Little things ("Little things, that run, and quail"). J. Stephens.—FaTh—LaT—LiSf—PrRh
Forgotten. Cynthia Rylant.—RyW
Forgotten girlhood, sels. Laura Riding
Around the corner.—HeR
Children ("Children sleep at night"). HoR
In Laddery street herself.—HeR
Into Laddery Street.—HeR
Forks. See Tableware
Forms of praise. Lillian Morrison.—LiSf
The forsaken, sels. Duncan Campbell Scott
"Once in the winter".—DoNw
The forsaken merman. Matthew Arnold.—BlO
Forster, Frederick J.
The lobsters and the fiddler crab.—PrRh
Forsyth, Sarah
My Christmas, mum's Christmas.—HaO
Forsythia bush. Lilian Moore.—MoSn
Fortune telling
"If you sneeze on Monday, you sneeze for danger." Mother Goose.—AlH
"Married when the year is new." Mother Goose.—LoR
"Monday's child is fair of face." Mother Goose.—DaC—DeM—FaW—LoR
"One I love." Mother Goose.—DeM
"Rich man, poor man, beggarman, thief." Mother Goose.—LoR—PlSc
Forty mermaids. Dennis Lee.—RuI
Forty performing bananas. Jack Prelutsky.—PrNk
Forty Seventh Street crash. X. J. Kennedy.—KeF
The fossil raindrops. Harriet Prescott Spofford.—HaOf
Fossils
The black fern. L. Norris.—LiSf
Crystals like blood. H. MacDiarmid.—HeR
Dinosaurs ("Their feet, planted into tar"). M. C. Livingston.—HoDi
The fossil raindrops. H. P. Spofford.—HaOf
Fossils. L. Moore.—HoDi—MoSn
Fossils. Lilian Moore.—HoDi—MoSn
Foul shot. Edwin A. Hoey.—PrRh
The fountain. James Russell Lowell.—HaOf
"Four and twenty tailors went to kill a snail." Mother Goose.—DaC
The four dears. Ebenezer Elliot.—PlSc
"Four ducks on a pond." William Allingham.—BlO
Four foot feat. Arnold Adoff.—AdA
Four little foxes. Lew Sarett.—PrRh
Four seasons ("Spring is showery, flowery, bowery"). Unknown.—PrRh
The four seasons ("Summer"). Jack Prelutsky.—PrRh
"Four-way stop." Myra Cohn Livingston.—KeK
"Four years ago I walk through the jungles." See Min Trang

Fourteen ways of touching the Peter ("You can push"). George MacBeth.—ChC
The **fourteenth** day of Adar. Barbara Juster Esbensen.—LiPj
The **Fourth**. Shel Silverstein.—LiSf
Fourth of July
  The brownies' celebration. P. Cox.—HaOf
  The Fourth. S. Silverstein.—LiSf
  Fourth of July ("Hurrah for the fourth of July"). M. C. Livingston.—LiCe
  The fourth of July. J. Prelutsky.—PrWi
  Fourth of July ("Tonight the air explodes"). B. J. Esbensen.—EsCs
  Fourth of July night ("Just see those pinwheels whirling round"). D. Aldis.—HoSi—LiSf
  Fourth of July night ("The little boat at anchor"). C. Sandburg.—HoRa
  A rocket in my pocket. Unknown.—PrRh
Fourth of July ("Hurrah for the fourth of July"). Myra Cohn Livingston.—LiCe
The **fourth** of July. Jack Prelutsky.—PrWi
Fourth of July ("Tonight the air explodes"). Barbara Juster Esbensen.—EsCs
Fourth of July night ("Just see those pinwheels whirling round"). Dorothy Aldis.—HoSi—LiSf
Fourth of July night ("The little boat at anchor"). Carl Sandburg.—HoRa
Fox, Siv Cedering
  "In the morning."—JaT
  Nightmares.—LiWa
  "Once I dreamt I was the snow."—LiSf
Fox dancing. Suzanne Knowles.—HeR
"A **fox** went out in a hungry plight." See Mister Fox
Foxes
  The arctic fox. T. Hughes.—HuU
  Four little foxes. L. Sarett.—PrRh
  Fox dancing. S. Knowles.—HeR
  Mister Fox. Unknown.—BlO
  Ol' red thief. E. Farjeon.—FaE
  "Put your finger in." Unknown.—RaT
  The sycophantic fox and the gullible raven. G. W. Carryl.—HaOf
  The vixen. J. Clare.—HeR
"**Frail** the white rose and frail are." See A flower given to my daughter
Frame for a picture. Eve Merriam.—MeF
Francis, Colin
  Tony O.—BlO
Francis, Cynthia B.
  Popsicles.—HoMu
Francis, J. G.
  "An elephant sat on some kegs."—BrT
  The genial grimalkin.—BrT
Francis, Robert
  The base stealer.—CoN—LiSf—PrRh
  Bouquets.—JaD
  Boy at a certain age.—JaD
  The bulldozer.—JaPo
  Cats ("Cats walk neatly").—JaD
  The dandelion gatherer.—JaPo
  Fisherman.—JaPo
  Glass.—JaD
  The house remembers.—JaD
  Light casualties.—JaPo
  Now that your shoulders reach my shoulders.—JaS
  Salt ("Salt for white").—FaTh
  Swimmer.—JaD
  While I slept.—KeK
Francis of Assisi, Saint
  "Lord, make me an instrument of thy peace."—LaT

Francis of Assisi, Saint (about)
  Saint Francis and the sow. G. Kinnell.—HeR
Frankie and Johnny. Unknown.—HeR
"**Frankie** and Johnny were lovers." See Frankie and Johnny
Franz Dominguez. Mel Glenn.—GlC
Fraser, Hermia
  The rousing canoe song.—DoNw
Fraser, Kathleen
  Broom balancing.—PrRh
  Follow the leader.—PrRh
  Poem in which my legs are accepted.—McL
  Wrestling.—HoBf—PrRh
Frau Bauman, Frau Schmidt, and Frau Schwartze. Theodore Roethke.—PlSc
Fraulein reads instructive rhymes. Maxine Kumin.—JaPi
"The **freak** is the other." See Celebrating the freak
Freckles. Aileen Fisher.—HoSu
Fred. Eleanor Farjeon.—FaE
"**Fred** likes creatures." See Fred
Freddy. Dennis Lee.—PrRh
"A **free** bird leaps." See Caged birds
Free union, sels. André Breton
  "My wife whose hair is a brush fire".—KoT
Freedom
  "As I lay asleep in Italy." From The mask of anarchy. P. B. Shelley.—HeR
  Caged birds. M. Angelou.—AnS
  The child and the bird. E. Farjeon.—FaE
  The cormorant's tale. P. Fleischman.—FlI
  Fist fight. D. Cockrell.—JaPi
  "Oh, isn't it a pity, such a pretty girl as I." H. H. Robinson.—PlSc
  "Oh my school notebooks." From Liberty. P Éluard.—KoT
  Passover. M. C. Livingston.—LiCe
  To dark eyes dreaming. Z. K. Snyder.—PrRh
Freeman, Carol
  "Christmas morning i."—KeK
Freeman, Mary E. Wilkins
  Blue-eyed Mary.—HaOf
  Marm Grayson's guests.—HaOf
  "The ostrich is a silly bird."—HaOf—KeK
  A pretty ambition.—HaOf
French. Eleanor Farjeon.—FaE
French language
  French. E. Farjeon.—FaE
  Innuendo. D. McCord.—McAs
Freneau, Philip
  Columbus to Ferdinand.—HaOf
The **fresh** air. Harold Monro.—LiIl
"The **fresh** air moves like water round a boat. See The fresh air
Fresh paint. Eve Merriam.—MeF
Freuchen, Peter
  The mother's song ("It is so still in the house" tr. by.—HaO
Friday, Ann
  The wish ("Each birthday wish").—PrRa
"**Friday** came and the circus was there." See T circus
Friebert, Stuart
  My father's heart.—JaS
Fried, Elliot
  Amtrak.—JaPo
  The man who owned cars.—JaG
Friend, Robert
  From my mother's house, tr. by.—StG
Friend ("Do you know Paul, Paul Pine (he nine)"). Felice Holman.—LiIl
Friend ("When"). Lilian Moore.—LiIl
Friend dog. Arnold Adoff.—HoDl

"**Friend**, I have watched you down the mountain."
See A parting
Friend or foe. Eleanor Farjeon.—FaE
The **friendly** beasts. Unknown.—LiIl
The **friendly** cinnamon bun. Russell Hoban.—LiIl
"The **friendly** cow, all red and white." See The
cow
"**Friendly** Fredrick Fuddlestone." Arnold Lobel.—
LoWr
A **friendly** mouse. Harry Behn.—HoCb
Friends. See Friendship
Friends. William Stafford.—JaPo
Friendship
Absent friend. C. Zolotow.—ZoE
Agnes Snaggletooth. X. J. Kennedy.—KeF—LiIl
Alex Garber. M. Glenn.—GlCd
Alfred Corning Clark. R. Lowell.—HeR
Amanda ("This girl, Amanda"). A. Turner.—
TuS
Anna playing in a graveyard. C. Gilman.—HaOf
"As the sun came up, a ball of red."
Unknown.—LiIl
Atop. P. Redcloud.—HoBf
Bad day. M. Ridlon.—HoBf
Beth Rossiter and. M. Glenn.—GlCd
"Blow, blow, thou winter wind." From As you
like it. W. Shakespeare.—HoUn
Brenda Stewart. M. Glenn.—GlC
Brian Nichols. M. Glenn.—GlCd
Captain Spud and his first mate, Spade. J.
Ciardi.—HaOf
Certain choices. R. Shelton.—JaPi
Coming from Kansas. M. C. Livingston.—LiWo
"De las islas Puerto Rico." Unknown.—LiIl
Discovery. H. Behn.—HoCb
Douglas Kearney. M. Glenn.—GlCd
The enemy's portrait. T. Hardy.—PlEd
The Erie Canal. Unknown.—LiIl
Everett Anderson's friend. L. Clifton.—LiIl
False start. C. Zolotow.—ZoE
Familiar friends. J. S. Tippett.—HoDl
Family affairs. M. Angelou.—AnS
Fifty-fifty. C. Sandburg.—LiIl
First love ("We fell in love at 'Journey for
Margaret'"). J. Hemschemeyer.—JaPi
For a friend. T. Kooser.—JaG
For Laura. M. C. Livingston.—HoBf
Friend ("Do you know Paul, Paul Pine (he's
nine)"). F. Holman.—LiIl
Friend ("When"). L. Moore.—LiIl
Friend dog. A. Adoff.—HoDl
Friends. W. Stafford.—JaPo
Friendship ("I've discovered a way to stay
friends forever"). S. Silverstein.—CoN—LiIl
Friendship ("Like a quetzal plume, a fragrant
flower"). Unknown.—LiIl
"Friendship is like china." Unknown.—LiIl
The funny house. M. Hillert.—HoBf
Girl who's moved around. X. J. Kennedy.—
KeF
Great things have happened. A. Nowlan.—JaG
Harvey. J. Viorst.—ViI
Hug o' war. S. Silverstein.—CoN—PrRh
"I had a hippopotamus, I loved him as a
friend." From I had a hippopotamus. P.
Barrington.—LiIl
"I have friends." C. Thornton.—LiIl
I met this guy who died. G. Corso.—JaPi
"Jenny White and Johnny Black." E. Farjeon.—
FaE
Letter to a friend. L. Moore.—LiIl—MoSn
Letters from Sicily. E. Di Pasquale.—LiIl
Lines for a friend who left. J. Logan.—JaD

Making a friend. M. C. Livingston.—HoDl
Mario Benedetto. M. Glenn.—GlCd
The marmalade man makes a dance to mend
us. N. Willard.—LiIl
"Mary Lorenz." M. C. Livingston.—LiWo
Maurice. G. Brooks.—HoBf
Millions of strawberries. G. Taggard.—LiIl—LiSf
"Misery is when your." L. Hughes.—LiIl
Missing you. C. Zolotow.—HoBf—LiIl
My dragon. X. J. Kennedy.—PrRa
My teddy bear ("A teddy bear is a faithful
friend"). M. Chute.—PrRa
Neighbors ("The Cobbles live in the house next
door"). M. A. Hoberman.—LiIl
A new friend. M. A. Anderson.—FrP
The new girl. C. Zolotow.—ZoE
Nicole Harris. M. Glenn.—GlCd
Now lift me close. W. Whitman.—JaD
Oath of friendship. Unknown, fr. the Chinese.—
KoT
"Of the islands, Puerto Rico." Unknown.—LiIl
The old familiar faces. C. Lamb.—HcR
The owl's bedtime story. R. Jarrell.—LiIl
A parting. Wang Wei.—LiIl
People ("Some people talk and talk"). C.
Zolotow.—PrRh—ZoE
Poem ("I loved my friend"). L. Hughes.—
CoN—HoBf—HuDk—JaD—LiIl—LiSf
A poison tree. W. Blake.—HeR
"Pussy can sit by the fire and sing." R.
Kipling.—DaC
Puzzle ("My best friend's name is Billy"). A.
Spilka.—LiIl—PrRh
The question ("If I could teach you how to
fly"). D. Lee.—LiIl
"Read up and down." Unknown.—LiIl
"Remember the M." Unknown.—LiIl
A riddle ("Once when I was very scared"). C.
Zolotow.—CoN
Scott Garber. M. Glenn.—GlCd
Secret talk. E. Merriam.—LiIl
Sensitive Sydney. W. Irvin.—LiIl
Seumas Beg. J. Stephens.—BlO
Sheila Franklin. M. Glenn.—GlC
Since Hanna moved away. J. Viorst.—HoBf—
PrRh—ViI
"Sing hey, sing hey." Mother Goose.—LiIl
Skilly Oogan. R. Hoban.—LiIl
Sleep over. M. C. Livingston.—LiWo
Someone I like. C. Zolotow.—ZoE
The song of a dream. Unknown.—LiIl
Steve. C. Rylant.—RyW
Taking leave of a friend. Rihaku.—HeR
The telephone. E. Field.—JaPo
The telephone call. J. Prelutsky.—HoBf
"There are gold ships." Unknown.—LiIl
There once was a puffin. F. P. Jaques.—CoN—
FrP
Three. E. Coatsworth.—LiIl
Today is Saturday. Z. K. Snyder.—LiIl
Tomorrow. M. Strand.—JaG—JaPo
Two friends. N. Giovanni.—GiSp—LiIl
A valentine for my best friend. J. Prelutsky.—
PrIv
"We are talking about." A. Adoff.—AdA
"We could be friends." M. C. Livingston.—LiIl
What Johnny told me. J. Ciardi.—LiIl
"When, in disgrace with fortune and men's
eyes." From Sonnets. W. Shakespeare.—HoUn
With my foot in my mouth. D. Lee.—LiIl
Wrestling. K. Fraser.—HoBf—PrRh
"You smiled." C. O'John.—LiIl

Friendship ("I've discovered a way to stay friends forever"). Shel Silverstein.—CoN—Lill
Friendship ("Like a quetzal plume, a fragrant flower"). Unknown, tr. by John Bierhorst.—Lill
"Friendship is like china." Unknown.—Lill
Frightening. Claudia Lewis.—PrRh
"Fritters used to say, there is poetry in neckties." From Heavy and light. Carl Sandburg.—HoRa
Frizzing. John Ciardi.—CiD
The frog ("Be kind and tender to the frog"). Hilaire Belloc.—CoN—LiSf—PrRh
"The frog." See Frog
Frog. N. M. Bodecker.—BoSs
The frog ("What a wonderful bird the frog are"). Unknown.—CoN—HeR
"A frog and a flea." Cynthia Mitchell.—PrRa
The frog and the mouse. Mother Goose.—BlPi
The frog on the log. Ilo Orleans.—PrRa
"Froggie, froggie." Unknown.—DeD
Frogs and toads
  "Ancient pool." Basho.—KeK
  At the garden gate. D. McCord.—Lill
  A big turtle. Unknown.—PrRa
  Bullfrogs. D. A. Evans.—JaPi
  "Bullfrogs, bullfrogs on parade." J. Prelutsky.—PrRi
  Colita de rana. Unknown.—GrT
  First song. G. Kinnell.—JaG
  The frog ("Be kind and tender to the frog"). H. Belloc.—CoN—LiSf—PrRh
  Frog. N. M. Bodecker.—BoSs
  The frog ("What a wonderful bird the frog are"). Unknown.—CoN—HeR
  "A frog and a flea." C. Mitchell.—PrRa
  The frog and the mouse. Mother Goose.—BlPi
  The frog on the log. I. Orleans.—PrRa
  "Froggie, froggie." Unknown.—DeD
  Frog's lullaby. C. Pomerantz.—PoA
  "Great frog race." I. H. Finlay.—KeK
  "Hopping frog, hop here and be seen." C. G. Rossetti.—BlO
  "If you chance to be crossing." Unknown.—DeD
  "I'm nobody, who are you." E. Dickinson.—HaOf—LiSf—PrRh—TrM
  Little frog tail. Unknown.—GrT
  "May rains." Sanpu.—KoT
  Noblesse oblige. C. T. Wright.—JaPi
  Odd ("That was"). L. Moore.—MoSn
  "An old silent pond." Basho.—LiSf
  The polliwog. A. Guiterman.—PrRh
  Small frogs. L. Norris.—LiSf
  The soggy frog. J. Prelutsky.—PrSr
  Song of the spring peeper. J. Yolen.—YoR
  Song of the tree frogs. L. Moore.—MoSn
  Spring cries. C. Sandburg.—HoRa
  "There was a small pig from Woonsocket." A. Lobel.—LoB
  The tin frog. R. Hoban.—FaTh—PrRh
  A toad. E. A. Allen.—HaOf
  The toad ("I met a little woman"). E. Coatsworth.—PrRa
  The toad ("In day of old, those far off times"). R. S. Oliver.—PrRh
  The toad and the rabbit. J. Martin.—PrRa
  "The tree frog." J. T. Moore.—PrRh
  Tree toad. Unknown.—CoN
  "What is the opposite of a prince." R. Wilbur.—LiSf—LiWa
"Frogs in the marsh and frogs in the stream." See Canticle of spring
"Frogs jump." See Jump or jiggle

Frog's lullaby. Charlotte Pomerantz.—PoA
"From a birch." P. Wolny.—JaD
From a childhood. Rainer Maria Rilke.—KoT
From A child's Christmas in Wales, sels. Dylan Thomas
  Ghost story.—HaO
From a prayer for the novice at the close of his initiation. Unknown.—BiSp
From a prayer of the shooting chant. Unknown.—BiSp
From a prayer summoning the novice for his initiation. Unknown.—BiSp
From a railway carriage. Robert Louis Stevenson.—PrRh
From an airplane, sels. Harry Behn
  "Night settles on earth".—HoSs
"From breakfast on through all the day." See The land of Nod
From Council Bluffs to Omaha. Myra Cohn Livingston.—LiWo
"From either side of Wheelers' walk." See Sentries
"From friendly Squanto, wise in all things wild." See At the first Thanksgiving
"From gallery grave and the hunt of a wren king." From Thanksgiving for a habitat. Wystan Hugh Auden.—PlEd
"From ghoulies and ghosties." From A Cornish litany. Unknown.—HoCr—LiSf
  Things that go bump in the night.—CoN
  A Cornish litany.—LiWa
"From groves of spice." See Cradle song
"From her perch of beauty." See Avec merci, mother
"From his pouch he took his colors." From The song of Hiawatha. Henry Wadsworth Longfellow.—PlEd
"From in back of our couch." See An unexplained ouch
"From my brother's bed." See Night eyes
"From my city bed in the dawn I see a raccoon." See Science fiction
"From my friend Joey." See Mario Benedetto
From my mother's house. Leah Goldberg, tr. by Robert Friend.—StG
"From my mother's sleep I fell into the state." See The death of the ball turret gunner
"From number nine, Penwiper Mews." Edward Gorey.—BrT
  Number nine, Penwiper Mews.—PrRh
"From out of a wood a cuckoo did fly." See Carol of the birds
"From Prince Atsumichi." See Love
"From Table Isle." Unknown, tr. by Geoffrey Bownas and Anthony Thwaite.—FaTh
"From the dark yard by the sheep barn the cock crowed." See The henyard round
"From the field behind our house, a low howling." See Back country
"From the hag and hungry goblin." See Mad Tom's song
"From the half." See The approach of the storm
"From the old camping place." See Song of a ghost
"From the private ease of Mother's womb." See Baby world
"From the top of a bridge." See The river is a piece of sky
"From troubles of the world." See Ducks
"From Victoria I can go." See Victoria
"From where I stand now." See 12 October

Froman, Robert
  Puzzle ("Map of a city with streets meeting at center").—LiSf
  Skyscratcher.—LiSf
  Undefeated.—LiIl
Frontier and pioneer life. See also Cowboys
  Alphabet 1727. From The New England Primer. Unknown.—HaOf
  At the first Thanksgiving. X. J. Kennedy.—LiTp
  Buffalo dusk. C. Sandburg.—HaOf—HoRa—LiSf—PrRh
  The buffalo skinners. Unknown.—HeR
  The first Thanksgiving ("For a long time"). B. J. Esbensen.—LiTp
  The first Thanksgiving ("When the Pilgrims"). J. Prelutsky.—CoN—PrIt
  The gift outright. R. Frost.—KoS
  Indian names. L. H. Sigourney.—HaOf
  Peregrine White and Virginia Dare. S. V. Benét, and R. C. Benét.—HaOf
  The shooting of Dan McGrew. R. W. Service.—DoNw—HeR
Frost, Frances
  Maple feast.—PrRh
  "Morning is a little lass."—ChG
  Night heron.—PrRh
  The sandpiper ("At the edge of tide").—PrRh
  Squirrel in the rain.—PrRa
  White season.—LiSf
Frost, Robert
  Acquainted with the night.—KoS
  Beyond words.—KeK
  Birches.—HeR—KoS
  The birthplace.—PlEd
  Canis major.—KeK—KoS
  Come in.—KoS
  Departmental.—KoS
  Desert places.—HeR
  Devotion.—KoS
  A drumlin woodchuck.—KoS
  Dust of snow.—KoS—LiSf—PrRh
  Fire and ice.—KoS
  Fireflies in the garden.—KoS—PrRh
  Gathering leaves.—HeR—KoS
  Ghost house.—LiWa
  The gift outright.—KoS
  House fear.—LiWa
  Hyla brook.—KoS
  The impulse.—PlAs
  In hardwood groves.—KoS
  The kitchen chimney.—PlEd
  The last word of a bluebird (as told to a child).—KoS—LiSf
  A late walk.—KoS
  Leaves compared with flowers.—KoS
  The lockless door.—LiWa
  A lone striker.—PlSc
  Looking for a sunset bird in winter.—KoS
  Mending wall.—KoS
  A minor bird.—KoS
  Nothing gold can stay.—KoS
  Now close the windows.—KoS
  On a tree fallen across the road.—HeR
  One guess.—KoS
  Out, out.—HeR
  The oven bird.—KoS
  A passing glimpse.—KoS
  The pasture.—KoS—KoT—LiSf
  A patch of old snow.—KoS
  A peck of gold.—KoS
  Plowmen.—PlSc
  A prayer in spring.—LaT
  Questioning faces.—KoS

Range-finding.—HeR
The road not taken.—KoS
The rose family.—HaOf—KoS
The runaway ("Once, when the snow of the year was beginning to fall").—KoS—LiSf
The secret sits.—KoS—LiSf
The span of life.—HoDl
Spring pools.—KoS
Stopping by woods on a snowy evening.—CoN—HaOf—HeR—KoS—KoT—LiSf—PrRh
A time to talk.—LiIl
To the thawing wind.—KoS
Tree at my window.—KoS
A young birch.—KoS
Frost
  Frost ("The frost moved up the window-pane"). E. J. Pratt.—DoNw
  Frost ("Frost on my window"). G. Johnston.—DoNw
  Frost ("How does/the plain"). V. Worth.—WoSp
  Jack Frost ("Rustily creak the crickets, Jack Frost came down"). C. Thaxter.—HaOf
  Jack Frost ("Someone painted pictures"). H. B. Davis.—PrRa
  Splinter. C. Sandburg.—HaOf—HoRa—KeK
  "Winter etches windowpanes, fingerpaints in white." M. C. Livingston.—LiCs
  Winter.—BaS
Frost ("The frost moved up the window-pane"). Edwin John Pratt.—DoNw
Frost ("Frost on my window"). George Johnston.—DoNw
Frost ("How does/the plain"). Valerie Worth.—WoSp
"The **frost** is on the ground, Jenny." See Robin to Jenny
"The **frost** moved up the window-pane." See Frost
"The **frost** of the moon fell over my floor." See Six green singers
"**Frost** on my window." See Frost
"A **frosty** Christmas eve." See Noel, Christmas eve, 1913
Fruit. See also names of fruits, as Blueberries
  "Andrew was an apple thief." A. Lobel.—LoWr
  Fruited rainbow. C. J. Egita.—HoMu
Fruited rainbow. Charles J. Egita.—HoMu
"**Fruits** of orange, yellow, red." See Fruited rainbow
Fry, Nan
  Apple ("At the center, a dark star").—JaPo
  Snow ("Drifting we wake").—JaPo
Fudging the issue. Eve Merriam.—MeF
Fufuka, Karama
  Basketball star.—PrRh
  Lil' bro'.—PrRh
"**Full** fathom five thy father lies." From The tempest. William Shakespeare.—HoUn
  Ariel's song.—BlO
"**Full** imagined, I suppose." See For my father on his birthday
Full moon, rising. Jonathan Holden.—JaG
Full moon, Santa Barbara. Sara Teasdale.—HaOf
"**Full** of oatmeal." See Miss Norma Jean Pugh, first grade teacher
Full of the moon. Karla Kuskin.—HoDl
Fuller, Roy
  Bringing up babies.—PrRh
  Christmas day ("Small girls on trikes").—HaO
  Horrible things.—CoOu
  Meetings and absences.—CoOu
Fulton, Alice
  Days through starch and bluing.—JaG
  The gone years.—JaS

Fulton, Alice—*Continued*
  The great aunts of my childhood.—JaS
"**Fumble-John** they call him." See Why
Fun. Leroy F. Jackson.—PrRa
Funerals. See also Death; Grief
  At the funeral of great aunt Mary. R. Bly.—JaS
  Aunt Gladys's home movie no. 31, Albert's funeral. J. W. Miller.—JaS
  Ballad of the man who's gone. L. Hughes.—PlAs
  Bells for John Whiteside's daughter. J. C. Ransom.—HeR
  Death of an old seaman. L. Hughes.—HuDk
  Departmental. R. Frost.—KoS
  The hearse song. Unknown.—HeR
  Irish wake. L. Hughes.—HuDk
  "Nobody loses all the time." E. E. Cummings.—HeR
  The sea ritual. G. Darley.—LiWa
  The shooting of John Dillinger outside the Biograph Theater, July 22, 1934. D. Wagoner.—HeR
  "Who killed Cock Robin." Mother Goose.—LoR
The **funny** house. Margaret Hillert.—HoBf
The **funny** old man and his wife. Unknown
"A **funny** thing about a chair." See The chair
"The **furred** magnificence, the precious stones." See Epiphany, for the artist
Furry bear. Alan Alexander Milne.—FrP
"The **furs** are put in the water." See A song of the coyoteway
"The **fury** and terror." See The storm
The **fury** of aerial bombardment. Richard Eberhart.—HeR
"**Fury** said to a mouse." From Alice's adventures in Wonderland. Lewis Carroll.—KeK
Futility. Wilfred Owen.—HeR
Future hero. X. J. Kennedy.—KeF
"**Fuzzy** wuzzy, creepy crawly." Lillian Schulz.—PrRa
"**Fuzzy** Wuzzy was a bear." Unknown.—CoN
Fyleman, Rose
  The birthday child.—FrP
  December ("All the months go past").—PrRa
  The goblin.—CoN
  Mary Middling.—PrRa
  Mice.—CoN—FrP—LiSf—PrRa—PrRh
  Singing time.—ChG—FrP—PrRa

G

G. Hilaire Belloc.—FaW
"**G** is a grumbler gruff." See A grumbler gruff
"**G** is for dear little Gustave." See G is for Gustave
G is for Gustave. Isabel Frances Bellows.—BrT
"**G** stands for Gnu, whose weapons of defense." See G
Gaelic lullaby. Unknown.—ChB
Gág, Wanda
  The A B C bunny.—LiSf
Gail Larkin. Mel Glenn.—GlC
"**Gaily** afloat." Arnold Lobel.—LoWr
Galente garden II. Juan Ramón Jiménez, tr. by H. R. Hays.—LiWa
The **gallant** highwayman. James De Mille.—DoNw
The **gallivanting** gecko. Jack Prelutsky.—PrZ
"The **gallivanting** gecko's ways." See The gallivanting gecko

"A **gallon** of." See Cumulus clouds
"**Gallop** up the instant stair." See Air on an escalator
Galoshes. Rhoda W. Bacmeister.—CoN
Gamblers and gambling
  Dirge. K. Fearing.—HeR
  A hero in the land of dough. R. Clairmont.—KeK
  On the cards and the dice. Sir W. Raleigh.—HeR
  Twin aces. K. Wilson.—JaPi
"A **game** called Kick the Can, which used to last about a month." See We used to play
"The **game** was ended, and the noise at last had died." See Football
Games. See also Nursery play; also names of games, as Baseball
  Croquet. D. Huddle.—JaS
  Dangerous. D. Aldis.—PrRa
  Follow the leader. K. Fraser.—PrRh
  Good sportsmanship. R. Armour.—KeK
  Grab-bag. H. H. Jackson.—HaOf
  Harvey always wins. J. Prelutsky.—CoN
  He ("Some bite off the others"). V. Popa.—HeR
  Hide and seek ("Someone hides from someone"). V. Popa.—HeR
  Hide and seek ("The trees are tall, but the moon small"). R. Graves.—CoN—KeK
  Hide and seek ("When I am alone, and quite alone"). A. B. Shiffrin.—FrP—PrRa
  Hug o' war. S. Silverstein.—CoN—PrRh
  In the park ("Two old-timers"). E. Merriam.—MeF
  In the park ("When you've"). L. Moore.—MoSn
  Jacks. V. Worth.—WoSp
  Marbles ("They are his planets"). J. LaBombard.—JaT
  The nail. V. Popa.—HeR
  No girls allowed. J. Prelutsky.—PrRh
  The old man's toes. E. Farjeon.—FaE
  On the cards and the dice. Sir W. Raleigh.—HeR
  One-upmanship. M. Chaikin.—CoN
  The rose thieves. V. Popa.—HeR
  Sneaky Sue. J. Prelutsky.—PrNk
  Stickball. V. Schonborg.—PrRh
  Wrestling. K. Fraser.—HoBf—PrRh
The **gap** in the cedar. Roy Scheele.—JaPi
Garage sale. Karl Shapiro.—JaPi
Garbage
  The city dump. F. Holman.—HoSs—PrRh
  Drumpp the grump. J. Prelutsky.—PrNk
  Garbage truck. M. Ridlon.—HoCl
  Junk. R. Wilbur.—PlSc
  Quest. E. Merriam.—MeF
  Sarah Cynthia Sylvia Stout would not take the garbage out. S. Silverstein.—HaOf—LiSf
  "There was a poor pig on the street." A. Lobel.—LoB
Garbage truck. Marci Ridlon.—HoCl
García Lorca, Federico
  The little mute boy.—HeR
  "Mr. Lizard is crying."—KoT
  The moon rises.—KoT
  Silly song.—KoT
  The six strings.—HeR
  Snail ("They have brought me a snail").—FaTh
"The **garden** fence bedewed with the mist." See Chilly dawn
"**Garden**, grow." See To any garden
The **garden** hose. Beatrice Janosco.—CoN
The **garden** in the dark. Eleanor Farjeon.—FaE
The **garden** of love. William Blake.—HeR

The **garden** seat. Thomas Hardy.—HeR
"A **gardener**, Tobias Baird." See The headless gardener
Gardeners. See Gardens and gardening
Gardens and gardening
  Box, for L.M.B. M. C. Livingston.—LiMp
  Burning the gate. E. Farjeon.—FaE
  Capability Brown. W. Cowper.—PlSc
  "The cherries' garden gala." J. Prelutsky.—PrNk
  Corn and beans. C. Sandburg.—HoRa
  Crow wonders. L. Moore.—MoSn
  The dying garden. H. Nemerov.—JaPi
  Frau Bauman, Frau Schmidt, and Frau Schwartze. T. Roethke.—PlSc
  The garden hose. B. Janosco.—CoN
  The garden in the dark. E. Farjeon.—FaE
  The garden seat. T. Hardy.—HeR
  The gate in the wall. E. Farjeon.—FaE
  Girls in the garden. E. Farjeon.—FaE
  A gopher in the garden. J. Prelutsky.—PrZ
  The headless gardener. I. Serraillier.—LiSf
  The little brown celery. G. MacBeth.—FaTh
  Little seeds. E. H. Minarik.—PrRa
  "Mary, Mary, quite contrary." Mother Goose.—DaC—DeM—FaW—LoR
  Maytime magic. M. Watts.—PrRh
  Mr. Bidery's spidery garden. D. McCord.—PrRh
  Mr. Potts. H. Behn.—HoCb
  Mother's garden. M. C. Livingston.—LiWo
  The mummies. M. Kumin.—JaPi
  My aunt. T. Hughes.—LiWa
  Nocturn cabbage. C. Sandburg.—HoRa
  "Old Quin Queeribus." N. B. Turner.—PrRh
  "Once, when the sky was very near the earth." N. Belting.—LiSf
  Poems. G. Gildner.—JaPi
  Rock gardener. X. J. Kennedy.—KeF
  The second birth of roses. E. Farjeon.—FaE
  The seeds of love. Unknown.—PlAs
  Snow in the garden. E. Farjeon.—FaE
  A spike of green. B. Baker.—PrRa
  The start. E. Farjeon.—FaE
  "Summer fattens melons up, grow berries plump and sweet." M. C. Livingston.—LiCs
  Summer fountains. E. Farjeon.—FaE
  Sweet herbs. E. Farjeon.—FaE
  This poem is for Nadine. P. B. Janeczko.—JaG
  This year, next year. E. Farjeon.—FaE
  To a butterfly. W. Wordsworth.—DaC
  To any garden. E. Farjeon.—FaE
  Tommy. G. Brooks.—HoSi
  Undine's garden. H. Behn.—HoCb
  Weeds. C. Zolotow.—ZoE
  Why ("We zoomed"). P. Redcloud.—HoMu
  Window boxes. E. Farjeon.—FaE
  The witch's garden. L. Moore.—MoSn
Gardner, John
  The lizard ("The lizard is a timid thing").—PrRh
Gardner, Martin
  Barbershop.—PrRh
  Soap ("Just look at those hands").—PrRh
Garland, Hamlin
  A Dakota wheat field.—HaOf
  Prairie fires.—HaOf
Garthwaite, Wymond
  Peter and Wendy.—PrRa
Gary, Irving. Mel Glenn.—GlCd
"The **gas** gauge." See Journey's end
Gasztold, Carmen Bernos de
  The prayer of the cat.—ChC—LiSf
  The prayer of the dog.—HoDl
  The prayer of the little ducks.—LaT
  The prayer of the little pig.—LiSf
  The prayer of the monkey.—LaT
The **gate** in the wall. Eleanor Farjeon.—FaE
Gates
  Angelica the doorkeeper. Unknown.—HeR
  At the garden gate. D. McCord.—LiIl
  Burning the gate. E. Farjeon.—FaE
  The gate in the wall. E. Farjeon.—FaE
"**Gather** up." See Litany
Gathering leaves. Robert Frost.—HeR—KoS
Gathering the bones together. Gregory Orr.—JaPi
Gatty, Alfred Scott
  The three little pigs.—DaC
Gay, Zhenya
  "In the summer we eat."—PrRa
The **gazelle** calf. David Herbert Lawrence.—HeR
"The **gazelle** calf, O my children." See The gazelle calf
Gazelles. See Antelopes
Geese
  And stands there sighing. E. Coatsworth.—KeK
  Autumn song of the goose. J. Yolen.—YoR
  Flight ("A hound sound"). L. Moore.—MoSn
  Flyaway. B. J. Esbensen.—EsCs
  "The giggling gaggling gaggle of geese." J. Prelutsky.—PrZ
  "Go tell Aunt Rhody." Unknown.—LiSf
    "Go and tell Aunt Nancy".—BlO
  Goose. T. Hughes.—HuU
  The goose and the gander. Unknown.—HeR
  "Goosey, goosey gander." Mother Goose.—BlQ—DeM—FaW—LoR
  "Grandfather Gander flew over the land." J. Prelutsky.—PrRi
  "Gray goose and gander." Mother Goose.—AlH—LoR
  Lost ("What happened in the sky"). L. Moore.—MoSn
  The misapprehended goose. O. Herford.—BrT
  Old grey goose. H. Behn.—HoCb
  "Old Mother Goose." Mother Goose.—DeM—LoR
  "Something told the wild geese." R. Field.—CoN—CoOu—HaOf—LiSf—PrRh
  "There was an old man of Dunluce." E. Lear.—LiH
  "There was an old person of Nice." E. Lear.—LiH
  "Three gray geese in a green field grazing." Mother Goose.—LoR
  "When the rain raineth." Unknown.—HeR
  "Why does it snow." L. E. Richards.—HaOf
  "Wild goose, wild goose." Issa.—KoT
  "Wire, briar, limber lock." Mother Goose.—DaC
"**Geese** keep dry." See Drippy weather
Gems. See Precious stones
General delivery. Cynthia Rylant.—RyW
General store. Rachel Field.—FaW
Genesis, sels. Bible/Old Testament
  "And the whole earth was of one language, and of one speech".—PlEd
The **genial** grimalkin. J. G. Francis.—BrT
The **genie**. Ann Stanford.—LiWa
Genies
  The genie. A. Stanford.—LiWa
"**Gentle** giant dinosaur." See To brontosaurus, a gentle giant dinosaur
"**Gentle** hunter." See Leopard
"**Gently** dip, but not too deep." See Celanta at the well of life
"**Gently**, gently, the wind blows." Kazue Mizumura.—FaTh

Genuine poem, found on a blackboard in a bowling alley in Story City, Iowa. Ted Kooser.—KeK
Geography
Geography. E. Farjeon.—FaE
"New York is in North Carolina." J. Prelutsky.—PrNk
Geography. Eleanor Farjeon.—FaE
Geology. See also Rocks and stones
Fossils. L. Moore.—HoDi—MoSn
Geometry. See Mathematics
George. Nikki Giovanni.—GiSp
Georgia
A Georgia song. M. Angelou.—AnS
A **Georgia** song. Maya Angelou.—AnS
Georgie. Unknown.—PlAs
"**Georgie** Porgie, pudding and pie." Mother Goose.—DeM—FaW—LoR
The **germ**. Ogden Nash.—HeR
German slumber song. Unknown, tr. by Louis Untermeyer.—BaH
Germs
The germ. O. Nash.—HeR
The microbe. H. Belloc.—LiSf
Things on a microscope slide. X. J. Kennedy.—FaTh
Gertrude. Gwendolyn Brooks.—LiSf
Gestures
Adam's apple. C. Barks.—JaPo
"**Get** a trap, set a trap." See Trap
Get 'em here. Lee Bennett Hopkins.—HoMu
"**Get** set, ready now, jump right in." See Rope rhyme
Get up and bar the door. Unknown.—BlO—PlAs
"**Get** up get up." See The clock ticks
"**Get** up, get up, you lazyhead." Unknown.—CoN
Slugabed.—DaC
"**Get** well, get well, little frog tail." See Little frog tail
Getting out of bed. Eleanor Farjeon.—ChG—FaE
Ghalib, Mirza
Ghazal XII.—McL
Ghazal XII. Mirza Ghalib, tr. by William Stanley Merwin and Aijaz Abmad.—McL
Ghost ("More gruesome than any groan"). Eve Merriam.—MeHa
Ghost ("There is a ghost"). Christian Morgenstern, tr. by William De Witt Snodgrass and Lore Segal.—LiWa
Ghost house. Robert Frost.—LiWa
"The **ghost** is gone in rags." From Five ghost songs. Unknown.—KoT
The **ghost** of the cargo boat. Pablo Neruda, tr. by Donald D. Walsh.—LiWa
Ghost sounds. Unknown.—HoCr
Ghost story. From From A child's Christmas in Wales. Dylan Thomas.—HaO
The **ghostly** grocer of Grumble Grove. Jack Prelutsky.—PrSr
"A **ghostly** snow." See Night snow
Ghosts
Afreet. D. McCord.—LiWa
"Ah, the roofs." From Five ghost songs. Unknown, fr. the Ambo people of Africa.—KoT
At the keyhole. W. De la Mare.—BlO
A ballad of Christmas. W. De la Mare.—HaO
El caballo. J. M. Eguren.—LiSf
Call them back. C. Petrakos.—JaG
Campsite. B. J. Esbensen.—EsCs
Colonel Fazackerley. C. Causley.—CoOu—PrRh
The cruise of the Mystery. C. Thaxter.—HaOf

Daniel Webster's horses. E. Coatsworth.—HaOf
The dark house. Unknown.—CoN
"Doris Drummond sneaked a look." X. J. Kennedy.—KeB
"The dove stays in the garden." From Five ghost songs. Unknown, fr. the Ambo people of Africa.—KoT
Down below. J. Aiken.—LiWa
The empty house. R. Hoban.—LiWa
"Fog, fog." From Songs of the ghost dance. Unknown, fr. the Paiute Indian.—LiWa
"From ghoulies and ghosties." From A Cornish litany. Unknown.—HoCr—LiSf
Things that go bump in the night.—CoN
A Cornish litany.—LiWa
The garden seat. T. Hardy.—HeR
Ghost ("More gruesome than any groan"). E. Merriam.—MeHa
Ghost ("There is a ghost"). C. Morgenstern.—LiWa
Ghost house. R. Frost.—LiWa
"The ghost is gone in rags." From Five ghost songs. Unknown, fr. the Ambo people of Africa.—KoT
The ghost of the cargo boat. P. Neruda.—LiWa
Ghost sounds. Unknown.—HoCr
Ghost story. From From A child's Christmas in Wales. D. Thomas.—HaO
The ghostly grocer of Grumble Grove. J. Prelutsky.—PrSr
Ghosts ("A cold and starry darkness moans"). H. Behn.—HoCr—PrRh
Ghosts ("Those houses haunt in which we leave"). E. Jennings.—JaPo
Gluskap's hound. T. G. Roberts.—DoNw
The great auk's ghost. R. Hodgson.—KeK—PrRh
Halloween ("The moon is full and"). C. Zolotow.—ZoE
A Halloween ghost story. B. J. Esbensen.—EsCs
Haunted house. V. Worth.—LiWa
The haunted oven. X. J. Kennedy.—LiWa
The haunted palace. E. A. Poe.—LiWa
Haunted room. S. Cassedy.—CaR
The highwayman. A. Noyes.—LiSf
"Hist whist." E. E. Cummings.—LiSf—PrRh
The horse. J. M. Eguren.—LiSf—LiWa
The horseman. W. De la Mare.—PrRh
House. E. Merriam.—MeHa
House fear. R. Frost.—LiWa
The house of hospitalities. T. Hardy.—HeR
"I have no rattles." From Five ghost songs. Unknown, fr. the Ambo people of Africa.—KoT
In the old house. J. Aiken.—LiWa
"The island of Yorrick." N. M. Bodecker.—LiWa
The juniper tree. W. Watson.—DoNw
The king's son. T. Boyd.—PlAs
The knee. C. Morgenstern.—HeR
The listeners. W. De la Mare.—LiWa
"Look at that." L. Moore.—MoSn
My father's ghost. D. Wagoner.—JaS
The new house. V. Rutsala.—JaG
Night piece. R. R. Patterson.—LiWa
Night scare. J. Viorst.—ViI
Nothing ("Whsst, and away, and over the green"). W. De la Mare.—LiWa
The old wife and the ghost. J. Reeves.—HoCr
"The only ghost I ever saw." E. Dickinson.—LiWa
Our little ghost. L. M. Alcott.—HaOf

Ghosts—*Continued*
The phantom horsewoman. T. Hardy.—LiWa
Phantoms on the steppe. A. Pushkin.—LiWa
Prayer of the ghost. Unknown, fr. the Winnebago Indian.—BiSp
"The rocks are ringing." From Songs of the ghost dance. Unknown, fr. the Paiute Indian.—LiWa
The sands of Dee. C. Kingsley.—BlO
Sea-change. J. Masefield.—HeR
"See how it circles." From Five ghost songs. Unknown, fr. the Ambo people of Africa.—KoT
Sentimental conversation. P. Verlaine.—LiWa
Silent hill. Z. K. Snyder.—LiWa
Skeleton and spirit. Unknown.—HoCr
Some one. W. De la Mare.—FrP—LiSf—PrRh
"Something is there." L. Moore.—LiWa—PrRh
Something silky. J. Prelutsky.—PrNk
Song of a ghost. Unknown, fr. the Wintu Indian.—BiSp
Song of two ghosts. Unknown, fr. the Omaha Indian.—BiSp
Southern mansion. A. Bontemps.—LiWa
Spirits. V. H. Cruz.—LiWa
Sweet William's ghost. Unknown.—PlAs
"There is a dust from the whirlwind." From Songs of the ghost dance. Unknown, fr. the Paiute Indian.—LiWa
"Three little ghostesses." Mother Goose.—DeM—FaW
    Three ghostesses.—PrRh
An unexplained ouch. X. J. Kennedy.—KeF
The unquiet grave ("So cold the wintry winds do blow"). Unknown.—PlAs
The unquiet grave ("The wind doth blow today, my love"). Unknown.—HeR
The voice. W. De la Mare.—LiWa
Wall shadows. C. Sandburg.—LiWa
The wandering spectre. Unknown.—HeR
    The ghost's song.—BlO
The whale ghost. L. Moore.—MoSn
"The whirlwind." From Songs of the ghost dance. Unknown, fr. the Paiute Indian.—LiWa
"Who's in the next room." T. Hardy.—LiWa
The wicked hawthorn tree. W. B. Yeats.—LiWa
The wife of Usher's well ("There lived a lady, a lady gay"). Unknown.—PlAs
The wife of Usher's well ("There lived a wife at Usher's well"). Unknown.—HeR—PlAs
The wind has wings. Unknown.—DoNw
"The wind stirs the willows." From Songs of the ghost dance. Unknown, fr. the Paiute Indian.—LiWa
Windy nights ("Whenever the moon and stars are set"). R. L. Stevenson.—DaC—KeK—LaW—LiSf—PrRh
Wraith. E. S. Millay.—LiWa
Zoe and the ghosts. D. Weslowski.—JaPo
hosts ("A cold and starry darkness moans"). Harry Behn.—HoCr—PrRh
hosts ("Those houses haunt in which we leave"). Elizabeth Jennings.—JaPo
he ghost's song. See The wandering spectre
he ghoul. Jack Prelutsky.—HaOf
giant." See Jungle gym
The **giant** brontosaurus." See Brontosaurus
giant came into my dream." See Dreamscape
giant hand inside my heart." See Mending
he **giant** is great." Unknown.—TrM

"The **giant** Jim, great giant grim." Mother Goose.—LoR
"The **giant** mouth." See Construction
Giants
"Ants live here." L. Moore.—PrRa
The bean stalk. E. S. Millay.—LiWa
Curses to fling at a giant. From A throw of threes. E. Merriam.—MeF
Dreamscape. L. M. Fisher.—HoDi
"The giant is great." Unknown.—TrM
"The giant Jim, great giant grim." Mother Goose.—LoR
"Hickenthrift and Hickenloop." X. J. Kennedy.—LiWa
Huffer and Cuffer. J. Prelutsky.—PrSr
"I want my breakfast." E. Merriam.—MeBl
In the orchard. J. Stephens.—LiWa
The sleeping giant. D. Hall.—JaPi
The sleepy giant. C. E. Carryl.—CoOu
A small discovery. J. A. Emanuel.—LiSf
"There was a maid on Scrabble Hill." Mother Goose.—LoR
Gibbons, Orlando
"The silver swan, who living had no note."—HeR
Gibson, Douglas
January ("The snow has melted now").—HaO
White cat in moonlight.—ChC
    Cat in the moonlight.—LaW
Gibson, Walker
Advice to travelers.—JaPo
    Before starting.—KeK
    Before starting. See Advice to travelers
Gibson, Wilfrid Wilson
Flannan Isle.—BlO
The **gift**. Ed Ochester.—JaD—JaPi
The **gift** outright. Robert Frost.—KoS
The **gift** to be simple. Howard Moss.—JaPi
Gift with the wrappings off. Mary Elizabeth Counselman.—PrRh
Gifts and giving. See also Thankfulness
Advent 1955. Sir J. Betjeman.—HaO
Afterthought. E. Jennings.—HaO
Annar-Mariar's Christmas shopping. E. Farjeon.—FaE
Betsy Jane's sixth birthday. A. Noyes.—LiIl
Buying a puppy. L. Norris.—LiIl—LiSf
Cat, Christmas. V. Worth.—LiCa
Chinese new year. Unknown.—LiNe
Christmas chime. X. J. Kennedy.—LiCp
Christmas 1970. S. Milligan.—HaO
Christmas shopping. L. MacNeice.—HaO
Christmas thank you's. M. Gowar.—HaO
December, prayer to St. Nicholas. J. Heath-Stubbs.—HaO
First foot. I. Serraillier.—LiNe
"For a companion." Shiki.—FaTh
For the children or the grown-ups. Unknown.—HaO
For them. E. Farjeon.—FaE
The gift. E. Ochester.—JaD—JaPi
Gift with the wrappings off. M. E. Counselman.—PrRh
Gifts from my grandmother. E. M. Almedingen.—StG
Giving potatoes. A. Mitchell.—HeR
Good King Wenceslas. Unknown.—RoC
Greensleeves. Unknown.—KoT
"Hang up the baby's stocking." Unknown.—HaO
"Hush, little baby, don't say a word." Mother Goose.—BaH—ChB—DeM—LaW—LoR
    The mocking bird ("Hush up, baby").—LiSf

Gifts and giving.—*Continued*
I sought all over the world. J. Tagliabue.—JaPi
"I will give my love an apple without e'er a core." Unknown.—HeR
   I will give my love an apple.—BlO
Kaleidoscope ("Chock full boxes, packages"). X. J. Kennedy.—LiCp
"Little girl, little girl, where have you been." Mother Goose.—AlH—DeM
Mother's chocolate valentine. J. Prelutsky.—PrIv
"Oh, dear, what can the matter be." Mother Goose.—FaW—LoR
   "O, dear, what can the matter be".—DeM
Old Jack Noman. E. Thomas.—BlO
Old people working (garden, car). G. Brooks.—PlSc
Otto. G. Brooks.—LiSf
Overheard on a saltmarsh. H. Monro.—LiSf—LiWa
The pleasing gift. Unknown.—BrT
Riddle song ("I gave my love a cherry that had no stone"). Unknown.—HeR
Roman presents. Martial.—HaO
A Roman thank you letter. Martial.—HaO
Stocking time. E. Farjeon.—FaE
Surprises. J. C. Soule.—PrRh
Thank you note. J. Viorst.—ViI
"There was a ship a-sailing." Mother Goose.—RoC
   "I saw a ship a-sailing".—CoN
Tide and time. R. McGough.—JaT
The true tale of grandfather Penny. E. Farjeon.—FaE
The twelve days of Christmas. Unknown.—RoC
   "The first day of Christmas".—LoR
A visit from St. Nicholas ("'Twas the night before Christmas, when all through the house"). C. C. Moore.—CoN—HaO—HaOf—LiCp—LiSf—PrRh—RoC
"What can I give him." C. G. Rossetti.—LiCp
   My gift.—LaT
Gifts from my grandmother. Edith Martha Almedingen.—StG
"The **giggling** gaggling gaggle of geese." Jack Prelutsky.—PrZ
Gilbert, Celia
Portrait of my mother on her wedding day.—JaD
Gilbert, William Schwenck
The Mikado, sels.
   "A wandering minstrel I".—PlAs
Mr. Wells. See The sorcerer
The pirates of Penzance, sels.
   The policeman's lot.—PlSc
The policeman's lot. See The pirates of Penzance
A professor called Chesterton.—BrT
The sorcerer, sels.
   Mr. Wells.—LiWa
"A wandering minstrel I." See The Mikado
Gildner, Gary
Around the kitchen table.—JaS
First practice.—JaPi
Letter to a substitute teacher.—JaPi
My father after work.—JaPi
Poems.—JaPi
Gilman, Caroline
Anna playing in a graveyard.—HaOf
The boat ("Oh, see my little boat").—HaOf
The dead sister.—HaOf
The **gingerbread** man. See "Smiling girls, rosy boys"

"The **gingham** dog and the calico cat." See The duel
Gingko trees
Simile, willow and ginkgo. E. Merriam.—MeSk
Ginsberg, Allen
The lion for real.—HeR
Gioia, Dana
The Sunday news.—JaG
Giotto's tower. Henry Wadsworth Longfellow.—PlEd
Giovanni, Nikki
Barbara poems.—GiSp
Basketball.—GiSp—PrRh
The boy in the barbershop.—GiSp
Chester's wisdom.—GiSp
Covers.—HoSu—PrRa
"Daddies."—GiSp
Dance poem.—GiSp—LiSf
Dreams ("I get up at seven o'clock").—GiSp
The drum.—GiSp—LiSf
Education.—GiSp
Ego tripping.—JaPi
Fear.—GiSp
For Deena.—GiSp
George.—GiSp
A heavy rap.—GiSp
If ("If he could climb a tree").—GiSp
James Shell's snowball stand.—GiSp
Kidnap poem.—JaG
Let's take a nap.—GiSp
Mattie Lou at twelve.—GiSp
Mrs. Martha Jean Black.—GiSp
"Mommies."—GiSp
Mommies do.—GiSp
One of the problems of play.—GiSp
Parents never understand.—GiSp
Poem for Debbie.—GiSp
Poem for Ntombe Iayo (at five weeks of age).—GiSp
Poem for Rodney.—GiSp—LiSf
"The reason I like chocolate."—PrRh
Shirley and her son.—GiSp
Shopping.—GiSp
Sleep.—GiSp
Some things are funny like that.—GiSp
Springtime.—GiSp
Stars ("In science today we learned").—GiSp—KeK
Ten years old ("I paid my 30¢ and rode by the bus").—GiSp—LiSf
Trips.—GiSp
Two friends.—GiSp—LiIl
"Yvonne."—GiSp
Gipsies. See Gypsies
Giraffe ("How lucky"). Valerie Worth.—WoSp
Giraffe ("I like."). N. M. Bodecker.—BoSs
"The **giraffe**." From Three animals. Ron Padgett.—KoT
Giraffe ("When I invite the giraffe to dine"). William Jay Smith.—LiIl
Giraffes
The dizzy giraffe. Unknown.—BrT
The elephant and the giraffe. C. O. Carter.—BrT
Giraffe ("How lucky"). V. Worth.—WoSp
Giraffe ("I like."). N. M. Bodecker.—BoSs
"The giraffe." From Three animals. R. Padgett.—KoT
Giraffe ("When I invite the giraffe to dine"). W. J. Smith.—LiIl
Giraffes. M. A. Hoberman.—LiSf
Giraffes don't huff. K. Kuskin.—PrRa
Long shadow story. L. Moore.—MoSn

Girls and girlhood.—*Continued*
"There was a little girl, and she had a little curl." Mother Goose.—DeM—LoR
    Jemima.—DaC
    Jemima (". . . and she wore a little curl").—ChG
    "There was a little girl, who had a little curl".—PrRh (at. to H. W. Longfellow)
To Mistress Isabel Pennell. J. Skelton.—KoT
Triolet against sisters. P. McGinley.—HaOf—KeK
Two friends. N. Giovanni.—GiSp—LiIl
The violet. W. Wordsworth.—ChG
Vision by Sweetwater. J. C. Ransom.—HeR
Weaving at the window. Wang Chien.—PlSc
"What are little girls made of." Mother Goose.—FaW
    Natural history.—DaC
    "What are little girls made of, made of".—AlH
What has happened to Lulu. C. Causley.—KeK
Why run. N. Smaridge.—PrRh
Wild thyme. E. Farjeon.—FaE
"Yvonne." N. Giovanni.—GiSp
Girls can, too. Lee Bennett Hopkins.—PrRh
Girls in the garden. Eleanor Farjeon.—FaE
Girls' names. Eleanor Farjeon.—FaE—LiSf
Girl's prayer to thunder during a storm. Unknown.—BiSp
Girl's song. Unknown, tr. by Willard R. Trask.—McL
"**Give** ear my children to my words." See John Rogers' exhortation to his children
"**Give** me my scallop-shell of quiet." See The passionate man's pilgrimage
"**Give** me something to eat." See Poor crow
"**Give** us courage, O Lord, to stand up." Alan Paton.—LaT
Giving. See Gifts and giving
Giving potatoes. Adrian Mitchell.—HeR
"**Giving** thanks giving thanks." Eve Merriam.—LiTp—MeF
"**Glad** Christmas comes, and every hearth." See December
"**Glad** that I live am I." See A little song of life
Glaser, Isabel Joshlin
How the end might have been.—HoDi
"What if."—HoDi
Glass
Glass. R. Francis.—JaD
Glass walling. N. M. Bodecker.—BoPc
The magnifying glass. W. De la Mare.—BlO
Upon Fairford windows. R. Corbett.—PlEd
Glass. Robert Francis.—JaD
The **glass** canoe. John Ciardi.—CiD
"**Glass** covers windows." See Covers
"The **glass** has been falling all the afternoon." See Storm warnings
"**Glass** in the gutter." See Trouble in town
A **glass** of beer. James Stephens.—HeR
Glass walling. N. M. Bodecker.—BoPc
Glassco, John
Lullaby ("Sleep sleep beneath the old wind's eye"), tr. by.—DoNw
"The **gleeful** evil wolverine." See The wolverine
Glenn, Mel
Adam Whitney.—GlC
Alex Garber.—GlCd
Alison Ford.—GlC
Allen Greshner.—GlC
Amanda Butler.—GlCd
Amy Pines.—GlC
Angelino Falco.—GlCd

Anna Montalvo.—GlC
Annie Scarella.—GlC
Arlene Lasky.—GlCd
Barbara Sutton.—GlCd
Barry Owens.—GlC
Benjamin Heywood.—GlC
Bernard Pearlman.—GlC
Beth Rossiter and.—GlCd
Billy Paris.—GlC
Brandon Dale.—GlCd
Brenda Stewart.—GlC
Brian Nichols.—GlC
Candie Brewer.—GlCd
Carl Immerman.—GlC
Carla Spooner.—GlCd
Carlos Rodriguez.—GlCd
Carolyn Warren.—GlCd
Carrie Pearson.—GlC
Catherine Heath.—GlC
Cecilia Dowling.—GlCd
Charlie Wallinsky.—GlC
Christine Leader.—GlC
Christopher Conti.—GlC
Clint Reynolds.—GlCd
Craig Blanchard.—GlCd
Crystal Rowe.—GlCd
Cynthia Leonard.—GlCd
Dana Moran.—GlCd
Danielle O'Mara.—GlCd
Danny Vargas.—GlC
Darcy Tanner.—GlC
David Eberhoff.—GlC
David Klein.—GlCd
Dominique Blanco.—GlC
Donald Kaminsky.—GlC
Donna Vasquez.—GlC
Dora Antonopolis.—GlC
Dorothy Osmond.—GlCd
Douglas Kearney.—GlCd
Eleanor Paine.—GlC
Elizabeth McKenzie.—GlCd
Ellen Winters.—GlC
Eric Theodore.—GlC
Ernest Mott.—GlC
Faith Plotkin.—GlC
Franz Dominguez.—GlC
Gail Larkin.—GlC
Gary Irving.—GlCd
Gordon Matthews.—GlC
Grace DeLorenzo.—GlC
Greg Hoffman.—GlCd
Harvey Persky.—GlCd
Hayes Iverson.—GlCd
Heather Yarnell.—GlCd
Helen Price.—GlC
Hildy Ross.—GlC
Howie Bystrom.—GlCd
Ian Sinclair.—GlCd
Isabel Navarro.—GlCd
James Petrie.—GlCd
Jason Talmadge.—GlC
Jay Stone.—GlCd
Jeanette Jaffe.—GlC
Jennie Tang.—GlCd
Jessica Berg.—GlCd
Jill Le Claire.—GlC
Jodi Kurtz.—GlC
Joel Feit.—GlC
Jose Cruz.—GlCd
Joy McNair.—GlC
Juan Pedro Carrera.—GlCd
Julie Snow.—GlC
Justin Faust.—GlCd

Glenn, Mel—*Continued*
Keith Jordan.—GlC
Kevin McDonald.—GlC
Kurt Benoit.—GlCd
Lance Perkins.—GlCd
Lauren Jones.—GlC
Laurie Allen.—GlC
Leigh Hamilton.—GlCd
Lisa Goodman.—GlC
Louise Coyle.—GlCd
Mandy Bailer.—GlCd
Marcy Mannes.—GlCd
Maria Preosi.—GlC
Marie Yeagerman.—GlC
Mario Benedetto.—GlCd
Marvin Pickett.—GlC
Mary Beth Collier.—GlCd
Mary Gilardi.—GlCd
Mary Louise Donahue.—GlCd
Meredith Piersall.—GlCd
Michael Ravenall.—GlC
Michelle Church.—GlCd
Miguel DeVega.—GlCd
Min Trang.—GlCd
Mitchell Chapin.—GlC
Monica Zindell.—GlC
Nancy Soto.—GlC
Neil Winningham.—GlCd
Nicole Harris.—GlCd
Nolan Davis.—GlCd
Norman Moskowitz.—GlC
Orlando Martinez.—GlC
Pamela Atkinson.—GlC
Paul Hewitt.—GlCd
Peter Quincy.—GlC
Rachel Ferrara.—GlCd
Raymond Crystal.—GlC
Rhonda Winfrey.—GlC
Rickie Miller.—GlC
Robert Ashford.—GlCd
Robin Gold.—GlC
Ronnie Evans.—GlCd
Rosemarie Stewart.—GlC
Russell Hodges.—GlCd
Sanford Evans Pierce.—GlC
Saul Steiner.—GlC
Scott Garber.—GlCd
Shari Morrow.—GlC
Sharon Vail and.—GlCd
Sheila Franklin.—GlC
Song Vu Chin.—GlC
Stacey Fowler.—GlC
Stella Kolsky.—GlC
Stuart Rieger.—GlC
Susan Tulchin.—GlC
Thomas Kearns.—GlC
Tina DeMarco.—GlC
Todd Michaels.—GlCd
Veronica Castell.—GlCd
Vinnie Robustelli.—GlCd
Wendy Tarloff.—GlCd
"Glinting on the roadway." See The magical picture
"Glittering bridge." See The bridge
Gloire. N. M. Bodecker.—BoPc
"Glory be to God for dappled things." See Pied beauty
"Glory, Halleluiah." See Prayer meeting
Glowworm ("He studies very late"). François Dodat, tr. by Bert Meyers and Odette Meyers.—FaTh
Glowworm ("Never talk down to a glowworm"). David McCord.—CoN—FaW—McAs

Glowworms. See Fireflies
Gluck, Louise
Portrait ("A child draws the outline of a body").—JaS
Glue
"Snickering like crazy, Sue." X. J. Kennedy.—KeB
Super goopy glue. J. Prelutsky.—PrNk
Gluskap's hound. Theodore Goodridge Roberts.—DoNw
The **glutton.** Karl Shapiro.—JaD
Gluttony
Eat-it-all Elaine. K. Starbird.—LiSf—PrRh
The fat man. V. Rutsala.—JaD
The glutton. K. Shapiro.—JaD
"Hannah Bantry, in the pantry." Mother Goose.—LoR
Jake O'Leary's Thanksgiving. K. Starbird.—LiTp
"Mary had a little lamb (it was a greedy glutton)." Unknown.—PaM
The mouse and the cake. E. Cook.—DaC
The pigs. E. Poulsson.—PrRa
The pizza. O. Nash.—HoMu—PrRh
"Robbin and Bobbin." Mother Goose.—LoR
"Sammy Smith would drink and eat." Mother Goose.—FaW
"She said she wasn't hungry." Unknown.—TrM
This is just to say. W. C. Williams.—KeK—PrRh
Too much. Unknown.—BrT
The **gnat.** Eugene Rudzewicz.—JaT
Gnat on my paper. Richard Eberhart.—JaD
Gnats
Accidentally. M. Kumin.—PrRh
The gnat. E. Rudzewicz.—JaT
Gnat on my paper. R. Eberhart.—JaD
"Gnats are gnumerous." See The gnat
The **gnome.** Harry Behn.—HoCb—HoCr
Gnome matter. Carolyn Wells.—BrT
Gnomes. See Fairies
The **gnomes.** Beth Bentley.—PlSc
Gnus
G. H. Belloc.—FaW
The refractory gnu. Unknown.—BrT
"Go and ask Robin to bring the girls over." See Vision by Sweetwater
"Go and tell Aunt Nancy". See "Go tell Aunt Rhody"
"Go back to where we left the bikes." See Where am I
Go from my window. Unknown.—PlAs
"Go, go." See No man on any moon
"Go pet a kitten, pet a dog." See Who to pet and who not to
"Go, soul, the body's guest." See The lie
"Go tell Aunt Rhody." Unknown.—LiSf
"Go and tell Aunt Nancy".—BlO
"Go tell him to clear me one acre of ground." See The elfin knight
"Go to bed first." Unknown.—BaH—FrP
"Go to bed late." Mother Goose.—LoR
Go wind. Lilian Moore.—MoSn
"Go wind, blow." See Go wind
The **goat.** Unknown.—CoOu
Goats
The goat. Unknown.—CoOu
"Hiking in the Rockies, Midge." X. J. Kennedy.—KeB
"Once upon a time there was an old goat." C. Watson.—WaC
Gobble gobble. Jack Prelutsky.—PrIt
Gobbledy-gobble. Felice Holman.—LiTp
Gobbolino, the witch's cat. G. C. Westcott.—ChC

The **goblin**. Rose Fyleman.—CoN
"The **goblin** has a wider mouth." See How to tell goblins from elves
"A **goblin** lives in our house." See The goblin
Goblins. See Fairies
"**Goblins** on the doorstep." See This is Halloween
God. See also Faith
"All things bright and beautiful." C. F. Alexander.—DaC—PrRh
"And God stepped out on space." From The creation. J. W. Johnson.—LaT
"And the whole earth was of one language, and of one speech." From Genesis. Bible/Old Testament.—PlEd
Bermudas. A. Marvell.—HeR
Caliban in the coal mines. L. Untermeyer.—LaT
Calvary. From Song for the cloth. W. B. Yeats.—HeR
The creation, complete. J. W. Johnson.—LiSf
The destruction of Sennacherib. Lord Byron.—HeR—PlAs
Drawing. M. L'Engle.—LaT
Evening ("The day is past, the sun is set"). T. Miller.—DaC
Father Gilligan. W. B. Yeats.—PlAs
"God be in my head." Unknown.—LaT
"God who made the earth." S. B. Rhodes.—LaT
"The hand that rounded Peter's dome." From The problem. R. W. Emerson.—PlEd
Holiness. C. Rylant.—RyW
"I see white and black, Lord." M. Boyd.—LaT
"I thank you God for most this amazing." E. E. Cummings.—LaT
John Rogers' exhortation to his children. J. Rogers.—HaOf
The lamb ("Little lamb, who made thee"). W. Blake.—LiSf
"Loving heavenly Father, who takes care of us all." M. Kitson.—LaT
Ma Lord. L. Hughes.—HuDk
My bath. M. L'Engle.—LaT
My cat Jeoffry. From Jubilate Agno. C. Smart.—BlO—HeR
    "For I will consider my cat Jeoffry".—KoT
O beauteous one. Unknown, fr. the Egyptian.—KoT
Pied beauty. G. M. Hopkins.—HeR—KoT
A prayer to go to paradise with the donkeys. F. Jammes.—HeR—LiSf
Prayer to the moon. Unknown.—LaT
Psalm 23 ("The Lord is my shepherd, I shall not want"). From The book of psalms. Bible/Old Testament.—LiSf
    Psalm 23 ("The Lord to me a shepherd is").—HaOf
Psalm 24. From The book of psalms. Bible/Old Testament.—LiSf
Psalm 100. From The book of psalms. Bible/Old Testament.—LiSf—LiTp
Psalm 103. From The book of psalms. Bible/Old Testament.—LiSf
Psalm 121. From The book of psalms. Bible/Old Testament.—HaOf
Samantha speaking. D. McCord.—LiTp
Sicilian thanksgiving on the feast of Saint John the Baptist. E. Di Pasquale.—LiTp
Sinner. L. Hughes.—HuDk
Song for the sun that disappeared behind the rainclouds. Unknown, fr. the Hottentot people of Africa.—KoT

Television. M. L'Engle.—LaT
They ask, is God, too, lonely. C. Sandburg.—LiIl
Trustworthiness. N. M. Bodecker.—BoPc
The tyger. W. Blake.—BlO—HeR—KoT
    The tiger.—LiSf
"When the night is wild." E. Vipont.—LaT
"The whole universe is full of God." Y. Emre.—McL
"**God** be in my head." Unknown.—LaT
"**God** bless all those I love." Unknown.—LaT
"**God** bless the animals I love." Elfrida Vipont.—LaT
"**God** bless the master of this house." Mother Goose.—DeM
"**God** bless us every one." See Tiny Tim's prayer
"**God** bless your house this holy night." See This holy night
"**God** created cat and asked." Unknown.—ChC
"**God** help me." See Barry Owens
"**God,** help us to face up to what." See Directions, please
"**God,** keep all claw-denned alligators." See Prayer for reptiles
"**God** made the bees." Mother Goose.—BlO—LoR—PlSc
"**God** put the cougar on the mountain." See Puma
"**God** rest that wicked woman." See Song for the clatter-bones
"**God,** though this life is but a wraith." See Prayer
"**God,** we don't like to complain." See Caliban in the coal mines
"**God** who made the earth." Sarah Betts Rhodes.—LaT
Goddard, Kate Cox
    High heeled shoes.—FrP
    Near and far.—FrP
    Woolly blanket.—FrP
Godden, Rumer
    The prayer of the cat, tr. by.—ChC—LiSf
    The prayer of the little pig, tr. by.—LiSf
Godmother. Phyllis B. Morden.—PrRh
Gods and goddesses
    The hammer. C. Sandburg.—HoRa
"**Goes.**" See The year
Goethe, Johann Wolfgang von
    The erl-king.—LiWa
    Faust, sels.
        "The limits of the sphere of dream".—LiWa
    "The limits of the sphere of dream." See Faust
Goffstein, M. B.
    "Oh this day."—CoN
"**Goin'** down de road, Lawd." See Bound no'th blues
Going away. Howard Nemerov.—JaD
Going barefoot. Aileen Fisher.—FiW
Going in ("Every day alone whittles me"). Marge Piercy.—JaD
Going into dream. Eleanor Farjeon.—FaE
Going steady. Ian Serraillier.—LiVp
Going to bed. Eleanor Farjeon.—FaE
Going to sleep in the country. Howard Moss.—JaD
Going up ("Space suit Sammy"). John Travers Moore.—PrRh
"**Going** up the river." Unknown.—PlAs
Gold (metal)
    By the Klondike River. A. Coren.—CoOu
    Ye ancient Yuba miner of the days of '49. S. C. Upham.—PlAs
"**Gold** as morning, still as sheaves." See Enchanted summer

The **gold** nest. Robert Wallace.—JaPo
The **gold-tinted** dragon. Karla Kuskin.—PrRa
Goldberg, Leah
From my mother's house.—StG
The **golden** cat. Eleanor Farjeon.—FaE
"The **golden** crocus reaches up." See The crocus
The **golden** hive. Harry Behn.—HoCb
"The **golden-rod** is yellow." See September
"**Golden** slumbers kiss your eyes." See A cradle song
The **Golden** Vanity ("A ship I have got in the north country"). Unknown.—BlO
The Golden Vanity ("Now Jack he had a ship in the north counterie").—PlAs
The Golden Vanity ("Now Jack he had a ship in the north counterie"). See The Golden Vanity ("A ship I have got in the north country")
Goldfish
"A B C D goldfish." Unknown.—CoN
Goldsmith, Oliver
Elegy on the death of a mad dog, complete.—PlAs
Elegy on the death of a mad dog, sels.
"A kind and gentle heart he had".—TrM
"A kind and gentle heart he had." See Elegy on the death of a mad dog
The **golf** links. Sarah N. Cleghorn.—KeK
"The **golf** links lie so near the mill." See The golf links
Goliath. Spike Milligan.—TrM
Gom, Leona
All.—JaS
Gone ("I've looked behind the shed"). David McCord.—HoDl—JaT
Gone ("Wind rattles the apples"). Ralph Pomeroy.—JaD
"**Gone** the three ancient ladies." See Frau Bauman, Frau Schmidt, and Frau Schwartze
The **gone** years. Alice Fulton.—JaS
"**Goneys** an' gullies an' all o' the birds o' the sea." See Sea-change
Gonzales Martinez, Enrique
Balada de la loca fortuna.—LiSf
The ballad of mad fortune.—LiSf
"**Good** afternoon, Sir Smashum Uppe." See Sir Smashum Uppe
Good and bad children. Robert Louis Stevenson.—BlO—DaC
"**Good,** better, best." See Comparatives
Good chew. N. M. Bodecker.—BoPc
"A **good** child, a good child." Mother Goose.—LoR
Good egg. N. M. Bodecker.—BoPc
"**Good** egg, her favorite words." See Mac
Good King Wenceslas. Unknown.—RoC
"**Good** King Wenceslas looked out." See Good King Wenceslas
The **good** mooly cow. Eliza Lee Follen.—HaOf
"**Good** morning." See Argument
Good morning ("Good morning, nurse, good morning, cook"). Eleanor Farjeon.—FaE
Good morning ("One day I saw a downy duck"). Muriel Sipe.—FrP—PrRa
"**Good** morning now." See For good morning
"**Good** morning, nurse, good morning, cook." See Good morning
Good-morning poems. See Wake-up poems
"**Good** morrow to you, Valentine." Mother Goose.—DeM
Good neighbors. May Justus.—PrRa
"**Good** night." See Bedtime

Good night ("Little baby, lay your head"). Jane Taylor.—ChB
Good night ("Many ways to spell good night"). Carl Sandburg.—HoRa
Good night ("This day's done"). Aileen Fisher.—FrP
Good night ("We turn out the lights"). Charlotte Zolotow.—ZoE
"**Good** night, good night." See Again, good night
Good night, good night. Dennis Lee.—PrRa
"**Good** night, good night." Victor Hugo.—LaT
Good-night poems. See Bedtime; Lullabies
"**Good** night, sleep tight." Mother Goose.—LoR
"**Good** old mother fairie." See To mother fairie
"**Good** people all, of every sort." See Elegy on the death of a mad dog, complete
A **good** play. Robert Louis Stevenson.—DaC
Good sportsmanship. Richard Armour.—KeK
"**Good** sportsmanship we hail, we sing." See Good sportsmanship
Good thinking. Unknown.—BrT
"A **good** week, we sing." See Havdalah
Good will to men. Dorothy Brown Thompson.—HaO
A **good** woman feeling bad. Maya Angelou.—AnS
"**Goodby** is a loose word, a yellow ribbon." See Different kinds of goodby
"**Goodby** my winter suit." N. M. Bodecker.—PrRh
Goodbye ("My mother, poor woman, lies tonight"). Galway Kinnell.—JaS
Goodbye ("Seven cats and seven mice"). John Ciardi.—CiD
The **goodbye** ("This endsaying, moon pried loose"). Myra Sklarew.—JaG
Goodbye six, hello seven. Judith Viorst.—ViI
Goodness. See Conduct of life
Goodnight, little people. Thomas Hood.—FrP
Goodnight moon. Margaret Wise Brown.—FaW
Goodrich, Samuel
"Higglety, pigglety, pop."—FaW (unat.)—PrRa—PrRh
"The **goofy** moose, the walking house-frame." See Mooses
The **goops.** See Table manners ("The goops they lick their fingers")
"The **goops** they lick their fingers." See Table manners
Goose. Ted Hughes.—HuU
The **goose** and the gander. Unknown.—HeR
Gooseberries. Peter Wild.—JaD
"**Gooseberry.**" Eve Merriam.—MeBl
"**Goosey,** goosey gander." Mother Goose.—BlQ—DeM—FaW—LoR
A **gopher** in the garden. Jack Prelutsky.—PrZ
Gophers
A gopher in the garden. J. Prelutsky.—PrZ
Gorbanyevskaya, Natalya
"Don't touch me, I scream at passers by."—McL
Gordon Matthews. Mel Glenn.—GlC
Gorey, Edward
"From number nine, Penwiper Mews."—BrT
Number nine, Penwiper Mews.—PrRh
Lord Cray.—PrRh
Gorillas. See Apes and monkeys
"**Gosnold,** watch out with that match." X. J. Kennedy.—KeB
Gospel according to Luke, sels. Bible/New Testament
"And there were in the same country shepherds".—LiCp
Gossamer. Eleanor Farjeon.—FaE

Gossip
  Portrait by a neighbor. E. S. Millay.—HaOf— LiSf
"Got me a special place." See Martin Luther King
Gotlieb, Phyllis
  A. See A bestiary of the garden for children who should know better
  A bestiary of the garden for children who should know better, sels.
    A.—DoNw
    R.—DoNw
    S.—DoNw
    W ("The wasp's a kind of buzzing cousin").—DoNw
    Z.—DoNw
  "How and when and where and why."—DoNw
  R. See A bestiary of the garden for children who should know better
  S. See A bestiary of the garden for children who should know better
  W ("The wasp's a kind of buzzing cousin"). See A bestiary of the garden for children who should know better
  Z. See A bestiary of the garden for children who should know better
Gould, Hannah F.
  The dying child's request.—HaOf
  The spider ("One biting winter morning").— HaOf
Government
  The four dears. E. Elliot.—PlSc
  An ode to the framers of the Frame Bill. Lord Byron.—PlSc
Gowar, Mick
  Christmas thank you's.—HaO
Gozzano, Guido
  The most beautiful.—KoT
Grab-bag. Helen Hunt Jackson.—HaOf
Grace DeLorenzo. Mel Glenn.—GlC
Gracious goodness. Marge Piercy.—JaPi
Graddon, Dorothy
  The wind ("What can the matter be").—CoOu
Graduation
  Arlene Lasky. M. Glenn.—GlCd
  Carlos Rodriguez. M. Glenn.—GlCd
  Helen Price. M. Glenn.—GlC
  Jessica Berg. M. Glenn.—GlCd
  Min Trang. M. Glenn.—GlCd
  Stuart Rieger. M. Glenn.—GlC
Graffiti
  Hello, graffiti. A. Turner.—TuS
  Observing a vulgar name on the plinth of an ancient statue. W. S. Landor.—PlEd
  Street painting. A. Turner.—TuS
Graham, Harry
  Grandpapa.—PrRh
  Tender heartedness.—PrRh
  Uncle.—PrRh
Grahame, Kenneth
  Carol of the field mice.—RoC
  Ducks' ditty.—CoN—LiSf—PrRh
Grain. See names of Grain, as wheat
Grammar lesson. Linda Pastan.—JaPi
"Gramps held the rooster." See Killing the rooster
The **grand** county fair. Jack Prelutsky.—PrWi
"Grand-dads." Eleanor Farjeon.—FaE
"The grand old Duke of York." Mother Goose.— LiSf
"The grandfather." See Grandfather clock
"Grandfather." Myra Cohn Livingston.—LiWo
Grandfather clock. Myra Cohn Livingston.—LiWo
"Grandfather Gander flew over the land." Jack Prelutsky.—PrRi

"The **grandfather** I never knew." Myra Cohn Livingston.—LiWo
"Grandfather, I wish I were already old." See The passing years
"Grandfather never went to school." See The legacy II
"Grandfather Penny." See The true tale of grandfather Penny
"A grandfather poem." William J. Harris.—StG
Grandfathers
  At grandfather's. C. B. Bates.—HaOf
  Deep in the mountains. Saibara.—StG
  The gnomes. B. Bentley.—PlSc
  Gooseberries. P. Wild.—JaD
  "Grand-dads." E. Farjeon.—FaE
  "Grandfather." M. C. Livingston.—LiWo
  "The grandfather I never knew." M. C. Livingston.—LiWo
  "A grandfather poem." W. J. Harris.—StG
  Grandfather's heaven. N. S. Nye.—JaS
  Grandpa dropped his glasses. L. F. Jackson.— PrRh
  Grandpapa. H. Graham.—PrRh
  Grandparents' houses. M. Van Doren.—StG
  Grandpa's lullaby. C. Pomerantz.—PoA
  Grandpa's picture. P. Ruffin.—JaS
  "I look at this picture of that old man." From Afternoon in Waterloo Park. G. Dumas.—StG
  In grandfather's glasses. P. Peters.—JaS
  In January, 1962. T. Kooser.—JaPi
  Ladybugs. P. Shumaker.—JaT
  The legacy II. L. V. Quintana.—StG
  Manners ("My grandfather said to me"). E. Bishop.—HeR—JaG
  My grandfather burning cornfields. R. Sauls.— JaS
  My grandfather dying. T. Kooser.—JaS
  My grandfather in search of moonshine. G. E. Lyon.—JaG
  Norman Moskowitz. M. Glenn.—GlC
  The passing years. R. Elsland.—StG
  A real story. L. Pastan.—JaS
  Rocking chair. R. Morgan.—JaPo
  The shark ("Oh what a lark to fish for shark"). J. J. Bell.—PrRh
  Shooting crows. D. Huddle.—JaG
  Still finding out. A. Adoff.—AdA
  The true tale of grandfather Penny. E. Farjeon.—FaE
  Zuni grandfather. Unknown.—StG
Grandfather's heaven. Naomi Shihab Nye.—JaS
"Grandfathers, here, eat, may I become a woman, and may." See Prayer of the youngest daughter, with an offering of crumbs
Grandma. Ann Turner.—TuS
"Grandma Bear from Delaware." Jack Prelutsky.— PrRi
Grandma chooses her plot at the county cemetery. Paul Ruffin.—JaG
"Grandma knows." See Grandma
"Grandma's bonnet flutters to her head." See Grandma's Easter bonnet
Grandma's Easter bonnet. Bobbi Katz.—LiE
Grandma's lost balance. Sydney Dayre.—HaOf
Grandma's lullaby. Charlotte Pomerantz.—PoA
The **grandmother.** Wendell Berry.—JaD—PlSc
Grandmother. Henry Carlile.—JaD
Grandmother Grace. Ronald Wallace.—JaG
Grandmother Jackson. David Jackson.—HaO
"Grandmother of mine." See Zuni grandmother
"Grandmother, you gave me the wealth of detail." See Gifts from my grandmother

Grandmothers
Basket. M. C. Livingston.—LiWo
Both my grandmothers. E. Field.—JaS
Daguerreotype of a grandmother. C. T. Wright.—JaS
Days through starch and bluing. A. Fulton.—JaG
Fat Lena's recipe for crocodile soup. P. Janowitz.—JaT
Fletcher Avenue. M. C. Livingston.—LiWo
From my mother's house. L. Goldberg.—StG
Gifts from my grandmother. E. M. Almedingen.—StG
Grandma. A. Turner.—TuS
"Grandma Bear from Delaware." J. Prelutsky.—PrRi
Grandma chooses her plot at the county cemetery. P. Ruffin.—JaG
Grandma's Easter bonnet. B. Katz.—LiE
Grandma's lost balance. S. Dayre.—HaOf
Grandma's lullaby. C. Pomcrantz. PoA
The grandmother. W. Berry.—JaD—PlSc
Grandmother. H. Carlile.—JaD
Grandmother Grace. R. Wallace.—JaG
Grandmother Jackson. D. Jackson.—HaO
Great-grandma. C. Shields.—JaS
Great Grandma Ida. A. Adoff.—AdA
Growing old. R. Henderson.—PrRh
The hill. M. C. Livingston.—LiWo
I know we can go back so far. A. Adoff.—AdA
"It's happy Thanksgiving." J. Prelutsky.—PrIt
The kitchen (for my grandmother). W. Bedford.—StG
The last words of my English grandmother. W. C. Williams.—HeR
Lineage. M. Walker.—StG
Mardi Gras. J. Nolan.—JaS
My grandmother had bones. J. Hemschemeyer.—JaD
Nanny. M. C. Livingston.—LiWo
A new pencil. E. Merriam.—MeF
New year's advice from my Cornish grandmother. X. J. Kennedy.—LiNe
"Oma was sixty three when I was born." From Afternoon in Waterloo Park. G. Dumas.—StG
Remedies. G. Soto.—JaS
A room in the past. T. Kooser.—JaS
Seashell ("My father's mother"). V. Worth.—WoSp
Victorian grandmother. M. Lockwood.—JaPi
What grandma knew. E. Field.—JaPi
When my grandmother died. S. Cornish.—JaPi
When the ambulance came. R. Morgan.—JaS
White autumn. R. Morgan.—JaS
Yonosa house. R. T. Smith.—JaS
You owe them everything. J. Allman.—PlSc
Zuni grandmother. Unknown.—StG
"Grandmother's basket." See Basket
Grandpa bear's lullaby. Jane Yolen.—PrRh
Grandpa dropped his glasses. Leroy F. Jackson.—PrRh
"Grandpa dropped his glasses once." See Grandpa dropped his glasses
Grandpapa. Harry Graham.—PrRh
"Grandpapa fell down a drain." See Grandpapa
Grandparents. See Grandfathers; Grandmothers
Grandparents' houses. Mark Van Doren.—StG
Grandpa's lullaby. Charlotte Pomerantz.—PoA
Grandpa's picture. Paul Ruffin.—JaS
"Granite and marble." See Homage to Paul Mellon, I. M. Pei, their gallery, and Washington City
Granny Grizer. Jack Prelutsky.—PrNk

"Granny Grizer, greedy miser." See Granny Grizer
Grapes
Taste of purple. L. B. Jacobs.—PrRh
"Grapes hang purple." See Taste of purple
Grass
Cut grass. P. Larkin.—HeR
Grass. C. Sandburg.—HoRa
Grasshoppers. J. Clare.—KoT
Green riders. R. Field.—FaTh
Green stems. M. W. Brown.—PrRh
Lawnmower. V. Worth.—HoCl
Something better. D. McCord.—McAs
Spring grass. C. Sandburg.—LiSf
Summer grass. C. Sandburg.—LiSf
The underworld. M. Lavington.—PrRa
Grass. Carl Sandburg.—HoRa
"The grass is always greener on the next date, I think." See Eric Theodore
"Grass path lasts." Anita Virgil.—KeK
The grasshopper. David McCord.—LiSf
The grasshopper and the elephant. See Way down south
"Grasshopper green." Nancy Dingman Watson.—PrRa
"The grasshopper, the grasshopper." See An explanation of the grasshopper
Grasshoppers
An explanation of the grasshopper. V. Lindsay.—PrRa
The grasshopper. D. McCord.—LiSf
"Grasshopper green." N. D. Watson.—PrRa
Grasshoppers. J. Clare.—KoT
"Little Miss Tucket." Mother Goose.—LoR
On the grasshopper and the cricket. J. Keats.—KoT
Way down south. Unknown.—PrRa—PrRh
The grasshopper and the elephant.—CoOu
Grasshoppers. John Clare.—KoT
"Grasshoppers go in many a thrumming spring." See Grasshoppers
Gratitude. See Thankfulness
Gravel paths. Patricia Hubbell.—HoSs
Graves, Robert
The Allansford pursuit.—HeR
Carol of patience.—HaO
Epitaph on an unfortunate artist.—TrM
Flying crooked.—HeR
The forbidden play.—LiSf
Henry and Mary.—LiSf
Hide and seek ("The trees are tall, but the moon small").—CoN—KeK
It was all very tidy.—HeR
The legs.—HeR
Lollocks.—HeR
Mad Tom's song.—HeR
The magical picture.—LiSf
Nature's lineaments.—HeR
The pumpkin.—LiWa—PrRh
The six badgers.—LiSf—LiWa
Warning to children.—BlO
Welsh incident.—LiWa
Graves. See also Epitaphs
After looking into a book belonging to my great-grandfather, Eli Eliakim Plutzik. H. Plutzik.—HeR
Anna playing in a graveyard. C. Gilman.—HaOf
Be merry. Unknown.—HeR
"Call for the robin redbreast and the wren." From The white devil. J. Webster.—HeR
A dirge.—BlO
A child's grave marker. T. Kooser.—JaG
A city graveyard. J. C. Oates.—JaD
Cool tombs. C. Sandburg.—HoRa

Graves.—*Continued*
Grandma chooses her plot at the county cemetery. P. Ruffin.—JaG
Grass. C. Sandburg.—HoRa
The hill. M. C. Livingston.—LiWo
The hill above the mine. M. Cowley.—PlSc
In a country cemetery in Iowa. T. Kooser.—JaD
The knight's tomb. S. T. Coleridge.—HeR
One rose of stone. K. Wilson.—JaG
The unquiet grave ("So cold the wintry winds do blow"). Unknown.—PlAs
The unquiet grave ("The wind doth blow today, my love"). Unknown.—HeR
Up North Second. M. C. Livingston.—LiWo
"With fairest flowers." From Cymbeline. W. Shakespeare.—HeR
Yew. M. C. Livingston.—LiMp
Yugoslav cemetery. C. T. Wright.—JaD
Graveyards. See Graves
Gray, Olivia
"Ancient pool", tr. by.—KeK
Gray (color)
Grayness. C. Zolotow.—ZoE
"It is grey out." K. Kuskin.—LiSf
"**Gray** goose and gander." Mother Goose.—AlH—LoR
Gray thrums. Clara Boty Bates.—HaOf
Grayness. Charlotte Zolotow.—ZoE
Grazing locomotives. Archibald MacLeish.—JaPo
"**Great** A, little a." Mother Goose.—DeM—LoR
Great and strong. Miroslav Holub, tr. by George Theiner.—HeR
The **great** auk's ghost. Ralph Hodgson.—KeK—PrRh
"The **great** auk's ghost rose on one leg." See The great auk's ghost
"**Great-aunt** Anna." See Harney Street
The **great** aunts of my childhood. Alice Fulton.—JaS
"**Great** balls of fire, Amanda Rose." See Television nose
The **great** beyond. Cynthia Rylant.—RyW
Great Britain. See England
"**Great** bubble eyed one." See Song for calling rain
The **great** figure. William Carlos Williams.—KoT
"**Great** frog race." Ian Hamilton Finlay.—KeK
Great-grandma. Carol Shields.—JaS
Great Grandma Ida. Arnold Adoff.—AdA
"**Great** Grandma Ida came from a small village." See Great Grandma Ida
"**Great** Grandma Ida came from a small village in Poland." See Borders
The **great** house. Edwin Muir.—PlEd
Great Lakes suite, complete. James Reaney
Lake Erie.—DoNw
Lake Huron.—DoNw
Lake Michigan.—DoNw
Lake Ontario.—DoNw
Lake St. Clair.—DoNw
Lake Superior.—DoNw
"**Great** one, austere." See Prayer before work
"The **great** Overdog." See Canis major
The **great** panjandrum. Samuel Foote.—BlO
"The **great** sea." Unknown, tr. by Harry Behn.—LiSf
Great things have happened. Alden Nowlan.—JaG
"**Great,** wide, beautiful, wonderful world." William Brighty Rands.—TrM
"The **greatest** ace of video space." See Zany Zapper Zockke
"**Greatly** shining." See Wind and silver

Greece
Doves of Dodona. P. Fleischman.—FlI
Monastery on Athos. R. Lattimore.—PlEd
On a landscape of Sestos. From A visit to the art gallery. C. Baker.—PlEd
On seeing the Elgin Marbles. J. Keats.—PlEd
Greed
By the Klondike River. A. Coren.—CoOu
Cooney Potter. E. L. Masters.—PlSc
Granny Grizer. J. Prelutsky.—PrNk
"The **greedy** man is he who sits." Mother Goose.—LoR
Griselda. E. Farjeon.—FaE
The mosquito knows. D. H. Lawrence.—HeR—PrBb
The mouse and the cake. E. Cook.—DaC
"My sister she works in a laundry." Unknown.—TrM
"Said the scorpion of hate." C. Sandburg.—HoRa
"There dwelt an old woman at Exeter." Mother Goose.—LoR
"The **greedy** man is he who sits." Mother Goose.—LoR
"A **greedy** small lassie once said." See Too much
Green, Matthew
"Though pleased to see the dolphins play."—TrM
Green (color)
Green ("The dawn was apple green"). D. H. Lawrence.—PrBb
Green ("Ducklings"). L. Moore.—MoSn
Green ("Green is a good color"). C. Zolotow.—ZoE
Saint Patrick's day. M. C. Livingston.—LiCe
The wearin' o' the green. Unknown.—PlAs
Wearing of the green. A. Fisher.—PrRh
Green ("The dawn was apple green"). David Herbert Lawrence.—PrBb
Green ("Ducklings"). Lilian Moore.—MoSn
Green ("Green is a good color"). Charlotte Zolotow.—ZoE
"**Green.**" See Saint Patrick's day
"**Green** as a seedling the one lane shines." See City traffic
"**Green** broom." Unknown.—BlO
"**Green** Buddhas." See Watermelons
The **green** bushes. Unknown.—PlAs
Green candles. Humbert Wolfe.—PrRh
"**Green** cat eyes." See Halloween
"The **green** cockleburs." Richard Wright.—KeK
"**Green** fire, mist in the air." See To cure epilepsy
"**Green** is a good color." See Green
"**Green** is go." See Yellow
Green riders. Rachel Field.—FaTh
"The **green** screen door." See How about
Green stems. Margaret Wise Brown.—PrRh
The **Green** Willow Tree. Unknown.—PlAs
"The **green** worm sleeps in silk." See Where do you sleep
Greenaway, Kate
Little wind.—PrRa
On the bridge.—PrRh
Susan Blue.—FrP
Greener grass. Frank Steele.—JaPi
Greenfield, Eloise
Aunt Roberta.—LiSf
Harriet Tubman.—LiSf
Moochie.—CoN
Rope rhyme.—LiSf
Way down in the music.—LiSf
Greenhouse. Sylvia Cassedy.—CaR

Greenhouses
Greenhouse. S. Cassedy.—CaR
Greensleeves. Unknown.—KoT
"**Greensleeves** was all my joy." See Greensleeves
Greenwood, Theresa
Psalm of a black mother.—LaT
Greetings. See also Wake-up poems
Country greeting. F. Steele.—JaPi
"One misty, moisty morning." Mother Goose.—
ChG—DeM—FaW—LoR—PrRh
Greg Hoffman. Mel Glenn.—GlCd
Gregory, Augusta
Donal Og, tr. by.—HeR
"**Gregory** Griggs, Gregory Griggs." Mother
Goose.—BlQ—DeM—LoR
The **Gresford** disaster. Unknown.—PlAs
Grey (color). See Gray (color)
"**Grey** as a mouse." See Oliphaunt
"**Grey** clouds jostle the tops." See Exchange
"A **greyhound** should be headed like a snake."
See The properties of a good greyhound
Grief. See also Laments; Melancholy
"Break, break, break." A. Tennyson.—BlO—
HeR
Cousin Ella goes to town. G. E. Lyon.—JaS
Donal Og. Unknown.—HeR
Girl's song. Unknown.—McL
Ha'nacker Mill. H. Belloc.—HeR
Lines for a friend who left. J. Logan.—JaD
My mother's death. J. Hemschemeyer.—JaS
On my first sonne. B. Jonson.—HeR
Poem ("I loved my friend"). L. Hughes.—
CoN—HoBf—HuDk—JaD—LiIl—LiSf
Stopping by home. D. Huddle.—JaG
Swahili love song. Unknown.—McL
"When my dog died." F. Littledale.—CoN
The **grief** of cafeterias. John Updike.—JaPo
Griffin, Susan
Nineteen pieces for love, sels.
"Trying to say".—McL
Perversity.—McL
"Trying to say." See Nineteen pieces for love
"**Griffin** calls to come and kiss him goodnight."
See Bearhug
Grigson, Geoffrey
"Clothes make no sound when I tread ground",
tr. by.—HeR
"I puff my breast out, my neck swells", tr.
by.—HeR
"White is my neck, head yellow, sides", tr.
by.—HeR
The wise men ask the children the way, tr.
by.—HaO
"**Grill** me some bones, said the cobbler." See At
the keyhole
"**Grimes** golden greening yellow transparent." See
Counting-out rhyme
Griselda. Eleanor Farjeon.—FaE
Griselda Gratz. Jack Prelutsky.—PrNk
"**Griselda** Gratz kept sixty cats." See Griselda
Gratz
"**Griselda** is greedy, I'm sorry to say." See
Griselda
Grist mills. See Millers and mills
The **grizzly** bear ("I see a bear"). Ted Hughes.—
HuU
Grizzly bear ("If you ever, ever, ever meet a
grizzly bear"). Mary Austin.—CoOu—LiSf
The **groaning** board. Pink.—FaW (unat.)—TrM
Grocery stores. See also Shops and shopkeepers
Supermarket. F. Holman.—LiSf
Gross, Ronald
"Yield."—KeK

"**Gross** innocent." From Elephant. Pablo
Neruda.—KoT
Grossberg, Shlomit
Prayer ("What shall I ask you for God").—LaT
"**Grotesque** gnome." See Weeping mulberry
Ground hog day. Lilian Moore.—PrRh
"**Ground** hog sleeps." See Ground hog day
Ground-squirrel song. Unknown.—KoT
Groundhog Day
Ground hog day. L. Moore.—PrRh
Groundhogs. See Woodchucks
"**Groundsel.**" Eleanor Farjeon.—FaE
Growing old. Rose Henderson.—PrRh
Growing up. See also Childhood recollections;
Children and childhood
Accomplishments. C. Macdonald.—JaD
Adolescence. G. Orr.—JaPi
Advice to my son. P. Meinke.—JaPi
After many springs. L. Hughes.—HuDk
The Aga Khan. S. Orlen.—JaPi
Agnes Snaggletooth. X. J. Kennedy.—KeF—LiIl
Alison Ford. M. Glenn.—GlC
All. L. Gom.—JaS
Amanda Butler. M. Glenn.—GlCd
An American boyhood. J. Holden.—JaPi
Angelino Falco. M. Glenn.—GlCd
Arlene Lasky. M. Glenn.—GlCd
As I grew older. L. Hughes.—HuDk
Autobiographia literaria. F. O'Hara.—KoT
Autobiography. L. MacNeice.—HeR
Band practice. C. Rylant.—RyW
Barbie doll. M. Piercy.—JaD
Before breakup on the Chena outside Fairbanks.
D. McElroy.—JaPi
Before play. V. Popa.—HeR
Big. D. Aldis.—PrRa
Big house. M. C. Livingston.—LiWo
The biplane. S. Orlen.—JaG
Birthdays. M. A. Hoberman.—PrRa
The birthplace. R. Frost.—PlEd
Brandon Dale. M. Glenn.—GlCd
Brother ("You still carry"). R. Shelton.—JaS
Brothers. R. Currie.—JaPi
Brown penny. W. B. Yeats.—McL
Carlos Rodriguez. M. Glenn.—GlCd
Catherine Heath. M. Glenn.—GlC
Chicago, summer past. R. Snyder.—JaPi
Childhood. F. Cornford.—KeK
A common light. S. Orlen.—JaS
Crayon house. M. Rukeyser.—PlEd
Dana Moran. M. Glenn.—GlCd
Death's blue-eyed girl. L. Pastan.—JaPo
Departing words to a son. R. Pack.—JaG
Donald Kaminsky. M. Glenn.—GlC
Empty holds a question. P. Folk.—JaG
"A father sees a son nearing manhood." C.
Sandburg.—HoRa
First kiss. J. Holden.—JaG
First song. G. Kinnell.—JaG
The first tooth. C. Lamb, and M. Lamb.—
DaC—PrRh
Five years old. M. L. Allen.—FrP—PrRa
For my daughter ("She often lies with her
hands behind her head"). R. Koertge.—JaS
For young men growing up to help themselves.
Unknown, fr. the Cherokee Indian.—BiSp
Forever. E. Merriam.—MeSk
From a prayer for the novice at the close of
his initiation. Unknown, fr. the Zuni
Indian.—BiSp
From a prayer summoning the novice for his
initiation. Unknown, fr. the Zuni Indian.—
BiSp

"**Growltiger** was a bravo cat, who travelled on
a barge." See Growltiger's last stand
Growltiger's last stand. Thomas Stearns Eliot.—
HaOf
Grubby grebbles. Jack Prelutsky.—PrB
"The **gruesome** ghoul, the grisly ghoul." See The
ghoul
A **grumbler** gruff. Oliver Herford.—BrT
"The **guard** has a right to despair." See In
galleries
Guernsey, Bruce
The apple.—JaPo
June twenty-first.—JaPo
Guests
The compassionate fool. N. Cameron.—HeR
The crocodile ("A crocodile once dropped a
line"). O. Herford.—BrT—HaOf
First foot. I. Serraillier.—LiNe
The flattered flying fish. E. V. Rieu.—PrRh
Giraffe ("When I invite the giraffe to dine").
W. J. Smith.—LiII
"The lands around my dwelling." Unknown.—
LiII
Marm Grayson's guests. M. E. W. Freeman.—
HaOf
Some one to tea. E. Farjeon.—FaE
Thanksgiving ("Pilgrims"). M. C. Livingston.—
LiCe
Vestibule. S. Cassedy.—CaR
Guide to the ruins. Howard Nemerov.—PlEd
"**Guido,** I wish that you and Lapo and I." See
Sonnet
Guilt
Boat stealing. From The prelude. W.
Wordsworth.—HeR
The cold heaven. W. B. Yeats.—HeR
Long John Brown and little Mary Bell. W.
Blake.—HeR
Owl ("Who"). E. Merriam.—MeHa
"There was a man of double deed."
Unknown.—HeR
This is just to say. W. C. Williams.—KeK—
PrRh
"**Guises,** disguises." See Mask
"The **guitar.**" See The six strings
Guitars
The six strings. F. García Lorca.—HeR
Guiterman, Arthur
The ambiguous dog.—HoDl
Ancient history.—HaOf—KeK
Chums.—FrP—PrRa
Habits of the hippopotamus.—CoOu—HaOf—
PrRh
Harvest home.—PrRh
House blessing ("Bless the four corners of this
house").—LaT
Nocturne.—LaW
On the vanity of earthly greatness.—HaOf—
TrM
The polliwog.—PrRh
Routine.—PrRh—TrM
The starlighter.—LaW
"The **gull,** it is said." See Magic words to the
gull
"A **gull,** up close." See Seagulls
Gulls
Cape Ann. From Landscapes. T. S. Eliot.—HeR
Magic words to the gull. Unknown, fr. the
Netsilik Eskimo.—BiSp
Sea gull. E. Coatsworth.—PrRh
Seagulls. J. Updike.—JaPi
Sunset blues. M. Kumin.—HoSe
Gumble. Michael Dugan.—PrRh

"The **gumble** lives behind the door." See Gumble
Gundersheimer, Karen
"Happy winter, steamy tub."—PrRa
Gunn, Thom
Baby song.—HeR
The cherry tree.—JaPi
The idea of trust.—JaPi
Slow waker.—JaS
Guns. See also Hunters and hunting
Channel firing. T. Hardy.—HeR
"**Gus** is the cat at the theatre door." See Gus,
the theatre cat
Gus, the theatre cat. Thomas Stearns Eliot.—HaOf
Gussie's Greasy Spoon. Jack Prelutsky.—PrNk
Guthrie, James
Last song.—LaW
Guthrie, Woodrow Wilson
Turkey in the corn.—KeK
Gutierrez, Linda
"Now I love you", tr. by.—McL
"A **guy** asked two jays at St. Louis." See Two
jays at St. Louis
Gypsies
The gypsies. M. C. Livingston.—LiWo
The gypsy laddies. Unknown.—BlO
Meg Merrilies. J. Keats.—BlO—LiSf
"My mother said I never should." Mother
Goose.—BlO—DeM
The pedlar's caravan. W. B. Rands.—BlO
Wild thyme. E. Farjeon.—FaE
The **gypsies.** Myra Cohn Livingston.—LiWo
The **gypsy** laddies. Unknown.—BlO

H

"**Ha,** ha, ha, fat Hans Schneider." See Fat Hans
Schneider
"**Había** una viejita." See La viejita
The **habit** of perfection. Gerard Manley
Hopkins.—HeR
Habits
Habits of the hippopotamus. A. Guiterman.—
CoOu—HaOf—PrRh
Jimmy Jet and his TV set. S. Silverstein.—
HaOf—LiSf—PrRh
Meditatio. E. Pound.—LiSf
Miss Hepzibah. E. Merriam.—MeSk
Mr. Kartoffel. J. Reeves.—PrRh
Routine. A. Guiterman.—PrRh—TrM
"There was an old person whose habits." E.
Lear.—LiH
Hurtful habits.—BrT
Habits of the hippopotamus. Arthur Guiterman.—
CoOu—HaOf—PrRh
"**Had** he and I but met." See The man he killed
"**Had** I known that the heart." See Prescience
"**Had** me a cat, the cat pleased me." See
Fiddle-i-fee
"**Had** perfect pitch." See Aunt Melissa
The **hag.** Robert Herrick.—BlO—LiWa
"The **hag** is astride." See The hag
Haggadah, sels. Unknown
An only kid.—LiPj
Hahn, Meyer
Tishab Be-Av.—LiPj
Yom Ha-Azma'ut.—LiPj
Hahn, Steve
October ("The whole world dances").—JaPo
Haida Indians. See Indians of the Americas—
Haida

"**Hamelin** town's in Brunswick." See The pied
  piper of Hamelin
Hamer, Richard
  A charm ("O wen, wen, O little wennikins"),
    tr. by.—HeR
Hamlet, sels. William Shakespeare
  "How should I your true love know".—PlAs
  "There is a willow grows aslant a brook".—
    HeR
    "There is a willow grows aslant the
      brook".—HoUn
  "The time is out of joint, O cursed spite".—
    TrM
  "To be, or not to be, that is the question".—
    HoUn
  "Tomorrow is Saint Valentine's day".—LiSf—
    LiVp
    Song.—CoN
Hammarskjöld, Dag
  "If only I may grow firmer, simpler."—LaT
The **hammer.** Carl Sandburg.—HoRa
Hamsters
  Hamsters. M. Ridlon.—HoSu—PrRa
  Hamsters. Marci Ridlon.—HoSu—PrRa
  "Hamsters are the nicest things." See Hamsters
Ha'nacker Mill. Hilaire Belloc.—HeR
Hand-clapping rhyme ("Did you eever, iver,
  ever"). See "Did you eever, iver, over"
"The **hand** goes up." See Country greeting
"**Hand** in hand, they are marching." See The
  children
"The **hand** that aches for the pitchfork heft." See
  Work
"The **hand** that rounded Peter's dome." From The
  problem. Ralph Waldo Emerson.—PlEd
"The **hand** that signed a paper felled a city."
  Dylan Thomas.—HeR
Handicapped. See Blind; Cripples; Deafness;
  Insanity
Hands
  Accomplishments. C. Macdonald.—JaD
  "Before goodbye." P. Wolny.—JaPo
  Country greeting. F. Steele.—JaPi
  "The fisherman's hands." N. Valen.—ChC
  "The hand that signed a paper felled a city."
    D. Thomas.—HeR
  "I look at this picture of that old man." From
    Afternoon in Waterloo Park. G. Dumas.—StG
  Mark's fingers. M. O'Neill.—PrRh
  Mittens. B. J. Esbensen.—EsCs
  Seashell ("My father's mother"). V. Worth.—
    WoSp
  Stonecarver. C. Oles.—JaS
  Ten fingers. Unknown.—PrRa
  Thumb. P. Dacey.—JaPo—KeK
"**Handsawwwwwwwwwww.**" Richard Lebovitz.—
  KeK
"A **handsome** young airman lay dying." See The
  dying airman
"A **handsome** young gent down in Fla." See A
  helpful nurse
"**Handy-dandy,** maple candy." Clyde Watson.—
  WaC
A **handy** guide. Unknown.—BrT
"A **handy** old guide from the Bosphorous." See
  A handy guide
"**Handy** spandy, Jack-a-Dandy." Mother Goose.—
  BlQ—LoR
"**Hang** up the baby's stocking." Unknown.—HaO
"**Hanging** their harps upon the willows." See Yom
  Ha-Azma'ut
Hangings. See Executions; Lynchings; Suicide

"**Hannah** Bantry, in the pantry." Mother Goose.—
  LoR
Hansi. Harry Behn.—HoCb—HoDl
Hanukkah
  At Hannukah. M. C. Livingston.—LiSf
  Dreidel song. E. Rosenzweig.—PrRa
  Dreidl. J. P. Lewis.—LiPj
  First night of Hanukkah. R. Boston.—LiPj
  Light another candle. M. Chaikin.—CoN
  Light the festive candles for Hanukkah. A.
    Fisher.—PrRh
"**Hanukkah,** Hanukkah." See Dreidl
Hanzlik, Josef
  Clap your hands for Herod.—HaO
Happiness
  "Ah, a monster's lot is merry." J. Prelutsky.—
    PrNk
  "And the days are not full enough." E.
    Pound.—HeR
  Anticipations. From A throw of threes. E.
    Merriam.—MeF
  Beggar boy. L. Hughes.—HuDk
  A blessing. J. Wright.—McL
  Bliss. E. Farjeon.—FaE—PrRh
  The brown thrush. L. Larcom.—HaOf
  The celestial surgeon. R. L. Stevenson.—DaC
  Christopher Conti. M. Glenn.—GlC
  Conjugation. P. Hubbell.—LiIl
  Convalescence. N. Coward.—KoT
  Crocodile ("The crocodile wept bitter tears"). W.
    J. Smith.—HaOf
  Day's work a-done. W. Barnes.—PlSc
  Delight of being alone. D. H. Lawrence.—PrBb
  Eskimo chant. Unknown.—DoNw
  Eternity. W. Blake.—HeR
  The fiddler of Dooney. W. B. Yeats.—LiSf
  First song. G. Kinnell.—JaG
  For the moment. P. Reverdy.—KoT
  Fun. L. F. Jackson.—PrRa
  The gift. E. Ochester.—JaD—JaPi
  Happiness. W. Dickey.—JaPi
  The happy heart. T. Dekker.—HeR
  Happy thought. R. L. Stevenson.—ChG—
    PrRa—PrRh
  How to paint a perfect Christmas. M. Holub.—
    HaO
  In a train. R. Bly.—KoT
  Joy. L. Hughes.—HuDk
  Joyful. R. Burgunder.—PrRa—PrRh
  Laughter. M. Waddington.—DoNw
  A little song of life. L. W. Reese.—HaOf
  Living with children. J. W. Miller.—JaG
  Many mansions. D. H. Lawrence.—PrBb
  "Oh I have dined on this delicious day." R.
    Snyder.—JaT
  On the house of a friend. J. Logan.—JaD
  "One thing work gives." From Reverdure. W.
    Berry.—PlSc
  The painters. J. Hemschemeyer.—JaPi
  Pillows. From A throw of threes. E. Merriam.—
    MeF
  "Piping down the valleys wild." W. Blake.—
    CoOu—LiSf
    Introduction to Songs of innocence.—PrRh
  Poem in October. D. Thomas.—HeR
  A prayer in spring. R. Frost.—LaT
  "The reason I like chocolate." N. Giovanni.—
    PrRh
  Sensation. A. Rimbaud.—KoT
  The smile. W. Blake.—HeR
  Sonnet. Dante Alighieri.—HeR—KoT
  The telephone. E. Field.—JaPo
  To my father. R. Pomeroy.—JaD

Hate—*Continued*

I hate Harry. M. Chaikin.—PrRh
"I saw a little girl I hate." A. Spilka.—PrRh
    A little girl I hate.—BeD
"If they hate me." A. Adoff.—AdA
The lie ("Today, you threaten to leave me").
    M. Angelou.—AnS
Mean Maxine. J. Prelutsky.—PrNk
Mean song. E. Merriam.—LiSf
On love. K. Tamekane.—McL
"Said the scorpion of hate." C. Sandburg.—
    HoRa
Willy wet-leg. D. H. Lawrence.—HeR
The winter moon ("I hit my wife and went
    out and saw"). T. Kyozo.—McL
"You smiled." C. O'John.—LiIl

Hathaway, James B.

What the stone dreams.—JaG

Hats

"All my hats." R. J. Margolis.—MaS
Colored hats. From Tender buttons. G. Stein.—
    KoT
Good thinking. Unknown.—BrT
Grandma's Easter bonnet. B. Katz.—LiE
"I put my hat upon my head." S. Johnson.—
    KeK
Mr. and Mrs. Spikky Sparrow. E. Lear.—LiH
"Mistress Pratt." A. Lobel.—LoWr
Old King Cabbage. R. K. Munkittrick.—HaOf
The quangle wangle's hat. E. Lear.—CoOu—
    LiH—LiIl
"The scroobious snake." From An animal
    alphabet. E. Lear.—LiH
A second stanza for Dr. Johnson. D. Hall.—
    KeK
The theater hat. C. Wells.—BrT
"There was a young lady of Dorking." E.
    Lear.—LiH
"There was a young lady whose bonnet." E.
    Lear.—LiH
"There was a young person in red." E. Lear.—
    LiH
"There was an old man of Dee-side." E.
    Lear.—LiH
"There was an old man of Thames Ditton."
    E. Lear.—LiH
"Timmy Tatt, Timmy Tatt." J. Prelutsky.—PrRi
While you were chasing a hat. L. Moore.—
    MoSn
Winter's tale. N. Farber.—FaTh
"Yankee Doodle came to town." Mother
    Goose.—DeM
      "Yankee Doodle went to town".—LoR

Hatton, Joseph

Christmas bills.—HaO

Haunted house. Valerie Worth.—LiWa
The **haunted** oven. X. J. Kennedy.—LiWa
The **haunted** palace. Edgar Allan Poe.—LiWa
Haunted room. Sylvia Cassedy.—CaR
Havasupai Indians. See Indians of the Americas—
    Havasupai
Havdalah. Carol Adler.—LiPj
"**Have** mercy, Lord." See Sinner
Have over the water to Florida. Unknown.—PlAs
"**Have** over the water to Floryda." See Have over
    the water to Florida
Have you ever seen. Unknown.—PrRh
"**Have** you ever seen a sheet on a river bed."
    See Have you ever seen
"**Have** you ever smelled summer." See That was
    summer

"**Have** you heard of the wonderful one-hoss shay."
    See The deacon's masterpiece
"**Have** you heard what happened to Ricky Rose."
    See Do you feel sorry for him
"**Have** you noted the white areas." Carlyle
    Reedy.—JaPo
"**Have** you seen them come." See White oak
"**Have** you tasted icicles." See Icicles
"**Having** little kids around, they say, is truly
    bliss." See Did you
"**Having** looked long at two garden rows." See
    Corn and beans
Having words. Eve Merriam.—MeSk
The **hawk.** George Mackay Brown.—HeR

Hawker, Robert Stephen

The mystic Magi.—HaO

Hawks

Eagle song. Unknown, fr. the Papago Indian.—
    BiSp
The hawk. G. M. Brown.—HeR
Hurt hawks. R. Jeffers.—HeR
The osprey. T. Hughes.—HuU
Sea-hawk. R. Eberhart.—HeR
The sparrow hawk. R. Hoban.—LiSf—PrRh
The watchers. P. Fleischman.—FlI
"While we dazed onlookers gawk." X. J.
    Kennedy.—KeB
The windhover, to Christ our Lord. G. M.
    Hopkins.—HeR

Hay, Sara Henderson

For a dead kitten.—ChC
Interview ("Yes, this is where she lived before
    she won").—HaOf

Hay

The barn ("While we unloaded the hay from
    the truck, building"). W. Berry.—PlEd
Hay song. L. Moore.—MoSn
"Willy boy, Willy boy, where are you going."
    Mother Goose.—DeM
Hay song. Lilian Moore.—MoSn

Hayden, Robert

Those winter Sundays.—JaD

Hayes, H. R.

My voice, tr. by.—LiSf
Hayes Iverson. Mel Glenn.—GlCd
Hazardous occupations. Carl Sandburg.—PlSc

Hazo, Samuel

Between you and me.—JaG
To a blind student who taught me to see.—JaG

He ("Has never written me a letter himself").
    Ronald Koertge.—JaS
He ("Some bite off the others"). Vasco Popa, tr.
    by Anne Pennington.—HeR
He and she. See "He was a rat, and she was
    a rat"
"He built a mud-wall'd hovel, where he kept."
    From Peter Grimes. George Crabbe.—PlSc
"He built himself a house." See Fairy tale
"He clasps the crag with crooked hands." See The
    eagle
"He comes from afar." See Air traveler
"He comes gusting out of the house." See Spring
    storm
"He didn't bark at anything." See My dog
"He found a formula for drawing comic rabbits."
    See Epitaph on an unfortunate artist
"He gave her some kind of elixir." See A mean
    trick
"He gave silver shoes to the rabbit." See Blake
    leads a walk on the Milky Way
"He had a falcon on his wrist." See Love me,
    love my dog

"He hadn't been right." See Whitley at three o'clock

"He has, by his wife's reckoning, failed so often." See Trying

"He has dust in his eyes and a fan for a wing." See One guess

"He has sprouted, he has burgeoned." See Inanna's song

"He has two antennae." See Gnat on my paper

He, haw, haw, hum. Mother Goose.—BlPi

He hears the cry of the sedge. William Butler Yeats.—HeR

"He is coming." See Christmas eve

"He is gone now." See For Mugs

"He is old, two weeks to eighty." See Blue sparks in dark closets

"He is sherrier." See The thinnest shadow

"He is so small, he does not know." See Six weeks old

"He killed the noble Mudjokivis." See The modern Hiawatha

"He longs to open his arms, we can see that." See My father's heart

"He looked at her with eyes full of passion." See Catherine Heath

"He loves me." Mother Goose.—DeM—LoR

"He opens his eyes with a cry of delight." See A child's Christmas day

"He played by the river when he was young." See Washington

"He received from some thoughtful relations." See The pleasing gift

He remembers forgotten beauty. William Butler Yeats.—McL

"He rose at dawn and, fired with hope." See The sailor boy

He runs into an old acquaintance. Alden Nowlan.—JaG

"He said he had been a soldier." Dorothy Wordsworth.—PlSc

"He said he was tired and sore all day." See Uncle Mells and the witches' tree

"He sat at the Algonquin, smoking a cigar." See At the Algonquin

"He sat upon the rolling deck." See Sailor

"He saw the portrait of his enemy, offered." See The enemy's portrait

"He scattered tarantulas over the roads." See The devil in Texas

"He seemed to know the harbour." See The shark

"He sent his love a valentine." David McCord.—LiVp

"He sipped at a weak hock and seltzer." See The arrest of Oscar Wilde at the Cadogan Hotel

"He sits and begs, he gives a paw." See Chums

He sits down on the floor of a school for the retarded. Alden Nowlan.—JaG

"He stands with his forefeet on the drum." See Two performing elephants

"He startles awake, his eyes are full of white light." See The hermit wakes to bird sounds

"He steps down from the dark train, blinking, stares." See Ten days leave

"He studies very late." See Glowworm

"He tells you when you've got on too much lipstick." See The perfect husband

"He that hears always, hear my cries, as my tears drop to." See Young man's prayer to the spirits

"He thought he saw a buffalo." See The mad gardener's song

"He thought he saw an elephant." See The mad gardener's song

"He threw the shroud about his head." See John Donne's statue

"He travels after a winter sun." See Tilly

"He waits perpetually crouched, teeth." See Mean Rufus throw-down

He was. Richard Wilbur.—PlSc

"He was a big man, says the size of his shoes." See Abandoned farmhouse

"He was a rat, and she was a rat." Unknown.—BlO

He and she.—BlPi

What became of them.—HaOf

"He was as old as old could be." See Danny Murphy

"He was older and." See Passage

"He wastes time walking and telling the air, I am superior even to the wind." From Sketch of a poet. Carl Sandburg.—HoRa

"He who binds himself to joy." See Eternity

"He worshiped me." See And the princess was astonished to see the ugly frog turn into a handsome prince

"He wouldn't come at first." See Making a friend

"Head bumper." Unknown.—RaT

Headland, Isaac Taylor
"Ladybug, ladybug", tr. by.—FaW
"Old Mr. Chang", tr. by.—FaW
"On the top of a mountain", tr. by.—FaW
"On the top of the mount", tr. by.—FaW
"There's a cow on the mountain", tr. by.—FaW

The **headless** gardener. Ian Serraillier.—LiSf

"A **headless** squirrel, some blood." See A day begins

Heads
"As I was going out one day." Mother Goose.—LoR
Celanta at the well of life. From The old wives' tale. G. Peele.—BlO
Song for the head.—HeR
Doctor Emmanuel. J. Reeves.—PrRh
"From number nine, Penwiper Mews." E. Gorey.—BrT
Number nine, Penwiper Mews.—PrRh
The hare and the pig. L. J. Bridgman.—PrRh
The headless gardener. I. Serraillier.—LiSf
"I left my head." L. Moore.—MoSn
In a museum cabinet. M. Swenson.—LiWa
It makes no difference to me. J. Ciardi.—CiD
"I've got an incredible headache." J. Prelutsky.—PrNk
"My brother's head should be replaced." J. Prelutsky.—PrNk
My fishbowl head. X. J. Kennedy.—KeF
The seed ("Someone sows someone"). V. Popa.—HeR
"There was a young person of Ayr." E. Lear.—KeK—LiH
"There was an old person of Dutton." E. Lear.—LiH

The **health-food** diner. Maya Angelou.—AnS

Heaney, Seamus
The names of the hare, tr. by.—HeR
Scaffolding.—JaG
Sweeney praises the trees, tr. by.—HeR
Valediction.—JaPo

Heap on more wood. Sir Walter Scott.—HaO

"**Heap** on more wood, the wind is chill." See Heap on more wood

"**Heaps** of headlights." See Passing by the junkyard

"**Hear** the sledges with the bells." See The bells
"**Hear** the voice of the Bard." William Blake.—HeR
Hearing. See Sounds
"**Hearken** all ye, 'tis the feast o' Saint Stephen." See The feast o' Saint Stephen
Hearn, Emily
   Jigsaw puddle.—BeD
Hearn, Michael Patrick
   In the library ("You're right").—CoN
   Rhinos purple, hippos green.—PrRh
The **hearse** song. Unknown.—HeR
Heart. Joan LaBombard.—JaPo
"The **heart** can think of no devotion." See Devotion
Heart crown and mirror. Guillaume Apollinaire.—KoT
"The **heart** goes out ahead." See Poem of the mother
"A **heart** that's been broken." Maureen Owen.—McL
"**Heart** we will forget him." Emily Dickinson.—McL
The **heart's** location. Peter Meinke.—JaG
A **hearty** cook. Roy Blount.—BrT
"A **hearty** old cook of Lithonia." See A hearty cook
Heat
   August ("In waves of heat"). R. Scheele.—JaPo
   August heat. Unknown.—HoSi—PrRa
   Drought. B. J. Esbensen.—EsCs
   Excursion. E. Merriam.—MeF
   Summer. F. Asch.—CoN—PrRh
   Too hot. J. Prelutsky.—PrWi
   Warmth. B. Sutter.—JaG
Heath, Gertrude E.
   The merry crocodile.—BrT
Heath-Stubbs, John
   December, prayer to St. Nicholas.—HaO
   February.—HaO
   January ("Under a white coverlet of snow").—HaO
   Winter cricket.—HaO
"A **heathen** named Min, passing by." See Tra-la-larceny
Heather Yarnell. Mel Glenn.—GlCd
Heaven
   Ah, sunflower. W. Blake.—HeR
   The big rock candy mountains ("On a summer's day in the month of May, a burly little bum come a-hiking"). Unknown.—KeK
      The big rock candy mountains ("One evening as the sun went down").—KoT
   Birches. R. Frost.—HeR—KoS
   The dead sister. C. Gilman.—HaOf
   The dying child's request. H. F. Gould.—HaOf
   Grandfather's heaven. N. S. Nye.—JaS
   Heaven. G. Herbert.—KoT
   If there are any heavens. E. E. Cummings.—JaD
   Judgement day. L. Hughes.—HuDk
   One step from an old dance. D. Helwig.—DoNw
   The passionate man's pilgrimage. Sir W. Raleigh.—HeR
   Poem for my father's ghost. M. Oliver.—JaS
   A prayer to go to paradise with the donkeys. F. Jammes.—HeR—LiSf
   Request of a dying child. L. H. Sigourney.—HaOf
   Samantha speaking. D. McCord.—LiTp
Heaven. George Herbert.—KoT
Heaven-haven. Gerard Manley Hopkins.—HeR

Heavy and light, sels. Carl Sandburg
   "Fritters used to say, there is poetry in neckties".—HoRa
A **heavy** rap. Nikki Giovanni.—GiSp
Hecht, Anthony
   Application for a grant.—PlSc
   More light, more light.—HeR
"**Hector** Protector was dressed all in green." Mother Goose.—AlH—DeM—LoR
"The **hedge**." Charlotte Zolotow.—ZoE
"The **hedgehog**.." See Hedgehog
Hedgehog. N. M. Bodecker.—BoSs
The **hedgehog**. J. J. Bell.—PrRh
"The **hedgehog** sleeps beneath the hedge." See The hedgehog
Heel ("The sun inside me lights a flame"). Eleanor Farjeon.—FaE
Heide, Florence Parry
   Rocks.—CoN
   "What's that."—HoCr—PrRh
"**Heigh** ho." See Heigh ho April
Heigh ho April. Eleanor Farjeon.—FaE
"**Heigh** ho, mistletoe." N. M. Bodecker.—BoSs
The **height** of the ridiculous. Oliver Wendell Holmes.—HaOf
Heine, Heinrich
   The loreley.—LiWa
   The wise men ask the children the way.—HaO
Held in suspense. X. J. Kennedy.—KeF
"**Helen**, my cousin, says she still has the scar." See Helen's scar
Helen Price. Mel Glenn.—GlC
Helen's scar. Alden Nowlan.—JaS
Helicopters
   Flight plan. J. Merchant.—HoCl—PrRh
Hell
   The curst wife. Unknown.—PlAs
   The devil in Texas. Unknown.—HeR
   The farmer's curst wife. Unknown.—PlAs
   "Methought that I had broken from the Tower." From Richard III. W. Shakespeare.—HeR
   Strange meeting ("It seemed that out of battle I escaped"). W. Owen.—HeR
   "Then to the bar, all they drew near." From The day of doom. M. Wigglesworth.—HaOf
Hellerstein, Kathryn
   Shavuot, for Jessica.—LiPj
"**Hello**." See Allen Greshner
Hello, graffiti. Ann Turner.—TuS
"**Hello**, hello, hello, sir." See Jump-rope rhyme
"**Hello**, Towzer, what's he after." See Child and dog
"**Hello** young sailor." See Martial choreograph
Help ("Firemen, firemen"). X. J. Kennedy.—PrRh
A **helpful** nurse. Unknown.—BrT
Helwig, David
   One step from an old dance.—DoNw
Hemp, Christine E.
   To build a poem.—JaG
   To my blood sister.—JaS
Hemschemeyer, Judith
   The dirty billed freeze footy.—JaS
   First love ("We fell in love at 'Journey for Margaret'").—JaPi
   Flight ("One day you were there, the next day gone").—JaPo
   My grandmother had bones.—JaD
   My mother's death.—JaS
   The painters.—JaPi
   Strawberries ("The first time I went to the fields alone").—JaD
   "That summer."—JaPo

Hemschemeyer, Judith—*Continued*
  This love.—JaG
  We interrupt this broadcast.—JaS
The **hen** ("The hen is a ferocious fowl"). Lord Alfred Douglas.—PrRh
The **hen** ("In the waiting room of the railway"). Christian Morgenstern, tr. by William De Witt Snodgrass and Lore Segal.—HeR
The **hen** and the carp. Ian Serraillier.—CoOu—LiSf
"The **hen** is a ferocious fowl." See The hen
Henderson, Rose
  Growing old.—PrRh
Henley, William Ernest
  Invictus.—HeR
Henri, Raymond
  At the woodpile.—PlSc
  The bridge from Brooklyn, sels.
    "Roebling, his life and mind reprieved enough".—PlEd
  Chartres. See View of the cathedral
  Duomo, Milan. See View of the cathedral
  "Roebling, his life and mind reprieved enough." See The bridge from Brooklyn
  View of the cathedral, sels.
    Chartres.—PlEd
    Duomo, Milan.—PlEd
Henrietta Snetter. Jack Prelutsky.—PrNk
"**Henrietta** Snetter knit a sweater in the night." See Henrietta Snetter
Henry and Mary. Robert Graves.—LiIl—LiSf
Henry IV, Part I, sels. William Shakespeare
  "All furnish'd, all in arms".—HoUn
Henry V, sels. William Shakespeare
  "This day is call'd the feast of Crispian".—HoUn
  "Yon island carrions desperate of their bones".—HeR
Henry VIII, King of England (about)
  Tudor portrait. R. Lattimore.—PlEd
Henry VIII, sels. William Shakespeare
  "Orpheus with his lute made trees".—HoUn
"**Henry** was a young king." See Henry and Mary
Henry's market. Cynthia Rylant.—RyW
The **hens**. Elizabeth Madox Roberts.—HaOf—LiSf
The **henyard** round. Donald Hall.—JaPi
"**Her** aunties trains of satin don." See Jenny
"**Her** body, smooth and sleek, stands." See Vinnie Robustelli
"**Her** face like a rain-beaten stone on the day she rolled off." See Elegy
"**Her** father lov'd me, oft invited me." From Othello. William Shakespeare.—HoUn
"**Her** honey fur pointed down her back." See Marmalade lost
"**Her** lute hangs shadowed in the apple tree." See A sea spell for a picture
"**Her** strong enchantments failing." Alfred Edward Housman.—KeK
Herbert, George
  Heaven.—KoT
Herbert, Zbigniew
  A devil.—HeR
  Two drops.—HeR
Herbert Glerbett. Jack Prelutsky.—PrRh
"**Herbert** Glerbett, rather round." See Herbert Glerbett
Herbs
  Catnip. V. Worth.—LiCa
  "Rosemary green." Mother Goose.—AlH
  Sweet herbs. E. Farjeon.—FaE
Here ("I am a man now"). Ronald Stuart Thomas.—HeR

Here ("In this spot"). Charlotte Zolotow.—ZoE
"**Here**." See Magic spell to turn a woman's heart
"**Here**." See Tu Bi-Shevat
"**Here** all we see." Walter De la Mare.—PrRa
"**Here** am I, little jumping Joan." Mother Goose.—BlQ—DeM—FaW—LiSf—LoR
  Little jumping Joan.—CoN
"**Here** are no signs of festival." See African Christmas
"**Here** be naked boys." See Autumn crocus
"**Here** come a dozen kangaroos." See How much is a gross
"**Here** come real stars to fill the upper skies." See Fireflies in the garden
"**Here** come the." See Song of the tree frogs
"**Here** comes a mouse." Clyde Watson.—WaC
"**Here** comes a tidbit." Clyde Watson.—WaC
"**Here** comes the moon." See The moon
"**Here**, Dana, let me show you my room." See Dorothy Osmond
"**Here** further up the mountain slope." See The birthplace
"**Here** goes a turtle up the hill." Unknown.—RaT
"**Here**, grandfathers, eat, and whoever had good luck in." See Offering to deceased hunters
"**Here** I am where you see me." See River's song
"**Here**, in my parents' home." See Visit
"**Here**, in the withered arbor, like the arrested wind." See Statue and birds
"**Here** is a building." See For you
"**Here** is a child who presses his head to the ground." See The windows
"**Here** is how I eat a fish." See Eating fish
"**Here** is the ancient floor." See The self-unseeing
"**Here** is the fossil." See The black fern
"**Here** is the nose that smelled something sweet." Clyde Watson.—WaC
"**Here** is the reply made by Benny." See Raisin bread
"**Here** is the story." See Freddy
"**Here** is the train to Glasgow." See The train to Glasgow
"**Here** it comes." See Frightening
Here it is. Ann Turner.—TuS
"**Here** it is, the tobacco, I am certain that you O ghost, are." See Prayer of the ghost
"**Here**, I've almost caught one." See Butterflies
"**Here** lies." See Tombstone
Here lies a lady. John Crowe Ransom.—HeR
"**Here** lies a lady of beauty and high degree." See Here lies a lady
"**Here** lies a most beautiful lady." See An epitaph
"**Here** lies Fred." Unknown.—DaC
"**Here** lies old Hobson, death hath broke his girt. John Milton.—PlSc
"**Here** lies the noble warrior that never blunte sword." See Epitaph on the Earl of Leiceste
"**Here** lies, whom hound did ne'er pursue." Se Epitaph on a hare
"**Here** living and the stone." See Duomo, Mila
"**Here** on my field." See A song of the cor dance
"**Here** she comes." Deborah Chandra.—LiNe
"**Here** sits the Lord Mayor." See The city sho
"**Here** sits the Lord Mayor." Mother Goose.—Ra
"**Here** the crow starves, here the patient stag. See Rannoch, by Glencoe
"**Here** we are all, by day, by night we a hurled." See Dreams
"**Here** we are, all dressed up to honor death See At the funeral of great aunt Mary

"Hermit crabs and cranberry." See Sea shore shanty
The **hermit** wakes to bird sounds. Maxine Kumin.—JaPi
Hermits
The hermit wakes to bird sounds. M. Kumin.—JaPi
Single. N. M. Bodecker.—BoPc
A **hero** in the land of dough. Robert Clairmont.—KeK
Herod, King (about)
A ballad of Christmas. W. De la Mare.—HaO
Clap your hands for Herod. J. Hanzlik.—HaO
Innocent's song. C. Causley.—HaO
Lully, lulla. Unknown.—KoT
Heroes and heroines. See also names of heros, as Washington, George
Adventures of Isabel. O. Nash.—CoN—CoOu—HaOf—PrRh
Alabama earth. L. Hughes.—HuDk
"All furnish'd, all in arms." From Henry IV, Part I. W. Shakespeare.—HoUn
Barbara Frietchie. J. G. Whittier.—HaOf
The bold pedlar and Robin Hood. Unknown.—PlAs
Casey at the bat. E. L. Thayer.—HaOf
The death of Admiral Benbow. Unknown.—BlO
Excelsior. H. W. Longfellow.—HaOf
Folk tune. R. Wilbur.—PlAs
Harriet Tubman. E. Greenfield.—LiSf
Jesse James. Unknown.—PlAs
John Henry ("When John Henry was a little tiny baby"). Unknown.—KeK
  John Henry ("John Henry was a lil baby").—PlAs
  John Henry ("When John Henry was a little babe").—LiSf
Lincoln monument, Washington. L. Hughes.—HuDk
Lochinvar. Sir W. Scott.—PlAs
Miss M.F.H.E.I.I. Jones. K. Kuskin.—LiIl
Paul Revere's ride. H. W. Longfellow.—HaOf
Peter Quincy. M. Glenn.—GlC
Robin Hood and the Bishop of Hereford. Unknown.—BlO
"Some talk of Alexander, and some of Hercules." Unknown.—TrM
The statues in the public gardens. H. Nemerov.—PlEd
"This day is call'd the feast of Crispian." From Henry V. W. Shakespeare.—HoUn
The wild colonial boy. Unknown.—PlAs
"Would you hear of an old-fashion'd sea-fight." From Song of myself. W. Whitman.—HeR
Heroism. See Courage; Heroes and heroines
Heron ("In the copper marsh"). Philip Booth.—JaPo
Heron ("Only / fools / pursue"). Valerie Worth.—WoSp
The **heron** ("The sun's an iceberg"). Ted Hughes.—HuU
Herons
Fishing Blue Creek. R. Scheele.—JaPo
Heron ("In the copper marsh"). P. Booth.—JaPo
Heron ("Only / fools / pursue"). V. Worth.—WoSp
The heron ("The sun's an iceberg"). T. Hughes.—HuU
Look up. A. Turner.—TuS
Night heron. F. Frost.—PrRh
"**Herons** and sweeps." Edward Lear.—LiH

Herrick, Robert
The argument of his book.—KoT
The beggar to Mab, the fairie Queen.—LiWa
Ceremony upon Candlemas eve.—HaO
Charmes.—LiWa
Dreams ("Here we are all, by day, by night we are hurled").—KeK
The fairies ("If ye will with Mab find grace").—BlO
The hag.—BlO—LiWa
How marigolds came yellow.—KoT
How violets came blue.—KoT
The spell.—LiWa
A ternary of littles, upon a pipkin of jelly sent to a lady.—KoT
To daffodils.—KoT
Upon Julia's clothes.—KoT
Yule log.—HaO
Hershenson, Miriam
"Husbands and wives."—CoN
"He's gone." See Nothing
"He's nothing much but fur." See A kitten
"He's pulling on his boots." See Outside
"He's shy Buck McLeish says." See Buying the dog
"He's up early for breakfast." See David in April
Hesitating ode. Miklós Radnóti, tr. by Steven Polgar and Stephen Berg and S. J. Marks.—McL
Hesse, Herman
Sometimes ("Sometimes, when a bird cries out").—LiWa
Hewitt, Geof
In like a lion.—JaPo
Hey, Phil
For Sue.—JaPo
Old clothes.—JaG
Sweetheart.—JaG
The true ballad of the great race to Gilmore City.—JaPi
"**Hey**." See A left-handed poem
Hey, bug. Lilian Moore.—PrRh
"**Hey**, bug, stay." See Hey, bug
"**Hey**, cackle, hey." See The witch's song
"**Hey** diddle diddle, the cat and the fiddle." Mother Goose.—AlH—DeM—FaW—LiSf—LoR
"**Hey**, Missy Sinkins." See Missy Sinkins
"**Hey**, my lad, ho, my lad." See Welcome to the new year
Hey, my pony. Eleanor Farjeon.—FaE
"**Hey**, sidewalk pacers." See Just for one day
"**Hey** there, brontosaurus." See To the skeleton of a dinosaur in the museum
"**Hey**, this little kid gets roller skates." See 74th Street
Heyen, William
The dark ("I am glad of that other life").—PlEd
Driving at dawn.—PlSc
The mill ("Over the harbor at St. James").—PlEd
Heywood, Thomas
"Pack, clouds, away, and welcome, day."—BlO
Hibernation
"All animals like me." R. Souster.—DoNw
The black bear ("The bear's black bulk"). T. Hughes.—HuU
Hard to bear. T. Jenks.—HaOf
Mrs. Brownish Beetle. A. Fisher.—FiW
Song of the spring peeper. J. Yolen.—YoR
Wake up call. B. J. Esbensen.—EsCs

Hiccups
"Hickup, hickup, go away." Mother Goose.—LoR
"Hick-a-more, hack-a-more." Mother Goose.—LiSf
"Hickenthrift and Hickenloop." X. J. Kennedy.—LiWa
"Hickety, pickety, my black hen." Mother Goose.—DeM—LoR
"Hickory dickory dock." Mother Goose.—DeM—FaW—LoR
"Hickup, hickup, go away." Mother Goose.—LoR
Hicky, Daniel Whitehead
To an aviator.—PrRh
Hidden. Eleanor Farjeon.—FaE
Hide and seek ("Someone hides from someone"). Vasco Popa, tr. by Anne Pennington.—HeR
Hide and seek ("The trees are tall, but the moon small"). Robert Graves.—CoN—KeK
Hide and seek ("When I am alone, and quite alone"). A. B. Shiffrin.—FrP—PrRa
Hide and seek shadow. Margaret Hillert.—PrRa
"Hide not, hide not." See The rousing canoe song
Hiding. Dorothy Aldis.—LiSf
"Hie upon Hielands." See Bonny George Campbell
Hiebert, Paul
Steeds.—DoNw
Higgins, Alice
Swimming.—PrRa
Higgins, Frederick Robert
Song for the clatter-bones.—HeR
"Higgledy-piggledy." See Easter disaster
"Higgledy piggledy." Dennis Lee.—LiSf
"Higglety, pigglety, pop." Samuel Goodrich.—FaW (unat.)—PrRa—PrRh
"High adventure." See Maps
High and low. John Banister Tabb.—BrT
"A **high** blow tousled all the yachts." See September, last day at the beach
"High diddle doubt, my candle's out." Mother Goose.—DeM
High heeled shoes. Kate Cox Goddard.—FrP
"High, high in the branches." See The ferns
"High, high up." See Widow's walk
"Higher and higher." See Ice skating
"Higher than a house." Mother Goose.—LiSf
"Highway turnpike thruway mall." See A charm for our time
The **highwayman.** Alfred Noyes.—LiSf
Highways. See Roads and streets
The **hiker.** Eve Merriam.—LiSf
Hiking. See Camping and hiking
"Hiking in the Rockies, Midge." X. J. Kennedy.—KeB
Hikmet, Nazim
Things I didn't know I loved.—McL
A **hikoka** in a hikoki. Charlotte Pomerantz.—PoI
Hildy Ross. Mel Glenn.—GlC
The **hill.** Myra Cohn Livingston.—LiWo
The **hill** above the mine. Malcolm Cowley.—PlSc
"A **hill** full, a hole full." Mother Goose.—LiSf
Hillert, Margaret
About feet.—PrRh
And suddenly spring.—HoSi
Blowing bubbles.—PrRa
Dinosaur.—HoDi
The funny house.—HoBf
Hide and seek shadow.—PrRa
Just me.—PrRh
My teddy bear ("A teddy bear is nice to hold").—PrRa
Surprise ("I tip my glass to take a drink").—HoMu

Thanksgiving ("I feel so stuffed inside my skin").—HoSi
Hills. See Mountains
"The **hills** lie over the water." See The hills over the water
The **hills** over the water. Eleanor Farjeon.—FaE
Hine, Daryl
Lady Sara Bunbury sacrificing to the Graces, by Reynolds.—PlEd
"Hinnikin Minnikin." Jack Prelutsky.—PrRi
"Hip hop hoppity, hip hop hoppity." See The rabbit
"A **hippo** decided one day." See Ballet
Hippopotami
Ballet. Unknown.—BrT
Habits of the hippopotamus. A. Guiterman.—CoOu—HaOf—PrRh
The hippopotamus ("Behold the hippopotamus"). O. Nash.—CoOu
Hippopotamus ("The hippopotamus"). N. M. Bodecker.—BoSs
The hippopotamus ("The huge hippopotamus hasn't a hair"). J. Prelutsky.—PrRh—PrZ
The hippopotamus ("I shoot the hippopotamus"). H. Belloc.—FaW
Hippopotamus ("See the handsome hippopotamus"). J. Cole.—CoN
"I had a hippopotamus, I loved him as a friend." From I had a hippopotamus. P. Barrington.—LiIl
The **hippopotamus** ("Behold the hippopotamus"). Ogden Nash.—CoOu
"The **hippopotamus.**" See Hippopotamus
Hippopotamus ("The hippopotamus"). N. M. Bodecker.—BoSs
The **hippopotamus** ("The huge hippopotamus hasn't a hair"). Jack Prelutsky.—PrRh—PrZ
The **hippopotamus** ("I shoot the hippopotamus"). Hilaire Belloc.—FaW
Hippopotamus ("See the handsome hippoppotamus"). Joanna Cole.—CoN
"The **hippopotamus** is strong." See Habits of the hippopotamus
The **hired** man's way. John Kendrick Bangs.—HaOf
His dog. Richard J. Margolis.—MaS
His dream of the sky land, a farewell poem, sels. Li Po, tr. by Shigeyoshi Obata
"The seafarers tell of the eastern Isle of Bliss".—LiWa
"His eyes are green and his nose is brown." See The king of the hobbledygoblins
"His figure's not noted for grace." See The wild boarder
"His gimpy leg was testimony to." See Old Doc
"His hands were talented for intricate transactions." See With a posthumous medal
His highness's dog. See Engraved on the collar of a dog, which I gave to his Royal Highness
His legs ran about. Ted Hughes.—McL
His lunch basket. Doug Cockrell.—JaPi
"His nose is short and scrubby." See My dog
"His proper name was Peter Sweet." See The reformed pirate
"A **hiss,** a gulp, where are you, Niles." X. J. Kennedy.—KeB
"Hist whist." Edward Estlin Cummings.—LiSf—PrRh
An **historic** moment. William J. Harris.—KeK
History. See also Explorers and exploration; Frontier and pioneer life; also names of countries
Ancient history. A. Guiterman.—HaOf—KeK

Hollo, Anselm
Troll chanting, tr. by.—LiWa
"Hollow as." See Yew
Holly and mistletoe. Eleanor Farjeon.—FaE
"The **holly** and the ivy." Unknown.—RoC
Holly trees
Holly and mistletoe. E. Farjeon.—FaE
"The holly and the ivy." Unknown.—RoC
Holman, Felice
At the top of my voice.—HoSu
Bedtime ("Now the mouse goes to his hole").—LaW
The city dump.—HoSs—PrRh
Easter habits.—LiE
Friend ("Do you know Paul, Paul Pine (he's nine)").—LiIl
Gobbledy-gobble.—LiTp
Halloween witches.—LiSf—LiWa
I can fly.—CoN—PrRh
Leave me alone.—PrRh
Loneliness.—LiIl
Lullaby ("The trees now look scary").—LaW
"My toe."—FaTh
Night sounds.—LaW
Sulk.—PrRh
Supermarket.—LiSf
They're calling.—LiSf—PrRh
Who am I.—FaTh—LiSf
Wild day at the shore.—HoSe
The year.—LiNe
Holmes, Oliver Wendell
The deacon's masterpiece.—HaOf
The height of the ridiculous.—HaOf
Holub, Miroslav
Bullfight.—HeR
Fairy tale ("He built himself a house").—HeR
The fly ("She sat on a willow-trunk").—HeR
Great and strong.—HeR
A history lesson.—HeR
How to paint a perfect Christmas.—HaO
Holy days. Valerie Worth.—LiPj
The **holy** innocents. Robert Lowell.—HaO
"**Holy** water come and bring." See The spell
Holz, Arno
Phantasus, 1, 8.—LiCp
Homage to Paul Mellon, I. M. Pei, their gallery, and Washington City. William Meredith.—PlEd
Homage to Wren. Louis MacNeice.—PlEd
Home. Jean Jaszi.—PrRa
Home and family life
Address to a child during a boisterous winter evening. D. Wordsworth.—BlO
All. L. Gom.—JaS
"All my hats." R. J. Margolis.—MaS
Always room for one more. S. N. Leodhas.—LiSf
The anniversary. W. Dickey.—JaG
Arm wrestling with my father. J. Driscoll.—JaG
Around the kitchen table. G. Gildner.—JaS
Aunt Elsie's night music. M. Oliver.—JaS
Aunt Gladys's home movie no. 31, Albert's funeral. J. W. Miller.—JaS
Baking day. R. Joseph.—JaS
Bearhug. M. Ondaatje.—JaPo
The birthplace. R. Frost.—PlEd
Brother ("You still carry"). R. Shelton.—JaS
Business as usual. M. Vinz.—JaS
Cassius. C. Rylant.—RyW
The children's hour. H. W. Longfellow.—HaOf
Cookout night. D. Aldis.—HoMu
Dad and the cat and the tree. K. Wright.—CoOu

Daddy fell into the pond. A. Noyes.—PrRh
Danny Vargas. M. Glenn.—GlC
Den. S. Cassedy.—CaR
Did you. W. Cole.—PrRh
The dirty billed freeze footy. J. Hemschemeyer.—JaS
Dora Antonopolis. M. Glenn.—GlC
Ellen Winters. M. Glenn.—GlC
Eviction. L. Clifton.—CoN
Family cups. S. Orlen.—JaS
Family needs. Unknown.—LiSf
Family reunion ("Sunlight glints off the chrome of many cars"). J. W. Miller.—JaS
Family reunion ("Thanksgiving day, our family"). X. J. Kennedy.—LiTp
The field. D. Huddle.—JaS
The first tooth. C. Lamb, and M. Lamb.—DaC—PrRh
From my mother's house. L. Goldberg.—StG
Gail Larkin. M. Glenn.—GlC
The gift. E. Ochester.—JaD—JaPi
The gone years. A. Fulton.—JaS
Grandparents' houses. M. Van Doren.—StG
Held in suspense. X. J. Kennedy.—KeF
Help ("Firemen, firemen"). X. J. Kennedy.—PrRh
Here it is. A. Turner.—TuS
His lunch basket. D. Cockrell.—JaPi
A history of the pets. D. Huddle.—JaPo
A home without a cat. M. Twain.—ChC
Home, you're where it's warm inside. J. Prelutsky.—PrRh
A house of readers. J. W. Miller.—JaPo
The house remembers. R. Francis.—JaD
Houses ("Time and the weather wear away"). D. Justice.—JaPo—PlEd
Housing starts. P. Davison.—PlEd
"I had a little hen, the prettiest ever seen." Mother Goose.—DeM—LoR
"In both the families." A. Adoff.—AdA
In our one family. A. Adoff.—AdA
In the music. R. Currie.—JaT
Into Laddery Street. From Forgotten girlhood. L. Riding.—HeR
"It's happy Thanksgiving." J. Prelutsky.—PrIt
Jason Talmadge. M. Glenn.—GlC
Jigsaw puzzle. R. Hoban.—CoN
The journey. D. Ignatow.—JaPi
June twenty-first. B. Guernsey.—JaPo
Justin Faust. M. Glenn.—GlCd
Keziah. G. Brooks.—PrRa—PrRh
The king of cats sends a postcard to his wife. N. Willard.—HaOf
The kitchen (for my grandmother). W. Bedford.—StG
Lantern. G. Soto.—JaS
"Lena." M. C. Livingston.—LiWo
Lessons ("My teacher taught me to add."). R. J. Margolis.—MaS
Listening to grownups quarreling. R. Whitman.—CoN—KeK
The little maid. A. M. Wells.—HaOf
Little orphant Annie. J. W. Riley.—HaOf
Living with children. J. W. Miller.—JaG
Marcy Mannes. M. Glenn.—GlCd
Marie Yeagerman. M. Glenn.—GlC
Marm Grayson's guests. M. E. W. Freeman.—HaOf
Michelle Church. M. Glenn.—GlCd
Mitchell Chapin. M. Glenn.—GlC
Monica Zindell. M. Glenn.—GlC
Mummy slept late and Daddy fixed breakfast. J. Ciardi.—LiSf—PrRh

Home and family life—*Continued*
"My sister she works in a laundry." Unknown.—TrM
Night fun. J. Viorst.—PrRa—ViI
Norman Moskowitz. M. Glenn.—GlC
110 year old house. E. Ochester.—JaPi
Our house. D. B. Thompson.—PrRh
The painters. J. Hemschemeyer.—JaPi
Pamela Atkinson. M. Glenn.—GlC
Party. M. C. Livingston.—LiWo
The piano ("I sit on the edge"). F. Davey.—DoNw
The portrait ("My mother never forgave my father"). S. Kunitz.—JaPi
"Puss came dancing out of a barn." Mother Goose.—DeM
Rickie Miller. M. Glenn.—GlC
Robert of Lincoln. W. C. Bryant.—HaOf
Rosemarie Stewart. M. Glenn.—GlC
The runaway ("I made peanut butter sandwiches"). B. Katz.—PrRh
"Say not of me that weakly I declined." R. L. Stevenson.—PlEd
Shooting crows. D. Huddle.—JaG
Sleepless nights. Zolotow. Charlotte.—ZoE—ZoE
The snow-filled nest. R. T. Cooke.—HaOf
Some things don't make any sense at all. J. Viorst.—PrRh—ViI
A song of the corn dance. Unknown, fr. the Papago Indian.—BiSp
Stark county holidays. M. Oliver.—JaS
Stella Kolsky. M. Glenn.—GlC
Stopping by home. D. Huddle.—JaG
Sunday funnies. A. Keiter.—JaD
Susan Tulchin. M. Glenn.—GlC
Ten days leave. W. D. W. Snodgrass.—JaPi
Thanksgiving ("The tides in my eyes are heavy"). P. Booth.—JaS
"There is so much." A. Adoff.—AdA
Those winter Sundays. R. Hayden.—JaD
Timothy Winters. C. Causley.—HeR
To a sad daughter. M. Ondaatje.—JaG
Toward dark. C. Zolotow.—ZoE
Turkey in the corn. W. W. Guthrie.—KeK
Twin aces. K. Wilson.—JaPi
Two people ("She reads the paper"). E. Merriam.—PrRh
Up in the pine. N. D. Watson.—PrRh
The very nicest place. Unknown.—PrRa
Visit. V. Coccimiglio.—JaS
Voices. A. Turner.—TuS
Watching the new year's eve party through the staircase. J. P. Lewis.—LiNe
We interrupt this broadcast. J. Hemschemeyer.—JaS
"When daddy carves the turkey." J. Prelutsky.—PrIt
When father carves the duck. E. V. Wright.—CoN
"When I was home last Christmas." R. Jarrell.—PlAs
Zimmer's street. P. Zimmer.—JaT
Home cooking cafe. Greg Field.—JaPo
The **home** place. Robert Currie.—JaPo
A **home** without a cat. Mark Twain.—ChC
"A **home** without a cat, and a well-fed." See A home without a cat
"**Home**, you are a special place." See Home, you're where it's warm inside
Home, you're where it's warm inside. Jack Prelutsky.—PrRh
Homesick blues. Langston Hughes.—HuDk

Homesickness
Halfway where I'm going. C. Zolotow.—ZoE
Homesick blues. L. Hughes.—HuDk
Juan Pedro Carrera. M. Glenn.—GlCd
The Lake Isle of Innisfree. W. B. Yeats.—LiSf
"My heart's in the Highlands, my heart is not here." R. Burns.—BlO
Homework ("Homework sits on top of Sunday, squashing Sunday flat"). Russell Hoban.—PrRh
Homework ("What is it about homework"). Jane Yolen.—PrRh
"**Homework**, oh homework." Jack Prelutsky.—PrNk
"**Homework** sits on top of Sunday, squashing Sunday flat." See Homework
"**Hominy**, succotash, raccoon, moose." See Where do these words come from
Honesty. See Truthfulness and falsehood
Honey. See also Bees
"**Honeybees** are very tricky." See Bees
Honig, Edwin
"What changes, my love."—JaPo
Hood, Thomas
Choosing their names.—DaC
Goodnight, little people.—FrP
"I remember, I remember."—DaC
The lay of the labourer.—PlSc
No ("No sun, no moon").—BlO
The song of the shirt.—PlSc
"A **hop**, a skip, and off you go." See Dancing
"**Hop** away." See Bedtime
"**Hop** skip jump." See The rabbit skip
Hope, Alec Derwent
Tiger ("The paper tigers roar at noon").—HeR
Hope
The darkling thrush. T. Hardy.—HeR
Dreams ("Hold fast to dreams"). L. Hughes.—HuDk—LiSf—PrRh
Fantasia ("I dream"). E. Merriam.—MeSk
The heart's location. P. Meinke.—JaG
Hope. L. Hughes.—HaOf—HoSu—LiIl
"I heard a bird sing." O. Herford.—CoN—LiSf—PrRh
"Let there be new flowering." L. Clifton.—JaPo
Mirage. C. G. Rossetti.—McL
"My Shalom, my peace, is hidden in every broad smile." M. Cohn.—LaT
A plagued journey. M. Angelou.—AnS
Sentimental conversation. P. Verlaine.—LiWa
Spring and all. G. Bauer.—JaPo
A story that could be true. W. Stafford.—CoN—JaG—KeK
To a sad daughter. M. Ondaatje.—JaG
Work without hope. S. T. Coleridge.—PlSc
Youth ("We have tomorrow"). L. Hughes.—HuDk
Hope. Langston Hughes.—HaOf—HoSu—LiIl
"The **hope** I dreamed of was a dream." See Mirage
Hopi Indians. See Indians of the Americas—Hopi
Hopkins, Gerard Manley
"As kingfishers catch fire, dragonflies draw flame."—HeR
Binsey poplars, felled 1879.—HeR
Cuckoo. See "Repeat that, repeat that"
Duns Scotus's Oxford.—PlEd
The habit of perfection.—HeR
Heaven-haven.—HeR
Inversnaid.—HeR
"Moonless darkness stands between."—HaO
Moonrise.—HeR
On St. Winefred.—PlSc

Hopkins, Gerard Manley—*Continued*
Pied beauty.—HeR—KoT
"Repeat that, repeat that."—HeR
   Cuckoo.—KoT
Spring ("Nothing is so beautiful as spring").—
   HeR
Spring and fall.—HeR
The starlight night.—LiWa
The windhover, to Christ our Lord.—HeR
The woodlark.—HeR
Hopkins, Lee Bennett
City blockades.—HoSs
The day after Christmas.—HoSi
Get 'em here.—HoMu
Girls can, too.—PrRh
"In the pitch of the night."—HoCr
Last laugh.—HoSu
"The merry-go-round horse."—HoSi
The museum door.—HoDi
My name.—LiSf
Night bear.—HoSu
On an August day.—HoSe
Puppy ("We bought our puppy").—HoDl
Questions ("If cookies come in boxes").—HoMu
Tricia's fish.—HoBf
"**Hopping** frog, hop here and be seen." Christina
   Georgina Rossetti.—BlO
Hoppity. Alan Alexander Milne.—CoN
Hops. Boris Pasternak.—KoT
Horae Canonicae, sels. Wystan Hugh Auden
   Sext.—PlSc
Hornets. See Wasps
"**Horribeloved**   Klaubautermann."   See
   Klabauterwife's letter
Horrible things. Roy Fuller.—CoOu
Horsburgh, Wilma
The train to Glasgow.—CoOu
The **horse**. Jose Maria Eguren, tr. by Cheli
   Durán.—LiSf—LiWa
A **horse** and a flea and three blind mice."
   Unknown.—CoN
Whoops.—PrRh
Horse chestnut. Myra Cohn Livingston.—LiMp
The **horse** from 200 B.C." See In the museum
A **horse** I am, whom bit." See The Trojan Horse
Horseback ride. Siddie Joe Johnson.—HoBf
The **horseman**. Walter De la Mare.—PrRh
Horses. See also Rides and riding—Horse
All the pretty little horses. Unknown.—KoT
   All the pretty horses.—ChB
At grass. P. Larkin.—HeR
"Beside the road." Basho.—KoT
Birth of the foal. F. Juhasz.—HeR
A blessing. J. Wright.—McL
El caballo. J. M. Eguren.—LiSf
The face of the horse. N. A. Zabolotsky.—HeR
Foal. M. B. Miller.—LiSf
Future hero. X. J. Kennedy.—KeF
The horse. J. M. Eguren.—LiSf—LiWa
The horses. E. Muir.—HeR
"The horses of the sea." C. G. Rossetti.—CoN
"I had a little hobby horse." Mother Goose.—
   LoR
"I had a little pony." Mother Goose.—BlO—
   DaC—DeM
In the museum. C. Zolotow.—ZoE
It starts toward me. Unknown, fr. the Navajo
   Indian.—BiSp
John Cook. Unknown.—BlO
The milk cart pony. E. Farjeon.—FaE
Minnie Morse. K. Starbird.—LiSf
Names of horses. D. Hall.—McL
New York City, 1935. G. Corso.—JaPi

On a horse carved in wood. D. Hall.—PlEd
On buying a horse. Unknown.—HeR
The runaway ("Once, when the snow of the
   year was beginning to fall"). R. Frost.—
   KoS—LiSf
"Shoe the little horse." Unknown.—RaT
Songs of the horse society. Unknown, fr. the
   Sioux Indian.—BiSp
A sporty young person. Unknown.—BrT
Steeds. P. Hiebert.—DoNw
To ride. P. Éluard.—KoT
The Trojan Horse. W. Drummond.—PlEd
War god's horse song. Unknown.—HeR—KoT
The white horse. D. H. Lawrence.—KeK—
   KoT—PrBb
White horses. E. Farjeon.—FaE
The white stallion. G. Owen.—KeK
The wild, the free. Lord Byron.—PrRh
The **horses**. Edwin Muir.—HeR
"The **horses** of the sea." Christina Georgina
   Rossetti.—CoN
"The **horses** of the sea, remember." See On a
   horse carved in wood
"The **horses** of the sun that played so long on
   hill and plain." See Autumn rain
"The **horses**, the pigs." See Familiar friends
"The **hose**." See Hose
Hose. Valerie Worth.—LiSf
Hoskins, Katherine
The Byfield rabbit.—PlSc
Hospital barge at Cerisy. Wilfred Owen.—HeR
Hospitals
For the sisters of the Hôtel Dieu. A. M.
   Klein.—DoNw
The new mothers. C. Shields.—JaS
"**Hot** cross buns, hot cross buns." Mother
   Goose.—DeM—FaW—LoR
"**Hot** dogs with sauerkraut." See Get 'em here
"**Hot**, languid." See Nocturne for late summer
Hot line. Louella Dunann.—PrRh
"**Hot** sun, cool fire, tempered with sweet air." See
   Bethsabe's song
"**Hot** wintry." See Candy cane
Hotels
"If ever you go to Dolgelly." T. Hughes.—TrM
In the motel. X. J. Kennedy.—JaS—PrRh
"Little Queen Pippin once built a hotel."
   Mother Goose.—BlPi
The **hound**. Kaye Starbird.—KeK
"A **hound** sound." See Flight
"**Hounds** charging from one wall to another." See
   Insomnia
"**Hours** late and afraid to go in." See Lantern
House. Eve Merriam.—MeHa
House blessing ("Bless the four corners of this
   house"). Arthur Guiterman.—LaT
House blessing ("May it be delightful, my house").
   Unknown.—LiSf
The **house** cat. Annette Wynne.—PrRa
"The **house** cat sits." See The house cat
House coming down. Eleanor Farjeon.—FaE
House fear. Robert Frost.—LiWa
House, for sale. Leonard Clark.—PrRh
"**House** full, yard full." Mother Goose.—CoN
House hunters. Eleanor Farjeon.—FaE
House-hunting. David Wagoner.—JaD
"The **house** I go to in my dream." George
   Barker.—CoOu
"The **house** inside still looks like a house." See
   Moving
"The **house** is inhabited by squirrels." See The
   abandoned house
"The **house** is so quiet now." See The vacuum

The **house** mouse. Jack Prelutsky.—PrRa—PrZ
House noises. X. J. Kennedy.—KeF
The **house** of hospitalities. Thomas Hardy.—HeR
A **house** of readers. Jim Wayne Miller.—JaPo
"The **house** of the mouse." Lucy Sprague Mitchell.—CoN
The **house** remembers. Robert Francis.—JaD
"**House** silent." See In the old house
House song to the east. Unknown.—KoT
"**House** to let." Mother Goose.—AlH
The **house-wreckers**. Charles Reznikoff.—HoSs—KeK
"The **house-wreckers** have left the door and a staircase." See The house-wreckers
Housekeepers and housekeeping
  The ballad of Befana. P. McGinley.—PlAs
  Broom. V. Worth.—WoSp
  Dainty Dottie Dee. J. Prelutsky.—PrNk
  For the little girl who asked why the kitchen was so bright. J. Ulmer.—JaT
  Held in suspense. X. J. Kennedy.—KeF
  "I married a wife by the light of the moon." Mother Goose.—LoR
  "My mother had a maid call'd Barbara." From Othello. W. Shakespeare.—HoUn—PlAs
  Portrait by a neighbor. E. S. Millay.—HaOf—LiSf
  "She sweeps with many-colored brooms." E. Dickinson.—PlSc
  "Who can find a virtuous woman, for her price is far above rubies." From Proverbs. Bible/Old Testament.—PlSc
  You owe them everything. J. Allman.—PlSc
Houses ("Houses are faces"). Aileen Fisher.—CoN
Houses ("Time and the weather wear away"). Donald Justice.—JaPo—PlEd
Houses and dwellings
  The abandoned house. P. Hubbell.—LiWa
  "After the palaces." From A nobleman's house. M. Sarton.—PlEd
  "After weeks of watching the roof leak." G. Snyder.—KeK
  Always room for one more. S. N. Leodhas.—LiSf
  Ann's house. D. Lourie.—JaD
  Architectural masks. T. Hardy.—PlEd
  August ("Deep in the wood I made a house"). K. Pyle.—HaOf
  The ballad of Rudolph Reed. G. Brooks.—HeR
  The beaver ("The beaver is fat"). J. Prelutsky.—PrZ
  Big house. M. C. Livingston.—LiWo
  The buildings. W. Berry.—PlEd
  The ceiling. T. Roethke.—KeK—PlEd
  Crayon house. M. Rukeyser.—PlEd
  The cricket kept the house. E. M. Thomas.—HaOf
  Den. S. Cassedy.—CaR
  A drumlin woodchuck. R. Frost.—KoS
  Edenhall. S. Coolidge.—HaOf
  The empty house. R. Hoban.—LiWa
  Fire ("This morning on the opposite shore of the river"). W. Carpenter.—JaPi
  Fletcher Avenue. M. C. Livingston.—LiWo
  The floor and the ceiling. W. J. Smith.—HaOf
  For the rebuilding of a house. W. Berry.—PlEd
  For you. K. Kuskin.—LiVp
  The funny house. M. Hillert.—HoBf
  Ghost house. R. Frost.—LiWa
  Ghosts ("Those houses haunt in which we leave"). E. Jennings.—JaPo

Gone ("Wind rattles the apples"). R. Pomeroy.—JaD
Grandparents' houses. M. Van Doren.—StG
The great house. E. Muir.—PlEd
Haunted house. V. Worth.—LiWa
Haunted room. S. Cassedy.—CaR
House. E. Merriam.—MeHa
House blessing ("Bless the four corners of this house"). A. Guiterman.—LaT
House blessing ("May it be delightful, my house"). Unknown, fr. the Navajo Indian.—LiSf
House coming down. E. Farjeon.—FaE
House fear. R. Frost.—LiWa
House, for sale. L. Clark.—PrRh
House-hunting. D. Wagoner.—JaD
House noises. X. J. Kennedy.—KeF
"The house of the mouse." L. S. Mitchell.—CoN
The house remembers. R. Francis.—JaD
House song to the east. Unknown, fr. the Navajo Indian.—KoT
"House to let." Mother Goose.—AlH
The house-wreckers. C. Reznikoff.—HoSs—KeK
Houses ("Houses are faces"). A. Fisher.—CoN
Houses ("Time and the weather wear away"). D. Justice.—JaPo—PlEd
Housing starts. P. Davison.—PlEd
I am home, said the turtle. J. Ciardi.—CiD
"I know some lonely houses off the road." E. Dickinson.—LiWa
"I wish that my room had a floor." G. Burgess.—HaOf
Ice. C. G. D. Roberts.—DoNw—PrRh
In the old house. J. Aiken.—LiWa
Incident ("Charley Coleman told me this"). K. Kopp.—JaG
Keep. S. Cassedy.—CaR
"The lands around my dwelling." Unknown.—LiIl
Late, passing prairie farm. W. Stafford.—JaG
Lavinia Nink. J. Prelutsky.—PrNk
The listeners. W. De la Mare.—LiWa
"Little King Boggen, he built a fine hall." Mother Goose.—BlPi—LoR
Looking both ways. J. O. Wayne.—JaG
Mending the adobe. H. Carruth.—JaPi—PlEd
Moving ("The house inside still looks like a house"). F. Steele.—JaG
My house is red. Mother Goose.—BlPi
The new house. V. Rutsala.—JaG
October nights in my cabin. N. M. Bodecker.—BoSs
The old woman ("You know the old woman"). B. Potter.—CoN—PrRa
"Oma was sixty three when I was born." From Afternoon in Waterloo Park. G. Dumas.—StG
On the house of a friend. J. Logan.—JaD
110 year old house. E. Ochester.—JaPi
Our house. D. B. Thompson.—PrRh
Out in the country, back home. J. D. Marion.—JaPo
Parlor. S. Cassedy.—CaR
Passing the Masonic home for the aged. H. Scott.—JaPo
Prayer for this house. L. Untermeyer.—LaT
"Put the pine tree in its pot by the doorway." N. Belting.—LiIl
The queer little house. Mother Goose.—BlPi
Recycled. L. Moore.—MoSn
Red flower. A. Turner.—TuS
Roof. S. Cassedy.—CaR
A secret place. J. W. Steinbergh.—LiIl

How to get there. Bonnie Nims.—PrRh
How to get through the memorial service. Richard J. Margolis.—LiPj
How to kill. Keith Douglas.—HeR
How to paint a perfect Christmas. Miroslav Holub, tr. by George Theiner and Ian Milner.—HaO
How to see deer. Philip Booth.—JaPi
How to solve a problem. Eve Merriam.—MeF
How to stay up late. X. J. Kennedy.—KeF
How to tell goblins from elves. Monica Shannon.—PrRh
How to treat elves. Morris Bishop.—HaOf
How to watch statues. X. J. Kennedy.—KeF
How to write a letter. Elizabeth Turner.—DaC
"How very quiet things can be." See Just three
How violets came blue. Robert Herrick.—KoT
"How will you your Christmas keep." See Keeping Christmas
Howard. Alan Alexander Milne.—BrT
Howes, Barbara
  Cardinal ("With deep snow").—JaD
  Cat on couch.—JaD
  The dressmaker's dummy as scarecrow.—JaD
  Portrait of the boy as artist.—JaD
  Returning to Store Bay.—JaPi
"However it came, this great house has gone down." See The great house
Howie Bystrom. Mel Glenn.—GlCd
Howitt, Mary
  The spider and the fly.—CoOu—DaC
Hsin Ch'i-chi
  Written at the Po-shan monastery.—LiIl
Hubbell, Patricia
  The abandoned house.—LiWa
  Bedtime ("Hop away").—HoSu
  Chant of the awakening bulldozers.—HoCl
  Concrete mixers.—PrRh
  Conjugation.—LiIl
  The fairies ("See the fairies dancing in").—LiWa
  First love ("I remember sadness").—LiSf
  Gravel paths.—HoSs
  Message from a mouse, ascending in a rocket.—LiSf—PrRh
  Old dog.—HoDl
  Our washing machine.—HoCl—LiSf—PrRh
  Prayer for reptiles.—LaT
  Sea fairies.—HoCr
  Shadows.—JaT
  When dinosaurs ruled the earth ("Brontosaurus, diplodocus, gentle trachodon").—HoDi—LiSf
"Huckleberry, gooseberry, raspberry pie." Clyde Watson.—PrRh
Huddle, David
  Croquet.—JaS
  The field.—JaS
  A history of the pets.—JaPo
  Icicle ("I smacked you in the mouth for no good reason").—JaS
  "In white tie."—JaS
  Kitchen tables.—JaS
  Mrs. Green.—JaPo
  My brother flies over low.—JaT
  Shooting crows.—JaG
  Stopping by home.—JaG
Huff, Barbara A.
  The library ("It looks like any building").—PrRh
"Huffer, a giant ungainly and gruff." See Huffer and Cuffer
Huffer and Cuffer. Jack Prelutsky.—PrSr
Hug o' war. Shel Silverstein.—CoN—PrRh

"The huge hippopotamus hasn't a hair." See The hippopotamus
"Huge, perfect creatures move across the screen." See Bijou
"Huge upon the hazy plain." See Grazing locomotives
Hughes, Langston
  African dance.—HuDk
  After many springs.—HuDk
  Alabama earth.—HuDk
  April rain song.—CoN—HaOf—HuDk—LiSf—PrRh
  As I grew older.—HuDk
  Aunt Sue's stories.—HuDk
  Autumn thought.—HuDk
  Baby.—HuDk
  Ballad of the man who's gone.—PlAs
  Beggar boy.—HuDk
  A black Pierrot.—HuDk
  Bound no'th blues.—HuDk
  Carol of the brown king.—LiCp
  City, complete ("In the morning the city").—FrP—PrRh
  City, sels.
    "In the morning the city".—HoSs
  Death of an old seaman.—HuDk
  The dream keeper.—HuDk
  Dream variation.—HuDk
  Dreams ("Hold fast to dreams").—HuDk—LiSf—PrRh
  Dressed up.—HuDk
  Ennui.—HaOf
  Fairies ("Out of the dust of dreams").—HuDk
  Feet o' Jesus.—HuDk
  Homesick blues.—HuDk
  Hope.—HaOf—HoSu—LiIl
  I, too.—HuDk
  "In the morning the city." See City
  Irish wake.—HuDk
  Joy.—HuDk
  Judgement day.—HuDk
  Juke box love song.—KoT
  Lincoln monument, Washington.—HuDk
  Litany.—LaT
  Long trip.—HuDk
  Lullaby ("My little dark baby").—HuDk
  Ma Lord.—HuDk
  Mexican market woman.—HuDk—PlSc
  Minstrel man.—HuDk
  "Misery is when your."—LiIl
  Miss Blues'es child.—KoT
  Mother to son.—CoN—HaOf—HuDk—LiSf
  My people.—HuDk
  The Negro.—HuDk
  Negro dancers.—HuDk
  The Negro speaks of rivers.—HaOf—HuDk—LiSf
  Night and morn.—HuDk
  Parisian beggar woman.—HuDk
  Passing love.—HuDk
  Po' boy blues.—HuDk
  Poem ("I loved my friend").—CoN—HoBf—HuDk—JaD—LiIl—LiSf
  Prayer ("I ask you this").—HuDk
  Prayer meeting.—HuDk
  Quiet girl.—HuDk
  Reasons why.—HuDk
  Sailor.—HuDk
  Sea calm.—HuDk
  "Sea charm."—HuDk
  Seascape.—HuDk
  Share-croppers.—PlSc
  Sinner.—HuDk

Human race.—*Continued*
The innocent. D. Levertov.—KeK
Is wisdom a lot of language. C. Sandburg.—HoRa
Kyrie Eleison. J. Aiken.—LiE
"The labouring poor, in spite of double pay." From The true-born Englishman. D. Defoe.—PlSc
Landscape. E. Merriam.—KeK—MeSk
A living. D. H. Lawrence.—PrBb
The man he killed. T. Hardy.—HeR
The man with the hoe. E. Markham.—PlSc
Man's image. D. H. Lawrence.—PrBb
Many mansions. D. H. Lawrence.—PrBb
The measure of man. E. Merriam.—MeSk
Meditatio. E. Pound.—LiSf
Mending wall. R. Frost.—KoS
Metamorphoses ("These people, with their illegible diplomas"). H. Nemerov.—PlEd
The mosquito knows. D. H. Lawrence.—HeR—PrBb
My people. L. Hughes.—HuDk
Neighbors ("They live alone"). D. A. Evans.—JaPi
No man on any moon. C. Lewis.—LiSf
"O heart, small urn." From The walls do not fall. H. D.—McL
On a tree fallen across the road. R. Frost.—HeR
On seeing the Elgin Marbles. J. Keats.—PlEd
The outwit song. D. Hoffman.—PlSc
Owl ("The diet of the owl is not"). X. J. Kennedy.—KeF
People ("I like people quite well"). D. H. Lawrence.—PrBb
People ("Some people talk and talk"). C. Zolotow.—PrRh—ZoE
Psalm 103. From The book of psalms. Bible/Old Testament.—LiSf
Rain forest, Papua, New Guinea. M. C. Livingston.—LiMp
Rape poem. M. Piercy.—JaPi
Remember. A. Adoff.—AdA
Routine. A. Guiterman.—PrRh—TrM
Sanford Evans Pierce. M. Glenn.—GlC
The secret sits. R. Frost.—KoS—LiSf
Self-pity. D. H. Lawrence.—HeR
Sext. From Horae Canonicae. W. H. Auden.—PlSc
Simple song. M. Piercy.—McL
Some people. R. Field.—CoN—PrRh
Some people I know. J. Prelutsky.—PrRh
Sometimes ("Sometimes, when a bird cries out"). H. Hesse.—LiWa
A song ("I am of the earth and the earth is of me"). A. Adoff.—AdA
Song ("Sweet beast, I have gone prowling"). W. D. W. Snodgrass.—McL
Song of the rabbits outside the tavern. E. Coatsworth.—HaOf
The song of the shirt. T. Hood.—PlSc
Soup. C. Sandburg.—HaOf—HoRa
Southbound on the freeway. M. Swenson.—CoN—LiSf
The stolen child. W. B. Yeats.—LiWa
Talk ("I wish people, when you sit near them"). D. H. Lawrence.—PrBb
Television. M. L'Engle.—LaT
Things I didn't know I loved. N. Hikmet.—McL
To a blind student who taught me to see. S. Hazo.—JaG

Two masks unearthed in Bulgaria. W. Meredith.—PlEd
Waiting both. T. Hardy.—KoT
Wanting. Unknown.—KeK
"The way I see any hope for later." A. Adoff.—AdA
The whale ghost. L. Moore.—MoSn
What there is. K. Patchen.—McL
"The **humanities** 5 section man." See Whom do you visualize as your reader
"**Humbert,** hiking Moonshine Hill." X. J. Kennedy.—KeB
Humdrum. Carl Sandburg.—HoRa
Humility
Lisa Goodman. M. Glenn.—GlC
A prayer to go to paradise with the donkeys. F. Jammes.—HeR—LiSf
Snake ("A snake came to my water-trough"). D. H. Lawrence.—HeR
The **hummer.** William Matthews.—JaT
Humming-bird ("I can imagine, in some otherworld"). David Herbert Lawrence.—HeR—PrBb
Humming birds. Betty Sage.—PrRa
Hummingbird ("Cried a scientist watching this creature dart by"). X. J. Kennedy.—KeF
The **hummingbird** ("The hummingbird, he has no song"). Michael Flanders.—PrRh
The **hummingbird** ("The ruby throated hummingbird"). Jack Prelutsky.—PrZ
"The **hummingbird,** he has no song." See The hummingbird
Hummingbirds
Humming-bird ("I can imagine, in some otherworld"). D. H. Lawrence.—HeR—PrBb
Humming birds. B. Sage.—PrRa
Hummingbird ("Cried a scientist watching this creature dart by"). X. J. Kennedy.—KeF
The hummingbird ("The hummingbird, he has no song"). M. Flanders.—PrRh
The hummingbird ("The ruby throated hummingbird"). J. Prelutsky.—PrZ
Humor
April fool. M. C. Livingston.—LiCe
The court jester's last report to the King. J. Prelutsky.—PrSr
Delayed action. C. Morgenstern.—HeR
The height of the ridiculous. O. W. Holmes.—HaOf
The joke. Unknown.—PrRh
Laughing backwards. J. Hall.—JaG
Sensitive Sydney. W. Irvin.—LiIl
The **humorous** ant. Oliver Herford.—BrT
"**Humps** are lumps." See Lumps
"**Humpty** Dumpty." Michael Rosen.—BeD
"**Humpty** Dumpty sat on a wall." Mother Goose.—DeM—FaW—LoR
Humpty Dumpty's poem. See Humpty Dumpty's recitation
Humpty Dumpty's recitation. From Through the looking glass. Lewis Carroll.—KoT
Humpty Dumpty's poem.—BlO
"A **hundred.**" See Water lily
A **Hungarian** nursery rhyme. Unknown, tr. by Matyas Sarkozi and C. Day Lewis.—FaW
Hungarian nursery rhymes. See Nursery rhymes—Hungarian
Hunger
Alligator pie. D. Lee.—FaW—JaT—PrRh
Chocolate cake. J. Prelutsky.—PrMp
Grab-bag. H. H. Jackson.—HaOf
"Here comes a tidbit." C. Watson.—WaC

"I am the family face." See Heredity
"I am the flotz, I gobble dots." See The flotz
"I am the king of Magla and Vlaga." See The king of Magla and Vlaga
"I am the magical mouse." See The magical mouse
"I am the medicine." Unknown.—BiSp
"I am the old one here." See Desert tortoise
"I am the only me I am." See Me I am
"I am the rose of Sharon, and the lily of the valleys." From The Song of Solomon. Bible/Old Testament.—McL
"I am the running girl." Arnold Adoff.—LiSf
"I am the sister of him." See Little
"I am the toy-maker, I have brought from the town." See The toy-maker
"I am the Turquoise Woman's son." See War god's horse song
"I am the wizard jaguar." See To keep animals out of the cornfield
"I am tired of this barn, said the colt." See The barn
"I am troubled by the blank fields, the speechless graves." See After looking into a book belonging to my great-grandfather, Eli Eliakim Plutzik
"I am trying to decide to go swimming." See The wind is blowing west
"I am very fond of bugs." See Bugs
"I and Pangur Ban, my cat." See Pangur Ban
I answer an SOS. X. J. Kennedy.—KeF
"I arise from dreams of thee." See Indian serenade
"I arise from rest with movements swift." See Introduction to life
"I ask you this." See Prayer
"I asked her, is Aladdin's lamp." See The sorceress
"I asked my mother for fifteen cents". See "I asked my mother for fifty cents."
"I asked my mother for fifty cents." Mother Goose.—PrRh
"I asked my mother for fifteen cents".—LiSf
"I asked the little boy who cannot see." Unknown.—CoOu
I ate too much. Jack Prelutsky.—PrIt
"I ate too much turkey." See I ate too much
"I awoke in the midsummer not-to-call night, in the white and." See Moonrise
"I beg my bones to be good but." See The poet
I bended unto me. Thomas Edward Brown.—CoN
"I bended unto me a bough of may." See I bended unto me
"I, Bertolt Brecht, came out of the black forests." See Of poor B. B.
"I bet I can hold my breath." See One-upmanship
"I bought a box of chocolate hearts." See Mother's chocolate valentine
"I bought a dozen new-laid eggs." Mother Goose.—LoR
"I burned my life, that I might find." See The alchemist
"I call everyone." See The fat man
"I called to the wind." Kyorai, tr. by Harry Behn.—LiSf—LiWa
"I came home and found a lion in my living room." See The lion for real
"I came to a forest so deep and wide." See Sometimes there is no easy answer
I can be a tiger. Mildred Leigh Anderson.—PrRa
I can do my hair. Arnold Adoff.—AdA
"I can do my hair short." See I can do my hair

"I can feel." See The new girl
I can fly. Felice Holman.—CoN—PrRh
"I can fly, of course." See I can fly
"I can get through a doorway without any key." See The wind
"I can imagine, in some otherworld." See Humming-bird
"I can read the pictures." See Worlds I know
"I can remember lying." See Sunday funnies
"I can run faster than any gazelle." See A heavy rap
"I can still see my father sitting in front of the TV." See Mitchell Chapin
"I can talk." See Trilingual
"I cannot explain the sadness." See The loreley
I cannot forget you. Unknown, tr. by Frances Densmore.—Lill—LiSf
"I cannot grow." Wystan Hugh Auden.—HeR
"I cannot see fairies." See Fairies
"I can't fall asleep." See Falling asleep
"I can't get enoughsky." See The Lizzie Pitofsky poem
"I can't go walking." See I can be a tiger
"I can't stand Willy wet-leg." See Willy wet-leg
"I can't talk about it." See Carla Spooner
"I can't tell my father." See Grace DeLorenzo
"I can't tell you exactly when love begins." See Brian Nichols
"I can't understand." See Weeds
I caught a fish. Betram Murray.—CoOu
"I caught a little fish one day." See I caught a fish
"I caught a tremendous fish." See The fish
"I caught this morning morning's minion, kingdom of daylight's." See The windhover, to Christ our Lord
"I chopped down the house that you had been saving to live in next summer." See Variations on a theme by William Carlos Williams
"I climbed a mountain three feet high." See It makes no difference to me
"I come from haunts of coot and hern." See The brook
"I come from the city of Boston." Unknown.—TrM
"I come more softly than a bird." Mary Austin.—LiSf
"I come to school an hour before everyone else." See Rickie Miller
"I come to work as well as play." See The March wind
"I could see bruises or shadows." See My grandfather dying
"I could take the Harlem night." See Juke box love song
"I counted them, and now I look through the door." See My father's ghost
"I cross the old bridge." See The rumbly night train
"I cut out a lot because school's a gigantic bore." See Faith Plotkin
"I dance the shape that dazzles in your head." See Box, for L.M.B.
"I did not see a mermaid." Siddie Joe Johnson.—LiSf
"I didn't give her a good-bye kiss." See Grandmother Grace
"I do not like a rainy day." See Rainy day
I do not like the rat. Jack Prelutsky.—PrNk
"I do not like the way you slide." See Egg thoughts, soft boiled

"I have been in bed for hours." Jack Prelutsky.—PrMp
"I have been one acquainted with the night." See Acquainted with the night
"I have desired to go." See Heaven-haven
"I have eaten." See This is just to say
"I have friends." Cheryl Thornton.—LiIl
"I have had playmates, I have had companions." See The old familiar faces
"I have heard, said a maid of Montclair." See Opportunity's knock
"I have hopped, when properly wound up, the whole length." See The tin frog
"I have lived and I have loved." Unknown.—KoT
"I have made the sun." See Song of creation
"I have my whole wedding planned out." See Leigh Hamilton
"I have no rattles." From Five ghost songs. Unknown.—KoT
"I have often been told, said the horse." See The thoroughbred horse
"I have searched my thesaurus through." See Be my non-Valentine
"I have seen." See The hammer
"I have seen mothers cradling dead babies in their arms." See Song Vu Chin
"I have seen schools in seven different states." See Veronica Castell
"I have taken up the dulcimer again." See Widow to her son
"I have ten little fingers." See Ten fingers
"I have the fore." See A song
"I have this neat truck." See Last word
"I have thought of beaches, fields." See Bundles
"I have to be nice." See Bert
"I have to jump up." See Wide awake
"I have to take my little brother." See Lil' bro'
"I have two dashing, prancing steeds." See Steeds
"I have wished a bird would fly away." See A minor bird
"I hear a sudden cry of pain." See The snare
I hear America singing. Walt Whitman.—LiSf—PlSc
"I hear America singing, the varied carols I hear." See I hear America singing
"I hear eating." See Night fun
"I hear it." See The train
"I heard a bird sing." Oliver Herford.—CoN—LiSf—PrRh
"I heard a cow low, a bonnie cow low." See The Queen of Elfan's nourice
"I heard a horseman." See The horseman
"I heard a mouse." See The mouse
"I heard of poor." See Poor
"I heard the bells on Christmas Day." Henry Wadsworth Longfellow.—CoN
Christmas bells.—HaO
"I heard the old, old men say." See The old men admiring themselves in the water
"I hid my love when young while I." See Song
I hid you. Miklós Radnóti, tr. by Steven Polgar and Stephen Berg and S. J. Marks.—McL
"I hid you for a long time." See I hid you
"I hit my wife and went out and saw." See The winter moon
"I hope the old Romans." See Ancient history
"I hunt." See Photographer
I, Icarus. Alden Nowlan.—DoNw
"I imagined the bombs and fighters." See Air raid
"I inherited forty acres from my Father." See Cooney Potter

"I is for ignorant Ida." See Ignorant Ida
"I joy." See Conjugation
"I keep bottle caps." See Keepsakes
"I keep seeing your car in the streets." See The little brother poem
"I knew a tiny sandpiper." See A certain sandpiper
"I knocked the green alarm clock." See A quick hush
"I know a bank where the wild thyme blows." From A midsummer night's dream. William Shakespeare.—HoUn
"I know a bloke." See Egg talk
"I know a busy fisherman." See Sky net
"I know a little cupboard." See The cupboard
I know a man. Peggy Steele.—JaPo
"I know a man who never." See I know a man
"I know a young fellow." See The half lullaby
"I know a young girl who can speak." See A warning
"I know I have lost my train." Mother Goose.—LoR
Joshua Lane.—DaC
I know I'm sweet, but. John Ciardi.—CiD
"I know it's not fashionable to admit I like reading." See Saul Steiner
"I know it's time." See Shopping
"I know no greater delight that the sheer delight of being alone." See Delight of being alone
"I know some lonely houses off the road." Emily Dickinson.—LiWa
"I know that a divorce is supposed to be." See Justin Faust
I know the rules. Arnold Adoff.—AdA
"I know the rules and I am what I am." See I know the rules
I know we can go back so far. Arnold Adoff.—AdA
"I know what I feel like." See Changing
"I know why, getting up in the cold dawn." See To a daughter with artistic talent
"I know you are not happy with me, Poppa." See Dora Antonopolis
"I leant upon a coppice gate." See The darkling thrush
"I left my head." Lilian Moore.—MoSn
"I left the castle of my mer-king father." See And although the little mermaid sacrificed everthing to win the love of the prince, the prince, alas, decided to wed another
"I lift the toilet seat." See Surprise
"I like." See Giraffe
"I like." See Night creature
"I like arroz y habichuelas." Charlotte Pomerantz.—PoI
"I like biscuit." See Boasting
"I like crawlers." See When it come to bugs
"I like fish, said the Mermaid." From Song. Elizabeth Coatsworth.—HoCr
"I like fish, toy tik ka." See Toy tik ka
"I like little pussy." Mother Goose.—LoR
Pussy.—DaC
"I love little pussy".—DeM
"I like my body when it is with your." Edward Estlin Cummings.—McL
"I like my fingers." See Mark's fingers
"I like people quite well." See People
"I like relativity and quantum theories." See Relativity
"I like the names." See Indian of the plains
"I like the town on rainy nights." See Rainy nights

"I put my hat upon my head." Samuel Johnson.—KeK

"I put on my aqua-lung and plunge." See The diver

"I put the seed into the ground." See Tommy

"I quarreled with my brother." See The quarrel

"I raised a great hullabaloo." Unknown.—PrRh

"I ran along the yellow sand." See Pete at the seashore

"I ran to the church." See Journey back to Christmas

"I rather like new clothes." See New clothes and old

"I read the papers all the time." See Jay Stone

"I really didn't notice that he had a funny nose." See And then the prince knelt down and tried to put the glass slipper on Cinderella's foot

"I really don't have time to breathe." See Heather Yarnell

"I remember, gracious, graceful moon." See To the moon

"I remember how, /long ago, I found." See Crystals like blood

"I remember, I remember." Thomas Hood.—DaC

"I remember or remember hearing." See Once upon a great holiday

"I remember sadness." See First love

I ride an old paint. Unknown.—LiSf

"I ride an old paint and I lead an old dan." See I ride an old paint

"I ride the horse that is the sea." See Song for a surf rider

"I rise on Sugar-loaf Mountain." See Molasses river

"I rode my pony one summer day." See The errand

"I said, why should a pyramid." See The innovator

"I sat down on my blanket." See Sand

"I saw a donkey." See The donkey

"I saw a famous man eating soup." See Soup

"I saw a gnome." See The gnome

"I saw a great scholar, apparently thinking." Maude Crint.—TrM

"I saw a jolly hunter." Charles Causley.—CoOu

"I saw a little girl I hate." Arnold Spilka.—PrRh
A little girl I hate.—BeD

"I saw a little snail." See Little snail

"I saw a little spider." See Spider

"I saw a peacock with a fiery tail." Unknown.—BlO—HeR

"I saw a proud, mysterious cat." See The mysterious cat

"I saw a robin." See All on a Christmas morning

"I saw a ship a-sailing". See "There was a ship a-sailing"

"I saw a ship a-sailing." Mother Goose.—DeM—LiSf—LoR—RuI

I saw a stable. Mary Elizabeth Coleridge.—HaO

"I saw a stable, low and bare." See I saw a stable

"I saw a star slide down the sky." See The falling star

"I saw Esau kissing Kate." See Esau and Kate

"I saw him brought into Emergency." See Empty holds a question

"I saw nine red horsemen ride over the plain." See Nine red horsemen

"I saw on the slant hill a putrid lamb." See For a lamb

"I saw on the snow." See Merry Christmas

"I saw the clock in Wells." See The wonderful clock

"I saw the devil walking down the lane." See The devil's bag

"I saw the moon." See Flying

"I saw the roofs of Elfin town." See Elfin town

"I saw the sidewalk catch the measles." See Sidewalk measles

"I saw this much from the window." See The gap in the cedar

"I saw thousands of pumpkins last night." See The pumpkin tide

I saw three ships. Unknown.—RoC

"I saw three ships come sailing by." Mother Goose.—LoR

"I saw three ships come sailing in." See I saw three ships

"I saw three ships go sailing by." See The north ship

"I saw you toss the kites on high." See The wind

I, says the poem. Eve Merriam.—MeSk

"I, says the poem arrogantly." See I, says the poem

"I scream you scream." See Ice cream chant

"I scuff." See Sulk

"I see a bear." See The grizzly bear

"I see the moon." Mother Goose.—ChB—CoN—DaC—DeM—FaW—LoR—PrRa

"I see their knavery, this is to make an ass of me, to fright me." From A midsummer night's dream. William Shakespeare.—HoUn

"I see white and black, Lord." Malcolm Boyd.—LaT

"I seem." See The actor

"I sent my mother copies of my poems in print." See Poems

"I sent you this bluebird of the name of Joe." See Happiness

"I set a little Christmas tree." See The Christmas tree

"I shall dance tonight." See Celebration

"I shall remember chuffs the train." See Lost

"I shoot the hippopotamus." See The hippopotamus

"I should like, said the vase from the china-store." See The toys talk of the world

"I should like to buy you a birthday present, said Billy." See Betsy Jane's sixth birthday

"I shouldn't tell you this, but." See First night of Hanukkah

I show the daffodils to the retarded kids. Constance Sharp.—JaD

"I simply can't tell you how glad I am." See Marmalade

"I simply do not know why I." See Apple pie

I sing for the animals. Unknown.—KoT

"I sing of a maiden." Unknown.—RoC

"I sing of brooks, of blossoms, birds, and bowers." See The argument of his book

"I sit beside old retired Italians." See Park

"I sit down on the floor of a school for the retarded." See He sits down on the floor of a school for the retarded

"I sit here in these stocks." See In Weatherbury stocks

"I sit on the edge." See The piano

"I slip and I slide." See Icy

"I smacked you in the mouth for no good reason." See Icicle

"I sometimes think I'd rather crow." See To be or not to be

I sought all over the world. John Tagliabue.—JaPi

I went hungry on Thanksgiving. Jack Prelutsky.—PrIt
"I went out to the hazel wood." See The song of wandering Aengus
"I went to a party." See The rose on my cake
"I went to look for Joy." See Joy
"I went to play with Billy, he." See What Johnny told me
"I went to the animal fair." See The animal fair
"I went to the garden of love." See The garden of love
"I went to the museum." See The museum
"I went to the park." See The balloon
"I went to the school." See Some things are funny like that
"I went to Wyoming one day in the spring." Jack Prelutsky.—PrRi
"I went up a high hill." Mother Goose.—DeM
"I went up one pair of stairs." Mother Goose.—DeM—LoR
"I whispered, I am too young." See Brown penny
"I will always love you." See Poem to Franz Kline
"I will arise and go now, and go to Innisfree." See The Lake Isle of Innisfree
"I will be a lion." See Wild beasts
"I will be the gladdest thing." See Afternoon on a hill
"I will gather the sunshine in my hands." See Down on my tummy
I will give my love an apple. See "I will give my love an apple without e'er a core"
"I will give my love an apple without e'er a core." Unknown.—HeR
I will give my love an apple.—BlO
"I will give you the key." Arnold Lobel.—LoWr
"I will go with my father a-ploughing." Joseph Campbell.—LiSf
"I will lose you, it is written." See The sweater
"I will not play at tug o' war." See Hug o' war
"I will sing the song of the sky." See Chief's song
"I will write you a letter." See I think
"I wish." Lilian Moore.—MoSn
"I wish I could meet the man that knows." John Ciardi.—PrRh
"I wish I lived in a caravan." See The pedlar's caravan
"I wish people, when you sit near them." See Talk
"I wish that I didn't have freckles on my face." See Bertha's wish
"I wish that my room had a floor." Gelett Burgess.—HaOf
"I wish to buy a dog, she said." See On buying a dog
I wonder. Charlotte Zolotow.—HoSu
"I wonder as into bed I creep." See Sweet dreams
"I wonder if ever." See The bride
"I wonder if the elephant." See Pete at the zoo
"I wonder this." See Mirror
"I wonder what it might be like." See Undine's garden
"I wonder why Dad is so thoroughly mad." Jack Prelutsky.—PrNk
"I would go round and round." See Lonely Monday
"I would like to dive." See The diver
"I would liken you." See Quiet girl
"I would rather be myself." See Written at the Po-shan monastery
I wouldn't. John Ciardi.—JaT
I wouldn't be afraid. Judith Viorst.—ViI

"I wouldn't be afraid to fight a demon or a dragon." See I wouldn't be afraid
"I wouldn't blame a beetle-bug." See Drippy day
"I write what I know on one side of the paper." See Paper II
"I wrote my name on the sidewalk." See My name
"I wrote some lines once on a time." See The height of the ridiculous
Ian Sinclair. Mel Glenn.—GlCd
Ice
  Birches. R. Frost.—HeR—KoS
  Fire and ice. R. Frost.—KoS
  Goodbye ("Seven cats and seven mice"). J. Ciardi.—CiD
  Ice. C. G. D. Roberts.—DoNw—PrRh
  The icebound swans. Unknown.—LaT
  Icy. R. W. Bacmeister.—PrRa
  Metamorphosis ("When water turns to ice does it remember"). C. Sandburg.—HoRa
  Nine mice. J. Prelutsky.—PrNk
  Weather report. L. Moore.—MoSn
Ice. Charles G. D. Roberts.—DoNw—PrRh
Ice cream
  Bleezer's ice cream. J. Prelutsky.—PrNk
  Doing a good deed. J. Ciardi.—CiD
  Herbert Glerbett. J. Prelutsky.—PrRh
  Ice cream. P. Wild.—JaPi
  Ice cream chant. Unknown.—CoN
  The ice cream ocean. J. M. Shaw.—RuI
  "Into Mother's slide trombone." X. J. Kennedy.—KeB
  The Kool-Kup. C. Rylant.—RyW
  Maid of Manila. Unknown.—BrT
  Mickey Jones. X. J. Kennedy.—KeF
  Popsicles. C. B. Francis.—HoMu
Ice cream. Peter Wild.—JaPi
Ice cream chant. Unknown.—CoN
The ice cream ocean. John Mackay Shaw.—RuI
The ice-king. A. B. Demille.—DoNw
Ice skating
  Ice skating. S. Liatsos.—HoSu
Ice skating. Sandra Liatsos.—HoSu
The icebound swans. Unknown, tr. by Seán O'Faoláin.—LaT
The ichthyosaurus. Unknown.—BrT
Icicle ("I smacked you in the mouth for no good reason"). David Huddle.—JaS
Icicle ("An icy stabbing so quickly done"). Eve Merriam.—MeHa
Icicles
  Icicle ("An icy stabbing so quickly done"). E. Merriam.—MeHa
  Icicles. B. J. Esbensen.—EsCs
  "Lives in winter." Mother Goose.—CoN—LiSf
Icicles. Barbara Juster Esbensen.—EsCs
"Ickle ockle, blue bockle." Mother Goose.—BlQ—DeM
Icy. Rhoda W. Bacmeister.—PrRa
"An icy stabbing so quickly done." See Icicle
"I'd like to be a lighthouse." Rachel Field.—HoSe—PrRa
"I'd like to bunch your lips." See Valentine thoughts for Mari
"I'd like to thank you, but I feel." See Trying to write thank-you letters
"I'd love to sit." See The shadow tree
"I'd much rather sit there in the sun." See Song
"I'd never dine on dinosaurs." Jack Prelutsky.—PrNk
I'd never eat a beet. Jack Prelutsky.—PrNk
"I'd never eat a beet, because." See I'd never eat a beet

"**I'd** not despoil the linnet's nest." See The bird's nest
"**I'd** rather be a peasant." See The light heart
"**I'd** want her eyes to fill with wonder." Kenneth Patchen.—McL
The **idea** of trust. Thom Gunn.—JaPi
"The **idea** of trust, or." See The idea of trust
Ideals. See also Ambition; Conduct of life; Dreams
   Adam Whitney. M. Glenn.—GlC
   "Beautification." N. M. Bodecker.—BoPc
   Dreams ("Hold fast to dreams"). L. Hughes.—HuDk—LiSf—PrRh
   Excelsior. H. W. Longfellow.—HaOf
   Jerusalem. From Milton. W. Blake.—HeR
   Teacher talk. A. Turner.—TuS
   Trustworthiness. N. M. Bodecker.—BoPc
Idiosyncratic. Eve Merriam.—MeSk
The **idiot.** Keith Wilson.—JaPi
Idleness. See Laziness
If ("If he could climb a tree"). Nikki Giovanni.—GiSp
If ("If I had a trunk like a big elephant"). John Kendrick Bangs.—HaOf
If ("If the pie crust"). N. M. Bodecker.—BoPc
"**If** a pig wore a wig." Christina Georgina Rossetti.—LiSf
"**If** all the seas were one sea." Mother Goose.—CoOu—FaW—LoR
"**If** all the whole world's taxicabs." See Valentine
"**If** all the world and love were young." See The nymph's reply to the shepherd
"**If** all the world was apple pie." Mother Goose.—LoR
"**If** all the world was paper." Mother Goose.—FaW
"**If** all the world were paper." Mother Goose.—BlO—CoN—KoT
"**If** babies could speak they'd tell mother or nurse." See Bringing up babies
"**If** bees stay at home." Mother Goose.—DeM
"**If** birthdays happened once a week." See Birthdays
"**If** Candlemas be fine and clear." See At Candlemas
"**If** chickens roll in the sand." Mother Goose.—LoR
"**If** cookies come in boxes." See Questions
"**If** ever there lived a Yankee lad." See Darius Green and his flying-machine
"**If** ever you go to Dolgelly." Thomas Hughes.—TrM
"**If** ever you go to the North Countree." See Edenhall
"**If** he could climb a tree." See If
"**If** I." See Wouldn't you
"**If** I could borrow a rocket ship." See The best part of going away is going away from you
"**If** I could only be a cloud." See For a cloud
"**If** I could see a little fish." See On the bridge
"**If** I could teach you how to fly." See The question
"**If** I could wish." See Wish
"**If** I eat one more piece of pie, I'll die." See Pie problem
"**If** I had a hundred dollars to spend." See The animal store
"**If** I had a million lives to live." See Humdrum
"**If** I had a paka." Charlotte Pomerantz.—PoI
"**If** I had a trunk like a big elephant." See If
"**If** I had a wish." See A wish

"**If** I have faltered more or less." See The celestial surgeon
"**If** I lost my little cat, I should be sad without it." Mother Goose.—ChC
"**If** I might be an ox." Unknown.—HeR
"**If** I run." See Lance Perkins
"**If** I serve one more piece of chicken." See Todd Michaels
"**If** I should ever by chance grow rich." Edward Thomas.—BlO
"**If** I were a bear." See Furry bear
If **I** were a fish. Alison Winn.—BeD
If **I** were a king. Alan Alexander Milne.—CoOu
"**If** I were a tree." See Open house
"**If** I were bigger than anyone." Ruth Harnden.—PrRa
"**If** I were in charge of the world." Judith Viorst.—ViI
"**If** I were swimming." See Forty mermaids
"**If** I were the Prime Minister of Britain." See I don't like you
"**If** I'd as much money as I could spend." Mother Goose.—FaW—LoR
"**If** it can't be out on the hill somewhere." See Grandma chooses her plot at the county cemetery
"**If** it was sunlight shining." Jack Prelutsky.—PrMp
"**If** it wasn't for me, Jimmy." See Nicole Harris
"**If** Nancy Hanks." See Nancy Hanks, 1784-1818
"**If** no one ever marries me." Laurence Alma-Tadema.—DaC—PrRh—TrM
"**If** once you have slept on an island." Rachel Field.—PrRh
"**If** only." See Swahili love song
"**If** only I may grow firmer, simpler." Dag Hammarskjöld.—LaT
"**If** people came to know where my king's palace is." See Fairyland
If **pigs** could fly. James Reeves.—CoOu
"**If** pigs could fly, I'd fly a pig." See If pigs could fly
"**If** restless, let little words." See How to get through the memorial service
"**If** sunlight fell like snowflakes." See Sunflakes
"**If** the blues would let me." See Miss Blues'es child
"**If** the flowers want to grow." See The city
"**If** the ocean was milk." Unknown.—LiIl
"**If** the ocean waves could ever be." See The ice cream ocean
"**If** the picture ever moved at all." See Grandpa's picture
"**If** the pie crust." See If
If **there** are any heavens. Edward Estlin Cummings.—JaD
"**If** there are any heavens my mother will (all by herself)." See If there are any heavens
"**If** there is going to be a nuclear winter." See Ian Sinclair
"**If** they hate me." Arnold Adoff.—AdA
"**If** this comes creased and creased again and soiled." See Pocket poem
If **turkeys** thought. Jack Prelutsky.—PrIt
"**If** turkeys thought, they'd run away." See If turkeys thought
If **we** didn't have birthdays. Dr. Seuss.—PrRh
"**If** we didn't have birthdays, you wouldn't be you." See If we didn't have birthdays
"**If** we shadows have offended." From A midsummer night's dream. William Shakespeare.—HoUn

"**In** winter I get up at night." See Bed in summer
"**In** winter, when the fields are white." See Humpty Dumpty's recitation
"**In** wintertime." See Greenhouse
"**In** Xanadu did Kubla Khan." See Kubla Khan
"**In** youth we dream of death." See Hardy perennial
Inanna's song. Unknown, tr. by Diane Wolkstein and Samuel Noab Kramer.—McL
Inca Indians. See Indians of the Americas—Inca
Incantation to Oedipus. John Dryden.—LiWa
"**Incey-wincey** spider climbed the water spout." Mother Goose.—LoR
Incident ("Charley Coleman told me this"). Karl Kopp.—JaG
Incident ("Once riding in old Baltimore"). Countee Cullen.—CoN—HaOf—KeK
Incidents in the life of my uncle Arly. Edward Lear.—LiH
"**Indeed.**" See A prayer of the midwinter hunt
Independence
Gail Larkin. M. Glenn.—GlC
Windy day. N. M. Bodecker.—BoPc
Independence day. See Fourth of July
India. W. J. Turner.—BlO
India rubber. Eleanor Farjeon.—FaE
Indian names. Lydia Huntley Sigourney.—HaOf
Indian of the plains. Myra Cohn Livingston.—LiWo
Indian serenade. Percy Bysshe Shelley.—KoT
Indian summer. See Autumn
Indian summer ("Along the line of smoky hills"). Wilfred Campbell.—DoNw
Indian summer ("Raise the curtain"). Barbara Juster Esbensen.—EsCs
Indian summer ("These are the days when early"). Harry Behn.—HoCb
Indians of the Americas
About Indians. J. Ciardi.—CiD
At the first Thanksgiving. X. J. Kennedy.—LiTp
Atop. P. Redcloud.—HoBf
"From his pouch he took his colors." From The song of Hiawatha. H. W. Longfellow.—PlEd
Indian names. L. H. Sigourney.—HaOf
Indian of the plains. M. C. Livingston.—LiWo
"O great spirit." Unknown, fr. the American Indian.—LaT
The rousing canoe song. H. Fraser.—DoNw
Ute Mountain. C. Tomlinson.—HeR
Where do these words come from. C. Pomerantz.—PoI
"The white man drew a small circle in the sand." C. Sandburg.—HoRa
Indians of the Americas—Acoma
"Nicely while it is raining." Unknown, fr. the Acoma Indian.—LiSf
Indians of the Americas—Anambe
Woman's prayer. Unknown, fr. the Anambe Indian.—BiSp
Indians of the Americas—Apache
A prayer of the girls' puberty ceremony. Unknown, fr. the Jicarilla Apache.—BiSp
A song of the girls' puberty ceremony ("When the earth was made"). Unknown, fr. the White Mountain Apache.—BiSp
A song of the girls' puberty ceremony ("You will be running to the four corners of the universe"). Unknown, fr. the Mescalero Apache.—BiSp

Indians of the Americas—Arapaho
Prayer before eating. Unknown, fr. the Arapaho Indian.—BiSp
Prayer of an old man at a young man's change of name. Unknown, fr. the Arapaho Indian.—BiSp
Indians of the Americas—Arekuna
Magic spell for a difficult birth. Unknown, fr. the Arejuna Indian.—BiSp
Magic spell for an approaching storm. Unknown, fr. the Arekuna Indian.—BiSp
Magic spell to turn a woman's heart. Unknown, fr. the Arekuna Indian.—BiSp
Indians of the Americas—Arikara
Prayer ("They have cleared away the place where the corn is to be"). Unknown, fr. the Arikara Indian.—BiSp
Indians of the Americas—Aztec
Confession of sin. Unknown, fr. the Aztec Indian.—BiSp
Cradlesong for Ahuitzotl. Unknown, fr. the Aztec Indian.—BiSp
For chest pain. Unknown, fr. the Aztec Indian.—BiSp
Friendship ("Like a quetzal plume, a fragrant flower"). Unknown.—LiIl
Magic spell for finding a woman. Unknown, fr. the Aztec Indian.—BiSp
Prayer of the midwife to the Goddess of Water. Unknown, fr. the Aztec Indian.—BiSp
Prayer to the deceased ("My child, you have toiled through life and come to the end"). Unknown, fr. the Aztec Indian.—BiSp
Prayer to the sun, for quick travel. Unknown, fr. the Aztec Indian.—BiSp
The song of a dream. Unknown.—LiIl
To keep animals out of the cornfield. Unknown, fr. the Seneca Indian.—BiSp
A widow's lament. Unknown, fr. the Aztec Indian.—BiSp
Indians of the Americas—Blackfeet
Girl's prayer to thunder during a storm. Unknown, fr. the Blackfeet Indian.—BiSp
Medicine man's prayer. Unknown, fr. the Blackfeet Indian.—BiSp
Indians of the Americas—Cagaba
Song ("Our mother of the growing fields, our mother of the streams"). Unknown, fr. the Cagaba Indian.—BiSp
Indians of the Americas—Cherokee
For putting a woman's family to sleep. Unknown, fr. the Cherokee Indian.—BiSp
For young men growing up to help themselves. Unknown, fr. the Cherokee Indian.—BiSp
This is to frighten a storm. Unknown, fr. the Cherokee Indian.—BiSp
To fix the affections. Unknown, fr. the Cherokee Indian.—BiSp
To make the road seem short. Unknown, fr. the Cherokee Indian.—BiSp
Indians of the Americas—Chippewa
The approach of the storm. Unknown, fr. the Chippewa Indian.—KoT
Initiation songs. Unknown, fr. the Chippewa Indian.—BiSp
Man's song ("It is my form and person that makes me great"). Unknown, fr. the Chippewa Indian.—BiSp
"Once in the winter." From The forsaken. D. C. Scott.—DoNw
Woman's song. Unknown, fr. the Chippewa Indian.—BiSp

Indians of the Americas—Creek
Lullaby ("Baby, sleep, sleep, sleep"). Unknown, fr. the Creek Indian.—BiSp
Indians of the Americas—Crow
Crazy dog prayer. Unknown, fr. the Crow Indian.—BiSp
Young man's prayer to the spirits. Unknown, fr. the Crow Indian.—BiSp
Indians of the Americas—Eskimo
"Do not weep, little one." Unknown, fr. the Eskimo.—LiSf
The dream ("Last night I dreamed of you"). Unknown, fr. the Ammassalik Eskimo.—BiSp
Eskimo chant. Unknown.—DoNw
"Far, far will I go." Unknown, fr. the Eskimo.—LiSf
For subduing a walrus. Unknown, fr. the Ammassalik Eskimo.—BiSp
"The great sea." Unknown.—LiSf
"I am afraid." Unknown, fr. the Eskimo.—LiWa
Introduction to life. Unknown, fr. the Iglulik Eskimo.—BiSp
"The lands around my dwelling." Unknown.—LiIl
Magic words to the gull. Unknown, fr. the Netsilik Eskimo.—BiSp
Manerathiak's song. Unknown.—DoNw
The mother's song ("It is so still in the house"). Unknown.—HaO
The song of Kuk-ook, the bad boy. Unknown, fr. the Eskimo.—KoT
Song to the child. Unknown, fr. the West Greenland Eskimo.—BiSp
"That woman down there beneath the sea." Unknown, from the Eskimo.—LiWa
"There is fear in." Unknown.—LiSf
To quiet a raging storm. Unknown, fr. the Copper Eskimo.—BiSp
Weather incantation. Unknown, fr. the Iglulik Eskimo.—BiSp
Words to a sick child. Unknown, fr. the Iglulik Eskimo.—BiSp
Words to call up game. Unknown, fr. the Iglulik Eskimo.—BiSp
Indians of the Americas—Flathead
Life song. Unknown, fr. the Flathead Indian.—BiSp
Indians of the Americas—Haida
Song for smooth waters. Unknown, fr. the Haida Indian.—BiSp
Indians of the Americas—Havasupai
Prayer to the sun. Unknown, fr. the Havasupai Indian.—BiSp
Indians of the Americas—Hopi
The owl ("The owl hooted and told of"). Unknown, fr. the Hopi Indian.—KoT
"Puva, puva, puva." Unknown, fr. the Hopi Indian.—KoT
Woman's prayer to the sun, for a newborn girl. Unknown, fr. the Hopi Indian.—BiSp
Indians of the Americas—Inca
Song ("In an accessible place"). Unknown, fr. the Inca Indian.—BiSp
Indians of the Americas—Kiowa
Crazy dog song. Unknown, fr. the Kiowa Indian.—BiSp
Lullaby ("Baby swimming down the river"). Unknown, fr. the Kiowa Indian.—BiSp
Indians of the Americas—Kwakiutl
Boatman's prayer for smooth waters. Unknown, fr. the Kwakiutl Indian.—BiSp

Man's song ("Like pain of fire runs down my body my love to you"). Unknown, fr. the Kwakiutl Indian.—BiSp
Prayer of a man to twin children. Unknown, fr. the Kwakiutl Indian.—BiSp
Prayer of the black bear. Unknown, fr. the Kwakiutl Indian.—BiSp
Prayer to the migratory birds. Unknown, fr. the Kwakiutl Indian.—BiSp
Song for calling rain. Unknown, fr. the Kwakiutl Indian.—BiSp
Song of parents who want to wake up their son. Unknown, fr. the Kwakiutl Indian.—KoT
Song to a son. Unknown, fr. the Kwakiutl Indian.—BiSp
Indians of the Americas—Makah
I cannot forget you. Unknown.—LiIl—LiSf
Indians of the Americas—Maya
Harvester's prayer, with an offering of copal. Unknown, fr. the Kekchi Maya.—BiSp
Prayer before felling to clear a cornfield. Unknown, fr. the Kekchi Maya.—BiSp
To cure epilepsy. Unknown, fr. the Tzotzil Maya.—BiSp
Traveler's prayer, with an offering of copal. Unknown, fr. the Kekchi Maya.—BiSp
Indians of the Americas—Mazatec
"I am the medicine." Unknown, fr. the Mazatec Indian.—BiSp
Indians of the Americas—Mbya
Cradlesong ("Sleep, little one, your father is bringing"). Unknown, fr. the Mbya Indian.—BiSp
Morning prayer to the creator. Unknown, fr. the Mbya Indian.—BiSp
Indians of the Americas—Modoc
Dream songs. Unknown, fr. the Modoc Indian.—BiSp
Prayer before the first meal in a new summer camp. Unknown, fr. the Modoc Indian.—BiSp
Indians of the Americas—Navajo
From a prayer of the shooting chant. Unknown, fr. the Navajo Indian.—BiSp
Ground-squirrel song. Unknown, fr. the Navajo Indian.—KoT
House song to the east. Unknown, fr. the Navajo Indian.—KoT
"In beauty may I walk." Unknown.—HeR
It starts toward me. Unknown, fr. the Navajo Indian.—BiSp
Mother's prayer for a girl. Unknown, fr. the Navajo Indian.—BiSp
"My great corn plants." Unknown, fr. the Navajo Indian.—LiSf
Prayer to a dead buck. Unknown, fr. the Navajo Indian.—BiSp
"The sacred blue corn-seed I am planting." From Songs in the garden of the house god. Unknown.—LiTp
A song of the coyoteway. Unknown, fr. the Navajo Indian.—BiSp
Song of the flood. Unknown, fr. the Navajo Indian.—KoT
There are no people song. Unknown, fr. the Navajo Indian.—KoT
Thunder song. Unknown, fr. the Navajo Indian.—BiSp
War god's horse song. Unknown.—HeR—KoT
Indians of the Americas—Nootka
Prayer to the whale. Unknown, fr. the Nootka Indian.—BiSp

"Inevitable, of course, very old now, she." See Elegy for Delina
Infant sorrow. William Blake.—HeR
Infants. See Babies
Infinity. See also Eternity; Space and space travel
A backwards journey. P. K. Page.—DoNw
Key. E. Merriam.—MeHa
Inge, Charles Cuthbert
A certain young gourmet.—BrT
Ingratitude. See Thankfulness
Inheritance. See Heritage
Initiation songs. Unknown.—BiSp
Injustice
Blacklisted. C. Sandburg.—PlSc
Blowin' in the wind. B. Dylan.—KeK
Brother, can you spare a dime. E. Y. Harburg.—PlAs—PlSc
The golf links. S. N. Cleghorn.—KeK
London. W. Blake.—HeR
The rain it raineth. C. Bowen.—CoN
Song, to the men of England. P. B. Shelley.—PlSc
The innkeeper's wife. Clive Sansom.—HaO
Innocence
Brief innocence. M. Angelou.—AnS
The holy innocents. R. Lowell.—HaO
Innocence. P. Kavanagh.—HeR
The innocent. D. Levertov.—KeK
Innocence. Patrick Kavanagh.—HeR
The innocent. Denise Levertov.—KeK
Innocent's song. Charles Causley.—HaO
The innovator. Stephen Vincent Benét.—PlEd
Inns and taverns
The boar and the dromedar. H. Beissel.—DoNw
Tarantella. H. Belloc.—HeR
Innuendo. David McCord.—McAs
The inquest. William Henry Davies.—HeR
The inquisitive leopard. Oliver Herford.—BrT
Insanity
The fist. D. Walcott.—McL
The mad gardener's song ("He thought he saw an elephant"). From Sylvie and Bruno. L. Carroll.—HeR
Mad gardener's song ("He thought he saw a buffalo").—CoOu
Mad Tom's song. R. Graves.—HeR
An old looney. Unknown.—BrT
"There is a willow grows aslant a brook." From Hamlet. W. Shakespeare.—HeR
"There is a willow grows aslant the brook".—HoUn
"There was a man and he was mad." Unknown.—HeR
Inscriptions. See Epitaphs
"Inscriptions in my yearbook." See Stuart Rieger
Insects. See also names of insects, as Ants
About feet. M. Hillert.—PrRh
Bookish. A. Fisher.—FiW
The bug ("And when the rain had gone away"). M. Barrows.—PrRh
"A bug sat in a silver flower." K. Kuskin.—PrRh
Bugs. K. Kuskin.—HoSu
But I wonder. A. Fisher.—PrRa
The butterfly's ball. W. Roscoe.—CoOu—PrRh
Clock-a-clay. J. Clare.—BlO
Cockroaches. K. Starbird.—PrRh
Crawler. E. Merriam.—MeHa
Hey, bug. L. Moore.—PrRh
"How and when and where and why." P. Gotlieb.—DoNw
"Hurt no living thing." C. G. Rossetti.—FaTh—HoSu—PrRh

Interlude. K. Shapiro.—JaD
Like a bug. A. Fisher.—FiW
"Little black bug." M. W. Brown.—CoN—FrP
The minimal. T. Roethke.—FaTh—HeR
My window screen. X. J. Kennedy.—KeF
The underworld. M. Lavington.—PrRa
Weevil. N. M. Bodecker.—BoSs
When all the world's asleep. A. E. Posey.—PrRa
When it come to bugs. A. Fisher.—FiW
Why run. N. Smaridge.—PrRh
Inside. Eleanor Farjeon.—FaE
"Inside my fuzzy mittens." See Mittens
"The inside of a whirlpool." See Warning
"Inside the wolf's fang, the mountain of heather." See Amulet
Insomnia
Falling asleep. I. Serraillier.—FaW
"I'm awake, I'm awake." J. Prelutsky.—PrMp
Insomnia ("Hounds charging from one wall to another"). J. C. Oates.—JaD
Insomnia ("The moon in the bureau mirror"). E. Bishop.—McL
Insomnia ("Where is that plain door"). M. Piercy.—JaD
Insomnia the gem of the ocean. J. Updike.—JaD
Insomniac. M. Angelou.—AnS
Rain ("I was having trouble sleeping"). J. Prelutsky.—PrMp
Sleepless nights. Zolotow. Charlotte.—ZoE—ZoE
Insomnia ("Hounds charging from one wall to another"). Joyce Carol Oates.—JaD
Insomnia ("The moon in the bureau mirror"). Elizabeth Bishop.—McL
Insomnia ("Where is that plain door"). Marge Piercy.—JaD
Insomnia the gem of the ocean. John Updike.—JaD
Insomniac. Maya Angelou.—AnS
Inspiration
Impeccable conception. M. Angelou.—AnS
The lion for real. A. Ginsberg.—HeR
Saint Francis and the sow. G. Kinnell.—HeR
A true account of talking to the sun at Fire Island ("The sun woke me this morning loud"). F. O'Hara.—HeR—KoT
Insults
Be my non-Valentine. E. Merriam.—MeSk
Blubber lips. J. Daniels.—JaT
"Don't worry if your job is small." Unknown.—PrRh
Double barreled ding dong bat. D. Lee.—PrRh
"Fatty, Fatty, boom a latty." Unknown.—PrRh
Floccinaucinihilipilification. E. Merriam.—MeSk
Having words. E. Merriam.—MeSk
"I never forget a face." G. Marx.—TrM
A penny valentine. Unknown.—LiVp
Similes for two political characters of 1819. P. B. Shelley.—HeR
A valentine for my best friend. J. Prelutsky.—PrIv
Intelligence
Brain. C. Barks.—JaPo
Pocket calculator. B. Katz.—HoCl
The thoroughbred horse. O. Herford.—BrT
Interlude. Karl Shapiro.—JaD
"An interplanetary torpedo." See The muskellunge
Interruption to a journey. Norman MacCaig.—HeR
Interview ("What would you like to be"). Eve Merriam.—MeSk

erview ("Yes, this is where she lived before she won"). Sara Henderson Hay.—HaOf
to a forest." Otsuju, tr. by Harry Behn
to a world where children shriek like suns." See On a child who lived one minute
o fish. Sheryl L. Nelms.—JaG
o Laddery Street. From Forgotten girlhood. Laura Riding.—HeR
ito Mother's slide trombone." X. J. Kennedy.—KeB
ito the bit flaked sugar snow." See Maple feast
ito the endless dark." See City lights
ito the room." See Nearly
ito the sunshine." See The fountain
roduction to life. Unknown.—BiSp
roduction to Songs of innocence. See "Piping down the valleys wild"
e intruders. James Reeves.—CoOu
e invention of the telephone. Peter Klappert.—JaPo
ventions. See Inventors and inventions
eutors and inventions
Darius Green and his flying-machine. J. T. Trowbridge.—HaOf
The deacon's masterpiece. O. W. Holmes.—HaOf
An historic moment. W. J. Harris.—KeK
The invention of the telephone. P. Klappert.—JaPo
"It was John Walker." Unknown.—TrM
Kermit Keene. J. Prelutsky.—PrSr
"Michael built a bicycle." J. Prelutsky.—PrNk
My uncle Dan. T. Hughes.—LiSf
Philbert Phlurk. J. Prelutsky.—PrSr
versnaid. Gerard Manley Hopkins.—HeR
victus. William Ernest Henley.—HeR
nvisible and out of sight." See Late night flight
vitation to a fish. Unknown.—BrT
vitation to a mouse. Eleanor Farjeon.—FaE
vitations
"Bat, bat, come under my hat." Mother Goose.—LoR
"Boys and girls, come out to play." Mother Goose.—DeM—LiSf—LoR
    "Girls and boys, come out to play".—AlH—ChB—DaC
Come in. R. Frost.—KoS
Forest: an invitation. M. C. Livingston.—LiMp
Invitation to a fish. Unknown.—BrT
Invitation to a mouse. E. Farjeon.—FaE
The pasture. R. Frost.—KoS—KoT—LiSf
To a squirrel at Kyle-na-no. W. B. Yeats.—BlO—LiSf—PrRh
Who calls. F. C. Sayers.—LiSf
vocation of the U'wannami, Part III, sels. Unknown
"Cover my earth mother four times with many flowers".—LaT
wa
From Council Bluffs to Omaha. M. C. Livingston.—LiWo
Iowa land. M. Bell.—PlSc
Madrid, Iowa. R. Ikan.—JaPo
wa land. Marvin Bell.—PlSc
car, Dahlov
Fishes' evening song.—PrRh
eland
Brennan on the moor. Unknown.—PlAs
Saint Patrick's day. M. C. Livingston.—LiCe
The sons of liberty. Unknown.—PlAs
The wearin' o' the green. Unknown.—PlAs
eson, Barbara
Don't go, Jo.—BaS

Irish wake. Langston Hughes.—HuDk
Irish yew. Myra Cohn Livingston.—LiMp
"The iron wolf, the iron wolf." See Wolf
An irritating creature. Jack Prelutsky.—PrNk
Irvin, Wallace
Sensitive Sydney.—LiIl
"Is a caterpillar ticklish." See Only my opinion
"Is Easter just a day of hats." From Easter morning. David McCord.—LiE
"Is he friend or is he foe." See Friend or foe
"Is is far to go." C. Day Lewis.—PlAs
"Is it coffee for breakfast." See Breakfast
"Is it, I wonder, a rum thing." See The boy
Is it nice to be wise. N. M. Bodecker.—BoPc
"Is it robin o'clock." Eve Merriam.—MeBl
"Is my craving so outlandish." See The perfect turkey sandwich
"Is that Mr. Riley, can anyone tell." Pat Rooney.—TrM
"Is that you, Willy, well, hello." See Ding-a-ling
"Is the ability to be." See Youth
"Is there anybody there, said the traveler." See The listeners
"Is there nothing to be said about the cockroach which is kind." See Cockroach
"Is this the sum of her, or was she human." See Daguerreotype of a grandmother
"Is what we all say." See A cliche
Is wisdom a lot of language. Carl Sandburg.—HoRa
Isabel. Unknown, tr. by George T. Lanigan.—DoNw
"Isabel met an enormous bear." See Adventures of Isabel
Isabel Navarro. Mel Glenn.—GlCd
"Isabel of the lily-white hand." See Isabel
Ise, Lady
Sleeping with someone who came in secret.—McL
Islam
Lepanto. G. K. Chesterton.—HeR
"The island of Yorrick." N. M. Bodecker.—LiWa
Islands
"If once you have slept on an island." R. Field.—PrRh
"The island of Yorrick." N. M. Bodecker.—LiWa
The Lake Isle of Innisfree. W. B. Yeats.—LiSf
The most beautiful. G. Gozzano.—KoT
A sea-chantey. D. Walcott.—HeR
"Islands and peninsulas, continents and capes." See Geography
"Isn't it foolish to dash off outside." See Footnote
"Isn't it strange." See French
"Isn't it strange some people make." See Some people
Israel
Both my grandmothers. E. Field.—JaS
Holy days. V. Worth.—LiPj
Song for Dov Shamir. D. Abse.—LaT
Issa
"Once upon a time."—LiWa
"One person."—KoT
"Seeking in my hut."—FaTh
"Well, hello down there."—FaTh—LiIl—LiSf
"Wild goose, wild goose."—KoT
"The wren."—CoN
"It appeared inside our classroom." See The creature in the classroom
"It began." See The man who owned cars
"It blew." Mother Goose.—LoR
"It cannot be seen, cannot be felt." John Ronald Reuel Tolkien.—LiSf

"It digs the air with green blades." See Tulip
"It doesn't breathe." See My nose
"It doesn't do to push too hard." See Sometimes it pays to back up
"It fell about the Martinmas time." See Get up and bar the door
"It fell in the city." Eve Merriam.—BaS—MeBl—PrRa
"It glistens on this wall." See Fresh paint
"It hard to love." See Short love poem
"It has a head like a cat, feet like a cat." Unknown.—CoN
"It has been estimated that." See The measure of man
"It has snowed." See Love letter
"It is a God-damned lie to say that these." See Another epitaph on an army of mercenaries
"It is a steadfast soldier." See Heart
"IT is a useful word." See Basic for irresponsibility
"It is a wonder foam is so beautiful." See Spray
"It is Christmas day in the workhouse." See In the workhouse
"It is grey out." Karla Kuskin.—LiSf
"It is late last night the dog was speaking of you." See Donal Og
"It is my form and person that makes me great." See Man's song
"It is nice to read." Onitsura, tr. by Harry Behn.—LiSf
"It is not growing like a tree." Ben Jonson.—HeR
"It is quite unfair to be." See Elephant
"It is raining, its cold." See A Hungarian nursery rhyme
"It is so peaceful on the ceiling." See Sleeping on the ceiling
It is so still. Jack Prelutsky.—PrMp
"It is so still in the house." See The mother's song
"It is so still, so still tonight." See It is so still
"It is summer, city summer." See Chicago, summer past
"It is the last of the ninth, two down, bases loaded, seventh." See The lady pitcher
"It is very dark." See Winter night
"It is what he does not know." See On a squirrel crossing the road in autumn, in New England
"It isn't proper, I guess you know." See Read this with gestures
"It lacks." See Office
"It lies." See Walking past the school at night
"It looks like any building." See The library
It makes no difference to me. John Ciardi.—CiD
"It never occurred to me, never." See The meeting
"It ought to come in April." See Wearing of the green
"It rained in my sleep." See September
"It rains and it pours." Arnold Lobel.—LoWr
It really wasn't too bad. John Ciardi.—CiD
"It seemed that out of battle I escaped." See Strange meeting
"It seems a day." See Nutting
"It seems to me that school sails along like a ship." See Raymond Crystal
"It sifts from leaden sieves." See The snow
"It snew all night, by the next noon." See Frizzing
"It started in kindergarten when the teacher." See Susan Tulchin
"It starts." See Broom
It starts toward me. Unknown.—BiSp

"It sushes." See Cynthia in the snow
"It swings upon the leafless tree." See The snow-filled nest
"It takes talent to fail gym three times." See Joel Feit
"It turned out." See After his death
"It was a cold and wintry night." Unknown.—TrM
"It was a' for our rightfu' king." Robert Burns.—PlAs
"It was a gallant highwayman." See The gallant highwayman
"It was a little captive cat." See The singing cat
"It was a long time ago." See As I grew older
"It was a lover and his lass." From As you like it. William Shakespeare.—HeR—HoUn—KoT
"It was a rainbow impossibly." See Prisms (altea)
"It was a refractory gnu." See The refractory gnu
"It was about the deep of night." See A ballad of Christmas
It was all very tidy. Robert Graves.—HeR
"It was almost easy to say goodby." See The soldiers returning
"It was dark but when I blinked." See Sleep
"It was easy." See How I escaped from the labyrinth
"It was in the night that I awoke, I, the woman, looking for." See A widow's lament
"It was John Walker." Unknown.—TrM
"It was late in the night when the Squire came home." See The gypsy laddies
"It was many and many a year ago." See Annabel Lee
"It was my thirtieth year to heaven." See Poem in October
"It was on a Wesnesday night, the moon was shining bright." See Jesse James
"It was six men of Indostan." See The blind men and the elephant
"It was the arrival of the kings." See The adoration of the Magi
"It was the schooner Hesperus." See The wreck of the Hesperus
"It was too lonely for her there." See The impulse
"It was your smell that, for a day after, I carried with me." See The anniversary
"It went many years." See The lockless door
"It will not hurt me when I am old." See Moonlight
Italy
  Giotto's tower. H. W. Longfellow.—PlEd
  In galleries. R. Jarrell.—PlEd
  The old bridge at Florence. H. W. Longfellow.—PlEd
  Venice. H. W. Longfellow.—PlEd
"It's." See Nan
"It's a kitchen, its curtains fill." See A room in the past
"It's a singular thing that Ned." See Ned
"It's a sun day." See Sun day
"It's a very odd thing." See Miss T.
"It's about." See Analysis of baseball
"It's all very well, said Peter to Mike." See Peter
"It's always." See The dark
"It's an old box camera." See Camera
"It's been a good day." See Playing
"It's been so long since I headed for East Mountain." See Thinking of East Mountain
"It's Christmas Day, I did not get." See Otto
"It's cold, cold, cold." See Before the bath
"Its echoes." See Haunted house

"It's eleven o'clock." Nancy Chambers.—PrRa
Its fangs were red. Jack Prelutsky.—PrNk
"Its fangs were red with bloody gore." See Its fangs were red
"Its former green is blue and thin." See The garden seat
"It's full of the moon." See Full of the moon
"It's fun turning somersaults." See Somersaults
"It's funny." See My puppy
"It's funny how beetles." See Upside down
"It's funny to look at a hurrying hound." See The hound
It's Halloween. Jack Prelutsky.—CoN
"It's Halloween, it's Halloween." See It's Halloween
"It's happy Thanksgiving." Jack Prelutsky.—PrIt
"It's hard to catch quiet." See Catching quiet
"It's hard to explain how I feel." See Gary Irving
"It's hard to say I'm sorry." See Apology
"It's just an old alley cat." See The stray cat
"It's midnight, not a moon is out." See The midnightmouse
"Its name linking." See Starfish
"It's never too early." See Advertisement for a divertissement
"It's no go the merrygoround, it's no go the rickshaw." See Bagpipe music
"It's nothing when I look again." See At sunrise
"It's of a famous highwayman a story I will tell." See Brennan on the moor
"Its quick soft silver bell beating, beating." See Auto wreck
It's raining. Guillaume Apollinaire.—KoT
"It's raining in the city." See Umbrellas
"It's raining, it's pouring." Mother Goose.—DaC—DeM—LoR
"It's raining, it's raining." Mother Goose.—LoR
"It's raining women's voices as if they were dead even in the memory." See It's raining
"It's snowing, it's snowing." Jack Prelutsky.—PrIs
"It's so good to talk with somebody." See He runs into an old acquaintance
"It's so still." See Spruce woods
"It's still inside me." See My mother's death
"It's such a." See Ennui
"It's such a little thing to weep." Emily Dickinson.—HeR
"It's such a shock, I almost screech." See Two sad
"It's the first storm of the winter." See Subway psalm
"It's the middle of November." See The middle of November
"It's the might it's the fight." See A football game
"It's too easy to." See Jessica Berg
"It's Valentine's day." Jack Prelutsky.—PrIv
"It's Valentine's day, so I'll create." See My special cake
"It's very hard to be polite." See Under the table manners
"I've a field with nothing in it." See This year, next year
"I've been out walking." See First January walk
"I've been planning to tell you." See Hesitating ode
"I've been scolded. Madeleine L'Engle.—LaT
"I've been workin' on the railroad." Unknown.—PlSc
"I've colored a picture with crayons." See Crayons
"I've come back." See Past love
"I've discovered a way to stay friends forever." See Friendship

I've got a dog. Unknown.—PrRh
"I've got a dog as thin as a rail." See I've got a dog
"I've got a mule, her name is Sal." See The Erie Canal
"I've got a rocket." See A rocket in my pocket
"I've got an incredible headache." Jack Prelutsky.—PrNk
I've got an itch. Jack Prelutsky.—PrNk
"I've got an itch, a wretched itch." See I've got an itch
"I've got the children to tend." See Woman work
"I've got the wiggly wiggles today." See Wiggly giggles
"I've heard him, my first blackbird." See The first blackbird
"I've just come up." Joso.—KoT
"I've just had an astounding dream as I lay in the straw." See Minstrel's song
"I've known rivers." See The Negro speaks of rivers
"I've looked behind the shed." See Gone
"I've no tooth to sing you the song." See Pat Cloherty's version of the Maisie
"I've often heard my mother say." See The unknown color
"I've scratched the measles, itched the pox." Unknown.—TrM
"I've seen." See The tree on the corner
"I've sung you, ninna nanna." See Grandpa's lullaby
"I've watched you now a full half hour." See To a butterfly
Ivy
    Arson. L. Moore.—MoSn
Izumi, Lady
    Love ("From Prince Atsumichi").—McL

J

J. Prior, Esq. N. M. Bodecker.—LiSf
Jabbering in school. Eleanor Farjeon.—FaE
Jabberwocky. From Through the looking glass. Lewis Carroll.—CoN—HeR—KoT—LiSf—PrRh
Jacaranda. Myra Cohn Livingston.—FaTh—LiMp
Jack. Charles Henry Ross.—DaC—PrRh
"Jack and Jill went up the hill." Mother Goose.—DeM—FaW—LiSf—LoR
"Jack be nimble." Mother Goose.—DeM—LoR
Jack Frost ("Rustily creak the crickets, Jack Frost came down"). Celia Thaxter.—HaOf
Jack Frost ("Someone painted pictures"). Helen Bayley Davis.—PrRa
"Jack-o'-lantern." Eve Merriam.—MeHa
Jack-o'-lanterns. See Pumpkins
"Jack Sprat could eat no fat." Mother Goose.—AlH—DeM—FaW—LoR
Jack was every inch a sailor. Unknown.—DoNw
"Jackknife swandive gainer twist." See Elegy for a diver
Jacks. Valerie Worth.—WoSp
Jackson, David
    Grandmother Jackson.—HaO
Jackson, Helen Hunt
    Grab-bag.—HaOf
    September ("The golden-rod is yellow").—HaOf
Jackson, Leroy F.
    Bella by the sea.—PrRh
    Fun.—PrRa

Jackson, Leroy F.—*Continued*
    Grandpa dropped his glasses.—PrRh
    How a puppy grows.—PrRa
Jackson, Stonewall (about)
    Barbara Frietchie. J. G. Whittier.—HaOf
"The **Jackson** Five beamed." See George
Jacobs, Frank
    The bat ("Bats are creepy, bats are scary").—
    PrRh
Jacobs, Leland B.
    Keepsakes.—HoSu
    Queenie.—PrRh
    Subway train.—HoCl—HoSu
    Taste of purple.—PrRh
    That May morning.—ChG—PrRh
Jaffray, Norman R.
    Beatnik limernik.—BrT
    Sliding scale.—BrT
"**Jagged** light, blue and bright." Clyde Watson.—
    WaC
Jake O'Leary's Thanksgiving. Kaye Starbird.—
    LiTp
James, Jesse (about)
    Jesse James. Unknown.—PlAs
"**James** James." See Disobedience
James Petrie. Mel Glenn.—GlCd
James Shell's snowball stand. Nikki Giovanni.—
    GiSp
Jamie Douglas. Unknown.—PlAs
Jammes, Francis
    A prayer to go to paradise with the donkeys.—
    HeR—LiSf
Jammy. Elizabeth Ripley.—BrT
Jams and jellies
    "While the fruit boils, Mom sends Lars." X.
    J. Kennedy.—KeB
Jane Seagrim's party. Leonard Nathan.—JaG
"**Jane** won't touch a caterpillar." See Why run
Janeczko, Paul B.
    Teresa's red Adidas.—JaT
    This poem is for Nadine.—JaG
Janet waking. John Crowe Ransom.—HeR
Janosco, Beatrice
    The garden hose.—CoN
Janowitz, Phyllis
    Fat Lena's recipe for crocodile soup.—JaT
January
    First January walk. E. Di Pasquale.—LiNe
    January ("In January"). From Chicken soup
    with rice. M. Sendak.—HoSi—PrRa
    January ("The days are short"). J. Updike.—
    PrRh
    January ("The snow has melted now"). D.
    Gibson.—HaO
    January ("Under a white coverlet of snow"). J.
    Heath-Stubbs.—HaO
    January thaw. E. Merriam.—MeF
January ("The days are short"). John Updike.—
    PrRh
January ("In January"). From Chicken soup with
    rice. Maurice Sendak.—HoSi—PrRa
January ("The snow has melted now"). Douglas
    Gibson.—HaO
January ("Under a white coverlet of snow"). John
    Heath-Stubbs.—HaO
"**January** brings the snow". See A calendar
"**January,** by this fire I warm my hands." See
    Labours of the months
"**January** first isn't new year's." See Happy new
    year, anyway
January one. David McCord.—LiNe
January thaw. Eve Merriam.—MeF

Japanese language
    A hikoka in a hikoki. C. Pomerantz.—PoI
Jaques, Florence Page
    Dragonfly ("A dragonfly").—PrRa
    There once was a puffin.—CoN—FrP
Jarrell, Randall
    Bats ("A bat is born").—CoN—HaOf
    The bird of night.—KeK—LiSf
    The chipmunk's day.—HaOf—PrRh
    The death of the ball turret gunner.—HeR
    In galleries.—PlEd
    The mockingbird ("Look one way and the sun
    is going down").—LiSf
    Moving ("Some of the sky is grey and some
    of it is white").—JaD
    "My aunt kept turnips in a flock."—LiSf
    The owl's bedtime story.—LiIl
    A sick child.—LiSf
    A war ("There set out, slowly, for a different
    world").—JaD
    "When I was home last Christmas."—PlAs
Jason Talmadge. Mel Glenn.—GlC
Jaszi, Jean
    Home.—PrRa
    Lullaby ("The moon and the stars and the wind
    in the sky").—LaW
Jauss, David
    For my son, born during an ice storm.—JaS
    On certain mornings everything is sensual.—JaG
    Sounding.—JaS
Jay Stone. Mel Glenn.—GlCd
Jays
    "The judicious jubilant jay." From An animal
    alphabet. E. Lear.—LiH
"**Jealous** girls these sometimes were." See How
    marigolds came yellow
Jealousy. See also Envy
    And some more wicked thoughts. J. Viorst.—
    ViI
    Binnorie. Unknown.—PlAs
    Frankie and Johnny. Unknown.—HeR
    How marigolds came yellow. R. Herrick.—KoT
    Maria Preosi. M. Glenn.—GlC
    More wicked thoughts. J. Viorst.—ViI
    Rosemarie Stewart. M. Glenn.—GlC
    The Sunday news. D. Gioia.—JaG
    Zebra and leopard. N. M. Bodecker.—BoSs
"**Jean** said, no." See Secret
Jeanette Jaffe. Mel Glenn.—GlC
Jeffers, Robinson
    Hurt hawks.—HeR
"**Jellicle** cats come out tonight." See The song
    of the Jellicles
"**Jelly** Belly bit." See The dreadful doings of Jelly
    Belly
"**Jelly** Jill loves Weasel Will." Jack Prelutsky.—
    PrIv
Jellyfish
    The jellyfish. O. Nash.—RuI
    "Jellyfish stew." J. Prelutsky.—PrNk
The **jellyfish.** Ogden Nash.—RuI
"**Jellyfish** stew." Jack Prelutsky.—PrNk
Jemima. See "There was a little girl, and she had
    a little curl"
Jemima (". . . and she wore a little curl"). See
    "There was a little girl, and she had a little
    curl"
Jenks, Tudor
    An accommodating lion.—HaOf
    Hard to bear.—HaOf

Jenner, Edward (about)
What Jenner said on hearing in Elysium that complaints had been made of his having a statue in Trafalgar Square. S. Brooks.—PlEd
Jennie Tang. Mel Glenn.—GlCd
"Jennifer Jill has the brainiest of all the brains." See More wicked thoughts
Jennings, Elizabeth
Afterthought.—HaO
Ago.—JaG
Father to son.—JaG
Ghosts ("Those houses haunt in which we leave").—JaPo
Rembrandt's late self portraits.—PlEd
Song for a departure.—JaG
Thinking of love.—JaG
Winter love.—JaPo
Jenny. Eleanor Farjeon.—FaE
Jenny kiss'd me. Leigh Hunt.—CoN
"Jenny kiss'd me when we met." See Jenny kiss'd me
"Jenny White and Johnny Black." Eleanor Farjeon.—FaE
"Jeremiah, blow the fire." Mother Goose.—BlQ
Jerome, Saint (about)
"If I lost my little cat, I should be sad without it." Mother Goose.—ChC
"Jerome was a dizzy giraffe." See The dizzy giraffe
"Jerry Hall." Mother Goose.—DeM—LoR
"Jerry has freckles." See Freckles
Jerusalem
Tishab Be-Av. M. Hahn.—LiPj
Yom Ha-Azma'ut. M. Hahn.—LiPj
Jerusalem. From Milton. William Blake.—HeR
Jesse James. Unknown.—PlAs
Jessica Berg. Mel Glenn.—GlCd
Jessica Jane. May Justus.—PrRh
"Jessica Jane is the kind of cook." See Jessica Jane
"The jester walked in the garden." See The cap and bells
Jesus Christ (about). See also Christianity; Christmas; Easter
The adoration of the Magi. C. Pilling.—HaO
"And there were in the same country shepherds." From Gospel according to Luke. Bible/New Testament.—LiCp
"Away in a manger." Unknown.—RoC
Ballad of the bread man. C. Causley.—HeR
The burning babe. R. Southwell.—HaO—HeR
Carol ("Mary laid her child among"). N. Nicholson.—HaO
A carol for Christmas eve. E. Farjeon.—FaE
The cherry-tree carol. Unknown.—LiE
"Joseph was an old man" .—HaO
Child's carol. E. Farjeon.—FaE
Christmas ("The bells of waiting advent ring"). Sir J. Betjeman.—HaO
A Christmas carol ("The Christ-child lay on Mary's lap"). G. K. Chesterton.—HaO
A Christmas carol ("The Christ-child lay on Mary's heart").—RoC
Christmas day ("Last night in the open shippen"). A. Young.—HaO—RoC
A Christmas hymn. R. Wilbur.—HaO
The crib. R. Finch.—HaO
The ending of the year. E. Farjeon.—FaE
Feet o' Jesus. L. Hughes.—HuDk
The first Christmas eve. H. Behn.—HoCb
For all. E. Farjeon.—FaE
The friendly beasts. Unknown.—LiIl
The holy innocents. R. Lowell.—HaO

I saw a stable. M. E. Coleridge.—HaO
"I sing of a maiden." Unknown.—RoC
"In the bleak midwinter." C. G. Rossetti.—RoC
A Christmas carol.—DaC
The innkeeper's wife. C. Sansom.—HaO
Journey back to Christmas. G. Denn.—HaO
Journey of the Magi. T. S. Eliot.—HaO
A manger song. E. Farjeon.—FaE
Mary's burden. E. Farjeon.—FaE
Mary's song. C. Causley.—HaO
The mystic Magi. R. S. Hawker.—HaO
Now every child. E. Farjeon.—FaE
"O little town of Bethlehem." P. Brooks.—RoC (unat.)
O simplicitas. M. L'Engle.—HaO
The passionate man's pilgrimage. Sir W. Raleigh.—HeR
Los pastores. E. Agnew.—LiCp
The pilgrim ("Father, I have launched my bark"). E. C. Embury.—HaOf
Psalm of a black mother. T. Greenwood.—LaT
The rocking carol. Unknown.—RoC
"Shall I to the byre go down." E. Farjeon.—FaE
"The shepherd and the king." E. Farjeon.—FaE
The shepherd's tale. R. Ponchon.—HaO
Silent night. J. Mohr.—RoC (unat.)
Wake up. Unknown.—FaE
"What can I give him." C. G. Rossetti.—LiCp
My gift.—LaT
"Jesus, our brother, kind and good." See The friendly beasts
"A jet screams and climbs." See Jetstream
Jetstream. Lilian Moore.—MoSn
Jewelry
The broken wedding ring. Unknown.—PlAs
Jewels. See Precious stones
Jewett, Sarah Orne
A country boy in winter.—HaOf
Jewish holidays
At Hannukah. M. C. Livingston.—LiSf
Dreidel song. E. Rosenzweig.—PrRa
Dreidl. J. P. Lewis.—LiPj
First night of Hanukkah. R. Boston.—LiPj
The fourteenth day of Adar. B. J. Esbensen.—LiPj
Havdalah. C. Adler.—LiPj
Holy days. V. Worth.—LiPj
How to get through the memorial service. R. J. Margolis.—LiPj
Light another candle. M. Chaikin.—CoN
Light the festive candles for Hanukkah. A. Fisher.—PrRh
"Pharaoh's horses were closing in behind us." From Passover 1970. R. Whitman.—LiPj
Rosh Hashanah eve. H. Philip.—LiPj
Shavuot, for Jessica. K. Hellerstein.—LiPj
Simhat Torah. R. H. Marks.—LiPj
Sukkot. R. H. Marks.—LiPj
Supermarket Shabbat. R. J. Margolis.—LiPj
Tishab Be-Av. M. Hahn.—LiPj
Tu Bi-Shevat. M. C. Livingston.—LiPj
Yom Ha-Azma'ut. M. Hahn.—LiPj
Jigsaw puddle. Emily Hearn.—BeD
Jigsaw puzzle. Russell Hoban.—CoN
"Jill came from the fair." Eleanor Farjeon.—FaE
"Jill is so straight, I can't stand it." See Brenda Stewart
Jill Le Claire. Mel Glenn.—GlC
"Jilliky Jolliky Jelliky Jee." Jack Prelutsky.—PrRi
Jim at the corner. Eleanor Farjeon.—FaE
Jim Desterland. Hyam Plutzik.—HeR
"Jim was a sailor." See Jim at the corner

Jim, who ran away from his nurse, and was eaten by a lion. Hilaire Belloc.—LiSf
Jiménez, Juan Ramón
 Galente garden II.—LiWa
 My voice.—LiSf
 Winter song.—LiWa
Jimmy Jet and his TV set. Shel Silverstein.—HaOf—LiSf—PrRh
"**Jimmy** Jones was skin and bones." See The dangers of taking baths
Jimmy's dad. Cynthia Rylant.—RyW
"**Jimmy's** dad worked for." See Jimmy's dad
Jittery Jim. William Jay Smith.—PrRh
Joan's door. Eleanor Farjeon.—FaE
Job, sels. Bible/Old Testament
 "Surely there is a mine for silver".—PlSc
"**Job** Davies, eighty-five." See Lore
Jodi Kurtz. Mel Glenn.—GlC
Joe. David McCord.—BaS
Joel Feit. Mel Glenn.—GlC
Joe's snow clothes. Karla Kuskin.—BaS
John. N. M. Bodecker.—PrRh
John Barleycorn. Robert Burns.—HeR—PlAs
John Brown's body, sels. Stephen Vincent Benét
 Melora's song.—PlAs
John Cook. Unknown.—BlO
"**John** Cook he had a little grey mare." See John Cook
"**John** could take his clothes off." See John
John Donne's statue. John Peale Bishop.—PlEd
John Grumlie. Unknown.—PlSc
"**John** Grumlie swore by the light o' the moon." See John Grumlie
John Henry ("When John Henry was a little tiny baby"). Unknown.—KeK
 John Henry ("John Henry was a lil baby").—PlAs
 John Henry ("When John Henry was a little babe").—LiSf
John Henry ("John Henry was a lil baby"). See John Henry ("When John Henry was a little tiny baby")
John Henry ("When John Henry was a little babe"). See John Henry ("When John Henry was a little tiny baby")
John Kinsella's lament for Mrs. Mary Moore. William Butler Yeats.—HeR
John Mouldy. Walter De la Mare.—HeR
John Quincy Adams. Stephen Vincent Benét and Rosemary Carr Benét.—HaOf
John Rogers' exhortation to his children. John Rogers.—HaOf
John, Tom, and James. Charles Henry Ross.—PrRh
"**John** was a bad boy, and beat a poor cat." See John, Tom, and James
"**John** while swimming in the ocean." X. J. Kennedy.—KeB
"**Johnnie** Crack and Flossie Snail." From Under Milk Wood. Dylan Thomas.—LiSf—PrRh
Johnny. Marci Ridlon.—PrRa
"**Johnny** Crow." See Johnny Crow's garden
Johnny Crow's garden. L. Leslie Brooke.—FaW
"**Johnny** had a black horse." Jack Prelutsky.—PrRi
"**Johnny,** Johnny, let go of that crab." See At the beach
"**Johnny** was acting." See Bad day
Johnny's the lad I love. Unknown.—PlAs
"**John's** manners at the table." See The visitor
Johnson, Don
 For Wilma.—JaG

Johnson, Hannah Lyons
 "That cheerful snowman."—BaS
Johnson, James Weldon
 "And God stepped out on space." See The creation
 The creation, complete.—LiSf
 The creation, sels.
  "And God stepped out on space".—LaT
Johnson, Pauline
 The train dogs.—DoNw
Johnson, Pyke
 The toucan.—CoN
Johnson, Samuel
 "I put my hat upon my head."—KeK
Johnson, Siddie Joe
 Horseback ride.—HoBf
 "I did not see a mermaid."—LiSf
"**Johnson** Prior." See J. Prior, Esq
Johnston, George
 Eating fish.—DoNw
 Flight ("All day long the clouds go by").—DoNw
 Frost ("Frost on my window").—DoNw
 The huntress.—DoNw
 O earth, turn!—DoNw
"**Joined** the band." See Band practice
The joke. Unknown.—PrRh
"**The joke** you just told isn't funny one bit." See The joke
"**Jolly** March wind." Eleanor Farjeon.—FaE
The jolly miller. Unknown.—DaC
"**A jolly** old sow once lived in a sty." See The three little pigs
"**A jolly** young artist called Bruno." See Bruno
A jolly young chemist. Unknown.—BrT
"**A jolly** young chemistry tough." See A jolly young chemist
Jonas, Gerald
 In passing.—JaT
Jonathan Bing. Beatrice Curtis Brown.—PrRh
Jones, D. G. (Douglas Gordon)
 After midnight.—DoNw
Jonson, Ben
 "Doing, a filthy pleasure is, and short", tr. by.—McL
 "It is not growing like a tree."—HeR
 The masque of queens, sels.
  "What our dame bids us do".—LiWa
 On my first sonne.—HeR
 "Slow, slow, fresh fount, keepe time with my salt teares."—HeR
 "What our dame bids us do." See The masque of queens
 Witches' charm.—BlO—HeR
 The witches' sabbath.—LiWa
Jordan, David Starr
 Food for a cat.—BrT
Jose Cruz. Mel Glenn.—GlCd
Joseph, Jenny
 Warning ("When I am an old woman I shall wear purple").—JaG
Joseph, Rosemary
 Baking day.—JaS
Joseph, Saint (about)
 Ballad of the bread man. C. Causley.—HeR
 The cherry-tree carol. Unknown.—LiE
  "Joseph was an old man" .—HaO
 Pilgrims in Mexico. Unknown.—HaO
 Take heart, sweet Mary. Unknown.—FaE
  In the town.—HaO
"**Joseph** fell a'dreaming." Eleanor Farjeon.—FaE
"**Joseph** was an old man" . See The cherry-tree carol

Josephine. Alexander Resnikoff.—PrRh
"Josephine, Josephine." See Josephine
Joshua Lane. See "I know I have lost my train"
Joso
"I've just come up."—KoT
"That duck, bobbing up."—LiSf—LiWa
Journal, sels. Edna St. Vincent Millay
"In the evening I would sit".—PlSc
The journey. David Ignatow.—JaPi
Journey back to Christmas. Gwen Denn.—HaO
Journey of the Magi. Thomas Stearns Eliot.—HaO
Journey's end. N. M. Bodecker.—BoPc
"The jowls of his belly crawl and swell like the
sea." See The glutton
Joy. See also Happiness
Joy. Langston Hughes.—HuDk
Joy McNair. Mel Glenn.—GlC
Joy of an immigrant, a thanksgiving. Emanuel Di
Pasquale.—LiTp
Joyce, James
A flower given to my daughter.—HeR
On the beach at Fontana.—HeR
Tilly.—HeR
Joyful. Rose Burgunder.—PrRa—PrRh
József, Attila
The seventh.—HeR
"J's the jumping jay walker." Phyllis McGinley.—
PrRh
Juan Pedro Carrera. Mel Glenn.—GlCd
Jubilate Agno, sels. Christopher Smart
My cat Jeoffrey.—BlO—HeR
"For I will consider my cat Jeoffry".—KoT
Judaism. See also Jewish holidays
At Hannukah. M. C. Livingston.—LiSf
Judas (about)
A ballad of Christmas. W. De la Mare.—HaO
Judgement day. Langston Hughes.—HuDk
"The judicious jubilant jay." From An animal
alphabet. Edward Lear.—LiH
Jugglers
Broom balancing. K. Fraser.—PrRh
Clara Cleech. J. Prelutsky.—PrNk
Hazardous occupations. C. Sandburg.—PlSc
The performing seal. R. Field.—PrRh
"Jugglers keep six bottles in the air." See
Hazardous occupations
Juhasz, Ferenc
Birth of the foal.—HeR
Juke box love song. Langston Hughes.—KoT
Julian barely misses Zimmer's brains. Paul
Zimmer.—JaG
Julie Snow. Mel Glenn.—GlC
"Julius Caesar made a law." Mother Goose.—
FaW
July
Back yard, July night. W. Cole.—KeK
A July goodbye. Richard J. Margolis.—MaS
July the first. Robert Currie.—JaPi
"A jumbled sight." See Paperclips
The jumblies. Edward Lear.—BlO—LiH
Jump or jiggle. Evelyn Beyer.—FrP—PrRa
Jump-rope rhyme. Unknown.—CoN
Jump-rope rhymes
Brooklyn bridge. W. J. Smith.—KeK
"Down in yonder meadow where the green
grass grows." Unknown.—DaC
"House to let." Mother Goose.—AlH
Jump-rope rhyme. Unknown.—CoN
Red-dress girl. A. Turner.—TuS
Rope rhyme. E. Greenfield.—LiSf
Skip rope rhyme for our time. E. Merriam.—
MeF

"Teddy bear, teddy bear." Unknown.—CoN—
PrRa
"The jump shot, it's all in the wrist." See Nothing
but net
Jumping. See also Jump-rope rhymes
"The acrobats are jumping around."
Unknown.—DeD
In the motel. X. J. Kennedy.—JaS—PrRh
"Jack be nimble." Mother Goose.—DeM—LoR
Jump or jiggle. E. Beyer.—FrP—PrRa
The rabbit skip. M. W. Brown.—FrP
Tumbling. Unknown.—DaC
"A jumping bean." See Jumping bean
Jumping bean. Mary Ann Hoberman.—FaTh
June
"Calm weather in June." Mother Goose.—LoR
Firefly ("On a June night"). C. Zolotow.—ZoE
I think. J. Schuyler.—KoT
June ("Everything is light"). B. J. Esbensen.—
EsCs
June ("Now is the ox-eyed daisy out"). J.
Reaney.—DoNw
June twenty-first. B. Guernsey.—JaPo
Poem in June. M. Acorn.—DoNw
June ("Everything is light"). Barbara Juster
Esbensen.—EsCs
June ("Now is the ox-eyed daisy out"). James
Reaney.—DoNw
June twenty-first. Bruce Guernsey.—JaPo
Jungle gym. Sylvia Cassedy.—CaR
The jungle husband. Stevie Smith.—HeR
Jungles and jungle life
India. W. J. Turner.—BlO
The jungle husband. S. Smith.—HeR
Monkeyland. S. Weöres.—HeR
On the Congo. H. E. Martinson.—HeR
Rain forest, Papua, New Guinea. M. C.
Livingston.—LiMp
The juniper tree. Wilfred Watson.—DoNw
Junk. Richard Wilbur.—PlSc
Junk and junkyards
In passing. G. Jonas.—JaT
Junkyards. J. L. Rayford.—JaPo
Passing by the junkyard. C. J. Egita.—HoSs
"Junk mail, junk mail." See Skip rope rhyme for
our time
Junkyards. Julian Lee Rayford.—JaPo
"Just a herd of Negroes." See Share-croppers
"Just as I reached out my hand." See False start
"Just because I loves you." See Reasons why
"Just because she wants to, Greer." X. J.
Kennedy.—KeB
"Just before." See Party
"Just before bed." See The mother's tale
Just before springtime. Judith Viorst.—ViI
"Just before the high time of autumn." See Proud
torsos
"Just beyond my reaching." See Slave coffle
Just for one day. Lillian Morrison.—PrRh
"Just look at those hands." See Soap
Just me. Margaret Hillert.—PrRh
"Just now." See The warning
"Just off the highway to Rochester, Minnesota."
See A blessing
"Just once." See That day
"Just see those pinwheels whirling round." See
Fourth of July night
Just three. William Wise.—PrRa
Just watch. Myra Cohn Livingston.—PrRa
"Just what is it." See Closet
"Just when I'm ready to." See Naughty soap song
Justice, Donald
Anonymous drawing.—PlEd

Kennedy, X. J.—*Continued*
Father and mother.—PrRh
"Feeling famished, Lester fried."—KeB
First one out of bed.—KeF
Flashlight ("Tucked tight in bed, the day all gone").—KeF
Flying uptown backwards.—KeF
"For a harmless April rain."—KeB
Forty Seventh Street crash.—KeF
Future hero.—KeF
Girl who's moved around.—KeF
"Gosnold, watch out with that match."—KeB
Halloween disguises.—KeF
The haunted oven.—LiWa
Held in suspense.—KeF
Help ("Firemen, firemen").—PrRh
"Hickenthrift and Hickenloop."—LiWa
"Hiking in the Rockies, Midge."—KeB
"A hiss, a gulp, where are you, Niles."—KeB
House noises.—KeF
How to stay up late.—KeF
How to watch statues.—KeF
"Humbert, hiking Moonshine Hill."—KeB
Hummingbird ("Cried a scientist watching this creature dart by").—KeF
"Hurry, Doctor, greedy Greg's."—KeB
I answer an SOS.—KeF
"Ignatz Mott ignored the rule."—KeB
"In a kangaroo one day."—KeB
"In the bakery Diane."—KeB
In the motel.—JaS—PrRh
"Into Mother's slide trombone."—KeB
"John while swimming in the ocean."—KeB
"Just because she wants to, Greer."—KeB
Kaleidoscope ("Chock full boxes, packages").—LiCp
"Keep a hand on your dream."—JaPi
"King Tut."—LiSf
Lasagna.—JaPo
Late night flight.—KeF
Lighting a fire.—FaTh—KeF
"Lightning, that's an old wives' tale."—KeB
"Louise, a whiz at curling hair."—KeB
"Mama Bear, you'll never miss."—KeB
"The man with the tan hands."—KeF
Maturity.—KeF
"Meaning well, Minerva Jean."—KeB
Mickey Jones.—KeF
Mingled yarns.—HaOf
Mixed-up kid.—KeF
Mixed-up school.—JaT
Mole ("A point-nosed half-pint parcel, eyes").—KeF
Moonwalk.—BaS—KeF
Mother's nerves.—PrRh
Muddy sneakers.—KeF
My dragon.—PrRa
My fishbowl head.—KeF
My window screen.—KeF
New year's advice from my Cornish grandmother.—LiNe
"Noticing an open-doored."—KeB
Old-timer.—KeF
"On a bet, foolhardy Sam."—KeB
On a boxer.—JaPo
On a child who lived one minute.—JaD
"On Halloween, when ghosts go boo."—KeB
"On his motorbike Lars stands."—KeB
"On the old mill's rotten roof."—KeB
"One winter night in August."—HaOf
"Over Mom's piano keys."—KeB
Owl ("The diet of the owl is not").—KeF
"Panic struck flight nine oh nine."—KeB

Paperclips.—FaTh
"Paul, in Aunt Pru's prune surprise."—KeB
Pick your own.—KeF
"Playing soccer, Plato Foley."—KeB
Porcupine pa.—KeF
Presents from the flood.—KeF
A quick hush.—KeF
"Rain into river."—KeF
Rock gardener.—KeF
Roofscape.—KeF
Sea horse and a sawhorse.—RuI
"The secret joy of diving bells."—KeF
Sentries.—KeF
"Sleeping bag and all, Fritz Fry."—KeB
Sleepy schoolbus.—KeF
"Snickering like crazy, Sue."—KeB
"Snowflake souffle."—BaS
Spring storm ("Our old fat tiger cat").—KeF
A sprung trap.—KeF
"Stealing eggs, Fritz ran afoul."—KeB
"Stephanie, that little stinker."—KeB
Summer milk.—KeF
Teacher ("My teacher looked at me and frowned").—KeF
Tear.—KeF
Television nose.—KeF
Ten billion crows.—KeF
These three.—LiE
Things on a microscope slide.—FaTh
"Thinking it hard candy, Rube."—KeB
To a forgetful wishing well.—KeF
To Dorothy on her exclusion from the Guinness Book of World Records.—JaPi
Trouble in town.—KeF
Trying to make time on a country highway.—KeF
Trying to write thank-you letters.—KeF
Two of a kind.—KeF
An unexplained ouch.—KeF
Unpopular Rex.—KeF
Unusual shoelaces.—JaT—LiSf
Valentine ("If all the whole world's taxicabs").—KeF—LiVp
"Vince released a jar of vermin."—KeB
The whales off Wales.—HaOf—RuI
"Where will we run to."—KeF
"While the fruit boils, Mom sends Lars."—KeB
"While we dazed onlookers gawk."—KeB
Who to pet and who not to.—HoSu
"Wilburforce Fong."—KeF
"With the garden sprinkler Brett."—KeB
Kennel. Eleanor Farjeon.—FaE
"Kennel's my castle." See Kennel
Kentucky babe. Unknown.—LaW
The **kept** secret. Unknown.—BrT
Keremes, Constance Andrea
At the table.—HoMu
Ocean treasures.—HoSe
Sand castle.—HoSe
Kermit Keene. Jack Prelutsky.—PrSr
"Kermit Keene, unkempt though clean." See Kermit Keene
Kerr's ass. Patrick Kavanagh.—HeR
The **Kerry** loon. Eleanor Farjeon.—FaE
Kevin McDonald. Mel Glenn.—GlC
Key. Eve Merriam.—MeHa
Key West, Florida
Christmas in Key West. J. Ciardi.—LiCp
Keys
"I will give you the key." A. Lobel.—LoWr
Key. E. Merriam.—MeHa

Keys—*Continued*
"This is the key of the kingdom." Mother Goose.—LoR
   This is the key.—BlO
Keziah. Gwendolyn Brooks.—PrRa—PrRh
Kherdian, David
   That day.—PlSc
Kidnap poem. Nikki Giovanni.—JaG
Kikaku
   "A bantam rooster."—KeK
The Kilkenny cats ("There wanst was two cats in Kilkenny"). See "There were once two cats of Kilkenny"
Killing the rooster. Sheryl L. Nelms.—JaS
Kilmer, Joyce
   Easter ("The air is like a butterfly").—PrRh
"A kind and gentle heart he had." From Elegy on the death of a mad dog. Oliver Goldsmith.—TrM
The kind armadillo. Oliver Herford.—BrT
Kindness. See also Animals—Care; Sympathy
   Aunt Ruth. M. C. Livingston.—LiWo
   Carrie Pearson. M. Glenn.—GlC
   Charlotte Bronte. S. Coolidge.—HaOf
   Doing a good deed. J. Ciardi.—CiD
   Feet o' Jesus. L. Hughes.—HuDk
   For the sisters of the Hôtel Dieu. A. M. Klein.—DoNw
   For them. E. Farjeon.—FaE
   The frog ("Be kind and tender to the frog"). H. Belloc.—CoN—LiSf—PrRh
   Good King Wenceslas. Unknown.—RoC
   He sits down on the floor of a school for the retarded. A. Nowlan.—JaG
   The hired man's way. J. K. Bangs.—HaOf
   "Hurt no living thing." C. G. Rossetti.—FaTh—HoSu—PrRh
   I answer an SOS. X. J. Kennedy.—KeF
   "I never spake bad word, nor did ill turn." From Pericles. W. Shakespeare.—HoUn
   The kind armadillo. O. Herford.—BrT
   A legend of the Northland. P. Cary.—HaOf
   Little things ("Little things, that run, and quail"). J. Stephens.—FaTh—LaT—LiSf—PrRh
   Marie Yeagerman. M. Glenn.—GlC
   "The neighbors are not fond of me." J. Prelutsky.—PrNk
   The raggedy man. J. W. Riley.—HaOf
   The rescue. C. Rylant.—RyW
   Travelers. J. Miles.—KeK
   Trees ("Trees are the kindest things I know"). H. Behn.—HoCb
   The week after. E. Farjeon.—FaE
Kindness to animals. Laura E. Richards.—CoN
Kineo mountain. Celeste Turner Wright.—JaPi
King, Ben
   The pessimist.—BlO
   That cat.—ChC
King, Paul
   Manerathiak's song, tr. by.—DoNw
   The wind has wings, tr. by.—DoNw
King, Martin Luther (about)
   Martin Luther King. M. C. Livingston.—LiSf—PrRh
   Martin Luther King day. M. C. Livingston.—LiCe
The king. Unknown.—BrT
"King and Queen of the pelicans we." See The pelican chorus
"The king asked." See The king's breakfast
"King Fisher courted Lady Bird." See The king-fisher song

The king-fisher song. From Sylvie and Bruno. Lewis Carroll.—BlO
King Lear, sels. William Shakespeare
   "This is the foul fiend Flibbertigibbet, he begins at".—LiWa
The king of cats sends a postcard to his wife. Nancy Willard.—HaOf
The king of Magla and Vlaga. Charlotte Pomerantz.—PoI
The king of the hobbledygoblins. Laura E. Richards.—HaOf
"The king of the yellow butterflies." Vachel Lindsay.—HaOf
"A king, on assuming his reign." See The king
King palm. Myra Cohn Livingston.—LiMp
King Rufus. Y. Y. Segal, tr. by Miriam Waddington.—DoNw
"The king sent for his wise men all." See W
"The king sits in Dumferling town." See Sir Patrick Spens
"The king sits in Dunfermline toun." See Sir Patrick Spens
"The king sits in Dunfermline town." See Sir Patrick Spens
"King Tut." X. J. Kennedy.—LiSf
Kingfisher. Eleanor Farjeon.—FaE
Kings. See Rulers
Kings, sels. Bible/Old Testament
   "And Hiram of Tyre sent his servants unto Solomon, for he had".—PlEd
"Kings." See A history lesson
The king's breakfast. Alan Alexander Milne.—FaW—LiSf
"Kings came riding." Charles Williams.—HaO
The king's son. Thomas Boyd.—PlAs
"The kings who slept in the caves are awake and out." See The National Gallery
Kingsley, Charles
   The river's song.—DaC
   The sands of Dee.—BlO
   Young and old.—DaC
Kinnell, Galway
   Crying.—CoN—KeK
   First song.—JaG
   Goodbye ("My mother, poor woman, lies tonight").—JaS
   "Looking at your face."—JaPo
   Saint Francis and the sow.—HeR
Kiowa Indians. See Indians of the Americas—Kiowa
Kipling, Rudyard
   Danny Deever.—PlAs
   Eddi's service.—HaO
   "I am the cat that walks by himself."—ChC
   "Pussy can sit by the fire and sing."—DaC
   A smugglers' song.—BlO
   The white seal's lullaby.—ChB
Kirkup, James
   Baby's drinking song.—CoN
   The lonely scarecrow.—BlO
   The shepherd's tale, tr. by.—HaO
   The winter moon ("I hit my wife and went out and saw"), tr. by.—McL
Kirkwood, Judith
   Last born.—JaS
Kirsten. Ted Berrigan.—KoT
Kissing
   The amorous señor. O. Nash.—BrT
   El beso de mama. Unknown.—GrT
   Carl Immerman. M. Glenn.—GlC
   Cat kisses. B. Katz.—PrRa
   Cecilia. Unknown.—DoNw

Kissing—*Continued*
"Did you eever, iver, over." Unknown.—KeK
    Hand-clapping rhyme ("Did you eever, iver, ever").—CoN
"Doing, a filthy pleasure is, and short." Petronius Arbiter.—McL
"Down in yonder meadow where the green grass grows." Unknown.—DaC
Esau and Kate. Unknown.—PaM
First kiss. J. Holden.—JaG
"Georgie Porgie, pudding and pie." Mother Goose.—DeM—FaW—LoR
Jenny kiss'd me. L. Hunt.—CoN
Laurie Allen. M. Glenn.—GlC
Mama's kiss. Unknown.—GrT
The mistletoe. J. Prelutsky.—PrRa
"Oh no." J. Prelutsky.—PrIv
Popsicles. C. B. Francis.—HoMu
The kitchen chimney. Robert Frost.—PlEd
The **kitchen** (for my grandmother). William Bedford.—StG
A kitchen memory. Roy Scheele.—JaS
Kitchen song. Jeannine Dobbs.—JaS
Kitchen tables. David Huddle.—JaS
Kitchens
"Alas, alas, for Miss Mackay." Mother Goose.—FaW—LoR
Around the kitchen table. G. Gildner.—JaS
Chocolate milk. R. Padgett.—KoT
Dangerous. D. Aldis.—PrRa
For the little girl who asked why the kitchen was so bright. J. Ulmer.—JaT
Here it is. A. Turner.—TuS
The kitchen chimney. R. Frost.—PlEd
The kitchen (for my grandmother). W. Bedford.—StG
A kitchen memory. R. Scheele.—JaS
Kitchen song. J. Dobbs.—JaS
The old wife and the ghost. J. Reeves.—HoCr
A room in the past. T. Kooser.—JaS
Kitchenware
The toaster ("A silver scaled dragon with jaws flaming red"). W. J. Smith.—PrRh
The **kite** ("How bright on the blue"). Harry Behn.—HoCb—LiSf
A **kite** ("I often sit and wish that I"). Unknown.—PrRa
Kites
The donkey ("I had a donkey, that was all right"). T. Roethke.—HaOf—PrRa
The kite ("How bright on the blue"). H. Behn.—HoCb—LiSf
A kite ("I often sit and wish that I"). Unknown.—PrRa
"Melvin Martin Riley Smith." D. McCord.—McAs
Mr. Skinner. N. M. Bodecker.—FaW—LiSf
Paper dragons. S. A. Schmeltz.—PrRh
"Sky." R. Roseliep.—KeK
"This is baby's trumpet." Unknown.—DeD
To a red kite. L. Moore.—MoSn
Tree house. T. Kooser.—JaPo
Two ways to look at kites. B. J. Esbensen.—EsCs
Windy day. N. M. Bodecker.—BoPc
Kitson, Margaret
"Loving heavenly Father, who takes care of us all."—LaT
A **kitten** ("He's nothing much but fur"). Eleanor Farjeon.—ChC—FaE
The **kitten** ("The trouble with a kitten is that"). Ogden Nash.—ChC—JaD

The **kitten** and the falling leaves. William Wordsworth.—BlO—ChC
"**Kitten**, my kitten." See My kitten
Kittens. See Cats
Kittens. Myra Cohn Livingston.—LiWo
"The **kitten's** in the dairy." See For Mary and her kitten
Kitty. Doug McLeod.—ChC
"**Kitty** caught a caterpillar." Jack Prelutsky.—PrRi
Kitty cornered. Eve Merriam.—ChC
Klabauterwife's letter. Christian Morgenstern, tr. by William De Witt Snodgrass and Lore Segal.—LiWa
Klappert, Peter
The invention of the telephone.—JaPo
Klauber, Edgar
On buying a dog.—CoN
Klein, Abraham Moses
Bandit.—DoNw
For the sisters of the Hôtel Dieu.—DoNw
Orders.—DoNw
Psalm of the fruitful field.—DoNw
Knappert, Jan
Swahili love song, tr. by.—McL
The **knee.** Christian Morgenstern, tr. by William De Witt Snodgrass and Lore Segal.—HeR
"The **knees.**" See Cadenza
Knies, Elisabeth
Absence ("You have withdrawn").—JaG
"A **knight** came riding from the east." Unknown.—BlO
Knights and knighthood
"All furnish'd, all in arms." From Henry IV, Part I. W. Shakespeare.—HoUn
La belle dame sans merci ("O, what can ail thee, knight at arms"). J. Keats.—HeR—LiWa—PlAs
A brave knight. M. M. Dodge.—BrT
Flowers in the valley. Unknown.—BlO
The knight's tomb. S. T. Coleridge.—HeR
Lepanto. G. K. Chesterton.—HeR
Lochinvar. Sir W. Scott.—PlAs
Sir Bedivere Bors. F. B. Opper.—BrT
Sir Blushington Bloone. J. Prelutsky.—PrNk
"Sir Eglamour, that worthy Knight." Unknown.—BlO
Three knights from Spain. Unknown.—BlO
The three ravens. Unknown.—PlAs
The twa corbies. Unknown.—HeR—PlAs
The **knight's** tomb. Samuel Taylor Coleridge.—HeR
Knister, Raymond
White cat.—DoNw
Knitted things. Karla Kuskin.—HoCr—KeK
The **knitters.** Padraic Colum.—PlSc
Knitting
Henrietta Snetter. J. Prelutsky.—PrNk
Knitted things. K. Kuskin.—HoCr—KeK
The knitters. P. Colum.—PlSc
"**Knock,** knock, anybody there." Clyde Watson.—LiSf
"**Knock** on the door." Mother Goose.—DeM
The **knockout.** Lillian Morrison.—PrRh
Knotholes. David McCord.—McAs
Know him. N. M. Bodecker.—BoPc
"**Know** the word by heart." See Theory of poetry
Know your true worth. Unknown.—BrT
Knowledge
The blind men and the elephant. J. G. Saxe.—CoOu—HaOf
Cadenza. C. Sandburg.—HoRa
Discovery. H. Behn.—HoCb
Grandma. A. Turner.—TuS

Kuskin, Karla—*Continued*
To you.—LiVp
"When a cat is asleep."—JaT
When I went out.—CoN
"Where have you been dear."—CoN
Winter clothes.—PrRh
Kuzma, Greg
For my father on his birthday.—JaS
Sometimes ("I am afraid of being crushed in the pincers").—JaPi
Kwakiutl Indians. See Indians of the Americas—Kwakiutl
Kyorai
"I called to the wind."—LiSf—LiWa
Kyozo, Tagaki
The winter moon ("I hit my wife and went out and saw").—McL
Kyrie Eleison. Joan Aiken.—LiE

L

LaBombard, Joan
Heart.—JaPo
Marbles ("They are his planets").—JaT
To my daughter riding in the circus parade.—JaG
Labor. See Work
Labor day
Labor day. M. C. Livingston.—LiCe
Labor day. Myra Cohn Livingston.—LiCe
Laborers of the Work
"The **labouring** poor, in spite of double pay." From The true-born Englishman. Daniel Defoe.—PlSc
Labours of the months. Unknown.—PlSc
"**Lacking** an imagination of my own, I rely on Billy's." See Peter Quincy
"**Ladies** and gentlemen." Mother Goose.—DeM
Lady-birds. See Beetles
Lady-bugs. See Beetles
"The **lady** director is a gentle guide, but." See Changsha shoe factory
A **lady** named Psyche. Unknown.—BrT
The **lady** pitcher. Cynthia Macdonald.—JaPi
The **lady** said. Arnold Adoff.—AdA
"The **lady** said, what are you going to be." See The lady said
Lady Sara Bunbury sacrificing to the Graces, by Reynolds. Daryl Hine.—PlEd
A **lady** track star. Roy Blount.—BrT
"A **lady** track star from Toccoa." See A lady track star
"**Lady,** weeping at the crossroads." Wystan Hugh Auden.—PlAs
"A **lady** who lived at Bordeaux." Unknown.—BrT
"A **lady** who lived in Uganda." See The panda
"A **lady** whose name was Miss Hartley." See Miss Hartley
"**Lady** with the frilled blouse." See Valediction
Ladybird, ladybird. Emily Brontë.—CoOu
"**Ladybird,** ladybird, fly away home/ Night is approaching." See Ladybird, ladybird
"**Ladybird,** ladybird, fly away home/ Your house is on fire." Mother Goose.—LoR
Ladybirds. See Beetles
"**Ladybug.**" See Going barefoot
Ladybug ("Little ladybug"). Charlotte Zolotow.—ZoE
Ladybug ("A small speckled visitor"). Joan Walsh Anglund.—PrRh

Ladybug ("A tiny island"). Francois Dodat, tr. by Bert Meyers and Odette Meyers.—FaTh
"**Ladybug,** ladybug." Unknown, tr. by Isaac Taylor Headland.—FaW
Ladybugs. See Beetles
Ladybugs. Peggy Shumaker.—JaT
The **lady's** farewell. Nuno Fernandez Torneol, tr. by Yvor Winters.—PlAs
Laing, Dilys
The farm hands.—PlSc
Lair. Eve Merriam.—MeHa
"A **laird,** a lord." Unknown.—PlSc
The **lake** ("Rippling green and gold and brown"). Harry Behn.—HoCb
The **lake** ("This winter day"). Barbara Juster Esbensen.—EsCs
Lake Erie. From Great Lakes suite. James Reaney.—DoNw
"**Lake** Erie is weary." See Lake Erie
Lake Huron. From Great Lakes suite. James Reaney.—DoNw
The **Lake** Isle of Innisfree. William Butler Yeats.—LiSf
Lake Michigan. From Great Lakes suite. James Reaney.—DoNw
Lake Ontario. From Great Lakes suite. James Reaney.—DoNw
Lake St. Clair. From Great Lakes suite. James Reaney.—DoNw
Lake Superior. From Great Lakes suite. James Reaney.—DoNw
"The **lake** was covered all over." Dorothy Wordsworth.—KeK
Lakes and ponds
The ballad of Semmerwater. W. Watson.—BlO
The boats. C. Zolotow.—ZoE
The cove. D. McCord.—McAs
Daddy fell into the pond. A. Noyes.—PrRh
Dusk ("Dusk over the lake"). J. Harrison.—JaT
Dusk in the country. H. E. Martinson.—HeR
The lake ("Rippling green and gold and brown"). H. Behn.—HoCb
The lake ("This winter day"). B. J. Esbensen.—EsCs
Lake Erie. From Great Lakes suite. J. Reaney.—DoNw
Lake Huron. From Great Lakes suite. J. Reaney.—DoNw
Lake Michigan. From Great Lakes suite. J. Reaney.—DoNw
Lake Ontario. From Great Lakes suite. J. Reaney.—DoNw
Lake St. Clair. From Great Lakes suite. J. Reaney.—DoNw
Lake Superior. From Great Lakes suite. J. Reaney.—DoNw
"The lake was covered all over." D. Wordsworth.—KeK
Lost ("Desolate and lone"). C. Sandburg.—HoRa
The mill-pond. E. Thomas.—HeR
The muskellunge. T. Hughes.—HuU
Perseid meteor shower. B. J. Esbensen.—EsCs
Plop. R. J. Margolis.—MaS
The pond. C. Zolotow.—ZoE
"Running lightly over spongy ground." T. Roethke.—HeR
Spring pools. R. Frost.—KoS
Summer's end ("In the still pond"). E. Merriam.—MeF
Lamb, Charles. See also next entry
The old familiar faces.—HeR

Language.—*Continued*
"Little girl, be careful what you say." C. Sandburg.—HoRa
Lulu, Lulu, I've a lilo. C. Pomerantz.—PoI
Metaphor. E. Merriam.—MeSk
Nym and graph. E. Merriam.—MeSk
Ornithology. E. Farjeon.—FaE
The reformed pirate. T. G. Roberts.—DoNw
Simile, willow and ginkgo. E. Merriam.—MeSk
Singular indeed. D. McCord.—HaOf
Stars ("In science today we learned"). N. Giovanni.—GiSp—KeK
Town meeting or 'hey man, don't speak so good'. N. M. Bodecker.—BoPc
Trilingual. A. Adoff.—AdA
The true ballad of the great race to Gilmore City. P. Hey.—JaPi
Verbs. E. Farjeon.—FaE
"Waterwheels in whirl." I. H. Finlay.—KeK
"Well, it's partly the shape of the thing." Unknown.—KeK
Yes, it's raining. C. Pomerantz.—PoI
Lanigan, George T.
Isabel, tr. by.—DoNw
Threnody.—DoNw
"The **lanky** hank of a she in the inn over there." See A glass of beer
Lantern. Gary Soto.—JaS
Lao Tse
"To become an archer."—KeK
"**Lap** I, swimming . . . laps." See Greg Hoffman
Lapage, Geoffry
Mr. Giraffe.—CoOu
Larcom, Lucy
The brown thrush.—HaOf
Dumpy ducky.—HaOf
In the tree-top.—HaOf
Spring whistles.—HaOf
The volunteer's Thanksgiving.—HaOf
Large bad picture. Elizabeth Bishop.—PlEd
"The **lariat** snaps, the cowboy rolls." See The closing of the rodeo
Larkin, Philip
At grass.—HeR
Cut grass.—HeR
Days.—HeR
The explosion.—HeR
First sight.—CoN
Livings, sels.
"Seventy feet down".—HeR
The north ship.—HeR
"Seventy feet down." See Livings
Toads revisited.—PlSc
Larks
Answer to a child's question. S. T. Coleridge.—BlO
"Hark, hark, the lark at heaven's gate sings." From Cymbeline. W. Shakespeare.—BlO—HoUn
The skylark. C. G. Rossetti.—DaC
"Up with me, up with me into the clouds." From To a skylark. W. Wordsworth.—KoT
The woodlark. G. M. Hopkins.—HeR
Lasagna. X. J. Kennedy.—JaPo
Last born. Judith Kirkwood.—JaS
The **last** cry of the damp fly. Dennis Lee.—CoN
Last day of school ("Look out"). Barbara Juster Esbensen.—EsCs
The **last** day of school ("On the last day of school"). Jack Prelutsky.—PrWi
The **last** days of November, and everything so green." See The volunteer's Thanksgiving
The **last** decision. Maya Angelou.—AnS

"The **last** dinosaur." Victoria Day Najjar.—HoDi
Last laugh. Lee Bennett Hopkins.—HoSu
The **last** leaf. Harry Behn.—HoCb
"A **last** love." See Recovery
"**Last** night." See March twenty-first
"**Last** night and the night before." Mother Goose.—AlH
"**Last** night, by the Klondike River." See By the Klondike River
"**Last** night I dreamed of you." See The dream
"**Last** night in the open shippen." See Christmas day
Last rites. Christina Georgina Rossetti.—PrRh
Last song. James Guthrie.—LaW
"**Last** summer I couldn't swim at all." See A year later
"**Last** week my brother jumped from the roof of our." See Stella Kolsky
Last word. Richard J. Margolis.—MaS
The **last** word of a bluebird (as told to a child). Robert Frost.—KoS—LiSf
The **last** words of my English grandmother. William Carlos Williams.—HeR
"**Latch**, latch." Eve Merriam.—MeBl
"**Late** at night and in secret." See Elizabeth McKenzie
"**Late** lies the wintry sun a-bed." See Winter time
The **late** mother. Cynthia Macdonald.—JaPi
Late night flight. X. J. Kennedy.—KeF
"**Late** November, driving to Wichita." See For a friend
"**Late** one night in Kalamazoo." Jack Prelutsky.—PrRi
Late, passing prairie farm. William Stafford.—JaG
A **late** spring. Philip Booth.—JaPi
A **late** walk. Robert Frost.—KoS
Latin. Eleanor Farjeon.—FaE
Latin language
Latin. E. Farjeon.—FaE
Lattimore, Richmond
Dislike of tasks.—PlSc
The father ("Once a gay wit, subsequently a wretched instructor").—PlEd
Max Schmitt in a single scull.—PlEd
Monastery on Athos.—PlEd
Tudor portrait.—PlEd
Laughing backwards. Jim Hall.—JaG
"The **laughing** hyena's behavior is strange." See The hyena
Laughlin, James
You came as a thought.—JaG
Laughter
"Alicia Patricia." N. M. Bodecker.—BoSs
Bursting. D. Aldis.—HoBf
Delayed action. C. Morgenstern.—HeR
The dirty billed freeze footy. J. Hemschemeyer.—JaS
The funny old man and his wife. Unknown.
The height of the ridiculous. O. W. Holmes.—HaOf
Laughing backwards. J. Hall.—JaG
Laughter. M. Waddington.—DoNw
Minstrel man. L. Hughes.—HuDk
The smile. W. Blake.—HeR
Three tickles. D. Lee.—PrRa
"When the green woods laugh." W. Blake.—KoT
Wiggly giggles. S. J. Crossen.—PrRh
Laughter. Miriam Waddington.—DoNw
"The **laughter** of the lesser lynx." See The lesser lynx
Laundresses and laundrymen. See Laundry
Laundromat. David McCord.—HoCl

Laundry
"At the laundromat Liz Meyer." X. J. Kennedy.—KeB
Days through starch and bluing. A. Fulton.—JaG
Laundromat. D. McCord.—HoCl
"Look at that." L. Moore.—MoSn
Muddy sneakers. X. J. Kennedy.—KeF
"The old woman must stand." Mother Goose.—DeM
"The old woman stands at the tub, tub, tub." Mother Goose.—LoR
Our washing machine. P. Hubbell.—HoCl—LiSf—PrRh
Partners. L. Moore.—MoSn
"Stocking and shirt." J. Reeves.—CoOu
"Swish, swash." E. Merriam.—MeBl
"They that wash on Monday." Mother Goose.—BlO
"A wolf is at the laundromat." J. Prelutsky.—PrNk
Lauren Jones. Mel Glenn.—GlC
Laurie Allen. Mel Glenn.—GlC
"**Lavender** blue and rosemary green." Mother Goose.—LoR
"**Lavender's** blue, diddle diddle". See "Lavender's blue, dilly, dilly"
"**Lavender's** blue, dilly, dilly." Mother Goose.—DaC
"Lavender's blue, diddle diddle".—DeM
Lavington, Margaret
The underworld.—PrRa
Lavinia Nink. Jack Prelutsky.—PrNk
"**Lavinia** Nink lives serenely." See Lavinia Nink
Law
The inquest. W. H. Davies.—HeR
An ode to the framers of the Frame Bill. Lord Byron.—PlSc
"The **lawnmower**." See Lawnmower
Lawnmower. Valerie Worth.—HoCl
Lawns and lawn care. See also Grass
Lawrence, David Herbert
Bavarian gentians.—KoT
Butterfly ("Butterfly, the wind blows sea-ward, strong beyond the garden wall").—KoT
Delight of being alone.—PrBb
Eagle in New Mexico, sels.
  "Toward the sun, towards the south-west".—HeR
"Elephants in the circus."—PrBb
Elephants plodding.—PrBb
The gazelle calf.—HeR
Green ("The dawn was apple green").—PrBb
Humming-bird ("I can imagine, in some otherworld").—HeR—PrBb
Little fish ("The tiny fish enjoy themselves").—HeR—KoT—PrBb
A living.—PrBb
Lizard ("A lizard ran out on a rock and looked up, listening").—HeR
Man and bat.—HeR
Man's image.—PrBb
Many mansions.—PrBb
Mosquito ("When did you start your tricks").—HeR
The mosquito knows.—HeR—PrBb
Mountain lion.—HeR
Peacock.—KoT
People ("I like people quite well").—PrBb
Piano ("Softly, in the dusk, a woman is singing to me").—HeR
The rainbow ("Even the rainbow has a body").—PrBb

Relativity.—PrBb
Roses.—PrBb
Salt ("Salt is scorched water that the sun has scorched").—PrBb
Sea-weed.—HeR—HoSe—PrBb
Self-pity.—HeR
Snake ("A snake came to my water-trough").—HeR
Song ("Up in the high").—PrBb
Space.—PrBb
Spray.—PrBb
Sunset ("There is a band of dull gold in the west and say what you like").—PrBb
Talk ("I wish people, when you sit near them").—PrBb
The third thing.—PrBb
"Toward the sun, towards the south-west." See Eagle in New Mexico
Two performing elephants.—HeR
The white horse.—KeK—KoT—PrBb
Willy wet-leg.—HeR
"**Lay** me on an anvil, O God." See Prayers of steel
The **lay** of the labourer. Thomas Hood.—PlSc
"**Lay** your sleeping head, my love." See Lullaby
Layton, Irving
Song for Naomi.—DoNw
"A spider danced a cosy jig."—DoNw
Laziness
"After weeks of watching the roof leak." G. Snyder.—KeK
"A diller, a dollar, a ten o'clock scholar." Mother Goose.—DaC—DeM—FaW—LiSf—LoR
  Ten o'clock scholar.—ChG
"Elsie Marley is grown so fine." Mother Goose.—AlH—ChG—DeM
  "Elsie Marley has grown so fine".—LoR
"Get up, get up, you lazyhead." Unknown.—CoN
  Slugabed.—DaC
Getting out of bed. E. Farjeon.—ChG—FaE
"I'm really not lazy." A. Spilka.—PrRh
Lazy Mary. Unknown.—LiSf
The lazy people. S. Silverstein.—CoN
The lazy pussy. P. Cox.—HaOf
"The lazy woman." Unknown.—DeD
The nothing doings. J. Prelutsky.—PrNk
Roger the dog. T. Hughes.—PrRh
Song ("I'd much rather sit there in the sun"). R. Krauss.—PrRh
Sunning. J. S. Tippett.—LiSf—PrRh
"There was a slow pig from Decatur." A. Lobel.—LoB
Lazy Mary. Unknown.—LiSf
"**Lazy** Mary, will you get up." See Lazy Mary
The **lazy** people. Shel Silverstein.—CoN
The **lazy** pussy. Palmer Cox.—HaOf
A **lazy** thought. Eve Merriam.—HoSs
"**Lazy** witch." Myra Cohn Livingston.—PrRh
"The **lazy** woman." Unknown.—DeD
Le Gallienne, Richard
Brooklyn Bridge at dawn.—LiSf
Lead. Eleanor Farjeon.—FaE
The **leaden-eyed**. Vachel Lindsay.—HeR
"**Leaf**." See Artichoke
"A **leaf** bug comes from an egg in June." See Cockroaches
"**Lean** your ladder light." See In a starry orchard
Leaning on a limerick. Eve Merriam.—BrT—MeSk
Lear, Edward
An animal alphabet, complete.—HeR

Lear, Edward—*Continued*
An animal alphabet, sels.
"The fizzgiggious fish".—LiH
"The judicious jubilant jay".—LiH
"The melodious meritorious mouse".—LiH
"The rural runcible raven".—LiH
"The scroobious snake".—LiH
"The tumultuous tom-tommy tortoise".—LiH
"The umbrageous umbrella maker".—LiH
"The worrying whizzing wasp".—LiH
"The zigzag zealous zebra".—LiH
"A bridge engineer, Mister Crumpett."—KeK
"Calico pie."—BlO—LiH
"Chimnies and wings."—LiH
The courtship of the Yonghy-Bonghy-Bo.—LiH
The dong with a luminous nose.—LiH
The duck and the kangaroo.—LiH—LiIl
A fatal mistake.—BrT
"The fizzgiggious fish." See An animal alphabet
"Herons and sweeps."—LiH
"How pleasant to know Mr. Lear."—LiH
Hurtful habits. See "There was an old person whose habits"
Incidents in the life of my uncle Arly.—LiH
"The judicious jubilant jay." See An animal alphabet
The jumblies.—BlO—LiH
Limerick. See "There was an old person of Dean"
"The melodious meritorious mouse." See An animal alphabet
Mr. and Mrs. Spikky Sparrow.—LiH
The new vestments.—PrRh
The old man of the Hague. See "There was an old man of the Hague"
An old man of the Nile. See "There was an old man of the Nile"
Old man with a beard. See "There was an old man with a beard"
The old man with a gong. See "There was an old man with a gong"
An old person of Cromer.—BrT
An old person of Tring. See "There was an old person of Tring"
An old person of Ware. See "There was an old person of Ware"
The owl and the pussycat.—BlO—CoN—FaW—KoT—LiH—LiSf—PrRh
The pelican chorus.—LiH
"The pobble who has no toes."—FaW—LiH
The pobble.—BlO
"Puddings and beams."—LiH
The quangle wangle's hat.—CoOu—LiH—LiIl
Rice and mice. See "There was an old person of Ewell"
"The rural runcible raven." See An animal alphabet
"The scroobious snake." See An animal alphabet
The table and the chair.—LiH—LiSf
Tea by the sea.—BrT
"There is a young lady, whose nose."—FaW—LiH
"There was a young lady of Bute."—LiH
"There was a young lady of Dorking."—LiH
"There was a young lady of Firle."—LiH
"There was a young lady of Greenwich."—LiH
"There was a young lady of Norway."—FaW
"There was a young lady of Poole."—LiH
"There was a young lady of Portugal."—LiH
"There was a young lady of Turkey."—LiH

"There was a young lady of Tyre."—LiH
The young lady of Tyre.—BrT
"There was a young lady of Wales."—LiH
"There was a young lady of Welling."—LiH
"There was a young lady whose bonnet."—LiH
"There was a young lady whose chin."—LiH
"There was a young lady whose eyes."—LiH
"There was a young lady whose nose."—LiH
"There was a young person in green."—LiH
"There was a young person in red."—LiH
"There was a young person of Ayr."—KeK—LiH
"There was a young person of Crete."—LiH
"There was an old lady of Chertsey."—BlO—FaW
"There was an old lady of France."—LiH
"There was an old man at a junction."—LiH
"There was an old man in a barge."—FaW—LiH—RuI
"There was an old man in a marsh."—LiH
"There was an old man in a tree."—LiH—LiH—LiH—LiSf
"There was an old man of Apulia."—LiH
"There was an old man of Blackheath."—LiH
"There was an old man of Bohemia."—LiH
"There was an old man of Calcutta."—LiH
"There was an old man of Cape Horn."—LiH
"There was an old man of Coblenz."—LiH
"There was an old man of Dee-side."—LiH
"There was an old man of Dumblane."—LiH
"There was an old man of Dumbree."—LiH
"There was an old man of Dunluce."—LiH
"There was an old man of Dunrose."—LiH
"There was an old man of El Hums."—LiH
"There was an old man of Hong Kong."—LiH
"There was an old man of Kilkenny."—LiH
"There was an old man of Melrose."—LiH
"There was an old man of Messina."—LiH
"There was an old man of Thames Ditton."—LiH
"There was an old man of the Hague."—LiH—LiSf
The old man of the Hague.—BrT
"There was an old man of the isles."—LiH
"There was an old man of the Nile."—FaW
An old man of the Nile.—BrT
"There was an old man of the South."—LiH
"There was an old man of the West."—LiH
"There was an old man of Thermopylae."—FaW
"There was an old man of Toulouse."—LiH
"There was an old man of West Dumpet."—LiH
"There was an old man of Whitehaven."—LiH
"There was an old man on a hill."—LiH
"There was an old man on the border."—LiH
"There was an old man, on whose nose."—LiH
"There was an old man who said, how."—BlO
"There was an old man who said, hush."—KeK—LiH
"There was an old man who said, well."—LiH—LiSf
"There was an old man whose despair."—LiH
"There was an old man with a beard."—CoOu—FaW—LiH—LiSf—PrRh
Old man with a beard.—CoN
"There was an old man with a beard, who sat."—LiH
"There was an old man with a flute."—LiH
"There was an old man with a gong."—LiH
The old man with a gong.—BrT
"There was an old man with a nose."—LiH

Lear, Edward—*Continued*
"There was an old person of Anerley."—LiH
"There was an old person of Bangor."—LiH
"There was an old person of Bar."—LiH
"There was an old person of Bree."—LiH
"There was an old person of Brigg."—LiH
"There was an old person of Bromley."—LiH
"There was an old person of Bude."—LiH
"There was an old person of Cassel."—LiH
"There was an old person of Chili."—LiH
"There was an old person of Crowle."—LiH
"There was an old person of Deal."—LiH
"There was an old person of Dean."—BlO—
    FaTh—LiH
    Limerick.—HoMu
"There was an old person of Down."—LiH
"There was an old person of Dutton."—LiH
"There was an old person of Ems."—LiH
"There was an old person of Ewell."—LiH
    Rice and mice.—BrT
"There was an old person of Fife."—LiH
"There was an old person of Filey."—LiH
"There was an old person of Grange."—LiH
"There was an old person of Gretna."—LiH
"There was an old person of Hurst."—LiH
"There was an old person of Hyde."—LiH
"There was an old person of Ibreem."—LiH
"There was an old person of Jodd."—LiH
"There was an old person of Mold."—LiH
"There was an old person of Newry."—LiH
"There was an old person of Nice."—LiH
"There was an old person of Peru."—LiH
"There was an old person of Pett."—LiH
"There was an old person of Philoe."—LiH
"There was an old person of Pinner."—LiH
"There was an old person of Rheims."—LiH
"There was an old person of Sestri."—LiH
"There was an old person of Skye."—KeK—
    LiH
"There was an old person of Spain."—LiH
"There was an old person of Tring."—LiH
    An old person of Tring.—BrT (unat.)
"There was an old person of Ware."—LiH
    An old person of Ware.—PrRa
"There was an old person of Wilts."—LiH
"There was an old person of Woking."—LiH
"There was an old person whose habits."—LiH
    Hurtful habits.—BrT
"The tumultuous tom-tommy tortoise." See An
    animal alphabet
"The umbrageous umbrella maker." See An
    animal alphabet
"Wafers and bears."—LiH
"The worrying whizzing wasp." See An animal
    alphabet
The young lady of Tyre. See "There was a
    young lady of Tyre"
"The zigzag zealous zebra." See An animal
    alphabet
Lear, Edward (about)
"How pleasant to know Mr. Lear." E. Lear.—
    LiH
Learning. Judith Viorst.—ViI
Leave me alone. Felice Holman.—PrRh
Leaves
    April ("The young cherry trees"). L. Pastan.—
        JaPi
    Beech leaves. J. Reeves.—CoOu
    Buds. E. Coatsworth.—FaTh
    December leaves. K. Starbird.—BaS
    "Down, down." E. Farjeon.—CoN—FaE
    The elm tree. E. Farjeon.—FaE
    Gathering leaves. R. Frost.—HeR—KoS

In hardwood groves. R. Frost.—KoS
The kitten and the falling leaves. W.
    Wordsworth.—BlO—ChC
The last leaf. H. Behn.—HoCb
Leaves ("My green leaves are more beautiful").
    F. Asch.—CoN
Leaves ("Now when a branch hangs out its
    leaves"). E. Farjeon.—FaE
The leaves ("The world is weeping leaves
    today"). C. Zolotow.—ZoE
Leaves compared with flowers. R. Frost.—KoS
The leaves in a frolic. Unknown.—CoOu
Maple. M. C. Livingston.—LiMp
Markings. F. Steele.—JaPi
New sounds. L. Moore.—HoSi—MoSn
October ("October turned my maple's leaves to
    gold"). T. B. Aldrich.—PrRh
One last little leaf. J. Prelutsky.—PrIs
Quaking aspen. E. Merriam.—MeF
Reply to the question, how can you become
    a poet. E. Merriam.—JaD
Robins. V. Worth.—WoSp
September ("Something is bleeding"). L.
    Moore.—MoSn
"This leaf." B. S. De Regniers.—HoSi
Willow yellow. L. Moore.—MoSn
Leaves ("My green leaves are more beautiful").
    Frank Asch.—CoN
Leaves ("Now when a branch hangs out its
    leaves"). Eleanor Farjeon.—FaE
The leaves ("The world is weeping leaves today").
    Charlotte Zolotow.—ZoE
"The leaves are fading and falling." See
    November
Leaves compared with flowers. Robert Frost.—
    KoS
"The leaves had a wonderful frolic." See The
    leaves in a frolic
The leaves in a frolic. Unknown.—CoOu
Leavetaking. Eve Merriam.—HoSi—MeSk
Lebovitz, Richard
    "Handsawwwwwwwwwwww."—KeK
Lee, B. J.
    Eight witches.—PrRh
    Troll trick.—HoCr
Lee, Dennis
    Alligator pie.—FaW—JaT—PrRh
    Double barreled ding dong bat.—PrRh
    The dreadful doings of Jelly Belly.—PrRa
    Forty mermaids.—RuI
    Freddy.—PrRh
    Good night, good night.—PrRa
    "Higgledy piggledy."—LiSf
    The last cry of the damp fly.—CoN
    Lying on things.—BaS
    The muddy puddle.—PrRh
    The question ("If I could teach you how to
        fly").—LiIl
    "Silverly."—PrRa
    Skyscraper.—PrRa
    There was a man.—KeK
    Three tickles.—PrRa
    Tony Baloney.—PrRh
    "Windshield wipers."—DoNw
    With my foot in my mouth.—LiIl
Lee, J. B.
    Clumsy.—BrT
Lee, Laurie
    Christmas landscape.—HaO
"Left foot." Eve Merriam.—MeBl
A left-handed poem. Eve Merriam.—MeSk
"Left, right." See Markings, the period
"Left! Right! march the waves." See Lake Ontario

Leftovers. Jack Prelutsky.—PrIt
The leg. Karl Shapiro.—JaD
"Leg over leg." Mother Goose.—RaT
The legacy II. Leroy V. Quintana.—StG
Legend. Judith Wright.—HeR
A legend of the Northland. Phoebe Cary.—HaOf
Legends
  Bifocal. W. Stafford.—HeR
  Legend. J. Wright.—HeR
Legs
  The amputation. H. Sorrells.—JaD
  Bullfrogs. D. A. Evans.—JaPi
  The leg. K. Shapiro.—JaD
  The legs. R. Graves.—HeR
  The octopus ("Tell me, O octopus, I begs"). O.
    Nash.—HeR—LiSf
  Poem in which my legs are accepted. K.
    Fraser.—McL
"Legs." See Poem in which my legs are accepted
The legs. Robert Graves.—HeR
LeGuin, Ursula K.
  The child on the shore.—KeK
Leigh, Henry S.
  The twins ("In form and feature, face and
    limb").—PrRh
Leigh Hamilton. Mel Glenn.—GlCd
"Lemonade ran out when the pitcher broke." Eve
  Merriam.—MeBl
Lemonade stand. Myra Cohn Livingston.—LiWo
"Lena." Myra Cohn Livingston.—LiWo
L'Engle, Madeleine
  Bedtime ("Good night").—LaT
  Drawing.—LaT
  I've been scolded.—LaT
  Morning ("Dear Lord my God").—LaT
  My bath.—LaT
  O simplicitas.—HaO
  Our food.—LaT
  Playing.—LaT
  Television.—LaT
Lenora. Unknown.—BrT
Lenski, Lois
  "Sing a song of people."—PrRh
"A lentil, a lentil, a lentil, a stone." See The
  woman cleaning lentils
Leodhas, Sorche Nic
  Always room for one more.—LiSf
Leopard ("Eons ago, when the earth was still
  yeasty"). Gretchen Kreps.—PrRh
Leopard ("Gentle hunter"). Unknown, tr. by Ulli
  Beier.—HeR
Leopard in the zoo. Charlotte Zolotow.—ZoE
"A leopard when told that benzine." See The
  inquisitive leopard
Leopardi, Giacomo
  To the moon ("I remember, gracious, graceful
    moon").—KoT
Leopards
  The inquisitive leopard. O. Herford.—BrT
  Leopard ("Eons ago, when the earth was still
    yeasty"). G. Kreps.—PrRh
  Leopard ("Gentle hunter"). Unknown.—HeR
  Leopard in the zoo. C. Zolotow.—ZoE
  Zebra and leopard. N. M. Bodecker.—BoSs
Lepan, Douglas
  Black bear ("Sweet-mouth, honey-paws, hairy
    one!").—DoNw
Lepanto. Gilbert Keith Chesterton.—HeR
The lesser lynx. Emile Victor Rieu.—PrRh
A lesson for mamma. Sydney Dayre.—HaOf
A lesson in manners. John Ciardi.—CiD
Lessons ("My teacher taught me to add.").
  Richard J. Margolis.—MaS

Lessons ("William the conqueror, ten sixty six").
  Eleanor Farjeon.—FaE
"Let all the family gather." See Light another
  candle
"Let it be anywhere." See For her
"Let me fetch sticks." See Bliss
"Let me see if Philip can." See The story of
  fidgety Philip
"Let me tell to you the story." See Los pastores
"Let me tell you." See Sunday
"Let my girl friend wear designer jeans." See Amy
  Pines
"Let not young souls be smothered out before."
  See The leaden-eyed
Let others share. Edward Anthony.—PrRh
"Let others share your toys, my son." See Let
  others share
"Let the limerick form be rehoised." See Leaning
  on a limerick
"Let the rain kiss you." See April rain song
"Let them." See Elm
"Let there be new flowering." Lucille Clifton.—
  JaPo
"Let us have winter loving that the heart." See
  Winter love
"Let us walk in the white snow." See Velvet
  shoes
Let X equal half. J. F. Wilson.—BrT
"Let's go." See Sled run
"Let's go see old Abe." See Lincoln monument,
  Washington
"Let's marry said the cherry." N. M. Bodecker.—
  LiSf
Let's take a nap. Nikki Giovanni.—GiSp
"Let's write a poem about lazy people." See The
  lazy people
The letter. Alfred Tennyson.—KoT
A letter from home. Mary Oliver.—JaS
Letter to a dead father. Richard Shelton.—JaD
Letter to a friend. Lilian Moore.—LiIl—MoSn
Letter to a substitute teacher. Gary Gildner.—JaPi
Letter to statues. John Malcolm Brinnin.—PlEd
"The letter you sent me touched my heart." See
  Thank you for your letter
Letters and letter writing
  "Bee, I'm expecting you." E. Dickinson.—KoT
  Burning love letters. H. Moss.—JaD
  Cecilia Dowling. M. Glenn.—GlCd
  The dual site. M. Hamburger.—PlAs
  The fisherman writes a letter to the mermaid.
    J. Aiken.—LiWa
  For Laura. M. C. Livingston.—HoBf
  How to write a letter. E. Turner.—DaC
  I think. J. Schuyler.—KoT
  The jungle husband. S. Smith.—HeR
  The king of cats sends a postcard to his wife.
    N. Willard.—HaOf
  Klabauterwife's letter. C. Morgenstern.—LiWa
  The letter. A. Tennyson.—KoT
  A letter from home. M. Oliver.—JaS
  Letter to a dead father. R. Shelton.—JaD
  Letter to a friend. L. Moore.—LiIl—MoSn
  Letter to a substitute teacher. G. Gildner.—JaPi
  Letter to statues. J. M. Brinnin.—PlEd
  Letters from Sicily. E. Di Pasquale.—LiIl
  Love letter. L. Pastan.—JaD
  Love letters, unmailed. E. Merriam.—JaD
  The river-merchant's wife, a letter ("While my
    hair was still cut straight across my
    forehead"). E. Pound.—HeR—KoT
  A Roman thank you letter. Martial.—HaO
  Sweetheart. P. Hey.—JaG

Life.—*Continued*

Delight of being alone. D. H. Lawrence.—PrBb
Departmental. R. Frost.—KoS
Disintegration. R. Shelton.—JaD
Dominique Blanco. M. Glenn.—GlC
Don't let me. A. Turner.—TuS
"Don't let my life grow dull, Lord." E. M. Shields.—LaT
The dream keeper. L. Hughes.—HuDk
Dreams ("Hold fast to dreams"). L. Hughes.—HuDk—LiSf—PrRh
The drum. N. Giovanni.—GiSp—LiSf
The dual site. M. Hamburger.—PlAs
Elegy for himself. C. Tichborne.—HeR
Even such is time. Sir W. Raleigh.—HeR
Fairy tale ("He built himself a house"). M. Holub.—HeR
Family reunion ("Sunlight glints off the chrome of many cars"). J. W. Miller.—JaS
"A father sees a son nearing manhood." C. Sandburg.—HoRa
"Fear no more the heat o' the sun." From Cymbeline. W. Shakespeare.—HeR—HoUn
"Fear no more the heat o' th' sun".—PlAs
Flux. R. Eberhart.—JaPi
For my father on his birthday. G. Kuzma.—JaS
For the moment. P. Reverdy.—KoT
"The force that through the green fuse drives the flower." D. Thomas.—HeR
Forget about it. R. Currie.—JaS
Full moon, rising. J. Holden.—JaG
Galente garden II. J. R. Jiménez.—LiWa
The gift. E. Ochester.—JaD—JaPi
Going in ("Every day alone whittles me"). M. Piercy.—JaD
Grammar lesson. L. Pastan.—JaPi
Grandma. A. Turner.—TuS
The grandmother. W. Berry.—JaD—PlSc
Happiness. W. Dickey.—JaPi
Happy thought. R. L. Stevenson.—ChG—PrRa—PrRh
He runs into an old acquaintance. A. Nowlan.—JaG
The heart's location. P. Meinke.—JaG
"I cannot grow." W. H. Auden.—HeR
"I have lived and I have loved." Unknown.—KoT
I know the rules. A. Adoff.—AdA
If ("If he could climb a tree"). N. Giovanni.—GiSp
If ("If the pie crust"). N. M. Bodecker.—BoPc
"If you are not." Mother Goose.—LoR
"In beauty may I walk." Unknown.—HeR
In school-days. J. G. Whittier.—HaOf
In the cafe. R. Borson.—JaPo
In time of 'the breaking of nations'. T. Hardy.—HeR
Incidents in the life of my uncle Arly. E. Lear.—LiH
Infant sorrow. W. Blake.—HeR
Irish wake. L. Hughes.—HuDk
Isabel Navarro. M. Glenn.—GlCd
"It is not growing like a tree." B. Jonson.—HeR
"It's such a little thing to weep." E. Dickinson.—HeR
Jay Stone. M. Glenn.—GlCd
Jigsaw puzzle. R. Hoban.—CoN
Joy. L. Hughes.—HuDk
The keeper. W. Carpenter.—JaPi
Laurie Allen. M. Glenn.—GlC
The leaden-eyed. V. Lindsay.—HeR
Letter to a friend. L. Moore.—LiIl—MoSn

Life song. Unknown, fr. the Flathead Indian.—BiSp
Lines for an old man. T. S. Eliot.—HeR
A little song of life. L. W. Reese.—HaOf
A living. D. H. Lawrence.—PrBb
The lockless door. R. Frost.—LiWa
A lone striker. R. Frost.—PlSc
Looking at quilts. M. Piercy.—PlSc
Lore. R. S. Thomas.—HeR
"A man of words and not of deeds." Mother Goose.—AlH—BlO
Mary Beth Collier. M. Glenn.—GlCd
The meeting. H. Moss.—JaG
The mill ("The spoiling daylight inched along the bar-top"). R. Wilbur.—JaPi
Minstrel man. L. Hughes.—HuDk
Miracles. W. Whitman.—LiSf
Mr. Kartoffel. J. Reeves.—PrRh
Monkeyland. S. Weöres.—HeR
Moonlight ("It will not hurt me when I am old"). S. Teasdale.—JaG
Morning light. E. Farjeon.—FaE
Mother to son. L. Hughes.—CoN—HaOf—HuDk—LiSf
A new pencil. E. Merriam.—MeF
1937 Ford convertible. T. McKeown.—JaPo
November. A. Cary.—HaOf
An old cat's confessions. C. P. Cranch.—HaOf
On learning to adjust to things. J. Ciardi.—HaOf—KeK
"Our revels now are ended." From The tempest. W. Shakespeare.—HeR
Pangur Ban. Unknown.—ChC—HeR
The passionate man's pilgrimage. Sir W. Raleigh.—HeR
Past ("I have all these parts stuffed in me"). A. Adoff.—AdA—JaT
People ("I like people quite well"). D. H. Lawrence.—PrBb
The pilgrim ("I fasted for some forty days on bread and buttermilk"). W. B. Yeats.—HeR
A plagued journey. M. Angelou.—AnS
The pretty ploughboy. Unknown.—PlAs
A psalm of life. H. W. Longfellow.—HaOf
Reflexes. M. Bell.—JaS
Religion. M. Malloy.—LaT
Return. M. Vinz.—JaG
The road not taken. R. Frost.—KoS
Routine. A. Guiterman.—PrRh—TrM
Russell Hodges. M. Glenn.—GlCd
Salt pilgrimage. Unknown, fr. the Papago Indian.—BiSp
Shirley and her son. N. Giovanni.—GiSp
Simhat Torah. R. H. Marks.—LiPj
Sketch ("Holding a picture up to the wall"). R. Farnsworth.—JaG
"So, we'll go no more a-roving." Lord Byron.—KoT
The soldiers returning. R. Shelton.—JaG
"Solomon Grundy." Mother Goose.—AlH—FaW—LoR—PrRh
Some night again. W. Stafford.—JaG
Some things are funny like that. N. Giovanni.—GiSp
A song ("I am of the earth and the earth is of me"). A. Adoff.—AdA
Song ("Lovely, dark, and lonely one"). L. Hughes.—HuDk
Song ("Wind and wave and star and sea"). D. McCord.—McAs
Song's eternity. J. Clare.—PlAs
Space. D. H. Lawrence.—PrBb

Life.—*Continued*

"Splashing water, lantern grass." Unknown.—DeD

Stark county holidays. M. Oliver.—JaS

Stars ("In science today we learned"). N. Giovanni.—GiSp—KeK

Statues. R. Wilbur.—PlEd

The statues in the public gardens. H. Nemerov.—PlEd

The stolen child. W. B. Yeats.—LiWa

Storm warnings. A. Rich.—JaG

Stupid old myself. R. Hoban.—PrRh

Terror. N. M. Bodecker.—BoPc

There isn't time. E. Farjeon.—FaE

There once was an owl. J. Ciardi.—LiSf

They ask, is God, too, lonely. C. Sandburg.—LiIl

Things I didn't know I loved. N. Hikmet.—McL

"This life." N. M. Bodecker.—BoPc

Thoughts on getting out of a nice warm bed in an ice cold house to go to the bathroom at three o'clock in the morning. J. Viorst.—ViI

Thumbprint ("Almost reluctant, we approach the block"). C. T. Wright.—JaPi

The time is. E. Merriam.—MeSk

To a blind student who taught me to see. S. Hazo.—JaG

To build a poem. C. E. Hemp.—JaG

To daffodils. R. Herrick.—KoT

To my children, fearing for them. W. Berry.—JaS

To the moon ("I remember, gracious, graceful moon"). G. Leopardi.—KoT

Today. F. O'Hara.—KoT

"Tomorrow, and tomorrow, and tomorrow." From Macbeth. W. Shakespeare.—HoUn

The top and the tip. C. Zolotow.—PrRa—ZoE

The toys talk of the world. K. Pyle.—HaOf

Transformations. T. Hardy.—HeR

Tree at my window. R. Frost.—KoS

Trees ("I am looking at trees"). W. S. Merwin.—JaPo

Trees ("To be a giant and keep quiet about it"). H. Nemerov.—JaPi

A true account of talking to the sun at Fire Island ("The sun woke me this morning loud"). F. O'Hara.—HeR—KoT

Uncle Claude. D. A. Evans.—JaS

Variations on a theme. M. Vinz.—JaPi

The village blacksmith. H. W. Longfellow.—HaOf

The village green. E. Farjeon.—FaE

The walnut tree. D. McCord.—HaOf

Warning to children. R. Graves.—BlO

The ways of living things. J. Prelutsky.—PrRh

"Well, so that is that, now we must dismantle the tree." From For the time being. W. H. Auden.—HaO

What grandma knew. E. Field.—JaPi

What there is. K. Patchen.—McL

"When that I was and a little tiny boy." From Twelfth night. W. Shakespeare.—HoUn

"The whole universe is full of God." Y. Emre.—McL

Why ("Fumble-John they call him"). A. Turner.—TuS

Why I never went into politics. R. Shelton.—JaS

The wicked hawthorn tree. W. B. Yeats.—LiWa

"The wind suffers of blowing." L. Riding.—HeR

Winding road. L. Moore.—MoSn

The woman cleaning lentils. Zehrd.—FaTh

Woman work. M. Angelou.—PlSc

Working girls. C. Sandburg.—PlSc

The writer. R. Wilbur.—JaS

The wrong start. M. Chute.—PrRh

Youth ("Is the ability to be"). R. Shelton.—JaD

Life—Conduct of life. See Conduct of life

Life—Life after death. See Immortality

"**Life** is peachy." See Nut

"**Life** is simple and gay." See For the moment

Life song. Unknown.—BiSp

"**Lift** your winter face." See Now that spring is here

Light

At sunrise. N. M. Bodecker.—BoPc

The bridge ("A bridge"). L. Moore.—MoSn

Caliban in the coal mines. L. Untermeyer.—LaT

The coming of light. M. Strand.—JaPo

December eclipse. M. Lockwood.—JaPi

Flashlight ("My flashlight tugs me"). J. Thurman.—BeD—LiSf

Fletcher Avenue. M. C. Livingston.—LiWo

Full moon, Santa Barbara. S. Teasdale.—HaOf

Leaves ("Now when a branch hangs out its leaves"). E. Farjeon.—FaE

Photographer. P. Booth.—PlEd

Poppies. R. Scheele.—JaPo

Prisms (altea). P. Dacey.—JaPi

Shimmerings. From A throw of threes. E. Merriam.—MeF

Sun on rain. L. Moore.—MoSn

Sun tiger. H. Behn.—HoCb

Sunflakes. F. Asch.—CoN

"There's a certain slant of light." E. Dickinson.—HeR

Tunnel ("Tunnel coming"). J. Thurman.—LiSf

Turner's sunrise. H. Bevington.—PlEd

Winter dark. L. Moore.—MoSn

Light another candle. Miriam Chaikin.—CoN

Light casualties. Robert Francis.—JaPo

The **light** heart. Eleanor Farjeon.—FaE

"The **light** in them stands as clear as water." See Poppies

"**Light** is a vehicle for shadows." See Wonders of the world

Light the festive candles for Hanukkah. Aileen Fisher.—PrRh

"**Light** the first of eight tonight." See Light the festive candles for Hanukkah

"**Light** the lamps up, lamplighter." Eleanor Farjeon.—FaE

"**Light** things falling, I think of rain." See Light casualties

"The **light** was burning very dim." See In the night

"A **light** white, a disgrace, an ink spot, a rosy charm." See A petticoat

Lighthouses

Flannan Isle. W. W. Gibson.—BlO

"I'd like to be a lighthouse." R. Field.—HoSe—PrRa

Skerryvore. R. L. Stevenson.—PlEd

Lighting a fire. X. J. Kennedy.—FaTh—KeF

Lightning. See Thunder and lightning

"The **lightning** and thunder." George MacDonald.—KeK

Lightning bugs. See Fireflies

"**Lightning** rides." P. Wolny.—JaPo

"**Lightning,** that's an old wives' tale." X. J. Kennedy.—KeB

Lights and lighting. See also Candles; Lighthouses

Lights and lighting.—*Continued*
City lights. R. Field.—PrRh
Flashlight ("My flashlight tugs me"). J. Thurman.—BeD—LiSf
"Light the lamps up, lamplighter." E. Farjeon.—FaE
The lights at night. E. Farjeon.—FaE
"Night settles on earth." From From an airplane. H. Behn.—HoSs
The oil lamp. W. J. Smith.—BrT
Where are you now. M. B. Miller.—PrRh
The **lights** at night. Eleanor Farjeon.—FaE
"**Like** a bird grown weak in a land." See Joy of an immigrant, a thanksgiving
Like a bug. Aileen Fisher.—FiW
"**Like** a drummer's brush." See Rain
"**Like** a nest." See Asparagus
"**Like** a quetzal plume, a fragrant flower." See Friendship
"**Like** liquid gold the wheat-field lies." See A Dakota wheat field
"**Like** pain of fire runs down my body my love to you." See Man's song
"**Like** rain it sounded till it curved." Emily Dickinson.—HeR
"**Like** rusted shower-heads at beach resorts." See Wintered sunflowers
"**Like** some kind of ruin, but domed." See In a museum cabinet
"**Like** the shore's alternation of door wave." See Crows
Likes and dislikes
Cat mystery. B. S. De Regniers.—DeT
Cats and dogs ("Some like cats, and some like dogs"). N. M. Bodecker.—PrRa
Egg thoughts, soft boiled. R. Hoban.—BeD—PrRh
   Soft boiled egg.—CoN
"Flowers are a silly bunch." A. Spilka.—PrRh
Giraffes. M. A. Hoberman.—LiSf
The health-food diner. M. Angelou.—AnS
"Hector Protector was dressed all in green." Mother Goose.—AlH—DeM—LoR
Horrible things. R. Fuller.—CoOu
I do not like the rat. J. Prelutsky.—PrNk
"I do not like thee, Doctor Fell." Mother Goose.—DeM—LoR
I don't like you. K. Wright.—CoOu
I'd never eat a beet. J. Prelutsky.—PrNk
James Petrie. M. Glenn.—GlCd
Keith Jordan. M. Glenn.—GlCd
The king's breakfast. A. A. Milne.—FaW—LiSf
"Molly, my sister, and I fell out." Mother Goose.—DeM
   "Mollie, my sister, and I fell out".—LoR
No ("No, I refuse to"). J. Viorst.—ViI
"Pease porridge hot." Mother Goose.—FaW—LiSf—LoR
People ("Some people talk and talk"). C. Zolotow.—PrRh—ZoE
Rainy day. W. Wise.—PrRa
"The reason I like chocolate." N. Giovanni.—PrRh
S. From A bestiary of the garden for children who should know better. P. Gotlieb.—DoNw
"There was a young lady of Kent." Unknown.—LiIl
Two people ("She reads the paper"). E. Merriam.—PrRh
Wanting. Unknown.—KeK
Weeds. C. Zolotow.—ZoE
When it come to bugs. A. Fisher.—FiW

With my foot in my mouth. D. Lee.—LiIl
"Xenobia Phobia." E. Merriam.—MeBl
Lil' bro'. Karama Fufuka.—PrRh
Lilies
Water lily. V. Worth.—WoSp
"**Lilla** was as fair a child." See The tale of Lilla
Lilliput. Eleanor Farjeon.—FaE
Limerick, Ireland (about)
Hail to the town of Limerick. L. Reed.—BrT
Limerick. See "There was an old person of Dean"
A **limerick** of frankness. X. Y. Z.—BrT
Limericks
An all American guard. Unknown.—BrT
The amorous señor. O. Nash.—BrT
Antonio. L. E. Richards.—BrT—HaOf—PrRh
An apple a day ("I must eat an apple, said Link"). L. Blair.—BrT
At a modernist school. M. Bishop.—BrT
An atrocious pun. Unknown.—BrT—PrRh
The autograph bore. O. Herford.—BrT
Bad manners. Unknown.—BrT
Ballet. Unknown.—BrT
The bath-bunny. From A baker's dozen of wild beasts. C. Wells.—HaOf
Beatnik limernik. N. R. Jaffray.—BrT
Beautiful Bella. Unknown.—BrT
A beggarly bear. C. Wells.—BrT
Bengal. Unknown.—CoOu
Beulah Louise. W. J. Smith.—BrT
"Blessed Lord, what it is to be young." D. McCord.—CoN—KeK
The bored ostrich. Unknown.—BrT
A brave knight. M. M. Dodge.—BrT
"A bridge engineer, Mister Crumpett." E. Lear.—KeK
Bruno. Unknown.—BrT
The careless zookeeper. Unknown.—BrT
The car's in the hall. M. Bishop.—BrT
A cat in despondency. Unknown.—PrRh
Caught stealing a dahlia. Unknown.—BrT
A certain young gourmet. C. C. Inge.—BrT
Church bells. B. Braley.—BrT
Cider inside her. Unknown.—BrT
Clumsy. J. B. Lee.—BrT
"A coloratura named Luna." J. F. Wilson.—BrT
The conservative owl. O. Herford.—BrT
The corn-pone-y. From A baker's dozen of wild beasts. C. Wells.—HaOf
A corpulent pig. M. Wood, and H. Wood.—BrT
The cream-puffin. From A baker's dozen of wild beasts. C. Wells.—HaOf
"Cried a man on the Salisbury Plain." M. C. Livingston.—KeK
Crockett. W. J. Smith.—BrT
The crocodile ("A crocodile once dropped a line"). O. Herford.—BrT—HaOf
The curate's cat. Unknown.—BrT
"Curiosity's not in me head." From On reading, four limericks. M. C. Livingston.—MeF
Curious Charlie. I. F. Bellows.—BrT
A difficult guest. C. W. Rankin.—BrT
Dirt dumping. M. Twain.—BrT
The disobliging bear. C. Wells.—BrT
The dizzy giraffe. Unknown.—BrT
Dizzy McPete. Unknown.—PaM
Double entendre. J. F. Wilson.—BrT
The dragon. C. Wells.—BrT
The Easter bunny. J. Ciardi.—LiE
Edser. S. Milligan.—BrT
The elephant and the giraffe. C. O. Carter.—BrT
"An elephant sat on some kegs." J. G. Francis.—BrT

Limericks—*Continued*

Skeleton and spirit. Unknown.—HoCr
The skunk to the gnu. G. Neyroud.—BrT
Sliding scale. N. R. Jaffray.—BrT
The smart little bear ("Teacher Bruin said, cub, bear in mind"). M. Fenderson.—BrT
Sole-hungering camel. O. Herford.—BrT
Spell it. Unknown.—BrT
A sporty young person. Unknown.—BrT
Squeaky shoes. Unknown.—BrT
Stop. L. Blair.—BrT
A strong feeling for poultry. R. J. Blount.—BrT
A strong minded lady. M. Bishop.—BrT
Such foolish old dames. S. S. Stinson.—BrT
The sultan. Unknown.—BrT
Suppressed. Unknown.—BrT
The surgeon and the ape. Unknown.—BrT
Table manners ("When you turn down your glass it's a sign"). J. M. Flagg.—BrT
Tact ("Quoth at me once, pray relieve"). O. Herford.—BrT
Tall. Unknown.—BrT
Tea by the sea. E. Lear.—BrT
The theater hat. C. Wells.—BrT
"There came an old woman from France." Mother Goose.—DeM
"There dwelt an old woman at Exeter." Mother Goose.—LoR
"There is a young lady, whose nose." E. Lear.—FaW—LiH
"There is a young reindeer named Donder." J. P. Lewis.—LiCp
"There was a cold pig from North Stowe." A. Lobel.—LoB
"There was a fair pig from Cohoes." A. Lobel.—LoB
"There was a fast pig from East Flushing." A. Lobel.—LoB
"There was a fat man of Bombay." Mother Goose.—LoR
"There was a fat pig from Savannah." A. Lobel.—LoB
"There was a light pig from Montclair." A. Lobel.—LiIl—LoB
"There was a loud pig from West Wheeling." A. Lobel.—LoB
"There was a pale pig from Spokane." A. Lobel.—LoB
"There was a plain pig, far from pretty." A. Lobel.—LoB
"There was a poor pig on the street." A. Lobel.—LoB
"There was a rich pig from Palm Springs." A. Lobel.—LoB
"There was a rude pig from Duluth." A. Lobel.—LoB
"There was a sad pig with a tail." A. Lobel.—LoB
"There was a shy pig by a wall." A. Lobel.—LoB
"There was a sick pig with a cold." A. Lobel.—LoB
"There was a slow pig from Decatur." A. Lobel.—LoB
"There was a small pig from Woonsocket." A. Lobel.—LoB
"There was a small pig who wept tears." A. Lobel.—LoB—PrRa
"There was a smart pig who was able." A. Lobel.—LoB
"There was a stout pig from Oak Ridge." A. Lobel.—LoB
"There was a strange pig in the park." A. Lobel.—LoB
"There was a tough pig from Pine Bluff." A. Lobel.—LoB
"There was a vague pig from Glens Falls." A. Lobel.—LoB
"There was a warm pig from Key West." A. Lobel.—LoB
"There was a wet pig from Fort Wayne." A. Lobel.—LoB
"There was a young belle of old Natchez." O. Nash.—KeK
"There was a young bugler named Breen." Unknown.—TrM
"There was a young farmer of Leeds." Mother Goose.—LoR
"There was a young lady from Lynn." Unknown.—KeK
 A young lady of Lynn ("There was a young lady of Lynn").—PrRh
"There was a young lady named Bright." Unknown.—LiSf
"There was a young lady of Bute." E. Lear.—LiH
"There was a young lady of Crete." Unknown.—CoOu
 A young lady of Crete.—BrT
"There was a young lady of Dorking." E. Lear.—LiH
"There was a young lady of Firle." E. Lear.—LiH
"There was a young lady of Greenwich." E. Lear.—LiH
"There was a young lady of Kent." Unknown.—LiIl
"There was a young lady of Niger." Unknown.—FaW
"There was a young lady of Norway." E. Lear.—FaW
"There was a young lady of Poole." E. Lear.—LiH
"There was a young lady of Portugal." E. Lear.—LiH
"There was a young lady of Turkey." E. Lear.—LiH
"There was a young lady of Twickenham." O. Herford.—KeK
"There was a young lady of Tyre." E. Lear.—LiH
 The young lady of Tyre.—BrT
"There was a young lady of Wales." E. Lear.—LiH
"There was a young lady of Welling." E. Lear.—LiH
"There was a young lady whose bonnet." E. Lear.—LiH
"There was a young lady whose chin." E. Lear.—LiH
"There was a young lady whose eyes." E. Lear.—LiH
"There was a young lady whose nose." E. Lear.—LiH
"There was a young man at St. Kitts." Mother Goose.—LoR
"There was a young man from the city." Unknown.—TrM
"There was a young man so benighted." Unknown.—TrM
"There was a young person in green." E. Lear.—LiH
"There was a young person in red." E. Lear.—LiH

Limericks—*Continued*

"There was a young person of Ayr." E. Lear.—KeK—LiH

"There was a young person of Crete." E. Lear.—LiH

"There was a young pig from Chanute." A. Lobel.—LoB

"There was a young pig from Moline." A. Lobel.—LoB

"There was a young pig from Nantucket." A. Lobel.—LoB

"There was a young pig from Schenectady." A. Lobel.—LoB

"There was a young pig who, in bed." A. Lobel.—LoB

"There was a young pig whose delight." A. Lobel.—LoB

"There was an old lady named Crockett." W. J. Smith.—KeK

"There was an old lady of Chertsey." E. Lear.—BlO—FaW

"There was an old lady of France." E. Lear.—LiH

"There was an old man at a junction." E. Lear.—LiH

"There was an old man from Peru." Unknown.—CoOu—KeK

An old man from Peru.—BrT—CoN

"There was an old man in a barge." E. Lear.—FaW—LiH—RuI

"There was an old man in a marsh." E. Lear.—LiH

"There was an old man in a tree." E. Lear.—LiH—LiH—LiH—LiSf

"There was an old man of Apulia." E. Lear.—LiH

"There was an old man of Blackheath." E. Lear.—LiH

"There was an old man of Bohemia." E. Lear.—LiH

"There was an old man of Calcutta." E. Lear.—LiH

"There was an old man of Cape Horn." E. Lear.—LiH

"There was an old man of Coblenz." E. Lear.—LiH

"There was an old man of Dee-side." E. Lear.—LiH

"There was an old man of Dumblane." E. Lear.—LiH

"There was an old man of Dumbree." E. Lear.—LiH

"There was an old man of Dunluce." E. Lear.—LiH

"There was an old man of Dunrose." E. Lear.—LiH

"There was an old man of El Hums." E. Lear.—LiH

"There was an old man of Hong Kong." E. Lear.—LiH

"There was an old man of Kilkenny." E. Lear.—LiH

"There was an old man of Melrose." E. Lear.—LiH

"There was an old man of Messina." E. Lear.—LiH

"There was an old man of Thames Ditton." E. Lear.—LiH

"There was an old man of the Hague." E. Lear.—LiH—LiSf

The old man of the Hague.—BrT

"There was an old man of the isles." E. Lear.—LiH

"There was an old man of the Nile." E. Lear.—FaW

An old man of the Nile.—BrT

"There was an old man of the South." E. Lear.—LiH

"There was an old man of the West." E. Lear.—LiH

"There was an old man of Thermopylae." E. Lear.—FaW

"There was an old man of Tobago." Mother Goose.—LoR

"There was an old man of Toulouse." E. Lear.—LiH

"There was an old man of West Dumpet." E. Lear.—LiH

"There was an old man of Whitehaven." E. Lear.—LiH

"There was an old man on a hill." E. Lear.—LiH

"There was an old man on the border." E. Lear.—LiH

"There was an old man, on whose nose." E. Lear.—LiH

"There was an old man who said, how." E. Lear.—BlO

"There was an old man who said, hush." E. Lear.—KeK—LiH

"There was an old man who said, well." E. Lear.—LiH—LiSf

"There was an old man whose despair." E. Lear.—LiH

"There was an old man with a beard." E. Lear.—CoOu—FaW—LiH—LiSf—PrRh

Old man with a beard.—CoN

"There was an old man with a beard, who sat." E. Lear.—LiH

"There was an old man with a flute." E. Lear.—LiH

"There was an old man with a gong." E. Lear.—LiH

The old man with a gong.—BrT

"There was an old man with a nose." E. Lear.—LiH

"There was an old person of Anerley." E. Lear.—LiH

"There was an old person of Bangor." E. Lear.—LiH

"There was an old person of Bar." E. Lear.—LiH

"There was an old person of Bree." E. Lear.—LiH

"There was an old person of Brigg." E. Lear.—LiH

"There was an old person of Bromley." E. Lear.—LiH

"There was an old person of Bude." E. Lear.—LiH

"There was an old person of Cassel." E. Lear.—LiH

"There was an old person of Chili." E. Lear.—LiH

"There was an old person of Crowle." E. Lear.—LiH

"There was an old person of Deal." E. Lear.—LiH

"There was an old person of Dean." E. Lear.—BlO—FaTh—LiH

Limerick.—HoMu

"There was an old person of Down." E. Lear.—LiH

Limericks—*Continued*

"There was an old person of Dutton." E. Lear.—LiH

"There was an old person of Ems." E. Lear.—LiH

"There was an old person of Ewell." E. Lear.—LiH
Rice and mice.—BrT

"There was an old person of Fife." E. Lear.—LiH

"There was an old person of Filey." E. Lear.—LiH

"There was an old person of Grange." E. Lear.—LiH

"There was an old person of Gretna." E. Lear.—LiH

"There was an old person of Hurst." E. Lear.—LiH

"There was an old person of Hyde." E. Lear.—LiH

"There was an old person of Ibreem." E. Lear.—LiH

"There was an old person of Jodd." E. Lear.—LiH

"There was an old person of Mold." E. Lear.—LiH

"There was an old person of Newry." E. Lear.—LiH

"There was an old person of Nice." E. Lear.—LiH

"There was an old person of Peru." E. Lear.—LiH

"There was an old person of Pett." E. Lear.—LiH

"There was an old person of Philoe." E. Lear.—LiH

"There was an old person of Pinner." E. Lear.—LiH

"There was an old person of Rheims." E. Lear.—LiH

"There was an old person of Sestri." E. Lear.—LiH

"There was an old person of Skye." E. Lear.—KeK—LiH

"There was an old person of Spain." E. Lear.—LiH

"There was an old person of Tring." E. Lear.—LiH
An old person of Tring.—BrT (unat.)

"There was an old person of Ware." E. Lear.—LiH
An old person of Ware.—PrRa

"There was an old person of Wilts." E. Lear.—LiH

"There was an old person of Woking." E. Lear.—LiH

"There was an old person whose habits." E. Lear.—LiH
Hurtful habits.—BrT

"There was an old pig from New York." A. Lobel.—LoB

"There was an old pig from South Goshen." A. Lobel.—LoB

"There was an old pig from Van Nuys." A. Lobel.—LoB

"There was an old pig in a chair." A. Lobel.—LoB

"There was an old pig with a clock." A. Lobel.—LoB

"There was an old pig with a pen." A. Lobel.—LoB—LoB

"There was an old soldier of Bister." Mother Goose.—LoR

"There was an old woman of Gloucester." Mother Goose.—LoR

"There was an old woman of Harrow." Mother Goose.—LoR

"There was an old woman of Surrey." Mother Goose.—LoR

"There were once two cats of Kilkenny." Mother Goose.—DeM
The cats of Kilkenny.—PrRh
The Kilkenny cats ("There wanst was two cats in Kilkenny").—ChC

"There's wonderful family called Stein." Unknown.—TrM

The thoroughbred horse. O. Herford.—BrT

A thrifty soprano. O. Nash.—BrT

A thrifty young fellow. Unknown.—BrT

Tired of waiting. Unknown.—BrT

'Tis strange. E. Field.—BrT

A token of attachment. J. A. Strawson.—BrT

Too much. Unknown.—BrT

Tra-la-larceny. O. Herford.—BrT

A troupial. M. Brackcr.—BrT

The twins ("When twins came, their father, Dan Dunn"). B. Braley.—BrT

Two jays at St. Louis. F. G. Christgau.—BrT

Uncertain what to wear. W. J. Smith.—BrT

A vaporish maiden. M. Bishop.—BrT

A very polite man. Unknown.—BrT

A warning ("I know a young girl who can speak"). M. A. Webber.—BrT

Weeping ash. M. C. Livingston.—LiMp

A well informed wight. O. Herford.—BrT

A what-is-it. R. M. Stuart, and A. B. Paine.—BrT

When a jolly young fisher. Unknown.—RuI

"When I sat next the Duchess at tea." Unknown.—TrM

Who's next. Unknown.—BrT

The wild boarder. K. Cox.—BrT

A wild worm. C. Wells.—BrT

Wilhelmj. R. J. Burdette.—BrT

"A woman named Mrs. S. Claus." J. P. Lewis.—LiCp

The yak ("There was a most odious yak"). T. Roethke.—LiSf

A young curate of Kidderminster. Unknown.—BrT

A young fellow from Boise. J. Straley.—BrT

A young fellow named Shear. J. Ciardi.—BrT

A young girl of Asturias. Unknown.—BrT

A young lady from Cork. O. Nash.—BrT

A young lady from Delaware. Unknown.—BrT

A young lady named Sue. Unknown.—BrT

A young lady of Ealing. Unknown.—BrT

A young lady of Munich. Unknown.—BrT

A young lady of Oakham. Unknown.—BrT

A young lady of Wilts. Unknown.—BrT

A young man on a journey. Unknown.—BrT

A young man who loved rain. W. J. Smith.—BrT

"A young person of precious precocity." From On reading, four limericks. M. C. Livingston.—MeF

A young school mistress. Unknown.—BrT

Zephyr. Unknown.—BrT

"The **limits** of the sphere of dream." From Faust. Johann Wolfgang von Goethe, tr. by Percy Bysshe Shelley.—LiWa

Lim'ricks and puns. Unknown.—BrT

Lincoln, Abraham (about)
Abraham Lincoln 1809-1865. S. V. Benét, and R. C. Benét.—LiSf
Lincoln. N. B. Turner.—PrRh
Lincoln monument, Washington. L. Hughes.—HuDk
Lincoln Park. M. C. Livingston.—LiWo
Nancy Hanks, 1784-1818. S. V. Benét, and R. C. Benét.—CoN
O captain, my captain. W. Whitman.—HaOf
Presidents' day. M. C. Livingston.—LiCe
"When lilacs last in the dooryard bloom'd." W. Whitman.—HeR
Lincoln. Nancy Byrd Turner.—PrRh
Lincoln monument, Washington. Langston Hughes.—HuDk
Lincoln Park. Myra Cohn Livingston.—LiWo
"Lincoln was a long man." See Abraham Lincoln 1809-1865
Lindsay, Vachel
An explanation of the grasshopper.—PrRa
"Factory windows are always broken."—HaOf
The flower-fed buffaloes.—HaOf—HeR
"The king of the yellow butterflies."—HaOf
The leaden-eyed.—HeR
The little turtle.—CoN—FrP—HaOf—LiSf—PrRa
"The moon's the north wind's cooky."—CoN—HaOf—LaW—LiSf—PrRa—PrRh
The mysterious cat.—HaOf—LiSf
The potatoes dance.—LiSf
The sea serpent chantey.—LiWa
The sorceress.—LiWa
Lineage. Margaret Walker.—StG
Lines for a friend who left. John Logan.—JaD
Lines for an old man. Thomas Stearns Eliot.—HeR
Lines on a small potato. Margaret Fishback.—HoDi
Lines written for Gene Kelly to dance to, sels. Carl Sandburg
"Spring is when the grass turns green and glad".—HoRa
Link, Lenore M.
Holding hands.—CoN—PrRa—PrRh
Link rhymes. See Build-on rhymes
"The lion." See Lion
Lion ("The lion"). N. M. Bodecker.—BoSs
The **lion** ("The lion has a golden mane"). Jack Prelutsky.—PrRh—PrZ
Lion ("The lion, ruler over all the beasts"). William Jay Smith.—PrRh
The **lion** ("The lion, the lion, he dwells in the waste"). Hilaire Belloc.—FaW
"The **lion** and the unicorn." Mother Goose.—AlH—DaC—DeM—FaW
The **lion** for real. Allen Ginsberg.—HeR
"The **lion** has a golden mane." See The lion
"Lion-hunger, tiger-leap!" See The way of Cape Race
"The **lion,** ruler over all the beasts." See Lion
"The **lion,** the lion, he dwells in the waste." See The lion
Lions
An accommodating lion. T. Jenks.—HaOf
"Clara, little curlylocks." A. Lobel.—LoWr
Jim, who ran away from his nurse, and was eaten by a lion. H. Belloc.—LiSf
Lion ("The lion"). N. M. Bodecker.—BoSs
The lion ("The lion has a golden mane"). J. Prelutsky.—PrRh—PrZ

Lion ("The lion, ruler over all the beasts"). W. J. Smith.—PrRh
The lion ("The lion, the lion, he dwells in the waste"). H. Belloc.—FaW
"The lion and the unicorn." Mother Goose.—AlH—DaC—DeM—FaW
The lion for real. A. Ginsberg.—HeR
The musical lion. O. Herford.—BrT—HaOf
"On Halloween, when ghosts go boo." X. J. Kennedy.—KeB
"There was a young man from the city." Unknown.—TrM
Tutankhamen. W. Dickey.—JaPi
Lipsitz, Lou
Winter twilight.—JaG
Lisa Goodman. Mel Glenn.—GlC
"Listen." See Spectacular
"Listen." Lilian Moore.—CoN
"Listen, children, listen, won't you come into the night." See Who calls
"Listen my children, and you shall hear." See Paul Revere's ride
"Listen, my dream." See Medicine man's prayer
"Listen, O now you are coming in rut, ha, I am exceedingly." See This is to frighten a storm
"Listen, that's mother singing and playing." See After tea
"Listen, the hay bells tinkle as the cart." See The holy innocents
"Listen to a cornstalk." See Corn talk
"Listen to me, as when ye heard our father." See Canadian boat-song
The **listeners.** Walter De la Mare.—LiWa
Listening. Aileen Fisher.—CoN
Listening to Beethoven on the Oregon coast. Henry Carlile.—JaPi
Listening to grownups quarreling. Ruth Whitman.—CoN—KeK
Litany. Langston Hughes.—LaT
Litter. See Garbage
Little ("I am the sister of him"). Dorothy Aldis.—CoN
Little ("Little wind little sun"). David McCord.—McAs
"Little baby, full of glee." Unknown.—DeD
"Little baby, lay your head." See Good night
"Little Betty Blue lost her holiday shoe." Mother Goose.—DeM—LoR
Little Billee. William Makepeace Thackeray.—BlO
Little bird ("Little bird, little bird"). Julia Cunningham.—FaTh
Little bird ("Little hurt bird"). Charlotte Zolotow.—ZoE
"Little bird, little bird." See Little bird
Little bird ("Once I saw a little bird"). Mother Goose.—ChG
"Once I saw a little bird".—DeM—FrP
The **little** birds. Unknown.—CoN
"The little birds sit in their nest and beg." See The little birds
"Little bit o' bread and no cheese." See Yellowhammer
"Little bits of soft boiled egg." Fay Maschler.—PrRh
"Little black bug." Margaret Wise Brown.—CoN—FrP
"Little black dog." See Little short legs
"A little black thing among the snow." See The chimney sweeper
"The little blessed Earth that turns." See O earth, turn!

"A **little** blood, more or less, he said." See Great and strong

"**Little** Blue Ben." Mother Goose.—BlQ—DeM

"**Little** Bo-Peep has lost her sheep." Mother Goose.—DeM—LoR

"The **little** boat at anchor." See Fourth of July night

"Der **little** boids is on der wing." Unknown.—TrM

The **little** boy and the old man. Shel Silverstein.—PrRh

Little boy blue. Eugene Field.—HaOf

"**Little** Boy Blue, come blow your horn." Mother Goose.—LoR

"A **little** boy, laid sick and low." See The dying child's request

"A **little** boy stood on the corner." See December

"The **little** boy was looking for his voice." See The little mute boy

"**Little** boys and little maidens." See Little catkins

The **little** brother poem. Naomi Shihab Nye.—JaS

Little brother puts his doll to sleep. Charlotte Pomerantz.—PoA

A **little** brown bird. Mother Goose.—BlPi

"A **little** brown bird built a little brown nest." See A little brown bird

The **little** brown celery. George MacBeth.—FaTh

"**Little** brown house mouse, laugh and leap." See The house mouse

"A **little** buoy said, Mother, deer." See A misspelled tail

"A **little** bush." See Little bush

Little bush. Elizabeth Madox Roberts.—LiSf

The **little** cat. Unknown, tr. by Helen Waddell.—ChC

"The **little** caterpillar creeps." See Cocoon

Little catkins. Alexander Blok, tr. by Babette Deutsch.—LiE

"The **little** chicks say, peep, peep, peep." See The chicks

"**Little** child, your mother's breasts are full of milk." See Words to a sick child

"**Little** children far away." See Near and far

"**Little** Clotilda." Unknown.—PrRh

"A **little** cock sparrow sat on a green tree." Mother Goose.—LoR

"A little cock sparrow sat on a tree".—DaC

"A **little** cock sparrow sat on a tree". See "A little cock sparrow sat on a green tree"

"**Little** crocus." See Crocus

Little Dimity. William Jay Smith.—LiSf

Little donkey close your eyes. Margaret Wise Brown.—LaW

"**Little** donkey on the hill." See Little donkey close your eyes

"**Little** drop of dew." See A dewdrop

"**Little** drops of water". See Little things ("Little drops of water")

Little elegy. Elinor Wylie.—LiIl

The **little** elf. John Kendrick Bangs.—CoN—HaOf—PrRa

The **little** elfman. See The little elf

The **little** elfman. See The little elf

The **little** factory girl to a more fortunate playmate. Unknown.—PlSc

"**Little** fellow, you're amusing." See Song of the ogres

Little fish ("Little fish move in the water, swim, swim, swim"). Unknown.—GrT

Little fish ("The tiny fish enjoy themselves"). David Herbert Lawrence.—HeR—KoT—PrBb

"The **little** fish are silent." See Fish

"**Little** fish move in the water, swim, swim, swim." See Little fish

"**Little** flocks of peaceful clouds." See The black cloud

"**Little** fly." See The fly

"A **little** forward a little back." See Ways of winding a watch

Little frog tail. Unknown.—GrT

"**Little** girl, be careful what you say." Carl Sandburg.—HoRa

"A **little** girl called Sile Javotte." See Christmas 1970

A **little** girl I hate. See "I saw a little girl I hate"

"**Little** girl, little girl, where have you been." Mother Goose.—AlH—DeM

"The **little** girl saw her first troop parade and asked." Carl Sandburg.—HoRa

"A **little** girl says." See A date

The **little** Hiawatha. From The song of Hiawatha. Henry Wadsworth Longfellow.—CoOu

The **little** hill. Harry Behn.—HoCb

"**Little** hurt bird." See Little bird

"**Little** Jack Horner." Mother Goose.—DeM—FaW—LoR

"**Little** Jack Sprat." Mother Goose.—BlQ

"The **little** Jesus came to town." See A Christmas folk song

"**Little** Jesus, sweetly sleep, do not stir." See The rocking carol

"**Little** jewel, stop crying." See Cradlesong for Ahuitzotl

Little jumping Joan. See "Here am I, little jumping Joan"

"A **little** kid." See Halloween

"**Little** King Boggen, he built a fine hall." Mother Goose.—BlPi—LoR

"**Little** King Pippin." Mother Goose.—DeM

"**Little** lad, little lad." See Towards Babylon

"**Little** ladybug." See Ladybug

"**Little** lamb, who made thee." See The lamb

"A **little** light is going by." See Firefly

"**Little**, littler, littlest sprite." See Elf

The **little** maid. Anna Maria Wells.—HaOf

The **little** man ("As I was walking up the stair"). Hughes Mearns.—PrRh

I met a man ("As I was going up the stair").—CoOu (unat.)

The **little** man and maid. Unknown.—DaC

"**Little** marble boy." James Wright.—PlEd

"**Little** Mary Bell had a fairy in a nut." See Long John Brown and little Mary Bell

"**Little** Miss Lily." Mother Goose.—LoR

"**Little** Miss Muffet." Mother Goose.—DeM—FaW—LiSf—LoR

"**Little** Miss Muffet discovered a tuffet." See The embarrassing episode of Little Miss Muffet

"**Little** Miss Tucket." Mother Goose.—LoR

"A **little** monkey goes like a donkey that means to say." See A dog

A **little** more cider. Unknown.—KeK

The **little** mute boy. Federico García Lorca, tr. by William Stanley Merwin.—HeR

"**Little** Nanny Etticoat." Mother Goose.—DeM—LiSf—LoR

"The **little** old-fashioned girl." See At grandfather's

The **little** old lady. Unknown.—GrT

"A **little** old woman." See Behind the waterfall

"A **little** old woman." See Good neighbors

"**Little** orange cat." Charlotte Zolotow.—ZoE

Little orphant Annie. James Whitcomb Riley.—HaOf

"**Little** orphant Annie's come to our house to stay." See Little orphant Annie

"**Little** pictures." Arnold Lobel.—LoWr

"**Little** pink pig in Arkansas." Jack Prelutsky.—PrRi

The **little** plant. Unknown.—BlPi

"**Little** Poll Parrot." Mother Goose.—DeM

The parrot in the garret.—BlPi

"**Little** Polly Flinders." Mother Goose.—AlH—DeM—FaW—LoR

"**Little** poppies, little hell flames." See Poppies in July

"A **little** puff boat." See Out for a ride

"**Little** Queen Pippin once built a hotel." Mother Goose.—BlPi

"**Little** Robin Redbreast." Mother Goose.—DaC

"A **little** saint best fits a little shrine." See A ternary of littles, upon a pipkin of jelly sent to a lady

"A **little** seed." See Maytime magic

Little seeds. Else Holmelund Minarik.—PrRa

"**Little** seeds we sow in spring." See Little seeds

"**Little** ships must keep the shore." Mother Goose.—LoR

Little short legs. Cynthia Rylant.—RyW

"**Little** silk worms, if you please." Unknown.—DeD

Little snail. Hilda Conkling.—LiSf

A **little** song of life. Lizette Woodworth Reese.—HaOf

"A **little** sparrow." See First surf

"**Little** square of earth." See Undefeated

A **little** talk. Unknown.—PrRa

Little talk. Aileen Fisher.—FiW

"**Little** Tee Wee." Mother Goose.—DeM—FaW—LoR—RuI

Little things, importance of
  Answers. A. Fisher.—LiSf
  Fable ("The mountain and the squirrel"). R. W. Emerson.—HaOf
  "Flower in the crannied wall." A. Tennyson.—FaTh
  For silence. R. Bond.—LaT
  "For want of a nail the shoe was lost." Mother Goose.—FaW—LoR
  Gnat on my paper. R. Eberhart.—JaD
  Green stems. M. W. Brown.—PrRh
  "Hurt no living thing." C. G. Rossetti.—FaTh—HoSu—PrRh
  Interlude. K. Shapiro.—JaD
  Lilliput. E. Farjeon.—FaE
  Lines on a small potato. M. Fishback.—HoDi
  Little ("Little wind little sun"). D. McCord.—McAs
  Little things ("Little things, that run, and quail"). J. Stephens.—FaTh—LaT—LiSf—PrRh
  Little things ("Little drops of water"). J. A. Carney.—DaC
    "Little drops of water".—LoR (unat.)
  "The lowest of trees have tops, the ant her gall." Sir E. Dyer.—HeR
  The minimal. T. Roethke.—FaTh—HeR
  Mushrooms. S. Plath.—HeR
  Oz. E. Merriam.—MeSk
  "Please God, take care of little things." E. Farjeon.—LaT
  The red wheelbarrow. W. C. Williams.—KoT
  "(Sitting in a tree)." E. E. Cummings.—FaTh
  A ternary of littles, upon a pipkin of jelly sent to a lady. R. Herrick.—KoT

Tittle and jot, jot and tittle. E. Merriam.—MeSk

"To see a world in a grain of sand." From Auguries of innocence. W. Blake.—PrRh
  To see a world.—KeK

Under the ground. R. W. Bacmeister.—PrRa

Little things ("Little things, that run, and quail"). James Stephens.—FaTh—LaT—LiSf—PrRh

Little things ("Little drops of water"). Julia A. Carney.—DaC

"**Little** drops of water".—LoR (unat.)

"**Little** things that crawl and creep." See Green stems

"**Little** things, that run, and quail." See Little things

"**Little** Tom Tucker." Mother Goose.—AlH

"**Little** Tommy Tittlemouse." Mother Goose.—AlH—BlPi—DeM—FaW—LoR

"**Little** Tommy Tucker." Mother Goose.—DeM—FaW—LoR

Little tortillas. Unknown.—GrT

"**Little** tortillas for Mama." See Little tortillas

"The **little** toy dog is covered with dust." See Little boy blue

"**Little** tree." Edward Estlin Cummings.—CoN—HaO—LiSf

"**Little** trees like pencil strokes." See Scene

Little trotty wagtail. John Clare.—BlO—CoOu—HeR

"**Little** trotty wagtail, he went in the rain." See Little trotty wagtail

The **little** turtle. Vachel Lindsay.—CoN—FrP—HaOf—LiSf—PrRa

"**Little** white boats." See The boats

"The **little** white mermaidens live in the sea." See The mermaidens

Little wind. Kate Greenaway.—PrRa

"**Little** wind, blow on the hill-top." See Little wind

"**Little** wind little sun." See Little

Littledale, Freya
  "When my dog died."—CoN

"**Live** lizard, dead lizard." See Witches' menu

"**Lives** in winter." Mother Goose.—CoN—LiSf

Livesay, Dorothy
  Abracadabra.—DoNw

A **living**. David Herbert Lawrence.—PrBb

"**Living** over a garage." See Mr. Dill

Living tenderly. May Swenson.—HaOf

Living with children. Jim Wayne Miller.—JaG

Livings, sels. Philip Larkin
  "Seventy feet down".—HeR

Livingston, Myra Cohn
  An angry valentine.—LiVp
  April fool.—LiCe
  At Hannukah.—LiSf
  Aunt Evelyn.—LiWo
  Aunt Flora (envoi).—LiWo
  Aunt Ruth.—LiWo
  Aunts and uncles.—LiWo
  "Autumn calls the winning toss, passes for a gain."—LiCs
  "Autumn leaves a fringe of frost when pumpkins turn to gold."—LiCs
  "Autumn scuffs across the earth, leaves it patched and brown."—LiCs
  Bald cypress.—LiMp
  Basket.—LiWo
  Bats ("Versa says").—LiWo
  Beech, to owl.—LiMp
  Bert.—LiWo
  Big house.—LiWo
  Birches, Doheny Road.—LiMp

Livingston, Myra Cohn—*Continued*
Birthday ("When he asked for the moon").—
  LiCe
Box, for L.M.B.—LiMp
Bristlecone pine.—LiMp
Car wash.—CoN—HoCl
Christmas eve ("He is coming").—LiCe
Christmas play.—LiWo
Clouds ("Today").—LiSi
Columbus day.—LiCe
Coming from Kansas.—LiWo
Coming storm.—LiSi
Construction ("And every time I pass").—HoSs
Construction job.—HoCl
"Cried a man on the Salisbury Plain."—KeK
"Curiosity's not in me head." See On reading,
  four limericks
The dark ("It's always").—LiWo
Dinosaurs ("Their feet, planted into tar").—
  HoDi
Doll.—LiWo
Douglas fir.—LiMp
Down on my tummy.—HoSi
Downpour.—HoSu
Dream ("The sandman put it in his sack").—
  LaW
Easter, for Penny.—LiCe
Elm ("Let them").—LiMp
English oak.—LiMp
Father ("Carrying my world").—CoN
Flame of the forest, midnight.—LiMp
Fletcher Avenue.—LiWo
For Laura.—HoBf
For Mugs.—HoDl
Forest: an invitation.—LiMp
"Four-way stop."—KeK
Fourth of July ("Hurrah for the fourth of
  July").—LiCe
From Council Bluffs to Omaha.—LiWo
"Grandfather."—LiWo
Grandfather clock.—LiWo
"The grandfather I never knew."—LiWo
The gypsies.—LiWo
Halloween ("Green cat eyes").—LiCe
Harney Street.—LiWo
The hill.—LiWo
History ("And I'm thinking how to get out").—
  PrRh
Horse chestnut.—LiMp
Hungry morning.—HoSi
"If you don't know the meaning of snook." See
  On reading, four limericks
"If you're apt to be ravenous, look." See On
  reading, four limericks
"In quiet night."—LaW
Indian of the plains.—LiWo
Irish yew.—LiMp
Jacaranda.—FaTh—LiMp
Just watch.—PrRa
King palm.—LiMp
Kittens.—LiWo
Labor day.—LiCe
"Lazy witch."—PrRh
Lemonade stand.—LiWo
"Lena."—LiWo
Lincoln Park.—LiWo
Lonesome.—LiIl
Making a friend.—HoDl
Maple.—LiMp
The marionettes.—LiWo
Martin Luther King.—LiSf—PrRh
Martin Luther King day.—LiCe
"Mary Lorenz."—LiWo

Math class.—FaTh
May Day.—LiWo
Memorial day.—LiCe
Mimosa.—LiMp
Mr. Pratt.—PrRh
The monkey puzzle.—LiMp
Monterey cypress, Point Lobos.—LiMp
Moon ("Why is").—LiSi
Morning sky.—LiSi
Mosquitoes ("Out on the porch").—LiWo
Mother's garden.—LiWo
My cousins' dollhouse.—LiWo
My dog ("He didn't bark at anything").—HoSu
My star.—LaW
"My valentine."—LiCe
Nanny.—LiWo
New planting, shopping mall.—LiMp
New year's eve.—LiCe
New year's eve, Opelousas, Louisiana ("Every
  one on Franklin Street").—LiNe
New year's eve, Opelousas, Louisiana
  ("Everyone on Franklin Street").—LiNe
"The night."—LaW
Noon.—LiSi
Old Sam.—LiWo
On reading, four limericks, complete.
    "Curiosity's not in me head".—MeF
    "If you don't know the meaning of
      snook".—MeF—MeF
    "If you're apt to be ravenous, look".—
      MeF—MeF
    "A young person of precious precocity".—
      MeF
Party.—LiWo
Passover.—LiCe
A penny valentine, tr. by.—LiVp
The planets.—LiSi
Poor.—KeK
Prayer ("Thank you for the sun").—LaT
Presidents' day.—LiCe
Rain ("Some nights").—LiSi
Rain forest, Papua, New Guinea.—LiMp
Reflections ("In the mirror").—FrP
Saint Patrick's day.—LiCe
Saturday.—LiWo
Secret door.—LiWo
Secret passageway.—LiWo
74th Street.—LiSf
Shagbark hickory.—LiMp
Shell ("When it was time").—LiWo
Shooting stars.—LiSi
Sierra redwoods, highway 101.—LiMp
Silver maple.—LiMp
Sleep over.—LiWo
Smog.—LiSi
Snow ("Trembling").—LiSi
"Spring brings out her baseball bat, swings it
  through the air."—LiCs
"Spring pipes at the peeper frogs, mocks the
  mockingbird."—LiCs
"Spring skips lightly on a thin crust of
  snow."—LiCs
"Spring skips lightly on a thin crust of snow,
  pokes her."—LiCs
Stars ("No one").—LiSi
Storm ("You must").—LiSi
"Summer blasts off fireworks, fuses them with
  red."—LiCs
"Summer fattens melons up, grow berries plump
  and sweet."—LiCs
"Summer wades the waters where distant
  islands gleam."—LiCs
Sunset ("Now you").—LiSi

Lobsters
  The lobsters and the fiddler crab. F. J. Forster.—PrRh
  The lobsters and the fiddler crab. Frederick J. Forster.—PrRh
  "The lobsters came ashore one night." See The lobsters and the fiddler crab
"The local groceries are all out of broccoli." See Song against broccoli
Lochinvar. Sir Walter Scott.—PlAs
"Lock the place in your heart." Zindzi Mandela.—McL
Locked doors. From A throw of threes. Eve Merriam.—MeF
"Locked up, inside." See Feline
The **lockless** door. Robert Frost.—LiWa
Locklin, Gerald
  Poop ("My daughter, Blake, is in kindergarten").—JaS
  Since you seem intent.—JaG
Locksley Hall, sels. Alfred Tennyson
  "Make me feel the wild pulsation that I felt before the strife".—PlSc
Lockwood, Margo
  December eclipse.—JaPi
  Victorian grandmother.—JaPi
  Wind flowers.—JaD
The **locust.** Unknown, tr. by A. Marre Trask and Willard R. Trask.—HeR
The **locust** tree in flower. William Carlos Williams.—KoT
Locusts
  The locust. Unknown.—HeR
  "The locusts' wings say, throng, throng." From Blessings on gentle folk. Unknown.—StG
  "The locusts' wings say, throng, throng." From Blessings on gentle folk. Unknown, tr. by Arthur Waley.—StG
Loewinsohn, Ron
  My sons.—JaD
"The **loft.**" See Loft
Loft. Sylvia Cassedy.—CaR
Logan, John
  Lines for a friend who left.—JaD
  On the house of a friend.—JaD
Lollocks. Robert Graves.—HeR
London, England
  Buckingham Palace. A. A. Milne.—FaW
  The city show. E. Farjeon.—FaE
  Composed upon Westminster bridge, Sept. 3, 1802. W. Wordsworth.—PlEd
    Composed on Westminster bridge.—LiSf
  Homage to Wren. L. MacNeice.—PlEd
  The lights at night. E. Farjeon.—FaE
  London. W. Blake.—HeR
  "London Bridge is falling down." Mother Goose.—PlEd
    "London bridge is broken down".—LoR
London. William Blake.—HeR
"**London** bridge is broken down". See "London Bridge is falling down"
"**London** Bridge is falling down." Mother Goose.—PlEd
  "London bridge is broken down".—LoR
London sparrow. Eleanor Farjeon.—FaE
Lone dog ("I'm a lean dog, a keen dog, a wild dog, and lone"). Irene Rutherford McLeod.—HoDl—LiSf—PrRh
A **lone** striker. Robert Frost.—PlSc
Loneliness
  Absence ("Lamplight lies in a ring"). P. Meinke.—JaPo
  Absent friend. C. Zolotow.—ZoE

Acquainted with the night. R. Frost.—KoS
Alone ("I was alone the other day"). D. Aldis.—FaW
The apparition. T. Roethke.—PlAs
Arm wrestling with my father. J. Driscoll.—JaG
Bound no'th blues. L. Hughes.—HuDk
Bundles. C. Sandburg.—HoRa
"Calico pie." E. Lear.—BlO—LiH
Canticle. D. Shapiro.—KoT
Charlotte Bronte. S. Coolidge.—HaOf
The courtship of the Yonghy-Bonghy-Bo. E. Lear.—LiH
The cricket kept the house. E. M. Thomas.—HaOf
Dear reader. P. Meinke.—JaPi
The departure. F. Steele.—JaG—JaPo
Desert places. R. Frost.—HeR
Disintegration. R. Shelton.—JaD
A dog ("I am alone"). C. Zolotow.—HoDl
Dominique Blanco. M. Glenn.—GlC
The dong with a luminous nose. E. Lear.—LiH
Ellen Winters. M. Glenn.—GlC
For Laura. M. C. Livingston.—HoBf
For Wilma. D. Johnson.—JaG
The forsaken merman. M. Arnold.—BlO
Grammar lesson. L. Pastan.—JaPi
Hope. L. Hughes.—HaOf—HoSu—LiIl
I cannot forget you. Unknown.—LiIl—LiSf
The impulse. R. Frost.—PlAs
It's raining. G. Apollinaire.—KoT
"Keep a poem in your pocket." B. S. De Regniers.—PrRh
Little elegy. E. Wylie.—LiIl
Loneliness. F. Holman.—LiIl
Lonely Monday. J. P. Lewis.—LiIl
Lonesome. M. C. Livingston.—LiIl
Looking at a picture on an anniversary. T. Hardy.—PlEd
Lost ("Desolate and lone"). C. Sandburg.—HoRa
Lost ("I shall remember chuffs the train"). H. Behn.—HoCb
The lost cat. E. V. Rieu.—ChC—LiSf
Miss Blues'es child. L. Hughes.—KoT
Missing the children. P. Zimmer.—JaS
Missing you. C. Zolotow.—HoBf—LiIl
The musk-ox. T. Hughes.—HuU
My life has turned to blue. M. Angelou.—AnS
Napoleon. W. De la Mare.—HeR
Neighbors ("They live alone"). D. A. Evans.—JaPi
The owl ("Downhill I came, hungry, and yet not starved"). E. Thomas.—HeR
The owl's bedtime story. R. Jarrell.—LiIl
Pete at the zoo. G. Brooks.—LiIl
Poem ("I loved my friend"). L. Hughes.—CoN—HoBf—HuDk—JaD—LiIl—LiSf
Poet in residence at a county school. D. Welch.—JaG
Prescience. M. Angelou.—AnS
A sad song about Greenwich Village. F. Park.—PrRh
Separation ("Each day"). P. Wolny.—JaD
Shaker, why don't you sing. M. Angelou.—AnS
Since Hanna moved away. J. Viorst.—HoBf—PrRh—ViI
Single. N. M. Bodecker.—BoPc
Snowy benches. A. Fisher.—BaS—HoSi, KeK
Someone I like. C. Zolotow.—ZoE
Song ("Reading about the Wisconsin weeping willow"). R. Krauss.—McL
Sunday morning lonely. L. Clifton.—FaW
The telephone. E. Field.—JaPo

Loneliness—*Continued*
"That summer." J. Hemschemeyer.—JaPo
They ask, is God, too, lonely. C. Sandburg.—LiIl
"They say you're staying in a mountain temple." Tu Fu.—KoT
Thinking of love. E. Jennings.—JaG
Tomorrow. M. Strand.—JaG—JaPo
"Too slow." L. Morrison.—LiIl
Unwanted. E. Field.—JaPi
Valediction. S. Heaney.—JaPo
"Western wind, when wilt thou blow." Unknown.—KeK—McL
"What is the opposite of two." R. Wilbur.—LiIl
    The opposite of two.—PrRh
When I was lost. D. Aldis.—PrRh
"The wind blows out of the gates of the day." From The land of heart's desire. W. B. Yeats.—HeR
The wolf ("When the pale moon hides and the wild wind wails"). G. R. Durston.—PrRh
Woman's song. Unknown, fr. the Chippewa Indian.—BiSp
Loneliness. Felice Holman.—LiIl
Lonely Monday. J. Patrick Lewis.—LiIl
The lonely scarecrow. James Kirkup.—BlO
"A lonely sparrow." Kazue Mizumura.—LiSf
"Lonely the sea-bird lies at her rest." See Calvary
Lonesome. Myra Cohn Livingston.—LiIl
"Lonesome all alone." See Lonesome
Long, Elizabeth Ellen
    Rain clouds.—PrRh
Long distance. William Stafford.—LiWa
Long gone. Jack Prelutsky.—PrRh—PrZ
Long Green Hill. Eleanor Farjeon.—FaE
Long John Brown and little Mary Bell. William Blake.—HeR
Long shadow story. Lilian Moore.—MoSn
Long trip. Langston Hughes.—HuDk
"The long yellow branches." See The dancers
Longfellow, Henry Wadsworth
    The children's hour.—HaOf
    Christmas bells. See "I heard the bells on Christmas Day"
    Excelsior.—HaOf
    "From his pouch he took his colors." See The song of Hiawatha
    Giotto's tower.—PlEd
    "I heard the bells on Christmas Day."—CoN
        Christmas bells.—HaO
    The little Hiawatha. See The song of Hiawatha
    The old bridge at Florence.—PlEd
    Paul Revere's ride.—HaOf
    A psalm of life.—HaOf
    The song of Hiawatha, sels.
        "From his pouch he took his colors".—PlEd
        The little Hiawatha.—CoOu
    Venice.—PlEd
    The village blacksmith.—HaOf
    The wreck of the Hesperus.—HaOf
Look. Charlotte Zolotow.—PrRa—ZoE
"Look ahead, look astern, look the weather and the lee." See The coasts of high Barbary
"Look, and keep very still." See Keep still
"Look at all those monkeys." Spike Milligan.—CoOu
"Look at itsy-bitsy Mitzi." See The pizza
"Look at me move." See The amputee soldier
"Look at pretty little kitty." See Kitty
"Look at that." Lilian Moore.—MoSn
"Look at the little sandpiper." See The sandpiper

"Look at the stars, look, look up at the skies." See The starlight night
"Look at them flit." See Fish
"Look at us." See Bike ride
"Look how / last year's." See Robins
"Look, how the clouds are flying south." See The snow-man
"Look in the caves at the edge of the sea." See Sea fairies
"Look, my baby's standing there." See Baby stands
"Look one way and the sun is going down." See The mockingbird
"Look out." See Last day of school
"Look out how you use proud words." See Primer lesson
Look up. Ann Turner.—TuS
"Look up." See King palm
Looking at a picture on an anniversary. Thomas Hardy.—PlEd
Looking at quilts. Marge Piercy.—PlSc
"Looking at your face." Galway Kinnell.—JaPo
Looking both ways. Jane O. Wayne.—JaG
Looking down in the rain. Barbara Juster Esbensen.—EsCs
Looking for a sunset bird in winter. Robert Frost.—KoS
"Looking for something in the Sunday paper." See The Sunday news
Looking forward. Robert Louis Stevenson.—DaC
"Looking in a thicket." See Sweetheart
"Looking like all outdoors." See For Richard Chase
Looks are deceiving. Beatrice Schenk De Regniers.—DeT
The loon. Ted Hughes.—HuU
"A loon." See Woman's song
"The loon, the loon." See The loon
Loons
    The Kerry loon. E. Farjeon.—FaE
    The loon. T. Hughes.—HuU
    Three. E. Coatsworth.—LiIl
"Loose and limber." Arnold Lobel.—LoWr
Loots, Barbara Kunz
    Mountain wind.—PrRh
Lopez, Alonzo
    Celebration.—LiIl
"Lopsided." See English oak
"Lord." See The prayer of the cat
"Lord." See The prayer of the dog
"Lord." See The prayer of the little pig
Lord Cray. Edward Gorey.—PrRh
"Lord God." See Drawing
"The Lord is my shepherd, I shall not want." See Psalm 23
"Lord Jesus." Graham Salmon.—LaT
"Lord, make me an instrument of thy peace." Saint Francis of Assisi.—LaT
"Lord of sea and earth and air." See Prayer for the pilot
Lord Randal. Unknown.—PlAs
"Lord, the snowful sky." See Sailor's carol
"The Lord to me a shepherd is." See Psalm 23
"Lord, you have given us." See Our food
Lore. Ronald Stuart Thomas.—HeR
The loreley. Heinrich Heine, tr. by Aaron Kramer.—LiWa
"Loss of weight." See Near drowning
Lost ("Desolate and lone"). Carl Sandburg.—HoRa
Lost ("I have a little turtle"). David McCord.—McAs
Lost ("I shall remember chuffs the train"). Harry Behn.—HoCb

Love—*Continued*

"I am the rose of Sharon, and the lily of the valleys." From The Song of Solomon. Bible/Old Testament.—McL

I cannot forget you. Unknown.—LiIl—LiSf

"I cannot grow." W. H. Auden.—HeR

"I dream'd a dream tonight." From Romeo and Juliet. W. Shakespeare.—HoUn

"I had a young man." Mother Goose.—AlH

"I have lived and I have loved." Unknown.—KoT

I hid you. M. Radnóti.—McL

I know a man. P. Steele.—JaPo

"I like my body when it is with your." E. E. Cummings.—McL

"I love coffee." Mother Goose.—LoR

"I love you." C. Sandburg.—HoRa

"I love you, I love you." Unknown.—PrRh

"I love you more than applesauce." J. Prelutsky.—PrIv

"I made a giant valentine." J. Prelutsky.—PrIv

"I met her as a blossom on a stem." From The dream. T. Roethke.—McL

"I see their knavery, this is to make an ass of me, to fright me." From A midsummer night's dream. W. Shakespeare.—HoUn

I sought all over the world. J. Tagliabue.—JaPi

"I sow hempseed." Unknown.—LiVp

I want to say your name. L. S. Senghor.—KoT

"I will give my love an apple without e'er a core." Unknown.—HeR

    I will give my love an apple.—BlO

"Ickle ockle, blue bockle." Mother Goose.—BlQ—DeM

"I'd want her eyes to fill with wonder." K. Patchen.—McL

If ("If he could climb a tree"). N. Giovanni.—GiSp

"If I might be an ox." Unknown, from the Ethiopian Galla tribe.—HeR

"If no one ever marries me." L. Alma-Tadema.—DaC—PrRh—TrM

"If the ocean was milk." Unknown.—LiIl

"If you love me, love me true." Mother Goose.—LoR

"If you were a pot." A. Lobel.—LoWr

I'm going to Georgia. Unknown.—PlAs

The impulse. R. Frost.—PlAs

"In a cavern, in a canyon." P. Dehn.—KeK

In like a lion. G. Hewitt.—JaPo

In school-days. J. G. Whittier.—HaOf

"In the touch of this bosom there worketh a spell." From Christabel. S. T. Coleridge.—HeR

In the workhouse. G. R. Sims.—HaO

In Weatherbury stocks. T. Hardy.—PlAs

Inanna's song. Unknown.—McL

Indian serenade. P. B. Shelley.—KoT

Innocence. P. Kavanagh.—HeR

Insomnia ("The moon in the bureau mirror"). E. Bishop.—McL

Isabel. Unknown.—DoNw

"It was a lover and his lass." From As you like it. W. Shakespeare.—HeR—HoUn—KoT

Jamie Douglas. Unknown.—PlAs

Jeanette Jaffe. M. Glenn.—GlC

"Jelly Jill loves Weasel Will." J. Prelutsky.—PrIv

Jennie Tang. M. Glenn.—GlCd

Jimmy's dad. C. Rylant.—RyW

John Kinsella's lament for Mrs. Mary Moore. W. B. Yeats.—HeR

Johnny's the lad I love. Unknown.—PlAs

Joy. L. Hughes.—HuDk

Juke box love song. L. Hughes.—KoT

The juniper tree. W. Watson.—DoNw

The kangaroo's courtship. J. Yolen.—LiVp

Kevin McDonald. M. Glenn.—GlC

Kidnap poem. N. Giovanni.—JaG

The king of Magla and Vlaga. C. Pomerantz.—PoI

Kirsten. T. Berrigan.—KoT

Kurt Benoit. M. Glenn.—GlCd

"Lady, weeping at the crossroads." W. H. Auden.—PlAs

The lady's farewell. N. Fernandez Torneol.—PlAs

Lament. G. Roberts.—JaG

"Lavender blue and rosemary green." Mother Goose.—LoR

"Lavender's blue, dilly, dilly." Mother Goose.—DaC

    "Lavender's blue, diddle diddle".—DeM

"Let there be new flowering." L. Clifton.—JaPo

The letter. A. Tennyson.—KoT

Letter to a dead father. R. Shelton.—JaD

Letter to a substitute teacher. G. Gildner.—JaPi

Letter to statues. J. M. Brinnin.—PlEd

The lie ("Today, you threaten to leave me"). M. Angelou.—AnS

Litany. L. Hughes.—LaT

The little man and maid. Unknown.—DaC

The Lizzie Pitofsky poem. J. Viorst.—ViI

Lochinvar. Sir W. Scott.—PlAs

"Lock the place in your heart." Z. Mandela.—McL

Locked doors. From A throw of threes. E. Merriam.—MeF

Long John Brown and little Mary Bell. W. Blake.—HeR

Looking at a picture on an anniversary. T. Hardy.—PlEd

Lord Randal. Unknown.—PlAs

Love ("From Prince Atsumichi"). Lady Izumi.—McL

Love ("I love you, I like you"). W. J. Smith.—PrRh

Love at sea. J. P. Lewis.—LiVp

"Love comes quietly." R. Creeley.—McL

"Love is not love until love's vulnerable." From The dream. T. Roethke.—McL

Love letter. L. Pastan.—JaD

Love letters, unmailed. E. Merriam.—JaD

"Love wears roses' elegance." Sister Bertke, Hermitess of Utrecht.—McL

"Love, you alone have been with us." Rumi.—McL

"The lowest of trees have tops, the ant her gall." Sir E. Dyer.—HeR

Lowlands. Unknown.—PlAs

The lowlands of Holland. Unknown.—PlAs

Lullaby ("Lay your sleeping head, my love"). W. H. Auden.—McL

Magic spell for finding a woman. Unknown, fr. the Aztec Indian.—BiSp

Magic spell to turn a woman's heart. Unknown, fr. the Arekuna Indian.—BiSp

The maid freed from the gallows. Unknown.—PlAs

Mama is a sunrise. E. T. Hunt.—LiSf

The man who owned cars. E. Fried.—JaG

Man's song ("It is my form and person that makes me great"). Unknown, fr. the Chippewa Indian.—BiSp

Love—*Continued*

Scott Garber. M. Glenn.—GlCd
Sea chest. C. Sandburg.—HoRa
Seagulls. J. Updike.—JaPi
"See how she leans her cheek upon her hand." From Romeo and Juliet. W. Shakespeare.—HoUn
The seeds of love. Unknown.—PlAs
Seizure. Sappho.—McL
Sensation. A. Rimbaud.—KoT
Sentimental conversation. P. Verlaine.—LiWa
Separation ("Each day"). P. Wolny.—JaD
Separation ("Your absence has gone through me"). W. S. Merwin.—LiIl
September, last day at the beach. R. Tillinghast.—JaG
Shaker, why don't you sing. M. Angelou.—AnS
"Shall I compare thee to a summer's day?" From Sonnets. W. Shakespeare.—HoUn
She and I. N. Cameron.—HeR
"She came toward me in a flowing air." From The dream. T. Roethke.—McL
"She held her body steady in the wind." From The dream. T. Roethke.—McL
"She listens to the waves resound." A. Lobel.—LoWr
She moved through the fair. P. Colum.—PlAs
The shooting of Dan McGrew. R. W. Service.—DoNw—HeR
Short love poem. J. Viorst.—ViI
Simple song. M. Piercy.—McL
Since Hanna moved away. J. Viorst.—HoBf—PrRh—ViI
"Since there's no help, come, let us kiss and part." M. Drayton.—HeR
Since you seem intent. G. Locklin.—JaG
Siren chorus. G. Darley.—LiWa
Sleeping with someone who came in secret. Lady Ise.—McL
So long. W. Stafford.—JaPo
"So, we'll go no more a-roving." Lord Byron.—KoT
Some night again. W. Stafford.—JaG
Someone's face. J. Ciardi.—PrRa
Song ("Desire for a woman took hold of me in the night"). Unknown, tr. fr. the Azande.—McL
Song ("Dew on the bamboos"). Unknown.—McL
Song ("Did you see me walking by the Buick Repairs"). F. O'Hara.—KoT
Song ("Early morning dawning green"). Unknown, fr. the Quechua Indian.—BiSp
Song ("I hid my love when young while I"). J. Clare.—HeR
Song ("In an accessible place"). Unknown, fr. the Inca Indian.—BiSp
Song ("O lady, when the tipped cup of the moon blessed you"). T. Hughes.—McL
Song ("Reading about the Wisconsin weeping willow"). R. Krauss.—McL
Song ("Sweet beast, I have gone prowling"). W. D. W. Snodgrass.—McL
Song for Dov Shamir. D. Abse.—LaT
The song of wandering Aengus. W. B. Yeats.—BlO—KoT—LiWa
Songs for a colored singer. E. Bishop.—HeR
Sonnet. Dante Alighieri.—HeR—KoT
Sonnet for my father. D. Justice.—JaD
The sound of rain. D. A. Evans.—JaG
Sounding. D. Jauss.—JaS
Sounds of the day. N. MacCaig.—HeR

Spring and all. G. Bauer.—JaPo
A spring song of Tzu-Yeh. H. Yen.—McL
"Stop all the clocks, cut off the telephone." W. H. Auden.—HeR
Stopping by home. D. Huddle.—JaG
Strawberries ("There were never strawberries"). E. Morgan.—McL
Subway psalm. A. Nowlan.—JaS
"Sukey, you shall be my wife." Mother Goose.—DaC—DeM
Sunday ("The mint bed is in"). J. Schuyler.—KoT
The Sunday news. D. Gioia.—JaG
Surfaces. P. Meinke.—JaS
Susie's enzyme poem. P. Zimmer.—JaPo
Swahili love song. Unknown.—McL
The sweater. G. Orr.—JaPo
Sweet William's ghost. Unknown.—PlAs
Sweetheart. P. Hey.—JaG
Swimmer. R. Francis.—JaD
Tam Lin ("O, I forbid you, maidens a'"). Unknown.—PlAs
    Tamlane (". . . maidens all").—LiWa
Tam Lin ("She's ta'en her petticoat by the band"). Unknown.—PlAs
Tarantella. H. Belloc.—HeR
"Tell me, tell me, Sarah Jane." C. Causley.—HoSe—LiSf
Ten week wife. R. Donovan.—JaS
Thank you for your letter. Ch'ao Li-houa.—LiIl
"There is so much." A. Adoff.—AdA
"There once was a king." Unknown.—FaW
Things I didn't know I loved. N. Hikmet.—McL
Thinking of love. E. Jennings.—JaG
"This is a poem to my son Peter." P. Meinke.—JaD
This love. J. Hemschemeyer.—JaG
"This lunar beauty." W. H. Auden.—HeR
Those winter Sundays. R. Hayden.—JaD
Three knights from Spain. Unknown.—BlO
Three moments. S. R. Sherman.—JaD
The three ravens. Unknown.—PlAs
"Tickly, tickly, on your knee." Mother Goose.—DeM
To a suitor. M. Angelou.—AnS
To an isle in the water. W. B. Yeats.—KoT
To carry on living. Y. Amichai.—McL
To Dorothy. M. Bell.—JaPi
To Dorothy on her exclusion from the Guinness Book of World Records. X. J. Kennedy.—JaPi
To Ellen. C. Stetler.—JaPo
To fix the affections. Unknown, fr. the Cherokee Indian.—BiSp
To my blood sister. C. E. Hemp.—JaS
To my father. R. Pomeroy.—JaD
To you. K. Kuskin.—LiVp
Together. P. Engle.—PrRh
"Tommy Trot, a man of law." Mother Goose.—DeM
Truelove. M. Van Doren.—PlAs
"Trying to say." From Nineteen pieces for love. S. Griffin.—McL
The tryst. W. De la Mare.—PlAs
The twelve days of Christmas. Unknown.—RoC
    "The first day of Christmas".—LoR
Two drops. Z. Herbert.—HeR
Two people ("She reads the paper"). E. Merriam.—PrRh
The two sisters. Unknown.—PlAs
An undefined tenderness. J. Oppenheimer.—JaPo

Lowlands. Unknown.—PlAs
The **lowlands** of Holland. Unknown.—PlAs
Luck
    Balada de la loca fortuna. E. Gonzales Martinez.—LiSf
    The ballad of mad fortune. E. Gonzales Martinez.—LiSf
    Edenhall. S. Coolidge.—HaOf
    "I found a four leaf clover." J. Prelutsky.—PrNk
    "I never had a piece of toast." J. Payn.—TrM
    New year's advice from my Cornish grandmother. X. J. Kennedy.—LiNe
    "Nobody loses all the time." E. E. Cummings.—HeR
    Opportunity's knock. M. Bishop.—BrT
    "See a pin and pick it up." Mother Goose.—DeM—LoR
    "Something old, something new." Mother Goose.—LoR
    "Lucy Locket lost her pocket." Mother Goose.—DeM—LoR
Lullabies
    All the pretty little horses. Unknown.—KoT
        All the pretty horses.—ChB
    All through the night ("Sleep, my babe, lie still and slumber"). Unknown.—DaC
    All through the night ("Sleep, my child, and peace attend thee"). Sir H. Boulton.—ChB
    "All tucked in and roasty toasty." C. Watson.—LaW—WaC
    April rain song. L. Hughes.—CoN—HaOf—HuDk—LiSf—PrRh
    Arullo. Unknown.—GrT
    Benue lullaby. M. Brennan.—LaW
    "Bye, baby bunting." Mother Goose.—LoR
        "By, baby bunting".—DeM
    A Christmas lullaby. E. Farjeon.—FaE
    Cradle song ("From groves of spice"). S. Naidu.—ChB
    A cradle song ("Golden slumbers kiss your eyes"). T. Dekker.—BlO
    A cradle song ("Sweet dreams, form a shade"). W. Blake.—HaO—RoC
    Cradlesong ("Sleep, little one, your father is bringing"). Unknown, fr. the Mbya Indian.—BiSp
    Cradlesong for Ahuitzotl. Unknown, fr. the Aztec Indian.—BiSp
    "Dance, little baby, dance up high." Mother Goose.—ChB—DeM
    "Do not weep, little one." Unknown, fr. the Eskimo.—LiSf
    "Fie fie." E. Farjeon.—FaE
    Frog's lullaby. C. Pomerantz.—PoA
    Gaelic lullaby. Unknown.—ChB
    German slumber song. Unknown.—BaH
    "Go to bed first." Unknown.—BaH—FrP
    Good night ("Little baby, lay your head"). J. Taylor.—ChB
    Good night, good night. D. Lee.—PrRa
    Grandma's lullaby. C. Pomerantz.—PoA
    Grandpa bear's lullaby. J. Yolen.—PrRh
    Grandpa's lullaby. C. Pomerantz.—PoA
    The half lullaby. C. Pomerantz.—PoA
    "Hush-a-bye, baby, on the tree top." Mother Goose.—BaH—DeM
    "Hush, baby, my dolly, I pray you." Mother Goose.—DeM
    "Hush, little baby, don't say a word." Mother Goose.—BaH—ChB—DeM—LaW—LoR
        The mocking bird ("Hush up, baby").—LiSf

Hush 'n' bye. Unknown.—LaW
"Hushabye my darling." C. Watson.—LaW—PrRa—WaC
"I see the moon." Mother Goose.—ChB—CoN—DaC—DeM—FaW—LoR—PrRa
In the tree-top. L. Larcom.—HaOf
Kentucky babe. Unknown.—LaW
Lullaby ("Baby, sleep, sleep, sleep"). Unknown, fr. the Creek Indian.—BiSp
Lullaby ("Baby swimming down the river"). Unknown, fr. the Kiowa Indian.—BiSp
Lullaby ("Flowers are closed and lambs are sleeping"). C. G. Rossetti.—LaW
Lullaby ("Lay your sleeping head, my love"). W. H. Auden.—McL
Lullaby ("The moon and the stars and the wind in the sky"). J. Jaszi.—LaW
Lullaby ("My little dark baby"). L. Hughes.—HuDk
Lullaby ("Sh sh what do you wish"). E. Merriam.—LaW—MeSk
Lullaby ("Shlof, sleep through the night"). C. Pomerantz.—PoI
Lullaby ("Sleep, my child"). Unknown.—GrT
Lullaby ("Sleep sleep beneath the old wind's eye"). G. Vigneault.—DoNw
Lullaby ("Someone would like to have you for her child"). Unknown, fr. the Akan people of Africa.—KoT—LaW
Lullaby ("Sweet love, everything"). S. Kowit.—JaT
Lullaby ("The trees now look scary"). F. Holman.—LaW
"Lullaby and good night." Unknown.—ChB
Lully, lulla. Unknown.—KoT
Manhattan lullabye. N. Farber.—HoSs
"Minnie and Winnie." A. Tennyson.—ChB—KoT
The mother sings. E. Farjeon.—FaE
The mouse's lullaby. P. Cox.—HaOf
"Puva, puva, puva." Unknown, fr. the Hopi Indian.—KoT
Raindrops ("Raindrops a-falling from the skies"). Unknown, fr. the Slovak.—LaW
"Rock-a-bye, baby, on the treetop." Mother Goose.—BaH—ChB—DaC—LoR
"Rock-a-bye baby, thy cradle is green." Mother Goose.—AlH—LiSf
"Rock, rock, sleep, my baby." C. Watson.—CoN—LaW
"Rockabye baby, so sweet and so fair." Unknown.—LaW
The rocking carol. Unknown.—RoC
"Silverly." D. Lee.—PrRa
"Sleep, baby, sleep, thy father guards the sheep." Mother Goose.—Dem—LoR
"Sleep, baby, sleep, thy father watches the sheep." Unknown, fr. the German.—BaH—LaW
Sleep now and rest. Unknown, fr. the Russian.—LaW
Sleep, sleep, my little one. Unknown.—LaW
Song for Susannah, a lullaby. D. Hardie.—JaT
Sweet and low. From The princess. A. Tennyson.—BlO—ChB
Sweet ass. E. Farjeon.—FaE
"This is baby ready for a nap." Unknown.—RaT
"Where should a baby rest." Mother Goose.—BaH
The white seal's lullaby. R. Kipling.—ChB

Lullabies—*Continued*

Wynken, Blynken, and Nod. E. Field.—CoN—DaC—HaOf

"You spotted snakes with double tongue." From A midsummer night's dream. W. Shakespeare.—BlO—HoUn—LiWa

Lullaby ("Baby, sleep, sleep, sleep"). Unknown.—BiSp

Lullaby ("Baby swimming down the river"). Unknown.—BiSp

Lullaby ("Flowers are closed and lambs are sleeping"). Christina Georgina Rossetti.—LaW

Lullaby ("Lay your sleeping head, my love"). Wystan Hugh Auden.—McL

Lullaby ("The moon and the stars and the wind in the sky"). Jean Jaszi.—LaW

Lullaby ("My little dark baby"). Langston Hughes.—HuDk

Lullaby ("Sh sh what do you wish"). Eve Merriam.—LaW—MeSk

Lullaby ("Shlof, sleep through the night"). Charlotte Pomerantz.—PoI

Lullaby ("Sleep, my child"). Unknown.—GrT

Lullaby ("Sleep sleep beneath the old wind's eye"). Gilles Vigneault, tr. by John Glassco.—DoNw

Lullaby ("Someone would like to have you for her child"). Unknown.—KoT—LaW

A **lullaby.** See "Speak roughly to your little boy"

Lullaby ("Sweet love, everything"). Steve Kowit.—JaT

Lullaby ("The trees now look scary"). Felice Holman.—LaW

"Lullaby and good night." Unknown.—ChB

"Lulled by rumble, babble, beep." See Manhattan lullabye

Lully, lulla. Unknown.—KoT

"Lully, lulla, thou little tiny child." See Lully, lulla

Lulu, Lulu, I've a lilo. Charlotte Pomerantz.—PoI

Lumps. Judith Thurman.—PrRh

La **luna.** Unknown.—GrT

"Lunging, plunging through the woods." See Lair

"Lydia and Shirley have." See Two friends

"Lying atop." See Atop

"Lying in the grass." Charlotte Zolotow.—ZoE

Lying on things. Dennis Lee.—BaS

Lyly, John

What bird so sings.—BlO

Lynchings

The faking boy. Unknown.—HeR

A **lynx.** Ted Hughes.—HuU

Lynxes

The lesser lynx. E. V. Rieu.—PrRh

A **lynx.** T. Hughes.—HuU

Lyon, George Ella

Birth.—JaS

Catechisms, talking with a four year old.—JaS

Cousin Ella goes to town.—JaS

My grandfather in search of moonshine.—JaG

A testimony.—JaG

M

"Ma baby lives across de river." See Wide river

"Ma, don't throw that shirt out." Jack Prelutsky.—PrNk

Ma Lord. Langston Hughes.—HuDk

"Ma Lord ain't no stuck-up man." See Ma Lord

Mabel, remarkable Mabel. Jack Prelutsky.—PrNk

Mac. Mark Vinz.—JaS

Macavity, the mystery cat. Thomas Stearns Eliot.—ChC—CoOu—HaOf—HeR—LiSf

"Macavity's a mystery cat, he's called the Hidden Paw." See Macavity, the mystery cat

MacBeth, George

Fourteen ways of touching the Peter ("You can push").—ChC

The little brown celery.—FaTh

Snowdrops.—HaO

Macbeth, sels. William Shakespeare

"Double, double, toil and trouble".—HoUn
    Song of the witches.—PrRh

"Thrice the brinded cat hath mew'd".—HeR—LiSf—LiWa

"Tomorrow, and tomorrow, and tomorrow".—HoUn

"The weird sisters, hand in hand".—HoUn

MacCaig, Norman

After his death.—HeR

Aunt Julia.—HeR

Interruption to a journey.—HeR

Praise of a collie.—HeR

Sleet.—HaO

Sounds of the day.—HeR

McCord, David

Afreet.—LiWa

All day long.—McAs

At the garden gate.—LiIl

August 28.—HoSi—McAs

"Bananas and cream."—FaW—HoMu

"Blessed Lord, what it is to be young."—CoN—KeK

"Books fall open."—HaOf

Cake.—HoMu

A Christmas package, sels.
    "My stocking's where".—PrRh

Christmas prayer.—LiCp

Cocoon.—HaOf—McAs

Come Christmas.—LiCp

The cove.—McAs

Crickets ("All busy punching tickets").—CoN—FaTh—LiSf—McAs

The door.—McAs

Easter morning, sels.
    "Is Easter just a day of hats".—LiE

Epitaph on a waiter.—JaPo

"Every time I climb a tree." See Five chants

Far away.—McAs

Five chants, sels.
    "Every time I climb a tree".—CoN—FaW—LiSf—PrRh

Forget it.—McAs

Glowworm ("Never talk down to a glowworm").—CoN—FaW—McAs

Gone ("I've looked behind the shed").—HoDl—JaT

The grasshopper.—LiSf

"He sent his love a valentine."—LiVp

I want you to meet.—McAs

Innuendo.—McAs

"Is Easter just a day of hats." See Easter morning

January one.—LiNe

Joe.—BaS

Knotholes.—McAs

Laundromat.—HoCl

Little ("Little wind little sun").—McAs

Lost ("I have a little turtle").—McAs

"Melvin Martin Riley Smith".—McAs

Mr. Bidery's spidery garden.—PrRh

"My stocking's where." See A Christmas package

McCord, David—*Continued*
Notice.—McAs
"On Halloween, what bothers some." See
 Witch's broom notes
"The pickety fence."—BeD—CoN—FaW—LiSf
Pome ("Hlo").—McAs
Rain song.—McAs
Samantha speaking.—LiTp
Secret.—McAs
Singular indeed.—HaOf
Snail ("This sticky trail").—McAs
Snowman.—McAs—PrRa
Something better.—McAs
Song ("Wind and wave and star and sea").—
 McAs
Song of the train.—CoN—HoCl
The star in the pail.—LiSf
"This is my rock."—CoN
Tiggady Rue.—LiWa
"To walk in warm rain."—PrRh
Tomorrows.—McAs
The walnut tree.—HaOf
"When I was christened."—HaOf—KeK
Wintry.—McAs
Witch's broom notes, sels.
 "On Halloween, what bothers some".—HoSi
Yellow ("Green is go").—FrP—PrRh
McCullers, Carson
Slumber party.—HoBf
MacDiarmid, Hugh
Another epitaph on an army of mercenaries.—
 HeR
Crystals like blood.—HeR
Perfect.—HeR
Scotland small.—HeR
The weapon.—HeR
Macdonald, Cynthia
Accomplishments.—JaD
Celebrating the freak.—JaPi
The lady pitcher.—JaPi
The late mother.—JaPi
MacDonald, George
"The lightning and thunder."—KeK
"Where did you come from, baby dear."—DaC
The wind and the moon.—PrRa
MacDonald, Marie Bruckman
The 'skeeter and Peter.—BrT
Macdonald, Mary
The alligator.—PrRh
MacDonnell, A. A.
An imprecation against foes and sorcerers, tr.
 by.—LiWa
McElroy, David
Before breakup on the Chena outside
 Fairbanks.—JaPi
Nocturn at the institute.—JaPi
Ode to a dead Dodge.—JaD
McFadden, David
Elephant ("In his travels, the elephant").—
 DoNw
McGee, Shelagh
"Wanted, a witch's cat."—ChC—PrRh
McGinley, Phyllis
The adversary.—HaOf
The ballad of Befana.—PlAs
Daylight saving time.—PrRh
E.—FrP
"J's the jumping jay walker."—PrRh
Trinity Place.—PlSc
Triolet against sisters.—HaOf—KeK
"We're racing, racing down the walk."—PrRh
McGough, Roger
The fight of the year.—HaO

Tide and time.—JaT
McGowan, John
Mister alley cat.—ChC
Machinery. See also names of machines, as
 Clocks
The ballad of Newington Green. J. Aiken.—LiSf
Construction ("The giant mouth"). L. Moore.—
 MoSn
Darius Green and his flying-machine. J. T.
 Trowbridge.—HaOf
John Henry ("When John Henry was a little
 tiny baby"). Unknown.—KeK
 John Henry ("John Henry was a lil
  baby").—PlAs
 John Henry ("When John Henry was a
  little babe").—LiSf
Lawnmower. V. Worth.—HoCl
Man and machine. R. Morgan.—JaS
The musician at his work. R. Currie.—JaS
Nightmare number three. S. V. Benét.—PlSc
An ode to the framers of the Frame Bill. Lord
 Dyron.—PlSc
Our washing machine. P. Hubbell.—HoCl—
 LiSf—PrRh
The power shovel. R. Bennett.—HoCl
A time for building. M. C. Livingston.—HoSs
The toaster ("A silver-scaled dragon with jaws
 flaming red"). W. J. Smith.—LiSf—PrRa
Tractor. V. Worth.—HoCl
"McIntosh apple." Steven Kroll.—PrRh
McKeown, Tom
1937 Ford convertible.—JaPo
"The **mackerel-man** drives down the street." See
 A pretty ambition
MacLeish, Archibald
Grazing locomotives.—JaPo
Theory of poetry.—JaD
McLennan, William
Cecilia, tr. by.—DoNw
McLeod, Doug
Kitty.—ChC
McLeod, Irene Rutherford
Lone dog ("I'm a lean dog, a keen dog, a wild
 dog, and lone").—HoDl—LiSf—PrRh
MacNeice, Louis
Apple blossom.—HeR
Autobiography.—HeR
Bagpipe music.—HeR
Christmas shopping.—HaO
Homage to Wren.—PlEd
The National Gallery.—PlEd
Poussin.—PlEd
The streets of Laredo ("O, early one morning
 I walked out like Agag").—PlAs
Macpherson, Jay
Egg.—DoNw
Mad dog. Cynthia Rylant.—RyW
The **mad** gardener's song ("He thought he saw
 an elephant"). From Sylvie and Bruno. Lewis
 Carroll.—HeR
Mad gardener's song ("He thought he saw a
 buffalo").—CoOu
Mad gardener's song ("He thought he saw a
 buffalo"). See The mad gardener's song ("He
 thought he saw an elephant")
Mad Tom's song. Robert Graves.—HeR
Madrid, Iowa. Ron Ikan.—JaPo
Maggie. See A shaggy dog
"**Maggie** and Milly and Molly and May." Edward
 Estlin Cummings.—HeR—HoSe—PrRh
Magi
The adoration of the Magi. C. Pilling.—HaO
The ballad of Befana. P. McGinley.—PlAs

Magi—*Continued*
Camels of the kings. L. Norris.—HaO
Carol of patience. R. Graves.—HaO
Carol of the brown king. L. Hughes.—LiCp
Journey of the Magi. T. S. Eliot.—HaO
"Kings came riding." C. Williams.—HaO
The mystic Magi. R. S. Hawker.—HaO
Los pastores. E. Agnew.—LiCp
The riding of the kings. E. Farjeon.—FaE
The three drovers. J. Wheeler.—RoC
Twelfth night ("Our candles, lit, re-lit, have gone down now"). P. Scupham.—HaO
We three kings. Unknown.—RoC
The wise men ask the children the way. H. Heine.—HaO

Magic. See also Charms; Enchantment
The abominable baseball bat. X. J. Kennedy.—LiWa
Abracadabra. D. Livesay.—DoNw
The alchemist ("Sail of Claustra, Aelis, Azalais"). E. Pound.—LiWa
And the princess was astonished to see the ugly frog turn into a handsome prince. J. Viorst.—ViI
The ballad of the harp-weaver. E. S. Millay.—LiSf—LiWa
Barbarossa. F. Ruckert.—LiWa
"Be not afeard, the isle is full of noises." From The tempest. W. Shakespeare.—HeR
C is for charms. E. Farjeon.—LiWa
Cat ("By the fire, like drifting reddish goldfish"). J. Cocteau.—LiCa
Celanta at the well of life. From The old wives' tale. G. Peele.—BlO
Song for the head.—HeR
Charmes. R. Herrick.—LiWa
Enchantment. H. Behn.—HoCb
Fable ("Pity the girl with the crystal hair"). J. Aiken.—LiWa
"Far over the misty mountains cold." J. R. R. Tolkien.—LiWa
From a prayer of the shooting chant. Unknown, fr. the Navajo Indian.—BiSp
The genie. A. Stanford.—LiWa
An imprecation against foes and sorcerers. From Atharva Veda. Unknown.—LiWa
Incantation to Oedipus. J. Dryden.—LiWa
Magic spell for a difficult birth. Unknown, fr. the Arejuna Indian.—BiSp
Magical eraser. S. Silverstein.—LiWa
The magical mouse. K. Patchen.—KeK
The magical picture. R. Graves.—LiSf
Medicine man's prayer. Unknown, fr. the Blackfeet Indian.—BiSp
Merlin. E. Muir.—HeR
Merlin and the snake's egg. L. Norris.—LiWa
Miraculous Mortimer. J. Prelutsky.—PrNk
Mr. Wells. From The sorcerer. W. S. Gilbert.—LiWa
On a night of snow. E. Coatsworth.—ChC—HaOf
The paint box. E. V. Rieu.—PrRh
The pumpkin. R. Graves.—LiWa—PrRh
Queer things. J. Reeves.—LiWa
The six badgers. R. Graves.—LiSf—LiWa
The song of wandering Aengus. W. B. Yeats.—BlO—KoT—LiWa
Sonnet. Dante Alighieri.—HeR—KoT
The spell. R. Herrick.—LiWa
Spirits. V. H. Cruz.—LiWa
Strange tree. E. M. Roberts.—LiWa
"That woman down there beneath the sea." Unknown, from the Eskimo.—LiWa

The toad ("In day of old, those far off times"). R. S. Oliver.—PrRh
Welsh incident. R. Graves.—LiWa
"The wizard messes up his bench." Unknown.—TrM
Z is for Zoroaster ("How mighty a wizard"). E. Farjeon.—LiWa
"The **magic** of the day is the morning." See Ballad of the morning streets
Magic spell for a difficult birth. Unknown.—BiSp
Magic spell for an approaching storm. Unknown.—BiSp
Magic spell for finding a woman. Unknown.—BiSp
Magic spell to turn a woman's heart. Unknown.—BiSp
Magic words to the gull. Unknown.—BiSp
Magical eraser. Shel Silverstein.—LiWa
The **magical** mouse. Kenneth Patchen.—KeK
The **magical** picture. Robert Graves.—LiSf
"**Magical** prognosticator." See Halloween witches
Magnet. Valerie Worth.—KeK
Magnetism
Magnet. V. Worth.—KeK
The **magnificent** bull. Unknown.—KoT
The **magnifying** glass. Walter De la Mare.—BlO
The **maid** freed from the gallows. Unknown.—PlAs
Maid of Manila. Unknown.—BrT
"The **maiden** caught me in the wild." See The crystal cabinet
"A **maiden** caught stealing a dahlia." See Caught stealing a dahlia
"The **maiden** trees their locks to dress." See Girls in the garden
Mail and mailcarriers. See also Letters and letter writing
General delivery. C. Rylant.—RyW
"Postman, postman." A. Lobel.—LoWr
Skip rope rhyme for our time. E. Merriam.—MeF
"Too slow." L. Morrison.—LiIl
"**Main** Street, yessir, let me see." See How I helped the traveler
Maine
Up north. N. M. Bodecker.—BoPc
"The **major** quirk of Philbert Phlurk." See Philbert Phlurk
"A **major,** with wonderful force." See An atrocious pun
"**Make** a joyful noise unto the Lord, all ye lands." See Psalm 100
Make-believe
Adventure. H. Behn.—HoCb
Adventures of Isabel. O. Nash.—CoN—CoOu—HaOf—PrRh
Aunt Leaf. M. Oliver.—JaT
Baby's baking. E. Stein.—PrRa
Bernard Pearlman. M. Glenn.—GlC
Block city. R. L. Stevenson.—CoN—PlEd
Brian O'Linn. Unknown.—HeR
Busy. A. A. Milne.—LiSf
The centaur. M. Swenson.—LiSf
The cooky-nut trees. A. B. Paine.—HaOf
The duel. E. Field.—FaW—HaOf—PrRh
Fairy tale ("He built himself a house"). M. Holub.—HeR
Fairyland. Sir R. Tagore.—LiWa
Fernando. M. Ridlon.—CoN—PrRh
For a cloud. E. Farjeon.—FaE
The funny house. M. Hillert.—HoBf
Going up ("Space suit Sammy"). J. T. Moore.—PrRh

Make-believe—*Continued*
I can be a tiger. M. L. Anderson.—PrRa
I can fly. F. Holman.—CoN—PrRh
I caught a fish. B. Murray.—CoOu
The ice cream ocean. J. M. Shaw.—RuI
"I'd like to be a lighthouse." R. Field.—HoSe—PrRa
If ("If I had a trunk like a big elephant"). J. K. Bangs.—HaOf
"If all the world were paper." Mother Goose.—BlO—CoN—KoT
"If you could be small." From Square as a house. K. Kuskin.—FaTh
Imaginary room. S. Cassedy.—CaR
Jenny. E. Farjeon.—FaE
The jumblies. E. Lear.—BlO—LiH
Kate and I. S. N. Tarrant.—JaT
The land of Counterpane. R. L. Stevenson.—CoN
The land of Nod. R. L. Stevenson.—ChB—DaC
The land of story books. R. L. Stevenson.—DaC
Little bush. E. M. Roberts.—LiSf
Make believe. H. Behn.—HoCb
The man who sang the sillies. J. Ciardi.—HaOf
The marrog. R. C. Scriven.—PrRh
"My father he died, but I can't tell you how." Unknown.—BlO
My sister Jane. T. Hughes.—CoOu—LiSf
Narcissa. G. Brooks.—CoN
"Oak leaf plate." M. A. Hoberman.—FaTh
Office. S. Cassedy.—CaR
The old salt. J. Ciardi.—CiD
"One day when we went walking." V. Hobbs.—PrRh
Open house. A. Fisher.—PrRa
Pirate story. R. L. Stevenson.—DaC
Pretending. B. Katz.—PrRa
Science fiction. R. Wittemore.—KeK
A sick child. R. Jarrell.—LiSf
Skilly Oogan. R. Hoban.—LiII
That's what we'd do. M. M. Dodge.—HaOf
They're calling. F. Holman.—LiSf—PrRh
Tip toe tail. D. Willson.—CoN
What should I see. E. Farjeon.—FaE
Where goblins dwell. J. Prelutsky.—PrRh
Wild beasts. E. Stein.—FrP—PrRa
Make believe. Harry Behn.—HoCb
"Make me, dear Lord, polite and kind." See A child's prayer
"Make me feel the wild pulsation that I felt before the strife." From Locksley Hall. Alfred Tennyson.—PlSc
"Make me, O Lord, thy spinning wheel compleate." See Huswifery
Makers. Nancy Dingman Watson.—PrRa
Making a friend. Myra Cohn Livingston.—HoDl
Malam, Charles
Steam shovel.—CoN—PrRh
The maldive shark. Herman Melville.—HeR
Malloy, Merrit
Religion.—LaT
Mama." See Silly song
Mama Bear, you'll never miss." X. J. Kennedy.—KeB
Mama got out and fussed." See Education
Mama is a sunrise. Evelyn Tooley Hunt.—LiSf
Mama is black." See I am
Mama is chocolate, you must be swirls." See Flavors (1)
Mama's kiss. Unknown.—GrT
Mammals are a varied lot." See Dogs and cats and bears and bats

Man. See Human race
Man. Ann Turner.—TuS
Man and bat. David Herbert Lawrence.—HeR
Man and machine. Robert Morgan.—JaS
The man he killed. Thomas Hardy.—HeR
"A man hired by John Smith and Co." See Dirt dumping
"The man in the moon came tumbling down." Mother Goose.—BaH—DeM—LoR
"The man in the moon looked out of the moon." Mother Goose.—DeM
"The man in the wilderness asked me". See "The man in the wilderness asked of me"
"The man in the wilderness asked of me." Mother Goose.—DaC—FaW
  "The man in the wilderness asked me".—LoR
"Man may work from sun to sun." Unknown.—PlSc
A man of action. Charles Stetler.—JaG
"A man of words and not of deeds." Mother Goose.—AlH—BlO
"A man on his own in a car." See Meditation on the A30
"Man outside." See To quiet a raging storm
"The man said." See An historic moment
"A man said to me at the fair." See The market
"A man should never earn his living." See A living
The man that had little to say. John Ciardi.—BeD
"The man the hare has met." See The names of the hare
"A man was sitting underneath a tree." See Seumas Beg
"The man who lies on his back under huge trees." See Breathing space July
The man who owned cars. Elliot Fried.—JaG
The man who sang the sillies. John Ciardi.—HaOf
The man with the hoe. Edwin Markham.—PlSc
"The man with the tan hands." X. J. Kennedy.—KeF
Mandela, Zindzi
"Lock the place in your heart."—McL
The mandrill. Conrad Aiken.—PrRh
Mandry, Kathy
Drink a garden.—HoMu
Mandy Bailer. Mel Glenn.—GlCd
Manerathiak's song. Unknown, tr. by Raymond De Coccola and Paul King.—DoNw
A manger song. Eleanor Farjeon.—FaE
Manhattan lullabye. Norma Farber.—HoSs
Manitou. Ron Ikan.—JaPo
Mannahatta. Walt Whitman.—PlEd
Manners
Apology ("It's hard to say I'm sorry"). J. Viorst.—ViI
"Arbuckle Jones." P. Wesley-Smith.—JaT
The compassionate fool. N. Cameron.—HeR
Dinnertime. R. J. Margolis.—MaS
Don't leave the spoon in the syrup. N. M. Bodecker.—BoSs
The embarrassing episode of Little Miss Muffet. G. W. Carryl.—HaOf
Exploding gravy. X. J. Kennedy.—LiSf
The gallant highwayman. J. De Mille.—DoNw
How to eat a poem. E. Merriam.—MeSk
"I eat my peas with honey." Unknown.—CoN—CoOu—PrRh
  Peas ("I always eat peas with honey").—FaW
If ("If I had a trunk like a big elephant"). J. K. Bangs.—HaOf

Margossian, Marzbed—*Continued*
The woman cleaning lentils, tr. by.—FaTh
"**Maria** intended a letter to write." See How to write a letter
Maria Preosi. Mel Glenn.—GlC
"**Marian.**" See Sleep over
Marie Yeagerman. Mel Glenn.—GlC
Marigold. John Haines.—JaPo
Marigolds
How marigolds came yellow. R. Herrick.—KoT
Marigold. J. Haines.—JaPo
Marigolds. C. Zolotow.—ZoE
Marigolds. Charlotte Zolotow.—ZoE
Mario Benedetto. Mel Glenn.—GlCd
Marion, Jeff Daniel
Out in the country, back home.—JaPo
The **marionettes.** Myra Cohn Livingston.—LiWo
La **mariposa** linda. Unknown.—GrT
The **mark.** Eleanor Farjeon.—FaE
Markers. Frank Steele.—JaG
The **market.** James Stephens.—PlAs
Markets and marketing. See also Grocery stores; Shops and shopkeepers
"As I was going to Banbury." Mother Goose.—DeM
Bags of meat. T. Hardy.—HeR
Mexican market woman. L. Hughes.—HuDk—PlSc
"To market, to market, to buy a fat pig." Mother Goose.—DeM—FaW—LiSf—LoR—RaT
When Jane goes to market. E. Farjeon.—FaE
Markham, Edwin
The man with the hoe.—PlSc
Markings. Frank Steele.—JaPi
Markings, the comma. Eve Merriam.—MeSk
Markings, the exclamation. Eve Merriam.—MeSk
Markings, the period. Eve Merriam.—MeSk
Markings, the question. Eve Merriam.—MeSk
Markings, the semicolon. Eve Merriam.—MeSk
Marks, R. H.
Simhat Torah.—LiPj
Sukkot.—LiPj
Marks, S. J.
Charm ("With trembling eyes"), tr. by.—McL
Hesitating ode, tr. by.—McL
I hid you, tr. by.—McL
Mark's fingers. Mary O'Neill.—PrRh
Marlowe, Christopher
The passionate shepherd to his love.—HeR—KoT
Marm Grayson's guests. Mary E. Wilkins Freeman.—HaOf
Marmalade. Eleanor Farjeon.—FaE
Marmalade lost. Ruth Whitman.—LiCa
The **marmalade** man makes a dance to mend us. Nancy Willard.—LiII
Marquis, Don
Pete at the seashore.—HoDl
Marriage. See also Married life; Weddings
Betrothed. L. Bogan.—McL
Marriage contract. V. Rutsala.—JaD
The river-merchant's wife, a letter ("While my hair was still cut straight across my forehead"). E. Pound.—HeR—KoT
Marriage contract. Vern Rutsala.—JaD
Married life
All the way back. L. Riding.—HeR
The anniversary. W. Dickey.—JaG
Blue Springs, Georgia. R. Young.—JaG
The bonny bride of Kent. E. Farjeon.—FaE
"Brave news is come to town." Mother Goose.—DeM—LoR

The curst wife. Unknown.—PlAs
"Eaper Weaper, chimbley sweeper." Mother Goose.—AlH
Epigrams. J. V. Cunningham.—HeR
The farmer's curst wife. Unknown.—PlAs
Get up and bar the door. Unknown.—BlO—PlAs
Good neighbors. M. Justus.—PrRa
The grandmother. W. Berry.—JaD—PlSc
The hardness scale. J. Peseroff.—McL
How about. S. L. Nelms.—JaS
"Husbands and wives." M. Hershenson.—CoN
"I had a little husband." Mother Goose.—AlH—BlQ—FaW—LoR
"I married a wife by the light of the moon." Mother Goose.—LoR
"I married a wife on Sunday." A. Lobel.—LoWr
The impulse. R. Frost.—PlAs
"In Golden Gate Park that day." L. Ferlinghetti.—HeR
"Jack Sprat could eat no fat." Mother Goose.—AlH—DeM—FaW—LoR
Jamie Douglas. Unknown.—PlAs
John Grumlie. Unknown.—PlSc
Klabauterwife's letter. C. Morgenstern.—LiWa
Lenora. Unknown.—BrT
Marriage contract. V. Rutsala.—JaD
A matter of principle. N. M. Bodecker.—BoPc
Meditation on the A30. Sir J. Betjeman.—HeR
Mrs. Kriss Kringle. E. M. Thomas.—HaOf
"My wife whose hair is a brush fire." From Free union. A. Breton.—KoT
"Needles and pins, needles and pins." Mother Goose.—AlH
The old man who lived in the woods. Unknown.—CoOu
"On Saturday night I lost my wife." Mother Goose.—LoR
On the eve of our anniversary. G. Margolis.—JaS
One of the boys. P. Dacey.—JaS
The perfect husband. O. Nash.—JaD
"Peter, Peter, pumpkin eater." Mother Goose.—DeM—FaW—LoR
Rickie Miller. M. Glenn.—GlC
Robert of Lincoln. W. C. Bryant.—HaOf
She and I. N. Cameron.—HeR
Songs for a colored singer. E. Bishop.—HeR
Surfaces. P. Meinke.—JaS
Ten week wife. R. Donovan.—JaS
Trying. L. Nathan.—JaS
The two sweethearts. E. Farjeon.—FaE
"Up and down Pie Street." Mother Goose.—AlH
The vacuum. H. Nemerov.—HeR
Washing windows. P. Wild.—JaS
The wife wrapt in wether's skin. Unknown.—PlAs
The winter moon ("I hit my wife and went out and saw"). T. Kyozo.—McL
"A woman named Mrs. S. Claus." J. P. Lewis.—LiCp
"**Married** when the year is new." Mother Goose.—LoR
The **marrog.** R. C. Scriven.—PrRh
Marsh, Corinna
Before the bath.—FrP—PrRa
Marshall, Catherine See Marshall, Peter, and Marshall, Catherine
Marshall, Peter. See also next entry
"O Lord, save us."—LaT

Matthews, William
  The hummer.—JaT
  In memory of the Utah stars.—JaPi
Mattie Lou at twelve. Nikki Giovanni.—GiSp
Maturity. X. J. Kennedy.—KeF
"**Maureen** came out of Ireland with her double
  cutting tongue." See City under water
Maurice. Gwendolyn Brooks.—HoBf
"**Maurice** must move away." See Maurice
Max Schmitt in a single scull. Richmond
  Lattimore.—PlEd
May
  Alibazan. L. E. Richards.—HaOf
  Cows. J. Reeves.—BlO—CoN
  "The fair maid who, the first of May." Mother
    Goose.—AlH
  For a dance. E. Farjeon.—FaE
  "I stood in the Maytime meadows."
    Unknown.—KoT
  May. J. Updike.—HaOf
  May Day. M. C. Livingston.—LiWo
  May first, two inches of snow. B. J.
    Esbensen.—EsCs
  May meadows. E. Farjeon.—FaE
  May night. S. Teasdale.—HoSi
  "May rains." Sanpu.—KoT
  The Mayers' song. Unknown.—PlAs
  Maytime magic. M. Watts.—PrRh
  Men working. E. S. Millay.—PlSc
  Phillida and Coridon. N. Breton.—KoT
  Summer fountains. E. Farjeon.—FaE
  Sun and wind. E. Farjeon.—FaE
  That May morning. L. B. Jacobs.—ChG—PrRh
May. John Updike.—HaOf
"**May** a gnat swallow you." See Curses to fling
  at a giant
May Day. Myra Cohn Livingston.—LiWo
"**May** evil sorcery be given the wink." See From
  a prayer of the shooting chant
May first, two inches of snow. Barbara Juster
  Esbensen.—EsCs
"**May** I, for my own self, song's truth reckon."
  See The seafarer
"**May** I give birth to Pollen Girl, may I give
  birth to Cornbeetle." See Mother's prayer for
  a girl
"**May** it be delightful, my house." See House
  blessing
May meadows. Eleanor Farjeon.—FaE
May night. Sara Teasdale.—HoSi
"**May** nothing evil cross this door." See Prayer
  for this house
"**May** rains." Sanpu.—KoT
"**May** the Milky Way enter my father's fading
  eyes." See To my father
"**May** you be renewed." See A prayer of the girls'
  puberty ceremony
"**Maybe** he dreamed of." See Retired farmer
"**Maybe** it's so." See Snail's pace
"**Maybe** life was better." See Thoughts on getting
  out of a nice warm bed in an ice cold house
  to go to the bathroom at three o'clock in
  the morning
The **Mayers'** song. Unknown.—PlAs
Maytime magic. Mabel Watts.—PrRh
Mazatec Indians. See Indians of the Americas—
  Mazatec
Mbya Indians. See Indians of the Americas—
  Mbya
Me ("As long as I live"). Walter De la Mare.—
  PrRh
Me ("My nose is blue"). Karla Kuskin.—PrRh
"**Me** an' ma baby's." See Negro dancers

Me I am. Jack Prelutsky.—PrRh
"**Me** is better." See Flavors (3)
The **meadow** mouse. Theodore Roethke.—HeR—
  LiSf
Meadows. See Fields
The **meal.** Karla Kuskin.—PrRa
Meals. See Breakfast; Food and eating
Mean Maxine. Jack Prelutsky.—PrNk
Mean Rufus throw-down. David Smith.—JaT
Mean song. Eve Merriam.—LiSf
A **mean** trick. Unknown.—BrT
"The **meanest** girl I've ever met." See Wicked
  thoughts
"The **meanest** trick I ever knew." See A low trick
"**Meaning** well, Minerva Jean." X. J. Kennedy.—
  KeB
Mearns, Hughes
  The little man ("As I was walking up the
    stair").—PrRh
    I met a man ("As I was going up the
      stair").—CoOu (unat.)
  The perfect reactionary.—CoN
Measles. Kaye Starbird.—PrRh
Measure for measure, sels. William Shakespeare
  "Aye, but to die, and go we know not
    where."—HeR
The **measure** of man. Eve Merriam.—MeSk
Measurement. A. M. Sullivan.—PrRh
Le **medecin** malgre lui. William Carlos
  Williams.—PlSc
Medicine
  "I am the medicine." Unknown, fr. the Mazatec
    Indian.—BiSp
  Medicine songs. Unknown, fr. the Sioux
    Indian.—BiSp
  Remedies. G. Soto.—JaS
Medicine man's prayer. Unknown.—BiSp
Medicine songs. Unknown.—BiSp
Meditatio. Ezra Pound.—LiSf
Meditation on the A30. Sir John Betjeman.—HeR
Meditations of a parrot. John Ashbery.—KoT
Meditations of a tortoise dozing under a rosetree
  near a beehive at noon while a dog scampers
  about and a cuckoo calls from a distant
  wood. Emile Victor Rieu.—LiSf
Medusa
  Perseid meteor shower. B. J. Esbensen.—EsCs
  The statue of Medusa. W. Drummond.—PlEd
"**Meet** ladybug." See I want you to meet
"**Meet** me my love, meet me my love." See The
  juniper tree
Meet neat Rosie De Fleet. Unknown.—BrT
Meet-on-the-road ("Now, pray, where are you
  going, said Meet-on-the-road"). Unknown.—
  BlO
  Meet-on-the-road ("Now, pray, where are you
    going, child").—KoT
Meet-on-the-road ("Now, pray, where are you
  going, child"). See Meet-on-the-road ("Now,
  pray, where are you going, said
  Meet-on-the-road")
"**Meet** the lazy nothing doings." See The nothing
  doings
The **meeting.** Howard Moss.—JaG
Meeting Mary. Eleanor Farjeon.—FaE
Meetings and absences. Roy Fuller.—CoOu
"**Meg.**" See Meg's egg
Meg Merrilies. John Keats.—BlO—LiSf
Meg's egg. Mary Ann Hoberman.—PrRh
Meigs, Mildred
  Pirate Don Durk of Dowdee.—CoOu

Memories.—*Continued*
Sweetheart. P. Hey.—JaG
Tarantella. H. Belloc.—HeR
Ten days leave. W. D. W. Snodgrass.—JaPi
"Tippetty Witchet." E. Farjeon.—FaE
To my daughter riding in the circus parade. J. Labombard.—JaG
To the moon ("I remember, gracious, graceful moon"). G. Leopardi.—KoT
Victorian grandmother. M. Lockwood.—JaPi
A visit from Alphonse. P. Zimmer.—JaG
What do they do to you in distant places. M. Bell.—JaPi
"When lilacs last in the dooryard bloom'd." W. Whitman.—HeR
When the ambulance came. R. Morgan.—JaS
Widow to her son. R. T. Smith.—JaS
Memories of Verdun. Alan Dugan.—HeR
Memory. See Forgetfulness; Memories
Memory of my father. Patrick Kavanagh.—HeR
Men—portraits. See People—portraits—men
"The **men** laughed and baaed like sheep." See Memories of Verdun
Men may talk of country Christmasses. Philip Massinger.—HaO
"**Men** may talk of country Christmasses and court gluttony." See Men may talk of country Christmasses
"**Men** of England, wherefore plough." See Song, to the men of England
Men working. Edna St. Vincent Millay.—PlSc
The **mendacious** mole. Oliver Herford.—BrT
Mending. Judith Viorst.—ViI
Mending the adobe. Hayden Carruth.—JaPi—PlEd
Mending wall. Robert Frost.—KoS
Mendings. Muriel Rukeyser.—PlSc
Mental retardation
Children not kept at home. J. C. Oates.—JaD
He sits down on the floor of a school for the retarded. A. Nowlan.—JaG
I show the daffodils to the retarded kids. C. Sharp.—JaD
My dim-wit cousin. T. Roethke.—JaD
Meogo, Pero
Cossante.—PlAs
Merchant, Jane
Flight plan.—HoCl—PrRh
"A **merchant** addressing a debtor." See Persuasive go-gebtor
Merchants. See Shops and shopkeepers
Mercy. See Sympathy
Meredith, William
The fishvendor.—PlSc
Homage to Paul Mellon, I. M. Pei, their gallery, and Washington City.—PlEd
Two masks unearthed in Bulgaria.—PlEd
Meredith Piersall. Mel Glenn.—GlCd
Merlin
Merlin. E. Muir.—HeR
Merlin and the snake's egg. L. Norris.—LiWa
Merlin. Edwin Muir.—HeR
Merlin and the snake's egg. Leslie Norris.—LiWa
The **mermaid,** complete. Alfred Tennyson.—DaC—LiWa—LiWa
The **mermaid,** sels. Alfred Tennyson
"Who would be".—HoCr
A **mermaid** song. James Reeves.—LiSf
The **mermaidens.** Laura E. Richards.—HaOf
Mermaids and mermen
And although the little mermaid sacrificed everthing to win the love of the prince, the prince, alas, decided to wed another. J. Viorst.—ViI

Burning bright. L. Morrison.—FaTh
The fisherman writes a letter to the mermaid. J. Aiken.—LiWa
The forsaken merman. M. Arnold.—BlO
Forty mermaids. D. Lee.—RuI
"I did not see a mermaid." S. J. Johnson.—LiSf
"I like fish, said the Mermaid." From Song. E. Coatsworth.—HoCr
The loreley. H. Heine.—LiWa
The mermaid, complete. A. Tennyson.—DaC—LiWa—LiWa
A mermaid song. J. Reeves.—LiSf
The mermaidens. L. E. Richards.—HaOf
Mermaid's music. J. Yolen.—RuI
A sea spell for a picture. D. G. Rossetti.—LiWa
Siren chorus. G. Darley.—LiWa
Song of the mermaids and mermen. Sir W. Scott.—LiWa
Undersea. M. Chute.—RuI
"Who would be." From The mermaid. A. Tennyson.—HoCr
Mermaid's music. Jane Yolen.—RuI
"A **mermaid's** tears." See Burning bright
Mermen. See Mermaids and mermen
Merriam, Eve
Advertisement for a divertissement.—MeSk
Alarm clock.—MeSk
Anticipations. See A throw of threes
"Apple."—MeHa
Apple joys. See A throw of threes
Argument.—MeSk
Artichoke ("Leaf").—MeF
Basic for further irresponsibility.—MeSk
Basic for irresponsibility.—MeSk
Bat ("Bats in the belfry").—MeHa
Be my non-Valentine.—MeSk
"Bella had a new umbrella."—MeBl
"Berries on the bushes."—MeBl
"Bertie, Bertie."—MeBl
Beware of the doggerel.—MeSk
Beware, or be yourself.—MeSk
Beyond sci-fi.—MeF
Butterflies.—MeF
"Cat cat cat on the bed."—MeBl
Catch a little rhyme.—HaOf
"Caterpillar."—MeBl
"Cat's tongue."—LiCa—MeBl
A charm for our time.—MeSk
City traffic.—LiSf—MeSk
A cliche.—MeSk
The clock ticks.—MeSk
Color.—MeSk
Conversation with myself.—MeSk
Counting-out rhyme ("Grimes golden greening yellow transparent").—KeK
Couplet countdown.—MeSk
Crawler.—MeHa
"Crick, crack."—MeBl
Cures for melancholy. See A throw of threes
Curses to fling at a giant. See A throw of threes
Demon.—MeHa
The dirty word.—MeSk
Disguises. See A throw of threes
Double trouble.—MeSk
Elf.—MeHa
End of winter.—MeSk
Excursion.—MeF
Fantasia ("I dream").—MeSk
Fiend.—MeHa
"The first day of spring."—MeF
"Five little monsters."—MeBl—PrRa
Floccinaucinihilipilification.—MeSk

Merriam, Eve—*Continued*
Trap.—MeHa
Two people ("She reads the paper").—PrRh
Umbilical.—HoCl—MeSk—PrRh
Umbrella ("Umbrella, umbrella").—MeHa
"Up in the attic there's a great big trunk."—MeBl
Urbanity.—MeSk
Uses for a fog. See A throw of threes
Vacation ("I am Paul Bunyan").—MeSk
Viper.—MeHa
Ways of winding a watch.—MeSk
"What in the world."—PrRh
Which Washington.—CoN
Why I did not reign.—MeSk
Windshield wiper.—KeK
Winter alphabet.—MeSk
Witchery.—MeHa
Witness.—MeSk
Word bird.—MeSk
"Xenobia Phobia." MeBl
Xylophone.—MeHa
Yeast.—MeHa
Zero.—MeHa
"**Merrily** swinging on brier and weed." See Robert of Lincoln
"**Merry** are the bells, and merry would they ring." Mother Goose.—LiSf—LoR
Merry Christmas. Aileen Fisher.—PrRh
The **merry** crocodile. Gertrude E. Heath.—BrT
"The **merry-go-round** horse." Lee Bennett Hopkins.—HoSi
Merry-go-rounds
"The merry-go-round horse." L. B. Hopkins.—HoSi
The **merry** pieman's song. John Bennett.—LiIl
Merwin, William Stanley
"Deep in love", tr. by.—McL
Ghazal XII, tr. by.—McL
The little mute boy, tr. by.—HeR
"Love, you alone have been with us", tr. by.—McL
Road.—JaPo
Sea monster.—LiWa
Separation ("Your absence has gone through me").—LiIl
Trees ("I am looking at trees").—JaPo
White summer flower.—JaD
"The whole universe is full of God", tr. by.—McL
The windows.—JaD
You have what I look for, tr. by.—McL
Message from a caterpillar. Lilian Moore.—LiSf—MoSn
Message from a mouse, ascending in a rocket. Patricia Hubbell.—LiSf—PrRh
Metamorphoses ("These people, with their illegible diplomas"). Howard Nemerov.—PlEd
Metamorphosis ("When water turns to ice does it remember"). Carl Sandburg.—HoRa
Metaphor (about)
Bruises. C. Barks.—JaPo
A cliche. E. Merriam.—MeSk
Metaphor. E. Merriam.—MeSk
Metaphor man. E. Merriam.—MeSk
Metaphor. Eve Merriam.—MeSk
"The **metaphor** man." See Metaphor man
Metaphor man. Eve Merriam.—MeSk
Meteors
Perseid meteor shower. B. J. Esbensen.—EsCs
"**Methought** that I had broken from the Tower." From Richard III. William Shakespeare.—HeR

Metz, Roberta
Exactly.—FaTh
The **mewlips**. John Ronald Reuel Tolkien.—LiWa
Mexican-American war. See United States—History—Mexican-American war
Mexican market woman. Langston Hughes.—HuDk—PlSc
Meyers, Bert
Glowworm ("He studies very late"), tr. by.—FaTh
Meyers, Odette
Crab, tr. by.—FaTh
Glowworm ("He studies very late"), tr. by.—FaTh
Ladybug ("A tiny island"), tr. by.—FaTh
Mice
The bat ("By day the bat is cousin to the mouse"). T. Roethke.—HaOf—LiSf—LiWa—PrRh
"Boing, boing, squeak." J. Prelutsky.—PrNk
The cat ("One gets a wife, one gets a house"). O. Nash.—ChC
The cat who aspired to higher things. X. J. Kennedy.—JaT
Cats and dogs ("Some like cats, and some like dogs."). N. M. Bodecker.—BoSs
The city mouse and the garden mouse. C. G. Rossetti.—CoN
The country mouse and the city mouse. R. S. Sharpe.—DaC
"Dormy, dormy dormouse." Mother Goose.—BlPi
Field mouse to kitchen mouse. E. Coatsworth.—FrP
A friendly mouse. H. Behn.—HoCb
The frog and the mouse. Mother Goose.—BlPi
"Fury said to a mouse." From Alice's adventures in Wonderland. L. Carroll.—KeK
"Here comes a mouse." C. Watson.—WaC
"Here's a little mouse." E. E. Cummings.—KoT
"Hickory dickory dock." Mother Goose.—DeM—FaW—LoR
The house mouse. J. Prelutsky.—PrRa—PrZ
"The house of the mouse." L. S. Mitchell.—CoN
"I raised a great hullabaloo." Unknown.—PrRh
"I saw a ship a-sailing." Mother Goose.—DeM—LiSf—LoR—RuI
I wouldn't. J. Ciardi.—JaT
Invitation to a mouse. E. Farjeon.—FaE
"Little black bug." M. W. Brown.—CoN—FrP
"Little Poll Parrot." Mother Goose.—DeM
The parrot in the garret.—BlPi
Loft. S. Cassedy.—CaR
The magical mouse. K. Patchen.—KeK
The meadow mouse. T. Roethke.—HeR—LiSf
"The melodious meritorious mouse." From An animal alphabet. E. Lear.—LiH
Merry Christmas. A. Fisher.—PrRh
Message from a mouse, ascending in a rocket. P. Hubbell.—LiSf—PrRh
Mice. R. Fyleman.—CoN—FrP—LiSf—PrRa—PrRh
Mice in the hay. L. Norris.—HaO
The midnightmouse. C. Morgenstern.—HeR
The mouse ("I heard a mouse"). E. Coatsworth.—HaOf
The mouse ("I'm only a poor little mouse, ma'am"). L. E. Richards.—HaOf
The mouse and the cake. E. Cook.—DaC
Mouse dinner. A. Fisher.—FaTh
The mouse's courting song. Unknown.—PlAs

Milkmen—*Continued*
Summer milk. X. J. Kennedy.—KeF
Milky Way
Blake leads a walk on the Milky Way. N. Willard.—HaOf
The Milky Way. B. J. Esbensen.—EsCs
The Milky Way. Barbara Juster Esbensen.—EsCs
The **mill** ("Over the harbor at St. James"). William Heyen.—PlEd
The **mill** ("The spoiling daylight inched along the bar-top"). Richard Wilbur.—JaPi
The **mill-pond**. Edward Thomas.—HeR
Millay, Edna St. Vincent
Afternoon on a hill.—CoN—HaOf—KoT
The ballad of the harp-weaver.—LiSf—LiWa
The bean stalk.—LiWa
Counting-out rhyme ("Silver bark of beech, and sallow").—KoT
"In the evening I would sit." See Journal
Journal, sels.
"In the evening I would sit".—PlSc
Men working.—PlSc
Portrait by a neighbor.—HaOf—LiSf
Recuerdo.—LiSf
Travel.—HaOf—PrRh
"What lips my lips have kissed, and where, and why."—McL
Wraith.—LiWa
Miller, Jim Wayne
Aunt Gladys's home movie no. 31, Albert's funeral.—JaS
Family reunion ("Sunlight glints off the chrome of many cars").—JaS
For Richard Chase.—JaG
A house of readers.—JaPo
Living with children.—JaG
Rechargeable dry cell poem.—JaG
Spring storm ("He comes gusting out of the house").—JaG
Miller, Mary Britton
Cat ("The black cat yawns").—ChC—LiSf—PrRh
Foal.—LiSf
Shore.—PrRa
They've all gone south.—PrRh
The universe ("There is the moon, there is the sun").—PrRh
Where are you now.—PrRh
Miller, Thomas
Evening ("The day is past, the sun is set").—DaC
Millers and mills
Bingo. Unknown.—KoT
"Blow, wind, blow." Mother Goose.—DeM—LoR
Five eyes. W. De la Mare.—ChC
"God made the bees." Mother Goose.—BlO—LoR—PlSc
The jolly miller. Unknown.—DaC
Two of a kind. X. J. Kennedy.—KeF
"When the wind blows." Mother Goose.—LoR
"The **miller's** mill-dog lay at the mill-door." See Bingo
"**Millicent** can play the flute." See Broom balancing
Milligan, Spike
"A baby sardine."—CoOu
"Cat will rhyme with hat."—ChC
Christmas 1970.—HaO
Edser.—BrT
Goliath.—TrM
"Look at all those monkeys."—CoOu
My sister Laura.—CoN—FaW—PrRa

"On the ning nang nong."—PrRh
Teeth.—TrM
"Tell me, little woodworm."—PrRa
"A thousand hairy savages."—CoOu—PrRh
"You must never bath in an Irish stew."—PrRh
A **million** candles. Jack Prelutsky.—PrMp
"A **million** candles fill the night." See A million candles
Millions of strawberries. Genevieve Taggard.—Lill—LiSf
Mills, Dorothy
Hair.—BeD
Mills. See Millers and mills
Milne, Alan Alexander
At the zoo ("There are lions and roaring tigers, and enormous camels and things").—FrP
Buckingham Palace.—FaW
Busy.—LiSf
Disobedience.—CoN
Furry bear.—FrP
Halfway down.—PrRa
Hoppity.—CoN
Howard.—BrT
If I were a king.—CoOu
The king's breakfast.—FaW—LiSf
"The more it snows."—CoN—PrRa—PrRh
Puppy and I.—CoOu—FrP
Solitude ("I have a house where I go").—LiSf
Teddy bear.—CoOu
Twinkletoes.—ChG
Milne, Ewart
Diamond cut diamond.—LiSf
Milner, Ian
Clap your hands for Herod, tr. by.—HaO
How to paint a perfect Christmas, tr. by.—HaO
Milner, Jarmila
Bullfight, tr. by.—HeR
Milner-Gulland, Robin
Colors, tr. by.—McL
"Under the dawn I wake my two-wheel friend", tr. by.—Lill
Waiting ("My love will come"), tr. by.—McL
Miłosz, Czesław
A devil, tr. by.—HeR
Milton, John
"Here lies old Hobson, death hath broke his girt."—PlSc
Milton, sels. William Blake
Jerusalem.—HeR
Mimosa. Myra Cohn Livingston.—LiMp
Min Trang. Mel Glenn.—GlCd
Minarik, Else Holmelund
Little seeds.—PrRa
"When mosquitoes make a meal."—PrRh
The **mince-python**. From A baker's dozen of wild beasts. Carolyn Wells.—HaOf
"The **mince-python's** a crusty old beast." See The mince-python
Mind. See also Wisdom
The alchemist ("I burned my life, that I might find"). L. Bogan.—McL
Brain. C. Barks.—JaPo
Knowledge. E. Farjeon.—FaE
A rabbit as king of the ghosts. W. Stevens.—KoT
Mine. Lilian Moore.—MoSn
"**Mine** eye and heart are at a mortal war." From Sonnets. William Shakespeare.—PlEd
"**Mine** eye hath play'd the painter, and hath steel'd." From Sonnets. William Shakespeare.—PlEd
"**Mine** the forest." See Forest: an invitation

Minerals
The hardness scale. J. Peseroff.—McL
Miners. See Mines and mining
Mines and mining
Caliban in the coal mines. L. Untermeyer.—LaT
The case for the miners. S. Sassoon.—PlSc
Clementine. Unknown.—KeK—LiSf
  Oh, my darling Clementine.—PlAs
Driving through coal country in Pennsylvania. J. Holden.—JaG
The explosion. P. Larkin.—HeR
The Gresford disaster. Unknown.—PlAs
The hill above the mine. M. Cowley.—PlSc
"I am going to California." Unknown.—PlAs
"In the coal pit, or the factory." J. Skipsey.—PlSc
Seeing the elephant. Unknown.—PlAs
"Surely there is a mine for silver." From Job. Bible/Old Testament.—PlSc
Working in the mines. Unknown.—PlAs
Ye ancient Yuba miner of the days of '49. S. C. Upham.—PlAs
"Mingled." See Subway rush hour
Mingled yarns. X. J. Kennedy.—HaOf
The **minimal.** Theodore Roethke.—FaTh—HeR
Minnie. Eleanor Farjeon.—FaE
"Minnie and Winnie." Alfred Tennyson.—ChB—KoT
"Minnie can't make her mind up." See Minnie
Minnie Morse. Kaye Starbird.—LiSf
A **minor** bird. Robert Frost.—KoS
Minstrel man. Langston Hughes.—HuDk
Minstrel's song. Ted Hughes.—HaO
"The mint bed is in." See Sunday
"Mips and ma the mooly moo." From Praise to the end. Theodore Roethke.—HeR
Miracles
Miracles. W. Whitman.—LiSf
Rollo's miracle. P. Zimmer.—JaG
"A spider danced a cosy jig." I. Layton.—DoNw
Miracles. Walt Whitman.—LiSf
Miraculous Mortimer. Jack Prelutsky.—PrNk
"Miraculous Mortimer, master magician." See Miraculous Mortimer
Mirage. Christina Georgina Rossetti.—McL
Mirror. Sylvia Cassedy.—CaR
"The mirror cared less and less at the last, but." See At the grave of my brother
"Mirror land, a meeting place." See Magic spell for finding a woman
"Mirror, mirror, over the sink." Arnold Lobel.—LoWr
"Mirror, mirror, tell me." Mother Goose.—DaC—LoR
Mirrors. See also Reflections (mirrored)
Beware, do not read this poem. I. Reed.—LiWa
Conversation with myself. E. Merriam.—MeSk
From my mother's house. L. Goldberg.—StG
Heart crown and mirror. G. Apollinaire.—KoT
"In the mirror." E. Fleming.—CoOu
The magical picture. R. Graves.—LiSf
Man's image. D. H. Lawrence.—PrBb
Mirror. S. Cassedy.—CaR
"Mirror, mirror, over the sink." A. Lobel.—LoWr
"Mirror, mirror, tell me." Mother Goose.—DaC—LoR
Nolan Davis. M. Glenn.—GlCd
Reflections ("In the mirror"). M. C. Livingston.—FrP

Robert, who is often a stranger to himself. G. Brooks.—PrRa
Throckmorton Thratte. J. Prelutsky.—PrNk
The **misapprehended** goose. Oliver Herford.—BrT
Mischief
Abracadabra. D. Livesay.—DoNw
Elf. E. Merriam.—MeHa
Fiend. E. Merriam.—MeHa
Lollocks. R. Graves.—HeR
"Misery is when your." Langston Hughes.—LiIl
Misnomer. Eve Merriam.—PrRh
Miss Bitter. N. M. Bodecker.—CoN
Miss Blues'es child. Langston Hughes.—KoT
"Miss Dinah when she goes to church." See A little more cider
Miss Hartley. William Jay Smith.—BrT
Miss Hepzibah. Eve Merriam.—MeSk
"Miss Hepzibah has a mania." See Miss Hepzibah
Miss Hocket. Unknown.—BrT
Miss M.F.H.E.I.I. Jones. Karla Kuskin.—LiIl
Miss Norma Jean Pugh, first grade teacher. Mary O'Neill.—PrRh
Miss T. Walter De la Mare.—CoN—CoOu—LiSf
Miss Tibbles. Ian Serraillier.—LiCa
"Miss Tibbles is my kitten, white." See Miss Tibbles
Miss Tillie McLush. Joseph S. Newman.—BrT
Missing my daughter. Stephen Spender.—JaS
Missing the children. Paul Zimmer.—JaS
Missing you. Charlotte Zolotow.—HoBf—LiIl
Mississippi River
Mississippi sounding calls. Unknown.—LiSf
Mississippi sounding calls. Unknown.—LiSf
A **misspelled** tail. Elizabeth T. Corbett.—HaOf
Missy Sinkins. Eleanor Farjeon.—FaE
Mist. See Fog
"The mist-foot man who forms within my cellars." See Nightfall
"A mist of snowflakes swirling in the street." See Quilt song
Mister alley cat. John McGowan.—ChC
Mr. and Mrs. Spikky Sparrow. Edward Lear.—LiH
"Mister Beedle Baddlebug." See Tea party
Mr. Bidery's spidery garden. David McCord.—PrRh
Mr. Dill. Cynthia Rylant.—RyW
"Mr. East gave a feast." Mother Goose.—DeM
Mister Fox. Unknown.—BlO
Mr. 'Gator. N. M. Bodecker.—CoN—CoOu—FaW—LiSf
Mr. Giraffe. Geoffry Lapage.—CoOu
"Mr. Ibister." Mother Goose.—BlPi
Mr. Kartoffel. James Reeves.—PrRh
"Mr. Kartoffel's a whimsical man." See Mr. Kartoffel
Mr. Lafon. Cynthia Rylant.—RyW
"Mr. Lizard is crying." Federico García Lorca.—KoT
"Mr. MacGregor says." See That's Gloria
"Mr. Matthews, how come you're still here." See Cynthia Leonard
Mr. Potts. Harry Behn.—HoCb
Mr. Pratt. Myra Cohn Livingston.—PrRh
"Mr. Pratt has never left." See Mr. Pratt
Mr. Pyme. Harry Behn.—HoCb
Mr. Rabbit. Dixie Willson.—FrP
"Mr. Rabbit has a habit." See Mr. Rabbit
Mr. Skinner. N. M. Bodecker.—FaW—LiSf
"Mr. T." See The artist
Mr. Wells. From The sorcerer. William Schwenck Gilbert.—LiWa

Mr. Wells. Elizabeth Madox Roberts.—KeK
Mistletoe
  "Heigh ho, mistletoe." N. M. Bodecker.—BoSs
  Holly and mistletoe. E. Farjeon.—FaE
  The mistletoe. J. Prelutsky.—PrRa
  The **mistletoe.** Jack Prelutsky.—PrRa
Mrs. Brownish Beetle. Aileen Fisher.—FiW
Mrs. Green. David Huddle.—JaPo
Mrs. Kriss Kringle. Edith M. Thomas.—HaOf
Mrs. Martha Jean Black. Nikki Giovanni.—GiSp
"**Mrs.** Peck Pigeon." Eleanor Farjeon.—CoN—
  CoOu—FaE—LiSf
"**Mistress** Pratt." Arnold Lobel.—LoWr
Mitchell, Adrian
  Autobahnmotorwayautoroute.—HeR
  Giving potatoes.—HeR
  Watch your step, I'm drenched.—HeR
Mitchell, Cynthia
  "A frog and a flea."—PrRa
Mitchell, Lucy Sprague
  "The house of the mouse."—CoN
Mitchell Chapin. Mel Glenn.—GlC
The **mitten** song. Marie Louise Allen.—CoN—
  PrRa
Mittens
  The mitten song. M. L. Allen.—CoN—PrRa
  Mittens. B. J. Esbensen.—EsCs
  The modern Hiawatha. G. A. Strong.—PrRh
  "Three little kittens lost their mittens." Mother
    Goose.—DeM
    The three little kittens.—HaOf
    "Three little kittens, they lost their
      mittens".—LoR
Mittens. Barbara Juster Esbensen.—EsCs
"**Mix** a pancake." Christina Georgina Rossetti.—
  CoN—FrP—LiSf—PrRa
  The pancake.—ChG
Mixed-up kid. X. J. Kennedy.—KeF
Mixed-up school. X. J. Kennedy.—JaT
Miyoshi, Sekiya
  "What are days for." See The world is day
    breaking
  The world is day breaking, sels.
    "What are days for".—BeD
Mizumura, Kazue
  "Gently, gently, the wind blows."—FaTh
  "A lonely sparrow."—LiSf
  Please bird.—BaS
  "Snow makes a new land."—LiSf
  "Who tossed those golden coins."—FaTh—LiSf
Moberg, Verne
  At Annika's place, tr. by.—CoN
  Best, tr. by.—CoN
  Once, tr. by.—CoN
A **mock** miracle. Oliver Herford.—BrT
The **mocking** bird ("Hush up, baby"). See "Hush,
  little baby, don't say a word"
The **mockingbird** ("Look one way and the sun
  is going down"). Randall Jarrell.—LiSf
Mockingbirds
  The actor. P. Fleischman.—FlI
  The mockingbird ("Look one way and the sun
    is going down"). R. Jarrell.—LiSf
Modeling. See Sculpture and statues
A **modern** dragon. Rowena Bennett.—PrRa
The **modern** Hiawatha. George A Strong.—PrRh
Modern life. See also Atomic age
  After his death. N. MacCaig.—HeR
  Air on an escalator. J. Aiken.—LiSf
  Annie Scarella. M. Glenn.—GlC
  "As I walked out one evening." W. H.
    Auden.—HeR—PlAs
  At the bomb testing site. W. Stafford.—HeR

Autobahnmotorwayautoroute. A. Mitchell.—HeR
Bagpipe music. L. MacNeice.—HeR
Ballad of the bread man. C. Causley.—HeR
Basic for further irresponsibility. E. Merriam.—
  MeSk
Basic for irresponsibility. E. Merriam.—MeSk
"Beautification." N. M. Bodecker.—BoPc
Brother, can you spare a dime. E. Y.
  Harburg.—PlAs—PlSc
Butch Weldy. E. L. Masters.—PlSc
The case for the miners. S. Sassoon.—PlSc
A charm for our time. E. Merriam.—MeSk
Christine Leader. M. Glenn.—GlC
Christmas, 1924. T. Hardy.—HaO
Christmas shopping. L. MacNeice.—HaO
Christmas tree ("Stores and filling stations
  prefer a roof"). S. Cook.—HaO
City dawn. N. M. Bodecker.—BoPc
Clarence. S. Silverstein.—HaOf
The clock ticks. E. Merriam.—MeSk
Cocaine Lil and Morphine Sue. Unknown.—
  IlcR
Contemporary announcement. M. Angelou.—
  AnS
The crib. R. Finch.—HaO
December eclipse. M. Lockwood.—JaPi
Departmental. R. Frost.—KoS
Development. N. M. Bodecker.—BoPc
Dirge. K. Fearing.—HeR
Disillusionment of ten o'clock. W. Stevens.—
  HeR—KoT
Driving at dawn. W. Heyen.—PlSc
Ellen Winters. M. Glenn.—GlC
Everett Anderson's friend. L. Clifton.—LiIl
Fantasia ("I dream"). E. Merriam.—MeSk
Fear. N. Giovanni.—GiSp
Folk tune. R. Wilbur.—PlAs
For Richard Chase. J. W. Miller.—JaG
"Four-way stop." M. C. Livingston.—KeK
Garage sale. K. Shapiro.—JaPi
Girl who's moved around. X. J. Kennedy.—
  KeF
Glass walling. N. M. Bodecker.—BoPc
Going away. H. Nemerov.—JaD
A good woman feeling bad. M. Angelou.—AnS
Greener grass. F. Steele.—JaPi
The health-food diner. M. Angelou.—AnS
A history lesson. M. Holub.—HeR
I met this guy who died. G. Corso.—JaPi
Ian Sinclair. M. Glenn.—GlCd
"In Golden Gate Park that day." L.
  Ferlinghetti.—HeR
It was all very tidy. R. Graves.—HeR
Jimmy Jet and his TV set. S. Silverstein.—
  HaOf—LiSf—PrRh
Junk. R. Wilbur.—PlSc
Junkyards. J. L. Rayford.—JaPo
Just for one day. L. Morrison.—PrRh
Kyrie Eleison. J. Aiken.—LiE
Lake Erie. From Great Lakes suite. J.
  Reaney.—DoNw
Landscape. E. Merriam.—KeK—MeSk
Late night flight. X. J. Kennedy.—KeF
The man who owned cars. E. Fried.—JaG
Mashkin Hill. L. Simpson.—PlSc
Maurice. G. Brooks.—HoBf
Meditation on the A30. Sir J. Betjeman.—HeR
Mendings. M. Rukeyser.—PlSc
A modern dragon. R. Bennett.—PrRa
Morning after. M. Vinz.—JaPo
Moving ("Some of the sky is grey and some
  of it is white"). R. Jarrell.—JaD
Neuteronomy. E. Merriam.—MeSk

Modern life.—*Continued*
Night, landing at Newark. J. Holden.—JaPo
Nightmare number three. S. V. Benét.—PlSc
Nude reclining at word processor, in pastel. C. Conover.—JaG
Of poor B. B. B. Brecht.—HeR
Old Doc. M. Vinz.—JaPi
The outwit song. D. Hoffman.—PlSc
Peace walk. W. Stafford.—JaPi
Pigeon hole. N. M. Bodecker.—BoPc
Poem ("O sole mio, hot diggety, nix, I wather think I can"). F. O'Hara.—KoT
Poem for people who are understandably too busy to read poetry. S. Dunn.—JaG
The poem in the park. P. Davison.—JaG
The poem you asked for. L. Levis.—JaG
Quest. E. Merriam.—MeF
Questions ("If cookies come in boxes"). L. B. Hopkins.—HoMu
Radar. A. Ross.—JaD
Rain forest, Papua, New Guinea. M. C. Livingston.—LiMp
Raleigh was right. W. C. Williams.—HeR
Relations. N. M. Bodecker.—BoPc
Rhonda Winfrey. M. Glenn.—GlC
The Saginaw song. T. Roethke.—HeR
Signs. N. M. Bodecker.—BoPc
A simple need. N. M. Bodecker.—BoPc
Skip rope rhyme for our time. E. Merriam.—MeF
Some good things to be said for the iron age. G. Snyder.—KoT
Song ("I'm about to go shopping"). J. Schuyler.—KoT
Song form. A. Baraka.—KoT
Song of the open road. O. Nash.—JaPo
Song Vu Chin. M. Glenn.—GlC
Southeast Arkanasia. M. Angelou.—PlSc
Stars ("In science today we learned"). N. Giovanni.—GiSp—KeK
The streets of Laredo ("O, early one morning I walked out like Agag"). L. MacNeice.—PlAs
Supermarket. F. Holman.—LiSf
The telephone. E. Field.—JaPo
Telephone poles ("They have been with us a long time"). J. Updike.—JaPi—PlSc
Television. M. L'Engle.—LaT
Television nose. X. J. Kennedy.—KeF
Think tank. E. Merriam.—HoCl—MeSk
"This little pig built a spaceship." F. Winsor.—PrRh
Tiempo muerto. R. Alonso.—PlSc
The toad ("In day of old, those far off times"). R. S. Oliver.—PrRh
Toads revisited. P. Larkin.—PlSc
Urbanity. E. Merriam.—MeSk
Us. D. Ignatow.—JaPo
War ("Each day the terror wagon"). R. Shelton.—JaPo
Weekend glory. M. Angelou.—AnS
Why ("We zoomed"). P. Redcloud.—HoMu
Wild west. M. Vinz.—JaPi
Willis Beggs. E. L. Masters.—PlSc
The witch's cat. I. Serraillier.—LiWa
With a posthumous medal. J. M. Brinnin.—PlSc
Witness. E. Merriam.—MeSk
"Yield." R. Gross.—KeK
Modoc Indians. See Indians of the Americas—Modoc
Mohr, Joseph
Silent night.—RoC (unat.)
Molasses river. Richard Kendall Munkittrick.—HaOf

The **mole** ("The mole's a solitary soul"). Jack Prelutsky.—PrZ
Mole ("A point-nosed half-pint parcel, eyes"). X. J. Kennedy.—KeF
The **mole** and the eagle. Sarah Josepha Hale.—HaOf
"The **mole** is blind, and under ground." See The mole and the eagle
Moles
The mendacious mole. O. Herford.—BrT
The mole ("The mole's a solitary soul"). J. Prelutsky.—PrZ
Mole ("A point-nosed half-pint parcel, eyes"). X. J. Kennedy.—KeF
The mole and the eagle. S. J. Hale.—HaOf
"The **mole's** a solitary soul." See The mole
"**Mollie,** my sister, and I fell out". See "Molly, my sister, and I fell out"
"**Molly,** my sister, and I fell out." Mother Goose.—DeM
"Mollie, my sister, and I fell out".—LoR
"**Mom** came home one day." See Forgotten
"A **moment** in summer." Charlotte Zolotow.—HoSi—PrRh
"**Mommies.**" Nikki Giovanni.—GiSp
Mommies do. Nikki Giovanni.—GiSp
"**Mommy.**" See The mistletoe
Monasteries
Monastery on Athos. R. Lattimore.—PlEd
Monastery on Athos. Richmond Lattimore.—PlEd
Monday. See Days of the week—Monday
"**Monday's** child is fair of face." Mother Goose.—DaC—DeM—FaW—LoR
"**Mondays** sweating the flat smell." See Days through starch and bluing
Money. See also Wealth
Christmas bills. J. Hatton.—HaO
Economy. E. Farjeon.—FaE
Flummery. E. Merriam.—MeSk
"God made the bees." Mother Goose.—BlO—LoR—PlSc
"Huckleberry, gooseberry, raspberry pie." C. Watson.—PrRh
"I love sixpence, jolly little sixpence." Mother Goose.—DeM
"If I'd as much money as I could spend." Mother Goose.—FaW—LoR
The lost farthing. E. Farjeon.—FaE
"Lucy Locket lost her pocket." Mother Goose.—DeM—LoR
"Money is power, so said one." C. Sandburg.—HoRa
Money makes the marriage. Unknown.—BrT
Penny royal. E. Farjeon.—FaE
Persuasive go-gebtor. Unknown.—BrT
"Said the scorpion of hate." C. Sandburg.—HoRa
Smart. S. Silverstein.—PrRh
Spendthrift. N. Farber.—LiSf
Writing for money. E. Field.—JaPo
"**Money** is power, so said one." Carl Sandburg.—HoRa
Money makes the marriage. Unknown.—BrT
Monica Zindell. Mel Glenn.—GlC
"The **monkey** curled his tail about." See Before the monkey's cage
The **monkey** puzzle. Myra Cohn Livingston.—LiMp
"The **monkey** puzzle is a tree." See The monkey puzzle
Monkeyland. Sándor Weöres, tr. by Edwin Morgan.—HeR

Monkeys. See Apes and monkeys
"**Monkeys** in the forest." See Where
Monkhouse, Cosmo
  Master of arts.—BrT
Monro, Harold
  The fresh air.—LiIl
  Milk for the cat.—BlO
  Overheard on a saltmarsh.—LiSf—LiWa
"**A monster.**" See Cloud shadow
Monsters
  Adventures of Isabel. O. Nash.—CoN—CoOu—
    HaOf—PrRh
  "Ah, a monster's lot is merry." J. Prelutsky.—
    PrNk
  "The baby uggs are hatching." J. Prelutsky.—
    PrB
  The bath-bunny. From A baker's dozen of wild
    beasts. C. Wells.—HaOf
  Bedtime stories. L. Moore.—BeD—CoN—HoCr
    Bedtime story.—MoSn—PrRa
  "The bloders are exploding." J. Prelutsky.—
    PrNk
  The bogeyman. J. Prelutsky.—PrRh
  "The bogus boo." J. Reeves.—PrRh
  Bye bye. S. O'Huigin.—DoNw
  The cave beast greets a visitor. J. Prelutsky.—
    PrNk
  Cloud shadow. L. Moore.—JaT—MoSn
  Come see the thing. J. Prelutsky.—PrNk
  The corn-pone-y. From A baker's dozen of wild
    beasts. C. Wells.—HaOf
  Crawler. E. Merriam.—MeHa
  The cream-puffin. From A baker's dozen of
    wild beasts. C. Wells.—HaOf
  The creature in the classroom. J. Prelutsky.—
    PrB—PrRh
  "The diatonic dittymunch." J. Prelutsky.—PrNk
  The Dracula vine. T. Hughes.—HoCr
  The dreary dreeze. J. Prelutsky.—PrB
  Father and mother. X. J. Kennedy.—PrRh
  "Five little monsters." E. Merriam.—MeBl—
    PrRa
  The flimsy fleek. J. Prelutsky.—PrNk
  The flotz. J. Prelutsky.—PrNk
  "From ghoulies and ghosties." From A Cornish
    litany. Unknown.—HoCr—LiSf
    Things that go bump in the night.—CoN
    A Cornish litany.—LiWa
  The ghoul. J. Prelutsky.—HaOf
  Grubby grebbles. J. Prelutsky.—PrB
  Gumble. M. Dugan.—PrRh
  Happy birthday, dear dragon. J. Prelutsky.—
    PrNk
  Herbert Glerbett. J. Prelutsky.—PrRh
  Hide and seek ("The trees are tall, but the
    moon small"). R. Graves.—CoN—KeK
  In black chasms. L. Norris.—LiWa
  In the night ("The light was burning very
    dim"). E. M. Roberts.—LiWa
  "In the pitch of the night." L. B. Hopkins.—
    HoCr
  Its fangs were red. J. Prelutsky.—PrNk
  Jabberwocky. From Through the looking glass.
    L. Carroll.—CoN—HeR—KoT—LiSf—PrRh
  Kermit Keene. J. Prelutsky.—PrSr
  The kraken. A. Tennyson.—LiSf—LiWa
  Lair. E. Merriam.—MeHa
  Lollocks. R. Graves.—HeR
  The marrog. R. C. Scriven.—PrRh
  The mewlips. J. R. R. Tolkien.—LiWa
  The mince-python. From A baker's dozen of
    wild beasts. C. Wells.—HaOf

"The nimpy numpy numpity." J. Prelutsky.—
  PrB
Pet. E. Merriam.—MeHa
The quossible. J. Prelutsky.—PrB
Sea monster. W. S. Merwin.—LiWa
The sea serpent chantey. V. Lindsay.—LiWa
Singing on the moon. T. Hughes.—LiWa
Sleep. N. Giovanni.—GiSp
"The slithergadee has crawled out of the sea."
  S. Silverstein.—LiWa
  The slithergadee.—CoOu—PrRh
  Not me.—CoN—KeK
The slithery slitch. J. Prelutsky.—PrB
The smasheroo. J. Prelutsky.—PrB
The sneepies. J. Prelutsky.—PrB
The sneezysnoozer. J. Prelutsky.—PrB
"Something is there." L. Moore.—LiWa—PrRh
Song of the gloopy gloppers. J. Prelutsky.—
  PrNk
Song of the ogres. W. H. Auden.—PrRh
"The spangled pandemonium." P. Brown.—
  PrRh
A spooky sort of shadow. J. Prelutsky.—PrMp
Steam shovel. C. Malam.—CoN—PrRh
The stone troll. J. R. R. Tolkien.—LiSf
"There is a grey thing that lives in the tree
  tops." S. Crane.—LiWa
"There is a thing." J. Prelutsky.—PrNk
The troll. J. Prelutsky.—PrRh
The troll bridge. L. Moore.—MoSn
Troll chanting. From Kalevala. Unknown.—
  LiWa
Troll trick. B. J. Lee.—HoCr
Walking past the school at night. B. J.
  Esbensen.—EsCs
Welsh incident. R. Graves.—LiWa
"The wendigo. O. Nash.—PrRh
The wendigo. T. Hughes.—HuU
"What's that." F. P. Heide.—HoCr—PrRh
"When Dracula went to the blood bank." J.
  Prelutsky.—PrNk
"When I'm very nearly sleeping." J. Prelutsky.—
  PrMp
When young, the slyne. J. Prelutsky.—PrNk
"A wife was sitting at her reel ae night."
  Unknown.—BlO
The worst. S. Silverstein.—LiWa
The zoosher. J. Prelutsky.—PrNk
"**Montague** Michael." Unknown.—ChC
Monterey cypress, Point Lobos. Myra Cohn
  Livingston.—LiMp
Montgomery. Sam Cornish.—JaPi
Months. See also names of months, as January
  A calendar. S. Coleridge.—DaC—FrP
    "January brings the snow".—LiSf (unat.)
    The months.—PrRh
  Chicken soup with rice, complete. M. Sendak.—
    FaW
  January one. D. McCord.—LiNe
  Labours of the months. Unknown.—PlSc
  "Married when the year is new." Mother
    Goose.—LoR
  Oh calendar. J. P. Lewis.—LiNe
  "A swarm of bees in May." Mother Goose.—
    AlH—DaC
  "Thirty days hath September." Mother Goose.—
    DeM—LoR
    The months.—DaC
  Zodiac. E. Farjeon.—FaE
The **months.** See A calendar
The **months.** See "Thirty days hath September"
Monuments. See also Graves; Sculpture and
  statues

Monuments.—*Continued*
  "Roebling, his life and mind reprieved enough."
    From The bridge from Brooklyn. R. Henri.—
    PlEd
  The street fountain. E. Farjeon.—FaE
Moochie. Eloise Greenfield.—CoN
"Moochie likes to keep on playing." See Moochie
Moods
  Bad day. M. Ridlon.—HoBf
  Dust of snow. R. Frost.—KoS—LiSf—PrRh
  I'm in a rotten mood. J. Prelutsky.—PrNk
  Sulk. F. Holman.—PrRh
  "When, in disgrace with fortune and men's
    eyes." From Sonnets. W. Shakespeare.—HoUn
"Mooly cow, mooly cow, home from the wood."
  See The cow-boy's song
"Moom moom." See Troll chanting
Moon
  Aiken Drum. Mother Goose.—BlO—BlPi
  Auctioneer. C. Sandburg.—HoRa
  Autumn ("Summer's flurry"). H. Behn.—HoCb
  Birthday ("When he asked for the moon"). M.
    C. Livingston.—LiCe
  The cat and the moon. W. B. Yeats.—ChC—
    KoT—LiSf
  "Catch me the moon, daddy." G. Vitez.—LaW
  Day-time moon. D. Aldis.—FrP
  Delight of being alone. D. H. Lawrence.—PrBb
  The first. L. Moore.—MoSn
  Flying ("I saw the moon"). J. M. Westrup.—
    CoOu
  Full moon, rising. J. Holden.—JaG
  Full moon, Santa Barbara. S. Teasdale.—HaOf
  Full of the moon. K. Kuskin.—HoDl
  "I see the moon." Mother Goose.—ChB—
    CoN—DaC—DeM—FaW—LoR—PrRa
  In the field forever. R. Wallace.—JaPo
  Insomnia ("The moon in the bureau mirror").
    E. Bishop.—McL
  The Kerry loon. E. Farjeon.—FaE
  La luna. Unknown.—GrT
  "The man in the moon came tumbling down."
    Mother Goose.—BaH—DeM—LoR
  "The man in the moon looked out of the
    moon." Mother Goose.—DeM
  The moon ("Here comes the moon").
    Unknown.—GrT
  Moon ("I have a white cat whose name is
    Moon"). W. J. Smith.—ChC—LiCa—LiSf
  Moon ("Who knows why I stand and bay at
    her"). E. Farjeon.—FaE
  Moon ("Why is"). M. C. Livingston.—LiSi
  The moon and a cloud. W. H. Davies.—HeR
  Moon boat. C. Pomerantz.—PoA—PrRa
  "Moon-come-out." E. Farjeon.—FaE—PrRa
  "The moon is a bucket of suds." From Two
    moon fantasies. C. Sandburg.—HoRa
  "The Moon King's knife of silver bright."
    Unknown.—DeD
  The moon rises. F. García Lorca.—KoT
  Moon rondeau. C. Sandburg.—HoRa
  Moon witches. T. Hughes.—LiWa
  Moonlight ("The moon drips its light"). C.
    Zolotow.—ZoE
  Moonlight ("Now, look, the big moon shines").
    E. Farjeon.—FaE
  Moonrise. G. M. Hopkins.—HeR
  "The moon's the north wind's cooky." V.
    Lindsay.—CoN—HaOf—LaW—LiSf—PrRa—PrRh
  Moonwalk. X. J. Kennedy.—BaS—KeF
  "Naughty little brown mouse." J. Prelutsky.—
    PrRi

  New moon. E. Merriam.—MeF
  Nocturn cabbage. C. Sandburg.—HoRa
  "Now the swing is still." N. Virgilio.—KeK
  "O moon, why must you." Koyo.—LiSf
  Outside at night. C. Zolotow.—ZoE
  Prayer to the moon. Unknown.—LaT
  "Put the pine tree in its pot by the doorway."
    N. Belting.—LiIl
  Rags. J. Thurman.—HoSi—JaT
  River moons. C. Sandburg.—HoRa
  Rosh Hashanah eve. H. Philip.—LiPj
  Silver. W. De la Mare.—KoT—PrRh
  "Silverly." D. Lee.—PrRa
  Singing on the moon. T. Hughes.—LiWa
  Still night thoughts. Li Po.—KoT
  "Tell me, thou star, whose wings of light." P.
    B. Shelley.—KoT
  "There is fear in." Unknown.—LiSf
  "There was a man lived in the moon." Mother
    Goose.—LoR
  "There was a young man at St. Kitts." Mother
    Goose.—LoR
  To the moon ("Art thou pale for weariness").
    P. B. Shelley.—KoT
  To the moon ("I remember, gracious, graceful
    moon"). G. Leopardi.—KoT
  "Was ever a dream a drum." C. Sandburg.—
    HoRa
  White cat in moonlight. D. Gibson.—ChC
    Cat in the moonlight.—LaW
  Wind and silver. A. Lowell.—KeK
  The wind and the moon. G. MacDonald.—PrRa
  Winter moon ("How thin and sharp is the
    moon tonight"). L. Hughes.—HuDk—KeK—
    PrRh
  The winter moon ("I hit my wife and went
    out and saw"). T. Kyozo.—McL
  The witch's cat. I. Serraillier.—LiWa
"Moon." See The first
The moon ("Here comes the moon"). Unknown.—
  GrT
Moon ("I have a white cat whose name is
  Moon"). William Jay Smith.—ChC—LiCa—
  LiSf
Moon ("Who knows why I stand and bay at
  her"). Eleanor Farjeon.—FaE
Moon ("Why is"). Myra Cohn Livingston.—LiSi
"Moon." Karla Kuskin.—LiIl
The moon and a cloud. William Henry Davies.—
  HeR
"The moon and the stars and the wind in the
  sky." See Lullaby
Moon boat. Charlotte Pomerantz.—PoA—PrRa
"Moon boat, little, brave and bright." See Moon
  boat
"Moon-come-out." Eleanor Farjeon.—FaE—PrRa
"The moon drips its light." See Moonlight
"The moon in the bureau mirror." See Insomnia
"The moon is a bucket of suds." From Two
  moon fantasies. Carl Sandburg.—HoRa
"The moon is a dusty place." See Moon witches
"The moon is full and." See Halloween
"The moon is full, and so am I." See A strange
  meeting
"The moon is up." See Old Moll
"The Moon King's knife of silver bright."
  Unknown.—DeD
The moon rises. Federico García Lorca.—KoT
Moon rondeau. Carl Sandburg.—HoRa
"The moon shines bright." Mother Goose.—DeM
Moon witches. Ted Hughes.—LiWa

"**Moonless** darkness stands between." Gerard Manley Hopkins.—HaO
Moonlight ("It will not hurt me when I am old"). Sara Teasdale.—JaG
Moonlight ("The moon drips its light"). Charlotte Zolotow.—ZoE
Moonlight ("Now, look, the big moon shines"). Eleanor Farjeon.—FaE
"**Moonlight** in front of my bed." See Still night thoughts
Moonrise. Gerard Manley Hopkins.—HeR
"The **moon's** the north wind's cooky." Vachel Lindsay.—CoN—HaOf—LaW—LiSf—PrRa—PrRh
Moonshine. Walter De la Mare.—BrT
Moonwalk. X. J. Kennedy.—BaS—KeF
Moore, Clement C.
    A visit from St. Nicholas ("'Twas the night before Christmas, when all through the house").—CoN—HaO—HaOf—LiCp—LiSf—PrRh—RoC
Moore, John Travers
    Going up ("Space suit Sammy").—PrRh
    "The tree frog."—PrRh
Moore, Lilian
    "Ants live here."—PrRa
    Arson.—MoSn
    Beach stones.—FaTh—MoSn
    Bedtime stories.—BeD—CoN—HoCr
        Bedtime story.—MoSn—PrRa
    Bike ride.—LiSf—MoSn
    The bridge ("A bridge").—MoSn
    The chestnuts are falling.—MoSn
    Cloud shadow.—JaT—MoSn
    Construction ("The giant mouth").—MoSn
    Corn talk.—MoSn
    Crow wonders.—MoSn
    December 21.—MoSn
    Dragon smoke.—LiSf—MoSn—PrRa
    Dry spell.—MoSn
    Ecology (for George Ember).—MoSn
    Encounter.—MoSn
    Fence.—MoSn
    The first.—MoSn
    Flight ("A hound sound").—MoSn
    Fog lifting.—MoSn
    Foghorns.—HoSs—MoSn—PrRh
    Forsythia bush.—MoSn
    Fossils.—HoDi—MoSn
    Friend ("When").—LiI
    Go wind.—MoSn
    Green ("Ducklings").—MoSn
    Ground hog day.—PrRh
    Hay song.—MoSn
    Hey, bug.—PrRh
    Hurricane.—MoSn
    "I left my head."—MoSn
    "I wish."—MoSn
    In the fog.—MoSn
    In the park ("When you've").—MoSn
    In the sun.—MoSn
    Jetstream.—MoSn
    Letter to a friend.—LiI—MoSn
    "Listen."—CoN
    Long shadow story.—MoSn
    "Look at that."—MoSn
    Lost ("What happened in the sky").—MoSn
    Lost and found.—MoSn
    Message from a caterpillar.—LiSf—MoSn
    Mine.—MoSn
    Move over.—MoSn
    Mural on second avenue.—MoSn
    New sounds.—HoSi—MoSn
    Night creature.—MoSn

    Night snow.—MoSn
    Odd ("That was").—MoSn
    Partners.—MoSn
    Patriarchs.—MoSn
    Pigeons.—HoSs—MoSn—PrRh
    Rain ("Mud").—MoSn
    Rain pools.—MoSn
    Recess.—MoSn
    Recycled.—MoSn
    Reflections ("On this street").—LiSf—MoSn
    September ("Something is bleeding").—MoSn
    The Shawangunks, early April.—MoSn
    Snowy morning.—BaS—MoSn
    "Something is there."—LiWa—PrRh
    Song of the tree frogs.—MoSn
    Spectacular.—KeK
    Spider ("Spider's").—MoSn
    Squirrel ("The squirrel in the hickory tree's a").—MoSn
    Stampede.—MoSn
    Summer rain.—MoSn
    Sun day.—MoSn
    Sun on rain.—MoSn
    Sunset ("There's dazzle").—JaT—MoSn
    Telling time.—MoSn
    To a red kite.—MoSn
    To the skeleton of a dinosaur in the museum.—HoDi
    Tonight.—MoSn
    The tree on the corner.—MoSn
    Tree shadows ("The shadow of a").—MoSn
    The troll bridge.—MoSn
    True.—MoSn
    "Until I saw the sea."—CoN—HoSe—MoSn—PrRh
    Waking ("My secret way of waking").—BeD—PrRh
    Weather report.—MoSn
    Wet.—MoSn
    The whale ghost.—MoSn
    While you were chasing a hat.—MoSn
    Willow yellow.—MoSn
    Wind song ("When the wind blows").—MoSn
    Winding road.—MoSn
    Winter cardinal.—MoSn
    Winter dark.—MoSn
    The witch's garden.—MoSn
    The witch's song.—MoSn
    Woodpecker ("Small sounds").—MoSn
    Yellow weed.—MoSn
Moore, Marianne
    No swan so fine.—PlEd
    When I buy pictures.—PlEd
Moore, Rosalie
    Catalogue.—ChC—CoN
        Catalog.—LiCa
Moose
    About trapping in the North woods. J. Ciardi.—CiD
    Mooses. T. Hughes.—HuU
Mooses. Ted Hughes.—HuU
Morden, Phyllis B.
    Godmother.—PrRh
"**More** gruesome than any groan." See Ghost
"The **more** it snows." Alan Alexander Milne.—CoN—PrRa—PrRh
More light, more light. Anthony Hecht.—HeR
"**More** reminiscent than distressed, you say." See To a blind student who taught me to see
"**More** than anything I want to be an actress." See Rachel Ferrara
"**More** than he mourned for walking he grieved." See The amputation

Mother Goose—*Continued*
"An apple a day."—LoR
"Apple in the morning."—LoR
"Apple-pie, pudding and pancake."—AlH
"April weather."—LoR
"As I sat on a sunny bank."—DeM
"As I was going by Charing Cross."—BlO
"As I was going out one day."—LoR
"As I was going to Banbury."—DeM
"As I was going to St. Ives."—CoN—DeM—LoR
"As I was going to sell my eggs."—DaC—LoR
"As I was going up Pippen Hill."—AlH—LoR
    "As I was going up Pippin Hill".—BlO
"As round as an apple, as deep as a cup."—LiSf
"As the days grow longer."—LoR
"As Tommy Snooks and Bessy Brooks."—DeM—FaW—LoR
"At early morn the spiders spin."—LoR
"Awake, arise."—FaW
"Baa, baa, black sheep."—AlH—DeM—FaW—LiSf—LoR
"Baby and I."—AlH
"Barber, barber, shave a pig."—AlH—DeM—FaW—LoR
"Bat, bat, come under my hat."—LoR
"Bell horses, bell horses."—LoR
"Bessy Bell and Mary Gray."—BlPi
"Betty Botter bought some butter."—FaW—LoR
    Betty Botter.—PaM
"Birds of a feather flock together."—DaC
    "Birds of a feather will flock together".—LoR
"Blow, wind, blow."—DeM—LoR
"Bobby Shafto's gone to sea."—LoR
    "Bobby Shaftoe's gone to sea".—DeM
"The boughs do shake and the bells do ring."—DeM—LoR
"Bow, wow, wow."—DeM—LiSf
"Boys and girls, come out to play."—DeM—LiSf—LoR
    "Girls and boys, come out to play".—AlH—ChB—DaC
"Brave news is come to town."—DeM—LoR
"The brown owl sits in the ivy bush."—LoR
"Bye, baby bunting."—LoR
    "By, baby bunting".—DeM
"Calm weather in June."—LoR
"A cat came fiddling out of a barn."—FaW
"The cat sat asleep by the side of the fire."—LoR
"Catch her, crow."—RaT
The cats of Kilkenny. See "There were once two cats of Kilkenny"
"Charley Barley, butter and eggs."—DeM
"Charlie Warlie had a cow."—DeM
"Chook, chook, chook, chook, chook."—DeM—LoR—PrRa
"Christmas comes but once a year."—DeM—LoR
"Christmas is coming, the geese are getting fat."—DeM—LiCp—LiSf—LoR—RoC
    "Christmas is a-coming".—CoN
"Cobbler, cobbler, mend my shoe."—DaC—DeM—LoR
"Cock-a-doodle-doo."—DaC—DeM
    "Cock-a-doodle-do".—LoR
"The cock crows in the morn."—DeM—LoR
"The cock's on the roof top blowing his horn."—DeM
    "The cock's on the housetop blowing his horn".—LoR

"Cold and raw the north wind doth blow."—DeM
"Come, butter, come."—DeM
"Come, let's to bed."—BaH—FaW—LoR
"Cross-patch, draw the latch."—DeM—LoR
The cuckoo ("O, the cuckoo she's a pretty bird").—HeR
"Curly locks, curly locks."—AlH—DeM—LoR
"Daffy-down-dilly is new come to town."—DeM—LoR
    "Daffadowndilly".—CoN
"Dame Trot and her cat."—DeM
"Dance, little baby, dance up high."—ChB—DeM
"Dance to your daddy."—DeM—LiSf
"The daughter of the farrier."—DaC
"Davy Davy Dumpling."—LoR
    Davy Dumpling.—PrRa
"Dear, dear, what can the matter be."—DeM
"Desperate Dan."—AlH—FaW
"Dickery dickery dare."—BlQ—DeM—LoR
"Diddle, diddle, dumpling, my son John."—BaH—DeM—FaW—LiSf—LoR
"Diddlety, diddlety, dumpty."—LoR
"A diller, a dollar, a ten o'clock scholar."—DaC—DeM—FaW—LiSf—LoR
    Ten o'clock scholar.—ChG
"Ding dong bell."—AlH—DaC—DeM—FaW—LiSf—LoR
"Dingty diddledy, my mammy's maid."—LoR
    "Dingty diddlety".—DeM
"Doctor Foster went to Gloucester."—DaC—DeM—FaW—LoR
"Donkey, donkey, old and gray."—DaC—LoR
"Don't Care didn't care."—AlH—BlO
    Don't Care ("Don't Care, he didn't care").—DaC
"Dormy, dormy dormouse."—BlPi
"A duck and a drake."—LoR
"Eaper Weaper, chimbley sweeper."—AlH
"Eat an apple going to bed."—LoR
"Elsie Marley is grown so fine."—AlH—ChG—DeM
    "Elsie Marley has grown so fine".—LoR
"The fair maid who, the first of May."—AlH
"Far from home across the sea."—LoR
"A farmer went trotting upon his gray mare."—LiSf
"Fiddle-de-dee, fiddle-de-dee."—LoR
Fiddle-i-fee ("Had me a cat, the cat pleased me").—LiSf
    "I had a cat and the cat pleased me".—DeM
"First in a carriage."—DeM
"Fishes swim in water clear."—LoR
"Fishy, fishy in the brook."—LoR
"Flying-man, flying-man."—LoR
"For want of a nail the shoe was lost."—FaW—LoR
"Four and twenty tailors went to kill a snail."—DaC
The frog and the mouse.—BlPi
"Georgie Porgie, pudding and pie."—DeM—FaW—LoR
"The giant Jim, great giant grim."—LoR
The gingerbread man. See "Smiling girls, rosy boys"
"Girls and boys, come out to play". See "Boys and girls, come out to play"
"Go to bed late."—LoR
"God bless the master of this house."—DeM
"God made the bees."—BlO—LoR—PlSc

Mother Goose—*Continued*
"A good child, a good child."—LoR
"Good morrow to you, Valentine."—DeM
"Good night, sleep tight."—LoR
"Goosey, goosey gander."—BlQ—DeM—FaW—
    LoR
"The grand old Duke of York."—LiSf
"Gray goose and gander."—AlH—LoR
"Great A, little a."—DeM—LoR
"The greedy man is he who sits."—LoR
"Gregory Griggs, Gregory Griggs."—BlQ—
    DeM—LoR
"Handy spandy, Jack-a-Dandy."—BlQ—LoR
"Hannah Bantry, in the pantry."—LoR
"Hark, hark, the dogs do bark."—ChG—DeM—
    FaW—LoR
He, haw, haw, hum.—BlPi
"He loves me."—DeM—LoR
"Hector Protector was dressed all in green."—
    AlH—DeM—LoR
"Here am I, little jumping Joan."—BlQ—
    DeM—FaW—LiSf LoR
    Little jumping Joan.—CoN
"Here sits the Lord Mayor."—RaT
"Here we go round the mulberry bush."—
    DeM—LoR
    The mulberry bush.—DaC
"Here's Tom Thumb."—FaW
"Hey diddle diddle, the cat and the fiddle."—
    AlH—DeM—FaW—LiSf—LoR
"Hick-a-more, hack-a-more."—LiSf
"Hickety, pickety, my black hen."—DeM—LoR
"Hickory dickory dock."—DeM—FaW—LoR
"Hickup, hickup, go away."—LoR
"High diddle doubt, my candle's out."—DeM
"Higher than a house."—LiSf
"A hill full, a hole full."—LiSf
"Hoddley, poddley, puddles and fogs."—LoR
    "Hoddley, poddley, puddle and frogs".—
    DeM
"Hot cross buns, hot cross buns."—DeM—
    FaW—LoR
"House full, yard full."—CoN
"House to let."—AlH
"How many days has my baby to play."—LoR
"How many miles to Babylon."—FaW—LiSf—
    LoR
    "How many miles is it to Babylon".—DaC
"How much wood would a woodchuck
    chuck."—LiSf—LoR
"Humpty Dumpty sat on a wall."—DeM—
    FaW—LoR
"Hush-a-bye, baby, on the tree top."—BaH—
    DeM
"Hush, baby, my dolly, I pray you."—DeM
"Hush, little baby, don't say a word."—BaH—
    ChB—DeM—LaW—LoR
    The mocking bird ("Hush up, baby").—LiSf
"I am a little beggar girl."—AlH
"I asked my mother for fifty cents."—PrRh
    "I asked my mother for fifteen cents".—
    LiSf
"I bought a dozen new-laid eggs."—LoR
"I do not like thee, Doctor Fell."—DeM—LoR
"I had a cat and the cat pleased me". See
    Fiddle-i-fee ("Had me a cat, the cat pleased
    me")
"I had a dog."—DeM
"I had a little castle upon the sea sand."—FaW
"I had a little hen, the prettiest ever seen."—
    DeM—LoR
"I had a little hobby horse."—LoR

"I had a little husband."—AlH—BlQ—FaW—
    LoR
"I had a little nut tree."—DaC—DeM—FaW—
    LiSf—LoR
    A nut tree.—KoT
"I had a little pony."—BlO—DaC—DeM
"I had a young man."—AlH
"I had two pigeons bright and gay."—DeM
"I have a little sister, they call her
    Peep-peep."—LiSf
"I know I have lost my train."—LoR
    Joshua Lane.—DaC
"I like little pussy."—LoR
    Pussy.—DaC
    "I love little pussy".—DeM
"I love coffee."—LoR
"I love sixpence, jolly little sixpence."—DeM
"I married a wife by the light of the moon."—
    LoR
"I saw a ship a-sailing". See "There was a ship
    a-sailing"
"I saw a ship a-sailing."—DeM—LiSf—LoR—
    RuI
"I saw three ships come sailing by."—LoR
"I see the moon."—ChB—CoN—DaC—DeM—
    FaW—LoR—PrRa
"I went up a high hill."—DeM
"I went up one pair of stairs."—DeM—LoR
"Ickle ockle, blue bockle."—BlQ—DeM
"If all the seas were one sea."—CoOu—FaW—
    LoR
"If all the world was apple pie."—LoR
"If all the world was paper."—FaW
"If all the world were paper."—BlO—CoN—
    KoT
"If bees stay at home."—DaC—DeM
"If chickens roll in the sand."—LoR
"If I lost my little cat, I should be sad without
    it."—ChC
"If I'd as much money as I could spend."—
    FaW—LoR
"If wishes were horses."—LoR
"If you are not."—LoR
"If you love me, love me true."—LoR
"If you sneeze on Monday, you sneeze for
    danger."—AlH
"If you wish to live and thrive."—LoR
"I'll sing you a song."—LoR
"I'll tell you a story."—FaW
"In a cottage in Fife."—BlPi—LoR
"In marble halls as white as milk."—FaTh
    A riddle.—BlPi
"In spring I look gay."—LoR
"Incey-wincey spider climbed the water
    spout."—LoR
"It blew."—LoR
"It's raining, it's pouring."—DaC—DeM—LoR
"It's raining, it's raining."—LoR
"Jack and Jill went up the hill."—DeM—
    FaW—LiSf—LoR
"Jack be nimble."—DeM—LoR
"Jack Sprat could eat no fat."—AlH—DeM—
    FaW—LoR
Jemima. See "There was a little girl, and she
    had a little curl"
"Jeremiah, blow the fire."—BlQ
"Jerry Hall."—DeM—LoR
Joshua Lane. See "I know I have lost my train"
"Julius Caesar made a law."—FaW
The Kilkenny cats ("There wanst was two cats
    in Kilkenny"). See "There were once two cats
    of Kilkenny"
"Knock on the door."—DeM

"**Mother** has gone away, the night is black." See A drink of water
"A **mother** in old Alabama." See Beulah Louise
"**Mother**, may I go out to swim." Mother Goose.—DeM—LoR
"**Mother** of gods, father of gods, ancient God." See Confession of sin
The **mother** sings. Eleanor Farjeon.—FaE
Mother to son. Langston Hughes.—CoN—HaOf—HuDk—LiSf
Motherhood. See Mothers and motherhood
"**Mother's.**" See Mother's garden
Mothers. Anne Sexton.—JaS
Mothers and motherhood
  Accomplishments. C. Macdonald.—JaD
  The adversary. P. McGinley.—HaOf
  Against idleness. Unknown.—DaC
  "Ah, the roofs." From Five ghost songs. Unknown, fr. the Ambo people of Africa.—KoT
  All asleep 1 ("A lamb has a lambkin"). C. Pomerantz.—PoA
  All asleep 2 ("Hush, it's the hour"). C. Pomerantz.—PoA
  Amanda Butler. M. Glenn.—GlCd
  Around the corner. From Forgotten girlhood. L. Riding.—HeR
  The arrival of my mother. K. Wilson.—JaD
  At night ("In the dust are my father's beautiful hands"). R. Eberhart.—JaS
  Avec merci, mother. M. Angelou.—AnS
  Baking day. R. Joseph.—JaS
  The ballad of the harp-weaver. E. S. Millay.—LiSf—LiWa
  Bats ("A bat is born"). R. Jarrell.—CoN—HaOf
  El beso de mama. Unknown.—GrT
  Birth. G. E. Lyon.—JaS
  The buttercup field. E. Farjeon.—FaE
  The child on the shore. U. K. LeGuin.—KeK
  Dahn the plug 'ole. Unknown.—HeR
  Darcy Tanner. M. Glenn.—GlC
  A daughter's house. N. H. Richman.—JaG
  Disobedience. A. A. Milne.—CoN
  Easter, for Penny. M. C. Livingston.—LiCe
  Falling asleep. I. Serraillier.—FaW
  Fantasia ("I dream"). E. Merriam.—MeSk
  First love ("We fell in love at 'Journey for Margaret'"). J. Hemschemeyer.—JaPi
  Flavors (1) ("Mama is chocolate, you must be swirls"). A. Adoff.—AdA
  A friendly mouse. H. Behn.—HoCb
  From a childhood. R. M. Rilke.—KoT
  "I love you." C. Sandburg.—HoRa
  "I sing of a maiden." Unknown.—RoC
  "I was the child." V. S. Warren.—JaS
  If there are any heavens. E. E. Cummings.—JaD
  "In a kangaroo one day." X. J. Kennedy.—KeB
  In Weatherbury stocks. T. Hardy.—PlAs
  The inquest. W. H. Davies.—HeR
  Interview ("Yes, this is where she lived before she won"). S. H. Hay.—HaOf
  It really wasn't too bad. J. Ciardi.—CiD
  Kineo mountain. C. T. Wright.—JaPi
  A kitchen memory. R. Scheele.—JaS
  Kitchen song. J. Dobbs.—JaS
  Last born. J. Kirkwood.—JaS
  The late mother. C. Macdonald.—JaPi
  A lesson for mamma. S. Dayre.—HaOf
  A letter from home. M. Oliver.—JaS
  Louise Coyle. M. Glenn.—GlCd
  Mama is a sunrise. E. T. Hunt.—LiSf
  Mama's kiss. Unknown.—GrT
  A manger song. E. Farjeon.—FaE
  Mary Louise Donahue. M. Glenn.—GlCd
  Mary's burden. E. Farjeon.—FaE
  Melora's song. From John Brown's body. S. V. Benét.—PlAs
  Mending the adobe. H. Carruth.—JaPi—PlEd
  "Mommies." N. Giovanni.—GiSp
  Mommies do. N. Giovanni.—GiSp
  Monica Zindell. M. Glenn.—GlC
  Mother. K. Starbird.—JaT
  "Mother doesn't want a dog." J. Viorst.—PrRh—ViI
  The mother sings. E. Farjeon.—FaE
  Mother to son. L. Hughes.—CoN—HaOf—HuDk—LiSf
  Mothers. A. Sexton.—JaS
  Mother's garden. M. C. Livingston.—LiWo
  Mother's nerves. X. J. Kennedy.—PrRh
  Mother's prayer for a girl. Unknown, fr. the Navajo Indian.—BiSp
  The mother's song ("It is so still in the house"). Unknown.—HaO
  The mother's song ("She knew, the maiden mother knew"). E. Farjeon.—FaE
  My Christmas, mum's Christmas. S. Forsyth.—HaO
  My mother. C. Zolotow.—ZoE
  "My mother says I'm sickening." J. Prelutsky.—PrNk
  My mother's death. J. Hemschemeyer.—JaS
  Nancy Hanks, 1784-1818. S. V. Benét, and R. C. Benét.—CoN
  The new mothers. C. Shields.—JaS
  "Old Mother Shuttle." Mother Goose.—BlPi—LoR
  "Once in the winter." From The forsaken. D. C. Scott.—DoNw
  Our mother's tunes. E. Farjeon.—FaE
  Parents never understand. N. Giovanni.—GiSp
  "Pensive, on her dead gazing, I heard the Mother of All." W. Whitman.—HeR
  Poem for my mother. S. Cedering.—JaS
  Poem of the mother. M. Sklarew.—JaS
  Poems. G. Gildner.—JaPi
  The portrait ("My mother never forgave my father"). S. Kunitz.—JaPi
  Portrait of my mother on her wedding day. C. Gilbert.—JaD
  PTA ("Seemed like everybody's mother"). C. Rylant.—RyW
  Rock me to sleep. E. A. Allen.—HaOf
  Shari Morrow. M. Glenn.—GlC
  Sleepless nights. Zolotow. Charlotte.—ZoE—ZoE
  Some things don't make any sense at all. J. Viorst.—PrRh—ViI
  Song of triumph. L. Duncan.—HoBf
  Songs my mother taught me. D. Wagoner.—JaS
  Spoilt child. E. Farjeon.—FaE
  Stark county holidays. M. Oliver.—JaS
  Taught me purple. E. T. Hunt.—LiSf
  "There was an old woman who lived in a shoe." Mother Goose.—AlH—DeM—FaW—LoR
    "There was an old woman, she lived in a shoe".—BlPi
  "This mother cat." B. S. De Regniers.—DeT
  To mother fairie. A. Cary.—HaOf
  To my daughter riding in the circus parade. J. Labombard.—JaG
  Too many Daves. Dr. Seuss.—HaOf—PrRh
  "When I have a little girl." C. Zolotow.—ZoE
  While I slept. R. Francis.—KeK

Mothers and motherhood—*Continued*
The wife of Usher's well ("There lived a lady, a lady gay"). Unknown.—PlAs
The wife of Usher's well ("There lived a wife at Usher's well"). Unknown.—HeR—PlAs
Woman work. M. Angelou.—PlSc
"**Mothers** are hardest to forgive." See The adversary
Mother's chocolate valentine. Jack Prelutsky.—PrIv
Mother's day. See also Mothers and motherhood
On Mother's Day. A. Fisher.—CoN—PrRh
Mother's garden. Myra Cohn Livingston.—LiWo
Mother's nerves. X. J. Kennedy.—PrRh
Mother's prayer for a girl. Unknown.—BiSp
The **mother's** song ("It is so still in the house"). Unknown, tr. by Peter Freuchen.—HaO
The **mother's** song ("She knew, the maiden mother knew"). Eleanor Farjeon.—FaE
The **mother's** tale. Eleanor Farjeon.—FaE
Moths
The warning ("Just now"). A. Crapsey.—LiWa
Motorcycles
"On his motorbike Lars stands." X. J. Kennedy.—KeB
"The **mountain** and the squirrel." See Fable
Mountain brook. Elizabeth Coatsworth.—PrRh
Mountain lion. David Herbert Lawrence.—HeR
Mountain lions
Mountain lion. D. H. Lawrence.—HeR
Puma. T. Hughes.—HuU
"The **mountain** peaks put on their hoods." See Twilight song
Mountain wind. Barbara Kunz Loots.—PrRh
Mountains
The birthplace. R. Frost.—PlEd
Boulder, Colorado. X. J. Kennedy.—KeF
Crossing the Alps. From The prelude. W. Wordsworth.—HeR
December hills. B. J. Esbensen.—EsCs
Excelsior. H. W. Longfellow.—HaOf
Fable ("The mountain and the squirrel"). R. W. Emerson.—HaOf
Mountain wind. B. K. Loots.—PrRh
Rannoch, by Glencoe. From Landscapes. T. S. Eliot.—HeR
The Shawangunks, early April. L. Moore.—MoSn
A survey. W. Stafford.—HeR
Thinking of East Mountain. Li Po.—KoT
Ute Mountain. C. Tomlinson.—HeR
The **mouse** ("I heard a mouse"). Elizabeth Coatsworth.—HaOf
The **mouse** ("I'm only a poor little mouse, ma'am"). Laura E. Richards.—HaOf
The **mouse** and the cake. Eliza Cook.—DaC
Mouse dinner. Aileen Fisher.—FaTh
"A **mouse** doesn't dine." See Mouse dinner
"A **mouse** found a beautiful piece of plum cake." See The mouse and the cake
The **mouse's** courting song. Unknown.—PlAs
The **mouse's** lullaby. Palmer Cox.—HaOf
Mouse's nest. John Clare.—HeR
"A **mouth,** can blow or breathe." See Cardinal ideograms
Mouths
How to tell goblins from elves. M. Shannon.—PrRh
My mouth. A. Adoff.—PrRh
Popsicles. C. B. Francis.—HoMu
"**Move** him into the sun." See Futility
"**Move** into." See Grammar lesson
Move over. Lilian Moore.—MoSn

Movement. Denise Levertov.—McL
Movies
Aunt Gladys's home movie no. 31, Albert's funeral. J. W. Miller.—JaS
Bijou. V. Rutsala.—JaD
Double feature. T. Roethke.—JaD
Faith Plotkin. M. Glenn.—GlC
First kiss. J. Holden.—JaG
First love ("We fell in love at 'Journey for Margaret'"). J. Hemschemeyer.—JaPi
Russell Hodges. M. Glenn.—GlCd
Moving
Everett Anderson's friend. L. Clifton.—LiIl
Girl who's moved around. X. J. Kennedy.—KeF
Going away. H. Nemerov.—JaD
Maurice. G. Brooks.—HoBf
Moving ("The house inside still looks like a house"). F. Steele.—JaG
Moving ("Some of the sky is grey and some of it is white"). R. Jarrell.—JaD
Moving in winter. A. Rich.—JaD
A new friend. M. A. Anderson.—FrP
The new girl. C. Zolotow.—ZoE
Note to the previous tenants. J. Updike.—JaG
Since Hanna moved away. J. Viorst.—HoBf—PrRh—ViI
Sketch ("Holding a picture up to the wall"). R. Farnsworth.—JaG
A sprung trap. X. J. Kennedy.—KeF
Tulips and addresses. E. Field.—JaPi
Veronica Castell. M. Glenn.—GlCd
Moving ("The house inside still looks like a house"). Frank Steele.—JaG
Moving ("Some of the sky is grey and some of it is white"). Randall Jarrell.—JaD
Moving in winter. Adrienne Rich.—JaD
"The **mower's** in the meadow." See Hay song
Mowing. See also Harvests and harvesting
Cut grass. P. Larkin.—HeR
Lawnmower. V. Worth.—HoCl
When mowers pass. A. Fisher.—FiW
"Willy boy, Willy boy, where are you going." Mother Goose.—DeM
"**Ms.** Beecher said I don't know how." See Art class
Ms. Minnie McFinney. Unknown.—BrT
"**Ms.** Minnie McFinney, of Butte." See Ms. Minnie McFinney
"**Ms.** Whatchamacallit Thingamajig." Miriam Chaikin.—PrRh
"A **much** of motors." See Parking lot full
Muckers. Carl Sandburg.—PlSc
Mud
Jessica Jane. M. Justus.—PrRh
Mud ("Mud is very nice to feel"). P. C. Boyden.—CoN—PrRa—PrRh
Mud ("Your fingers can take"). B. J. Esbensen.—EsCs
The muddy puddle. D. Lee.—PrRh
Mud ("Mud is very nice to feel"). Polly Chase Boyden.—CoN—PrRa—PrRh
"**Mud.**" See Rain
Mud ("Your fingers can take"). Barbara Juster Esbensen.—EsCs
"**Mud** is very nice to feel." See Mud
The **muddy** puddle. Dennis Lee.—PrRh
Muddy sneakers. X. J. Kennedy.—KeF
"**Muddy** sneakers, make 'em clean." See Muddy sneakers
"**Muffle** the wind." See Orders
"**Muffled** thunder." See The sea

Muir, Edwin
 The child dying.—HeR
 The great house.—PlEd
 The horses.—HeR
 Mary Stuart.—HeR
 Merlin.—HeR
The **mulberry** bush. See "Here we go round the mulberry bush"
Mules
 "Ignatz Mott ignored the rule." X. J. Kennedy.—KeB
The **multilingual** mynah bird. Jack Prelutsky.—PrZ
"**Multiplication** is vexation." See Arithmetic
The **mummers**. Eleanor Farjeon.—FaE
Mummies
 The museum ("So we went to see this mummy"). A. Turner.—TuS
The **mummies**. Maxine Kumin.—JaPi
Mummy slept late and Daddy fixed breakfast. John Ciardi.—LiSf—PrRh
Munch, scls. Alexandra Wallner
 "Sunday is our roast beef day".—HoMu
"**Munching** a plum on." See To a poor old woman
Munday, Anthony
 Song ("Weep, weep, ye woodmen, wail").—BlO
The **mungle** and the munn. Jack Prelutsky.—PrNk
Munkittrick, Richard Kendall
 Molasses river.—HaOf
 Old King Cabbage.—HaOf
 The redingote and the vamoose.—HaOf
 The song of the owl.—HaOf
Mural on second avenue. Lilian Moore.—MoSn
Murder
 Another epitaph on an army of mercenaries. H. MacDiarmid.—HeR
 Binnorie. Unknown.—PlAs
 The bonny Earl of Moray ("Ye hielands and ye lawlands"). Unknown.—BlO
  The bonny earl of Murray ("Ye highlands and ye lawlands").—PlAs
 The brother ("O, know you what I have done"). T. Hardy.—PlAs
 The compassionate fool. N. Cameron.—HeR
 Danny Deever. R. Kipling.—PlAs
 Edward, Edward. Unknown.—PlAs
 "Farewell to barn and stack and tree." A. E. Housman.—PlAs
 Frankie and Johnny. Unknown.—HeR
 Icicle ("An icy stabbing so quickly done"). E. Merriam.—MeHa
 Lord Randal. Unknown.—PlAs
 Mary Stuart. E. Muir.—HeR
 The shooting of Dan McGrew. R. W. Service.—DoNw—HeR
 The two sisters. Unknown.—PlAs
Murgatroyd. Celeste Turner Wright.—JaS
Murphy, Richard
 Pat Cloherty's version of the Maisie.—HeR
Murray, Betram
 I caught a fish.—CoOu
"**Musetta** of the mountains." James Reeves.—LiSf
The **museum** ("I went to the museum"). Jack Prelutsky.—PrWi
The **museum** ("So we went to see this mummy"). Ann Turner.—TuS
The **museum** door. Lee Bennett Hopkins.—HoDi
"The **Museum** of Modern Art on West Fifty-third Street." See Tulips and addresses
Museums
 At the museum. J. M. Brinnin.—PlEd

Dinosaurs ("Their feet, planted into tar"). M. C. Livingston.—HoDi
A Floridian museum of art. R. Whittemore.—PlEd
In a museum cabinet. M. Swenson.—LiWa
In galleries. R. Jarrell.—PlEd
In the museum. C. Zolotow.—ZoE
Letter to statues. J. M. Brinnin.—PlEd
The most expensive picture in the world. H. Nemerov.—PlEd
The museum ("I went to the museum"). J. Prelutsky.—PrWi
The museum ("So we went to see this mummy"). A. Turner.—TuS
The museum door. L. B. Hopkins.—HoDi
The National Gallery. L. MacNeice.—PlEd
To the skeleton of a dinosaur in the museum. L. Moore.—HoDi
Tutankhamen. W. Dickey.—JaPi
Mushroom. Eve Merriam.—MeF
Mushrooms
 The elf and the dormouse. O. Herford.—PrRh
 Mushroom. E. Merriam.—MeF
 Mushrooms. S. Plath.—HeR
 The toadstool wood. J. Reeves.—FaTh—LiWa
Mushrooms. Sylvia Plath.—HeR
Music ("Can you dance"). Eleanor Farjeon.—FaE
Music ("When you wanted a piano"). Naomi Shihab Nye.—JaS
Music and musicians. See also Orchestras; Singing; also names of musical instruments, as Pianos; also names of muscians as Mozart, Wolfgang Amadeus
 At the St. Louis Institute of Music. R. Wallace.—JaG
 The ballad of the harp-weaver. E. S. Millay.—LiSf—LiWa
 Concert. R. Morgan.—JaT
 The dreaming of the bones. From Song for the cloth. W. B. Yeats.—HeR
 Dulcimer maker. C. Forché.—PlSc
 Fantasia ("The old grand piano"). L. Nathan.—JaPo
 The fiddler of Dooney. W. B. Yeats.—LiSf
 First song. G. Kinnell.—JaG
 Hit tune. Unknown.—BrT
 I know a man. P. Steele.—JaPo
 In the music. R. Currie.—JaT
 "Into Mother's slide trombone." X. J. Kennedy.—KeB
 The lobsters and the fiddler crab. F. J. Forster.—PrRh
 Mermaid's music. J. Yolen.—RuI
 Music ("Can you dance"). E. Farjeon.—FaE
 The musical maiden. Unknown.—BrT
 "My father played the melodeon." From A Christmas childhood. P. Kavanagh.—HeR
 A nuisance at home. Unknown.—BrT
 "O mistress mine, where are you roaming." From Twelfth night. W. Shakespeare.—HoUn
 Organ grinder. E. Farjeon.—FaE
 "Orpheus with his lute made trees." From Henry VIII. W. Shakespeare.—HoUn
 The piano ("I sit on the edge"). F. Davey.—DoNw
 Piano ("Red quince branch"). L. Russ.—JaPo
 Piano ("Softly, in the dusk, a woman is singing to me"). D. H. Lawrence.—HeR
 A piper. S. O'Sullivan.—LiSf
 "Piping down the valleys wild." W. Blake.—CoOu—LiSf
  Introduction to Songs of innocence.—PrRh

Music and musicians.—*Continued*
The rattle bag. D. Ap Gwilym.—HeR
Rocky Trailer's grandmother's garage. C. Rylant.—RyW
A sensitive man. M. Bishop.—BrT
The shooting of Dan McGrew. R. W. Service.—DoNw—HeR
A short note. E. Merriam.—MeSk
The six strings. F. García Lorca.—HeR
Spring whistles. L. Larcom.—HaOf
The tape. M. C. Livingston.—CoN
"There was a piper, he'd a cow." Mother Goose.—AlH
"There was a young bugler named Breen." Unknown.—TrM
"There was a young lady of Bute." E. Lear.—LiH
"There was a young lady of Tyre." E. Lear.—LiH
  The young lady of Tyre.—BrT
"There's music in a hammer." Unknown.—PrRa
"Tom, he was a piper's son." Mother Goose.—FaW—LiSf—LoR
"Tommy waved his stick about." Unknown.—TrM
Umbilical. E. Merriam.—HoCl—MeSk—PrRh
"A wandering minstrel I." From The Mikado. W. S. Gilbert.—PlAs
Way down in the music. E. Greenfield.—LiSf
We four lads. Unknown.—KeK
The weary blues. L. Hughes.—HuDk
Widow to her son. R. T. Smith.—JaS
The **musical** lion. Oliver Herford.—BrT—HaOf
The **musical** maiden. Unknown.—BrT
The **musician** at his work. Robert Currie.—JaS
Musicians. See Music and musicians
The **musk-ox.** Ted Hughes.—HuU
The **muskellunge.** Ted Hughes.—HuU
Muskrats
Ecology (for George Ember). L. Moore.—MoSn
"**Musky** mint." See Catnip
Muslim religion. See Islam
"**Must** we go inside there." See Vet
"A **muvver** was barfin' 'er biby one night." See Dahn the plug 'ole
"**My** accountant father." See Sum
"**My** age is three hundred and seventy two." See The sleepy giant
"**My** aspens dear, whose airy cages quelled." See Binsey poplars, felled 1879
"**My** aunt. Ted Hughes.—LiWa
"**My** aunt Bebe." See The Aga Khan
"**My** aunt kept turnips in a flock." Randall Jarrell.—LiSf
"**My** aunty Jean." See Tide and time
My baby brother. Jack Prelutsky.—PrNk
"**My** baby brother is so small." See My baby brother
"**My** baby, my burden." See Mary's burden
My bath. Madeleine L'Engle.—LaT
"**My** bath is the ocean." See My bath
"**My** beautiful picture of pirates and treasure." See Jigsaw puzzle
My bed is a boat. Robert Louis Stevenson.—ChB
"**My** bed is like a little boat." See My bed is a boat
"**My** best friend's name is Billy." See Puzzle
"**My** bird, why do you sing no more." See The child and the bird
"**My** birthday's in August." Jack Prelutsky.—PrWi
"**My** birthdays take so long to start." See Between birthdays

"**My** body a rounded stone." See Living tenderly
My brother. Marci Ridlon.—PrRh
My brother Bert. Ted Hughes.—PrRh
My brother flies over low. David Huddle.—JaT
"**My** brother is so bright." See Alex Garber
"**My** brother Jamie lost me all." See Mary Stuart
"**My** brother, learning how to dress." See Mixed-up kid
"**My** brother lost his bathing suit." Jack Prelutsky.—PrWi
"**My** brother shuffles through the door." See His dog
"**My** brother's head should be replaced." Jack Prelutsky.—PrNk
"**My** brother's worth about two cents." See My brother
"**My** bull is white like the silver fish in the river." See The magnificent bull
"**My** cat." See Cat
My cat. Judith Viorst.—ViI
"**My** cat." See Territory
"**My** cat died." See Poem about a special cat
"**My** cat has got no name." See Cat
"**My** cat is a tough hood." See My cat, Robin Hood
"**My** cat isn't stuck up." See My cat
My cat Jeoffrey. From Jubilate Agno. Christopher Smart.—BlO—HeR
  "For I will consider my cat Jeoffry".—KoT
My cat Mrs. Lick-a-chin. John Ciardi.—ChC
My cat, Robin Hood. Emanuel Di Pasquale.—LiCa
"**My** cat, washing her tail's tip, is a whorl." See Cat on couch
"**My** cheap toy lamp." See Child's song
"**My** child, you have toiled through life and come to the end." See Prayer to the deceased
My Christmas, mum's Christmas. Sarah Forsyth.—HaO
My cousin. Jack Prelutsky.—PrWi
"**My** cousin came to visit." See My cousin
My cousins' dollhouse. Myra Cohn Livingston.—LiWo
"**My** dad gave me one dollar bill." See Smart
"**My** Daddy baptized me." See A testimony
"**My** dame hath a lame, tame crane." Mother Goose.—LoR
"**My** daughter, Blake, is in kindergarten." See Poop
"**My** daughter is drawing a picture." See Art work
"**My** dear, do you know." See The babes in the wood
"**My** desk's at the back of the class." See The marrog
My dim-wit cousin. Theodore Roethke.—JaD
"**My** dim-wit cousin, saved by a death bed quaver." See My dim-wit cousin
My dog ("He didn't bark at anything"). Myra Cohn Livingston.—HoSu
My dog ("His nose is short and scrubby"). Marchette Chute.—FrP
"**My** dog, he is an ugly dog." Jack Prelutsky.—PrNk
"**My** dog's so furry I've not seen." See The hairy dog
My dragon. X. J. Kennedy.—PrRa
"**My** ducks are so funny, I think." See Peter and Wendy
"**My** enemy had bidden me as guest." See The compassionate fool
My father. Charlotte Zolotow.—ZoE
My father after work. Gary Gildner.—JaPi

"My father drinks, so I don't stay home much."
See Danny Vargas
"My father he died, but I can't tell you how."
Unknown.—BlO
"My father is tall." See My father
"My father owns the butcher shop." Unknown.—
PrRa—PrRh
"My father played the melodeon." From A
Christmas childhood. Patrick Kavanagh.—HeR
"My father teaches in a nearby junior high." See
Adam Whitney
"My father tells me." See Forever
"My father's father gave." See The gold nest
My father's ghost. David Wagoner.—JaS
My father's heart. Stuart Friebert.—JaS
"My father's mother." See Seashell
"My father's name is Frankenstein." See Father
and mother
"My Fathers sit on benches." See Song for the
old ones
My father's valentine. Jack Prelutsky.—PrIv
My fingers. Mary O'Neill.—KeK
"My fingers are antennae." See My fingers
My fishbowl head. X. J. Kennedy.—KeF
"My flashlight tugs me." See Flashlight
"My friend." See Song of two ghosts
"My friend and I have decided to write for
money." See Writing for money
"My friend Anna tells me to stay in school." See
Donna Vasquez
"My friend, who was a heroin addict." See
Certain choices
My gift. See "What can I give him"
My girl Maggie. N. M. Bodecker.—BoSs
"My golden cat has dappled sides." See The
golden cat
"My goodness, my goodness." See Christmas
"My grandfather." See Zuni grandfather
My grandfather burning cornfields. Roger Sauls.—
JaS
My grandfather dying. Ted Kooser.—JaS
My grandfather in search of moonshine. George
Ella Lyon.—JaG
"My grandfather said to me." See Manners
"My grandfather, the sun, you who walk yellow,
look down." See Prayer of an old man at
a young man's change of name
"My grandfather told me I had a choice." See
Grandfather's heaven
"My grandfather's picture sits on my desk." See
Norman Moskowitz
My grandmother had bones. Judith
Hemschemeyer.—JaD
"My grandmother had bones as delicate." See My
grandmother had bones
"My grandmothers were strong." See Lineage
"My great corn plants." Unknown.—LiSf
"My great-grandparents." See The hill
"My green leaves are more beautiful." See Leaves
"My happiness depends on an electric appliance."
See The telephone
"My head's a fishbowl full of fish." See My
fishbowl head
"My heart aches, and a drowsy numbness pains."
See Ode to a nightingale
"My heart is like a singing bird." See A birthday
My heart's in the Highlands, my heart is not
here." Robert Burns.—BlO
"My house is red. Mother Goose.—BlPi
"My house is red, a little house." See My house
is red
"My india rubber is the friend." See India rubber

My jacket old. Herman Melville.—PlSc
"My jacket old, with narrow seam." See My
jacket old
My kitten. Marchette Chute.—HoSu
"My kitty cat has nine lives." See Nine lives
"My learned friend and neighbor pig." Mother
Goose.—LoR
"My left upper." See After the dentist
My life has turned to blue. Maya Angelou.—AnS
"My little dark baby." See Lullaby
"My little Pink." Mother Goose.—LoR
"My little sister." William Wise.—PrRh
"My little snowman has a mouth." See Snowman
"My London Bridge." Arnold Lobel.—LoWr
My love. Richard Shelton.—JaG
"My love is like a cabbage." Unknown.—LiVp
"My love will come." See Waiting
"My magic is dead, said the witch, I'm
astounded." See The witch's cat
"My maid Mary." Mother Goose.—DeM
"My mom says I'm her sugarplum." See Some
things don't make any sense at all
My mother. Charlotte Zolotow.—ZoE
"My mother groan'd, my father wept." See Infant
sorrow
"My mother had a maid call'd Barbara." From
Othello. William Shakespeare.—HoUn—PlAs
"My mother hassled me about boys." See Shari
Morrow
"My mother is beautiful as a flapper." See
Among his effects we found a photograph
"My mother is peeling an apple over the sink."
See A kitchen memory
"My mother is soft." See My mother
"My mother, living in the past tense." See Louise
Coyle
"My mother never forgave my father." See The
portrait
"My mother, poor woman, lies tonight." See
Goodbye
"My mother said." See Against idleness
"My mother said I never should." Mother
Goose.—BlO—DeM
"My mother said, if just once more." See
Mother's nerves
"My mother saw my report card." See Marie
Yeagerman
"My mother says." See Mother
"My mother says I'm sickening." Jack
Prelutsky.—PrNk
"My mother taught me purple." See Taught me
purple
"My mother told me that boys are supposed to."
See Stacey Fowler
"My mother took me skating." Jack Prelutsky.—
PrIs
"My mother worries about my social life these
days." See Annie Scarella
"My mother's big green gravy boat." See
Exploding gravy
"My mother's big on little fears." See House
noises
"My mother's cigarette flares and fades." See June
twenty-first
My mother's death. Judith Hemschemeyer.—JaS
"My mother's got me bundled up." Jack
Prelutsky.—PrIs
"My mother's mother died." See From my
mother's house
"My mouse, my girl in gray, I speak to her."
See Afternoon
My mouth. Arnold Adoff.—PrRh

My name. Lee Bennett Hopkins.—LiSf
My name is. Pauline Clarke.—PrRh
"My name is Sluggery wuggery." See My name is
"My neighbor always buys a lamb." See Sicilian Easter Sunday
My nose. Dorothy Aldis.—PrRh
"My nose is blue." See Me
My, oh wow, book. Judith Viorst.—ViI
My old cat. Hal Summers.—ChC—KeK
"My old cat is dead." See My old cat
"My old red Schwinn had a carrier over the back fender." See Lament
"My only desire was to make myself over." See The outwit song
"My pants could maybe fall down when I dive off the diving board." See Fifteen, maybe sixteen, things to worry about
"My parents' plans for me include." See David Klein
"My parents think I'm sleeping." Jack Prelutsky.—PrMp
"My parents wanted me to go." See Keith Jordan
"My parents wanted me to go to this very." See James Petrie
My people. Langston Hughes.—HuDk
"My pillow won't tell me." See The apparition
"My poem would eat nothing." See The poem you asked for
"My poor old bones, I've only two." See The lonely scarecrow
"My pretty little pink, I once did think." See My pretty pink
My pretty pink. Mother Goose.—DaC
"My prime of youth is but a frost of cares." See Elegy for himself
My puppy. Aileen Fisher.—CoOu
"My room's a square and candle-lighted boat." See The country bedroom
"My secret way of waking." See Waking
My shadow. Robert Louis Stevenson.—CoOu—FaW
"My Shalom, my peace, is hidden in every broad smile." Margit Cohn.—LaT
"My shirt is a token and symbol." See Shirt
"My shoes are new and squeaky shoes." See New shoes
"My shoulders once were yours for riding." See Now that your shoulders reach my shoulders
"My sister had a slumber party." See Slumber party
"My sister is a sissy." Jack Prelutsky.—PrNk
My sister Jane. Ted Hughes.—CoOu—LiSf
My sister Laura. Spike Milligan.—CoN—FaW—PrRa
"My sister Laura's bigger than me." See My sister Laura
"My sister says." See Rhinos purple, hippos green
"My sister she works in a laundry." Unknown.—TrM
"My sister Stephanie's in love." See Weird
"My sister would never throw snowballs at butterflies." Jack Prelutsky.—PrIs
"My snowman has a noble head." Jack Prelutsky.—PrIs
"My snowman sadly bowed." See The snowman's lament
"My son." See Why I never went into politics
My sons. Ron Loewinsohn.—JaD
My special cake. Jack Prelutsky.—PrIv
"My spirit is too weak, mortality." See On seeing the Elgin Marbles

My star. Myra Cohn Livingston.—LaW
"My star comes out." See My star
"My stepfather was a hobo because he didn't know any better." See Open roads
"My stocking's where." From A Christmas package. David McCord.—PrRh
"My stomach's full of butterflies." See Dora Diller
"My street thunders like." See Zimmer's street
"My sun." See When the child is named
"My tail is not impressive." See Ode to the pig, his tail
"My tea is nearly ready and the sun has left the sky." See The lamplighter
"My teacher looked at me and frowned." See Teacher
"My teacher taught me to add." See Lessons
"My teacher's very special." See A valentine for my teacher
My teddy bear ("A teddy bear is a faithful friend"). Marchette Chute.—PrRa
My teddy bear ("A teddy bear is nice to hold"). Margaret Hillert.—PrRa
My teeth. Ed Ochester.—JaD
"My Thompson, least attractive character." See Elegy
"My toe." Felice Holman.—FaTh
My trouble with porringers and oranges. N. M. Bodecker.—BoSs
My uncle Dan. Ted Hughes.—LiSf
"My uncle Dan's an inventor." See My uncle Dan
"My Uncle Julius died." See Uncle Julius
"My uncle Paul of Pimlico." Mervyn Peake.—CoOu
"My valentine." Myra Cohn Livingston.—LiCe
My voice. Juan Ramón Jiménez, tr. by H. R. Hayes.—LiSf
"My whole life is going great, no complaints." See Christopher Conti
"My wife whose hair is a brush fire." From Free union. André Breton.—KoT
My window screen. X. J. Kennedy.—KeF
"My window screen, all crisscrossed wire." See My window screen
"My young love said to me, my brothers won't mind." See She moved through the fair
"Myra, Myra, sing song." See The Myra song
The Myra song. John Ciardi.—PrRh
Myrtle. Ted Kooser.—JaG
The mysterious cat. Vachel Lindsay.—HaOf—LiSf
The mystic Magi. Robert Stephen Hawker.—HaO

N

"N is for naughty young Nat." See Naughty young Nat
Naidu, Sarojini
    Cradle song ("From groves of spice").—ChB
The nail. Vasco Popa, tr. by Anne Pennington.—HeR
Nails
    "For want of a nail the shoe was lost." Mother Goose.—FaW—LoR
    The nail. V. Popa.—HeR
Najjar, Victoria Day
    "The last dinosaur."—HoDi
"Naked you came from Earth the mother, naked you return." See Prayer to the deceased
Nam. Mike Lowery.—JaPi
"Name, Brandon Dale." See Brandon Dale
"Nameless." See White summer flower

Nature.—*Continued*
Forest: an invitation. M. C. Livingston.—LiMp
The fresh air. H. Monro.—LiIl
Immalee. C. G. Rossetti.—BlO
In hardwood groves. R. Frost.—KoS
The intruders. J. Reeves.—CoOu
Inversnaid. G. M. Hopkins.—HeR
June ("Now is the ox-eyed daisy out"). J. Reaney.—DoNw
Keep still. E. Farjeon.—FaE
The little Hiawatha. From The song of Hiawatha. H. W. Longfellow.—CoOu
The minimal. T. Roethke.—FaTh—HeR
Nature is. J. Prelutsky.—PrRh
Nature's lineaments. R. Graves.—HeR
On a squirrel crossing the road in autumn, in New England. R. Eberhart.—JaPi
On the grasshopper and the cricket. J. Keats.—KoT
"Pensive, on her dead gazing, I heard the Mother of All." W. Whitman.—HeR
Psalm of the fruitful field. A. M. Klein.—DoNw
Range-finding. R. Frost.—HeR
Roses. D. H. Lawrence.—PrBb
A sea-chantey. D. Walcott.—HeR
The secret song. M. W. Brown.—HaOf—PrRh
Sensation. A. Rimbaud.—KoT
Song ("The sun is mine"). R. Hogg.—DoNw
There was a boy. From The prelude. W. Wordsworth.—HeR
A walk. N. A. Zabolotsky.—HeR
Written at the Po-shan monastery. Hsin Ch'i-chi.—LiIl
Nature and art. Oliver Herford.—BrT
Nature is. Jack Prelutsky.—PrRh
"Nature is the endless sky." See Nature is
"Nature responds so beautifully." See Roses
"Nature's decorations glisten." See Christmas day
"Nature's first green is gold." See Nothing gold can stay
Nature's lineaments. Robert Graves.—HeR
"Naughty little brown mouse." Jack Prelutsky.—PrRi
Naughty soap song. Dorothy Aldis.—PrRa
Naughty young Nat. Isabel Frances Bellows.—BrT
Navajo Indians. See Indians of the Americas—Navajo
Naval battles
The coasts of high Barbary. Unknown.—BlO
The death of Admiral Benbow. Unknown.—BlO
How do you do, Alabama. F. Wilson.—PlAs
Lepanto. G. K. Chesterton.—HeR
Roll, Alabama, roll. Unknown.—PlAs
"Would you hear of an old-fashion'd sea-fight." From Song of myself. W. Whitman.—HeR
"Nay nay nay." See Nightmare
Near and far. Kate Cox Goddard.—FrP
"Near dark." See The first hunt
Near drowning. Ralph Pomeroy.—JaD
"Near that rusty." See The apple tree
"Near the lilac bush." See Secret passageway
Nearly. Eleanor Farjeon.—FaE
"Nearly seven." See The new mothers
Ned ("It's a singular thing that Ned"). Eleanor Farjeon.—FaE
"Needing one, I invented her." See Aunt Leaf
Needles
"Old Mother Twitchett has but one eye." Mother Goose.—FaTh—LiSf
"Old Mother Twitchett had but one eye".—CoN
"Needles and pins, needles and pins." Mother Goose.—AlH

Neel, Alice (about)
Portrait by Alice Neel. A. Kramer.—PlEd
Nefertiti (about)
Queen Nefertiti. Unknown.—PrRh
The Negro. Langston Hughes.—HuDk
Negro dancers. Langston Hughes.—HuDk
The Negro speaks of rivers. Langston Hughes.—HaOf—HuDk—LiSf
Negroes. See Blacks
Neighbors
The ballad of Rudolph Reed. G. Brooks.—HeR
"Cross-patch, draw the latch." Mother Goose.—DeM—LoR
For Deena. N. Giovanni.—GiSp
Friend ("Do you know Paul, Paul Pine (he's nine)"). F. Holman.—LiIl
Man. A. Turner.—TuS
Mr. Dill. C. Rylant.—RyW
Mother. K. Starbird.—JaT
Neighbors ("The Cobbles live in the house next door"). M. A. Hoberman.—LiIl
Neighbors ("They live alone"). D. A. Evans.—JaPi
A new friend. M. A. Anderson.—FrP
Portrait by a neighbor. E. S. Millay.—HaOf—LiSf
Suburban. H. R. Coursen.—JaG
Neighbors ("The Cobbles live in the house next door"). Mary Ann Hoberman.—LiIl
Neighbors ("They live alone"). David Allan Evans.—JaPi
"The neighbors are not fond of me." Jack Prelutsky.—PrNk
"Neighbour, what was the sound I pray." See Wake up
Neil Winningham. Mel Glenn.—GlCd
Nelms, Sheryl L.
Cumulus clouds.—JaT
Edwin A. Nelms.—JaS
How about.—JaS
Into fish.—JaG
Killing the rooster.—JaS
Real talent.—JaT
Nemerov, Howard
Dandelions.—JaD
The dying garden.—JaPi
Elegy ("My Thompson, least attractive character").—JaPo
Going away.—JaD
Guide to the ruins.—PlEd
Metamorphoses ("These people, with their illegible diplomas").—PlEd
The most expensive picture in the world.—PlEd
The statues in the public gardens.—PlEd
Trees ("To be a giant and keep quiet about it").—JaPi
The vacuum.—HeR
Neruda, Pablo
Bestiary, sels.
"Fleas interest me so much".—FaTh
Elephant, sels.
"Gross innocent".—KoT
"Fleas interest me so much." See Bestiary
The ghost of the cargo boat.—LiWa
"Gross innocent." See Elephant
To the foot from its child.—HeR
Nest. Sylvia Cassedy.—CaR
Neuberger, Elsa
"Fleas interest me so much", tr. by.—FaTh
Neumeyer, Peter
Easter under the water.—LiE
Neuteronomy. Eve Merriam.—MeSk

"**Never**, in all your career of worrying, did you imagine." See The flying cat
Never mince words with a shark. Jack Prelutsky.—PrNk
"**Never** mind the rain." N. M. Bodecker.—HoSu
"**Never** said." See Adam's apple
"**Never** talk down to a glowworm." See Glowworm
"**Never** wondering." See Amoeba
New Brunswick, Canada
  "Sweet maiden of Passamaquoddy." J. De Mille.—DoNw
New clothes and old. Eleanor Farjeon.—BeD
A **new** cup and saucer. From Tender buttons. Gertrude Stein.—KoT
New day. N. M. Bodecker.—BoPc
New England
  Cape Ann. From Landscapes. T. S. Eliot.—HeR
  New England road. N. M. Bodecker.—BoPc
The **New** England boy's song about Thankgiving day. See Thanksgiving day
The **New** England Primer, sels. Unknown
  Alphabet 1727.—HaOf
New England road. N. M. Bodecker.—BoPc
New England verses, sels. Wallace Stevens
  Statue against a clear sky.—PlEd
A **new** friend. Marjorie Allen Anderson.—FrP
The **new** girl. Charlotte Zolotow.—ZoE
New Guinea
  Rain forest, Papua, New Guinea. M. C. Livingston.—LiMp
New Hampshire. From Landscapes. Thomas Stearns Eliot.—HeR
The **new** house. Vern Rutsala.—JaG
The **new** kid on the block. Jack Prelutsky.—PrNk
New love. Eve Merriam.—MeF
New Mexico
  "Toward the sun, towards the south-west." From Eagle in New Mexico. D. H. Lawrence.—HeR
New moon. Eve Merriam.—MeF
The **new** mothers. Carol Shields.—JaS
A **new** pencil. Eve Merriam.—MeF
New planting, shopping mall. Myra Cohn Livingston.—LiMp
"A **new** servant maid named Maria." See Fire
New shoes ("The first time in new shoes"). Eve Merriam.—MeF
New shoes ("My shoes are new and squeaky shoes"). Unknown.—BeD
New shoes ("When I am walking down the street"). Marjorie Seymour Watts.—FrP
A **new** song to sing about Jonathan Bing. Beatrice Curtis Brown.—FaW
New sounds. Lilian Moore.—HoSi—MoSn
"**New** sounds to." See New sounds
New suit. Eve Merriam.—MeF
"A **new** suit is crackly." See New suit
The **new** vestments. Edward Lear.—PrRh
New Year. See also Rosh Hashanah
  Beginning a new year means. R. Whitman.—LiNe
  The bell hill. J. Fields.—LiNe
  Chinese new year. Unknown.—LiNe
  Family needs. Unknown.—LiSf
  Farewell to the old year. E. Farjeon.—FaE
  First foot. I. Serraillier.—LiNe
  Happy new year. E. Merriam.—MeSk
  Happy new year, anyway. J. Cole.—CoN
  "Here she comes." D. Chandra.—LiNe
  "I saw three ships come sailing by." Mother Goose.—LoR
  January one. D. McCord.—LiNe

  Midnight ("After waiting up"). V. Worth.—LiNe
  New year ("After Christmas"). V. Worth.—LiNe
  The new year ("Here we bring new water from the well so clear"). Unknown.—HaO
    New Year's water.—LiSf
  "The new year lanterns." Unknown.—DeD
  New year song. T. Hughes.—HaO
  New year's advice from my Cornish grandmother. X. J. Kennedy.—LiNe
  New year's eve. M. C. Livingston.—LiCe
  New year's eve, Opelousas, Louisiana ("Every one on Franklin Street"). M. C. Livingston.—LiNe
  New year's eve, Opelousas, Louisiana ("Everyone on Franklin Street"). M. C. Livingston.—LiNe
  The new year's journey. J. Ridland.—LiNe
  News, news. E. Farjeon.—FaE
  Oh calendar. J. P. Lewis.—LiNe
  The old year. J. Clare.—HaO
  Promises. J. Yolen.—LiNe
  "Ring out, wild bells, to the wild sky." From In memoriam. A. Tennyson.—LiNe
  Rosh Hashanah eve. H. Philip.—LiPj
  Watching the new year's eve party through the staircase. J. P. Lewis.—LiNe
  Welcome to the new year. E. Farjeon.—FaE
  The year. F. Holman.—LiNe
New year ("After Christmas"). Valerie Worth.—LiNe
The **new** year ("Here we bring new water from the well so clear"). Unknown.—HaO
  New Year's water.—LiSf
"The **new** year lanterns." Unknown.—DeD
"The **new** year lives a long way off." See The new year's journey
New year song. Ted Hughes.—HaO
New year's advice from my Cornish grandmother. X. J. Kennedy.—LiNe
New year's eve. Myra Cohn Livingston.—LiCe
New year's eve, Opelousas, Louisiana ("Every one on Franklin Street"). Myra Cohn Livingston.—LiNe
New year's eve, Opelousas, Louisiana ("Everyone on Franklin Street"). Myra Cohn Livingston.—LiNe
The **new** year's journey. John Ridland.—LiNe
New Year's water. See The new year ("Here we bring new water from the well so clear")
New York City
  Awakening in New York. M. Angelou.—AnS
  The beginning. A. Turner.—TuS
  Brooklyn Bridge at dawn. R. Le Gallienne.—LiSf
  Manhattan lullabye. N. Farber.—HoSs
  Mannahatta. W. Whitman.—PlEd
  New York City, 1935. G. Corso.—JaPi
  "Roebling, his life and mind reprieved enough." From The bridge from Brooklyn. R. Henri.—PlEd
  To Brooklyn Bridge. H. Crane.—PlEd
  Tulips and addresses. E. Field.—JaPi
New York City, 1935. Gregory Corso.—JaPi
"**New** York is in North Carolina." Jack Prelutsky.—PrNk
Newbread. N. M. Bodecker.—BoPc
Newell, Peter
  Wild flowers ("Of what are you afraid, my child").—PrRh
Newman, Joseph S.
  Miss Tillie McLush.—BrT
  Serpentine verse.—BrT

News
"Brave news is come to town." Mother Goose.—DeM—LoR
"It is nice to read." Onitsura.—LiSf
Myrtle. T. Kooser.—JaG
News, news. E. Farjeon.—FaE
A patch of old snow. R. Frost.—KoS
The Sunday news. D. Gioia.—JaG
News, news. Eleanor Farjeon.—FaE
"News, news, I bring you good news." See News, news
Newspapers
Jay Stone. M. Glenn.—GlCd
The Sunday news. D. Gioia.—JaG
'Tis strange. E. Field.—BrT
Yesterday's paper. M. Watts.—PrRa
"Next." See X
Neyroud, Gerard
The skunk to the gnu.—BrT
Niagara Falls
Lake Erie. From Great Lakes suite. J. Reaney.—DoNw
"Nibble on a fiddle fern." See Spring diet
"Nicely while it is raining." Unknown.—LiSf
Nichio, Nakamo
The winter moon ("I hit my wife and went out and saw"), tr. by.—McL
Nicholas, Saint. See Santa Claus
"Nicholas Ned." Unknown.—CoN
Nicholas Nye. Walter De la Mare.—BlO
Nicholl, Louise Townsend
Architect.—PlEd
Nichols, Kevin
The feast of Stephen.—HaO
Nicholson, Norman
Carol ("Mary laid her child among").—HaO
Carol for the last Christmas eve.—HaO
Cowper's tame hare.—HeR
Shepherd's carol.—HaO
Nicole Harris. Mel Glenn.—GlCd
Nienhauser, William H.
Weaving at the window, tr. by.—PlSc
Night
Acquainted with the night. R. Frost.—KoS
After midnight. D. G. Jones.—DoNw
The arctic fox. T. Hughes.—HuU
Ashes. V. Popa.—HeR
At midnight. T. Kooser.—JaG
At night ("When night is dark"). A. Fisher.—LiSf—PrRa
Benue lullaby. M. Brennan.—LaW
Between the bars. E. Farjeon.—FaE
The bird of night. R. Jarrell.—KeK—LiSf
"Boys and girls, come out to play." Mother Goose.—DeM—LiSf—LoR
"Girls and boys, come out to play".—AlH—ChB—DaC
The bridge ("A bridge"). L. Moore.—MoSn
The bridge ("Glittering bridge"). C. Zolotow.—ZoE
Business as usual. M. Vinz.—JaS
Check. J. Stephens.—CoOu—PrRh
"The clouds I watched this afternoon." J. Prelutsky.—PrMp
The cottager to the infant. D. Wordsworth.—KoT
The country bedroom. F. Cornford.—BlO
Covers. N. Giovanni.—HoSu—PrRa
The dark ("I am glad of that other life"). W. Heyen.—PlEd
The dark ("It's always"). M. C. Livingston.—LiWo
Dial tone. F. Pollak.—JaPo

The dreaming of the bones. From Song for the cloth. W. B. Yeats.—HeR
The fireflies. C. Zolotow.—ZoE
Flashlight ("My flashlight tugs me"). J. Thurman.—BeD—LiSf
Foghorns. L. Moore.—HoSs—MoSn—PrRh
Fourth of July ("Tonight the air explodes"). B. J. Esbensen.—EsCs
Frost ("Frost on my window"). G. Johnston.—DoNw
The garden in the dark. E. Farjeon.—FaE
Good night ("Many ways to spell good night"). C. Sandburg.—HoRa
Good night, good night. D. Lee.—PrRa
Hymn to the sun. Unknown, fr. the Fang people of Africa.—KoT
"I am afraid." Unknown, fr. the Eskimo.—LiWa
"If it was sunlight shining." J. Prelutsky.—PrMp
In the night ("The light was burning very dim"). E. M. Roberts.—LiWa
In the night ("When I wake up and it is dark"). M. Chute.—HoSu
"In the pitch of the night." L. B. Hopkins.—HoCr
Insomnia ("The moon in the bureau mirror"). E. Bishop.—McL
Insomniac. M. Angelou.—AnS
It is so still. J. Prelutsky.—PrMp
Late night flight. X. J. Kennedy.—KeF
"Light the lamps up, lamplighter." E. Farjeon.—FaE
The lights at night. E. Farjeon.—FaE
May night. S. Teasdale.—HoSi
The middle of the night ("This is a song to be sung at night"). K. Kuskin.—LaW—PrRh
Midnight ("After waiting up"). V. Worth.—LiNe
Midnight ("Midnight's bell goes ting, ting, ting, ting, ting"). T. Middleton.—BlO
The midnightmouse. C. Morgenstern.—HeR
A million candles. J. Prelutsky.—PrMp
The mockingbird ("Look one way and the sun is going down"). R. Jarrell.—LiSf
Moon ("I have a white cat whose name is Moon"). W. J. Smith.—ChC—LiCa—LiSf
Moon boat. C. Pomerantz.—PoA—PrRa
"The moon shines bright." Mother Goose.—DeM
Moonlight ("Now, look, the big moon shines"). E. Farjeon.—FaE
"The night." M. C. Livingston.—LaW
Night ("The night is coming softly, slowly"). M. A. Hoberman.—PrRh
Night ("Stars over snow"). S. Teasdale.—LiSf
Night ("The sun descending in the west"). W. Blake.—ChB
Night ("Tonight the earth"). P. Marshall, and C. Marshall.—LaT
Night ("Up to bed, your head"). A. Adoff.—BeD
Night bear. L. B. Hopkins.—HoSu
"Night comes." B. S. De Regniers.—PrRa—PrRh
Night creature. L. Moore.—MoSn
Night eyes. R. J. Margolis.—MaS
Night game. L. Morrison.—LiSf
"The night is a big black cat." G. O. Clark.—PrRh
Night is here. J. Prelutsky.—PrMp
Night piece. R. R. Patterson.—LiWa
Night roof. A. Turner.—TuS
Night scare. J. Viorst.—ViI

Nine mice. Jack Prelutsky.—PrNk
"Nine mice on tiny tricycles." See Nine mice
Nine o'clock. From The wonder clock. Katharine Pyle.—HaOf
"Nine o'clock bell." See School bell
Nine red horsemen. Eleanor Farjeon.—FaE
Nineteen pieces for love, sels. Susan Griffin "Trying to say".—McL
1937 Ford convertible. Tom McKeown.—JaPo
No ("No, I refuse to"). Judith Viorst.—ViI
No ("No sun, no moon"). Thomas Hood.—BlO
"No bottom." See Mississippi sounding calls
"No breath of wind." See Snow
"No eagle flies through sun and rain." See The airplane
"No feet, snow." See The arctic fox
No girls allowed. Jack Prelutsky.—PrRh
No holes marred. Suzanne Douglas.—PrRh
"No, I refuse to." See No
"No, I won't turn orange." Jack Prelutsky.—PrNk
No man on any moon. Claudia Lewis.—LiSf
"No matter how hard I try to forget you." See I cannot forget you
"No matter what." See Number two
"No matter what." See Pigeon hole
"No matter what we are and who." See Routine
"No money to bury him." See Ballad of the man who's gone
"No more barefoot." See First day of school
"No more shall I work in the factory." See Factory girl
"No need even." See Library
"No need to squeeze out half a tube." See Toothsome
"No one." See Stars
"No one at Sam's place." See Patriarchs
"No one remembered when she first discovered God." See Grandmother
"No one sat in the chair." See Sundays visiting
"No one spells out the unwritten agreement." See Marriage contract
"No one spoke." Ryota.—KoT
"No one wants to hear about the war." See Nam
"No one was in the fields." See Tom's angel
"No room in the inn, of course." See What the donkey saw
"No shop does the bird use." Elizabeth Coatsworth.—HaOf
"No sooner does the sky grow dark." See The lights at night
"No sprouted wheat and soya shoots." See The health-food diner
"No sun, no moon." See No
No swan so fine. Marianne Moore.—PlEd
No talking shop. Minnie Leona Upton.—BrT
"No, the little girl said." See The crack of light
"No water so still as the." See No swan so fine
"No wonder Wendy's coat blew off." See Wendy in winter
Noah
The boa ("Allow me just one short remark"). J. J. Bell.—PrRh
Noah. R. Daniells.—DoNw
"When Noah loaded the ark as bidden." R. Beasley.—TrM
Noah. Roy Daniells.—DoNw
"Noble executors of the munificent testament." See Application for a grant
"Noble one, our great one, skirt of jade, jade that shines." See Prayer of the midwife to the Goddess of Water

A nobleman's house, sels. May Sarton "After the palaces".—PlEd
Noblesse oblige. Celeste Turner Wright.—JaPi
"Nobody comes to the graveyard on the hill." See The hill above the mine
"Nobody could believe." See My brother flies over low
"Nobody knows from whence he came." See Mr. Potts
"Nobody loses all the time." Edward Estlin Cummings.—HeR
"Nobody pays attention to me." See Lisa Goodman
"Nobody sees what I can see." See Just me
Nocturn at the institute. David McElroy.—JaPi
Nocturn cabbage. Carl Sandburg.—HoRa
Nocturne. Arthur Guiterman.—LaW
Nocturne for late summer. Barbara Juster Esbensen.—EsCs
Noel. Charlotte Zolotow.—ZoE
Noel, Christmas eve, 1913. Robert Bridges.—HaO
Noise. See Sounds
Noises. Aileen Fisher.—HoBf
Nolan, James
Mardi Gras.—JaS
Sum.—JaS
Nolan Davis. Mel Glenn.—GlCd
Nonsense. See also Limericks; also entries under Carroll, Lewis and Lear, Edward
Aiken Drum. Mother Goose.—BlO—BlPi
The alligator. M. Macdonald.—PrRh
Alligator pie. D. Lee.—FaW—JaT—PrRh
The animal fair. Unknown.—CoN—PrRh
"Anna Maria she sat on the fire." Mother Goose.—DeM
"As I was standing in the street." Unknown.—CoN—FaW
"As I was walking down the lake." Unknown.—DaC
"The baby uggs are hatching." J. Prelutsky.—PrB
Bandit. A. M. Klein.—DoNw
"Black-eyed Susan." N. M. Bodecker.—BoSs
The bluffalo. J. Yolen.—PrRh
The boar and the dromedar. H. Beissel.—DoNw
"Catch me and kiss me and say it again." C. Watson.—WaC
The ceiling. T. Roethke.—KeK—PlEd
"Cobwebs, cobwebs." C. Watson.—WaC
"Cock-a-doodle-doo." Mother Goose.—DaC—DeM
"Cock-a-doodle-do".—LoR
"The common cormorant or shag." Unknown.—BlO
The common cormorant.—PrRh (at. to Christopher Isherwood)
The contrary waiter. E. Parker.—PrRh
The cooky-nut trees. A. B. Paine.—HaOf
Cuckoo ("The cuckoo in our cuckoo clock"). J. Prelutsky.—PrNk
"Did you eever, iver, over." Unknown.—KeK
Hand-clapping rhyme ("Did you eever, iver, ever").—CoN
"Did you ever go fishing on a bright sunny day." Unknown.—PrRh
"Dilly Dilly Piccallilli." C. Watson.—CoN
Donkey riding. Unknown.—DaC—DoNw
The duel. E. Field.—FaW—HaOf—PrRh
Eletelephony. L. E. Richards.—CoN—CoOu—FaW—HaOf—LiSf—PrRh
The flimsy fleek. J. Prelutsky.—PrNk
The flotterzott. J. Prelutsky.—PrB

Nonsense.—*Continued*

"The folk who live in Backward Town." M. A. Hoberman.—HaOf—PrRh

"The grand old Duke of York." Mother Goose.—LiSf

The great panjandrum. S. Foote.—BlO

"The greedy man is he who sits." Mother Goose.—LoR

The hare and the pig. L. J. Bridgman.—PrRh

Herbert Glerbett. J. Prelutsky.—PrRh

"Hey diddle diddle, the cat and the fiddle." Mother Goose.—AlH—DeM—FaW—LiSf—LoR

"Hickup, hickup, go away." Mother Goose.—LoR

"Higgledy piggledy." D. Lee.—LiSf

"Higglety, pigglety, pop." S. Goodrich.—FaW (unat.)—PrRa—PrRh

"High diddle doubt, my candle's out." Mother Goose.—DeM

"A horse and a flea and three blind mice." Unknown.—CoN
    Whoops.—PrRh

Humpty Dumpty's recitation. From Through the looking glass. L. Carroll.—KoT
    Humpty Dumpty's poem.—BlO

"I asked my mother for fifty cents." Mother Goose.—PrRh
    "I asked my mother for fifteen cents".—LiSf

"I had a little husband." Mother Goose.—AlH—BlO—FaW—LoR

"I had a little nut tree." Mother Goose.—DaC—DeM—FaW—LiSf—LoR
    A nut tree.—KoT

"I saw a peacock with a fiery tail." Unknown.—BlO—HeR

"I wish that my room had a floor." G. Burgess.—HaOf

"If all the seas were one sea." Mother Goose.—CoOu—FaW—LoR

"If all the world was apple pie." Mother Goose.—LoR

"If all the world was paper." Mother Goose.—FaW

"If all the world were paper." Mother Goose.—BlO—CoN—KoT

"In a cottage in Fife." Mother Goose.—BlPi—LoR

"Johnnie Crack and Flossie Snail." From Under Milk Wood. D. Thomas.—LiSf—PrRh

Johnny Crow's garden. L. L. Brooke.—FaW

"Knock, knock, anybody there." C. Watson.—LiSf

"Latch, latch." E. Merriam.—MeBl

Lavinia Nink. J. Prelutsky.—PrNk

"Let's marry said the cherry." N. M. Bodecker.—LiSf

The little man ("As I was walking up the stair"). H. Mearns.—PrRh
    I met a man ("As I was going up the stair").—CoOu (unat.)

A little more cider. Unknown.—KeK

The lobsters and the fiddler crab. F. J. Forster.—PrRh

"McIntosh apple." S. Kroll.—PrRh

"The man in the wilderness asked of me." Mother Goose.—DaC—FaW
    "The man in the wilderness asked me".—LoR

"Master I have, and I am his man." Mother Goose.—AlH

"Mips and ma the mooly moo." From Praise to the end. T. Roethke.—HeR

Mr. Pyme. H. Behn.—HoCb

"Mother, may I go out to swim." Mother Goose.—DeM—LoR

"My father owns the butcher shop." Unknown.—PrRa—PrRh

"My mother said I never should." Mother Goose.—BlO—DeM

A new song to sing about Jonathan Bing. B. C. Brown.—FaW

"Nicholas Ned." Unknown.—CoN

Nonsense. J. Prelutsky.—PrRh

Nottamun Town. Unknown.—BlO

"Now I lay me down to sleep." Unknown.—TrM

Nut. N. M. Bodecker.—BoSs

"Oh that I were." Mother Goose.—FaW

"Old Mother Hubbard." Mother Goose.—DeM—FaW—LoR

"Old Quin Queeribus." N. B. Turner.—PrRh

The old woman of Norwich. Mother Goose.—DaC

"On the ning nang nong." S. Milligan.—PrRh

"One day a boy went walking." Mother Goose.—LoR

"One misty, moisty morning." Mother Goose.—ChG—DeM—FaW—LoR—PrRh

"One winter night in August." X. J. Kennedy.—HaOf

Ounce and Bounce. J. Prelutsky.—PrNk

"The owl, the eel, and the warming-pan." L. E. Richards.—HaOf

A peanut. Unknown.—HoSu
    Toot, toot.—PrRh

Pennies from heaven. J. Ciardi.—CiD

Poor old lady. Unknown.—HaOf—PrRh

"Poor old Penelope." J. Prelutsky.—LiSf

The ptarmigan. Unknown.—PrRh

"Pumberly Pott's unpredictable niece." J. Prelutsky.—PrRh

Punkydoodle and Jollapin. L. E. Richards.—HaOf

The purple cow. G. Burgess.—CoN—HaOf—LiSf—PrRh
    "I never saw a purple cow".—BlO

The redingote and the vamoose. R. K. Munkittrick.—HaOf

The reformed pirate. T. G. Roberts.—DoNw

"Rub-a-dub-dub." Mother Goose.—DaC—DeM—FaW—LoR—WaC

"Sally go round the sun." Mother Goose.—DeM—FaW—LoR

"Sam, Sam, the butcher man." Mother Goose.—DaC

"See, see, what shall I see." Mother Goose.—LoR

Sensitive, Seldom and Sad. M. Peake.—PrRh

Sing me a song of teapots and trumpets. N. M. Bodecker.—PrRh

Sir Blushington Bloone. J. Prelutsky.—PrNk

"Sleeping Charlie in the chair." A. Lobel.—LoWr

Snillies. J. Prelutsky.—PrNk

Sweetie Maguire. Unknown.—PaM

Tender heartedness. H. Graham.—PrRh

"There was a crooked man." Mother Goose.—DeM—FaW—LoR

There was a man. D. Lee.—KeK

"There was a man from nowhere." J. Ciardi.—CiD

Nonsense.—*Continued*
"There was a man, he went mad." Mother Goose.—LoR
"There was a man lived in the moon." Mother Goose.—LoR
"There was a man of Newington." Mother Goose.—FaW
"There was a young lady from Lynn." Unknown.—KeK
    A young lady of Lynn ("There was a young lady of Lynn").—PrRh
"There was an old woman called Nothing-at-all." Mother Goose.—LoR
    Nothing at all.—BlPi
"There was an old woman sat spinning." Mother Goose.—AlH—FaW
"There was an old woman tossed up in a basket." Mother Goose.—DaC—DeM—FaW—LiSf—LoR
"There were three jovial Welshmen." Mother Goose.—BlO—DeM
Three wise old women. E. T. Corbett.—HaOf
'Tis midnight. Unknown.—CoN
Uncanny Colleen. J. Prelutsky.—PrNk
"The underwater wibbles." J. Prelutsky.—PrNk
Unusual shoelaces. X. J. Kennedy.—JaT—LiSf
The village of Erith. Unknown.—LiWa
The Walloping Window-Blind. C. E. Carryl.—HaOf
Way down south. Unknown.—PrRa—PrRh
    The grasshopper and the elephant.—CoOu
"Went to the river, couldn't get across." Unknown.—FaW
"We're all in the dumps." Mother Goose.—BlO
When young, the slyne. J. Prelutsky.—PrNk
"William McTrimbletoe." Mother Goose.—BlQ
"You must never bath in an Irish stew." S. Milligan.—PrRh
Nonsense. Jack Prelutsky.—PrRh
"**Nonsense,** that's what makes no sense." See Nonsense
Noon. Myra Cohn Livingston.—LiSi
Nootka Indians. See Indians of the Americas—Nootka
Norman Moskowitz. Mel Glenn.—GlC
Norris, Leslie
"All night I've kept an eye." See The old dog's song
The black fern.—LiSf
Buying a puppy.—LiIl—LiSf
Camels of the kings.—HaO
In black chasms.—LiWa
Merlin and the snake's egg.—LiWa
Mice in the hay.—HaO
The old dog's song, complete.—LiSf
The old dog's song, sels.
    "All night I've kept an eye".—HoDl
The shepherd's dog.—HaO
Small frogs.—LiSf
North America. See names of countries, as United States
North and south. Charlotte Zolotow.—ZoE
North Atlantic, sels. Carl Sandburg
    "The sea is always the same".—HoRa
North pole. See Polar regions
The **north** ship. Philip Larkin.—HeR
"The **north** wind doth blow." Mother Goose.—BlO—CoOu—DeM—FaW—LiSf—LoR
    Poor robin.—RoC
The **nose** (after Gogol). Iain Crichton Smith.—HeR

"The **nose** knows, I hunt the wind." See Winter song of the weasel
"**Nose,** nose, jolly red nose." Mother Goose.—LoR
"The **nose** went away by itself." See The nose (after Gogol)
Nosegay. Elizabeth Coatsworth.—HaOf
Noses
"Be glad your nose is on your face." J. Prelutsky.—PrNk
The dong with a luminous nose. E. Lear.—LiH
My nose. D. Aldis.—PrRh
The nose (after Gogol). I. C. Smith.—HeR
"Nose, nose, jolly red nose." Mother Goose.—LoR
Noses. A. Fisher.—FaW
"Peter White will ne'er go right." Mother Goose.—AlH
    "Peter White will never go right".—LoR
"Sing a song of succotash." A. Lobel.—LoWr
Television nose. X. J. Kennedy.—KeF
"There is a young lady, whose nose." E. Lear.—FaW—LiH
"There was a man and he was mad." Unknown.—HeR
"There was a young lady whose nose." E. Lear.—LiH
"There was an old man in a barge." E. Lear.—FaW—LiH—RuI
"There was an old man of Dunrose." E. Lear.—LiH
"There was an old man of West Dumpet." E. Lear.—LiH
"There was an old man, on whose nose." E. Lear.—LiH
"There was an old man with a nose." E. Lear.—LiH
"There was an old person of Cassel." E. Lear.—LiH
"There was an old person of Tring." E. Lear.—LiH
    An old person of Tring.—BrT (unat.)
Noses. Aileen Fisher.—FaW
"**Not** all the time." See People
"**Not** being Breedlove, whose immortal skid." See To Dorothy on her exclusion from the Guinness Book of World Records
"**Not** every man has gentians in his house." See Bavarian gentians
"**Not** from Titania's court do I." See Hob gobbling's song
"**Not** in the cities, nor among fabricated towers." See Boulder dam
"**Not** just its." See Tinsel
Not me. See "The slithergadee has crawled out of the sea"
"**Not** single filmy threads." See A shower of cobwebs
"**Not** that my hand could make of stubborn stone." See Death-bed reflections of Michelangelo
"**Not** the lead, please not the lead." See Lead
Note to the previous tenants. John Updike.—JaC
Nothing
    Zero. E. Merriam.—MeHa
Nothing ("He's gone"). Eleanor Farjeon.—FaE
Nothing ("Whsst, and away, and over the green". Walter De la Mare.—LiWa
Nothing at all. See "There was an old woman called Nothing-at-all"
Nothing but net. Roy Scheele.—JaT
The **nothing** doings. Jack Prelutsky.—PrNk
Nothing gold can stay. Robert Frost.—KoS

"**Nothing** is more honest." See Good egg
"**Nothing** is so beautiful as spring." See Spring
Nothing more than a sister. Unknown.—BrT
"**Nothing** to do but work." See The pessimist
Notice. David McCord.—McAs
"**Notice** how." See Spring cleaning
Notice to myself. Eve Merriam.—MeF
"**Noticing** an open-doored." X. J. Kennedy.—KeB
Nottamun Town. Unknown.—BlO
"**Nouns** are the things I see and touch." See Verbs
November
  Cat, Thanksgiving. V. Worth.—LiTp
  The dying garden. H. Nemerov.—JaPi
  The middle of November. J. Prelutsky.—PrIt
  No ("No sun, no moon"). T. Hood.—BlO
  November. A. Cary.—HaOf
  November song. M. Vinz.—JaPi
  November the fifth. L. Clark.—CoOu
  The transparence of November. R. Borson.— JaPo
  The volunteer's Thanksgiving. L. Larcom.— HaOf
November. Alice Cary.—HaOf
November song. Mark Vinz.—JaPi
November the fifth. Leonard Clark.—CoOu
"**Now**." See After many springs
Now. Prince Redcloud.—HoSi
"**Now**." See Prayer for safe passage through enemy country
Now about tigers. John Ciardi.—CiD
"**Now** about tigers, notice please." See Now about tigers
"**Now** all the crab trees are in bloom." See Spring in Hampstead
"**Now** another day is breaking." See Morning prayer
"**Now** as the train bears west." See Night journey
"**Now** as the year turns toward its darkness." See Going away
"**Now** children may." See May
Now close the windows. Robert Frost.—KoS
"**Now** close the windows and hush all the fields." See Now close the windows
"**Now** comes the fisherman to terms." See Fisherman
"**Now** corn pushes past the foam." See Ode to a dead Dodge
"**Now** entertain conjecture of a time." William Shakespeare.—HeR
Now every child. Eleanor Farjeon.—FaE
"**Now** every child that dwells on earth." See Now every child
"**Now** every man at my request." Unknown.— HaO
"**Now** good night." See For good night
"**Now**, I am as beautiful as the very blossoms themselves." See For young men growing up to help themselves
"**Now** I can catch and throw a ball." See Big
"**Now** I go down here and bring up a moon." See Auctioneer
"**Now** I lay me down to sleep." Mother Goose.— ChB—DeM
"**Now** I love you." From Razon de amor. Pedro Salinas, tr. by Linda Gutierrez and Lawrence Pitketbly.—McL
"**Now**, in lean November." See Cat, Thanksgiving
"**Now** is my father." See Poem for my father's ghost
"**Now** is the ox-eyed daisy out." See June

"**Now** Jack he had a ship in the north counterie." See The Golden Vanity
"**Now**, leech, quickly you have just come undulating in." See To make the road seem short
Now lift me close. Walt Whitman.—JaD
"**Now** lift me close to your face till I whisper." See Now lift me close
"**Now**, look, the big moon shines." See Moonlight
"**Now** May has drawn her meadows up." See May meadows
"**Now** midnight's here." See Watching the new year's eve party through the staircase
"**Now** Mister Johnson had troubles of his own." See The cat came back
"**Now**, my friends, please hear." See The song of a dream
"**Now**, pray, where are you going, child." See Meet-on-the-road
"**Now**, pray, where are you going, said Meet-on-the-road." See Meet-on-the-road
"**Now** sleeps the crimson petal, now the white." From The princess. Alfred Tennyson.—McL
"**Now** that it is May, the sky stays light." See Shavuot, for Jessica
Now that spring is here. Barbara Juster Esbensen.—EsCs
"**Now** that the time has come wherein." See Advice from Poor Robin's almanack
Now that your shoulders reach my shoulders. Robert Francis.—JaS
"**Now** the day is over." Sabine Baring-Gould.— DaC—LaW
"**Now** the drowsy sun shine." See Evening
"**Now** the hungry lion roars." From A midsummer night's dream. William Shakespeare.—LiWa
"**Now** the mellowest sun of all." See The mellow time
"**Now** the mid-May brings." See Summer fountains
"**Now** the mouse goes to his hole." See Bedtime
"**Now** the summer is grown old." See Autumn
"**Now** the swing is still." Nicholas Virgilio.—KeK
"**Now** there comes." See New year song
"**Now**, 'twas twenty-five or thirty years since Jack first saw the light." See Jack was every inch a sailor
"**Now** when a branch hangs out its leaves." See Leaves
"**Now** winter, that mean polar bear." See All around the year
"**Now** you." See Sunset
"**Now** you are going, what can I do but wish you." See The poet's farewell to his teeth
"**Now** you have to promise." See Cousin Ella goes to town
Nowhere. Ann Turner.—TuS
Nowlan, Alden
  Great things have happened.—JaG
  He runs into an old acquaintance.—JaG
  He sits down on the floor of a school for the retarded.—JaG
  Helen's scar.—JaS
  I, Icarus.—DoNw
  Subway psalm.—JaS
Noyes, Alfred
  Betsy Jane's sixth birthday.—LiIl
  Daddy fell into the pond.—PrRh
  The highwayman.—LiSf
Nude reclining at word processor, in pastel. Carl Conover.—JaG
A **nuisance** at home. Unknown.—BrT

Ocean.—*Continued*
Sea calm. L. Hughes.—HuDk
A sea-chantey. D. Walcott.—HeR
"Sea charm." L. Hughes.—HuDk
Sea chest. C. Sandburg.—HoRa
"The sea is always the same." From North Atlantic. C. Sandburg.—HoRa
Sea monster. W. S. Merwin.—LiWa
The sea serpent chantey. V. Lindsay.—LiWa
Sea shell. A. Lowell.—PrRh
Sea-wash. C. Sandburg.—HaOf
Sea-weed. D. H. Lawrence.—HeR—HoSe—PrBb
Seashell ("This seashell is an ocean cove"). S. Liatsos.—HoSe
"Seventy feet down." From Livings. P. Larkin.—HeR
Siren chorus. G. Darley.—LiWa
Song for a surf rider. S. V. A. Allen.—HoSe
Song for smooth waters. Unknown, fr. the Haida Indian.—BiSp
Song of the mermaids and mermen. Sir W. Scott.—LiWa
"Summer wades the waters where distant islands gleam." M. C. Livingston.—LiCs
"Tell me, tell me, Sarah Jane." C. Causley.—HoSe—LiSf
"That woman down there beneath the sea." Unknown, from the Eskimo.—LiWa
"There was an old person of Bree." E. Lear.—LiH
"This is the hay that no man planted." E. Coatsworth.—HaOf
Undersea. M. Chute.—RuI
Undine's garden. H. Behn.—HoCb
"Until I saw the sea." L. Moore.—CoN—HoSe—MoSn—PrRh
Waking from a nap on the beach. M. Swenson.—CoN
The waves of the sea. E. Farjeon.—FaE
The way of Cape Race. E. J. Pratt.—DoNw
Whale ("When I swam underwater I saw a blue whale"). W. J. Smith.—RuI
The whale ghost. L. Moore.—MoSn
Young sea. C. Sandburg.—HoRa
"Ocean spirit." See Song for smooth waters
Ocean treasures. Constance Andrea Keremes.—HoSe
"Ocean waves rush in." See On an August day
Ocelots
"Saucy little ocelot." J. Prelutsky.—LiSf—PrSr
Ochester, Ed
Among his effects we found a photograph.—JaS
For my daughter ("This is the summer storm").—JaS
The gift.—JaD—JaPi
In the library ("The silent girl").—JaPi
My teeth.—JaD
110 year old house.—JaPi
Rowing.—JaS
October
October ("In October"). From Chicken soup with rice. M. Sendak.—PrRh
October ("October turned my maple's leaves to gold"). T. B. Aldrich.—PrRh
October ("The whole world dances"). S. Hahn.—JaPo
October nights in my cabin. N. M. Bodecker.—BoSs
Poem in October. D. Thomas.—HeR
October ("In October"). From Chicken soup with rice. Maurice Sendak.—PrRh

October ("October turned my maple's leaves to gold"). Thomas Bailey Aldrich.—PrRh
October ("The whole world dances"). Steve Hahn.—JaPo
October nights in my cabin. N. M. Bodecker.—BoSs
"October turned my maple's leaves to gold." See October
Octopus ("Marvel at the"). Valerie Worth.—WoSp
The **octopus** ("The octopus would surely be"). Sonja Delander.—RuI
The **octopus** ("Tell me, O octopus, I begs"). Ogden Nash.—HeR—LiSf
"The octopus would surely be." See The octopus
Octopuses
Love at sea. J. P. Lewis.—LiVp
Octopus ("Marvel at the"). V. Worth.—WoSp
The octopus ("The octopus would surely be"). S. Delander.—RuI
The octopus ("Tell me, O octopus, I begs"). O. Nash.—HeR—LiSf
Odd ("That was"). Lilian Moore.—MoSn
"The odd, friendless boy raised by four aunts." See Thumb
An **odd** old man in Hackensack. Unknown.—BrT
Ode to a dead Dodge. David McElroy.—JaD
Ode to a dressmaker's dummy. Donald Justice.—JaD
Ode to a nightingale. John Keats.—HeR
Ode to spring. Walter R. Brooks.—PrRa—PrRh
An **ode** to the framers of the Frame Bill. Lord Byron.—PlSc
Ode to the pig, his tail. Walter R. Brooks.—PrRh
Odors
The bonfire. E. Farjeon.—FaE
Catnip. V. Worth.—LiCa
Driving to the beach. J. Cole.—PrRh
The hound. K. Starbird.—KeK
I know a man. P. Steele.—JaPo
Mr. Wells. E. M. Roberts.—KeK
My mother. C. Zolotow.—ZoE
Nowhere. A. Turner.—TuS
Old dog. P. Hubbell.—HoDl
Skunk ("Skunk's football plods padded"). T. Hughes.—HuU
Skunk ("Sometimes, around/moonrise"). V. Worth.—WoSp
The skunk to the gnu. G. Neyroud.—BrT
Smell my fingers. D. B. Axelrod.—JaS
The smell of old newspapers is always stronger after sleeping in the sun. M. Lowery.—JaPi
Smells. K. Worth.—PrRh
That was summer. M. Ridlon.—CoN—LiSf
"There was a man." A. Lobel.—LoWr
Unpopular Rex. X. J. Kennedy.—KeF
Wharf. M. C. Livingston.—HoSe
Winter song of the weasel. J. Yolen.—YoR
"Of all the birds I know." See The toucan
"Of all the gay birds that ever I did see." Mother Goose.—LoR
"Of all the insects." See Crickets
"Of all the problems no one's solved." See Minnie Morse
"Of all the rides since the birth of time." See Skipper Ireson's ride
"Of all the secret places." See The sound of rain
"Of all the songs that birds sing." See Roosters and hens
"Of all the ways of traveling in earth and air and sea." See Flight plan
Of calico cats. Kirsty Seymour-Ure.—ChC

"Of inviting to dine, in Epirus." See A difficult guest
"Of one who grew up at Gallipoli." See War story
Of poor B. B. Bertolt Brecht, tr. by Michael Hamburger.—HeR
"Of that Medusa strange." See The statue of Medusa
"Of the islands, Puerto Rico." Unknown.—LiIl
Of the race. Arnold Adoff.—AdA
"Of the three Wise Men." See Carol of the brown king
"Of what are you afraid, my child." See Wild flowers
O'Faoláin, Seán
    The icebound swans, tr. by.—LaT
"Off the coast of Ireland." See Seascape
"Off we go on a piggyback ride." Clyde Watson.—WaC
Offering to deceased hunters. Unknown.—BiSp
Office. Sylvia Cassedy.—CaR
"The office feels like a sealed glass case today." See What grandma knew
"Oft, in the silence of the night." See Our little ghost
"O, Alison Gross that lives in yon tower." See Alison Gross
"O barn reality, I saw you swimming." See Iowa land
O beauteous one. Unknown.—KoT
"O beauteous one, O cow, O great one." See O beauteous one
"O beautiful." See A boat
"O, but I saw a solemn sight." See The wicked hawthorn tree
Oh calendar. J. Patrick Lewis.—LiNe
O captain, my captain. Walt Whitman.—HaOf
"O captain, my captain, our fearful trip is done." See O captain, my captain
"Oh come and see the wallaby." See The wallaby
"Oh crash." See The Fourth
"Oh dear, need I brush my hair." See Going to bed
"O, dear, what can the matter be". See "Oh, dear, what can the matter be"
"Oh, dear, what can the matter be." Mother Goose.—FaW—LoR
    "O, dear, what can the matter be".—DeM
"Oh, dear, what shall I do." See Boredom
"Oh, dearest grandpa, come and see." See The dead sister
"Oh, did your Granny sing the song." See Morning glory
"Oh do not fear the dreary dreeze." See The dreary dreeze
"Oh, do not tease the bluffalo." See The bluffalo
"O, early one morning I walked out like Agag." See The streets of Laredo
"O earth, turn! George Johnston.—DoNw
"O echo, echo." See Echo echo
"O, fare you well, sweet Ireland, whom I shall see no more." See The sons of liberty
"Oh for far-off monkeyland." See Monkeyland
"Oh, get you forth, my son Willy." See Marm Grayson's guests
"Oh, give us pleasure in the flowers today." See A prayer in spring
"O God, bless all the people for whom life is hard and difficult." William Barclay.—LaT
"Oh God, I thank you that you have made me as I am." William Barclay.—LaT
"Oh God, it's great." See Chocolate milk

"O god, my lord, mother, father, lord of the mountains and valleys." See Harvester's prayer, with an offering of copal
"O God, my mother, my father, lord of the hills." See Prayer before felling to clear a cornfield
"O God, O lord of the mountains and valleys, I have offered." See Traveler's prayer, with an offering of copal
"O great one, source of surprise." See Song to a son
"O great spirit." Unknown.—LaT
Oh hark. Eleanor Farjeon.—FaE
"Oh, hark, my darling, hark." See Oh hark
Oh have you heard. Shel Silverstein.—LiSf
"Oh have you heard it's time for vaccinations." See Oh have you heard
"Oh, have you heard the gallant news." From Western star. Stephen Vincent Benét.—PlAs
"O heart, small urn." From The walls do not fall. H. (Hilda Doolittle) D.—McL
"Oh, I can laugh and I can sing." See Whistling
"O, I forbid you, maidens a'." See Tam Lin
"O, I forbid you, maidens all." See Tam Lin
"Oh I have dined on this delicious day." Richard Snyder.—JaT
"Oh, I laugh to hear what grown folk." See Mrs. Kriss Kringle
"Oh I suppose I should." See Le medecin malgre lui
"Oh I want to." See Perversity
"Oh I'm Dirty Dan, the world's dirtiest man." See The dirtiest man in the world
"Oh, I'm goin' to sing a song, and I won't detain you long." See How do you do, Alabama
"Oh, isn't it a pity, such a pretty girl as I." Harriet Hanson Robinson.—PlSc
"Oh, it's fiddle-de-dum and fiddle-de-dee." See The dancing bear
"Oh, Johathan Bing, oh, Bingathan Jon." See A new song to sing about Jonathan Bing
"Oh, kangaroos, sequins, chocolate sodas." See Today
"Oh, king of the fiddle, Wilhelmj." See Wilhelmj
"O, know you what I have done." See The brother
"O lady, when the tipped cup of the moon blessed you." See Song
"O little soldier with the golden helmet." See Dandelion
"O little town of Bethlehem." Phillips Brooks.—RoC (unat.)
"O Lord, save us." Peter Marshall.—LaT
Oh, lovely, lovely, lovely. Unknown.—ChC
"Oh, Mabel, remarkable Mabel." See Mabel, remarkable Mabel
"Oh Madame Curie." See While dissecting frogs in biology class Scrut discovers the intricacies of the scooped neckline in his lab partner's dress
"Oh, make my bed in the warm air." See To carry on living
"O Mary, go and call the cattle home." See The sands of Dee
"O Merlin in your crystal cave." See Merlin
"O Mister Giraffe, you make me laugh." See Mr. Giraffe
"O mistress mine, where are you roaming." From Twelfth night. William Shakespeare.—HoUn
"O moon, why must you." Koyo, tr. by Harry Behn.—LiSf
"Oh mother." See Mothers

O'Hara, Frank
Autobiographia literaria.—KoT
Poem ("O sole mio, hot diggety, nix, I wather think I can").—KoT
Poem to Franz Kline.—McL
Song ("Did you see me walking by the Buick Repairs").—KoT
Today.—KoT
A true account of talking to the sun at Fire Island ("The sun woke me this morning loud").—HeR—KoT

Ohio
"Pick me poppies in Ohio." From Crossing Ohio when poppies bloom in Ashtabula. C. Sandburg.—HoRa

O'Huigin, Sean
Bye bye.—DoNw

Oil
Oil slick. J. Thurman.—HoSs—LiSf
The oil lamp. William Jay Smith.—BrT
Oil slick. Judith Thurman.—HoSs—LiSf

O'John, Calvin
"You smiled."—LiIl

O'Keefe, Adelaide
"The dog will come when he is called."—BlO

Oklahoma
Earthy anecdote. W. Stevens.—HeR—LiSf
Ol' red thief. Eleanor Farjeon.—FaE

"Old." See Ago
"Old Abram Brown is dead and gone." Mother Goose.—LoR

Old age. See also Childhood recollections; Youth and age
Ago. E. Jennings.—JaG
Aunt Elsie's night music. M. Oliver.—JaS
Aunt Roberta. E. Greenfield.—LiSf
The belly dancer in the nursing home. R. Wallace.—JaG
By the Exeter River. D. Hall.—PlAs
Charlie Wallinsky. M. Glenn.—GlC
Charwomen. B. Belitt.—PlSc
Childhood. F. Cornford.—KeK
Concert. R. Morgan.—JaT
Danny Murphy. J. Stephens.—CoOu
"Dear, dear, what can the matter be." Mother Goose.—DeM
Desert tortoise. B. Baylor.—PrRh
"Desperate Dan." Mother Goose.—AlH—FaW
"Do not go gentle into that good night." D. Thomas.—HeR
Edwin A. Nelms. S. L. Nelms.—JaS
Frau Bauman, Frau Schmidt, and Frau Schwartze. T. Roethke.—PlSc
The gnomes. B. Bentley.—PlSc
Going steady. I. Serraillier.—LiVp
Good neighbors. M. Justus.—PrRa
"Grand-dads." E. Farjeon.—FaE
Grandma's lost balance. S. Dayre.—HaOf
Growing old. R. Henderson.—PrRh
I dreamed that I was old. S. Kunitz.—JaG
In January, 1962. T. Kooser.—JaPi
In the basement of the Goodwill Store. T. Kooser.—JaG
In the park ("Two old-timers"). E. Merriam.—MeF
Jane Seagrim's party. L. Nathan.—JaG
Jim at the corner. E. Farjeon.—FaE
The last decision. M. Angelou.—AnS
The last words of my English grandmother. W. C. Williams.—HeR
Lines for an old man. T. S. Eliot.—HeR
The lockless door. R. Frost.—LiWa
"Looking at your face." G. Kinnell.—JaPo

Lore. R. S. Thomas.—HeR
Mac. M. Vinz.—JaS
Mending the adobe. H. Carruth.—JaPi—PlEd
Mexican market woman. L. Hughes.—HuDk—PlSc
Miss Hepzibah. E. Merriam.—MeSk
Mr. Potts. H. Behn.—HoCb
Moonlight ("It will not hurt me when I am old"). S. Teasdale.—JaG
My teeth. E. Ochester.—JaD
Old dog. P. Hubbell.—HoDl
"An old man stirs the fire to a blaze." From Wanderings of Oisin. W. B. Yeats.—HeR
The old men ("The fish has too many bones"). C. Reznikoff.—JaD
Old men ("People expect old men to die"). O. Nash.—HeR—JaD
The old men admiring themselves in the water. W. B. Yeats.—KeK
Old people working (garden, car). G. Brooks.—PlSc
Old-timer. X. J. Kennedy.—KeF
"Old woman, old woman." Mother Goose.—DeM
"Old woman, old woman, shall we go a-shearing." Mother Goose.—FaW—LoR
The one to grieve. R. Thomas.—JaG
Park ("I sit beside old retired Italians"). D. Ignatow.—JaPi
Passing the Masonic home for the aged. H. Scott.—JaPo
The passing years. R. Elsland.—StG
Patriarchs. L. Moore.—MoSn
Poem for my mother. S. Cedering.—JaS
The poet's farewell to his teeth. W. Dickey.—JaD
A prayer for rivers. K. Wilson.—JaG
A real story. L. Pastan.—JaS
Rembrandt's late self portraits. E. Jennings.—PlEd
Retired farmer. D. A. Evans.—JaPi
Rhymes ("We were talking about poems he had written"). F. Steele.—JaPo
Rocking chair. R. Morgan.—JaPo
A sad song about Greenwich Village. F. Park.—PrRh
Senex. Sir J. Betjeman.—HeR
The smell of old newspapers is always stronger after sleeping in the sun. M. Lowery.—JaPi
Some one to tea. E. Farjeon.—FaE
Song for the old ones. M. Angelou.—PlSc
The span of life. R. Frost.—HoDl
Stark county holidays. M. Oliver.—JaS
Stonecarver. C. Oles.—JaS
Stroke. M. Lowery.—JaPi
The sugar lady. F. Asch.—PrRh
A summer Christmas in Australia. D. Sladen.—HaO
"There was an old woman lived under a hill." Mother Goose.—DeM—LoR
The old woman (". . . lived under the hill").—BlPi
"Tommy's tears and Mary's fears." Mother Goose.—LoR
The two old gentlemen. R. Wallace.—JaD
Warning ("When I am an old woman I shall wear purple"). J. Joseph.—JaG
When the ambulance came. R. Morgan.—JaS
White autumn. R. Morgan.—JaS
"The wind has taken the damson tree." E. Farjeon.—FaE
You owe them everything. J. Allman.—PlSc

"An **old** astronomer there was." See A marvel

"**Old** Ben Bailey." See Done for

The **old** bridge at Florence. Henry Wadsworth Longfellow.—PlEd

An **old** cat's confessions. C. P. Cranch.—HaOf

"An **old** charcoal seller." Po Chu-yi, tr. by Eugene Eoyang.—PlSc

Old clothes. Phil Hey.—JaG

"An **old** couple living in Gloucester." See The lost girl

Old deep sing song. Carl Sandburg.—HoRa

"The **old** devil he came to a woodsman one day." See The curst wife

Old Doc. Mark Vinz.—JaPi

Old dog. Patricia Hubbell.—HoDl

"The **old** dog barks backward without getting up." See The span of life

"**Old** Dog lay in the summer sun." See Sunning

"**Old** dog, old dog." See Old dog

The **old** dog's song, complete. Leslie Norris.—LiSf

The **old** dog's song, sels. Leslie Norris
  "All night I've kept an eye".—HoDl

The **old** familiar faces. Charles Lamb.—HeR

An **old** fellow from Cleathe. Unknown.—BrT

Old florist. Theodore Roethke.—PlSc

"**Old** Friedrich Barbarossa." See Barbarossa

"**Old** friend, you." See Back from the word processing course, I say to my old typewriter

"The **old** grand piano." See Fantasia

Old grey goose. Harry Behn.—HoCb

"The **old** grey hearse goes rolling by." See The hearse song

Old Jack Noman. Edward Thomas.—BlO

The **old** king. Walter De la Mare.—PlAs

Old King Cabbage. Richard Kendall Munkittrick.—HaOf

"**Old** King Cole." Mother Goose.—DeM—FaW—LoR

The **old** lady from Dover. Carolyn Wells.—BrT

"**Old** lady in black bonnet." See Christmas chime

The **old** lady in Bumbletown. John Ciardi.—CiD

An **old** lady of Harrow. Unknown.—BrT

"**Old** leaves, the perfume of moldering." See Looking both ways

An **old** looney. Unknown.—BrT

An **old** man by Salt Lake. William Jay Smith.—BrT

Old man from Darjeeling. Unknown.—CoN

An **old** man from Peru. See "There was an old man from Peru"

Old man ocean. Russell Hoban.—LiSf

"**Old** man ocean, how do you pound." See Old man ocean

An **old** man of Hawaii. Unknown.—BrT

The **old** man of the Hague. See "There was an old man of the Hague"

An **old** man of the Nile. See "There was an old man of the Nile"

An **old** man of Toulon. William Jay Smith.—BrT

"**Old** man, put your hands on the sea and press it down." See Boatman's prayer for smooth waters

"An **old** man stirs the fire to a blaze." From Wanderings of Oisin. William Butler Yeats.—HeR

The **old** man who lived in the woods. Unknown.—CoOu

Old man with a beard. See "There was an old man with a beard"

The **old** man with a gong. See "There was an old man with a gong"

The **old** man's toes. Eleanor Farjeon.—FaE

"**Old** Meg she was a gipsy." See Meg Merrilies

The **old** men ("The fish has too many bones"). Charles Reznikoff.—JaD

Old men ("People expect old men to die"). Ogden Nash.—HeR—JaD

The **old** men admiring themselves in the water. William Butler Yeats.—KeK

"**Old** men beneath the mountain." See With a sliver of marble from Carrara

An **old** miser named Quince. John Ciardi.—BrT

"**Old** Mr. Chang." Unknown, tr. by Isaac Taylor Headland.—FaW

Old Moll. James Reeves.—LiWa

"**Old** Mother Goose." Mother Goose.—DeM—LoR

"**Old** Mother Hubbard." Mother Goose.—DeM—FaW—LoR

"**Old** Mother Shuttle." Mother Goose.—BlPi—LoR

"**Old** Mother Twitchett had but one eye". See "Old Mother Twitchett has but one eye"

"**Old** Mother Twitchett has but one eye." Mother Goose.—FaTh—LiSf

"Old Mother Twitchett had but one eye".—CoN

"**Old** Nellie is so very high." See Horseback ride

"The **old** Penobscot indian." See Flux

Old people working (garden, car). Gwendolyn Brooks.—PlSc

"**Old** people working, making a gift of garden." See Old people working (garden, car)

An **old** person of Cromer. Edward Lear.—BrT

An **old** person of Tring. See "There was an old person of Tring"

An **old** person of Ware. See "There was an old person of Ware"

"The **old** priest Peter Gilligan." See Father Gilligan

"**Old** Quin Queeribus." Nancy Byrd Turner.—PrRh

The **old** salt. John Ciardi.—CiD

Old Sam. Myra Cohn Livingston.—LiWo

"An **old** silent pond." Basho.—LiSf

"The **old** sun, the gold sun." See Sun and wind

The **old** Sussex road. Ian Serraillier.—CoN

Old-timer. X. J. Kennedy.—KeF

"**Old** Tom, he was a merry one." Arnold Lobel.—LoWr

The **old** wife and the ghost. James Reeves.—HoCr

Old wife's song. Eleanor Farjeon.—FaE

"**Old** witch winter." See December 21

The **old** wives' tale, sels. George Peele
  Celanta at the well of life.—BlO
  Song for the head.—HeR

The **old** woman ("You know the old woman"). Beatrix Potter.—CoN—PrRa

The **old** woman (". . . lived under the hill"). See "There was an old woman lived under a hill"

"The **old** woman must stand." Mother Goose.—DeM

The **old** woman of Norwich. Mother Goose.—DaC

"**Old** woman, old woman." Mother Goose.—DeM

"**Old** woman, old woman, shall we go a-shearing." Mother Goose.—FaW—LoR

"The **old** woman stands at the tub, tub, tub." Mother Goose.—LoR

Old women beside a church. Keith Wilson.—JaPi

The **old** year. John Clare.—HaO

"The **old** year's gone away." See The old year

"**Older** than." See Fossils

Oles, Carole
  Stonecarver.—JaS

Oliphaunt. John Ronald Reuel Tolkien.—LiSf—
PrRh
Oliver, Mary
Aunt Elsie's night music.—JaS
Aunt Leaf.—JaT
Beaver moon, the suicide of a friend.—JaG
A letter from home.—JaS
Poem for my father's ghost.—JaS
Stark county holidays.—JaS
Oliver, Robert S.
The toad ("In day of old, those far off
times").—PrRh
Olson, Elder
Nightfall.—JaD
"Oma was sixty three when I was born." From
Afternoon in Waterloo Park. Gerald
Dumas.—StG
Omaha Indians. See Indians of the Americas—
Omaha
Omens. See also Prophecies; Superstitions
The knowledgeable child. L. Strong. KeK
London. W. Blake.—HeR
Marm Grayson's guests. M. E. W. Freeman.—
HaOf
"Methought that I had broken from the
Tower." From Richard III. W. Shakespeare.—
HeR
Omens ("Early on the morning of Monday").
Unknown.—HeR
The omens ("The wind has changed, and all
the signs turned right"). A. Stanford.—LiWa
"There's a certain slant of light." E.
Dickinson.—HeR
The warning ("Just now"). A. Crapsey.—LiWa
Omens ("Early on the morning of Monday").
Unknown, tr. by A. Carmichael.—HeR
The **omens** ("The wind has changed, and all the
signs turned right"). Ann Stanford.—LiWa
"An **ominous** length uncoiling and thin." See The
rattlesnake
The **omnivorous** bookworm. Oliver Herford.—BrT
"**On** & between the blades of grass." See A
On a bad singer. Samuel Taylor Coleridge.—PrRh
"**On** a bet, foolhardy Sam." X. J. Kennedy.—KeB
On a bicycle, sels. Yevgeny Yevtushenko, tr. by
Robin Milner-Gulland and Peter Levi
"Under the dawn I wake my two-wheel
friend".—Lill
On a boxer. X. J. Kennedy.—JaPo
On a child who lived one minute. X. J.
Kennedy.—JaD
"**On** a flat road runs the well trained runner."
See The runner
On a horse carved in wood. Donald Hall.—PlEd
"**On** a June night." See Firefly
On a landscape of Sestos. From A visit to the
art gallery. Carlos Baker.—PlEd
"**On** a little piece of wood." See Mr. and Mrs.
Spikky Sparrow
"**On** a mountain of sugar candy." See Phantasus,
1, 8
On a night of snow. Elizabeth Coatsworth.—
ChC—HaOf
On a squirrel crossing the road in autumn, in
New England. Richard Eberhart.—JaPi
"**On** a summer's day in the month of May, a
burly little bum come a-hiking." See The big
rock candy mountains
On a Sunday. Charles Reznikoff.—JaD
"**On** a Sunday, when the place was closed." See
On a Sunday

On a tree fallen across the road. Robert Frost.—
HeR
"**On** a winter's night." See Three furry cats
On Addy Road. May Swenson.—JaG
On an August day. Lee Bennett Hopkins.—HoSe
On being much better than most and yet not
quite good enough (". . . a great swimmer
named Jack"). See About being very good and
far better than most but still not quite good
enough to take on the Atlantic Ocean ("There
was a fine swimmer named Jack")
"**On** blue summer evenings I'll go." See Sensation
On buying a dog. Edgar Klauber.—CoN
On buying a horse. Unknown.—HeR
On certain mornings everything is sensual. David
Jauss.—JaG
"**On** Christmas eve in Palestine." See Bethlehem
bells
"**On** Easter morn." See Easter
"**On** Elm and Main a dreamy cur has
recollected." See Madrid, Iowa
"**On** Hallow-Mass eve, ere you bounc ye to root."
See St. Swithin's chair
On Halloween. Aileen Fisher.—PrRa
"**On** Halloween, what bothers some." From
Witch's broom notes. David McCord.—HoSi
"**On** Halloween, when ghosts go boo." X. J.
Kennedy.—KeB
"**On** his deathbed my grandfather." See
Gooseberries
"**On** his last swing around." See Field work
"**On** his motorbike Lars stands." X. J.
Kennedy.—KeB
On his portrait. William Cowper.—PlEd
On learning to adjust to things. John Ciardi.—
HaOf—KeK
"**On** Lolham Brigs in wild and lonely mood." See
The flood
On love. Kyogoku Tamekane, tr. by Burton
Watson.—McL
"**On** May Day." See May Day
"**On** midsummer eve." See Midsummer eve
"**On** midsummer night the witches shriek." See
Owl
"**On** Monday my mother went for a ride." See
It really wasn't too bad
On Mother's Day. Aileen Fisher.—CoN—PrRh
On my applications. Arnold Adoff.—AdA
"**On** my applications I can put." See On my
applications
On my first sonne. Ben Jonson.—HeR
"**On** new year's eve, at your front door." See New
year's advice from my Cornish grandmother
"**On** new year's eve the snow came down." See
Promises
"**On** paper." See Beginning on paper
"**On** pianos and organs she lbs." See The musical
maiden
On reading, four limericks, complete. Myra Cohn
Livingston
"Curiosity's not in me head".—MeF
"If you don't know the meaning of snook".—
MeF—MeF
"If you're apt to be ravenous, look".—MeF—
MeF
"A young person of precious precocity".—MeF
On St. Winefred. Gerard Manley Hopkins.—PlSc
"**On** Saturday night I lost my wife." Mother
Goose.—LoR
"**On** Saturday night shall be my care." Mother
Goose.—AlH—LoR
"**On** Saturdays." See Saturday

Ondaatje, Michael—*Continued*
Buying the dog.—JaS
A dog in San Francisco.—JaG
To a sad daughter.—JaG
"One August day, it was as hot." See Too hot
"One be the nail another the pincers." See The nail
"One biting winter morning." See The spider
"One bliss for which." See Taboo to boot
"One by one the petals drop." See Summer's end
"One cannot have enough." See Soliloquy of a tortoise on revisiting the lettuce beds after an interval of one hour while supposed to be sleeping in a clump of hollyhocks
"One Christmas-time." From The prelude. William Wordsworth.—HeR
"One day." See The gift
"One day a boy went walking." Mother Goose.—LoR
"One day, a fine day, a high-flying-sky day." See The cat heard the cat-bird
"One day I saw a downy duck." See Good morning
"One day I so depressed." See The park
"One day I was out walking on the mountain." See The wild lumberjack
"One day in Oklahoma." Jack Prelutsky.—PrRi
"One day is swimming, who should I." See I answer an SOS
"One day the letters went to school." See The letters at school
"One day we took our lunches." See The circus parade
"One day when we went walking." Valine Hobbs.—PrRh
"One day you were there, the next day gone." See Flight
"One evening a goose, for a treat." See The misapprehended goose
"One evening as the sun went down." See The big rock candy mountains
"One evening (surely I was led by her)." See Boat stealing
"One fine night in a witch's cavern." See Gobbolino, the witch's cat
"One flower at a time, please." See Bouquets
"One for me and one for you." Clyde Watson.—WaC
"One for the money." Mother Goose.—LoR
"One gets a wife, one gets a house." See The cat
One guess. Robert Frost.—KoS
110 year old house. Ed Ochester.—JaPi
"One I have wounded, yonder he moves." See A song of the buffalo dance
"One I love." Mother Goose.—DeM
One inch tall. Shel Silverstein.—HaOf
One last little leaf. Jack Prelutsky.—PrIs
The **one-legged** colonel. Unknown.—BrT
"One letter stands for alphabet." See Alphabet
"One lives by commerce, said the guide." See Guide to the ruins
"One misty, moisty morning." Mother Goose.—ChG—DeM—FaW—LoR—PrRh
"One morning in August." Jack Prelutsky.—PrWi
One morning in May (the nightingale). Unknown.—PlAs
"One morning, one morning, one morning in May." See One morning in May (the nightingale)
"One mouse adds up to many mice." See Singular indeed

"One night." See Sleepless nights
"One night as I lay on my bed." See Death
One-night fair. Nancy Price.—JaG
"One night I dreamed." See The dream
"One night the brownies reached a mound." See The brownies' celebration
"One November morning clean and cold." See The elm tree
One o'clock. From The wonder clock. Katharine Pyle.—HaOf
One of the boys. Philip Dacey.—JaS
"One of the clock, and silence deep." See One o'clock
One of the problems of play. Nikki Giovanni.—GiSp
One of the years. William Stafford.—KeK
"One, one." Clyde Watson.—LiSf—WaC
"One person." Issa.—KoT
"One purple summer eve." Richard J. Margolis.—MaS
"One quick scratch." See Lighting a fire
One rose of stone. Keith Wilson.—JaG
"One Saturday night as we set sail." Unknown.—LiSf
"One scene as I bow to pour her coffee." See Vacation
"One shuts one eye." See Before play
One step from an old dance. David Helwig.—DoNw
"One thing has a shelving bank." See A drumlin woodchuck
"One thing work gives." From Reverdure. Wendell Berry.—PlSc
"One time I knew a real good boy." See Girl who's moved around
The **one** to grieve. Rudy Thomas.—JaG
"One traffic rule." See Traffic rule I
"One, two, buckle my shoe." See The late mother
"One, two, buckle my shoe." Mother Goose.—AlH—DaC—DeM—FaW—LiSf—LoR
"One, two, three, cho-." See Chocolate rhyme
"One, two, three, four." See First foot
"1, 2, 3, 4, 5". See "One, two, three, four, five"
"One, two, three, four, five." Mother Goose.—DaC—DeM
"1, 2, 3, 4, 5".—AlH—LiSf
One, two, three, gough ("To make some bread you must have dough"). Eve Merriam.—CoN—MeSk
"1-2-3 was the number he played but today the number came." See Dirge
One-upmanship. Miriam Chaikin.—CoN
"One wall." See Elevator
"One waxwing's wakened." See Morning
"One white foot, try him." See On buying a horse
"One who sees corn and is glad." See Chicken
"One winter night in August." X. J. Kennedy.—HaOf
"One without looks in tonight." See The fallow deer at the lonely house
O'Neill, Mary
Feelings about words.—PrRh
Mark's fingers.—PrRh
Miss Norma Jean Pugh, first grade teacher.—PrRh
My fingers.—KeK
Sound of water.—CoN
What is black.—CoN
What is orange.—PrRh
What is red.—PrRh
Onions
Why ("We zoomed"). P. Redcloud.—HoMu

Onitsura
"It is nice to read."—LiSf
"Only / fools / pursue." See Heron
"Only a litter." See Kaleidoscope
"Only a man harrowing clods." See In time of 'the breaking of nations'
"The only ghost I ever saw." Emily Dickinson.—LiWa
An only kid. From Haggadah. Unknown.—LiPj
"An only kid, an only kid." See An only kid
"The only light at this hour." See My grandfather burning cornfields
Only my opinion. Monica Shannon.—PrRa
Only teasing. Unknown.—BrT
"The only way I would follow God was if." See Mary Louise Donahue
Onomatopoeia and onomatopoeia II. Eve Merriam.—MeSk
Oodles of noodles. Lucia Hymes and James L. Hymes.—PrRh
"Opalescent fins on a trout." See Shimmerings
"Open-backed dumpy junktruck." See In passing
The open door. Elizabeth Coatsworth.—LiCa
"An open door says, come in." See Doors
Open doors. From A throw of threes. Eve Merriam.—MeF
Open house. Aileen Fisher.—PrRa
Open hydrant. Marci Ridlon.—PrRh
Open roads. David Donnell.—JaS
"Open the closet." See Coat hangers
Operatic Olivia. Isabel Frances Bellows.—BrT
Opossums
  Possum. N. M. Bodecker.—BoSs
Oppenheimer, Joel
  An undefined tenderness.—JaPo
Opper, Frederick B.
  Sir Bedivere Bors.—BrT
Opportunity's knock. Morris Bishop.—BrT
The opposite of two. See "What is the opposite of two"
Opposites
  Some opposites. R. Wilbur.—HaOf
  "What is the opposite of a prince." R. Wilbur.—LiSf—LiWa
  "What is the opposite of nuts." R. Wilbur.—LiSf
  "What is the opposite of two." R. Wilbur.—LiIl
    The opposite of two.—PrRh
Optimism. See Happiness; Laughter
"Or what is closer to the truth." See When I buy pictures
Orange (color)
  "No, I won't turn orange." J. Prelutsky.—PrNk
  What is orange. M. O'Neill.—PrRh
"Orange is a tiger lily." See What is orange
Oranges
  "No, I won't turn orange." J. Prelutsky.—PrNk
  Peeling an orange. E. Merriam.—MeF
  Urbanity. E. Merriam.—MeSk
"Oranges and lemons, say the bells of St. Clement's." Mother Goose.—DaC
The oratorical crab. Oliver Herford.—BrT
Orbiter 5 shows how earth looks from the moon. May Swenson.—LiSf
Orbit's end. N. M. Bodecker.—BoPc
Orchards
  He was. R. Wilbur.—PlSc
  In a starry orchard. N. Farber.—LiSf
"The orchestra of the dark tangled field." See The transparence of November
Orchestras. See also Music and musicians
  The ceremonial band. J. Reeves.
Order. N. M. Bodecker.—BoSs

Orders. Abraham Moses Klein.—DoNw
"Ordinary candy." See Valentine chocolates
Organ grinder. Eleanor Farjeon.—FaE
Orgel, Doris
  Written on an egg, tr. by.—LiE
Orlando Martinez. Mel Glenn.—GlC
Orleans, Ilo
  Change in the weather.—HoSu
  The frog on the log.—PrRa
  Poor shadow.—PrRa
  The shadow tree.—HoSi
Orlen, Steve
  The Aga Khan.—JaPi
  Big friend of the stones.—JaPi
  The biplane.—JaG
  A common light.—JaS
  Family cups.—JaS
Ornithology. Eleanor Farjeon.—FaE
Orphans
  Little orphant Annie. J. W. Riley.—HaOf
  A story that could be true. W. Stafford.—CoN—JaG—KeK
"Orpheus with his lute made trees." From Henry VIII. William Shakespeare.—HoUn
Orr, Gregory
  Adolescence.—JaPi
  Gathering the bones together.—JaPi
  The sweater.—JaPo
"Orson Porson." Arnold Lobel.—LoWr
"Orville Skinner." See Mr. Skinner
The osprey. Ted Hughes.—HuU
Ospreys. See Hawks
An ossified oyster. Carolyn Wells.—BrT
The ostrich. Jack Prelutsky.—PrZ
"The ostrich believes she is hidden from view." See The ostrich
"The ostrich is a silly bird." Mary E. Wilkins Freeman.—HaOf—KeK
"An ostrich who lived at the zoo." See The bored ostrich
Ostriches
  The bored ostrich. Unknown.—BrT
  The ostrich. J. Prelutsky.—PrZ
  "The ostrich is a silly bird." M. E. W. Freeman.—HaOf—KeK
O'Sullivan, Seumas
  A piper.—LiSf
Othello, sels. William Shakespeare
  "And let me the canakin clink, clink".—PlAs
  "Her father lov'd me, oft invited me".—HoUn
  "My mother had a maid call'd Barbara".—HoUn—PlAs
Otomo of Sakanone, Lady
  "Unknown love."—McL
Otsuju
  "Into a forest."
Otto. Gwendolyn Brooks.—LiSf
Ouch. Unknown.—BrT
Ough, or, the cross farmer. D. S. Martin.—BrT
Ounce and Bounce. Jack Prelutsky.—PrNk
The ounce of detention. Oliver Herford.—BrT
"Our blue planet." See Drought
"Our brains ache, in the merciless iced east winds that knive." See Exposure
"Our candles, lit, re-lit, have gone down now." See Twelfth night
"Our cat had kittens." See Kittens
"Our cat turns up her nose at mice." See The cat who aspired to higher things
"Our chairs drawn to one end of the living." See Aunt Gladys's home movie no. 31, Albert's funeral
"Our cherry tree." See Blow up

"The **owl**, the eel, and the warming-pan." Laura E. Richards.—HaOf
The **owl** ("There was an old owl who lived in an oak"). See "A wise old owl sat in an oak"
Owls
  Beech, to owl. M. C. Livingston.—LiMp
  The bird of night. R. Jarrell.—KeK—LiSf
  "The brown owl sits in the ivy bush." Mother Goose.—LoR
  The conservative owl. O. Herford.—BrT
  The frog on the log. I. Orleans.—PrRa
  "Of all the gay birds that ever I did see." Mother Goose.—LoR
  Oh hark. E. Farjeon.—FaE
  Owl ("The diet of the owl is not"). X. J. Kennedy.—KeF
  The owl ("Downhill I came, hungry, and yet not starved"). E. Thomas.—HeR
  Owl ("On midsummer night the witches shriek"). S. Read.—PrRh
  The owl ("The owl hooted and told of"). Unknown, fr. the Hopi Indian.—KoT
  The owl ("The owl is wary, the owl is wise"). J. Prelutsky.—PrZ
  The owl ("When cats run home and light is come"). A. Tennyson.—BlO—DaC
    Song, the owl.—LiSf
  Owl ("Who"). E. Merriam.—MeHa
  The owl and the pussycat. E. Lear.—BlO—CoN—FaW—KoT—LiH—LiSf—PrRh
  Owls ("Sun's down, sky's dark"). P. Fleischman.—FlI
  Owls ("Wait, the great horned owls"). W. D. W. Snodgrass.—JaPi
  The owl's bedtime story. R. Jarrell.—LiIl
  Questioning faces. R. Frost.—KoS
  The snowy owl. T. Hughes.—HuU
  The song of the owl. R. K. Munkittrick.—HaOf
  "Stealing eggs, Fritz ran afoul." X. J. Kennedy.—KeB
  Sweet Suffolk owl. T. Vautor.—HeR
  That's what we'd do. M. M. Dodge.—HaOf
  "There came a gray owl at sunset." Unknown.—LiWa
  There once was an owl. J. Ciardi.—LiSf
  There was a boy. From The prelude. W. Wordsworth.—HeR
  "There was a little boy went into a barn." Mother Goose.—DeM
  "There was an old man of Dumbree." E. Lear.—LiH
  "There was an old person of Crowle." E. Lear.—LiH
  "An unassuming owl." J. Prelutsky.—PrNk
  "A wise old owl sat in an oak." Mother Goose.—DeM—FaW—LoR
    "There was an old owl who lived in an oak".—BlPi
    The owl ("There was an old owl who lived in an oak").—DaC
  "A wolf." Unknown, fr. the Osage Indian.—PrRh
Owls ("Sun's down, sky's dark"). Paul Fleischman.—FlI
Owls ("Wait, the great horned owls"). William De Witt Snodgrass.—JaPi
The **owl's** bedtime story. Randall Jarrell.—LiIl
The **ox-tamer**. Walt Whitman.—HeR
Oxen. See Cattle
The **oxen** ("Christmas eve, and twelve of the clock"). Thomas Hardy.—HaO—HeR—RoC

Oxford, England
  Duns Scotus's Oxford. G. M. Hopkins.—PlEd
Oysters
  Crustration. N. M. Bodecker.—BoPc
  Do oysters sneeze. J. Prelutsky.—PrNk
  The exclusive old oyster. L. A. Steel.—BrT
  An ossified oyster. C. Wells.—BrT
  "Oysters." J. Prelutsky.—PrZ—RuI
"Oysters." Jack Prelutsky.—PrZ—RuI
Oz. Eve Merriam.—MeSk
Ozymandias. Percy Bysshe Shelley.—HeR

P

P., A. B.
  The scholastic mouse.—BrT
Pa ("When we got home, there was our old man"). Leo Dangel.—JaS
Pacheco, José Emilio
  Mosquitoes ("They are born in the swamps of sleeplessness").—FaTh
"Pacing back and forth between their restless." See What the stone dreams
Pack, Robert
  Departing words to a son.—JaG
  Waiting ("As in a thunderstorm at night").—JaG—JaPo
"Pack, clouds, away, and welcome, day." Thomas Heywood.—BlO
The **pack** rat. Jack Prelutsky.—PrZ
"The pack rat's day is spent at play." See The pack rat
Packard. David Barker.—JaD
"Packing." See Labor day
"Pada kisa." See Yes, it's raining
Padgett, Ron
  "The butterfly." See Three animals
  Chocolate milk.—KoT
  "The electric eel." See Three animals
  "The giraffe." See Three animals
  Three animals, complete.
    "The butterfly".—KoT
    "The electric eel".—KoT
    "The giraffe".—KoT
Page, Patricia K.
  A backwards journey.—DoNw
  The crow ("By the wave rising, by the wave breaking").—DoNw
Pain
  Isabel Navarro. M. Glenn.—GlCd
  Justin Faust. M. Glenn.—GlCd
  Minstrel man. L. Hughes.—HuDk
  "My toe." F. Holman.—FaTh
  The snare. J. Stephens.—BlO—LiSf
  Sometimes ("I am afraid of being crushed in the pincers"). G. Kuzma.—JaPi
  Sounds of the day. N. MacCaig.—HeR
  This love. J. Hemschemeyer.—JaG
  A visit from Alphonse. P. Zimmer.—JaG
Paine, Albert Bigelow
  The cooky-nut trees.—HaOf
  The dancing bear ("Oh, it's fiddle-de-dum and fiddle-de-dee").—HaOf
A **painful** love song. Yehuda Amichai.—McL
The **paint** box. Emile Victor Rieu.—PrRh
"Paint samples." See Bruises
The **painters.** Judith Hemschemeyer.—JaPi
Painters. Muriel Rukeyser.—PlEd
Painting and pictures
  Anonymous drawing. D. Justice.—PlEd
  Art class. X. J. Kennedy.—KeF

Painting and pictures—*Continued*
Art work. R. Wallace.—JaPo
As if you had never been. R. Eberhart.—PlEd
A backwards journey. P. K. Page.—DoNw
"Betwixt mine eye and heart a league is took." From Sonnets. W. Shakespeare.—PlEd
Cardinal ideograms. M. Swenson.—HaOf
A Chinese mural. From A visit to the art gallery. C. Baker.—PlEd
Coloring. H. Behn.—HoCb
Crayon house. M. Rukeyser.—PlEd
Crayons. M. Chute.—PrRa
The dark ("I am glad of that other life"). W. Heyen.—PlEd
"Don't let that horse." L. Ferlinghetti.—HeR
Drawing. M. L'Engle.—LaT
The enemy's portrait. T. Hardy.—PlEd
Epiphany, for the artist. E. Sewell.—PlEd
Frame for a picture. E. Merriam.—MeF
"From his pouch he took his colors." From The song of Hiawatha. H. W. Longfellow.—PlEd
How to paint a perfect Christmas. M. Holub.—HaO
"I look at this picture of that old man." From Afternoon in Waterloo Park. G. Dumas.—StG
Lady Sara Bunbury sacrificing to the Graces, by Reynolds. D. Hine.—PlEd
Large bad picture. E. Bishop.—PlEd
Looking at a picture on an anniversary. T. Hardy.—PlEd
Max Schmitt in a single scull. R. Lattimore.—PlEd
Metamorphoses ("These people, with their illegible diplomas"). H. Nemerov.—PlEd
"Mine eye hath play'd the painter, and hath steel'd." From Sonnets. W. Shakespeare.—PlEd
The most expensive picture in the world. H. Nemerov.—PlEd
Mural on second avenue. L. Moore.—MoSn
The National Gallery. L. MacNeice.—PlEd
On a landscape of Sestos. From A visit to the art gallery. C. Baker.—PlEd
On his portrait. W. Cowper.—PlEd
The paint box. E. V. Rieu.—PrRh
The painters. J. Hemschemeyer.—JaPi
Painters. M. Rukeyser.—PlEd
Portrait by Alice Neel. A. Kramer.—PlEd
Poussin. L. MacNeice.—PlEd
Rembrandt's late self portraits. E. Jennings.—PlEd
Rutherford McDowell. E. L. Masters.—PlEd
The sand painters. B. Belitt.—PlEd
A sea spell for a picture. D. G. Rossetti.—LiWa
Still life. W. De la Mare.—PlEd
Street painting. A. Turner.—TuS
To a daughter with artistic talent. P. Meinke.—JaPi
To an artist. R. Burns.—PlEd
Tudor portrait. R. Lattimore.—PlEd
Turner's sunrise. H. Bevington.—PlEd
Vincent Van Gogh. W. J. Smith.—PlEd
When I buy pictures. M. Moore.—PlEd
Witchcraft by a picture. J. Donne.—PlEd
Pamela Atkinson. Mel Glenn.—GlC
The **pancake**. See "Mix a pancake"
The **pancake** collector. Jack Prelutsky.—HaOf
The **panda**. William Jay Smith.—BrT
Pandas
The panda. W. J. Smith.—BrT
Pangur Ban. Unknown, tr. by Robin Flower.—ChC—HeR

"**Panic** struck flight nine oh nine." X. J. Kennedy.—KeB
Pansies. Charlotte Zolotow.—ZoE
"**Pansies** purple." See Pansies
The **panther**. Ogden Nash.—HaOf
"The **panther** is like a leopard." See The panther
Panthers
The panther. O. Nash.—HaOf
Pantomime. Eleanor Farjeon.—FaE
Papago Indians. See Indians of the Americas—Papago
Paper
Paper dragons. S. A. Schmeltz.—PrRh
Paper I. C. Sandburg.—HoRa
Paper II. C. Sandburg.—HoRa
Paperclips. X. J. Kennedy.—FaTh
Yesterday's paper. M. Watts.—PrRa
"**Paper** cups and paper plates." See Cookout night
Paper dragons. Susan Alton Schmeltz.—PrRh
Paper I. Carl Sandburg.—HoRa
Paper II. Carl Sandburg.—HoRa
"**Paper** is two kinds, to write on, to wrap with" See Paper I
"The **paper** tigers roar at noon." See Tiger
Paperclips. X. J. Kennedy.—FaTh
Parades
"Bullfrogs, bullfrogs on parade." J. Prelutsky.—PrRi
The circus ("Friday came and the circus was there"). E. M. Roberts.—LiSf
A circus garland. R. Field.—HaOf
The circus parade. K. Pyle.—HaOf
The city show. E. Farjeon.—FaE
The Easter parade. W. J. Smith.—LiE
"The little girl saw her first troop parade and asked." C. Sandburg.—HoRa
The Thanksgiving day parade. J. Prelutsky.—PrIt
To my daughter riding in the circus parade. J. Labombard.—JaG
"We each wore half a horse." J. Prelutsky.—PrNk
Paradise. See Heaven
Pardoner's tale blues. Patricia Beer.—PlAs
Parents and parenthood. See Fathers and fatherhood; Home and family life; Mothers and motherhood
"**Parents**, friends, teachers, on this special day." See Helen Price
Parents never understand. Nikki Giovanni.—GiSp
Paris, France
Parisian beggar woman. L. Hughes.—HuDk
Sleeping on the ceiling. E. Bishop.—KoT
Parisian beggar woman. Langston Hughes.—HuDk
Park, Frances
A sad song about Greenwich Village.—PrRh
Park ("I sit beside old retired Italians"). David Ignatow.—JaPi
The **park** ("One day I so depressed"). Ann Turner.—TuS
Parke, Walter
A person of note.—BrT
Parker, Edgar
The contrary waiter.—PrRh
Parking lot full. Eve Merriam.—HoCl
Parks
"In Golden Gate Park that day." L. Ferlinghetti.—HeR
In the park ("Two old-timers"). E. Merriam.—MeF
In the park ("When you've"). L. Moore.—MoSn
Lincoln Park. M. C. Livingston.—LiWo

Parks—*Continued*
 Park ("I sit beside old retired Italians"). D. Ignatow.—JaPi
 The park ("One day I so depressed"). A. Turner.—TuS
 The poem in the park. P. Davison.—JaG
 Saturday in the park. B. J. Esbensen.—EsCs
 Snowy benches. A. Fisher.—BaS—HoSi, KeK
 Statues. R. Wilbur.—PlEd
 The statues in the public gardens. H. Nemerov.—PlEd
 "There was a strange pig in the park." A. Lobel.—LoB
 Tunnel ("Tunnel in the park"). S. Cassedy.—CaR
Parlor. Sylvia Cassedy.—CaR
Parodies
 Father William. From Alice's adventures in Wonderland. L. Carroll.—LiSf—LiSf—PrRh
 "He was a rat, and she was a rat." Unknown.—BlO
  He and she.—BlPi
  What became of them.—HaOf
 "How doth the little crocodile." From Alice's adventures in Wonderland. L. Carroll.—BlO—HeR—KoT—LiSf
  The crocodile.—PrRh
 "I never had a piece of toast." J. Payn.—TrM
 "I put my hat upon my head." S. Johnson.—KeK
 "Mary had a little lamb (it was a greedy glutton)." Unknown.—PaM
 The modern Hiawatha. G. A. Strong.—PrRh
 "Now I lay me down to sleep." Unknown.—TrM
 A second stanza for Dr. Johnson. D. Hall.—KeK
 Song of the open road. O. Nash.—JaPo
 "This little pig built a spaceship." F. Winsor.—PrRh
 Twinkle, twinkle. From Alice's adventures in Wonderland. L. Carroll.—PrRa
 "Under a spreading gooseberry bush the village burglar lies." Unknown.—TrM
 Variations on a theme by William Carlos Williams. K. Koch.—KeK
 We four lads. Unknown.—KeK
Parrish, Elsie
 Some things that Easter brings.—PrRa
The **parrot** in the garret. See "Little Poll Parrot"
"Parrot with a pomegranate." Jack Prelutsky.—PrRi
Parrots
 "Little Poll Parrot." Mother Goose.—DeM
  The parrot in the garret.—BlPi
 Meditations of a parrot. J. Ashbery.—KoT
 "Parrot with a pomegranate." J. Prelutsky.—PrRi
 "There was an old woman of Gloucester." Mother Goose.—LoR
Parties
 Advertisement for a divertissement. E. Merriam.—MeSk
 Always room for one more. S. N. Leodhas.—LiSf
 Behavior of fish in an English tea garden. K. Douglas.—HeR
 Betty at the party. Unknown.—CoOu
 The butterfly's ball. W. Roscoe.—CoOu—PrRh
 Catholics. C. Rylant.—RyW
 Celebration. A. Lopez.—LiIl
 "The cherries' garden gala." J. Prelutsky.—PrNk

Girl sitting alone at party. D. Justice.—JaD
Happy birthday, dear dragon. J. Prelutsky.—PrNk
Jane Seagrim's party. L. Nathan.—JaG
Jennie Tang. M. Glenn.—GlCd
"Late one night in Kalamazoo." J. Prelutsky.—PrRi
"Little Clotilda." Unknown.—PrRh
"Mr. East gave a feast." Mother Goose.—DeM
"My birthday's in August." J. Prelutsky.—PrWi
New year's eve. M. C. Livingston.—LiCe
Party. M. C. Livingston.—LiWo
"Polly put the kettle on." Mother Goose.—DeM—FaW—LoR
The rose on my cake. K. Kuskin.—LiIl—LiSf
Slumber party. C. McCullers.—HoBf
Watching the new year's eve party through the staircase. J. P. Lewis.—LiNe
Parting
 Back from the word processing course, I say to my old typewriter. M. Blumenthal.—JaG
 "Before goodbye." P. Wolny.—JaPo
 The best part of going away is going away from you. J. Ciardi.—CiD
 Departing words to a son. R. Pack.—JaG
 The departure. F. Steele.—JaG—JaPo
 Don't go, Jo. B. Ireson.—BaS
 The dying child's request. H. F. Gould.—HaOf
 "Farewell to barn and stack and tree." A. E. Housman.—PlAs
 First, goodbye. J. Smith.—JaG
 Going away. H. Nemerov.—JaD
 The goodbye ("This endsaying, moon pried loose"). M. Sklarew.—JaG
 Grandmother Grace. R. Wallace.—JaG
 The impulse. R. Frost.—PlAs
 The lady's farewell. N. Fernandez Torneol.—PlAs
 Leavetaking. E. Merriam.—HoSi—MeSk
 "Lena." M. C. Livingston.—LiWo
 The lie ("Today, you threaten to leave me"). M. Angelou.—AnS
 A parting. Wang Wei.—LiIl
 Prelude to a parting. M. Angelou.—AnS
 Request of a dying child. L. H. Sigourney.—HaOf
 The send-off. W. Owen.—HeR
 Separation ("Your absence has gone through me"). W. S. Merwin.—LiIl
 September, last day at the beach. R. Tillinghast.—JaG
 "Since there's no help, come, let us kiss and part." M. Drayton.—HeR
 Since you seem intent. G. Locklin.—JaG
 Song for a departure. E. Jennings.—JaG
 Taking leave of a friend. Rihaku.—HeR
A **parting.** Wang Wei, tr. by Witter Bynner and Kan-Hu, Kiang.—LiIl
Partners. Lilian Moore.—MoSn
Party. Myra Cohn Livingston.—LiWo
"Pass the plate." Jane Yolen.—LiTp
Passage ("He was older and"). John M. Roderick.—JaG
Passage ("Remember"). Barbara Juster Esbensen.—EsCs
The **passenger** pigeon. Paul Fleischman.—FlI
Passing. Arnold Adoff.—AdA
Passing by the junkyard. Charles J. Egita.—HoSs
A **passing** glimpse. Robert Frost.—KoS
Passing love. Langston Hughes.—HuDk
Passing the Masonic home for the aged. Herbert Scott.—JaPo

The **passing** years. Reuben Elsland.—StG
The **passionate** man's pilgrimage. Sir Walter Raleigh.—HeR
The **passionate** pilgrim, sels. William Shakespeare "Crabbed age and youth cannot live together".—HoUn
The **passionate** shepherd to his love. Christopher Marlowe.—HeR—KoT
Passover
An only kid. From Haggadah. Unknown.—LiPj
Passover. M. C. Livingston.—LiCe
"Pharaoh's horses were closing in behind us." From Passover 1970. R. Whitman.—LiPj
Passover. Myra Cohn Livingston.—LiCe
Passover 1970, sels. Ruth Whitman "Pharaoh's horses were closing in behind us".—LiPj
Past. See Time—past
Past ("I have all these parts stuffed in me"). Arnold Adoff.—AdA—JaT
Past love. Anne Keiter.—JaG
Pastan, Linda
April ("The young cherry trees").—JaPi
Death's blue-eyed girl.—JaPo
Dido's farewell.—JaG
Grammar lesson.—JaPi
Love letter.—JaD
Poet ("At his right hand").—JaD
A real story.—JaS
September ("It rained in my sleep").—JaPi
Whom do you visualize as your reader.—JaPo
Pasternak, Boris
Hops.—KoT
"The **pastimes** of people." See Idiosyncratic
Los **pastores**. Edith Agnew.—LiCp
The **pasture**. Robert Frost.—KoS—KoT—LiSf
"**Pat-a-cake**, pat-a-cake, baker's man." Mother Goose.—DeM—LoR—RaT
Pat Cloherty's version of the Maisie. Richard Murphy.—HeR
A **patch** of old snow. Robert Frost.—KoS
Patchen, Kenneth
"I'd want her eyes to fill with wonder."—McL
The magical mouse.—KeK
What there is.—McL
Patience. See also Perseverance
Between birthdays. O. Nash.—CoOu
Heron ("Only / fools / pursue"). V. Worth.—WoSp
Patience. B. Katz.—PrRh
Patience. Bobbi Katz.—PrRh
Patmore, Coventry
An evening scene.—DaC
Paton, Alan
"Give us courage, O Lord, to stand up."—LaT
Patriarchs. Lilian Moore.—MoSn
A **patriot**. Langford Reed.—BrT
"A **patriot**, living at Ewell." See A patriot
Patriotism. See Fourth of July; Memorial day; names of countries, as United States;
"**Patron** of all those who do good by stealth." See December, prayer to St. Nicholas
Patterson, Raymond R.
Night piece.—LiWa
"**Patton** and Dick." See The marionettes
Paul Bunyan
"When Paul Bunyan was ill." W. Reaker.—KeK
Paul Hewitt. Mel Glenn.—GlCd
"**Paul**, in Aunt Pru's prune surprise." X. J. Kennedy.—KeB
Paul Revere's ride. Henry Wadsworth Longfellow.—HaOf

"**Paula** is the prettiest, the whole sixth grade agrees." See Who's who
Pawnee Indians. See Indians of the Americas—Pawnee
Payn, James
"I never had a piece of toast."—TrM
Payne, Anne Blackwell
At night ("When I go to bed at night").—ChB
Payne, Nina
"Chocolate cake."—PrRh
Tag along.—PrRh
Peace
Heaven-haven. G. M. Hopkins.—HeR
Kyrie Eleison. J. Aiken.—LiE
The Lake Isle of Innisfree. W. B. Yeats.—LiSf
"Lord, make me an instrument of thy peace." Saint Francis of Assisi.—LaT
"Make me feel the wild pulsation that I felt before the strife." From Locksley Hall. A. Tennyson.—PlSc
"My Shalom, my peace, is hidden in every broad smile." M. Cohn.—LaT
One step from an old dance. D. Helwig.—DoNw
Peace walk. W. Stafford.—JaPi
Prayer ("What shall I ask you for God"). S. Grossberg.—LaT
Raleigh was right. W. C. Williams.—HeR
"**Peace** upon earth, was said, we sing it." See Christmas, 1924
Peace walk. William Stafford.—JaPi
The **peach** ("There once was a peach on a tree"). Abbie Farwell Brown.—BrT
Peach ("Touch it to your cheek and it's soft"). Rose Rauter.—KeK
Peaches and peach trees
Canning time. R. Morgan.—JaS
The peach ("There once was a peach on a tree"). A. F. Brown.—BrT
Peach ("Touch it to your cheek and it's soft"). R. Rauter.—KeK
Sunset ("Yellow and pink as a peach"). E. Merriam.—MeF
Two sad. W. Cole.—PrRa
Peacock. David Herbert Lawrence.—KoT
"A **peacock** feather." Unknown.—DeD
Peacocks
Peacock. D. H. Lawrence.—KoT
"When the peacock loudly calls." Mother Goose.—LoR
Peake, Mervyn
"My uncle Paul of Pimlico."—CoOu
Sensitive, Seldom and Sad.—PrRh
A **peanut**. Unknown.—HoSu
Toot, toot.—PrRh
"A **peanut** sat on the railroad track." See A peanut
Peanuts
A peanut. Unknown.—HoSu
Toot, toot.—PrRh
The **pear** tree. Eleanor Farjeon.—FaE
"The **pear** tree, more dead than alive." See Markers
"**Pearly** and opaque boy, it was to you." See For my brother who died before I was born
Pears and pear trees
The pear tree. E. Farjeon.—FaE
Peas ("I always eat peas with honey"). See "I eat my peas with honey"
"**Pease** porridge hot." Mother Goose.—FaW—LiSf—LoR
A **peck** of gold. Robert Frost.—KoS
The **peddler**. Eleanor Farjeon.—FaE

Peddlers and vendors
Air balloons. E. Farjeon.—FaE
"As I was going to sell my eggs." Mother Goose.—DaC—LoR
The bold pedlar and Robin Hood. Unknown.—PlAs
The fishvendor. W. Meredith.—PlSc
The flower seller. E. Farjeon.—FaE
Garage sale. K. Shapiro.—JaPi
Get 'em here. L. B. Hopkins.—HoMu
"Hot cross buns, hot cross buns." Mother Goose.—DeM—FaW—LoR
"I gathered mosses in Easedale." D. Wordsworth.—PlSc
"If I'd as much money as I could spend." Mother Goose.—FaW—LoR
"In just." E. E. Cummings.—KeK—LiSf
James Shell's snowball stand. N. Giovanni.—GiSp
"The man with the tan hands." X. J. Kennedy.—KeF
Mexican market woman. L. Hughes.—HuDk—PlSc
The peddler. E. Farjeon.—FaE
The pedlar's caravan. W. B. Rands.—BlO
A pretty ambition. M. E. W. Freeman.—HaOf
"She sells sea shells on the seashore." Mother Goose.—LoR
"Simple Simon met a pieman." Mother Goose.—DeM—FaW—LiSf—LoR
"Smiling girls, rosy boys." Mother Goose.—LoR
The gingerbread man.—DaC
Strawberries ("Ripe, ripe strawberries"). E. Farjeon.—FaE
"Tired old peddler." A. Lobel.—LoWr
"Who'll buy my valley lilies." E. Farjeon.—FaE
The **pedlar's** caravan. William Brighty Rands.—BlO

Peele, George
Bethsabe's song. See The love of King David and fair Bethsabe
Celanta at the well of life. See The old wives' tale
The love of King David and fair Bethsabe, sels. Bethsabe's song.—HeR
The old wives' tale, sels.
Celanta at the well of life.—BlO
Song for the head.—HeR
Song for the head. See The old wives' tale—Celanta at the well of life
Peeling an orange. Eve Merriam.—MeF
"Peep-eye." Clyde Watson.—WaC
Pelican. N. M. Bodecker.—BoSs
The **pelican** chorus. Edward Lear.—LiH
Pelicanaries. J. Patrick Lewis.—JaPo
"Pelicanaries are homely birds." See Pelicanaries
Pelicans
Pelican. N. M. Bodecker.—BoSs
The pelican chorus. E. Lear.—LiH
"Ride a purple pelican." J. Prelutsky.—PrRi
Pencil and paint. Eleanor Farjeon.—FaE
Pencils
Magical eraser. S. Silverstein.—LiWa
A new pencil. E. Merriam.—MeF
"Pencils telling where the wind comes from." From Pencils. C. Sandburg.—HoRa
Pencils, sels. Carl Sandburg
"Pencils telling where the wind comes from".—HoRa
"Pencils telling where the wind comes from." From Pencils. Carl Sandburg.—HoRa
Pennies from heaven. John Ciardi.—CiD
Pennington, Anne

Angelica the doorkeeper, tr. by.—HeR
Ashes, tr. by.—HeR
Before play, tr. by.—HeR
Girl, tr. by.—HeR
He ("Some bite off the others"), tr. by.—HeR
Hide and seek ("Someone hides from someone"), tr. by.—HeR
The nail, tr. by.—HeR
The rose thieves, tr. by.—HeR
The seed ("Someone sows someone"), tr. by.—HeR
To a schoolboy, tr. by.—HeR
Pennsylvania
Driving through coal country in Pennsylvania. J. Holden.—JaG
"Penny, penny royal." See Penny royal
Penny royal. Eleanor Farjeon.—FaE
A **penny** valentine. Unknown, tr. by Myra Cohn Livingston.—LiVp
"Pensive, on her dead gazing, I heard the Mother of All." Walt Whitman.—HeR
People. See also Crowds; Human race
People—portraits. See also Boys and boyhood; Girls and girlhood
Abandoned farmhouse. T. Kooser.—JaD
"All the world's a stage." From As you like it. W. Shakespeare.—HeR—HoUn
Basic for further irresponsibility. E. Merriam.—MeSk
The belly dancer in the nursing home. R. Wallace.—JaG
Disguises. From A throw of threes. E. Merriam.—MeF
Disillusionment of ten o'clock. W. Stevens.—HeR—KoT
The fat man. V. Rutsala.—JaD
The glutton. K. Shapiro.—JaD
He sits down on the floor of a school for the retarded. A. Nowlan.—JaG
I hear America singing. W. Whitman.—LiSf—PlSc
Idiosyncratic. E. Merriam.—MeSk
"If you are not." Mother Goose.—LoR
"In a cottage in Fife." Mother Goose.—BlPi—LoR
"The labouring poor, in spite of double pay." From The true-born Englishman. D. Defoe.—PlSc
"A laird, a lord." Unknown.—PlSc
The leaden-eyed. V. Lindsay.—HeR
"Man may work from sun to sun." Unknown.—PlSc
The measure of man. E. Merriam.—MeSk
Meredith Piersall. M. Glenn.—GlCd
Neuteronomy. E. Merriam.—MeSk
People ("Some people talk and talk"). C. Zolotow.—PrRh—ZoE
Portrait by Alice Neel. A. Kramer.—PlEd
Portrait of the boy as artist. B. Howes.—JaD
Relations. N. M. Bodecker.—BoPc
"Rich man, poor man, beggarman, thief." Mother Goose.—LoR—PlSc
Shirley and her son. N. Giovanni.—GiSp
Some people. R. Field.—CoN—PrRh
Thumbprint ("On the pad of my thumb"). E. Merriam.—MeSk
Vacation ("I am Paul Bunyan"). E. Merriam.—MeSk
Wash in the street. A. Turner.—TuS
Witness. E. Merriam.—MeSk
You're. S. Plath.—HeR

People—portraits—men

"All furnish'd, all in arms." From Henry IV, Part I. W. Shakespeare.—HoUn
Application for a grant. A. Hecht.—PlSc
Art work. R. Wallace.—JaPo
Bird watcher. R. Wallace.—JaPo
Breathing space July. T. Tranströmer.—HeR
Elegy on the death of a mad dog, complete. O. Goldsmith.—PlAs
The enemy's portrait. T. Hardy.—PlEd
Epitaph on the Earl of Leicester. Sir W. Raleigh.—HeR
Fairy tale ("He built himself a house"). M. Holub.—HeR
For Richard Chase. J. W. Miller.—JaG
"Grandfather." M. C. Livingston.—LiWo
Great and strong. M. Holub.—HeR
"He wastes time walking and telling the air, I am superior even to the wind." From Sketch of a poet. C. Sandburg.—HoRa
Here ("I am a man now"). R. S. Thomas.—HeR
The hired man's way. J. K. Bangs.—HaOf
"How pleasant to know Mr. Lear." E. Lear.—LiH
In the basement of the Goodwill Store. T. Kooser.—JaG
"Is that Mr. Riley, can anyone tell." P. Rooney.—TrM
Lizard ("A lizard ran out on a rock and looked up, listening"). D. H. Lawrence.—HeR
Man and machine. R. Morgan.—JaS
Memory of my father. P. Kavanagh.—HeR
Men working. E. S. Millay.—PlSc
Metaphor man. E. Merriam.—MeSk
Mr. Dill. C. Rylant.—RyW
Mr. Lafon. C. Rylant.—RyW
On his portrait. W. Cowper.—PlEd
Owl ("The diet of the owl is not"). X. J. Kennedy.—KeF
The pilgrim ("I fasted for some forty days on bread and buttermilk"). W. B. Yeats.—HeR
The raggedy man. J. W. Riley.—HaOf
Rembrandt's late self portraits. E. Jennings.—PlEd
The return. E. Pound.—HeR
"Rich man, poor man, beggarman, thief." Mother Goose.—LoR—PlSc
Sam the shoe shop man. C. Rylant.—RyW
Senex. Sir J. Betjeman.—HeR
The shooting of John Dillinger outside the Biograph Theater, July 22, 1934. D. Wagoner.—HeR
Similes for two political characters of 1819. P. B. Shelley.—HeR
Southern Pacific. C. Sandburg.—HoRa
Spring storm ("He comes gusting out of the house"). J. W. Miller.—JaG
Sum. J. Nolan.—JaS
"There was a crooked man." Mother Goose.—DeM—FaW—LoR
The thinnest shadow. J. Ashbery.—KoT
Trying. L. Nathan.—JaS
Tudor portrait. R. Lattimore.—PlEd
Uncle Claude. D. A. Evans.—JaS
Unwanted. E. Field.—JaPi
The village blacksmith. H. W. Longfellow.—HaOf
Why ("Fumble-John they call him"). A. Turner.—TuS
Work gangs. C. Sandburg.—PlSc

People—portraits—women

Aunt Melissa. R. T. Smith.—JaS
The baite. J. Donne.—HeR
"The barge she sat in, like a burnish'd throne." From Antony and Cleopatra. W. Shakespeare.—HoUn
Behavior of fish in an English tea garden. K. Douglas.—HeR
Blackberry sweet. D. Randall.—KeK
Blue girls. J. C. Ransom.—HeR
Blue Springs, Georgia. R. Young.—JaG
Bridges and tunnels. B. Bentley.—PlEd
The buildings. W. Berry.—PlEd
Cadenza. C. Sandburg.—HoRa
Charwomen. B. Belitt.—PlSc
D.A.R. N. M. Bodecker.—BoPc
The dandelion gatherer. R. Francis.—JaPo
Days through starch and bluing. A. Fulton.—JaG
Eleanor Paine. M. Glenn.—GlC
Elegy for a woman who remembered everything. D. Wagoner.—JaD
Factory girl ("No more shall I work in the factory"). Unknown.—PlSc
The factory girl ("She wasn't the least bit pretty"). J. A. Phillips.—PlSc
The fair maid of Amsterdam. Unknown.—HeR
First love ("At his incipient sun"). S. Kunitz.—JaG
For Wilma. D. Johnson.—JaG
Frau Bauman, Frau Schmidt, and Frau Schwartze. T. Roethke.—PlSc
From my mother's house. L. Goldberg.—StG
Girl in a white coat. J. M. Brinnin.—PlSc
The girl writing her English paper. R. Wallace.—JaPi
A glass of beer. J. Stephens.—HeR
A good woman feeling bad. M. Angelou.—AnS
The grandmother. W. Berry.—JaD—PlSc
"Her strong enchantments failing." A. E. Housman.—KeK
Here lies a lady. J. C. Ransom.—HeR
I am Rose. G. Stein.—ChG—HaOf—KeK—PrRh
"I'd want her eyes to fill with wonder." K. Patchen.—McL
Impeccable conception. M. Angelou.—AnS
Jamie Douglas. Unknown.—PlAs
Jane Seagrim's party. L. Nathan.—JaG
John Kinsella's lament for Mrs. Mary Moore. W. B. Yeats.—HeR
The knitters. P. Colum.—PlSc
The lady pitcher. C. Macdonald.—JaPi
Lady Sara Bunbury sacrificing to the Graces, by Reynolds. D. Hine.—PlEd
"The lazy woman." Unknown.—DeD
The little old lady. Unknown.—GrT
Looking at quilts. M. Piercy.—PlSc
Love me, love my dog. I. V. Crawford.—DoNw
Mac. M. Vinz.—JaS
Mardi Gras. J. Nolan.—JaS
"Mary Lorenz." M. C. Livingston.—LiWo
"The master, the swabber, the boatswain, and I." From The tempest. W. Shakespeare.—HoUn
Mexican market woman. L. Hughes.—HuDk—PlSc
Miss Hepzibah. E. Merriam.—MeSk
Mrs. Kriss Kringle. E. M. Thomas.—HaOf
Mrs. Martha Jean Black. N. Giovanni.—GiSp
Montgomery. S. Cornish.—JaPi
"My wife whose hair is a brush fire." From Free union. A. Breton.—KoT
Myrtle. T. Kooser.—JaG

erfection—*Continued*
  Exactly. R. Metz.—FaTh
  The mark. E. Farjeon.—FaE
Perfection, of a kind, was what he was after."
    See Epitaph on a tyrant
Perfectly rounded yet how slender." See Boy at
    a certain age
he **performing** seal. Rachel Field.—PrRh
Perhaps if we are lucky." See Special request for
    the children of Mother Corn
ericles, sels. William Shakespeare
  "I never spake bad word, nor did ill turn".—
    HoUn
Permit me to present to you." See Super goopy
    glue
erseid meteor shower. Barbara Juster Esbensen.—
    EsCs
erseverance
  About being very good and far better than most
    but still not quite good enough to take on
    the Atlantic Ocean ("There was a fine
    swimmer named Jack"). J. Ciardi.—CiD
      On being much better than most and yet
        not quite good enough (". . . a great
        swimmer named Jack").—JaG
  Dislike of tasks. R. Lattimore.—PlSc
  Epitaph on an army of mercenaries. A. E.
    Housman.—HeR—PlSc
  For the young who want to. M. Piercy.—JaPi
  If ("If the pie crust"). N. M. Bodecker.—BoPc
  On a tree fallen across the road. R. Frost.—
    HeR
  Undefeated. R. Froman.—LiIl
  "Work, for the night is coming." A. L.
    Walker.—PlSc
  person of note. Walter Parke.—BrT
ersonal beauty. See Beauty, personal
ersuasive go-gebtor. Unknown.—BrT
erversity. Susan Griffin.—McL
os pescaditos. Unknown.—GrT
Los **pescaditos** andan en el agua, nadan, nadan,
    nadan." See Los pescaditos
eseroff, Joyce
  The hardness scale.—McL
essimism. See Despair; Melancholy
he pessimist. Ben King.—BlO
et. Eve Merriam.—MeHa
et rock. Cynthia Rylant.—RyW
A **pet** to pat, a pal of a pet." See Pet
ete at the seashore. Don Marquis.—HoDl
ete at the zoo. Gwendolyn Brooks.—LiIl
eter. Eleanor Farjeon.—FaE
eter and Wendy. Wymond Garthwaite.—PrRa
eter Grimes, sels. George Crabbe
  "He built a mud-wall'd hovel, where he
    kept".—PlSc
Peter, Peter, pumpkin eater." Mother Goose.—
    DeM—FaW—LoR
Peter Piper picked a peck of pickled peppers."
    Mother Goose.—FaW—LoR
eter Quincy. Mel Glenn.—GlC
Peter White will ne'er go right." Mother
    Goose.—AlH
  "Peter White will never go right".—LoR
Peter White will never go right". See "Peter
    White will ne'er go right"
eters, Patricia
  In grandfather's glasses.—JaS
etrakos, Chris
  Call them back.—JaG
etronius Arbiter
  "Doing, a filthy pleasure is, and short."—McL

Pets. See also Animals; also names of pets, as
    Cats
The animal store. R. Field.—LiSf
The badger. J. Clare.—HeR
Broken wing. E. Farjeon.—FaE
Buying a puppy. L. Norris.—LiIl—LiSf
Cassius. C. Rylant.—RyW
The cat ("One gets a wife, one gets a house").
    O. Nash.—ChC
A cat ("She had a name among the children").
    E. Thomas.—BlO
Cats and dogs ("Some like cats, and some like
    dogs."). N. M. Bodecker.—BoSs
"Charlie Warlie had a cow." Mother Goose.—
    DeM
Child and dog. E. Farjeon.—FaE
The child and the bird. E. Farjeon.—FaE
A child's pet. W. H. Davies.—HeR
Chums. A. Guiterman.—FrP—PrRa
The cormorant's tale. P. Fleischman.—FlI
A dog ("I am alone"). C. Zolotow.—HoDl
Dog ("Whether I'm Alsatian"). E. Farjeon.—FaE
"A dog is a pal, so friendly and fun." L. C.
    Briggs.—TrM
"The dog will come when he is called." A.
    O'Keefe.—BlO
The Dracula vine. T. Hughes.—HoCr
Epitaph on a hare. W. Cowper.—BlO
Fiddle-i-fee ("Had me a cat, the cat pleased
    me"). Mother Goose.—LiSf
  "I had a cat and the cat pleased me".—
    DeM
For Mugs. M. C. Livingston.—HoDl
The frog ("Be kind and tender to the frog").
    H. Belloc.—CoN—LiSf—PrRh
The goat. Unknown.—CoOu
Gone ("I've looked behind the shed"). D.
    McCord.—HoDl—JaT
Hamsters. M. Ridlon.—HoSu—PrRa
Hansi. H. Behn.—HoCb—HoDl
His dog. R. J. Margolis.—MaS
A history of the pets. D. Huddle.—JaPo
"I had a little pony." Mother Goose.—BlO—
    DaC—DeM
I made him welcome but he didn't stay. J.
    Ciardi.—CiD
"I made my dog a valentine." J. Prelutsky.—
    PrIv
"I wish." L. Moore.—MoSn
An irritating creature. J. Prelutsky.—PrNk
Janet waking. J. C. Ransom.—HeR
Just three. W. Wise.—PrRa
Kindness to animals. L. E. Richards.—CoN
Kittens. M. C. Livingston.—LiWo
Lost ("I have a little turtle"). D. McCord.—
    McAs
Lost and found. L. Moore.—MoSn
The lost cat. E. V. Rieu.—ChC—LiSf
"Mama Bear, you'll never miss." X. J.
    Kennedy.—KeB
Mary's lamb. S. J. Hale.—HaOf
  "Mary had a little lamb".—LoR (unat.)
The meadow mouse. T. Roethke.—HeR—LiSf
"Mother doesn't want a dog." J. Viorst.—
    PrRh—ViI
My brother Bert. T. Hughes.—PrRh
My cat. J. Viorst.—ViI
My cat Jeoffrey. From Jubilate Agno. C.
    Smart.—BlO—HeR
  "For I will consider my cat Jeoffry".—KoT
"My dame hath a lame, tame crane." Mother
    Goose.—LoR

Pies.—*Continued*

Jake O'Leary's Thanksgiving. K. Starbird.—LiTp
"Little Jack Horner." Mother Goose.—DeM—FaW—LoR
The nine little goblins. J. W. Riley.—HaOf
Pie problem. S. Silverstein.—PrRh
"The Queen of Hearts." Mother Goose.—DaC—DeM—LoR
"Simple Simon met a pieman." Mother Goose.—DeM—FaW—LiSf—LoR
"Sing a song of sixpence." Mother Goose.—AlH—DaC—DeM—FaW—LoR
"The Texan was mighty hungry." L. C. Briggs.—TrM
There's nothing to it. J. Ciardi.—CiD
Tra-la-larceny. O. Herford.—BrT
The **pig** ("The pig, if I am not mistaken"). Ogden Nash.—HeR
The **pig** ("The pig is not a nervous beast"). Roland Young.—PrRh
Pig ("With sun on his back and sun on his belly"). Paul Eluard.—KoT
"The **pig**, if I am not mistaken." See The pig
A **pig** is never blamed. Babette Deutsch.—PrRh
"A **pig** is never blamed in case." See A pig is never blamed
"The **pig** is not a nervous beast." See The pig
"**Pig'back** she brought me where the lake surrounded." See Kineo mountain
Pigeon hole. N. M. Bodecker.—BoPc

Pigeons

Brooms. X. J. Kennedy.—KeF
Carol of the birds. Unknown.—RoC
"The dove stays in the garden." From Five ghost songs. Unknown, fr. the Ambo people of Africa.—KoT
Doves and starlings. E. Farjeon.—FaE
Doves of Dodona. P. Fleischman.—FlI
"I had two pigeons bright and gay." Mother Goose.—DeM
"Mrs. Peck Pigeon." E. Farjeon.—CoN—CoOu—FaE—LiSf
"Parrot with a pomegranate." J. Prelutsky.—PrRi
The passenger pigeon. P. Fleischman.—FlI
Perfect. H. MacDiarmid.—HeR
Pigeons. L. Moore.—HoSs—MoSn—PrRh
Song ("I had a dove and the sweet dove died"). J. Keats.—BlO
Trinity Place. P. McGinley.—PlSc
Pigeons. Lilian Moore.—HoSs—MoSn—PrRh
"**Pigeons** are city folk." See Pigeons
"The **pigeons** that peck at the grass in Trinity Churchyard." See Trinity Place
"**Piggie** Wig and Piggie Wee." See The pigs
"A **piggish** young person from Leeds." Unknown.—KeK

Pigs

"Barber, barber, shave a pig." Mother Goose.—AlH—DeM—FaW—LoR
The boar and the dromedar. H. Beissel.—DoNw
A corpulent pig. M. Wood, and H. Wood.—BrT
"Dickery dickery dare." Mother Goose.—BlQ—DeM—LoR
Hog calling. R. Blount.—BrT
Hog calling competition. M. Bishop.—BrT—PrRh
"I had a little pig." Unknown.—PrRh
"If a pig wore a wig." C. G. Rossetti.—LiSf
If pigs could fly. J. Reeves.—CoOu
"Little Jack Sprat." Mother Goose.—BlQ

"Little pink pig in Arkansas." J. Prelutsky.—PrRi
Mary Middling. R. Fyleman.—PrRa
Ode to the pig, his tail. W. R. Brooks.—PrRh
The pig ("The pig, if I am not mistaken"). O. Nash.—HeR
The pig ("The pig is not a nervous beast"). R. Young.—PrRh
Pig ("With sun on his back and sun on his belly"). P. Éluard.—KoT
A pig is never blamed. B. Deutsch.—PrRh
The pigs. E. Poulsson.—PrRa
The prayer of the little pig. C. B. de Gasztold.—LiSf
"Put a piggy in a poke." C. Watson.—WaC
Saint Francis and the sow. G. Kinnell.—HeR
"Snickering like crazy, Sue." X. J. Kennedy.—KeB
"Sukey, you shall be my wife." Mother Goose.—DaC—DeM
"There was a cold pig from North Stowe." A. Lobel.—LoB
"There was a fair pig from Cohoes." A. Lobel.—LoB
"There was a fast pig from East Flushing." A. Lobel.—LoB
"There was a fat pig from Savannah." A. Lobel.—LoB
"There was a light pig from Montclair." A. Lobel.—LiIl—LoB
"There was a loud pig from West Wheeling." A. Lobel.—LoB
"There was a pale pig from Spokane." A. Lobel.—LoB
"There was a plain pig, far from pretty." A. Lobel.—LoB
"There was a poor pig on the street." A. Lobel.—LoB
"There was a rich pig from Palm Springs." A. Lobel.—LoB
"There was a rude pig from Duluth." A. Lobel.—LoB
"There was a sad pig with a tail." A. Lobel.—LoB
"There was a shy pig by a wall." A. Lobel.—LoB
"There was a sick pig with a cold." A. Lobel.—LoB
"There was a slow pig from Decatur." A. Lobel.—LoB
"There was a small pig from Woonsocket." A. Lobel.—LoB
"There was a small pig who wept tears." A. Lobel.—LoB—PrRa
"There was a smart pig who was able." A. Lobel.—LoB
"There was a stout pig from Oak Ridge." A. Lobel.—LoB
"There was a strange pig in the park." A. Lobel.—LoB
"There was a tough pig from Pine Bluff." A. Lobel.—LoB
"There was a vague pig from Glens Falls." A. Lobel.—LoB
"There was a warm pig from Key West." A. Lobel.—LoB
"There was a wet pig from Fort Wayne." A. Lobel.—LoB
"There was a young pig by a cradle." A. Lobel.—LoB
"There was a young pig from Chanute." A. Lobel.—LoB

Pigs—*Continued*

"There was a young pig from Moline." A. Lobel.—LoB

"There was a young pig from Nantucket." A. Lobel.—LoB

"There was a young pig from Schenectady." A. Lobel.—LoB

"There was a young pig who, in bed." A. Lobel.—LoB

"There was a young pig whose delight." A. Lobel.—LoB

"There was an old pig from New York." A. Lobel.—LoB

"There was an old pig from South Goshen." A. Lobel.—LoB

"There was an old pig from Van Nuys." A. Lobel.—LoB

"There was an old pig in a chair." A. Lobel.—LoB

"There was an old pig with a clock." A. Lobel.—LoB

"There was an old pig with a pen." A. Lobel.—LoB—LoB

"This little pig built a spaceship." F. Winsor.—PrRh

"This little pig found a hole in the fence." C. Watson.—WaC

"This little pig went to market." Mother Goose.—DeM—LoR
  "This little piggy".—RaT

The three little pigs. A. S. Gatty.—DaC

"To market, to market, to buy a fat pig." Mother Goose.—DeM—FaW—LiSf—LoR—RaT

"Tom, Tom, the piper's son." Mother Goose.—DeM—LoR

The unknown color. C. Cullen.—HaOf

The visitor. K. Pyle.—CoOu

Why pigs cannot write poems. J. Ciardi.—CiD

The **pigs**. Emilie Poulsson.—PrRa

"**Pigs** cannot write poems because." See Why pigs cannot write poems

Pilate, Pontius (about)

A ballad of Christmas. W. De la Mare.—HaO

"**Pile** the bodies high at Austerlitz and Waterloo." See Grass

The **pilgrim** ("Father, I have launched my bark"). Emma C. Embury.—HaOf

The **pilgrim** ("I fasted for some forty days on bread and buttermilk"). William Butler Yeats.—HeR

"**Pilgrims**." See Thanksgiving

Pilgrims in Mexico. Unknown.—HaO

Pilinszky, Janos

Fable ("Once upon a time").—HeR

Pilling, Christopher

The adoration of the Magi.—HaO

Pillows. From A throw of threes. Eve Merriam.—MeF

Pilots and piloting. See Airplanes and aviators

Pine trees

Bristlecone pine. M. C. Livingston.—LiMp

Irish yew. M. C. Livingston.—LiMp

Spruce woods. A. R. Ammons.—KeK

Up in the pine. N. D. Watson.—PrRh

Yew. M. C. Livingston.—LiMp

Ping-pong. Eve Merriam.—MeSk

"**Pinging** rain." See Weather report

Pink

The groaning board.—FaW (unat.)—TrM

Pink belly. Cynthia Rylant.—RyW

Pins

Safety pin. V. Worth.—FaTh—LiSf

"See a pin and pick it up." Mother Goose.—DeM—LoR

Pioneer life. See Frontier and pioneer life

The **pious** young priest. Unknown.—BrT

A **piper**. Seumas O'Sullivan.—LiSf

"A **piper** in the streets today." See A piper

Pipers

The pied piper of Hamelin. R. Browning.—LiSf

A piper. S. O'Sullivan.—LiSf

"Piping down the valleys wild." W. Blake.—CoOu—LiSf
  Introduction to Songs of innocence.—PrRh

"There was a piper, he'd a cow." Mother Goose.—AlH

"Tom, he was a piper's son." Mother Goose.—FaW—LiSf—LoR

"**Piping** down the valleys wild." William Blake.—CoOu—LiSf

Introduction to Songs of innocence.—PrRh

Pippa passes, sels. Robert Browning

"The year's at the spring".—ChG—LaT
  Pippa's song.—CoN

Pippa's song. See "The year's at the spring"

Pirate Don Durk of Dowdee. Mildred Meigs.—CoOu

Pirate story. Robert Louis Stevenson.—DaC

Pirates

Captain Kidd. S. V. Benét, and R. C. Benét.—RuI

The coasts of high Barbary. Unknown.—BlO

Pirate Don Durk of Dowdee. M. Meigs.—CoOu

Pirate story. R. L. Stevenson.—DaC

The reformed pirate. T. G. Roberts.—DoNw

The **pirates** of Penzance, sels. William Schwenck Gilbert

The policeman's lot.—PlSc

"**Pitiful** these crying swans tonight." See The icebound swans

Pitketbly, Lawrence

"Now I love you", tr. by.—McL

Pitt, William

"A strong nor'wester's blowing, Bill."—TrM

"**Pity** the girl with the crystal hair." See Fable

The **pizza**. Ogden Nash.—HoMu—PrRh

"**Pizza**, pickle." See Three tickles

Places. See also names of places, as Vermont

Adlestrop. E. Thomas.—BlO

From Council Bluffs to Omaha. M. C. Livingston.—LiWo

Interruption to a journey. N. MacCaig.—HeR

Keep. S. Cassedy.—CaR

"One Christmas-time." From The prelude. W. Wordsworth.—HeR

A secret place. J. W. Steinbergh.—LiIl

Places for an extra pocket. From A throw of threes. Eve Merriam.—MeF

Places to hide a secret message. From A throw of threes. Eve Merriam.—MeF

A **plagued** journey. Maya Angelou.—AnS

Planets. See also Moon; Space and space travel; World

The planets. M. C. Livingston.—LiSi

The **planets**. Myra Cohn Livingston.—LiSi

"**Plank**." See Recycled

Plans. Maxine Kumin.—HoSu

Plant-eater. Sandra Liatsos.—HoDi

Plants and planting. See also Gardens and gardening; also names of plants, as Dandelions

"And can the physician make sick men well." Unknown.—BlO

Play.—*Continued*

Ode to a dressmaker's dummy. D. Justice.—JaD
Office. S. Cassedy.—CaR
"Oh this day." M. B. Goffstein.—CoN
Oil slick. J. Thurman.—HoSs—LiSf
The old man's toes. E. Farjeon.—FaE
One of the problems of play. N. Giovanni.—GiSp
One-upmanship. M. Chaikin.—CoN
Open hydrant. M. Ridlon.—PrRh
"Out in the dark and daylight." A. Fisher.—BeD
"Over the garden wall." E. Farjeon.—FaE
Pete at the seashore. D. Marquis.—HoDl
Pink belly. C. Rylant.—RyW
Play. F. Asch.—CoN
Playing. M. L'Engle.—LaT
Pretending. B. Katz.—PrRa
Promises. J. Yolen.—LiNe
Puppy ("Catch and shake the cobra garden hose"). R. L. Tyler.—HoDl
Puppy and I. A. A. Milne.—CoOu—FrP
"Rain, rain, go away." Mother Goose.—DeM—LiSF—LoR
Read this with gestures. J. Ciardi.—BaS—PrRh
Recess. L. Moore.—MoSn
Red-dress girl. A. Turner.—TuS
"Ring-a-ring o' roses." Mother Goose.—DaC—DeM
    "Ring-a-ring-a-roses".—LoR
Roof. S. Cassedy.—CaR
Rural recreation. L. Morrison.—KeK
"Sally go round the sun." Mother Goose.—DeM—FaW—LoR
Sand castle. C. A. Keremes.—HoSe
Secret passageway. M. C. Livingston.—LiWo
A secret place. J. W. Steinbergh.—LiIl
Shore. M. B. Miller.—PrRa
Silly Sallie. W. De la Mare.—BlO
Sitting in the sand. K. Kuskin.—HoSe—HoSi
Sled run. B. J. Esbensen.—EsCs
Sneaky Sue. J. Prelutsky.—PrNk
Snow ("We'll play in the snow"). K. Kuskin.—BaS—PrRa
Snow print one, mystery. B. J. Esbensen.—EsCs
Some one to tea. E. Farjeon.—FaE
Somersaults. J. Prelutsky.—PrRa
Something better. D. McCord.—McAs
Song form. A. Baraka.—KoT
Springtime. N. Giovanni.—GiSp
Statues. R. Wilbur.—PlEd
Stickball. V. Schonborg.—PrRh
The swing. R. L. Stevenson.—CoN—FaW—FrP—LiSf
"Tambourine, tambourine." C. Watson.—WaC
That's what we'd do. M. M. Dodge.—HaOf
They're calling. F. Holman.—LiSf—PrRh
"This is baby's trumpet." Unknown.—DeD
Toboggan ride, down Happy Hollow. M. C. Livingston.—LiWo
Today is Saturday. Z. K. Snyder.—LiIl
Treasure. E. Farjeon.—FaE
Tumbling. Unknown.—DaC
"We built a castle near the rocks." J. W. Anglund.—PrRa
"We each wore half a horse." J. Prelutsky.—PrNk
We used to play. D. Welch.—JaPi
What I've been doing. E. Farjeon.—FaE
What Johnny told me. J. Ciardi.—LiIl
Wild beasts. E. Stein.—FrP—PrRa
The windows. W. S. Merwin.—JaD

With my foot in my mouth. D. Lee.—LiIl
Yesterday's paper. M. Watts.—PrRa
Play. Frank Asch.—CoN
"**Play** a thin tune." See New year's eve
"**Play** on the seashore." See Shore
Playing. Madeleine L'Engle.—LaT
"**Playing** soccer, Plato Foley." X. J. Kennedy.—KeB
Please bird. Kazue Mizumura.—BaS
"**Please** bird, don't go yet." See Please bird
"**Please,** everybody, look at me." See Five years old
"**Please** God, take care of little things." Eleanor Farjeon.—LaT
"**Please,** sir, I don't mean to be disrespectful." See Paul Hewitt
"**Please** your Grace, from out your store." See The beggar to Mab, the fairie Queen
The **pleasing** gift. Unknown.—BrT
"**Plenty** of love." Unknown.—LiVp
"**Plod,** plod." See Elephants plodding
Plop. Richard J. Margolis.—MaS
Ploughing on Sunday. Wallace Stevens.—HeR—KoT
"**Ploughman** ploughing a level field." See To a schoolboy
"A **plow,** they say, to plow the snow." See Plowmen
Plowmen. Robert Frost.—PlSc
The **plumppuppets.** Christopher Morley.—PrRh
Plutzik, Hyam
After looking into a book belonging to my great-grandfather, Eli Eliakim Plutzik.—HeR
And in the 51st year of that century, while my brother cried in the trench, while my enemy glared from the cave.—HeR
The dream about our master, William Shakespeare.—HeR
Jim Desterland.—HeR
Po' boy blues. Langston Hughes.—HuDk
Po Chu-yi
"An old charcoal seller."—PlSc
The **pobble.** See "The pobble who has no toes"
"The **pobble** who has no toes." Edward Lear.—FaW—LiH
The **pobble.**—BlO
Pocket calculator. Bobbi Katz.—HoCl
Pocket poem. Ted Kooser.—JaPo
Pockets
Places for an extra pocket. From A throw of threes. E. Merriam.—MeF
"Something's in my pocket." E. Merriam.—MeBl
"**Pods** of summer crowd around the door." See Fall wind
Poe, Edgar Allan
Annabel Lee.—HaOf
The bells.—HaOf
The haunted palace.—LiWa
The raven.—HaOf
Poem ("As the cat"). William Carlos Williams.—KeK—KoT
Poem ("I loved my friend"). Langston Hughes.—CoN—HoBf—HuDk—JaD—LiIl—LiSf
Poem ("O sole mio, hot diggety, nix, I wather think I can"). Frank O'Hara.—KoT
Poem about a special cat. Beatrice Schenk De Regniers.—DeT
The **poem** as striptease. Philip Dacey.—JaPo
Poem by a cat. Beatrice Schenk De Regniers.—DeT
Poem for a suicide. George Economou.—JaD
Poem for Debbie. Nikki Giovanni.—GiSp

Points of view—*Continued*
Thirteen ways of looking at a blackbird. W. Stevens.—HeR
To a blind student who taught me to see. S. Hazo.—JaG
The toys talk of the world. K. Pyle.—HaOf
A true account of talking to the sun at Fire Island ("The sun woke me this morning loud"). F. O'Hara.—HeR—KoT
"**Poised** between going on and back, pulled." See The base stealer
Poison
"Apple." E. Merriam.—MeHa
Lord Randal. Unknown.—PlAs
A poison tree. W. Blake.—HeR
Willie the poisoner. Unknown.—CoN
Poison ivy
The witch's garden. L. Moore.—MoSn
A **poison** tree. William Blake.—HeR
Poker
Twin aces. K. Wilson.—JaPi
The **polar** bear ("The polar bear by being white"). Jack Prelutsky.—PrZ
The **polar** bear ("The polar bear is unaware"). Hilaire Belloc.—LiSf
Polar bear ("The secret of the polar bear"). Gail Kredenser.—PrRa
"The **polar** bear by being white." See The polar bear
"The **polar** bear is unaware." See The polar bear
Polar regions
Eskimo chant. Unknown.—DoNw
The ice-king. A. B. Demille.—DoNw
A legend of the Northland. P. Cary.—HaOf
The train dogs. P. Johnson.—DoNw
The wolf cry. L. Sarett.—PrRh
Polgar, Steven
Charm ("With trembling eyes"), tr. by.—McL
Hesitating ode, tr. by.—McL
I hid you, tr. by.—McL
Police
"Policeman, policeman, don't take me." Mother Goose.—AlH
The policeman's lot. From The pirates of Penzance. W. S. Gilbert.—PlSc
The sheriff of Rottenshot. J. Prelutsky.—PrSr
"**Policeman,** policeman, don't take me." Mother Goose.—AlH
The **policeman's** lot. From The pirates of Penzance. William Schwenck Gilbert.—PlSc
Politeness. See Manners
Politics
An ode to the framers of the Frame Bill. Lord Byron.—PlSc
Sanford Evans Pierce. M. Glenn.—GlC
Similes for two political characters of 1819. P. B. Shelley.—HeR
The Vicar of Bray. Unknown.—PlAs
Pollak, Felix
Dial tone.—JaPo
Los pollitos. Unknown.—GrT
"**Los pollitos** dicen, pio, pio, pio." See Los pollitos
The **polliwog.** Arthur Guiterman.—PrRh
Pollution
City dawn. N. M. Bodecker.—BoPc
Journey's end. N. M. Bodecker.—BoPc
Lake St. Clair. From Great Lakes suite. J. Reaney.—DoNw
Quest. E. Merriam.—MeF
Smog. M. C. Livingston.—LiSi
"Where will we run to." X. J. Kennedy.—KeF

"**Polly** Barlor, in the parlor." Arnold Lobel.—LoWr
"**Polly,** Dolly, Kate, and Molly." Mother Goose.—LoR
"**Polly** put the kettle on." Mother Goose.—DeM—FaW—LoR
Pome ("Hlo"). David McCord.—McAs
Pomerantz, Charlotte
All asleep 1 ("A lamb has a lambkin").—PoA
All asleep 2 ("Hush, it's the hour").—PoA
Don't make a peep.—PoA
Door number four.—LiIl—PoI
Drowsy bees.—PoA
Frog's lullaby.—PoA
Grandma's lullaby.—PoA
Grandpa's lullaby.—PoA
The half lullaby.—PoA
A hikoka in a hikoki.—PoI
"Hush, my posy sleeps."—PoA
"I like arroz y habichuelas."—PoI
"If I had a paka."—PoI
The king of Magla and Vlaga.—PoI
Little brother puts his doll to sleep.—PoA
Lullaby ("Shlof, sleep through the night").—PoI
Lulu, Lulu, I've a lilo.—PoI
Moon boat.—PoA—PrRa
The puffin ("Warm and plump as fresh baked muffins").—PoA
The puppy's song.—PoA
"Roll gently, old dump truck."—PoA
The rumbly night train.—PoA
"The tamarindo puppy."—LiIl
Toy tik ka.—PoI
Trees ("Berkeboom").—PoI
Where do these words come from.—PoI
Yes, it's raining.—PoI
"You take the blueberry."—PoI
Pomeroy, Ralph
Between here and Illinois.—JaPi
Gone ("Wind rattles the apples").—JaD
Near drowning.—JaD
Snow ("Tilt, wilt").—JaPi
To my father.—JaD
Ponchon, Raoul
The shepherd's tale.—HaO
The **pond.** Charlotte Zolotow.—ZoE
"**Ponderous,** he wanders by the lake." See Prehistoric morning
Ponds. See Lakes and ponds
"**Pone,** pone, tata." See Rima de la hermana vestiendose
Ponies. See Horses
Poop ("My daughter, Blake, is in kindergarten"). Gerald Locklin.—JaS
Poor. Myra Cohn Livingston.—KeK
Poor but honest. Unknown.—HeR
Poor crow. Mary Mapes Dodge.—HaOf
"**Poor** little pigeon-toed Dimity Drew." See Little Dimity
"**Poor** Martha Snell has gone away." See Epitaph on Martha Snell
"**Poor** old Jonathan Bing." See Jonathan Bing
Poor old lady. Unknown.—HaOf—PrRh
"**Poor** old lady, she swallowed a fly." See Poor old lady
"**Poor** old Mr. Bidery." See Mr. Bidery's spidery garden
"**Poor** old Penelope." Jack Prelutsky.—LiSf
"**Poor** old Robinson Crusoe." Mother Goose.—LoR
"**Poor** potatoes underground." Jack Prelutsky.—PrRi
Poor robin. See "The north wind doth blow"

Poor shadow. Ilo Orleans.—PrRa
"**Poor** song." See The tape
"**Poor** tired Tim, it's sad for him." See Tired Tim
"The **poorest** juggler ever seen." See Clara Cleech
"**Pop** bottles pop-bottles." See Song of the pop-bottlers
Popa, Vasco
    Ashes.—HeR
    Before play.—HeR
    He ("Some bite off the others").—HeR
    Hide and seek ("Someone hides from someone").—HeR
    The nail.—HeR
    The rose thieves.—HeR
    The seed ("Someone sows someone").—HeR
"**Popcorn** crunches." See Crunch and lick
Pope, Alexander
    Engraved on the collar of a dog, which I gave to his Royal Highness.—KoT
        His highness's dog.—PrRh (unat.)
        Epigram engraved on the collar of a dog.—CoN—KeK
"**Poplars** are standing there still as death." See Southern mansion
Poppies
    "Pick me poppies in Ohio." From Crossing Ohio when poppies bloom in Ashtabula. C. Sandburg.—HoRa
    Poppies. R. Scheele.—JaPo
    Poppies in July. S. Plath.—HeR
    White summer flower. W. S. Merwin.—JaD
Poppies. Roy Scheele.—JaPo
Poppies in July. Sylvia Plath.—HeR
Popsicles. Cynthia B. Francis.—HoMu
"**Popsicles** give cool wet kisses." See Popsicles
The **porcupine**. Jack Prelutsky.—PrZ
"The **porcupine** is puzzled." See The porcupine
Porcupine pa. X. J. Kennedy.—KeF
Porcupines
    Friend ("When"). L. Moore.—LiII
    Hedgehog. N. M. Bodecker.—BoSs
    The hedgehog. J. J. Bell.—PrRh
    The porcupine. J. Prelutsky.—PrZ
"**Poring** over a book, or my sewing." See The gnomes
Porpoises. See Dolphins and porpoises
Porter, Anne
    Another Sarah.—KoT
"**Portion** of this yew." See Transformations
Portrait ("A child draws the outline of a body"). Louise Gluck.—JaS
The **portrait** ("My mother never forgave my father"). Stanley Kunitz.—JaPi
Portrait by a neighbor. Edna St. Vincent Millay.—HaOf—LiSf
Portrait by Alice Neel. Aaron Kramer.—PlEd
Portrait of my mother on her wedding day. Celia Gilbert.—JaD
Portrait of the boy as artist. Barbara Howes.—JaD
Portraits. See Painting and pictures; People—portraits
Poseidon
    On a horse carved in wood. D. Hall.—PlEd
Posey, Anita E.
    When all the world's asleep.—PrRa
Possesions. See Wealth
Possum. N. M. Bodecker.—BoSs
Possums. See Opossums
"The **possum's** tail." See Possum
A **post-mortem**. Siegfried Sassoon.—JaD
Posted as missing. John Masefield.—BlO

"The **poster** with my picture on it." See Unwanted
"The **postman** comes when I am still in bed." See A sick child
"**Postman,** postman." Arnold Lobel.—LoWr
Postmen. See Mail and mailcarriers
Potatoes
    Cold potato. R. J. Margolis.—MaS
    Giving potatoes. A. Mitchell.—HeR
    "Poor potatoes underground." J. Prelutsky.—PrRi
    The potatoes dance. V. Lindsay.—LiSf
The **potatoes** dance. Vachel Lindsay.—LiSf
Potter, Beatrix
    The old woman ("You know the old woman").—CoN—PrRa
Pottery. See Tableware
    The Byfield rabbit. K. Hoskins.—PlSc
Poulsson, Emilie
    The pigs.—PrRa
Pound, Ezra
    The alchemist ("Sail of Claustra, Aelis, Azalais").—LiWa
    "And the days are not full enough."—HeR
    Meditatio.—LiSf
    The return.—HeR
    The river-merchant's wife, a letter ("While my hair was still cut straight across my forehead").—HeR—KoT
    The seafarer, tr. by.—HeR
    Taking leave of a friend, tr. by.—HeR
"**Pour** yourself a glass." See Drink a garden
Poussin. Louis MacNeice.—PlEd
Poverty
    The ballad of the harp-weaver. E. S. Millay.—LiSf—LiWa
    Ballad of the man who's gone. L. Hughes.—PlAs
    Beggar boy. L. Hughes.—HuDk
    Brother, can you spare a dime. E. Y. Harburg.—PlAs—PlSc
    The burglar of Babylon. E. Bishop.—HeR
    The carol of the poor children. R. Middleton.—HaO
    The carol singers. E. Farjeon.—FaE
    The case for the miners. S. Sassoon.—PlSc
    The chimney sweeper ("A little black thing among the snow"). W. Blake.—HeR—PlSc
    Contemporary announcement. M. Angelou.—AnS
    Cousin Ella goes to town. G. E. Lyon.—JaS
    Dawn ("The soft grey of the distant hills"). Unknown.—PlSc
    Ennui. L. Hughes.—HaOf
    The factory girl ("She wasn't the least bit pretty"). J. A. Phillips.—PlSc
    For them. E. Farjeon.—FaE
    The golf links. S. N. Cleghorn.—KeK
    Grab-bag. H. H. Jackson.—HaOf
    The happy heart. T. Dekker.—HeR
    "He said he had been a soldier." D. Wordsworth.—PlSc
    "I am a little beggar girl." Mother Goose.—AlH
    In the workhouse. G. R. Sims.—HaO
    The lay of the labourer. T. Hood.—PlSc
    The leaden-eyed. V. Lindsay.—HeR
    The man with the hoe. E. Markham.—PlSc
    An ode to the framers of the Frame Bill. Lord Byron.—PlSc
    "An old charcoal seller." Po Chu-yi.—PlSc
    Poor. M. C. Livingston.—KeK
    Poor but honest. Unknown.—HeR
    The reminder. T. Hardy.—HaO

Poverty—*Continued*
Saturday's child. C. Cullen.—PlSc
Share-croppers. L. Hughes.—PlSc
Song ("Child, is thy father dead"). E. Elliot.—PlSc
The song of the shirt. T. Hood.—PlSc
Through a shop window. E. Farjeon.—FaE
Tiempo muerto. R. Alonso.—PlSc
Timothy Winters. C. Causley.—HeR
Trinity Place. P. McGinley.—PlSc
Vagabonds. L. Hughes.—PlSc
Wash in the street. A. Turner.—TuS
With a posthumous medal. J. M. Brinnin.—PlSc
"The **power** digger." See The power shovel
The **power** shovel. Rowena Bennett.—HoCl
Prairie fires. Hamlin Garland.—HaOf
Prairies
Prairie fires. H. Garland.—HaOf
"To make a prairie it takes a clover." E. Dickinson.—HaOf
Praise of a collie. Norman MacCaig.—HeR
Praise to the end, sels. Theodore Roethke
"Mips and ma the mooly moo".—HeR
Pratt, Edwin John
Frost ("The frost moved up the window-pane").—DoNw
The shark ("He seemed to know the harbour").—DoNw
The way of Cape Race.—DoNw
Praxiteles (about)
Spoken by Venus on seeing her statue done by Praxiteles. Unknown.—PlEd
Prayer ("Dear God"). Elizabeth M. Shields.—LaT
Prayer ("Dear heavenly Father"). Elizabeth M. Shields.—LaT
Prayer ("Dear heavenly Father, I often make mistakes"). Elizabeth M. Shields.—LaT
Prayer ("Father, Great Spirit, behold this boy, your ways he shall see"). Unknown.—BiSp
Prayer ("God, though this life is but a wraith"). Louis Untermeyer.—LaT
Prayer ("I ask you this"). Langston Hughes.—HuDk
Prayer ("Sun, we pray"). Unknown.—BiSp
Prayer ("Thank you for the sun"). Myra Cohn Livingston.—LaT
Prayer ("They have cleared away the place where the corn is to be"). Unknown.—BiSp
Prayer ("What shall I ask you for God"). Shlomit Grossberg.—LaT
Prayer before eating. Unknown.—BiSp
Prayer before felling to clear a cornfield. Unknown.—BiSp
Prayer before killing an eagle. Unknown.—BiSp
Prayer before the first meal in a new summer camp. Unknown.—BiSp
Prayer before work. May Sarton.—PlSc
Prayer for reptiles. Patricia Hubbell.—LaT
A **prayer** for rivers. Keith Wilson.—JaG
Prayer for safe passage through enemy country. Unknown.—BiSp
Prayer for smooth waters. Unknown.—BiSp
Prayer for the pilot. Cecil Roberts.—LaT
Prayer for this house. Louis Untermeyer.—LaT
A **prayer** in spring. Robert Frost.—LaT
Prayer meeting. Langston Hughes.—HuDk
Prayer of a man to twin children. Unknown.—BiSp
Prayer of an old man at a young man's change of name. Unknown.—BiSp
Prayer of the black bear. Unknown.—BiSp
The **prayer** of the cat. Carmen Bernos de Gasztold, tr. by Rumer Godden.—ChC—LiSf

The **prayer** of the dog. Carmen Bernos de Gasztold.—HoDl
Prayer of the ghost. Unknown.—BiSp
A **prayer** of the girls' puberty ceremony. Unknown.—BiSp
The **prayer** of the little ducks. Carmen Bernos de Gasztold.—LaT
The **prayer** of the little pig. Carmen Bernos de Gasztold, tr. by Rumer Godden.—LiSf
Prayer of the Mexican child. Unknown.—LaT
Prayer of the midwife to the Goddess of Water. Unknown.—BiSp
A **prayer** of the midwinter hunt. Unknown.—BiSp
The **prayer** of the monkey. Carmen Bernos de Gasztold.—LaT
Prayer of the youngest daughter, with an offering of crumbs. Unknown.—BiSp
Prayer to a dead buck. Unknown.—BiSp
A **prayer** to go to paradise with the donkeys. Francis Jammes, tr. by Richard Wilbur.—HeR—LiSf
Prayer to the corn mothers. Unknown.—BiSp
Prayer to the deceased ("My child, you have toiled through life and come to the end"). Unknown.—BiSp
Prayer to the deceased ("Naked you came from Earth the mother, naked you return"). Unknown.—BiSp
Prayer to the deceased ("We have muddied the waters for you"). Unknown.—BiSp
Prayer to the migratory birds. Unknown.—BiSp
Prayer to the moon. Unknown.—LaT
Prayer to the sun. Unknown.—BiSp
Prayer to the sun, for quick travel. Unknown.—BiSp
Prayer to the whale. Unknown.—BiSp
"**Prayer** unsaid, and Mass unsung." See The sea ritual
Prayers. See also Psalms
Bedtime ("Good night"). M. L'Engle.—LaT
Boatman's prayer for smooth waters. Unknown, fr. the Kwakiutl Indian.—BiSp
A child's prayer. J. B. Tabb.—LaT
Christmas prayer. D. McCord.—LiCp
Confession of sin. Unknown, fr. the Aztec Indian.—BiSp
"Cover my earth mother four times with many flowers." From Invocation of the U'wannami, Part III. Unknown, fr. the Zuni Indian.—LaT
Crazy dog prayer. Unknown, fr. the Crow Indian.—BiSp
"Dear Father." Unknown.—LaT
"Dear God." Unknown.—LaT
"Dear God, thank you for our toys." Unknown.—LaT
"Don't let my life grow dull, Lord." E. M. Shields.—LaT
Evening ("The day is past, the sun is set"). T. Miller.—DaC
"Every morning when I wake." From Under Milk Wood. D. Thomas.—LaT
"From ghoulies and ghosties." From A Cornish litany. Unknown.—HoCr—LiSf
Things that go bump in the night.—CoN
A Cornish litany.—LiWa
Girl's prayer to thunder during a storm. Unknown, fr. the Blackfeet Indian.—BiSp
"Give us courage, O Lord, to stand up." A. Paton.—LaT
"God be in my head." Unknown.—LaT
"God bless all those I love." Unknown.—LaT

Prayers.—*Continued*

"God who made the earth." S. B. Rhodes.—LaT

"Goosey, goosey gander." Mother Goose.—BlQ—DeM—FaW—LoR

Harvester's prayer, with an offering of copal. Unknown, fr. the Kekchi Maya.—BiSp

House blessing ("Bless the four corners of this house"). A. Guiterman.—LaT

"I see white and black, Lord." M. Boyd.—LaT

"I thank you God." From Thanksgiving. L. Driscoll.—LaT

"Lord Jesus." G. Salmon.—LaT

"Lord, make me an instrument of thy peace." Saint Francis of Assisi.—LaT

"Matthew, Mark, Luke and John, bless the bed that I lie on." Mother Goose.—DaC—DeM

Medicine man's prayer. Unknown, fr. the Blackfeet Indian.—BiSp

Morning ("Dear Lord my God"). M. L'Engle.—LaT

Morning prayer. O. Nash.—LaT

Morning prayer to the creator. Unknown, fr. the Mbya Indian.—BiSp

Mother's prayer for a girl. Unknown, fr. the Navajo Indian.—BiSp

"Now I lay me down to sleep." Mother Goose.—ChB—DeM

"Now the day is over." S. Baring-Gould.—DaC—LaW

"O God, bless all the people for whom life is hard and difficult." W. Barclay.—LaT

"Oh God, I thank you that you have made me as I am." W. Barclay.—LaT

"O great spirit." Unknown, fr. the American Indian.—LaT

"O Lord, save us." P. Marshall.—LaT

"O thou great Chief." Unknown.—LaT

Our food. M. L'Engle.—LaT

Playing. M. L'Engle.—LaT

"Please God, take care of little things." E. Farjeon.—LaT

Prayer ("Dear God"). E. M. Shields.—LaT

Prayer ("Dear heavenly Father"). E. M. Shields.—LaT

Prayer ("Dear heavenly Father, I often make mistakes"). E. M. Shields.—LaT

Prayer ("Father, Great Spirit, behold this boy, your ways he shall see"). Unknown, fr. the Sioux Indian.—BiSp

Prayer ("God, though this life is but a wraith"). L. Untermeyer.—LaT

Prayer ("Sun, we pray"). Unknown, fr. the Paviotso Indian.—BiSp

Prayer ("Thank you for the sun"). M. C. Livingston.—LaT

Prayer ("They have cleared away the place where the corn is to be"). Unknown, fr. the Arikara Indian.—BiSp

Prayer ("What shall I ask you for God"). S. Grossberg.—LaT

Prayer before eating. Unknown, fr. the Arapaho Indian.—BiSp

Prayer before felling to clear a cornfield. Unknown, fr. the Kekchi Maya.—BiSp

Prayer before killing an eagle. Unknown, fr. the Yokuts Indian.—BiSp

Prayer before the first meal in a new summer camp. Unknown, fr. the Modoc Indian.—BiSp

Prayer before work. M. Sarton.—PlSc

Prayer for reptiles. P. Hubbell.—LaT

Prayer for safe passage through enemy country. Unknown, fr. the Zuni Indian.—BiSp

Prayer for smooth waters. Unknown, fr. the Yahgan Indian.—BiSp

Prayer for the pilot. C. Roberts.—LaT

Prayer for this house. L. Untermeyer.—LaT

A prayer in spring. R. Frost.—LaT

Prayer meeting. L. Hughes.—HuDk

Prayer of a man to twin children. Unknown, fr. the Kwakiutl Indian.—BiSp

Prayer of an old man at a young man's change of name. Unknown, fr. the Arapaho Indian.—BiSp

Prayer of the black bear. Unknown, fr. the Kwakiutl Indian.—BiSp

The prayer of the cat. C. B. de Gasztold.—ChC—LiSf

The prayer of the dog. C. B. de Gasztold.—HoDl

Prayer of the ghost. Unknown, fr. the Winnebago Indian.—BiSp

A prayer of the girls' puberty ceremony. Unknown, fr. the Jicarilla Apache.—BiSp

The prayer of the little ducks. C. B. de Gasztold.—LaT

Prayer of the Mexican child. Unknown.—LaT

Prayer of the midwife to the Goddess of Water. Unknown, fr. the Aztec Indian.—BiSp

A prayer of the midwinter hunt. Unknown, fr. the Zuni Indian.—BiSp

The prayer of the monkey. C. B. de Gasztold.—LaT

Prayer to a dead buck. Unknown, fr. the Navajo Indian.—BiSp

A prayer to go to paradise with the donkeys. F. Jammes.—HeR—LiSf

Prayer to the corn mothers. Unknown, fr. the Tewa Indian.—BiSp

Prayer to the deceased ("My child, you have toiled through life and come to the end"). Unknown, fr. the Aztec Indian.—BiSp

Prayer to the deceased ("Naked you came from Earth the mother, naked you return"). Unknown, fr. the Omaha Indian.—BiSp

Prayer to the deceased ("We have muddied the waters for you"). Unknown, fr. the Tewa Indian.—BiSp

Prayer to the migratory birds. Unknown, fr. the Kwakiutl Indian.—BiSp

Prayer to the moon. Unknown.—LaT

Prayer to the sun. Unknown, fr. the Havasupai Indian.—BiSp

Prayer to the sun, for quick travel. Unknown, fr. the Aztec Indian.—BiSp

Prayer to the whale. Unknown, fr. the Nootka Indian.—BiSp

Prayers of steel. C. Sandburg.—HoRa

Simhat Torah. R. H. Marks.—LiPj

Song of the sky loom. Unknown, fr. the Tewa Indian.—LaT

"There was a rat, for want of stairs." Mother Goose.—DeM—LoR

Tiny Tim's prayer. From A Christmas carol. C. Dickens.—LaT

Traveler's prayer, with an offering of copal. Unknown, fr. the Kekchi Maya.—BiSp

A verse. M. B. Eddy.—LaT

"When the night is wild." E. Vipont.—LaT

"White floating clouds." Unknown, fr. the Sia Indian.—LaT

Woman's prayer. Unknown, fr. the Anambe Indian.—BiSp

Prayers.—*Continued*
> Woman's prayer to the sun, for a newborn girl. Unknown, fr. the Hopi Indian.—BiSp
> Young man's prayer to the spirits. Unknown, fr. the Crow Indian.—BiSp

Prayers of steel. Carl Sandburg.—HoRa

Praying mantis. Mary Ann Hoberman.—PrRh

Praying mantises
> Mantis. V. Worth.—WoSp
> Praying mantis. M. A. Hoberman.—PrRh

Precious stones. See also Jewelry
> Flint. C. G. Rossetti.—PrRh
> The hardness scale. J. Peseroff.—McL
> "Surely there is a mine for silver." From Job. Bible/Old Testament.—PlSc

"A **precocious**, impulsive young Mr." See Nothing more than a sister

Pregnancy
> Grace DeLorenzo. M. Glenn.—GlC

Prehistoric animals
> Brontosaurus. G. Kredenser.—PrRh
> Dinosaur. M. Hillert.—HoDi
> Dinosaur din. X. J. Kennedy.—LiSf
> Dinosaurs. V. Worth.—CoN—HoDi—LiSf
> Dinosaurs ("Their feet, planted into tar"). M. C. Livingston.—HoDi
> Dreamscape. L. M. Fisher.—HoDi
> Easter disaster. J. P. Lewis.—LiE
> Fossils. L. Moore.—HoDi—MoSn
> How the end might have been. I. J. Glaser.—HoDi
> The ichthyosaurus. Unknown.—BrT
> I'm glad I'm living now, not then. L. M. Fisher.—HoDi
> "The last dinosaur." V. D. Najjar.—HoDi
> Lines on a small potato. M. Fishback.—HoDi
> Long gone. J. Prelutsky.—PrRh—PrZ
> Painters. M. Rukeyser.—PlEd
> Plant-eater. S. Liatsos.—HoDi
> Prehistoric morning. F. Haraway.—HoDi
> Steam shovel. C. Malam.—CoN—PrRh
> To brontosaurus, a gentle giant dinosaur. L. M. Fisher.—HoDi
> To the skeleton of a dinosaur in the museum. L. Moore.—HoDi
> Unfortunately. B. Katz.—HoDi—PrRa
> "What if." I. J. Glaser.—HoDi
> "Whatever happened to the allosaurus." From Whatever happened to the dinosaurs. B. Most.—HoDi
> When dinosaurs ruled the earth ("Brontosaurus, diplodocus, gentle trachodon"). P. Hubbell.—HoDi—LiSf

Prehistoric morning. Fran Haraway.—HoDi

The prelude, sels. William Wordsworth
> Boat stealing.—HeR
> Crossing the Alps.—HeR
> "One Christmas-time".—HeR
> There was a boy.—HeR
> "Was it for this".—HeR

Prelude to a parting. Maya Angelou.—AnS

Prelutsky, Jack
> The aardvark.—PrZ
> Adelaide.—LiSf
> "Ah, a monster's lot is merry."—PrNk
> An alley cat with one life left.—PrNk
> "Alligators are unfriendly."—PrNk
> Alphabet stew.—PrRh
> The anteater ("An anteater can't eat a thing but an ant").—PrSr
> Archie B. McCall.—PrNk
> The armadillo.—PrZ
> "The baby uggs are hatching."—PrB

> Ballad of a boneless chicken.—PrNk
> "Baloney belly Billy."—PrNk
> "Be glad your nose is on your face."—PrNk
> The beaver ("The beaver is fat").—PrZ
> Bees ("Every bee").—PrZ
> The Bengal tiger.—PrZ
> "Betty ate a butternut."—PrRi
> The black bear ("In the summer, fall and spring").—PrZ
> Bleezer's ice cream.—PrNk
> "The bloders are exploding."—PrNk
> The bogeyman.—PrRh
> "Boing, boing, squeak."—PrNk
> Boring.—PrWi
> Bulgy Bunne.—PrNk
> "Bullfrogs, bullfrogs on parade."—PrRi
> The carpenter rages.—PrNk
> The catfish.—PrSr
> The cave beast greets a visitor.—PrNk
> The centipede ("The centipede with many feet").—PrSr
> "A certain lady kangaroo."—PrSr
> The chameleon.—PrZ
> The cheetah.—PrZ
> "The cherries' garden gala."—PrNk
> "Children, children everywhere."—PrRh
> The chipmunk.—PrZ
> Chocolate cake.—PrMp
> "Cincinnati Patty."—PrRi
> "City, oh, city."—PrRh
> Clara Cleech.—PrNk
> "The clouds I watched this afternoon."—PrMp
> Come see the thing.—PrNk
> The court jester's last report to the King.—PrSr
> The cow ("The cow mainly moos as she chooses to moo").—PrRh—PrZ
> A cow's outside.—PrNk
> The creature in the classroom.—PrB—PrRh
> The crocodile ("Beware the crafty crocodile").—PrZ
> Cuckoo ("The cuckoo in our cuckoo clock").—PrNk
> Daddy's football game.—PrIt
> Dainty Dottie Dee.—PrNk
> The darkling elves.—PrRh
> Dauntless Dimble.—PrNk
> A day in the country.—PrWi
> December days are short.—PrIs
> "The diatonic dittymunch."—PrNk
> Do oysters sneeze.—PrNk
> Dogs and cats and bears and bats.—PrRh
> Don't ever seize a weasel by the tail.—PrRh—PrZ
> Dora Diller.—PrNk
> The dreary dreeze.—PrB
> "A dromedary standing still."—PrZ
> Drumpp the grump.—PrNk
> "Early one morning on Featherbed Lane."—PrRi
> The egg ("If you listen very carefully, you' hear the").—PrZ
> "Eggs."—PrNk
> Electric eels.—PrZ
> Euphonica Jarre.—PrNk
> The first Thanksgiving ("When the Pilgrims").—CoN—PrIt
> Fish ("Fish have fins").—FrP—PrZ
> The flimsy fleek.—PrNk
> Floradora Doe.—PrNk
> The flotterzott.—PrB
> The flotz.—PrNk
> Forty performing bananas.—PrNk
> The four seasons ("Summer").—PrRh

Prelutsky, Jack—*Continued*
The fourth of July.—PrWi
The gallivanting gecko.—PrZ
The ghostly grocer of Grumble Grove.—PrSr
The ghoul.—HaOf
"The giggling gaggling gaggle of geese."—PrZ
Gobble gobble.—PrIt
A gopher in the garden.—PrZ
The grand county fair.—PrWi
"Grandfather Gander flew over the land."—PrRi
"Grandma Bear from Delaware."—PrRi
Granny Grizer.—PrNk
Griselda Gratz.—PrNk
Grubby grebbles.—PrB
Gussie's Greasy Spoon.—PrNk
Happy birthday, dear dragon.—PrNk
Harvey always wins.—CoN
Henrietta Snetter.—PrNk
Herbert Glerbett.—PrRh
"Hinnikin Minnikin."—PrRi
The hippopotamus ("The huge hippopotamus hasn't a hair").—PrRh—PrZ
Home, you're where it's warm inside.—PrRh
"Homework, oh homework."—PrNk
The house mouse.—PrRa—PrZ
Huffer and Cuffer.—PrSr
The hummingbird ("The ruby throated hummingbird").—PrZ
The hyena.—PrZ
"I am falling off a mountain."—PrNk
I am flying.—PrNk
I am freezing.—PrIs
"I am running in a circle."—PrNk
I ate too much.—PrIt
I do not like the rat.—PrNk
"I do not mind you, winter wind."—PrIs
"I found a four leaf clover."—PrNk
"I have been in bed for hours."—PrMp
"I love you more than applesauce."—PrIv
"I made a giant valentine."—PrIv
"I made my dog a valentine."—PrIv
"I only got one valentine."—PrIv
"I spied my shadow slinking."—PrNk
I toss them to my elephant.—PrNk
I went hungry on Thanksgiving.—PrIt
"I went to Wyoming one day in the spring."—PrRi
"I wonder why Dad is so thoroughly mad."—PrNk
"I'd never dine on dinosaurs."—PrNk
I'd never eat a beet.—PrNk
"If it was sunlight shining."—PrMp
If turkeys thought.—PrIt
"I'm a yellow-bill duck."—PrRi
"I'm awake, I'm awake."—PrMp
I'm bold, I'm brave.—PrNk
"I'm disgusted with my brother."—PrNk
I'm hungry.—PrRh
I'm in a rotten mood.—PrNk
I'm thankful.—PrNk
"I'm the single most wonderful person I know."—PrNk
An irritating creature.—PrNk
It is so still.—PrMp
Its fangs were red.—PrNk
It's Halloween.—CoN
"It's happy Thanksgiving."—PrIt
"It's snowing, it's snowing."—PrIs
"It's Valentine's day."—PrIv
"I've got an incredible headache."—PrNk
I've got an itch.—PrNk
"Jelly Jill loves Weasel Will."—PrIv
"Jellyfish stew."—PrNk

"Jilliky Jolliky Jelliky Jee."—PrRi
"Johnny had a black horse."—PrRi
"Justin Austin."—PrRi
Kermit Keene.—PrSr
"Kitty caught a caterpillar."—PrRi
The land of potpourri.—PrRh
The last day of school ("On the last day of school").—PrWi
"Late one night in Kalamazoo."—PrRi
Lavinia Nink.—PrNk
Leftovers.—PrIt
The lion ("The lion has a golden mane").—PrRh—PrZ
"Little pink pig in Arkansas."—PrRi
Long gone.—PrRh—PrZ
"Louder than a clap of thunder."—PrNk
"Ma, don't throw that shirt out."—PrNk
Mabel, remarkable Mabel.—PrNk
Me I am.—PrRh
Mean Maxine.—PrNk
"Michael built a bicycle."—PrNk
A microscopic topic.—PrNk
The middle of November.—PrIt
A million candles.—PrMp
Miraculous Mortimer.—PrNk
The mistletoe.—PrRa
The mole ("The mole's a solitary soul").—PrZ
Mother's chocolate valentine.—PrIv
The multilingual mynah bird.—PrZ
The mungle and the munn.—PrNk
The museum ("I went to the museum").—PrWi
My baby brother.—PrNk
"My birthday's in August."—PrWi
"My brother lost his bathing suit."—PrWi
"My brother's head should be replaced."—PrNk
My cousin.—PrWi
"My dog, he is an ugly dog."—PrNk
My father's valentine.—PrIv
"My mother says I'm sickening."—PrNk
"My mother took me skating."—PrIs
"My mother's got me bundled up."—PrIs
"My parents think I'm sleeping."—PrMp
"My sister is a sissy."—PrNk
"My sister would never throw snowballs at butterflies."—PrIs
"My snowman has a noble head."—PrIs
My special cake.—PrIv
Nature is.—PrRh
"Naughty little brown mouse."—PrRi
"The neighbors are not fond of me."—PrNk
Never mince words with a shark.—PrNk
The new kid on the block.—PrNk
"New York is in North Carolina."—PrNk
Night is here.—PrMp
"The nimpy numpy numpity."—PrB
Nine mice.—PrNk
No girls allowed.—PrRh
"No, I won't turn orange."—PrNk
Nonsense.—PrRh
The nothing doings.—PrNk
"Oh no."—PrIv
"Oh Pennington Poe."—PrRi
Oh, teddy bear.—PrNk
"One day in Oklahoma."—PrRi
One last little leaf.—PrIs
"One morning in August."—PrWi
The ostrich.—PrZ
Ounce and Bounce.—PrNk
"Our classroom has a mailbox."—PrIv
The owl ("The owl is wary, the owl is wise").—PrZ
"Oysters."—PrZ—RuI
The pack rat.—PrZ

Prelutsky, Jack—*Continued*
The pancake collector.—HaOf
"Parrot with a pomegranate."—PrRi
Philbert Phlurk.—PrSr
The polar bear ("The polar bear by being white").—PrZ
"Poor old Penelope."—LiSf
"Poor potatoes underground."—PrRi
The porcupine.—PrZ
"Pumberly Pott's unpredictable niece."—PrRh
The quossible.—PrB
The rabbit ("Hip hop hoppity, hip hop hoppity").—PrZ
Rain ("I was having trouble sleeping").—PrMp
"Ride a purple pelican."—PrRi
"Rudy rode a unicorn."—PrRi
"Rumpitty Tumpitty Rumpitty Tum."—PrRi
Sadie Snatt.—PrSr
Sand ("I sat down on my blanket").—PrWi
"Saucy little ocelot."—LiSf—PrSr
The seven sneezes of Cecil Snedde.—PrSr
Seymour Snorkle.—PrNk
Shadow thought.—PrIs
Sheep ("Sheep are gentle, shy and meek").—PrZ
The sheriff of Rottenshot.—PrSr
Sidney Snickke.—PrNk
Sir Blushington Bloone.—PrNk
Skeleton parade.—CoN—PrRa
The slithery slitch.—PrB
The smasheroo.—PrB
The snail ("The snail doesn't know where he's going").—FrP—PrZ
The snake ("Don't ever make").—PrZ
The snatchits.—PrB
Sneaky Sue.—PrNk
The sneepies.—PrB
The sneezysnoozer.—PrB
Snillies.—PrNk
A snowflake fell.—PrIs
The snowman's lament.—PrIs
The soggy frog.—PrSr
Some people I know.—PrRh
Somersaults.—PrRa
Something silky.—PrNk
Sometimes ("Sometimes I simply have to cry").—PrRa
Song of the gloopy gloppers.—PrNk
The spaghetti nut.—PrSr
"Spaghetti, spaghetti."—HoMu
A spooky sort of shadow.—PrMp
Stringbean Small.—PrNk
"Stuck in the snow."—PrIs
Super goopy glue.—PrNk
"Suzanna socked me Sunday."—PrNk
The telephone call.—HoBf
The Thanksgiving day parade.—PrIt
"There is a thing."—PrNk
"There's someone I know."—PrIv
The three toed sloth.—PrZ
Throckmorton Thratte.—PrNk
"Timble Tamble Turkey."—PrRi
"Timmy Tatt, Timmy Tatt."—PrRi
"Today is a day to crow about."—PrNk
"Today is very boring."—PrNk
"Tonight is impossibly noisy."—PrMp
Too hot.—PrWi
Toucans two.—PrZ
   Toucannery.—CoOu
The troll.—PrRh
The turtle.—PrZ
Twickham Tweer.—PrRh—PrSr
"The two horned black rhinoceros."—PrZ
"Two robins from Charlotte."—PrRi

"An unassuming owl."—PrNk
Uncanny Colleen.—PrNk
"The underwater wibbles."—PrNk
A valentine for my best friend.—PrIv
A valentine for my teacher.—PrIv
The wallaby.—PrZ
The walrus ("The widdly, waddly walrus").—PrZ
The ways of living things.—PrRh
"We each wore half a horse."—PrNk
We heard Wally wail.—PrNk
We need a hit.—PrWi
"What happens to the colors."—PrMp
"What nerve you've got, Minerva Mott."—PrNk
"When daddy carves the turkey."—PrIt
"When Dracula went to the blood bank."—PrNk
"When I'm very nearly sleeping."—PrMp
"When Molly Day wears yellow clothes."—PrRi
"When snowflakes are fluttering."—PrIs
"When Tillie ate the chili."—PrNk
When young, the slyne.—PrNk
Where goblins dwell.—PrRh
Whistling.—BeD—PrRa
"A white cloud floated like a swan."—PrRi
Winter signs.—PrIs
Winter's come.—PrIs
The wishbone.—PrIt
"A wolf is at the laundromat."—PrNk
Wrimples.—PrRh
The yak ("Yickity yackity, yickity yak").—PrRh—PrZ
"You need to have an iron rear."—PrNk
Yubbazubbies.—PrNk
Zany Zapper Zockke.—PrNk
The zebra ("The zebra is undoubtedly").—PrZ
Zoo doings.—PrZ
The zoosher.—PrNk

Premonitions. See Omens; Prophecies
Prescience. Maya Angelou.—AnS
Presents. See Gifts and giving
Presents from the flood. X. J. Kennedy.—KeF
Presidents' day. Myra Cohn Livingston.—LiCe
Press, John
African Christmas.—HaO
"Pretend you are a dragon." See Things to do if you are a subway
Pretending. Bobbi Katz.—PrRa
A **pretty** ambition. Mary E. Wilkins Freeman.—HaOf
The **pretty** butterfly. Unknown.—GrT
"Pretty John Watts." Mother Goose.—BlQ—LoR
Pretty little girl. Unknown.—GrT
The **pretty** ploughboy. Unknown.—PlAs
"Pretty, say when." See The dear girl
"A pretty young school mistress named Beauchamp." See A young school mistress
Price, Nancy
One-night fair.—JaG
Pride and vanity
Aunt Sponge and Aunt Spiker. R. Dahl.—PrRh
Between you and me. S. Hazo.—JaG
"The daughter of the farrier." Mother Goose.—DaC
Get up and bar the door. Unknown.—BlO—PlAs
"Gregory Griggs, Gregory Griggs." Mother Goose.—BlQ—DeM—LoR
"He wastes time walking and telling the air I am superior even to the wind." From Sketch of a poet. C. Sandburg.—HoRa
A heavy rap. N. Giovanni.—GiSp

Pride and vanity—*Continued*

The hen and the carp. I. Serraillier.—CoOu—LiSf

"I'm never as good as I want to be." N. M. Bodecker.—BoSs

"I'm the single most wonderful person I know." J. Prelutsky.—PrNk

In the workhouse. G. R. Sims.—HaO

Lake Superior. From Great Lakes suite. J. Reaney.—DoNw

"Little girl, be careful what you say." C. Sandburg.—HoRa

Man's image. D. H. Lawrence.—PrBb

Monica Zindell. M. Glenn.—GlC

My brother flies over low. D. Huddle.—JaT

On the vanity of earthly greatness. A. Guiterman.—HaOf—TrM

Pa ("When we got home, there was our old man"). L. Dangel.—JaS

Primer lesson. C. Sandburg.—HoRa

Proud Maisie. Sir W. Scott.—BlO—PlAs

The rapid. C. Sangster.—DoNw

Sounds of the day. N. MacCaig.—HeR

The spider and the fly. M. Howitt.—CoOu—DaC

The sycophantic fox and the gullible raven. G. W. Carryl.—HaOf

Teddy bear. A. A. Milne.—CoOu

'Tis strange. E. Field.—BrT

"Vain, vain, Mister McLain." A. Lobel.—LoWr

We real cool. G. Brooks.—KeK

The wizard in the well. H. Behn.—HoCb

"Prim and proper." See Parlor

Primer lesson. Carl Sandburg.—HoRa

"Prince Absalom and Sir Rotherham Redde." See Evening

Princes and princesses

And the princess was astonished to see the ugly frog turn into a handsome prince. J. Viorst.—ViI

Engraved on the collar of a dog, which I gave to his Royal Highness. A. Pope.—KoT

His highness's dog.—PrRh (unat.)

Epigram engraved on the collar of a dog.—CoN—KeK

Noblesse oblige. C. T. Wright.—JaPi

"What is the opposite of a prince." R. Wilbur.—LiSf—LiWa

The **princess**, sels. Alfred Tennyson

"Now sleeps the crimson petal, now the white".—McL

"The splendour falls on castle walls".—LiWa

Blow, bugle, blow.—LiSf

Song.—BlO

Sweet and low.—BlO—ChB

"The print is too small, distressing me." See The last decision

Prisms (altea). Philip Dacey.—JaPi

The **problem**, sels. Ralph Waldo Emerson

"The hand that rounded Peter's dome".—PlEd

"Proceed, great chief, with virtue on thy side." From To his excellency George Washington. Phillis Wheatley.—LiSf

Professions. See names of professions, as Doctors

A **professor** called Chesterton. William Schwenck Gilbert.—BrT

Progress

The flower-fed buffaloes. V. Lindsay.—HaOf—HeR

"From gallery grave and the hunt of a wren king." From Thanksgiving for a habitat. W. H. Auden.—PlEd

Landscape. E. Merriam.—KeK—MeSk

Mashkin Hill. L. Simpson.—PlSc

Progress. C. Martin.—JaPo

Rain forest, Papua, New Guinea. M. C. Livingston.—LiMp

Requiem for Sonora. R. Shelton.—JaPi

Train blues. P. Zimmer.—JaPo

Progress. Connie Martin.—JaPo

Prometheus unbound, sels. Percy Bysshe Shelley

"Canst thou imagine where those spirits live".—LiWa

"A prominent lady in Brooking." See Expert

Promises. Jane Yolen.—LiNe

The **properties** of a good greyhound. Dame Juliana Barners.—HeR

Prophecies. See also Omens

Auguries of innocence, complete. W. Blake.—HeR

Doves of Dodona. P. Fleischman.—FlI

"Hear the voice of the Bard." W. Blake.—HeR

Kubla Khan. S. T. Coleridge.—LiSf—LiWa—PlEd

Noah. R. Daniells.—DoNw

Proud Maisie. Sir W. Scott.—BlO—PlAs

The raven. E. A. Poe.—HaOf

A **proposal.** Mother Goose.—DaC

The **proud** engine. Unknown.—BrT

Proud Maisie. Sir Walter Scott.—BlO—PlAs

"Proud Maisie is in the wood." See Proud Maisie

Proud torsos. Carl Sandburg.—HoRa

Proverbs. See also Superstitions

"Birds of a feather flock together." Mother Goose.—DaC

"Birds of a feather will flock together".—LoR

"Here's little proverb that you surely ought to know." Unknown.—TrM

Oz. E. Merriam.—MeSk

Proverbs, sels. Bible/Old Testament

"Who can find a virtuous woman, for her price is far above rubies".—PlSc

Psalm 23 ("The Lord is my shepherd, I shall not want"). From The book of psalms. Bible/Old Testament.—LiSf

Psalm 23 ("The Lord to me a shepherd is").—HaOf

Psalm 23 ("The Lord to me a shepherd is"). See Psalm 23 ("The Lord is my shepherd, I shall not want")

Psalm 24. From The book of psalms. Bible/Old Testament.—LiSf

Psalm 100. From The book of psalms. Bible/Old Testament.—LiSf—LiTp

Psalm 103. From The book of psalms. Bible/Old Testament.—LiSf

Psalm 121. From The book of psalms. Bible/Old Testament.—HaOf

Psalm of a black mother. Theresa Greenwood.—LaT

A **psalm** of life. Henry Wadsworth Longfellow.—HaOf

Psalm of the fruitful field. Abraham Moses Klein.—DoNw

Psalms

Psalm 23 ("The Lord is my shepherd, I shall not want"). From The book of psalms. Bible/Old Testament.—LiSf

Psalm 23 ("The Lord to me a shepherd is").—HaOf

Psalm 24. From The book of psalms. Bible/Old Testament.—LiSf

Psalms—*Continued*
Psalm 100. From The book of psalms. Bible/Old Testament.—LiSf—LiTp
Psalm 103. From The book of psalms. Bible/Old Testament.—LiSf
Psalm 121. From The book of psalms. Bible/Old Testament.—HaOf
Psalm of a black mother. T. Greenwood.—LaT
A psalm of life. H. W. Longfellow.—HaOf
Psalm of the fruitful field. A. M. Klein.—DoNw
Subway psalm. A. Nowlan.—JaS
"**Psst**, psst." See Kitty cornered
PTA ("Seemed like everybody's mother"). Cynthia Rylant.—RyW
The **ptarmigan**. Unknown.—PrRh
"The **ptarmigan** is strange." See The ptarmigan
"**Puddings** and beams." Edward Lear.—LiH
Puddles
Jigsaw puddle. E. Hearn.—BeD
Looking down in the rain. B. J. Esbensen.—EsCs
"**Puddles** dry up." See January thaw
The **puffin** ("Upon this cake of ice is perched"). Robert Williams Wood.—PrRh
The **puffin** ("Warm and plump as fresh baked muffins"). Charlotte Pomerantz.—PoA
Puffins
The puffin ("Upon this cake of ice is perched"). R. W. Wood.—PrRh
The puffin ("Warm and plump as fresh baked muffins"). C. Pomerantz.—PoA
There once was a puffin. F. P. Jaques.—CoN—FrP
Puma. Ted Hughes.—HuU
"**Pumberly** Pott's unpredictable niece." Jack Prelutsky.—PrRh
The **pumpkin**. Robert Graves.—LiWa—PrRh
The **pumpkin** tide. Richard Brautigan.—HoSi
Pumpkins
Halloween disguises. X. J. Kennedy.—KeF
"Jack-o'-lantern." E. Merriam.—MeHa
"Peter, Peter, pumpkin eater." Mother Goose.—DeM—FaW—LoR
The pumpkin. R. Graves.—LiWa—PrRh
The pumpkin tide. R. Brautigan.—HoSi
The stranger in the pumpkin. J. Ciardi.—CoN
"**Punch** and Judy." Mother Goose.—LoR
Punctuation
"I saw a peacock with a fiery tail." Unknown.—BlO—HeR
Markings, the comma. E. Merriam.—MeSk
Markings, the exclamation. E. Merriam.—MeSk
Markings, the period. E. Merriam.—MeSk
Markings, the question. E. Merriam.—MeSk
Markings, the semicolon. E. Merriam.—MeSk
Punishment
The destruction of Sennacherib. Lord Byron.—HeR—PlAs
"Little Polly Flinders." Mother Goose.—AlH—DeM—FaW—LoR
"Methought that I had broken from the Tower." From Richard III. W. Shakespeare.—HeR
Punishment. Unknown.—BrT
"There was a man of double deed." Unknown.—HeR
"Three little kittens lost their mittens." Mother Goose.—DeM
The three little kittens.—HaOf
"Three little kittens, they lost their mittens".—LoR
We heard Wally wail. J. Prelutsky.—PrNk

What someone said when he was spanked on the day before his birthday. J. Ciardi.—PrRh
Punishment. Unknown.—BrT
Punkydoodle and Jollapin. Laura E. Richards.—HaOf
Puns
An atrocious pun. Unknown.—BrT—PrRh
"Fuzzy Wuzzy was a bear." Unknown.—CoN
Have you ever seen. Unknown.—PrRh
Only teasing. Unknown.—BrT
Punishment. Unknown.—BrT
Serpentine verse. J. S. Newman.—BrT
The smart little bear ("Teacher Bruin said, cub, bear in mind"). M. Fenderson.—BrT
Threnody. G. T. Lanigan.—DoNw
Tra-la-larceny. O. Herford.—BrT
The twins ("When twins came, their father, Dan Dunn"). B. Braley.—BrT
Puppets and marionettes
The marionettes. M. C. Livingston.—LiWo
"Put on your shoes and don't be late." Unknown.—DeD
Puppies. See Dogs
Puppy ("Catch and shake the cobra garden hose"). Robert L. Tyler.—HoDl
Puppy ("We bought our puppy"). Lee Bennett Hopkins.—HoDl
Puppy and I. Alan Alexander Milne.—CoOu—FrP
"The **puppy** chased the sunbeam." Ivy O. Eastwick.—PrRa
The **puppy's** song. Charlotte Pomerantz.—PoA
Purdy, Alfred
The rattlesnake.—DoNw
"The **pure** contralto sings in the organloft." From Song of myself. Walt Whitman.—KoT
Purim
The fourteenth day of Adar. B. J. Esbensen.—LiPj
The **purist**. Ogden Nash.—HaOf
Purple (color)
Grandpa dropped his glasses. L. F. Jackson.—PrRh
The purple cow. G. Burgess.—CoN—HaOf—LiSf—PrRh
"I never saw a purple cow".—BlO
Taste of purple. L. B. Jacobs.—PrRh
The **purple** cow. Gelett Burgess.—CoN—HaOf—LiSf—PrRh
"I never saw a purple cow".—BlO
"**Purr**." See Poem by a cat
Pushkin, Alexander
Phantoms on the steppe.—LiWa
"**Puss** came dancing out of a barn." Mother Goose.—DeM
Pussy. See "I like little pussy"
"**Pussy** can sit by the fire and sing." Rudyard Kipling.—DaC
"**Pussy** cat ate the dumplings." Mother Goose.—BlQ
"**Pussy** cat Mole jumped over a coal." Mother Goose.—DeM
"**Pussy**, pussy Baudrons." Unknown.—ChC
"**Pussy** sits beside the fire." Mother Goose.—LoR
Pussy willows. See Willow trees
Pussy willows. Aileen Fisher.—PrRa
"**Pussycat**, pussycat, where have you been." Mother Goose.—AlH—DeM—FaW—LoR
"**Put** a heading on your paper like this." See Donald Kaminsky
"**Put** a piggy in a poke." Clyde Watson.—WaC
"**Put** on your shoes and don't be late." Unknown.—DeD

"**Put** the pine tree in its pot by the doorway." Natalia Belting.—LiIl

"**Put** the rubber mouse away." See For a dead kitten

"**Put** your finger in." Unknown.—RaT

"**Putting** out the candles." See My father after work

"**Puva**, puva, puva." Unknown.—KoT

Puzzle ("Map of a city with streets meeting at center"). Robert Froman.—LiSf

Puzzle ("My best friend's name is Billy"). Arnold Spilka.—LiIl—PrRh

Puzzled. Carolyn Wells.—HaOf

Puzzles
 How I escaped from the labyrinth. P. Dacey.—JaPo
 Jigsaw puzzle. R. Hoban.—CoN
 Puzzle ("Map of a city with streets meeting at center"). R. Froman.—LiSf
 "Thinking it hard candy, Rube." X. J. Kennedy. KeB

Pyle, Katharine
 August ("Deep in the wood I made a house").—HaOf
 The circus parade.—HaOf
 Clever Peter and the ogress.—HaOf
 Nine o'clock. See The wonder clock
 One o'clock. See The wonder clock
 The toys talk of the world.—HaOf
 Two o'clock. See The wonder clock
 The visitor.—CoOu
 The wonder clock, sels.
  Nine o'clock.—HaOf
  One o'clock.—HaOf
  Two o'clock.—HaOf

Pyman, Avril
 Two sisters looking at baby brother, tr. by.—FaW

"The **pyramids** first, which in Egypt were laid." See The seven wonders of the ancient world

Q

"**Q** is a quoter who'll cite." See A quoter

"**Quack**, quack." See Ducks at dawn

Quack, quack. Dr. Seuss.—PrRa

"**Quack**, quack, quack." See Dumpy ducky

Quail in autumn. William Jay Smith.—JaPi

Quaking aspen. Eve Merriam.—MeF

The **quangle** wangle's hat. Edward Lear.—CoOu—LiH—LiIl

The **quarrel**. Eleanor Farjeon.—FaE

"**Quartered**." See The apple

"**Quarts** of ladybugs." See Ladybugs

"**Quasimodo** loomed." See For Wilma

Quatrain. Eve Merriam.—MeSk

Quechua Indians. See Indians of the Americas—Quechua

Queen Nefertiti. Unknown.—PrRh

The **Queen** of Elfan's nourice. Unknown.—PlAs

"The **Queen** of Hearts." Mother Goose.—DaC—DeM—LoR

"The **queen** of winter walks the land." See The talking of the trees

Queenie. Leland B. Jacobs.—PrRh

"**Queenie's** strong and Queenie's tall." See Queenie

Queens. See Rulers

Queens of the river. Claudia Lewis.—HoCl—LiSf

"**Queer** are the ways of a man I know." See The phantom horsewoman

A **queer** fellow named Woodin. Edward Bradley.—BrT

The **queer** little house. Mother Goose.—BlPi

Queer things. James Reeves.—LiWa

Quest. Eve Merriam.—MeF

Question ("Do you love me"). Unknown.—PrRh

The **question** ("If I could teach you how to fly"). Dennis Lee.—LiIl

The **question** ("People always say to me"). Karla Kuskin.—CoN

Questioning faces. Robert Frost.—KoS

Questions
 All I did was ask my sister a question. J. Ciardi.—CiD
 Blowin' in the wind. B. Dylan.—KeK
 Catechisms, talking with a four year old. G. E. Lyon.—JaS
 "A centipede was happy quite." Unknown.—BlO
  A centipede.—CoOu
 Engraved on the collar of a dog, which I gave to his Royal Highness. A. Pope.—KoT
  His highness's dog.—PrRh (unat.)
  Epigram engraved on the collar of a dog.—CoN—KeK
 "The man in the wilderness asked of me." Mother Goose.—DaC—FaW
  "The man in the wilderness asked me".—LoR
 The oven bird. R. Frost.—KoS
 Owl ("Who"). E. Merriam.—MeHa
 The question ("If I could teach you how to fly"). D. Lee.—LiIl
 The question ("People always say to me"). K. Kuskin.—CoN
 Questions ("Are you asleep yet."). R. J. Margolis.—MaS
 Questions ("If cookies come in boxes"). L. B. Hopkins.—HoMu
 Questions ("The questions they ask"). E. Farjeon.—FaE
 Questions ("Write it on the north wind"). E. Merriam.—MeHa
 Questions for an angel. From A throw of threes. E. Merriam.—MeF
 They ask, is God, too, lonely. C. Sandburg.—LiIl
 To be answered in our next issue. Unknown.—PrRh
 "To be, or not to be, that is the question." From Hamlet. W. Shakespeare.—HoUn
 Water lily. V. Worth.—WoSp
 "What happens to the colors." J. Prelutsky.—PrMp
 Who am I. F. Holman.—FaTh—LiSf

Questions ("Are you asleep yet."). Richard J. Margolis.—MaS

Questions ("If cookies come in boxes"). Lee Bennett Hopkins.—HoMu

Questions ("The questions they ask"). Eleanor Farjeon.—FaE

Questions ("Write it on the north wind"). Eve Merriam.—MeHa

Questions for an angel. From A throw of threes. Eve Merriam.—MeF

Questions for September. Barbara Juster Esbensen.—EsCs

"The **questions** they ask." See Questions

"The **quick** flick of a smile." See Edwin A. Nelms

A **quick** hush. X. J. Kennedy.—KeF

Quiet girl. Langston Hughes.—HuDk

Quiet room. Sylvia Cassedy.—CaR

"**Quietly** through the forest pries." See Sun tiger

Quilt song. Mark Vinz.—JaG
Quilts
  Looking at quilts. M. Piercy.—PlSc
  Quilt song. M. Vinz.—JaG
Quintana, Leroy V.
  The legacy II.—StG
"**Quiver** shiver." See The river
The **quossible**. Jack Prelutsky.—PrB
"The **quossible**, the quossible." See The quossible
"The **quote-throated**." See Word bird
A **quoter**. Oliver Herford.—BrT
"**Quoth** a cat to me once, pray relieve." See Tact
"**Quoth** the bookworm, I don't care one bit." See The omnivorous bookworm

R

R. From A bestiary of the garden for children who should know better. Phyllis Gotlieb.—DoNw
The **rabbit** ("Hip hop hoppity, hip hop hoppity"). Jack Prelutsky.—PrZ
The **rabbit** ("When they said the time to hide was mine"). Elizabeth Madox Roberts.—HaOf—PrRh
A **rabbit** as king of the ghosts. Wallace Stevens.—KoT
The **rabbit** skip. Margaret Wise Brown.—FrP
Rabbits
  A bunny romance. O. Herford.—HaOf
  The Byfield rabbit. K. Hoskins.—PlSc
  Cowper's tame hare. N. Nicholson.—HeR
  Done for. W. De la Mare.—BlO
  The Easter bunny. J. Ciardi.—LiE
  Easter habits. F. Holman.—LiE
  Epitaph on a hare. W. Cowper.—BlO
  Epitaph on an unfortunate artist. R. Graves.—TrM
  "Five little rabbits went out to walk." Unknown.—TrM
  Hares at play. J. Clare.—HeR
  "In the pitch of the night." L. B. Hopkins.—HoCr
  Interruption to a journey. N. MacCaig.—HeR
  Mr. Rabbit. D. Willson.—FrP
  The names of the hare. Unknown.—HeR
  R. From A bestiary of the garden for children who should know better. P. Gotlieb.—DoNw
  The rabbit ("Hip hop hoppity, hip hop hoppity"). J. Prelutsky.—PrZ
  The rabbit ("When they said the time to hide was mine"). E. M. Roberts.—HaOf—PrRh
  A rabbit as king of the ghosts. W. Stevens.—KoT
  The rabbit skip. M. W. Brown.—FrP
  "Rabbits are nice neighbors." Z. K. Snyder.—LiE
  "Round about there." Unknown.—RaT
  The snare. J. Stephens.—BlO—LiSf
  "The snow-shoe hare." T. Hughes.—HuU
  The snowy owl. T. Hughes.—HuU
  Song of the rabbits outside the tavern. E. Coatsworth.—HaOf
  The toad and the rabbit. J. Martin.—PrRa
  Two songs of a fool. W. B. Yeats.—HeR
  White season. F. Frost.—LiSf
"**Rabbits** are nice neighbors." Zilpha Keatley Snyder.—LiE
Raccoon. Kenneth Rexroth.—KeK
"**Raccoon.**" Charlotte Zolotow.—ZoE
"The **raccoon** wears a black mask." See Raccoon

Raccoons
  "Raccoon." C. Zolotow.—ZoE
  Raccoon. K. Rexroth.—KeK
  Science fiction. R. Wittemore.—KeK
Race relations
  Alabama earth. L. Hughes.—HuDk
  All the colors of the race. A. Adoff.—AdA
  "All the colors of the race are." A. Adoff.—AdA
  The ballad of Rudolph Reed. G. Brooks.—HeR
  Color. E. Merriam.—MeSk
  David Klein. M. Glenn.—GlCd
  Family affairs. M. Angelou.—AnS
  I am. A. Adoff.—AdA
  "I am making a circle for myself." A. Adoff.—AdA
  "I see white and black, Lord." M. Boyd.—LaT
  I, too. L. Hughes.—HuDk
  "In both the families." A. Adoff.—AdA
  Incident ("Once riding in old Baltimore"). C. Cullen.—CoN—HaOf—KeK
  Montgomery. S. Cornish.—JaPi
  Share-croppers. L. Hughes.—PlSc
  Subway rush hour. L. Hughes.—KeK
  Sum people. A. Adoff.—AdA
  "The way I see any hope for later." A. Adoff.—AdA
  "We are talking about." A. Adoff.—AdA
  "When they asked." A. Adoff.—AdA
Races and racing
  And some more wicked thoughts. J. Viorst.—ViI
  At grass. P. Larkin.—HeR
  Crystal Rowe. M. Glenn.—GlCd
  "The dragon boats, there they go." Unknown.—DeD
  "Great frog race." I. H. Finlay.—KeK
  The sidewalk racer. L. Morrison.—CoN—KeK—LiSf—PrRh
  The true ballad of the great race to Gilmore City. P. Hey.—JaPi
  "We're racing, racing down the walk." P. McGinley.—PrRh
  What do they do to you in distant places. M. Bell.—JaPi
  The women's 400 meters. L. Morrison.—LiSf
Rachel Ferrara. Mel Glenn.—GlCd
Racing. See Races and racing
"The **racing** flag whips out." See Markings, the exclamation
Radar
  Radar. A. Ross.—JaD
Radar. Alan Ross.—JaD
The **radiance**. Kabir, tr. by Robert Bly.—McL
Radio
  Umbilical. E. Merriam.—HoCl—MeSk—PrRh
Radish. N. M. Bodecker.—BoSs
"The **radish** is." See Radish
Radishes
  Radish. N. M. Bodecker.—BoSs
Radnóti, Miklós
  Charm ("With trembling eyes").—McL
  Hesitating ode.—McL
  I hid you.—McL
Ragged robin. Eleanor Farjeon.—FaE
The **raggedy** dog. Sherman Ripley.—PrRa
"The **raggedy** dog chased the raggedy cat." See The raggedy dog
The **raggedy** man. James Whitcomb Riley.—HaOf
Rags. Judith Thurman.—HoSi—JaT
"De **railroad** bridge's." See Homesick blues
"The **railroad** track is miles away." See Travel

Rain—*Continued*
"A sunshiny shower." Mother Goose.—DeM—LoR
"There was a wet pig from Fort Wayne." A. Lobel.—LoB
"To walk in warm rain." D. McCord.—PrRh
Umbrella ("Umbrella, umbrella"). E. Merriam.—MeHa
Umbrellas ("It's raining in the city"). M. Kumin.—HoSs
Umbrellas ("Umbrellas bloom"). B. J. Esbensen.—PrRa
"Vain, vain, Mister McLain." A. Lobel.—LoWr
"Walking in the rain." D. Saxon.—JaD
Watch your step, I'm drenched. A. Mitchell.—HeR
Weathers. T. Hardy.—BlO—DaC—HeR
"Western wind, when wilt thou blow." Unknown.—KeK—McL
"When clouds appear like rocks and towers." Mother Goose.—LoR
When I went out. K. Kuskin.—CoN
"When the peacock loudly calls." Mother Goose.—LoR
"When the rain raineth." Unknown.—HeR
"A white cloud floated like a swan." J. Prelutsky.—PrRi
Windshield wiper. E. Merriam.—KeK
"Windshield wipers." D. Lee.—DoNw
A young man who loved rain. W. J. Smith.—BrT
Rain ("I was having trouble sleeping"). Jack Prelutsky.—PrMp
Rain ("Like a drummer's brush"). Emanuel di Pasquale.—KeK
Rain ("Mud"). Lilian Moore.—MoSn
Rain ("The rain is raining all around"). Robert Louis Stevenson.—CoN—FaW—FrP
The rain. See "Rain on the green grass"
"The rain." See Rain pools
Rain ("Some nights"). Myra Cohn Livingston.—LiSi
"Rain before seven." Mother Goose.—DeM—LoR
Rain clouds. Elizabeth Ellen Long.—PrRh
"The rain comes in sheets." See Sudden storm
"Rain falling, what things do you grow." See River winding
Rain forest, Papua, New Guinea. Myra Cohn Livingston.—LiMp
"The rain has silver sandals." May Justus.—PrRh
Rain in the city. N. M. Bodecker.—BoPc
"Rain into river." X. J. Kennedy.—KeF
"The rain is chronic." See Dido's farewell
"The rain is clinging to the round rose cheek." See After rain
"The rain is driving silver nails." See Rain song
"Rain is good." See April
"The rain is raining all around." See Rain
The rain it raineth. Charles Bowen.—CoN
"The rain it raineth on the just." See The rain it raineth
"Rain on the green grass." Mother Goose.—DeM
The rain.—PrRa
Rain pools. Lilian Moore.—MoSn
"Rain, rain." See Sun after rain
"Rain, rain, go away." Mother Goose.—DeM—LiSF—LoR
Rain song. David McCord.—McAs
The rainbow ("Boats sail on the rivers"). Christina Georgina Rossetti.—DaC
The rainbow ("Even the rainbow has a body"). David Herbert Lawrence.—PrBb

Rainbow ("Oh, my pretty rainbow"). Eleanor Farjeon.—FaE
Rainbows
Bubbles. C. Sandburg.—HoRa—JaT
A factory rainbow. R. Saadi.—PlSc
Legend. J. Wright.—HeR
Prisms (altea). P. Dacey.—JaPi
The rainbow ("Boats sail on the rivers"). C. G. Rossetti.—DaC
The rainbow ("Even the rainbow has a body"). D. H. Lawrence.—PrBb
Rainbow ("Oh, my pretty rainbow"). E. Farjeon.—FaE
Send us a rainbow. Unknown, fr. the Nootka Indian.—LaT
The storm ("A perfect rainbow, a wide"). W. C. Williams.—JaPo
Sun after rain. N. Farber.—HoSu—PrRa
Sun on rain. L. Moore.—MoSn
Raindrops ("How brave a ladybug must be"). Aileen Fisher.—PrRa
Raindrops ("Raindrops a-falling from the skies"). Unknown.—LaW
"Raindrops a-falling from the skies." See Raindrops
Rainy day. William Wise.—PrRa
Rainy nights. Irene Thompson.—PrRh
"Raise the curtain." See Indian summer
Raisin bread. Lee Blair.—BrT
"A rake, a coat, a meadow, a mill." See Coloring
Raleigh, Sir Walter
"As you came from the holy land."—HeR
Epitaph on the Earl of Leicester.—HeR
Even such is time.—HeR
The lie ("Go, soul, the body's guest").—HeR
The nymph's reply to the shepherd.—HeR
On the cards and the dice.—HeR
The passionate man's pilgrimage.—HeR
Sir Walter Ralegh to his son.—HeR
Raleigh was right. William Carlos Williams.—HeR
Randall, Dudley
Blackberry sweet.—KeK
Rands, William Brighty
The cat of cats.—PrRh
"Great, wide, beautiful, wonderful world."—TrM
The pedlar's caravan.—BlO
Winifred Waters.—DaC
Range-finding. Robert Frost.—HeR
Rankin, Carroll Watson
A difficult guest.—BrT
Rannoch, by Glencoe. From Landscapes. Thomas Stearns Eliot.—HeR
Ransom, John Crowe
Bells for John Whiteside's daughter.—HeR
Blue girls.—HeR
Here lies a lady.—HeR
Janet waking.—HeR
Vision by Sweetwater.—HeR
Rape
Cynthia Leonard. M. Glenn.—GlCd
Rape poem. M. Piercy.—JaPi
Rape poem. Marge Piercy.—JaPi
Raphael (about)
Cardinal Bembo's epitaph on Raphael. P. Bembo, Cardinal.—PlEd
The rapid. Charles Sangster.—DoNw
"Rapunzel, Rapunzel." Mark Van Doren.—PlAs
Rare Willie drowned in Yarrow. Unknown.—PlAs
Rasmussen, Knud
Eskimo chant, tr. by.—DoNw
"The lands around my dwelling", tr. by.—LiIl
"There is fear in", tr. by.—LiSf

Rats
"He was a rat, and she was a rat."
Unknown.—BlO
He and she.—BlPi
What became of them.—HaOf
I do not like the rat. J. Prelutsky.—PrNk
The pack rat. J. Prelutsky.—PrZ
The pied piper of Hamelin. R. Browning.—LiSf
"Pretty John Watts." Mother Goose.—BlQ—
LoR
Rats. E. Farjeon.—FaE
"There was a rat, for want of stairs." Mother
Goose.—DeM—LoR
Rats. Eleanor Farjeon.—FaE
The **rattle** bag. Dafydd Ap Gwilym, tr. by Joseph
Clancy.—HeR
The **rattlesnake.** Alfred Purdy.—DoNw
Rauter, Rose
Peach ("Touch it to your cheek and it's
soft").—KeK
The **raven.** Edgar Allan Poe. HaOf
"A **raven** sat upon a tree." See The sycophantic
fox and the gullible raven
Rayford, Julian Lee
Junkyards.—JaPo
Raymond Crystal. Mel Glenn.—GlC
Razon de amor, sels. Pedro Salinas, tr. by Linda
Gutierrez and Lawrence Pitketbly
"Now I love you".—McL
Read, Sylvia
Owl ("On midsummer night the witches
shriek").—PrRh
Read. Ann Turner.—TuS
Read this with gestures. John Ciardi.—BaS—PrRh
"**Read** up and down." Unknown.—LiIl
"**Reader,** in your hand you hold." See Egg
Reading. See Books and reading
"**Reading** about the Wisconsin weeping willow."
See Song
Reading room the New York Public Library.
Richard Eberhart.—JaG
Reaker, Willie
"When Paul Bunyan was ill."—KeK
A **real** story. Linda Pastan.—JaS
Real talent. Sheryl L. Nelms.—JaT
Reaney, James
Clouds ("These clouds are soft fat horses").—
DoNw
Great Lakes suite, sels.
Lake Erie.—DoNw
Lake Huron.—DoNw
Lake Michigan.—DoNw
Lake Ontario.—DoNw
Lake St. Clair.—DoNw
Lake Superior.—DoNw
June ("Now is the ox-eyed daisy out").—DoNw
Lake Erie. See Great Lakes suite
Lake Huron. See Great Lakes suite
Lake Michigan. See Great Lakes suite
Lake Ontario. See Great Lakes suite
Lake St. Clair. See Great Lakes suite
Lake Superior. See Great Lakes suite
"The **reason** I clobbered." See With my foot in
my mouth
"The **reason** I like chocolate." Nikki Giovanni.—
PrRh
Reasons why. Langston Hughes.—HuDk
Rebus valentine. Unknown.—LiVp
Recess. Lilian Moore.—MoSn
Rechargeable dry cell poem. Jim Wayne Miller.—
JaG
Recovery. Maya Angelou.—AnS
Recuerdo. Edna St. Vincent Millay.—LiSf

Recycled. Lilian Moore.—MoSn
Red (color)
Cardinal ("Red as a shout"). B. J. Esbensen.—
EsCs
King Rufus. Y. Y. Segal.—DoNw
Red. C. Zolotow.—ZoE
Strike me pink. E. Merriam.—MeF
What is red. M. O'Neill.—PrRh
When Sue wears red. L. Hughes.—HuDk
Winter cardinal. L. Moore.—MoSn
Red. Charlotte Zolotow.—ZoE
"**Red** as a shout." See Cardinal
"**Red** brick building." See The song of the factory
worker
Red-dress girl. Ann Turner.—TuS
"The **red** fence." See Snow fence
Red flower. Ann Turner.—TuS
"**Red** is a good color." See Red
"**Red** is a sunset." See What is red
Red monkey. Unknown, tr. by Ulli Beier.—HeR
"**Red** quince branch." See Piano
A **red,** red rose. Robert Burns.—LiSf
"**Red** river, red river." See Virginia
Red roses. From Tender buttons. Gertrude
Stein.—KoT
"**Red** sky at night." Mother Goose.—DaC—DeM
"A red sky at night is a shepherd's delight".—
LoR
"A **red** sky at night is a shepherd's delight". See
"Red sky at night"
"**Red** stockings, blue stockings." Mother Goose.—
LoR
The **red** wheelbarrow. William Carlos Williams.—
KoT
The **red-wing** blackbird. William Carlos
Williams.—JaD
"The **red-winged** blackbird." See Bay bank
"**Redbird,** bluebird." See They've all gone south
Redcloud, Prince
And the.—BaS
Atop.—HoBf
Now.—HoSi
Why ("We zoomed").—HoMu
The **redingote** and the vamoose. Richard Kendall
Munkittrick.—HaOf
"The **redingote** sat in the hawthorn spray." See
The redingote and the vamoose
"The **reds** of fall." See Willow yellow
Reed, Ishmael
Beware, do not read this poem.—LiWa
Reed, Langford
Hail to the town of Limerick.—BrT
A patriot.—BrT
Reedy, Carlyle
"Have you noted the white areas."—JaPo
Reese, Lizette Woodworth
A Christmas folk song.—HaOf
A little song of life.—HaOf
A street scene.—HaOf
Reeves, James
Beech leaves.—CoOu
Bobadil.—LiSf
"The bogus boo."—PrRh
The ceremonial band
Cows.—BlO—CoN
Doctor Emmanuel.—PrRh
Fireworks ("They rise like sudden fiery
flowers").—CoOu
If pigs could fly.—CoOu
The intruders.—CoOu
A mermaid song.—LiSf
Mr. Kartoffel.—PrRh
"Musetta of the mountains."—LiSf

Restaurants—*Continued*
A mock miracle. O. Herford.—BrT
On a Sunday. C. Reznikoff.—JaD
Waiters. M. A. Hoberman.—PrRh
Retired farmer. David Allan Evans.—JaPi
Return. Mark Vinz.—JaG
The **return.** Ezra Pound.—HeR
Return of the village lad. Alfred Lichtenstein, tr. by Michael Hamburger.—StG
Returning to Store Bay. Barbara Howes.—JaPi
Revenge
Frankie and Johnny. Unknown.—HeR
The Golden Vanity ("A ship I have got in the north country"). Unknown.—BlO
The Golden Vanity ("Now Jack he had a ship in the north counterie").—PlAs
Meditation on the A30. Sir J. Betjeman.—HeR
The pied piper of Hamelin. R. Browning.—LiSf
Skipper Ireson's ride. J. G. Whittier.—HaOf
"Taffy was a Welshman." Mother Goose.—DeM—HeR—LoR
Reverdure, sels. Wendell Berry
"One thing work gives".—PlSc
Reverdy, Pierre
For the moment.—KoT
Revolution
D.A.R. N. M. Bodecker.—BoPc
Revolution—American. See United States—History—Revolution
"A **revolution.**" See D.A.R.
Rexroth, Kenneth
"Oh, who will shoe your pretty little foot."—PlAs
Raccoon.—KeK
Thank you for your letter, tr. by.—LiIl
Reznikoff, Charles
"About an excavation."—CoN—KeK
The house-wreckers.—HoSs—KeK
The old men ("The fish has too many bones").—JaD
On a Sunday.—JaD
"The **rhino** is a homely beast." See The rhinoceros
Rhinoceros. Mary Ann Hoberman.—LiSf
The **rhinoceros.** Ogden Nash.—CoOu
Rhinoceroses
"I went to Wyoming one day in the spring." J. Prelutsky.—PrRi
Rhinoceros. M. A. Hoberman.—LiSf
The rhinoceros. O. Nash.—CoOu
"The two horned black rhinoceros." J. Prelutsky.—PrZ
Rhinos purple, hippos green. Michael Patrick Hearn.—PrRh
Rhodes, Sarah Betts
"God who made the earth."—LaT
Rhonda Winfrey. Mel Glenn.—GlC
Rhyme ("I like to see a thunder storm"). Elizabeth Coatsworth.—PrRh
Rhyme ("Two legs will bear a marching man"). Eleanor Farjeon.—FaE
Rhymes (about)
Cake. D. McCord.—HoMu
Catch a little rhyme. E. Merriam.—HaOf
Morning at the Post Office. N. M. Bodecker.—BoPc
One, two, three, gough ("To make some bread you must have dough"). E. Merriam.—CoN—MeSk
Rhyme ("Two legs will bear a marching man"). E. Farjeon.—FaE

The tickle rhyme ("Who's that tickling my back, said the wall"). I. Serraillier.—CoN—CoOu—PrRh
W ("The king sent for his wise men all"). J. Reeves.—CoN—FaW
Rhymes ("Two respectable rhymes"). Y. Y. Segal, tr. by Miriam Waddington.—DoNw
Rhymes ("We were talking about poems he had written"). Frank Steele.—JaPo
"The **ribs** of leaves lie in the dust." See The coming of the cold
Rice and mice. See "There was an old person of Ewell"
Rich, Adrienne
Moving in winter.—JaD
Storm warnings.—JaG
"The **rich** and rare magnolia tree." See The daisies
The **rich** lady over the sea. Unknown.—PlAs
"**Rich** man, poor man, beggarman, thief." Mother Goose.—LoR—PlSc
Richard III, sels. William Shakespeare
"Methought that I had broken from the Tower".—HeR
Richards, Laura E.
Alibazan.—HaOf
Antonio.—BrT—HaOf—PrRh
Bobbily Boo and Wollypotump.—LiSf
Eletelephony.—CoN—CoOu—FaW—HaOf—LiSf—PrRh
Kindness to animals.—CoN
The king of the hobbledygoblins.—HaOf
The mermaidens.—HaOf
The mouse ("I'm only a poor little mouse, ma'am").—HaOf
"The owl, the eel, and the warming-pan."—HaOf
Punkydoodle and Jollapin.—HaOf
"The snail and the mouse."—PrRa
"Why does it snow."—HaOf
Richards, Michael
After Christmas.—HaO
Riches. See Wealth
Richman, Norma Hope
A daughter's house.—JaG
Poem to help my father.—JaS
"**Rickenbacker** flew a Spad Thirteen." L. C. Briggs.—TrM
Rickie Miller. Mel Glenn.—GlC
Riddell, Elizabeth
The train in the night.—LaW
A **riddle.** See "In marble halls as white as milk"
A **riddle** ("Once when I was very scared"). Charlotte Zolotow.—CoN
"A **riddle,** a riddle, as I suppose." Mother Goose.—LiSf
"**Riddle** cum diddle cum dido." See Kindness to animals
"**Riddle** me, riddle, what is that." Mother Goose.—LoR
"The **riddle** silently sees its image, it spins evening." See Dusk in the country
Riddle song ("I gave my love a cherry that had no stone"). Unknown.—HeR
Riddles
"Alive without breath." J. R. R. Tolkien.—LiSf
Answers. A. Fisher.—LiSf
"As I was going to St. Ives." Mother Goose.—CoN—DeM—LoR
"As round as an apple, as deep as a cup." Mother Goose.—LiSf

Ridlon, Marci—*Continued*
Fernando.—CoN—PrRh
Garbage truck.—HoCl
Hamsters.—HoSu—PrRa
Johnny.—PrRa
My brother.—PrRh
Open hydrant.—PrRh
That was summer.—CoN—LiSf
Threats.—FrP
Rieu, Emile Victor
The flattered flying fish.—PrRh
The lesser lynx.—PrRh
The lost cat.—ChC—LiSf
Meditations of a tortoise dozing under a rosetree near a beehive at noon while a dog scampers about and a cuckoo calls from a distant wood.—LiSf
The paint box.—PrRh
Sir Smashum Uppe.—PrRh
Soliloquy of a tortoise on revisiting the lettuce beds after an interval of one hour while supposed to be sleeping in a clump of hollyhocks.—PrRh
Two people ("Two people live in Rosamund").—PrRh
"**Right** here I was nearly killed one night in February." See Solitude
Right-of-way. Aileen Fisher.—FiW
Rihaku
Taking leave of a friend.—HeR
Riley, James Whitcomb
The days gone by.—HaOf
Little orphant Annie.—HaOf
The nine little goblins.—HaOf
The raggedy man.—HaOf
A wee little worm.—PrRh
Rilke, Rainer Maria
From a childhood.—KoT
"Oh this is the animal that never was." See The unicorn
Rose, oh pure contradiction.—KoT
The unicorn, sels.
"Oh this is the animal that never was".—KoT
Rima de chocolate. Unknown.—GrT
Rima de la hermana vestiendose. Unknown.—GrT
Rimbaud, Arthur
Dawn ("I embraced the summer dawn").—KoT
Sensation.—KoT
Vowels.—KoT
"**Ring-a-ring-a-roses**". See "Ring-a-ring o' roses"
"**Ring-a-ring** o' roses." Mother Goose.—DaC—DeM
"Ring-a-ring-a-roses".—LoR
"**Ring** out the old." See Happy new year
"**Ring** out, wild bells, to the wild sky." From In memoriam. Alfred Tennyson.—LiNe
"**Ring** the bell." Mother Goose.—RaT
"**Ring** the big bells." See Contemporary announcement
"A **ringing** tire iron." See Some good things to be said for the iron age
Rings. See Jewelry
Rio de Janiero, Brazil
The burglar of Babylon. E. Bishop.—HeR
Ríos, Alberto
Sundays visiting.—JaS
Riots
Trouble in town. X. J. Kennedy.—KeF
"**Ripe,** ripe strawberries." See Strawberries
Ripley, Elizabeth
Jammy.—BrT

Ripley, Sherman
The raggedy dog.—PrRa
"**Rippling** green and gold and brown." See The lake
"**Rise** up and look." See Sun for breakfast
"**Rise** up, rise up, my mate." See Autumn song of the goose
The **river** ("Quiver shiver"). Charlotte Zolotow.—ZoE
The **river** ("Winter"). Don Welch.—JaS
The **river** is a piece of sky. John Ciardi.—LiSf
The **river-merchant's** wife, a letter ("While my hair was still cut straight across my forehead"). Ezra Pound.—HeR—KoT
River moons. Carl Sandburg.—HoRa
River winding. Charlotte Zolotow.—PrRh
Rivers. See also names of rivers, as Mississippi River
In the deep channel. W. Stafford.—HeR
Indian names. L. H. Sigourney.—HaOf
Lake Huron. From Great Lakes suite. J. Reaney.—DoNw
Molasses river. R. K. Munkittrick.—HaOf
The Negro speaks of rivers. L. Hughes.—HaOf—HuDk—LiSf
On the Congo. H. E. Martinson.—HeR
A prayer for rivers. K. Wilson.—JaG
"Rain into river." X. J. Kennedy.—KeF
The rapid. C. Sangster.—DoNw
The river ("Quiver shiver"). C. Zolotow.—ZoE
The river ("Winter"). D. Welch.—JaS
The river is a piece of sky. J. Ciardi.—LiSf
River winding. C. Zolotow.—PrRh
The river's song. C. Kingsley.—DaC
River's song. H. Behn.—HoCb
"Runs all day and never walks." Mother Goose.—LiSf
"The tide in the rive." E. Farjeon.—BlO
Virginia. From Landscapes. T. S. Eliot.—HeR
"Was it for this." From The prelude. W. Wordsworth.—HeR
Weeping willow. M. C. Livingston.—LiMp
Wide river. L. Hughes.—HuDk
The **river's** song. Charles Kingsley.—DaC
River's song. Harry Behn.—HoCb
The **riveter.** Mabel Watts.—PrRh
Road. William Stanley Merwin.—JaPo
"The **road.**" See Winding road
The **road** not taken. Robert Frost.—KoS
Roads and streets
Autobahnmotorwayautoroute. A. Mitchell.—HeR
Baby. L. Hughes.—HuDk
"Beside the road." Basho.—KoT
Blind alley. E. Farjeon.—FaE
Bound no'th blues. L. Hughes.—HuDk
Breakin'. A. Turner.—TuS
City streets and country roads. E. Farjeon.—FaE
City traffic. E. Merriam.—LiSf—MeSk
Clean. A. Turner.—TuS
Close call. X. J. Kennedy.—KeF
Gloire. N. M. Bodecker.—BoPc
The great figure. W. C. Williams.—KoT
How I helped the traveler. J. Ciardi.—CiD
The idiot. K. Wilson.—JaPi
New England road. N. M. Bodecker.—BoPc
The old Sussex road. I. Serraillier.—CoN
"One day in Oklahoma." J. Prelutsky.—PrRi
The road not taken. R. Frost.—KoS
Sierra redwoods, highway 101. M. C. Livingston.—LiMp
Song of the open road. O. Nash.—JaPo
A street scene. L. W. Reese.—HaOf

Rodgers, William Robert
Carol ("Deep in the fading leaves of night").—HaO

Roebling, John (about)
"Roebling, his life and mind reprieved enough." From The bridge from Brooklyn. R. Henri.—PlEd
"**Roebling**, his life and mind reprieved enough." From The bridge from Brooklyn. Raymond Henri.—PlEd

Roethke, Theodore
The apparition.—PlAs
The bat ("By day the bat is cousin to the mouse").—HaOf—LiSf—LiWa—PrRh
The ceiling.—KeK—PlEd
The chair.—JaT
Child on top of a greenhouse.—KeK
The coming of the cold.—HaO
The cow ("There once was a cow with a double udder").—HaOf
Dinky.—HaOf—LiSf—PrRh
The donkey ("I had a donkey, that was all right").—HaOf—PrRa
Double feature.—JaD
The dream, sels.
　　"I met her as a blossom on a stem".—McL
　　"Love is not love until love's vulnerable".—McL
　　"She came toward me in a flowing air".—McL
　　"She held her body steady in the wind".—McL
Elegy ("Her face like a rain-beaten stone on the day she rolled off").—JaD
The flight ("At Woodlawn I heard the dead cry"). See The lost son
Frau Bauman, Frau Schmidt, and Frau Schwartze.—PlSc
"I met her as a blossom on a stem." See The dream
The lamb ("The lamb just says, I am").—LiSf
The lizard ("The time to tickle a lizard").—PrRh
The lost son, sels.
　　The flight ("At Woodlawn I heard the dead cry").—HeR
"Love is not love until love's vulnerable." See The dream
The meadow mouse.—HeR—LiSf
The minimal.—FaTh—HeR
"Mips and ma the mooly moo." See Praise to the end
My dim-wit cousin.—JaD
Night crow.—JaD
Night journey.—KeK
Old florist.—PlSc
Praise to the end, sels.
　　"Mips and ma the mooly moo".—HeR
"Running lightly over spongy ground."—HeR
The Saginaw song.—HeR
The serpent.—PrRh
"She came toward me in a flowing air." See The dream
"She held her body steady in the wind." See The dream
The sloth.—HaOf—PrRh
The visitant.—HeR
The waking ("I strolled across").—KoT
The yak ("There was a most odious yak").—LiSf
"**Roger** came to Beaver." See Pet rock

"**Roger** is a friend of mine, it was his idea." See Arf, said Sandy
Roger the dog. Ted Hughes.—PrRh
Rogers, John
John Rogers' exhortation to his children.—HaOf
Roll, Alabama, roll. Unknown.—PlAs
"**Roll** gently, old dump truck." Charlotte Pomerantz.—PoA
Roller-coasters
Flight of the roller-coaster. R. Souster.—DoNw
"**Rollo** says, I can bring down rain." See Rollo's miracle
Rollo's miracle. Paul Zimmer.—JaG
Roman presents. Martial, tr. by James Michie.—HaO
A **Roman** thank you letter. Martial, tr. by James Michie.—HaO
Romance. See also Adventure and adventurers; Knights and knighthood; Love
Rome, Italy
The eternal city. A. R. Ammons.—PlEd
Romeo and Juliet, sels. William Shakespeare
"I dream'd a dream tonight".—HoUn
"O, then, I see Queen Mab hath been with you".—LiWa
"See how she leans her cheek upon her hand".—HoUn
"She is the fairies' midwife, and she comes".—HeR
"What's in a name, that which we call a rose".—HoUn
Ronnie Evans. Mel Glenn.—GlCd
Roof. Sylvia Cassedy.—CaR
"The **roofs** over the shops." See Christmas eve
Roofscape. X. J. Kennedy.—KeF
A **room** in the past. Ted Kooser.—JaS
Rooms
Closet. S. Cassedy.—CaR
The country bedroom. F. Cornford.—BlO
Den. S. Cassedy.—CaR
Elevator. S. Cassedy.—CaR
Green candles. H. Wolfe.—PrRh
Haunted room. S. Cassedy.—CaR
"I wish that my room had a floor." G. Burgess.—HaOf
Imaginary room. S. Cassedy.—CaR
Keep. S. Cassedy.—CaR
Office. S. Cassedy.—CaR
Parlor. S. Cassedy.—CaR
Quiet room. S. Cassedy.—CaR
Vestibule. S. Cassedy.—CaR
Your room. S. Cassedy.—CaR
Rooney, Pat
"Is that Mr. Riley, can anyone tell."—TrM
Rooster. N. M. Bodecker.—BoSs
"The **rooster's**." See Rooster
Roosters and hens. Harry Behn.—HoCb
The **root** canal. Marge Piercy.—JaD
Rope. Eve Merriam.—MeHa
Rope and drum. Robert Currie.—JaS
Rope rhyme. Eloise Greenfield.—LiSf
"The **rope** swings in." See Red-dress girl
Ropes
Rope. E. Merriam.—MeHa
Roscoe, William
The butterfly's ball.—CoOu—PrRh
"**Rose** became madder." See Strike me pink
The **rose** family. Robert Frost.—HaOf—KoS
"The **rose** is a rose." See The rose family
"The **rose** is red, the violet's blue." Mother Goose.—DeM
Rose, oh pure contradiction. Rainer Maria Rilke.—KoT

"**Rose**, oh pure contradiction, joy." See Rose, oh pure contradiction
The **rose** on my cake. Karla Kuskin.—LiIl—LiSf
The **rose** thieves. Vasco Popa, tr. by Anne Pennington.—HeR
Roseliep, Raymond
  "Child."—KeK
  "Sky."—KeK
Rosemarie Stewart. Mel Glenn.—GlC
"**Rosemary** green." Mother Goose.—AlH
Rosen, Michael
  Before I count fifteen.—FaW
  Christmas dinner.—HaO
  Don't tell.—RoC
  Egg talk.—BeD
  "Humpty Dumpty."—BeD
  "I'm alone in the evening."—PrRh
  This ship.—FaW
Rosenzweig, Efraim
  Dreidel song.—PrRa
Roses
  A flower given to my daughter. J. Joyce.—HeR
  I am Rose. G. Stein.—ChG—HaOf—KeK—PrRh
  Red roses. From Tender buttons. G. Stein.—KoT
  The rose family. R. Frost.—HaOf—KoS
  Rose, oh pure contradiction. R. M. Rilke.—KoT
  The rose thieves. V. Popa.—HeR
  Roses. D. H. Lawrence.—PrBb
  The second birth of roses. E. Farjeon.—FaE
  Seven sisters roses. E. Farjeon.—FaE
  The sick rose. W. Blake.—HeR
  "What's in a name, that which we call a rose." From Romeo and Juliet. W. Shakespeare.—HoUn
Roses. David Herbert Lawrence.—PrBb
"**Roses** are red." Mother Goose.—DeM—LiVp—LoR
Rosh Hashanah
  Holy days. V. Worth.—LiPj
  Rosh Hashanah eve. H. Philip.—LiPj
Rosh Hashanah eve. Harry Philip.—LiPj
Ross, Abram Bunn
  Two in bed.—CoN
  "The way they scrub."—PrRa
Ross, Alan
  Radar.—JaD
Ross, Charles Henry
  Jack.—DaC—PrRh
  John, Tom, and James.—PrRh
Ross, W.W.E.
  The diver ("I would like to dive").—DoNw
  "There's a fire in the forest."—DoNw
Rossetti, Christina Georgina
  A birthday ("My heart is like a singing bird").—BlO—KoT
  "Brown and furry". See Caterpillar
  Caterpillar.—FrP—PrRh
    "Brown and furry".—LiSf
  A chill.—ChB
  A Christmas carol. See "In the bleak midwinter"
  The city mouse and the garden mouse.—CoN
  Flint.—PrRh
  "Hopping frog, hop here and be seen."—BlO
  "The horses of the sea."—CoN
  "Hurt no living thing."—FaTh—HoSu—PrRh
  "If a pig wore a wig."—LiSf
  Immalee.—BlO
  "In the bleak midwinter."—RoC
    A Christmas carol.—DaC
  Last rites.—PrRh

  Lullaby ("Flowers are closed and lambs are sleeping").—LaW
  Mirage.—McL
  "Mix a pancake."—CoN—FrP—LiSf—PrRa
    The pancake.—ChG
  My gift. See "What can I give him"
  The pancake. See "Mix a pancake"
  The rainbow ("Boats sail on the rivers").—DaC
  The skylark.—DaC
  The sound of the wind.—BlO—CoOu
  The swallow ("Fly away, fly away, over the sea").—DaC
  "What can I give him."—LiCp
    My gift.—LaT
  What is pink.—CoOu—DaC—PrRh
  "Who has seen the wind."—BlO—CoN—FrP—LiSf—PrRh
    The wind.—DaC
  The wind. See "Who has seen the wind"
Rossetti, Dante Gabriel
  A sea spell for a picture.—LiWa
  "Rosy Betsy, blue eyed Milly." See The willow wren
  "A rosy shield upon its back." See The dead crab
Rothenberg, Jerome K.
  "In beauty may I walk", tr. by.—HeR
  The seven, tr. by.—HeR
A **round**. Eve Merriam.—MeSk
"**Round** about, round about." Unknown.—RaT
"**Round** about the rosebush." Unknown.—RaT
"**Round** about there." Unknown.—RaT
"**Round** and round." Unknown.—RaT
"**Round** blank." See Zero
"**Round** the Maypole dance about." See For a dance
The **rousing** canoe song. Hermia Fraser.—DoNw
Routine. Arthur Guiterman.—PrRh—TrM
Rover. William Stafford.—JaT
"A **row** of pearls." See Seeds
"The **row** oficicles along the gutter." See Beyond words
Rowe, Albert
  Elegy for Delina.—ChC
  "Terry."—ChC
Rowing. Ed Ochester.—JaS
"**Rub-a-dub-dub**." Mother Goose.—DaC—DeM—FaW—LoR—WaC
"The **ruby** throated hummingbird." See The hummingbird
Ruckert, Friedrich
  Barbarossa.—LiWa
"**Ruda**, Ruda." See Woman's prayer
Rudolph is tired of the city. Gwendolyn Brooks.—PrRh
"**Rudolph** Reed was oaken." See The ballad of Rudolph Reed
"**Rudy** rode a unicorn." Jack Prelutsky.—PrRi
Rudzewicz, Eugene
  The gnat.—JaT
Ruffin, Paul
  Cleaning the well.—JaS
  Grandma chooses her plot at the county cemetery.—JaG
  Grandpa's picture.—JaS
Ruins. Harry Behn.—HoCb
Rukeyser, Muriel
  Crayon house.—PlEd
  Mendings.—PlSc
  Painters.—PlEd
Rulers. See also Princes and princesses; also names of rulers, as Mary, Queen of Scots
  "As I was going by Charing Cross." Mother Goose.—BlO

Rulers.—*Continued*

Barbarossa. F. Ruckert.—LiWa

"The barge she sat in, like a burnish'd throne." From Antony and Cleopatra. W. Shakespeare.—HoUn

Carol of the brown king. L. Hughes.—LiCp

Columbus to Ferdinand. P. Freneau.—HaOf

Engraved on the collar of a dog, which I gave to his Royal Highness. A. Pope.—KoT

His highness's dog.—PrRh (unat.)

Epigram engraved on the collar of a dog.— CoN—KeK

Epitaph on a tyrant. W. H. Auden.—HeR

"The hand that signed a paper felled a city." D. Thomas.—HeR

The haunted palace. E. A. Poe.—LiWa

"Hector Protector was dressed all in green." Mother Goose.—AlH—DeM—LoR

Henry and Mary. R. Graves.—LiIl—LiSf

History ("Willy, Willy, Harry, Steve"). Unknown.—DaC

"I am Queen Anne, of whom 'tis said." Unknown.—DaC

The ice-king. A. B. Demille.—DoNw

If I were a king. A. A. Milne.—CoOu

The innovator. S. V. Benét.—PlEd

The king. Unknown.—BrT

The king of Magla and Vlaga. C. Pomerantz.— PoI

The king of the hobbledygoblins. L. E. Richards.—HaOf

King Rufus. Y. Y. Segal.—DoNw

"King Tut." X. J. Kennedy.—LiSf

The king's breakfast. A. A. Milne.—FaW—LiSf

Kubla Khan. S. T. Coleridge.—LiSf—LiWa— PlEd

"Lavender blue and rosemary green." Mother Goose.—LoR

"Little King Boggen, he built a fine hall." Mother Goose.—BlPi—LoR

"Little King Pippin." Mother Goose.—DeM

Mary Stuart. E. Muir.—HeR

"The mighty emperor Ch'in Shih Huang." Unknown.—DeD

The old king. W. De la Mare.—PlAs

Old King Cabbage. R. K. Munkittrick.—HaOf

"Old King Cole." Mother Goose.—DeM— FaW—LoR

Ozymandias. P. B. Shelley.—HeR

The pelican chorus. E. Lear.—LiH

"Pussycat, pussycat, where have you been." Mother Goose.—AlH—DeM—FaW—LoR

Queen Nefertiti. Unknown.—PrRh

The Queen of Elfan's nourice. Unknown.—PlAs

"The Queen of Hearts." Mother Goose.—DaC— DeM—LoR

"Sing a song of sixpence." Mother Goose.— AlH—DaC—DeM—FaW—LoR

"There once was a king." Unknown.—FaW

Threnody. G. T. Lanigan.—DoNw

"When good king Arthur ruled this land." Mother Goose.—AlH

The wizard in the well. H. Behn.—HoCb

The yak ("For hours the princess would not play or sleep"). V. Sheard.—DoNw

Rules

The garden of love. W. Blake.—HeR

I know the rules. A. Adoff.—AdA

"My mother says I'm sickening." J. Prelutsky.— PrNk

No holes marred. S. Douglas.—PrRh

Reflection on ingenuity. O. Nash.—HeR

Rules ("All schools"). E. Farjeon.—FaE

Rules ("Do not jump on ancient uncles"). K. Kuskin.—PrRh

Signs. N. M. Bodecker.—BoPc

Traffic rule I. N. M. Bodecker.—BoPc

"When I have a little girl." C. Zolotow.—ZoE

Why I did not reign. E. Merriam.—MeSk

Rules ("All schools"). Eleanor Farjeon.—FaE

Rules ("Do not jump on ancient uncles"). Karla Kuskin.—PrRh

"**Rumbling** in the chimneys." See Windy nights

The **rumbly** night train. Charlotte Pomerantz.— PoA

Rumi

"Love, you alone have been with us."—McL

"**Rumpitty** Tumpitty Rumpitty Tum." Jack Prelutsky.—PrRi

Run a little. James Reeves.—PrRa

"**Run** a little this way." See Run a little

The **runaway** ("I made peanut butter sandwiches"). Bobbi Katz.—PrRh

Runaway ("I think today"). William Wise.—PrRa

The **runaway** ("Once, when the snow of the year was beginning to fall"). Robert Frost.—KoS— LiSf

The **runner**. Walt Whitman.—KeK

Runners and running

Crystal Rowe. M. Glenn.—GlCd

"I am the running girl." A. Adoff.—LiSf

A lady track star. R. Blount.—BrT

Run a little. J. Reeves.—PrRa

The runner. W. Whitman.—KeK

"Running lightly over spongy ground." T. Roethke.—HeR

What do they do to you in distant places. M. Bell.—JaPi

"**Running** down the tracks one day." See The rescue

"**Running** lightly over spongy ground." Theodore Roethke.—HeR

"**Runs** all day and never walks." Mother Goose.— LiSf

Rural recreation. Lillian Morrison.—KeK

"The **rural** runcible raven." From An animal alphabet. Edward Lear.—LiH

Russ, Lisa

Piano ("Red quince branch").—JaPo

Russell Hodges. Mel Glenn.—GlCd

"**Rusted** and without tires." See 1937 Ford convertible

"**Rustily** creak the crickets, Jack Frost came down." See Jack Frost

"The **rusty** spigot." See Onomatopoeia and onomatopoeia II

Ruth Luce and Bruce Booth. N. M. Bodecker.— BoSs

Rutherford McDowell. Edgar Lee Masters.—PlEd

Rutsala, Vern

Bijou.—JaD

The fat man.—JaD

Marriage contract.—JaD

The new house.—JaG

Sunday ("Up early while everyone sleeps").— JaD

The war of the worlds.—JaPi

The world ("I move back by shortcut").—JaPi

Rylant, Cynthia

Band practice.—RyW

Beaver ("Coming to it from the country").— RyW

The brain surgeon.—RyW

Cassius.—RyW

Rylant, Cynthia—*Continued*
  Catholics.—RyW
  Forgotten.—RyW
  General delivery.—RyW
  The great beyond.—RyW
  Henry's market.—RyW
  Holiness.—RyW
  Jimmy's dad.—RyW
  The Kool-Kup.—RyW
  Little short legs.—RyW
  Mad dog.—RyW
  Mike and Major.—RyW
  Mr. Dill.—RyW
  Mr. Lafon.—RyW
  Pet rock.—RyW
  Pink belly.—RyW
  PTA ("Seemed like everybody's mother").—RyW
  The rescue.—RyW
  Rocky Trailer's grandmother's garage.—RyW
  Sam the shoe shop man.—RyW
  Saved.—RyW
  Spelling bee.—RyW
  Steve.—RyW
  Swearing.—RyW
  Teenagers.—RyW
  Wax lips.—RyW
  The world ("Went to Florida once").—RyW
Ryota
  "No one spoke."—KoT
  "They look."—KoT

S

S. From A bestiary of the garden for children who should know better. Phyllis Gotlieb.—DoNw
Saadi, Rose
  A factory rainbow.—PlSc
Sabines, Jaime
  You have what I look for.—McL
"The **sacred** blue corn-seed I am planting." From Songs in the garden of the house god. Unknown.—LiTp
Sacrifices
  And although the little mermaid sacrificed everthing to win the love of the prince, the prince, alas, decided to wed another. J. Viorst.—ViI
The **sad** boy. Laura Riding.—HeR
A **sad** song about Greenwich Village. Frances Park.—PrRh
Sad sweet story. Norah Smaridge.—HoMu
Sadie Snatt. Jack Prelutsky.—PrSr
Sadness. See also Despair; Grief; Melancholy
  Anna playing in a graveyard. C. Gilman.—HaOf
  Being sad. O. V. Kanik.—McL
  Infant sorrow. W. Blake.—HeR
  Little bird ("Little bird, little bird"). J. Cunningham.—FaTh
  Poem ("I loved my friend"). L. Hughes.—CoN—HoBf—HuDk—JaD—LiIl—LiSf
  Since Hanna moved away. J. Viorst.—HoBf—PrRh—ViI
Safe ("Come, stir the fire"). James Walker.—HaO
Safe in bed. Mother Goose.—ChB

Safety
  Psalm 23 ("The Lord is my shepherd, I shall not want"). From The book of psalms. Bible/Old Testament.—LiSf
    Psalm 23 ("The Lord to me a shepherd is").—HaOf
  Psalm 121. From The book of psalms. Bible/Old Testament.—HaOf
Safety pin. Valerie Worth.—FaTh—LiSf
Sage, Betty
  Humming birds.—PrRa
The **Saginaw** song. Theodore Roethke.—HeR
Saibara
  Deep in the mountains.—StG
"**Said** a cat, as he playfully threw." See Only teasing
"**Said** a fellow from North Philadelphia." See Church bells
"**Said** a lachrymose Labrador seal." See The feminine seal
"**Said** a lady beyond Pompton Lakes." See The car's in the hall
"**Said** a lady who wore a swell cape." See Nature and art
"**Said** a maid, I will marry for lucre." See Money makes the marriage
"**Said** a rooster, I'd have you all know." See Know your true worth
"**Said** a saucy young skunk to a gnu." See The skunk to the gnu
"**Said** a sporty young person named Groat." See A sporty young person
"**Said** an asp to an adder named Rhea." See Serpentine verse
"**Said** Dorothy Hughes to Helen Hocking." William Jay Smith.—KeK
"**Said** Jan to Feb." See January one
"**Said** little Ruth Luce." See Ruth Luce and Bruce Booth
"**Said** the crab, 'tis not beauty or birth." See The oratorical crab
"**Said** the duck to the kangaroo." See The duck and the kangaroo
"**Said** the elephant to the giraffe." See The elephant and the giraffe
"**Said** the first little chicken." See Five little chickens
"**Said** the lion, on music I dote." See The musical lion
"**Said** the little boy, sometimes I drop my spoon." See The little boy and the old man
"**Said** the mole, you would never suppose." See The mendacious mole
"**Said** the mouse with scholastical hat." See The scholastic mouse
"**Said** the rabbit to the hop toad." See The toad and the rabbit
"**Said** the scorpion of hate." Carl Sandburg.—HoRa
"**Said** the shark to the flying fish over the phone." See The flattered flying fish
"**Said** the spider, in tones of distress." See The eternal feminine
"**Said** the table to the chair." See The table and the chair
"**Said** the turtle to the turkey." See The turkey's wattle
"**Said** the wind to the moon." See The wind and the moon
Sail, Lawrence
  Christmas night.—HaO

"**Sail** of Claustra, Aelis, Azalais." See The alchemist
Sailing. See Boats and boating; Ships
Sailor. Langston Hughes.—HuDk
The **sailor** boy. Alfred Tennyson.—PlAs
Sailors. See Seafaring life
Sailor's carol. Charles Causley.—HaO
"**St.** Dunstan, as the story goes." Mother Goose.—DeM—LoR
Saint Francis and the sow. Galway Kinnell.—HeR
Saint Patrick's Day
  Saint Patrick's day. M. C. Livingston.—LiCe
  The wearin' o' the green. Unknown.—PlAs
  Wearing of the green. A. Fisher.—PrRh
Saint Patrick's day. Myra Cohn Livingston.—LiCe
St. Paul's steeple. Unknown.—DaC
Saint Stephen's Day
  The feast o' Saint Stephen. R. Sawyer.—HaO
  The feast of Stephen. K. Nichols.—HaO
  Good King Wenceslas. Unknown.—RoC
  St. Stephen's day. P. Dickinson.—HaO
St. Stephen's day. Patric Dickinson.—HaO
St. Swithin's chair. Sir Walter Scott.—LiWa
St. Thomas. Ferdinand G. Christgau.—BrT
Saint Valentine's Day
  An angry valentine. M. C. Livingston.—LiVp
  Be my non-Valentine. E. Merriam.—MeSk
  Conversation hearts. V. Worth.—LiVp
  "Country bumpkin." C. Watson.—LiSf
  Going steady. I. Serraillier.—LiVp
  "Good morrow to you, Valentine." Mother Goose.—DeM
  "He sent his love a valentine." D. McCord.—LiVp
  "I made a giant valentine." J. Prelutsky.—PrIv
  "I made my dog a valentine." J. Prelutsky.—PrIv
  "I only got one valentine." J. Prelutsky.—PrIv
  "I sow hempseed." Unknown.—LiVp
  "It's Valentine's day." J. Prelutsky.—PrIv
  The kangaroo's courtship. J. Yolen.—LiVp
  Love at sea. J. P. Lewis.—LiVp
  Mother's chocolate valentine. J. Prelutsky.—PrIv
  My father's valentine. J. Prelutsky.—PrIv
  My special cake. J. Prelutsky.—PrIv
  "My valentine." M. C. Livingston.—LiCe
  "Our classroom has a mailbox." J. Prelutsky.—PrIv
  A penny valentine. Unknown.—LiVp
  "Phoebe in a rosebush." C. Watson.—CoN—WaC
  "The rose is red, the violet's blue." Mother Goose.—DeM
  "Roses are red." Mother Goose.—DeM—LiVp—LoR
  "There's someone I know." J. Prelutsky.—PrIv
  "Tomorrow is Saint Valentine's day." From Hamlet. W. Shakespeare.—LiSf—LiVp
    Song.—CoN
  Valentine ("Chipmunks jump and"). D. Hall.—CoN—McL
  Valentine ("I got a valentine from Timmy"). S. Silverstein.—PrRh
  Valentine ("If all the whole world's taxicabs"). X. J. Kennedy.—KeF—LiVp
  A valentine birthday. B. J. Esbensen.—LiVp
  Valentine chocolates. V. Worth.—LiVp
  A valentine for my best friend. J. Prelutsky.—PrIv
  A valentine for my teacher. J. Prelutsky.—PrIv
  Valentine thoughts for Mari. E. Di Pasquale.—LiVp

  Valentines. H. Dumas.—LiVp
Saints. See also names of saints, as Luke
  "Matthew, Mark, Luke and John, bless the bed that I lie on." Mother Goose.—DaC—DeM
  On St. Winefred. G. M. Hopkins.—PlSc
  "St. Dunstan, as the story goes." Mother Goose.—DeM—LoR
  Saint Francis and the sow. G. Kinnell.—HeR
  Upon Fairford windows. R. Corbett.—PlEd
Salesmen
  Archie B. McCall. J. Prelutsky.—PrNk
Salinas, Pedro
  "Now I love you." See Razon de amor
  Razon de amor, sels.
    "Now I love you".—McL
Sally and Manda. Alice B. Campbell.—FrP—PrRh
"**Sally** and Manda are two little lizards." See Sally and Manda
"**Sally** go round the sun." Mother Goose.—DeM—FaW—LoR
"**Sally** is gone that was so kindly." See Ha'nacker Mill
Salmon, Graham
  "Lord Jesus."—LaT
"The **salmon** lying in the depths of Llyn Llifon." See The ancients of the world
"A **salmon** remarked to his mate." See Sliding scale
Salt
  Salt ("Salt for white"). R. Francis.—FaTh
  Salt ("Salt is scorched water that the sun has scorched"). D. H. Lawrence.—PrBb
Salt ("Salt for white"). Robert Francis.—FaTh
Salt ("Salt is scorched water that the sun has scorched"). David Herbert Lawrence.—PrBb
"**Salt** for white." See Salt
"**Salt** is scorched water that the sun has scorched." See Salt
Salt pilgrimage. Unknown.—BiSp
"The **salty** wind." See By the sea
"**Sam** owned the Beaver Shoe Shop." See Sam the shoe shop man
"**Sam,** Sam, the butcher man." Mother Goose.—DaC
Sam the shoe shop man. Cynthia Rylant.—RyW
Samantha speaking. David McCord.—LiTp
"The **same** leaves over and over again." See In hardwood groves
"**Sammy** Smith would drink and eat." Mother Goose.—FaW
Samuel. Bobbi Katz.—PrRh
"**Sana,** sana colita de rana." See Colita de rana
Sand
  At the sea-side. R. L. Stevenson.—CoN—FaW
  Baby's baking. E. Stein.—PrRa
  Little things ("Little drops of water"). J. A. Carney.—DaC
    "Little drops of water".—LoR (unat.)
  Mine. L. Moore.—MoSn
  Rocks. F. P. Heide.—CoN
  Sand ("I sat down on my blanket"). J. Prelutsky.—PrWi
  Sand ("The sand is the sand, till you take it"). E. Farjeon.—FaE
  Sand castle. C. A. Keremes.—HoSe
  The sand painters. B. Belitt.—PlEd
  Sandpiper ("The roaring alongside he takes for granted"). E. Bishop.—HeR
  Sitting in the sand. K. Kuskin.—HoSe—HoSi
Sand ("I sat down on my blanket"). Jack Prelutsky.—PrWi

Sandburg, Carl—*Continued*
Working girls.—PlSc
Young sea.—HoRa
Sanders, Donald T.
Poem for Shane on her brother's birthday.—KoT
"The **sandman** put it in his sack." See Dream
"**Sandpaper** kisses." See Cat kisses
The **sandpiper** ("Across the lonely beach we flit"). Celia Thaxter.—HaOf
The **sandpiper** ("Along the sea edge, like a gnome"). Witter Bynner.—PrRh
The **sandpiper** ("At the edge of tide"). Frances Frost.—PrRh
The **sandpiper** ("Look at the little sandpiper"). Charlotte Zolotow.—FaTh—HoSe
Sandpiper ("The roaring alongside he takes for granted"). Elizabeth Bishop.—HeR
Sandpipers
A certain sandpiper. X. J. Kennedy.—JaT
The sandpiper ("Across the lonely beach we flit"). C. Thaxter.—HaOf
The sandpiper ("Along the sea edge, like a gnome"). W. Bynner.—PrRh
The sandpiper ("At the edge of tide"). F. Frost.—PrRh
The sandpiper ("Look at the little sandpiper"). C. Zolotow.—FaTh—HoSe
Sandpiper ("The roaring alongside he takes for granted"). E. Bishop.—HeR
"**Sandra** built a castle out of sand." See Sand castle
The **sands** of Dee. Charles Kingsley.—BlO
Sanford Evans Pierce. Mel Glenn.—GlC
Sangster, Charles
The rapid.—DoNw
Sanpu
"May rains."—KoT
Sansom, Clive
The innkeeper's wife.—HaO
Snowflakes ("And did you know").—HaO
Santa Ana. Unknown.—PlAs
Santa Claus
Christmas eve ("He is coming"). M. C. Livingston.—LiCe
Christmas prayer. D. McCord.—LiCp
December, prayer to St. Nicholas. J. Heath-Stubbs.—HaO
Don't tell. M. Rosen.—RoC
Mrs. Kriss Kringle. E. M. Thomas.—HaOf
Reindeer report. U. A. Fanthorpe.—HaO
A visit from St. Nicholas ("'Twas the night before Christmas, when all through the house"). C. C. Moore.—CoN—HaO—HaOf—LiCp—LiSf—PrRh—RoC
"A woman named Mrs. S. Claus." J. P. Lewis.—LiCp
Santa Fe sketches, sels. Carl Sandburg
"In April the little farmers go out in the foothills".—HoRa
Sappho
Seizure.—McL
"**Sarah** Cynthia Sylvia Stout." See Sarah Cynthia Sylvia Stout would not take the garbage out
Sarah Cynthia Sylvia Stout would not take the garbage out. Shel Silverstein.—HaOf—LiSf
Sarah Samantha. Unknown.—BrT
Sarett, Lew
Four little foxes.—PrRh
The wolf cry.—PrRh
Sargent, William D.
Wind wolves.—PrRh
Sarkozi, Matyas

A Hungarian nursery rhyme, tr. by.—FaW
Sarton, May
"After the palaces." See A nobleman's house
Boulder dam.—PlSc
A nobleman's house, sels.
"After the palaces".—PlEd
Prayer before work.—PlSc
Sassoon, Siegfried
The case for the miners.—PlSc
A post-mortem.—JaD
Satan. See Devil
Sato, Hiroaki
Deep in the mountains, tr. by.—StG
Love ("From Prince Atsumichi"), tr. by.—McL
Saturday. Myra Cohn Livingston.—LiWo
Saturday in the park. Barbara Juster Esbensen.—EsCs
Saturday's child. Countee Cullen.—PlSc
"**Saucy** little ocelot." Jack Prelutsky.—LiSf—PrSr
Saul Steiner. Mel Glenn.—GlC
Sauls, Roger
My grandfather burning cornfields.—JaS
Saved. Cynthia Rylant.—RyW
"**Saw** a movie about a girl in a Southern town." See Mad dog
"**Saw** a play once." See Morning
"The **sawmill** is here already." See Progress
Sawmills
Progress. C. Martin.—JaPo
Sawyer, Ruth
Christmas morn.—HaO—RoC
The feast o' Saint Stephen.—HaO
Saxe, John Godfrey
The blind men and the elephant.—CoOu—HaOf
Saxon, Dan
"Walking in the rain."—JaD
"**Say** not of me that weakly I declined." Robert Louis Stevenson.—PlEd
Sayers, Frances Clarke
Who calls.—LiSf
Scaffolding. Seamus Heaney.—JaG
Scannell, Vernon
Cat ("My cat has got no name").—ChC
"**Scant** is the holly." See The brown birds
Scarecrows
Crow wonders. L. Moore.—MoSn
The dressmaker's dummy as scarecrow. B. Howes.—JaD
The lonely scarecrow. J. Kirkup.—BlO
"Today is a day to crow about." J. Prelutsky.—PrNk
Scene. Charlotte Zolotow.—HoSi
Scheele, Roy
August ("In waves of heat").—JaPo
Dancer.—JaG
Fishing Blue Creek.—JaPo
The gap in the cedar.—JaPi
A kitchen memory.—JaS
Nothing but net.—JaT
Poppies.—JaPo
Schlichter, Norman C.
A sledding song.—FrP
Schmeltz, Susan Alton
Paper dragons.—PrRh
The **scholar.** Austin Clarke.—HeR
The **scholastic** mouse. A. B. P.—BrT
Schonborg, Virginia
Crowds.—PrRh
Stickball.—PrRh
School. See also Teachers and teaching
Allen Greshner. M. Glenn.—GlC
Alley cat school. F. Asch.—PrRh
Alphabet. E. Farjeon.—FaE

School.—*Continued*
"Snow makes a new land." K. Mizumura.—LiSf
Song to the ninth grade. P. C. Holahan.—PlAs
Spade Scharnweber. D. Welch.—JaPi
Steve. C. Rylant.—RyW
Stuart Rieger. M. Glenn.—GlC
Susan Tulchin. M. Glenn.—GlC
Timothy Winters. C. Causley.—HeR
Veronica Castell. M. Glenn.—GlCd
Walking past the school at night. B. J. Esbensen.—EsCs
We real cool. G. Brooks.—KeK
What the stone dreams. J. B. Hathaway.—JaG
"When for school o'er Little Field with its brook and wooden brig." From Remembrances. J. Clare.—PlSc
"When they asked." A. Adoff.—AdA
While dissecting frogs in biology class Scrut discovers the intricacies of the scooped neckline in his lab partner's dress. G. Roberts.—JaG
Whitley at three o'clock. J. Worley. JaG
Who's who. J. Viorst.—ViI
Why I did not reign. E. Merriam.—MeSk
Wiggly giggles. S. J. Crossen.—PrRh
Yawning. E. Farjeon.—FaE—PrRh
Zimmer in grade school. P. Zimmer.—KeK
School bell. Eleanor Farjeon.—FaE
"The school-bell rings." See Nine o'clock
School buses. Russell Hoban.—LiSf
School day. Charlotte Zolotow.—ZoE
"The school greets me like a series." See Poet in residence at a county school
School mornings. Richard J. Margolis.—MaS
The schoolbus comes before the sun. Robert Currie.—JaT—JaT
"A schoolma'am of much reputation." See No talking shop
The schoolmaster and the truants. John Brownjohn.—HaOf
"School's all right if you don't take it seriously." See Benjamin Heywood
Schulz, Lillian
"Fuzzy wuzzy, creepy crawly."—PrRa
Schuyler, James
I think.—KoT
Song ("I'm about to go shopping").—KoT
Sunday ("The mint bed is in").—KoT
Schwartz, Delmore
"I am cherry alive, the little girl sang."—KoT
I am cherry alive.—PrRh
Science
How everything happens (based on a study on the wave). M. Swenson.—LiSf
Mendings. M. Rukeyser.—PlSc
Relativity. D. H. Lawrence.—PrBb
The third thing. D. H. Lawrence.—PrBb
Science fiction. Reed Wittemore.—KeK
"A scissor." See Double trouble
Scollard, Clinton
The butterfly ("Up and down the air you float").—PrRa
"The score is tied." See Hayes Iverson
Scotland
"My heart's in the Highlands, my heart is not here." R. Burns.—BlO
Rannoch, by Glencoe. From Landscapes. T. S. Eliot.—HeR
Scotland small. H. MacDiarmid.—HeR
Scotland—History
"It was a' for our rightfu' king." R. Burns.—PlAs
Scotland small. Hugh MacDiarmid.—HeR

"Scotland small, our multiform, our infinite Scotland small." See Scotland small
"Scots steel tempered wi' Irish fire." See The weapon
Scott, Duncan Campbell
The forsaken, sels.
"Once in the winter".—DoNw
"Once in the winter." See The forsaken
Scott, Francis Reginald
Eclipse.—DoNw
Scott, Herbert
Passing the Masonic home for the aged.—JaPo
Scott, Peter Dale
Two drops, tr. by.—HeR
Scott, Sir Walter
The erl-king, tr. by.—LiWa
The fire ("The fire with well dried logs supplied").—HaO
Heap on more wood.—HaO
Lochinvar.—PlAs
Proud Maisie.—BlO—PlAs
St. Swithin's chair. LiWa
Song of the mermaids and mermen.—LiWa
Scott, Winfield Townley
Brief encounter.—JaG
To L.B.S.—JaD
Uses of poetry.—JaD
Scott Garber. Mel Glenn.—GlCd
Scottish nursery rhymes. See Nursery rhymes—Scottish
Scriven, R. C.
The marrog.—PrRh
"The scroobious snake." From An animal alphabet. Edward Lear.—LiH
"Scrubbed like a cube of sunlight." See The kitchen (for my grandmother)
"The scruffy one." See Hyena
Sculpture and statues
Box, for L.M.B. M. C. Livingston.—LiMp
Bronzes. C. Sandburg.—PlEd
A Calder. K. Shapiro.—PlEd
The Chicago Picasso. G. Brooks.—PlEd
A child's grave marker. T. Kooser.—JaG
Guide to the ruins. H. Nemerov.—PlEd
How to watch statues. X. J. Kennedy.—KeF
In the museum. C. Zolotow.—ZoE
John Donne's statue. J. P. Bishop.—PlEd
Letter to statues. J. M. Brinnin.—PlEd
"Little marble boy." J. Wright.—PlEd
No swan so fine. M. Moore.—PlEd
Observing a vulgar name on the plinth of an ancient statue. W. S. Landor.—PlEd
On a horse carved in wood. D. Hall.—PlEd
On seeing the Elgin Marbles. J. Keats.—PlEd
On the bust of Helen by Canova. Lord Byron.—PlEd
One rose of stone. K. Wilson.—JaG
Ozymandias. P. B. Shelley.—HeR
Sentries. X. J. Kennedy.—KeF
Spoken by Venus on seeing her statue done by Praxiteles. Unknown.—PlEd
Statue against a clear sky. From New England verses. W. Stevens.—PlEd
Statue and birds. L. Bogan.—PlEd
The statue of Medusa. W. Drummond.—PlEd
The statues in the public gardens. H. Nemerov.—PlEd
Tutankhamen. W. Dickey.—JaPi
Up North Second. M. C. Livingston.—LiWo
What Jenner said on hearing in Elysium that complaints had been made of his having a statue in Trafalgar Square. S. Brooks.—PlEd

Sculpture and statues—*Continued*
With a sliver of marble from Carrara. J. Wright.—PlEd
Scupham, Peter
Twelfth night ("Our candles, lit, re-lit, have gone down now").—HaO
"A scythe." See Markings, the question
Sea. See Ocean
The **sea** ("Behold the wonders of the mighty deep"). Unknown.—PrRh
The **sea** ("Muffled thunder"). Charlotte Zolotow.—ZoE
Sea calm. Langston Hughes.—HuDk
Sea-change. John Masefield.—HeR
A **sea-chantey.** Derek Walcott.—HeR
"Sea charm." Langston Hughes.—HuDk
Sea chest. Carl Sandburg.—HoRa
Sea fairies. Patricia Hubbell.—HoCr
"Sea go dark, dark with wind." See Wild iron
Sea gull. Elizabeth Coatsworth.—PrRh
"The sea gull curves his wings." See Sea gull
Sea-hawk. Richard Eberhart.—HeR
Sea horse and a sawhorse. X. J. Kennedy.—RuI
"A sea horse saw a sawhorse." See Sea horse and a sawhorse
Sea horses
Sea horse and a sawhorse. X. J. Kennedy.—RuI
"Sea horses leaping and laughing." See Easter under the water
"The sea is a wilderness of waves." See Long trip
"The sea is always the same." From North Atlantic. Carl Sandburg.—HoRa
"The sea is never still." See Young sea
"The sea is ringed around with hills." See Home
Sea life. See names of sea life, as Whales
Sea monster. William Stanley Merwin.—LiWa
The **sea** ritual. George Darley.—LiWa
The **sea** serpent chantey. Vachel Lindsay.—LiWa
Sea shell. Amy Lowell.—PrRh
The **sea** shell. Harry Behn.—HoCb
"Sea shell, sea shell." See Sea shell
The **sea** shore. Harry Behn.—HoCb
Sea shore shanty. Bobbi Katz.—HoSe
Sea slant. Carl Sandburg.—HoRa
A **sea** spell for a picture. Dante Gabriel Rossetti.—LiWa
Sea-wash. Carl Sandburg.—HaOf
"The sea-wash never ends." See Sea-wash
Sea-weed. David Herbert Lawrence.—HeR—HoSe—PrBb
"Sea-weed sways and sways and swirls." See Sea-weed
The **seafarer.** Unknown, tr. by Ezra Pound.—HeR
"The seafarers tell of the eastern Isle of Bliss." From His dream of the sky land, a farewell poem. Li Po, tr. by Shigeyoshi Obata.—LiWa
Seafaring life. See also Fishers and fishing; Pirates; Ships
Boatman's prayer for smooth waters. Unknown, fr. the Kwakiutl Indian.—BiSp
"Bobby Shafto's gone to sea." Mother Goose.—LoR
"Bobby Shaftoe's gone to sea".—DeM
Captain Spud and his first mate, Spade. J. Ciardi.—HaOf
The coasts of high Barbary. Unknown.—BlO
The cruise of the Mystery. C. Thaxter.—HaOf
Death of an old seaman. L. Hughes.—HuDk
Donkey riding. Unknown.—DaC—DoNw
"Far from home across the sea." Mother Goose.—LoR

The fisherman writes a letter to the mermaid. J. Aiken.—LiWa
Ghost ("There is a ghost"). C. Morgenstern.—LiWa
Jack was every inch a sailor. Unknown.—DoNw
Jim at the corner. E. Farjeon.—FaE
Klabauterwife's letter. C. Morgenstern.—LiWa
Little Billee. W. M. Thackeray.—BlO
The lowlands of Holland. Unknown.—PlAs
The marvel. K. Douglas.—HeR
"The master, the swabber, the boatswain, and I." From The tempest. W. Shakespeare.—HoUn
The most beautiful. G. Gozzano.—KoT
Pat Cloherty's version of the Maisie. R. Murphy.—HeR
Prayer for smooth waters. Unknown, fr. the Yahgan Indian.—BiSp
Sailor. L. Hughes.—HuDk
The sailor boy. A. Tennyson.—PlAs
Sailor's carol. C. Causley.—HaO
Sea-change. J. Masefield.—HeR
The sea ritual. G. Darley.—LiWa
Sea shell. A. Lowell.—PrRh
A sea spell for a picture. D. G. Rossetti.—LiWa
The seafarer. Unknown.—HeR
Seascape. L. Hughes.—HuDk
Sheep ("When I was once in Baltimore"). W. H. Davies.—HeR
Sing me a song. R. L. Stevenson.—PlAs
A smugglers' song. R. Kipling.—BlO
Song for smooth waters. Unknown, fr. the Haida Indian.—BiSp
Song of the mermaids and mermen. Sir W. Scott.—LiWa
Stormalong. Unknown.—PlAs
The Walloping Window-Blind. C. E. Carryl.—HaOf
The wandering albatross. P. Fleischman.—FlI
Water-front streets. L. Hughes.—HuDk
"A wet sheet and a flowing sea." A. Cunningham.—BlO
Young sea. C. Sandburg.—HoRa
Seagulls. See Gulls
Seagulls. John Updike.—JaPi
"Seagulls' crying." See Sunset blues
Seal. William Jay Smith.—LiSf—PrRh—RuI
Seals (animals)
An evening seal. T. Hughes.—HuU
The feminine seal. O. Herford.—BrT
The performing seal. R. Field.—PrRh
Seal. W. J. Smith.—LiSf—PrRh—RuI
The white seal's lullaby. R. Kipling.—ChB
Seamen. See Seafaring life
"Searched, we wait to fly." See Sparrow in an airport
"Searching for souvenirs among some rubble." See A post-mortem
Seascape. Langston Hughes.—HuDk
Seashell ("My father's mother"). Valerie Worth.—WoSp
Seashell ("This seashell is an ocean cove"). Sandra Liatsos.—HoSe
"A seashell is a castle." See Shell castles
Seashells. See Shells
Seashore. See Shore
"Season of mists and mellow fruitfulness." See To autumn
Season song. Unknown, tr. by Flann O'Brien.—HeR
Seasons. See also names of seasons, as Autumn; also names of months, as January
Autumn rain. E. Farjeon.—FaE

Self—*Continued*

Full moon, rising. J. Holden.—JaG

"Great, wide, beautiful, wonderful world." W. B. Rands.—TrM

Hide and seek ("When I am alone, and quite alone"). A. B. Shiffrin.—FrP—PrRa

"The house I go to in my dream." G. Barker.—CoOu

"I am making a circle for myself." A. Adoff.—AdA

I know the rules. A. Adoff.—AdA

"I think the real color is behind the color." A. Adoff.—AdA

"I'm nobody, who are you." E. Dickinson.—HaOf—LiSf—PrRh—TrM

In Laddery street herself. From Forgotten girlhood. L. Riding.—HeR

Just me. M. Hillert.—PrRh

The keeper. W. Carpenter.—JaPi

The lady said. A. Adoff.—AdA

"Maggie and Milly and Molly and May." E. E. Cummings.—HeR—HoSe—PrRh

Me ("As long as I live"). W. De la Mare.—PrRh

Me ("My nose is blue"). K. Kuskin.—PrRh

Me I am. J. Prelutsky.—PrRh

Mirror. S. Cassedy.—CaR

Nolan Davis. M. Glenn.—GlCd

O earth, turn! G. Johnston.—DoNw

"O thou great Chief." Unknown.—LaT

On my applications. A. Adoff.—AdA

Past ("I have all these parts stuffed in me"). A. Adoff.—AdA—JaT

People ("I like people quite well"). D. H. Lawrence.—PrBb

Robert Ashford. M. Glenn.—GlCd

Robert, who is often a stranger to himself. G. Brooks.—PrRa

Song ("The sun is mine"). R. Hogg.—DoNw

A story that could be true. W. Stafford.—CoN—JaG—KeK

That's Gloria. A. Turner.—TuS

"There was a little woman." Mother Goose.—DeM

Thumbprint ("On the pad of my thumb"). E. Merriam.—MeSk

Trees ("To be a giant and keep quiet about it"). H. Nemerov.—JaPi

Who am I. F. Holman.—FaTh—LiSf

"The wind suffers of blowing." L. Riding.—HeR

Written at the Po-shan monastery. Hsin Ch'i-chi.—LiIl

Self-pity. David Herbert Lawrence.—HeR

The **self-unseeing.** Thomas Hardy.—HeR

Selfishness

The clod and the pebble. W. Blake.—HeR

Let others share. E. Anthony.—PrRh

The mouse and the cake. E. Cook.—DaC

A **senator.** Unknown.—BrT

"A **senator,** Rex Asinorum." See A senator

The **send-off.** Wilfred Owen.—HeR

Send us a rainbow. Unknown.—LaT

Sendak, Maurice

Chicken soup with rice, complete.—FaW

Chicken soup with rice, sels.

January ("In January").—HoSi—PrRa

October ("In October").—PrRh

January ("In January"). See Chicken soup with rice

October ("In October"). See Chicken soup with rice

Seneca Indians. See Indians of the Americas—Seneca

Senex. Sir John Betjeman.—HeR

Senghor, Léopold Sédar

I want to say your name.—KoT

"**Senior** year should be a breeze." See Rhonda Winfrey

Sensation. Arthur Rimbaud.—KoT

Senses. See also Odors; Sight; Sounds; Taste; Touch

The habit of perfection. G. M. Hopkins.—HeR

I show the daffodils to the retarded kids. C. Sharp.—JaD

Sensible Sue. N. M. Bodecker.—BoPc

The **sensitive** cat. Alice Brown.—BrT

A **sensitive** man. Morris Bishop.—BrT

Sensitive, Seldom and Sad. Mervyn Peake.—PrRh

"**Sensitive,** Seldom and Sad are we." See Sensitive, Seldom and Sad

Sensitive Sydney. Wallace Irvin.—LiIl

Sentimental conversation. Paul Verlaine, tr. by Lloyd Alexander.—LiWa

The **sentimentalist.** Edward Field.—JaPo

Sentries. X. J. Kennedy.—KeF

Separation ("Each day"). P. Wolny.—JaD

Separation ("Your absence has gone through me"). William Stanley Merwin.—LiIl

September

Crickets ("All busy punching tickets"). D. McCord.—CoN—FaTh—LiSf—McAs

Questions for September. B. J. Esbensen.—EsCs

September ("The breezes taste"). J. Updike.—KeK

September ("I already know where Africa is"). L. Clifton.—HoSi—LiSf

September ("It rained in my sleep"). L. Pastan.—JaPi

September ("Something is bleeding"). L. Moore.—MoSn

September, last day at the beach. R. Tillinghast.—JaG

September ("The breezes taste"). John Updike.—KeK

September ("The golden-rod is yellow"). Helen Hunt Jackson.—HaOf

September ("I already know where Africa is"). Lucille Clifton.—HoSi—LiSf

September ("It rained in my sleep"). Linda Pastan.—JaPi

September ("Something is bleeding"). Lilian Moore.—MoSn

September, last day at the beach. Richard Tillinghast.—JaG

Sequoia trees

"Johnny had a black horse." J. Prelutsky.—PrRi

"When Paul Bunyan was ill." W. Reaker.—KeK

Serbo-Croatian language

Yes, it's raining. C. Pomerantz.—PoI

Sergeant, Howard

Soft landings.—CoOu

The **serpent.** Theodore Roethke.—PrRh

Serpentine verse. Joseph S. Newman.—BrT

Serraillier, Ian

The diver ("I put on my aqua-lung and plunge").—FaW

Falling asleep.—FaW

First foot.—LiNe

Going steady.—LiVp

The headless gardener.—LiSf

The hen and the carp.—CoOu—LiSf

Miss Tibbles.—LiCa

The old Sussex road.—CoN

"**Shari** and I have known each other since the fourth." See Sheila Franklin
Shari Morrow. Mel Glenn.—GlC
The **shark** ("He seemed to know the harbour"). Edwin John Pratt.—DoNw
The **shark** ("Oh what a lark to fish for shark"). J. J. Bell.—PrRh
The **shark** ("A treacherous monster"). Lord Alfred Douglas.—PrRh
Sharks
    About the teeth of sharks. J. Ciardi.—HaOf
    The maldive shark. H. Melville.—HeR
    Never mince words with a shark. J. Prelutsky.—PrNk
    The shark ("He seemed to know the harbour"). E. J. Pratt.—DoNw
    The shark ("Oh what a lark to fish for shark"). J. J. Bell.—PrRh
    The shark ("A treacherous monster"). Lord A. Douglas.—PrRh
    The sick shark. M. Bishop.—BrT
Sharon Vail and. Mel Glenn.—GlCd
Sharp, Constance
    I show the daffodils to the retarded kids.—JaD
Sharpe, Richard Scrafton
    The country mouse and the city mouse.—DaC
Shavuot, for Jessica. Kathryn Hellerstein.—LiPj
Shaw, John Mackay
    The ice cream ocean.—RuI
Shaw, Richard
    Cat's menu.—PrRh
The **Shawangunks**, early April. Lilian Moore.—MoSn
She and I. Norman Cameron.—HeR
"**She** and I, we thought and fought." See She and I
"**She** bounded o'er the graves." See Anna playing in a graveyard
"**She** came out of the field, low." See Rover
"**She** came to him in dreams--her ears." See Cowper's tame hare
"**She** came toward me in a flowing air." From The dream. Theodore Roethke.—McL
"**She** carefully regards her software, the amber." See Nude reclining at word processor, in pastel
"**She** died in the upstairs bedroom." See Death in Leamington
"**She** feels her presence as never." See The lost carnival
"**She** got off, according to the diary." See The arrival of my mother
"**She** had a name among the children." See A cat
"**She** had always loved to read, even." See White autumn
"**She** held her body steady in the wind." From The dream. Theodore Roethke.—McL
"**She** is the fairies' midwife, and she comes." From Romeo and Juliet. William Shakespeare.—HeR
"**She** knew the grades of all her neighbors' children." See Elegy for a woman who remembered everything
"**She** knew, the maiden mother knew." See The mother's song
"**She** listens to the waves resound." Arnold Lobel.—LoWr
"**She** lives in a garret." See A sad song about Greenwich Village
"**She** lives in Chicago." See Aunt Evelyn

She moved through the fair. Padraic Colum.—PlAs
"**She** must have been kicked unseen or brushed by a car." See Dog's death
"**She** often lies with her hands behind her head." See For my daughter
"**She** reads the paper." See Two people
"**She** said she wasn't hungry." Unknown.—TrM
"**She** sat on a willow-trunk." See The fly
"**She** sells sea shells on the seashore." Mother Goose.—LoR
"**She** sends me news of bluejays, frost." See A letter from home
"**She** sits by the sea in the clear, shining air." See A mermaid song
"**She** spent the day counting how many birds." See Exactly
"**She** spent three hundred and sixty four days a year." See Grandmother Jackson
"**She** stroked molten tones." See Yonosa house
"**She** sweeps with many-colored brooms." Emily Dickinson.—PlSc
"**She** talks about the decimal point." See Math class
"**She** took a last and simple meal." See The lost cat
"**She** waited eagerly on a park bench." See The poem in the park
"**She** was a small dog, neat and fluid." See Praise of a collie
"**She** was poor, but she was honest." See Poor but honest
"**She** wasn't the least bit pretty." See The factory girl
"**She** wouldn't believe." See Magical eraser
Sheard, Verna
    The yak ("For hours the princess would not play or sleep").—DoNw
"**Shed** a tear for Twickham Tweer." See Twickham Tweer
Sheep. See also Shepherds
    "Baa, baa, black sheep." Mother Goose.—AlH—DeM—FaW—LiSf—LoR
    A child's pet. W. H. Davies.—HeR
    First sight. P. Larkin.—CoN
    For a lamb. R. Eberhart.—HeR
    Henrietta Snetter. J. Prelutsky.—PrNk
    Lamb ("In Noah's"). N. M. Bodecker.—BoSs
    The lamb ("The lamb just says, I am"). T. Roethke.—LiSf
    The lamb ("Little lamb, who made thee"). W. Blake.—LiSf
    "Little Bo-Peep has lost her sheep." Mother Goose.—DeM—LoR
    "Mary had a little lamb (it was a greedy glutton)." Unknown.—PaM
    Mary's lamb. S. J. Hale.—HaOf
        "Mary had a little lamb".—LoR (unat.)
    Ol' red thief. E. Farjeon.—FaE
    Praise of a collie. N. MacCaig.—HeR
    Sheep ("Sheep are gentle, shy and meek"). J. Prelutsky.—PrZ
    Sheep ("When I was once in Baltimore"). W. H. Davies.—HeR
    Sicilian Easter Sunday. E. Di Pasquale.—LiE
    "Sleep, baby, sleep, thy father guards the sheep." Mother Goose.—Dem—LoR
    "Sleep, baby, sleep, thy father watches the sheep." Unknown, fr. the German.—BaH—LaW
    "A whistling girl and a flock of sheep." Mother Goose.—LoR

Sheep ("Sheep are gentle, shy and meek"). Jack Prelutsky.—PrZ
Sheep ("When I was once in Baltimore"). William Henry Davies.—HeR
"Sheep are gentle, shy and meek." See Sheep
"The sheep bell tolleth curfew time." See An evening scene
"The sheep upon the mountain." See A Christmas lullaby
"Sheeted in steel, embedded face to face." See At a low mass for two hot rodders
Sheila Franklin. Mel Glenn.—GlC
"The shell." See Shell
Shell ("The shell"). Sylvia Cassedy.—CaR
Shell ("When it was time"). Myra Cohn Livingston.—LiWo
Shell castles. Rowena Bennett.—HoSe
Shelley, Percy Bysshe
 "As I lay asleep in Italy." See The mask of anarchy
 "Canst thou imagine where those spirits live." See Prometheus unbound
 Indian serenade.—KoT
 "The limits of the sphere of dream", tr. by.—LiWa
 The mask of anarchy, sels.
  "As I lay asleep in Italy".—HeR
 Ozymandias.—HeR
 Prometheus unbound, sels.
  "Canst thou imagine where those spirits live".—LiWa
 Similes for two political characters of 1819.—HeR
 Song, to the men of England.—PlSc
 "Tell me, thou star, whose wings of light."—KoT
 To the moon ("Art thou pale for weariness").—KoT
 "A widow bird sate mourning for her love."—BlO
Shelley, Percy Bysshe (about)
 Memorabilia. R. Browning.—HeR
Shells
 Home. J. Jaszi.—PrRa
 Sea shell. A. Lowell.—PrRh
 The sea shell. H. Behn.—HoCb
 Seashell ("My father's mother"). V. Worth.—WoSp
 Seashell ("This seashell is an ocean cove"). S. Liatsos.—HoSe
 "She sells sea shells on the seashore." Mother Goose.—LoR
 Shell ("The shell"). S. Cassedy.—CaR
 Shell ("When it was time"). M. C. Livingston.—LiWo
 Shell castles. R. Bennett.—HoSe
Shelton, Richard
 Brother ("You still carry").—JaS
 Certain choices.—JaPi
 Disintegration.—JaD
 Letter to a dead father.—JaD
 My love.—JaG
 Requiem for Sonora.—JaPi
 The soldiers returning.—JaG
 War ("Each day the terror wagon").—JaPo
 Why I never went into politics.—JaS
 Wonders of the world.—JaD
 Youth ("Is the ability to be").—JaD
Shepherd, Nathaniel Graham
 Calling the roll.—HaOf
"The shepherd and the king." Eleanor Farjeon.—FaE

Shepherds. See also Sheep
 "And there were in the same country shepherds." From Gospel according to Luke. Bible/New Testament.—LiCp
 "Little Bo-Peep has lost her sheep." Mother Goose.—DeM—LoR
 "Little Boy Blue." Mother Goose.—LoR
 The passionate shepherd to his love. C. Marlowe.—HeR—KoT
 Los pastores. E. Agnew.—LiCp
 Phillida and Coridon. N. Breton.—KoT
 Psalm 23 ("The Lord is my shepherd, I shall not want"). From The book of psalms. Bible/Old Testament.—LiSf
  Psalm 23 ("The Lord to me a shepherd is").—HaOf
 "Red sky at night." Mother Goose.—DaC—DeM
  "A red sky at night is a shepherd's delight".—LoR
 Shepherd's carol. N. Nicholson.—HaO
 The shepherd's dog. L. Norris.—HaO
"Shepherds armed with staff and sling." See Carol of patience
Shepherd's carol. Norman Nicholson.—HaO
The **shepherd's** dog. Leslie Norris.—HaO
The **shepherd's** tale. Raoul Ponchon, tr. by James Kirkup.—HaO
The **sheriff** of Rottenshot. Jack Prelutsky.—PrSr
"The sheriff of Rottenshot, Jogalong Jim." See The sheriff of Rottenshot
Sherman, Frank Dempster
 Baseball.—HaOf
 Blossoms.—HaOf
Sherman, Susan R.
 Three moments.—JaD
Sherrard, Philip
 As much as you can, tr. by.—HeR
"She's ta'en her petticoat by the band." See Tam Lin
Shields, Carol
 Great-grandma.—JaS
 The new mothers.—JaS
Shields, Elizabeth M.
 "Don't let my life grow dull, Lord."—LaT
 Prayer ("Dear God").—LaT
 Prayer ("Dear heavenly Father").—LaT
 Prayer ("Dear heavenly Father, I often make mistakes").—LaT
Shiffrin, A. B.
 Hide and seek ("When I am alone, and quite alone").—FrP—PrRa
Shigeyoshi Obata
 "The seafarers tell of the eastern Isle of Bliss", tr. by.—LiWa
Shiki
 "For a companion."—FaTh
 "When my canary."—LiSf
Shimmerings. From A throw of threes. Eve Merriam.—MeF
"Shining in his stickiness and glistening with honey." See The friendly cinnamon bun
"Shining Japanese beetle." See Beetles
"The shiny coach squeaks and crawls over arid." See Amtrak
"A ship at sea." See Absent friend
"A ship I have got in the north country." See The Golden Vanity
Ships. See also Shipwrecks
 Absent friend. C. Zolotow.—ZoE
 "As I sat on a sunny bank." Mother Goose.—DeM
 The cruise of the Mystery. C. Thaxter.—HaOf

Ships.—*Continued*
Down below. J. Aiken.—LiWa
Frightening. C. Lewis.—PrRh
The ghost of the cargo boat. P. Neruda.—LiWa
The Golden Vanity ("A ship I have got in the north country"). Unknown.—BlO
    The Golden Vanity ("Now Jack he had a ship in the north counterie").—PlAs
The Green Willow Tree. Unknown.—PlAs
Hospital barge at Cerisy. W. Owen.—HeR
How do you do, Alabama. F. Wilson.—PlAs
"I saw a ship a-sailing." Mother Goose.—DeM—LiSf—LoR—RuI
I saw three ships. Unknown.—RoC
"I saw three ships come sailing by." Mother Goose.—LoR
"Little ships must keep the shore." Mother Goose.—LoR
The north ship. P. Larkin.—HeR
On the Congo. H. E. Martinson.—HeR
Queens of the river. C. Lewis.—HoCl—LiSf
Roll, Alabama, roll. Unknown.—PlAs
A sea-chantey. D. Walcott.—HeR
The sea serpent chantey. V. Lindsay.—LiWa
Sea slant. C. Sandburg.—HoRa
Seascape. L. Hughes.—HuDk
Sheep ("When I was once in Baltimore"). W. H. Davies.—HeR
The ships of Yule. B. Carman.—DoNw
Sketch ("The shadows of the ships"). C. Sandburg.—HoRa
The sound of the wind. C. G. Rossetti.—BlO—CoOu
"There are gold ships." Unknown.—LiIl
"There was a ship a-sailing." Mother Goose.—RoC
    "I saw a ship a-sailing".—CoN
This ship. M. Rosen.—FaW
"Three times round goes our gallant ship." Mother Goose.—LoR
The Walloping Window-Blind. C. E. Carryl.—HaOf
Water sport. N. M. Bodecker.—BoPc
The **ships** of Yule. Bliss Carman.—DoNw
Shipwrecks
The Golden Vanity ("A ship I have got in the north country"). Unknown.—BlO
    The Golden Vanity ("Now Jack he had a ship in the north counterie").—PlAs
The Green Willow Tree. Unknown.—PlAs
Listening to Beethoven on the Oregon coast. H. Carlile.—JaPi
"One Saturday night as we set sail." Unknown.—LiSf
Pat Cloherty's version of the Maisie. R. Murphy.—HeR
Posted as missing. J. Masefield.—BlO
Sir Patrick Spens ("The king sits in Dunfermline town"). Unknown.—BlO—PlAs
    Sir Patrick Spens (". . . Dunfermline toun").—HeR
    Sir Patrick Spence (". . . Dumferling town").—LiSf
Skipper Ireson's ride. J. G. Whittier.—HaOf
The wandering albatross. P. Fleischman.—FlI
The way of Cape Race. E. J. Pratt.—DoNw
The wreck of the Hesperus. H. W. Longfellow.—HaOf
Shirley and her son. Nikki Giovanni.—GiSp
Shirt. Carl Sandburg.—HoRa
"Shlof, sleep through the night." See Lullaby
"Shoe the little horse." Unknown.—RaT
Shoes. See Boots and shoes

Shoes. Valerie Worth.—JaT
Shooting. B. H. Fairchild.—JaT
Shooting crows. David Huddle.—JaG
The **shooting** of Dan McGrew. Robert William Service.—DoNw—HeR
The **shooting** of John Dillinger outside the Biograph Theater, July 22, 1934. David Wagoner.—HeR
Shooting stars. Myra Cohn Livingston.—LiSi
Shopping. See Markets and marketing; Peddlers and vendors; Shops and shopkeepers
Shopping. Nikki Giovanni.—GiSp
Shops and shopkeepers. See also names of shops, as Barbers and barbershops
Air on an escalator. J. Aiken.—LiSf
The animal store. R. Field.—LiSf
Annar-Mariar's Christmas shopping. E. Farjeon.—FaE
"Butterprint knocks on the milkshop door." C. Watson.—WaC
Door number four. C. Pomerantz.—LiIl—PoI
Elijah Snow. X. J. Kennedy.—KeF
Father ("You spent fifty-five years"). T. Kooser.—JaS
The fishvendor. W. Meredith.—PlSc
For a quick exit. N. Farber.—HoCl—KeK
General store. R. Field.—FaW
The ghostly grocer of Grumble Grove. J. Prelutsky.—PrSr
The gnomes. B. Bentley.—PlSc
Henry's market. C. Rylant.—RyW
Miss Tillie McLush. J. S. Newman.—BrT
"My father owns the butcher shop." Unknown.—PrRa—PrRh
Reflections ("On this street"). L. Moore.—LiSf—MoSn
Sam the shoe shop man. C. Rylant.—RyW
Shopping. N. Giovanni.—GiSp
"Smiling girls, rosy boys." Mother Goose.—LoR
    The gingerbread man.—DaC
Song against broccoli. R. Blount.—JaPo
Supermarket Shabbat. R. J. Margolis.—LiPj
The sweetstuff wife. E. Farjeon.—FaE
Through a shop window. E. Farjeon.—FaE
Wax lips. C. Rylant.—RyW
"A wee little boy has opened a store." Unknown.—DeD
Shore, Jane
Anthony.—JaD
Shore. See also Ocean
At the beach ("First I walked"). S. Liatsos.—HoSe
At the beach ("Johnny, Johnny, let go of tha crab"). J. Ciardi.—CiD
At the sea-side. R. L. Stevenson.—CoN—FaW
Baby's baking. E. Stein.—PrRa
"The beach at this evening full." Unknown.—JaT
Beach stones. L. Moore.—FaTh—MoSn
The bight, on my birthday. E. Bishop.—HeI
"Boxes on the beach are empty." From San scribblings. C. Sandburg.—HoSe
By the sea. C. Zolotow.—ZoE
A certain sandpiper. X. J. Kennedy.—JaT
"Come unto these yellow sands." From Th tempest. W. Shakespeare.—BlO—KoT
The crow ("By the wave rising, by the wav breaking"). P. K. Page.—DoNw
Devotion. R. Frost.—KoS
Down on my tummy. M. C. Livingston.—HoS
Driving to the beach. J. Cole.—PrRh
Flowers by the sea. W. C. Williams.—HeR
Foghorns. L. Moore.—HoSs—MoSn—PrRh

Shore.—*Continued*

For Sue. P. Hey.—JaPo

"From Table Isle." Unknown.—FaTh

Gracious goodness. M. Piercy.—JaPi

Home. J. Jaszi.—PrRa

"I had a little castle upon the sea sand." Mother Goose.—FaW

In the shadows of early sunlight. R. Wallace.—JaT

Listening to Beethoven on the Oregon coast. H. Carlile.—JaPi

The lobsters and the fiddler crab. F. J. Forster.—PrRh

"Maggie and Milly and Molly and May." E. E. Cummings.—HeR—HoSe—PrRh

Mine. L. Moore.—MoSn

Monterey cypress, Point Lobos. M. C. Livingston.—LiMp

"My brother lost his bathing suit." J. Prelutsky.—PrWi

On an August day. L. B. Hopkins.—HoSe

On the beach at Fontana. J. Joyce.—HeR

Pete at the seashore. D. Marquis.—HoDl

The picnic. D. Aldis.—FrP—PrRa

Returning to Store Bay. B. Howes.—JaPi

Sand ("I sat down on my blanket"). J. Prelutsky.—PrWi

Sand ("The sand is the sand, till you take it"). E. Farjeon.—FaE

Sand castle. C. A. Keremes.—HoSe

The sandpiper ("Across the lonely beach we flit"). C. Thaxter.—HaOf

The sandpiper ("Look at the little sandpiper"). C. Zolotow.—FaTh—HoSe

Sandpiper ("The roaring alongside he takes for granted"). E. Bishop.—HeR

The sea ("Muffled thunder"). C. Zolotow.—ZoE

A sea-chantey. D. Walcott.—HeR

Sea fairies. P. Hubbell.—HoCr

Sea-hawk. R. Eberhart.—HeR

The sea shell. H. Behn.—HoCb

The sea shore. H. Behn.—HoCb

Sea shore shanty. B. Katz.—HoSe

Sea-wash. C. Sandburg.—HaOf

Seagulls. J. Updike.—JaPi

September, last day at the beach. R. Tillinghast.—JaG

"Seventy feet down." From Livings. P. Larkin.—HeR

The shark ("A treacherous monster"). Lord A. Douglas.—PrRh

"She listens to the waves resound." A. Lobel.—LoWr

Shell ("The shell"). S. Cassedy.—CaR

Shore. M. B. Miller.—PrRa

Sitting in the sand. K. Kuskin.—HoSe—HoSi

Sketch ("The shadows of the ships"). C. Sandburg.—HoRa

A smugglers' song. R. Kipling.—BlO

Spray. D. H. Lawrence.—PrBb

Starfish ("Spined / with sparks"). V. Worth.—WoSp

Summer snow. C. Zolotow.—HoSe—ZoE

Sunset blues. M. Kumin.—HoSe

"There was a warm pig from Key West." A. Lobel.—LoB

"There was an old person of Hyde." E. Lear.—LiH

Treasure. E. Farjeon.—FaE

"Until I saw the sea." L. Moore.—CoN—HoSe—MoSn—PrRh

Waking from a nap on the beach. M. Swenson.—CoN

Water's edge. L. Morrison.—PrRh

Waves ("There's big waves and little waves"). E. Farjeon.—FaE

There are big waves.—CoOu

"Waves of the sea." A. Fisher.—HoSe

The waves of the sea. E. Farjeon.—FaE

"We built a castle near the rocks." J. W. Anglund.—PrRa

Wharf. M. C. Livingston.—HoSe

Wild day at the shore. F. Holman.—HoSe

The wind is blowing west. J. Ceravolo.—KoT

A year later. M. A. Hoberman.—HoSi

Shore. Mary Britton Miller.—PrRa

Short love poem. Judith Viorst.—ViI

A **short** note. Eve Merriam.—MeSk

"A **short** pause." See Markings, the comma

"The **shortest** fight." See The knockout

A **shower** of cobwebs. Gilbert White.—FaTh

Showers. Marchette Chute.—PrRa

Showers, clearing later in the day. Eve Merriam.—MeSk

"The **shrewdest** salesman anywhere." See Archie B. McCall

Shrews

Small, smaller ("I thought that I knew all there was to know"). R. Hoban.—FaTh—JaT

Shroud. George Mackay Brown.—HeR

The **shubble.** Walter De la Mare.—BrT

Shuckburg, Richard

Yankee Doodle ("Fath'r and I went down to camp").—PlAs

Yankee Doodle ("Father and I went down to camp").—LiSf (unat.)

Shumaker, Peggy

Ladybugs.—JaT

"**Shut** in from all the world without." From Snowbound. John Greenleaf Whittier.—HaO

"**Shy** one, shy one." See To an isle in the water

"**Si** monumentum requiris...the church in which we are sitting." See In memory of George Whitby, architect

Sia Indians. See Indians of the Americas—Sia

Sicilian Easter Sunday. Emanuel Di Pasquale.—LiE

Sicilian thanksgiving on the feast of Saint John the Baptist. Emanuel Di Pasquale.—LiTp

A **sick** child. Randall Jarrell.—LiSf

The **sick** rose. William Blake.—HeR

The **sick** shark. Morris Bishop.—BrT

Sickness

Among the narcissi. S. Plath.—HeR

Ancient history. A. Guiterman.—HaOf—KeK

Aunt Ruth. M. C. Livingston.—LiWo

The ceiling. T. Roethke.—KeK—PlEd

Colita de rana. Unknown.—GrT

Convalescence. N. Coward.—KoT

The destruction of Sennacherib. Lord Byron.—HeR—PlAs

Edwin A. Nelms. S. L. Nelms.—JaS

Fair warning. N. Smaridge.—HoSi

For chest pain. Unknown, fr. the Aztec Indian.—BiSp

The germ. O. Nash.—HeR

Here lies a lady. J. C. Ransom.—HeR

"I am the medicine." Unknown, fr. the Mazatec Indian.—BiSp

"I've got an incredible headache." J. Prelutsky.—PrNk

"I've scratched the measles, itched the pox." Unknown.—TrM

Sickness—*Continued*

The land of Counterpane. R. L. Stevenson.—CoN

The last words of my English grandmother. W. C. Williams.—HeR

Little frog tail. Unknown.—GrT

Measles. K. Starbird.—PrRh

My nose. D. Aldis.—PrRh

My, oh wow, book. J. Viorst.—ViI

Old Doc. M. Vinz.—JaPi

"One morning in August." J. Prelutsky.—PrWi

Poem to help my father. N. H. Richman.—JaS

Poppies in July. S. Plath.—HeR

Remedies. G. Soto.—JaS

The seven sneezes of Cecil Snedde. J. Prelutsky.—PrSr

A sick child. R. Jarrell.—LiSf

The sick rose. W. Blake.—HeR

Soups and juices. R. J. Margolis.—MaS

Stopping by home. D. Huddle.—JaG

Stroke. M. Lowery.—JaPi

To blow away a headache. Unknown, fr. the Uitoto Indian.—BiSp

To cure epilepsy. Unknown, fr. the Tzotzil Maya.—BiSp

"When old corruption first begun." W. Blake.—HeR

"When Paul Bunyan was ill." W. Reaker.—KeK

"The wicked who would do me harm." Unknown.—HeR

Words to a sick child. Unknown, fr. the Iglulik Eskimo.—BiSp

Sidewalk measles. Barbara M. Hales.—HoSi—HoSs

The **sidewalk** racer. Lillian Morrison.—CoN—KeK—LiSf—PrRh

Sidney Snickke. Jack Prelutsky.—PrNk

Siebert, Diane

Train song.—PrRh

Siebert, T. Lawrence

Casey Jones.—BlO (unat.)—PlAs

Sierra redwoods, highway 101. Myra Cohn Livingston.—LiMp

Sieves

The jumblies. E. Lear.—BlO—LiH

"A riddle, a riddle, as I suppose." Mother Goose.—LiSf

"**Sighing** high and again a sigh." See Weaving at the window

Sight

Grandpa dropped his glasses. L. F. Jackson.—PrRh

I am not a camera. W. H. Auden.—PlEd

"I asked the little boy who cannot see." Unknown.—CoOu

"Who has seen the wind." C. G. Rossetti.—BlO—CoN—FrP—LiSf—PrRh

The wind.—DaC

"The **sight** of his guests filled Lord Cray." See Lord Cray

A **sightseer** named Sue. Unknown.—BrT

Signs

Carol of the signs. E. Farjeon.—FaE

"Four-way stop." M. C. Livingston.—KeK

Signs. N. M. Bodecker.—BoPc

Song of the open road. O. Nash.—JaPo

Winter dark. L. Moore.—MoSn

Signs. N. M. Bodecker.—BoPc

Sigourney, Lydia Huntley

Indian names.—HaOf

Request of a dying child.—HaOf

Silence

Attic. S. Cassedy.—CaR

Catching quiet. M. Ridlon.—HoSs

Crossing the water. S. Plath.—HeR

The first snow ("There is a special kind of quiet"). C. Zolotow.—ZoE

Fish ("The little fish are silent"). A. S. Bourinot.—PrRa

For silence. R. Bond.—LaT

Full moon, Santa Barbara. S. Teasdale.—HaOf

Ghost ("More gruesome than any groan"). E. Merriam.—MeHa

The habit of perfection. G. M. Hopkins.—HeR

Just three. W. Wise.—PrRa

The listeners. W. De la Mare.—LiWa

The little mute boy. F. García Lorca.—HeR

Orders. A. M. Klein.—DoNw

Quiet room. S. Cassedy.—CaR

Silence. W. C. Williams.—JaT

Snowy morning. L. Moore.—BaS—MoSn

The white horse. D. H. Lawrence.—KeK—KoT—PrBb

Silence. William Carlos Williams.—JaT

"The **silent** girl." See In the library

Silent hill. Zilpha Keatley Snyder.—LiWa

Silent night. Joseph Mohr.—RoC (unat.)

"**Silent** night, holy night." See Silent night

The **silent** snake. Unknown.—ChG

Silent warnings. From A throw of threes. Eve Merriam.—MeF

Silkworms

"Little silk worms, if you please." Unknown.—DeD

"**Silly**." See Chameleon

Silly Sallie. Walter De la Mare.—BlO

"**Silly** Sallie, silly Sallie." See Silly Sallie

Silly song. Federico García Lorca.—KoT

"**Silly,** stupid, gawky elf." See A penny valentine

Silver (color)

Silver. W. De la Mare.—KoT—PrRh

Silver. Walter De la Mare.—KoT—PrRh

"**Silver** bark of beech, and sallow." See Counting-out rhyme

Silver maple. Myra Cohn Livingston.—LiMp

"A **silver** scaled dragon with jaws flaming red." See The toaster

"The **silver** swan, who living had no note." Orlando Gibbons.—HeR

"**Silverly.**" Dennis Lee.—PrRa

Silverstein, Shel

Clarence.—HaOf

The dirtiest man in the world.—HaOf

The Fourth.—LiSf

Friendship ("I've discovered a way to stay friends forever").—CoN—LiIl

Hug o' war.—CoN—PrRh

Jimmy Jet and his TV set.—HaOf—LiSf—PrRh

The lazy people.—CoN

The little boy and the old man.—PrRh

Magical eraser.—LiWa

Not me. See "The slithergadee has crawled out of the sea"

Oh have you heard.—LiSf

One inch tall.—HaOf

Pie problem.—PrRh

Sarah Cynthia Sylvia Stout would not take the garbage out.—HaOf—LiSf

"The slithergadee has crawled out of the sea."—LiWa

The slithergadee.—CoOu—PrRh

Not me.—CoN—KeK

Smart.—PrRh

Thumbs.—FaTh

Valentine ("I got a valentine from Timmy").—PrRh

Silverstein, Shel—*Continued*
The worst.—LiWa
Simhat Torah. R. H. Marks.—LiPj
Simic, Charles
Watermelons.—JaPo
Simile, willow and ginkgo. Eve Merriam.—MeSk
Similes for two political characters of 1819. Percy Bysshe Shelley.—HeR
A **simple** need. N. M. Bodecker.—BoPc
"**Simple** Simon met a pieman." Mother Goose.—DeM—FaW—LiSf—LoR
Simple song. Marge Piercy.—McL
Simpson, Louis
Carentan O Carentan.—HeR
Mashkin Hill.—PlSc
Simpson, Mark
X, oh X.—JaG
Sims, George R.
In the workhouse.—HaO
"**Since** Easter was a month ago." See Written on an egg
Since Hanna moved away. Judith Viorst.—HoBf—PrRh—ViI
"**Since** money talks." See Flummery
"**Since** there's no help, come, let us kiss and part." Michael Drayton.—HeR
"**Since** you have gone." See Three moments
Since you seem intent. Gerald Locklin.—JaG
"**Since** you seem intent on going away." See Since you seem intent
"**Sing** a song of people." Lois Lenski.—PrRh
"**Sing** a song of picnics." See Picnic day
"**Sing** a song of sixpence." Mother Goose.—AlH—DaC—DeM—FaW—LoR
"**Sing** a song of soapsuds." Clyde Watson.—WaC
"**Sing** a song of subways." Eve Merriam.—KeK—PrRh
"**Sing** a song of succotash." Arnold Lobel.—LoWr
"**Sing** a song of winter." See A sledding song
"**Sing** for your supper." Eleanor Farjeon.—FaE
"**Sing** hey, sing hey." Mother Goose.—LiIl
Sing me a song. Robert Louis Stevenson.—PlAs
"**Sing** me a song." See Sing me a song of teapots and trumpets
"**Sing** me a song of a lad that is gone." See Sing me a song
Sing me a song of teapots and trumpets. N. M. Bodecker.—PrRh
"**Sing,** sing, what shall I sing." Mother Goose.—DeM—LiCa—LoR
Sing, sing, what shall we sing." Arnold Lobel.—LoWr
Sing song." See Tag along
Singers. See Singing
Singing
After tea. E. Farjeon.—FaE
Brontosaurus. G. Kredenser.—PrRh
Caged birds. M. Angelou.—AnS
A carol for Christmas eve. E. Farjeon.—FaE
The carol singers. E. Farjeon.—FaE
The child and the bird. E. Farjeon.—FaE
The children's carol. E. Farjeon.—FaE—PrRh
"A coloratura named Luna." J. F. Wilson.—BrT
Elves and goblins. H. Behn.—HoCb
Euphonica Jarre. J. Prelutsky.—PrNk
Gertrude. G. Brooks.—LiSf
Humming birds. B. Sage.—PrRa
I hear America singing. W. Whitman.—LiSf—PlSc
"I went to Wyoming one day in the spring." J. Prelutsky.—PrRi
The ichthyosaurus. Unknown.—BrT
"I'll sing you a song." Mother Goose.—LoR

J. Prior, Esq. N. M. Bodecker.—LiSf
"Little Tom Tucker." Mother Goose.—AlH
"Little Tommy Tucker." Mother Goose.—DeM—FaW—LoR
The market. J. Stephens.—PlAs
A mermaid song. J. Reeves.—LiSf
"Merry are the bells, and merry would they ring." Mother Goose.—LiSf—LoR
A minor bird. R. Frost.—KoS
The musical lion. O. Herford.—BrT—HaOf
"My mother had a maid call'd Barbara." From Othello. W. Shakespeare.—HoUn—PlAs
Now every child. E. Farjeon.—FaE
On a bad singer. S. T. Coleridge.—PrRh
Operatic Olivia. I. F. Bellows.—BrT
Our mother's tunes. E. Farjeon.—FaE
Our vicar. Unknown.—BrT
Piano ("Softly, in the dusk, a woman is singing to me"). D. H. Lawrence.—HeR
The serpent. T. Roethke.—PrRh
"The silver swan, who living had no note." O. Gibbons.—HeR
"Sing, sing, what shall we sing." A. Lobel.—LoWr
The singing cat. S. Smith.—ChC
Singing in the spring. I. O. Eastwick.—PrRa
Singing on the moon. T. Hughes.—LiWa
Singing time. R. Fyleman.—ChG—FrP—PrRa
Six green singers. E. Farjeon.—FaE
The skylark. C. G. Rossetti.—DaC
The solitary reaper. W. Wordsworth.—BlO
A song of the girls' puberty ceremony ("When the earth was made"). Unknown, fr. the White Mountain Apache.—BiSp
Song's eternity. J. Clare.—PlAs
Songs my mother taught me. D. Wagoner.—JaS
Sun song. L. Hughes.—HuDk
"There was a loud pig from West Wheeling." A. Lobel.—LoB
"There was an old man of the isles." E. Lear.—LiH
"There was an old person of Tring." E. Lear.—LiH
An old person of Tring.—BrT (unat.)
A thrifty soprano. O. Nash.—BrT
"Through the house give glimmering light." From A midsummer night's dream. W. Shakespeare.—HoUn
Tree song. H. Behn.—HoCb
"A wandering minstrel I." From The Mikado. W. S. Gilbert.—PlAs
The wolf ("When the pale moon hides and the wild wind wails"). G. R. Durston.—PrRh
The **singing** cat. Stevie Smith.—ChC
Singing games. See Games
Singing in the spring. Ivy O. Eastwick.—PrRa
Singing on the moon. Ted Hughes.—LiWa
"**Singing** on the moon seems precarious." See Singing on the moon
"**Singing,** singing." See Winter song
Singing time. Rose Fyleman.—ChG—FrP—PrRa
Single. N. M. Bodecker.—BoPc
"The **single** clenched fist lifted and ready." See Choose
"**Single-eyed** to child and sunbeam." See Blue-eyed Mary
Singular indeed. David McCord.—HaOf
Sinner. Langston Hughes.—HuDk
The **Sioux.** Unknown.—BrT
Sioux Indians. See Indians of the Americas—Sioux
"**Sip** a little." See Baby's drinking song

Sipe, Muriel
   Good morning ("One day I saw a downy duck").—FrP—PrRa
"Sipping a Schlitz." See Bullfrogs
Sir Bedivere Bors. Frederick B. Opper.—BrT
"Sir Bedivere Bors was a chivalrous knight." See Sir Bedivere Bors
Sir Blushington Bloone. Jack Prelutsky.—PrNk
"Sir Blushington Bloone is a knight of the court." See Sir Blushington Bloone
"Sir Eglamour, that worthy Knight." Unknown.—BlO
Sir Patrick Spence (". . . Dumferling town"). See Sir Patrick Spens ("The king sits in Dunfermline town")
Sir Patrick Spens ("The king sits in Dunfermline town"). Unknown.—BlO—PlAs
   Sir Patrick Spens (". . . Dunfermline toun").—HeR
   Sir Patrick Spence (". . . Dumferling town").—LiSf
Sir Patrick Spens (". . . Dunfermline toun"). See Sir Patrick Spens ("The king sits in Dunfermline town")
Sir Smashum Uppe. Emile Victor Rieu.—PrRh
Sir Walter Ralegh to his son. Sir Walter Raleigh.—HeR
Siren chorus. George Darley.—LiWa
Sisters. See Brothers and sisters
Sisters. Eleanor Farjeon.—FaE
"Sisters are always drying their hair." See Triolet against sisters
Sister's dressing rhyme. Unknown.—GrT
"Sit." See In the sun
"Sit here." See A secret place
"Sitter Bitter." See Miss Bitter
"(Sitting in a tree)." Edward Estlin Cummings.—FaTh
"Sitting in an empty house." See A dog in San Francisco
Sitting in the sand. Karla Kuskin.—HoSe—HoSi
"Sitting in the sand and the sea comes up." See Sitting in the sand
Sitwell, Dame Edith
   Evening ("Prince Absalom and Sir Rotherham Redde").—PlAs
Sitwell, Sir Osbert
   Winter, the huntsman.—BlO
The six badgers. Robert Graves.—LiSf—LiWa
"The six-foot nest of the sea-hawk." See Sea-hawk
Six green singers. Eleanor Farjeon.—FaE
"Six little mice sat down to spin." Mother Goose.—DeM—LoR
The six strings. Federico García Lorca, tr. by Donald Hall.—HeR
Six weeks old. Christopher Morley.—PrRh
Size. See also People—size
   Elephant ("It is quite unfair to be"). A. Brownjohn.—CoOu
   The fly ("How large unto the tiny fly"). W. De la Mare.—CoOu
   Lake Superior. From Great Lakes suite. J. Reaney.—DoNw
   Measurement. A. M. Sullivan.—PrRh
   Teddy bear. A. A. Milne.—CoOu
   Yeast. E. Merriam.—MeHa
Skateboards and skateboarding
   The sidewalk racer. L. Morrison.—CoN—KeK—LiSf—PrRh
The skaters. John Gould Fletcher.—KeK

Skating
   The lake ("This winter day"). B. J. Esbensen.—EsCs
   "My mother took me skating." J. Prelutsky.—PrIs
   74th Street. M. C. Livingston.—LiSf
   The skaters. J. G. Fletcher.—KeK
   "We're racing, racing down the walk." P. McGinley.—PrRh
The 'skeeter and Peter. Marie Bruckman MacDonald.—BrT
"'Skeeters are a-humming on the honeysuckle vine." See Kentucky babe
Skeleton. Eve Merriam.—MeHa
Skeleton and spirit. Unknown.—HoCr
"A skeleton once in Khartoum." See Skeleton and spirit
Skeleton parade. Jack Prelutsky.—CoN—PrRa
Skeletons
   Flies. V. Worth.—WoSp
   In a museum cabinet. M. Swenson.—LiWa
   Skeleton. E. Merriam.—MeHa
   Skeleton and spirit. Unknown.—HoCr
   Skeleton parade. J. Prelutsky.—CoN—PrRa
"The skeletons are out tonight." See Skeleton parade
Skelton, John
   To Mistress Isabel Pennell.—KoT
Skerryvore. Robert Louis Stevenson.—PlEd
Sketch ("Holding a picture up to the wall"). Robert Farnsworth.—JaG
Sketch ("The shadows of the ships"). Carl Sandburg.—HoRa
Sketch of a poet, sels. Carl Sandburg
   "He wastes time walking and telling the air, I am superior even to the wind".—HoRa
"Skilled to pull wires, he baffles Nature's hope." See The boss
Skilly Oogan. Russell Hoban.—LiIl
"Skilly Oogan's no one you can see." See Skilly Oogan
"Skimming." See The sidewalk racer
Skin
   Beside the line of elephants. E. Becker.—PrRh
   Color. E. Merriam.—MeSk
   A cow's outside. J. Prelutsky.—PrNk
   "I think the real color is behind the color." A. Adoff.—AdA
   Just me. M. Hillert.—PrRh
   Rhinoceros. M. A. Hoberman.—LiSf
   Rhymes ("We were talking about poems he had written"). F. Steele.—JaPo
Skip rope rhyme for our time. Eve Merriam.—MeF
Skip to my Lou. Unknown.—LiSf
Skipper Ireson's ride. John Greenleaf Whittier.—HaOf
Skipping
   "Justin Austin." J. Prelutsky.—PrRi
   The rabbit skip. M. W. Brown.—FrP
   Red-dress girl. A. Turner.—TuS
   Skip to my Lou. Unknown.—LiSf
Skipsey, Joseph
   "In the coal pit, or the factory."—PlSc
"Skittish." See The women's 400 meters
Sklarew, Myra
   The goodbye ("This endsaying, moon pried loose").—JaG
   Poem of the mother.—JaS
Skunk ("Skunk's football plods padded"). Ted Hughes.—HuU
Skunk ("Sometimes, around/moonrise"). Valerie Worth.—WoSp

The **skunk** to the gnu. Gerard Neyroud.—BrT
Skunks
Skunk ("Skunk's football plods padded"). T. Hughes.—HuU
Skunk ("Sometimes, around/moonrise"). V. Worth.—WoSp
The skunk to the gnu. G. Neyroud.—BrT
Unpopular Rex. X. J. Kennedy.—KeF
"Skunk's football plods padded." See Skunk
Sky
The approach of the storm. Unknown, fr. the Chippewa Indian.—KoT
Back yard, July night. W. Cole.—KeK
Clouds ("Today"). M. C. Livingston.—LiSi
The cold heaven. W. B. Yeats.—HeR
Earth and sky. E. Farjeon.—FaE
Fog lifting. L. Moore.—MoSn
How strange it is. C. Lewis.—PrRh
"I'm glad the sky is painted blue." Unknown.— ChG—PrRh—TrM
  I'm glad.—FrP
In the field forever. R. Wallace.—JaPo
Jetstream. L. Moore.—MoSn
"The lightning and thunder." G. MacDonald.— KeK
The loaves. R. Everson.—JaT
"Lying in the grass." C. Zolotow.—ZoE
Manitou. R. Ikan.—JaPo
The moon and a cloud. W. H. Davies.—HeR
Morning sky. M. C. Livingston.—LiSi
New moon. E. Merriam.—MeF
Night roof. A. Turner.—TuS
Questions for September. B. J. Esbensen.—EsCs
Rags. J. Thurman.—HoSi—JaT
"Red sky at night." Mother Goose.—DaC— DeM
  "A red sky at night is a shepherd's delight".—LoR
The river is a piece of sky. J. Ciardi.—LiSf
School day. C. Zolotow.—ZoE
Shooting stars. M. C. Livingston.—LiSi
"Sky." R. Roseliep.—KeK
Skyscraper. D. Lee.—PrRa
Song ("Don't you ever"). Unknown, fr. the Nootka Indian.—BiSp
"There was an old woman tossed up in a basket." Mother Goose.—DaC—DeM—FaW— LiSf—LoR
"Three skies." C. Lewis.—LiSf
Until we built a cabin. A. Fisher.—LaW
"Who is the east." E. Dickinson.—KoT
"Sky." Raymond Roseliep.—KeK
"Sky flowers." See Two ways to look at kites
"The sky is." See Summer rain
"The sky is blue today." See Spring day
Sky net. Aileen Fisher.—FiW
The **skylark.** Christina Georgina Rossetti.—DaC
Skylarks. See Larks
Skyscraper. Dennis Lee.—PrRa
"Skyscraper, skyscraper." See Skyscraper
Skyscrapers
Boulder, Colorado. X. J. Kennedy.—KeF
City blockades. L. B. Hopkins.—HoSs
Glass walling. N. M. Bodecker.—BoPc
Skyscraper. D. Lee.—PrRa
Skyscrapers. R. Field.—FrP
Skyscratcher. R. Froman.—LiSf
Skyscrapers. Rachel Field.—FrP
"Skyscrapers made of earth, stones, trees." See Boulder, Colorado
Skyscratcher. Robert Froman.—LiSf
"Slack your rope, hangs-a-man."** See The maid freed from the gallows

Sladen, Douglas
A summer Christmas in Australia.—HaO
Slave coffle. Maya Angelou.—AnS
Slavery
Aunt Sue's stories. L. Hughes.—HuDk
The cruise of the Mystery. C. Thaxter.—HaOf
Harriet Tubman. E. Greenfield.—LiSf
"I was Harriet." A. Adoff.—AdA
Passing. A. Adoff.—AdA
Slave coffle. M. Angelou.—AnS
Still finding out. A. Adoff.—AdA
Sled run. Barbara Juster Esbensen.—EsCs
A **sledding** song. Norman C. Schlichter.—FrP
Sleds and sleighs
Atop. P. Redcloud.—HoBf
A country boy in winter. S. O. Jewett.—HaOf
Downhill. R. J. Margolis.—MaS
Sled run. B. J. Esbensen.—EsCs
A sledding song. N. C. Schlichter.—FrP
Toboggan ride, down Happy Hollow. M. C. Livingston.—LiWo
The train dogs. P. Johnson.—DoNw
Sleep. See also Bedtime; Dreams; Lullabies
Alarm clock. E. Merriam.—MeSk
"All animals like me." R. Souster.—DoNw
Awake. N. M. Bodecker.—BoPc
"The cat sat asleep by the side of the fire." Mother Goose.—LoR
Cats ("Cats sleep"). E. Farjeon.—PrRh
Circle sleeper. J. H. Marvin.—ChC
The dark ("I am glad of that other life"). W. Heyen.—PlEd
Dog ("Under a maple tree"). V. Worth.—HoDl
For putting a woman's family to sleep. Unknown, fr. the Cherokee Indian.—BiSp
"Girls a' weeping." E. Farjeon.—FaE
Going to sleep in the country. H. Moss.—JaD
"How cool it feels." Basho.—KoT
"Hush, my posy sleeps." C. Pomerantz.—PoA
"I have lived and I have loved." Unknown.— KoT
"I want to." B. S. De Regniers.—LaW
In the night ("When I wake up and it is dark"). M. Chute.—HoSu
In the old house. J. Aiken.—LiWa
"Little Boy Blue, come blow your horn." Mother Goose.—LoR
Lullaby ("Sleep sleep beneath the old wind's eye"). G. Vigneault.—DoNw
The middle of the night ("This is a song to be sung at night"). K. Kuskin.—LaW—PrRh
Mother cat's purr. J. Yolen.—PrRa
Ned ("It's a singular thing that Ned"). E. Farjeon.—FaE
Night piece. R. R. Patterson.—LiWa
The puppy's song. C. Pomerantz.—PoA
Rain ("I was having trouble sleeping"). J. Prelutsky.—PrMp
Sleeping on the ceiling. E. Bishop.—KoT
Sleeping outdoors. M. Chute.—LaW—PrRa
Sweet dreams. O. Nash.—CoOu
Waking at night. E. Farjeon.—FaE
"When a cat is asleep." K. Kuskin.—JaT
Where do you sleep. W. Engvik.—LaW
While I slept. R. Francis.—KeK
Sleep. Nikki Giovanni.—GiSp
"Sleep, baby, sleep, thy father guards the sheep." Mother Goose.—Dem—LoR
"Sleep, baby, sleep, thy father watches the sheep." Unknown.—BaH—LaW
"Sleep King Jesus." See Mary's song
"Sleep, little one, your father is bringing." See Cradlesong

Smith, William Jay—*Continued*
Lion ("The lion, ruler over all the beasts").—PrRh
Little Dimity.—LiSf
Love ("I love you, I like you").—PrRh
Miss Hartley.—BrT
Moon ("I have a white cat whose name is Moon").—ChC—LiCa—LiSf
The oil lamp.—BrT
An old man by Salt Lake.—BrT
An old man of Toulon.—BrT
The panda.—BrT
Quail in autumn.—JaPi
"Said Dorothy Hughes to Helen Hocking."—KeK
Seal.—LiSf—PrRh—RuI
Snail ("They have brought me a snail"), tr. by.—FaTh
"There was an old lady named Crockett."—KeK
The toaster ("A silver scaled dragon with jaws flaming red").—PrRh
Uncertain what to wear.—BrT
Unicorn ("The unicorn with the long white horn").—PrRh
Vincent Van Gogh.—PlEd
Whale ("When I swam underwater I saw a blue whale").—RuI
A young man who loved rain.—BrT
Smog. Myra Cohn Livingston.—LiSi
Smoke
The bonfire. E. Farjeon.—FaE
Dragon smoke. L. Moore.—LiSf—MoSn—PrRa
"A hill full, a hole full." Mother Goose.—LiSf
"House full, yard full." Mother Goose.—CoN
The smoke. E. Farjeon.—FaE
There are no people song. Unknown, fr. the Navajo Indian.—KoT
"What comes out of a chimney." Mother Goose.—LoR
The **smoke.** Eleanor Farjeon.—FaE
"**Smoky** with fog." See The fog
A **smugglers'** song. Rudyard Kipling.—BlO
"**Snaggle** tooth." See My girl Maggie
The **snail** ("At sunset, when the night-dews fall"). James Reeves.—BlO—FaTh
The **snail** ("The snail doesn't know where he's going"). Jack Prelutsky.—FrP—PrZ
The **snail** ("Snail upon the wall"). John Drinkwater.—CoOu
Snail ("They have brought me a snail"). Federico García Lorca, tr. by William Jay Smith.—FaTh
Snail ("This sticky trail"). David McCord.—McAs
"The **snail** and the mouse." Laura E. Richards.—PrRa
"The **snail** doesn't know where he's going." See The snail
"**Snail** upon the wall." See The snail
"A **snail,** who had a way, it seems." See The snail's dream
Snails
"Four and twenty tailors went to kill a snail." Mother Goose.—DaC
I don't like you. K. Wright.—CoOu
Little snail. H. Conkling.—LiSf
S. From A bestiary of the garden for children who should know better. P. Gotlieb.—DoNw
The snail ("At sunset, when the night-dews fall"). J. Reeves.—BlO—FaTh
The snail ("The snail doesn't know where he's going"). J. Prelutsky.—FrP—PrZ

The snail ("Snail upon the wall"). J. Drinkwater.—CoOu
Snail ("They have brought me a snail"). F. García Lorca.—FaTh
Snail ("This sticky trail"). D. McCord.—McAs
"The snail and the mouse." L. E. Richards.—PrRa
The snail's dream. O. Herford.—PrRh
Snail's pace. A. Fisher.—PrRa
"Well, hello down there." Issa.—FaTh—LiIl—LiSf
The **snail's** dream. Oliver Herford.—PrRh
Snail's pace. Aileen Fisher.—PrRa
The **snake** ("Don't ever make"). Jack Prelutsky.—PrZ
Snake ("A snake came to my water-trough"). David Herbert Lawrence.—HeR
"A **snake** came to my water-trough." See Snake
Snakes
"As I was walking down the lake." Unknown.—DaC
Asparagus. V. Worth.—WoSp
The boa ("Allow me just one short remark"). J. J. Bell.—PrRh
The garden hose. B. Janosco.—CoN
"A hiss, a gulp, where are you, Niles." X. J. Kennedy.—KeB
"Mother doesn't want a dog." J. Viorst.—PrRh—ViI
"A narrow fellow in the grass." E. Dickinson.—HaOf—HeR—LiSf
The rattlesnake. A. Purdy.—DoNw
"The scroobious snake." From An animal alphabet. E. Lear.—LiH
The serpent. T. Roethke.—PrRh
Serpentine verse. J. S. Newman.—BrT
The silent snake. Unknown.—ChG
The snake ("Don't ever make"). J. Prelutsky.—PrZ
Snake ("A snake came to my water-trough"). D. H. Lawrence.—HeR
"Snakes alive." A. Lobel.—LoWr
Springfield Mountain. Unknown.—PlAs
"There was an old man with a flute." E. Lear.—LiH
Viper. E. Merriam.—MeHa
"**Snakes** alive." Arnold Lobel.—LoWr
Snapshots. N. M. Bodecker.—BoPc
The **snare.** James Stephens.—BlO—LiSf
The **snatchits.** Jack Prelutsky.—PrB
Sneaky Bill. William Cole.—PrRh
Sneaky Sue. Jack Prelutsky.—PrNk
The **sneepies.** Jack Prelutsky.—PrB
"The **sneepies,** lying in a heap." See The sneepies
Sneeze. Maxine Kumin.—PrRa
Sneezing
Bandit. A. M. Klein.—DoNw
But I wonder. A. Fisher.—PrRa
"If you sneeze on Monday, you sneeze for danger." Mother Goose.—AlH
"Julius Caesar made a law." Mother Goose.—FaW
A queer fellow named Woodin. E. Bradley.—BrT
The seven sneezes of Cecil Snedde. J. Prelutsky.—PrSr
Sneeze. M. Kumin.—PrRa
The sneezysnoozer. J. Prelutsky.—PrB
The **sneezysnoozer.** Jack Prelutsky.—PrB
"The **sneezysnoozer** sneezes." See The sneezysnoozer

Snow.—*Continued*
  "This little house is sugar." L. Hughes.—CoN
  Winter sweetness.—HuDk—PrRa
Toboggan ride, down Happy Hollow. M. C. Livingston.—LiWo
Velvet shoes. E. Wylie.—LiSf
"Well, let's go." Basho.—KoT
When all the world is full of snow. N. M. Bodecker.—PrRh
"When snowflakes are fluttering." J. Prelutsky.—PrIs
"Why does it snow." L. E. Richards.—HaOf
"Winter etches windowpanes, fingerpaints in white." M. C. Livingston.—LiCs
  Winter.—BaS
Winter is tacked down. S. N. Weygant.—BaS
The winter moon ("I hit my wife and went out and saw"). T. Kyozo.—McL
Winter morning. O. Nash.—BaS
Winter's tale. N. Farber.—FaTh
Snow. Mary Ann Hoberman.—DaS
Snow ("Drifting we wake"). Nan Fry.—JaPo
The snow ("It sifts from leaden sieves"). Emily Dickinson.—DaC
Snow ("No breath of wind"). Walter De la Mare.—CoOu
Snow ("Oh the falling snow"). Eleanor Farjeon.—FaE
"Snow." See Snowflakes
Snow ("Tilt, wilt"). Ralph Pomeroy.—JaPi
Snow ("Trembling"). Myra Cohn Livingston.—LiSi
Snow ("We'll play in the snow"). Karla Kuskin.—BaS—PrRa
"Snow bright." See Noel
"Snow falling." See Snowfall
"Snow falling and night falling fast, oh, fast." See Desert places
Snow fence. Ted Kooser.—JaPo
The snow-filled nest. Rose Terry Cooke.—HaOf
"The snow has melted now." See January
Snow in the garden. Eleanor Farjeon.—FaE
"Snow kept on sifting through the night." See Moonwalk
"Snow makes a new land." Kazue Mizumura.—LiSf
"Snow makes whiteness where it falls." See First snow
The snow-man. Marian Douglas.—HaOf
Snow print one, mystery. Barbara Juster Esbensen.—EsCs
Snow print two, hieroglyphics. Barbara Juster Esbensen.—EsCs—FaTh
"The snow-shoe hare." Ted Hughes.—HuU
Snow stars. Barbara Juster Esbensen.—EsCs
Snow woman. Nancy Dingman Watson.—BaS
"Snow woman snow woman." See Snow woman
Snowball wind. Aileen Fisher.—BaS
"Snowballs are fun." See James Shell's snowball stand
Snowbound, sels. John Greenleaf Whittier
  "Shut in from all the world without".—HaO
Snowdrops. George MacBeth.—HaO
Snowfall. Eleanor Farjeon.—FaE
Snowfall ("Snow falling"). Artis Bernard.—CoN
The snowflake. Walter De la Mare.—FaTh—LiSf—PrRh
"Snowflake." See First snowflake
A snowflake fell. Jack Prelutsky.—PrIs
"A snowflake fell into my hand." See A snowflake fell
"Snowflake souffle." X. J. Kennedy.—BaS

Snowflakes ("And did you know"). Clive Sansom.—HaO
Snowflakes ("Snow"). Suk-Joong Yoon.—BaS
"The snowflakes fell, the first this year." See A lost snowflake
Snowman. David McCord.—McAs—PrRa
Snowman sniffles. N. M. Bodecker.—BoSs
The snowman's lament. Jack Prelutsky.—PrIs
Snowmen
  "My snowman has a noble head." J. Prelutsky.—PrIs
The snow-man. M. Douglas.—HaOf
Snow woman. N. D. Watson.—BaS
Snowman. D. McCord.—McAs—PrRa
Snowman sniffles. N. M. Bodecker.—BoSs
The snowman's lament. J. Prelutsky.—PrIs
"That cheerful snowman." H. L. Johnson.—BaS
The snowstorm. Kaye Starbird.—BaS
Snowy benches. Aileen Fisher.—BaS—HoSi, KeK
Snowy morning. Lilian Moore.—BaS—MoSn
The snowy owl. Ted Hughes.—HuU
"A snowy path for squirrel and fox." See The brook in February
Snyder, Gary
  "After weeks of watching the roof leak."—KeK
Some good things to be said for the iron age.—KoT
Snyder, Richard
  The aging poet, on a reading trip to Dayton, visits the Air Force Museum and discovers there a plane he once flew.—JaPi
Blue sparks in dark closets.—JaPi
Chicago, summer past.—JaPi
"Oh I have dined on this delicious day."—JaT
Sparrow in an airport.—JaPo
Wintered sunflowers.—JaPo
Snyder, Zilpha Keatley
  "Rabbits are nice neighbors."—LiE
Silent hill.—LiWa
To dark eyes dreaming.—PrRh
Today is Saturday.—LiIl
"So cold the wintry winds do blow." See The unquiet grave
"So far as I can see." See Meditations of a tortoise dozing under a rosetree near a beehive at noon while a dog scampers about and a cuckoo calls from a distant wood
"So great the pain." See On love
So long. William Stafford.—JaPo
"So low it used to seem almost." See Full moon, rising
"So many things happen." See The war of the worlds
"So much depends." See The red wheelbarrow
"So, nine crows to this April field." See Crows
"So proud in his furry robe." See Baboon
"So she went into the garden." See The great panjandrum
"So, so, spade and hoe." See Baby's baking
"So tall was a cowboy called Slouch." See Tall
So they went deeper into the forest. Roy Daniells.—DoNw
"So they went deeper into the forest, said Jacob Grimm." See So they went deeper into the forest
"So we went to see this mummy." See The museum
"So, we'll go no more a-roving." Lord Byron.—KoT
Soap
  Naughty soap song. D. Aldis.—PrRa

Some people. Rachel Field.—CoN—PrRh
"Some people are born to." See Meredith Piersall
Some people I know. Jack Prelutsky.—PrRh
"Some people I know like to chatter." See Some people I know
"Some people occasionally carry a camera." See David Eberhoff
"Some people own lots of land." See Shirley and her son
"Some people talk and talk." See People
"Some people talk in a telephone." See Thoughts on talkers
"Some primal termite knocked on wood." See The termite
"Some say the nightmare is." See Nightmares
"Some say the sun is a golden earring." Natalia Belting.—LiSf
"Some say the world will end in fire." See Fire and ice
Some sound advice from Singapore. John Ciardi.—LiSf
"Some talk of Alexander, and some of Hercules." Unknown.—TrM
Some things are funny like that. Nikki Giovanni.—GiSp
Some things don't make any sense at all. Judith Viorst.—PrRh—ViI
"Some things go to sleep in such a funny way." See How they sleep
Some things I know about cats. Beatrice Schenk De Regniers.—DeT
Some things that Easter brings. Elsie Parrish.—PrRa
"Some things will never change although." See Far trek
Some uses for poetry. Eve Merriam.—MeSk
"Some very nice persons have no use for things." See Ruins
"Some whirled scythes through the thick oats." See The farm hands
"Some words clink." See Feelings about words
"Somebody's coming to tea today." See Some one to tea
"Someday I'm going to have a store." See General store
"Someday when we're older." See Big house
"Someone." See Mural on second avenue
"Someone be a rose tree." See The rose thieves
"Someone hides from someone." See Hide and seek
Someone I like. Charlotte Zolotow.—ZoE
"Someone I like is far away." See Someone I like
"Someone new has come to stay." See Everett Anderson's friend
"Someone painted pictures." See Jack Frost
"Someone runs about." See Bullfight
"Someone sows someone." See The seed
"Someone told me someone said." See A lesson in manners
"Someone would like to have you for her child." See Lullaby
"Someone's been up here nights." See In a country cemetery in Iowa
Someone's face. John Ciardi.—PrRa
"Someone's face was all frowned shut." See Someone's face
"Somersault eve." See Holidays
Somersaults. Jack Prelutsky.—PrRa
"Something." See In one place
Something about me. Unknown.—PrRa
Something better. David McCord.—McAs

"Something goes wrong with my synthetic brain." See The case for the miners
"Something is bleeding." See September
"Something is there." Lilian Moore.—LiWa—PrRh
"Something old, something new." Mother Goose.—LoR
"Something points us." See Campsite
Something silky. Jack Prelutsky.—PrNk
"Something silky, scarcely there." See Something silky
"Something told the wild geese." Rachel Field.—CoN—CoOu—HaOf—LiSf—PrRh
"Something vague waxes or wanes." See Lines for a friend who left
"Something's come over pumpkins." See Halloween disguises
"Something's in my pocket." Eve Merriam.—MeBl
Sometimes ("I am afraid of being crushed in the pincers"). Greg Kuzma.—JaPi
Sometimes ("Sometimes I simply have to cry"). Jack Prelutsky.—PrRa
Sometimes ("Sometimes, when a bird cries out"). Herman Hesse, tr. by Robert Bly.—LiWa
"Sometimes." See Teased
"Sometimes, around/moonrise." See Skunk
"Sometimes I am an unseen." See Cat
"Sometimes, I felt the sun." See Psalm of a black mother
"Sometimes I simply have to cry." See Sometimes
"Sometimes I watch the moon at night." See The moon and a cloud
"Sometimes, I'm sorry, but sometimes." See Yawning
Sometimes it pays to back up. John Ciardi.—CiD
Sometimes poems. Judith Viorst.—ViI
"Sometimes poems are." See Sometimes poems
"Sometimes the night is not enough, I rise remembering." See The biplane
Sometimes there is no easy answer. John Ciardi.—CiD
"Sometimes, tired, I imagine your death." See To L.B.S.
"Sometimes up out of this land." See Bifocal
"Sometimes want makes touch too much." See Warmth
"Sometimes, when a bird cries out." See Sometimes
"Sometimes when I see the bare arms of trees in the evening." See The bare arms of trees
"Sometimes when I watch my brother." See On the sidelines
"Sometimes when I'm lonely." See Hope
"Sometimes when you watch the fire." See Long distance
"Sometimes you come on a whole." See Driving through coal country in Pennsylvania
"Somewhere between." See Howie Bystrom
"Somewhere between the flume ride." See Wendy Tarloff
"Somewhere in the night." See At midnight
"A somnolent & furry heap." See R
"Son, said my mother." See The ballad of the harp-weaver
Song ("Child, is thy father dead"). Ebenezer Elliot.—PlSc
Song, sels. Elizabeth Coatsworth
  "I like fish, said the Mermaid".—HoCr
Song ("Desire for a woman took hold of me in the night"). Unknown.—McL
Song ("Dew on the bamboos"). Unknown, tr. by Edward Powys Mathers.—McL

Song to the ninth grade. Pamela Crawford Holahan.—PlAs
Song Vu Chin. Mel Glenn.—GlC
Songs. See also Singing
Song's eternity. John Clare.—PlAs
Songs for a colored singer. Elizabeth Bishop.—HeR
Songs in the garden of the house god, sels. Unknown
"The sacred blue corn-seed I am planting".—LiTp
Songs my mother taught me. David Wagoner.—JaS
Songs of the corn dance. Unknown.—BiSp
Songs of the ghost dance, complete. Unknown
"Fog, fog".—LiWa
"The rocks are ringing".—LiWa
"There is a dust from the whirlwind".—LiWa
"The whirlwind".—LiWa
"The wind stirs the willows".—LiWa
Songs of the horse society. Unknown.—BiSp
Sonnet. Dante Alighieri, tr. by Kenneth Koch. HeR—KoT
Sonnet for my father. Donald Justice.—JaD
Sonnets, sels. William Shakespeare
"Betwixt mine eye and heart a league is took".—PlEd
"Mine eye and heart are at a mortal war".—PlEd
"Mine eye hath play'd the painter, and hath steel'd".—PlEd
"Shall I compare thee to a summer's day?".—HoUn
"When, in disgrace with fortune and men's eyes".—HoUn
"When my love swears that she is made of truth".—HoUn
Sons
"A father sees a son nearing manhood." C. Sandburg.—HoRa
For my son, born during an ice storm. D. Jauss.—JaS
Song to a son. Unknown, fr. the Kwakiutl Indian.—BiSp
The sons of liberty. Unknown.—PlAs
"Soon as Caesar, our dog, spied that fox-fur scarf." See An awful moment
The sorcerer, sels. William Schwenck Gilbert
Mr. Wells.—LiWa
"Sorcerers, they've turned." See Living with children
The sorceress. Vachel Lindsay.—LiWa
Sorrells, Helen
The amputation.—JaD
Sorrow. See Grief
Soto, Gary
Lantern.—JaS
Remedies.—JaS
Stars ("At dusk the first stars appear").—JaT
Soul. See also Death; Immortality
The cold heaven. W. B. Yeats.—HeR
The devil's bag. J. Stephens.—LiWa
The lie ("Go, soul, the body's guest"). Sir W. Raleigh.—HeR
Sea-change. J. Masefield.—HeR
The six strings. F. García Lorca.—HeR
Soule, Jean Conder
Surprises.—PrRh
A sound. From Tender buttons. Gertrude Stein.—KoT
"A sound-alike." See Nym and graph
The sound of night. Maxine Kumin.—JaD
The sound of rain. David Allan Evans.—JaG

The sound of the wind. Christina Georgina Rossetti.—BlO—CoOu
Sound of water. Mary O'Neill.—CoN
"The sound of water is." See Sound of water
"Sound the flute." See Spring
Sounding. David Jauss.—JaS
Sounds
"Ancient pool." Basho.—KeK
Apple ("At the center, a dark star"). N. Fry.—JaPo
"Be not afeard, the isle is full of noises." From The tempest. W. Shakespeare.—HeR
The bed. C. Zolotow.—ZoE
The bells. E. A. Poe.—HaOf
The blacksmiths. Unknown.—HeR
The brook. A. Tennyson.—BlO
The brook in February. C. G. D. Roberts.—DoNw
Celery. O. Nash.—JaT—PrRh
Closet. S. Cassedy.—CaR
Cockpit in the clouds. D. Dorrance.—PrRh
"Creeping Jenny." E. Farjeon.—FaE
Cynthia in the snow. G. Brooks.—BaS—HoSi—LiSf
The dark ("It's always"). M. C. Livingston.—LiWo
Dinosaur din. X. J. Kennedy.—LiSf
Ears hear. L. Hymes, and J. L. Hymes.—PrRa
Encounter. L. Moore.—MoSn
Fish ("Look at them flit"). M. A. Hoberman.—PrRa
Foghorns. L. Moore.—HoSs—MoSn—PrRh
The fresh air. H. Monro.—LiIl
Gray thrums. C. B. Bates.—HaOf
The great figure. W. C. Williams.—KoT
"Handsawwwwwwwwwwww." R. Lebovitz.—KeK
House noises. X. J. Kennedy.—KeF
"I asked the little boy who cannot see." Unknown.—CoOu
Icicles. B. J. Esbensen.—EsCs
"I'm a prickly crab." E. Merriam.—MeBl
"In quiet night." M. C. Livingston.—LaW
It is so still. J. Prelutsky.—PrMp
Jim Desterland. H. Plutzik.—HeR
Kitty cornered. E. Merriam.—ChC
Lake Ontario. From Great Lakes suite. J. Reaney.—DoNw
Lost ("I shall remember chuffs the train"). H. Behn.—HoCb
"Louder than a clap of thunder." J. Prelutsky.—PrNk
New sounds. L. Moore.—HoSi—MoSn
Night sounds. F. Holman.—LaW
Nocturne. A. Guiterman.—LaW
Noises. A. Fisher.—HoBf
Now that spring is here. B. J. Esbensen.—EsCs
October nights in my cabin. N. M. Bodecker.—BoSs
Old deep sing song. C. Sandburg.—HoRa
"An old silent pond." Basho.—LiSf
Onomatopoeia and onomatopoeia II. E. Merriam.—MeSk
Owls ("Wait, the great horned owls"). W. D. W. Snodgrass.—JaPi
The people upstairs. O. Nash.—PrRh
"The pickety fence." D. McCord.—BeD—CoN—FaW—LiSf
Quaking aspen. E. Merriam.—MeF
Rain ("Like a drummer's brush"). E. di Pasquale.—KeK
Rain song. D. McCord.—McAs
The rattle bag. D. Ap Gwilym.—HeR

Sounds—*Continued*

"Repeat that, repeat that." G. M. Hopkins.—HeR

Cuckoo.—KoT

Seashell ("This seashell is an ocean cove"). S. Liatsos.—HoSe

Shell ("When it was time"). M. C. Livingston.—LiWo

The silent snake. Unknown.—ChG

Snowy morning. L. Moore.—BaS—MoSn

Some good things to be said for the iron age. G. Snyder.—KoT

Song of the pop-bottlers. M. Bishop.—FaW—KeK

Song of the train. D. McCord.—CoN—HoCl

A sound. From Tender buttons. G. Stein.—KoT

The sound of night. M. Kumin.—JaD

Sound of water. M. O'Neill.—CoN

"The sounds in the evening." E. Farjeon.—FaE

"The sounds in the morning." E. Farjeon.—FaE

Sounds of the day. N. MacCaig.—HeR

Spring night in Lo-yang, hearing a flute. Li Po.—KoT

Sunset ("Before I left my spot"). D. A. Evans.—JaPo

"Tommy waved his stick about." Unknown.—TrM

"Tonight is impossibly noisy." J. Prelutsky.—PrMp

The train. C. Zolotow.—ZoE

The train in the night. E. Riddell.—LaW

An unexplained ouch. X. J. Kennedy.—KeF

Vowels. A. Rimbaud.—KoT

Walking with your eyes shut. W. Stafford.—JaG

"Who has seen the wind." C. G. Rossetti.—BlO—CoN—FrP—LiSf—PrRh

The wind.—DaC

Wild iron. A. Curnow.—HeR

Wind song ("When the wind blows"). L. Moore.—MoSn

Windy nights ("Whenever the moon and stars are set"). R. L. Stevenson.—DaC—KeK—LaW—LiSf—PrRh

"The **sounds** in the evening." Eleanor Farjeon.—FaE

"The **sounds** in the morning." Eleanor Farjeon.—FaE

"**Sounds** like big." See Waking from a nap on the beach

Sounds of the day. Norman MacCaig.—HeR

Soup

"Beautiful soup, so rich and green." From Alice's adventures in wonderland. L. Carroll.—BlO

Turtle soup.—HoMu—PrRh

Chicken soup with rice, complete. M. Sendak.—FaW

Fat Lena's recipe for crocodile soup. P. Janowitz.—JaT

January ("In January"). From Chicken soup with rice. M. Sendak.—HoSi—PrRa

Seymour Snorkle. J. Prelutsky.—PrNk

Soup. C. Sandburg.—HaOf—HoRa

The story of Augustus who would not have any soup. H. Hoffman.—PrRh

Soup. Carl Sandburg.—HaOf—HoRa

Soupault, Philippe

Sporting goods.—KoT

Soups and juices. Richard J. Margolis.—MaS

"**Sour**." See Bald cypress

Souster, Raymond

"All animals like me."—DoNw

Flight of the roller-coaster.—DoNw

The worm ("Don't ask me how he managed").—DoNw

Southbound on the freeway. May Swenson.—CoN—LiSf

Southeast Arkanasia. Maya Angelou.—PlSc

Southern mansion. Arna Bontemps.—LiWa

Southern Pacific. Carl Sandburg.—HoRa

Southwell, Robert

The burning babe.—HaO—HeR

The **sower**. William Cowper.—PlSc

"**Soy** chiquita, soy bonita." See Chiquita bonita

Space. David Herbert Lawrence.—PrBb

Space and space travel

The first. L. Moore.—MoSn

Going up ("Space suit Sammy"). J. T. Moore.—PrRh

How strange it is. C. Lewis.—PrRh

Last laugh. L. B. Hopkins.—HoSu

Message from a mouse, ascending in a rocket. P. Hubbell.—LiSf—PrRh

"Naughty little brown mouse." J. Prelutsky.—PrRi

The new year's journey. J. Ridland.—LiNe

No man on any moon. C. Lewis.—LiSf

"Noticing an open-doored." X. J. Kennedy.—KeB

Orbiter 5 shows how earth looks from the moon. M. Swenson.—LiSf

Orbit's end. N. M. Bodecker.—BoPc

Soft landings. H. Sergeant.—CoOu

Southbound on the freeway. M. Swenson.—CoN—LiSf

Space. D. H. Lawrence.—PrBb

"Three skies." C. Lewis.—LiSf

The universe ("There is the moon, there is the sun"). M. B. Miller.—PrRh

"**Space** man, space man." See Soft landings

"**Space**, of course, is alive." See Space

"**Space** suit Sammy." See Going up

"A **spade**, a rake, a hoe." See The lay of the labourer

Spade Scharnweber. Don Welch.—JaPi

"**Spade** Scharnweber was a white Watusi, his mother." See Spade Scharnweber

"**Spades** take up leaves." See Gathering leaves

"**Spaghetti**." See A round

The **spaghetti** nut. Jack Prelutsky.—PrSr

"**Spaghetti**, spaghetti." Jack Prelutsky.—HoMu

The **span** of life. Robert Frost.—HoDl

"The **spangled** pandemonium." Palmer Brown.—PrRh

Spanish language

"I like arroz y habichuelas." C. Pomerantz.—PoI

Spanish nursery rhymes. See Nursery rhymes—Spanish

The **sparrow** hawk. Russell Hoban.—LiSf—PrRh

Sparrow in an airport. Richard Snyder.—JaPo

A **sparrow** in winter. N. M. Bodecker.—BoSs

"**Sparrow**, you little brown gutter-mouse." See London sparrow

Sparrows

"Footprints of a sparrow." N. M. Bodecker.—BaS—BoSs

"A little cock sparrow sat on a green tree." Mother Goose.—LoR

"A little cock sparrow sat on a tree".—DaC

London sparrow. E. Farjeon.—FaE

"A lonely sparrow." K. Mizumura.—LiSf

Mr. and Mrs. Spikky Sparrow. E. Lear.—LiH

Sparrow in an airport. R. Snyder.—JaPo

A sparrow in winter. N. M. Bodecker.—BoSs

Sparrows—*Continued*
Sparrows. P. Fleischman.—FlI
They've all gone south. M. B. Miller.—PrRh
Sparrows. Paul Fleischman.—FlI
"**Sparrows** everywhere." See Sparrows
"**Speak** gently, spring, and make no sudden sound." See Four little foxes
"**Speak** of this to no one." See Sleeping with someone who came in secret
"**Speak** roughly to your little boy." From Alice's adventures in Wonderland. Lewis Carroll.—BlO
  A lullaby.—PrRh
"**Speaking** of cows." Kaye Starbird.—LiSf
A **special** dictionary to help you understand cats. Beatrice Schenk De Regniers.—DeT
Special request for the children of Mother Corn. Unknown.—BiSp
"A **speckled** cat and a tame hare." See Two songs of a fool
Spectacular. Lilian Moore.—KeK
Speech
  Beware of speaker. N. M. Bodecker.—BoPc
  The child in the rug. J. Haines.—JaD
  Sarah Samantha. Unknown.—BrT
  Town meeting or 'hey man, don't speak so good'. N. M. Bodecker.—BoPc
Speed
  "Swift things are beautiful." E. Coatsworth.—LiSf
  "There was a young lady named Bright." Unknown.—LiSf
"The **speedy** cheetah loves to run." See The cheetah
The **spell.** Robert Herrick.—LiWa
Spell it. Unknown.—BrT
A **spell** of weather. Eve Merriam.—MeSk
Spelling
  Alphabet. E. Farjeon.—FaE
  Bananananananananana. W. Cole.—PrRh
  "The electric eel." From Three animals. R. Padgett.—KoT
  "The giraffe." From Three animals. R. Padgett.—KoT
  The gnat. E. Rudzewicz.—JaT
  India rubber. E. Farjeon.—FaE
  A misspelled tail. E. T. Corbett.—HaOf
  Nym and graph. E. Merriam.—MeSk
  One, two, three, gough ("To make some bread you must have dough"). E. Merriam.—CoN—MeSk
  Ough, or, the cross farmer. D. S. Martin.—BrT
  Spell it. Unknown.—BrT
  Spelling bee. C. Rylant.—RyW
  A tail of the see. E. T. Corbett.—HaOf
  We heard Wally wail. J. Prelutsky.—PrNk
  Why I did not reign. E. Merriam.—MeSk
Spelling bee. Cynthia Rylant.—RyW
Spender, Stephen
  Daybreak.—JaD
  Missing my daughter.—JaS
  To my daughter.—JaD
"**Spending** beyond their income on gifts for Christmas." See Christmas shopping
Spendthrift. Norma Farber.—LiSf
Spices
  "Amelia mixed the mustard." A. E. Housman.—PrRh
  "Nose, nose, jolly red nose." Mother Goose.—LoR
  "Peter Piper picked a peck of pickled peppers." Mother Goose.—FaW—LoR

Spider ("I saw a little spider"). Aileen Fisher.—FiW
The **spider** ("One biting winter morning"). Hannah F. Gould.—HaOf
Spider ("Spider's"). Lilian Moore.—MoSn
Spider ("With what voice"). Basho.—KoT
The **spider** and the fly. Mary Howitt.—CoOu—DaC
"A **spider** danced a cosy jig." Irving Layton.—DoNw
"The **spider** in its web of gray." See Ambush
Spider Reeves. Henry Carlile.—JaPi
"The **spider** works across the wall." See The huntress
Spiders. See also Cobwebs
  "After the rains." N. M. Bodecker.—BoSs
  Ambush. E. Farjeon.—FaE
  "At early morn the spiders spin." Mother Goose.—LoR
  The embarrassing episode of Little Miss Muffet. G. W. Carryl.—HaOf
  The eternal feminine. O. Herford.—BrT
  Gossamer. E. Farjeon.—FaE
  The huntress. G. Johnston.—DoNw
  "If you wish to live and thrive." Mother Goose.—LoR
  "Incey-wincey spider climbed the water spout." Mother Goose.—LoR
  "Little Miss Muffet." Mother Goose.—DeM—FaW—LiSf—LoR
  Sky net. A. Fisher.—FiW
  Spider ("I saw a little spider"). A. Fisher.—FiW
  The spider ("One biting winter morning"). H. F. Gould.—HaOf
  Spider ("Spider's"). L. Moore.—MoSn
  Spider ("With what voice"). Basho.—KoT
  The spider and the fly. M. Howitt.—CoOu—DaC
"**Spider's.**" See Spider
"The **spike** of daffodil." See The start
A **spike** of green. Barbara Baker.—PrRa
Spilka, Arnold
  "Don't tell me that I talk too much."—PrRh
  "Flowers are a silly bunch."—PrRh
  "I saw a little girl I hate."—PrRh
    A little girl I hate.—BeD
  "I'm really not lazy."—PrRh
  A little girl I hate. See "I saw a little girl I hate"
  Puzzle ("My best friend's name is Billy").—LiIl—PrRh
  "Slippery Sam."—PrRa
"**Spin** a coin, spin a coin." See Queen Nefertiti
"**Spined** / with sparks." See Starfish
Spirit. See Soul
Spirits. See Ghosts
Spirits. Victor Hernandez Cruz.—LiWa
"**Splash,** splosh." See If I were a fish
"**Splashing** water, lantern grass." Unknown.—DeD
"The **splendour** falls on castle walls." From The princess. Alfred Tennyson.—LiWa
  Blow, bugle, blow.—LiSf
  Song.—BlO
Splinter. Carl Sandburg.—HaOf—HoRa—KeK
"**Splish** splosh, February fill the dike." See February
Spofford, Harriet Prescott
  The fossil raindrops.—HaOf
"The **spoiling** daylight inched along the bar-top." See The mill
Spoilt child. Eleanor Farjeon.—FaE
Spoken by Venus on seeing her statue done by Praxiteles. Unknown.—PlEd

A **spooky** sort of shadow. Jack Prelutsky.—PrMp
Sporting goods. Philippe Soupault.—KoT
Sports. See also Athletes and athletics; Games; also names of games, as Baseball; also names of sports, as Fishers and fishing
First practice. G. Gildner.—JaPi
Football. W. Mason.—KeK
Good sportsmanship. R. Armour.—KeK
In memory of the Utah stars. W. Matthews.—JaPi
Jill Le Claire. M. Glenn.—GlC
Joel Feit. M. Glenn.—GlC
A **sporty** young person. Unknown.—BrT
Spray. David Herbert Lawrence.—PrBb
Spring. See also March; April; May; also Seasons
After many springs. L. Hughes.—HuDk
All around the year. X. J. Kennedy.—KeF
And suddenly spring. M. Hillert.—HoSi
Another Sarah. A. Porter.—KoT
"Bee, I'm expecting you." E. Dickinson.—KoT
Canticle of spring. H. Behn.—HoCb
Cardinal ("With deep snow"). B. Howes.—JaD
A charm for spring flowers. R. Field.—LiSf
Coloring. H. Behn.—HoCb
Crows ("When the high/snows lie worn"). V. Worth.—WoSp
Dan. C. Sandburg.—HoDl
The dancers. C. Zolotow.—ZoE
A day begins. D. Levertov.—JaD
Early spring. P. Whalen.—JaT
Easter habits. F. Holman.—LiE
Elm buds. C. Sandburg.—HoRa
End of winter. E. Merriam.—MeSk
Feline. R. Wallace.—JaT
The fight of the year. R. McGough.—HaO
"The first day of spring." E. Merriam.—MeF
First gathering. E. Farjeon.—FaE
First one out of bed. X. J. Kennedy.—KeF
The flower-fed buffaloes. V. Lindsay.—HaOf—HeR
Forsythia bush. L. Moore.—MoSn
"Four ducks on a pond." W. Allingham.—BlO
Four little foxes. L. Sarett.—PrRh
The fourteenth day of Adar. B. J. Esbensen.—LiPj
"Goodby my winter suit." N. M. Bodecker.—PrRh
Green ("Ducklings"). L. Moore.—MoSn
Here ("In this spot"). C. Zolotow.—ZoE
"Here we come a-piping." Unknown.—BlO
House hunters. E. Farjeon.—FaE
"In April the little farmers go out in the foothills." From Santa Fe sketches. C. Sandburg.—HoRa
"In just." E. E. Cummings.—KeK—LiSf
In like a lion. G. Hewitt.—JaPo
"In the fields of spring." Unknown.—LiIl
"Is it robin o'clock." E. Merriam.—MeBl
"It was a lover and his lass." From As you like it. W. Shakespeare.—HeR—HoUn—KoT
Johnny's the lad I love. Unknown.—PlAs
Just before springtime. J. Viorst.—ViI
A late spring. P. Booth.—JaPi
Letter to a friend. L. Moore.—LiIl—MoSn
Little catkins. A. Blok.—LiE
Little seeds. E. H. Minarik.—PrRa
The locust tree in flower. W. C. Williams.—KoT
March. E. Coatsworth.—FaW—PrRh
March twenty-first. B. J. Esbensen.—EsCs
"March winds and April showers." Mother Goose.—DaC—DeM
May. J. Updike.—HaOf

May meadows. E. Farjeon.—FaE
May night. S. Teasdale.—HoSi
Missing the children. P. Zimmer.—JaS
Nothing gold can stay. R. Frost.—KoS
November. A. Cary.—HaOf
Now that spring is here. B. J. Esbensen.—EsCs
Ode to spring. W. R. Brooks.—PrRa—PrRh
Passage ("Remember"). B. J. Esbensen.—EsCs
A patch of old snow. R. Frost.—KoS
Patriarchs. L. Moore.—MoSn
A prayer in spring. R. Frost.—LaT
The pretty ploughboy. Unknown.—PlAs
Pussy willows. A. Fisher.—PrRa
The Shawangunks, early April. L. Moore.—MoSn
Singing in the spring. I. O. Eastwick.—PrRa
Smells. K. Worth.—PrRh
Snowdrops. G. MacBeth.—HaO
Song of the spring peeper. J. Yolen.—YoR
Song of the tree frogs. L. Moore.—MoSn
Song to the ninth grade. P. C. Holahan.—PlAs
Spring ("Bluebird and"). R. Bye.—KoT
Spring ("I'm shouting"). K. Kuskin.—LiSf—PrRh
Spring ("Nothing is so beautiful as spring"). G. M. Hopkins.—HeR
Spring ("Sound the flute"). W. Blake.—FrP—KoT—LiSf
Spring ("Spring, the sweet spring, is the year's pleasant king"). T. Nashe.—BlO—CoOu
Spring, sweet spring.—KoT
Spring again. R. Wallace.—JaPo
Spring and all. G. Bauer.—JaPo
"Spring brings out her baseball bat, swings it through the air." M. C. Livingston.—LiCs
Spring cleaning. B. J. Esbensen.—EsCs
Spring cries. C. Sandburg.—HoRa
Spring day. C. Zolotow.—ZoE
Spring fever. B. J. Esbensen.—EsCs
Spring flowers. H. Behn.—HoCb
Spring gale. N. M. Bodecker.—BoSs
Spring grass. C. Sandburg.—LiSf
Spring in Hampstead. E. Farjeon.—FaE
Spring is. B. Katz.—PrRh
"Der spring is sprung." Unknown.—TrM
"Spring is when the grass turns green and glad." From Lines written for Gene Kelly to dance to. C. Sandburg.—HoRa
Spring morning in Boston's south end. N. M. Bodecker.—BoPc
Spring night in Lo-yang, hearing a flute. Li Po.—KoT
"Spring pipes at the peeper frogs, mocks the mockingbird." M. C. Livingston.—LiCs
Spring rain. M. Chute.—FrP—PrRh
"Spring skips lightly on a thin crust of snow." M. C. Livingston.—LiCs
"Spring skips lightly on a thin crust of snow, pokes her." M. C. Livingston.—LiCs
A spring song of Tzu-Yeh. H. Yen.—McL
Spring whistles. L. Larcom.—HaOf
The spring wind. C. Zolotow.—PrRa—ZoE
Springtime. N. Giovanni.—GiSp
The sun on Easter day. N. Farber.—LiE
Swedes. E. Thomas.—HeR
The talking of the trees. E. Farjeon.—FaE
"Terry." A. Rowe.—ChC
To the thawing wind. R. Frost.—KoS
Up north. N. M. Bodecker.—BoPc
Wake up call. B. J. Esbensen.—EsCs
Water-front streets. L. Hughes.—HuDk
We like March. E. Dickinson.—KoT
Weathers. T. Hardy.—BlO—DaC—HeR

Spring.—*Continued*
Weird. J. Viorst.—ViI
When. D. Aldis.—PrRh
"When daffodils begin to peer." From The winter's tale. W. Shakespeare.—PlAs
"When the almond blossoms." E. Farjeon.—FaE
"When things were as fine as could possibly be." J. Byrom.—TrM
Who calls. F. C. Sayers.—LiSf
Wind stories. B. J. Esbensen.—EsCs
Winter cricket. J. Heath-Stubbs.—HaO
"Winter wakes to changing wind, gives a little cry." M. C. Livingston.—LiCs
The worm ("Don't ask me how he managed"). R. Souster.—DoNw
The worm ("When the earth is turned in spring"). R. Bergengren.—ChG—PrRh
Written in March. W. Wordsworth.—CoN—DaC
"The year's at the spring." From Pippa passes. R. Browning.—ChG LaT
Pippa's song.—CoN
Spring ("Bluebird and"). Reed Bye.—KoT
Spring ("I'm shouting"). Karla Kuskin.—LiSf—PrRh
Spring ("Nothing is so beautiful as spring"). Gerard Manley Hopkins.—HeR
Spring ("Sound the flute"). William Blake.—FrP—KoT—LiSf
Spring ("Spring, the sweet spring, is the year's pleasant king"). Thomas Nashe.—BlO—CoOu
Spring, sweet spring.—KoT
Spring again. Ronald Wallace.—JaPo
Spring and all. Grace Bauer.—JaPo
Spring and fall. Gerard Manley Hopkins.—HeR
"**Spring** approaches, blowing east." See On the eve of our anniversary
"**Spring** brings out her baseball bat, swings it through the air." Myra Cohn Livingston.—LiCs
Spring cleaning. Barbara Juster Esbensen.—EsCs
Spring cries. Carl Sandburg.—HoRa
Spring day. Charlotte Zolotow.—ZoE
Spring diet. Nancy Dingman Watson.—LiSf
Spring fever. Barbara Juster Esbensen.—EsCs
Spring flowers. Harry Behn.—HoCb
Spring gale. N. M. Bodecker.—BoSs
Spring grass. Carl Sandburg.—LiSf
"**Spring** grass, there is a dance to be danced." See Spring grass
Spring in Hampstead. Eleanor Farjeon.—FaE
Spring is. Bobbi Katz.—PrRh
"The **spring** is fresh and fearless." See May night
"The **spring** is not so beautiful there." See Water-front streets
"**Spring** is showery, flowery, bowery." See Four seasons
"Der **spring** is sprung." Unknown.—TrM
"**Spring** is the promise." See Blessings
"**Spring** is when." See Spring is
"**Spring** is when the grass turns green and glad." From Lines written for Gene Kelly to dance to. Carl Sandburg.—HoRa
Spring morning in Boston's south end. N. M. Bodecker.—BoPc
Spring night in Lo-yang, hearing a flute. Li Po.—KoT
"**Spring** pipes at the peeper frogs, mocks the mockingbird." Myra Cohn Livingston.—LiCs
Spring pools. Robert Frost.—KoS
Spring rain. Marchette Chute.—FrP—PrRh

"**Spring** skips lightly on a thin crust of snow." Myra Cohn Livingston.—LiCs
"**Spring** skips lightly on a thin crust of snow, pokes her." Myra Cohn Livingston.—LiCs
A **spring** song of Tzu-Yeh. Hsiao Yen, tr. by Jan W. Walls.—McL
Spring storm ("He comes gusting out of the house"). Jim Wayne Miller.—JaG
Spring storm ("Our old fat tiger cat"). X. J. Kennedy.—KeF
Spring, sweet spring. See Spring ("Spring, the sweet spring, is the year's pleasant king")
"**Spring,** the sweet spring, is the year's pleasant king." See Spring
Spring whistles. Lucy Larcom.—HaOf
The **spring** wind. Charlotte Zolotow.—PrRa—ZoE
Springfield Mountain. Unknown.—PlAs
Springtime. Nikki Giovanni.—GiSp
"The **sprinkler** twirls." See August
Sprod, G. N.
Request number.—TrM
Spruce woods. Archie Randolph Ammons.—KeK
A **sprung** trap. X. J. Kennedy.—KeF
"**Spry,** wry, and gray as these March sticks." See Among the narcissi
Square as a house, sels. Karla Kuskin
"If you could be small".—FaTh
"**Squat.**" See Mushroom
Squeaky shoes. Unknown.—BrT
"**Squeezing** round a bend, train shrieks." See Flying uptown backwards
"**Squelch** and squirt and squiggle." See Showers
Squirrel ("The squirrel in the hickory tree's a"). Lilian Moore.—MoSn
The **squirrel.** Unknown.—PrRa
"The **squirrel** in his shirt." See Ground-squirrel song
"The **squirrel** in the hickory tree's a." See Squirrel
Squirrel in the rain. Frances Frost.—PrRa
Squirrels
The abandoned house. P. Hubbell.—LiWa
The bear and the squirrels. C. P. Cranch.—HaOf
Fable ("The mountain and the squirrel"). R. W. Emerson.—HaOf
Ground-squirrel song. Unknown, fr. the Navajo Indian.—KoT
Joe. D. McCord.—BaS
On a squirrel crossing the road in autumn, in New England. R. Eberhart.—JaPi
Squirrel ("The squirrel in the hickory tree's a"). L. Moore.—MoSn
The squirrel. Unknown.—PrRa
Squirrel in the rain. F. Frost.—PrRa
To a squirrel at Kyle-na-no. W. B. Yeats.—BlO—LiSf—PrRh
"A **stable** lamp is lighted." See A Christmas hymn
Stacey Fowler. Mel Glenn.—GlC
Stafford, William
At the bomb testing site.—HeR
At the grave of my brother.—JaS
Bifocal.—HeR
Fall journey.—JaS
Fall wind ("Pods of summer crowd around the door").—JaPo
Friends.—JaPo
In the deep channel.—HeR
Late, passing prairie farm.—JaG
Long distance.—LiWa
One of the years.—KeK
Peace walk.—JaPi
Rover.—JaT

Stafford, William—*Continued*
So long.—JaPo
Some night again.—JaG
A story that could be true ("If you were exchanged in the cradle and").—CoN
A survey.—HeR
Vacation ("One scene as I bow to pour her coffee").—JaPi
Walking west.—HeR
Walking with your eyes shut.—JaG
The well rising.—HeR
"The **stair** carpet is Turkey red." See On the staircase
Stairs
Halfway down. A. A. Milne.—PrRa
The house-wreckers. C. Reznikoff.—HoSs—KeK
A housewife. Unknown.—BrT
On the staircase. E. Farjeon.—FaE
"**Stale** moon, climb down." See Rosh Hashanah eve
Stallworthy, John
War story.—JaD
Stampede. Lilian Moore.—MoSn
"**Stand** still." See In the fog
"**Standing** in the hall against the." See Listening to grownups quarreling
Stanford, Ann
The bear.—LiWa
The genie.—LiWa
The omens ("The wind has changed, and all the signs turned right").—LiWa
"**Stanley** the fierce." Judith Viorst.—ViI
The **star.** Jane Taylor.—CoN—DaC—FrP—LiSf—PrRa—PrRh
  "Tinkle, twinkle, little star".—ChB—DeM (unat.)—TrM
The **star** in the pail. David McCord.—LiSf
"**Star** light, star bright." Mother Goose.—DaC—DeM—FaW—LiSf
Wishing poem.—CoN
"A **star** looks down at me." See Waiting both
"**Star** Nadine, Golden Spear, Gypsum King." See Queens of the river
"**Star** over all." See Christmas tree
Starbird, Kaye
Cockroaches.—PrRh
December leaves.—BaS
"Don't ever cross a crocodile."—LiSf
Eat-it-all Elaine.—LiSf—PrRh
The hound.—KeK
Jake O'Leary's Thanksgiving.—LiTp
Measles.—PrRh
Minnie Morse.—LiSf
Mother.—JaT
The snowstorm.—BaS
"Speaking of cows."—LiSf
Wendy in winter.—PrRh
Starfish
Starfish ("Its name linking"). E. Merriam.—MeF
Starfish ("Spined / with sparks"). V. Worth.—WoSp
Starfish ("Its name linking"). Eve Merriam.—MeF
Starfish ("Spined / with sparks"). Valerie Worth.—WoSp
Stark county holidays. Mary Oliver.—JaS
The **starlight** night. Gerard Manley Hopkins.—LiWa
The **starlighter.** Arthur Guiterman.—LaW
Starlings
Doves and starlings. E. Farjeon.—FaE

Stars
And in the 51st year of that century, while my brother cried in the trench, while my enemy glared from the cave. H. Plutzik.—HeR
Ashes. V. Popa.—HeR
Blake leads a walk on the Milky Way. N. Willard.—HaOf
Blow the stars home. E. Farjeon.—FaE
"By'm bye." Unknown.—LaW
Cadenza. C. Sandburg.—HoRa
Canis major. R. Frost.—KeK—KoS
De koven. G. Brooks.—HoSu
The falling star. S. Teasdale.—HaOf—LiSf
February twilight. S. Teasdale.—HaOf—HoSi—PrRh
The fireflies. C. Zolotow.—ZoE
Fireflies in the garden. R. Frost.—KoS—PrRh
"Higher than a house." Mother Goose.—LiSf
"I have a little sister, they call her Peep-peep." Mother Goose.—LiSf
In a starry orchard. N. Farber.—LiSf
In the field forever. R. Wallace.—JaPo
"Light the lamps up, lamplighter." E. Farjeon.—FaE
A million candles. J. Prelutsky.—PrMp
The musk-ox. T. Hughes.—HuU
My star. M. C. Livingston.—LaW
"Once, when the sky was very near the earth." N. Belting.—LiSf
Shooting stars. M. C. Livingston.—LiSi
The star. J. Taylor.—CoN—DaC—FrP—LiSf—PrRa—PrRh
  "Tinkle, twinkle, little star".—ChB—DeM (unat.)—TrM
The star in the pail. D. McCord.—LiSf
"Star light, star bright." Mother Goose.—DaC—DeM—FaW—LiSf
Wishing poem.—CoN
Starfish ("Spined / with sparks"). V. Worth.—WoSp
The starlight night. G. M. Hopkins.—LiWa
The starlighter. A. Guiterman.—LaW
Stars ("At dusk the first stars appear"). G. Soto.—JaT
Stars ("Bright stars, light stars"). R. W. Bacmeister.—FrP
Stars ("I'm glad the stars are over me"). Unknown.—ChB
Stars ("In science today we learned"). N. Giovanni.—GiSp—KeK
Stars ("No one"). M. C. Livingston.—LiSi
Stars ("The stars are too many to count"). C. Sandburg.—HoRa
The stars, the dark, and the daisies. I. O. Eastwick.—LaW
"Tell me, thou star, whose wings of light." P. B. Shelley.—KoT
The universe ("There is the moon, there is the sun"). M. B. Miller.—PrRh
Until we built a cabin. A. Fisher.—LaW
Waiting both. T. Hardy.—KoT
"When I heard the learn'd astronomer." W. Whitman.—LiSf
"When the smoke of the clouds parted." From Bright conversation with Saint-Ex. C. Sandburg.—HoRa
Zodiac. E. Farjeon.—FaE
Stars ("At dusk the first stars appear"). Gary Soto.—JaT
Stars ("Bright stars, light stars"). Rhoda W. Bacmeister.—FrP

Stars ("I'm glad the stars are over me").
Unknown.—ChB
Stars ("In science today we learned"). Nikki
Giovanni.—GiSp—KeK
Stars ("No one"). Myra Cohn Livingston.—LiSi
Stars ("The stars are too many to count"). Carl
Sandburg.—HoRa
"Stars and atoms have no size." See Measurement
"The stars are too many to count." See Stars
"Stars over snow." See Night
The stars, the dark, and the daisies. Ivy O.
Eastwick.—LaW
The start. Eleanor Farjeon.—FaE
Starvation. Maya Angelou.—AnS
"The statue." See Up North Second
Statue against a clear sky. From New England
verses. Wallace Stevens.—PlEd
Statue and birds. Louise Bogan.—PlEd
The statue of Medusa. William Drummond.—
PlEd
Statues. See Sculpture and statues
Statues. Richard Wilbur.—PlEd
The statues in the public gardens. Howard
Nemerov.—PlEd
"Stay beautiful." See For poets
"Stay, stay, little sister." See Sister's dressing
rhyme
"Stays shut." See My mouth
"Stealing eggs, Fritz ran afoul." X. J. Kennedy.—
KeB
Steam shovel. Charles Malam.—CoN—PrRh
Steam shovels
Steam shovel. C. Malam.—CoN—PrRh
"Steam, summer, steam." See Night roof
Steeds. Paul Hiebert.—DoNw
Steel, Laura A.
The exclusive old oyster.—BrT
Steel
Prayers of steel. C. Sandburg.—HoRa
Steele, Frank
Country greeting.—JaPi
The departure.—JaG—JaPo
Greener grass.—JaPi
Markers.—JaG
Markings.—JaPi
Moving ("The house inside still looks like a
house").—JaG
Rhymes ("We were talking about poems he had
written").—JaPo
Shaggy dog story.—JaS
Steele, Peggy
I know a man.—JaPo
Stein, Evaleen
Baby's baking.—PrRa
Wild beasts.—FrP—PrRa
Stein, Gertrude
Colored hats. See Tender buttons
A dog ("A little monkey goes like a donkey
that means to say"). See Tender buttons
I am Rose.—ChG—HaOf—KeK—PrRh
A new cup and saucer. See Tender buttons
A petticoat. See Tender buttons
Red roses. See Tender buttons
A sound. See Tender buttons
Tender buttons, sels.
Colored hats.—KoT
A dog ("A little monkey goes like a donkey
that means to say").—KoT
A new cup and saucer.—KoT
A petticoat.—KoT
Red roses.—KoT
A sound.—KoT

An umbrella ("Coloring high means that the
strange reason is in front").—KoT
An umbrella ("Coloring high means that the
strange reason is in front"). See Tender
buttons
Steinbergh, Judith W.
A secret place.—LiIl
Stella Kolsky. Mel Glenn.—GlC
"Step in a ditch." Mother Goose.—LoR
"Step in a hole." Mother Goose.—LoR
"Step in the dirt." Mother Goose.—LoR
"Step on a crack." Mother Goose.—LoR
"Step on a nail." Mother Goose.—LoR
"Step on it, said Aunt Alice, for God's sake."
See The ascension, 1925
"Step one." See Development
Stepfather, a girl's song. Yusef Komunyakaa.—JaS
Stepfathers. See Fathers and fatherhood
"Stephanie, that little stinker." X. J. Kennedy.—
KeB
Stephens, James
Check.—CoOu—PrRh
Danny Murphy.—CoOu
The devil's bag.—LiWa
A glass of beer.—HeR
In the orchard.—LiWa
Little things ("Little things, that run, and
quail").—FaTh—LaT—LiSf—PrRh
The market.—PlAs
The secret.—LiWa
Seumas Beg.—BlO
The snare.—BlO—LiSf
The turn of the road.—LiWa
The wind ("The wind stood up, and gave a
shout").—KeK
"Stepping gingerly." See Cat in the snow
"Stern Master Munchem, rod in hand, stole out
of school one day." See The schoolmaster and
the truants
Stetler, Charles
Arf, said Sandy.—JaPo
A man of action.—JaG
To Ellen.—JaPo
Steve. Cynthia Rylant.—RyW
"Steve Meador moving to Beaver." See Steve
"Steven, your birth brought." See For my son,
born during an ice storm
Stevens, Wallace
The brave man.—LiSf
Disillusionment of ten o'clock.—HeR—KoT
Earthy anecdote.—HeR—LiSf
New England verses, sels.
Statue against a clear sky.—PlEd
Ploughing on Sunday.—HeR—KoT
A rabbit as king of the ghosts.—KoT
Statue against a clear sky. See New England
verses
Thirteen ways of looking at a blackbird.—HeR
Stevenson, Robert Louis
At the sea-side.—CoN—FaW
Bed in summer.—DaC—FaW
Block city.—CoN—PlEd
The celestial surgeon.—DaC
The cow ("The friendly cow, all red and
white").—BlO—CoN—FrP
From a railway carriage.—PrRh
Good and bad children.—BlO—DaC
A good play.—DaC
Happy thought.—ChG—PrRa—PrRh
The lamplighter.—PlSc
The land of Counterpane.—CoN
The land of Nod.—ChB—DaC
The land of story books.—DaC

Stevenson, Robert Louis—*Continued*
Looking forward.—DaC
My bed is a boat.—ChB
My shadow.—CoOu—FaW
Pirate story.—DaC
Rain ("The rain is raining all around").—CoN—
FaW—FrP
"Say not of me that weakly I declined."—PlEd
Sing me a song.—PlAs
Skerryvore.—PlEd
The swing.—CoN—FaW—FrP—LiSf
Time to rise.—ChG—DaC—FaW—FrP
Where go the boats.—CoN
The wind ("I saw you toss the kites on
high").—LiSf
Windy nights ("Whenever the moon and stars
are set").—DaC—KeK—LaW—LiSf—PrRh
Winter time.—DaC
Stewart, Anna Bird
Baby talk.—PrRh
Stickball. Virginia Schonborg.—PrRh
Still finding out. Arnold Adoff.—AdA
Still life. Walter De la Mare.—PlEd
Still night thoughts. Li Po.—KoT
"**Still** sits the school-house by the road." See In
school-days
"**Still,** still, stillness." See Loneliness
"**Still** unable to pronounce the months." See Ice
cream
Stillness
Feather or fur. J. Becker.—PrRh
"The lightning and thunder." G. MacDonald.—
KeK
Sea calm. L. Hughes.—HuDk
Sea-weed. D. H. Lawrence.—HeR—HoSe—PrBb
Spruce woods. A. R. Ammons.—KeK
Summer night. H. Behn.—HoCb
When all the world is full of snow. N. M.
Bodecker.—PrRh
Stinson, Sam S.
Such foolish old dames.—BrT
"**Stir** it in the brew." See Yeast
"**Stocking** and shirt." James Reeves.—CoOu
Stocking time. Eleanor Farjeon.—FaE
A **stocking** to fill. Eleanor Farjeon.—FaE
The **stolen** child. William Butler Yeats.—LiWa
Stone. Donald Justice.—JaT
The **stone** troll. John Ronald Reuel Tolkien.—LiSf
Stonecarver. Carole Oles.—JaS
Stones. See Precious stones; Rocks and stones
Stop. Lee Blair.—BrT
"**Stop** all the clocks, cut off the telephone."
Wystan Hugh Auden.—HeR
Stopping by home. David Huddle.—JaG
Stopping by woods on a snowy evening. Robert
Frost.—CoN—HaOf—HeR—KoS—KoT—LiSf—PrRh
"**Stores** and filling stations prefer a roof." See
Christmas tree
Stores and storekeepers. See Shops and shop-
keepers
Stories and storytelling
"And to think that I saw it on Mulberry
Street." Dr. Seuss.—FaW
Aunt Sue's stories. L. Hughes.—HuDk
Bedtime stories. L. Moore.—BeD—CoN—HoCr
Bedtime story.—MoSn—PrRa
City under water. E. Farjeon.—FaE
The cruise of the Mystery. C. Thaxter.—HaOf
Fairy tale ("They don't tell you"). B. J.
Esbensen.—EsCs
For Richard Chase. J. W. Miller.—JaG
Fossils. L. Moore.—HoDi—MoSn

"Her father lov'd me, oft invited me." From
Othello. W. Shakespeare.—HoUn
"I'll tell you a story." Mother Goose.—FaW
The land of story books. R. L. Stevenson.—
DaC
Little orphant Annie. J. W. Riley.—HaOf
Mingled yarns. X. J. Kennedy.—HaOf
Morning glory. E. Farjeon.—FaE
The mother's tale. E. Farjeon.—FaE
The oxen ("Christmas eve, and twelve of the
clock"). T. Hardy.—HaO—HeR—RoC
Request number. G. N. Sprod.—TrM
So they went deeper into the forest. R.
Daniells.—DoNw
A story that could be true. W. Stafford.—
CoN—JaG—KeK
Welsh incident. R. Graves.—LiWa
"What is the opposite of a prince." R.
Wilbur.—LiSf—LiWa
Worlds I know. M. C. Livingston.—LiWo
"Would you hear of an old-fashion'd sea-fight."
From Song of myself. W. Whitman.—HeR
Storks
"Ride a purple pelican." J. Prelutsky.—PrRi
The **storm** ("The fury and terror"). Elizabeth
Coatsworth.—HaOf
The **storm** ("A perfect rainbow, a wide"). William
Carlos Williams.—JaPo
Storm ("There has never been a wind"). Barbara
Juster Esbensen.—EsCs
Storm ("You must"). Myra Cohn Livingston.—
LiSi
Storm at night. Elizabeth Coatsworth.—LaW
"The **storm** came up so very quick." See Spring
rain
Storm warnings. Adrienne Rich.—JaG
Stormalong. Unknown.—PlAs
Storms. See also Rain; Snow; Thunder and light-
ning; Weather; Wind
The approach of the storm. Unknown, fr. the
Chippewa Indian.—KoT
"As the days grow longer." Mother Goose.—
LoR
The black cloud. W. H. Davies.—HeR
Blizzard. B. J. Esbensen.—EsCs
Charm ("With trembling eyes"). M. Radnóti.—
McL
Child frightened by thunderstorm. T. Kooser.—
KeK
Coming storm. M. C. Livingston.—LiSi
"Cover my earth mother four times with many
flowers." From Invocation of the U'wannami,
Part III. Unknown, fr. the Zuni Indian.—LaT
"For a harmless April rain." X. J. Kennedy.—
KeB
Hops. B. Pasternak.—KoT
Hurricane. L. Moore.—MoSn
"Jagged light, blue and bright." C. Watson.—
WaC
"Like rain it sounded till it curved." E.
Dickinson.—HeR
Magic spell for an approaching storm.
Unknown, fr. the Arekuna Indian.—BiSp
The mill-pond. E. Thomas.—HeR
The rescue. C. Rylant.—RyW
Rhyme ("I like to see a thunder storm"). E.
Coatsworth.—PrRh
The snowstorm. K. Starbird.—BaS
Spring gale. N. M. Bodecker.—BoSs
Spring rain. M. Chute.—FrP—PrRh
Stampede. L. Moore.—MoSn

Storms.—*Continued*
 The storm ("The fury and terror"). E. Coatsworth.—HaOf
 The storm ("A perfect rainbow, a wide"). W. C. Williams.—JaPo
 Storm ("There has never been a wind"). B. J. Esbensen.—EsCs
 Storm ("You must"). M. C. Livingston.—LiSi
 Storm at night. E. Coatsworth.—LaW
 Storm warnings. A. Rich.—JaG
 "A strong nor'wester's blowing, Bill." W. Pitt.—TrM
 Subway psalm. A. Nowlan.—JaS
 Sudden storm. E. Coatsworth.—HoSu
 A tail of the see. E. T. Corbett.—HaOf
 "There came a wind like a bugle." E. Dickinson.—HeR
 This is to frighten a storm. Unknown, fr. the Cherokee Indian.—BiSp
 Thunderstorm. H. Behn.—HoCb
 To quiet a raging storm. Unknown, fr. the Copper Eskimo.—BiSp
 To the thawing wind. R. Frost.—KoS
 Tornado. M. C. Livingston.—LiSi
 Umbrella ("Umbrella, umbrella"). E. Merriam.—MeHa
 Up north. N. M. Bodecker.—BoPc
 Waiting ("As in a thunderstorm at night"). R. Pack.—JaG—JaPo
 Weather report. L. Moore.—MoSn
 Wild iron. A. Curnow.—HeR
 The wreck of the Hesperus. H. W. Longfellow.—HaOf
The **story** of Augustus who would not have any soup. Heinrich Hoffman.—PrRh
The **story** of fidgety Philip. Heinrich Hoffman.—DaC
The **story** of Lava. David Allan Evans.—JaPi
A **story** that could be true ("If you were exchanged in the cradle and"). William Stafford.—CoN
Storytelling. See Stories and storytelling
"The **stove** was grey, the coal was gone." See Into Laddery Street
Straley, John
 A young fellow from Boise.—BrT
Strand, Mark
 The coming of light.—JaPo
 For her.—JaG
 Tomorrow.—JaG—JaPo
"**Strange** it was." See The first Christmas eve
Strange meeting ("It seemed that out of battle I escaped"). Wilfred Owen.—HeR
A **strange** meeting ("The moon is full, and so am I"). William Henry Davies.—BlO
"**Strange** shadows out." See Tonight
Strange tree. Elizabeth Madox Roberts.—LiWa
The **stranger** in the pumpkin. John Ciardi.—CoN
"The **stranger** in the pumpkin said." See The stranger in the pumpkin
The **strangers.** Audrey Alexandra Brown.—DoNw
Strawberries
 Millions of strawberries. G. Taggard.—LiIl—LiSf
 Strawberries ("The first time I went to the fields alone"). J. Hemschemeyer.—JaD
 Strawberries ("Ripe, ripe strawberries"). E. Farjeon.—FaE
 Strawberries ("There were never strawberries"). E. Morgan.—McL
Strawberries ("The first time I went to the fields alone"). Judith Hemschemeyer.—JaD

Strawberries ("Ripe, ripe strawberries"). Eleanor Farjeon.—FaE
Strawberries ("There were never strawberries"). Edwin Morgan.—McL
Strawson, J. Adair
 A token of attachment.—BrT
The **stray.** Barbara Euphan Todd.—ChC
The **stray** cat. Eve Merriam.—HoSs
"**Streaking.**" See Shooting stars
Streams
 The brook. A. Tennyson.—BlO
 The brook in February. C. G. D. Roberts.—DoNw
 Hyla brook. R. Frost.—KoS
 Mountain brook. E. Coatsworth.—PrRh
Street cries
 Get 'em here. L. B. Hopkins.—HoMu
 "Hot cross buns, hot cross buns." Mother Goose.—DeM—FaW—LoR
 "If I'd as much money as I could spend." Mother Goose.—FaW—LoR
 "I'll sing you a song." Mother Goose.—LoR
 The merry pieman's song. J. Bennett.—LiIl
 A pretty ambition. M. E. W. Freeman.—HaOf
 Strawberries ("Ripe, ripe strawberries"). E. Farjeon.—FaE
 "Who'll buy my valley lilies." E. Farjeon.—FaE
The **street** fountain. Eleanor Farjeon.—FaE
"The **street** is soon there." See To ride
Street painting. Ann Turner.—TuS
Street people
 Wash in the street. A. Turner.—TuS
 Why ("Fumble-John they call him"). A. Turner.—TuS
A **street** scene. Lizette Woodworth Reese.—HaOf
Streets. See Roads and streets
The **streets** of Laredo ("As I walked out in the streets of Laredo"). Unknown.—HeR—LiSf
 "As I walked out in the streets of Laredo".—PlAs
The **streets** of Laredo ("O, early one morning I walked out like Agag"). Louis MacNeice.—PlAs
Strength
 Elephant. Unknown.—HeR
 The grandmother. W. Berry.—JaD—PlSc
 Great and strong. M. Holub.—HeR
 John Henry ("When John Henry was a little tiny baby"). Unknown.—KeK
  John Henry ("John Henry was a lil baby").—PlAs
  John Henry ("When John Henry was a little babe").—LiSf
 Work. From Boy's will, joyful labor without pay, and harvest home. R. P. Warren.—PlSc
Strike me pink. Eve Merriam.—MeF
Strikes
 The case for the miners. S. Sassoon.—PlSc
 A lone striker. R. Frost.—PlSc
String
 The string of my ancestors. N. Nyhart.—JaS
 The string of my ancestors. Nina Nyhart.—JaS
Stringbean Small. Jack Prelutsky.—PrNk
"**Stringbean** Small was tall and trim." See Stringbean Small
Stroke. Mike Lowery.—JaPi
Strong, George A
 The modern Hiawatha.—PrRh
Strong, L.A.G. (Leonard Alfred George)
 The knowledgeable child.—KeK
A **strong** feeling for poultry. Roy, Jr. Blount.—BrT
A **strong** minded lady. Morris Bishop.—BrT

Swahili love song. Unknown, tr. by Jan Knappert.—McL

The **swallow** ("Fly away, fly away, over the sea"). Christina Georgina Rossetti.—DaC

The **swallow** ("Swallow, swallow, swooping free"). Ogden Nash.—PrRa

"**Swallow** it raw." See The dirty word

"**Swallow,** swallow, swooping free." See The swallow

Swallows

Dusk ("At dusk there are swallows"). P. Fleischman.—FlI

The swallow ("Fly away, fly away, over the sea"). C. G. Rossetti.—DaC

The swallow ("Swallow, swallow, swooping free"). O. Nash.—PrRa

Swamps

"Ah, a monster's lot is merry." J. Prelutsky.—PrNk

Bald cypress. M. C. Livingston.—LiMp

"**Swan** swam over the sea." Mother Goose.—LoR

Swans

"Clothes make no sound when I tread ground." From Three riddles from the Exeter book. Unknown.—HeR

The icebound swans. Unknown.—LaT

No swan so fine. M. Moore.—PlEd

"The silver swan, who living had no note." O. Gibbons.—HeR

"Swan swam over the sea." Mother Goose.—LoR

"The wild swan's call." Unknown.—DeD

"**Swans** sing before they die, 'twere no bad thing." See On a bad singer

"A **swarm** of bees in May." Mother Goose.—AlH—DaC

"**Swart** swarthy smiths besmattered with smoke." See The blacksmiths

Swearing. Cynthia Rylant.—RyW

The **sweater.** Gregory Orr.—JaPo

Swedes. Edward Thomas.—HeR

Sweeney praises the trees. Unknown, tr. by Seamus Heaney.—HeR

"**Sweep,** sweep." Mother Goose.—LoR

"A **sweet,** a delicate white mouse." See The waltzer in the house

Sweet and low. From The princess. Alfred Tennyson.—BlO—ChB

"**Sweet** and low, sweet and low." See Sweet and low

Sweet ass. Eleanor Farjeon.—FaE

"**Sweet** ass, go gently, go." See Sweet ass

"**Sweet** beast, I have gone prowling." See Song

Sweet dreams. Ogden Nash.—CoOu

"**Sweet** dreams, form a shade." See A cradle song

Sweet herbs. Eleanor Farjeon.—FaE

Sweet history. N. M. Bodecker.—BoPc

"**Sweet** love, everything." See Lullaby

"**Sweet** maiden of Passamaquoddy." James De Mille.—DoNw

"**Sweet-mouth,** honey-paws, hairy one!" See Black bear

Sweet Suffolk owl. Thomas Vautor.—HeR

"**Sweet** Suffolk owl, so trimly dight." See Sweet Suffolk owl

"**Sweet** William he married a wife." See The wife wrapt in wether's skin

Sweet William's ghost. Unknown.—PlAs

"**Sweeten** these bitter wild crabapples." See Crabapples

Sweetheart. Phil Hey.—JaG

Sweetie Maguire. Unknown.—PaM

"**Sweetly** sweetly singing." See Morning magic

The **sweetstuff** wife. Eleanor Farjeon.—FaE

"The **sweetstuff** wife in the queer little shop." See The sweetstuff wife

Swenson, May

After the dentist.—JaD

Analysis of baseball.—KeK

Cardinal ideograms.—HaOf

Cat and the weather.—LiCa

The centaur.—LiSf

How everything happens (based on a study on the wave).—LiSf

In a museum cabinet.—LiWa

Living tenderly.—HaOf

On Addy Road.—JaG

Orbiter 5 shows how earth looks from the moon.—LiSf

The secret in the cat.—JaD

Southbound on the freeway.—CoN—LiSf

Waking from a nap on the beach.—CoN

Swift, Jonathan

AEIOU.—BlO

"**Swift** things are beautiful." Elizabeth Coatsworth.—LiSf

Swimmer. Robert Francis.—JaD

Swimming. Alice Higgins.—PrRa

Swimming and diving

About being very good and far better than most but still not quite good enough to take on the Atlantic Ocean ("There was a fine swimmer named Jack"). J. Ciardi.—CiD

On being much better than most and yet not quite good enough (". . . a great swimmer named Jack").—JaG

At the pool. B. J. Esbensen.—EsCs

"Bathing near Oahu, May." X. J. Kennedy.—KeB

The diver ("I put on my aqua-lung and plunge"). I. Serraillier.—FaW

The diver ("I would like to dive"). W. Ross.—DoNw

The diver ("This time I'll do it, Mommy, look"). A. Resnikoff.—FaW

Elegy for a diver. P. Meinke.—JaPi

A fish who could not swim. M. Kumin.—RuI

The great beyond. C. Rylant.—RyW

Greg Hoffman. M. Glenn.—GlCd

I answer an SOS. X. J. Kennedy.—KeF

In goes Robin. E. Farjeon.—FaE

Into fish. S. L. Nelms.—JaG

John Quincy Adams. S. V. Benét, and R. C. Benét.—HaOf

"John while swimming in the ocean." X. J. Kennedy.—KeB

Lament for the non-swimmers. D. Wagoner.—JaD

"Lightning, that's an old wives' tale." X. J. Kennedy.—KeB

Mandy Bailer. M. Glenn.—GlCd

"Mother, may I go out to swim." Mother Goose.—DeM—LoR

"My brother lost his bathing suit." J. Prelutsky.—PrWi

Near drowning. R. Pomeroy.—JaD

"One purple summer eve." R. J. Margolis.—MaS

"The pobble who has no toes." E. Lear.—FaW—LiH

The pobble.—BlO

Seal. W. J. Smith.—LiSf—PrRh—RuI

"The secret joy of diving bells." X. J. Kennedy.—KeF

Swimmer. R. Francis.—JaD

Swimming and diving—*Continued*
Swimming. A. Higgins.—PrRa
The waves of the sea. E. Farjeon.—FaE
The wind is blowing west. J. Ceravolo.—KoT
The women's 400 meters. L. Morrison.—LiSf
A year later. M. A. Hoberman.—HoSi
The **swing**. Robert Louis Stevenson.—CoN—
FaW—FrP—LiSf
A **swing** song. William Allingham.—FrP
"**Swing**, swing." See A swing song
Swinging
Birches. R. Frost.—HeR—KoS
The swing. R. L. Stevenson.—CoN—FaW—
FrP—LiSf
A swing song. W. Allingham.—FrP
The walnut tree. D. McCord.—HaOf
"The **swinging** mill bell changed its rate." See A
lone striker
"**Swish**, swash." Eve Merriam.—MeBl
The **sycophantic** fox and the gullible raven. Guy
Wetmore Carryl.—HaOf
Sylvie and Bruno, sels. Lewis Carroll
The king-fisher song.—BlO
The mad gardener's song ("He thought he saw
an elephant").—HeR
Mad gardener's song ("He thought he saw
a buffalo").—CoOu
Sympathy. See also Friendship; Kindness
Beaver moon, the suicide of a friend. M.
Oliver.—JaG
Sinner. L. Hughes.—HuDk

T

Tabb, John Banister
A child's prayer.—LaT
High and low.—BrT
The **table** and the chair. Edward Lear.—LiH—
LiSf
Table manners. See Manners
Table manners ("The goops they lick their
fingers"). Gelett Burgess.—FrP—HaOf—
PrRa—PrRh
The goops.—FaW
Table manners ("When you turn down your glass
it's a sign"). James Montgomery Flagg.—BrT
Tables
Kitchen tables. D. Huddle.—JaS
The table and the chair. E. Lear.—LiH—LiSf
Tableware
"Alas, alas, for Miss Mackay." Mother Goose.—
FaW—LoR
"I am learning." A. Adoff.—HoMu
Roman presents. Martial.—HaO
Seymour Snorkle. J. Prelutsky.—PrNk
"Trip upon trenchers, and dance upon dishes."
Mother Goose.—AlH
Taboo to boot. Ogden Nash.—HeR
Tact ("Quoth a cat to me once, pray relieve").
Oliver Herford.—BrT
"**Taddeo** Gaddi built me, I am old." See The old
bridge at Florence
Tadpoles. See Frogs and toads
"**Taffy**, the topaz coloured cat." See In honour
of Taffy Topaz
"**Taffy** was a Welshman." Mother Goose.—
DeM—HeR—LoR
Tag along. Nina Payne.—PrRh
Taggard, Genevieve
Millions of strawberries.—LiIl—LiSf

Tagliabue, John
The bare arms of trees.—JaPi
I sought all over the world.—JaPi
An unseen deer.—JaPi
Tagore, Sir Rabindranath
Fairyland.—LiWa
A **tail** of the see. Elizabeth T. Corbett.—HaOf
Tailors
"Four and twenty tailors went to kill a snail."
Mother Goose.—DaC
Tails
Before the monkey's cage. E. Becker.—PrRa
Don't ever seize a weasel by the tail. J.
Prelutsky.—PrRh—PrZ
"Little Bo-Peep has lost her sheep." Mother
Goose.—DeM—LoR
Ode to the pig, his tail. W. R. Brooks.—PrRh
Possum. N. M. Bodecker.—BoSs
"There was a sad pig with a tail." A. Lobel.—
LoB
"Three blind mice." Mother Goose.—AlH—
DeM—LoR
Tails and heads. Suzanne Knowles.—HeR
"**Take** a large olive, stone it and then stuff it
with a paste made of anchovy." See A dish
for a poet
"**Take** cake, a very easy rhyme for bake." See
Cake
Take heart, sweet Mary. Unknown, tr. by Eleanor
Farjeon.—FaE
In the town.—HaO
"**Take** heart, the journey's ended." See Take heart,
sweet Mary
"**Take** my face and give me yours." See Prayer
to the moon
"**Take** the back off the watch." See Time piece
"**Take** the leaf of a tree." See Reply to the
question, how can you become a poet
"**Take** your duffel bag and go." See A July
goodbye
Taking leave of a friend. Rihaku, tr. by Ezra
Pound.—HeR
Taking off. Unknown.—HoSu
"**Taking** off." See Beginning a new year means
The **tale** of Custard the dragon. Ogden Nash.—
HaOf
Custard the dragon.—CoOu
The **tale** of Lilla. Eleanor Farjeon.—FaE
"**Talent** is what they say." See For the young who
want to
Talk ("I wish people, when you sit near them").
David Herbert Lawrence.—PrBb
Talk with a poet. Helen Bevington.—PlSc
Talking
Adam's apple. C. Barks.—JaPo
Brian Nichols. M. Glenn.—GlCd
Catechisms, talking with a four year old. G.
E. Lyon.—JaS
Cockatoo. N. M. Bodecker.—BoSs
"Don't tell me that I talk too much." A.
Spilka.—PrRh
Fifty-fifty. C. Sandburg.—LiIl
Fish ("The little fish are silent"). A. S.
Bourinot.—PrRa
Floradora Doe. J. Prelutsky.—PrNk
A heavy rap. N. Giovanni.—GiSp
Jabbering in school. E. Farjeon.—FaE
A limerick of frankness. X. Y. Z.—BrT
The man that had little to say. J. Ciardi.—BeD
Manual system. C. Sandburg.—HoRa
The multilingual mynah bird. J. Prelutsky.—PrZ
Secret talk. E. Merriam.—LiIl

Talking—*Continued*
Some people I know. J. Prelutsky.—PrRh
Talk ("I wish people, when you sit near them").
    D. H. Lawrence.—PrBb
Talking. J. Viorst.—ViI
The telephone. E. Field.—JaPo
The telephone call. J. Prelutsky.—HoBf
"There was an old woman of Gloucester."
    Mother Goose.—LoR
Thoughts on talkers. W. R. Brooks.—PrRh
A time to talk. R. Frost.—LiIl
Trilingual. A. Adoff.—AdA
"A wise old owl sat in an oak." Mother
    Goose.—DeM—FaW—LoR
    "There was an old owl who lived in an
        oak".—BlPi
    The owl ("There was an old owl who lived
        in an oak").—DaC
"Yip yap rattletrap." C. Watson.—PrRh
Talking. Judith Viorst.—ViI
The **talking** of the trees. Eleanor Farjeon.—FaE
"Tall." See Douglas fir
Tall. Unknown.—BrT
"Tall as a foxglove spire, on tiptoe." See Fox
    dancing
"Tall building." See Skyscratcher
"The tall ferns shivered." See How the end might
    have been
Tam Lin ("O, I forbid you, maidens a'").
    Unknown.—PlAs
    Tamlane (". . . maidens all").—LiWa
Tam Lin ("She's ta'en her petticoat by the band").
    Unknown.—PlAs
"The tamarindo puppy." Charlotte Pomerantz.—
    LiIl
"Tambourine, tambourine." Clyde Watson.—WaC
Tamekane, Kyogoku
    On love.—McL
Tamlane (". . . maidens all"). See Tam Lin ("O,
    I forbid you, maidens a'")
"Tangled over a stone wall grows." See Spring
    flowers
The **tape**. Myra Cohn Livingston.—CoN
Tarantella. Hilaire Belloc.—HeR
Tarrant, Susan Navarre
    Kate and I.—JaT
Tarrier's song. Unknown.—PlAs
"A tarsier worked as a waiter." See The contrary
    waiter
Taste
    Chocolate chocolate. A. Adoff.—PrRh
    Icicles. B. J. Esbensen.—EsCs
    Oh the toe test. N. Farber.—PrRh
    Peach ("Touch it to your cheek and it's soft").
        R. Rauter.—KeK
    Taste of purple. L. B. Jacobs.—PrRh
    Thumbs. S. Silverstein.—FaTh
    The worm ("When the earth is turned in
        spring"). R. Bergengren.—ChG—PrRh
Taste of purple. Leland B. Jacobs.—PrRh
Taught me purple. Evelyn Tooley Hunt.—LiSf
Taunts. See Insults
Taverns. See Inns and taverns
'The taxi halts before a pale museum." See Letter
    to statues
Taxicabs
    Taxis. R. Field.—LiSf
    Valentine ("If all the whole world's taxicabs").
        X. J. Kennedy.—KeF—LiVp
Taxis. Rachel Field.—LiSf
Taylor, Edward
    Huswifery.—PlSc

Taylor, Eric Clough
    Catmint.—ChC
Taylor, Jane
    Good night ("Little baby, lay your head").—
        ChB
    The star.—CoN—DaC—FrP—LiSf—PrRa—
        PrRh
        "Tinkle, twinkle, little star".—ChB—DeM
            (unat.)—TrM
Tea by the sea. Edward Lear.—BrT
Tea parties
    "Polly put the kettle on." Mother Goose.—
        DeM—FaW—LoR
    Some one to tea. E. Farjeon.—FaE
    Tea party. H. Behn.—LiSf
    "When I sat next the Duchess at tea."
        Unknown.—TrM
Tea party. Harry Behn.—LiSf
Teacher ("My teacher looked at me and
    frowned"). X. J. Kennedy.—KeF
Teacher ("Teacher's tall and teacher's short").
    Eleanor Farjeon.—FaE
"Teacher Bruin said, cub, bear in mind." See The
    smart little bear
"Teacher say, be what you can be." See Teacher
    talk
Teacher talk. Ann Turner.—TuS
Teachers and teaching. See also School
    Adam Whitney. M. Glenn.—GlC
    At the St. Louis Institute of Music. R.
        Wallace.—JaG
    Cecilia Dowling. M. Glenn.—GlCd
    Charlie Wallinsky. M. Glenn.—GlC
    The creature in the classroom. J. Prelutsky.—
        PrB—PrRh
    Dr. Foster. Unknown.—DaC
    Empty holds a question. P. Folk.—JaG
    A fish who could not swim. M. Kumin.—RuI
    For Richard Chase. J. W. Miller.—JaG
    Franz Dominguez. M. Glenn.—GlC
    "From his pouch he took his colors." From
        The song of Hiawatha. H. W. Longfellow.—
        PlEd
    I show the daffodils to the retarded kids. C.
        Sharp.—JaD
    In school-days. J. G. Whittier.—HaOf
    Jeanette Jaffe. M. Glenn.—GlC
    Letter to a substitute teacher. G. Gildner.—JaPi
    Miss Norma Jean Pugh, first grade teacher. M.
        O'Neill.—PrRh
    Nine o'clock. From The wonder clock. K.
        Pyle.—HaOf
    Paul Hewitt. M. Glenn.—GlCd
    Poet in residence at a county school. D.
        Welch.—JaG
    The purist. O. Nash.—HaOf
    Saint Francis and the sow. G. Kinnell.—HeR
    The schoolmaster and the truants. J.
        Brownjohn.—HaOf
    Taught me purple. E. T. Hunt.—LiSf
    Teacher ("My teacher looked at me and
        frowned"). X. J. Kennedy.—KeF
    Teacher ("Teacher's tall and teacher's short").
        E. Farjeon.—FaE
    Teacher talk. A. Turner.—TuS
    A valentine for my teacher. J. Prelutsky.—PrIv
    What the stone dreams. J. B. Hathaway.—JaG
    "When I heard the learn'd astronomer." W.
        Whitman.—LiSf
    Whitley at three o'clock. J. Worley.—JaG
    A young school mistress. Unknown.—BrT
"Teacher's tall and teacher's short." See Teacher

"The **teachers** think I'm sick." See Joy McNair
Teapots. See Tableware
Tear. X. J. Kennedy.—KeF
"A **teardrop** in your eye." See Tear
"**Tearing** the skin carelessly." See Peeling an orange
Tears
  Burning bright. L. Morrison.—FaTh
  "Slow, slow, fresh fount, keepe time with my salt teares." B. Jonson.—HeR
  Small rains. N. M. Bodecker.—BoSs
  Tear. X. J. Kennedy.—KeF
  "Tommy's tears and Mary's fears." Mother Goose.—LoR
  Why ("We zoomed"). P. Redcloud.—HoMu
Teasdale, Sara
  The falling star.—HaOf—LiSf
  February twilight.—HaOf—HoSi—PrRh
  Full moon, Santa Barbara.—HaOf
  May night.—HoSi
  Moonlight ("It will not hurt me when I am old").—JaG
  Night ("Stars over snow").—LiSf
Teased. Richard J. Margolis.—MaS
Teddy bear. Alan Alexander Milne.—CoOu
"A **teddy** bear is a faithful friend." See My teddy bear
"A **teddy** bear is nice to hold." See My teddy bear
Teddy bear poem. Judith Viorst.—ViI
"**Teddy** bear, teddy bear." Unknown.—CoN—PrRa
Teenagers. Cynthia Rylant.—RyW
Teeth
  About the teeth of sharks. J. Ciardi.—HaOf
  After the dentist. M. Swenson.—JaD
  "Although he didn't like the taste." A. Lobel.—LoWr
  Carl Immerman. M. Glenn.—GlC
  The first tooth. C. Lamb, and M. Lamb.—DaC—PrRh
  I went hungry on Thanksgiving. J. Prelutsky.—PrIt
  My girl Maggie. N. M. Bodecker.—BoSs
  My teeth. E. Ochester.—JaD
  An old fellow from Cleathe. Unknown.—BrT
  The poet's farewell to his teeth. W. Dickey.—JaD
  The root canal. M. Piercy.—JaD
  Ruth Luce and Bruce Booth. N. M. Bodecker.—BoSs
  Teeth. S. Milligan.—TrM
  "Thirty white horses upon a red hill." Mother Goose.—CoN—LiSf
  Toothsome. N. Smaridge.—PrRa
Teeth. Spike Milligan.—TrM
"**Teevo** cheevo cheevio chee." See The woodlark
The **telephone.** Edward Field.—JaPo
The **telephone** call. Jack Prelutsky.—HoBf
Telephone poles ("Close by, / they're stolid"). Valerie Worth.—WoSp
Telephone poles ("They have been with us a long time"). John Updike.—JaPi—PlSc
Telephones
  Allen Greshner. M. Glenn.—GlC
  The cable ship. H. E. Martinson.—HeR
  Central. T. Kooser.—JaPi
  Cotton. H. E. Martinson.—HeR
  Dial tone. F. Pollak.—JaPo
  Eletelephony. L. E. Richards.—CoN—CoOu—FaW—HaOf—LiSf—PrRh
  He ("Has never written me a letter himself"). R. Koertge.—JaS
  Hot line. L. Dunann.—PrRh

The invention of the telephone. P. Klappert.—JaPo
  Lonesome. M. C. Livingston.—LiIl
  Long distance. W. Stafford.—LiWa
  Manual system. C. Sandburg.—HoRa
  "Phone girl, I'm sorry I gave you the wrong number." C. Sandburg.—HoRa
  The telephone. E. Field.—JaPo
  The telephone call. J. Prelutsky.—HoBf
  Telephone poles ("Close by, / they're stolid"). V. Worth.—WoSp
  "We could be friends." M. C. Livingston.—LiIl
Television
  Clarence. S. Silverstein.—HaOf
  Daddy's football game. J. Prelutsky.—PrIt
  Fear. N. Giovanni.—GiSp
  Jimmy Jet and his TV set. S. Silverstein.—HaOf—LiSf—PrRh
  Late night flight. X. J. Kennedy.—KeF
  Michelle Church. M. Glenn.—GlCd
  Mitchell Chapin. M. Glenn.—GlC
  A simple need. N. M. Bodecker.—BoPc
  Television. M. L'Engle.—LaT
  Television nose. X. J. Kennedy.—KeF
  The Thanksgiving day parade. J. Prelutsky.—PrIt
  Urbanity. E. Merriam.—MeSk
  The winning of the TV west. J. T. Alexander.—PrRh
  "With the garden sprinkler Brett." X. J. Kennedy.—KeB
Television. Madeleine L'Engle.—LaT
Television nose. X. J. Kennedy.—KeF
"**Tell** me." See Horse chestnut
"**Tell** me a story." See Bedtime stories
"**Tell** me a story, Father, please do." See Request number
"**Tell** me again." See Wind stories
"**Tell** me, daughter, my pretty daughter." See Cossante
"**Tell** me, little woodworm." Spike Milligan.—PrRa
"**Tell** me not, in mournful numbers." See A psalm of life
"**Tell** me, O octopus, I begs." See The octopus
"**Tell** me, tell me, Sarah Jane." Charles Causley.—HoSe—LiSf
"**Tell** me, thou star, whose wings of light." Percy Bysshe Shelley.—KoT
"**Tell** me, you anti-saints, why glass." See Upon Fairford windows
Telling time. Lilian Moore.—MoSn
The **tempest,** sels. William Shakespeare
  "Be not afeard, the isle is full of noises".—HeR
  "Come unto these yellow sands".—BlO—KoT
  "Full fathom five thy father lies".—HoUn
    Ariel's song.—BlO
  "The master, the swabber, the boatswain, and I".—HoUn
  "Our revels now are ended".—HeR
  "Where the bee sucks, there suck I".—BlO—HoUn—KoT
Temple of the muses. Beth Bentley.—PlEd
Ten billion crows. X. J. Kennedy.—KeF
"**Ten** billion crows with cracking bills." See Ten billion crows
Ten days leave. William De Witt Snodgrass.—JaPi
Ten fingers. Unknown.—PrRa
Ten kinds. Mary Mapes Dodge.—PrRh
"**Ten** little mice sat in a barn to spin." Mother Goose.—DaC

Ten o'clock scholar. See "A diller, a dollar, a ten o'clock scholar"
"Ten tired tortoises." See Ten to one
Ten to one. Ivy O. Eastwick.—PrRa
Ten week wife. Rhoda Donovan.—JaS
Ten years old ("I paid my 30¢ and rode by the bus"). Nikki Giovanni.—GiSp—LiSf
Tender buttons, sels. Gertrude Stein
  Colored hats.—KoT
  A dog ("A little monkey goes like a donkey that means to say").—KoT
  A new cup and saucer.—KoT
  A petticoat.—KoT
  Red roses.—KoT
  A sound.—KoT
  An umbrella ("Coloring high means that the strange reason is in front").—KoT
Tender heartedness. Harry Graham.—PrRh
Tennis
  "At the tennis court, Paul Pest." X. J. Kennedy.—KeB
  Its tangs were red. J. Prelutsky.—PrNk
Tennyson, Alfred
  Blow, bugle, blow. See The princess—"The splendour falls on castle walls"
  "Break, break, break."—BlO—HeR
  The brook.—BlO
  The city child.—DaC
  The eagle.—BlO—CoN—LiSf—PrRh
  "Flower in the crannied wall."—FaTh
  In memoriam, sels.
    "Ring out, wild bells, to the wild sky".—LiNe
  The kraken.—LiSf—LiWa
  The letter.—KoT
  Locksley Hall, sels.
    "Make me feel the wild pulsation that I felt before the strife".—PlSc
  "Make me feel the wild pulsation that I felt before the strife." See Locksley Hall
  The mermaid, complete.—DaC—LiWa—LiWa
  The mermaid, sels.
    "Who would be".—HoCr
  "Minnie and Winnie."—ChB—KoT
  "Now sleeps the crimson petal, now the white." See The princess
  The owl ("When cats run home and light is come").—BlO—DaC
    Song, the owl.—LiSf
  The princess, sels.
    "Now sleeps the crimson petal, now the white".—McL
    "The splendour falls on castle walls".—LiWa
    Blow, bugle, blow.—LiSf
    Song.—BlO
    Sweet and low.—BlO—ChB
  "Ring out, wild bells, to the wild sky." See In memoriam
  The sailor boy.—PlAs
  Song. See The princess—"The splendour falls on castle walls"
  Song, the owl. See The owl ("When cats run home and light is come")
  "The splendour falls on castle walls." See The princess
  Sweet and low. See The princess
  The throstle.—DaC
  "Who would be." See The mermaid
Tents
  The chap who disappeared. J. Ciardi.—CiD
"Terence McDiddler." Mother Goose.—BlO—DeM—LoR

Teresa's red Adidas. Paul B. Janeczko.—JaT
The termite. Ogden Nash.—HaOf—KeK
Termites
  The termite. O. Nash.—HaOf—KeK
A ternary of littles, upon a pipkin of jelly sent to a lady. Robert Herrick.—KoT
"The terraces rise and fall." See Going to sleep in the country
Territory. Jean Chapman.—ChC
Terror. N. M. Bodecker.—BoPc
"Terrors are to come, the earth." See To my children, fearing for them
"Terry." Albert Rowe.—ChC
A testimony. George Ella Lyon.—JaG
Tewa Indians. See Indians of the Americas—Tewa
"The Texan was mighty hungry." L. C. Briggs.—TrM
Texas
  The devil in Texas. Unknown.—HeR
  "In the long flat panhandle of Texas." C. Sandburg.—HoRa
  "The Texan was mighty hungry." L. C. Briggs.—TrM
Thackeray, William Makepeace
  Little Billee.—BlO
Thackeray, William Makepeace
  At the zoo ("First I saw the white bear").—CoN
Thank you. Lily Breek.—LaT
"Thank you." See Thanksgiving
"Thank you for leaving the bar of soap." See Note to the previous tenants
"Thank you for the sun." See Prayer
Thank you for your letter. Ch'ao Li-houa, tr. by Kenneth Rexroth.—LiIl
"Thank you, friend, that you did not make me walk about in vain." See Prayer of the black bear
"Thank you, Lord, for silence." See For silence
Thank you note. Judith Viorst.—ViI
"Thank you sun, for being here." See Thank you
Thankfulness
  Blake leads a walk on the Milky Way. N. Willard.—HaOf
  "Blow, blow, thou winter wind." From As you like it. W. Shakespeare.—HoUn
  Carlos Rodriguez. M. Glenn.—GlCd
  Christmas 1970. S. Milligan.—HaO
  Christmas thank you's. M. Gowar.—HaO
  "Come, ye thankful people, come." G. J. Elvey.—LiTp
  The first Thanksgiving ("When the Pilgrims"). J. Prelutsky.—CoN—PrIt
  For silence. R. Bond.—LaT
  "Giving thanks giving thanks." E. Merriam.—LiTp—MeF
  Happy thought. R. L. Stevenson.—ChG—PrRa—PrRh
  "I thank you God." From Thanksgiving. L. Driscoll.—LaT
  "I thank you God for most this amazing." E. E. Cummings.—LaT
  I'm thankful. J. Prelutsky.—PrNk
  Joy of an immigrant, a thanksgiving. E. Di Pasquale.—LiTp
  Noel, Christmas eve, 1913. R. Bridges.—HaO
  "Oh God, I thank you that you have made me as I am." W. Barclay.—LaT
  The owl ("Downhill I came, hungry, and yet not starved"). E. Thomas.—HeR
  Pied beauty. G. M. Hopkins.—HeR—KoT
  The poem you asked for. L. Levis.—JaG

"There was a poor pig on the street." Arnold Lobel.—LoB
"There was a powder the druggist had." See Reflexes
"There was a professor called Chesterton." See A professor called Chesterton
"There was a queer fellow named Woodin." See A queer fellow named Woodin
"There was a rat, for want of stairs." Mother Goose.—DeM—LoR
"There was a rich lady lived over the sea." See The rich lady over the sea
"There was a rich pig from Palm Springs." Arnold Lobel.—LoB
"There was a rude pig from Duluth." Arnold Lobel.—LoB
"There was a sad pig with a tail." Arnold Lobel.—LoB
"There was a serpent who had to sing." See The serpent
"There was a ship a-sailing." Mother Goose.—RoC
"I saw a ship a-sailing".—CoN
"There was a ship a-sailing off North America." See The Green Willow Tree
"There was a shy pig by a wall." Arnold Lobel.—LoB
"There was a sick pig with a cold." Arnold Lobel.—LoB
"There was a sightseer named Sue." See A sightseer named Sue
"There was a slow pig from Decatur." Arnold Lobel.—LoB
"There was a small maiden named Maggie." See A shaggy dog
"There was a small pig from Woonsocket." Arnold Lobel.—LoB
"There was a small pig who wept tears." Arnold Lobel.—LoB—PrRa
"There was a smart pig who was able." Arnold Lobel.—LoB
"There was a stout pig from Oak Ridge." Arnold Lobel.—LoB
"There was a strange pig in the park." Arnold Lobel.—LoB
"There was a time when I could fly, I swear it." See I, Icarus
"There was a tough pig from Pine Bluff." Arnold Lobel.—LoB
"There was a vague pig from Glens Falls." Arnold Lobel.—LoB
"There was a warm pig from Key West." Arnold Lobel.—LoB
"There was a wee house in the heather." See Always room for one more
"There was a wet pig from Fort Wayne." Arnold Lobel.—LoB
"There was a witch." See Two witches
"There was a witch who knitted things." See Knitted things
"There was a woman loved a man." See Sea chest
"There was a young belle of old Natchez." Ogden Nash.—KeK
"There was a young bugler named Breen." Unknown.—TrM
"There was a young curate of Kidderminster." See A young curate of Kidderminster
"There was a young farmer of Leeds." Mother Goose.—LoR
"There was a young fellow from Boise." See A young fellow from Boise

"There was a young fellow from Tyne." See Tired of waiting
"There was a young fellow named Hall." See A fellow named Hall
"There was a young fellow named Shear." See A young fellow named Shear
"There was a young fellow named West." See Suppressed
"There was a young girl of Asturias." See A young girl of Asturias
"There was a young hopeful named Sam." See Jammy
"There was a young lady from Ayr." See Squeaky shoes
"There was a young lady from Cork." See A young lady from Cork
"There was a young lady from Del." See A young lady from Delaware
"There was a young lady from Lynn." Unknown.—KeK
A young lady of Lynn ("There was a young lady of Lynn").—PrRh
"There was a young lady named Bright." Unknown.—LiSf
"There was a young lady named Sue." See A young lady named Sue
"There was a young lady of Bute." Edward Lear.—LiH
"There was a young lady of Crete." Unknown.—CoOu
A young lady of Crete.—BrT
"There was a young lady of Dorking." Edward Lear.—LiH
"There was a young lady of Ealing." See A young lady of Ealing
"There was a young lady of Firle." Edward Lear.—LiH
"There was a young lady of Greenwich." Edward Lear.—LiH
"There was a young lady of Kent." Unknown.—LiIl
"There was a young lady of Munich." See A young lady of Munich
"There was a young lady of Newington Green." See The ballad of Newington Green
"There was a young lady of Niger." Unknown.—FaW
"There was a young lady of Norway." Edward Lear.—FaW
"There was a young lady of Oakham." See A young lady of Oakham
"There was a young lady of Poole." Edward Lear.—LiH
"There was a young lady of Portugal." Edward Lear.—LiH
"There was a young lady of Rheims." See Moonshine
"There was a young lady of Ryde." See Cider inside her
"There was a young lady of Turkey." Edward Lear.—LiH
"There was a young lady of Twickenham." Oliver Herford.—KeK
"There was a young lady of Tyre." Edward Lear.—LiH
The young lady of Tyre.—BrT
"There was a young lady of Wales." Edward Lear.—LiH
"There was a young lady of Welling." Edward Lear.—LiH
"There was a young lady of Wilts." See A young lady of Wilts

"There was an old man of the Nile." Edward Lear.—FaW
An old man of the Nile.—BrT
"There was an old man of the South." Edward Lear.—LiH
"There was an old man of the West." Edward Lear.—LiH
"There was an old man of Thermopylae." Edward Lear.—FaW
"There was an old man of Tobago." Mother Goose.—LoR
"There was an old man of Toulon." See An old man of Toulon
"There was an old man of Toulouse." Edward Lear.—LiH
"There was an old man of West Dumpet." Edward Lear.—LiH
"There was an old man of Whitehaven." Edward Lear.—LiH
"There was an old man on a hill." Edward Lear.—LiH
"There was an old man on the border." Edward Lear.—LiH
"There was an old man, on whose nose." Edward Lear.—LiH
"There was an old man said, I fear." See The shubble
"There was an old man who lived in the woods." See The old man who lived in the woods
"There was an old man who said, how." Edward Lear.—BlO
"There was an old man who said, hush." Edward Lear.—KeK—LiH
"There was an old man who said, well." Edward Lear.—LiH—LiSf
"There was an old man whose despair." Edward Lear.—LiH
"There was an old man with a beard." Edward Lear.—CoOu—FaW—LiH—LiSf—PrRh
Old man with a beard.—CoN
"There was an old man with a beard, who sat." Edward Lear.—LiH
"There was an old man with a flute." Edward Lear.—LiH
"There was an old man with a gong." Edward Lear.—LiH
The old man with a gong.—BrT
"There was an old man with a nose." Edward Lear.—LiH
"There was an old owl who lived in an oak". See "A wise old owl sat in an oak"
"There was an old peddler." See The peddler
"There was an old person of Anerley." Edward Lear.—LiH
"There was an old person of Bangor." Edward Lear.—LiH
"There was an old person of Bar." Edward Lear.—LiH
"There was an old person of Bree." Edward Lear.—LiH
"There was an old person of Brigg." Edward Lear.—LiH
"There was an old person of Bromley." Edward Lear.—LiH
"There was an old person of Bude." Edward Lear.—LiH
"There was an old person of Cassel." Edward Lear.—LiH
"There was an old person of Chili." Edward Lear.—LiH
"There was an old person of Cromer." See An old person of Cromer

"There was an old person of Crowle." Edward Lear.—LiH
"There was an old person of Deal." Edward Lear.—LiH
"There was an old person of Dean." Edward Lear.—BlO—FaTh—LiH
Limerick.—HoMu
"There was an old person of Down." Edward Lear.—LiH
"There was an old person of Dutton." Edward Lear.—LiH
"There was an old person of Ems." Edward Lear.—LiH
"There was an old person of Ewell." Edward Lear.—LiH
Rice and mice.—BrT
"There was an old person of Fife." Edward Lear.—LiH
"There was an old person of Filey." Edward Lear.—LiH
"There was an old person of Grange." Edward Lear.—LiH
"There was an old person of Gretna." Edward Lear.—LiH
"There was an old person of Hurst." Edward Lear.—LiH
"There was an old person of Hyde." Edward Lear.—LiH
"There was an old person of Ibreem." Edward Lear.—LiH
"There was an old person of Jodd." Edward Lear.—LiH
"There was an old person of Mold." Edward Lear.—LiH
"There was an old person of Newry." Edward Lear.—LiH
"There was an old person of Nice." Edward Lear.—LiH
"There was an old person of Peru." Edward Lear.—LiH
"There was an old person of Pett." Edward Lear.—LiH
"There was an old person of Philoe." Edward Lear.—LiH
"There was an old person of Pinner." Edward Lear.—LiH
"There was an old person of Putney." See Tea by the sea
"There was an old person of Rheims." Edward Lear.—LiH
"There was an old person of Sestri." Edward Lear.—LiH
"There was an old person of Skye." Edward Lear.—KeK—LiH
"There was an old person of Spain." Edward Lear.—LiH
"There was an old person of Tring." Edward Lear.—LiH
An old person of Tring.—BrT (unat.)
"There was an old person of Ware." Edward Lear.—LiH
An old person of Ware.—PrRa
"There was an old person of Wilts." Edward Lear.—LiH
"There was an old person of Woking." Edward Lear.—LiH
"There was an old person who said." See The oil lamp
"There was an old person whose habits." Edward Lear.—LiH
Hurtful habits.—BrT

"There's always." See Cat, Christmas
"There's an irritating creature." See An irritating creature
"There's big waves and little waves." See Waves
"There's dazzle." See Sunset
"There's music in a hammer." Unknown.—PrRa
"There's no one as immaculate." See Dainty Dottie Dee
"There's no one mean as mean Maxine." See Mean Maxine
"There's nothing so golden." See Buttercups
There's nothing to it. John Ciardi.—CiD
"There's pudding in the pantry." See Invitation to a mouse
"There's room in the bus." See Jittery Jim
"There's someone at the door, said gold candlesticks." See Green candles
"There's someone I know." Jack Prelutsky.—PrIv
"There's something about me." See Something about me
"There's that smell of the boats." See Wharf
"There's the man who sells balloons." See Air balloons
"There's wonderful family called Stein." Unknown.—TrM
"These are supposed to be the best years of my life." See Dominique Blanco
"These are the beds." From The bed book. Sylvia Plath.—PrRh
"These are the days when early." See Indian summer
"These buildings are too close to me." See Rudolph is tired of the city
"These carved and glowing crowds." See Chartres
"These children playing at statues fill." See Statues
"These clouds are soft fat horses." See Clouds
"These golden heads, these common suns." See Dandelions
"These Gothic windows, how they wear me out." See The young glass-stainer
"These, in the day when heaven was falling." See Epitaph on an army of mercenaries
"These people, with their illegible diplomas." See Metamorphoses
"These pools that, though in forests, still reflect." See Spring pools
These three. X. J. Kennedy.—LiE
"These three on Friday." See These three
"These walls they knew those shadows." See Wall shadows
"These white-clay pits of Byfield." See The Byfield rabbit
"They all climbed up on a high board fence." See The nine little goblins
"They all laughed when I told them." See Last laugh
"They always said, what a pretty little girl you are." See Mattie Lou at twelve
"They are born in the swamps of sleeplessness." See Mosquitoes
"They are his planets." See Marbles
"They are making a creche at the Saturday morning classes." See The crib
They ask, is God, too, lonely. Carl Sandburg.—LiLl
"They ask me to handle bronzes." See Bronzes
"They brought a bouquet of thistles." See Thistle
"They brought me ambrotypes." See Rutherford McDowell
"They built the front, upon my word." See The building of a new church

"They call Mrs. Black the mother." See Mrs. Martha Jean Black
"They call us common." See The common egret
"They called it." See Passing
"They chop down 100-ft trees." See Goliath
"They cloud the mirror, when I put them on." See In grandfather's glasses
"They come in ones and twos and threes." See The carol singers
"They didn't want me to have this job." See Mandy Bailer
"They don't tell you." See Fairy tale
"They gathered around and told him not to do it." See Noah
"They had pulled her out of the river, she was dead." See Along the river
"They have been with us a long time." See Telephone poles
"They have brought me a snail." See Snail
"They have cleared away the place where the corn is to be." See Prayer
"They have taken the gable from the roof of clay." See Swedes
"They hunt, the velvet tigers in the jungle." See India
"THEY is another useful word." See Basic for further irresponsibility
"They laughed at one I loved." See Innocence
"They live alone." See Neighbors
"They look." Ryota.—KoT
"They must have magnets in them, set." See Grandparents' houses
"They named it Aultgraat—Ugly Burn." See Black rock of Kiltearn
"They never feel they can be well in the water." See Lament for the non-swimmers
"They put ma body in de ground." See Judgement day
"They rise like sudden fiery flowers." See Fireworks
"They said don't go to the playground after school." See Pink belly
"They say the wells." See Winter news
"They say you're staying in a mountain temple." Tu Fu.—KoT
"They shall know my surprise in the morning." See Flame of the forest, midnight
"They should never have built a barn there, at all." See The barn
"They slew a god in a valley." See Gluskap's hound
"They talk to each other on Christmas eve." See Earth and sky
"They tell me I talk too much." See Talking
"They tell of a hunter named Shephard." See A hunter named Shephard
"They that wash on Monday." Mother Goose.—BlO
"They used to tell me I was building a dream." See Brother, can you spare a dime
"They went out to sea in a sieve, they did." See The jumblies
"They're building a skyscraper." See Building a skyscraper
They're calling. Felice Holman.—LiSf—PrRh
"They're calling, Nan." See They're calling
"They're changing guard at Buckingham Palace." See Buckingham Palace
"They're pulling down the house." See House coming down
"They're still my grown-ups." See We interrupt this broadcast

They've all gone south. Mary Britton Miller.—PrRh
"They've put a fountain in the road." See The street fountain
"They've taken in the furniture." See A new friend
Thibaudeau, Colleen
Balloon ("As / big / as").—DoNw
The clock tower.—DoNw
Thieves
"Andrew was an apple thief." A. Lobel.—LoWr
Boat stealing. From The prelude. W. Wordsworth.—HeR
Caught stealing a dahlia. Unknown.—BrT
"Dingty diddledy, my mammy's maid." Mother Goose.—LoR
  "Dingty diddlety".—DeM
"I know some lonely houses off the road." E. Dickinson.—LiWa
The idea of trust. T. Gunn.—JaPi
"Last night and the night before." Mother Goose.—AlH
"Policeman, policeman, don't take me." Mother Goose.—AlH
"The Queen of Hearts." Mother Goose.—DaC—DeM—LoR
Red monkey. Unknown.—HeR
The rose thieves. V. Popa.—HeR
"Stealing eggs, Fritz ran afoul." X. J. Kennedy.—KeB
"Taffy was a Welshman." Mother Goose.—DeM—HeR—LoR
"There was a man and he had naught." Mother Goose.—LoR
Thomas Kearns. M. Glenn.—GlC
"Tom, Tom, the piper's son." Mother Goose.—DeM—LoR
"Under a spreading gooseberry bush the village burglar lies." Unknown.—TrM
"Thin rain, whom are you haunting." See Wraith
"Thin streams." See The Shawangunks, early April
"The thing about a shark is—teeth." See About the teeth of sharks
"A thing Dylan Thomas once said." See Talk with a poet
"The thing is." See A new pencil
Things I didn't know I loved. Nazim Hikmet, tr. by Randy Blasing and Mutlu Konuk.—McL
Things on a microscope slide. X. J. Kennedy.—FaTh
"Things remember me." See A field poem
Things that go bump in the night. See "From ghoulies and ghosties"
Things to do if you are a subway. Bobbi Katz.—HoSs—PrRh
"The things to draw with compasses." See Circles
"Think as I think, said a man." Stephen Crane.—KeK
"Think how a peacock in a forest of high trees." See Peacock
"Think, said the robin." See Bird talk
Think tank. Eve Merriam.—HoCl—MeSk
"Think thinktank think." See Think tank
"Thinking it hard candy, Rube." X. J. Kennedy.—KeB
Thinking of East Mountain. Li Po.—KoT
Thinking of love. Elizabeth Jennings.—JaG
The thinnest shadow. John Ashbery.—KoT
The third thing. David Herbert Lawrence.—PrBb
Thirst
The street fountain. E. Farjeon.—FaE

Thirteen ways of looking at a blackbird. Wallace Stevens.—HeR
"Thirty days hath September." Mother Goose.—DeM—LoR
  The months.—DaC
"Thirty white horses upon a red hill." Mother Goose.—CoN—LiSf
"This." See Memorial day
"This ancient hag." See Mexican market woman
"This big cat." Beatrice Schenk De Regniers.—DeT
"This black scrap from Viet Nam." See Nocturn at the institute
"This calls for a toast, she hates." See Jane Seagrim's party
"This cat, see, yellow." See Tom cat
"This clock." See Clock
"This cloud of smoke in other hours." See The bonfire
"This country." See Us
"This darksome burn, horseback brown." See Inversnaid
"This day is call'd the feast of Crispian." From Henry V. William Shakespeare.—HoUn
"This day's done." See Good night
"This decorous, nineteenth century." See Croquet
"This empty man came, see." See Don't let me
"This endsaying, moon pried loose." See The goodbye
"This face in the mirror." See Conversation with myself
"This face you got." See Phizzog
"This girl, Amanda." See Amanda
"This girlchild was born as usual." See Barbie doll
This holy night. Eleanor Farjeon.—FaE
"This is a poem to my son Peter." Peter Meinke.—JaD
"This is a song to be sung at night." See The middle of the night
"This is baby ready for a nap." Unknown.—RaT
"This is baby's trumpet." Unknown.—DeD
This is Halloween. Dorothy Brown Thompson.—PrRh
This is just to say. William Carlos Williams.—KeK—PrRh
"This is my Carnac, whose unmeasured dome." Henry David Thoreau.—PlEd
"This is my heart as I travel all over, my spirit, my life and living." See Life song
"This is my rock." David McCord.—CoN
"This is the bridge." See The troll bridge
"This is the day the circus comes." See A circus garland
"This is the foul fiend Flibbertigibbet, he begins at." From King Lear. William Shakespeare.—LiWa
"This is the hay that no man planted." Elizabeth Coatsworth.—HaOf
"This is the house that Jack built." Mother Goose.—LoR
This is the key. See "This is the key of the kingdom"
"This is the key of the kingdom." Mother Goose.—LoR
  This is the key.—BlO
"This is the plaza of Paradise." See Marigold
"This is the saga of Cecil Snedde." See The seven sneezes of Cecil Snedde
"This is the song of Kuk-ook, the bad boy." See The song of Kuk-ook, the bad boy
"This is the story." See Sensible Sue

"This is the story of my desire." See Salt pilgrimage
"This is the summer storm." See For my daughter
"This is the way the ladies ride." Mother Goose.—DeM
"This is the weather the cuckoo likes." See Weathers
"This is the week when Christmas comes." See In the week when Christmas comes
"This is the wind's doing." See Partners
This is to frighten a storm. Unknown.—BiSp
"This is where it begins." See The beginning
"This lamp in my window." Arnold Lobel.—LoWr
"This leaf." Beatrice Schenk De Regniers.—HoSi
"This life." N. M. Bodecker.—BoPc
"This little boy found an egg." See Finding an egg
"This little bug." See Bookish
"This little cow." Unknown.—RaT
"This little fellow was naughty, they say." Unknown.—DeD
"This little girl was traveling unattached, as they say." See Travelers
"This little house is sugar." Langston Hughes.—CoN
    Winter sweetness.—HuDk—PrRa
"This little man lived all alone." Mother Goose.—LoR
"This little pelican could." See Pelican
"This little pig built a spaceship." Frederick Winsor.—PrRh
"This little pig found a hole in the fence." Clyde Watson.—WaC
"This little pig went to market." Mother Goose.—DeM—LoR
    "This little piggy".—RaT
"This little piggy". See "This little pig went to market"
This love. Judith Hemschemeyer.—JaG
"This love is a bruise." See This love
"This lunar beauty." Wystan Hugh Auden.—HeR
"'This midnight, and the setting sun." See 'Tis midnight
"This midnight dream whispered to me." See The dream about our master, William Shakespeare
"This morning." See Variations on a theme
"This morning." See Wake up call
"This morning a cat got." See Dad and the cat and the tree
"This morning on the opposite shore of the river." See Fire
"This morning they are putting away the whales." See Autumn
"This mother cat." Beatrice Schenk De Regniers.—DeT
"This much, I think." See Morning at the Post Office
"This old King of Dorchester." See The ceremonial band
"This person in the gaudy clothes." See Captain Kidd
"This place is not ours." See The new house
This poem is for Nadine. Paul B. Janeczko.—JaG
"This seashell is an ocean cove." See Seashell
This ship. Michael Rosen.—FaW
"This ship in the dock was at the end of its trip." See This ship
"This small." See Magnet

"This star is only an angury of the morning." See And in the 51st year of that century, while my brother cried in the trench, while my enemy glared from the cave
"This sticky trail." See Snail
"This summer I went." See The grand county fair
"This summer we dare, we climb, we." See At the pool
"This sunny wind is only air." See March wind
"This term I don't have a lunch period." See Billy Paris
"This thing all things devour." John Ronald Reuel Tolkien.—LiSf
"This time I'll do it, Mommy, look." See The diver
"This time let me steer." See Downhill
"This wallpaper has lines that rise." See Missing my daughter
"This was the moment when before." See BC, AD.
"This water is so clear." See The fisherman writes a letter to the mermaid
"This winter day." See The lake
"This worker is a fearless one." See The riveter
This year, next year. Eleanor Farjeon.—FaE
Thistle. Nikolai Alekseevich Zabolotsky, tr. by Daniel Weissbort.—HeR
"Thistle and darnel and dock grew there." See Nicholas Nye
Thistles
    Thistle. N. A. Zabolotsky.—HeR
Thomas, Dylan
    "Do not go gentle into that good night."—HeR
    "Every morning when I wake." See Under Milk Wood
    "The force that through the green fuse drives the flower."—HeR
    From A child's Christmas in Wales, sels. Ghost story.—HaO
    Ghost story. See From A child's Christmas in Wales
    "The hand that signed a paper felled a city."—HeR
    "Johnnie Crack and Flossie Snail." See Under Milk Wood
    Poem in October.—HeR
    Under Milk Wood, sels.
        "Every morning when I wake".—LaT
        "Johnnie Crack and Flossie Snail".—LiSf—PrRh
Thomas, Edith M.
    The cricket kept the house.—HaOf
    Mrs. Kriss Kringle.—HaOf
Thomas, Edward
    Adlestrop.—BlO
    "As the team's head-brass flashed out on the turn."—HeR
    The barn ("They should never have built a barn there, at all").—PlEd
    A cat ("She had a name among the children").—BlO
    Cock-crow.—HeR
    The combe.—HeR
    "If I should ever by chance grow rich."—BlO
    The mill-pond.—HeR
    Old Jack Noman.—BlO
    Out in the dark.—HeR
    The owl ("Downhill I came, hungry, and yet not starved").—HeR
    Swedes.—HeR
    The unknown bird.—HeR

Thomas, Ronald Stuart
 The ancients of the world.—HeR
 Here ("I am a man now").—HeR
 Lore.—HeR
Thomas, Rudy
 The one to grieve.—JaG
Thomas Kearns. Mel Glenn.—GlC
Thomas Rymer ("True Thomas lay on Huntlie
  bank"). Unknown.—HeR
 Thomas Rymer (". . . o'er yond grassy
  bank").—PlAs
Thomas Rymer (". . . o'er yond grassy bank").
  See Thomas Rymer ("True Thomas lay on
  Huntlie bank")
Thompson, Dorothy Brown
 Good will to men.—HaO
 Maps.—PrRh
 Our house.—PrRh
 This is Halloween.—PrRh
 Wish ("If I could wish").—PrRa
Thompson, Irene
 Rainy nights.—PrRh
"Thonah, Thonah." See Thunder song
Thoreau, Henry David
 Epitaph on an engraver.—PlEd
 "This is my Carnac, whose unmeasured
  dome."—PlEd
Thornton, Cheryl
 "I have friends."—LiIl
The **thoroughbred** horse. Oliver Herford.—BrT
"Those dressed in blue." Mother Goose.—LoR
"Those houses haunt in which we leave." See
  Ghosts
Those winter Sundays. Robert Hayden.—JaD
"Thou that diest, thou that never diest." See The
  week after
"Though buds still speak in hints." See
  Field-glasses
"Though pleased to see the dolphins play."
  Matthew Green.—TrM
"Though the house had burned years ago." See
  The two old gentlemen
"Though three men dwell on Flannan Isle." See
  Flannan Isle
Thought. See also Mind
 Aunt Roberta. E. Greenfield.—LiSf
 A cliche. E. Merriam.—MeSk
 Colored hats. From Tender buttons. G. Stein.—
  KoT
 Encounter. L. Moore.—MoSn
 "Evening hushes." E. Farjeon.—FaE
 "I saw a great scholar, apparently thinking." M.
  Crint.—TrM
 The meeting. H. Moss.—JaG
 My fishbowl head. X. J. Kennedy.—KeF
 A new cup and saucer. From Tender buttons.
  G. Stein.—KoT
 A petticoat. From Tender buttons. G. Stein.—
  KoT
 A sound. From Tender buttons. G. Stein.—KoT
 Think tank. E. Merriam.—HoCl—MeSk
 Tree at my window. R. Frost.—KoS
 "Where have you been dear." K. Kuskin.—CoN
Thoughts. Peter Marshall and Catherine
  Marshall.—LaT
"Thoughts in a math class." See Bernard
  Pearlman
Thoughts on getting out of a nice warm bed in
  an ice cold house to go to the bathroom at
  three o'clock in the morning. Judith Viorst.—
  ViI
Thoughts on talkers. Walter R. Brooks.—PrRh

"A thousand hairy savages." Spike Milligan.—
  CoOu—PrRh
Threats. Marci Ridlon.—FrP
Three. Elizabeth Coatsworth.—LiIl
"Three ancient men in Bethlehem's cave." See
  The mystic Magi
Three animals, complete. Ron Padgett
 "The butterfly".—KoT
 "The electric eel".—KoT
 "The giraffe".—KoT
Three birds flying. Eve Merriam.—MeSk
"Three blind mice." Mother Goose.—AlH—
  DeM—LoR
Three children. Unknown.—DaC
"Three children sliding on the ice." See Three
  children
The **three** drovers. John Wheeler.—RoC
"Three each day, seven days a week." Mother
  Goose.—LoR
Three furry cats. Beatrice Schenk De Regniers.—
  DeT
Three ghostesses. See "Three little ghostesses"
"Three gray geese in a green field grazing."
  Mother Goose.—LoR
"Three jolly gentlemen." See The huntsmen
Three knights from Spain. Unknown.—BlO
"Three little ghostesses." Mother Goose.—DeM—
  FaW
 Three ghostesses.—PrRh
The **three** little kittens. See "Three little kittens
  lost their mittens"
"Three little kittens lost their mittens." Mother
  Goose.—DeM
 The three little kittens.—HaOf
 "Three little kittens, they lost their mittens".—
  LoR
"Three little kittens, they lost their mittens". See
  "Three little kittens lost their mittens"
The **three** little pigs. Alfred Scott Gatty.—DaC
"Three lovely notes he whistled, too soft to be
  heard." See The unknown bird
Three moments. Susan R. Sherman.—JaD
"Three of us afloat in the meadow by the swing."
  See Pirate story
"Three practical farmers from back of the dale."
  See Shepherd's carol
The **three** ravens. Unknown.—PlAs
Three riddles from the Exeter book, complete.
  Unknown, tr. by Geoffrey Grigson
 "Clothes make no sound when I tread
  ground".—HeR
 "I puff my breast out, my neck swells".—HeR
 "White is my neck, head yellow, sides".—HeR
"Three skies." Claudia Lewis.—LiSf
"Three things there be that prosper up apace."
  See Sir Walter Ralegh to his son
Three tickles. Dennis Lee.—PrRa
"Three times round goes our gallant ship."
  Mother Goose.—LoR
The **three** toed sloth. Jack Prelutsky.—PrZ
"The three toed sloth is in a deep." See The
  three toed sloth
"The three-toed tree toad." See Nocturne
"Three weeks gone and the combatants gone." See
  Vergissmeinicht
"Three wise men of Gotham." Mother Goose.—
  DeM—FaW—LoR
Three wise old women. Elizabeth T. Corbett.—
  HaOf
"Three wise old women were they, were they."
  See Three wise old women

"**Three** young rats with black felt hats." Mother Goose.—DeM
Threnody. George T. Lanigan.—DoNw
"**Thrice** the brinded cat hath mew'd." From Macbeth. William Shakespeare.—HeR—LiSf—LiWa
"**Thrice** tosse these oaken ashes in the ayre." Thomas Campion.—LiWa
Thrift
  Economy. E. Farjeon.—FaE
  A thrifty soprano. O. Nash.—BrT
  A thrifty young fellow. Unknown.—BrT
A **thrifty** soprano. Ogden Nash.—BrT
"A **thrifty** soprano of Hingham." See A thrifty soprano
A **thrifty** young fellow. Unknown.—BrT
"A **thrifty** young fellow of Shoreham." See A thrifty young fellow
Throckmorton Thratte. Jack Prelutsky.—PrNk
"**Throckmorton** Thratte has charm and class." See Throckmorton Thratte
The **throstle.** Alfred Tennyson.—DaC
Through a shop window. Eleanor Farjeon.—FaE
"**Through** all the frozen winter." See Smells
"**Through** brush and love-vine, well blooded." See Boy wandering in Simms' valley
"**Through** his iron glades." See Winter, the huntsman
"**Through** moonlight's milk." See White cat in moonlight
"**Through** the house give glimmering light." From A midsummer night's dream. William Shakespeare.—HoUn
"**Through** the house what busy joy." See The first tooth
Through the looking glass, sels. Lewis Carroll
  Humpty Dumpty's recitation.—KoT
      Humpty Dumpty's poem.—BlO
  Jabberwocky.—CoN—HeR—KoT—LiSf—PrRh
  The walrus and the carpenter.—BlO—LiSf
A **throw** of threes, complete. Eve Merriam
  Anticipations.—MeF
  Apple joys.—MeF
  Cures for melancholy.—MeF
  Curses to fling at a giant.—MeF
  Disguises.—MeF
  Holidays.—MeF
  Lands where no one can live.—MeF
  Locked doors.—MeF
  Open doors.—MeF
  Pillows.—MeF
  Places for an extra pocket.—MeF
  Places to hide a secret message.—MeF
  Questions for an angel.—MeF
  Shimmerings.—MeF
  Silent warnings.—MeF
  Uses for a fog.—MeF
The **thrush's** nest. John Clare.—BlO
Thumb. Philip Dacey.—JaPo—KeK
"The **thumb,** for a summer's promise." See The sand painters
"**Thumbkin** Bumpkin, jolly and stout." Clyde Watson.—WaC
Thumbprint ("Almost reluctant, we approach the block"). Celeste Turner Wright.—JaPi
Thumbprint ("On the pad of my thumb"). Eve Merriam.—MeSk
Thumbs
  The mitten song. M. L. Allen.—CoN—PrRa
  Thumb. P. Dacey.—JaPo—KeK
  Thumbprint ("On the pad of my thumb"). E. Merriam.—MeSk
  Thumbs. S. Silverstein.—FaTh

Thumbs. Shel Silverstein.—FaTh
"**Thumbs** in the thumb place." See The mitten song
Thunder and lightning
  Girl's prayer to thunder during a storm. Unknown, fr. the Blackfeet Indian.—BiSp
  "I never speak a word." M. Austin.—LiSf
  "Jagged light, blue and bright." C. Watson.—WaC
  "Lightning rides." P. Wolny.—JaPo
  "Lightning, that's an old wives' tale." X. J. Kennedy.—KeB
  Thunder dragon. H. Behn.—HoCb
  Thunder song. Unknown, fr. the Navajo Indian.—BiSp
  "Winter's thunder." Mother Goose.—LoR
Thunder dragon. Harry Behn.—HoCb
"**Thunder** has nested in the grass all night." See Child frightened by thunderstorm
Thunder song. Unknown.—BiSp
Thunderstorm. Harry Behn.—HoCb
Thurman, Judith
  Flashlight ("My flashlight tugs me").—BeD—LiSf
  Lumps.—PrRh
  Oil slick.—HoSs—LiSf
  Rags.—HoSi—JaT
  Tunnel ("Tunnel coming").—LiSf
  Zebra ("White sun").—PrRh
"**Thursday** was baking day in our house." See Baking day
Thwaite, Anthony
  "From Table Isle", tr. by.—FaTh
"**Thy** cradle was a manger." See For all
Tichborne, Chidiock
  Elegy for himself.—HeR
"**Tick** tick tick tick tick tick tick." See Toaster time
The **tickle** rhyme ("Who's that tickling my back, said the wall"). Ian Serraillier.—CoN—CoOu—PrRh
"**Tickly,** tickly, on your knee." Mother Goose.—DeM
Tide and time. Roger McGough.—JaT
"The **tide** in the rive." Eleanor Farjeon.—BlO
Tides
  "The beach at this evening full." Unknown.—JaT
  The pumpkin tide. R. Brautigan.—HoSi
  Sea-wash. C. Sandburg.—HaOf
  "The tide in the rive." E. Farjeon.—BlO
"The **tides** in my eyes are heavy." See Thanksgiving
"The **tidy** woman." Unknown.—DeD
Tiempo muerto. Ricardo Alonso.—PlSc
"The **tiger** / has swallowed." See Tiger
Tiger ("The paper tigers roar at noon"). Alec Derwent Hope.—HeR
Tiger ("The tiger / has swallowed"). Valerie Worth.—WoSp
The **tiger** ("The tiger, on the other hand, is kittenish and mild"). Hilaire Belloc.—FaW
The **tiger.** See The tyger
"The **tiger** is in the tiger-pit." See Lines for an old man
"The **tiger,** on the other hand, is kittenish and mild." See The tiger
"**Tiger,** sunflowers, king of cats." See The marmalade man makes a dance to mend us
A **tiger** tale. John Bennett.—HaOf
Tigers
  The Bengal tiger. J. Prelutsky.—PrZ
  India. W. J. Turner.—BlO

Tigers—*Continued*
Now about tigers. J. Ciardi.—CiD
Sun tiger. H. Behn.—HoCb
"There was a young lady of Niger."
    Unknown.—FaW
Tiger ("The paper tigers roar at noon"). A. D.
    Hope.—HeR
Tiger ("The tiger / has swallowed"). V.
    Worth.—WoSp
The tiger ("The tiger, on the other hand, is
    kittenish and mild"). H. Belloc.—FaW
A tiger tale. J. Bennett.—HaOf
The tyger. W. Blake.—BlO—HeR—KoT
    The tiger.—LiSf
Tiggady Rue. David McCord.—LiWa
"**Till** they tangled and seemed to trip and lie
    down." See His legs ran about
Tillinghast, Richard
September, last day at the beach.—JaG
Tilly. James Joyce.—HeR
"**Tilt,** wilt." See Snow
"**Timble** Tamble Turkey." Jack Prelutsky.—PrRi
Time. See also Change
"After the palaces." From A nobleman's house.
    M. Sarton.—PlEd
"As I walked out one evening." W. H.
    Auden.—HeR—PlAs
BC, AD. U. A. Fanthorpe.—HaO
"Bell horses, bell horses." Mother Goose.—LoR
The black fern. L. Norris.—LiSf
"Break, break, break." A. Tennyson.—BlO—
    HeR
Burning the gate. E. Farjeon.—FaE
Daylight saving time. P. McGinley.—PrRh
Days. P. Larkin.—HeR
The days gone by. J. W. Riley.—HaOf
The empty house. R. Hoban.—LiWa
Even such is time. Sir W. Raleigh.—HeR
Fall wind ("Pods of summer crowd around the
    door"). W. Stafford.—JaPo
The garden seat. T. Hardy.—HeR
Grass. C. Sandburg.—HoRa
The great house. E. Muir.—PlEd
Guide to the ruins. H. Nemerov.—PlEd
He remembers forgotten beauty. W. B. Yeats.—
    McL
Houses ("Time and the weather wear away").
    D. Justice.—JaPo—PlEd
How time goes. J. Ciardi.—CiD
Humming-bird ("I can imagine, in some
    otherworld"). D. H. Lawrence.—HeR—PrBb
"Is it robin o'clock." E. Merriam.—MeBl
"It is not growing like a tree." B. Jonson.—
    HeR
"Loveliest of trees, the cherry now." A. E.
    Housman.—HeR
    Loveliest of trees.—BlO
May meadows. E. Farjeon.—FaE
The mill ("The spoiling daylight inched along
    the bar-top"). R. Wilbur.—JaPi
The National Gallery. L. MacNeice.—PlEd
The nymph's reply to the shepherd. Sir W.
    Raleigh.—HeR
The old men admiring themselves in the water.
    W. B. Yeats.—KeK
The old year. J. Clare.—HaO
On the vanity of earthly greatness. A.
    Guiterman.—HaOf—TrM
On Wenlock Edge. A. E. Housman.—HeR
Ozymandias. P. B. Shelley.—HeR
The river ("Winter"). D. Welch.—JaS
Rock me to sleep. E. A. Allen.—HaOf
A room in the past. T. Kooser.—JaS

The sand painters. B. Belitt.—PlEd
"Shall I compare thee to a summer's day?"
    From Sonnets. W. Shakespeare.—HoUn
Slowly. J. Reeves.—BlO
Snapshots. N. M. Bodecker.—BoPc
Storm warnings. A. Rich.—JaG
Sweet history. N. M. Bodecker.—BoPc
Telling time. L. Moore.—MoSn
There isn't time. E. Farjeon.—FaE
There once was an owl. J. Ciardi.—LiSf
"This thing all things devour." J. R. R.
    Tolkien.—LiSf
This year, next year. E. Farjeon.—FaE
Thumbprint ("Almost reluctant, we approach
    the block"). C. T. Wright.—JaPi
The time is. E. Merriam.—MeSk
"The time is out of joint, O cursed spite."
    From Hamlet. W. Shakespeare.—TrM
"Tomorrow, and tomorrow, and tomorrow."
    From Macbeth. W. Shakespeare.—HoUn
Tomorrows. D. McCord.—McAs
"Two brothers are we." A. Lobel.—LoWr
Two masks unearthed in Bulgaria. W.
    Meredith.—PlEd
Waiting both. T. Hardy.—KoT
Wild thyme. E. Farjeon.—FaE
"**Time** and the weather wear away." See Houses
A **time** for building. Myra Cohn Livingston.—
    HoSs
The **time** is. Eve Merriam.—MeSk
"The **time** is out of joint, O cursed spite." From
    Hamlet. William Shakespeare.—TrM
"The **time** it took he could have." See The
    invention of the telephone
"The **time** my brothers." See Regrets
Time piece. William Cole.—JaPo
"**Time** runs wild on the hilltops." See Wild thyme
"**Time** ticks." See Telling time
Time to rise. Robert Louis Stevenson.—ChG—
    DaC—FaW—FrP
A **time** to talk. Robert Frost.—LiIl
"The **time** to tickle a lizard." See The lizard
Timesweep, sels. Carl Sandburg
    "There is only one horse on the earth".—HoRa
"The **timid** corn-pone-y's heart fluttered." See The
    corn-pone-y
"**Timmy** Tatt, Timmy Tatt." Jack Prelutsky.—PrRi
"**Timothy** Tompkins had turnips and tea." See
    The meal
Timothy Winters. Charles Causley.—HeR
"**Timothy** Winters comes to school." See Timothy
    Winters
The **tin** frog. Russell Hoban.—FaTh—PrRh
Tina DeMarco. Mel Glenn.—GlC
"**Tinker,** tailor." Mother Goose.—PlSc
"**Tinkle,** twinkle, little star". See The star
Tinsel. Valerie Worth.—LiCp
"The **tiny** fish enjoy themselves." See Little fish
"A **tiny** island." See Ladybug
Tiny Tim's prayer. From A Christmas carol.
    Charles Dickens.—LaT
Tip toe tail. Dixie Willson.—CoN
Tippett, James S.
Building a skyscraper.—CoOu
Ducks at dawn.—ChG
Ducks in the rain.—PrRa
Familiar friends.—HoDl
Sunning.—LiSf—PrRh
Trains.—FrP
Up in the air.—HoSu
"**Tippetty** Witchet." Eleanor Farjeon.—FaE
Tired of waiting. Unknown.—BrT
"**Tired** old peddler." Arnold Lobel.—LoWr

Tired Tim. Walter De la Mare.—CoN—PrRh
The tired tree. Eleanor Farjeon.—FaE
"The tires on my bike are flat." See Since Hanna moved away
'Tis midnight. Unknown.—CoN
'Tis strange. Eugene Field.—BrT
"'Tis strange how the newspapers honor." See 'Tis strange
"'Tis the week before Christmas and every night." See For the children or the grown-ups
Tishab Be-Av. Meyer Hahn.—LiPj
Tittle and jot, jot and tittle. Eve Merriam.—MeSk
Tlingit Indians. See Indians of the Americas—Tlingit
To a blind student who taught me to see. Samuel Hazo.—JaG
To a butterfly. William Wordsworth.—DaC
To a daughter with artistic talent. Peter Meinke.—JaPi
To a forgetful wishing well. X. J. Kennedy.—KeF
"To a king who had." See King Rufus
To a poor old woman. William Carlos Williams.—KoT
To a red kite. Lilian Moore.—MoSn
To a sad daughter. Michael Ondaatje.—JaG
To a schoolboy. Unknown, tr. by Anne Pennington.—HeR
To a skylark, sels. William Wordsworth
    "Up with me, up with me into the clouds".—KoT
To a squirrel at Kyle-na-no. William Butler Yeats.—BlO—LiSf—PrRh
To a suitor. Maya Angelou.—AnS
"To all those who warned me against dangers I was." See Laurie Allen
To an artist. Robert Burns.—PlEd
To an aviator. Daniel Whitehead Hicky.—PrRh
To an isle in the water. William Butler Yeats.—KoT
"To and fro." See Haunted room
To any garden. Eleanor Farjeon.—FaE
To autumn. John Keats.—HeR
"To be a giant and keep quiet about it." See Trees
"To be a second class scout." See Cold potato
To be answered in our next issue. Unknown.—PrRh
To be or not to be. Unknown.—PrRh
"To be, or not to be, that is the question." From Hamlet. William Shakespeare.—HoUn
"To become an archer." Lao Tse, tr. by Jose Garcia Villa.—KeK
To blow away a headache. Unknown.—BiSp
To brontosaurus, a gentle giant dinosaur. Lillian M. Fisher.—HoDi
To Brooklyn Bridge. Hart Crane.—PlEd
To build a poem. Christine E. Hemp.—JaG
"To call our sight vision." See I am not a camera
To carry on living. Yehuda Amichai.—McL
"To conquer skyscrapers." See Uses for a fog
To cure epilepsy. Unknown.—BiSp
To daffodils. Robert Herrick.—KoT
To dark eyes dreaming. Zilpha Keatley Snyder.—PrRh
To Dorothy. Marvin Bell.—JaPi
To Dorothy on her exclusion from the Guinness Book of World Records. X. J. Kennedy.—JaPi
To Ellen. Charles Stetler.—JaPo
To Evan. Richard Eberhart.—JaD
"To fashion a room." See Imaginary room
To fix the affections. Unknown.—BiSp

"To fling my arms wide." See Dream variation
"To get into life." See Mosquito
"To give advice I hesitate." R. Beasley.—TrM
"To grocery store cats." See Dedication
"To have been a little ill." See Convalescence
To his excellency George Washington, sels. Phillis Wheatley
    "Proceed, great chief, with virtue on thy side".—LiSf
"To Johnny a box." See Johnny
To keep animals out of the cornfield. Unknown.—BiSp
"To know the inhabiting reasons." See For the rebuilding of a house
To L.B.S. Winfield Townley Scott.—JaD
"To lace my shoes." See Unusual shoelaces
"To leave my home country." See Juan Pedro Carrera
"To let father vacuum the rug under her chair." See Held in suspense
"To make a knothole." See Knotholes
"To make a prairie it takes a clover." Emily Dickinson.—HaOf
"To make some bread you must have dough." See One, two, three, gough
To make the road seem short. Unknown.—BiSp
"To make your candles last for aye." Mother Goose.—DeM
"To market, to market, to buy a fat pig." Mother Goose.—DeM—FaW—LiSf—LoR—RaT
"To me that man equals a god." See Seizure
"To Meath of the pastures." See A drover
To Michaelmas daisies. Eleanor Farjeon.—FaE
To Mistress Isabel Pennell. John Skelton.—KoT
To mother fairie. Alice Cary.—HaOf
To my blood sister. Christine E. Hemp.—JaS
To my children, fearing for them. Wendell Berry.—JaS
To my daughter. Stephen Spender.—JaD
To my daughter riding in the circus parade. Joan Labombard.—JaG
To my father. Ralph Pomeroy.—JaD
To my Lady Rogers, the authors wiues mother, how Doctor Sherwood commended her house in Bathe. Sir John Harington.—PlEd
"To my twin who lives in a cruel country." See The dual site
"To paint without a palette." See Some uses for poetry
To quiet a raging storm. Unknown.—BiSp
"To raise an iron tree." See A Calder
To ride. Paul Éluard.—KoT
"To see." See Oh calendar
To see a world. See "To see a world in a grain of sand"
"To see a world in a grain of sand." See Auguries of innocence, complete
"To see a world in a grain of sand." From Auguries of innocence. William Blake.—PrRh
To see a world.—KeK
"To shower at sea." See Water sport
"To sup." See To sup like a pup
To sup like a pup. Dorothy W. Baruch.—HoDl
To the fly in my drink. David Wagoner.—JaD
To the foot from its child. Pablo Neruda, tr. by Alastair Reid.—HeR
To the moon ("Art thou pale for weariness"). Percy Bysshe Shelley.—KoT
To the moon ("I remember, gracious, gracious moon"). Giacomo Leopardi.—KoT
To the skeleton of a dinosaur in the museum. Lilian Moore.—HoDi

Tongue-twisters—*Continued*
"She sells sea shells on the seashore." Mother Goose.—LoR
Song of the pop-bottlers. M. Bishop.—FaW—KeK
"Swan swam over the sea." Mother Goose.—LoR
Tea party. H. Behn.—LiSf
The tooter. Unknown.—PaM
Toucans two. J. Prelutsky.—PrZ
Toucannery.—CoOu
Tree toad. Unknown.—CoN
The tutor. C. Wells.—PrRh
Two witches. A. Resnikoff.—PrRh
Weather. Unknown.—DaC—PrRh
The whales off Wales. X. J. Kennedy.—HaOf—RuI
What a to-do. Unknown.—DaC

Tongues
"Cat's tongue." E. Merriam.—LiCa—MeBl
Looks are deceiving. B. S. De Regniers.—DeT
Tonight. Lilian Moore. MoSn
"Tonight is impossibly noisy." Jack Prelutsky.—PrMp
"Tonight is the night." See Hallowe'en
"Tonight the air explodes." See Fourth of July
"Tonight the earth." See Night
"Tonight, the first snow." See November song
"Tonight the wind gnaws." See Christmas landscape
"Tonight, thriller was." See Beware, do not read this poem
Tony Baloney. Dennis Lee.—PrRh
"Tony Baloney is fibbing again." See Tony Baloney
Tony O. Colin Francis.—BlO
"Tony said, boys are better." See Girls can, too
Too hot. Jack Prelutsky.—PrWi
Too many cats. Beatrice Schenk De Regniers.—DeT
Too many Daves. Dr. Seuss.—HaOf—PrRh
Too much. Unknown.—BrT
"Too slow." Lillian Morrison.—LiIl
Toot, toot. See A peanut
The tooter. Unknown.—PaM
"A tooter who tooted the flute." See The tooter
Toothsome. Norah Smaridge.—PrRa
The top and the tip. Charlotte Zolotow.—PrRa—ZoE

Topiary
Box, for L.M.B. M. C. Livingston.—LiMp
Tornado. Myra Cohn Livingston.—LiSi

Tornadoes
Tornado. M. C. Livingston.—LiSi
Tortillitas. Unknown.—GrT
"Tortillitas para Mama." See Tortillitas
Tortoises. See Turtles and tortoises
The toucan. Pyke Johnson.—CoN
Toucannery. See Toucans two

Toucans
The toucan. P. Johnson.—CoN
Toucans two. J. Prelutsky.—PrZ
Toucannery.—CoOu
Toucans two. Jack Prelutsky.—PrZ
Toucannery.—CoOu

Touch
Cat kisses. B. Katz.—PrRa
"Cat's tongue." E. Merriam.—LiCa—MeBl
Love letters, unmailed. E. Merriam.—JaD
My fingers. M. O'Neill.—KeK
On certain mornings everything is sensual. D. Jauss.—JaG
Prelude to a parting. M. Angelou.—AnS

"Running lightly over spongy ground." T. Roethke.—HeR
Warmth. B. Sutter.—JaG
"Touch blue." Mother Goose.—LoR
"Touch it to your cheek and it's soft." See Peach
"Tough Captain Spud and his first mate, Spade." See Captain Spud and his first mate, Spade
"A tourist came in from Orbitville." See Southbound on the freeway
Toward dark. Charlotte Zolotow.—ZoE
"Toward the sun, towards the south-west." From Eagle in New Mexico. David Herbert Lawrence.—HeR
Towards Babylon. Unknown.—ChG
"Towards not being." See Movement

Tower of Babel
"And the whole earth was of one language, and of one speech." From Genesis. Bible/Old Testament.—PlEd
"Towery city and branchy between towers." See Duns Scotus's Oxford
Town meeting or 'hey man, don't speak so good'. N. M. Bodecker.—BoPc
Towns. See also Cities and city life; also names of towns, as Jerusalem
Beaver ("Coming to it from the country"). C. Rylant.—RyW
General delivery. C. Rylant.—RyW
New England road. N. M. Bodecker.—BoPc
The toy-maker. Padraic Colum.—PlSc
Toy tik ka. Charlotte Pomerantz.—PoI

Toys
Block city. R. L. Stevenson.—CoN—PlEd
A child's Christmas day. Unknown.—HaO
"Dear God, thank you for our toys." Unknown.—LaT
"Deep in the rippling spring." M. Ushida.—KeK
Dreidel song. E. Rosenzweig.—PrRa
The duel. E. Field.—FaW—HaOf—PrRh
For the children or the grown-ups. Unknown.—HaO
"I had a little hobby horse." Mother Goose.—LoR
I'm thankful. J. Prelutsky.—PrNk
Kaleidoscope ("Only a litter"). V. Worth.—WoSp
Last word. R. J. Margolis.—MaS
Letty's globe. C. T. Turner.—CoOu
Little boy blue. E. Field.—HaOf
Magnet. V. Worth.—KeK
Maturity. X. J. Kennedy.—KeF
My teddy bear ("A teddy bear is a faithful friend"). M. Chute.—PrRa
My teddy bear ("A teddy bear is nice to hold"). M. Hillert.—PrRa
"Roll gently, old dump truck." C. Pomerantz.—PoA
"Smiling girls, rosy boys." Mother Goose.—LoR
The gingerbread man.—DaC
Teddy bear poem. J. Viorst.—ViI
"Teddy bear, teddy bear." Unknown.—CoN—PrRa
The tin frog. R. Hoban.—FaTh—PrRh
The toy-maker. P. Colum.—PlSc
The toys talk of the world. K. Pyle.—HaOf
Where go the boats. R. L. Stevenson.—CoN
The toys talk of the world. Katharine Pyle.—HaOf
Tra-la-larceny. Oliver Herford.—BrT
Track. Tomas Tranströmer, tr. by Robert Bly.—HeR

Tractor. Valerie Worth.—HoCl
"The **tractor** rests." See Tractor
Trade. See Markets and marketing; Peddlers and vendors; Shops and shopkeepers; names of occupations, as Carpenter;
Traffic
    City traffic. E. Merriam.—LiSf—MeSk
    Close call. X. J. Kennedy.—KeF
    Forty Seventh Street crash. X. J. Kennedy.—KeF
    Freddy. D. Lee.—PrRh
    "J's the jumping jay walker." P. McGinley.—PrRh
    Meditation on the A30. Sir J. Betjeman.—HeR
    Traffic rule I. N. M. Bodecker.—BoPc
    Trying to make time on a country highway. X. J. Kennedy.—KeF
Traffic rule I. N. M. Bodecker.—BoPc
The **train**. Charlotte Zolotow.—ZoE
Train blues. Paul Zimmer.—JaPo
The **train** dogs. Pauline Johnson.—DoNw
The **train** in the night. Elizabeth Riddell.—LaW
"A **train** is a dragon that roars through the dark." See A modern dragon
"The **train** keeps on." See The train melody
The **train** melody. Charlotte Zolotow.—ZoE
Train song. Diane Siebert.—PrRh
The **train** to Glasgow. Wilma Horsburgh.—CoOu
Trains. See Railroads
Trains. James S. Tippett.—FrP
"**Trains** and boats and cars and wagons." See Halfway where I'm going
"The **trains** they come and go." See Hello, graffiti
Transformations. Thomas Hardy.—HeR
The **transparence** of November. Roo Borson.—JaPo
Tranströmer, Tomas
    Breathing space July.—HeR
    Solitude ("Right here I was nearly killed one night in February").—HeR
    Track.—HeR
Trap. Eve Merriam.—MeHa
Trapped mouse. Julia Cunningham.—FaTh
Trappers and trapping. See Hunters and hunting
Trash. See Garbage
"The **trash** cans." See The day after Christmas
Trask, A. Marre
    The locust, tr. by.—HeR
Trask, Willard R.
    Girl's song, tr. by.—McL
    The locust, tr. by.—HeR
Travel. See also Adventure and adventurers; Seafaring life; Wayfaring life; also names of modes of travel, as Railroads
    Advice to travelers. W. Gibson.—JaPo
        Before starting.—KeK
    Air traveler. L. Morrison.—PrRh
    The ambitious ant. A. R. Wells.—HaOf
    Amtrak. E. Fried.—JaPo
    "As I was going to St. Ives." Mother Goose.—CoN—DeM—LoR
    Autobahnmotorwayautoroute. A. Mitchell.—HeR
    Blake leads a walk on the Milky Way. N. Willard.—HaOf
    Bound no'th blues. L. Hughes.—HuDk
    "Conductor, when you receive a fare." N. Brooks.—TrM
    Crossing the Alps. From The prelude. W. Wordsworth.—HeR
    Driving to the beach. J. Cole.—PrRh
    "Far, far will I go." Unknown, fr. the Eskimo.—LiSf
    Far trek. J. Brady.—PrRh

A Floridian museum of art. R. Whittemore.—PlEd
The flying cat. N. S. Nye.—JaT
Ford pickup. D. A. Evans.—JaPo
From a railway carriage. R. L. Stevenson.—PrRh
Ghost ("There is a ghost"). C. Morgenstern.—LiWa
Halfway where I'm going. C. Zolotow.—ZoE
The hills over the water. E. Farjeon.—FaE
Home cooking cafe. G. Field.—JaPo
How I helped the traveler. J. Ciardi.—CiD
"How many miles to Babylon." Mother Goose.—FaW—LiSf—LoR
    "How many miles is it to Babylon".—DaC
"I am going to California." Unknown.—PlAs
"I went up a high hill." Mother Goose.—DeM
I wonder. C. Zolotow.—HoSu
"If ever you go to Dolgelly." T. Hughes.—TrM
In a train. R. Bly.—KoT
"In August once." K. Kuskin.—LiCa
The jumblies. E. Lear.—BlO—LiH
The king of cats sends a postcard to his wife. N. Willard.—HaOf
Life song. Unknown, fr. the Flathead Indian.—BiSp
Long trip. L. Hughes.—HuDk
Manitou. R. Ikan.—JaPo
Maps. D. B. Thompson.—PrRh
Nanny. M. C. Livingston.—LiWo
Night journey. T. Roethke.—KeK
Night, landing at Newark. J. Holden.—JaPo
"O mistress mine, where are you roaming." From Twelfth night. W. Shakespeare.—HoUn
A passing glimpse. R. Frost.—KoS
Prayer to the sun, for quick travel. Unknown, fr. the Aztec Indian.—BiSp
Salt pilgrimage. Unknown, fr. the Papago Indian.—BiSp
The ships of Yule. B. Carman.—DoNw
Sparrow in an airport. R. Snyder.—JaPo
"There is no frigate like a book." E. Dickinson.—HaOf
To make the road seem short. Unknown, fr. the Cherokee Indian.—BiSp
Tony O. C. Francis.—BlO
Track. T. Tranströmer.—HeR
Train song. D. Siebert.—PrRh
Travel. E. S. Millay.—HaOf—PrRh
Travelers. J. Miles.—KeK
Traveler's prayer, with an offering of copal. Unknown, fr. the Kekchi Maya.—BiSp
Trying to make time on a country highway. X. J. Kennedy.—KeF
Tunnel ("Tunnel coming"). J. Thurman.—LiSf
Vacation ("One scene as I bow to pour her coffee"). W. Stafford.—JaPi
Victoria. E. Farjeon.—BlO
Water sport. N. M. Bodecker.—BoPc
"When I set out for Lyonesse." T. Hardy.—HeR
Winding road. L. Moore.—MoSn
"Windshield wipers." D. Lee.—DoNw
"You, north must go." Unknown.—DaC
Travel. Edna St. Vincent Millay.—HaOf—PrRh
Travelers. Josephine Miles.—KeK
Traveler's prayer, with an offering of copal. Unknown.—BiSp
"A **traveling** fair pitched by our pasture gate." See One-night fair
"A **treacherous** monster." See The shark
"**Tread**." See Catsnest
Treasure. Eleanor Farjeon.—FaE

Tree at my window. Robert Frost.—KoS
"Tree at my window, window tree." See Tree at my window
"The tree frog." John Travers Moore.—PrRh
Tree house. Ted Kooser.—JaPo
The tree in the wood. Unknown.—LiSf
The tree on the corner. Lilian Moore.—MoSn
Tree shadows ("All hushed the trees are waiting"). Unknown.—ChB
Tree shadows ("The shadow of a"). Lilian Moore.—MoSn
Tree song. Harry Behn.—HoCb
"The tree the tempest with a crash of wood." See On a tree fallen across the road
Tree toad. Unknown.—CoN
"A tree toad loved a she toad." See Tree toad
Treece, Henry
Conquerors.—JaG
Trees. See also Christmas trees; Forests and forestry; also names of kinds of trees, as Oak trees
Art class. X. J. Kennedy.—KeT
Bald cypress. M. C. Livingston.—LiMp
The bare arms of trees. J. Tagliabue.—JaPi
Binsey poplars, felled 1879. G. M. Hopkins.—HeR
A Calder. K. Shapiro.—PlEd
Counting-out rhyme ("Silver bark of beech, and sallow"). E. S. Millay.—KoT
Deep in the mountains. Saibara.—StG
Douglas fir. M. C. Livingston.—LiMp
"Evening hushes." E. Farjeon.—FaE
"Every time I climb a tree." From Five chants. D. McCord.—CoN—FaW—LiSf—PrRh
Flame of the forest, midnight. M. C. Livingston.—LiMp
Girls in the garden. E. Farjeon.—FaE
Goliath. S. Milligan.—TrM
I bended unto me. T. E. Brown.—CoN
"I had a little nut tree." Mother Goose.—DaC—DeM—FaW—LiSf—LoR
A nut tree.—KoT
In one place. R. Wallace.—JaPi
"In spring I look gay." Mother Goose.—LoR
In the park ("When you've"). L. Moore.—MoSn
Irish yew. M. C. Livingston.—LiMp
"It is not growing like a tree." B. Jonson.—HeR
Jacaranda. M. C. Livingston.—FaTh—LiMp
King palm. M. C. Livingston.—LiMp
Leaves compared with flowers. R. Frost.—KoS
The locust tree in flower. W. C. Williams.—KoT
Mimosa. M. C. Livingston.—LiMp
The monkey puzzle. M. C. Livingston.—LiMp
Monterey cypress, Point Lobos. M. C. Livingston.—LiMp
New planting, shopping mall. M. C. Livingston.—LiMp
On a tree fallen across the road. R. Frost.—HeR
Open house. A. Fisher.—PrRa
The pear tree. E. Farjeon.—FaE
A poison tree. W. Blake.—HeR
Progress. C. Martin.—JaPo
Proud torsos. C. Sandburg.—HoRa
Quaking aspen. E. Merriam.—MeF
Rain forest, Papua, New Guinea. M. C. Livingston.—LiMp
The shadow tree. I. Orleans.—HoSi
Shagbark hickory. M. C. Livingston.—LiMp
Sierra redwoods, highway 101. M. C. Livingston.—LiMp

Song ("Reading about the Wisconsin weeping willow"). R. Krauss.—McL
The song of the fir. E. Farjeon.—FaE
Spring in Hampstead. E. Farjeon.—FaE
Spring pools. R. Frost.—KoS
Strange tree. E. M. Roberts.—LiWa
Sweeney praises the trees. Unknown.—HeR
The tale of Lilla. E. Farjeon.—FaE
The talking of the trees. E. Farjeon.—FaE
Telephone poles ("They have been with us a long time"). J. Updike.—JaPi—PlSc
Thumbprint ("Almost reluctant, we approach the block"). C. T. Wright.—JaPi
The tired tree. E. Farjeon.—FaE
Transformations. T. Hardy.—HeR
Tree at my window. R. Frost.—KoS
The tree in the wood. Unknown.—LiSf
The tree on the corner. L. Moore.—MoSn
Tree shadows ("All hushed the trees are waiting"). Unknown.—ChB
Tree shadows ("The shadow of a"). L. Moore.—MoSn
Tree song. H. Behn.—HoCb
Trees ("Berkeboom"). C. Pomerantz.—PoI
Trees ("I am looking at trees"). W. S. Merwin.—JaPo
Trees ("The oak is called the king of trees"). S. Coleridge.—DaC—PrRh
Trees ("To be a giant and keep quiet about it"). H. Nemerov.—JaPi
Trees ("Trees are the kindest things I know"). H. Behn.—HoCb
Trees ("The trees toss their long branches"). C. Zolotow.—ZoE
Trees, the seeds. M. C. Livingston.—LiMp
Tu Bi-Shevat. M. C. Livingston.—LiPj
"Under the greenwood tree." From As you like it. W. Shakespeare.—HoUn—KoT—LiSf
The walnut tree. D. McCord.—HaOf
Weeping ash. M. C. Livingston.—LiMp
Weeping mulberry. M. C. Livingston.—LiMp
"When the almond blossoms." E. Farjeon.—FaE
"Who has seen the wind." C. G. Rossetti.—BlO—CoN—FrP—LiSf—PrRh
The wind.—DaC
The wicked hawthorn tree. W. B. Yeats.—LiWa
"The wind has taken the damson tree." E. Farjeon.—FaE
Yew. M. C. Livingston.—LiMp
Trees ("Berkeboom"). Charlotte Pomerantz.—PoI
Trees ("I am looking at trees"). William Stanley Merwin.—JaPo
Trees ("The oak is called the king of trees"). Sara Coleridge.—DaC—PrRh
Trees ("To be a giant and keep quiet about it"). Howard Nemerov.—JaPi
Trees ("Trees are the kindest things I know"). Harry Behn.—HoCb
Trees ("The trees toss their long branches"). Charlotte Zolotow.—ZoE
"The trees are tall, but the moon small." See Hide and seek
"Trees are the kindest things I know." See Trees
"The trees ask me." See Who am I
"Trees in the old days used to stand." See Carentan O Carentan
"A tree's leaves may be ever so good." See Leaves compared with flowers
"The trees now look scary." See Lullaby
Trees, the seeds. Myra Cohn Livingston.—LiMp
"The trees toss their long branches." See Trees
"Trembling." See Snow

The **turn** of the road. James Stephens.—LiWa
"**Turn** to right, turn to left." See Witches' spells
Turner, Ann
  Amanda ("This girl, Amanda").—TuS
  The beginning.—TuS
  Breakin'.—TuS
  Clean.—TuS
  Don't let me.—TuS
  Grandma.—TuS
  Halloween ("A little kid").—TuS
  Hello, graffiti.—TuS
  Here it is.—TuS
  Look up.—TuS
  Man.—TuS
  Morning ("Saw a play once").—TuS
  The museum ("So we went to see this mummy").—TuS
  Night roof.—TuS
  Nowhere.—TuS
  The park ("One day I so depressed").—TuS
  People leaves.—TuS
  Read.—TuS
  Red-dress girl.—TuS
  Red flower.—TuS
  Street painting.—TuS
  Sunday ("Let me tell you").—TuS
  Teacher talk.—TuS
  That's Gloria.—TuS
  Tom cat.—TuS
  Voices.—TuS
  Wash in the street.—TuS
  Why ("Fumble-John they call him").—TuS
  The zoo ("The zoo is a wonderful place").—TuS
Turner, Charles Tennyson
  Letty's globe.—CoOu
Turner, Elizabeth
  How to write a letter.—DaC
Turner, Nancy Byrd
  Lincoln.—PrRh
  "Old Quin Queeribus."—PrRh
  Washington.—PrRh
  When young Melissa sweeps.—CoN
Turner, Steve
  "Christmas is really for the children."—HaO
Turner, W. J.
  India.—BlO
Turner, Joseph Mallord William (about)
  Turner's sunrise. H. Bevington.—PlEd
Turner's sunrise. Helen Bevington.—PlEd
The **turtle**. Jack Prelutsky.—PrZ
Turtle soup. See "Beautiful soup, so rich and green"
"The **turtle's** always been inclined." See The turtle
Turtles and tortoises
  A big turtle. Unknown.—PrRa
  Desert tortoise. B. Baylor.—PrRh
  I am home, said the turtle. J. Ciardi.—CiD
  The little turtle. V. Lindsay.—CoN—FrP—HaOf—LiSf—PrRa
  Living tenderly. M. Swenson.—HaOf
  Lost ("I have a little turtle"). D. McCord.—McAs
  Meditations of a tortoise dozing under a rosetree near a beehive at noon while a dog scampers about and a cuckoo calls from a distant wood. E. V. Rieu.—LiSf
  Soliloquy of a tortoise on revisiting the lettuce beds after an interval of one hour while supposed to be sleeping in a clump of hollyhocks. E. V. Rieu.—PrRh
  "The tumultuous tom-tommy tortoise." From An animal alphabet. E. Lear.—LiH
  The turtle. J. Prelutsky.—PrZ

Zimmer and his turtle sink the house. P. Zimmer.—JaPi
"The **tusks** that clashed in mighty brawls." See On the vanity of earthly greatness
Tutankhamen. William Dickey.—JaPi
The **tutor.** Carolyn Wells.—PrRh
"A **tutor** who tootled the flute." See The tutor
The **twa** corbies. Unknown.—HeR—PlAs
Twain, Mark
  Dirt dumping.—BrT
  A home without a cat.—ChC
"'**Twas** all along the Binder Line." See Sensitive Sydney
"'**Twas** brillig, and the slithy toves." See Jabberwocky
"'**Twas** early one morning in the month of May." See The green bushes
"'**Twas** in the moon of winter time." See The Huron carol
"'**Twas** not as lonesome as it might have been." See The cricket kept the house
"'**Twas** the night before Christmas, when all through the house." See A visit from St. Nicholas
"**Tweedledum** and Tweedledee." Mother Goose.—AlH—DeM—FaW—LoR
Twelfth night ("Our candles, lit, re-lit, have gone down now"). Peter Scupham.—HaO
Twelfth night, sels. William Shakespeare
  "Come away, come away, death".—PlAs
  "O mistress mine, where are you roaming".—HoUn
  "When that I was and a little tiny boy".—HoUn
The **twelve** days of Christmas. Unknown.—RoC
  "The first day of Christmas".—LoR
The **twelve** elf. Christian Morgenstern, tr. by William De Witt Snodgrass and Lore Segal.—LiWa
"The **twelve** elf raises his left hand." See The twelve elf
"**Twelve** huntsmen with horns and hounds." Mother Goose.—AlH
12 October. Myra Cohn Livingston.—CoN—LiSf—PrRh
"**Twenty** men stand watching the muckers." See Muckers
"**Twenty-nine-letter** word meaning action or habit." See Floccinaucinihilipilification
Twickham Tweer. Jack Prelutsky.—PrRh—PrSr
Twilight song. John Hunter-Duvar.—DoNw
Twin aces. Keith Wilson.—JaPi
"**Twinkle** Toes." Arnold Lobel.—LoWr
Twinkle, twinkle. From Alice's adventures in Wonderland. Lewis Carroll.—PrRa
"**Twinkle,** twinkle, little bat." See Twinkle, twinkle
"**Twinkle,** twinkle, little star." See The star
Twinkletoes. Alan Alexander Milne.—ChG
Twins
  The dual site. M. Hamburger.—PlAs
  "I'm disgusted with my brother." J. Prelutsky.—PrNk
  Prayer of a man to twin children. Unknown, fr. the Kwakiutl Indian.—BiSp
  The twins ("In form and feature, face and limb"). H. S. Leigh.—PrRh
  The twins ("When twins came, their father, Dan Dunn"). B. Braley.—BrT
  The twins ("In form and feature, face and limb"). Henry S. Leigh.—PrRh
  The twins ("When twins came, their father, Dan Dunn"). Berton Braley.—BrT

U

Uncle Julius. Richard J. Margolis.—MaS
Uncle Mells and the witches' tree. Elizabeth Madox Roberts.—LiWa
"Uncle, whose inventive brains." See Uncle
Uncles
Aunts and uncles. M. C. Livingston.—LiWo
Door number four. C. Pomerantz.—LiIl—PoI
In the music. R. Currie.—JaT
Incidents in the life of my uncle Arly. E. Lear.—LiH
Manners ("I have an uncle I don't like"). M. G. Van Rensselaer.—PrRh
My uncle Dan. T. Hughes.—LiSf
"My uncle Paul of Pimlico." M. Peake.—CoOu
"Nobody loses all the time." E. E. Cummings.—HeR
Uncle. H. Graham.—PrRh
Uncle Claude. D. A. Evans.—JaS
Uncle Julius. R. J. Margolis.—MaS
"An uncontrollable night." See Fist fight
Undefeated. Robert Froman.—LiIl
An undefined tenderness. Joel Oppenheimer.—JaPo
"An undefined tenderness came." See An undefined tenderness
"Under a low sky." See Silence
"Under a maple tree." See Dog
"Under a spreading chestnut-tree." See The village blacksmith
"Under a spreading gooseberry bush the village burglar lies." Unknown.—TrM
"Under a toadstool." See The elf and the dormouse
"Under a white coverlet of snow." See January
"Under all her topsails she trembled like a stag." See Posted as missing
"Under fingers of blood." See An evening seal
Under Milk Wood, sels. Dylan Thomas
"Every morning when I wake".—LaT
"Johnnie Crack and Flossie Snail".—LiSf—PrRh
"Under my hood I have a hat." See Winter clothes
"Under pared moons." See The horse
"Under the boulders." See What should I see
"Under the dark is a star." See Sleeping outdoors
"Under the dawn I wake my two-wheel friend." From On a bicycle. Yevgeny Yevtushenko, tr. by Robin Milner-Gulland and Peter Levi.—LiIl
"Under the dining room light." See Business as usual
"Under the greenwood tree." From As you like it. William Shakespeare.—HoUn—KoT—LiSf
Under the ground. Rhoda W. Bacmeister.—PrRa
"Under the lightly leaved." See On the house of a friend
"Under the parabola of a ball." See How to kill
Under the table manners. Unknown.—ChC
"Underneath my belt." See When I was lost
Undersea. Marchette Chute.—RuI
"The underwater wibbles." Jack Prelutsky.—PrNk
Underwood, Edna Worthley
The ballad of mad fortune, tr. by.—LiSf
The underworld. Margaret Lavington.—PrRa
Undine's garden. Harry Behn.—HoCb
An unexplained ouch. X. J. Kennedy.—KeF
"Unfastened." See Perseid meteor shower
Unfortunately. Bobbi Katz.—HoDi—PrRa
"Unfriendly friendly universe." See The child dying
The unicorn, sels. Rainer Maria Rilke
"Oh this is the animal that never was".—KoT

Unicorn ("The unicorn with the long white horn"). William Jay Smith.—PrRh
The unicorn ("While yet the Morning Star"). Ella Young.—LiSf
"The unicorn with the long white horn." See Unicorn
Unicorns
"I stood in the Maytime meadows." Unknown.—KoT
"The lion and the unicorn." Mother Goose.—AlH—DaC—DeM—FaW
"Oh this is the animal that never was." From The unicorn. R. M. Rilke.—KoT
"Rudy rode a unicorn." J. Prelutsky.—PrRi
The strangers. A. A. Brown.—DoNw
Unicorn ("The unicorn with the long white horn"). W. J. Smith.—PrRh
The unicorn ("While yet the Morning Star"). E. Young.—LiSf
United States
Clint Reynolds. M. Glenn.—GlCd
The gift outright. R. Frost.—KoS
I hear America singing. W. Whitman.—LiSf—PlSc
I, too. L. Hughes.—HuDk
Indian names. L. H. Sigourney.—HaOf
"Said the scorpion of hate." C. Sandburg.—HoRa
Us. D. Ignatow.—JaPo
Wild west. M. Vinz.—JaPi
United States—History. See also Explorers and exploration; Frontier and pioneer life; Immigration and emigration
United States—History—Revolution
A farewell to Kingsbridge. Unknown.—PlAs
Paul Revere's ride. H. W. Longfellow.—HaOf
"Proceed, great chief, with virtue on thy side." From To his excellency George Washington. P. Wheatley.—LiSf
The rich lady over the sea. Unknown.—PlAs
The sons of liberty. Unknown.—PlAs
Yankee Doodle ("Fath'r and I went down to camp"). R. Shuckburg.—PlAs
Yankee Doodle ("Father and I went down to camp").—LiSf (unat.)
United States—History—War of 1812
Lake Michigan. From Great Lakes suite. J. Reaney.—DoNw
United States—History—Mexican-American war
Santa Ana. Unknown.—PlAs
United States—History—Civil War
Barbara Frietchie. J. G. Whittier.—HaOf
The Battle of Shiloh. Unknown.—PlAs
How do you do, Alabama. F. Wilson.—PlAs
Lincoln monument, Washington. L. Hughes.—HuDk
Melora's song. From John Brown's body. S. V. Benét.—PlAs
O captain, my captain. W. Whitman.—HaOf
Roll, Alabama, roll. Unknown.—PlAs
The volunteer's Thanksgiving. L. Larcom.—HaOf
"When lilacs last in the dooryard bloom'd." W. Whitman.—HeR
United States—History—Vietnam War
Nam. M. Lowery.—JaPi
Nocturn at the institute. D. McElroy.—JaPi
Song Vu Chin. M. Glenn.—GlC
Universe. See Space and space travel
The universe ("There is the moon, there is the sun"). Mary Britton Miller.—PrRh

Universe ("The universe is all the skies"). Eleanor Farjeon.—FaE
"The universe is all the skies." See Universe
The unknown bird. Edward Thomas.—HeR
The unknown color. Countee Cullen.—HaOf
"Unknown love." Lady Otomo of Sakanone, tr. by Willis Barnstone.—McL
Unmeasured tempo. Maya Angelou.—AnS
"Uno, dos, tres, cho-." See Rima de chocolate
Unpopular Rex. X. J. Kennedy.—KeF
The unquiet grave ("So cold the wintry winds do blow"). Unknown.—PlAs
The unquiet grave ("The wind doth blow today, my love"). Unknown.—HeR
An unseen deer. John Tagliabue.—JaPi
"An unseen deer through seen shadows leaps through my heart." See An unseen deer
Untermeyer, Louis
  Caliban in the coal mines.—LaT
  German slumber song, tr. by.—BaH
  Prayer ("God, though this life is but a wraith").—LaT
  Prayer for this house.—LaT
"Until I can earn me a shilling a year." See Economy
"Until I saw the sea." Lilian Moore.—CoN—HoSe—MoSn—PrRh
Until we built a cabin. Aileen Fisher.—LaW
Unusual shoelaces. X. J. Kennedy.—JaT—LiSf
"An unusual thing called a troupial." See A troupial
Unwanted. Edward Field.—JaPi
"Up and down Pie Street." Mother Goose.—AlH
"Up and down the air you float." See The butterfly
"Up early while everyone sleeps." See Sunday
"Up from the meadows rich with corn." See Barbara Frietchie
"The up front ones are marvelous." See My teeth
Up in the air. James S. Tippett.—HoSu
"Up in the attic there's a great big trunk." Eve Merriam.—MeBl
"Up in the green orchard there is a green tree." Mother Goose.—LoR
"Up in the high." See Song
"Up in the morning's no' for me." Robert Burns.—BlO
Up in the pine. Nancy Dingman Watson.—PrRh
"Up into the silence the green." Edward Estlin Cummings.—KoT
Up north. N. M. Bodecker.—BoPc
Up North Second. Myra Cohn Livingston.—LiWo
"Up on their brooms the witches stream." See The-ride-by-nights
"Up the airy mountain." See The fairies
"Up the street." See The old man's toes
"Up through the fog came the Frisky Dog." See Love at sea
"Up through the ground." See First one out of bed
"Up to bed, your head." See Night
"Up, up, ye dames, and lasses gay." See Hunting song
"Up with me, up with me into the clouds." From To a skylark. William Wordsworth.—KoT
"Up with you, lazybones." See Getting out of bed
Updike, John
  August ("The sprinkler twirls").—HaOf—PrRh
  Commencement, Pingree School.—JaS
  Dog's death.—JaPi
  The grief of cafeterias.—JaPo
  Insomnia the gem of the ocean.—JaD

January ("The days are short").—PrRh
May.—HaOf
Note to the previous tenants.—JaG
Seagulls.—JaPi
September ("The breezes taste").—KeK
Sunday rain.—JaD
Telephone poles ("They have been with us a long time").—JaPi—PlSc
Upham, Samuel C.
  Ye ancient Yuba miner of the days of '49.—PlAs
Upon Fairford windows. Richard Corbett.—PlEd
Upon Julia's clothes. Robert Herrick.—KoT
"Upon my bedroom windowsill." See Nest
"Upon Paul's steeple stands a tree." See St. Paul's steeple
"Upon the level field behold." See Baseball
"Upon the village green." See The village green
"Upon this cake of ice is perched." See The puffin
Upside down ("A field of clouds"). Rose Burgunder.—LiSf
Upside down ("It's funny how beetles"). Aileen Fisher.—BeD—FiW
"Upstairs." Sylvia Cassedy.—CaR
"The upstairs room." See Secret door
Upton, Minnie Leona
  No talking shop.—BrT
"Upward a gull." See Wild day at the shore
Urbanity. Eve Merriam.—MeSk
Us. David Ignatow.—JaPo
Uses for a fog. From A throw of threes. Eve Merriam.—MeF
Uses of poetry. Winfield Townley Scott.—JaD
Ushida, May
  "Deep in the rippling spring."—KeK
Usk. From Landscapes. Thomas Stearns Eliot.—HeR
Ute Mountain. Charles Tomlinson.—HeR

V

Vacation
  August ("The sprinkler twirls"). J. Updike.—HaOf—PrRh
  Boring. J. Prelutsky.—PrWi
  A day in the country. J. Prelutsky.—PrWi
  Driving to the beach. J. Cole.—PrRh
  Home. J. Jaszi.—PrRa
  "In August once." K. Kuskin.—LiCa
  In the motel. X. J. Kennedy.—JaS—PrRh
  The last day of school ("On the last day of school"). J. Prelutsky.—PrWi
  Leavetaking. E. Merriam.—HoSi—MeSk
  No talking shop. M. L. Upton.—BrT
  Sea shore shanty. B. Katz.—HoSe
  Vacation ("I am Paul Bunyan"). E. Merriam.—MeSk
  Vacation ("One scene as I bow to pour her coffee"). W. Stafford.—JaPi
Vacation ("I am Paul Bunyan"). Eve Merriam.—MeSk
Vacation ("One scene as I bow to pour her coffee"). William Stafford.—JaPi
"Vacation is over." See Leavetaking
The vacuum. Howard Nemerov.—HeR
Vagabonds. See Gypsies; Wayfaring life
Vagabonds. Langston Hughes.—PlSc
"Vain, vain, Mister McLain." Arnold Lobel.—LoWr

Valaitis, Laura
A field poem.—JaG
Valediction. Seamus Heaney.—JaPo
Valen, Nanine
"The fisherman's hands."—ChC
Valentine ("Chipmunks jump and"). Donald Hall.—CoN—McL
Valentine ("I got a valentine from Timmy"). Shel Silverstein.—PrRh
Valentine ("If all the whole world's taxicabs"). X. J. Kennedy.—KeF—LiVp
A **valentine** birthday. Barbara Juster Esbensen.—LiVp
Valentine chocolates. Valerie Worth.—LiVp
A **valentine** for my best friend. Jack Prelutsky.—PrIv
A **valentine** for my teacher. Jack Prelutsky.—PrIv
"**Valentine**, O valentine." See Going steady
Valentine thoughts for Mari. Emanuel Di Pasquale.—LiVp
Valentines. Henry Dumas.—LiVp
Valentine's Day. See Saint Valentine's Day
Vallejo, Cesar
España, aparta de me este Caliz, sels. Masses.—HeR
Masses. See España, aparta de me este Caliz
Vampires. See Monsters
Van Doren, Mark
Grandparents' houses.—StG
Midwife cat.—ChC
"Rapunzel, Rapunzel."—PlAs
Truelove.—PlAs
Van Eck, Alice
A football game.—PrRh
Van Gogh, Vincent (about)
Vincent Van Gogh. W. J. Smith.—PlEd
Van Rensselaer, Mariana Griswold
Manners ("I have an uncle I don't like").—PrRh
Vanderbilt, Sanderson
December ("A little boy stood on the corner").—HoSi
A **vaporish** maiden. Morris Bishop.—BrT
Variations on a theme. Mark Vinz.—JaPi
Variations on a theme by William Carlos Williams. Kenneth Koch.—KeK
Vautor, Thomas
Sweet Suffolk owl.—HeR
Vedder, Miriam
Epitaph for a persian kitten.—ChC
Vegetables. See also Food and eating; Gardens and gardening; also names of vegetables, as Potatoes
Asparagus. V. Worth.—WoSp
Song against broccoli. R. Blount.—JaPo
Vegetables. E. Farjeon.—FaE
Vegetables. Eleanor Farjeon.—FaE
Velvet shoes. Elinor Wylie.—LiSf
Vendors. See Peddlers and vendors
Venice, Italy
Venice. H. W. Longfellow.—PlEd
Venice. Henry Wadsworth Longfellow.—PlEd
Verbs. Eleanor Farjeon.—FaE
Vergissmeinicht. Keith Douglas.—HeR
Verlaine, Paul
Sentimental conversation.—LiWa
Vern. Gwendolyn Brooks.—HoDl—LiIl—LiSf
Veronica Castell. Mel Glenn.—GlCd
"**Versa** says." See Bats
Verse. See Poets and poetry
A **verse.** Mary Baker Eddy.—LaT
Verses of the same song, sels. Wendell Berry
"And my love has come to me".—McL

The **very** nicest place. Unknown.—PrRa
A **very** polite man. Unknown.—BrT
"A **very** polite man named Hawarden." See A very polite man
"**Very**, very queer things have been happening to me." See Queer things
Vestibule. Sylvia Cassedy.—CaR
Vet. Eleanor Farjeon.—FaE
The **Vicar** of Bray. Unknown.—PlAs
Victoria. Eleanor Farjeon.—BlO
Victorian grandmother. Margo Lockwood.—JaPi
Video games
Zany Zapper Zockke. J. Prelutsky.—PrNk
La **viejita.** Unknown.—GrT
"**Viene** por las calles." See El caballo
Vietnam war. See United States—History—Vietnam War
Vietnamese language
Toy tik ka. C. Pomerantz.—PoI
The **view** from father's porch. Celeste Turner Wright.—JaS
View of the cathedral, sels. Raymond Henri
Chartres.—PlEd
Duomo, Milan.—PlEd
Viewing the waterfall at Mount Lu. Li Po.—KoT
Vigneault, Gilles
Lullaby ("Sleep sleep beneath the old wind's eye").—DoNw
"A **vigorous** matron of Baxter." See Hog calling
Villa, Jose Garcia
"To become an archer", tr. by.—KeK
The **village** blacksmith. Henry Wadsworth Longfellow.—HaOf
The **village** green. Eleanor Farjeon.—FaE
Village life
The clock tower. C. Thibaudeau.—DoNw
The village green. E. Farjeon.—FaE
Zuni grandmother. Unknown.—StG
The **village** of Erith. Unknown.—LiWa
"**Villagers** all, this frosty tide." See Carol of the field mice
The **villain.** William Henry Davies.—HeR
"**Vince** released a jar of vermin." X. J. Kennedy.—KeB
Vincent Van Gogh. William Jay Smith.—PlEd
Vinnie Robustelli. Mel Glenn.—GlCd
Vinz, Mark
Business as usual.—JaS
The children ("Hand in hand, they are marching").—JaD
The fat boy.—JaT
Mac.—JaS
Morning after.—JaPo
November song.—JaPi
Old Doc.—JaPi
Quilt song.—JaG
Return.—JaG
Variations on a theme.—JaPi
Wild west.—JaPi
The **violet.** William Wordsworth.—ChG
"A **violet** by a mossy stone." See The violet
Violets
How violets came blue. R. Herrick.—KoT
The violet. W. Wordsworth.—ChG
"**Violets**, daffodils." See Nosegay
Violinists. See Fiddlers and fiddling
Viorst, Judith
And although the little mermaid sacrificed everthing to win the love of the prince, the prince, alas, decided to wed another.—ViI
And some more wicked thoughts.—ViI
And the princess was astonished to see the ugly frog turn into a handsome prince.—ViI

Viorst, Judith—*Continued*
And then the prince knelt down and tried to put the glass slipper on Cinderella's foot.—ViI
Apology ("It's hard to say I'm sorry").—ViI
Bertha's wish.—ViI
Fifteen, maybe sixteen, things to worry about.—ViI
Goodbye six, hello seven.—ViI
Harvey.—ViI
I wouldn't be afraid.—ViI
"If I were in charge of the world."—ViI
I'm not.—ViI
Just before springtime.—ViI
Learning.—ViI
The Lizzie Pitofsky poem.—ViI
Mending.—ViI
More wicked thoughts.—ViI
"Mother doesn't want a dog."—PrRh—ViI
My cat.—ViI
My, oh wow, book.—ViI
Night fun.—PrRa—ViI
Night scare.—ViI
Nightmare ("Beautiful beautiful Beverly").—ViI
No ("No, I refuse to").—ViI
Remember me.—ViI
Secrets.—ViI
Short love poem.—ViI
Since Hanna moved away.—HoBf—PrRh—ViI
Some things don't make any sense at all.—PrRh—ViI
Sometimes poems.—ViI
"Stanley the fierce."—ViI
Summer's end ("One by one the petals drop").—ViI
Talking.—ViI
Teddy bear poem.—ViI
Thank you note.—ViI
Thoughts on getting out of a nice warm bed in an ice cold house to go to the bathroom at three o'clock in the morning.—ViI
Weird.—ViI
What price glory.—ViI
Who's who.—ViI
Wicked thoughts.—ViI
Viper. Eve Merriam.—MeHa
"Viper, viper." See Viper
Vipont, Elfrida
"God bless the animals I love."—LaT
"When the night is wild."—LaT
Virgil, Anita
"Grass path lasts."—KeK
Virgilio, Nicholas
"Now the swing is still."—KeK
Virginia
"Oh, have you heard the gallant news." From Western star. S. V. Benét.—PlAs
Virginia. From Landscapes. T. S. Eliot.—HeR
Virginia. From Landscapes. Thomas Stearns Eliot.—HeR
Vision by Sweetwater. John Crowe Ransom.—HeR
Visions. See also Dreams
Auguries of innocence, complete. W. Blake.—HeR
The burning babe. R. Southwell.—HaO—HeR
Columbus day. M. C. Livingston.—LiCe
The hills over the water. E. Farjeon.—FaE
"I have been in bed for hours." J. Prelutsky.—PrMp
Jim Desterland. H. Plutzik.—HeR
Kubla Khan. S. T. Coleridge.—LiSf—LiWa—PlEd
Martin Luther King day. M. C. Livingston.—LiCe

Strange meeting ("It seemed that out of battle I escaped"). W. Owen.—HeR
"To make a prairie it takes a clover." E. Dickinson.—HaOf
"To see a world in a grain of sand." From Auguries of innocence. W. Blake.—PrRh
To see a world.—KeK
Tudor portrait. R. Lattimore.—PlEd
Visit. Vic Coccimiglio.—JaS
A **visit** from Alphonse. Paul Zimmer.—JaG
A **visit** from St. Nicholas ("'Twas the night before Christmas, when all through the house"). Clement C. Moore.—CoN—HaO—HaOf—LiCp—LiSf—PrRh—RoC
A **visit** to the art gallery, sels. Carlos Baker
A Chinese mural.—PlEd
On a landscape of Sestos.—PlEd
The **visitant.** Theodore Roethke.—HeR
The **visitor.** Katharine Pyle.—CoOu
Vitez, Griger
"Catch me the moon, daddy."—LaW
The **vixen.** John Clare.—HeR
The **voice.** Walter De la Mare.—LiWa
"The **voice** of the last cricket." See Splinter
"Voiceless it cries." John Ronald Reuel Tolkien.—LiSf
Voices
Euphonica Jarre. J. Prelutsky.—PrNk
For a mocking voice. E. Farjeon.—LiSf
Hog calling competition. M. Bishop.—BrT—PrRh
"Into a forest." Otsuju.
The little mute boy. F. García Lorca.—HeR
Long distance. W. Stafford.—LiWa
My voice. J. R. Jiménez.—LiSf
On a bad singer. S. T. Coleridge.—PrRh
Spider ("With what voice"). Basho.—KoT
The unknown bird. E. Thomas.—HeR
The voice. W. De la Mare.—LiWa
Voices. A. Turner.—TuS
"Your little voice." E. E. Cummings.—McL
Voices. Ann Turner.—TuS
The **volunteer's** Thanksgiving. Lucy Larcom.—HaOf
Vowels. Arthur Rimbaud.—KoT
Voznesensky, Andrei
War ("With the open eyes of their dead fathers").—HeR
The **vulture.** Hilaire Belloc.—PrRh
"The **vulture** eats between his meals." See The vulture
Vultures
The vulture. H. Belloc.—PrRh
The watchers. P. Fleischman.—FlI

W

W ("The king sent for his wise men all"). James Reeves.—CoN—FaW
W ("The wasp's a kind of buzzing cousin"). From A bestiary of the garden for children who should know better. Phyllis Gotlieb.—DoNw
"W was a wild worm." See A wild worm
Waddell, Helen
The little cat, tr. by.—ChC
Waddington, Miriam
King Rufus, tr. by.—DoNw
Laughter.—DoNw
Rhymes ("Two respectable rhymes"), tr. by.—DoNw
"Wae's me, wae's me." See The wandering spectre

"**Wafers** and bears." Edward Lear.—LiH
Wagoner, David
   Elegy for a woman who remembered everything.—JaD
   House-hunting.—JaD
   Lament for the non-swimmers.—JaD
   My father's ghost.—JaS
   The shooting of John Dillinger outside the Biograph Theater, July 22, 1934.—HeR
   Songs my mother taught me.—JaS
   To the fly in my drink.—JaD
Waily, waily. Unknown.—PlAs
"**Wait**, the great horned owls." See Owls
Waiters. Mary Ann Hoberman.—PrRh
Waiters and waitresses
   The contrary waiter. E. Parker.—PrRh
   "An epicure, dining at Crewe." Unknown.—CoN
   Epitaph on a waiter. D. McCord.—JaPo
   Mary Beth Collier. M. Glenn.—GlCd
   Waiters. M. A. Hoberman.—PrRh
Waiting
   At the Algonquin. H. Moss.—JaPi
   How to see deer. P. Booth.—JaPi
   The juniper tree. W. Watson.—DoNw
   "One person." Issa.—KoT
   Waiters. M. A. Hoberman.—PrRh
   Waiting ("As in a thunderstorm at night"). R. Pack.—JaG—JaPo
   Waiting ("Dreaming of honeycombs to share"). H. Behn.—HoCb—HoSi
   Waiting ("My love will come"). Y. Yevtushenko.—McL
   Waiting both. T. Hardy.—KoT
Waiting ("As in a thunderstorm at night"). Robert Pack.—JaG—JaPo
Waiting ("Dreaming of honeycombs to share"). Harry Behn.—HoCb—HoSi
Waiting ("My love will come"). Yevgeny Yevtushenko, tr. by Robin Milner-Gulland and Peter Levi.—McL
Waiting both. Thomas Hardy.—KoT
"**Wake**." See Snowy morning
Wake up. Unknown, tr. by Eleanor Farjeon.—FaE
Wake up call. Barbara Juster Esbensen.—EsCs
Wake-up poems. See also Morning
   Alarm clock. E. Merriam.—MeSk
   "Awake, arise." Mother Goose.—FaW
   El beso de mama. Unknown.—GrT
   "The cock crows in the morn." Mother Goose.—DeM—LoR
   "Cocks crow in the morning." Unknown.—DaC
   "The day has come." Unknown.—DeD
   For good morning. E. Farjeon.—FaE
   "Get up, get up, you lazyhead." Unknown.—CoN
      Slugabed.—DaC
   Getting out of bed. E. Farjeon.—ChG—FaE
   Good morning ("Good morning, nurse, good morning, cook"). E. Farjeon.—FaE
   "Hark, hark, the lark at heaven's gate sings." From Cymbeline. W. Shakespeare.—BlO—HoUn
   Mama's kiss. Unknown.—GrT
   Ned ("It's a singular thing that Ned"). E. Farjeon.—FaE
   Singing time. R. Fyleman.—ChG—FrP—PrRa
   Song of parents who want to wake up their son. Unknown, fr. the Kwakiutl Indian.—KoT
   "The sounds in the morning." E. Farjeon.—FaE
   "The sun came up this morning." C. Watson.—WaC
   Sun for breakfast. N. Farber.—HoSu

Time to rise. R. L. Stevenson.—ChG—DaC—FaW—FrP
Waking ("My secret way of waking"). L. Moore.—BeD—PrRh
Waking at night. E. Farjeon.—FaE
Wide awake. M. C. Livingston.—PrRa
The **waking** ("I strolled across"). Theodore Roethke.—KoT
Waking ("My secret way of waking"). Lilian Moore.—BeD—PrRh
Waking at night. Eleanor Farjeon.—FaE
Waking from a nap on the beach. May Swenson.—CoN
"**Waking** into an early world." See Sunrise and sun
Waking, the love poem sighs. Jim Hall.—JaG
Walcott, Derek
   The fist.—McL
   A sea-chantey.—HeR
Wales
   The Gresford disaster. Unknown.—PlAs
   Usk. From Landscapes. T. S. Eliot.—HeR
   Welsh incident. R. Graves.—LiWa
Waley, Arthur
   "The locusts' wings say, throng, throng", tr. by.—StG
A **walk**. Nikolai Alekseevich Zabolotsky, tr. by Daniel Weissbort.—HeR
Walker, Annie L.
   "Work, for the night is coming."—PlSc
Walker, James
   Safe ("Come, stir the fire").—HaO
Walker, Margaret
   Lineage.—StG
Walkers with the dawn. Langston Hughes.—HuDk
Walking
   Acquainted with the night. R. Frost.—KoS
   The amputation. H. Sorrells.—JaD
   "As Tommy Snooks and Bessy Brooks." Mother Goose.—DeM—FaW—LoR
   At midnight. T. Kooser.—JaG
   At the beach ("First I walked"). S. Liatsos.—HoSe
   Baby stands. E. Farjeon.—FaE
   Beech leaves. J. Reeves.—CoOu
   Blake leads a walk on the Milky Way. N. Willard.—HaOf
   Cats ("Cats walk neatly"). R. Francis.—JaD
   Coati-mundi. W. J. Smith.—LiIl
   "Doctor Foster went to Gloucester." Mother Goose.—DaC—DeM—FaW—LoR
   First January walk. E. Di Pasquale.—LiNe
   "For a companion." Shiki.—FaTh
   Galoshes. R. W. Bacmeister.—CoN
   "Grand-dads." E. Farjeon.—FaE
   Gravel paths. P. Hubbell.—HoSs
   "In beauty may I walk." Unknown.—HeR
   The intruders. J. Reeves.—CoOu
   "Jenny White and Johnny Black." E. Farjeon.—FaE
   "J's the jumping jay walker." P. McGinley.—PrRh
   Jump or jiggle. E. Beyer.—FrP—PrRa
   A late walk. R. Frost.—KoS
   Laughing backwards. J. Hall.—JaG
   The legs. R. Graves.—HeR
   Long Green Hill. E. Farjeon.—FaE
   Look up. A. Turner.—TuS
   New sounds. L. Moore.—HoSi—MoSn
   "One day when we went walking." V. Hobbs.—PrRh
   The passing years. R. Elsland.—StG
   "See, saw, sacaradown." Mother Goose.—LoR

Walking—*Continued*
Sensation. A. Rimbaud.—KoT
"Step in a ditch." Mother Goose.—LoR
"Step in a hole." Mother Goose.—LoR
"Step in the dirt." Mother Goose.—LoR
"Step on a crack." Mother Goose.—LoR
"Step on a nail." Mother Goose.—LoR
A strange meeting ("The moon is full, and so am I"). W. H. Davies.—BlO
The table and the chair. E. Lear.—LiH—LiSf
"There was an old man of Melrose." E. Lear.—LiH
"There was an old person of Deal." E. Lear.—LiH
"There was an old soldier of Bister." Mother Goose.—LoR
"Three young rats with black felt hats." Mother Goose.—DeM
"To walk in warm rain." D. McCord.—PrRh
Twinkletoes. A. A. Milne.—ChG
Upside down ("It's funny how beetles"). A. Fisher.—BeD—FiW
Velvet shoes. E. Wylie.—LiSf
A walk. N. A. Zabolotsky.—HeR
Walkers with the dawn. L. Hughes.—HuDk
"Walking in the rain." D. Saxon.—JaD
Walking past the school at night. B. J. Esbensen.—EsCs
Walking west. W. Stafford.—HeR
Watch your step, I'm drenched. A. Mitchell.—HeR
"**Walking** around in the park." See Toads revisited
"**Walking** at night in a hat fitted with twelve candles." See Vincent Van Gogh
"**Walking** in the rain." Dan Saxon.—JaD
Walking past the school at night. Barbara Juster Esbensen.—EsCs
Walking west. William Stafford.—HeR
Walking with your eyes shut. William Stafford.—JaG
Wall shadows. Carl Sandburg.—LiWa
The **wallaby**. Jack Prelutsky.—PrZ
Wallace, Robert
Bird theater.—JaT
Dog's song.—JaT
Girl in front of the bank.—JaD
The girl writing her English paper.—JaPi
The gold nest.—JaPo
In one place.—JaPi
In the field forever.—JaPo
In the shadows of early sunlight.—JaT
Tulip.—JaPo
The two old gentlemen.—JaD
Wallace, Ronald
Art work.—JaPo
At the St. Louis Institute of Music.—JaG
The belly dancer in the nursing home.—JaG
Bird watcher.—JaPo
Feline.—JaT
Grandmother Grace.—JaG
Spring again.—JaPo
Tunes for bears to dance to.—JaG
Wallner, Alexandra
Munch, sels.
"Sunday is our roast beef day".—HoMu
"Sunday is our roast beef day." See Munch
The **Walloping** Window-Blind. Charles Edward Carryl.—HaOf
Walls, Jan W.
A spring song of Tzu-Yeh, tr. by.—McL

Walls
Architectural masks. T. Hardy.—PlEd
Fresh paint. E. Merriam.—MeF
The gate in the wall. E. Farjeon.—FaE
Mending wall. R. Frost.—KoS
"The mighty emperor Ch'in Shih Huang." Unknown.—DeD
"Over the garden wall." E. Farjeon.—FaE
Scaffolding. S. Heaney.—JaG
Wall shadows. C. Sandburg.—LiWa
The **walls** do not fall, sels. H. (Hilda Doolittle) D.
"O heart, small urn".—McL
"**Walnut** in a walnut shell." See Bye baby walnut
The **walnut** tree. David McCord.—HaOf
Walnuts and walnut trees
Bye baby walnut. N. Farber.—FaTh
The walnut tree. D. McCord.—HaOf
The **walrus** ("The walrus lives on icy floors"). Michael Flanders.—PrRh
The **walrus** ("The widdly, waddly walrus"). Jack Prelutsky.—PrZ
The **walrus** and the carpenter. From Through the looking glass. Lewis Carroll.—BlO—LiSf
"The **walrus**, I harpoon it." See For subduing a walrus
"The **walrus** lives on icy floors." See The walrus
Walruses
For subduing a walrus. Unknown, fr. the Ammassalik Eskimo.—BiSp
The walrus ("The walrus lives on icy floors"). M. Flanders.—PrRh
The walrus ("The widdly, waddly walrus"). J. Prelutsky.—PrZ
The walrus and the carpenter. From Through the looking glass. L. Carroll.—BlO—LiSf
Walsh, Donald D.
The ghost of the cargo boat, tr. by.—LiWa
The **waltzer** in the house. Stanley Kunitz.—PrRh
The **wanderer**. Wystan Hugh Auden.—HeR
The **wandering** albatross. Paul Fleischman.—FlI
"A **wandering** minstrel I." From The Mikado. William Schwenck Gilbert.—PlAs
The **wandering** spectre. Unknown.—HeR
The ghost's song.—BlO
Wanderings of Oisin, sels. William Butler Yeats
"An old man stirs the fire to a blaze".—HeR
Wang Chien
Weaving at the window.—PlSc
Wang Wei
A parting.—LiIl
"**Wanted**, a witch's cat." Shelagh McGee.—ChC—PrRh
Wanting. Unknown.—KeK
"**Wanting** to lie down on a bed." See One of the boys
War. See also Soldiers; Weapons; also subdivisions under countries, as United States/History/Civil War
Air raid. P. Wild.—JaPi
Another epitaph on an army of mercenaries. H. MacDiarmid.—HeR
"As I lay asleep in Italy." From The mask of anarchy. P. B. Shelley.—HeR
"As the team's head-brass flashed out on the turn." E. Thomas.—HeR
The Battle of Shiloh. Unknown.—PlAs
Blue cuckoo. Unknown.—HeR
Carentan O Carentan. L. Simpson.—HeR
Channel firing. T. Hardy.—HeR
Conquerors. H. Treece.—JaG

War.—*Continued*

The death of the ball turret gunner. R. Jarrell.—HeR

The destruction of Sennacherib. Lord Byron.—HeR—PlAs

The dirty word. E. Merriam.—MeSk

Epitaph on an army of mercenaries. A. E. Housman.—HeR—PlSc

Exposure. W. Owen.—HeR

Fantasia ("I dream"). E. Merriam.—MeSk

The fly ("She sat on a willow-trunk"). M. Holub.—HeR

The fury of aerial bombardment. R. Eberhart.—HeR

Grass. C. Sandburg.—HoRa

"The hand that signed a paper felled a city." D. Thomas.—HeR

A history lesson. M. Holub.—HeR

The horses. E. Muir.—HeR

Hospital barge at Cerisy. W. Owen.—HeR

In time of 'the breaking of nations'. T. Hardy.—HeR

"It was a' for our rightfu' king." R. Burns.—PlAs

"Let there be new flowering." L. Clifton.—JaPo

The lowlands of Holland. Unknown.—PlAs

"Make me feel the wild pulsation that I felt before the strife." From Locksley Hall. A. Tennyson.—PlSc

The man he killed. T. Hardy.—HeR

Memorial day. M. C. Livingston.—LiCe

Mendings. M. Rukeyser.—PlSc

More light, more light. A. Hecht.—HeR

Napoleon. W. De la Mare.—HeR

O, what is that sound. W. H. Auden.—PlAs

A post-mortem. S. Sassoon.—JaD

Radar. A. Ross.—JaD

Range-finding. R. Frost.—HeR

Rannoch, by Glencoe. From Landscapes. T. S. Eliot.—HeR

Santa Ana. Unknown.—PlAs

The send-off. W. Owen.—HeR

The soldiers returning. R. Shelton.—JaG

Song of the dying gunner A.A.I. C. Causley.—PlAs

The sons of liberty. Unknown.—PlAs

Strange meeting ("It seemed that out of battle I escaped"). W. Owen.—HeR

Ten days leave. W. D. W. Snodgrass.—JaPi

"This day is call'd the feast of Crispian." From Henry V. W. Shakespeare.—HoUn

War ("Each day the terror wagon"). R. Shelton.—JaPo

A war ("There set out, slowly, for a different world"). R. Jarrell.—JaD

War ("With the open eyes of their dead fathers"). A. Voznesensky.—HeR

The war of the worlds. V. Rutsala.—JaPi

War story. J. Stallworthy.—JaD

"When howitzers began." H. Carruth.—JaPi

War ("Each day the terror wagon"). Richard Shelton.—JaPo

A war ("There set out, slowly, for a different world"). Randall Jarrell.—JaD

War ("With the open eyes of their dead fathers"). Andrei Voznesensky, tr. by William Jay Smith and Vera Dunham.—HeR

War god's horse song. Unknown, tr. by Louis Watchman.—HeR—KoT

War of 1812. See United States—History—War of 1812

The war of the worlds. Vern Rutsala.—JaPi

War story. John Stallworthy.—JaD

"Warblers." Paul Fleischman.—FlI

"Warm and plump as fresh baked muffins." See The puffin

Warmth. Barton Sutter.—JaG

Warner, Sylvia Townsend

The dear girl.—PlAs

A **warning** ("I know a young girl who can speak"). Mary A. Webber.—BrT

Warning ("The inside of a whirlpool"). John Ciardi.—RuI

The **warning** ("Just now"). Adelaide Crapsey.—LiWa

Warning ("When I am an old woman I shall wear purple"). Jenny Joseph.—JaG

Warning to children. Robert Graves.—BlO

Warnings

Beware, do not read this poem. I. Reed.—LiWa

"Beware of dog." N. M. Bodecker.—BoSs

The crocodile ("Beware the crafty crocodile"). J. Prelutsky.—PrZ

Fair warning. N. Smaridge.—HoSi

Silent warnings. From A throw of threes. E. Merriam.—MeF

The troll. J. Prelutsky.—PrRh

Warning ("The inside of a whirlpool"). J. Ciardi.—RuI

The warning ("Just now"). A. Crapsey.—LiWa

Warning to children. R. Graves.—BlO

Warren, Robert Penn

Boy wandering in Simms' valley.—JaD

Boy's will, joyful labor without pay, and harvest home, sels.

Work.—PlSc

Work. See Boy's will, joyful labor without pay, and harvest home

Warren, Valerie S.

"I was the child."—JaS

"The **warthog**." See Warthog

Warthog. N. M. Bodecker.—BoSs

Warthogs

Warthog. N. M. Bodecker.—BoSs

"Was ever a dream a drum." Carl Sandburg.—HoRa

"Was it for this." From The prelude. William Wordsworth.—HeR

"Was that me jabbering." See Jabbering in school

"Was the love between them." See His lunch basket

Wash in the street. Ann Turner.—TuS

"Wash me and comb me." Unknown.—BaH

Washing. See Bathing; Laundry

"A **washing** hangs upon the line." See Songs for a colored singer

Washing windows. Peter Wild.—JaS

Washington, Booker T. (about)

Alabama earth. L. Hughes.—HuDk

Washington, D.C.

Homage to Paul Mellon, I. M. Pei, their gallery, and Washington City. W. Meredith.—PlEd

Washington, George (about)

Presidents' day. M. C. Livingston.—LiCe

"Proceed, great chief, with virtue on thy side." From To his excellency George Washington. P. Wheatley.—LiSf

Washington. N. B. Turner.—PrRh

Which Washington. E. Merriam.—CoN

Washington. Nancy Byrd Turner.—PrRh

Wasps

"At the tennis court, Paul Pest." X. J. Kennedy.—KeB

I'm bold, I'm brave. J. Prelutsky.—PrNk

Waves
"The horses of the sea." C. G. Rossetti.—CoN
How everything happens (based on a study on
the wave). M. Swenson.—LiSf
Lake Ontario. From Great Lakes suite. J.
Reaney.—DoNw
The sea ("Muffled thunder"). C. Zolotow.—ZoE
Song for a surf rider. S. V. A. Allen.—HoSe
Spray. D. H. Lawrence.—PrBb
Surf. L. Morrison.—CoN—KeK
Waves ("There's big waves and little waves").
E. Farjeon.—FaE
There are big waves.—CoOu
"Waves of the sea." A. Fisher.—HoSe
The waves of the sea. E. Farjeon.—FaE
Waves ("There's big waves and little waves").
Eleanor Farjeon.—FaE
There are big waves.—CoOu
The **waves** of the sea. Eleanor Farjeon.—FaE
"Waves of the sea." Aileen Fisher.—HoSe
"Waves want." See Surf
Wax lips. Cynthia Rylant.—RyW
"The **way** / jacks nest." See Jacks
"The **way** a crow." See Dust of snow
"**Way** back in eighty-two or three." See The
dreadful fate of naughty Nate
Way down in the music. Eloise Greenfield.—LiSf
Way down south. Unknown.—PrRa—PrRh
The grasshopper and the elephant.—CoOu
"**Way** down south where bananas grow." See Way
down south
"The **way** I see any hope for later." Arnold
Adoff.—AdA
The **way** of Cape Race. Edwin John Pratt.—
DoNw
"The **way** the sun on Easter day." See The sun
on Easter day
"The **way** they scrub." Abram Bunn Ross.—PrRa
Wayfaring life
The wanderer. W. H. Auden.—HeR
Wayne, Jane O.
Looking both ways.—JaG
The **ways** of living things. Jack Prelutsky.—PrRh
Ways of winding a watch. Eve Merriam.—MeSk
"**Wayward** things." See Orbit's end
"**We**." See Clap your hands for Herod
"**We** all look on with anxious eyes." See When
father carves the duck
"**We** always love the cradle." See Rocking chair
"**We** are." See Trees, the seeds
"**We** are glad to be here." See Prayer before the
first meal in a new summer camp
"**We** are gloppers, gloopy gloppers." See Song of
the gloopy gloppers
"**We** are in Wieser, Idaho." See Home cooking
cafe
"**We** are light." See Laughter
"**We** are talking about." Arnold Adoff.—AdA
"**We** are the bulldozers, bulldozers, bulldozers."
See Chant of the awakening bulldozers
"**We** are the desperate." See Vagabonds
"**We** are the highway guard, the radar eye." See
Sierra redwoods, highway 101
"**We** are the poor children, come out to see the
sights." See The carol of the poor children
"**We** are three brethren come from Spain." See
Three knights from Spain
"**We** are very little creatures." See AEIOU
"**We** borrowed the loan of Kerr's big ass." See
Kerr's ass
"**We** both stood." See Encounter
"**We** bought our puppy." See Puppy

"**We** brought a rug for sitting on." See The picnic
"**We** built a castle near the rocks." Joan Walsh
Anglund.—PrRa
"**We** built a ship upon the stair." See A good
play
"**We** buried him high on the windy hill." See
Death of an old seaman
"**We** can go back so far." See I know we can
go back so far
"**We** cannot go to the country." See Raleigh was
right
"**We** cannot say that crickets sing." See Crickets
"**We** caroused." See I met this guy who died
"**We** choose to say goodbye against our will." See
Departing words to a son
"**We** climbed to the pond." See Small frogs
"**We** come to your doorstep." See A carol for
Christmas eve
"**We** could." See The American dilemma
"**We** could be friends." Myra Cohn Livingston.—
LiIl
"**We** dance." See Simhat Torah
"**We** dance round in a ring and suppose." See
The secret sits
"**We** don't remember, we weren't." See Spring
fever
"**We** drove out to the country." See A day in
the country
"**We** each wore half a horse." Jack Prelutsky.—
PrNk
"**We** feed the birds in winter." See Joe
"**We** fell in love at 'Journey for Margaret'." See
First love
"**We** fished up the Atlantic Cable one day
between the Barbadoes." See The cable ship
"**We** flung gravel out in arcs then cut for trees."
See Before breakup on the Chena outside
Fairbanks
"**We** found a little bird in spring." See Broken
wing
We four lads. Unknown.—KeK
"**We** four lads from Liverpool are." See We four
lads
"**We** got our mail." See General delivery
"**We** had expected everything but revolt." See
Nightmare number three
"**We** had shepherds." See Christmas play
"**We** have a crazy mixed-up school." See
Mixed-up school
"**We** have a nice clean new green lawn." See
Something better
"**We** have been helping with the cake." See Day
before Christmas
"**We** have muddied the waters for you." See
Prayer to the deceased
"**We** have once more caught." See The bear
"**We** have tomorrow." See Youth
"**We** have two ducks, one blue, one black." See
Quack, quack
"**We** haven't eaten the grape." See Letters from
Sicily
We heard Wally wail. Jack Prelutsky.—PrNk
"**We** heard Wally wail through the whole." See
We heard Wally wail
We interrupt this broadcast. Judith
Hemschemeyer.—JaS
"**We** invite him to die." See Colobus monkey
"**We** lean across the kitchen table." See Arm
wrestling with my father
We like March. Emily Dickinson.—KoT
"**We** like March, his shoes are purple." See We
like March

"We live the same, our way." See Bad guys
"We mask our faces." See On Halloween
"We mustn't pick the garden flowers." See Wildflowers
We need a hit. Jack Prelutsky.—PrWi
"We need a hit, my teammates said." See We need a hit
"We play that we are soldiers." See Noises
We real cool. Gwendolyn Brooks.—KeK
"We real cool, we." See We real cool
"We saw thee come in, a wee naked babe." See Farewell to the old year
"We stand in line all morning long to see it." See The most expensive picture in the world
"We started early, just as soon." See Today is Saturday
"We stretched a rope between two trees." See The funny house
"We swallow the odors of Southern cities." See A Georgia song
"We, the." See Birches, Doheny Road
We three kings. Unknown.—RoC
"We turn out the lights." See Good night
We used to play. Don Welch.—JaPi
"We were all sitting round the table." See Christmas dinner
"We were counted not in thousands." See The passenger pigeon
"We were just three." See Three
"We were not even out of sight of land." See Sea monster
"We were talking about poems he had written." See Rhymes
"We were talking about the great things." See Great things have happened
"We were very tired, we were very merry." See Recuerdo
"We who play under the pines." See Song of the rabbits outside the tavern
"We wondered what our walk should mean." See Peace walk
"We zoomed." See Why
Wealth. See also Money
  Alfred Corning Clark. R. Lowell.—HeR
  Balada de la loca fortuna. E. Gonzales Martinez.—LiSf
  The ballad of mad fortune. E. Gonzales Martinez.—LiSf
  By the Klondike River. A. Coren.—CoOu
  Dorothy Osmond. M. Glenn.—GlCd
  Fire ("This morning on the opposite shore of the river"). W. Carpenter.—JaPi
  The happy heart. T. Dekker.—HeR
  "If I should ever by chance grow rich." E. Thomas.—BlO
  The ships of Yule. B. Carman.—DoNw
  Shirley and her son. N. Giovanni.—GiSp
  "There was an old man of Kilkenny." E. Lear.—LiH
"A wealthy dromedar." See The boar and the dromedar
The weapon. Hugh MacDiarmid.—HeR
Weapons. See also names of weapons, as Guns
  The weapon. H. MacDiarmid.—HeR
The wearin' o' the green. Unknown.—PlAs
"Wearing her yellow rubber slicker." See Myrtle
Wearing of the green. Aileen Fisher.—PrRh
The weary blues. Langston Hughes.—HuDk
Weasels
  Don't ever seize a weasel by the tail. J. Prelutsky.—PrRh—PrZ
  Winter song of the weasel. J. Yolen.—YoR

Weather. See also Clouds; Dew; Fog; Rain; Rainbows; Seasons; Snow; Storms; Wind
  "April weather." Mother Goose.—LoR
  At Candlemas. C. Causley.—HaO
  A calendar. S. Coleridge.—DaC—FrP
    "January brings the snow".—LiSf (unat.)
    The months.—PrRh
  "Calm weather in June." Mother Goose.—LoR
  Change in the weather. I. Orleans.—HoSu
  Clouds ("These clouds are soft fat horses"). J. Reaney.—DoNw
  "If bees stay at home." Mother Goose.—DaC—DeM
  "It blew." Mother Goose.—LoR
  "March winds and April showers." Mother Goose.—DaC—DeM
  "My learned friend and neighbor pig." Mother Goose.—LoR
  "Never mind the rain." N. M. Bodecker.—HoSu
  "One misty, moisty morning." Mother Goose.—ChG—DeM—FaW—LoR—PrRh
  "Rain before seven." Mother Goose.—DeM—LoR
  "Red sky at night." Mother Goose.—DaC—DeM
    "A red sky at night is a shepherd's delight".—LoR
  Showers, clearing later in the day. E. Merriam.—MeSk
  A spell of weather. E. Merriam.—MeSk
  Storm warnings. A. Rich.—JaG
  "This little man lived all alone." Mother Goose.—LoR
  Thunderstorm. H. Behn.—HoCb
  Weather. Unknown.—DaC—PrRh
  Weather incantation. Unknown, fr. the Iglulik Eskimo.—BiSp
  Weather report. L. Moore.—MoSn
  Weathers. T. Hardy.—BlO—DaC—HeR
Weather. Unknown.—DaC—PrRh
Weather incantation. Unknown.—BiSp
Weather report. Lilian Moore.—MoSn
Weathers. Thomas Hardy.—BlO—DaC—HeR
Weathervanes
  "I puff my breast out, my neck swells." From Three riddles from the Exeter book. Unknown.—HeR
Weavers and weaving
  The ballad of the harp-weaver. E. S. Millay.—LiSf—LiWa
  Huswifery. E. Taylor.—PlSc
  "Six little mice sat down to spin." Mother Goose.—DeM—LoR
  Song of the weaving woman. Yuan Chen.—PlSc
  Weaving at the window. Wang Chien.—PlSc
Weaving at the window. Wang Chien, tr. by William H. Nienhauser.—PlSc
Webber, Mary A.
  A warning ("I know a young girl who can speak").—BrT
Webster, A. W.
  On the wrong side.—BrT
Webster, John
  "Call for the robin redbreast and the wren." See The white devil
  A dirge. See The white devil—"Call for the robin redbreast and the wren"
  The white devil, sels.
    "Call for the robin redbreast and the wren".—HeR
    A dirge.—BlO

Weddings
"Beat the drum, beat the drum." Unknown.—DeD
The bonny bride of Kent. E. Farjeon.—FaE
The bride ("I wonder if ever"). C. Zolotow.—ZoE
The bride ("In she goes"). E. Farjeon.—FaE
The broken wedding ring. Unknown.—PlAs
"Fiddle-de-dee, fiddle-de-dee." Mother Goose.—LoR
Leigh Hamilton. M. Glenn.—GlCd
"Let's marry said the cherry." N. M. Bodecker.—LiSf
Lochinvar. Sir W. Scott.—PlAs
"Married when the year is new." Mother Goose.—LoR
The mouse's courting song. Unknown.—PlAs
"Oh, Mother, I shall be married." Mother Goose.—BlQ—LoR
"On Saturday night shall be my care." Mother Goose.—AlH—LoR
"Puss came dancing out of a barn." Mother Goose.—DeM
"Something old, something new." Mother Goose.—LoR
"A **wee** little boy has opened a store." Unknown.—DeD
A **wee** little worm. James Whitcomb Riley.—PrRh
"A **wee** little worm in a hickory nut." See A wee little worm
The **wee** wee man. Unknown.—PlAs
"**Wee** Willie Winkie runs through the town." Mother Goose.—DeM—LoR
Weeds. See also names of weeds, as Dandelions
"The green cockleburs." R. Wright.—KeK
Inversnaid. G. M. Hopkins.—HeR
My aunt. T. Hughes.—LiWa
Weeds. C. Zolotow.—ZoE
Yellow weed. L. Moore.—MoSn
Weeds. Charlotte Zolotow.—ZoE
The **week** after. Eleanor Farjeon.—FaE
Weekend glory. Maya Angelou.—AnS
"**Weekends**, the battered yellow bus." See Sleepy schoolbus
"**Weep**, weep, ye woodmen, wail." See Song
Weeping ash. Myra Cohn Livingston.—LiMp
Weeping mulberry. Myra Cohn Livingston.—LiMp
Weeping willow. Myra Cohn Livingston.—LiMp
"A **weevil**." See Weevil
Weevil. N. M. Bodecker.—BoSs
Weird. Judith Viorst.—ViI
"The **weird** sisters, hand in hand." From Macbeth. William Shakespeare.—HoUn
Weissbort, Daniel
"Don't touch me, I scream at passers by", tr. by.—McL
The face of the horse, tr. by.—HeR
Thistle, tr. by.—HeR
A walk, tr. by.—HeR
Welch, Don
Poet in residence at a county school.—JaG
Welch, Don
The river ("Winter").—JaS
Spade Scharnweber.—JaPi
We used to play.—JaPi
"**Welcome**, supernatural ones, we have come to meet alive." See Prayer to the migratory birds
Welcome to the new year. Eleanor Farjeon.—FaE
"**Well**, hello down there." Issa, tr. by Harry Behn.—FaTh—LiIl—LiSf
"**Well** I can't 'cause." See Parents never understand

A **well** informed wight. Oliver Herford.—BrT
"**Well**, it's partly the shape of the thing." Unknown.—KeK
"**Well**, let's go." Basho.—KoT
"**We'll** play in the snow." See Snow
The **well** rising. William Stafford.—HeR
"The **well** rising without sound." See The well rising
"**Well**, so that is that, now we must dismantle the tree." From For the time being. Wystan Hugh Auden.—HaO
"**Well**, son, I'll tell you." See Mother to son
Welles, Winifred
Behind the waterfall.—LiSf
Wells, Amos R.
The ambitious ant.—HaOf
The considerate crocodile.—HaOf
Wells, Anna Maria
The cow-boy's song.—HaOf
The little maid.—HaOf
Wells, Carolyn
A baker's dozen of wild beasts, sels.
The bath-bunny.—HaOf
The corn-pone-y.—HaOf
The cream-puffin.—HaOf
The mince-python.—HaOf
The bath-bunny. See A baker's dozen of wild beasts
A beggarly bear.—BrT
The corn-pone-y. See A baker's dozen of wild beasts
The cream-puffin. See A baker's dozen of wild beasts
The disobliging bear.—BrT
The dragon.—BrT
Gnome matter.—BrT
The happy hyena.—BrT
A marvel.—HaOf
The mince-python. See A baker's dozen of wild beasts
The old lady from Dover.—BrT
An ossified oyster.—BrT
Puzzled.—HaOf
The theater hat.—BrT
The tutor.—PrRh
A wild worm.—BrT
Wells
"As round as an apple, as deep as a cup." Mother Goose.—LiSf
At grandfather's. C. B. Bates.—HaOf
Celanta at the well of life. From The old wives' tale. G. Peele.—BlO
Song for the head.—HeR
Cleaning the well. P. Ruffin.—JaS
"Ding dong bell." Mother Goose.—AlH—DaC—DeM—FaW—LiSf—LoR
The grasshopper. D. McCord.—LiSf
To a forgetful wishing well. X. J. Kennedy.—KeF
Welsh incident. Robert Graves.—LiWa
The **wendigo**. Ted Hughes.—HuU
"The **wendigo**." Ogden Nash.—PrRh
"The **wendigo's** tread." See The wendigo
Wendy in winter. Kaye Starbird.—PrRh
Wendy Tarloff. Mel Glenn.—GlCd
"**Went** to Florida once." See The world
"**Went** to the river, couldn't get across." Unknown.—FaW
Weöres, Sándor
Monkeyland.—HeR
"**We're** all in the dumps." Mother Goose.—BlO
"**We're** burning up the old blue garden gate." See Burning the gate

"We're forty performing bananas." See Forty performing bananas

"Were he composer, he would surely write." See Portrait of the boy as artist

"We're racing, racing down the walk." Phyllis McGinley.—PrRh

"We're rolling on the living room floor." See Shaggy dog story

"We're sinking into beds of lights that." See Night, landing at Newark

"Were you ever in Quebec." See Donkey riding

Wesley-Smith, Peter
"Arbuckle Jones."—JaT

Weslowski, Dieter
Zoe and the ghosts.—JaPo

"The west was getting out of gold." See Looking for a sunset bird in winter

Westcott, G. C.
Gobbolino, the witch's cat.—ChC

Western star, sels. Stephen Vincent Benét
"Oh, have you heard the gallant news".—PlAs

"Western wind, when wilt thou blow." Unknown.—KeK—McL

Westrup, J. M.
Flying ("I saw the moon").—CoOu

Wet. Lilian Moore.—MoSn

"A wet sheet and a flowing sea." Allan Cunningham.—BlO

"Wet wet wet." See Wet

"We've laughed until my cheeks are tight." See Bursting

Wevill, David
Birth of the foal, tr. by.—HeR

Weygant, Sister Noemi
Winter is tacked down.—BaS

"Wha you been, Lord Randal, my son." See Lord Randal

Whale ("A whale is stout about the middle"). Mary Ann Hoberman.—RuI

Whale ("When I swam underwater I saw a blue whale"). William Jay Smith.—RuI

"The whale can swallow." See A zoo without bars

The **whale** ghost. Lilian Moore.—MoSn

"Whale, I want you to come near me, so that I will get hold of." See Prayer to the whale

"A whale is stout about the middle." See Whale

Whalen, Philip
Early spring.—JaT

Whalers. See Whales

Whales
Autumn ("This morning they are putting away the whales"). W. Carpenter.—JaPi

"Down the blowhole of a whale." X. J. Kennedy.—KeB

Jack was every inch a sailor. Unknown.—DoNw

Prayer to the whale. Unknown, fr. the Nootka Indian.—BiSp

Whale ("A whale is stout about the middle"). M. A. Hoberman.—RuI

Whale ("When I swam underwater I saw a blue whale"). W. J. Smith.—RuI

The whale ghost. L. Moore.—MoSn

The whales off Wales. X. J. Kennedy.—HaOf—RuI

A zoo without bars. N. M. Bodecker.—BoSs

The **whales** off Wales. X. J. Kennedy.—HaOf—RuI

Wharf. Myra Cohn Livingston.—HoSe

"What a drag it must be for you." See Susie's enzyme poem

"What a pity, when a man looks at himself in a glass." See Man's image

"What a to-do. Unknown.—DaC

"What a to-do to die today." See What a to-do

"What a wonderful bird the frog are." See The frog

"What about caterpillars." See About caterpillars

"What angel fell here." See Snow print one, mystery

"What are all the seasons to me." See Dragonfly's summer song

"What are days for." See Days

"What are days for." From The world is day breaking. Sekiya Miyoshi.—BeD

"What are little boys made of." Mother Goose.—FaW

"What are little boys made of, made of".—AlH—DeM

Natural history.—DaC

"What are little boys made of, made of". See "What are little boys made of"

"What are little girls made of." Mother Goose.—FaW

Natural history.—DaC

"What are little girls made of, made of".—AlH

"What are little girls made of, made of". See "What are little girls made of"

"What are pussycats good for." See Cats are good for something

"What are the bugles blowin' for, said Files-on-Parade." See Danny Deever

"What are the signs of zodiac." See Zodiac

"What are you able to build with your blocks." See Block city

What became of them. See "He was a rat, and she was a rat"

What bird so sings. John Lyly.—BlO

"What bird so sings, yet so does wail." See What bird so sings

"What can I give him." Christina Georgina Rossetti.—LiCp

My gift.—LaT

"What can lambkins do." See A chill

"What can the matter be." See The wind

"What changes, my love." Edwin Honig.—JaPo

"What comes out of a chimney." Mother Goose.—LoR

"What could have frightened them away." See Fairies

"What did they feel, those twenty odd." See Temple of the muses

"What did you hear." See Advent, a carol

"What do caterpillars do." See Caterpillars

"What do people think about." See Aunt Roberta

What do they do to you in distant places. Marvin Bell.—JaPi

"What, do they suppose that everything has been said that can be said." See Christmas

"What does the old dog say." See The old dog's song, complete

What grandma knew. Edward Field.—JaPi

"What happened in the sky." See Lost

"What happens to the colors." Jack Prelutsky.—PrMp

"What has happened, is this me." See Waking at night

What has happened to Lulu. Charles Causley.—KeK

"What has happened to Lulu, mother." See What has happened to Lulu

"What have I been doing, then." See What I've been doing

"What have you picked up, baby on the shore." See Treasure

What he saw. Robert Currie.—JaS
"What I had never imagined, your return." See Brief encounter
"What I remember about that day." See Eviction
"What if." Isabel Joshlin Glaser.—HoDi
"What in the world." Eve Merriam.—PrRh
"What is ambition, 'tis a glorious cheat." See Ambition
"What is being rejected." See Barbara Sutton
What is black. Mary O'Neill.—CoN
A what-is-it. Ruth McEnery Stuart and Albert Bigelow Paine.—BrT
"What is it about homework." See Homework
"What is it you're mumbling, old Father, my Dad." See By the Exeter River
What is orange. Mary O'Neill.—PrRh
What is pink. Christina Georgina Rossetti.—CoOu—DaC—PrRh
"What is pink, a rose is pink." See What is pink
"What is poetry, who knows." See Poetry
What is red. Mary O'Neill.—PrRh
"What is song's eternity." See Song's eternity
"What is the difference." See Color
"What is the matter, grandmother dear." See Grandma's lost balance
"What is the opposite of a prince." Richard Wilbur.—LiSf—LiWa
"What is the opposite of nuts." Richard Wilbur.—LiSf
"What is the opposite of riot." See Some opposites
"What is the opposite of two." Richard Wilbur.—LiIl
  The opposite of two.—PrRh
"What is the world, O soldiers." See Napoleon
"What is there for us two." See Fifty-fifty
"What is there within this beggar lad." See Beggar boy
"What is this stone he's laid upon my bones." See Epitaph
"What is under the grass." See Under the ground
What I've been doing. Eleanor Farjeon.—FaE
What Jenner said on hearing in Elysium that complaints had been made of his having a statue in Trafalgar Square. Shirley Brooks.—PlEd
What Johnny told me. John Ciardi.—LiIl
"What jolly things are farms." See Farms
"What lips my lips have kissed, and where, and why." Edna St. Vincent Millay.—McL
"What lovely names for girls there are." See Girls' names
"What nerve you've got, Minerva Mott." Jack Prelutsky.—PrNk
"What our dame bids us do." From The masque of queens. Ben Jonson.—LiWa
What price glory. Judith Viorst.—ViI
"What ran under the rosebush." See Could it have been a shadow
"What shall I ask you for God." See Prayer
"What shall I plant in my little herb border." See Sweet herbs
"What shall I wear for the Easter parade." See The Easter parade
What should I see. Eleanor Farjeon.—FaE
What someone said when he was spanked on the day before his birthday. John Ciardi.—PrRh
"What sort of things are seen in the class-room." See Class-room
"What splendid names for boys there are." See Boys' names
What the donkey saw. U. A. Fanthorpe.—HaO

"What the horriblest thing you've seen." See Horrible things
What the stone dreams. James B. Hathaway.—JaG
What there is. Kenneth Patchen.—McL
"What this country needs." See A simple need
"What treasures lie beneath." See Ocean treasures
"What way does the wind come, what way does he go." See Address to a child during a boisterous winter evening
"What weighs the littlest." See Answers
"What, what, what." See Threnody
"What will they say." See Remember me
"What will you find at the edge of the world." See Landscape
"What will you ride on." See Hey, my pony
"What worlds of wonder are our books." See Books
"What would you like to be." See Interview
What Zimmer would be. Paul Zimmer.—JaPi
"Whatever happened to the allosaurus." From Whatever happened to the dinosaurs. Bernard Most.—HoDi
Whatever happened to the dinosaurs, sels. Bernard Most
  "Whatever happened to the allosaurus".—HoDi
"Whatever he does, you have to do too." See Follow the leader
"Whatever it is you're missing, whatever." See Call them back
"Whatever one toucan can do." See Toucans two
"What's behind the museum door." See The museum door
"What's half of nothing, I have no pie." See There's nothing to it
"What's in a name, that which we call a rose." From Romeo and Juliet. William Shakespeare.—HoUn
"What's ornithology, pray can you tell." See Ornithology
"What's that." Florence Parry Heide.—HoCr—PrRh
"What's the good of a wagon." See The gold-tinted dragon
"What's the news of the day." Mother Goose.—LoR
"What's the oldest thing that's living." See Catechisms, talking with a four year old
"What's the score." See The baseball player
Wheat
  A Dakota wheat field. H. Garland.—HaOf
  The four dears. E. Elliot.—PlSc
Wheatley, Phillis
  "Proceed, great chief, with virtue on thy side." See To his excellency George Washington
  To his excellency George Washington, sels. "Proceed, great chief, with virtue on thy side".—LiSf
Wheeler, John
  The three drovers.—RoC
Wheelock, John Hall
  Ballad.—PlAs
"When." See Friend
When. Dorothy Aldis.—PrRh
"When." See True
"When." See When my grandmother died
"When a beetle." See Right-of-way
"When a bird flips his tail in getting his balance on a tree." See Many mansions
"When a cat has its tail." See A special dictionary to help you understand cats
"When a cat is asleep." Karla Kuskin.—JaT

"When I told my mother she didn't look well." See Darcy Tanner

"When I wake up and it is dark." See In the night

"When I was a baby you sang me soft Spanish lullabies." See Anna Montalvo

"When I was a child." See Autobiographia literaria

"When I was a child of, say, seven." See A backwards journey

"When I was a little boy." Mother Goose.—DeM—LoR

"When I was a little girl." See Tina DeMarco

"When I was at the party." See Betty at the party

"When I was christened." David McCord.—HaOf—KeK

"When I was down beside the sea." See At the sea-side

"When I was home de." See Po' boy blues

"When I was home last Christmas." Randall Jarrell.—PlAs

"When I was just a little boy." See The ships of Yule

"When I was little maid." See The little maid

When I was lost. Dorothy Aldis.—PrRh

"When I was once in Baltimore." See Sheep

"When I was past such thinking." See You came as a thought

"When I was seven." See Growing up

"When I was sick and lay abed." See The land of Counterpane

"When I was small." See Clean

"When I was small I'm sure I heard." See The fairy and the bird

"When I was very small and lonely." See The sea shell

"When I was young, and the day." See Poem to help my father

"When I was young the world was a little pond." See Return of the village lad

"When I was younger, mothers didn't let me play with." See Ernest Mott

"When I wear my football jersey to class." See Marvin Pickett

"When I went into my room, at mid-morning." See Man and bat

"When I went out." See A spike of green

When I went out. Karla Kuskin.—CoN

"When I went out to see the sun." See When I went out

"When icicles hang by the wall." From Love's labour's lost. William Shakespeare.—HoUn Winter.—BlO

"When I'm tucked in bed." See Storm at night

"When I'm very nearly sleeping." Jack Prelutsky.—PrMp

"When in danger." Unknown.—TrM

"When, in disgrace with fortune and men's eyes." From Sonnets. William Shakespeare.—HoUn

"When Indians are sleepy." See About Indians

When it come to bugs. Aileen Fisher.—FiW

"When it was October." See Mrs. Brownish Beetle

"When it was time." See Shell

"When it's hot." See Summer

"When it's time." See Listening

"When Jack's a very good boy". See "When Jacky's a good boy"

"When Jacky's a good boy." Mother Goose.—DeM—FaW

"When Jack's a very good boy".—LoR

"When Jacky's a very good boy".—AlH

"When Jacky's a very good boy". See "When Jacky's a good boy"

"When Jake O'Leary." See Jake O'Leary's Thanksgiving

When Jane goes to market. Eleanor Farjeon.—FaE

"When Jane goes to market she wears a pink gown." See When Jane goes to market

"When John Henry was a little babe." See John Henry

"When John Henry was a little tiny baby." See John Henry

"When Julius Caesar was a child." See Latin

"When Letty had scarce passed her third glad year." See Letty's globe

"When Levin mowed Mashkin Hill." See Mashkin Hill

"When lilacs last in the dooryard bloom'd." Walt Whitman.—HeR

"When little Fred went to bed." Mother Goose.—DeM

"When little heads weary have gone to bed." See The plumppuppets

"When Mickey Jones." See Mickey Jones

"When Molly Day wears yellow clothes." Jack Prelutsky.—PrRi

"When mosquitoes make a meal." Else Holmelund Minarik.—PrRh

"When most students didn't know the Midwest from the." See Sanford Evans Pierce

"When mountain rocks and leafy trees." See Nature's lineaments

When mowers pass. Aileen Fisher.—FiW

"When Mr. Croxford." See At the St. Louis Institute of Music

"When my arms wrap you round I press." See He remembers forgotten beauty

"When my brother Tommy." See Two in bed

"When my canary." Shiki.—LiSf

"When my dog died." Freya Littledale.—CoN

"When my English teacher told me it was my turn to give a speech." See Nancy Soto

"When my father died." See Between here and Illinois

When my grandmother died. Sam Cornish.—JaPi

"When my house is full of flowers the brightness." See Ann's house

"When my love swears that she is made of truth." From Sonnets. William Shakespeare.—HoUn

"When my mother died I was very young." See The chimney sweeper

"When my mother found my birth control pills." See Monica Zindell

"When my parents went away on a short vacation." See Danielle O'Mara

"When my sister, Debbie, went away to college." See Jodi Kurtz

"When night is dark." See At night

"When Noah loaded the ark as bidden." R. Beasley.—TrM

"When nothing is happening." See How everything happens (based on a study on the wave)

"When old corruption first begun." William Blake.—HeR

"When our hound dog Rex." See Unpopular Rex

"When over the flowery, sharp pasture's." See Flowers by the sea

"When Paul Bunyan was ill." Willie Reaker.—KeK

"When people call this beast to mind." See The elephant

"When pigeons clutter up July." See Brooms
"When President John Quincy." See John Quincy Adams
"When rain falls gray and unabating." See A different door
"When Rhonda read one of her poems in class." See Eleanor Paine
"When searching for." See Glass walling
"When she comes slip footing." See Mama is a sunrise
"When singing songs of scariness." See The worst
"When skies are low." N. M. Bodecker.—BoSs
"When snowflakes are fluttering." Jack Prelutsky.—PrIs
"When somewhere life." See Beaver moon, the suicide of a friend
"When Spanky goes." See Basketball
"When spring gales." See Up north
When Sue wears red. Langston Hughes.—HuDk
"When summer smells like apples." See Back to school
"When supper time is almost come." See Milking time
"When Susanna Jones wears red." See When Sue wears red
"When that I was and a little tiny boy." From Twelfth night. William Shakespeare.—HoUn
"When the Alabama's keel was laid." See Roll, Alabama, roll
"When the almond blossoms." Eleanor Farjeon.—FaE
When the ambulance came. Robert Morgan.—JaS
"When the ambulance came for Grandma." See When the ambulance came
"When the bat's on the wing and the bird's in the tree." See The starlighter
"When the battle was over." See Masses
When the child is named. Unknown.—BiSp
"When the clock strikes five but it's only four." See Wrimples
"When the corn stands yellow in September." See Harvest
"When the crows fly away." See My love
"When the earth is turned in spring." See The worm
"When the earth was made." See A song of the girls' puberty ceremony
"When the green woods laugh." William Blake.—KoT
"When the hare and the pig had some pleasure to plan." See The hare and the pig
"When the heat of the summer." See A dragonfly
"When the high/snows lie worn." See Crows
"When the landfills all are full." See Quest
"When the last of gloaming's gone." See The shadow
"When the moon." See Ghost sounds
"When the moon comes up." See The moon rises
"When the neat white." See Duck
"When the night begins to fall." See Where are you now
"When the night is wild." Elfrida Vipont.—LaT
"When the organ grinder turns his organ handle." See Organ grinder
"When the pale moon hides and the wild wind wails." See The wolf
"When the peacock loudly calls." Mother Goose.—LoR
"When the Pilgrims." See The first Thanksgiving
"When the present has latched its postern behind my tremulous stay." See Afterwards
"When the rain raineth." Unknown.—HeR

"When the smoke of the clouds parted." From Bright conversation with Saint-Ex. Carl Sandburg.—HoRa
"When the summer sun is blazing." See I toss them to my elephant
"When the sun." See Twinkletoes
"When the sun is strong." See In August
"When the tea is brought at five o'clock." See Milk for the cat
"When the turkey gobble gobbles." See Gobble gobble
"When the wind blows." See Wind song
"When the wind blows." Mother Goose.—LoR
"When the wind is in the east." Mother Goose.—DeM
"When the world vanishes, I will come back." See Some night again
"When there are minds to heal, and you." See Girl in a white coat
"When there dawns a certain star." See Child's carol
"When there's hardly a breath of wind to stir." See Green riders
"When these small." See Beach stones
"When they asked." Arnold Adoff.—AdA
"When they go out walking the Sioux." See The Sioux
"When they pull my clock tower down." See The clock tower
"When they said the time to hide was mine." See The rabbit
"When things were as fine as could possibly be." John Byrom.—TrM
"When this cat wants breakfast." See Early breakfast
"When Tillie ate the chili." Jack Prelutsky.—PrNk
"When trees did show no leaves." See The ending of the year
"When twilight comes to Prairie Street." See The winning of the TV west
"When twins came, their father, Dan Dunn." See The twins
"When walking in a tiny rain." See Vern
"When water turns to ice does it remember." See Metamorphosis
"When we are going toward someone we say." See Simple song
"When we are like." Yvonne Caroutch, tr. by Carl Hermey.—McL
"When we got home, there was our old man." See Pa
"When we lived in a city." See Until we built a cabin
"When we're." See Dangerous
"When we're playing tag." See No girls allowed
"When we've emptied." See The whale ghost
"When winter scourged the meadow and the hill." See Ice
"When winter was half over." See Another Sarah
"When you are in bed and it's cold outside." See Pretending
"When you break your heart it changes." See End song
"When you fly in a plane." See Flying
"When you go away." See The departure
"When you talk to a monkey." Rowena Bennett.—PrRa
"When you think me dreaming, chin on paws." See Wolf
"When you turn down your glass it's a sign." See Table manners
"When you visit the barber." See Barbershop

"When you wanted a piano." See Music
"When you watch for." See Feather or fur
When young Melissa sweeps. Nancy Byrd Turner.—CoN
"When young Melissa sweeps a room." See When young Melissa sweeps
When young, the slyne. Jack Prelutsky.—PrNk
"When young, the slyne, from noon to nine." See When young, the slyne
"When your face." See Colors
"When you're a duck like me it's impossible." See The duck
"When you've." See In the park
"Whenas in silks my Julia goes." See Upon Julia's clothes
"Whence came the crimson on the daisy's tip." See The mark
"Whence got ye your soft, soft eyes of the mother, O soft eyed." See A manger song
"Whenever I go fishing." See Tricia's fish
"Whenever Pa neglects to shave." See Porcupine pa
"Whenever someone asks me what I want to be." See A hikoka in a hikoki
"Whenever the moon and stars are set." See Windy nights
"Whenever they come from Kansas." See Coming from Kansas
"Whenever we would open, there he stood." See Murgatroyd
"Whenever you see the hearse go by." See Be merry
"Whenever you're sitting and reading a book." See Cats love books
Where. Walter De la Mare.—BaH
Where am I. Richard J. Margolis.—MaS
"Where are you going, child, so far away." See Going into dream
"Where are you going, my father." See Song of farewell to the deceased
Where are you now. Mary Britton Miller.—PrRh
"Where did they start, those well-marked." See Footprints
"Where did you come from, baby dear." George MacDonald.—DaC
"Where dips the rocky highland." See The stolen child
"Where do insects go at night." See When all the world's asleep
Where do these words come from. Charlotte Pomerantz.—PoI
Where do you sleep. William Engvik.—LaW
"Where gates say Pick Your Own, and trees." See Pick your own
Where go the boats. Robert Louis Stevenson.—CoN
Where goblins dwell. Jack Prelutsky.—PrRh
"Where have you been dear." Karla Kuskin.—CoN
"Where he stood in boots in water to his calves." See The fishvendor
"Where I bend over." See Weeping willow
"Where I stood still, whirring." See Two of a kind
"Where is another sweet as my sweet." See The letter
"Where is that plain door." See Insomnia
"Where is the grave of Sir Arthur O'Kellyn." See The knight's tomb
"Where should a baby rest." Mother Goose.—BaH

"Where the bee sucks, there suck I." From The tempest. William Shakespeare.—BlO—HoUn—KoT
"Where the lone wind on the hilltop." See The empty house
"Where the pools are bright and deep." See A boy's song
"Where the remote Bermudas ride." See Bermudas
"Where the wind blows." See The wind
"Where the working bee still hums." See The second birth of roses
"Where the world is grey and lone." See The ice-king
"Where will we run to." X. J. Kennedy.—KeF
"Wherever there's sun a cat is sunning." See Cats know what's good
"Whether I'm Alsatian." See Dog
"Whether the weather be fine." See Weather
"Which is the cosiest voice." See Gray thrums
"Which one of you did this." See Can't win
"Which to prefer." See Shoes
Which Washington. Eve Merriam.—CoN
"Which, which." See Witchery
"Which will you have, a ball or a cake." See Choosing
While dissecting frogs in biology class Scrut discovers the intricacies of the scooped neckline in his lab partner's dress. George Roberts.—JaG
While I slept. Robert Francis.—KeK
"While I slept, while I slept and the night grew colder." See While I slept
"While I watch the Christmas blaze." See The reminder
"While joy gave clouds the light of stars." See The villain
"While my hair was still cut straight across my forehead." See The river-merchant's wife, a letter
"While snows the window panes bedim." See December
"While the fruit boils, Mom sends Lars." X. J. Kennedy.—KeB
"While we dazed onlookers gawk." X. J. Kennedy.—KeB
"While we unloaded the hay from the truck, building." See The barn
"While we were together." See A painful love song
"While yet the Morning Star." See The unicorn
While you were chasing a hat. Lilian Moore.—MoSn
"While you were still asleep." See For the little girl who asked why the kitchen was so bright
"Whip-poor-will." Paul Fleischman.—FII
"A whippet." See Beware of the doggerel
Whippoorwills
    "Whip-poor-will." P. Fleischman.—FII
Whirlpools
    Warning ("The inside of a whirlpool"). J. Ciardi.—RuI
"The whirlwind." From Songs of the ghost dance. Unknown.—LiWa
"Whiskers of style." Arnold Lobel.—LoWr
Whiskey
    John Barleycorn. R. Burns.—HeR—PlAs
"Whisky, frisky." See The squirrel
"Whistle, daughter, whistle." Mother Goose.—LoR
Whistling
    Spring whistles. L. Larcom.—HaOf

Wind—*Continued*

"Days that the wind takes over." K. Kuskin.—HoSi

The dreaming of the bones. From Song for the cloth. W. B. Yeats.—HeR

Fall wind ("Everything is on the run"). A. Fisher.—HoSi

Fall wind ("Pods of summer crowd around the door"). W. Stafford.—JaPo

A field poem. L. Valaitis.—JaG

"Gently, gently, the wind blows." K. Mizumura.—FaTh

Go wind. L. Moore.—MoSn

"Hinnikin Minnikin." J. Prelutsky.—PrRi

Hurricane. L. Moore.—MoSn

"I called to the wind." Kyorai.—LiSf—LiWa

"I do not mind you, winter wind." J. Prelutsky.—PrIs

"I think that the root of the wind is water." E. Dickinson.—IIcR

Illinois farmer. C. Sandburg.—HoRa

"Jolly March wind." E. Farjeon.—FaE

The leaves in a frolic. Unknown.—CoOu

"Like rain it sounded till it curved." E. Dickinson.—HeR

Little wind. K. Greenaway.—PrRa

The March wind. Unknown.—PrRh

March wind. H. Behn.—HoCb

"The moon's the north wind's cooky." V. Lindsay.—CoN—HaOf—LaW—LiSf—PrRa—PrRh

Mountain wind. B. K. Loots.—PrRh

"The north wind doth blow." Mother Goose.—BlO—CoOu—DeM—FaW—LiSf—LoR
   Poor robin.—RoC

Now close the windows. R. Frost.—KoS

On Wenlock Edge. A. E. Housman.—HeR

Quaking aspen. E. Merriam.—MeF

Rags. J. Thurman.—HoSi—JaT

The secret. J. Stephens.—LiWa

Small dark song. P. Dacey.—JaPo

Snowball wind. A. Fisher.—BaS

The sound of the wind. C. G. Rossetti.—BlO—CoOu

The spring wind. C. Zolotow.—PrRa—ZoE

"Stocking and shirt." J. Reeves.—CoOu

The storm ("A perfect rainbow, a wide"). W. C. Williams.—JaPo

A strong wind. A. Clarke.—HeR

Sun and wind. E. Farjeon.—FaE

Sweet and low. From The princess. A. Tennyson.—BlO—ChB

"Tell me, thou star, whose wings of light." P. B. Shelley.—KoT

"There came a wind like a bugle." E. Dickinson.—HeR

Thunderstorm. H. Behn.—HoCb

Two ways to look at kites. B. J. Esbensen.—EsCs

The unknown color. C. Cullen.—HaOf

"Until I saw the sea." L. Moore.—CoN—HoSe—MoSn—PrRh

The villain. W. H. Davies.—HeR

"Voiceless it cries." J. R. R. Tolkien.—LiSf

"Western wind, when wilt thou blow." Unknown.—KeK—McL

"When the wind blows." Mother Goose.—LoR

"When the wind is in the east." Mother Goose.—DeM

While you were chasing a hat. L. Moore.—MoSn

"The whirlwind." From Songs of the ghost dance. Unknown, fr. the Paiute Indian.—LiWa

"Who has seen the wind." C. G. Rossetti.—BlO—CoN—FrP—LiSf—PrRh
   The wind.—DaC

Wild iron. A. Curnow.—HeR

The wind ("I can get through a doorway without any key"). J. Reeves.—PrRh

The wind ("I saw you toss the kites on high"). R. L. Stevenson.—LiSf

The wind ("What can the matter be"). D. Graddon.—CoOu

The wind ("Where the wind blows"). E. Farjeon.—FaE

The wind ("The wind stood up, and gave a shout"). J. Stephens.—KeK

The wind and the moon. G. MacDonald.—PrRa

"The wind blows out of the gates of the day." From The land of heart's desire. W. B. Yeats. HeR

"The wind has taken the damson tree." E. Farjeon.—FaE

The wind has wings. Unknown.—DoNw

Wind song ("When the wind blows"). L. Moore.—MoSn

Wind song ("Wind now commences to sing"). Unknown, fr. the Pima Indian.—LiSf

"The wind stirs the willows." From Songs of the ghost dance. Unknown, fr. the Paiute Indian.—LiWa

Wind stories. B. J. Esbensen.—EsCs

"A wind that rose." E. Dickinson.—HeR

"The wind took up the northern things." E. Dickinson.—KoT

Wind wolves. W. D. Sargent.—PrRh

The windhover, to Christ our Lord. G. M. Hopkins.—HeR

Windy nights ("Rumbling in the chimneys"). R. Bennett.—KeK

Windy nights ("Whenever the moon and stars are set"). R. L. Stevenson.—DaC—KeK—LaW—LiSf—PrRh

Windy trees. A. R. Ammons.—JaPo

Wouldn't you. J. Ciardi.—PrRa

Z. From A bestiary of the garden for children who should know better. P. Gotlieb.—DoNw

The **wind** ("I can get through a doorway without any key"). James Reeves.—PrRh

The **wind** ("I saw you toss the kites on high"). Robert Louis Stevenson.—LiSf

The **wind** ("What can the matter be"). Dorothy Graddon.—CoOu

The **wind** ("Where the wind blows"). Eleanor Farjeon.—FaE

"The **wind**." See While you were chasing a hat

The **wind**. See "Who has seen the wind"

The **wind** ("The wind stood up, and gave a shout"). James Stephens.—KeK

Wind and silver. Amy Lowell.—KeK

The **wind** and the moon. George MacDonald.—PrRa

"**Wind** and wave and star and sea." See Song

"The **wind** billowing out the seat of my britches." See Child on top of a greenhouse

"The **wind** blows out of the gates of the day." From The land of heart's desire. William Butler Yeats.—HeR

"The **wind** doth blow today, my love." See The unquiet grave

Wind flowers. Margo Lockwood.—JaD

"The **wind** has changed, and all the signs turned right." See The omens

"The **wind** has such a rainy sound." See The sound of the wind

"The **wind** has taken the damson tree." Eleanor Farjeon.—FaE

"The **wind** has twisted the roof from an old house." See House-hunting

The **wind** has wings. Unknown, tr. by Raymond De Coccola and Paul King.—DoNw

The **wind** is blowing west. Joseph Ceravolo.—KoT

"The **wind** may blow the snow about." See A country boy in winter

"**Wind** now commences to sing." See Wind song

"**Wind** rattles the apples." See Gone

Wind song ("When the wind blows"). Lilian Moore.—MoSn

Wind song ("Wind now commences to sing"). Unknown.—LiSf

"The **wind** stirs the willows." From Songs of the ghost dance. Unknown.—LiWa

"The **wind** stood up, and gave a shout." See The wind

Wind stories. Barbara Juster Esbensen.—EsCs

"The **wind** suffers of blowing." Laura Riding.—HeR

"A **wind** that rose." Emily Dickinson.—HeR

"The **wind** took up the northern things." Emily Dickinson.—KoT

"The **wind** was a torrent of darkness." See The highwayman

"The **wind** was blowing over the moors." See Charlotte Bronte

"The **wind** was throwing snowballs." See Snowball wind

"**Wind** whines and whines the shingle." See On the beach at Fontana

"**Wind**, wind, give me back my feather." See The child on the shore

Wind wolves. William D. Sargent.—PrRh

Windfalls. Eleanor Farjeon.—FaE

"**Windfalls** under the apple tree." See Windfalls

The **windhover,** to Christ our Lord. Gerard Manley Hopkins.—HeR

Winding road. Lilian Moore.—MoSn

Windmills. See Millers and mills

Window. Carl Sandburg.—HoRa

"A **window** box of pansies." See Window boxes

Window boxes. Eleanor Farjeon.—FaE

"The **window** screen." See Sunday rain

Windows

"Factory windows are always broken." V. Lindsay.—HaOf

My window screen. X. J. Kennedy.—KeF

Now close the windows. R. Frost.—KoS

Questioning faces. R. Frost.—KoS

Reflections ("On this street"). L. Moore.—LiSf—MoSn

Sunday rain. J. Updike.—JaD

"This lamp in my window." A. Lobel.—LoWr

Tree at my window. R. Frost.—KoS

Upon Fairford windows. R. Corbett.—PlEd

Washing windows. P. Wild.—JaS

Window. C. Sandburg.—HoRa

Window boxes. E. Farjeon.—FaE

X. S. Cassedy.—CaR

Zebra ("White sun"). J. Thurman.—PrRh

The **windows**. William Stanley Merwin.—JaD

"**Windrush** down the timber chutes." See Mountain wind

Winds. See Wind

"The **winds** of March were sleeping." See And suddenly spring

"The **winds** they did blow." Mother Goose.—DeM—LoR

Windshield wiper. Eve Merriam.—KeK

"**Windshield** wipers." Dennis Lee.—DoNw

"The **windshield** wipers clear an arc." See Girl in front of the bank

Windy day. N. M. Bodecker.—BoPc

Windy nights ("Rumbling in the chimneys"). Rodney Bennett.—KeK

Windy nights ("Whenever the moon and stars are set"). Robert Louis Stevenson.—DaC—KeK—LaW—LiSf—PrRh

"**Windy** shadows race." See The little hill

Windy trees. Archie Randolph Ammons.—JaPo

Wine

"Come, thou monarch of the vine." From Antony and Cleopatra. W. Shakespeare.—HoUn

Wings

Dragonfly's summer song. J. Yolen.—YoR

Questions for an angel. From A throw of threes. E. Merriam.—MeF

Wings. A. Fisher.—PrRa

Wings. Aileen Fisher.—PrRa

"**Wings** like pistols flashing at his sides." See The sparrow hawk

Wingtip. Carl Sandburg.—HoRa

Winifred Waters. William Brighty Rands.—DaC

"**Winifred** Waters sat and sighed." See Winifred Waters

Winn, Alison

If I were a fish.—BeD

Winnebago Indians. See Indians of the Americas—Winnebago

"**Winnie** Whiney, all things grieve her." See Ten kinds

The **winning** of the TV west. John T. Alexander.—PrRh

Winsor, Frederick

"This little pig built a spaceship."—PrRh

Winter. See also December; January; February; also Seasons; Snow

"All animals like me." R. Souster.—DoNw

All around the year. X. J. Kennedy.—KeF

At Candlemas. C. Causley.—HaO

Bed in summer. R. L. Stevenson.—DaC—FaW

Beyond winter. R. W. Emerson.—PrRh

Birches, Doheny Road. M. C. Livingston.—LiMp

The brook in February. C. G. D. Roberts.—DoNw

The brown birds. E. Farjeon.—FaE

Christmas card. T. Hughes.—HaO

"Cold and raw the north wind doth blow." Mother Goose.—DeM

The coming of the cold. T. Roethke.—HaO

A country boy in winter. S. O. Jewett.—HaOf

Crows ("When the high/snows lie worn"). V. Worth.—WoSp

Daniel Webster's horses. E. Coatsworth.—HaOf

The darkling thrush. T. Hardy.—HeR

December 21. L. Moore.—MoSn

Dragon smoke. L. Moore.—LiSf—MoSn—PrRa

End of winter. E. Merriam.—MeSk

Exposure. W. Owen.—HeR

The fallow deer at the lonely house. T. Hardy.—BlO—HeR—KoT

The fight of the year. R. McGough.—HaO

First snowfall ("Out of the grey"). B. J. Esbensen.—BaS—EsCs

Winter.—*Continued*
First snowflake. N. M. Bodecker.—BoSs
Greenhouse. S. Cassedy.—CaR
Ground hog day. L. Moore.—PrRh
The heron ("The sun's an iceberg"). T.
  Hughes.—HuU
Holly and mistletoe. E. Farjeon.—FaE
Hungry morning. M. C. Livingston.—HoSi
I am freezing. J. Prelutsky.—PrIs
"I heard a bird sing." O. Herford.—CoN—
  LiSf—PrRh
Ice. C. G. D. Roberts.—DoNw—PrRh
In January, 1962. T. Kooser.—JaPi
"In the bleak midwinter." C. G. Rossetti.—RoC
  A Christmas carol.—DaC
"It was a cold and wintry night." Unknown.—
  TrM
January ("The days are short"). J. Updike.—
  PrRh
Joe. D. McCord.—BaS
Kate and I. S. N. Tarrant.—JaT
The lake ("This winter day"). B. J. Esbensen.—
  EsCs
Looking for a sunset bird in winter. R. Frost.—
  KoS
Markers. F. Steele.—JaG
The Milky Way. B. J. Esbensen.—EsCs
The mitten song. M. L. Allen.—CoN—PrRa
Mittens. B. J. Esbensen.—EsCs
"My mother's got me bundled up." J.
  Prelutsky.—PrIs
"The north wind doth blow." Mother Goose.—
  BlO—CoOu—DeM—FaW—LiSf—LoR
  Poor robin.—RoC
November. A. Cary.—HaOf
November song. M. Vinz.—JaPi
On a night of snow. E. Coatsworth.—ChC—
  HaOf
"Once in the winter." From The forsaken. D.
  C. Scott.—DoNw
Owls ("Wait, the great horned owls"). W. D.
  W. Snodgrass.—JaPi
Passage ("Remember"). B. J. Esbensen.—EsCs
Passing the Masonic home for the aged. H.
  Scott.—JaPo
Pencil and paint. E. Farjeon.—FaE
Questioning faces. R. Frost.—KoS
Quilt song. M. Vinz.—JaG
Robin to Jenny. E. Farjeon.—FaE
Safe ("Come, stir the fire"). J. Walker.—HaO
Scene. C. Zolotow.—HoSi
The Shawangunks, early April. L. Moore.—
  MoSn
"Shut in from all the world without." From
  Snowbound. J. G. Whittier.—HaO
Sled run. B. J. Esbensen.—EsCs
Song of the rabbits outside the tavern. E.
  Coatsworth.—HaOf
The talking of the trees. E. Farjeon.—FaE
"There is fear in." Unknown.—LiSf
"There was a cold pig from North Stowe." A.
  Lobel.—LoB
Thirteen ways of looking at a blackbird. W.
  Stevens.—HeR
"This little house is sugar." L. Hughes.—CoN
  Winter sweetness.—HuDk—PrRa
This poem is for Nadine. P. B. Janeczko.—JaG
Those winter Sundays. R. Hayden.—JaD
Turner's sunrise. H. Bevington.—PlEd
"Up in the morning's no' for me." R. Burns.—
  BlO

Waiting ("Dreaming of honeycombs to share").
  H. Behn.—HoCb—HoSi
Weather report. L. Moore.—MoSn
Wendy in winter. K. Starbird.—PrRh
Wet. L. Moore.—MoSn
"When icicles hang by the wall." From Love's
  labour's lost. W. Shakespeare.—HoUn
  Winter.—BlO
White season. F. Frost.—LiSf
Windfalls. E. Farjeon.—FaE
Winter alphabet. E. Merriam.—MeSk
"Winter blows a blizzard, rages with a gale."
  M. C. Livingston.—LiCs
Winter cardinal. L. Moore.—MoSn
Winter clothes. K. Kuskin.—PrRh
Winter cricket. J. Heath-Stubbs.—HaO
Winter dark. L. Moore.—MoSn
Winter day. C. Zolotow.—ZoE
Winter days. G. Owen.—HaO
"Winter etches windowpanes, fingerpaints in
  white." M. C. Livingston.—LiCs
  Winter.—BaS
Winter is tacked down. S. N. Weygant.—BaS
Winter moon ("How thin and sharp is the
  moon tonight"). L. Hughes.—HuDk—KeK—
  PrRh
Winter morning. O. Nash.—BaS
Winter news. J. Haines.—JaPo
Winter night ("As I lie in bed I hear"). M.
  Chute.—LaW
Winter night ("It is very dark"). H. Behn.—
  HoCb
Winter signs. J. Prelutsky.—PrIs
Winter song. J. R. Jiménez.—LiWa
Winter song of the weasel. J. Yolen.—YoR
Winter, the huntsman. Sir O. Sitwell.—BlO
Winter time. R. L. Stevenson.—DaC
Winter twilight. L. Lipsitz.—JaG
"Winter wakes to changing wind, gives a little
  cry." M. C. Livingston.—LiCs
Winter's come. J. Prelutsky.—PrIs
Winter's tale. N. Farber.—FaTh
"Winter's thunder." Mother Goose.—LoR
Wintry. D. McCord.—McAs
"Winter." See The river
Winter. See "When icicles hang by the wall"
Winter. See "Winter etches windowpanes,
  fingerpaints in white"
Winter alphabet. Eve Merriam.—MeSk
"Winter and summer, whatever the weather." See
  The floor and the ceiling
"Winter blows a blizzard, rages with a gale."
  Myra Cohn Livingston.—LiCs
Winter cardinal. Lilian Moore.—MoSn
Winter clothes. Karla Kuskin.—PrRh
Winter cricket. John Heath-Stubbs.—HaO
Winter dark. Lilian Moore.—MoSn
"Winter dark comes early." See Winter dark
Winter day. Charlotte Zolotow.—ZoE
Winter days. Gareth Owen.—HaO
"Winter etches windowpanes, fingerpaints in
  white." Myra Cohn Livingston.—LiCs
  Winter.—BaS
"Winter has a pencil." See Pencil and paint
"Winter has come to the old folks' home." See
  Passing the Masonic home for the aged
Winter is tacked down. Sister Noemi Weygant.—
  BaS
"Winter is the king of snowmen." See Winter
  morning
Winter love. Elizabeth Jennings.—JaPo

Winter moon ("How thin and sharp is the moon tonight"). Langston Hughes.—HuDk—KeK—PrRh

The winter moon ("I hit my wife and went out and saw"). Tagaki Kyozo, tr. by James Kirkup and Nakamo Nichio.—McL

Winter morning. Ogden Nash.—BaS

Winter news. John Haines.—JaPo

Winter night ("As I lie in bed I hear"). Marchette Chute.—LaW

Winter night ("It is very dark"). Harry Behn.—HoCb

"The winter owl banked just in time to pass." See Questioning faces

Winter signs. Jack Prelutsky.—PrIs

"Winter signs are everywhere." See Winter signs

Winter song. Juan Ramón Jiménez, tr. by H.R. Hayes.—LiWa

Winter song of the weasel. Jane Yolen.—YoR

"The winter sun stays close to me." See Shadow thought

Winter sweetness. See "This little house is sugar"

Winter, the huntsman. Sir Osbert Sitwell.—BlO

Winter time. Robert Louis Stevenson.—DaC

Winter twilight. Lou Lipsitz.—JaG

"Winter wakes to changing wind, gives a · little cry." Myra Cohn Livingston.—LiCs

Wintered sunflowers. Richard Snyder.—JaPo

Winters, Yvor
  Cossante, tr. by.—PlAs
  The lady's farewell, tr. by.—PlAs

Winter's come. Jack Prelutsky.—PrIs

"Winter's come, the trees are bare." See Winter's come

Winter's tale. Norma Farber.—FaTh

The winter's tale, sels. William Shakespeare
  "When daffodils begin to peer".—PlAs

"Winter's thunder." Mother Goose.—LoR

Wintry. David McCord.—McAs

Wintu Indians. See Indians of the Americas—Wintu

"Wire, briar, limber lock." Mother Goose.—DaC

Wisdom. See also Mind
  Black dog. C. Zolotow.—ZoE
  The blind men and the elephant. J. G. Saxe.—CoOu—HaOf
  "The brown owl sits in the ivy bush." Mother Goose.—LoR
  Channel firing. T. Hardy.—HeR
  Chester's wisdom. N. Giovanni.—GiSp
  Girl in a white coat. J. M. Brinnin.—PlSc
  Is it nice to be wise. N. M. Bodecker.—BoPc
  Is wisdom a lot of language. C. Sandburg.—HoRa
  The legacy II. L. V. Quintana.—StG
  Now about tigers. J. Ciardi.—CiD
  Owl ("The diet of the owl is not"). X. J. Kennedy.—KeF
  Pangur Ban. Unknown.—ChC—HeR
  The pilgrim ("I fasted for some forty days on bread and buttermilk"). W. B. Yeats.—HeR
  Reflection on ingenuity. O. Nash.—HeR
  Small, smaller ("I thought that I knew all there was to know"). R. Hoban.—FaTh—JaT
  What grandma knew. E. Field.—JaPi
  "A wise old owl sat in an oak." Mother Goose.—DeM—FaW—LoR
    "There was an old owl who lived in an oak".—BlPi
    The owl ("There was an old owl who lived in an oak").—DaC
  The wizard in the well. H. Behn.—HoCb

Wise, William
  Just three.—PrRa
  "My little sister."—PrRh
  Rainy day.—PrRa
  Runaway ("I think today").—PrRa

The wise men ask the children the way. Heinrich Heine, tr. by Geoffrey Grigson.—HaO

"A wise old owl sat in an oak." Mother Goose.—DeM—FaW—LoR
  "There was an old owl who lived in an oak".—BlPi
  The owl ("There was an old owl who lived in an oak").—DaC

The wish ("Each birthday wish"). Ann Friday.—PrRa

Wish ("If I could wish"). Dorothy Brown Thompson.—PrRa

A wish ("If I had a wish"). Eleanor Farjeon.—FaE

The wishbone. Jack Prelutsky.—PrIt

"Wishbone, wishbone." See The wishbone

Wishes and wishing
  Bertha's wish. J. Viorst.—ViI
  Birthday ("When he asked for the moon"). M. C. Livingston.—LiCe
  Factory girl ("No more shall I work in the factory"). Unknown.—PlSc
  The falling star. S. Teasdale.—HaOf—LiSf
  "The house I go to in my dream." G. Barker.—CoOu
  The ice-king. A. B. Demille.—DoNw
  If I were a fish. A. Winn.—BeD
  If I were a king. A. A. Milne.—CoOu
  "If I were in charge of the world." J. Viorst.—ViI
  "If wishes were horses." Mother Goose.—LoR
  Leaves ("My green leaves are more beautiful"). F. Asch.—CoN
  "Oh that I were." Mother Goose.—FaW
  Old wife's song. E. Farjeon.—FaE
  The passing years. R. Elsland.—StG
  The pedlar's caravan. W. B. Rands.—BlO
  Silly song. F. García Lorca.—KoT
  "Star light, star bright." Mother Goose.—DaC—DeM—FaW—LiSf
    Wishing poem.—CoN
  To a forgetful wishing well. X. J. Kennedy.—KeF
  To my daughter riding in the circus parade. J. Labombard.—JaG
  "Touch blue." Mother Goose.—LoR
  "What comes out of a chimney." Mother Goose.—LoR
  White horses. E. Farjeon.—FaE
  The wish ("Each birthday wish"). A. Friday.—PrRa
  Wish ("If I could wish"). D. B. Thompson.—PrRa
  A wish ("If I had a wish"). E. Farjeon.—FaE
  The wishbone. J. Prelutsky.—PrIt
  The yak ("For hours the princess would not play or sleep"). V. Sheard.—DoNw

Wishing. See Dreams; Wishes and wishing

Wishing poem. See "Star light, star bright"

"Wisselton, wasselton, who lives here." See Wassailing song

The witch, sels. Thomas Middleton
  "Black spirits and white, red spirits and gray".—LiWa

"The witch flew out on Hallowe'en." See Oh, lovely, lovely, lovely

The witch, the witch. Eleanor Farjeon.—FaE—PrRh

Wizards—*Continued*
Fable ("Pity the girl with the crystal hair"). J. Aiken.—LiWa
"The fabulous wizard of Oz." Unknown.—BrT
"The limits of the sphere of dream." From Faust. J. W. von Goethe.—LiWa
Lost and found. L. Moore.—MoSn
Merlin. E. Muir.—HeR
Mr. Wells. From The sorcerer. W. S. Gilbert.—LiWa
The wizard in the well. H. Behn.—HoCb
"The wizard messes up his bench." Unknown.—TrM
Z is for Zoroaster ("How mighty a wizard"). E. Farjeon.—LiWa
"**Woke,** the old king of Cumberland." See The old king
Wolf ("The iron wolf, the iron wolf"). Ted Hughes.—HuU
The **wolf** ("When the pale moon hides and the wild wind wails"). Georgia Roberts Durston.—PrRh
Wolf ("When you think me dreaming, chin on paws"). Eleanor Farjeon.—FaE
"A **wolf.**" Unknown.—PrRh
The **wolf** cry. Lew Sarett.—PrRh
"A **wolf** is at the laundromat." Jack Prelutsky.—PrNk
Wolfe, Humbert
Autumn, sels.
"Come, let us draw the curtains".—LiIl
The blackbird.—LiSf—PrRh
"Come, let us draw the curtains." See Autumn
Green candles.—PrRh
Wolkstein, Diane
Inanna's song, tr. by.—McL
Wolny, P.
"Before goodbye."—JaPo
"From a birch."—JaD
"Lightning rides."—JaPo
Separation ("Each day").—JaD
The **wolverine.** Ted Hughes.—HuU
Wolverines
The wolverine. T. Hughes.—HuU
Wolves
Amulet. T. Hughes.—HuU
A boat ("O beautiful"). R. Brautigan.—KeK
Fable ("Once upon a time"). J. Pilinszky.—HeR
A song of the coyoteway. Unknown, fr. the Navajo Indian.—BiSp
Wolf ("The iron wolf, the iron wolf"). T. Hughes.—HuU
The wolf ("When the pale moon hides and the wild wind wails"). G. R. Durston.—PrRh
Wolf ("When you think me dreaming, chin on paws"). E. Farjeon.—FaE
The wolf cry. L. Sarett.—PrRh
"A wolf is at the laundromat." J. Prelutsky.—PrNk
The **woman** cleaning lentils. Zehrd, tr. by Diana Der Hovanessian and Marzbed Margossian.—FaTh
"A **woman** named Mrs. S. Claus." J. Patrick Lewis.—LiCp
Woman work. Maya Angelou.—PlSc
"**Woman,** you'll never credit what." See The shepherd's tale
Woman's prayer. Unknown.—BiSp
Woman's prayer to the sun, for a newborn girl. Unknown.—BiSp
Woman's song. Unknown.—BiSp
Women—portraits. See People—portraits—women

The **women's** 400 meters. Lillian Morrison.—LiSf
The **wonder** clock, sels. Katharine Pyle
Nine o'clock.—HaOf
One o'clock.—HaOf
Two o'clock.—HaOf
The **wonderful** clock. Eleanor Farjeon.—FaE
Wonders of the World
The seven wonders of the ancient world. Unknown.—PlEd
Wonders of the world. Richard Shelton.—JaD
Wood, Harnie See Wood, Marnie, and Wood, Harnie
Wood, Marnie, and Wood, Harnie
A corpulent pig.—BrT
Wood, Robert Williams
The puffin ("Upon this cake of ice is perched").—PrRh
Wood
At the woodpile. R. Henri.—PlSc
Dulcimer maker. C. Forché.—PlSc
English oak. M. C. Livingston.—LiMp
"How much wood would a woodchuck chuck." Mother Goose.—LiSf—LoR
I know a man. P. Steele.—JaPo
Recycled. L. Moore.—MoSn
"Tell me, little woodworm." S. Milligan.—PrRa
The termite. O. Nash.—HaOf—KeK
"A **woodchuck** who'd chucked lots of wood." See Double entendre
Woodchucks
Double entendre. J. F. Wilson.—BrT
A drumlin woodchuck. R. Frost.—KoS
Ground hog day. L. Moore.—PrRh
"How much wood would a woodchuck chuck." Mother Goose.—LiSf—LoR
The **woodlark.** Gerard Manley Hopkins.—HeR
Woodpecker ("Small sounds"). Lilian Moore.—MoSn
Woodpecker ("Woodpecker is rubber-necked"). Ted Hughes.—HuU
The **woodpecker** ("The woodpecker pecked out a little round hole"). Elizabeth Madox Roberts.—HaOf—LiSf
Woodpecker in disguise. Grace Taber Hallock.—PrRa
"**Woodpecker** is rubber-necked." See Woodpecker
"The **woodpecker** pecked out a little round hole." See The woodpecker
"**Woodpecker** taps at the apple tree." See Woodpecker in disguise
Woodpeckers
A legend of the Northland. P. Cary.—HaOf
On Addy Road. M. Swenson.—JaG
Woodpecker ("Small sounds"). L. Moore.—MoSn
Woodpecker ("Woodpecker is rubber-necked"). T. Hughes.—HuU
The woodpecker ("The woodpecker pecked out a little round hole"). E. M. Roberts.—HaOf—LiSf
Woodpecker in disguise. G. T. Hallock.—PrRa
Yellowhammer. E. Farjeon.—FaE
Woods. See Forests and forestry
Woolly bear caterpillar ("Caterpillar, have a care"). Aileen Fisher.—FiW
Woolly bear caterpillar ("Darkness comes early"). Barbara Juster Esbensen.—EsCs
Woolly blanket. Kate Cox Goddard.—FrP
A **word.** See "A word is dead"
Word bird. Eve Merriam.—MeSk
"A **word** is dead." Emily Dickinson.—KeK
A word.—LiSf—PrRh
"A **word** sticks in the wind's throat." See Apology

Words

Advertisement for a divertissement. E. Merriam.—MeSk
AEIOU. J. Swift.—BlO
After looking into a book belonging to my great-grandfather, Eli Eliakim Plutzik. H. Plutzik.—HeR
Alphabet stew. J. Prelutsky.—PrRh
Argument. E. Merriam.—MeSk
Baby talk. A. B. Stewart.—PrRh
Basic for further irresponsibility. E. Merriam.—MeSk
Basic for irresponsibility. E. Merriam.—MeSk
Be my non-Valentine. E. Merriam.—MeSk
Beware of speaker. N. M. Bodecker.—BoPc
Beware, or be yourself. E. Merriam.—MeSk
Beyond words. R. Frost.—KeK
Blum. D. Aldis.—FrP—LiSf
The Byfield rabbit. K. Hoskins.—PlSc
A charm for our time. E. Merriam.—MeSk
A cliche. E. Merriam.—MeSk
"Could mortal lip divine." E. Dickinson.—HeR
Different kinds of goodby. C. Sandburg.—HoRa
The dirty word. E. Merriam.—MeSk
"Doris Drummond sneaked a look." X. J. Kennedy.—KeB
English. E. Farjeon.—FaE
Feelings about words. M. O'Neill.—PrRh
Floccinaucinihilipilification. E. Merriam.—MeSk
Flummery. E. Merriam.—MeSk
Frizzing. J. Ciardi.—CiD
Fudging the issue. E. Merriam.—MeF
Glass. R. Francis.—JaD
Grammar lesson. L. Pastan.—JaPi
"A grandfather poem." W. J. Harris.—StG
Having words. E. Merriam.—MeSk
Heart crown and mirror. G. Apollinaire.—KoT
"If I had a paka." C. Pomerantz.—PoI
"Is it robin o'clock." E. Merriam.—MeBl
Is wisdom a lot of language. C. Sandburg.—HoRa
Jabberwocky. From Through the looking glass. L. Carroll.—CoN—HeR—KoT—LiSf—PrRh
Lessons ("My teacher taught me to add."). R. J. Margolis.—MaS
The lie ("Today, you threaten to leave me"). M. Angelou.—AnS
"Little girl, be careful what you say." C. Sandburg.—HoRa
Misnomer. E. Merriam.—PrRh
My trouble with porringers and oranges. N. M. Bodecker.—BoSs
Nym and graph. E. Merriam.—MeSk
"Oh my school notebooks." From Liberty. P. Éluard.—KoT
"On the first snowfall." E. Merriam.—MeF
One, two, three, gough ("To make some bread you must have dough"). E. Merriam.—CoN—MeSk
Onomatopoeia and onomatopoeia II. E. Merriam.—MeSk
Ornithology. E. Farjeon.—FaE
Pangur Ban. Unknown.—ChC—HeR
Ping-pong. E. Merriam.—MeSk
Pome ("Hlo"). D. McCord.—McAs
Poop ("My daughter, Blake, is in kindergarten"). G. Locklin.—JaS
Primer lesson. C. Sandburg.—HoRa
The purist. O. Nash.—HaOf
Read. A. Turner.—TuS
Rebus valentine. Unknown.—LiVp
Rhymes ("Two respectable rhymes"). Y. Y. Segal.—DoNw

Rollo's miracle. P. Zimmer.—JaG
A short note. E. Merriam.—MeSk
Singular indeed. D. McCord.—HaOf
Skerryvore. R. L. Stevenson.—PlEd
Snow ("Tilt, wilt"). R. Pomeroy.—JaPi
Strike me pink. E. Merriam.—MeF
"Sweet maiden of Passamaquoddy." J. De Mille.—DoNw
Think tank. E. Merriam.—HoCl—MeSk
To build a poem. C. E. Hemp.—JaG
Toy tik ka. C. Pomerantz.—PoI
Uses of poetry. W. T. Scott.—JaD
Verbs. E. Farjeon.—FaE
Where do these words come from. C. Pomerantz.—PoI
Word bird. E. Merriam.—MeSk
"A word is dead." E. Dickinson.—KeK
A word.—LiSf—PrRh
Worlds I know. M. C. Livingston.—LiWo
A young curate of Kidderminster. Unknown.—BrT
"Words can be stuffy, sticky as glue." See Alphabet stew
"Word's gane to the kitchen." See Mary Hamilton
"Words of a poem should be glass." See Glass
Words to a sick child. Unknown.—BiSp
Words to call up game. Unknown.—BiSp
Wordsworth, Dorothy
Address to a child during a boisterous winter evening.—BlO
The cottager to the infant.—KoT
"He said he had been a soldier."—PlSc
"I gathered mosses in Easedale."—PlSc
"The lake was covered all over."—KeK
Wordsworth, William
Boat stealing. See The prelude
Composed upon Westminster bridge, Sept. 3, 1802.—PlEd
Composed on Westminster bridge.—LiSf
Crossing the Alps. See The prelude
Daffodils, sels.
"I wandered lonely as a cloud".—BlO—KoT
"I wandered lonely as a cloud." See Daffodils
The kitten and the falling leaves.—BlO—ChC
Nutting.—HeR
"One Christmas-time." See The prelude
The prelude, sels.
Boat stealing.—HeR
Crossing the Alps.—HeR
"One Christmas-time".—HeR
There was a boy.—HeR
"Was it for this".—HeR
The solitary reaper.—BlO
There was a boy. See The prelude
To a butterfly.—DaC
To a skylark, sels.
"Up with me, up with me into the clouds".—KoT
"Up with me, up with me into the clouds." See To a skylark
The violet.—ChG
"Was it for this." See The prelude
Written in March.—CoN—DaC
Work
"Ah leave my harp and me alone." Unknown.—LoR
"All work and no play makes Jack a dull boy." Mother Goose.—LoR
Blacklisted. C. Sandburg.—PlSc
The blacksmiths. Unknown.—HeR
The boss. J. R. Lowell.—PlSc
Brandon Dale. M. Glenn.—GlCd

World
All day long. D. McCord.—McAs
"All things bright and beautiful." C. F. Alexander.—DaC—PrRh
Amulet. T. Hughes.—HuU
"And God stepped out on space." From The creation. J. W. Johnson.—LaT
The argument of his book. R. Herrick.—KoT
Beyond sci-fi. E. Merriam.—MeF
Bifocal. W. Stafford.—HeR
The black fern. L. Norris.—LiSf
Breathing space July. T. Tranströmer.—HeR
Catch it. E. Farjeon.—FaE
Columbus to Ferdinand. P. Freneau.—HaOf
The creation, complete. J. W. Johnson.—LiSf
Crossing the Alps. From The prelude. W. Wordsworth.—HeR
Earth and sky. E. Farjeon.—FaE
Ego tripping. N. Giovanni.—JaPi
Enchanted summer. H. Behn.—HoCb
Fire and ice. R. Frost.—KoS
Fog lifting. L. Moore.—MoSn
For a dewdrop. E. Farjeon.—FaE
Fossils. L. Moore.—HoDi—MoSn
Geography. E. Farjeon.—FaE
Gifts from my grandmother. E. M. Almedingen.—StG
"Giving thanks giving thanks." E. Merriam.—LiTp—MeF
"Great, wide, beautiful, wonderful world." W. B. Rands.—TrM
Green ("Ducklings"). L. Moore.—MoSn
Happy thought. R. L. Stevenson.—ChG—PrRh
The hills over the water. E. Farjeon.—FaE
How everything happens (based on a study on the wave). M. Swenson.—LiSf
"If all the seas were one sea." Mother Goose.—CoOu—FaW—LoR
"I'm glad the sky is painted blue." Unknown.—ChG—PrRh—TrM
I'm glad.—FrP
Immalee. C. G. Rossetti.—BlO
Inversnaid. G. M. Hopkins.—HeR
Landscape. E. Merriam.—KeK—MeSk
The lie ("Go, soul, the body's guest"). Sir W. Raleigh.—HeR
Little things ("Little drops of water"). J. A. Carney.—DaC
"Little drops of water".—LoR (unat.)
Lumps. J. Thurman.—PrRh
Makers. N. D. Watson.—PrRa
Manitou. R. Ikan.—JaPo
May meadows. E. Farjeon.—FaE
Measurement. A. M. Sullivan.—PrRh
Miracles. W. Whitman.—LiSf
The mole and the eagle. S. J. Hale.—HaOf
"The Moon King's knife of silver bright." Unknown.—DeD
Morning light. E. Farjeon.—FaE
The musk-ox. T. Hughes.—HuU
My bath. M. L'Engle.—LaT
Nature is. J. Prelutsky.—PrRh
O earth, turn! G. Johnston.—DoNw
Orbiter 5 shows how earth looks from the moon. M. Swenson.—LiSf
Pied beauty. G. M. Hopkins.—HeR—KoT
Prayer before felling to clear a cornfield. Unknown, fr. the Kekchi Maya.—BiSp
Psalm 24. From The book of psalms. Bible/Old Testament.—LiSf
Rain forest, Papua, New Guinea. M. C. Livingston.—LiMp

The rainbow ("Boats sail on the rivers"). C. G. Rossetti.—DaC
Relativity. D. H. Lawrence.—PrBb
Requiem for Sonora. R. Shelton.—JaPi
River winding. C. Zolotow.—PrRh
River's song. H. Behn.—HoCb
Season song. Unknown.—HeR
The secret song. M. W. Brown.—HaOf—PrRh
The snowy owl. T. Hughes.—HuU
A song ("I am of the earth and the earth is of me"). A. Adoff.—AdA
Song ("Our mother of the growing fields, our mother of the streams"). Unknown, fr. the Cagaba Indian.—BiSp
Song of the sky loom. Unknown, fr. the Tewa Indian.—LaT
Song of the spring peeper. J. Yolen.—YoR
"Splashing water, lantern grass." Unknown.—DeD
Starfish ("Its name linking"). E. Merriam.—MeF
"Tell me, thou star, whose wings of light." P. B. Shelley.—KoT
Thank you. L. Breek.—LaT
"There is only one horse on the earth." From Timesweep. C. Sandburg.—HoRa
The third thing. D. H. Lawrence.—PrBb
"This is the key of the kingdom." Mother Goose.—LoR
This is the key.—BlO
"To see a world in a grain of sand." From Auguries of innocence. W. Blake.—PrRh
To see a world.—KeK
The top and the tip. C. Zolotow.—PrRa—ZoE
A true account of talking to the sun at Fire Island ("The sun woke me this morning loud"). F. O'Hara.—HeR—KoT
12 October. M. C. Livingston.—CoN—LiSf—PrRh
Universe ("The universe is all the skies"). E. Farjeon.—FaE
"Up into the silence the green." E. E. Cummings.—KoT
"Walking in the rain." D. Saxon.—JaD
The ways of living things. J. Prelutsky.—PrRh
What is pink. C. G. Rossetti.—CoOu—DaC—PrRh
"Where will we run to." X. J. Kennedy.—KeF
Wonders of the world. R. Shelton.—JaD
The world ("The world is big"). B. Young.—PrRa
"The year's at the spring." From Pippa passes. R. Browning.—ChG—LaT
Pippa's song.—CoN
The **world** ("I move back by shortcut"). Vern Rutsala.—JaPi
The **world** ("Went to Florida once"). Cynthia Rylant.—RyW
The **world** ("The world is big"). Barbara Young.—PrRa
"The **world** is big." See The world
The **world** is day breaking, sels. Sekiya Miyoshi "What are days for".—BeD
"The **world** is rolling around for all the young people, so let's." See Song
"The **world** is so full of a number of things." See Happy thought
"The **world** is spinning madly." See Spring gale
"The **world** is weeping leaves today." See The leaves
"The **world** seems cold today." See Winter day
Worlds I know. Myra Cohn Livingston.—LiWo

"**You** have." See Noon
"**You** have anti-freeze in the car, yes." See Christmas card
"**You** have put your two hands upon me, and your mouth." See Betrothed
"**You** have to be brainy, not drippy." See Spell it
You have what I look for. Jaime Sabines, tr. by William Stanley Merwin.—McL
"**You** have withdrawn." See Absence
"**You** know the old woman." See The old woman
"**You** let down, from arched." See Family affairs
"**You** made healing as you wanted us to make bread and poems." See Mendings
"**You** may call, you may call." See The bad kittens
"**You** may not believe it, for hardly could I." See The pumpkin
"**You** may not (carrot) all for me." See Rebus valentine
"**You** may quarrel with centipedes, quibble with seals." See Never mince words with a shark
"**You** must." See Storm
"**You** must never bath in an Irish stew." Spike Milligan.—PrRh
"**You** must remember to remember." See Supermarket Shabbat
"**You** need not see what someone is doing." See Sext
"**You** need to have an iron rear." Jack Prelutsky.—PrNk
"**You**, north must go." Unknown.—DaC
You on the tower. Thomas Hardy.—PlSc
"**You** on the tower of my factory." See You on the tower
You owe them everything. John Allman.—PlSc
"**You** read the New York Times." See Alfred Corning Clark
"**You** round a curve." See Out in the country, back home
"**You** said you would kill it this morning." See Pheasant
"**You** say there were no people." See There are no people song
"**You** see before you an icing of skin." See The root canal
"**You** see this Christmas tree all silver gold." See Come Christmas
"**You** see this prom." See Ronnie Evans
"**You** send me your poems." See The conspiracy
"**You** should never squeeze a weasel." See Don't ever seize a weasel by the tail
"**You** sit with hands folded." See Girl sitting alone at party
"**You** smiled." Calvin O'John.—LiIl
"**You** spent fifty-five years." See Father
"**You** spotted snakes with double tongue." From A midsummer night's dream. William Shakespeare.—BlO—HoUn—LiWa
"**You** still carry." See Brother
"**You** take any junkyard." See Junkyards
"**You** take the blueberry." Charlotte Pomerantz.—PoI
"**You** tell me over the telephone about your world." See The fist upstairs
"**You** want to know what kind of week it's been." See Isabel Navarro
"**You** who have grown so intimate with stars." See To an aviator
"**You** whose day it is." See Send us a rainbow

"**You** will be running to the four corners of the universe." See A song of the girls' puberty ceremony
"**You** would think the fury of aerial bombardment." See The fury of aerial bombardment
"**You** wouldn't listen to my wordless temperance lecture." See To the fly in my drink
"**You'd** be surprised how short the roads." See Windy trees
"**You'd** think that by the end of June they'd." See School buses
"**You'll** find, in French, that couplet's a little word." See Couplet countdown
"**You'll** find me in the laundromat." See Laundromat
"**You'll** find whene'er the new year come." See Family needs
Young, Al
For poets.—JaD
Young, Andrew
Black rock of Kiltearn.—HeR
Christmas day ("Last night in the open shippen").—HaO—RoC
The dead crab.—HeR
Field-glasses.—HeR
Young, Barbara
The world ("The world is big").—PrRa
Young, Ella
The unicorn ("While yet the Morning Star").—LiSf
Young, Ree
Blue Springs, Georgia.—JaG
Young, Roland
The flea.—PrRh
The pig ("The pig is not a nervous beast").—PrRh
Young and old. Charles Kingsley.—DaC
A **young** birch. Robert Frost.—KoS
"The **young** cherry trees." See April
A **young** curate of Kidderminster. Unknown.—BrT
A **young** fellow from Boise. John Straley.—BrT
A **young** fellow named Shear. John Ciardi.—BrT
A **young** girl of Asturias. Unknown.—BrT
The **young** glass-stainer. Thomas Hardy.—PlSc
"A **young** kangaroo, Miss Hocket." See Miss Hocket
A **young** lady from Cork. Ogden Nash.—BrT
A **young** lady from Delaware. Unknown.—BrT
A **young** lady named Sue. Unknown.—BrT
A **young** lady of Crete. See "There was a young lady of Crete"
A **young** lady of Ealing. Unknown.—BrT
A **young** lady of Lynn ("There was a young lady of Lynn"). See "There was a young lady from Lynn"
A **young** lady of Munich. Unknown.—BrT
A **young** lady of Oakham. Unknown.—BrT
The **young** lady of Tyre. See "There was a young lady of Tyre"
A **young** lady of Wilts. Unknown.—BrT
A **young** man on a journey. Unknown.—BrT
"A **young** man on a journey had met her." See A young man on a journey
A **young** man who loved rain. William Jay Smith.—BrT
Young man's prayer to the spirits. Unknown.—BiSp
"A **young** person of precious precocity." From On reading, four limericks. Myra Cohn Livingston.—MeF
A **young** school mistress. Unknown.—BrT

Z

Zabolotsky, Nikolai Alekseevich—*Continued*
  A walk.—HeR
Zany Zapper Zockke. Jack Prelutsky.—PrNk
Zebra ("White sun"). Judith Thurman.—PrRh
The **zebra** ("The zebra is undoubtedly"). Jack
  Prelutsky.—PrZ
Zebra and leopard. N. M. Bodecker.—BoSs
"The **zebra** is undoubtedly." See The zebra
Zebras
  The zebra ("The zebra is undoubtedly"). J.
    Prelutsky.—PrZ
  Zebra and leopard. N. M. Bodecker.—BoSs
  "The zigzag zealous zebra." From An animal
    alphabet. E. Lear.—LiH
  "Zebras want polka dots." See Zebra and leopard
Zebus
  Zoo doings. J. Prelutsky.—PrZ
Zehrd
  The woman cleaning lentils.—FaTh
Zephyr. Unknown.—BrT
"**Zephyr**, the lovely wind of summer." See Z
Zero. Eve Merriam.—MeHa
"The **zigzag** zealous zebra." From An animal
  alphabet. Edward Lear.—LiH
Zimmer, Paul
  Julian barely misses Zimmer's brains.—JaG
  Missing the children.—JaS
  Rollo's miracle.—JaG
  Susie's enzyme poem.—JaPo
  Train blues.—JaPo
  A visit from Alphonse.—JaG
  What Zimmer would be.—JaPi
  Zimmer and his turtle sink the house.—JaPi
  Zimmer in fall.—JaPo
  Zimmer in grade school.—KeK
  Zimmer's street.—JaT
Zimmer and his turtle sink the house. Paul
  Zimmer.—JaPi
Zimmer in fall. Paul Zimmer.—JaPo
Zimmer in grade school. Paul Zimmer.—KeK
Zimmer's street. Paul Zimmer.—JaT
Zinnias. Valerie Worth.—CoN
"**Zinnias**, stout and stiff." See Zinnias
Zodiac (signs of)
  Zodiac. E. Farjeon.—FaE
Zodiac. Eleanor Farjeon.—FaE
Zoe and the ghosts. Dieter Weslowski.—JaPo
Zolotow, Charlotte
  Absent friend.—ZoE
  Again, good night.—ZoE
  The apple tree.—ZoE
  Autumn ("Now the summer is grown old").—
    ZoE
  The bed.—ZoE
  Beetles.—ZoE
  Black dog.—ZoE
  Blue.—ZoE
  The boats.—ZoE
  The bride ("I wonder if ever").—ZoE
  The bridge ("Glittering bridge").—ZoE
  Buttercups.—ZoE
  By the sea.—ZoE
  "Candlelight and moth wings."—ZoE
  The cardinal ("After the snow stopped").—ZoE
  Contrast.—ZoE
  Crocus ("Little crocus").—ZoE
  The dancers.—ZoE
  A date.—ZoE
  A dog ("I am alone").—HoDl
  Eight o'clock.—ZoE
  False start.—ZoE
  The fireflies.—ZoE
  Firefly ("On a June night").—ZoE

The first snow ("There is a special kind of
  quiet").—ZoE
The fly ("I was sitting on the porch").—ZoE
The fog.—ZoE
Good night ("We turn out the lights").—ZoE
Grayness.—ZoE
Green ("Green is a good color").—ZoE
Halfway where I'm going.—ZoE
Halloween ("The moon is full and").—ZoE
"The hedge."—ZoE
Here ("In this spot").—ZoE
I wonder.—HoSu
In the museum.—ZoE
Ladybug ("Little ladybug").—ZoE
The leaves ("The world is weeping leaves
  today").—ZoE
Leopard in the zoo.—ZoE
Little bird ("Little hurt bird").—ZoE
"Little orange cat."—ZoE
Look.—PrRa—ZoE
"Lying in the grass."—ZoE
Marigolds.—ZoE
Missing you.—HoBf—LiIl
"A moment in summer."—HoSi—PrRh—ZoE
Moonlight ("The moon drips its light").—ZoE
My father.—ZoE
My mother.—ZoE
The new girl.—ZoE
Noel.—ZoE
North and south.—ZoE
Outside at night.—ZoE
Pansies.—ZoE
People ("Some people talk and talk").—PrRh—
  ZoE
The pond.—ZoE
"Raccoon."—ZoE
Red.—ZoE
A riddle ("Once when I was very scared").—
  CoN
The river ("Quiver shiver").—ZoE
River winding.—PrRh
The sandpiper ("Look at the little
  sandpiper").—FaTh—HoSe
Scene.—HoSi
School day.—ZoE
The sea ("Muffled thunder").—ZoE
Someone I like.—ZoE
Spring day.—ZoE
The spring wind.—PrRa—ZoE
Summer snow.—HoSe—ZoE
The top and the tip.—PrRa—ZoE
Toward dark.—ZoE
The train.—ZoE
The train melody.—ZoE
Trees ("The trees toss their long branches").—
  ZoE
Weeds.—ZoE
"When I have a little girl."—ZoE
Winter day.—ZoE
Yellow ("Yellow is a good color").—ZoE
Zolotow. Charlotte
  Sleepless nights.—ZoE—ZoE
Zoo ("For comfort and pleasure"). Sylvia
  Cassedy.—CaR
The **zoo** ("The zoo is a wonderful place"). Ann
  Turner.—TuS
Zoo doings. Jack Prelutsky.—PrZ
"The **zoo** is a wonderful place." See The zoo
A **zoo** without bars. N. M. Bodecker.—BoSs
"**Zooming** across the sky." See Up in the air
Zoos
  At the zoo ("First I saw the white bear"). W.
    M. Thackeray.—CoN

Zoos—*Continued*

At the zoo ("There are lions and roaring tigers, and enormous camels and things"). A. A. Milne.—FrP

The careless zookeeper. Unknown.—BrT

Leopard in the zoo. C. Zolotow.—ZoE

Nature and art. O. Herford.—BrT

Pete at the zoo. G. Brooks.—LiIl

A sightseer named Sue. Unknown.—BrT

Zoo ("For comfort and pleasure"). S. Cassedy.—CaR

The zoo ("The zoo is a wonderful place"). A. Turner.—TuS

Zoo doings. J. Prelutsky.—PrZ

A zoo without bars. N. M. Bodecker.—BoSs

The **zoosher**. Jack Prelutsky.—PrNk

Zuni grandfather. Unknown.—StG

Zuni grandmother. Unknown.—StG

Zuni Indians. See Indians of the Americas—Zuni

DIRECTORY OF PUBLISHERS
AND DISTRIBUTORS

Atheneum. Atheneum, c/o Macmillan Publishing Co., 866 Third Ave., New York, NY 10022.

Bradbury. Bradbury Press, Inc., Affiliate of Macmillan, Inc., 866 Third Ave., New York, NY 10022.

Collins. William Collins Sons & Company Ltd., 14 St. James's Place, London SW1A 1PS England.

Crowell. Thomas Y. Crowell, c/o Harper and Row, 10 E. 53rd St., New York, NY 10022.

Crown. Crown Publishers, Inc., 225 Park Ave., New York, NY 10003.

Delacorte. Delacorte Press/Dell Publishing Co., Inc., 666 Fifth Ave., New York, NY 10103.

Dial. Dial Books for Young Readers, Division of NAL Penguin, Inc., 2 Park Ave., New York, NY 10016.

Doubleday. Doubleday, 666 Fifth Ave., New York, NY 10103.

Dutton. E. P. Dutton, Division of NAL Penguin, Inc., 2 Park Ave., New York, NY 10016.

Faber. Faber and Faber, 50 Cross St., Winchester, MA 01890.

Farrar. Farrar, Straus & Giroux, Inc., 19 Union Square West, New York, NY 10003.

Greenwillow. Greenwillow Books, Division of William Morrow and Co., Inc., 105 Madison Ave., New York, NY 10016.

Harcourt. Harcourt Brace Jovanovich, Inc., 1250 Sixth Ave., San Diego, CA 92101.

Harper. Harper and Row, Publishers, Inc., 10 E. 53rd St., New York, NY 10022.

Hill. Hill and Wang, Division of Farrar, Straus & Giroux, Inc., 19 Union Square West, New York, NY 10003.

Holiday. Holiday House, Inc., 18 East 53rd St., New York, NY 10022.

Holt. Holt, Rinehart and Winston Inc., Subsidiary of Harcourt Brace Jovanovich, Inc., 1627 Woodland Ave., Austin, TX 78741.

Houghton. Houghton Mifflin Co., One Beacon St., Boston, MA 02108.

Knopf. Alfred A. Knopf Inc., Subsidiary of Random House Inc., 201 E. 50th St., New York, NY 10022.

Lippincott. Lippincott Junior Books, c/o Harper and Row, 10 East 53rd St., New York, NY 10022.

Little. Little, Brown, and Company, Subsidiary of Time Inc., 34 Beacon St., Boston, MA 02108.

Lothrop. Lothrop, Lee and Shepard Books, Division of William Morrow & Co., Inc., 105 Madison Ave., New York, NY 10016.

Macmillan. Macmillan Publishing Co., 866 Third Ave., New York, NY 10022.

Morrow. Morrow Junior Books, Division of William Morrow & Co., Inc., 105 Madison Ave., New York, NY 10016.

Orchard. Orchard Books, Division of Franklin Watts, Inc., 387 Park Ave. S., New York, NY 10016.

Oxford. Oxford University Press Inc., 200 Madison Ave., New York, NY 10016; 70 Wynford Drive, Don Mills, Ontario ON M3C 1J9 Canada.

Putnam. Philomel/Putnam, 51 Madison Ave., New York, NY 10010.

Random House. Random House Inc., 201 E. 50th St., New York, NY 10022.

Scott. Scott, Foresman & Co., Subsidiary of Time Inc., 1900 East Lake Ave., Glenview, IL 60025.

Scribner. c/o Macmillan Publishing Co., 866 Third Ave., New York, NY 10022.

Stemmer House. Stemmer House Publishers Inc., 2627 Caves Rd., Owings Mill, MD 21117.

Viking. Viking Penguin Inc., 40 W. 23rd St., New York, NY 10010.

Westminster. Westminster Press, 925 Chestnut St., Philadelphia, PA 19107.